PERSPECTIVES ON THE SOCIAL ORDER
Readings in Sociology

H. LAURENCE ROSS
Professor of Sociology and Law
University of Denver

SECOND EDITION

McGRAW-HILL BOOK COMPANY
New York
St. Louis
San Francisco
Toronto
London
Sydney

PERSPECTIVES ON THE SOCIAL ORDER

Readings in Sociology

Cover and part opening art are by Crosby/Fletcher/Forbes, London, England.

To My Parents

FOREWORD

The editor of this successful book has invited me to prepare a brief Foreword to the second edition, as he did for the first. Once more I am happy to accept the invitation. It is indeed an unusual compliment. For *Perspectives on the Social Order,* as its title suggests, has a close relationship to my own book, *The Social Order,* now also in its second edition. *Perspectives* was, and is, particularly appropriate as a supplement to *The Social Order.* In this second edition Professor Ross has shifted his selections somewhat, discarding those from the first that seemed perhaps no longer at the peak of their effectiveness, and adding new ones that bring fresh points of view, or new evidence, or both, to the ever-fascinating subject that is the study of society. In this edition, as in the earlier one, his choices exhibit a high degree of sociological sophistication and discrimination.

The close and, I hope, fruitful relationship between our two books finds continuing expression in this new and revised edition of *Perspectives.* The organization of the materials is the same in both places. Professor Ross has preserved the same sequence in his chapters and has used the same chapter titles. He has also adopted most of the conceptual apparatus of *The Social Order.* This is apparent throughout but most especially in the treatment of social organization and social differentiation. It is good to know that there is a growing consensus about the organization of sociological knowledge.

It should be said that, although *Perspectives on the Social Order* was prepared with *The Social Order* in mind, this second edition of the former is in no sense dependent upon the latter. Among the many virtues of this collection of readings is that it can be used with other introductory texts as well. It can also serve as an independent text for those instructors who prefer to develop their own plan of presentation.

This second edition of *Perspectives on the Social Order,* in short, appears again in its own right as a superior pedagogical instrument. The editor has a clear conception of the nature and meaning of contemporary sociology and communicates this conception with vigor and precision. He knows that the first and most fundamental task of a general and introductory book in sociology is to acquaint the student with the recurrences and regularities in the affairs of society, to suggest to him that social life is not at all a random and haphazard series of events but rather something that exhibits patterns of interaction and that these patterns, in turn, constitute an essential part of the social structure. His emphasis from the outset is upon this structure, this basic order, that society exhibits, the order that it is thus the task of sociology to discover and disclose. It is the existence of this order, as the editor says in his initial sentences, that makes possible the explanation of the daily routines in which we all indulge and of the social relationships we have with our fellows. He shows how systematic observation differs from common sense in giving an account of these relationships, and he indicates by precept and example the importance of rigorous methods of investigation and of sound research designs.

The selections Professor Ross offers us now include both classical and contemporary authors. He has wisely decided not to present them in snippets so small that they fail to satisfy—and this, incidentally, is one of the distinctive features of his book. The selections are complete essays in themselves and are presented, as nearly as possible, as the authors wrote them.

To these selections Professor Ross has added his own perceptive comment. He writes first of all a general introduction to each chapter and then introduces separately each of the selections within the chapter and summarizes for the student the content of the selection. Finally, and most helpfully, he mentions on a number of occasions the criticisms that have been made of an author's treatment of his theme, and he offers his own considered judgment of their cogency. The result is a lively collection, one that gives both substance and animation to the introductory course, one that quickly engages the attention of the reader, and one that rewards him with a comprehensive view of the field of sociology. The editor knows, as all good teachers do, that one should never overestimate the knowledge of his students, nor underestimate their intelligence. His book exhibits a firm understanding of this principle.

Most impressive of all is the editor's appreciation of the role of sociology as part—indeed an almost indispensable part—of a general education. Sociology is increasingly taking its proper place among the liberal arts. As do other liberal arts—history, literature, and philosophy—it liberates the student from the provincialisms of time, place, and circumstance. It lends perspective not only to the social order but to human life itself. This is the sense and this the spirit that inform this new book of readings, and for these gifts the students who use it will owe a pleasant debt to their editor.

Robert Bierstedt

PREFACE

This collection of sociological literature is intended for use as either a basic or a supplementary text for the college course in general sociology. My goal has been to provide materials which not only will interest and inform the student, but which will illustrate the range and diversity of our science. Classical statements are balanced where possible by modern commentaries and theoretical essays by empirical research. Moreover, although most of the selections are by academic sociologists, I have drawn freely from the works of biologists, anthropologists, historians, psychologists, economists, and political scientists where their writings bear on sociological concerns.

The selections are of professional caliber, but they have been chosen to be interesting and comprehensible to the liberal arts student who has had no previous experience with sociology or other quantitative social sciences. Some selections will be more meaningful to the quantitatively trained student, but all can be read without difficulty by the student who lacks this training.

With few exceptions, articles and chapters from books are reproduced here in their entirety, including original footnotes and references, so that the scholarship and "flavor" of the original sources can be experienced by the reader of this collection.

The book is organized along the lines sketched by Robert Bierstedt in his text, *The Social Order*, which I consider one of the best solutions to the problem of organizing the complex body of current sociological thought. I have borrowed freely from Professor Bierstedt's work for terminology and theoretical orienta-

tion, and this book will make a particularly suitable companion to his charming and scholarly text.

Each chapter begins with a general statement that places the following selections within the broader concerns they have been chosen to represent. In turn, each selection is preceded by an introduction which includes an abstract as an indented passage, remarks on the origin of the selection and its place in current discussion, as well as my opinion of the strengths and weaknesses of the argument. Technical terms not defined here are explained in footnotes to the text. An Inventory of Concepts at the back of the volume indexes the terms for which a definition is provided either in the selections or in the introductory materials.

This revised and enlarged edition contains nineteen new selections. About one-third of the book has been changed, the changes being based on my own and my colleagues' experience with the first edition, including its use as a supplementary text for the national *Sunrise Semester* television program. I have tried to retain the most instructive and best-liked selections and to replace material that turned out to be unclear, unconvincing, or obsolete. I hope that the teachers and students who use this book will enjoy it and that it helps to attract a few new recruits to the task of building the science of society. Most of all, I hope that it contributes to its readers a measure of insight into their own society and thus into themselves.

H. Laurence Ross
Newfane, Vermont

CONTENTS

Part 1

INTRODUCTION

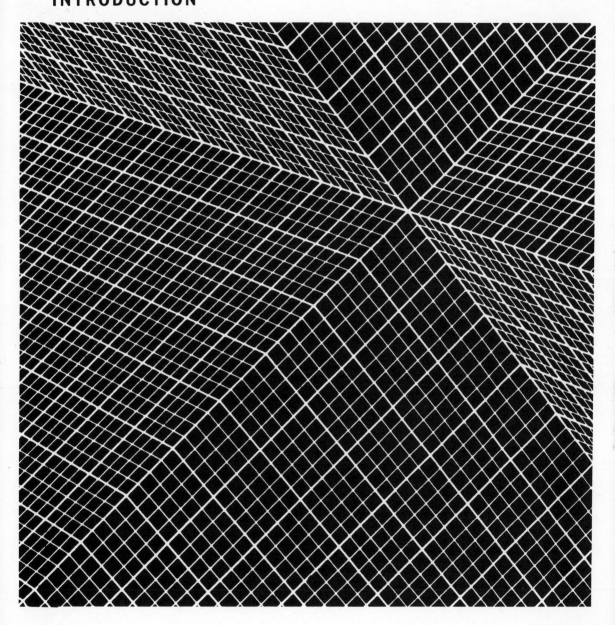

Chapter 1

THE NATURE OF SOCIOLOGY

THE SOCIOLOGIST AND HIS WORK
Selection 1

THE SUBJECT MATTER OF SOCIOLOGY
Selection 2

THE DESIGN OF SOCIOLOGICAL RESEARCH
Selection 3

RESEARCH DESIGN EXEMPLIFIED
Selection 4

Sociology is the scientific study of human behavior in groups. Its aim is to discover regularities and order in this behavior and to express these discoveries as theoretical "laws" or generalizations that succinctly describe a wide variety of behavior.

A large part of sociology, though by no means all of it, is concerned with things that are very familiar to us: the routines of our daily existence. To enjoy sociology and to experience its real excitement, it is necessary to look at our everyday experiences in a new light. They must be seen as part of a social order that cannot be taken for granted, but that must be investigated and explained. The most ordinary of daily routines requires such impressive regulation of individual needs and such precise coordination of one person's actions with those of others that its achievement can be considered among the wonders of the world.

Modern Americans should not find it very difficult to take this new view. We live in a civilization that is among the most complex in the history of mankind. Consider the degree of coordination necessary to manufacture and distribute the ordinary commodities of everyday purchase: soap, breakfast cereals, and the hundreds of other items we take for granted. Consider the intricacies of interaction that result in a number of students and one professor coming together in exactly the same room at nearly the same time, again and again throughout the school year. That these arrangements are relatively effortless for the individuals involved is further testimony to the accomplishment that constitutes the social order.

Since everyone participates in social relations of many kinds, knowledge concerning the social order is not a monopoly of sociology. In addition to the theory and systematic research of scientific sociology, there exist the broad generalizations and insights of common sense, as well as the academic school of thought known as social philosophy.

Common sense, or "folk sociology," is the body of beliefs concerning the facts

3

and reasons of social life that are held by the layman. The average man is not a stupid observer, but neither is he systematic. The generalizations of common sense have a tendency to be overstated, oversimplified, and supported by provincial or parochial evidence. Not uncommonly, they are contrary to most objective facts. However, the reader should not be surprised if many of the discoveries of sociology sound like common sense. For one thing, common sense often takes both sides of an issue, so that it is supported no matter how the facts may lie. If like attracts like, and opposites attract, common sense will certainly be shown to be right (and wrong) on all occasions. Again, many sociological statements sound exactly like common sense if one is not able to make the distinction between a carefully limited generalization, supported by systematic observation, and an exaggerated, unsupported, and irresponsible statement of essentially the same principle. Finally, some commonsense observations do turn out to be reasonably stated and in accord with the facts, and scientific sociology can indicate which ones these are.

Social philosophy is the product of intelligent speculation. Men have been considering the social order since the beginning of recorded history. The works of such thinkers as Plato, Aristotle, Saint Thomas, Machiavelli, Hobbes, and Rousseau suggest the great intellectual talent that has been devoted to understanding social behavior in the philosophical tradition. The methods of investigation used by these social philosophers were less systematic and dependable than those available today, but many of their insights have been confirmed by the more recently available research techniques. Thus, it is not surprising if parts of sociology sound like restatements of Aristotle or Hobbes, who if living in this day would very likely be considered sociologists.

The science of sociology became differentiated from social philosophy by following a program roughly sketched out by Auguste Comte in the mid-nineteenth century. Comte, and sociologists since, believed that an understanding of the social order would come more rapidly if investigators applied the scientific procedure of systematic observation to the study of society. In this procedure, assertions of fact are tested by rigorous methods, and the search for facts is directed by theories that derive in turn from previous investigations. Sociology has grown enormously since it was suggested by Comte. It has produced brilliant theories by scholars it can call its own, such as Emile Durkheim and Max Weber, as well as many new techniques for knowing more precisely the facts of the social order. If, in comparison with other fields of knowledge, sociology is still a young and undeveloped science, this state of affairs should be regarded as a challenge and an opportunity. Even the layman and beginning student can add significantly to sociological knowledge by a brilliant idea or a well-designed piece of research. At a time in history when the power of mass extermination has become available to complex social organizations, sociology may be ranked among the most consequential of intellectual disciplines.

The selections in this introductory chapter define sociology and the work of the sociologist, indicate both the focus and the scope of the discipline, and discuss the research procedures by which the propositions of sociological theory are tested in the world of facts. Selection 1, by Peter L. Berger, attempts to correct some misconceptions concerning what a sociologist does, and to substitute a more realistic image. Selection 2 is a classic work by Emile Durkheim, who was one of the founders of modern sociology. In this work Durkheim specifies the central subject matter of sociology in contrast to other social sciences. In Selection 3, Samuel A. Stouffer discusses the things that make studies good or bad and offers some practical advice on designing research. Selection 4, by H. Laurence Ross and Donald T. Campbell, shows how research can be done in a situation in which the classical experimental method of science cannot be used.

THE SOCIOLOGIST AND HIS WORK

Sociology is one of the least understood of academic disciplines. Not only do most people have little information concerning what sociology is and what sociologists do, but the ideas that they do have are frequently either dated or distorted. This selection by Peter L. Berger refutes some of the inaccurate images that exist, and proposes a definition of the sociological enterprise that is particularly relevant to the liberal arts student. Professor Berger invites you to the study of sociology, sketching broadly the outlines of what is to come and warning of intellectual perils as well as pleasures in the process.

The sociologist is not a social uplifter. Neither does he provide the intellectual basis for the practice of social work, nor is he a social reformer. These images of the sociologist are inaccurate because they presuppose that knowledge is on the side of the "good," whereas in fact the meaning of knowledge depends on the intentions as well as the skill of the user. Furthermore, although sociology has developed considerable knowledge that could be of use in social reform, the social work movement has been built more on the basis of psychiatric than sociological theory.

More up-to-date images of the sociologist depict him as a compiler of data, a methodologist, or as a detached observer and cynical manipulator of men. Although these images are not entirely without foundation, they represent distortions that are neither accurate nor fair. At best they represent the work of sociology when it is badly done.

A better definition of a sociologist would be someone who is concerned with understanding society in a disciplined way. The discipline involved is adherence to the rules of science. But this definition does not explain why a sociologist pursues his work. The principal motivation of the sociologist is curiosity, not in the idle sense but rather with commitment. The sociologist is the man who is burning with curiosity to understand human interaction, whether exotic or hum-drum, extraordinary or apparently trivial; for even the routines of everyday life, when approached with the guide of discipline, can offer unexpected, even shocking, revelations.

Berger's treatment of sociology, in his words "as an individual pastime," is admittedly somewhat one-sided. He gives little stress to the fact that sociology is also a collective enterprise, a body of theory buttressed by controlled observations, continually increasing in scale and sophistication. He might give more emphasis to the striving of sociologists to build and develop a great intellectual edifice, as well as to satisfy their own individual curiosities, however serious these might be. Nonetheless, the image he proposes is very pertinent to the role of sociology in a liberal arts education.

Liberal arts education is directed to developing the independent mind and free spirit, and here the study of sociology offers an important opportunity. Sociology has this message, in brief, to impart to the liberal arts student: the limitations on human action are nearly always of human origin. Only rarely do the "givens" of geography, biology, or innate psychological capacity set limits to what men can do. The principal restraints are those of culture, applied to our behavior by social forces in such a way that we are seldom conscious of this. The first step in achieving freedom is to understand the origin and nature of the forces that affect us. To know them is to be able to question them and to evaluate their demands in terms of our considered needs and goals as ethical and rational beings. If we understand these cultural imperatives, and judge them good and proper, we can obey with the knowledge that we are serving our ends in an effective manner. If, on the other hand, we judge certain of them to be evil, we are able to exercise our freedom to resist them. The free and independent man, the ideal product of a liberal arts education, is not necessarily the nonconformist, but the person who selects conformity or nonconformity to particular demands on the basis of informed reflection. The appreciation, knowledge, and understanding of the social order that are obtained from the study of sociology may be a priceless advantage in this task of the educated man.

Selection 1
FROM INVITATION TO SOCIOLOGY
Peter L. Berger

There are very few jokes about sociologists. This is frustrating for the sociologists, especially if they compare themselves with their more favored second cousins, the psychologists, who have pretty much taken over that sector of American humor that used to be occupied by clergymen. A psychologist, introduced as such at a party, at once finds himself the object of considerable attention and uncomfortable mirth. A sociologist in the same circumstance is likely to meet with no more of a reaction than if he had been announced as an insurance salesman. He will have to win his attention the hard way, just like everyone else. This is annoying and unfair, but it may also be instructive. The dearth of jokes about sociologists indicates, of course, that they are not as much part of the popular imagination as psychologists have become. But it probably also indicates that there is a certain ambiguity in the images that people do have of them. It may thus be a good starting point for our considerations to take a closer look at some of these images.

If one asks undergraduate students why they are taking sociology as a major, one often gets the reply, "because I like to work with people." If one then goes on to ask such students about their occupational future, as they envisage it, one often hears that they intend to go into social work. Of this more in a moment. Other answers are more vague and general, but all indicate that the student in question would rather deal with people than with things. Occupations mentioned in this connection include personnel work, human relations in industry, public relations, advertising, com-

munity planning or religious work of the unordained variety. The common assumption is that in all these lines of endeavor one might "do something for people," "help people," "do work that is useful for the community." The image of the sociologist involved here could be described as a secularized version of the liberal Protestant ministry, with the YMCA secretary perhaps furnishing the connecting link between sacred and profane benevolence. Sociology is seen as an up-to-date variation on the classic American theme of "uplift." The sociologist is understood as one professionally concerned with edifying activities on behalf of individuals and of the community at large.

One of these days a great American novel will have to be written on the savage disappointment this sort of motivation is bound to suffer in most of the occupations just mentioned. There is moving pathos in the fate of these likers of people who go into personnel work and come up for the first time against the human realities of a strike that they must fight on one side of the savagely drawn battle lines, or who go into public relations and discover just what it is that they are expected to put over in what experts in the field have called "the engineering of consent," or who go into community agencies to begin a brutal education in the politics of real estate speculation. But our concern here is not with the despoiling of innocence. It is rather with a particular image of the sociologist, an image that is inaccurate and misleading.

It is, of course, true that some Boy Scout types have become sociologists. It is also true that a benevolent interest in people could be the biographical starting point for sociological studies. But it is important to point out that a malevolent and misanthropic outlook could serve just as well. Sociological insights are valuable to anyone concerned with action in society. But this action need not be particularly humanitarian. Some American sociologists today are employed by governmental agencies seeking to plan more livable communities for the nation. Other American sociologists are employed by governmental agencies concerned with wiping communities of hostile nations off the map, if and when the necessity should arise. Whatever the moral implications of these respective activities may be, there is no reason why interesting sociological studies could not be carried on in both. Similarly, criminology, as a special field within sociology, has uncovered valuable information about processes of crime in modern society. This information is equally valuable for those seeking to fight crime as it would be for those interested in promoting it. The fact that more criminologists have been employed by the police than by gangsters can be ascribed to the ethical bias of the criminologists themselves, the public relations of the police and perhaps the lack of scientific sophistication of the gangsters. It has nothing to do with the character of the information itself. In sum, "working with people" can mean getting them out of slums or getting them into jail, selling them propaganda or robbing them of their money (be it legally or illegally), making them produce better automobiles or making them better bomber pilots. As an image of the sociologist, then, the phrase leaves something to be desired, even though it may serve to describe at least the initial impulse as a result of which some people turn to the study of sociology.

Some additional comments are called for in connection with a closely related image of the sociologist as a sort of theoretician for social work. This image is understandable in view of the development of sociology in America. At least one of the roots of American sociology is to be found in the worries of social workers confronted with the massive problems following in the wake of the industrial revolution— the rapid growth of cities and of slums within them, mass immigration, mass movements of people, the disruption of traditional ways of life and the resulting disorientation of individuals caught in these processes. Much sociological research has been spurred by this sort of concern. And so it is still quite customary for undergraduate students planning to go into social work to major in sociology.

Actually, American social work has been far more influenced by psychology than by sociology in the development of its "theory." Very probably this fact is not unrelated to what was previously said about the relative status of sociology and psychology in the popular imagination. Social workers have had to fight an uphill battle for a long time to be recognized as "professionals," and to get the prestige, power and (not least) pay that such recognition entails. Looking around for a "professional" model to emulate, they found that of the psychiatrist to be the most natural. And so contemporary social workers receive their "clients" in an office, conduct fifty-minute "clinical interviews" with them, record the interviews in quadruplicate and discuss them with a hierarchy of "supervisors." Having adopted the outward paraphernalia of the psychiatrist, they naturally also adopted his ideology. Thus contemporary American social-work "theory" consists very largely of a somewhat bowdlerized version of psychoanalytic psychology, a sort of poor man's Freudianism that serves to legitimate the social worker's claim to help people in a "scientific" way. We are not interested here in investigating the "scientific" validity of this synthetic doctrine. Our point is that not only does it have very little to do with sociology, but it is marked, indeed, by a singular obtuseness with regard to social reality. The identification of sociology with social work in the minds of many people is somewhat a phenomenon of "cultural lag," dating from the period when as yet pre-"professional" social workers dealt with poverty rather than with libidinal frustration, and did so without the benefit of a dictaphone.

But even if American social work had not jumped on the bandwagon of popular psychologism the image of the sociologist as the social worker's theoretical mentor would be misleading. Social work, whatever its theoretical rationalization, is a certain *practice* in society. Sociology is not a practice, but an *attempt to understand*. Certainly this understanding may have use for the practitioner. For that matter, we would contend that a more profound grasp of sociology would be of great use to the social worker and that such grasp would obviate the necessity of his descending into the mythological depths of the "subconscious" to explain matters that are typically quite conscious, much more simple and, indeed, *social* in nature. But there is nothing inherent in the sociological enterprise of trying to understand society that necessarily leads to this practice, or to any other. Sociological understanding can be recommended to social workers, but also to salesmen, nurses, evangelists and politicians—in fact, to anyone whose goals involve the manipulation of men, for whatever purpose and with whatever moral justification.

This conception of the sociological enterprise is implied in the classic statement by Max Weber, one of the most important figures in the development of the field, to the effect that sociology is "value-free." Since it will be necessary to return to this a number of times later, it may be well to explicate it a little further at this point. Certainly the statement does *not* mean that the sociologist has or should have no values. In any case, it is just about impossible for a human being to exist without any values at all, though, of course, there can be tremendous variation in the values one may hold. The sociologist will normally have many values as a citizen, a private person, a member of a religious group or as an adherent of some other association of people. But within the limits of his activities as a sociologist there is one fundamental value only—that of scientific integrity. Even there, of course, the sociologist, being human, will have to reckon with his convictions, emotions and prejudices. But it is part of his intellectual training that he tries to understand and control these as *bias* that ought to be eliminated, as far as possible, from his work. It goes without saying that this is not always easy to do, but it is not impossible. The sociologist tries to see what is there. He may have many hopes or fears concerning what he may find. But he will try to see regardless of hopes or fears. It is thus an act of pure perception, as pure as humanly limited means allow, toward which sociology strives.

An analogy may serve to clarify this a little more. In any political or military conflict it is of advantage to capture the information used by the intelligence organs of the opposing side. But this is so only because good intelligence consists of information free of bias. If a spy does his reporting in terms of the ideology and ambitions of his superiors, his reports are useless not only to the enemy, if the latter should capture them, but also to the spy's own side. It has been claimed that one of the weaknesses of the espionage apparatus of totalitarian states is that spies report not what they find but what their superiors want to hear. This, quite evidently, is bad espionage. The good spy reports what is there. Others decide what should be done as a result of his information. The sociologist is a spy in very much the same way. His job is to report as accurately as he can about a certain social terrain. Others, or he himself in a role other than that of sociologist, will have to decide what moves ought to be made in that terrain. We would stress strongly that saying this does *not* imply that the sociologist has no responsibility to ask about the goals of his employers or the use to which they will put his work. But this asking is not sociological asking. It is asking the same questions that any man ought to ask himself about his actions in society. Again, in the same way, biological knowledge can be employed to heal or to kill. This does not mean that the biologist is free of responsibility as to which use he serves. But when he asks himself about this responsibility, he is not asking a biological question.

Another image of the sociologist, related to the two already discussed, is that of social reformer. Again, this image has historical roots, not only in America but also in Europe. Auguste Comte, the early nineteenth-century French philosopher who invented the name of the discipline, thought of sociology as the doctrine of progress, a secularized successor to theology as the mistress of the sciences. The sociologist in this view plays the role of arbiter of all branches of knowledge for the welfare of men. This notion, even when stripped of its more fantastic pretensions, died especially hard in the development of French sociology. But it had its repercussions in America too, as when, in the early days of American sociology, some transatlantic disciples of Comte seriously suggested in a memorandum to the president of Brown University that all the departments of the latter should be reorganized under the department of sociology. Very few sociologists today, and probably none in this country, would think of their role in this way. But something of this conception survives when sociologists are expected to come up with blueprints for reform on any number of social issues.

It is gratifying from certain value positions (including some of this writer's) that sociological insights have served in a number of instances to improve the lot of groups of human beings by uncovering morally shocking conditions or by clearing away collective illusions or by showing that socially desired results could be obtained in more humane fashion. One might point, for example, to some applications of sociological knowledge in the penological practice of Western countries. Or one might cite the use made of sociological studies in the Supreme Court decision of 1954 on racial segregation in the public schools. Or one could look at the applications of other sociological studies to the humane planning of urban redevelopment. Certainly the sociologist who is morally and politically sensitive will derive gratification from such instances. But, once more, it will be well to keep in mind that what is at issue here is not sociological understanding as such but certain applications of this understanding. It is not difficult to see how the same understanding could be applied with opposite intentions. Thus the sociological understanding of the dynamics of racial prejudice can be applied effectively by those promoting intragroup hatred as well as by those wanting to spread tolerance. And the sociological understanding of the nature of human solidarity can be employed in the service of both totalitarian and democratic regimes. It is sobering to realize that the same processes that generate consensus can be manipulated by a social group worker in a summer camp in the Adirondacks and by a Communist brainwasher in a prisoner camp in China. One may readily grant that the sociologist can sometimes be called upon to give advice when it comes to changing certain social conditions deemed undesirable. But the image of the sociologist as social reformer suffers from the same confusion as the image of him as social worker.

If these images of the sociologist all have an element of "cultural lag" about them, we can now turn to some other images that are of more recent date and refer themselves to more recent developments in the discipline. One such image is that of the sociologist as a gatherer of statistics about human behavior. The sociologist is here seen essentially as an aide-de-camp to an IBM machine. He goes out with a questionnaire, interviews people selected at random, then goes home, enters his tabulations onto innumerable punch cards, which are then fed into a machine. In all of this, of course, he is supported by a large staff and a very large budget. Included in this image is the implication that the results of all this effort are picayune, a pedantic restatement of what everybody knows anyway. As one observer remarked pithily, a sociologist is a fellow who spends $100,000 to find his way to a house of ill repute.

This image of the sociologist has been strengthened in the public mind by the activities of many agencies that might well be called parasociological, mainly agencies concerned with public opinion and market trends. The pollster has become a well-known figure in American life, importuning people about their views from foreign policy to toilet paper. Since the methods used in the pollster business bear close resemblance to sociological research, the growth of this image of the sociologist is understandable. The Kinsey studies of American sexual behavior have probably greatly augmented the impact of this image. The fundamental sociological question, whether concerned with premarital petting or with Republican votes or with the incidence of gang knifings, is always presumed to be "how often?" or "how many?" Incidentally the very few jokes current about sociologists usually relate to this statistical image (which jokes had better be left to the imagination of the reader).

Now it must be admitted, albeit regretfully, that this image of the sociologist and his trade is not altogether a product of fantasy. Beginning shortly after World War I, American sociology turned rather resolutely away from theory to an intensive preoccupation with narrowly circumscribed empirical studies. In connection with this turn, sociologists increasingly refined their research techniques. Among these, very naturally, statistical techniques figured prominently. Since about the mid-1940s there has been a revival of interest in sociological theory, and there are good indications that this tendency away from a narrow empiricism is continuing to gather momentum. It remains true, however, that a goodly part of the sociological enterprise in this country continues to consist of little studies of obscure fragments of social life, irrelevant to any broader theoretical concern. One glance at the table of contents of the major sociological journals or at the list of papers read at sociological conventions will confirm this statement.

The political and economic structure of American academic life encourages this pattern, and not only in sociology. Colleges and universities are normally administered by very busy people with little time or inclination to delve into the esoterica produced by their scholarly employees. Yet these administrators are called upon to make decisions concerning the hiring and firing, promotion and tenure of their faculty personnel. What criteria should they use in these decisions? They cannot be expected to read what their professors write, having no time for such activities and, especially in the more technical disciplines, lacking the necessary qualifications to judge the material. The opinions of immediate colleagues of the professors in question are suspect *a priori*, the normal academic institution being a jungle of bitter warfare between faculty factions, none of which can be relied upon for an objective judgment of members of either his own or an opposing group. To ask the views of students would be even more uncertain procedure. Thus the administrators are left with a number of equally unsatisfactory options. They can go on the principle that the institution is one happy family, in which every member advances steadily up the status ladder regardless of merit. This has been tried often enough, but becomes ever more difficult in an age of competition for the favor of the public and the funds of foundations. Another option is to rely on the advice of one clique, chosen on some more or less rational basis. This creates obvious political difficulties for the administrator of a group chronically defensive about its independence. The third option, the one most common today, is to fall back on the criterion of productivity as used in the business world. Since it is very difficult indeed to judge the productivity of a scholar with whose field one is not well acquainted, one must somehow try to find out how acceptable the scholar is to unprejudiced colleagues in his field. It is then assumed that such acceptability can be deduced from the number of books or articles that publishers or editors of professional publications are willing to accept from the man in question. This forces scholars to concentrate on work that can easily and speedily be converted into a respectable little article likely to be accepted for publication in a professional journal. For sociologists this means some little empirical study of a nar-

rowly confined topic. In most instances such studies will require the application of statistical techniques. Since most professional journals in the field are suspicious of articles that do not contain at least some statistical material, this tendency is further strengthened. And so eager young sociologists stranded somewhere in hinterland institutions, yearning for the richer pastures of the better universities, supply us with a steady stream of little statistical studies of the dating habits of their students, the political opinions of the surrounding natives or the class system of some hamlet within commuting distance of their campus. It might be added here that this system is not quite so terrible as it may seem to the newcomer to the field, since its ritual requirements are well known to all concerned. As a result, the sensible person reads the sociological journals mainly for the book reviews and the obituaries, and goes to sociological meetings only if he is looking for a job or has other intrigues to carry on.

The prominence of statistical techniques in American sociology today has, then, certain ritual functions that are readily understandable in view of the power system within which most sociologists have to make a career. In fact, most sociologists have little more than a cookbook knowledge of statistics, treating it with about the same mixture of awe, ignorance and timid manipulation as a poor village priest would the mighty Latin cadences of Thomist theology. Once one has realized these things, however, it should be clear that sociology ought not to be judged by these aberrations. One then becomes, as it were, sociologically sophisticated about sociology, and enabled to look beyond the outward signs to whatever inward grace may be hidden behind them.

Statistical data by themselves do not make sociology. They become sociology only when they are sociologically interpreted, put within a theoretical frame of reference that is sociological. Simple counting, or even correlating different items that one counts, is not sociology. There is almost no sociology in the Kinsey reports. This does not mean that the data in these studies are not true or that they cannot be relevant to sociological understanding. They are, taken by themselves, raw materials that can be used in sociological interpretation. The interpretation, however, must be broader than the data themselves. So the sociologist cannot arrest himself at the frequency tables of premarital petting or extramarital pederasty. These enumerations are meaningful to him only in terms of their much broader implications for an understanding of institutions and values in our society. To arrive at such understanding the sociologist will often have to apply statistical techniques, especially when he is dealing with the mass phenomena of modern social life. But sociology consists of statistics as little as philology consists of conjugating irregular verbs or chemistry of making nasty smells in test tubes.

Another image of the sociologist current today and rather closely related to that of statistician is the one that sees him as a man mainly concerned in developing a scientific methodology that he can then impose on human phenomena. This image is frequently held by people in the humanities and presented as proof that sociology is a form of intellectual barbarism. One part of this criticism of sociology by the *littérateurs* is often a scathing commentary on the outlandish jargon in which much sociological writing is couched. By contrast, of course, the one who makes these criticisms offers himself as a guardian of the classical traditions of humane learning.

It would be quite possible to meet such criticism by an argument *ad hominem.* Intellectual barbarism seems to be fairly evenly distributed in the main scholarly disciplines dealing with the phenomenon "man." However, it is undignified to argue *ad hominem,* so we shall readily admit that, indeed, there is much that passes today under the heading of sociology that is justly called barbarian, if that word is intended to denote an ignorance of history and philosophy, narrow expertise without wider horizons, a preoccupation with technical skills, and total insensitivity to the uses of language. Once more, these elements can themselves be understood sociologically in terms of certain characteristics of contemporary academic life. The competition for prestige and jobs in fields rapidly becoming more and more complex forces specialization that all too frequently leads to a depressing parochialism of interests. But it would again be inaccurate to identify sociology with this much more pervasive intellectual trend.

Sociology has, from its beginnings, understood itself as a science. There has been much controversy about the precise meaning of this self-definition. For instance, German sociologists have emphasized the difference between the social and the natural sciences much more strongly than their French or American colleagues. But the allegiance of sociologists to the scientific ethos has meant everywhere a willingness to be bound by certain scientific canons of procedure. If the sociologist remains faithful to his calling, his statements must be arrived at through the observation of certain rules of evidence that allow others to check on or to repeat or to develop his findings further. It is this scientific discipline that often supplies the motive for reading a sociological work as against, say, a novel on the same topic that might describe matters in much more impressive and convincing language. As sociologists tried to develop their scientific rules of evidence, they were compelled to reflect upon methodological problems. This is why methodology is a necessary and valid part of the sociological enterprise.

At the same time it is quite true that some sociologists, especially in America, have become so preoccupied with methodological questions that they have ceased to be interested in society at all. As a result, they have found out nothing of significance about any aspect of social life, since in science as in love a concentration on technique is quite likely to lead to impotence. Much of this fixation on methodology can be explained in terms of the urge of a relatively new discipline to find acceptance on the academic scene. Since science is an almost sacred entity among Americans in general and American academicians in particular, the desire to emulate the procedures of the older natural sciences is very strong among the newcomers in the marketplace of erudition. Giving in to this desire, the experimental psychologists, for instance, have succeeded to such an extent that their studies have commonly nothing more to do with anything that human beings are or do. The irony of this process lies in the fact that natural scientists themselves have been giving up the very positivistic dogmatism that their emulators are still straining to adopt. But this is not our concern here. Suffice it to say that sociologists have succeeded in avoiding some of the more grotesque exaggerations of this "methodism," as compared with some fields close by. As they become more secure in their academic status, it may be expected that this methodological inferiority complex will diminish even further.

The charge that many sociologists write in a barbaric dialect must also be admitted with similar reservations. Any scientific discipline must develop a terminology. This is self-evident for a discipline such as, say, nuclear physics that deals with matters unknown to most people and for which no words exist in common speech. However, terminology is possibly even more important for the social sciences, just because their subject matter *is* familiar and just because words *do* exist to denote it. Because we are well acquainted with the social institutions that surround us, our perception of them is imprecise and often erroneous. In very much the same way most of us will have considerable difficulty giving an accurate description of our parents, husbands or wives, children or close friends. Also, our language is often (and perhaps blessedly) vague and confusing in its references to social reality. Take for an example the concept of *class*, a very important one in sociology. There must be dozens of meanings that this term may have in common speech—income brackets, races, ethnic groups, power cliques, intelligence ratings, and many others. It is obvious that the sociologist must have a precise, unambiguous definition of the concept if his work is to proceed with any degree of scientific rigor. In view of these facts, one can understand that some sociologists have been tempted to invent altogether new words to avoid the semantic traps of the vernacular usage. We would contend, then, that some of these neologisms have been necessary. We would also contend, however, that most sociology can be presented in intelligible English with but a little effort and that a good deal of contemporary "sociologese" can be understood as a self-conscious mystification. Here again, however, we are confronted with an intellectual phenomenon that affects other fields as well. There may be a connection with the strong influence of German academic life in a formative period in the development of American universities. Scientific profundity was gauged by the ponderousness of scientific language. If scientific prose was unintelligible to any but the narrow circle of initiates to the field in question, this was *ipso facto* proof of its intellectual respectability. Much American

scholarly writing still reads like a translation from the German. This is certainly regrettable. It has little to do, however, with the legitimacy of the sociological enterprise as such.

Finally, we would look at an image of the sociologist not so much in his professional role as in his being, supposedly, a certain kind of person. This is the image of the sociologist as a detached, sardonic observer, and a cold manipulator of men. Where this image prevails, it may represent an ironic triumph of the sociologist's own efforts to be accepted as a genuine scientist. The sociologist here becomes the self-appointed superior man, standing off from the warm vitality of common existence, finding his satisfactions not in living but in coolly appraising the lives of others, filing them away in little categories, and thus presumably missing the real significance of what he is observing. Further, there is the notion that, when he involves himself in social processes at all, the sociologist does so as an uncommitted technician, putting his manipulative skills at the disposal of the powers that be.

This last image is probably not very widely held. It is mainly held by people concerned for political reasons with actual or possible misuses of sociology in modern societies. There is not very much to say about this image by way of refutation. As a general portrait of the contemporary sociologist it is certainly a gross distortion. It fits very few individuals that anyone is likely to meet in this country today. The problem of the political role of the social scientist is, nevertheless, a very genuine one. For instance, the employment of sociologists by certain branches of industry and government raises moral questions that ought to be faced more widely than they have been so far. These are, however, moral questions that concern all men in positions of responsibility in modern society. The image of the sociologist as an observer without compassion and a manipulator without conscience need not detain us further here. By and large, history produces very few Talleyrands. As for contemporary sociologists, most of them would lack the emotional equipment for such a role, even if they should aspire to it in moments of feverish fantasy.

How then are we to conceive of the sociologist? In discussing the various images of him that abound in the popular mind we have already brought out certain elements that would have to go into our conception. We can now put them together. In doing so, we shall construct what sociologists themselves call an "ideal type." This means that what we delineate will not be found in reality in its pure form. Instead, one will find approximations to it and deviations from it, in varying degrees. Nor is it to be understood as an empirical average. We would not even claim that all individuals who now call themselves sociologists will recognize themselves without reservations in our conception, nor would we dispute the right of those who do not so recognize themselves to use the appellation. Our business is not excommunication. We would, however, contend that our "ideal type" corresponds to the self-conception of most sociologists in the mainstream of the discipline, both historically (at least in this century) and today.

The sociologist, then, is someone concerned with understanding society in a disciplined way. The nature of this discipline is scientific. This means that what the sociologist finds and says about the social phenomena he studies occurs within a certain rather strictly defined frame of reference. One of the main characteristics of this scientific frame of reference is that operations are bound by certain rules of evidence. As a scientist, the sociologist tries to be objective, to control his personal preferences and prejudices, to perceive clearly rather than to judge normatively. This restraint, of course, does not embrace the totality of the sociologist's existence as a human being, but is limited to his operations *qua* sociologist. Nor does the sociologist claim that his frame of reference is the only one within which society can be looked at. For that matter, very few scientists in any field would claim today that one should look at the world only scientifically. The botanist looking at a daffodil has no reason to dispute the right of the poet to look at the same object in a very different manner. There are many ways of playing. The point is not that one denies other people's games but that one is clear about the rules of one's own. The game of the sociologist, then, uses scientific rules. As a result, the sociologist must be clear in his own mind as to the meaning of these rules. That is, he must concern himself with methodological questions. Methodology does not constitute his goal. The latter, let us recall once more, is the attempt to understand society. Methodology helps in reaching this goal. In order to understand society, or that segment of it that he is studying at the moment, the sociologist will use a variety of means. Among these are statistical techniques. Statistics can be very useful in answering certain sociological questions. But statistics does not constitute sociology. As a scientist, the sociologist will have to be concerned with the exact significance of the terms he is using. That is, he will have to be careful about terminology. This does not have to mean that he must invent a new language of his own, but it does mean that he cannot naïvely use the language of everyday discourse. Finally, the interest of the sociologist is primarily theoretical. That is, he is interested in understanding for its own sake. He may be aware of or even concerned with the practical applicability and consequences of his findings, but at that point he leaves the sociological frame of reference as such and moves into realms of values, beliefs and ideas that he shares with other men who are not sociologists.

We daresay that this conception of the sociologist would meet with very wide consensus within the discipline today. But we would like to go a little bit further here and ask a somewhat more personal (and therefore, no doubt, more controversial) question. We would like to ask not only what it is that the sociologist is doing but also what it is that drives him to it. Or, to use the phrase Max Weber used in a similar connection, we want to inquire a little into the nature of the sociologist's demon. In doing so, we shall evoke an image that is not so much ideal-typical in the above sense but more confessional in the sense of personal commitment. Again, we are not interested in excommunicating anyone. The game of sociology goes on in a spacious playground. We are just describing a little more closely those we would like to tempt to join our game.

We would say then that the sociologist (that is, the one we would really like to invite to our game) is a person intensively, endlessly, shamelessly interested in the doings of men. His natural habitat is all the human gathering places of the world, wherever men come together. The sociologist may be interested in many other things. But his consuming interest remains in the world of men, their institutions, their history, their passions. And since he is interested in men, nothing that men do can be altogether tedious for him. He will naturally be interested in the events that engage men's ultimate beliefs, their moments of tragedy and grandeur and ecstasy. But he will also be fascinated by the commonplace, the everyday. He will know reverence, but this reverence will not prevent him from wanting to see and to understand. He may sometimes feel revulsion or contempt. But this also will not deter him from wanting to have his questions answered. The sociologist, in his quest for understanding, moves through the world of men without respect for the usual lines of demarcation. Nobility and degradation, power and obscurity, intelligence and folly—these are equally *interesting* to him, however unequal they may be in his personal values or tastes. Thus his questions may lead him to all possible levels of society, the best and the least known places, the most respected and the most despised. And, if he is a good sociologist, he will find himself in all these places because his own questions have so taken possession of him that he has little choice but to seek for answers.

It would be possible to say the same things in a lower key. We could say that the sociologist, but for the grace of his academic title, is the man who must listen to gossip despite himself, who is tempted to look through keyholes, to read other people's mail, to open closed cabinets. Before some otherwise unoccupied psychologist sets out now to construct an aptitude test for sociologists on the basis of sublimated voyeurism, let us quickly say that we are speaking merely by way of analogy. Perhaps some little boys consumed with curiosity to watch their maiden aunts in the bathroom later become inveterate sociologists. This is quite uninteresting. What interests us is the curiosity that grips any sociologist in front of a closed door behind which there are human voices. If he is a good sociologist, he will want to open that door, to understand these voices. Behind each closed door he will anticipate some new facet of human life not yet perceived and understood.

The sociologist will occupy himself with matters that others regard as too sacred or as too distasteful for dispassionate investigation. He will find rewarding the company of priests or of prostitutes, depending not on his personal preferences but on the questions he happens to be asking at the moment. He will also concern himself with matters that others may find much too boring. He will be interested in the human interaction that goes with warfare or with great intellectual discoveries, but also in the relations between people employed in a restaurant or between a group of little girls playing with their dolls. His main focus of attention is not the ultimate significance of what men do, but the action in itself, as another example of the infinite richness of human conduct. So much for the image of our playmate.

In these journeys through the world of men the sociologist will inevitably encounter other professional Peeping Toms. Sometimes these will resent his presence, feeling that he is poaching on their preserves. In some places the sociologist will meet up with the economist, in others with the political scientist, in yet others with the psychologist or the ethnologist. Yet chances are that the questions that have brought him to these same places are different from the ones that propelled his fellow-trespassers. The sociologist's questions always remain essentially the same: "What are people doing with each other here?" "What are their relationships to each other?" "How are these relationships organized in institutions?" "What are the collective ideas that move men and institutions?" In trying to answer these questions in specific instances, the sociologist will, of course, have to deal with economic or political matters, but he will do so in a way rather different from that of the economist or the political scientist. The scene that he contemplates is the same human scene that these other scientists concern themselves with. But the sociologist's angle of vision is different. When this is understood, it becomes clear that it makes little sense to try to stake out a special enclave within which the sociologist will carry on business in his own right. Like Wesley the sociologist will have to confess that his parish is the world. But unlike some latter-day Wesleyans he will gladly share this parish with others. There is, however, one traveler whose path the sociologist will cross more often than anyone else's on his journeys. This is the historian. Indeed, as soon as the sociologist turns from the present to the past, his preoccupations are very hard indeed to distinguish from those of the historian. However, we shall leave this relationship to a later part of our considerations. Suffice it to say here that the socio-logical journey will be much impoverished unless it is punctuated frequently by conversation with that other particular traveler.

Any intellectual activity derives excitement from the moment it becomes a trail of discovery. In some fields of learning this is the discovery of worlds previously unthought and unthinkable. This is the excitement of the astronomer or of the nuclear physicist on the antipodal boundaries of the realities that man is capable of conceiving. But it can also be the excitement of bacteriology or geology. In a different way it can be the excitement of the linguist discovering new realms of human expression or of the anthropologist exploring human customs in faraway countries. In such discovery, when undertaken with passion, a widening of awareness, sometimes a veritable transformation of consciousness, occurs. The universe turns out to be much more wonderfull than one had ever dreamed. The excitement of sociology is usually of a different sort. Sometimes, it is true, the sociologist penetrates into worlds that had previously been quite unknown to him—for instance, the world of crime, or the world of some bizarre religious sect, or the world fashioned by the exclusive concerns of some group such as medical specialists or military leaders or advertising executives. However, much of the time the sociologist moves in sectors of experience that are familiar to him and to most people in his society. He investigates communities, institutions and activities that one can read about every day in the newspapers. Yet there is another excitement of discovery beckoning in his investigations. It is not the excitement of coming upon the totally unfamiliar, but rather the excitement of finding the familiar becoming transformed in its meaning. The fascination of sociology lies in the fact that its perspective makes us see in a new light the very world in which we have lived all our lives. This also constitutes a transformation of consciousness. Moreover, this transformation is more relevant existentially than that of many other intellectual disciplines, because it is more difficult to segregate in some special compartment of the mind. The astronomer does not live in the remote galaxies, and the nuclear physicist can, outside his laboratory, eat and laugh and marry and vote without thinking about the insides of the atom. The geologist looks at rocks only at appropriate times, and the linguist speaks English with his wife. The sociologist lives in society, on the job and off it. His own life, inevitably, is part of his subject matter. Men being what they are, sociologists too manage to segregate their professional insights from their everyday affairs. But it is a rather difficult feat to perform in good faith.

The sociologist moves in the common world of men, close to what most of them would call real. The categories he employs in his analyses are only refinements of the categories by which other men live—power, class, status, race, ethnicity. As a result, there is a deceptive simplicity and obviousness about some sociological investigations. One reads them, nods at the familiar scene, remarks that one has heard all this before and don't people have better things to do than to waste their time on truisms—until one is suddenly brought up against an insight that radically questions everything one had previously assumed about this familiar scene. This is the point at which one begins to sense the excitement of sociology.

Let us take a specific example. Imagine a sociology class in a Southern college where almost all the students are white Southerners. Imagine a lecture on the subject of the racial system of the South. The lecturer is talking here of matters that have been familiar to his students from the time of their infancy. Indeed, it may be that they are much more familiar with the minutiae of this system than he is. They are quite bored as a result. It seems to them that he is only using more pretentious words to describe what they already know. Thus he may use the term "caste," one commonly used now by American sociologists to describe the Southern racial system. But in explaining the term he shifts to traditional Hindu society, to make it clearer. He then goes on to analyze the magical beliefs inherent in caste tabus, the social dynamics of commensalism and connubium, the economic interests concealed within the system, the way in which religious beliefs relate to the tabus, the effects of the caste system upon the industrial development of the society and vice versa —all in India. But suddenly India is not very far away at all. The lecture then goes back to its Southern theme. The familiar now seems not quite so familiar any more. Questions are raised that are new, perhaps raised angrily, but raised all the same. And at least some of the students have begun to understand that there are functions involved in this business of race that they have not read about in the newspapers (at least not those in their home-towns) and that their parents have not told them—partly, at least, because neither the newspapers nor the parents knew about them.

It can be said that the first wisdom of soci-ology is this—things are not what they seem. This too is a deceptively simple statement. It ceases to be simple after a while. Social reality turns out to have many layers of meaning. The discovery of each new layer changes the per-ception of the whole.

Anthropologists use the term "culture shock" to describe the impact of a totally new cul-ture upon a newcomer. In an extreme instance such shock will be experienced by the West-ern explorer who is told, halfway through din-ner, that he is eating the nice old lady he had been chatting with the previous day—a shock with predictable physiological if not moral consequences. Most explorers no longer en-counter cannibalism in their travels today. However, the first encounters with polygamy or with puberty rites or even with the way some nations drive their automobiles can be quite a shock to an American visitor. With the shock may go not only disapproval or disgust but a sense of excitement that things can *really* be that different from what they are at home. To some extent, at least, this is the excitement of any first travel abroad. The experience of sociological discovery could be described as "culture shock" minus geographical displace-ment. In other words, the sociologist travels at home—with shocking results. He is unlikely to find that he is eating a nice old lady for din-ner. But the discovery, for instance, that his own church has considerable money invested in the missile industry or that a few blocks from his home there are people who engage in cultic orgies may not be drastically different in emotional impact. Yet we would not want to imply that sociological discoveries are al-ways or even usually outrageous to moral sen-timent. Not at all. What they have in common with exploration in distant lands, however, is

the sudden illumination of new and unsus-pected facets of human existence in society. This is the excitement and, as we shall try to show later, the humanistic justification of so-ciology.

People who like to avoid shocking discov-eries, who prefer to believe that society is just what they were taught in Sunday School, who like the safety of the rules and the maxims of what Alfred Schuetz has called the "world-taken-for-granted," should stay away from so-ciology. People who feel no temptation before closed doors, who have no curiosity about hu-man beings, who are content to admire sce-nery without wondering about the people who live in those houses on the other side of that river, should probably also stay away from sociology. They will find it unpleasant or, at any rate, unrewarding. People who are in-terested in human beings only if they can change, convert or reform them should also be warned, for they will find sociology much less useful than they hoped. And people whose interest is mainly in their own conceptual con-structions will do just as well to turn to the study of little white mice. Sociology will be satisfying, in the long run, only to those who can think of nothing more entrancing than to watch men and to understand things human.

It may now be clear that we have, albeit deliberately, understated the case in the title of this chapter. To be sure, sociology is an individual pastime in the sense that it inter-ests some men and bores others. Some like to observe human beings, others to experiment with mice. The world is big enough to hold all kinds and there is no logical priority for one interest as against another. But the word "pastime" is weak in describing what we mean. Sociology is more like a passion. The sociological perspective is more like a demon that possesses one, that drives one compell-ingly, again and again, to the questions that are its own. An introduction to sociology is, therefore, an invitation to a very special kind of passion. No passion is without its dangers. The sociologist who sells his wares should make sure that he clearly pronounces a *caveat emptor* quite early in the transaction.

THE SUBJECT MATTER OF SOCIOLOGY

This selection is by one of the first of Comte's countrymen to rally to the standard of sociology. It poses and attempts to answer the question, "Is there a special subject matter of sociology?"

The selection was written at a time of great self-consciousness on the part of the sociological profession. Comte had already distinguished between sociology and its philosophical ancestry, but Emile Durkheim and his colleagues felt the need further to delineate the new science from the other sciences of man, specifically biology and psychology. In *The Rules of the Sociological Method*, from which this selection is drawn, Durkheim proposed that there exists a set of phenomena that are specifically social and that cannot be explained by principles applicable to individuals. Biological and psychological explanations for these phenomena are thus ruled out, and specifically social explanations are required. These social phenomena comprise the distinctive subject matter of sociology.

> Social phenomena are the principles of behavior—ways of doing and ways of being—that characterize a group. They can be recognized by their coercive power, which is most evident when a group member tries to resist these principles. Although social phenomena have effects on the behavior of all group members, they are external to individuals, as in law and custom. Their expression in the behavior of individuals is affected by biological and psychological peculiarities that "contaminate" the social phenomena. The pure effects of social phenomena are therefore to be distinguished from those of biology and psychology through the study of rates or averages, which balance out individual peculiarities.
>
> Although some social phenomena take the form of transitory forces or "social currents," the majority are traditional and established, and are learned by the individual through childhood education. Because the individual therefore desires to behave in accordance with the principles of behavior accepted in his society, he is usually unaware of their constraint. However, social phenomena are nonetheless real. They can be studied independently of individuals, and this study is the proper concern of the science of sociology.

Some sociologists have dissented from Durkheim's extreme "sociological realism," which insists on the externality of social phenomena and which accords the individual a negligible or nonexistent contribution to them. (The opposing point of view is stressed in the "great man" theories of history.) However, modern sociologists generally agree with the proposition that there is a realm of phenomena that is distinctly social, that centers in law and custom, and that cannot efficiently be explained in terms of psychological or biological principles. This is the subject matter of sociology.

Selection 2
FROM THE RULES OF THE SOCIOLOGICAL METHOD
Emile Durkheim

Before trying to discover the method that best suits the study of social phenomena, it is essential to know just what these are. The question is all the more important as this term is employed rather imprecisely. It is commonly used to designate almost every phenomenon which occurs within a society as long as it offers, in a general sense, some social interest. However, by this reckoning, there are practically no human events which could not be called "social." Every individual drinks, sleeps, eats, and thinks, and it is to society's every interest that these functions are performed regularly. If, however, these phenomena were social, sociology would have no real subject matter of its own, and its field of study would

Translated by Judith Atkins Ross from *Les Règles de la Méthode Sociologique* by Emile Durkheim, 1895.

be indistinguishable from those of biology and psychology.

In reality, though, there is, in every society, a circumscribed group of phenomena which are clearly distinguished from those studied by the natural sciences. When I fulfill my role as brother, husband, or citizen, when I carry out obligations which I have incurred, I am discharging duties that are defined by law and custom apart from myself and my actions. Even when these obligations match my own feelings, and I am subjectively aware of their reality, this reality still remains objective—for I didn't create these duties and roles; they were learned. Just think how often we happen not to know the details of certain of our responsibilities and, in order to learn them, must consult the law and its authorized representatives. Similarly, the religious beliefs and observances of the church-goer are ready-made and waiting for him at birth. Since they existed before him, they therefore exist independently of him. The language I use to express my thoughts, the currency I employ to pay my debts, the instruments of credit I utilize in my business dealings, the practices followed by my profession, etc., all exist independently of the uses I make of them. If you take all the elements which form a society one by one, this will hold true for each of them.

So, then, we see here different ways of behaving, thinking, and feeling, all of which share this remarkable characteristic of existing independently of the individual mind. These types of behavior or thought not only exist outside of the individual, but they are endowed with an imperious and persuasive power by which they impress themselves on him, whether or not he wills it. Of course, when I willingly conform to them, this pressure is felt very little or not at all, since it is not necessary. But this pressure is still an inherent part of these phenomena, the proof of which is that this coercive power asserts itself as soon as I try to resist it. If I attempt to violate the law, it reacts so as to prevent my action, if there is time; to negate it (or possibly to rectify it) if already carried out; or to have me punished, if there is no other way to atone. As for important customs not embodied in the law, the public conscience restricts all offensive actions by keeping a close watch on the citizens' conduct and by using non-legal penalties.

In other cases, the constraint is less powerful, but it still exists. If I flaunt the usual social conventions—for instance, if I utterly ignore the customs of dress followed by my country or social class—the resultant isolation and the laughter I provoke produce the same effects, though somewhat reduced in force, as an actual punishment. In other respects this constraint remains effective but in an indirect form. I am not obliged to speak my native language to my own countrymen, nor to use legal currency, but it is impossible to do otherwise. If I tried to avoid these necessities my attempt would fail dismally. As a businessman, nothing prevents me from using eighteenth-century methods and procedures, but if I did, it would mean certain bankruptcy. Even when I can in fact free myself from these regulations and conventions, and violate them successfully, it is never without having to struggle against them. Even when they are overcome, their restraining power is felt by the resistance they have offered. There are no innovations, however successful, which have not come up against opposition of this sort.

We have, then, a set of phenomena, which consists of various ways of behaving, thinking, and feeling, existing independently of the individual and endowed with a persuasive power, or authority, by which they force themselves on him. Consequently, they cannot possibly be confused with either biological phenomena, which consist of organic processes, or with psychological phenomena, which exist only in and through the individual mind. Therefore, this new system constitutes a separate order of things, and the term "social" must be accorded to and reserved for these phenomena.

This term is appropriate, for obviously, since these phenomena are not based on the individual, they must derive from society—either society as a whole, or one of the groups which are included in the broader term, such as religious affiliations, political or literary movements, professional bodies, etc. Then again, the qualification applies to these phenomena alone; for the term "social" has a special significance only when it describes things that do not belong in any category of phenomena already specified and listed. It follows that these social phenomena form the proper domain of sociological study.

It is possible that the word "constraint,"

which we mentioned in defining these phenomena, might frighten off the zealous partisans of free will. They advocate the absolute self-determination of the individual, and find that man's dignity is slighted whenever he is made to feel less than completely his own master. Nowadays, however, it is generally acknowledged that most of our ideas and attitudes do not originate within ourselves, but come to us from the outside. They are able to penetrate our consciousness only by exercising a strong persuasive power. That is the whole meaning of our definition. We know, too, that social constraint is not necessarily incompatible with individuality.[1]

Since the examples we cited previously (legal and moral rules, religious dogma, monetary systems, etc.) all consist of established beliefs and practices, one might be led to think that social phenomena exist only as an aspect of an established social organization. But there are other phenomena that lack these crystallized forms, and yet that have the same objectivity and the same influence over the individual. These may be called "social currents" or mass emotions. For instance, the great waves of enthusiasm, indignation, or pity which sweep through a crowd do not originate in any one particular mind. They come to each of us from without and are liable to carry us away in spite of ourselves. In giving way wholeheartedly to these emotions, I may not feel the insistent pressure they exert on me, but the pressure becomes apparent as soon as I try to resist them. When a man tries to oppose a crowd demonstration, the very emotions he wants to repulse turn against him. Now, if this external power of coercion asserts itself so firmly in cases of resistance, then, whether or not we are aware of it, it must also exist when no resistance is offered. In such cases, we are victims of the illusion of having ourselves created something which actually forced itself on us from without.

Though the willingness with which we allow ourselves to be carried away may mask the pressure to which we have been subjected, it does not abolish this pressure (in the same way that air does not become any less heavy because we do not ordinarily feel its weight). Even if we have spontaneously gone along with the mass emotion, the impression we have received is very different from what we should have experienced had we been alone.

Once the crowd disperses, once the social currents have ceased to influence us, and we are alone again, the emotions that swept over us may seem strange and even unreal. They might even horrify us by seeming so contrary to our "true nature." We realize, then, that these emotions and feelings were impressed on us to a far greater degree than they were generated by us. Thus, a group of people who are perfectly harmless for the most part may be drawn into lynchings, riots, and other atrocities when gathered into a mob. What we say about these transitory outbursts applies equally to the more permanent currents of opinion on religious, political, literary, or artistic matters which constantly develop around us—in society as a whole, or within more limited groups.

Our definition of the social phenomenon as existing independently of the individual, and exerting a power of constraint over him, can be confirmed by a typical example from everyday life—the way in which children are raised. Examining the facts as they are and have always been, one immediately sees that all education consists of a continual effort to impose certain modes of behavior on the child. We teach him ways of seeing, feeling, and acting which he could never acquire spontaneously. From the very beginning of his life we insist that he eat, drink, and sleep regularly: we require him to be clean, quiet, and obedient. Later on, we compel him to be considerate of others, to respect social customs and conventions, to work hard, etc. If, with time, this pressure ceases to be apparent, it is because it gradually gives rise to habits and tendencies which render such constraint unnecessary, yet which do not replace it, since constraint remains the source of these habits.

It is true that, according to Spencer, a rational education ought to condemn such methods, and allow the child to develop in complete freedom. As this theory of education has never been practiced by any known group, however, it remains simply a personal expression of opinion, and does not contradict the observations I have just made. These observations are particularly interesting when one considers the real object of education, which is the socialization* of the individual. This learning process shows in microcosm the historical development of the social being. The pressure

* Acquisition of culture (see Chapter 7).—Ed.

to which the child is submitted is the pressure of the social environment, which tends to fashion him in its own image through the medium of parents and teachers.

A social phenomenon cannot be defined by its universality. The fact that the same thought is found in every mind, or that a movement is repeated by every individual, doesn't necessarily make it a social phenomenon. If sociologists in the past have been satisfied to cite this universal quality in a definition of social phenomena, they have mistakenly confused them with what might be called their individual expressions. Actually, it is the collective* aspect of the beliefs, tendencies, and practices of a group that characterizes social phenomena. The individual manifestations of collective behavior are something else again. This duality is plainly demonstrated by the fact that these two orders of phenomena are often found dissociated from one another. In fact, some of these ways of acting and thinking acquire, through repetition, a certain rigidity of form which serves to crystallize them and which isolates this behavior from the particular acts that reflect it. Some collective behavior thus assumes a perceptible form, so to speak, and constitutes a reality in its own right, quite distinct from the individual phenomena which make it up. A social phenomenon is not only inherent in the successive acts it engenders but, by a prerogative wholly lacking in the biological field, it can be permanently expressed in a formula or model, which can then be repeated by word of mouth, transmitted through education, or defined in writing. Such is the origin and nature of legal and social rules, popular sayings and proverbs, the professions of faith which set forth religious or political beliefs, the aesthetic standards drawn up by artistic or literary movements, etc. None of these can be entirely reproduced in any of their individual applications since social phenomena can exist in theory alone, even without actually being applied.

Of course, this dissociation we have been discussing may not always be clearly evident. The very fact of its obvious existence in the numerous and important cases just cited, though, is sufficient to prove that a social phenomenon is something quite distinct from its

* This word in Durkheim connotes "obligatory." —Ed.

individual manifestations. Even when this dissociation is not readily visible, certain methodological devices may help to disclose it. It is really essential to do so, if we want to separate the social phenomenon from its alloys and examine it in a pure state. There are certain currents of opinion, whose intensity varies with time and place, which impel one group toward a high number of marriages, for example, another toward more suicides, or more or fewer births, etc. These currents are clearly social phenomena. At the first sight they seem inseparable from the forms they take in individual cases, but statistics furnish us with the means of isolating them. They are, in fact, represented with considerable precision by birth, marriage, and suicide rates—that is, by the number obtained by dividing the average annual total of marriages, births, and suicides, by the number of men who are of an age to marry, beget children, or commit suicide.[2] Since each of these figures includes all the individual cases indiscriminately, the particular circumstances which may have had a share in the production of the phenomenon are neutralized and, consequently, do not contribute to its determination. The rate obtained, then, expresses a certain state of the "group mind."

These rates are social phenomena, detached from all foreign components. Their individual manifestations are, of course, to a certain extent social, since they partly reproduce a social model. Each of these manifestations, however, depends a great deal on the mental and physical make-up of the individual and the particular circumstances in which he finds himself. Strictly speaking, then, they are not really social phenomena. The sociologist finds these individual acts of interest, yet they do not form the immediate subject matter of sociology. We could call them socio-psychological, since they belong to two fields of study at once. We find similar compound phenomena in biological organisms, which are in turn studied by the inter-disciplinary natural sciences, such as biochemistry, for example.

One might object that a phenomenon can be social only if it is common to all members of society or, at least, to most of them—that is, only if it is generalized. This may be true, but it is general because it is collective (that is, more or less obligatory) and certainly not collective because it is general. The social phenomenon is a group condition which is found repeated in every individual because it has been imposed on him. It is found in each part because it exists in the whole, rather than in the whole because it exists in the parts. This becomes particularly evident in the beliefs and practices which have been handed down to us, ready-made, by previous generations. We accept and adopt them because, being collective and venerable, they are invested with a special authority that our education has taught us to recognize and respect. It should be noted that the vast majority of social phenomena reach us in this way. Even when the social phenomenon is partly dependent on our direct collaboration, its nature remains unchanged. The mass emotion that surges suddenly through a crowd is not simply the expression of what all the individuals feel in common; it is something quite different, as we have already shown. Such emotion is the result of people being together. It is a product of the actions, reactions and interactions among individuals in a group. If the mass emotion is echoed by each person, it is by virtue of the special force of its collective origin. If all hearts beat in tempo it is not because of a spontaneous and pre-established agreement, but rather because the same force propels them in the same direction. Each one is carried along by all.

We now reach the point where we can present and delineate the domain of sociology with some precision. It comprises only a limited group of phenomena. A social phenomenon is recognized by the externalized power of coercion it exercises, or is capable of exercising, over individuals. The presence of this power is in turn recognized either by the existence of a specific sanction, or by the resistance offered to the individual effort that tends to violate it. However, we can also define a social phenomenon by its diffusion within a group, provided that care is taken to add, as a second essential characteristic, that its existence remains independent of the individual forms it assumes in this diffusion. The last criterion may be easier to apply, in certain cases, than the first. Constraint is easy to ascertain when it is expressed externally through some direct reaction of society, as is the case in law, custom, beliefs, conventions, even in fashions and taste. But when it is only indirect, like the constraint exercised by an economic organization, it is not so readily perceived. Universality, in combination with an external objectivity, may be

easier to establish. The second part of our definition of social phenomena will be seen, then, as merely an expansion of the first; for if a mode of behavior whose existence is exterior to the human mind becomes universal, this can be brought about only by an application of coercive pressure by the group.[3]

All the phenomena on which our definition is based have, so far, been "ways of doing," or modes of behavior. There are also, however, "ways of being"; that is, phenomena exhibited in a pattern or structure. These diverse phenomena (e.g., distribution of population, channels of communications, kinds of housing, etc.) present the same characteristic by which we defined the others. The social structure is imposed on the individual in the same way as the behavioral phenomena which we discussed earlier. When we want to know how a society is divided politically, of what these divisions are composed, or what sort of coalition exists among them, physical inspection or geographic observations will be of no help in reaching an answer. These divisions are social even though they have a certain physical basis. We are able to understand this organization only through a study of public law, for it is determined by the law, just as our domestic and civil relations are. This political organization is therefore no less obligatory than the phenomena mentioned earlier. If the population crowds into our cities, instead of scattering throughout the countryside, it is because of a social tendency, a collective drive, which imposes this geographic concentration on individuals. We can no more arbitrarily choose the style of our houses than the type of clothing we do or do not wear; at least, both are equally obligatory. The direction and extent of internal migrations and commerce are determined by the means of communications available. Consequently, it should be necessary to add just one more category to the list of things we have enumerated which present the distinctive sign of a social phenomenon. This addition would be the concept "ways of being." Since the list was not meant to be rigorously exhaustive, this addition would not be absolutely essential.

In fact, it may not even be necessary, for these ways of being, or social structure, are really just a consolidation of social behavior (ways of doing). The political structure of a society is merely the manner in which the component segments have become accustomed to living with one another. If their relationships traditionally have been intimate, the different segments tend to fuse with one another or, in the contrary case, to retain their separate identities. The kind of dwelling is simply the type of house which our peers, and to some extent our ancestors, have been accustomed to building. Means of communications are just the channels which the regular shuttling of commerce and migration have developed. Certainly, if these structural or anatomical° phenomena (ways of being) were alone in presenting this permanence they could be considered a separate category. However, a legal regulation is no less permanent than an architectural style, yet the law is a physiological phenomenon (way of doing). A simple moral principle is, assuredly, more flexible than a professional custom, a fashion, or a fad,

° The terms "anatomical" and "physiological" are used in analogy to the biological study of structure and function.—Ed.

yet its forms are much more rigid. There is, then, a continuous range of nuances between the extremes marked by society's most structured phenomena and those free-flowing social tendencies which have not yet formed a definite pattern. These varying degrees of consolidation are the only differences that exist between them. Both are just life, more or less crystallized in form. It may be advisable to reserve the term "anatomical" for phenomena that concern the sub-stratum of society. It should be kept in mind, however, that they are similar in nature to the other social phenomena. Our definition will then include the relevant facts if we say: "A social phenomenon is every mode of behavior, fixed or not, that is capable of exerting an externalized power of constraint on the individual," or again, "every mode of behavior that is general throughout a given society, while at the same time existing in its own right, independent of its individual manifestations."[4]

Notes

[1] This is not to say that all constraint is normal. We will return to this point, farther on.

[2] It should be noted that suicides take place only at certain age levels, and vary in frequency according to age.

[3] It will be seen how this definition of a social phenomenon differs from the one on which M. Tarde bases his ingenious system. First of all, we want to state that our research has nowhere led us to observe that dominant influence, in the origin and development of collective phenomena, which M. Tarde attributes to imitation. Moreover, it seems to follow from our definition (which is not a theory, but a simple résumé of observed data) not

only that imitation does not always express the essential and characteristic features of a social phenomenon, but, in fact, that it never expresses them at all. Certainly, every social phenomenon is imitated—as we have just indicated, it has a tendency to become general—but that is because the phenomenon is social, i.e. compulsory. Its power of extension is not the cause, but the result of its sociological nature. Still, if only social phenomena produced this result, imitation might serve, if not to explain them, at least to define them. But an individual condition that sets off a sequence of effects remains just as complete a whole. Moreover, one may question the validity of using the term "imitation" to describe the dissemination

of a phenomenon due to a coercive influence. With this single expression, then, very different phenomena, which ought to be distinguished, are being confused.

[4] This close relationship between life and structure, organ and function, may easily be established in sociology, because of the existence of a whole series of directly observable intermediate stages, which show the connection between the extremes. Biology lacks this expedient, but it may be that the sociological inductions in this matter could be applied to biology as well. In other words, perhaps, in organisms as well as in societies, only differences in degree exist between the two orders of phenomena.

THE DESIGN OF SOCIOLOGICAL RESEARCH

In a discipline that accepts the scientific method as its guide, asserted facts must be supported by evidence of their validity. The performance of a classical experiment is a familiar and acceptable demonstration of this type. Classical experiments are by no means impossible in social science, and many have been performed. However, they tend to be rare in sociology, partly because of the difficulty and expense of experimenting upon groups, and partly because of fear that the experimental situation will "react" upon the human participants, causing the results to be valid only for groups upon which an experiment is being performed. For instance, people participating in a study designed to test the prejudice-reducing effect of a film may guess that they are in an experimental situation, and try to "help" the investigator by changing their answers to a questionnaire measuring their prejudice. The results would obviously be misleading.

It has been established that there are forms of investigation other than the classical experiment that will provide acceptable scientific evidence. However, nonexperimental forms of study often contain hazards that may lead to incorrect conclusions. In this selection, Samuel A. Stouffer discusses some nonexperimental research designs common in sociology and warns against their improper use. He also discusses the relationship of scientific method to scientific theory and raises the criterion of importance, as well as technical competence, in judging research.

The promise of social science has been slow in fulfillment. The reason for this failure is not the complexity of data and lack of objectivity mentioned by various critics, but rather the presence in social science of poor methods of investigation, leading to the acceptance of theories without adequate evidence. A source of this situation is the demand in our society for quick and ready answers, coupled with a lack of demand for rigorous proof.

The classical experiment is generally valid, but is seldom used. Alternative research designs may be easier, but the researcher must be alert to the weaknesses of these designs. Moreover, the researcher must be careful, having done a valid study, not to claim more generality for the results than the sample procedure and research conditions legitimately permit.

Good, valid research is usually expensive. To justify investing scarce resources in a project, the research must have importance in addition to validity. The best way to assure the importance of research is to direct it to testing theory. Particularly likely to be important is that study which investigates the contradictory claims of two competing theories, so that if the predictions yielded by one theory must be rejected, those of another theory are supported. Research that is limited to a few well-defined variables is more likely to succeed than a study concerning a large number of vaguely defined variables.

The exhortation in this paper to produce studies that are both valid and important expresses the ideal goal of all scientific research. One should not, however, gain from this paper the impression that the controlled experiment is the only proper method for the conduct of valid research. Even a very deficient research design, if it is the only one possible in the circumstances and it is interpreted with caution, may be of great value. Moreover, many deficient nonexperimental designs can be patched up by special **ad hoc** methods to yield validity as great as that of classical experiments. Stouffer rightly insists that the sociologist must be aware of possible deficiencies in order to correct for them, but partial knowledge, if recognized as such, is preferable to no knowledge at all.

Selection 3
SOME OBSERVATIONS ON STUDY DESIGN
Samuel A. Stouffer

As a youth I read a series of vigorous essays in the *Century Magazine* by its editor, the late Glenn Frank. His theme was that the natural sciences had remade the face of the earth; now had arrived the age of the social sciences. The same techniques which had worked their miracles in physics, chemistry, and biology should, in competent hands, achieve equally dazzling miracles in economics, political science, and sociology. That was a long time ago. The disconcerting fact is that people are writing essays just like that today. Of course, the last two decades have seen considerable progress in social science—in theory, in technique, and in the accumulation of data. It is true that the number of practitioners is pitifully few; only a few hundred research studies are reported annually in sociology, for example, as compared with more than twenty thousand studies summarized annually in *Biological Abstracts*. But the bright promise of the period when Frank was writing has not been fulfilled.

Two of the most common reasons alleged for slow progress are cogent, indeed.

The data of social science are awfully complex, it is said. And they involve values which sometimes put a strain on the objectivity of the investigator even when they do not incur resistance from the vested interests of our society. However, an important part of the trouble has very little to do with the subject matter of social science as such but, rather, is a product of our own bad work habits. That is why this paper on the subject of study design may be relevant. So much has been spoken and written on this topic that I make no pretense to originality. But in the course of a little experience, especially in an effort during the war to apply social psychology to military problems, and in an undertaking to nurture a new program of research in my university, I have encountered some frustrations which perhaps can be examined with profit.

A basic problem—perhaps *the* basic problem —lies deeply imbedded in the thoughtways of our culture. This is the implicit assumption

Reprinted from *American Journal of Sociology,* 55:4, 1950, pp. 355–361, with permission of the publisher.

that anybody with a little common sense and a few facts can come up at once with the correct answer on any subject. Thus the newspaper editor or columnist, faced with a column of empty space to fill with readable English in an hour, can speak with finality and authority on any social topic, however complex. He might not attempt to diagnose what is wrong with his sick cat; he would call a veterinarian. But he knows precisely what is wrong with any social institution and the remedies.

In a society which rewards quick and confident answers and does not worry about how the answers are arrived at, the social scientist is hardly to be blamed if he conforms to the norms. Hence, much social science is merely rather dull and obscure journalism; a few data and a lot of "interpretation." The fact that the so-called "interpretation" bears little or no relation to the data is often obscured by academic jargon. If the stuff is hard to read, it has a chance of being acclaimed as profound. The rewards are for the answers, however tediously expressed, and not for rigorously marshaled evidence.

In the army no one would think of adopting a new type of weapon without trying it out exhaustively on the firing range. But a new idea about handling personnel fared very differently. The last thing anybody ever thought about was trying out the idea experimentally. I recall several times when we had schemes for running an experimental tryout of an idea in the sociopsychological field. Usually one of two things would happen: the idea would be rejected as stupid without a tryout (it may have been stupid, too) or it would be seized on and applied generally and at once. When the provost marshal wanted us to look into the very low morale of the MP's, our attitude surveys suggested that there was room for very much better selectivity in job assignment. There were routine jobs like guarding prisoners which could be given to the duller MP's, and there were a good many jobs calling for intelligence, discretion, and skill in public relations. We thought that the smarter men might be assigned to these jobs and that the prestige of these jobs would be raised further if a sprinkling of returned veterans with plenty of ribbons and no current assignment could be included among them. We proposed a trial program of a reassignment system in a dozen MP outfits for the purpose of comparing the resulting morale with that in a dozen matched outfits which were left untouched. Did we get anywhere? No. Instead, several of our ideas were put into effect immediately throughout the army without any prior testing at all.

The army cannot be blamed for behavior like that. In social relations it is not the habit in our culture to demand evidence for an idea; plausibility is enough.

To alter the folkways, social science itself must take the initiative. We must be clear in our own minds what proof consists of, and we must, if possible, provide dramatic examples of the advantages of relying on something more than plausibility. And the heart of our problem lies in study design *in advance*, such that the evidence is not capable of a dozen alternative interpretations.

Basically, I think it is essential that we always keep in mind the model of a controlled experiment, even if in practice we may have to deviate from an ideal model. Take the simple accompanying diagram. The test of

	Before	After	After − Before
Experimental group	x_1	x_2	$d = x_2 - x_1$
Control group	x_1'	x_2'	$d' = x_2' - x_1'$

whether a difference d is attributable to what we think it is attributable to is whether d is significantly larger than d'.

We used this model over and over again during the war to measure the effectiveness of orientation films in changing soldiers' attitudes. These experiences are described in Volume III of our *Studies in Social Psychology in World War II*.[1]

One of the troubles with using this careful design was that the effectiveness of a single film when thus measured turned out to be so slight. If, instead of using the complete experimental design, we simply took an unselected sample of men and compared the attitudes of those who said they had seen a film with those who said they had not, we got much more impressive differences. This was more rewarding to us, too, for the management wanted to

believe the films were powerful medicine. The gimmick was the selective fallibility of memory. Men who correctly remembered seeing the films were likely to be those most sensitized to their message. Men who were bored or indifferent may have actually seen them but slept through them or just forgot.

Most of the time we are not able or not patient enough to design studies containing all four cells as in the diagram above. Sometimes we have only the top two cells, as in the accompanying diagram. In this situation we have

x_1	x_2	$d = x_2 - x_1$

two observations of the same individuals or groups taken at different times. This is often a very useful design. In the army, for example, we would take a group of recruits, ascertain their attitudes, and restudy the same men later. From this we could tell whose attitudes changed and in what direction (it was almost always for the worse, which did not endear us to the army!). But exactly what factors in the early training period were most responsible for deterioration of attitudes could only be inferred indirectly.

The panel study[*] is usually more informative than a more frequent design, which might be pictured thus:

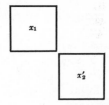

Here at one point in time we have one sample, and at a later point in time we have another sample. We observe that our measure, say, the mean, is greater for the recent sample than for the earlier one. But we are precluded from observing which men or what type of men shifted. Moreover, there is always the disturbing possibility that the populations in our two samples were initially different; hence the differences might not be attributable to conditions taking place in the time interval between the two observations. Thus we would study a group of soldiers in the United States and

[*] The design described immediately above.—Ed.

later ask the same questions of a group of soldiers overseas. Having matched the two groups of men carefully by branch of service, length of time in the army, rank, etc., we hoped that the results of the study would approximate what would be found if the same men could have been studied twice. But this could be no more than a hope. Some important factors could not be adequately controlled, for example, physical conditions. Men who went overseas were initially in better shape on the average than men who had been kept behind; but, if the follow-up study was in the tropics, there was a chance that unfavorable climate already had begun to take its toll. And so it went. How much men overseas changed called for a panel study as a minimum if we were to have much confidence in the findings.

A very common attempt to get the results of a controlled experiment without paying the price is with the design that might be as shown in the accompanying diagram. This is

usually what we get with correlation analysis. We have two or more groups of men whom we study at the same point in time. Thus we have men in the infantry and men in the air corps and compare their attitudes. How much of the difference between x'_2 and x_2 we can attribute to experience in a given branch of service and how much is a function of attributes of the men selected for each branch we cannot know assuredly. True, we can try to rule out various possibilities by matching; we can compare men from the two branches with the same age and education, for example. But there is all too often a wide-open gate through which other uncontrolled variables can march.

Sometimes, believe it or not, we have only one cell:

When this happens, we do not know much of anything. But we can still fill pages of social science journals with "brilliant analysis" if we use plausible conjecture in supplying missing cells from our imagination. Thus we may find that the adolescent today has wild ideas and

conclude that society is going to the dogs. We fill in the dotted cell representing our own yesterdays with hypothetical data, where x_1 represents us and x_2 our offspring. The tragicomic

part is that most of the public, including, I fear, many social scientists, are so acculturated that they ask for no better data.

I do not intend to disparage all research not conforming to the canons of the controlled experiment. I think that we will see more of full experimental design in sociology and social psychology in the future than in the past. But I am well aware of the practical difficulties of its execution, and I know that there are numberless important situations in which it is not feasible at all. What I am arguing for is awareness of the limitations of a design in which crucial cells are missing.

Sometimes by forethought and patchwork we can get approximations which are useful if we are careful to avoid overinterpretation. Let me cite an example:

In Europe during the war the army tested the idea of putting an entire platoon of Negro soldiers into a white infantry outfit. This was done in several companies. The Negroes fought beside white soldiers. After several months we were asked to find out what the white troops thought about the innovation. We found that only 7 per cent of the white soldiers in companies with Negro platoons said they disliked the idea very much, whereas 62 per cent of the white soldiers in divisions without Negro troops said they would dislike the idea very much if it were tried in their outfits. We have:

	Before	After
Experimental		7%
Control		62%

Now, were these white soldiers who fought beside Negroes men who were naturally more favorable to Negroes than the cross-section of white infantrymen? We did not think so, since, for example, they contained about the same proportion of southerners. The point was of some importance, however, if we were to make the inference that actual experience with

Negroes reduced hostility from 62 to 7 per cent. As a second-best substitute, we asked the white soldiers in companies with Negro platoons if they could recall how they felt when the innovation was first proposed. It happens that 67 per cent said they were initially opposed to the idea. Thus we could tentatively fill in a missing cell and conclude that, under the conditions obtaining, there probably had been a marked change in attitude.

Even if this had been a perfectly controlled experiment, there was still plenty of chance to draw erroneous inferences. The conclusions apply only to situations closely approximating those of the study. It happens, for example, that the Negroes involved were men who volunteered to leave rear-area jobs for combat duty. If other Negroes had been involved, the situation might have been different. Moreover, they had white officers. One army colonel who saw this study and whom I expected to ridicule it because he usually opposed innovations, surprised me by offering congratulations. "This proves," he said, "what I have been arguing in all my thirty years in the army—that niggers will do all right if you give 'em white officers!" Moreover, the study applied only to combat experience. Other studies would be needed to justify extending the findings to noncombat or garrison duty. In other words, one lone study, however well designed, can be a very dangerous thing if it is exploited beyond its immediate implications.

Now experiments take time and money, and there is no use denying that we in social science cannot be as prodigal with the replications as the biologist who can run a hundred experiments simultaneously by growing plants in all kinds of soils and conditions. The relative ease of experimentation in much—not all —of natural science goes far to account for the difference in quality of proof demanded by physical and biological sciences, on the one hand, and social scientists, on the other.

Though we cannot always design neat experiments when we want to, we can at least keep the experimental model in front of our eyes and behave cautiously when we fill in missing cells with dotted lines. But there is a further and even more important operation we can perform in the interest of economy. That lies in our choice of the initial problem.

Professor W. F. Ogburn always told his students to apply to a reported research conclusion the test, "How do you know it?" To this wise advice I should like to add a further question: "What of it?" I suspect that if before designing a study we asked ourselves, more conscientiously than we do, whether or not the study really is important, we would economize our energies for the few studies which are worth the expense and trouble of the kind of design I have been discussing.

Can anything be said about guides for selecting problems? I certainly think so. That is where theory comes in and where we social scientists have gone woefully astray.

Theory has not often been designed with research operations in mind. Theory as we have it in social science serves indispensably as a very broad frame of reference or general orientation. Thus modern theories of culture tell us that it is usually more profitable to focus on the learning process and the content of what is learned rather than on innate or hereditary traits. But they do not provide us with sets of interrelated propositions which can be put in the form: if x_1, given x_2, and x_3, then there is strong probability that we get x_4. Most of our propositions of that form, sometimes called "theory," are likely to be *ad hoc* common-sense observations which are not deducible from more general considerations and which are of the same quality as the observation, "If you stick your hand in a fire and hold it there, you will get burned."

Now in view of the tremendous cost in time and money of the ideal kind of strict empirical research operations, it is obvious that we cannot afford the luxury of conducting them as isolated fact-finding enterprises. Each should seek to be some sort of *experimentum crucis,* and, with rare exceptions, that will only happen if we see its place *beforehand* in a more general scheme of things. Especially, we need to look for situations where two equally plausible hypotheses deducible from more general theory lead to the expectation of different consequences. Then, if our evidence supports one and knocks out the other, we have accomplished something.

The best work of this sort in our field is probably being done today in laboratory studies of learning and of perception. I do not know of very good sociological examples. Yet in sociology experiments are possible. One of the most exciting, for example, was that initiated long before the war by Shaw and Mc-

Kay to see whether co-operative effort by adult role models within a delinquent neighborhood would reduce juvenile delinquency. So many variables are involved in a single study like that that it is not easy to determine which were crucial. But there was theory behind the study, and the experimental design provided for controlling at least some variables.

It may be that in sociology we will need much more thinking and many more descriptive studies involving random ratlike movements on the part of the researcher before we can even begin to state our problems so that they are in decent shape for fitting into an ideal design. However, I think that we can reduce to some extent the waste motion of the exploratory period if we try to act as if we have some a priori ideas and keep our eyes on the possible relevance of data to these ideas. This is easier said than done. So many interesting rabbit tracks are likely to be uncovered in the exploratory stages of research that one is tempted to chase rabbits all over the woods and forget what his initial quarry was.

Exploratory research is of necessity fumbling, but I think that the waste motion can be reduced by the self-denying ordinance of deliberately limiting ourselves to a few variables at a time. Recently two of my colleagues and myself have been doing a little exploratory work on a problem in the general area of social mobility. We started by tabulating some school records of fifty boys in the ninth grade of one junior high school and then having members of our seminar conduct three or four interviews with each boy and his parents. We had all the interviews written up in detail, and we had enough data to fill a book—with rather interesting reading, too. But it was a very wasteful process because there were just too many intriguing ideas. We took a couple of ideas which were deducible from current general theory and tried to make some simple fourfold tables. It was obvious that, with a dozen variables uncontrolled, such tables meant little or nothing. But that led us to a second step. Now we are trying to collect school records and a short questionnaire on two thousand boys. We will not interview all these boys and their parents in detail. But, with two thousand cases to start with, we hope to take a variable in which we are interested and find fifty boys who are plus on it and fifty

who are minus, yet who are approximately alike on a lot of other things. A table based on such matched comparisons should be relatively unambiguous. We can take off from there and interview those selected cases intensively to push further our exploration of the nexus between theory and observation. This, we think, will be economical, though still exploratory. Experimental manipulation is far in the future in our problem, but we do hope we can conclude the first stage with a statement of some hypotheses susceptible to experimental verification.

I am not in the least deprecating exploratory work. But I do think that some orderliness is indicated even in the bright dawn of a youthful enterprise.

One reason why we are not more orderly in our exploratory work is that all too often what is missing is a sharp definition of a given variable, such that, if we wanted to take a number of cases and even throw them into a simple fourfold table, we could.

Suppose we are studying a problem in which one of the variables we are looking for is overprotection or overindulgence of a child by his mother. We have a number of case histories or questionnaires. Now how do we know whether we are sorting them according to this variable or not? The first step, it would seem, is to have some way of knowing whether we are sorting them along any single continuum, applying the same criteria to each case. But to know this we need to have built into the study the ingredients of a scale. Unless we have some such ingredients in our data, we are defeated from the start. This is why I think the new interest social scientists are taking in scaling techniques is so crucially important to progress. In particular, the latent-structure theory developed by Paul F. Lazarsfeld, which derives Louis Guttman's scale as an important special case, is likely to be exceedingly useful, for it offers criteria by which we can make a small amount of information go a long way in telling us the logical structure of a supposed variable we are eager to identify. The details of Guttman's and Lazarsfeld's work[2] are likely to promote a good deal of attack and controversy. Our hope is that this will stimulate others to think such problems out still better and thus make their work obsolete as rapidly as possible.

Trying to conduct a social science investigation without good criteria for knowing whether a particular variable may be treated as a single dimension is like trying to fly without a motor in the plane. Students of the history of invention point out that the reason why the airplane, whose properties had been pretty well thought out by Leonardo da Vinci, was so late in development was the unavailability of a light-weight power plant, which had to await the invention of the internal combustion motor. We are learning more and more how to make our light-weight motors in social science, and that augurs well for the future. But much work is ahead of us. In particular, we desperately need better projective techniques and better ways of getting respondents to reveal attitudes which are too emotionally charged to be accessible to direct questioning. Schemes like the latent-structure theory of Lazarsfeld should speed up the process of developing such tests.

I have tried to set forth the model of the controlled experiment as an ideal to keep in the forefront of our minds even when by necessity some cells are missing from our design. I have also tried to suggest that more economy and orderliness are made possible, even in designing the exploratory stages of a piece of research—by using theory in advance to help us decide whether a particular inquiry would be important if we made it; by narrowing down the number of variables; and by making sure that we can classify our data along a particular continuum, even if only provisionally. And a central, brooding hope is that we will have the modesty to recognize the difference between a promising idea and proof.

Oh, how we need that modesty! The public expects us to deal with great problems like international peace, full employment, maximization of industrial efficiency. As pundits we can pronounce on such matters; as citizens we have a duty to be concerned with them; but as social scientists our greatest achievement now will be to provide a few small dramatic examples that hypotheses in our field can be stated operationally and tested crucially. And we will not accomplish that by spending most of our time writing or reading papers like this one. We will accomplish it best by rolling up our sleeves and working at the intricacies of design of studies which, though scientifically strategic, seem to laymen trivial compared with the global concerns of the atomic age. Thereby, and only thereby, I believe, can we some day have the thrilling sense of having contributed to the structure of a social science which is cumulative.

Notes

[1] Carl I. Hovland, Arthur A. Lumsdaine, and Fred D. Sheffield, *Experiments in Mass Communication* (Princeton: Princeton University Press, 1949).

[2] Samuel A. Stouffer, Louis Guttman, Edward A. Suchman, Paul F. Lazarsfeld, Shirley A. Star, and John A. Clausen, *Measurement and Prediction* (Princeton: Princeton University Press, 1949).

RESEARCH DESIGN EXEMPLIFIED

This selection continues the discussion of research strategies in social science. It is based on a systematic exploration of the important opportunity for research which occurs when a change is introduced into a situation in which records have been kept over a period of time. In our record-keeping society this is very common. For instance, industrial organizations usually keep output records, clubs keep statistics on attendance at meetings, tax receipts are recorded by governments, and, most prominently, a wide variety of data concerning various characteristics of the population is kept by the United States Bureau of the Census. Not only are such records common, but we can furthermore assume that matters deemed worthy of being recorded are also important, at least in the eyes of the record gatherer. Finally, these matters to which records pertain are frequently the subject of planned change. The industrial organization tries new techniques to increase output, the club introduces programs to reduce absenteeism at meetings, and governments try various programs to increase tax compliance.

The deliberate introduction of a measure intended to produce change is an opportunity for the researcher to see whether particular social variables are related in a causal manner. However, as planned change is seldom introduced randomly, the logic of classical experimental design cannot be used, and various problems occur in the interpretation of observed relationships. The theme of this selection is that dependable analyses and evaluations can be made in this situation if appropriate procedures are applied to the data, and if the interpretations are guarded to allow for known weaknesses in the study design.

Connecticut traffic fatalities of the 1950s are examined to determine whether the 1955 crackdown on speeders affected highway deaths. Two separate research designs are utilized. In the first, the highway death rate in Connecticut after the crackdown is compared with the rate prior to the crackdown, both series extending over a number of years. The second design compares the Connecticut experience for several years before and after the crackdown with the experience of a group of nearby and similar states for the same period. Some slight evidence is found for the hypothesis that the death rate in Connecticut was affected by the crackdown. Clear evidence is found concerning some unforeseen and undesired results of the crackdown, including an increase in driving while one's license is suspended. The methodology of quasi-experimentation employed in this study is suggested as a useful model for appraising the effects of legal and other social changes.

The Connecticut speed crackdown is an example of a large class of situations which can and ought to be studied by social scientists. At the present time, some needed statistical methods are still in the process of development, and estimation of the role of instability in any apparent change is still difficult. In fact, an earlier unpublished analysis of these same data failed to show any evidence that the crackdown reduced deaths, because it seemed so likely that the apparent reduction was entirely an artifact of the instability of the death rates. The more sensitive and more appropriate techniques used here now indicate the presence of an effect, albeit a small one, which cannot be explained in terms of instability.

The social sciences are an underdeveloped field of knowledge but, as this article attempts to demonstrate, the frontiers are close and penetrable. Much information reposes in easily available files, and even the beginning student can undertake analyses like these and become a collaborator in building the science of society. The authors of this article are optimists concerning the possibility of accumulating information and developing the repertory of factually grounded propositions on which a mature social science will have to rely.

Selection 4

THE CONNECTICUT SPEED CRACKDOWN: A STUDY OF THE EFFECTS OF LEGAL CHANGE

H. Laurence Ross and Donald T. Campbell

In 1955, the state of Connecticut introduced a campaign to reduce highway fatalities through enforcement of speed-limit laws. We report here the results of a study of this campaign,

Published for the first time in the second edition of *Perspectives on the Social Order.*

with two goals in mind. First, with our methodology we wish to illustrate some pitfalls of uncritical interpretations of change and to demonstrate some more dependable ways in which to evaluate the effects of changes in law and other systems of social control. Second, although our findings are limited to the case at hand, we wish to suggest some problems and unforeseen results that may accompany attempts to change behavior by law enforcement.

Automobile accidents caused 324 deaths in Connecticut in 1955. This was a record high for the decade of the fifties. As the hazardous Christmas holidays approached, Governor Abraham Ribicoff initiated an unprecedented attempt to control traffic deaths by law enforcement, in the form of a crackdown on speeders. He acted in the belief that excess speed was a common contributing factor in traffic deaths, that control of speed would result in diminished fatalities, and that this control could be accomplished by enforcing speed limits. On December 23, Governor Ribicoff announced that in the future all persons convicted of speeding in Connecticut would have their licenses suspended for thirty days on the first offense, with longer periods of suspension for repeating offenders. The decree was put into force through the Governor's power of appointment over local judges, who were told that reappointment in 1957 would be denied to those who appeared lax in conviction of speeders, or who did not recommend to the Motor Vehicle Department the suspension of drivers' licenses for this offense.

In the first three months of 1956, license suspensions for speeding numbered 2,855, an increase of almost 2,700 over the corresponding period in 1955. There were 10 fewer fatalities, and 765 fewer arrests for speeding. The Governor was quoted as saying: "This is positive proof that operators are not only driving slower, but are driving better."

By the end of June there were 22 fewer fatalities than in the first six months of 1955, representing a 15 per cent reduction. Suspensions for speeding had risen from 231 to 5,398, and arrests had declined from 4,377 to 2,735. Ribicoff announced: "Connecticut has succeeded in stopping the upward surge in highway deaths, and in the first six months of this year, contrary to the national trend, we have saved lives. Fewer people died on the highways this year than in the same period last year, in Connecticut. We did it by enforcing the law, something the safety experts said couldn't be done because the people wouldn't be behind it."

In the late summer Connecticut experienced a very high number of traffic fatalities, and by the beginning of September deaths almost equaled those of the previous year. However, fatalities were fewer in the fall, and by the end of the year Connecticut counted a total of 284 traffic deaths, as compared with 324 in 1955. Governor Ribicoff concluded: "With the saving of forty lives in 1956, a reduction of 12.3 per cent from the 1955 motor vehicle death toll, we can say the program is definitely worthwhile."

Our study of the Connecticut speed crackdown is based on analysis of mileage death rates, i.e., the number of deaths per 100 million miles driven in the state. This corrects for the fact that more deaths would be expected in Connecticut during the decade merely because more miles were being driven.

Figure 1 presents the mileage death rates for Connecticut for the years 1955 and 1956, on which Governor Ribicoff based his claims for the effectiveness of his program. If we think of these data as similar to a classical experiment, the 1955 data constitute a pretest, the crackdown is like an experimental treatment, and the 1956 data constitute a posttest.[1] Governor Ribicoff believed the difference between the pretest and the posttest to be the effect of the treatment, an inference that might be valid if the study had truly been a classical experiment, subject to controls and randomization of extraneous variables. As the

Figure 1   Pre- and Posttest Measures of Connecticut Traffic Fatalities per 100 Million Vehicle Miles

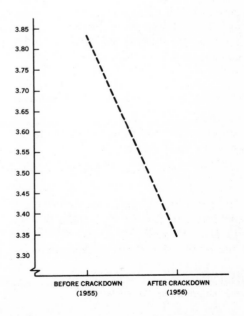

BEFORE CRACKDOWN	AFTER CRACKDOWN
(1955)	(1956)

latter was not the case, this situation, which we term "quasi-experimental," requires independent evidence to rule out several possible alternative explanations of the observed difference. Some of these, briefly stated, are as follows:

1. History. This term denotes specific events, other than the treatment, occurring between the pretest and posttest, which might independently account for the change. For instance, 1956 might have had less snow and ice than 1955, this fact rather than the speed crackdown producing the lower death rate.

2. Maturation. This term is taken from psychology, where it refers to changes correlated with the passage of time per se, such as growing older or more tired. Its use is not limited to organic changes, however. "Maturation" may refer to any general, secular, time-linked changes not the result of discrete events. Potential causes of the change in the Connecticut death rate subsumed under this heading are improved roads and more competent medical care.

3. Testing. A change may occur as a result of the pretest, even without the treatment. In the present instance, the assessment of the death rate for 1955 constitutes the pretest. It is conceivable that publicizing the high death rate for that year may have changed driver caution, and hence changed the death rates for the following year.

4. Instrumentation. This term refers to a shifting of the measuring instrument independent of any change in the phenomenon measured. Such changes are common in sociology, for example, artificial rises in crime rates which occur due to changes in the administration of police records.

5. Regression. Statistical theory tells us that when a group is selected for study because of extreme scores on one test, their scores on a subsequent test will tend to be less extreme, merely as a statistical artifact. As high accident rates for 1955 were cited to justify the crackdown, lower rates for 1956 would be expected due to regression.

6. Instability. A ubiquitous problem in quasi-experimentation is to distinguish "true" changes in a measure from random changes due either to a small population base on which observations are made or to large numbers of change-producing events which, taken individually, we have called history.

The plausibility of these alternative explanations can be evaluated by the systematic use of series of data which are commonly available to the researcher in the situations similar to this. If data are gathered for the years directly prior to and following the treatment, they are usually available for other years as well. A fairly long sequence of observations before and after the treatment allows us to apply the logic of the quasi-experimental model termed the Interrupted Time-series Design. Figure 2 presents the relevant data for Connecticut.

The data of Figure 2 help us to evaluate maturation and, on certain assumptions, testing as causes of the observed change of Figure 1. For these explanations to be plausible, the observed change should be part of a long-term, secular trend. They would be implausible—and our preferred explanation in terms of the treatment would be more plausible—if an abrupt change took place at the time of treatment and nowhere else in the series. Unfortunately for Governor Ribicoff's claims, the changes in 1955–1956 seem to be well in ac-

Figure 2   Interrupted Time-series Presentation of Connecticut Traffic Fatalities per 100 Million Vehicle Miles

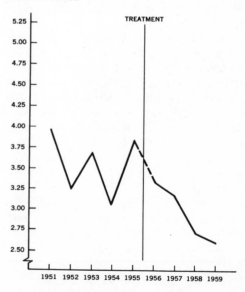

cord with these alternative explanations. The fact that 1955–1956 is the third abrupt downward jump in five years, and the smallest of the three, certainly argues against imputing any special causal effects to events occurring at that point.

The likelihood of regression is also supported by the data of Figure 2. The largest upswing in the series occurs in 1954–1955, just prior to the crackdown. This peak is seen even more strongly in the raw death statistics, presented for comparison in Figure 2a. It thus seems quite likely that the high figures of 1955 caused the crackdown, and thus less likely that the crackdown caused the low figures of 1956, for such a drop would have been predicted on grounds of regression in any case.

The graphic presentation of the precrackdown years provides evidence of the general instability of the accidental death rate and makes the supposed effect of Figure 1 now look trivial. Box and Tiao[2] have developed an analytical technique for estimating and making inferences about change in the level of a nonstationary time series, and this technique was applied to our data (in monthly units) by Gene V. Glass.[3] The test was unable to show a significant shift at the time of the crackdown.

In the case at hand it was possible to improve on the methodology discussed up to

Figure 3   Multiple Time-series Comparing Connecticut Fatalities with Those of Four Comparable States

now by constructing a type of control group of adjacent and similar states: New York, Massachusetts, Rhode Island, and New Jersey. This is a Multiple Time-series Design. It provides a quasi-experimental control for history, which is not possible with single Interrupted Time-series, and acts as an additional check on maturation, testing, and instrumentation. The data are presented in Figure 3. A significant fact in this comparison is that prior to the crackdown Connecticut's rate is rising relative to the other states, but afterwards its rate is falling. Glass' analysis applied to these data does show a statistically significant reduction in fatalities associated with the speed crackdown. However, the change appears minute, and the continuing possibility of regression as a cause of the shift renders enthusiastic support of the hypothesis very difficult.

Some additional analyses were made to illustrate further the use of time-series methodology, and to show that the crackdown had a real effect in the legal system and that it produced some unanticipated and unintended consequences. No control-state figures were obtained, but the single-state time series are quite convincing.

Figure 4 provides evidence that the crackdown was put into effect as indicated by a

Figure 2a   Interrupted Time-series Presentation of Traffic Deaths in Connecticut (Raw Figures)

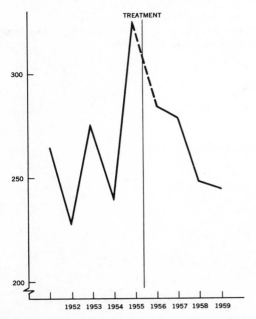

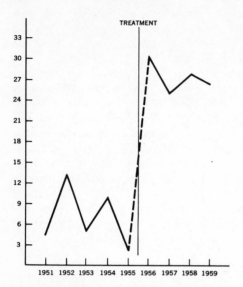

Figure 4   Suspensions of Licenses for Speeding, as a Percentage of All Suspensions

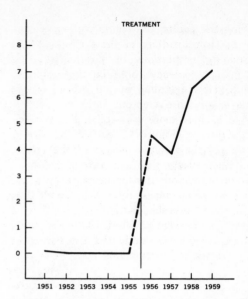

Figure 6   Arrested while Driving with a Suspended License, as a Percentage of Suspensions

great increase in suspensions of licenses for speeding.

Figure 5 plots the percentage which speeding violations constitute of all traffic violations. This shows a decline, ostensibly due to greater conformity to speed limits, although it is also likely that policemen and prosecutors were more willing to overlook minor infractions or to charge them as something else.

Figure 6 concerns persons whose licenses were further suspended because they were convicted of driving with a suspended license. As a percentage of all suspensions, this jumps

from an almost consistent zero to some 4 to 6 per cent. Our interpretation of this phenomenon is that automobile transportation has become a virtual necessity for many residents of the diffusely settled megalopolitan region that includes Connecticut and that these people are willing to risk very severe punishments in order to continue daily routines that involve driving.

Figure 7 shows a reaction of the legal system to the administratively imposed crackdown. Even with fewer speeding violations

Figure 5   Speeding Violations, as a Percentage of All Traffic Violations

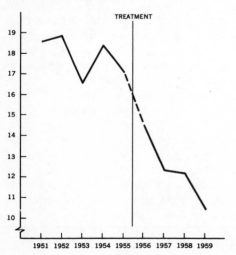

Figure 7   Percentage of Speeding Violations Judged Not Guilty

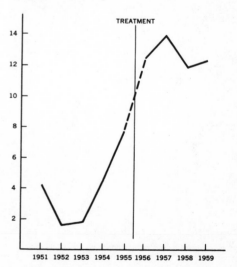

reaching the courts, the courts were more lenient in their handling of these cases, as expressed by proportions of not-guilty judgments. Such leniency could be the result of more generous handling by judges and prosecutors or of more vigorous defenses by the accused because more is at stake. The two effects shown in Figures 6 and 7 indicate a vitiation of the punitive effects of the crackdown in a society that acknowledges dependence on automobile transportation.

In conclusion, our analysis has shown that the Connecticut crackdown on speeding was a substantial enforcement effort, though its most punitive aspects were mitigated in practice by fewer arrests and convictions and by a willingness of some people to drive with suspended licenses. As to its effects, we are forced to conclude that they comprised no substantial reduction in traffic fatalities.

More important, we believe, than the specific findings of the study is the methodology here exemplified. While the social scientist cannot as a rule truly experiment on a societal scale, abrupt focused social change is continually going on, especially in the legal realm, and it can be evaluated by the careful researcher despite the lack of classical controls. We hope that familiarity with quasi-experimental techniques such as Time–series will increase the ambitions as well as the results of sociologists who study societal changes.

Notes

[1] Quasi-experimental methodology is discussed in, e.g., Donald T. Campbell and Julian S. Stanley, "Experimental and Quasi-experimental Designs for Research on Teaching," in Nathan L. Gage, Ed., *Handbook of Research on Teaching*, Chicago: Rand McNally, 1963, pp. 171–246; Donald T. Campbell, "From Description to Experimentation: Interpreting Trends as Quasi-experiments," in Chester W. Harris, Ed., *Problems in Measuring Change*, Madison: University of Wisconsin Press, 1963; Donald T. Campbell and Keith N. Clayton, "Avoiding Regression Effects in Panel Studies of Communication Impact," *Studies in Public Communication*, No. 3, Chicago: Department of Sociology, University of Chicago, 1961, pp. 99–118, reprinted in Bobbs-Merrill Reprints in Sociology as S–353.

[2] E. P. Box and G. C. Tiao, "A Change in Level of a Nonstationary Time Series," *Biometrika*, 52 (1965), pp. 181–192.

[3] Gene V. Glass, "Analysis of Data on the Connecticut Speeding Crackdown as a Time-series Quasi-experiment," Research Paper #1, Laboratory of Educational Research, University of Colorado, July, 1967.

Part 2

THE NATURAL CONDITIONS
OF HUMAN SOCIETY

Chapter 2

THE GEOGRAPHIC FACTOR

CLIMATE AND SOCIAL LIFE
Selection 5

TOPOGRAPHY AND SOCIAL LIFE
Selection 6

It seems reasonable to begin the study of the social order with consideration of some of life's "givens," the natural conditions that both make life possible and restrict the forms that it can take. Human societies consist of creatures with particular physical, chemical, and biological properties, existing in an environment that likewise has physical, chemical, and biological characteristics. The properties of man's body and environment set limits on the possible varieties of behavior. In this chapter, certain of these limits are considered under the heading of the geographic factor; others are discussed in the following two chapters concerning the biological and demographic factors.

By the geographic factor is meant those conditions relevant to human behavior that result from the physical and chemical characteristics of the Earth, on which all known societies exist. This "factor" is actually an extremely complex combination of many variables, among them temperature, rainfall, condition of the soil, location with respect to land and water, and length of days and seasons; it is not possible to discuss them in any detail in a general work like this. The two selections included in this chapter should be considered merely as examples of thinking about the social order in geographic terms.

Theories relating social life to geography in the broadest sense are common in the history of social philosophy. Perhaps most notable have been those relating social traits to climate, exemplified by a large part of Montesquieu's *Spirit of the Laws* (1748) and Henry Thomas Buckle's *History of Civilization in England* (1857). Other theories have concerned the relative location of land and water masses, natural resources, and natural cycles such as days, months, and seasons. In general these theories tend to be unacceptable because they are overstated. Many are one-factor explanations attributing the whole of a civilization to a single condition such as temperature. Moreover, they often fail to acknowledge the fact that environment not only has effects on society, but is itself affected by society, as will be shown in the following selections.

Modern sociologists reject theories of the geographic factor as determining social life, but few would dispute the idea that it influences the social order. Some observed social uniformities seem most reasonably explained in terms of the geographic factor. Climate, for example, explains why people do not wear thin, light clothing in any part of the Arctic. However, the influence of the geographic factor on social life must be understood as being relative to the state of man's tools for coping with the environment. A climate or location that is completely forbidding to a society with few tools may be merely uncomfortable to members of a different society with better tools; it may be quite compatible with a civilization that possesses enormous resources of inanimate power capable of heating the polar air or watering the desert. Again, man's control of fire has in some ways eliminated the social effects of the natural seasons, and electric lighting has done the same for the distinction between day and night.

In Selection 5, Julian Steward discusses a group of American Indians that has a very rudimentary type of social organization. He finds the sources of their condition in the climate of the area in which they live, which is so dry that a dispersed and migratory pattern of life is necessary for survival. Selection 6, by H. W. Gilmore, is a study of the effect of land elevation upon the physical and social structure of the city of New Orleans.

CLIMATE AND SOCIAL LIFE

The role usually conceded to the geographic factor is to set limits or boundaries upon possible variations in the social order. These limits are, however, not absolute, but relative to the state of technology. In consequence of this fact, the best contemporary examples of strong geographical influence are found in anthropological descriptions of societies possessed of "primitive" technology. Such is the case of the Shoshone Indians, the subjects of this selection.

The Shoshone Indians were native to the Great Basin, an arid, elevated region, between mountains, contained mainly in Utah and Nevada. The Great Basin is hot in summer and cold in winter, with very little water available at any time. For these reasons it can be said to contain the most inhospitable climatic conditions found anywhere, on a large scale, in the United States. Julian Steward believes that the unfavorable environment accounts for the very rare type of social structure found among the Shoshone, who lived in isolated migratory groups of one or a few families without the clans, tribes, and nations that are typical among human groups.

> Foods found in the Great Basin are scarce and vary in amount and location from year to year. Indians in this area, therefore, lived in groups of no more than a few families that were not only isolated from other groups but migratory, depending on the food supply. They came into contact with other groups only during the fall and winter when they went into the mountains to gather pine nuts or during occasional cooperative hunts when game was temporarily plentiful. The Indians' ability for and pleasure in social interaction was demonstrated by their coordination of the hunts and intervisitation when they were in proximity, but a permanent social organization (for instance, tribes) based on these occasional meetings was impossible because the groups involved were different on each occasion.
>
> The effect of the distinctive environment of the Shoshone was apparent in their institutions, such as property rights and religion. When disputes occurred, they took place between families and were settled without intervention by others. The Shoshone knew neither crime nor warfare, which are meaningless terms for people who do not recognize a corporate community that can be offended and take punitive action.

Steward notes elsewhere that the rather rudimentary social organization described here is paralleled among the Eskimos and in several South American tribes. These groups are widely scattered and have little in common other than a harsh environment that is reluctant to yield food and other resources to people with primitive technologies. His thesis is further supported by the observation that more hospitable environments generally house more complex societies, and that the beginnings of the very complex societies called civilizations are uniformly found in highly fertile areas, such as the Nile Valley.

While admitting the strength of Steward's argument in this case, one should note that the Great Basin today provides impressive evidence for the influence of technology in overcoming environmental limitations on society. The Mormons who migrated to the Great Basin in search of religious freedom brought with them the knowledge of how best to utilize the available water and how to obtain more of it from subsurface origins. In consequence, the barren steppes that could support no more than a handful of Indians now produce abundant fruits and vegetables, which are exported to distant markets. More than a quarter-million people presently live in pleasant, tree-shaded cities by the shore of the lifeless Great Salt Lake.

Selection 5
FROM THEORY OF CULTURE CHANGE
Julian Steward

The Shoshonean-speaking Indians—the Ute, Western Shoshoni, and Northern Paiute of western Colorado, Utah, Nevada, and eastern Oregon and California—acquired most of their hunting and gathering techniques from other peoples, but their general adaptation to the intermontane steppes and deserts was so distinctive that they constitute a special culture area usually called the Great Basin or Basin-Plateau area. In a quantitative sense, this culture was extremely simple. An "element list," which breaks the culture down into details such as basket weaves and shapes, religious beliefs, social practices, and other details, includes a total of about 3,000 items. By comparison, the U. S. forces landing at Casa Blanca during World War II unloaded 500,000 items of material equipment alone. The total "elements" of modern American culture would probably run to several million.

Shoshonean culture, however, is of interest for the nature of its organization as much as for its quantitative simplicity. Virtually all cultural activities were carried out by the family in comparative isolation from other families. A contrast with modern America helps clarify this point. In the United States today, people are highly specialized workers in an economic system geared to national and international patterns; education is increasingly standard-

ized and the community or state takes over this function from the family when the child is six years old or younger; health practices are dictated largely by research carried out on an international scale and in part administered by the state and community; recreation more and more involves the consumption of products made by national organizations; religious worship is carried on in national or international churches. These growing functions of the community, state, and nation increasingly relieve the family of functions it performed in earlier historical periods. It is perhaps difficult to imagine that a family, alone and unaided, could obtain virtually all the food it consumed; manufacture all its clothing, household goods, and other articles; rear and train its children without assistance; take care of its sick except in time of crisis; be self-sufficient in its religious activities; and, except on special occasions, manage its own recreation. Why this was so in the case of the Shoshoneans is explainable largely in terms of their cultural ecological adaptations.*

Owing to the nature of the natural environment of the Great Basin area and to the simple hunting and gathering techniques for exploiting it, it was inevitable that the individual family or at the most two or three related families should live in isolation during most of

Reprinted from *Theory of Culture Change* by Julian Steward (Urbana: University of Illinois Press, 1955), with permission of the publisher.

* Adaptations of way of life to the environment. —Ed.

the year. "Family" in this case signifies the nuclear, biological or bilateral family, consisting of mother, father, and children. Unlike many primitive peoples, the Shoshoneans were not organized in extended family or lineage groups and, although, as we shall see subsequently, the immediate family was frequently enlarged through plural spouses and different families were closely allied by marriage, the functioning unit was the nuclear family, augmented only by a grandparent, aunt, or uncle who otherwise would be homeless.

Environment and resources

The natural resources which were exploitable by Shoshonean culture were so limited that the population was extremely sparse. In the more fertile portions of this area there was perhaps one person to five square miles, while in the vast stretches of nearly waterless terrain the ratio was one to fifty or even one hundred square miles. The mean for the whole area was one person to between twenty or thirty square miles.

The territory once inhabited by the Shoshonean Indians is extremely arid, but technically most of it is classified as "steppe" rather than true "desert" although there are large areas devoid of vegetation. The country consists of large arid valleys lying between mountain ranges which run north and south. These valleys are from five to twenty miles wide and twenty to eighty miles long. The greater portion of the Shoshonean habitat lies within the Great Basin, a vast area of interior drainage between the Wasatch Mountains of Utah and the Sierra Nevada Range of California and Oregon, but it also includes portions of the Columbia River Plateau of Idaho and eastern Oregon and the Colorado River Plateau of eastern Utah and western Colorado.

The flora and fauna of all these areas are very similar. There are several biotic zones,* which set the basic conditions for a society equipped only with very simple hunting and gathering techniques. In the valleys, which lie between 4,000 and 6,000 feet elevation, the low rainfall—five to twenty inches a year—together with high evaporation supports a predominantly xerophytic vegetation,† that is, such drought-resisting plants as sagebrush and

* Zones of plant and animal life.—Ed.
† Plants suited to a dry climate.—Ed.

greasewood. This vegetation has very limited value to human beings or animals. Plants bearing edible seeds and roots occur in some abundance immediately along the stream banks, but, except in favored areas, such as the piedmont of the Wasatch Mountains and the Sierra Nevada Mountains, the streams are small and widely-spaced. In the Great Basin, the streams end in saline marshes or lakes. In the vast sandy areas between the streams, the quantity of edible plants depends directly upon rainfall, which varies from year to year and from place to place. These plants only afforded small quantities of food for the Indians, and they could not support game in herds comparable to the bison of the Great Plains or the caribou of the far north. The two species of greatest importance to the Indians were antelope and rabbits. These not only supplied meat and skins, but the communal hunts in which they were sometimes taken were among the few collective cultural activities. The numbers of both species, however, were limited, and the hunts were infrequent.

It is impossible to estimate the quantitative importance of different animal foods in the valley zone, but the Shoshoneans probably ate more rats, mice, gophers, locusts, ants, ant eggs, larvae of flies which breed in the salt lakes, snakes, and lizards than large game. In the rivers, such as the Owyhee, John Day, Crooked, Snake, Truckee, Carson, Walker, and Humboldt rivers, fish were an important supplement to other foods, but the runs were seasonal, the quantity did not compare with that of fish in coastal rivers, and the fish were evidently not suited for preservation and storage.

The zone of piñon and juniper trees lies between about 6,000 and 8,000 or 9,000 feet. This zone is largely restricted to the flanks of the mountain ranges since most valleys lie below this altitude. The juniper had little value to the Indians except for its wood, but the piñon (Pinus monophylla in the north, Pinus edulis in the south), which occurred throughout the Shoshonean area to a little north of the Humboldt River in Nevada, yielded pine nuts which were the most important of all food species. North of the piñon area, the seeds of certain other species of pines were eaten, but they were a relatively minor item in the diet. Since there was greater rainfall in the piñon-juniper belt than in the valleys, this zone afforded more seeds, roots, and grasses, and it had more game, especially deer. But it constitutes only a small portion of the total area, and the growing season is short. A few mountain ranges rise above 8,000 or 9,000 feet into the zone of the ponderosa pine, where vegetation is lush and where mountain sheep as well as deer were hunted.

The Shoshonean tribes were of necessity gatherers of vegetable foods and lower forms of animal life rather than hunters. They utilized nearly a hundred species of wild plants. The more important of these yielded small, hard-shelled seeds, which were collected in conical basketry containers, roasted with live coals in shallow baskets, ground on flat stones or metates, and eaten from basketry bowls. In the higher altitudes and latitudes where rainfall is greater, roots were relatively more important as food. When seeds and roots could not be had, especially in early spring, leafy vegetables or greens from many plants were eaten.

Socially fragmenting effect of the cultural ecology

All of the plant and animal foods had in common the extremely important characteristic that the place and quantity of their occurrence from year to year were unpredictable, owing largely to variations in rainfall. A locality might be very fertile one year and attract large numbers of families, but offer little food for several years thereafter. Few localities had foods in sufficient quantity and reliability to permit permanent settlements. Throughout most of the area, the families were concerned predominantly with warding off potential starvation by moving from place to place. These movements were determined by reports from friends or relatives about the probable quantities of foods to be had. Families from different localities would assemble at places where food was temporarily plentiful, but, owing to the impossibility of storing large quantities of food for the future, they soon dispersed to seek elsewhere.

The typical Shoshoni family living in the piñon area of Nevada traveled alone or with one or two related families during the spring and summer, seeking seeds, roots, various small mammals, rodents, insects, larvae, and other edible items. In the late summer when a family heard reports that the pine nuts seemed

very promising in a certain portion of a mountain range, it arranged its travels so as to arrive in that locality in late October or early November, when the first frosts would have opened the cones and made the nuts ready to harvest. Other families who had also been foraging for food within a radius of perhaps twenty to thirty miles of that locality came there for the same reason.

In gathering the pine nuts, each family restricted itself by common understanding to a limited area, because there were so many pine nuts in the locality as a whole that no one could gather them all before they dropped and because each family could harvest more if it worked alone. The different families remained from several hundred yards to a mile or more apart. Each gathered pine nuts as rapidly as it could and stored them in earth caches. If the harvest was good, it might support the family throughout most of the winter.

The winter encampment consisted of perhaps twenty or thirty families within easy visiting distance of one another. Early spring generally found the people suffering more or less acutely from hunger. The families then had to go their separate ways to forage for greens, game, and any other foods they could find. Throughout spring and summer, the migrations of a particular family, although limited in general to the terrain it knew well, were determined almost week to week by its knowledge of available foods. It might learn that sand grass seeds were promising in one place, rabbits numerous elsewhere, fly larvae abundant in a certain lake, and antelope ready for a communal hunt under a shaman or medicine man over in the next valley.

Although the pine nut was perhaps the most important factor in determining the whereabouts of the winter encampment and which families would be associated in it, most other foods had a very similar effect in causing seasonal variations in interfamilial contacts. Owing to yearly and local variations in rainfall, the whereabouts of other wild seed and root crops and animal resources was unpredictable. Rabbits might be so numerous in a portion of a valley in a given year that people would assemble from considerable distances to hold a communal hunt. Several years might then follow before it was worth while to hold another such hunt in the same place, whereas rabbits were ready for a hunt in an adjoining valley the next year. The same was true of antelope. A co-operative hunt would so reduce the antelope that it required eight or ten years for their number to be restored. Even such foods as grasshoppers and locusts, or "Mormon crickets," were unpredictable. In certain years locusts occurred in such numbers as to be a major source of food to the Indians—and a plague to the modern farmers—and then during several years they were of no importance.

A limitation of the value of animal products was the absence of preservation and storing techniques. Rabbits, antelope, and fish might afford more meat than the people who assembled to take them could eat, but after a few days or weeks, they spoiled. Fish, unlike other animal species, occurred with some annual regularity in fixed places. During runs, a considerable number of families came from far and wide to fish for a few weeks, after which they had to disperse in search of other foods. Had the Shoshoneans been able to dry and smoke fish, like the Northwest Coast Indians, it is possible that fairly large permanent populations might have developed along certain of the better fishing streams and lakes. In the absence of this possibility, the winter inhabitants of these areas were limited to the few families who used fish as a supplement to other foods. Consequently, the effect of fishing resources on social groups was like that of other foods: it permitted large aggregates of people to assemble for short periods and it helped tide a small number of local families over the winter.

Shoshonean society was affected not only by the erratic and unpredictable occurrence of practically all principal foods and by the limited technical skills for harvesting and storing most of them, but it was also shaped by the predominant importance of wild vegetable products, which put a premium upon family separatism rather than upon co-operation. Anyone who has gathered wild berries in a party knows that he can pick far more if he finds a patch of his own. Unlike certain forms of hunting—for example, collective rabbit drives or antelope hunts—participation of many persons in seed and root gathering not only failed to increase the per capita harvest, but it generally decreased it so greatly that individual families preferred to forage alone so as not to compete with other families.

The competitive aspect of seed and root gathering together with the erratic annual occurrence of practically all principal foods and the inability of the people to store foods in any locality in sufficient amount to permit considerable numbers of families to remain there for a major portion of the year, all contributed to the fragmentation of Shoshonean society into nuclear family units, which moved about the country seasonally and annually in an unpredictable itinerary.

Property

The concept of property rights among the Shoshoneans was directly related to their mode of life. These Indians assumed that rights to exclusive use of anything resulted from work expended by particular individuals or groups and from habitual use. This is a rather obvious, simple, and practical concept, and it seems to have entailed a minimum of conflict.

In most parts of the area, natural resources were available to anyone. The seeds gathered by a woman, however, belonged to her because she had done the work of converting a natural resource into something that could be directly consumed. If a man made a bow or built a house, these were his, although prior to making objects of them, the trees he utilized belonged to no one. Any family might fish in a certain river or stream, but if a group of families built a fish weir, it alone had the right to use that weir.

When a number of families came into potential conflict in the utilization of natural resources, the same principle held. In seed gathering, it was "first come, first served." The families which entered a seed plot or piñon grove selected the best portion and, by virtue of having started to work on it, had prior rights. Other families gathered pine nuts elsewhere, which was reasonable and necessary because if they gathered in competition with the first family, all would have harvested less. In rabbit drives, the person who clubbed or shot a rabbit or who owned the net which caught it had first claim. In deer or mountain sheep hunting, the man whose arrow first entered the game was entitled to the skin and the choice portions of the meat.

This principle of property rights was essential to survival in the Shoshonean area. Owing to the erratic annual and local occurrence of foods, the arbitrary exclusion of territorially delimited groups of families from utilization of other territories would have caused starvation and death. With few exceptions, the habitat of most families always provided such uncertain subsistence that the territorial interpenetration of families living in different localities was necessary to the survival of all. The absence of property claims of local groups to delimitable areas of natural resources upon which work had not been expended was the corollary of the fragmented nature of Shoshonean society.

In a few portions of the Great Basin, such as Owens Valley in eastern California, which was occupied by Northern Paiute, the many streams flowing from the high Sierra Nevada Range afforded food resources which were comparatively so abundant and reliable that each family could be reasonably certain of finding enough to eat within one or two days' travel from a permanent village. Instead of wandering an unpredictable course determined by the vicissitudes of nature, these families were able to make forays from permanent headquarters. Habitual use of resources within readily accessible portions of the terrain led to the concept that each local village or group of villages had exclusive rights to resources within bounded areas. This economic stability and permanent residence of a particular group of families provided a basis for association, leadership, and organization in band groups.

Co-operation and leadership as integrating factors

The typical Shoshonean family was independent and self-sufficient during the greater part of the year, perhaps during 80 or 90 percent of the time. It subsisted and fulfilled most cultural functions with little assistance from other families. It probably could have survived in complete isolation.

But human history provides no instances in which nuclear families had progeny and perpetuated their culture without associating with and intermarrying with other families. Moreover, nuclear families have always co-operated with other families in various ways. Since this is so, the Shoshoneans, like other fragmented family groups, represent a family level of sociocultural integration only in a relative sense. It is relative in that most societies having a higher level of integration possess patterns of cooperation and leadership among a perma-

nent membership. I classify the Shoshoneans as an exemplification of a family level of sociocultural integration because in the few forms of collective activity the same group of families did not co-operate with one another or accept the same leader on successive occasions. By another definition, however, it might be entirely permissible to view this everchanging membership and leadership as a special form of suprafamilial integration. While the Shoshoneans represent a family level of sociocultural integration in a relative sense, their suprafamilial patterns of integration involved no permanent social groups of fixed membership despite several kinds of interfamilial co-operation.

Collective hunting. The most important cooperation consisted of collective hunts. In these hunts, rabbits, antelope, deer, and mud hens were the principal species taken. Communal hunts could be held, however, only when there was sufficient game, when a considerable number of families could assemble, and when an appropriate leader was available. Under these circumstances, co-operation yielded many times the quantity of game that individuals, expending the same effort, could take alone.

The principal collective hunt was the rabbit drive. It could be held fairly often, and it yielded not only meat which could be consumed during a short period but furs which, cut into long strips and twisted, were woven into robes and blankets. The only distinctive technical feature of these drives was a net of about the height and mesh of a modern tennis net but often several hundred feet long. A number of these nets were placed end to end to form a huge semicircle. Men, women, children, and dogs beat the brush over a wide area, gradually closing in so that rabbits which were not clubbed or shot by the drivers became entangled in the nets, where they were killed.

Custom determined the several crucial aspects of the drive and the division of game. Experienced men—in recent years called rather appropriately "rabbit bosses"—were given supreme authority to co-ordinate all activities in this fairly complex operation. They chose the locality of the drive, directed disposition of nets, regulated the drivers, and divided the game according to customary understandings.

Anyone who killed a rabbit with a bow or throwing stick in the course of the drive could claim it. Since, however, only a few families owned rabbit nets, net owners received a somewhat greater portion of the rabbits caught in the nets.

In spite of the rather rigid direction of these drives, there were several reasons why they did not bring about permanent integration or cohesion of territorial or social groups of fixed membership. First, drives were held only when rabbits were sufficiently numerous in a particular locality. Second, participants in the drive consisted of families who, because of the rather fortuitous annual occurrence of seeds and other foods in one place or another, happened to be in the locality where the drive was worth holding. Third, the drive was held only if an experienced leader and families owning nets happened to be present. Since the occurrence of these factors was rather haphazard, since the place, the participants, and the leaders were never quite the same in successive years, the drives provided only temporary bonds between independent families. A given family was under no obligation whatever to participate in a drive with a fixed group of families under a permanent leader. And, since the "rabbit boss" held authority only during the drive, the family paid little heed to him in other times, places, and contexts.

The communal antelope hunt had a social function like that of the rabbit drive. It was held in any given locality at intervals of several years and the participants consisted of those families which happened to be in the vicinity. It was held less frequently than the rabbit drive because it took much longer for the antelope herds to recover their number. A major difference in form rather than function between the rabbit drive and the antelope hunt is that whereas the former were led by men of experience and prestige—qualifications which anyone might develop—the latter were led by "antelope shamans." According to Shoshonean belief, these men were qualified less by their practical ability—though no doubt they were far from incompetent—than by their possession of supernatural power which enabled them to charm the antelope into a state of helplessness.

The practical procedures in the antelope drives were as appropriate to the situation as those in the rabbit hunts. The people built a brush corral from which wings, consisting of piles of brush or stones, extended outward a half mile or so. Drivers spread out several miles from the corral, formed a line across the valley, and slowly closed in, urging the antelope between the wings and into the corral. Antelope differ from rabbits in that they not only flee from something threatening but they are drawn by curiosity toward strange objects. The antelope shaman evidently became one of the chief functionaries in native Shoshonean culture because his role combined this peculiarity of antelope with a basic belief about sickness. It was thought by many primitive peoples, including the Shoshoneans, that sickness might be caused by loss of one's soul. While the antelope shaman was not a curer of human ills, he was thought to possess the power to capture the souls of antelope before the hunt began and thus irresistibly to draw them into the corral, where he stood during the drive.

The shaman's authority was very great during these drives, but he had no voice in other activities. Moreover, even this socioreligious leadership like the lay authority found in rabbit drives failed to integrate social groups of fixed membership.

The other hunting activities involved much less co-operation than rabbit and antelope drives. Mud hen hunts were held only by small groups in the lake areas, while deer drives, held in the mountains, were infrequent and involved few persons.

Dancing, gambling, and visiting. The interfamilial associations of the Shoshonean Indians had to be adapted, as previously shown, to the exigencies of obtaining food by means of the techniques known to them. Although these families foraged throughout most of the year in isolation, their contacts with other families over many generations had contributed certain social patterns which strengthened bonds between them.

Whenever groups of Shoshonean families were together, they carried out certain recreational activities, such as dancing and gambling. Dancing, although popular, was originally limited to the circle dance, a performance in which men and women formed a circle and side-stepped to the accompaniment of singing.

Gambling games were extremely numerous and included several forms of dice, the handgame, sports such as racing and hockey, and games of skill such as the hoop-and-pole game and archery. Both dancing and games, however, could be held only when local abundance of food, such as rabbits, locusts, antelope, or pine nuts, made large gatherings possible. After a rabbit or antelope drive, for instance, people might dance and gamble for several days until the meat supply was exhausted, when each family had to go its separate way in the unending food quest.

Interfamilial contacts were not limited to such formalized activities as hunting, dancing, and gambling. Visiting was an important integrating fact since people were always eager to associate with one another whether or not they danced and gambled. They preferred to visit with relatives, but when food was plentiful, a large number of unrelated families could assemble.

Hostilities and warfare. In aboriginal times most of the Shoshonean people had no national or tribal warfare. There were no territorial rights to be defended, no military honors to be gained, and no means of organizing groups of individuals for concerted action. When war parties of neighboring peoples invaded their country, the Shoshoneans ran away more often than they fought.

Hostilities generally consisted of feuds, not organized military action, and they resulted largely from the suspicion of witchcraft and from woman-stealing. They were therefore as often intratribal as intertribal. Death was generally ascribed to supernatural causes, especially to shamans, whose normally beneficent power had turned bad, perhaps even without the shaman's knowledge, and it was avenged by slaying the suspect. Usually, the malignant shaman was identified either as the person who had treated the deceased or as a member of a somewhat distant group. Accusations of witchcraft were rarely directed against relatives because kinship relations were too important to be endangered. It was, in fact, one of the most important kinship obligations to avenge the death of a relative. Once revenge had been taken, a series of reprisals and counter-reprisals might follow. These were purely personal and could not involve defin-able suprafamilial groups, for such groups did not exist. . . .

Religion. Religion integrated families with one another only to a minor degree. Shoshonean culture lacked collective social and economic activities and common interests, except the communal hunts, dancing, and gaming previously mentioned. There was no functional need for ceremonialism dedicated to group purposes and led by priests holding a definite office. The communal antelope hunt was directed by a special shaman, but this leader did not serve any permanent group.

The relationship between human beings and supernatural powers was conceived largely as a matter of individual concern. Every person hoped to acquire a supernatural power or guardian spirit. This power, manifest in the form of animals, plants, clouds, mountains, and other natural phenomena, came to him in dreams and gave him special abilities, such as gambling luck, hunting skill, endurance, and others of benefit to himself alone. Shamans' powers differed from those of ordinary persons mainly in the ability to cure sickness in other people. The shaman did not lead group ceremonies. His curing performances might attract large numbers of families which happened to be in the vicinity because they liked not only to watch his singing, dancing, trance, laying-on-of-hands, and other rites but to visit other families. Shamans were influential because their curing abilities gave them prestige while their presumed capacity for practicing black magic made them feared, but they carried no specific authority.

A minor collective religious activity designed for the common good was the circle dance, which, according to the belief of some of the Western Shoshoni, promoted general fertility and benefited everyone. Harris (1940) reported that the Tosavits or White Knife Shoshoni of northern Nevada held group ceremonies for general welfare. It is more likely, however, that the principal feature of such ceremonies was the circle dance, which was held by whatever families came together at various stages of their food quest, and that the religious aspect was secondary and incidental to the recreational purpose. The "dance boss" was certainly not a religious leader. Similarly, the bear dance of the Ute was primarily recreational and only secondarily religious in heralding the spring season and providing protection against bears. Its leader, like that of the circle dance, was a layman.

Winter encampments. The only prolonged accessibility of families to one another occurred in the winter encampments. These winter quarters have sometimes been called villages, but they were not tightly nucleated settlements which constituted organized communities. Instead, family houses were widely scattered within productive portions of the piñon zone. The location of each household was determined primarily by its pine nut caches and secondarily by accessibility to wood and water. The scattered families were able to visit one another to dance, gamble, and exchange gossip, and the men occasionally co-operated in a deer or mountain sheep hunt. Although dances and collective hunts required co-ordination, the leaders had no authority outside the particular activity.

Other interfamilial and interpersonal relationships were determined by customary usage. Disputes and hostilities arising from such matters as murder, theft, wife-stealing, and other violations of custom were settled between families. None of these was a "crime" against the community, for the community did not exist in any corporate or legal sense. Violations of custom threatened families, not larger socially integrated units. Thus, the very concept of crime presupposes some kind of suprafamily level of integration, some collectivity, which has a common purpose that must be protected against antisocial behavior by its members.

In addition to the leaders of special activities, each village or local area of scattered winter houses usually had a man of some importance whom modern Shoshonean informants frequently call the "village chief." So far as "chief" implies permanent authority over an identifiable group, this term is a complete misnomer, for this man had no authority, and he served only one function. This function, however, was extremely important. It was to act as a clearing-house of information about where foods could be found. Since the Shoshoneans were constantly on the verge of starvation, especially at the end of winter, knowledge of where greens, seeds, rabbits, insects, and other foods were to be had made the repository of such information the most important person in the village.

The winter village cannot be considered a genuine suprafamilial form of social integration because it lacked permanent membership and even permanent location. Each year, families came from a general area to a locality of abundant pine nuts. Leaders were accepted by common consent to control such collective activities as required coordination. It was only in the few regions of uncommonly abundant and reliable food that a group of fixed membership occupied one or more permanent villages throughout most of the year and had a true village chief and permanent leaders of other activities.

TOPOGRAPHY AND SOCIAL LIFE

The geographic factor influences society on the small scale as well as on the large. One particularly interesting example of this effect is seen in the study of the structure of cities. This selection discusses the unusual case of New Orleans, where relatively minor differences in the altitude of the terrain are reflected in impressive differences in land usage.

This study is addressed to the generalization, originally formulated on the basis of studying Chicago, that as cities grow, the newest and best residences tend to be situated at the periphery. The oldest residences, near the center, degenerate into slums until they are replaced by the offices and stores of the expanding commercial core. This process typically results in the distribution of populations in a pattern roughly of concentric rings. Slum dwellers tend to live in a circle immediately around the city center, the well-to-do in a suburban ring, and the ordinary citizens in a band between these. Although many exceptions to this pattern have been noted, the generalization is a fair approximation to the reality of most American cities studied to this time. Gilmore's observations of New Orleans show a rather different pattern, which he finds to be related to the city's unusual geography, as well as to its peculiar history.

New Orleans is a city composed of Creoles (descendants of the original French and Spanish settlers), of their Negro servants, of now dominant settlers from the Eastern states, and of various later immigrant groups. If the ring hypothesis were applied to New Orleans, one would expect to find the Creoles and the Old Americans living at the periphery, and the Negroes and other immigrants in slums near the core. Rather, until recently, the Creoles lived in the virtual center of the city and the Old Americans lived in a distinct but close-by area. The Negroes lived on the periphery of both areas, and the other immigrants adjoined the Creoles on the opposite side of the city from the Old Americans. As the city grew, the various areas expanded outward, but the better-off members of the Creole and particularly the Old American groups frequently remained in the downtown locations. The schematic diagram below indicates the location of the various groups.

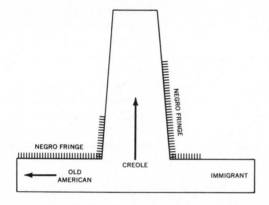

The T-formation noted here is caused by the fact that slight declines in elevation of this sea-level city resulted in swamps that were unsuitable for pleasant dwellings until efficient drainage was introduced, well into the twentieth century. The two wealthier, but conflicting, groups seized the higher and more desirable land, and developed it in two of the three possible directions for expansion. The third arm of development went by default to the middle-level Negroes. As this form of development resulted in very inconvenient travel distances for the newer residential areas, the central areas remained relatively more desirable than in other cities, and deterioration was retarded until the sentimental value of historic edifices guaranteed the survival of the central areas as prestigeful residential locations.

The development of effective drainage techniques and more efficient modes of transportation in the twentieth century cited in this selection illustrates how technology can react upon the geographical factor and reduce its influence. Perhaps if these technological skills had been available during the early years of New Orleans, its physical and social structure might more strongly have resembled that of Chicago. However, it is interesting to note that the technology which was introduced relatively late in the development of the city had a fairly minimal effect. The French quarter and the Garden District continue to attract the well-to-do, based no longer on their geographic superiority, but on sentiment and symbolism related to antiquity. The early response of the city to the peculiarities of its geographical environment set constraints on future development that will doubtless be felt for many years after the direct effect of geography has been eliminated.

Selection 6

THE OLD NEW ORLEANS AND THE NEW: A CASE FOR ECOLOGY

H. W. Gilmore

New Orleans is sufficiently different from the general run of American cities to make it an interesting laboratory for studying ecological principles evolved on the basis of data from other cities. Its topography, on casual observation, appears to be rather similar to that of Chicago, or of any number of plains cities. Yet in certain respects its topography is very different, and uniquely, it has been changed fundamentally during the history of the city. In its population history it has shown evidence of the processes of accommodation and assimilation of minority groups characteristic of other cities plus long-standing patterns of accommodation of racial groups which assimilated very slowly or not at all. As a result of these complex factors, ecological maps of New Orleans look like a crazy-quilt to sociologists acquainted with the ecology of conventional American cities. Actually, however, the city is not without an ecological pattern and this pattern is not difficult to see once the city's topography and history of ethnic groups are understood.

As was said above, the topography of the city is in some respects typical but in other respects it is unique. The city is located on a strip of land roughly five to seven miles wide between Lake Pontchartrain on the north and the Mississippi River on the south. Though eighty miles from the gulf, this land, like all land in the area, was built up by a long process of sedimentation. Therefore, in contrast to inland areas, the higher land is found along streams or where streams once existed while the lowest land is found farther away from the streams. Thus, while the land may appear to be perfectly flat, a contour map shows that the land ranges from fifteen feet above to two feet below mean gulf-level.

The highest land in the city is found along the river and ranges from five to fifteen feet above mean gulf-level. Passing north from the river, the altitude declines to two feet below gulf-level. The low area, however, is transversed by "ridges" where bayous are or have

Reprinted from *American Sociological Review*, 9:4, 1944, pp. 385–394, with permission of Mrs. H. W. Gilmore and the publisher.

been. Thus there is Metairie Ridge, two feet above sea-level running east and west almost parallel with the river and about half way between the river and the lake. There is also a ridge about two feet above gulf-level, running north-south from the end of Bayou St. John to the river, passing the lower end of the French quarter. We will call this Esplanade Ridge. This ridge divides the city into what may be conceived as two saucers sitting edge to edge, the other edges being formed by Metairie Ridge and the high land along the river. Each saucer is two feet below sea-level at its center and is from two to fifteen feet above sea-level at its periphery. Until relatively modern times the centers of these saucers were swamps and habitation was feasible only along the rims of the saucers. It is in terms, therefore, of the struggle of the nationality groups for residential space around the edges of the saucers that the ecology of the city is to be understood.

Creole New Orleans

New Orleans, of course, was settled by the French. Presumably the particular site was selected because they wanted an inland water route to the gulf coast of the present state of Mississippi where they already had a settlement at Biloxi. Such a route was available through Bayou St. John, Lake Pontchartrain and a series of lakes and bayous which link this lake to the gulf. A short and easy portage between the river and Bayou St. John was provided by Esplanade Ridge which was already in use for this purpose by the Indians when the French explorations and settlement were made. The settlement originated at the junction of Esplanade Ridge and the river and as it expanded it did so mostly to the west where the land was higher than it was to the east. This is the area that is now known as the French Quarter.

Like the settlers in most colonies, the early French settlers of New Orleans were a rather motley lot. They came from various walks of life and various stations in France and probably are not to be considered as coming primarily from any particular social element of

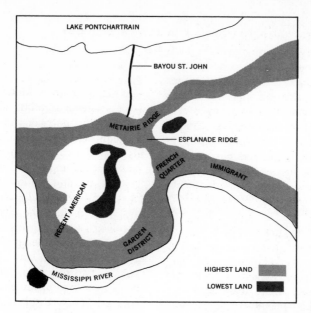

the homeland. After a period of frontier hardship, however, they began to be moulded into a quite distinctive and homogeneous group. The French government followed a very liberal policy of land grants to individuals with the result that most of the early settlers became big land holders. This policy was continued by the Spanish government when this territory passed into the hands of that nation. Thus under both France and Spain, there was a tendency for government officials and military personnel sent out to the colony to acquire sizeable land holdings usually without having to purchase them. On these holdings the French established plantations worked with slave labor and rapidly attained prosperity on this basis. Most of them, however, continued to live in the city, particularly during the winter and if they lived on their plantations at all they did so in the summer. Their city life was based almost as much on slave labor and the labor of free Negroes as was their plantation life. Thus at the time of the Louisiana Purchase there were twice as many Negroes as whites in the city. As time went on these French plantation owners came to refer to themselves as Creoles and they will be so referred to in the remainder of this paper. The term itself does not refer to land ownership but merely to unmixed descendants of French or Spanish settlers. This prosperous, land-endowed group, plentifully supplied with colored labor, and gathering in the city for a winter of leisure, made a very favorable situa-

tion for an elegant social life. The city being also the colonial capital made this almost inevitable. Such a development seems to have taken place in a large way from 1743 when the great marquis, Pierre François de Rigaud, Marquis de Vaudreuil, came as governor of Louisiana. He and his wife were accustomed to life in the royal courts of Europe and apparently sought with considerable success to set up a similarly pretentious society in New Orleans. Once established, this pattern was continued by succeeding governors, French and Spanish, with the exception of a brief period under General ("Bloody") O'Reilly who was sent by Spain to suppress a revolt against Spanish rule.

Spanish rule does not seem to have altered the situation in any significant way. The Spanish made no attempt to colonize New Orleans or Louisiana. They did make a half-hearted attempt to teach Spanish in the colony but it attained very indifferent success. For the most part, Spanish officials and military men seem to have found the Creole social life much to their taste and to have been accepted by the Creoles into that social life. Thus they came nearer being assimilated by the Creoles than the reverse. In reality many of them did marry Creoles and others received land grants, established plantations and became part of the Creole aristocracy.

Thus, prior to the Louisiana Purchase, the city was dominated by this Creole landed aristocracy centered around the colonial capital. It was a typical Estate pattern. The emphasis was on inherited wealth in the form of land. There was a law of primogeniture with the surplus sons placed in professions or the government service and stress was laid on social life or leisure time pursuits instead of occupational attainment.

The following description by a French traveler, C. C. Robin, of a reception given in 1803 may give a glimpse of the life of these Creoles prior to the Louisiana Purchase:

> The Louisiana Ladies appeared there with a magnificence that was astonishing in such a colony, and that magnificence could be compared with what is most brilliant in our principal towns in France. The stature of the ladies, generally tall, and their fair complexion, which was set off to advantage by their light dresses adorned with flowers and rich embroideries, gave a fairy-like appearance to these festivities. The last one especially astonished me by its magnificence. After the tea, the concert, the dances, the guests descended at midnight into a hall where, on a table of sixty to eighty covers rose from the midst of rocks the temple of Good Faith, surrounded with columns and surmounted by a dove; underneath was the statue of the allegorical goddess. But further, outside of that hall, the brilliance of the lights attracted the guests under an immense gallery closed by awnings. Forty to fifty dishes, served in different styles, were offered to the choice of four or five hundred guests who were assembled in little groups.[1]

In addition to the Creoles and the Negroes, there were other nationality groups in the city prior to the nineteenth century. A number of Germans had come to the Louisiana territory during the John Law boom in the 1720's and after unsuccessful attempts at settlement on the Arkansas River had settled in the vicinity of New Orleans. Also French immigrants came from Santo Domingo as a result of slave uprisings and from France as a result of the French Revolution during the latter part of the eighteenth and early part of the nineteenth century. Most of these groups were unable to get large land grants and hence did not become plantation owners. In large part they seem to have become dairymen and truck gardeners though many of them also became artisans. There were also, of course, some representatives of numerous other nationalities but they can be ignored in an ecological study.

With this information before us, let us try to get a picture of the city at the time of the Louisiana Purchase in 1803. It contained only 8,475 population (census of 1805) and covered a correspondingly small area. The heart of the city was what is now known as the French Quarter, bounded by Canal Street, Rampart Street, Esplanade Avenue and the river. In this area were the government buildings, what business there was and the homes of the Creoles. The slaves were housed on the premises of their owners so far as possible. Since most of the Negroes, whether free or slave, were employed in service around the homes of the Creoles, and hours were long and travel was by foot, the Creoles desired them to live close to their homes. Thus those who could not be quartered on the premises formed a residential fringe around the Creole section. Outside this Negro zone was the immigrant truck gardening and dairying zone, the latter using land which was too swampy for residence or cultivation but usable as pasture. On the high land adjacent to the river and east of the city this trucking zone expanded into a considerable area. Outside of this area were plantations wherever the land was high enough to permit cultivation. Thus there were plantations along Bayou St. John and along the river on both sides of the city.

Creole-American conflict

Up to the Louisiana Purchase the infiltration of Americans into New Orleans had been small. They came in and out with the shipping and there were some permanent residents but in some degree immigration of Americans had been held back by unfavorable Spanish laws. With the Louisiana Purchase, however, the dam was breached and the tide began to flow. Thus within the five year period from 1805–1810 there was a 125 per cent increase in the white population of the city, and a large part of this increase undoubtedly was American.

These incoming Americans were a sharp contrast to the polished, wealthy Creoles with their elegant social life. While as a group the Americans who came to New Orleans were perhaps not as crude as the American frontiersmen in the open country, certainly they had among them many who were just that crude. In fact the river men who floated down the Mississippi on barges and were known locally as the Kentucks were just as crude and rough and ready as the frontiersmen in any part of the country. Thus in New Orleans, the spreading American frontier ran into a culture which, on a basis of manners and fine appearance at least, was superior to its own; the only case of its kind in American history.

The difference in degree of cultural refinement, however, was not the only difference between the Creoles and the Americans. The Creoles, it will be remembered, laid stress on family tradition, hereditary wealth, leisure and social position. The American, on the other hand, had as his sun god the self-made man. The individual who had been born free and equal, had through his own initiative, industry and thrift gained wealth or success, was the man to be worshiped whether he was the son of a prince, a millionaire, a beggar, a criminal or a simple frontier woodchopper. Thus the two had basically different social philosophies as well as social systems; neither understood the philosophy of the other and neither was much impressed if he did understand. Also the fact that the Creoles were Catholic whereas most of the Americans were Protestant did little to foster mutual affection. Language differences of course increased these tensions, and furthermore, the question which language would be the official language, was an issue of serious moment.

On the basis of their culture, their wealth and their numbers in a more normal situation, the Americans might have been expected to have assumed the role of a minority group but, as usual, New Orleans was not a normal situation. The Americans were representatives of the nation which had just purchased Louisiana and now controlled the government and they were in no psychological mood to be a minority group. Nor was the government in any mood to insist on their playing a minority role. Thus from the beginning, to the tune of much conflict, overt and covert, with the Creoles, they were forced by the factors of the situation into a position somewhat better than that of a minority group.

The course of events brought a rapid improvement in their situation. The passage of the Louisiana Territory into the hands of the United States ended all barriers to commerce on the Mississippi River and brought a rapid commercial development in New Orleans. The Creoles with their philosophy of hereditary wealth and leisurely social life, had never had much taste for the make or break drive for efficiency characteristic of the commercial world and they did not take to it now. Since most of the tillable land was already held by the Creoles, most of the Americans had little chance of establishing themselves as landlords. In any event, the uncertainties, the big stakes and the competition of the business world, had a natural appeal to the worshipers of the self-made man, and they rapidly took over the competitive area as their special domain.

Thus the port figures for the first six months in 1803 show that the shipping was already largely in American hands even before the Louisiana Purchase. Of the 153 cargo ships entering the Mississippi during that period 93 were American, 58 were Spanish and 2 were French.[2] Similarly, Vincent Nolte who visited New Orleans in 1806, three years after the Purchase, informs us that the mercantile system was made up of four or five French establishments founded during the French rule, three Scotch counting-houses, one German concern and eight or ten commission houses lately opened by young American merchants from New York, Philadelphia and Baltimore.[3]

This near-monopoly on the thriving commerce of the port city rapidly brought prosperity to the Americans and along with it brought a rapid increase in their numbers. With their nationality status thus backed by wealth and numbers, the Americans increasingly challenged the Creoles for the leadership role, culture or no culture, and the struggle between the two groups grew in severity and bitterness.

Ecology of the Old New Orleans

This struggle made inevitable an ecological separation of the two groups. The first Americans did live and have their business in the French Quarter but the crowded conditions plus the Creole-American struggle brought growing pressure for them to go elsewhere. Being so heavily engaged in commerce, it was imperative that they stay on the high land along the river but the fact that they moved west instead of east of the French Quarter was perhaps the result of the Marigny affair.

About 1822 two Americans, James H. Caldwell and Samuel J. Peters, planning to develop a succession of warehouses and cotton presses and other important enterprises (hotel, gas works and water works, etc.), approached Bernard de Marigny with a proposition to buy the whole of his extensive property along the Elysian Field Section. The Creole was extremely unwilling to deal with the Americans, whom he disliked intensely, but was finally persuaded to do so, for a stipulated sum. When the necessary legal documents had been drawn up to conclude the sale, Mrs. Marigny failed to appear at the notary's office. Her signature was necessary to ratify the sale and Marigny used her absence as an excuse to prevent the sale. Infuriated, Mr. Peters is said to have cried out to the Creole: "I shall live, by God, to see the day when rank grass shall choke up the streets of your old faubourg."

. . . Outraged but not discouraged, the two pioneers transferred their interests above Canal Street. They felt that the Americans would be glad to congregate there since they would be separate from those whom they regarded as their oppressors. With the assistance of other local American capitalists a considerable part of the holdings of Jean Gravier was purchased.[4]

Whether or not this event is a full explanation, at any rate from about this time on an American section did grow rapidly to the west of the French Quarter. Into this section moved both American residents and American business. This movement was particularly rapid in the early 30's and a survey made by a local newspaper in 1834 showed that about three fifths of the "merchants," two fifths of the "retailers" and four fifths of the "brokers" were by that time in the American section.[5] Thus the city quickly evolved a pattern with the business section around Canal Street as the center, the Creole section to the east and the American residential section to the west of this. Each of these residential areas had Negro slaves living on the premises and a horseshoe shaped fringe of Negro residences around it with the open side of the horseshoe being towards the business section. Outside of this was the trucking-dairying zone.

The strife which produced this residential segregation was manifest in a severe degree in political circles. The Creoles, considering themselves the settlers of Louisiana, felt the government belonged to them, and the Americans, considering that they had purchased Louisiana, felt the government was theirs. The Creoles had been accustomed to use government positions to support their sons who could not inherit land under primogeniture, and the Americans had no inclination to use tax funds to support Creole families. In contrast the Americans wanted the government to build all sorts of facilities which would be of aid to commerce, and the Creoles were not interested in being taxed to bring prosperity to the Americans. These differences were so great that as the two factions attained near equality numerically and financially one government could no longer contain them. Thus in 1836 New Orleans was divided into three municipalities, having one mayor but for all practical purposes having separate governments. In the center was the Creole city bounded on the east by Esplanade Avenue and on the west by Canal Street. To the east of it was the immigrant truck gardening city and to the west of the Creole section was the American municipality. In all three cases the river was the southern boundary and the lake was the northern boundary.

This separation of the city into three municipalities practically established Canal Street and Esplanade Avenue as national boundary lines. It became a matter of honor and of loyalty to one's cause to live on the proper side of these streets; those who moved into enemy territory were viewed askance if not actually as deserters. And after more than a century these definitions have by no means disappeared.

With this division the American municipality launched an almost extravagant program of public improvements. Old wharves were improved and new ones were built, streets were paved, public schools were developed and public buildings were constructed. Accompanying this was a growing prosperity and a rapid inflow of white population. Thus the white population in the whole city (three municipalities combined) increased from 21,281 in 1830, to 59,519 in 1840, and 91,431 in 1850. Meanwhile there were no more Negroes in the city at the end of this period than at the beginning.

A significant part of this influx of white population was Irish workmen. The growth in commerce and shipping brought laboring jobs and the public works program of the American municipality meant the need for many workmen. To meet these needs there was virtually no local labor supply. There were not enough free Negroes, slaves were too expensive, and the immigrants were happily employed in their crafts and agricultural pursuits. As a result, outside laborers were brought in and these for the most part were Irish immigrants.

This growth in population with the influx of a new immigrant element brought an expansion and reshuffling of the residential areas in the American section. With their mounting wealth the American elements were in a position to move farther out and build themselves new homes. South was the river, north were the swamps, and to the east were the business section and Creole land. Their logical move, therefore, was toward the strip of higher land adjacent to the river, and this move they made, developing a pretentious residential section with large homes and spacious grounds. This section has since been known as the Garden District. At the time it was built, it equaled or surpassed anything the Creoles possessed either in the city or on their plantations, and doubtless served to give the Americans a psychological compensation for their lack of "culture" and family background as compared with the Creoles.

This move of the Americans meant that the Negro residential fringe and the truck gardening zone had to be invaded and pushed out farther. It was the beginning of a process which continued up to relatively recent times both in the Creole and American sections. While in both cases the invasion did take place, the succession was not completed, particularly with reference to the Negro residences, for in all of the older sections of the city today there are scattered small groups of Negro residences which are remnants of a once solid Negro residential zone. Also in moving out the Americans deserted their old residences. Since the Irish were working for the Americans, they were not welcomed in other sections of the city, and being laborers, they needed no land to cultivate. Thus they were

glad enough to get the discarded residences and New Orleans gave birth to what has since been known as the Irish Channel.

As the city grew, the Creole area, being adjacent to the central business section, tended to deteriorate and this, with a natural increase in Creole population, created pressure for that group to move out also. If the Americans had their fate sealed as to where they might move, so also did the Creoles. To move east meant crossing the national boundary line of Esplanade Avenue and invading the immigrant truck gardening section and this would violate their pride and honor. To the west was Canal Street, the central business section and the unthinkable American section. Their only recourse was to move out Esplanade Ridge to Bayou St. John, and here today New Orleans has lovely old homes which are a product of this period. The migration process in this area was similar to that in the American section with some significant differences. The invasion process was about the same but the tendency of the Creoles to stay in the French Quarter in spite of deterioration was much greater. Thus there resulted an extraordinarily large number of what in other cities would be called marooned families, and there are in that area today many homes which are still owned and occupied by descendants of the families who originally built them.

Due to administrative and financial difficulties, the three municipalities were recombined into one in 1855, but by that time the ecological pattern was firmly fixed. Esplanade Avenue and Canal Street were made and the Creole section limited to Esplanade Ridge while the American section was confined to its ridge west of the city.

The strips of habitable land on these ridges were rather narrow and any tendency of these residential areas to widen was quickly checked by the swamps or the river. Therefore, expansion could only take place by building farther and farther out along these ridges. Such building, however, meant greater and greater distances from the central business section, and greater distance meant serious inconvenience when travel was by walking, bicycle or horse and buggy. In the American section, where the growth had been the greatest, the distances became so great as practically to reach the toleration point. Thus further expansion was made with a minimum of land and a minimum of added distance. This was done by making the yards inconveniently small and building the houses close together. Economically, of course, this was reflected in very high land values.

The immigrant truck-gardening section to the east of the city seems to have had, by comparison, relatively few growing pains. Being engaged in agriculture, the residents were not densely settled and, as the city developed, the population turned more and more to non-agricultural occupations. There was little accretion to this area by migration, and the rate of natural increase was not enough to take up for residential uses the land which was thrown out of cultivation. Thus while other sections were crying for land, this section had land to spare. As a result, land in this section became a quick-sand for real estate speculators who knew land but did not know New Orleans. For the same reason there was a plentiful supply of land on that side of town for military uses during the First and Second World Wars.

Thus up to the early part of this century the basic ecological pattern of the city was T-shaped. The T was formed by the intersection of Esplanade Ridge and the ridge running along the river. The French Quarter (original French settlement) was approximately at the intersection of this T. The immigrant truck-gardening area was at the east end of the cross bar and on the west end were the central business section, the Irish Channel and the Garden District (American section), respectively. The newer Creole area was on the leg of the T, Esplanade Ridge, running vertically to the river. All of these were long narrow rectangular shaped areas, strung out along the top of the ridges, flanked on both sides by the swamps or the river. The American section and the Creole area were fringed by horseshoe shaped residential areas for Negroes and outside of these was a truck-gardening and dairying zone. The latter used land which was dry enough to cultivate or pasture but too low for residential use.

The new ecology

During the present century several developments have been taking place which have been materially altering this ecological pattern. About 1910 the city began to attain success in a long effort at artificial drainage of surface water. The city had early used canals and drainage ditches to hasten the flow of water from the ridges to the swamps. Then in the latter part of the last century it tried canals with windmill powered pumps to drain lower sections. These pumps were found inadequate and in 1903 they were replaced by electric-powered centrifugal pumps. These were an improvement but still did not have the capacity necessary for a city with the heavy rainfall which New Orleans has. Finally in 1917 a large screw type of electric pump, something like a ship's propeller installed in a large pipe, was developed and this proved adequate to the task. With these pump developments went a gradual improvement in surface and underground drainage facilities. From small beginnings this system was thus expanded until today it has a pumping capacity of 16½ billion gallons per day (24 hours), enough water to cover eighty square miles of land one foot deep. As a result, the water level was gradually lowered until by the 1930's all of the former swamp areas were as effectively drained as the higher areas.

The development of this drainage system ecologically had the effect of changing the topography of the city. In virtually no place in the city is the change of altitude sudden enough that there is any visible difference between high land and low land. With drainage, therefore, the land, for ecological purposes, is perfectly flat and as far as topography is concerned it is all equally desirable for building purposes. Hence the barrier which the swamps had formerly been to residential expansion was now removed and the residential areas began to respond accordingly. The American section most strikingly turned squarely north away from the river and directly toward the center of a former swamp. Thus during the past two decades, census tracts which are in the former swamp area show population increases of from 700 to 1400 per cent. The Creole section correspondingly spread out in both directions from the Bayou St. John area, though the population pressure here was not nearly so great as in the American section.

About the time these drainage developments were taking place transportation developments were in process which also had marked effects on the ecological pattern. So far as this city is concerned probably the most important transportation development was the street car. Like other social developments, this one cannot be very specifically dated. Horse-drawn cars and steam "dummies," of course, date well back into the past century. The successful electric car was not developed until about 1885 and its effect on the ecology of the city was not very evident until well into the present century. While the street car aided greatly in relieving pressures in the American and Creole sections, probably its most pronounced effect was on the Negro residential fringe. With the street car available it was no longer necessary for the Negroes to live so close to where they worked. In other words, the electric street car made the Negro residential fringe obsolete. As a result, this fringe began to disappear. In its stead, large Negro residential areas began to develop back towards the central business section in the formerly swampy areas between the white residential sections. This concentration has in turn attracted to these areas schools and other facilities for Negroes which are an incentive for more Negroes to move there.

The automobile which had such profound effects on most American cities had a relatively small effect on New Orleans. It augmented the effect of the street car in a number of ways but since it was not commonly used by Negroes and other poor elements in the population, it created no new trends related to these residential areas. The only part of the city where there was sufficient residential pressure to make a demand for residential suburbs was the American side of the city, and here the outlying areas were so swampy that this was impractical. There did develop on the west end of Metairie Ridge, over in an adjoining parish a suburb known as Metarie. However, the 1940 census still showed New Orleans as ranking among the lowest cities in the country in the proportion of its population living in the metropolitan area outside the official city.

In general, the drainage system, the street car and the automobile combined have created a tendency for New Orleans to shift from its former ecological pattern to a zone system similar to that recognized in other cities. However, this pattern is by no means yet completed and it seems likely it will not soon be completed. Vast areas of the city are still socially taboo to large elements of the population and these do not conform to a symmetrical zone pattern. In addition, on the American side of the city, the drainage did not provide enough land to bring the price of building lots down to what would be considered elsewhere as "reasonable." Therefore, building new homes is still expensive and as a result old ones are not recklessly discarded. Consequently the "nice" old residential areas do not deteriorate except under the greatest of duress. And by the time the natural pressures for deterioration have become sufficiently great these areas have accumulated enough tradition to make them antiques. Thus the French Quarter is now protected by special legislation designed to prevent invasion and deterioration. Under this protection it has actually been undergoing a restoration with middle and upper class Americans moving in. Correspondingly the Garden District has tenaciously remained respectable. The 1940 rent map shows that this district is still one of the high rent areas of the city. Very high order rooming houses are about the only degradation it has yet suffered and to date it has not needed special legislation to protect it. However, should that necessity come, its antiquity is such that it will doubtless be museumized in the legislative halls.

In summary, the ecological pattern of New Orleans up to the present century was primarily the result of its topography. This pattern was set by the ridges and limited by the swamps and the river. In the historical process, sections of these ridges were occupied by the different nationality groups and came to be considered their special domain. Due to the ethnic conflicts and status differences between these nationality groups the social definitions of these areas became very strong and highly emotionalized. As a result of the division of the city into three municipalities in 1836 Canal Street became the accepted boundary line between the American section and the Creole section and Esplanade Avenue became the dividing line between the Creole area and the immigrant area. With the development of the drainage system during the present century the swamps disappeared and this land became as well drained as the ridges. Therefore, with the land being so nearly flat, today there is no visible difference between the low land and the high. Thus for all practical purposes topography as an ecological factor has disappeared except for outer limits set by the Mississippi River, Lake Pontchartrain and outlying swamps. In this situation the ecological pattern is tending to respond to modern transportation facilities and develop in the direction of a symmetrical zone pattern. The social definitions of the different areas carried over from the previous era, however, are proving very strong and resistant to change. This resistance is further increased by the fact that suitable land is not available for developing extensive suburbs which would make inevitable the deterioration of the old areas. Therefore, the old areas tend to be preserved and occupied by the same groups as formerly, and wherever necessary protective legislation is provided to facilitate this preservation.

Notes

[1] Fortier, Alcie, *History of Louisiana*, New York, 1904, II, pp. 240–241. Nellie Warner Price, "Le Spectacle de la Rue St. Pierre," *Louisiana Historical Quarterly* I, p. 218.

[2] *Annals of Congress, Seventh Congress—Second Session*, Washington, 1851, p. 1525.

[3] *Biographical and Historical Memories of Louisiana*, Chicago, 1892, I, p. 30.

[4] Klein, Selma L., Social Interaction of the Creoles and Anglo-Americans in New Orleans, 1803–1860, M. S. Thesis, Department of Sociology, Tulane University, 1940, pp. 35–36.

[5] *The Bee*, May 29, 1935.

Chapter 3

THE BIOLOGICAL FACTOR

HUMAN ABILITIES
Selection 7

HEALTH AND ILLNESS
Selection 8

The biological factor, like the geographic, is a conglomerate, affecting social life in different ways and by different means. One aspect of biological influence on human behavior is the abilities and limitations associated with the human body. Here, as in the discussion of the geographic factor, sociologists stress the influence of social factors upon the biological, as well as the opposite. The superior height and weight of modern Americans, compared with previous generations as well as the European populations from which they originate, is a simple example. Clothing, weapons, etc., are illustrations of the way in which the limitations of man's frail constitution are transcended.

From another point of view, biology affects the social order because men live in an environment that contains other biological creatures. Living creatures affect man's life in a great variety of ways. They are the source of all man's food; they provide the raw materials, such as wood and textiles, for the majority of artifacts with which man surrounds himself; for most of human history, they have directly or indirectly provided the major source of power in man's technology; and they have also been among the most formidable enemies man has had to face in the struggle for survival. Here again, the relationship between the biological and the social is two-way. The horse population of the world rose and fell with the development of human society. Man's great cities have immensely increased the number and prosperity of creatures like the rat and the housefly. On the other hand, many deadly germs have joined the dodo in extinction through man's agency.

The selections that follow exemplify thought about the social order in biological terms. Selection 7, by Weston LaBarre, indicates the aspects of man's biological constitution that have enabled him to engage in a "new kind of evolution." Selection 8, by Irving Kenneth Zola, discusses the social nature of the judgment of health and illness, and shows the effect of a people's way of life on their interpretation and evaluation of bodily events.

HUMAN ABILITIES

In his book *The Human Animal*, Weston LaBarre traces the evolution of man and then proceeds to relate various aspects of man's social life to his biological needs. This selection presents LaBarre's conception of the biological characteristics that most fundamentally distinguish man from other animals and that lay the foundations for specifically human behavior. The selection should be read in the light of LaBarre's observation that man is, relative to other animals, a physically unspecialized creature. Evolution is described as a series of responses of organisms to new environments, entered because they offer possibilities of additional food or safety from natural enemies. The usual method of adaptation to the new environments is physical specialization caused by genetic mutation, illustrated by the wings of flying birds and the neck of the giraffe which enables him to nibble from the "unreachable" treetops. The disadvantage of physical specialization is that once it occurs it is irreversible. A paw (unspecialized) can evolve into a wing, a flipper, or a hoof (specialized), but the reverse process does not seem to happen. The specialized animal is accordingly restricted to a specialized environment to which it may be superbly adapted, but from which it cannot escape if the need should arise. An extensive and rapid change in the environment leaves the specialized inhabitant extinct as a species.

> Man is a relatively unspecialized animal who rather closely resembles his primate ancestors except for the form of his foot, which is specialized for erect, bipedal walking. However, given hands, freed from the necessity of aid in locomotion, and coupled with intelligence and stereoscopic vision, man has achieved a better adjustment to his environment than any other animal. Man can be seen as the end point of biological evolution, since adjustment to the environment is achieved in his hands through tools, rather than through further biological specialization. This new form of evolution (recognized as technological evolution by sociologists) is generally quicker and more satisfactory than biological evolution, and it lacks the disadvantages that physical specialization entails.

LaBarre supports his thesis that man is "the best animal" by citing man's superiority in numbers to other large mammals and his "discovery" of walking, which, unlike all other such evolutionary innovations, has not been followed by a proliferation of species (but rather by a proliferation of technology).

The introduction to this chapter suggested that biology, like geography, is a limiting factor for the social order. The import of LaBarre's thesis is that these limits are very broad and are being increased through man's development of increasingly better tools with which to adapt to new environments. This terrestrial animal, a descendent of tree dwellers, has become in many ways better adapted to water and air than the fishes and birds. Moreover, man is the only animal capable of surviving in that most hostile of environments, outer space.

Selection 7
FROM THE HUMAN ANIMAL
Weston LaBarre

Early man was an earth-bound ape, with empty hands. But it was these same empty hands that changed completely the whole

manner of evolution in man and made him unique beyond all comparison with any other living creature. Seen in its separate aspects, the human hand is nothing special. Five-toed paws were part of the original pattern of lungs and legs of even the early amphibians, and they are thoroughly commonplace in later land animals descended from the amphibians. For man to have five fingers would be the usual thing to expect: it is the pterodactyl's little-finger flying, the bat's long-fingered wing-hand, the bird's arm-wing, and the whale's handflippers that are the anatomically clever, the functionally spectacular, variations on the basic pentadactyl* theme. Human hands are not unusual, either, as the freed limbs of bipedal† animals: there are plenty of instances of this, from reptilian dinosaurs to marsupial kangaroos and mammalian jerboas. Nor is the hand unique as a grasping organ in man: many of the tree-living primates were even four-handed, and thus two up on man—whose specialized foot has lost just about all its one-time prehensile skill.

The uniqueness of man's hand is functional, not physical. Of course his primate ancestors' sojourn in the trees did greatly improve the grasping ability of the old amphibian-reptilian-mammalian paw. It is also true that the fully opposable thumb in man is a further improvement on the primate hand. But in purely physical terms, monkey hands could probably do nearly everything a man's hands could. The main significance of the human hand lies in its being one member of a functional complex of hands, brains, and eyes.

When man, heir of four limbs, uses only two of them for walking, his clever primate hands are then finally freed from use in any kind of locomotion whatever. They can now be used for purely exploratory grasping. The advantages of this are not to be underestimated. Some New World monkeys, it is true, have prehensile‡ tails, but these are still largely locomotor in function; besides, the tail has the grave disadvantage of not being ordinarily in the monkey's field of vision. A better case of exploratory prehensility is the elephant's trunk—perhaps significantly combined, as is man's hand, with great intelligence. But the elephant's trunk is mainly used for feeding; and, besides, there is only one of them. Nor do elephants have stereoscopic vision,§ to put together a muscular with a visual space-sense. Still, a sensitive grasping trunk is not to be sneezed at as a biological advantage. At least in the past, the elephant family had the

adaptive radiation¶ that often shows up in a successful animal type; for elephant-like creatures once made themselves at home in a variety of environments from Siberia to Sumatra, from England to Africa, and from Saskatchewan to South America. But judgment must respect the fact that all of these are extinct, some of them with man's assistance, except for the elephants of Africa and of Southeast Asia —and these too are dying out.

Emancipated hands are not enough: many dinosaurs had them, but they lacked sufficient brains. Intelligence is not enough: elephants have a great deal of intelligence behind their trunks, but they do not have stereoscopic sight; the prehensile-tailed monkeys are intelligent too, and they have stereoscopic vision as well, but they do not ordinarily see their tails. Stereoscopic eyes are not enough either: for the intelligent, tree-living apes have them, with color vision and the yellow spot in the retina to boot. It is the combination that counts. Man has paired grasping organs, fully in his field of vision and wholly freed from locomotor duties, in a stereoscopic-sighted, big-brained mammal —and these add up to the answer.

Anaxagoras claimed that man had brains because he had hands, but Aristotle argued that man had hands because he had brains. When the implications of these statements are better understood and the dust of battle has settled a bit, modern anthropologists are inclined to give the decision to Anaxagoras rather than to Aristotle. But hands, brains, and eyes are a case, really, of hens-and-eggs causality; nor did it all begin, strictly speaking, with man. For in all primate evolution they influence each other mutually and develop progressively together; and the ability to "monkey with things" that man got from his primate ancestors is still one of the keystones of human nature. Certainly such hands and eyes and brains put an animal into closer object-relationship with reality and enlarge the animal ego in the technical sense of increasing awareness and testing of reality. Very literally, such an animal as man has more contacts with reality.

But when we remember the conflict of brains and snout for possession of the skull (the total size of which is limited by pelvic birth), it is probable that the mouth is also part of the hand-brain-eye complex. Eating is

---

* Five-fingered.—Ed.
† Two-footed.—Ed.
‡ Grasping.—Ed.
§ Arrangement of the eyes to allow perception of depth.—Ed.

¶ Generating additional species of the same general type.—Ed.

just as much a function of the primate hand as are tree-acrobatics. Food, as much as safety, both available in the trees, probably took the primates originally into the trees. And at least some students believe that food available on the ground brought them down again—after a refashioning of locomotion itself in the service of nutrition. When primary grasping with the snout is given up, the sense of smell is less important as a guide. But if snout-smelling gives pleasure in feeding, hands will now share in the pleasurable accomplishment of the basic organic satisfaction, eating. While smell still plays a large role in eating enjoyment, the relative insignificance of the snout anatomically and of smell functionally indicates that they are overshadowed in man.

The matter is probably more complex than this. It should be remembered that grasping the mother's fur is part of the association of food and security in primate babies. It is significant too that in human babies the two major reflexes fully prepared at birth are the "sucking reflex" and the "grasping reflex" (such that a baby can actually support its weight and hang from a bar tightly grasped in its hands). Also, one gets the decided impression in watching older babies that half the fun of eating lies in playing with the food. All in all, it seems quite probable that human hands have an "erotized" interest in handling things, which is borrowed from their pleasurable association with feeding. Anatomically, man has obviously moved beyond a mere nutritional "oral" interest in his environment. His hands show a controlling, manipulative concern with non-nutritional *objects*, with a desire and an ability to coerce reality beyond his own body and body-contents, or potential body-contents like food; just as, similarly, the permanent human breast and heightened sexuality evidence a persistent and organically rooted inter-individual interest in other *persons*.

In this hand-brain-mouth-eye complex, the close brain-eye tie-up is quite clear: we have only to look at the large optic lobe in the brain of later animals to see this. The brain-hand nexus is very evident neurologically, for the nerve-supply of the hand is almost fantastically rich—even in so archaic a sense as touch, the hand (as compared, say, with the thigh, the leg, or the back) is developed in discrimination and sensitivity to an extravagant degree. The hand-eye connection is easily appreciated on study of muscle-sense, stereoscopic seeing, and space-awareness in man. The hand-mouth relationship is shown in several ways. The newborn human baby is very undeveloped neurologically, that is, many of its nerves do not grow to make final connections with muscles until a couple of years after birth; and, in this context, the neurological maturity of the sucking and that of the grasping reflexes is particularly striking. Furthermore, the representation of the lips in the cerebral cortex is quite enormous in comparison with other parts of the body. Also, in a baby old enough to sit up, anything that the eye can see and the hand can grasp is immediately sent to the mouth for consultation and confirmation.

The price in irreversible specialization in his foot, which man has paid for this new significance of the hand, seems a small one indeed when its advantages are noted. For it must be admitted that the human foot is now as hopelessly specialized as the limbs and appendages of most other warm-blooded creatures, and it is difficult to imagine its ever being useful for anything but bipedal walking. The accidents of evolution rarely give an animal a chance for more than one or perhaps two adaptive specializations of any organ: the more exactly and efficiently an organ is adapted anatomically to some special aspect of the environment, the more fatally dependent it is on the accidents of environmental change. The large-scale extinction of animal species in the past fully illustrates this fact. It is as if that species goes farthest which holds off its physical specializations as long as possible; it can then build its own minor specialization on as large a collection of prior major animal accomplishments as possible.

But this suggests a greater planning and self-consciousness in organisms than is really visible in evolution. The value to organisms of getting a hold on things must be a general one, for it is found in many kinds of animals. The general idea of hands has been stumbled on again and again in evolution, from crabs and scorpions and their claws to the various back-boned animals (the two-legged dinosaurs, and "three-legged" wallabies and kangaroo rats) that sit or stand up to use their front paws in holding things. In this light, the hand in man is a venture backed by the biological capital of all the long line of body patents to which he is the heir, in the main line of amphibians, reptiles, mammals, and primates. But the double arch of the human foot—that came from changing from the land to the trees and then back again from the trees to the ground—shows that man's line has already taken all his probable chances at adaptive specialization of the hind limbs. As far as the foot is concerned, man is now in the same evolutionary boat as every other specialized animal: an adaptation, once made, is a hostage to fortune and a commitment to future evolutionary fate. The human foot has "had it."

The great bargain that this specialization represents in man, however, removes him from any comparison with any other animal. The human hand is the adaptation to end all adaptations: *the emancipated hand has emancipated man from any other organic evolution whatsoever.* With man, genetic evolution and organic experiments have come to an end. Without involving the animal body and its slow, blind genetic mechanisms, man's hands make the tools and the machines which render his own further physical evolution unnecessary; they replace the slow, cumbrous, expensive, uncertain, and painful mechanism of organic evolution with the swift, conscious, biologically free, and painless making of machines.

Nothing like this has ever happened before in evolution. Machines not only can do man's flying, diving, and superhuman seeing and hearing for him, but also *they do his evolving for him.* (Indeed, in a cybernetic "feed-back" machine like a thermostat—in which the results of its action are automatically scanned by the machine to correct and modify its future action according to man's preconceived, built-in intentions—man is already creating a quasi-organism, with one sense and a part-brain, after his own image. Nor does it invite disrespect to realize that with his brain man can build mathematical thinking machines better than his own for their particular purpose.) The critical fact is that the making of machines is done with no narrow and irreversible commitment whatever of man's body. With human hands, the old-style evolution by body adaptation is obsolete. All previous animals had been subject to the *autoplastic** evolution of their self-substance, committing their bodies to experimental adaptations in a blind genetic gamble for survival. The stakes in this game

* Changing the form of the body, as contrasted with *alloplastic*.—Ed.

were high: life or death. Man's evolution, on the other hand, is through *alloplastic* experiments with objects outside his own body and is concerned only with the products of his hands, brains, and eyes—and not with his body itself. True, a flaw in the design of an experimental jet plane may kill a pilot, but that does not make the human race extinct or even wipe out aeronautical engineers as a species.

It is an error to suppose that a spider's web is in this sense a "tool." For, besides being instinctive (a genetically given function), the spider web is merely an autoplastic extension into space of its own non-living substance or metaplasm. No more is a bird's nest a "tool," since neither insight nor intuition and neither memory nor experience plays any part in this instinctual activity. Even the most generous interpretation would allow temporary or accidental nonce "tools" only to anthropoids. But then these tools are not socially hereditary, for the best that apes have is insight or imitation-by-contiguity, and not human culture.

It is not only the genetic freedom of man's new kind of evolution that is significant; one has to consider also the fantastic speed of it as well. It took millions and millions of years from fish to whale to evolve a warm-blooded marine mammal: but man evolved submarines from dream to actuality in a mere few centuries and at no genetic price in physical specialization. It took innumerable genera of birds uncountable eons since *Archaeopteryx* for their autoplastic experimentation with flying: but man, in only some fifty years since Kitty Hawk, flies not only as well as birds but actually far better. In objective physical terms of speed, altitude, and range, man already flies faster than sound (something no bird will ever do with moving wings), higher than any bird (since birds must breathe the open air), and farther than even the most miraculous migratory bird (with its settled complex of methods, materials, and metabolism). Even by the admittedly crude evolutionary criterion of gross size, man's airplanes are even now far larger and far heavier than any eagle or condor, whereas a bird as large as an ostrich is already permanently grounded. Man makes a new model of plane and tinkers with its mechanical "bugs" much more cheaply biologically and more efficiently and quickly than any bird can modify its form by evolution.

Since man's machines evolve now, not anatomical man, he has long since gone outside

his own individual skin in his functional relatedness to the world. The real evolutionary
unit now is not man's mere body; it is "all-
mankind's-brains-together-with-all-the-extra-
bodily-materials-that-come-under-the-manipu-
lation-of-their-hands." Man's very physical ego
is expanded to encompass everything within
reach of his manipulating hands, within sight
of his searching eyes, and within the scope of
his restless brain. An airplane is part of a
larger kinaesthetic and functional self; it is a
larger ownership of reality by the questing ego
of life. And airplanes are biologically cheap.
For, as unconcernedly as a man changes an
auger for a reamer in an electric drill, he exchanges the joystick of a plane for the driving
wheel of a car. Without being, through spe-

cialization, a biological amputee, he attaches
all sorts of prosthetic devices* to his limbs. This
evolution-by-prosthesis is uniquely human and
uniquely freed from the slowness of reproduction and of evolutionary variation into blind
alleys from which there is no retreat. Man,
with tools as his projected body and machines
the prosthetic creatures of his hands, is not
merely a promising animal biologically: he
makes every other animal wholly obsolete, except as they serve *his* purposes of prosthetic
metabolism, locomotion, manufacture of materials and of biological medicines.

* Literally, artificial extensions, such as wooden
legs.—Ed.

HEALTH AND ILLNESS

The effect of biology upon human behavior is obvious in the area of disease and
health. What is less obvious is the effect of social factors upon the health-related
functioning of the body. Anthropologists have documented an amazing variety
of normal and abnormal bodily functions that are influenced by the social
environment, including such seemingly automatic functions as heartbeat and
breathing. The role of society, through personality, in the increasing number of
disorders labeled psychosomatic, is an important one. Social factors are also
responsible for creating conditions that retard or facilitate the actions of micro-
organisms, for example through more or less adequate clothing, shelter, diet, etc.
Perhaps most impressive among social factors influencing health is the science
of medicine, which has rendered many of the scourges of the past utterly unknown in the technologically advanced parts of the world today.

The interaction between biological and social factors in the matter of health
and illness is illustrated in this selection in the context of how people evaluate
their physical state. Were doctors to formulate a model of a healthy man, practically nobody could be found who would fit the model; yet most people feel
sick or unhealthy only at infrequent intervals. The judgment of health or illness
is a socially influenced judgment, which biological factors affect but do not
completely determine. This fact is demonstrated in the selection by comparing
the reactions of people of Irish and Italian background to what medically are the
same conditions.

A condition may be defined as illness by some people and not by others.
Two reasons can be suggested for this fact. First, where an abnormality, by
medical definition, is very widespread in a population it can be considered
normal by members of that population. Second, the abnormality may be
relatively uncommon, but explanations other than sickness may be utilized
to interpret it.

In a comparison of Americans of Irish and Italian extraction, it was found
that the Irish were more likely to deny pain, and to limit and underestimate their difficulties. The Irish felt less pain, counted fewer symptoms,
and believed that their condition affected their social life less than did the
Italians. This contrast held even in a group in which objective physical
conditions as judged by doctors were approximately equal. The number
and extent of symptoms complained of by the Italians is part of an Italian

response to problems generally, i.e. by expressiveness and expansiveness. Similarly, the Irish understatement and restraint in face of physical ailments is part and parcel of their more general controlling and suppressive response to problems.

The selection raises, but does not answer, the question of whether the difference between the two groups in reported pain is a matter of how they feel or how they report their feelings. Although there are probably no important neurological differences between the two groups, it is quite possible that the social forces bearing on the Irish are strong enough to render the conscious sensation of pain less for them than for the Italians. To the extent that this is the case, it is an impressive testimonial to the power of social forces. Before rejecting this interpretation, the reader should consider carefully the impact of social pressures on seemingly straightforward behavior, as discussed in Selection 20.

Selection 8
CULTURE AND SYMPTOMS: AN ANALYSIS OF PATIENTS' PRESENTING COMPLAINTS
Irving Kenneth Zola

The conception of disease

In most epidemiological studies,* the definition of disease is taken for granted. Yet today's chronic disorders do not lend themselves to such easy conceptualization and measurement as did the contagious disorders of yesteryear. That we have long assumed that what constitutes disease is a settled matter is due to the tremendous medical and surgical advances of the past half-century. After the current battles against cancer, heart disease, cystic fibrosis and the like have been won, Utopia, a world without disease, would seem right around the next corner. Yet after each battle a new enemy seems to emerge. So often has this been the pattern, that some have wondered whether life without disease is attainable.[1]

Usually the issue of life without disease has been dismissed as a philosophical problem—a dismissal made considerably easier by our general assumptions about the statistical distribution of disorder. For though there is a grudging recognition that each of us must go sometime, illness is generally assumed to be a relatively infrequent, unusual, or abnormal phenomenon. Moreover, the general kinds of

Reprinted from *American Sociological Review,* 31:5, 1966, pp. 615–630, with permission of the author and the publisher.

* Studies of the incidence, distribution, and control of disease in a population.—Ed.

statistics used to describe illness support such an assumption. Specifically diagnosed conditions, days out of work, and doctor visits do occur for each of us relatively infrequently. Though such statistics represent only treated illness, we rarely question whether such data give a true picture. Implicit is the further notion that people who do not consult doctors and other medical agencies (and thus do not appear in the "illness" statistics) may be regarded as healthy.

Yet studies have increasingly appeared which note the large number of disorders escaping detection. Whether based on physicians' estimates[2] or on the recall of lay populations,[3] the proportion of untreated disorders amounts to two-thirds or three-fourths of all existing conditions.[4] The most reliable data, however, come from periodic health examinations and community "health" surveys.[5] At least two such studies have noted that as much as 90 percent of their apparently healthy sample has some physical aberration or clinical disorder.[6] Moreover, neither the type of disorder, nor the seriousness by objective medical standards, differentiated those who felt sick from those who did not. In one of the above studies, even of those who felt sick, only 40 percent were under medical care.[7] It seems that the more intensive the investigation, the higher the prevalence of clinically serious but previously undiagnosed and untreated disorders.

Such data as these give an unexpected statistical picture of illness. Instead of it being a relatively infrequent or abnormal phenomenon, the empirical reality may be that illness, defined as the presence of clinically serious symptoms, is the statistical norm.[8] What is particularly striking about this line of reasoning is that the statistical notions underlying many "social" pathologies are similarly being questioned. A number of social scientists have noted that the basic acts or deviations, such as law-breaking, addictive behaviors, sexual "perversions" or mental illness, occur so frequently in the population[9] that were one to tabulate all the deviations that people possess or engage in, virtually no one could escape the label of "deviant."

Why are so relatively few potential "deviants" labelled such or, more accurately, why do so few come to the attention of official agencies? Perhaps the focus on how or why a particular deviation arose in the first place might be misplaced; an equally important issue for research might be the individual and societal reaction to the deviation once it occurs.[10] Might it then be the differential response to deviation rather than the prevalence of the deviation which accounts for many reported group and subgroup differences? A similar set of questions can be asked in regard to physical illness. Given that the prevalence of clinical abnormalities is so high and the rate of acknowledgment so low, how representative are "the treated" of all those with a particular condition? Given further that what is treated seems unrelated to what would usually be thought the objective situation, i.e., seriousness, disability and subjective discomfort, is it possible that some selective process is operating in what gets counted or tabulated as illness?

The interplay of culture and "symptoms"

Holding in abeyance the idea that many epidemiological differences may in fact be due to as yet undiscovered etiological* forces, we may speculate on how such differences come to exist, or how a selective process of attention may operate. Upon surveying many cross-cultural comparisons of morbidity,† we concluded that there are at least two ways in which signs ordinarily defined as indicating problems in one population may be ignored in others.[11] The first is related to the actual prevalence of the sign, and the second to its congruence with dominant or major value-orientations.

In the first instance, when the aberration is fairly widespread, this, in itself, might constitute a reason for its not being considered "symptomatic" or unusual. Among many Mexican-Americans in the Southwestern United States, diarrhea, sweating, and coughing are everyday experiences,[12] while among certain groups of Greeks trachoma is almost universal.[13] Even within our own society, Koos has noted that, although lower back pain is a quite common condition among lower-class women, it is not considered symptomatic of any disease or disorder but part of their expected everyday existence.[14] For the population where the particular condition is ubiquitous, the condition is perceived as the normal state.[15] This does not mean that it is considered "good" (although instances have been noted where not having the endemic condition was considered abnormal)[16] but rather that it is natural and inevitable and thus to be ignored as being of no consequence. Because the "symptom" or condition is omnipresent (it always was and always will be) there simply exists for such populations or cultures no frame of reference according to which it could be considered a deviation.[17]

In the second process, it is the "fit" of certain signs with a society's major values which accounts for the degree of attention they receive. For example, in some non-literate societies there is anxiety-free acceptance of and willingness to describe hallucinatory experiences. Wallace noted that in such societies the fact of hallucination per se is seldom disturbing; its content is the focus of interest. In Western society, however, with its emphasis on rationality and control, the very admission of hallucinations is commonly taken to be a grave sign and, in some literature, regarded as the essential feature of psychosis.[18] In such instances it is not the sign itself or its frequency which is significant but the social context within which it occurs and within which it is perceived and understood. Even more explicit working of this process can be seen in the interplay of "symptoms" and social rules. Tiredness, for example, is a physical sign which is not only ubiquitous but a correlate of

* Causal.—Ed.
† Illness.—Ed.

a vast number of disorders. Yet amongst a group of the author's students who kept a calendar noting all bodily states and conditions, tiredness, though often recorded, was rarely cited as a cause for concern. Attending school and being among peers who stressed the importance of hard work and achievement, almost as an end in itself, tiredness, rather than being an indication of something being wrong was instead positive proof that they were doing right. If they were tired, it must be because they had been working hard. In such a setting tiredness would rarely, in itself, be either a cause for concern, a symptom, or a reason for action or seeking medical aid.[19] On the other hand, where arduous work is not gratifying in and of itself, tiredness would more likely be a matter for concern and perhaps medical attention.[20]

Also illustrative of this process are the divergent perceptions of those bodily complaints often referred to as "female troubles."[21] Nausea is a common and treatable concomitant of pregnancy, yet Margaret Mead records no morning sickness among the Arapesh; her data suggest that this may be related to the almost complete denial that a child exists, until shortly before birth.[22] In a Christian setting, where the existence of life is dated from conception, nausea becomes the external sign, hope and proof that one is pregnant. Thus in the United States, this symptom is not only quite widespread but is also an expected and almost welcome part of pregnancy. A quite similar phenomenon is the recognition of dysmenorrhea.* While Arapesh women reported no pain during menstruation, quite the contrary is reported in the United States.[23] Interestingly enough the only consistent factor related to its manifestation among American women was a learning one—those that manifested it reported having observed it in other women during their childhood.[24]

From such examples as these, it seems likely that the degree of recognition and treatment of certain gynecological problems may be traced to the prevailing definition of what constitutes "the necessary part of the business of being a woman."[25] That such divergent definitions are still operative is shown by two recent studies. In the first, 78 mothers of lower socioeconomic status were required to keep health calendars over a four-week period. Despite the

instruction to report all bodily states and dysfunctions, only 14 noted even the occurrence of menses or its accompaniments.[26] A second study, done on a higher socioeconomic group yielded a different expression of the same phenomenon. Over a period of several years the author collected four-week health calendars from students. The women in the sample had at least a college education and virtually all were committed to careers in the behavioral sciences. Within this group there was little failure to report menses; very often medication was take. for the discomforts of dysmenorrhea. Moreover, this group was so psychologically sophisticated or self-conscious that they interpreted or questioned most physical signs or symptoms as attributable to some psychosocial stress. There was only one exception—dysmenorrhea. Thus, even in this "culturally advantaged" group, this seemed a sign of a bodily condition so ingrained in what one psychiatrist has called "the masochistic character of her sex" that the woman does not ordinarily subject it to analysis.

In the opening section of this paper, we presented evidence that a selective process might well be operating in what symptoms are brought to the doctor. We also noted that it might be this selective process and not an etiological one which accounts for the many unexplained or over-explained epidemiological differences observed between and within societies.[27] (There may even be no "real" differences in the prevalence rates of many deviations.[28]) Such selective processes are probably present at all the stages through which an individual and his condition must pass before he ultimately gets counted as "ill." In this section we have focused on one of these stages, the perception of a particular bodily state as a symptom, and have delineated two possible ways in which the culture or social setting might influence the awareness of something as abnormal and thus its eventual tabulation in medical statistics.

Sample selection and methodology

The investigation to be reported here is not an attempt to prove that the foregoing body of reasoning is correct but rather to demonstrate the fruitfulness of the orientation in understanding the problems of health and illness. This study reports the existence of a selective process in what the patient "brings" to a doc-

* Painful menstruation.—Ed.

tor. The selectiveness is analyzed not in terms of differences in diseases but rather in terms of differences in responses to essentially similar disease entities.

Specifically, this paper is a documentation of the influence of "culture" (in this case ethnic-group membership) on "symptoms" (the complaints a patient presents to his physician). The measure of "culture" was fairly straightforward. The importance of ethnic groups in Boston, where the study was done, has been repeatedly documented;[29] ethnicity seemed a reasonable urban counterpart of the cultures so often referred to in the previous pages. The sample was drawn from the outpatient clinics of the Massachusetts General Hospital and the Massachusetts Eye and Ear Infirmary; it was limited to those new patients of both sexes between 18 and 50 who were white, able to converse in English, and of either Irish Catholic, Italian Catholic, or Anglo-Saxon Protestant background.[30] These were the most numerous ethnic groups in the clinics; together they constituted approximately fifty percent of all patients. The actual interviewing took place at the three clinics to which these patients were most frequently assigned (the three largest out-patient clinics): The Eye Clinic, the Ear, Nose and Throat Clinic, and the Medical Clinic.

In previous research the specific method of measuring and studying symptoms has varied among case record analysis, symptom check lists, and interviews. The data have been either retrospective or projective, that is, requesting the subject either to recall symptoms experienced during a specific time period or to choose symptoms which would bother him sufficiently to seek medical aid.[31] Such procedures do not provide data on the complaints which people actually bring to a doctor, a fact of particular importance in light of the many investigations pointing to the lack of, and distortions in, recall of sickness episodes.[32] An equally serious problem is the effect of what the doctor, medicine-man or health expert may tell the patient on the latter's subsequent perceptions of and recall about his ailment.[33] We resolved these problems by restricting the sample to new patients on their first medical visit to the clinics and by interviewing them during the waiting period before they were seen by a physician.[34]

The primary method of data-collection was a focused open-ended interview dealing with the patient's own or family's responses to his presenting complaints. Interspersed throughout the interview were a number of more objective measures of the patient's responses—checklists, forced-choice comparisons, attitudinal items, and scales. Other information included a demographic background questionnaire, a review of the medical record, and a series of ratings by each patient's examining physician as to the primary diagnosis, the secondary diagnosis, the potential seriousness, and the degree of clinical urgency (i.e., the necessity that the patient be seen immediately) of the patient's presenting complaint.

The patient and his illness

The data are based on a comparison between 63 Italians (34 female, 29 male) and 81 Irish (42 female, 39 male), who were new admissions to the Eye, the Ear, Nose and Throat, and the Medical Clinics of the Massachusetts General Hospital and the Massachusetts Eye and Ear Infirmary, seen between July, 1960, and February, 1961.[35] The mean age of each ethnic group (male and female computed separately) was approximately thirty-three. While most patients were married, there was, in the sample, a higher proportion of single Irish men—a finding of other studies involving the Irish[36] and not unexpected from our knowledge of Irish family structure.[37] Most respondents had between 10 and 12 years of schooling, but only about 30 percent of the males claimed to have graduated from high school as compared with nearly 60 percent of the females. There were no significant differences on standard measures of social class, though in education, social class, occupation of the breadwinner in the patient's family, and occupation of the patient's father, the Irish ranked slightly higher.[38] The Italians were overwhelmingly American-born children of foreign parents: about 80 percent were second generation while 20 percent were third. Among the Irish about 40 percent were second generation, 30 percent third, and 30 percent fourth.

With regard to general medical coverage, there were no apparent differences between the ethnic groups. Approximately 62 percent of the sample had health insurance, a figure similar to the comparable economic group in the Rosenfeld survey of Metropolitan Boston.[39] Sixty percent had physicians whom they would call family doctors. The Irish tended more than the Italians to perceive themselves as having poor health, claiming more often they had been seriously ill in the past. This was consistent with their reporting of the most recent visit to the doctor: nine of the Irish but none of the Italians claimed to have had a recent major operation (e.g., appendectomy) or illness (e.g., pneumonia). Although there were no differences in the actual seriousness of their present disorders (according to the doctor's ratings) there was a tendency for the examining physician to consider the Irish as being in more urgent need of treatment. It was apparent that the patients were not in the throes of an acute illness, although they may have been experiencing an acute episode. There was a slight tendency for the Irish, as a group, to have had their complaints longer. More significantly, the women of both groups claimed to have borne their symptoms for a longer time than the men.

In confining the study to three clinics, we were trying not only to economize but also to limit the range of illnesses. The latter was necessary for investigating differential responses to essentially similar conditions.[40] Yet at best this is only an approximate control. To resolve this difficulty, after all initial comparisons were made between the ethnic groups as a whole, the data were examined for a selected subsample with a specific control for diagnosis. This subsample consisted of matched pairs of one Irish and one Italian of the same sex, who had the same primary diagnosis, and whose disorder was of approximately the same duration and was rated by the examining physician as similar in degree of "seriousness." Where numbers made it feasible, there was a further matching on age, marital status, and education. In all, thirty-seven diagnostically matched pairs (18 female and 19 male) were created; these constituted the final test of any finding of the differential response to illness.[41]

Location and quality of presenting complaints. In the folklore of medical practice, the supposed opening question is, "Where does it hurt?" This query provides the starting-point of our analysis—the perceived location of the patient's troubles. Our first finding is that more Irish than Italians tended to locate their chief problem in either the eye, the ear, the nose, or the throat (and more so for females than for

Table 1   Distribution of Irish and Italian Clinic Admissions by Location of Chief Complaint

Location of complaint	Italian	Irish*
Eye, ear, nose or throat	34	61
Other parts of the body	29	17
Total	63	78

Note: $\chi^2 = 9.31$, p < .01.
* Since 3 Irish patients (two women, one man) claimed to be asymptomatic, no location could be determined from their viewpoint.

males). The same tendency was evident when all patients were asked what they considered to be the most important part of their body and the one with which they would be most concerned if something went wrong. Here, too, significantly more Irish emphasized difficulties of the eye, the ear, the nose, or the throat. That this reflected merely a difference in the conditions for which they were seeking aid is doubtful since the two other parts of the body most frequently referred to were heart and "mind" locations, and these represent only 3 percent of the primary diagnoses of the entire sample. In the retesting of these findings on diagnostically matched pairs, while there were a great many ties, the general directions were still consistent.[42] Thus even when Italians had a diagnosed eye or ear disorder, they did not locate their chief complaints there, nor did they focus their future concern on these locations.

Pain, the commonest accompaniment of illness, was the dimension of patients' symptoms to which we next turned. Pain is an especially interesting phenomenon since there is considerable evidence that its tolerance and perception are not purely physiological responses and do not necessarily reflect the degree of objective discomfort induced by a particular disorder or experimental procedure.[43] In our study not only did the Irish more often than

Table 2   Distribution of Irish and Italian Clinic Admissions by Part of the Body Considered Most Important

Most important part of the body	Italian	Irish
Eye, ear, nose or throat	6	26
Other parts of the body	57	55
Total	63	81

Note: $\chi^2 = 10.50$, p < .01.

Table 3   Distribution of Irish and Italian Clinic Admissions by Presence of Pain in Their Current Illness

Presence of pain	Italian	Irish
No	27	54
Yes	36	27
Total	63	81

Note: $\chi^2 = 10.26$, p < .01.

the Italians deny that pain was a feature of their illness but this difference held even for those patients with the same disorder.[44] When the Irish were asked directly about the presence of pain, some hedged their replies with qualifications. ("It was more a throbbing than a pain . . . not really pain, it feels more like sand in my eye.") Such comments indicated that the patients were reflecting something more than an objective reaction to their physical conditions.

While there were no marked differences in the length, frequency or noticeability of their symptoms, a difference did emerge in the ways in which they described the quality of the physical difficulty embodied in their chief complaint. Two types of difficulty were distinguished; one was of a more limited nature and emphasized a circumscribed and specific dysfunctioning; the second emphasized a difficulty of a grosser and more diffuse quality.[45] When the patients' complaints were analyzed according to these two types, proportionately more Irish described their chief problem in terms of specific dysfunction while proportionately more Italians spoke of a diffuse difficulty. Once again, the findings for diagnostically matched pairs were in the predicted direction.[46]

Table 4   Distribution of Irish and Italian Clinic Admissions by Quality of Physical Difficulty Embodied in Chief Complaint

Quality of physical difficulty	Italian	Irish[*]
Problems of a diffuse nature	43	33
Problems of a specific nature	20	45
Total	63	78

Note: $\chi^2 = 9.44$, p < .01.
* Since 3 Irish patients (two women, one man) claimed to be asymptomatic, no rating of the quality of physical difficulty could be determined from their viewpoint.

Diffuse versus specific reactions. What seems to emerge from the above is a picture of the Irish limiting and understating their difficulties and the Italians spreading and generalizing theirs. Two other pieces of information were consistent with this interpretation: first, an enumeration of the symptoms an individual presented—a phenomenon which might reflect how diffusely the complaint was perceived; second, the degree to which each patient felt his illness affected aspects of life other than purely physical behavior.

The first measure of this specific-diffuse dimension—number of distinguishable symptoms[47]—was examined in three ways: (1) the total number presented by each patient; (2) the total number of different bodily areas in which the patient indicated he had complaints, e.g., back, stomach, legs; (3) the total number of different qualities of physical difficulty embodied in the patient's presenting complaints.[48] The ethnic differences were consistent with the previous findings. Compared to the Irish, the Italians presented significantly more symptoms, had symptoms in significantly more bodily locations, and noted significantly more types of bodily dysfunction.[49]

The second analysis, the degree to which a patient felt his illness affected his more general well-being, was derived from replies to three questions: (1) Do you think your symptoms affected how you got along with your family? (2) Did you become more irritable? (3) What would you say has bothered you

Table 5   Distribution of Irish and Italian Clinic Admissions by Number of Presenting Complaints[*]

Number of presenting complaints	Italian	Irish
Zero	0	3
One	5	21
Two	15	22
Three	14	16
Four	10	7
Five	9	7
Six or more	10	5
Total	63	81

Note: p < .001.
* The Mann-Whitney U-test was used. Probabilities were computed for one-tailed tests. They are, however, slightly "conservative"; with a correction for ties, the probabilities or levels of significance would have been even lower. See Siegel, op. cit., pp. 116–127.

most about your symptoms?[50] An admission of irritability scale was created by classifying an affirmative response to any of the three questions as an admission that the symptoms affected extraphysical performance. As seen in Table 6, the Irish were more likely than the Italians to state that their disorders had not affected them in this manner. Here again the asides by the Irish suggested that their larger number of negative responses by the Irish reflected considerable denial rather than a straightforward appraisal of their situation.

To examine these conclusions in a more rigorous manner, we turned to our subsample of matched diagnostic pairs. In general, the pattern and direction of the hypotheses were upheld.[51] Thus, even for the same diagnosis, the Italians expressed and complained of more symptoms, more bodily areas affected, and more kinds of dysfunctions, than did the Irish, and more often felt that their symptoms affected their interpersonal behavior.

The composite on page 72 offers a final illustration of how differently these patients reacted to and perceived their illnesses. Each set of responses was given by an Italian and an Irish patient of similar age and sex with a disorder of approximately the same duration and with the same primary and secondary diagnosis (if there was one). In the first two cases, the Irish patient focused on a specific malfunctioning as the main concern while the Italian did not even mention this aspect of the problem but went on to mention more diffuse qualities of his condition. The last four responses contrast the Italian and Irish response to questions of pain and interpersonal relations.

Sociocultural communication

What has so far been demonstrated is the systematic variability with which bodily conditions may be perceived and communicated.

Table 6 Distribution of Irish and Italian Clinic Admissions by Responses to Three Questions concerning Admission of Irritability and Effect of Symptoms on Interpersonal Behavior

Response pattern	Italian	Irish
No on all three questions	22	47
Yes on at least one question	41	34
Total	63	81

Note: $\chi^2 = 7.62$, $p < .01$.

Until now the empirical findings have been presented without interpretation. Most of the data are quite consistent with those reported by other observers.[52] Although no data were collected in our investigation on the specific mechanics of the interplay between being a member of a specific subculture and the communication of "symptoms," some speculation on this seems warranted.

In theorizing about the interplay of culture and symptoms particular emphasis was given to the "fit" of certain bodily states with dominant value orientations. The empirical examples for the latter were drawn primarily from data on social roles. Of course, values are evident on even more general levels, such as formal and informal societal sanctions and the culture's orientation to life's basic problems. With an orientation to problems usually goes a preferred solution or way of handling them.[53] Thus a society's values may also be reflected in such preferred solutions. One behavioral manifestation of this is defense mechanisms—a part of the everyday way individuals have of dealing with their everyday stresses and strains.[54] We contend that illness and its treatment (from taking medicine to seeing a physician) is one of these everyday stresses and strains, an anxiety-laden situation which calls forth coping of defense mechanisms.[55] From this general reasoning, we would thus speculate that Italian and Irish ways of communicating illness may reflect major values and preferred ways of handling problems within the culture itself.[56]

For the Italians, the large number of symptoms and the spread of the complaints, not only throughout the body but into other aspects of life, may be understood in terms of their expressiveness and expansiveness so often missing in sociological, historical, and fictional writing.[57] And yet their illness behavior seems to reflect something more than lack of inhibition, and valuation of spontaneity. There is something more than real in their behavior, a "well-seasoned, dramatic emphasis to their lives." In fact, clinicians have noted that this openness is deceptive. It only goes so far and then. . . . Thus this Italian overstatement of "symptoms" is not merely an expressive quality but perhaps a more general mechanism, their special way of handling problems—a defense mechanism we call dramatization. Dynamically dramatization seems to cope with anxiety by repeatedly overexpressing it and thereby dis-

Diagnosis	Question of Interviewer	Irish Patient	Italian Patient
1. Presbyopis and hyperopia [Far-sightedness.—Ed.]	What seems to be the trouble?	I can't see to thread a needle or read a paper.	I have a constant headache and my eyes seem to get all red and burny.
	Anything else?	No, I can't recall any.	No, just that it lasts all day long and I even wake up with it sometimes.
2. Myopia [Near-sightedness.—Ed.]	What seems to be the trouble?	I can't see across the street.	My eyes seem very burny, especially the right eye. . . . Two or three months ago I woke up with my eyes swollen. I bathed it and it did go away but there was still the burny sensation.
	Anything else?	I had been experiencing headaches, but it may be that I'm in early menopause.	Yes, there always seems to be a red spot beneath this eye. . . .
	Anything else?	No.	Well, my eyes feel very heavy . . . at night they bother me most.
3. Otitis externa A.D. [Ear inflammation.—Ed.]	Is there any pain?	There's a congestion . . . but it's a pressure not really a pain.	Yes . . . if I rub it, it disappears. . . . I had a pain from my shoulder up to my neck and thought it might be a cold.
4. Pharyngitis [Throat inflammation.—Ed.]	Is there any pain?	No, maybe a slight headache but nothing that lasts.	Yes, I have had a headache a few days. Oh, yes, every time I swallow it's annoying.
5. Presbyopis and hyperopia	Do you think the symptoms affected how you got along with your family? your friends?	No, I have had loads of trouble. I can't imagine this bothering me.	Yes, when I have a headache, I'm very irritable, very tense, very short-tempered.
6. Deafness, hearing loss.	Did you become more irritable?	No, not me . . . maybe everybody else but not me.	Oh, yes . . . the least little thing aggravates me . . . and I take it out on the children.

sipating it. Anne Parsons delineates this process in a case study of a schizophrenic woman. Through a process of repetition and exaggeration she was able to isolate and defend herself from the destructive consequences of her own psychotic breakdown. Thus Anne Parsons concludes:

> . . . rather than appearing as evidence for the greater acceptance of id impulses the greater dramatic expression of Southern Italian culture might be given a particular place among the ego mechanisms, different from but in this respect fulfilling the same function as the emphasis on rational mastery of the objective or subjective world which characterizes our own culture (U.S.A.).[58]

While other social historians have noted the Italian flair for show and spectacle, Barzini has most explicitly related this phenomenon to the covering up of omnipresent tragedy and poverty, a way of making their daily lives bearable, the satisfactory ersatz for the many things they lack.

> The most easily identifiable reasons why the Italians love their own show. . . . First of all they do it to tame and prettify savage nature, to make life bearable, dignified, significant and pleasant for others, and themselves. They do it then for their own private ends; a good show makes a man *simpatico* to powerful people, helps him get on in the world and obtain what he wants, solves many problems, lubricates the wheels of society, protects him from the envy of his enemies and the arrogance of the mighty—they do it to avenge themselves on unjust fate.[59]

Through many works on the Southern Italian there seems to run a thread—a valued and preferred way of handling problems shown in the tendency toward dramatization. The experience of illness provides but another stage.

But if the Italian view of life is expressed through its fiestas, for the Irish it is expressed through its fasts.[60] Their life has been depicted as one of long periods of plodding routine followed by episodes of wild adventure, of lengthy postponement of gratification of sex and marriage, interspersed with brief immediate satisfactions like fighting and carousing. Perhaps it is in recognition of the expected and limited nature of such outbursts that the most common Irish outlet, alcoholism, is often referred to as "a good man's weakness." Life

was black and long-suffering, and the less said the better.[61]

It is the last statement which best reflects the Irish handling of illness. While in other contexts the ignoring of bodily complaints is merely descriptive of what is going on, in Irish culture it seems to be the culturally prescribed and supported defense mechanism—singularly most appropriate for their psychological and physical survival.[62] When speaking of the discomfort caused by her illness, one stated, "I ignore it like I do most things." In terms of presenting complaints this understatement and restraint was even more evident. It could thus be seen in their seeming reluctance to admit they have any symptoms at all, in their limiting their symptoms to the specific location in which they arose and finally in their contention that their physical problems affected nothing of their life but the most minute physical functioning. The consistency of the Irish illness behavior with their general view of life is shown in two other contexts. First it helped perpetuate a self-fulfilling prophecy. Thus their way of communicating complaints, while doing little to make treatment easy, did assure some degree of continual suffering and thus further proof that life is painful and hard (that is, "full of fasts").[63] Secondly, their illness behavior can be linked to the sin and guilt ideology which seems to pervade so much of Irish society. For, in a culture where restraint is the modus operandi, temptation is ever-present and must be guarded against. Since the flesh is weak, there is a concomitant expectation that sin is likely. Thus, when unexpected or unpleasant events take place, there is a search for what they did or must have done wrong. Perhaps their three most favored locations of symptoms (the eyes, ears and throat) might be understood as symbolic reflections of the more immediate source of their sin and guilt—what they should not have seen; what they should not have heard; and what they should not have said.

In these few paragraphs, we have tried to provide a theoretical link between membership in a cultural group and the communication of bodily complaints. The illness behavior of the Irish and the Italians has been explained in terms of two of the more generally prescribed defense mechanisms of their respective cultures—with the Irish handling their troubles by denial and the Italians theirs by dramatization.[64]

Qualifications and implications

The very fact that we speak of trends and statistical significance indicates the tentativeness of this study. In particular, the nature of sample selection affected the analysis of certain demographic variables since the lack of significant differences in some cases may be due to the small range available for comparison. Thus, there were no Italians beyond the third generation and few in the total sample who had gone to college. When comparisons were made within this small range (for example, only within the second generation or only within the high-school group) there were, with but one exception, no significant differences from previously reported findings.[65] Despite the limitations cited, it can be stated with some confidence that, of the variables capable of analysis, sociocultural ones were the most significant. When a correlational analysis (and within this, a cluster analysis) was performed on all the codable and quantifiable material (including the demographic data, the health behaviors and attitude scales) the variable which consistently correlated most highly with the "illness behaviors" reported in this study was ethnic group membership.

There is one final remark about our sample selection which has ramifications, not for our data analysis, but rather for our interpretation. We are dealing here with a population who had decided to seek or were referred for medical aid at three clinics. Thus we can make no claim that in a random selection of Irish, they will be suffering primarily from eye, ear, nose, and throat disorders or even locate their chief symptoms there. What we are claiming is that there are significant differences in the way people present and react to their complaints, not that the specific complaints and mechanisms we have cited are necessarily the most common ones. (We would, of course, be surprised if the pattern reported here did not constitute one of the major ones.) Another difficulty in dealing with this population is the duration of the patients' disorders. Since the majority of these patients have had their conditions for some time, one may wonder if similar differences in perception would exist for more acute episodes, or whether the very length of time which the people have borne their problems has allowed for coloration by sociocultural factors. As a result of this we can

only raise the issues as to whether the differences reported here between members of a cultural group exist only at a particular stage of their illness, or reflect more underlying and enduring cultural concerns and values.[66]

While there has long been recognition of the subjectivity and variability of a patient's reporting of his symptoms, there has been little attention to the fact that this reporting may be influenced by systematic social factors like ethnicity. Awareness of the influence of this and similar factors can be of considerable aid in the practical problems of diagnosis and treatment of many diseases, particularly where the diagnosis is dependent to a large extent on what the patient is able and willing, or thinks important enough, to tell the doctor.[67] The physician who is unaware of how the patient's background may lead him to respond in certain ways, may, by not probing sufficiently, miss important diagnostic cues, or respond inappropriately to others.[68]

The documentation of sociocultural differences in the perception of and concern with certain types of "symptoms" has further implications for work in preventive medicine and public health. It has been found in mental health research that there is an enormous gulf between lay and professional opinion as to when mental illness is present, as well as when and what kind of help is needed.[69] If our theorizing is correct, such differences reflect not merely something inadequately learned (that is, wrong medical knowledge) but also a solidly embedded value system.[70] Such different frames of reference would certainly shed light on the failures of many symptom-based health campaigns. Often these campaigns seem based on the assumption that a symptom or sign is fairly objective and recognizable and that it evokes similar levels of awareness and reaction. Our study adds to the mounting evidence which contradicts this position by indicating, for example, the systematic variability in response to even the most minor aches and pains.

The discerning of reactions to minor problems harks back to a point mentioned in the early pages of this report. For, while sociologists, anthropologists, and mental health workers have usually considered sociocultural factors to be etiological factors in the creation of specific problems, the interpretative emphasis in this study has been on how sociocultural background may lead to different definitions and responses to essentially the same experience. The strongest evidence in support of this argument is the different ethnic perceptions for essentially the same disease. While it is obvious that not all people react similarly to the same disease process, it is striking that the pattern of response can vary with the ethnic background of the patient. There is little known physiological difference between ethnic groups which would account for the differing reactions. In fact, the comparison of the matched diagnostic groups led us to believe that, should diagnosis be more precisely controlled, the differences would be even more striking.

The present report has attempted to demonstrate the fruitfulness of an approach which does not take the definition of abnormality for granted. Despite its limitations, our data seem sufficiently striking to provide further reason for re-examining our traditional and often rigid conceptions of health and illness, of normality and abnormality, of conformity and deviance. Symptoms, or physical aberrations, are so widespread that perhaps relatively few, and a biased selection at best, come to the attention of official treatment agencies like doctors, hospitals and public health agencies. There may even be a sense in which they are part and parcel of the human condition. We have thus tried to present evidence showing that the very labelling and definition of a bodily state as a symptom or as a problem is, in itself, part of a social process. If there is a selection and definitional process, then focusing solely on reasons for deviation (the study of etiology) and ignoring what constitutes a deviation in the eyes of the individual and his society may obscure important aspects of our understanding and eventually our philosophies of treatment and control of illness.[71]

Notes

[1] Rene Dubos, *Mirage of Health*, Garden City, New York: Anchor, 1961. On more philosophical grounds, William A. White, in *The Meaning of Disease*, Baltimore: Williams and Wilkins, 1926, arrives at a similar conclusion.

[2] R. J. F. H. Pinsett, *Morbidity Statistics from General Practice*, Studies of Medical Population, No. 14, London, H.M.S.O., 1962; P. Stocks, *Sickness in the Population of England and Wales*, 1944–1947, Studies of Medical Populations, No. 2, London, H.M.S.O., 1944; John Horder and Elizabeth Horder, "Illness in General Practice," *Practitioner*, 173 (August, 1954), pp. 177–185.

[3] Charles R. Hoffer and Edgar A. Schuler, "Measurement of Health Needs and Health Care," *American Sociological Review*, 13 (December, 1948), pp. 719–724; Political and Economic Planning, *Family Needs and the Social Services*, George Allen and Unwin, Ltd., London, 1961; Leonard S. Rosenfeld, Jacob Katz and Avedis Donabedian, *Medical Care Needs and Services in the Boston Metropolitan Area*, Boston: Medical Care Evaluation Studies, Health, Hospitals, and Medical Care Division, United Community Services of Metropolitan Boston, 1957.

[4] That these high figures of disorder include a great many minor problems is largely irrelevant. The latter are nevertheless disorders, clinical entities, and may even be the precursors of more medically serious difficulties.

[5] See for example, Commission on Chronic Illness, *Chronic Illness in a Large City*, Cambridge: Harvard University Press, 1957; Kendall A. Elsom, Stanley Schor, Thomas W. Clark, Katherine O. Elsom, and John P. Hubbard, "Periodic Health Examination—Nature and Distribution of Newly Discovered Disease in Executives," *Journal of the American Medical Association*, 172 (January, 1960), pp. 55–61; John W. Runyan, Jr., "Periodic Health Maintenance Examination—I. Business Executives," *New York State Journal of Medicine*, 59 (March, 1959), pp. 770–774; Robert E. Sandroni, "Periodic Health Maintenance Examination—III. Industrial Employees," *New York State Journal of Medicine*, 59 (March, 1959), pp. 778–781; C. J. Tupper and M. B. Becket, "Faculty Health Appraisal, University of Michigan," *Industrial Medicine and Surgery*, 27 (July, 1958), pp. 328–332; Leo Wade, John Thorpe, Thomas Elias, and George Bock, "Are Periodic Health Examinations Worth-while?" *Annals of Internal Medicine*, 56 (January, 1962), pp. 81–93. For questionnaire studies, see Paul B. Cornely and Stanley K. Bigman, *Cultural Considerations in Changing Health Attitudes*, Department of Preventive Medicine and Public Health, College

of Medicine, Howard University, Washington, D.C., 1961; and for more general summaries, J. Wister Meigs, "Occupational Medicine," *New England Journal of Medicine*, 264 (April, 1961), pp. 861–867; George S. Siegel, *Periodic Health Examinations—Abstracts from the Literature*, Public Health Service Publication No. 1010, Washington, D.C.: U.S. Government Printing Office, 1963.

6 See Innes H. Pearse and Lucy H. Crocker, *The Peckham Experiment*, London: George Allen and Unwin, Ltd., 1949; *Biologists in Search of Material*, Interim Reports of the Work of the Pioneer Health Center, Peckham, London: Faber and Faber, 1938; Joseph E. Schenthal, "Multiphasic Screening of the Well Patient," *Journal of the American Medical Association*, 172 (January, 1960), pp. 51–64.

7 Pearse and Crocker, *op. cit.*

8 Consider the following computation of Hinkle *et al.* They noted that the average lower-middle-class male between the ages of 20 and 45 experiences over a 20-year period approximately one life-endangering illness, 20 disabling illnesses, 200 non-disabling illnesses and 1,000 symptomatic episodes. These total 1,221 episodes over 7,305 days or one new episode every six days. And this figure takes no account of the duration of a particular condition, nor does it consider any disorder of which the respondent may be unaware. In short, even among a supposedly "healthy" population scarcely a day goes by wherein they would not be able to report a symptomatic experience. Lawrence E. Hinkle, Jr., Ruth Redmont, Norman Plummer, and Harold G. Wolff, "An Examination of the Relation between Symptoms, Disability, and Serious Illness in Two Ho-

mogeneous Groups of Men and Women," *American Journal of Public Health*, 50 (September, 1960), pp. 1327–1336.

9 See Fred J. Murphy, Mary M. Shirley, and Helen L. Witmer, "The Incidence of Hidden Delinquency," *American Journal of Orthopsychiatry*, 16 (October, 1946), pp. 686–696; Austin L. Porterfield, *Youth in Trouble*, Fort Worth: Leo Potishman Foundation, 1949; James F. Short and F. Ivan Nye, "Extent of Unrecorded Delinquency," *Journal of Criminal Law, Criminology, and Police Science*, 49 (December, 1958), pp. 296–302; James S. Wallerstein and Clement J. Wyle, "Our Law-abiding Lawbreakers," *Probation*, 25 (April, 1947), pp. 107–112; Alfred C. Kinsey, Wardell B. Pomeroy, and Clyde C. Martin, *Sexual Behavior in the Human Male*, Philadelphia: W. B. Saunders, 1953; Stanton Wheeler, "Sex Offenses: A Sociological Critique," *Law and Contemporary Problems*, 25 (Spring, 1960), pp. 258–278; Leo Srole, Thomas S. Langer, Stanley T. Michael, Marvin K. Opler, and Thomas A. C. Rennie, *Mental Health in the Metropolis*, New York: McGraw-Hill, 1962; Dorothea C. Leighton, John S. Harding, David B. Macklin, Allister M. MacMillan and Alexander H. Leighton, *The Character of Danger*, New York: Basic Books, Inc., 1963.

10 As seen in the work of: Howard S. Becker, *Outsiders*, Glencoe, Illinois: The Free Press, 1963; Kai T. Erikson, "Notes on the Sociology of Deviance," *Social Problems*, 9 (Spring, 1962), pp. 307–314; Erving Goffman, *Stigma—Notes on the Management of Spoiled Identity*, Englewood Cliffs, New Jersey: Prentice-Hall, 1963; Wendell Johnson, *Stuttering*, Minneapolis: University of Minnesota Press, 1961; John I. Kitsuse, "Societal Reaction to

Deviant Behavior: Problems of Theory and Method," in Howard S. Becker (ed.) *The Other Side*, Glencoe, Illinois: The Free Press, 1964, pp. 87–102; Edwin M. Lemert, *Social Pathology*, New York: McGraw-Hill, 1951; Thomas J. Scheff, "The Societal Reaction to Deviance: Ascriptive Elements in the Psychiatric Screening of Mental Patients in a Midwestern State," *Social Problems*, 11 (Spring, 1964), pp. 401–413.

11 Here we are dealing solely with factors influencing the perception of certain conditions as symptoms. A host of other factors influence a second stage in this process, i.e., once perceived as a symptom, what, if anything, is done. See, for example, Edward S. Suchman, "Stages of Illness and Medical Care," *Journal of Health and Human Behavior*, 6 (Fall, 1965), pp. 114–128. Such mechanisms, by determining whether or not certain conditions are treated, would also affect their over- or under-representation in medical statistics.

12 Margaret Clark, *Health in the Mexican-American Culture*, Berkeley: University of California Press, 1958.

13 Richard H. Blum, *The Management of the Doctor-Patient Relationship*, New York: McGraw-Hill, 1960, p. 11.

14 Earl L. Koos, *The Health of Regionsville*, New York: Columbia University Press, 1954.

15 Erwin W. Ackerknecht, "The Role of Medical History in Medical Education," *Bulletin of History of Medicine*, 21 (March-April, 1947), pp. 135–145; Allan B. Raper, "The Incidence of Peptic Ulceration in some African Tribal Groups," *Transactions of the Royal Society of Tropical Medicine and Hygiene*, 152 (November, 1958), pp. 535–546.

[16] For example, Ackerknecht, *op. cit.* noted that pinto (dichromic spirochetosis), a skin disease, was so common among some South American tribes that the few single men who were not suffering from it were regarded as pathological to the degree of being excluded from marriage.

[17] It is no doubt partly for this reason that many public health programs founder when transported in toto to a foreign culture. In such a situation, when an outside authority comes in and labels a particularly highly prevalent condition a disease, and, as such, both abnormal and preventable, he is postulating an external standard of evaluation which for the most part, is incomprehensible to the receiving culture. To them it simply has no cognitive reality.

[18] Anthony F. C. Wallace, "Cultural Determinants of Response to Hallucinatory Experience," *Archives of General Psychiatry*, 1 (July, 1959), pp. 58–69. With the increased use of LSD, psychedelics, and so forth, within our own culture such a statement might have to be qualified.

[19] For the specific delineation of this process, I am grateful to Barbara L. Carter, "Nonphysiological Dimensions of Health and Illness," Brandeis University, Waltham, 1965.

[20] Dr. John D. Stoeckle, in a personal communication, has noted that such a problem is often the presenting complaint of the "trapped housewife" syndrome. For detail on the latter see Betty Friedan, *The Feminine Mystique*, New York: Dell, 1963; and Richard E. Gordon, Katherine K. Gordon, and Max Gunther, *The Split-level Trap*, New York: Dell, 1962. We realize, of course, that tiredness here might be more related to depression than any degree of physical exertion. But this does not alter how it is perceived and reacted to once it occurs.

[21] This section on "female troubles" was suggested by the following readings: Simone de Beauvoir, *The Second Sex*, New York: Knopf, 1957; Helene Deutsch, *The Psychology of Women*, New York: Grune and Stratton, 1944; and Margaret Mead, *Male and Female*, New York: Morrow, 1949.

[22] Margaret Mead, *Sex and Temperament in Three Primitive Societies*, New York: Mentor, 1950.

[23] Mead, *op. cit.*, 1949. As far as the Arapesh are concerned, Mead does note that this lack of perception may be related to the considerable self-induced discomfort prescribed for women during menstruation.

[24] Reported in Mead, *ibid.* The fact that one has to learn that something is painful or unpleasant has been noted elsewhere. Mead reports that in causalgia a given individual suffers and reports pain because she is aware of uterine contractions and not because of the occurrence of these contractions. Becker, *op. cit.*, 1963, and others studying addictive behaviors have noted not only that an individual has to learn that the experience is pleasurable but also that a key factor in becoming addicted is the recognition of the association of withdrawal symptoms with the lack of drugs. Among medical patients who had been heavily dosed and then withdrawn, even though they experience symptoms as a result of withdrawal, they may attribute them to their general convalescent aches and pains. Stanley Schacter and Jerome Singer, "Cognitive, Social, and Physiological Determinants of Emotional State," *Psychological Review*, 69 (September, 1962), pp. 379–387, have recently reported a series of experiments where epinephrine-injected subjects defined their mood as euphoria or anger depending on whether they spent time with a euphoric or angry stooge. Subjects without injections reported no such change in mood responding to these same social situations. This led them to the contention that the diversity of human emotional experiences stems from differential labelling of similar physical sensations.

[25] A term used by Drs. R. Green and K. Dalton, as quoted in Hans Selye, *The Stress of Life*, New York: McGraw-Hill, 1956, p. 177.

[26] John Kosa, Joel Alpert, M. Ruth Pickering, and Robert J. Haggerty, "Crisis and Family Life: A Re-examination of Concepts," *The Wisconsin Sociologist*, 4 (Summer, 1965), pp. 11–19.

[27] For example, Saxon Graham, "Ethnic Background and Illness in a Pennsylvania County," *Social Problems*, 4 (July, 1956), pp. 76–81, noted a significantly higher incidence of hernia among men whose backgrounds were Southern European (Italy or Greece) as compared with Eastern European (Austria, Czechoslovakia, Russia or Poland). Analysis of the occupations engaged in by these groups revealed no evidence that the Southern Europeans in the sample were more engaged in strenuous physical labor than the Eastern Europeans. From what is known of tolerance to hernia, we suggest that, for large segments of the population, there may be no differences in the actual incidence and prevalence of hernia but that in different groups different perceptions of the same physical signs may lead to dissimilar ways of handling them. Thus the Southern Europeans in

Graham's sample may have been more concerned with problems in this area of the body, and have sought aid more readily (and therefore appear more frequently in the morbidity statistics). Perhaps the Southern Europeans are acting quite rationally and consistently while the other groups are so threatened or ashamed that they tend to deny or mask such symptoms and thus keep themselves out of the morbidity statistics.

[28] In studying the rates of peptic ulcer among African tribal groups Raper, op. cit., first confirmed the stereotype that it was relatively infrequent among such groups and therefore that it was associated (as many had claimed) with the stresses and strains of modern living. Yet when he relied not on reported diagnosis but on autopsy data, he found that the scars of peptic ulcer were no less common than in Britain. He concluded: "There is no need to assume that in backward communities peptic ulcer does not develop; it is only more likely to go undetected because the conditions that might bring it to notice do not exist."

[29] Oscar Handlin, Race and Nationality in American Life, Garden City, New York: Doubleday, 1957; Oscar Handlin, Boston's Immigrants, Cambridge: Harvard University Press, 1959.

[30] Ethnicity was ascertained by the responses to several questions: what the patients considered their nationality to be; the birthplaces of themselves, their parents, their maternal and paternal grandparents; and, if the answers to all of these were American, they were also asked whence their ancestors originated. For details, see Irving Kenneth Zola, Sociocultural Factors in the Seeking of Medical Aid, unpublished doctoral dissertation, Harvard University, Department of Social Relations, 1962.

[31] The range of methods includes: case research analysis—Berta Fantl and Joseph Schiro, "Cultural Variables in the Behavior Patterns and Symptom Formation of 15 Irish and 15 Italian Female Schizophrenics," International Journal of Social Psychiatry, 4 (Spring, 1959), pp. 245–253; check lists—Cornerly and Bigman, op. cit.; standardized questionnaires—Sydney H. Croog, "Ethnic Origins and Responses to Health Questionnaires," Human Organization, 20 (Summer, 1961), pp. 65–69; commitment papers—John B. Enright and Walter R. Jaeckle, "Psychiatric Symptoms and Diagnosis in Two Subcultures," International Journal of Social Psychiatry, 9 (Winter, 1963), pp. 12–17; interview and questionnaire—Graham, op. cit.; Mark Zborowski, "Cultural Components in Response to Pain," Journal of Social Issues, 8 (Fall, 1952), pp. 16–30; interview and psychological tests—Marvin K. Opler and Jerome L. Singer, "Ethnic Differences in Behavior and Psychopathology; Italian and Irish," International Journal of Social Psychiatry, 2 (Summer, 1956), pp. 11–12; observation—Clark, op. cit.; and Lyle Saunders, op. cit.

[32] See Jacob J. Feldman, "The Household Interview Survey as a Technique for the Collection of Morbidity Data," Journal of Chronic Diseases, 11 (May, 1960), pp. 535–557; Theodore D. Woolsey, "The Health Survey," presented at the session, "The Contributions of Research in the Field of Health," 1959 AAPOR Conference, May, 1959, Lake George, New York.

[33] Charles Kadushin, "The Meaning of Presenting Problems: A Sociology of Defenses," paper read at the 1962 annual meeting of the American Sociological Association.

[34] This particular methodological choice was also determined by the nature of the larger study, that is, how patients decided to seek medical aid, where the above-mentioned problems loom even larger. While only new admissions were studied, a number of patients had been referred by another medical person. Subsequent statistical analysis revealed no important differences between this group and those for whom the Massachusetts General Hospital or the Massachusetts Eye and Ear Infirmary was the initial source of help.

[35] Forty-three Anglo-Saxons were also interviewed but are not considered in this analysis. They were dropped from this report because they differed from the Irish and Italians in various respects other than ethnicity: they included more students, more divorced and separated, more people living away from home, and more downwardly mobile; they were of higher socioeconomic and educational level, and a majority were fourth generation and beyond.

[36] Opler and Singer, op. cit.

[37] Conrad M. Arensberg and Solon T. Kimball, Family and Community in Ireland, Cambridge: Harvard University Press, 1948.

[38] In Warner's terms (W. Lloyd Warner, Social Class in America, Chicago: Science Research Associates, 1949), the greatest number of patients was in Class V. Only a small proportion of new Irish and Italian patients were what might be traditionally labelled as charity cases, although by some criteria they

were perhaps "medically indigent."

[39] Rosenfeld, *op. cit.*

[40] This is similar to Zborowski's method, in his study of pain reactions, of confining his investigations to patients on certain specified wards. *Op. cit.*

[41] These pairs included some eighteen distinct diagnoses: conjunctivitis; eyelid disease (e.g., blepharitis); myopia; hyperopia; vitreous opacities; impacted cerumen; external otitis; otitis media; otosclerosis; deviated septum; sinusitis; nasopharyngitis; allergy; thyroid; obesity; functional complaints; no pathology; psychological problems.

To give some indication of the statistical significance of these comparisons, a sign test was used. For the sign test, a "tie" occurs when it is not possible to discriminate between a matched pair on the variable under study, or when the two scores earned by any pair are equal. All tied cases were dropped from the analysis, and the probabilities were computed only on the total N's excluding ties. In our study there were many ties. In the nature of our hypotheses, as will appear subsequently, a tie means that at least one member of the pair was in the predicted direction. Despite this problem, the idea of a diagnostically matched pair was retained because it seemed to convey the best available test of our data. Because there were specific predictions as to the direction of differences, the probabilities were computed on the basis of a one-tailed sign test. This was used to retest the findings of Tables 1–6. See Sidney Siegel, *Non-parametric Statistics for the Behavioral Sciences*, New York: McGraw-Hill, 1956, pp. 68–75.

[42] For the prediction that the

Irish would locate their chief complaint, in eye, ear, nose or throat, and the Italians in some other part, 8 matched diagnostic pairs were in favor of the hypothesis, 1 against, 28 ties ($p = .02$); for the same with respect to most important part of the body there were 12 in favor of the hypothesis, 2 against, 23 ties ($p = .006$).

[43] William P. Chapman and Chester M. Jones, "Variations in Cutaneous and Visceral Pain Sensitivity in Normal Subjects," *Journal of Clinical Investigation*, 23 (January, 1944), pp. 81–91; James D. Hardy, Harold G. Wolff, and Helen Goodell, *Pain Sensations and Reactions*, Baltimore: Williams and Wilkins, 1952; Ronald Melzack, "The Perception of Pain," *Scientific American*, 204 (February, 1961), pp. 41–49; Harry S. Olin and Thomas P. Hackett, "The Denial of Chest Pain in 32 Patients with Acute Myocardial Infection," *Journal of the American Medical Association*, 190 (December, 1964), pp. 977–981; Zborowski, *op. cit.*

[44] For the prediction that Italians would admit the presence of pain and the Irish would deny it, 16 matched diagnostic pairs were in favor of the hypotheses, 0 against, 21 ties ($p = .001$).

[45] Complaints of the first type emphasized a somewhat limited difficulty and dysfunction best exemplified by something specific, e.g., an organ having gone wrong in a particular way. The second type seemed to involve a more attenuated kind of problem whose location and scope were less determinate, and whose description was finally more qualitative and less measurable.

[46] For the prediction that the Italians would emphasize a diffuse difficulty and the Irish a

specific one, there were 10 diagnostically matched pairs in favor, 0 against, 27 ties ($p = .001$).

[47] This number could be zero, as in a situation where the patient denied the presence of any difficulty, but others around him disagreed and so made the appointment for him or "forced" him to see a doctor.

[48] Qualities of physical difficulty were categorized under nine headings.

[49] The distributions for these two tables closely resemble those of Table 5 ($p = .018$ for bodily locations; $p = .003$ for types of bodily dysfunctions).

[50] For the latter question, the patient was presented with a card on which were listed eight aspects of illness and/or symptoms which might bother him. One of these statements was, "That it made you irritable and difficult to get along with."

[51] For the prediction that the Italians would have more symptoms in all instances there were: for total number, 24 matched diagnostic pairs in favor of hypotheses, 7 against, 6 ties ($p = .005$); for number of different locations, 16 in favor, 5 against, 16 ties ($p = .013$); for number of different qualities of physical difficulties, 22 in favor, 9 against, 6 ties ($p = .025$). For the prediction that Italians would admit irritability and Irish would deny it, there were 17 in favor, 6 against, 14 ties ($p = .017$).

[52] The whole specific-diffuse pattern and the generalizing-withholding illness behavior dovetails neatly with the empirical findings of Opler and Singer, *op. cit.*, Fantl and Schiro, *op. cit.*, and Paul Barrabee and Otto von Mering, "Ethnic Variations in Mental

Stress in Families with Psychotic Children" *Social Problems*, 1 (October, 1953), pp. 48–53. The specific emphasis on expressiveness has been detailed especially by Zborowski, *op. cit.* and the several studies of Italian mental patients done by Anne Parsons, "Some Comparative Observations on Ward Social Structure: Southern Italy, England, and the United States," *Tipografia dell'Ospedale Psichiatrico*, Napoli, April, 1959; "Family Dynamics in Southern Italian Schizophrenics," *Archives of General Psychiatry*, 3 (November, 1960), pp. 507–518; "Patriarchal and Matriarchal Authority in the Neapolitan Slum," *Psychiatry*, 24 (May, 1961), pp. 109–121. The contrast on number of symptoms has been noted by Croog, *op. cit.*, and Graham, *op. cit.*

53 Florence R. Kluckhohn, "Dominant and Variant Value Orientations," in *Personality in Nature, Society and Culture*, Clyde Kluckhohn, Henry A. Murray and David M. Schneider (eds.) New York: Knopf, 2nd ed., 1956, pp. 342–357; Florence R. Kluckhohn and Fred L. Strodtbeck, *Variations in Value Orientations*, Evanston, Illinois: Row Peterson, 1961; John Spiegel, "Some Cultural Aspects of Transference and Countertransference," in *Individual and Family Dynamics*, Jules H. Masserman (ed.), New York: Greene and Stratton, 1959, pp. 160–182; John P. Spiegel, "Conflicting Formal and Informal Roles in Newly Acculturated Families," in *Disorders of Communication*, Vol. XLII, Research Publications, Association for Research in Nervous and Mental Disease, 1964, pp. 307–316; John P. Spiegel and Florence R. Kluckhohn, "The Influence of the Family and Cultural Values on the Mental Health and Illness of the In-

dividual," Unpublished Progress Report of Grant M-971, U. S. Public Health Service.

54 Anna Freud, *The Ego and the Mechanisms of Defense*, London: Hogarth, 1954.

55 That illness is almost an everyday problem is shown by the data in our opening section on the prevalence of illness. That illness and its concomitants are anxiety-laden is suggested by the findings of many studies on patient delay. Barbara Blackwell, "The Literature of Delay in Seeking Medical Care for Chronic Illnesses," *Health Education Monographs*, No. 16, 1963, pp. 3–32; Bernard Kutner, Henry B. Malcover and Abraham Oppenheim, "Delay in the Diagnosis and Treatment of Cancer," *Journal of Chronic Diseases*, 7 (January, 1958), pp. 95–120; *Journal of Health and Human Behavior*, 2 (Fall, 1961), pp. 171–178.

56 Speculation as to why the Italians and the Irish, with similar problems of hardship and poverty, should develop dissimilar ways of handling such problems is beyond the scope of this paper.

57 In addition to the references cited in footnotes 52 and 53, we have drawn our picture from many sociological, literary, and historical works. A complete bibliography is available on request. For the compilation and annotation of many of these references I am particularly indebted to Mrs. Marlene Hindley.

58 Anne Parsons, *Psychiatry, op. cit.*, p. 26.

59 Luigi Barzini, *The Italians*, New York: Bantam, 1965, p. 104.

60 In addition to the papers in footnote 52, Arensberg and

Kimball, *op. cit.*, remains the classic reference work.

61 The ubiquitous comic spirit, humor, and wit for which the Irish are famous can be regarded in part as a functional equivalent of the dramatization by Italians. It is a cover, a way of isolating life's hardships, and at the same time a preventive of deeper examination and probing. Also, while their daily life was endowed with great restrictions, their fantasy life was replete with great richness (tales of the "wee folk").

62 Spiegel and Kluckhohn, *op. cit.*, state that the Irishman's major avenue of relief from his oppressive sense of guilt lies in his almost unlimited capacity for denial. This capacity they claim is fostered by the perception in the rural Irish of a harmonic blending between man and nature. Such harmonizing of man and nature is further interpreted as blurring the elements of causality, thus allowing for continually shifting the responsibility for events from one person to another, and even from a person to animistically conceived forces. Thus denial becomes not only a preferred avenue of relief but also one supported and perhaps elicited by their perception of their environment.

63 Their "fantasying" and their "fasting" might be reflected in the serious illness they claim to have had in the past, and the dire consequences they forecast for their future. We do not know for a fact that the Irish had more serious illnesses than the Italians, but merely that they claimed to. The Italians might well have had similar conditions but did not necessarily consider them serious.

64 The Anglo-Saxons complete the circle with an emphasis on neutralizing their anxiety.

[65] The previously reported ethnic differences with respect to presenting complaints did begin to blur. The Italian and the Irish males tended to "move" toward the "middle position" of the Anglo-Saxon Protestant group. In many of the major comparisons of this study, the Anglo-Saxon group occupied a position midway between the responses of the two other ethnic groups, though generally closer to the Irish. For example, when asked about the presence of pain some 70 per cent of the Irish males denied it, as compared to almost 60 per cent of the Anglo-Saxon males, and 40 per cent of the Italian males.

[66] Such a problem was explicitly stated and investigated by Ellen Silver, "The Influence of Culture on Personality: A Comparison of the Irish and Italians with Emphasis on Fantasy Behavior," Mimeographed, Harvard University, 1958, in her attempted replication of the Opler and Singer work, *op. cit.,* and was emphasized by the somewhat ambiguous findings of Rena S. Grossman, "Ethnic Differences in the Apperception of Pain," unpublished undergraduate honors thesis, Department of Social Relations, Radcliffe College, 1964, in her replication of Zborowski's findings, *op. cit.,* on a non-hospitalized population.

[67] Several examples are more fully delineated in Irving Kenneth Zola, "Illness Behavior of the Working Class: Implications and Recommendations," in Arthur B. Shostak and William Gombert (eds.), *Blue Collar World,* Englewood Cliffs, New Jersey: Prentice-Hall, 1964, pp. 350–361.

[68] This may be done to such an extreme that it is the physician's response which creates epidemiological differences. Such a potential situation was noted using data from the present study and is detailed in Irving Kenneth Zola, "Problems of Communication, Diagnosis, and Patient Care: The Interplay of Patient, Physician, and Clinic Organization," *Journal of Medical Education,* 38 (October, 1963), pp. 829–838.

[69] The explanations for such differences have, however, more often emphasized negative aspects of the respondents' background—their lower education, lower socioeconomic status, lesser psychological sophistication, and greater resistance and antipathy—by virtue of their membership in certain racial and cultural minorities. See Bernard Bergen, "Social Class, Symptoms, and Sensitivity to Descriptions of Mental Illness—Implications for Programs of Preventive Psychiatry," unpublished doctoral dissertation, Harvard University, 1962; Elaine Cumming and John Cumming, *Closed Ranks: An Experiment in Mental Health Education,* Cambridge: Harvard University Press, 1957; Howard E. Freeman and Gene G. Kassebaum, "Relationship of Education and Knowledge to Opinions about Mental Illness," *Mental Hygiene,* 44 (January, 1960), pp. 43–47; Gerald Gurin, Joseph Veroff, and Sheila Feld, *Americans View their Mental Health,* New York: Basic Books, 1960; Jum C. Nunnally, *Popular Conceptions of Mental Health,* New York: Holt, Rinehart & Winston, 1961; Glenn V. Ramsey and Melita Seipp, "Attitudes and Opinions concerning Mental Illness," *Psychiatric Quarterly,* 22 (July, 1949), pp. 1–17; Elmo Roper and Associates, *People's Attitudes concerning Mental Health,* New York: Private Publication, 1950; Shirley Star, "The Public's Ideas about Mental Illness," paper presented to the Annual Meeting of the National Association for Mental Health, Indianapolis, 1955; Shirley Star, "The Place of Psychiatry in Popular Thinking," paper presented at the annual meeting of the American Association for Public Opinion Research, Washington, D.C., 1957; Julian L. Woodward, "Changing Ideas on Mental Illness and Its Treatment," *American Sociological Review,* 16 (August, 1951), pp. 443–454.

[70] This approach is evident in such works as Stanley King, *op. cit.;* Clyde Kluckhohn, "Culture and Behavior," in Gardner Lindzey, *Handbook of Social Psychology,* Cambridge: Addison-Wesley, 1954, Vol. 2, pp. 921–976; Walter B. Miller, "Lower Class Culture as a Generating Milieu of Gang Delinquency," *Journal of Social Issues,* 14 (July, 1958), pp. 5–19; Marvin K. Opler, *Culture, Psychiatry and Human Values,* Springfield, Illinois: Charles C. Thomas, 1956; Marvin K. Opler, *Culture and Mental Health,* New York: Macmillan, 1959; Benjamin D. Paul, *Health, Culture, and Community—Case Studies of Public Reactions to Health Programs,* New York: Russell Sage Foundation, 1955; Lyle Saunders, *Cultural Differences and Medical Care,* New York: Russell Sage Foundation, 1954; Henry J. Wegroksi, "A Critique of Cultural and Statistical Concepts of Abnormality," in Clyde Kluckhohn, Henry A. Murray, and David M. Schneider, *Personality in Nature, Society, and Culture,* New York: Knopf, revised edition, 1956, pp. 691–701.

[71] This is spelled out from various points of view in such works as: Samuel Butler, *Erewhon,* New York: Signet, 1961; Rene Dubos, *op. cit.;* Joseph D. Lohman (participant), "Juvenile Delinquency: Its Dimensions, Its Conditions, Techniques of Control, Proposals for Action," Subcommit-

tee on Juvenile Delinquency of the Senate Committee on Labor and Public Welfare, 86th Congress, S. 765, S. 1090, S. 1314, Spring, 1959, p. 268; Talcott Parsons, "Social Change and Medical Organization in the United States: A Sociological Perspective," *Annals of the American Academy of Political and Social Science,* 346 (March, 1963), pp. 21–34; Edwin M. Schur, *Crimes without Victims —Deviant Behavior and Public Policy,* Englewood, New Jersey: Prentice-Hall, 1965; Thomas Szasz, *The Myth of Mental Illness,* New York: Hoeber-Harper, 1961; Thomas Szasz, *Law, Liberty, and Psychiatry,* New York: Macmillan, 1963; Irving Kenneth Zola, "Problems for Research—Some Effects of Assumptions Underlying Sociomedical Investigations," in Gerald Gordon (editor), *Proceedings, Conference on Medical Sociology and Disease Control, National Tuberculosis Association,* 1966, pp. 9–17.

Chapter 4

THE DEMOGRAPHIC FACTOR

POPULATION AND RESOURCES
Selection 9

**POLITICAL IMPLICATIONS OF
THE DEMOGRAPHIC FACTOR**
Selection 10

SOCIAL INFLUENCES ON POPULATION GROWTH
Selection 11

Size, distribution, and composition of population have long been recognized as significant influences on the social order by both social philosophers and sociologists. Consider, for example, the differences between a group of two people and a group of three. Folk wisdom tells us about this situation that "two's company, three's a crowd." The sociologist Georg Simmel noted that a group of two cannot have a majority; it either divides evenly or is unanimous, and therefore is much less stable and more inclined to dissolve when faced with serious differences of opinion. The reader can furthermore note from his own experience how groups differ depending on whether they contain members of one or both sexes, age peers or people of different ages, and whether the members are physically close or scattered.

On a macroscopic level, great size, density, and heterogeneity of a population are associated with urbanism, and the opposites of these traits with a rural or folk existence. Many sociologists believe that the traits associated with urbanism produce a life style that includes, among other things, sophistication and rationality, segregation, indirect political representation, and mass movements.

The most prominent aspect of sociological interest in the demographic factor, and the exclusive one in the following selections, concerns size of population in relation to resources for sustaining it. This issue was first raised in modern times by Thomas Malthus, and it has achieved in the mid-twentieth century the status of a major social problem. The essence of Malthus' thesis (see Selection 9) is that the population size must be limited in proportion to the food resources available, if not by social factors reducing births, then by the biological factor through increasing deaths. The main line of demographic discussion since Malthus has centered about this thesis, but it includes more refined notions of the resources needed to support population—not only food, but water, fuels, timber, metals, and ultimately, living space.

The demographic experience of the industrial West suggests one possible model for the social control of population. An initially small population in which the number of births and the number of deaths were both high grew enormously as death rates declined with improvements in medicine and public health technology. But eventually the birth rate also declined, and population growth moderated. Were population growth in nonindustrial countries to follow this model, Malthusian pessimism would be unjustified. However, many of to-day's "underdeveloped" areas show no sign of lower birth rates, while their populations continue to expand rapidly. The causes of the decline in births in Europe and America are not completely known, and some students of demography fear that they were closely related to cultural factors present there and not elsewhere—for instance, admiration of chastity and dislike of unwed motherhood. Moreover, a time lag appears to be necessary between the decline in deaths and the decline in births, during which a growing population must be fed and otherwise supported; but this may be an economic impossibility in many parts of the world. In some countries of southeast Asia and the circum-Caribbean area, "overpopulation" is already a reality.

Detailed facts about the world's population have become relatively available in recent years, mainly through the efforts of the United Nations. The "neo-Malthusians," those who look at these facts pessimistically, appear to be in the majority among demographers. They are able to formulate impressive and cataclysmic population projections from present demographic facts, based on the mathematics of compound interest. Obviously, pessimistic projections of population that "predict" a time in which the world will contain standing room only are not meant to be taken literally. Rather they provide convincing evidence that the growth of human population will of necessity have to stop at some future time. The alternative methods of achieving this population control remain those stated by Malthus: fewer births or more deaths.

Selection 9 is Malthus' classic statement of the problem of balance between population and resources. Selection 10, by Philip Hauser, restates the problem in the light of contemporary knowledge and shows its weighty consequences in the realm of international relations. In Selection 11, J. Mayone Stycos investigates how family structure and other social factors react upon the demographic factor in one developing society.

POPULATION AND RESOURCES

This selection, from Thomas Malthus' *Essay on the Principle of Population*, was written well before the beginning of scientific sociology. Its author was a clergyman, who wrote for the political purpose of defeating extension of government aid to the poor. It is reproduced here because, on the basis of originality, simplicity, and clarity of argument, it has endured as the classic statement of the influence of population on the social order. In addition, the work gains in importance because it poses a social problem that has not been solved to this day.

In the late eighteenth century, the prevailing intellectual climate of Europe was one of great optimism, exemplified by the works of Godwin and Condorcet, disciples of the French Enlightenment. Great humanitarian revolutions had just been accomplished, and the day of the common man was dawning, while the subsequent evils of the Industrial Revolution that so angered Marx were not yet clearly apparent. Aside from the gloomy Malthus, few could see in the sunny skies of the future the clouds of what is today called the population explosion.

> When unhindered, population increases in a geometric progression, doubling at least every twenty-five years. Population requires food in order to exist, and an arithmetic progression, adding a constant amount of food to a society's supply every twenty-five years, is the most that can be expected from such factors as farming the land more intensively. If population and food behave thus there must come a point where food resources are only

barely adequate for the population on hand. At this point, large-scale starvation will be felt.

If population does not in fact increase at the geometric rate, it is because its growth is hindered by factors called checks. These checks influence the size of population either through increasing the number of deaths or decreasing the number of births in a society. Factors that increase deaths, and are thus considered undesirable, are called positive checks. If positive checks are not to operate, births must be decreased by preventive checks, chief among which is moral restraint in sexual relations.

The poor are limited in their contribution to population growth by the fact that they cannot support children. Aid to the poor would only remove this positive check and allow the population to grow, in the end producing a larger population, working for lower wages (since labor would be more plentiful), and as miserable as ever. The solution to the population problem is to educate the poor to adopt moral restraint.

Malthus can be shown to have been wrong on many specific issues. Perhaps his most serious miscalculation was the main point of the *Essay*. Contrary to what he wrote, in Western Europe at that time and generally through modern history, the poor have produced more children than the rich, despite their misery. Furthermore, Malthus ignored the possibility that contraception could do the same thing as moral restraint, although as a minister he might have felt constrained by religious principles from mentioning this. However, in many important matters Mathus can be shown to have been correct. His estimate of unchecked population growth now appears to be rather conservative. Although his estimate of resource growth has not been accepted, few people would propose that in the long run food can increase as fast as population. Thus, the *Essay* poses a real problem for all societies.

It is important to note that Malthus saw the relationship of population to society in very modern terms. Population has great consequences for society, but society can in turn influence the principle of population. Moreover, the application of technology to the environment, while it cannot reverse the principle of population, can delay its impact. In procedure as well as substance the *Essay* is a superb sociological study.

Selection 9
FROM AN ESSAY ON THE PRINCIPLE OF POPULATION
Thomas Malthus

In an inquiry concerning the improvement of society, the mode of conducting the subject which naturally presents itself, is,

1. To investigate the causes that have hitherto impeded the progress of mankind toward happiness; and,

2. To examine the probability of the total or partial removal of these causes in the future.

To enter fully into this question, and to

Reprinted from *An Essay on the Principle of Population* by Thomas Malthus, 5th ed., 1817.

enumerate all the causes that have hitherto influenced human improvement, would be much beyond the power of an individual. The principal object of the present essay is to examine the effects of one great cause intimately united with the very nature of man; which, though it has been constantly and powerfully operating since the commencement of society, has been little noticed by the writers who have treated this subject. The facts which establish the existence of this cause have, indeed, been repeatedly stated and acknowledged; but its natural and necessary effects have been almost totally overlooked; though probably among these effects may be reckoned a very considerable portion of that vice and misery, and of that unequal distribution of the bounties of nature, which it has been the unceasing object of the enlightened philanthropist in all ages to correct.

The cause to which I allude, is the constant tendency in all animated life to increase beyond the nourishment prepared for it.

It is observed by Dr. Franklin, that there is no bound to the prolific nature of plants or animals, but what is made by their crowding and interfering with each other's means of subsistence. Were the face of the earth, he says, vacant of other plants, it might be gradually sowed and overspread with one kind only, as for instance with fennel: and were it empty of other inhabitants, it might in a few ages be replenished from one nation only, as for instance with Englishmen.[1]

This is incontrovertibly true. Through the animal and vegetable kingdoms Nature has scattered the seeds of life abroad with the most profuse and liberal hand; but has been comparatively sparing in the room and the nourishment necessary to rear them. The germs of existence contained in this earth, if they could freely develop themselves, would fill millions of worlds in the course of a few thousand years. Necessity, that imperious, all-pervading law of nature, restrains them within the prescribed bounds. The race of plants and the race of animals shrink under this great restrictive law; and man cannot by any efforts of reason escape from it.

In plants and irrational animals, the view of the subject is simple. They are all impelled by a powerful instinct to the increase of their species; and this instinct is interrupted by no doubts about providing for their offspring. Wherever therefore there is liberty, the power of increase is exerted; and the superabundant effects are repressed afterwards by want of room and nourishment.

The effects of this check on man are more complicated. Impelled to the increase of his species by an equally powerful instinct, reason interrupts his career, and asks him whether he may not bring beings into the world, for whom he cannot provide the means of support. If he attend to this natural suggestion, the restriction too frequently produces vice. If he hear it not, the human race will be constantly endeavouring to increase beyond the means of subsistence. But as, by that law of our nature which makes food necessary to the life of man, population can never actually increase beyond the lowest nourishment capable of supporting it, a strong check on population, from the difficulty of acquiring food, must be constantly in operation. This difficulty must fall somewhere, and must necessarily be severely felt in some or other of the various forms of misery, or the fear of misery, by a large portion of mankind.

That population has this constant tendency to increase beyond the means of subsistence, and that it is kept to its necessary level by these causes, will sufficiently appear from a review of the different states of society in which man has existed. But, before we proceed to this review, the subject will, perhaps, be seen in a clearer light, if we endeavour to ascertain what would be the natural increase of population, if left to exert itself with perfect freedom; and what might be expected to be the rate of increase in the productions of the earth, under the most favourable circumstances of human industry.

It will be allowed that no country has hitherto been known, where the manners were so pure and simple, and the means of subsistence so abundant, that no check whatever has existed to early marriages from the difficulty of providing for a family, and that no waste of the human species has been occasioned by vicious customs, by towns, by unhealthy occupations, or too severe labour. Consequently in no state that we have yet known, has the power of population been left to exert itself with perfect freedom.

Whether the law of marriage be instituted, or not, the dictate of nature and virtue seems to be an early attachment to one woman; and where there were no impediments of any kind in the way of an union to which such an attachment would lead, and no causes of depopulation afterwards, the increase of the human species would be evidently much greater than any increase which has been hitherto known.

In the northern states of America, where the means of subsistence have been more ample, the manners of the people more pure, and the checks to early marriages fewer, than in any of the modern states of Europe, the population has been found to double itself, for above a century and a half successively, in less than twenty-five years.[2] Yet, even during these periods, in some of the towns, the deaths exceeded the births,[3] a circumstance which clearly proves that, in those parts of the country which supplied this deficiency, the increase must have been much more rapid than the general average.

In the back settlements, where the sole employment is agriculture, and vicious customs and unwholesome occupations are little known, the population has been found to double itself in fifteen years.[4] Even this extraordinary rate of increase is probably short of the utmost power of population. Very severe labour is requisite to clear a fresh country; such situations are not in general considered as particularly healthy; and the inhabitants, probably, are occasionally subject to the incursions of the Indians, which may destroy some lives, or at any rate diminish the fruits of their industry.

According to a table of Euler, calculated on a mortality of 1 in 36, if the births be to the deaths in the proportion of 3 to 1, the period of doubling will be only 12 years and 4-5ths.[5] And this proportion is not only a possible supposition, but has actually occurred for short periods in more countries than one.

Sir William Petty supposes a doubling possible in so short a time as ten years.[6]

But, to be perfectly sure that we are far within the truth, we will take the slowest of these rates of increase, a rate in which all concurring testimonies agree, and which has been repeatedly ascertained to be from procreation only.

It may safely be pronounced, therefore, that population, when unchecked, goes on doubling itself every twenty-five years, or increases in a geometrical ratio.

The rate according to which the productions of the earth may be supposed to increase, it will not be so easy to determine. Of this, however, we may be perfectly certain, that the ratio of their increase must be totally of a different nature from the ratio of the increase of population. A thousand millions are just as easily doubled every twenty-five years by the power of population as a thousand. But the food to support the increase from the greater number will by no means be obtained with the same facility. Man is necessarily confined in room. When acre has been added to acre till all the fertile land is occupied, the yearly increase of food must depend upon the melioration of the land already in possession. This is a fund, which, from the nature of all soils, instead of increasing, must be gradually diminishing. But population, could it be supplied with food, would go on with unexhausted vigour; and the increase of one period would furnish the power of a greater increase the next, and this without any limit.

From the accounts we have of China and Japan, it may be fairly doubted, whether the best directed efforts of human industry could double the produce of these countries even once in any number of years. There are many parts of the globe, indeed, hitherto uncultivated, and almost unoccupied; but the right of exterminating, or driving into a corner where they must starve, even the inhabitants of these thinly-peopled regions, will be questioned in a moral view. The process of improving their minds and directing their industry would necessarily be slow; and during this time, as population would regularly keep pace with the increasing produce, it would rarely happen that a great degree of knowledge and industry would have to operate at once upon rich unappropriated soil. Even where this might take place, as it does sometimes in new colonies, a geometrical ratio increases with such extraordinary rapidity, that the advantage could not last long. If the United States of America continue increasing, which they certainly will do, though not with the same rapidity as formerly, the Indians will be driven further and further back into the country, till the whole race is ultimately exterminated, and the territory is incapable of further extension.

These observations are, in a degree, applicable to all the parts of the earth, where the soil is imperfectly cultivated. To exterminate the inhabitants of the greatest part of Asia and Africa, is a thought that could not be admitted for a moment. To civilize and direct the industry of the various tribes of Tartars and Negroes, would certainly be a work of considerable time, and of variable and uncertain success.

Europe is by no means so fully peopled as it might be. In Europe there is the fairest chance that human industry may receive its best direction. The science of agriculture has been much studied in England and Scotland; and there is still a great portion of uncultivated land in these countries. Let us consider, at what rate the produce of this island might be supposed to increase under circumstances the most favourable to improvement.

If it be allowed, that by the best possible

policy, and great encouragements to agriculture, the average produce of the island could be doubled in the first twenty-five years, it will be allowing, probably, a greater increase than could with reason be expected.

In the next twenty-five years, it is impossible to suppose that the produce could be quadrupled. It would be contrary to all our knowledge of the properties of land. The improvement of the barren parts would be a work of time and labour; and it must be evident to those who have the slightest acquaintance with agricultural subjects, that in proportion as cultivation extended, the additions that could yearly be made to the former average produce must be gradually and regularly diminishing. That we may be the better able to compare the increase of population and food, let us make a supposition, which, without pretending to accuracy, is clearly more favourable to the power of production in the earth, than any experience we have had of its qualities will warrant.

Let us suppose that the yearly additions which might be made to the former average produce, instead of decreasing, which they certainly would do, were to remain the same; and that the produce of this island might be increased every twenty-five years, by a quantity equal to what it at present produces. The most enthusiastic speculator cannot suppose a greater increase than this. In a few centuries it would make every acre of land in the island like a garden.

If this supposition be applied to the whole earth, and if it be allowed that the subsistence for man which the earth affords might be increased every twenty-five years by a quantity equal to what it at present produces, this will be supposing a rate of increase much greater than we can imagine that any possible exertions of mankind could make it.

It may be fairly pronounced, therefore, that, considering the present average state of the earth, the means of subsistence, under circumstances the most favourable to human industry, could not possibly be made to increase faster than in an arithmetical ratio.

The necessary effects of these two different rates of increase, when brought together, will be very striking. Let us call the population of this island eleven millions; and suppose the present produce equal to the easy support of such a number. In the first twenty-five years the population would be twenty-two millions, and the food being also doubled, the means of subsistence would be equal to this increase. In the next twenty-five years, the population would be forty-four millions, and the means of subsistence only equal to the support of thirty-three millions. In the next period the population would be eighty-eight millions, and the means of subsistence just equal to the support of half that number. And, at the conclusion of the first century, the population would be a hundred and seventy-six millions, and the means of subsistence only equal to the support of fifty-five millions, leaving a population of a hundred and twenty-one millions totally unprovided for.

Taking the whole earth, instead of this island, emigration would of course be excluded; and, supposing the present population equal to a thousand millions, the human species would increase as the numbers 1, 2, 4, 8, 16, 32, 64, 128, 256, and subsistence as 1, 2, 3, 4, 5, 6, 7, 8, 9. In two centuries the population would be to the means of subsistence as 256 to 9; in three centuries as 4096 to 13, and in two thousand years the difference would be almost incalculable.

In this supposition no limits whatever are placed to the produce of the earth. It may increase for ever, and be greater than any assignable quantity; yet still the power of population being in every period so much superior, the increase of the human species can only be kept down to the level of the means of subsistence by the constant operation of the strong law of necessity, acting as a check upon the greater power.

The ultimate check to population appears then to be a want of food, arising necessarily from the different ratios according to which population and food increase. But this ultimate check is never the immediate check, except in cases of actual famine.

The immediate check may be stated to consist in all those customs, and all those diseases, which seem to be generated by a scarcity of the means of subsistence; and all those causes, independent of this scarcity, whether of a moral or physical nature, which tend prematurely to weaken and destroy the human frame.

These checks to population, which are constantly operating with more or less force in every society, and keep down the number to the level of the means of subsistence, may be classed under two general heads—the preventive, and the positive checks.

The preventive check, as far as it is voluntary, is peculiar to man, and arises from that distinctive superiority in his reasoning faculties, which enables him to calculate distant consequences. The checks to the indefinite increase of plants and irrational animals are all either positive, or, if preventive, involuntary. But man cannot look around him, and see the distress which frequently presses upon those who have large families; he cannot contemplate his present possessions or earnings, which he now nearly consumes himself, and calculate the amount of each share, when with very little addition they must be divided, perhaps, among seven or eight, without feeling a doubt whether, if he follow the bent of his inclinations, he may be able to support the offspring which he will probably bring into the world. In a state of equality, if such can exist, this would be the simple question. In the present state of society other considerations occur. Will he not lower his rank in life, and be obliged to give up in great measure his former habits? Does any mode of employment present itself by which he may reasonably hope to maintain a family? Will he not at any rate subject himself to greater difficulties, and more severe labour, than in his single state? Will he not be unable to transmit to his children the same advantages of education and improvement that he had himself possessed? Does he even feel secure that, should he have a large family, his utmost exertions can save them from rags and squalid poverty, and their consequent degradation in the community? And may he not be reduced to the grating necessity of forfeiting his independence, and of being obliged to the sparing hand of Charity for support?

These considerations are calculated to prevent, and certainly do prevent, a great number of persons in all civilized nations from pursuing the dictate of nature in an early attachment to one woman.

If this restraint does not produce vice, it is undoubtedly the least evil that can arise from the principle of population. Considered as a restraint on a strong natural inclination, it must be allowed to produce a certain degree of temporary unhappiness; but evidently slight, compared with the evils which result from any of the other checks to population; and merely of the same nature as many other sacrifices of temporary to permanent gratification, which it is the business of a moral agent continually to make.

When this restraint produces vice, the evils which follow are but too conspicuous. A promiscuous intercourse to such a degree as to prevent the birth of children seems to lower, in the most marked manner, the dignity of human nature. It cannot be without its effect on men, and nothing can be more obvious than its tendency to degrade the female character, and to destroy all its most amiable and distinguishing characteristics. Add to which, that among those unfortunate females, with which all great towns abound, more real distress and aggravated misery are, perhaps, to be found, than in any other department of human life.

When a general corruption of morals, with regard to the sex, pervades all the classes of society, its effects must necessarily be, to poison the springs of domestic happiness, to weaken conjugal and parental affection, and to lessen the united exertions and ardour of parents in the care and education of their children;—effects which cannot take place without a decided diminution of the general happiness and virtue of the society; particularly as the necessity of art in the accomplishment and conduct of intrigues, and in the concealment of their consequences, necessarily leads to many other vices.

The positive checks to population are extremely various, and include every cause, whether arising from vice or misery, which in any degree contributes to shorten the natural duration of human life. Under this head, therefore, may be enumerated all unwholesome occupations, severe labour and exposure to the seasons, extreme poverty, bad nursing of children, great towns, excesses of all kinds, the whole train of common diseases and epidemics, wars, plague, and famine.

On examining these obstacles to the increase of population which I have classed under the heads of preventive and positive checks, it will appear that they are all resolvable into moral restraint, vice, and misery.

Of the preventive checks, the restraint from marriage which is not followed by irregular gratifications may properly be termed moral restraint.[7]

Promiscuous intercourse, unnatural passions, violations of the marriage bed, and improper arts to conceal the consequences of irregular connexions, are preventive checks that clearly come under the head of vice.

Of the positive checks, those which appear to arise unavoidably from the laws of nature, may be called exclusively misery; and those which we obviously bring upon ourselves, such as wars, excesses, and many others which it would be in our power to avoid, are of mixed nature. They are brought upon us by vice, and their consequences are misery.[8]

The sum of all these preventive and positive checks, taken together, forms the immediate check to population; and it is evident that, in every country where the whole of the procreative power cannot be called into action, the preventive and the positive checks must vary inversely as each other; that is, in countries either naturally unhealthy, or subject to a great mortality, from whatever cause it may arise, the preventive check will prevail very little. In those countries, on the contrary, which are naturally healthy, and where the preventive check is found to prevail with considerable force, the positive check will prevail very little, or the mortality be very small.

In every country some of these checks are, with more or less force, in constant operation; yet notwithstanding their general prevalence, there are few states in which there is not a constant effort in the population to increase beyond the means of subsistence. This constant effort as constantly tends to subject the lower classes of society to distress, and to prevent any great permanent melioration of their condition.

These effects, in the present state of society, seem to be produced in the following manner. We will suppose the means of subsistence in any country just equal to the easy support of its inhabitants. The constant effort towards population, which is found to act even in the most vicious societies, increases the number of people before the means of subsistence are increased. The food, therefore, which before supported eleven millions, must now be divided among eleven millions and a half. The poor consequently must live much worse, and many of them be reduced to severe distress. The number of labourers also being above the proportion of work in the market, the price of labour must tend to fall, while the price of provisions would at the same time tend to rise.

The labourer therefore must do more work, to earn the same as he did before. During this season of distress, the discouragements to marriage and the difficulty of rearing a family are so great, that population is nearly at a stand. In the mean time, the cheapness of labour, the plenty of labourers, and the necessity of an increased industry among them, encourage cultivators to employ more labour upon their land, to turn up fresh soil, and to manure and improve more completely what is already in tillage, till ultimately the means of subsistence may become in the same proportion to the population, as at the period from which we set out. The situation of the labourer being then again tolerably comfortable, the restraints to population are in some degree loosened; and, after a short period, the same retrograde and progressive movements, with respect to happiness, are repeated.

This sort of oscillation will not probably be obvious to common view; and it may be difficult even for the most attentive observer to calculate its periods. Yet that, in the generality of old states, some alternation of this kind does exist, though in a much less marked, and in a much more irregular manner, than I have described it, no reflecting man, who considers the subject deeply, can well doubt.

One principal reason why this oscillation has been less remarked, and less decidedly confirmed by experience than might naturally be expected, is, that the histories of mankind which we possess are, in general, histories only of the higher classes. We have not many accounts that can be depended upon, of the manners and customs of that part of mankind, where these retrograde and progressive movements chiefly take place. A satisfactory history of this kind, of one people and of one period, would require the constant and minute attention of many observing minds in local and general remarks on the state of the lower classes of society, and the causes that influenced it; and, to draw accurate inferences upon this subject, a succession of such historians for some centuries would be necessary. This branch of statistical knowledge has of late years, been attended to in some countries,[9] and we may promise ourselves a clearer insight into the internal structure of human society from the progress of these inquiries. But the science may be said yet to be in its infancy, and many of the objects, on which it would be desirable to have information, have been either omitted or not stated with sufficient accuracy. Among these, perhaps, may be reckoned the proportion of the number of adults to the number of marriages; the extent to which vicious customs have prevailed in consequence of the restraints upon matrimony; the comparative mortality among the children of the most distressed part of the community, and of those who live rather more at their ease; the variations in the real price of labour; the observable differences in the state of the lower classes of society, with respect to ease and happiness, at different times during a certain period; and very accurate registers of births, deaths, and marriages, which are of the utmost importance in this subject.

A faithful history, including such particulars, would tend greatly to elucidate the manner in which the constant check upon population acts; and would probably prove the existence of the retrograde and progressive movements that have been mentioned; though the times of their vibration must necessarily be rendered irregular from the operation of many interrupting causes; such as, the introduction or failure of certain manufactures; a greater or less prevalent spirit of agricultural enterprise; years of plenty, or years of scarcity; wars, sickly seasons, poor-laws, emigration, and other causes of a similar nature.

A circumstance which has, perhaps, more than any other, contributed to conceal this oscillation from common view, is the difference between the nominal and real price of labour. It very rarely happens that the nominal price of labour universally falls; but we well know that it frequently remains the same, while the nominal price of provisions has been gradually rising. This, indeed, will generally be the case, if the increase of manufactures and commerce be sufficient to employ the new labourers that are thrown into the market, and to prevent the increased supply from lowering the money-price.[10] But an increased number of labourers receiving the same money-wages will necessarily, by their competition, increase the money-price of corn. This is, in fact, a real fall in the price of labour; and, during this period, the condition of the lower classes of the community must be gradually growing

worse. But the farmers and capitalists are growing rich from the real cheapness of labour. Their increasing capitals enable them to employ a greater number of men; and, as the population had probably suffered some check from the greater difficulty of supporting a family, the demand for labour, after a certain period, would be great in proportion to the supply, and its price would of course rise, if left to find its natural level; and thus the wages of labour, and consequently the condition of the lower classes of society, might have progressive and retrograde movements, though the price of labour might never nominally fall.

In savage life, where there is no regular price of labour, it is little to be doubted that similar oscillations take place. When population has increased nearly to the utmost limits of the food, all the preventive and the positive checks will naturally operate with increased force. Vicious habits with respect to the sex will be more general, the exposing of children more frequent, and both the probability and fatality of wars and epidemics will be considerably greater; and these causes will probably continue their operation till the population is sunk below the level of the food; and then the return to comparative plenty will again produce an increase, and, after a certain period, its further progress will again be checked by the same causes.[11]

But without attempting to establish these progressive and retrograde movements in different countries, which would evidently require more minute histories than we possess, and which the progress of civilization naturally tends to counteract, the following propositions are intended to be proved:—

1. Population is necessarily limited by the means of subsistence.

2. Population invariably increases where the means of subsistence increase, unless prevented by some very powerful and obvious checks.[12]

3. These checks, and the checks which repress the superior power of population, and keep its effects on a level with the means of subsistence, are all resolvable into moral restraint, vice, and misery.

Notes

[1] Franklin's Miscell. p. 9.

[2] It appears, from some recent calculations and estimates, that from the first settlement of America, to the year 1800, the periods of doubling have been but very little above twenty years. See a note on the increase of American population in Book ii. chap. xi [of this *Essay*].

[3] Price's Observ. on Revers. Pay. Vol. i. p. 274. Edit. 4to.

[4] Id. p. 282.

[5] See this table at the end of chap. iv. book ii.

[6] Polit. Arith. p. 14.

[7] It will be observed, that I here use the term *moral* in its most confined sense. By moral restraint I would be understood to mean a restraint from marriage, from prudential motives, with a conduct strictly moral during the period of this restraint; and I have never intentionally deviated from this sense. When I have wished to consider the restraint from marriage unconnected with its consequences, I have either called it prudential restraint, or a part of the preventive check, of which indeed it forms the principal branch.

In my review of the different stages of society, I have been accused of not allowing sufficient weight in the prevention of population to moral restraint; but when the confined sense of the term, which I have here explained, is adverted to, I am fearful that I shall not be found to have erred much in this respect. I should be very glad to believe myself mistaken.

[8] As the general consequence of vice is misery, and as this consequence is the precise reason why an action is termed vicious, it may appear that the term misery alone would be here sufficient, and that it is superfluous to use both. But the rejection of the term vice would introduce a considerable confusion into our language and ideas. We want it particularly to distinguish those actions, the general tendency of which is to produce misery, and which are therefore prohibited by the commands of the Creator, and the precepts of the moralist, although, in their immediate or individual effects, they may produce perhaps exactly the contrary. The gratification of all our passions in its immediate effect is happiness, not misery; and, in individual instances, even the remote consequences (at least in this life) may possibly come under the same denomination. There may have been some irregular connexions with women, which have added to the happiness of both parties, and have injured no one. These individual actions therefore cannot come under the head of misery. But they are still evidently vicious, because an action is so denominated, which violates an express precept, founded upon its general tendency to produce misery, whatever may be its individual effect; and no person can doubt the general tendency of an illicit intercourse between sexes, to injure the happiness of society.

[9] The judicious questions which Sir John Sinclair circulated in Scotland, and the valuable accounts which he has collected in that part of the island, do him the highest honour; and these accounts will ever remain an extraordinary monument of the learning, good sense, and general information of the clergy of Scotland. It is to be regretted that the adjoining parishes are not put together in the work, which would have assisted the memory both in attaining and recollecting the state of particular districts. The repetitions and contradictory opinions which occur are not in my opinion so objectionable; as, to the result of such testimony, more faith may be given than we could possibly give to the testimony of any individual. Even were this result drawn for us by some master hand, though much valuable time would undoubtedly be saved, the information would not be so satisfactory. If, with a few subordinate improvements, this work had contained accurate and complete registers for the last 150 years, it would have been inestimable, and would have exhibited a better picture of the internal state of a country than has yet been presented to the world. But this last most essential improvement no diligence could have effected.

[10] If the new labourers thrown yearly into the market should find no employment but in agriculture, their competition might so lower the money-price of labour, as to prevent the increase of population from occasioning an effective demand for more corn; or, in other words, if the landlords and farmers could get nothing but an additional quantity of agricultural labour in exchange for any additional produce which they could raise, they might not be tempted to raise it.

[11] Sir James Steuart very justly compares the generative faculty to a spring loaded with a variable weight, (Polit. Econ. vol. i. b.i.c. 4. p. 20.) which would of course produce exactly that kind of oscillation which has been mentioned. In the first book of his Political Economy, he has explained many parts of the subject of population very ably.

[12] I have expressed myself in this cautious manner, because I believe there are some instances, where population does not keep up to the level of the means of

subsistence. But these are extreme cases; and, generally speaking, it might be said, that,

2. Population always increases where the means of subsistence increase.

3. The checks which repress the superior power of popula-

tion, and keep its effects on a level with the means of subsistence, are all resolvable into moral restraint, vice, and misery.

It should be observed, that, by an increase in the means of subsistence, is here meant such an increase as will enable the

mass of the society to command more food. An increase might certainly take place, which in the actual state of a particular society would not be distributed to the lower classes, and consequently would give no stimulus to population.

POLITICAL IMPLICATIONS OF THE DEMOGRAPHIC FACTOR

Interest in the problems raised by Malthus was relatively slack during the balance of the nineteenth century and the beginning of the twentieth. Shortly after the publication of his essay on population, world food supply was greatly increased by harvests from the rich American continent, and Malthus's cry began to sound very much like "Wolf!" More significantly, the birth rate in the industrial West began to decline, and population growth moderated. Just prior to World War II, the growth of many countries in the West was negligible, and some countries, notably France, were actually declining in population.

Following World War II, however, a new note of crisis appeared in discussions of population, for two reasons. The less ominous, but symbolically more important, development was renewed population growth in the West. High birth rates in industrial countries, at first dismissed by demographers as a temporary phenomenon related to the war, showed no signs of diminution with passing years. Large numbers of children created unexpected demands for houses with extra bedrooms, for schools and colleges, and for employment opportunities. An intrinsically more important development on the global level was a decline in death rates, as techniques for improving health spread to non-Western societies, with resultant world population growth on a scale unknown in man's history. Demographers began to use the term "explosion," and the ghost of Malthus walked among them.

Philip M. Hauser here explains the source of the demographers' "emotionally surcharged language" with reference to current population trends. He suggests that the presence of large, relatively deprived, populations in specific nations may have serious consequences for world peace.

The rate of world population growth has been rising drastically in recent years, and is expected to go higher yet. By the end of the century, Malthus's hypothetical doubling of population every twenty-five years may be realized in fact on a world basis. This poses a problem which, in the short run, is not of avoiding starvation so much as of raising standards of living outside of Europe and North America. Little would be accomplished by a better distribution of goods among nations, since there is relatively little to distribute. The problem can be solved only by creating a larger total product.

At present, the countries with the lowest levels of living have the highest rates of population increase, which makes the task of raising standards of living most difficult in the very places where it is most urgent. The increasing urbanization of population merely concentrates the problem.

This situation will present temptations for the overpopulated poor nations to embark on projects for territorial expansion. Asia, the Middle East, Latin America, and Africa are the most likely trouble spots, but difficulties in these areas will involve the United States and Russia as well.

Raising the standard of living in deprived nations requires control over population increase, which in practice means the establishment of some kind of limitation of births. This in turn means that the people of the world must learn, desire, and possess the means to control the numbers of their children.

Hauser's argument can be termed "neo-Malthusian," but it is broader in its implications than would be a simple restatement of Malthus using modern data. Hauser is concerned not with starvation, which is still mostly a long-range problem, but with the standard of living, which is a problem of the immediate present. The consequences of population pressures in remote areas are linked to world peace and to the safety of the best-fed of Western nations.

Population restriction is not a welcome policy in most societies. Americans will be quick to note that limitation of the number of children concerns an area that is traditionally considered to be private in our society, and that it conflicts with secular as well as religious beliefs concerning the value of human life. Although similar conflicts are met in nearly all societies in the world, the alternative to this policy, increasing the number of deaths, is even more patently considered undesirable. The demographers' facts indicate that large-scale limitation of the number of children is not only necessary; it is a future inevitability.

Selection 10
DEMOGRAPHIC DIMENSIONS OF WORLD POLITICS
Philip M. Hauser

Politics in general, as well as world politics, is a branch of engineering—social engineering—not of science. Yet the consideration of the demographic aspects of world politics is not an inappropriate subject for a scientific journal. It is the purpose of this article to point to ways in which the findings of the science of demography illuminate various aspects of the world political scene.

There are various ways in which this subject can be developed, but I have arbitrarily chosen to discuss population factors in relation to politics, broadly conceived, on the global and on the international levels, respectively. By "global" problems I mean those that concern the earth as a whole; by "international" problems I mean those that arise among the various political subdivisions of the globe.

Global considerations

There is no world government charged with the task of achieving world order and performing other civil governmental functions for the earth as a whole. This, however, does not mean that there are no political problems of a global, as distinguished from an international,

Reprinted from *Science*, 131:3414, 1960, pp. 1641–1647, by permission of the author and the publisher.

character. Some such global problems are in fact dealt with by the United Nations and its specialized agencies, which are, of course, organizations of individual sovereign nations rather than organs of world government. Examples of global problems—problems which transcend and cannot be contained within national boundaries—include health, weather, fallout, and the newly emergent problems of outer space. It is easy to demonstrate that the contemporary rate of world population growth also constitutes a global problem—one which would be of great concern to a world government if we had one, and one which is of increasing concern to various organs of the United Nations and the specialized agencies.

Although the first complete census of mankind has yet to be taken, it is possible to reconstruct, with reasonable accuracy, the history of world population growth. This history may be encapsulated in the following estimates of the population of the earth: at the end of the Neolithic period in Europe (8000 to 7000 B.C.)[1] 10 million; at the beginning of the Christian era, 200 to 300 million; at the beginning of the modern era (1650), 500 million; in 1950, 2.5 billion.

These four numbers constitute a measurement of one of the most dramatic aspects of man's existence on the globe, and they explain the purple language of the demographer in describing the changes in rates of population growth during the modern era as a "demographic revolution" or "population explosion."[2]

The basis for the demographer's emotionally surcharged language may be summarized as follows.

1. The present population of the world could be produced from an initial population of two dozen individuals increasing at the rate of 0.02 percent per year over a period of 100,-000 years, and man has been on the earth for at least 200,000 to 1 million years.

2. The rate of population growth has increased enormously over the three centuries of the modern era (1650–1950), during which time it averaged about 0.5 percent per year. Over this period the rate of growth increased from about 0.3 percent per year between 1650 and 1750 to 0.9 percent per year between 1900 and 1950. World population growth averaged 1 percent per year between 1930 and 1940.

Now, a 1-percent return per year, even compounded, would by our standards represent a meager return on investment. But it constitutes a fantastically rapid rate of population increase. One hundred persons multiplying at 1 percent per year, not over the period of 200,000 to 1 million years of man's occupancy of this globe but merely for the 5000 years of human history, would have produced a contemporary population of 2.7 billion persons per square foot of land surface of the earth! Such an exercise in arithmetic, although admittedly dramatic and propagandistic, is also a conclusive way of demonstrating that a 1 percent per year increase in world population could not have taken place for very long in the past; nor can it continue for very long into the future.

The demographer's concern is not based only on considerations of the past. It is even more justified by postwar developments in population growth.

Since the end of World War II the rate of population increase has continued to accelerate and has reached a level of about 1.7 percent per year. There is justification, indeed, for pointing to a new population explosion in the wake of World War II of a greater magnitude than that previously observed. At the rate of world population increase for the period 1800–1850, for example, the present population would double in 135 years; at the 1900–

1950 rate, in 67 years; and at the postwar rate, in only 42 years.

Projection of the post-World War II rate of increase gives a population of one person per square foot of the land surface of the earth in less than 800 years. It gives a population of 50 billions (the highest estimate of the population-carrying capacity of the globe ever calculated by a responsible scholar) in less than 200 years! This estimate, by geochemist Harrison Brown,[3] is based on the assumptions that developments in the capturing of solar or nuclear energy will produce energy at a cost so low that it would be feasible to obtain all the "things" we need from rock, sea, and air, and that mankind would be content to subsist largely on food products from "algae farms and yeast factories!"

Moreover, the United Nations estimates of future world population indicate even further acceleration in the rate of world population growth during the remainder of this century. Between 1950 and 1975 the average annual percentage of increase, according to the United Nations "medium" assumptions, may be 2.1 percent, and between 1975 and 2000, almost 2.6 percent.[4] Such rates of increase would double the population about every 33 and 27 years, respectively.

It is considerations of this type that would make it necessary for a world government to exercise forethought and planning, which constitute rational decision making, in facing the future. This, of course, is the purpose of the projections. The figures do not show what the future population of the world will be—for the world could not support such populations. They do demonstrate that man, as a culture-building animal, has created an environment in which the rhythm of his own reproduction has been modified in such a manner as to point to crisis possibilities.

Crisis possibilities

The crisis possibilities are of several forms, each posing major world political problems. The first, we may note, is the ultimate crisis, which would result from the fact that the globe is finite[5] and that living space would be exhausted. Unless one is prepared to argue that future technological developments will enable man to colonize other globes,[6] it is clear that present rates of population increase must come to a halt by reason of lack of space.

No facts or hopes as to man's ability to increase his food production and to increase other types of goods and services can indefinitely increase man's *lebensraum* (or could do so even if we accept the absurd assumption that man, at terrific cost, could burrow into the earth, live in man-made layers above it, or live on the seas).

In the short run, let us say to 1975 or to 2000, world population will be confined to much more manageable numbers. The United Nations projects, on the basis of its medium assumptions, a world population of about 3.8 billion by 1975 and 6.3 billion by 2000.[1]

In the short run there is no problem of exhausting the space on the globe, nor is there reason to fear serious decreases in world per capita food supply, as is evidenced by projections of The Food and Agricultural Organization and others concerning foodstuffs.[7] But there is great reason to be pessimistic about the possibility of greatly increasing the average world level of living during the remainder of this century.

In 1950, world per capita income was estimated at $223.[8, 9] In North America, per capita income was $1100. Had each person on the globe enjoyed the North American level of living in 1950, as measured by per capita income, the aggregate world product in 1950 would have supported only 500 million persons, as contrasted with the actual world population of 2.5 billion. For average world income to have matched income in North America, aggregate income would have had to be increased about fivefold. To bring world per capita income by 1975 to the level enjoyed in North America in 1950 would require about a 7.5-fold increase of the 1950 level in 25 years. To do the same by 2000 would require a 12-fold increase in the 1950 world income within 50 years.

Even if the more modest income level of Europe ($380 per capita in 1950) were set as the target, great increases in productivity would be necessary, because of prospective rates of population increase, to raise average world income to the required level by 1975 or 2000. To achieve this goal by 1975, world income would have to be increased 2.5-fold over the 1950 level, and to achieve it by 2000, the required increase would be greater than fourfold. A decline in the rate of world population growth to that of the period 1800 to 1850—namely, to 0.5 percent—would decrease by

three-fourths and four-fifths, respectively, the projected world-income requirements for attaining this goal by 1975 or 2000.

These considerations not only show the enormous difficulty of materially increasing the world level of living on the basis of present rates of population increase but indicate, also, the weakness of the argument that a solution to the population problem is to be found in more equitable distribution of the world's food supply or of goods and services in general.[10] The equitable distribution of world income in 1950 would, to be sure, have raised the per capita income of Latin America by 31 percent; of Africa, almost threefold, and of Asia, four- to fivefold, but it would still have produced a per capita income per annum of $223, only one-fifth that in North America and only three-fifths that in Europe (exclusive of the U.S.S.R.). The miserably low level of living of most of the world's population is attributable not so much to maldistribution as to low aggregate product, the result of the low productivity of most of the world's peoples.

These political problems of a global character may perhaps be better understood through consideration of their international aspects, special attention being given to the plight of the two-thirds of the world's population resident in the underdeveloped areas of the world, in Asia, Africa, and Latin America.

International considerations

The short-run implications of present rates of world population growth are manifest in specific forms and in varying degrees of intensity among the various regional and national subdivisions of the globe. The distribution of the world's population and of the world's utilized resources, manifest in differentials in levels of living, is the result, of course, of millennia of human history. The demographic dimensions of international politics may best be comprehended against the background of differences among peoples in levels of living and the significance of these differences at this juncture in world history.[8, 11, 12] (Table 1).

To note the extremes, North America in 1950, with about 16 percent of the earth's land surface, contained less than 9 percent of the world's population but about 43 percent of the world's income. Asia, in contrast, with about the same proportion of the world's land

Table 1 Population, Income, and Energy Consumed per Capita, by Continent, about 1950. Source of data, United Nations, except where otherwise indicated.

Area	TOTAL POPULATION No. (thousands)	%	AGGREGATE INCOME Dollars* (millions)	%	Per capita income ($)	Energy consumed per capita (kw-hr)†
World	2497	100.0	556	100.0	223	1676
Africa	199	8.0	15	2.7	75	686
North America	219	8.8	241	43.3	1100	10,074
South America	112	4.5	19	3.4	170	741
Asia	1380	55.3	69	12.4	50	286
Europe (exclusive of U.S.S.R.)	393	15.7	149	26.8	380	3117
U.S.S.R.	181	7.2	56	10.1	310	1873
Oceania	13	0.5	7	1.3	560	3543

* See Notes 8 and 9.
† See Note 33.

surface (18 percent), had 55 percent of the world's population but only 12 percent of the world's income. Per capita income in Asia was at a level of about $50 per year as contrasted with a level of $1100 in North America. Despite the fact that such comparisons are subject to considerable error,[13] there is no doubt that a tremendous difference in per capita income existed, of a magnitude perhaps as great as 20 to 1.

The major factor underlying this difference is indicated by the contrast in the difference in nonhuman energy consumed in North America and Asia, respectively—over 10,000 kilowatt-hours per capita per year for the former in contrast to less than 300 for the latter. The availability of nonhuman energy for the production of goods and services is perhaps the best single measurement available of differences in capital investment, know-how, and technology which account for the great differences in productivity and, consequently, in the size of the aggregate product available for distribution.

The other relatively underdeveloped continents of the world also had relatively low shares of world income as compared with their proportions of world population. Africa, with a per capita income of about $75 per year, and South America, with $170, were also well below not only the level for North America ($1100) but also the levels for Europe (exclusive of the U.S.S.R.) ($380), the U.S.S.R. ($310), and Oceania ($560). There is a high correlation among these areas between per capita income and amount of non-human energy consumed (Table 1).

These differences in levels of living, as it turns out, are in general inversely related to present and prospective rates of population increase. The populations of the relatively underdeveloped continents of the world are increasing at a more rapid rate than those of the economically advanced continents[4, 14] (Table 2). Between 1950 and 1975, to use the medium projections of the United Nations, while the population of Northern America is increasing at an average annual rate of 1.7 percent and that of Europe, at 1.2 percent, that of Asia will be growing at an average annual rate of 2.4 percent, that of Africa at 2.1 percent, and that of Latin America at 3.4 percent. Between 1975 and 2000, while the rate of increase for Northern America will average 1.2 percent per year and that for Europe, 1.0 percent, the rate for Asia will be 3.0 percent, that for Africa 2.8 percent, and that for Latin America 3.8 percent, a rate at which the population would double about every 18 years.

As I have indicated above, rapid increase in world population imposes a severe burden on efforts to raise levels of living. It is easy to demonstrate that the burden would become an impossible one for the economically underdeveloped areas should their rates of population increase follow the trends indicated in the United Nations projections.

For example, Asia, merely to maintain her present low level of living, must increase her aggregate product by 60 percent between 1950 and 1975, and by an additional 75 percent between 1975 and 2000. To raise her per capita income to the European level for 1950

Table 2 Estimated Population and Population Increases, by Continent, 1900 to 2000[4]

Area	POPULATION (MILLION)					AV. ANNUAL INCREASE (%)[*]			
	1900	1925	1950	1975	2000	1900–1925	1925–1950	1950–1975	1975–2000
World	1550	1907	2497	3828	6267	0.9	1.2	2.1	2.6
Africa	120	147	199	303	517	0.9	1.4	2.1	2.8
Northern America	81	126	168	240	312	2.2	1.3	1.7	1.2
Latin America	63	99	163	303	592	2.3	2.6	3.4	3.8
Asia	857	1020	1380	2210	3870	0.8	1.4	2.4	3.0
Europe (including U.S.S.R.)	423	505	574	751	947	0.8	0.6	1.2	1.0
Oceania	6	10	13	21	29	2.3	1.4	2.4	1.6

* Arithmetic mean of percentage of increase for 25-year periods.

while continuing to experience her rapid population growth, Asia would have to increase her 1950 aggregate income 12-fold by 1975 and 21-fold by 2000. Africa, to do the same, must increase her aggregate income eightfold by 1975 and 13-fold by 2000, and Latin America would have to increase her aggregate income fourfold by 1975 and eightfold by 2000.[15]

To achieve a per capita income equal to that of Northern America in 1950 while experiencing the projected population growth, Asia would have to increase her aggregate income 35-fold by 1975 and 62-fold by 2000. Africa, to achieve a similar goal, would require 22-fold and 38-fold increases, respectively, in aggregate income, and Latin America, 12-fold and 23-fold increases.

These considerations provide additional justification for the use by the demographer of the phrase *population explosion*; and they certainly indicate the hopeless task which confronts the underdeveloped areas in their efforts to achieve higher levels of living while experiencing rapid population growth. The control of rates of population growth would unquestionably decrease the magnitude of the task of achieving higher levels of living in the underdeveloped areas, especially in those with populations that are large relative to resources.[16]

Increasingly large proportions of the population in the underdeveloped areas of the world are becoming concentrated in urban places. The continued acceleration in the rate of world urbanization during the first half of this century was mainly attributable to urbanization in the underdeveloped areas, which proceeded at a pace considerably above that in

the developed areas.[17] I have had occasion to make projections of the urban population of the world and of Asia to 1975; these are presented in Table 3 as illustrative of what is in prospect in the underdeveloped areas of the globe.[18] For the rate of urbanization in Latin America and Africa is, also, accelerating.

The projections for Asia indicate that in the 25 years between 1950 and 1975, in cities either of 100,000 and over or of 20,000 and over, urban population will increase by at least two-thirds and may perhaps triple. The lower projection is based on the assumption that the proportion of urban population in Asia will be the same in 1975 as it was in 1950. Under this assumption the projected increase would result from total population growth alone. But if it is assumed that the rate of urbanization in Asia will increase as it did between 1900 and 1950 while the total population continues to grow at the rate projected by the United Nations, then tripling of Asia's urban population is indicated.

Thus, while the nations of Asia are attempting to improve their miserable urban living conditions, their urban populations will continue to increase explosively—perhaps to triple within a period of less than one generation.

In the economically more advanced nations of the world, urbanization is both an antecedent and a consequent of technological advance and of a high level of living—a symbol of man's mastery over nature. In the underdeveloped nations, however, urbanization represents instead the transfer of rural poverty from an over-populated and unsettled countryside to a mass urban setting. In the economically underdeveloped areas of the world, ur-

Table 3 Summary of Projections of Urban Population for the World and for Asia, 1975[18]

Cities (category)	POPULATION (MILLIONS) PROJECTION FOR 1975		1950	ESTIMATE OF INCREASE IN POPULATION, 1950–1975 (MILLIONS)		ESTIMATE OF INCREASE IN POPULATION, 1950–1975 (%)		PROPORTION OF TOTAL POPULATION IN CITIES Projection for 1975*	1950
	Upper	Lower		Upper	Lower	Upper	Lower		
The World									
100,000 and over	745	488	314	431	174	138	55	19	13
20,000 and over	1155	779	502	653	277	130	55	30	21
Asia									
100,000 and over	340	176	106	234	70	222	66	15	8
20,000 and over	544	283	170	374	113	220	66	25	13

* Figures are based on the "upper" projection, which assumes urbanization of an increasing proportion of the population.

banization is outpacing economic development and the city is more a symbol of mass misery and political instability than of man's conquest of nature.[17, 19]

The prospect for individual nations, while variable, is in general the same—one of explosive growth. Between 1955 and 1975, according to the United Nations medium projections, the population of China will increase by 294 million persons and that of India, by 177 million.[4, 20] That of Pakistan will increase by 45 million persons, and that of Indonesia, by 40 million, in these 20 years. Japan, although she has now greatly slowed down her rate of population growth, will, despite her already great population pressure, increase by an additional 27 million. To confine our attention to the Far East for the moment, smaller countries with the most explosive increases include South Korea, Taiwan, and Ceylon. Each of these nations is faced with a task of tremendous proportions merely to maintain her present level of living, let alone to greatly increase it while continuing to grow at the projected rates.

Political instability

What will happen if the underdeveloped areas in Asia are frustrated in their efforts to attain a higher standard of living?

Warren S. Thompson devotes his latest book to providing an answer to this question.[21] The larger of these nations are not apt to remain hungry and frustrated without noting the rela-

tively sparsely settled areas in their vicinities—the nations in the South-East Asian peninsula: Burma, Thailand, and the newly formed free countries of Indochina, Laos, Cambodia, and Vietnam. (Vietminh, that is, North Vietnam, is already engulfed by Communist China.) Even parts of thinly settled Africa may be subject to the aggressive action of the larger and hungrier nations as feelings of population pressure mount. Moreover, Communist China, the largest nation in the world by far, faced with the greatest absolute population increases to add to her already heavy burdens in striving for economic development, may not confine her attention only to the smaller nations within her reach. Her present actions relative to her boundaries with India and possible tensions over her boundaries with the U.S.S.R. contain explosive possibilities.

It is Thompson's conclusion that the larger nations in the Far East, including Japan, India, and Pakistan as well as China, may resort to force to achieve access to additional resources under sufficient population pressure. The smaller countries may not be able to resort to force but are almost certain to require outside aid to prevent chaos. Furthermore, while neither Indonesia nor the Philippines is in a position to be aggressive or is easily accessible to aggressors, both, under mounting population pressures, are likely to continue to experience growing internal political instability.

Population pressure as a factor in political

instability is not confined to the Far East. Populations of the Middle East and North Africa —the Muslim area (exclusive of Pakistan)— may increase from 119 million in 1955 to 192 million by 1975, an increase of 73 million or 61 percent in 20 years.[4] As Irene Taeuber has noted, this is an area "where internal instabilities and conflicts of religious and ethnic groups create recurrent crises for the region and world." Taeuber observes that the immediate political instabilities in this area are attributable more to "diversities among the peoples and the nations than to population pressure or population growth."[22] But she points to the importance, in the decades that lie ahead, of economic advances to lessen tension in this region and to the barrier that rapid population growth may contribute to that development.

Latin America, although in large part still a sparsely settled area of the world, is already experiencing problems associated with rapid population growth which give promise of worsening. For Latin America, as has been reported above, is faced with a population increase of 86 percent between 1950 and 1975 and of 95 percent, almost a doubling, between 1975 and 2000.[4, 23] Especially difficult in Latin America are the problems posed by accelerating rates of urbanization. Recent measurements of rate of urban growth in Latin America indicated that of 15 countries for which data were available, urban population in one, Venezuela, was increasing at 7 percent per year, a rate which produces a doubling about every 10 years; seven had growth rates which would double their population in less than 18 years; and only two (Chile and Bolivia) had rates of urban growth of less than 1 percent per year.[10, 24] Growth rates (total and urban) of the magnitude which Latin America is experiencing are likely to add appreciably to the difficulty of raising living levels and are likely to worsen already existent political instabilities that threaten internal order and may affect world peace.

Finally, a fourth region of political instability to which the population factor is a contributing element, and one where it will be increasingly manifest, is sub-Saharan Africa.[22, 25] Middle Africa is sparsely settled, but increasing knowledge about the area indicates high birth rates, decreasing death rates, and explosive growth. The United Nations projections indicate a population increase from 154 million in 1955 to about 202 million in 1975,

or an increase of 31 percent. The familiar syndrome of underdeveloped areas—malnutrition, disease, and urban and rural squalor on the one hand and aspirations for independence and economic development on the other—are now emergent in this most primitive continent of the globe. And here, as in the other underdeveloped areas, rapid population growth is likely to intensify political unrest.

In southern Africa another type of population problem is also a major element in a political problem that has grave implications for world order as well as for the stability of the Union of South Africa. This is the problem arising from the conflict between the indigenous people and European settlers manifest in apartheid. Rapid and differential rates of growth of native and European populations are likely to intensify rather than to allay conflict in southern Africa.

The tensions and political instabilities generated by explosive population growth in the economically underdeveloped nations have a special significance in the contemporary world, characterized by the bipolar conflict between the Free and Communist blocs and the efforts on the part of each to win the allegiance of the uncommitted nations of the world. This conflict has several demographic dimensions of importance.

The Free and Communist blocs

The first of these dimensions is evident in the way in which population is distributed among the three political blocs into which the world is divided. For in 1955, each of these political groups—the free nations, the Communist nations, and the uncommitted nations— had approximately the same population. The Free and the Communist blocs, respectively, each have much to gain in the struggle to win the allegiance of the uncommitted third of the world's people. This titanic competition is focused primarily on South and Southeast Asia at the present time, because the bulk of the world's politically uncommitted population is located there.

In this war for men's minds, the competition between free-world and Communist ideologies, each of the contestants has powerful weapons. Apart from military power, which I will leave out on the assumption that a nuclear stalemate exists, the key weapons of the Communists, as is daily attested to by their propaganda, are the exploitation of the wide gap between the levels of living of the "have" and "have-not" nations and the attribution of blame for the misery of the "have-not" nations on the imperialistic and colonial practices of the "have" powers. Needless to say, the fire of this propaganda is effectively fed by the frustration of the underdeveloped areas in their efforts to advance their levels of living, or in their efforts to win independence from imperial powers, where this is not yet accomplished.

The Communist bloc, with relatively little, but with increasing, surplus product, is attempting more and more to help the uncommitted nations in economic development. The U.S.S.R. may perhaps be departing from its postwar cold-war policy of trying to persuade uncommitted nations to accept its ideology by means either of internal coups or direct external aggression.

The chief weapon of the free nations, apart from the example of their free way of life, is, undoubtedly, the provision of assistance to the underdeveloped nations to help them achieve their economic goals.

Thus, the success or failure of underdeveloped areas to raise their levels of living has the most profound world political implications. The most important immediate international political question is the question of whether the free-world approach or the Communist approach is the more effective one for achieving economic development.

It is to be emphasized that this is not a rhetorical or hypothetical question. It is being answered by the course of events, the definitive test of achievement. It is being answered by what may be regarded as the most important experiments of all time—experiments under way in each of the three blocs of nations. A great race is on among the economically underprivileged nations to attain higher living levels—some by relatively free, and some by totalitarian and Communist, methods. The contests involve nations within each of the great political blocs, for within each of them both economically advanced and underdeveloped areas are to be found.[26]

The greatest single race under way is undoubtedly the race between the leaders of the Free and Communist blocs, respectively—that is, the United States and the U.S.S.R. The U.S.S.R. has certainly served notice that, by its methods, it hopes to surpass the level of living attained by the United States, and in the not too distant future. Overshadowed only by the direct contest between the United States and the U.S.S.R. is the race between India and Communist China,[27] a race of special and direct immediate interest to the underdeveloped areas. For these mammoth nations, the two largest in the world, are bending every effort to achieve higher living standards—one through the Communist approach and the other by democratic methods. The outcome of this race will be of great interest not only to the underdeveloped nations in the uncommitted bloc but also to those in the Free bloc—the underdeveloped nations in Latin America as well as those committed to the Free bloc in Asia and in Africa.

The international political situation, then, as described above, gives a special significance to explosive population growth. For present and future rates of population growth may, indeed, prevent underdeveloped nations from raising their levels of living. Simon Kuznets' examination of the evidence indicates that the gap between "have" and "have-not" nations is increasing rather than decreasing.[12] To the extent that underdeveloped nations are frustrated in their efforts to advance their living standards, they will, it may be presumed, be more open to the blandishments of the Communist bloc. Furthermore, if the underdeveloped Communist nations demonstrate that they can achieve more rapid economic progress than the underdeveloped free nations, the free way of life may well be doomed. Success or failure in this fateful contest may well hinge on the ability of the nations involved to decrease their rates of population growth.[28]

The alternatives

The "why" of the population increase, in an immediate sense, is readily identifiable. It is to be found in the great increase in "natural increase"—in the gap between fertility and mortality.[*1] Quite apart from the precise timing of changes in the relations between mortality and fertility, it is clear that explosive growth can be dampened only by decreasing natural increase. This is true for the world as a whole in the ultimate sense, with differences in timing for different parts of the world. For suggested solutions to the problems of present

* Birth and death rates.—Ed.

and prospective rates of population growth in the various subdivisions of the world through wealth, and similar means hold forth little promise, if any, even in the short run.[21]

There are only three ways to decrease natural increase: (i) by increasing the death rate; (ii) by decreasing the birth rate; and (iii) by some combination of the two.

Although it is true that decreased death rates were largely responsible for the population explosion in the past and are foreseen to be a large factor in the future, the adoption of a policy to increase mortality, or to diminish efforts to increase longevity, is unthinkable. Unless one is prepared to debate this, two of the three ways of decreasing natural increase are ruled out. For two of them involve an increase in death rates.

If longevity gains are to be retained, then, the only way to reduce explosive population growth is to decrease the birth rate. That is, the "death control" mankind has achieved can be retained only if it is accompanied by birth control. This proposition, even though it flows directly from the demographic facts of life, in view of prevalent value systems provokes heated debate of the type manifest in the press. Birth control has recently, indeed, made the front pages of the world press.

What is important about the value controversy under way is that it definitely affects global and international policy and action on matters of population and, therefore, on the crucial political problems involved. The most significant thing about all the available methods of birth control—a fact mainly obscured in the present public controversy—is that they are by no means adequate to the task of slowing down explosive world population increase, especially that in the underdeveloped areas. The great mass of mankind in the economically less advanced nations which are faced with accelerating rates of growth fail to limit their birth rates not because of the factors at issue in the controversy we are witnessing but because

they do not have the desire, the know-how, or the means to do so. The desire to control fertility, arising from recognition of the problem, is, however, increasing. Japan is already well down the road to controlling its birth rate, although by methods which are not enthusiastically endorsed either by the Japanese themselves or by other peoples. China, India, Pakistan, and Egypt[29] have population limitation programs under way or under serious consideration, and other underdeveloped areas are showing increasing interest in this problem.[30] The changes in value systems which will create mass motivation to adopt methods of family limitation are not easily brought about,[31] but they are at least under way.

Birth control methods in use in the economically more advanced nations are not, in the main, well adapted for use in the underdeveloped areas. But the results of increased research and experimentation with oral contraceptives are encouraging,[32] and there may soon be a breakthrough on obtaining adequate means for the task of limiting population growth in the underdeveloped areas.

Conclusion

The demographer and the increasing number of his allies, in directing attention to the implications of world population growth, are in fact pointing to major global and international political problems—problems that cannot be ignored. Needless to say, the solution to the problems is not to be found in appeals to the traditions of the past, sacred or secular. The solution is to be found in the policies and actions which man himself, as a rational animal, must work out and implement. The mind of man, which has conceived remarkable methods for increasing life expectancy, is probably ingenious enough to devise methods by which the population explosion can be controlled within the framework of man's diverse value systems.

Notes

[1] *Determinants and Consequences of Population Trends* (United Nations, New York, 1953), chap. 2.

[2] See the objection to this phrase in "Statement by Roman Catholic bishops of U.S. on birth control," New York *Times* (26 Nov. 1959).

[3] H. Brown, *The Challenge of Man's Future* (Viking, New York, 1954).

[4] *The Future Growth of World Population* (United Nations, New York, 1958).

5 This fact is ignored by Roman Catholic bishops [see New York *Times* (26 Nov. 1959)] and by the Pope [see "Pope denounces birth limitation," New York *Times*, 15 Dec. 1959)].

6 The impracticability of colonizing other planets is considered by G. Hardin [*J. Heredity* **50**, 2 (1959)].

7 W. H. Leonard, *Sci. Monthly* **85**, 113 (1957).

8 "National and Per Capita Income of 70 Countries in 1949," *U.N. Statist. Papers, Ser. E., No. 1* (United Nations, New York, 1950).

9 The calculations were made by using United Nations per capita income figures for each continent applied to revised United Nations estimates of 1950 population of continents to obtain revised aggregate income by continent and for the world, as shown in Table 1. A new world per capita figure of $223 was obtained, as compared with the published figure of $230.

10 For the Communist position see F. Lorimer, "Population policies and politics in the Communist world," in *Population and World Politics*, P. M. Hauser, Ed. (Free Press, Glencoe, Ill., 1958); for the Catholic position see "Pope denounces birth limitation," New York *Times* (15 Dec. 1959); for the Socialist position, see J. D. Bernal, "Population growth is no threat for a free society," *Natl. Guardian* (7 Dec. 1959) (extract from J. D. Bernal, *Science in History*).

11 W. S. Woytinsky and E. S. Woytinsky. *World Population and Production* (Twentieth Century Fund, New York, 1953).

12 S. Kuznets, "Regional economic trends and levels of living," in *Population and World Politics*, P. M. Hauser, Ed. (Free Press, Glencoe, Ill., 1958).

13 *Report on International Definition and Measurement of Standards and Levels of Living* (United Nations, New York, 1954).

14 Note the different definitions of area in Tables 1 and 2. In Table 2, which gives population projections to 1975 and 2000, "Northern America" includes only North America north of the Rio Grande; "Latin America" includes South America, Central America, and North America south of the Rio Grande. For the rough comparisons made, no adjustment of the data was necessary.

15 Calculations were based on revised data, as explained in [Note] 9. For Latin America the calculations were based on a comparison of estimated aggregate income for "Latin America" in 1950, per capita income for "South America" being used.

16 The "population problem" differs for areas with different ratios of population to resources; for example, see Political and Economic Planning, *World Population and Resources* (Essential Books, Fairlawn, N.J., 1955).

17 P. M. Hauser, "World and urbanization in relation to economic development and social change," in *Urbanization in Asia and Far East* (UNESCO, Calcutta, 1957), p. 57, based on work of K. Davis and H. Hertz.

18 ——, "Implications of population trends for regional and urban planning in Asia," UNESCO Working Paper No. 2, U.N. Seminar on Regional Planning. Tokyo, Japan (1958).

19 ——, Ed., "Urbanization in Latin America" (UNESCO, New York).

20 "The Population of South East Asia (Including Ceylon and China: Taiwan) 1950–1980," *U.N. Rept. No. 3 on Future Population Estimates by Sex and Age* (United Nations, New York, 1958).

21 W. S. Thompson, *Population and Progress in the Far East* (Univ. of Chicago Press, Chicago, 1959).

22 I. B. Taeuber, "Population and political instabilities in underdeveloped areas," in *Population and World Politics*, P. M. Hauser, Ed. (Free Press, Glencoe, Ill., 1958).

23 "The Population of Central America (Including Mexico), 1950–1980," *U.N. Rept. No. 1 on Future Population Estimates by Sex and Age* (United Nations, New York, 1954); "The Population of South America, 1950–1980," *U.N. Rept. No. 2 on Future Population Estimates by Sex and Age* (United Nations, New York, 1955).

24 "Demographic aspects of urbanization in Latin America," UNESCO Seminar on Urbanization Problems in Latin America, Santiago, Chile (1959).

25 *Social Implications of Industrialization in Africa South of the Sahara* (UNESCO, London, 1956).

26 K. Davis, "Population and power in the free world," in *Population and World Politics*, P. M. Hauser, Ed. (Free Press, Glencoe, Ill., 1958).

27 W. Lippmann, "China is No. 1 problem," Chicago *Sun-Times* (14 Dec. 1959); "To live India must change its way of life . . .," Chicago *Sun-Times* (15 Dec. 1959).

28 Nor is population a factor in political instability only in the underdeveloped areas. There are many other demographic

dimensions of world politics which cannot be treated here because of limitations of space. The authors of a recent symposium volume which it was my privilege to edit include further considerations of population as a factor in world politics. Especially pertinent are the articles by Kingsley Davis, Frank Lorimer, Irene Taeuber, and Quincy Wright, from which I have drawn material for this discussion.

[29] "Japan's population miracle,"

Population Bull. **15**, No. 7 (1959); "The race between people and resources—in the ECAFE region," pt. 1, *Population Bull.* **15**, No. 5, 89 (1959).

[30] *Asia and the Far East, Seminar on Population* (United Nations, New York, 1957).

[31] F. W. Notestein, "Knowledge, action, people," *University—A Princeton Magazine*, No. 2 (1959); P. Streit and P. Streit, "New light on India's worry," New York *Times Magazine* (13 Mar. 1960).

[32] See, for example, G. Pincus *et al., Science* **130**, 81 (1959); ——, "Field Trials with Norethnyodrel as an Oral Contraceptive (Worcester Foundation for Experimental Biology, Shrewsbury, Mass., in preparation).

[33] Data are based on the following: J. J. Spengler, *Proc. Am. Phil. Soc.* **95**, 53 (1951); original data (for 1937) from "Energy Resources of the World," *U.S. Dept. State Publ.* (Government Printing Office, Washington, D.C., 1949), pp. 102 ff.

SOCIAL INFLUENCES ON POPULATION GROWTH

As previously noted, one of the paradoxes raised by Malthusian theory is that the poor have children, although they are least able to afford them. It was this paradox that attracted the attention of J. Mayone Stycos in Puerto Rico during the 1950s. His selection contains a convincing explanation which is applicable in greater or lesser degree to many other societies in which population presses hard on resources, yet growth continues.

> Puerto Rico exemplifies the situation predicted by Malthus, in which there are barely enough resources to support the population. However, although the society is becoming more urban and industrial, and although families express preferences for fewer children, a high fertility rate continues.
>
> The paradox is explained by two sets of characteristics of the Puerto Rican family. First, although the position of women in this society leads them to desire family limitation, the position of men is opposed to it. The idea of *machismo* defines masculinity in terms of having children, and the superiority of men and inferiority of women in Puerto Rican society means that the man's preference prevails over that of the woman. Second, the individual family is able to escape some of the burdens entailed by the high birth rate by sharing the children's support with biological or ritual relatives.

The selection demonstrates that the demographic factor, like the geographic and biological, is far from being a "given" or fixed condition for society. Population is very much a product of social forces, and demographic changes are accomplished by social changes.

In terms of efforts to solve the Malthusian problem, Stycos' work suggests that fertility would decline if there were a way to put the cost of children more directly on the unit that produces them, for example by reducing the parents' opportunity to place them with relatives. Other sources of lower fertility might be an improvement of women's position in the family, or a lessening of the need for men to prove themselves masculine by having children. In one sense this is an optimistic thesis, countering the nasty inevitabilities that are suggested by Malthus' mathematical progressions, and pointing to the areas in which social change can be expected to have demographic effects. In another sense, however, Stycos' thesis appears pessimistic, for the phenomena that he indicates as causes of high fertility are cherished values, beliefs, and ways of doing things. Simple panaceas like education are unlikely to accomplish much if Stycos is correct, and changes in the places and of the magnitudes necessary to affect fertility are likely to be upsetting to extensive and fundamental parts of the society. When the fertility rate of Puerto Rico eventually declines, it will be an indication of the fact that profound changes are occurring throughout the social structure.

Selection 11
FAMILY AND FERTILITY IN PUERTO RICO
J. Mayone Stycos

The past decade's development program in Puerto Rico has aided but far from solved the island's population problem. With the present rate of natural increase at 29 (United States, 8) Puerto Rico's population will double by 1985 if the birth rate continues at its present rate. With a population density 15 times that of the United States, with a population characterized as "rural, landless and wage-earning," and with less than 1,000,000 acres of tillable land for its 2,100,000 inhabitants, Puerto Rico's "problem" is clearly Malthusian.

Various studies have aimed at providing information which could assist in effecting a rapid solution of the population problem. Insular and mainland anthropologists, economists and demographers have pursued research projects which have thrown valuable light on reduction of high fertility. Considerable research can still be profitably directed, however, at the institution most strategic to the regulation of fertility—the family. This paper, consequently, will describe and analyze the salient characteristics of the Puerto Rican family, in an attempt to establish the kind of hypotheses fruitful for research in the area of human fertility.

Background information

The considerable advances in industrialization made by the Popular Government in the past ten years have not yet altered Puerto Rico's status as an underdeveloped economy. In 1948 about 39 per cent of the labor force was directly engaged in farming.[1] Despite the

Reprinted from *American Sociological Review*, 17:5, 1952, pp. 572–580, with permission of the author and the publisher.

fact that real income has increased 80 per cent from 1940–1950,[2] three-quarters of the families of Puerto Rico still have an annual income under 1000 dollars, while 44 per cent earn less than 500 dollars.[3] While this is considerably higher than average incomes for families of other Caribbean islands, it ranks well below the income of our poorest states. The per capita income of Mississippi, for example, is twice that of Puerto Rico.

Unemployment is high, the yearly average usually totaling around 10 per cent of the labor force.[4] Yet this disguises the true picture, for sugar harvesting and refining is a seasonal occupation. Approximately three-quarters of the sugar workers are employed about 175 days a year, and the remainder work only about a hundred days during the peak harvest season.

While the insular economy is still strongly agrarian the situation is now changing, particularly with respect to urban migration. At the time of American occupation a half century ago, Puerto Rico's population was 14.5 per cent urban. Urbanization has grown steadily, accelerating in the past decade, and now stands at 60 per cent. Literacy rates have also increased greatly. While only one-fifth of the population over ten years of age could be classified as literate in 1900, three-fourths of the present day population can read and write.[5] Even in many rural areas, the degree of contact with the larger cities is such as to promote a degree of modernization not characteristic of Puerto Rico's agrarian economy of two or three decades ago.

We may assume too that family ideals are undergoing rapid change.[6] Whereas the *jibaro* once wanted "all the children that God sends," his ideal is now three,[7] and he feels that a family has the right to limit the number of its children.[8] Despite such changes Puerto Rico's birth rate has not dropped appreciably.

We are left with a difficult task—that of reconciling Puerto Rico's high fertility rate with the small-family preference among its population. Before attributing this anomaly solely to the relative absence within the lower class of technical means to achieve lower rates of fertility, it is desirable to examine those institutions and cultural patterns which may work counter to low fertility ideals. Two principal patterns help explain the relationship between family and fertility in Puerto Rico.

(1) Differential sex statuses and roles are such as to encourage family limitation on the part of the wife and to discourage it on the part of the husband. These roles and statuses are often sufficiently disparate to limit adequate communication between husband and wife on matters of family limitation; and to frustrate the wife's desires where such communication may exist.

(2) Subsequent to high fertility performance in a given family, certain individual and institutional mechanisms operate to alleviate the pressure of numbers on resources.

Differential sex statuses and roles

Rigorous subordination of the women is a normal concomitant of rural living where a sharp division of labor relegates wage-earning activities to the male. Spanish-Catholic patterns fit neatly this type of economy. The virginity cult,[9] fostered by religious ideology[10] and accompanied by severe limitations on the freedom of the female, helps to insure continuing dominance of the male in the economic and political spheres.

Even in the middle and upper class families where the subordination patterns are less emphasized[11] but none-the-less effective, male dominance is partly insured by secrecy on the part of husbands. There appears to be a great deal of separate sex recreation—a pattern of "going out with the boys," and illicit affairs. This privilege of privacy concerning the husband's business and pleasure enshrouds much of his life with mystery and enhances his role as an authority figure.

For the lower class the differential statuses and roles have other manifestations, the consequences of which have a more direct effect upon fertility. This is not because the double standard is more strictly enforced in the lower class but because there are fewer compensating institutions. For the lower class it is principally the combination of marginal economic subsistence and the disparate masculine and feminine statuses which succeed in aggravating the fertility rate. It is hypothecated that the discrepancy between male and female statuses and roles is widened subsequent to marriage, that this forestalls the establishing of adequate communication between the marital pair, and results not only in an unstable marital relationship, but in high rates of fertility.

In the pre-marital period the double standard takes several important manifestations. The society and particularly the males put a high premium on masculinity and virility. To be a *macho* (a virile male) is one of the dominant values which is inculcated into the male child and which continues to be valued in manhood.[12] This male ethic is supported by permissiveness in regard to behavior. The society allows the male a great deal of freedom for socio-sexual exploration with prostitutes and *mujeres baratas* (cheap women).

For the women precisely opposite proscriptions exist. The cult of virginity puts a premium on modesty and sublimation or repression of sexual drives. Relative to the lower class male her behavior is heavily circumscribed. She is surrounded by cultural obstacles to socio-sexual experimentation and her experience with males may be largely confined to her own kin. The male, tantalized by his erratic and expensive contacts with prostitutes, has a decided sexual appetite at marriage. But the woman, due to thorough childhood training, tends to regard sex as a necessary evil, and enters the marital relation with an attitude toward sex ranging from ignorance to revulsion.[13]

The already existent gap between the sexes may be further emphasized upon marriage. The male sexual interest may only serve to increase his wife's indifference or distaste. Also, his attempts to compartmentalize his sexual attitudes towards prostitutes and toward his wife (*una buena mujer*) may serve to increase his own conflict or frustration, and so result in diminished understanding between the sexes. The gulf is not only present with regard to sexuality but with regard to procreation as well. Here again it may be supposed that the male has more immediate gratifications to derive from children than does the woman.

For the lower class male there are few available channels for prestige. The most important, economic advancement, is unavailable to him. Due to the scarcity of land, the seasonal nature of employment, and the surplus of labor, he can scarcely provide the basic necessities of life for himself and his family.[14] Consequently, two of his chief sources of prestige are virility and fatherhood.

Machismo will provide him with respect from his peers, and being *un buen padre* respect from his community. Both show that despite his poverty he is after all a man. Thus the institutions which once had meaning for the survival of the species and for survival of the family unit have been exaggerated beyond their original meaning and now function as a perhaps compulsively desired substitute for masculine achievement in the economic world. *"Mira como la tengo"* (Look at what I have done to her) brags the lower class male about his pregnant wife, and the more pregnancies he can point to, the better he has proved his *machismo*.[15]

Economically derived prestige is not normally a part of the female expectations. She is not expected to provide for the family—the double standard places her firmly in the home as wife and mother, thereby protecting her against the frustrations attendant upon contact with the economic world. To be a *macho* (a positive demand) a man must continue to prove himself. For the female, however, the demand is negative: "Don't be a *machorra*" (a barren woman) and one child is sufficient to dispel all fears. She thus has none of the additional motivations for having a large family, and indeed must suffer the brunt of the hardships entailed in the production and rearing of children.

For such reasons we would expect that the woman would be more "small family minded" than the male. Hatt's study has shown this to be true, although the sex differences do not seem as marked as would seem likely from the foregoing analysis—6.6 per cent of the married women interviewed reported that their husbands desired more children than they, but only 1.8 per cent of the husbands wanted fewer.[16] On the basis of a number of such indices, Hatt concluded that "Women seem to have adopted what we might call the low fertility value system more strongly than their husbands."

Thus the evidence gives some support to the hypothesis that the female is more small family minded than the male. Why then, does she not utilize contraceptive techniques herself? Contraception is not employed because of the combination of male resistance to contraceptive techniques and male dominance includes the prerogative of initiating sex activity and of determining its frequency and form. This means not only that there will be a higher frequency of relations than the woman desires, but that usually contraceptives will not be used.

The woman, on the other hand, must not only meet the male sexual needs, but cannot resort to contraception for herself, for the premarital circumscriptions concerning sex information prevent a knowledge of birth control for large numbers of lower class women. Also, since the male controls the sexual situation, even if she desires contraception, she is not in a position to demand its implementation,[17] and in several ways the modesty complex, stemming from indoctrination with the virginity cult, impedes the use of birth control.

Modesty may reduce the likelihood that she discusses the matter with her husband ("Such things are not talked about"), and the modesty pattern plus the crowded bedroom of the lower class home discourage employing the usual methods designed for women. Also it discourages her from soliciting birth control information from clinics with male physicians.[18] Thus the gulf between the sexes is both manifested and then aggravated by the inability of the female to communicate or to realize her family ideals.

Given culturally reinforced sex and reproduction drives on the part of the male, given his reluctance to use contraception and the inability of his spouse to deny his wishes, the net result is a high degree of marital stress and a high rate of fertility. The high fertility pattern itself is both productive of further tension in the marital relationship, and of drastic personal and institutional means to alleviate the consequent psychological and economic hardships.[19] The now obvious pressure of family numbers upon scant resources may induce wives to resort to sterilization and sexual denial and may impel husbands to desertion or marital infidelity. Furthermore it may lead to a reliance upon the extended family to drain off the excess number of children.

Individual responses

Sterilization is one of the most popular birth control measures on the island. Though less than 3 per cent of the lower rental group mothers in Hatt's study had been sterilized, it is among this group that sterilization is becoming increasingly popular.[20] Cofresi found it to be the second most popularly used method of birth control for the lower income group, far out-ranking other methods.[21] Sterilization is popular because it obviates the necessity for contraception, is a sure technique which solves the problem of contraceptive defects and male caprice, and is a method upon which both parties can agree. The male who has proved his virility by several past pregnancies[22] can avoid the economic pressure of children without losing his pleasure or his sense of respect for his wife.

But sterilization may be considered too expensive, too difficult to arrange, or too dangerous. One other drastic technique may finally be used by the mother of a large family —that of complete sexual denial. The incidence of such a technique is not known but its frequency in a selected Puerto Rican town probably indicates that it is not uncommon. King, in reporting on 37 cases of women definitely willing to limit their families, cites example of 13 cases expressing "rather typical attitudes."[23] Five of these statements clearly indicate that sexual denial was employed. In two cases the women actually suggested that their husbands satisfy their sex urges by consorting with other women. In three of the cases the avoidance led to separation. We may speculate then, that the reputedly high rates of male promiscuity and desertion in the lower class may result not only from the desire to escape the responsibilities of a large number of children, but additionally from sexual denial on the part of the wife.

Institutional mechanisms: the extended family and familism

Because of easy shifting of funds and personnel from one nuclear family to another within a broad kinship system, it is largely the extended family that provides relief from the pressure of numbers upon resources. Before describing the shock-absorbing qualities of the extended family, it seems desirable to demonstrate to what extent such a structure exists in Puerto Rico.

There is some evidence indicating that as many extended kin live under the same roof

as the income permits. Thus, while fertility drops as income increases, *size of household* shows the opposite trend. Roberts and Stefani found that 17.5 per cent of the households in the less than 500 dollars yearly income group had one or two members only. In the 2000 dollar income bracket only 6 per cent had such small households.[24] The situation may be similar to the Chinese pattern, in which the large household is expected of all groups but practiced by those with means.[25]

Another evidence of familism is the extent to which children and relatives contribute to the family income. In only about half of the households is the father the sole source of support. Sons and daughters contribute to family income in about a quarter of the households, and relatives in about 5 per cent.[26] Since in both rural and urban areas (though more so in the former) the father tends to be the chief breadwinner in higher economic groups, it is clear that children and relatives play an important economic role in the lower class household. This is not to say, however, that they are more of an asset than a liability, for the statistics do not show how many children in a family help or how much they contribute.[27] On the other hand the figures do give some credence to the popular belief that children help provide for parents' old age. Less than 6 per cent of Robert's and Stefani's sample was composed of individuals sixty years of age and older, yet children are recorded as sole sources of support in about 8 per cent of the households. While this does not, of course, prove that these cases are actually supporting the aged, when considered along with Hatt's data showing that many parents think of their children as security for old age,[28] it seems likely that filial devotion is still strong in Puerto Rico.

Another index of familism is the degree to which the family relationships operate at the expense of the community. While no concrete data are available at this time, we may speculate that in rural areas the community is subordinate to the family. The jíbaro's sense of individualism with regard to property and marriage precludes much of a sense of community responsibility. For example workers in the new Title V Communities[29] report that their greatest difficulty in the successful organization of these rural villages is the lack of community spirit on the part of the participants. That kin solidarity operates to the exclusion of easy identification with non-kin strangers. Originators of a foster home care plan for homeless children a few years ago encountered powerful resistance on the part of donors who did not want their young relatives given to strangers and on the part of prospective caretakers who did not like taking "strangers" into their homes.[30] Finally, the cleavage between family and community is given particular emphasis by another characteristic of family living in Puerto Rico—the seeming lack of concern for privacy. Given the physically cramped living quarters of the lower class Puerto Rican (58 per cent of Puerto Rico's rural families average two or more per room),[31] the crowded sleeping quarters (76 per cent of the rural population sleep with three or more to a room, 39 per cent with 5 or more),[32] and the general intimacy of family members, it is not surprising that lower class Puerto Ricans in the United States startle social workers by their desire for interpersonal contacts and a seeming unconcern with privacy. This pattern may lead to an interesting end product—the standardization of the personalities of any given family. The usually high degree of interpersonal relationships, plus the wide range within the family toward whom these relations may be directed, may result in greater identification with the group than upon the mother or father, as is characteristic of the small, privacy-conscious nuclear family typical of industrial Western society. This greater degree of personality standardization within the family might contribute to tighter family organization or at least to greater dependence on the family— another pattern which would reinforce the familistic pattern at the expense of identification with the larger community.

We may conclude then that familism exists to a high degree in Puerto Rico. What specifically is its relation to fertility? Disregarding the fact of family economic pools, the relation occurs in the easy and frequent transferring of excess children from one nuclear family to another, within a structure of blood and ritual kin. Such informally adopted children are frequently taken by their god-parents—these latter are frequently ritual rather than blood kin. Since the institutions of ritual kin (*compadrazgo*) and informal adoption are among the few which articulate the family with non-kin,[33] both are here interpreted as devices for relieving the pressure of fertility, and as structurally significant institutions in the Puerto Rican family system.

Hijos de crianza and the compadrazgo system

Within the extended family in Puerto Rico, children are shifted around from home to relatives with a great deal of ease. The period for which a child is sent to a relative may vary from months to life. The latter case, in which parental rights and duties with respect to a child are handed over to the relative, is quite prevalent,[34] and the children in such a system are designated as *hijos de crianza*.

At the death of the father or mother of a family, it is quite usual in rural areas for the members to be dispersed to kin or ritual kin,[35] but such a family crisis is hardly needed for the adoption of children. For example, a very young child may be sent to live with a relative or friend who is better off economically, or to live with grandparents who may be lonely. The latter will informally adopt the child, feed and clothe it, and in return may expect it to assist in the housework.

Looking at the institution broadly we can hypothesize three functions. First, the pattern serves both as a manifestation of the extended family and a cohesive force in preserving and intensifying it. When one segment of the family has migrated to the city or to the United States, the *hijo de crianza* may form a bridge between a widening gap in extended family relations.[36] Second, it may have certain important functions for the donor of the child, serving both as a means of social mobility and as a kind of human investment which might bring dividends in old age. Given the sense of futility of improving his economic status that faces the average rural Puerto Rican, and given the tradition of respect and care for the aged kin, the giving of a child to a relative or friend of better status, preferably in the city or in the States, may be partly based on the estimation of the child's future value. The *hijo de crianza* may provide a wedge into urban society which the parents may eventually use for migration or at least support. Third, it can be seen as a means of giving a more equitable distribution of scarce goods— as a society's crude way of relieving population pressure in relation to resources. Since *hijos de crianza* are usually from homes poorer than those of the foster parents (except in cases of broken homes where children may be farmed out to class contemporaries), it can be assumed that this provides some relief for the lower class population pressure.

One of the most frequent institutional channels used for this transfer of children is *compadrazgo*. The god-father relationship, in the United States now an empty ritual, is a living, vital part of social relations among Puerto Ricans. It acts as a security mechanism for children in a land where life expectancy is low (46 years in 1940) and where economic security is always tenuous. If a family has an excess of children for which it desires a better way of life,[37] it is not unusual that a child or children be sent to a *compadre* whose economic position is slightly better.

Probably even more important for an understanding of the Puerto Rican family is the *compadre* relationship established between age contemporaries which binds the participants in a net of reciprocal aid and friendship. As country women say once they enter into such a relationship, *"Los siete sacramentos estan entre nosotros."* (The seven sacraments are between us.) Not only is the relation sacred, but it taboos fighting and quarreling and establishes reciprocal rights and obligations such as aid in time of sickness, and in economic and other crises. In a society where social mobility is encouraged and where the pattern of land tenure makes this virtually impossible for the bulk of the population, the *compadrazgo* system theoretically could form a convenient channel toward mobility. To what extent *compadrazgo* is used for such purposes is not known in any statistical sense, and would be an important area for research. What concerns us here is the fact that *compadrazgo* may be used where the individual feels insecure or dissatisfied with his present status. In such cases, the way out for the individual with Spanish heritage but without a history of community action or a high degree of community relations, is to deal with the situation in the only terms he knows—family terms. In effect he may extend his family to encompass non-blood-related individuals who will be bound by family mores. He may thus construct a large artificial family as an additional bulwark against ever-present misfortune in Puerto Rico.

Finally, *compadrazgo*, as *hijos de crianza*, may be used as a tool for cementing family relationships where these are threatened by mobility;[38] or it may be increasingly employed as a mechanism to wean the individual from the family and toward a more secular society.[39]

Summary

The discrepancy in lower class Puerto Rico between low fertility aspirations and high fertility performance can be partly explained by the dynamics of family life. It is hypothecated that the wide gulf between the sexes may become widened or aggravated upon marriage and result in a breakdown of adequate communication between the pair. The male is almost compulsively concerned with sex and procreation while the woman, at least relatively, is indifferent to birth. High fertility may result then, not from planning on the part of the parents, but as a natural by-product of an interpersonal situation in which the woman's effective role is minimal.

As palliatives both for the pressure of numbers on resources and for the psychological disequilibrium between the marital pair, certain individual and institutional mechanisms are operative. Sexual denial and sterilization are drastic personal means used to reduce fertility while desertion functions as an escape from it. The extended family, by means of informal adoption and through channels such as *compadrazgo*, serves to cushion the impact of high fertility on any given family. By a process of supply and demand, a situation is brought into equilibrium in a manner which relieves the situation of a particular family, though not that of the society.

The value of the foregoing paper will consist in its provision of an analytical model of the lower class Puerto Rican family which can be employed in research, particularly in the area of human fertility. It provides the researcher with the defined task of testing three areas of hypotheses: (1) The differential extent and quality of certain marital interrelationships and familial institutions among varying social groups in Puerto Rico; (2) The functional articulation of such patterns and institutions with other parts of society; (3) The relation between such patterns and institutions and the prevailing rates of fertility.

Notes

[1] Harvey S. Perloff, *Puerto Rico's Economic Future*, Chicago: University of Chicago Press, 1950, p. 54.

[2] *Economic Development of Puerto Rico*, Puerto Rico Planning Board, January 1951, p. 13.

[3] Lydia J. Roberts and Rosa Luisa Stefani, *Patterns of Living in Puerto Rican Families*, Rio Piedras: University of Puerto Rico, 1949, p. s.

[4] Harvey S. Perloff, *op. cit.*, p. 145.

[5] 1950 Census of Population, Preliminary Reports, Series PC–6, No. 12, Washington, D.C. May 1951, p. 7.

[6] The implications of changing family ideals and organization in Puerto Rico's rapidly industrializing economy are not considered in this short paper. Attention is concentrated on that large proportion of the population which has been least affected by the changes—the rural lower class. Additionally, such factors in family life as are considered are treated largely as *if* change were not occurring.

[7] Hatt's study of 13,000 Puerto Ricans disclosed that three or fewer children is the ideal for about 75 per cent of the population. Paul K. Hatt, *Background of Human Fertility in Puerto Rico: A Sociological Survey*, Princeton: Princeton University Press, 1952, Table 187, p. 219.

[8] Less than 13 per cent of Hatt's sample felt that no couple has the right to practice family limitations. *Ibid.*, Table 60, p. 79. In another recent study of 2,125 Puerto Rican women, it was found that religious scruples were mentioned in less than 5 per cent of the cases not employing birth control methods. Emilio Cofresi, *Realidad Poblacional de Puerto Rico*, San Juan: Imprenta Venezuela, 1951, Table 36, p. 95.

[9] A phrase used by Seigel to describe "a set of ideas and practices which . . . dominates the relationships between the sexes in Lajas and determines the role of the males and females in pre-marital and post-marital life." Morris Seigel, *A Puerto Rican Town*, 1948, unpublished, p. 148.

[10] Observers report that the popularity of the Virgin as a direct or inter-cessional object of prayer and ritual is increasing in Puerto Rico, probably at the expense of Christ and male saints. Whether or not the cult of the Virgin is increasing, its manifestations are easily evident all over the island.

[11] The inordinate number of "Queen" contests, particularly in the middle class, may represent the culture's response to the threat of the modern, competitive career woman. The queens appear to be chosen more for modesty and grace than for glamor, suggesting something of the Queen of Heaven, the Virgin Mary. The lavishness and publicity which accompanies such contests also suggests a channeling both of resources and ideals away from the utilitarian and toward the pure but useless.

[12] Dynamically, the strong emphasis on "being *macho*" may represent an effort on the part of the male to escape the strong mother-son bonds which have been formed as a result of the deficient role of the father in socialization. Patterns of desertion, drinking, separate sex recreation, etc., are a few of the lower class patterns which keep the father physically removed from the children. On the part of the female child these same absence patterns may lead to considerable fantasy, the consequent misconception of the male sex increasing the gap between masculine and feminine worlds.

[13] "So much is intercourse considered in terms of obligation (*un deber*) that one woman who enjoyed sexual intercourse 'for its own sake' was considered sick by the other women of the *barrio*." Eric Wolf, *Culture Change and Culture Stability in a Puerto Rican Coffee Community*, Cambridge: Eagle Enterprises (offset), 1951, p. 94.

[14] "Sixty-two per cent (of the population) have less than the amount needed to buy a minimum adequate diet ($140 per year)." Roberts and Stefani, *op. cit.*, p. 13.

[15] "The importance of beginning a family soon is a value rather more generally accepted throughout the society than are any principles with regard to either the size of the family or the acceptability of planning the family." Paul Hatt, *op. cit.* Hatt reports that such a large proportion of his sample felt that the first child should come "as soon as possible" that correlation with other factors was rendered impossible. *At this point both machorra and macho complexes coincide to insure a rapid first birth:* "(Because) working people here do not regard a marriage as truly consummated before the birth of the first child, consensually married couples will seek to have a child . . . within a year of their union." Sidney Mintz, *Canamelar, The Contemporary Culture of a Puerto Rican Pro-*

letariat, unpublished doctoral dissertation, 1950, Chap. VII, p. 21.

[16] Paul Hatt, *op. cit.,* Table 276, p. 324. It is possible that the high percentage (76.5) of women reporting the concurrence of their spouses on this item may be exaggerated by the desire to present a united front to the interviewer.

[17] Cofresi found that half of the failures to employ birth control methods were due either to ignorance on the part of the women or objections on the part of the husband. Emilio Cofresi, *op. cit.,* Table 36, p. 95.

[18] "A number of women expressed horror at the prospect of being subjected to a vaginal examination, particularly by a male physician. . . . Several women declared that they preferred a midwife, even though inadequately trained, to a male doctor whose services might be obtained free of charge, specifically because of shame at being seen by a man." Marguerite King, "Culture Aspects of Birth Control in Puerto Rico," *Human Biology,* Vol. 20 (February, 1948), p. 32.

[19] At this point class differentials operate to the disadvantage of the lower class. Whereas all classes see the small family as an ideal, it is the upper class which comes closest to achieving the ideal. Consequently, the greater frustration on the part of the lower class is more productive of this drastic palliative measure.

[20] P. Hatt, *op. cit.,* Table 318, p. 444. About 8 per cent of the "upper class" women had been sterilized; this rate is doubtlessly affected to some degree by their greater ability to pay a private fee and by the fact that lower class women usually have their children at home.

[21] Cofresi, *op. cit.,* Table 34, p. 90. From three to four thousand sterilizations are performed every year in Puerto Rico.

[22] Although the trend over the past thirty years has been toward earlier sterilization 86 per cent of the sterilizations of the women married between 1940 and 1947 occurred subsequent to at least two births. Hatt, *op. cit.,* Table 320, p. 446.

[23] Marguerite King, *op. cit.,* pp. 26–27.

[24] *Op. cit.,* Table V, p. 272. It is possible that a greater number of wage-earners in the upper income households have exaggerated the picture. Rosario's data by average monthly wage, however, show the same trend, the average number per household ranging from 5.3 to 6.7, as average monthly wage varies from 13.76 to 22.73 dollars. Jose C. Rosario, *The Development of the Puerto Rican Jibaro and His Present Attitude towards Society,* University of Puerto Rico, 1935, p. 85.

[25] Olga Lang, *Chinese Family and Society,* New Haven: Yale University Press, 1946.

[26] Roberts and Stefani, *op. cit.,* Table 12, p. 275.

[27] Unpaid family workers cannot be considered a major source of income in Puerto Rico. Whereas a total of 37 per cent of Hatt's household heads were engaged in agriculture, only 3.9 of the total male sample were classified as non-paid family workers.

[28] Roughly 47 per cent of Hatt's respondents mentioned assistance in old age when asked why they had not picked a smaller number for ideal size of family. Table 42, p. 59.

[29] A program initiated in the

early 40's, the Title V Communities or *Parcelas* are composed of a few hundred families, each with an acre or so of land for subsistence farming.

[30] Not only is it particularly humiliating to accept charity from non-kin but there appears to be an equal aversion or at least indifference to giving it. Philanthropy, as opposed to paternalism, is not a part of culture, for it is held that needy should be cared for by their "own people."

[31] Roberts, *op. cit.,* p. 52.

[32] *Ibid.,* p. 86.

[33] The neighborhood is of course another institution which articulates the family with non-kin, but little can be said of this with any certainty. Contradictory norms and behavior patterns exist with respect to the relation of family and neighbors. Some claim that there is a clear line between neighbor and relative and that reciprocal rights and obligations are more extensive with the latter. In other instances neighborhood ties parallel or exceed those of family. *"Quien es tu hermano? Tu vecino mas cercano."* (Who is your brother? Your closest neighbor.) Actually, the general situation may be such that there is a fine line between neighbor and relative. In country areas the visiting patterns are so liberal that people have a great deal to do with the socialization of their neighbors' children, to the extent that close bonds are formed between the former, the children, and the children's parents. In a transitional society such as Puerto Rico, the neighborhood may serve as a "weaning" institution which makes the transition from family to society less painful.

[34] Six and a half per cent of Puerto Rico's households have

one or more such informally adopted children. Additionally, 13.4 per cent have grandchildren, living in the home. Roberts and Stefani, *op. cit.*, Table 17, p. 279.

[35] "If a man who has a family and no property dies his brothers and sisters will either support the family, keeping it as a unit in their own homes, or will apportion the different members among themselves. . . . It is a rather common spectacle in the rural regions of Puerto Rico to see two or three children from a *compadre,* brother or sister joining an already numerous brood in another family." Jose C. Rosario, *op. cit.,* p. 81.

[36] Children are sent to urban centers for the enhanced levels of living and educational possibilities there. But city residents also send children back to the farm. City households have fewer *hijos de crianza* and grandchildren living with the family. See Roberts and Stefani, *op. cit.,* Table 17, p. 279.

[37] Levels of aspiration for children are high. About 80 per cent of the island's parents want their sons at least to complete high school, and only about three-quarters of one per cent want their sons to be laborers. Paul Hatt, *op. cit.,* Tables 56 and 58, pp. 75 and 77.

[38] ". . . *compadrazgo* . . . may be a valuable social mechanism even when families are quite unstable, and families or family heads geographically very mobile," Mintz, *op. cit.,* Chap. VI, p. 64. Mintz also states, however, without citing sufficient evidence, that *compadre* relationships break down if they cease to be face to face.

[39] "Where families are no longer tightly knit, all-encompassing networks of relationships, *compadrazgo* may be understood as a mechanism to facilitate the transition to a more individualized and less familistic type society." *Ibid.,* p. 65.

Chapter 5

THE MEANING OF CULTURE

INSTINCTUAL BEHAVIOR
Selection 12

CULTURAL BEHAVIOR
Selection 13

CULTURE AND EXPERIENCE
Selection 14

Geography, biology, and demography give partial but very incomplete explanations of the social order. They provide the material out of which life is constructed, and they set limitations on the forms that the social order can take, but with this material and within these limitations human societies ring many changes. The variation possible within the limits of biology and geography results in societies as different as the Soviets and Eskimos, or classical China and Saudi Arabia, or Switzerland and Tibet. Such differences as these are explained in sociology by reference to the concept of culture.

The term "culture" is an example of a word taken from ordinary discourse and given a special meaning in sociology and related sciences. As is common in these cases, even among social scientists the term retains a fuzziness around the edges that makes it difficult to define and compromises the precision that a scientific term should have for maximum usefulness. It is, however, so widely used and so powerful an explanatory concept that its understanding is necessary for the student of sociology.

The term in its social science usage comes close to what the layman calls "tradition." Cultural behavior is learned and shared as a result of membership in a group, and culture is an abstraction, from this behavior, of general principles according to which the behavior appears to be regulated.

Culture furnishes one way in which behavior is regulated, but it is not the only way. Many lower animals are social, living harmoniously in groups. The social behavior of these animals is chiefly regulated by instinct—that is, the behavior is shared, but not learned. Currently, sociology and anthropology are beginning to note rudiments of "cultural" behavior among some lower animals. However, the role of learned and shared behavior in the total behavioral repertory of these animals is very small as compared with humans, because of their lack of symbolic language, which is a superbly efficient transmitter of culture.

Culture descends from one generation to another, so that each generation can take advantage of the experience of the previous ones. In small, "primitive" groups, each member may know nearly all the cultural heritage of the group;

but in large, complex societies any one member will be a party to only a small proportion of the group's culture. The group as a whole, through an enduring social organization, enables its members to enjoy the benefits of an enormous amount of knowledge. Even in the simplest of societies, the cultural heritage represents many more experiences than an individual can have during his lifetime. Through culture, man has transcended his own life span, bequeathing to his dullest children far more wisdom than the most brilliant ape could ever hope to acquire before death.

Explanations of behavior in terms of culture are purely social explanations. It is not necessary to know anything about a given individual's personality or life experiences in order to predict behavior on cultural grounds. Such concepts as childhood trauma and obsessive-compulsive neurosis are irrelevant to these explanations, which are based upon knowledge of group memberships and of the cultures of groups. However, statements concerning culture, like nearly all sociological generalizations, are statistical, presumably valid for the group as a whole, but subject to possible error when applied to specific individual members of the group. In situations where cultural patterns are very rigid, such error is likely to be negligible. In the performance of the Catholic Mass, or at a military parade, cultural regulation of the minute details of the behavior of thousands of individuals provides a marvellous illustration of the social order.

The two following selections contrast the principles that guide social behavior among men, where cultural regulation is the rule, and among animals, where it is the exception. Selection 12, by Konrad Lorenz, provides extraordinary insight into the coordination of behavior in animal groups; the "stupid" breakdowns in this system demonstrate the severe limitations that are present in the regulation of social behavior by instinct. Selection 13, by Clyde Kluckhohn, shows that cultural regulation of social behavior, while perhaps not so completely reliable in many situations as instinct, is far more flexible and covers a far more extensive variety of situations than any instinctual system ever evolved. In Selection 14, Laura Bohannan illustrates the profound influence of cultural assumptions in forming human experience, and the difficulties which these may cause in communicating across cultural lines.

INSTINCTUAL BEHAVIOR

Some lower animals spend nearly their entire lives as isolated individuals, never engaging in social interaction with other members of their own species. Perhaps the most fortunate in this type of life are those, like some protozoans, that can reproduce without the necessity of sexual contact. Except for chance meetings due to their tendency to inhabit the same environment as others of their species, these individuals can survive from birth and leave descendants, in the total absence of their fellows. Other animals require the society of their species only for the brief moment of sexual contact, and for the rest of their lives they can do quite well by themselves.

In contrast, many lower animals, particularly among the insects and the vertebrates, live in groups and engage in social interaction. The complexity and smooth-running order of some of these groups, such as the bees, is legendary. Society in these cases, as with man, has survival value. By hunting together, wolves get more food per head than if they were to hunt separately. An isolated queen bee would die of starvation, and no new bees would be produced.

The existence of independent organisms in social life requires coordination of behavior, a symmetry of action appropriately timed. This is achieved by both human and other animal societies. Since the needs of both types are similar, and since the solutions of these needs are analogous, animal societies present many resemblances to human societies. Viewing animal societies from our human perspective, we have a tendency to attribute to their members the same feelings and psychological states that we experience, and to consider these groups as organized by the same principles as human societies. Konrad Lorenz, a naturalist with an interest in the social behavior of subhuman animals, demonstrates in this selection both the amazing degree of analogy between human and animal social behavior and the great differences in the reasons for this analogy.

Many animals resemble humans to the point of apparently possessing systems of morals that prevent them from harming members of their own group. Moreover, while men cannot be trusted always to obey the rules of their morality, the animals follow their "moral" principles to the letter.

An example is the sign of defeat that a losing wolf presents to a wolf that has vanquished him in battle. The loser drops his defenses and extends his neck, a most vulnerable part of the body, in a manner analogous to the human warrior's abandonment of shield and kneeling posture before the victor. The human victor has been known to decapitate his defeated opponent forthwith, but the vanquishing wolf is helpless to complete the kill.

The wolf's powerlessness in this situation is based on instinct. The instinct is functional in preserving the species, for if animals equipped with dangerous weapons such as teeth and claws were to use these on others of their species, the species would have little hope for survival. The problem with this animal "morality" is that it is not flexible. It relies on instinctual nervous circuits instead of culturally based principles of morality, which allow consideration and reflection. A number of "mistakes" end disastrously for one of the participants. In a situation in which we humans would see that a given cultural rule was obviously applicable, if the animal's instinctual apparatus fails to be activated, the niceties mentioned above are completely dispensed with, and nature appears "red in tooth and claw."

The intimate style of this passage should not obscure its scientific validity. Lorenz's argument is closely reasoned and is based on great familiarity with the wild creatures of which he speaks. His functional hypothesis that animal "morals" preserve the species is buttressed by observation of situations in which animals are enclosed together without the natural means of escape that are usually available to them. Here mutual destruction often results, supporting Lorenz's theory.

The reader should gain from this selection the idea that whereas instinctual and cultural means of regulating behavior may be functionally similar, instinctual regulation has the advantage of almost absolute certainty and the disadvantage of extreme rigidity and limitation. Cultural regulation of behavior, although never certain, has the advantage of flexibility and the possibility of great extension. Instincts are extremely slow to change, and they require biological mutations. Culture, basically social rather than biological, is highly adaptable and changes to some degree every day of our lives.

Selection 12
FROM KING SOLOMON'S RING
Konrad Z. Lorenz

It is early one Sunday morning at the beginning of March, when Easter is already in the air, and we are taking a walk in the Vienna forest whose wooded slopes of tall beeches can be equalled in beauty by few and surpassed by none. We approach a forest glade. The tall smooth trunks of the beeches soon give place to the Hornbeam which are clothed from top to bottom with pale green foliage. We now tread slowly and more carefully. Before we break through the last bushes and out of cover on to the free expanse of the meadow, we do what all wild animals and all good naturalists, wild boars, leopards, hunters and zoologists would do under similar circumstances: we reconnoitre, seeking, before we leave our cover, to gain from it the advantage which it can offer alike to hunter and hunted, namely, to see without being seen.

Here, too, this age-old strategy proves beneficial. We do actually see someone who is not yet aware of our presence, as the wind is blowing away from him in our direction: in the middle of the clearing sits a large fat hare. He is sitting with his back to us, making a big V with his ears, and is watching intently something on the opposite edge of the meadow. From this point, a second and equally large hare emerges and with slow, dignified hops, makes his way towards the first one. There follows a measured encounter, not unlike the meeting of two strange dogs. This cautious mutual taking stock soon develops into sparring. The two hares chase each other round, head to tail, in minute circles. This giddy rotating continues for quite a long time. Then suddenly, their pent-up energies burst forth into a battle royal. It is just like the outbreak of war, and happens at the very moment when the long mutual threatening of the hostile parties has forced one to the conclusion that neither dares to make a definite move. Facing each other, the hares rear up on their hind legs and, straining to their full height, drum furiously at each other with their fore pads. Now they clash in flying leaps and, at last,

to the accompaniment of squeals and grunts, they discharge a volley of lightning kicks, so rapidly that only a slow motion camera could help us to discern the mechanism of these hostilities. Now, for the time being, they have had enough, and they recommence their circling, this time much faster than before; then follows a fresh, more embittered bout. So engrossed are the two champions, that there is nothing to prevent myself and my little daughter from tiptoeing nearer, although that venture cannot be accomplished in silence. Any normal and sensible hare would have heard us long ago, but this is March and March Hares are mad! The whole boxing match looks so comical that my little daughter, in spite of her iron upbringing in the matter of silence when watching animals, cannot restrain a chuckle. That is too much even for March Hares—two flashes in two different directions and the meadow is empty, while over the battlefield floats a fistful of fluff, light as a thistledown.

It is not only funny, it is almost touching, this duel of the unarmed, this raging fury of the meek in heart. But are these creatures really so meek? Have they really got softer hearts than those of the fierce beasts of prey? If, in a zoo, you ever watched two lions, wolves or eagles in conflict, then, in all probability, you did not feel like laughing. And yet, these sovereigns come off no worse than the harmless hares. Most people have the habit of judging carnivorous and herbivorous animals by quite inapplicable moral criteria. Even in fairy-tales, animals are portrayed as being a community comparable to that of mankind, as though all species of animals were beings of one and the same family, as human beings are. For this reason, the average person tends to regard the animal that kills animals in the same light as he would the man that kills his own kind. He does not judge the fox that kills a hare by the same standard as the hunter who shoots one for precisely the same reason, but with that severe censure that he would apply to the gamekeeper who made a practice of shooting farmers and frying them for supper! The "wicked" beast of prey is branded as a murderer, although the fox's hunting is quite as legitimate and a great deal more necessary to his existence than is that of the gamekeeper, yet nobody regards the latter's "bag" as his prey, and only one author, whose own standards were indicted by the severest moral criticism, has dared to dub the fox-hunter "the unspeakable in pursuit of the uneatable"! In their dealing with members of their own species, the beasts and birds of prey are far more restrained than many of the "harmless" vegetarians.

Still more harmless than a battle of hares appears the fight between turtle- or ring-doves. The gentle pecking of the frail bill, the light flick of the fragile wing seems, to the uninitiated, more like a caress than an attack. Some time ago I decided to breed a cross between the African blond ring-dove and our own indigenous somewhat frailer turtle-dove, and, with this object, I put a tame, home-reared male turtle-dove and a female ring-dove together in a roomy cage. I did not take their original scrapping seriously. How could these paragons of love and virtue dream of harming one another? I left them in their cage and went to Vienna. When I returned, the next day, a horrible sight met my eyes. The turtle-dove lay on the floor of the cage; the top of his head and neck, as also the whole length of his back, were not only plucked bare of feathers, but so flayed as to form a single wound dripping with blood. In the middle of this gory surface, like an eagle on his prey, stood the second harbinger of peace. Wearing that dreamy facial expression that so appeals to our sentimental observer, this charming lady pecked mercilessly with her silver bill in the wounds of her prostrated mate. When the latter gathered his last resources in a final effort to escape, she set on him again, struck him to the floor with a light clap of her wing and continued with her slow pitiless work of destruction. Without my interference she would undoubtedly have finished him off, in spite of the fact that she was already so tired that she could hardly keep her eyes open. Only in two other instances have I seen similar horrible lacerations inflicted on their own kind by vertebrates: once, as an observer of the embittered fights of cichlid fishes who sometimes actually skin each other, and again as a field surgeon, in the late war, where the highest of all vertebrates perpetrated mass mutilations on members of his own species. But to return to our "harmless" vegetarians. The battle of the hares which we witnessed in the forest clearing would have ended in quite

as horrible a carnage as that of the doves, had it taken place in the confines of a cage where the vanquished could not flee the victor.

If this is the extent of the injuries meted out to their own kind by our gentle doves and hares, how much greater must be the havoc wrought amongst themselves by those beasts to whom nature has relegated the strongest weapons with which to kill their prey? One would certainly think so, were it not that a good naturalist should always check by observation even the most obvious-seeming inferences before he accepts them as truth. Let us examine that symbol of cruelty and voraciousness, the wolf. How do these creatures conduct themselves in their dealings with members of their own species? At Whipsnade, that zoological country paradise, there lives a pack of timber wolves. From the fence of a pine-wood of enviable dimensions we can watch their daily round in an environment not so very far removed from conditions of real freedom. To begin with, we wonder why the antics of the many woolly, fat-pawed whelps have not led them to destruction long ago. The efforts of one ungainly little chap to break into a gallop have landed him in a very different situation from that which he intended. He stumbles and bumps heavily into a wicked-looking old sinner. Strangely enough, the latter does not seem to notice it, he does not even growl. But now we hear the rumble of battle sounds! They are low, but more ominous than those of a dog-fight. We were watching the whelps and have therefore only become aware of this adult fight now that it is already in full swing.

An enormous old timber wolf and a rather weaker, obviously younger one are the opposing champions and they are moving in circles round each other, exhibiting admirable "footwork." At the same time, the bared fangs flash in such a rapid exchange of snaps that the eye can scarcely follow them. So far, nothing has really happened. The jaws of one wolf close on the gleaming white teeth of the other who is on the alert and wards off the attack. Only the lips have received one or two minor injuries. The younger wolf is gradually being forced backwards. It dawns upon us that the older one is purposely manoeuvring him towards the fence. We wait with breathless anticipation what will happen when he "goes to the wall". Now he strikes the wire netting, stumbles . . . and the old one is upon him. And now the incredible happens, just the opposite of what you would expect. The furious whirling of the grey bodies has come to a sudden standstill. Shoulder to shoulder they stand, pressed against each other in a stiff and strained attitude, both heads now facing in the same direction. Both wolves are growling angrily, the elder in a deep bass, the younger in higher tones, suggestive of the fear that underlies his threat. But notice carefully the position of the two opponents; the older wolf has his muzzle close, very close against the neck of the younger, and the latter holds away his head, offering unprotected to his enemy the bend of his neck, the most vulnerable part of his whole body! Less than an inch from the tensed neck-muscles, where the jugular vein lies immediately beneath the skin, gleam the fangs of his antagonist from beneath the wickedly retracted lips. Whereas, during the thick of the fight, both wolves were intent on keeping only their teeth, the one invulnerable part of the body, in opposition to each other, it now appears that the discomfited fighter proffers intentionally that part of his anatomy to which a bite must assuredly prove fatal. Appearances are notoriously deceptive, but in his case, surprisingly, they are not!

This same scene can be watched any time wherever street-mongrels are to be found. I cited wolves as my first example because they illustrate my point more impressively than the all-too-familiar domestic dog. Two adult male dogs meet in the street. Stiff-legged, with tails erect and hair on end, they pace towards each other. The nearer they approach, the stiffer, higher and more ruffled they appear, their advance becomes slower and slower. Unlike fighting cocks they do not make their encounter head to head, front against front, but make as though to pass each other, only stopping when they stand at last flank to flank, head to tail, in close juxtaposition. Then a strict ceremonial demands that each should sniff the hind regions of the other. Should one of the dogs be overcome with fear at this juncture, down goes his tail between his legs and he jumps with a quick, flexible twist, wheeling at an angle of 180 degrees thus modestly retracting his former offer to be smelt. Should the two dogs remain in an attitude of self-display, carrying their tails as rigid as standards, then the sniffing process may be of a long protracted nature. All may be solved amicably and there is still the chance that first one tail

and then the other may begin to wag with small but rapidly increasing beats and then this nerve-racking situation may develop into nothing worse than a cheerful canine romp. Failing this solution the situation becomes more and more tense, noses begin to wrinkle and to turn up with a vile, brutal expression, lips begin to curl, exposing the fangs on the side nearer the opponent. Then the animals scratch the earth angrily with their hind feet, deep growls rise from their chests, and, in the next moment, they fall upon each other with loud piercing yells.

But to return to our wolves, whom we left in a situation of acute tension. This was not a piece of inartistic narrative on my part, since the strained situation may continue for a great length of time which is minutes to the observer, but very probably seems hours to the losing wolf. Every second you expect violence and await with bated breath the moment when the winner's teeth will rip the jugular vein of the loser. But your fears are groundless, for it will not happen. In this particular situation, the victor will definitely not close on his less fortunate rival. You can see that he would like to, but he just cannot. A dog or wolf that offers its neck to its adversary in this way will never be bitten seriously. The other growls and grumbles, snaps with his teeth in the empty air and even carries out, without delivering so much as a bite, the movement of shaking something to death in the empty air. However, this strange inhibition from biting persists only so long as the defeated dog or wolf maintains his attitude of humility. Since the fight is stopped so suddenly by this action, the victor frequently finds himself straddling his vanquished foe in anything but a comfortable position. So to remain, with his muzzle applied to the neck of the "under-dog" soon becomes tedious for the champion, and, seeing that he cannot bite anyway, he soon withdraws. Upon this, the under-dog may hastily attempt to put distance between himself and his superior. But he is not usually successful in this, for, as soon as he abandons his rigid attitude of submission, the other again falls upon him like a thunderbolt and the victim must again freeze into his former posture. It seems as if the victor is only waiting for the moment when the other will relinquish his submissive attitude, thereby enabling him to give vent to his urgent desire to bite. But, luckily for the "under-dog," the top-dog at the close of the fight is overcome by the pressing need to leave his trade-mark on the battlefield, to designate it as his personal property—in other words, he must lift his leg against the nearest upright object. This right-of-possession ceremony is usually taken advantage of by the under-dog to make himself scarce.

By this commonplace observation, we are here, as so often, made conscious of a problem which is actual in our daily life and which confronts us on all sides in the most various forms. Social inhibitions of this kind are not rare, but so frequent that we take them for granted and do not stop to think about them. An old German proverb says that one crow will not peck out the eye of another and for once the proverb is right. A tame crow or raven will no more think of pecking at your eye than he will at that of one of his own kind. Often when Roah, my tame raven, was sitting on my arm, I purposely put my face so near to his bill that my open eye came close to its wickedly curved point. Then Roah did something positively touching. With a nervous, worried movement he withdrew his beak from my eye, just as a father who is shaving will hold back his razor blade from the inquisitive fingers of his tiny daughter. Only in one particular connection did Roah ever approach my eye with his bill during this facial grooming. Many of the higher, social birds and mammals, above all monkeys, will groom the skin of a fellow-member of their species in those parts of his body to which he himself cannot obtain access. In birds, it is particularly the head and the region of the eyes which are dependent on the attentions of a fellow. In my description of the jackdaw, I have already spoken of the gestures with which these birds invite one another to preen their head feathers. When, with half-shut eyes, I held my head sideways towards Roah, just as corvine birds do to each other, he understood this movement in spite of the fact that I have no head feathers to ruffle, and at once began to groom me. While doing so, he never pinched my skin, for the epidermis of birds is delicate and would not stand such rough treatment. With wonderful precision, he submitted every attainable hair to a dry-cleaning process by drawing it separately through his bill. He worked with the same intensive concentration that distinguishes the "lousing" monkey and the operating surgeon. This is not meant as a joke: the social grooming of monkeys, and particularly of anthropoid apes has not the object of catching vermin—these animals usually have none—and is not limited to the cleaning of the skin, but serves also more remarkable operations, for instance the dexterous removal of thorns and even the squeezing-out of small carbuncles.

The manipulations of the dangerous-looking corvine beak round the open eye of a man naturally appear ominous and, of course, I was always receiving warnings from onlookers at this procedure. "You never know—a raven is a raven—" and similar words of wisdom. I used to respond with the paradoxical observation that the warner was for me potentially more dangerous than the raven. It has often happened that people have been shot dead by madmen who have masked their condition with the cunning and pretence typical of such cases. There was always a possibility, though admittedly a very small one, that our kind adviser might be afflicted with such a disease. But a sudden and unpredictable loss of the eye-pecking inhibition in a healthy, mature raven is more unlikely by far than an attack by a well-meaning friend.

Why has the dog the inhibition against biting his fellow's neck? Why has the raven an inhibition against pecking the eye of his friend? Why has the ring-dove no such "insurance" against murder? A really comprehensive answer to these questions is almost impossible. It would certainly involve a *historical* explanation of the process by which these inhibitions have been developed in the course of evolution. There is no doubt that they have arisen side by side with the development of the dangerous weapons of the beast of prey. However, it is perfectly obvious why these inhibitions are necessary to all weapon-bearing animals. Should the raven peck, without compunction, at the eye of his nest-mate, his wife or his young, in the same way as he pecks at any other moving and glittering object, there would, by now, be no more ravens in the world. Should a dog or wolf unrestrainedly and unaccountably bite the neck of his pack-mates and actually execute the movement of shaking them to death, then his species also would certainly be exterminated within a short space of time.

The ring-dove does not require such an inhibition since it can only inflict injury to a much lesser degree, while its ability to flee is so well developed that it suffices to protect the bird even against enemies equipped with vastly better weapons. Only under the unnatural conditions of close confinement which deprive the losing dove of the possibility of flight does it become apparent that the ring-dove has no inhibitions which prevent it from injuring or even torturing its own kind. Many other "harmless" herbivores prove themselves just as unscrupulous when they are kept in narrow captivity. One of the most disgusting, ruthless and blood-thirsty murderers is an animal which is generally considered as being second only to the dove in the proverbial gentleness of its nature, namely the roe-deer. The roe-buck is about the most malevolent beast I know and is possessed, into the bargain, of a weapon, its antlers, which it shows mighty little restraint in putting into use. The species can "afford" this lack of control since the fleeing capacity even of the weakest doe is enough to deliver it from the strongest buck. Only in very large paddocks can the roe-buck be kept with females of his own kind. In smaller enclosures, sooner or later he will drive his fellows, females and young ones included, into a corner and gore them to death. The only "insurance against murder" which the roe-deer possesses, is based on the fact that the onslaught of the attacking buck proceeds relatively slowly. He does not rush with lowered head at his adversary as, for example, a ram would do, but he approaches quite slowly, cautiously feeling with his antlers for those of his opponent. Only when the antlers are interlocked and the buck feels firm resistance does he thrust with deadly earnest. According to the statistics given by W. T. Hornaday, the former director of the New York Zoo, tame deer cause yearly more serious accidents than captive lions and tigers, chiefly because an uninitiated person does not recognize the slow approach of the buck as an earnest attack, even when the animal's antlers have come dangerously near. Suddenly there follows, thrust upon thrust, the amazingly strong stabbing movement of the sharp weapon, and you will be lucky if you have time enough to get a good grip on the aggressor's antlers. Now there follows a wrestling-match in which the sweat pours and the hands drip blood, and in which even a very strong man can hardly obtain mastery over the roe-buck unless he succeeds in getting to the side of the beast and bending his neck backwards. Of course, one is

ashamed to call for help—until one has the point of an antler in one's body. So take my advice and if a charming, tame roe-buck comes playfully towards you, with a characteristic prancing step and flourishing his antlers gracefully, hit him, with your walking stick, a stone or the bare fist, as hard as you can, on the side of his nose, before he can apply his antlers to your person.

And now, honestly judged: who is really a "good" animal, my friend Roah to whose social inhibitions I could trust the light of my eyes, or the gentle ring-dove that in hours of hard work nearly succeeded in torturing its mate to death? Who is a "wicked" animal, the roe-buck who will slit the bellies even of females and young of his own kind if they are unable to escape him, or the wolf who cannot bite his hated enemy if the latter appeals to his mercy?

Now let us turn our mind to another question. Wherein consists the essence of all the gestures of submission by which a bird or animal of a social species can appeal to the inhibitions of its superior? We have just seen, in the wolf, that the defeated animal actually facilitates his own destruction by offering to the victor those very parts of his body which he was most anxious to shield as long as the battle was raging. All submissive attitudes with which we are so far familiar, in social animals, are based on the same principle: The supplicant always offers to his adversary the most vulnerable part of his body, or, to be more exact, that part *against which every killing attack is inevitably directed!* In most birds, this area is the base of the skull. If one jackdaw wants to show submission to another, he squats back on his hocks, turns away his head, at the same time drawing in his bill to make the nape of his neck bulge, and, leaning towards his superior, seems to invite him to peck at the fatal spot. Seagulls and herons present to their superior the top of their head, stretching their neck forward horizontally, low over the ground, also a position which makes the supplicant particularly defenceless.

With many gallinaceous birds, the fights of the males commonly end by one of the combatants being thrown to the ground, held down and then scalped as in the manner described in the ring-dove. Only one species shows mercy in this case, namely the turkey: and this one only does so in response to a specific submissive gesture which serves to forestall the intent of the attack. If a turkey-cock has had more than his share of the wild and grotesque wrestling-match in which these birds indulge, he lays himself with out-stretched neck upon the ground. Whereupon the victor behaves exactly as a wolf or dog in the same situation, that is to say, he evidently *wants* to peck and kick at the prostrated enemy, but simply cannot: he would if he could but he can't. So, still in threatening atti-tude, he walks round and round his prostrated rival, making tentative passes at him, but leav-ing him untouched.

This reaction—though certainly propitious for the turkey species—can cause a tragedy if a turkey comes to blows with a peacock, a thing which not infrequently happens in cap-tivity, since these species are closely enough related to "appreciate" respectively their mu-tual manifestations of virility. In spite of greater strength and weight the turkey nearly always loses the match, for the peacock flies better and has a different fighting technique. While the red-brown American is muscling himself up for the wrestling-match, the blue East-Indian has already flown above him and struck at him with his sharply pointed spurs. The turkey justifiably considers this infringe-ment of his fighting code as unfair and, al-though he is still in possession of his full strength, he throws in the sponge and lays himself down in the above depicted manner now. And a ghastly thing happens: the pea-cock does not "understand" this submissive gesture of the turkey, that is to say, it elicits no inhibition of his fighting drives. He pecks and kicks further at the helpless turkey, who, if nobody comes to his rescue, is doomed, for the more pecks and blows he receives, the more certainly are his escape reactions blocked by the psycho-physiological mechanism of the submissive attitude. It does not and cannot occur to him to jump up and run away.

The fact that many birds have developed special "signal organs" for eliciting this type of social inhibition, shows convincingly the blind instinctive nature and the great evolutionary age of these submissive gestures. The young of the water-rail, for example, have a bare red patch at the back of their head which, as they present it meaningly to an older and stronger fellow, takes on a deep red colour. Whether, in higher animals and man, social inhibitions of this kind are equally mechanical, need not for the moment enter into our consideration. Whatever may be the reasons that prevent the dominant individual from injuring the submis-sive one, whether he is prevented from doing so by a simple and purely mechanical reflex process or by a highly philosophical moral standard, is immaterial to the practical issue. The essential behaviour of the submissive as well as of the dominant partner remains the same: the humbled creature suddenly seems to lose his objections to being injured and re-moves all obstacles from the path of the killer, and it would seem that the very removal of these outer obstacles raises an insurmountable inner obstruction in the central nervous system of the aggressor.

And what is a human appeal for mercy after all? Is it so very different from what we have just described? The Homeric warrior who wishes to yield and plead mercy, discards hel-met and shield, falls on his knees and inclines his head, a set of actions which should make it easier for the enemy to kill, but, in reality, hinders him from doing so. As Shakespeare makes Nestor say of Hector:

Thou hast hung thy advanced sword i'
    the air,
Not letting it decline on the declined.

Even to-day, we have retained many sym-bols of such submissive attitudes in a number of our gestures of courtesy: bowing, removal of the hat, and presenting arms in military ceremonial. If we are to believe the ancient epics, an appeal to mercy does not seem to have raised an "inner obstruction" which was entirely insurmountable. Homer's heroes were certainly not as soft-hearted as the wolves of Whipsnade! In any case, the poet cites numer-ous instances where the supplicant was slaugh-tered with or without compunction. The Norse heroic sagas bring us many examples of similar failures of the submissive gesture and it was not till the era of knight-errantry that it was no longer considered "sporting" to kill a man who begged for mercy. The Christian knight is the first who, for reasons of traditional and religious morals, is as chivalrous as is the wolf from the depth of his natural impulses and inhibitions. What a strange paradox!

Of course, the innate, instinctive, fixed in-hibitions that prevent an animal from using his weapons indiscriminately against his own kind are only a functional analogy, at the most a slight foreshadowing, a genealogical prede-cessor of the social morals of man. The worker in comparative ethology does well to be very careful in applying moral criteria to animal behaviour. But here, I must myself own to harbouring sentimental feelings: I think it a truly magnificent thing that one wolf finds himself unable to bite the proffered neck of the other, but still more so that the other relies upon him for this amazing restraint. Mankind can learn a lesson from this, from the animal that Dante calls "la bestia senza pace." I at least have extracted from it a new and deeper understanding of a wonderful and often misunderstood saying from the Gospel which hitherto had only awakened in me feelings of strong opposition: "And unto him that smiteth thee on the one cheek offer also the other." (St. Luke vi, 26). A wolf has enlightened me: not so that your enemy may strike you again do you turn the other cheek toward him, but to make him unable to do it.

When, in the course of its evolution, a species of animals develops a weapon which may destroy a fellow-member at one blow, then, in order to survive, it must develop, along with the weapon, a social inhibition to prevent a usage which could endanger the existence of the species. Among the predatory animals, there are only a few which lead so solitary a life that they can, in general, forego such restraint. They come together only at the mating season when the sexual impulse outweighs all others, including that of aggression. Such unsociable hermits are the polar bear and the jaguar and, owing to the absence of these social inhibitions, animals of these species, when kept together in zoos, hold a sorry record for murdering their own kind. The system of special inherited impulses and inhibitions, together with the weapons with which a social species is provided by nature, form a complex which is carefully computed and self-regulating. All living beings have received their weapons through the same process of evolution that moulded their impulses and inhibitions; for the structural plan of the body and the system of behaviour of a species are parts of the same whole.

If such be Nature's holy plan,
Have I not reason to lament
What man has made of man?

Wordsworth is right: there is only one being in possession of weapons which do not grow on his body and of whose working plan, therefore, the instincts of his species know nothing and in the usage of which he has no correspondingly adequate inhibition. That being is man. With unarrested growth his weapons increase in monstrousness, multiplying horribly within a few decades. But innate impulses and inhibitions, like bodily structures, need time for their development, time on a scale in which geologists and astronomers are accustomed to calculate, and not historians. We did not receive our weapons from nature. We made them ourselves, of our own free will. Which is going to be easier for us in the future, the production of the weapons or the engendering of the feeling of responsibility that should go along with them, the inhibitions without which our race must perish by virtue of its own creations? We must build up these inhibitions purposefully for we cannot rely upon our instincts. Fourteen years ago, in November 1935, I concluded an article on "Morals and Weapons of Animals" which appeared in a Viennese journal, with the words, "The day will come when two warring factions will be faced with the possibility of each wiping the other out completely. The day may come when the whole of mankind is divided into two such opposing camps. Shall we then behave like doves or like wolves? The fate of mankind will be settled by the answer to this question." We may well be apprehensive.

CULTURAL BEHAVIOR

Man is not so unusual an animal that he is without instinctual behavior, if such behavior is defined as unlearned. However, man's instincts appear to be few and to have relatively limited social consequences.

There is a temptation to conclude that behavior is instinctual, and hence a result of the biological factor, when the behavior is widely distributed. It is necessary to exercise extreme caution before yielding to this temptation. Although no behavior can be considered instinctual unless it is found in all biologically normal human beings, behavior that is universal may still be the product of culture. An example is the incest taboo, the rule that the common man cannot have sexual relations with certain close relatives, which occurs in some form in all known human groups. A biological explanation of the incest taboo is ruled out by two facts: (1) Incest does occur among biologically normal people despite the presence of a taboo, and the taboo would not be necessary if there were an instinct against incest. (2) The taboo, while always prohibiting relations between some members of the inner or nuclear family, sometimes prohibits relations between people who are biologically related in the most tenuous sense, and it is hard to conceive of instincts that vary so from society to society. In consequence, sociologists believe that the source of the incest taboo is social and not biological.

This selection defines and illustrates the concept of culture, one of the most important concepts in contemporary social science.

> People in a given society behave in a way that is orderly, regular, and predictable to other members of the society. The everyday nature of this behavior and its widespread occurrence within a society encourage members of the society to attribute it to the biological nature of man.
>
> It is when one takes a comparative look at behavior, comparing what is prevalent within a given society with what is prevalent in different societies, or when one looks closely within a complex society and observes the differences among subgroups therein, that one is forced to reject the layman's biological explanations. If people are not everywhere sober in church and raucous at athletic events, if men need not be masculine, nor women feminine, then it may be concluded that these patterns of behavior have their origin within the society.
>
> Culture is the real source of most behavioral regularities. The selection explores its nature and functions and makes the important distinction between explicit culture, which is evident to the social scientist but not to the average man. The selection also points out the implications of a knowledge of culture for achieving practical goals within a society.

It is difficult to disagree with Kluckhohn's conclusion that cultural explanations are preferable to biological explanations of the social order. Indeed, man appears to be so much a product of his culture that it is impossible to envisage his survival without culture. One of the inescapable conclusions of social science is that as long as man has existed on earth he has had culture.

However, as powerful a concept as it is, culture is not the only social factor affecting behavior. Within the context of a given culture, the size and arrangement of groups will produce different behaviors. For this reason, culture, even when combined with biological and geographic factors, is not a sufficient explanation of the social order. Cultures contain different rules, some that are independent of others and some that are in direct contradiction. It is not always clear from cultural considerations alone which cultural alternatives are available in which situations and which ones are, in fact, applied. The rest of the story of the social order, insofar as it is known, comes under the heading of social organization.

Selection 13
FROM MIRROR FOR MAN
Clyde Kluckhohn

Why do the Chinese dislike milk and milk products? Why would the Japanese die willingly in a Banzai charge that seemed senseless to Americans? Why do some nations trace descent through the father, others through the mother, still others through both parents? Not because they were destined by God or Fate to different habits, not because the weather is different in China and Japan and the United States. Sometimes shrewd common sense has an answer that is close to that of the anthropologist: "because they were brought up that way." By "culture" anthropology means the total life way of a people, the social legacy the individual acquires from his group. Or culture can be regarded as that part of the environment that is the creation of man.

This technical term has a wider meaning than the "culture" of history and literature. A humble cooking pot is as much a cultural product as is a Beethoven sonata. In ordinary speech a man of culture is a man who can speak languages other than his own, who is familiar with history, literature, philosophy, or the fine arts. In some cliques that definition is still narrower. The cultured person is one who can talk about James Joyce, Scarlatti, and Picasso. To the anthropologist, however, to be human is to be cultured. There is culture in general, and then there are the specific cultures such as Russian, American, British, Hottentot, Inca. The general abstract notion serves to remind us that we cannot explain acts solely in terms of the biological properties of the people concerned, their individual past experience, and the immediate situation. The past experience of other men in the form of culture enters into almost every event. Each specific culture constitutes a kind of blueprint for all of life's activities.

One of the interesting things about human beings is that they try to understand themselves and their own behavior. While this has been particularly true of Europeans in recent times, there is no group which has not developed a scheme or schemes to explain man's

actions. To the insistent human query "why?" the most exciting illumination anthropology has to offer is that of the concept of culture. Its explanatory importance is comparable to categories such as evolution in biology, gravity in physics, disease in medicine. A good deal of human behavior can be understood, and indeed predicted, if we know a people's design for living. Many acts are neither accidental nor due to personal peculiarities nor caused by supernatural forces nor simply mysterious. Even those of us who pride ourselves on our individualism follow most of the time a pattern not of our own making. We brush our teeth on arising. We put on pants—not a loincloth or a grass skirt. We eat three meals a day—not four or five or two. We sleep in a bed—not in a hammock or on a sheep pelt. I do not have to know the individual and his life history to be able to predict these and countless other regularities, including many in the thinking process, of all Americans who are not incarcerated in jails or hospitals for the insane.

To the American woman a system of plural wives seems "instinctively" abhorrent. She cannot understand how any woman can fail to be jealous and uncomfortable if she must share her husband with other women. She feels it "unnatural" to accept such a situation. On the other hand, a Koryak woman of Siberia, for example, would find it hard to understand how a woman could be so selfish and so undesirous of feminine companionship in the home as to wish to restrict her husband to one mate.

Some years ago I met in New York City a young man who did not speak a word of English and was obviously bewildered by American ways. By "blood" he was as American as you or I, for his parents had gone from Indiana to China as missionaries. Orphaned in infancy, he was reared by a Chinese family in a remote village. All who met him found him more Chinese than American. The facts of his blue eyes and light hair were less impressive than a Chinese style of gait, Chinese arm and hand movements, Chinese facial expression, and Chinese modes of thought. The biological heritage was American, but the cultural training had been Chinese. He returned to China.

Another example of another kind: I once

knew a trader's wife in Arizona who took a somewhat devilish interest in producing a cultural reaction. Guests who came her way were often served delicious sandwiches filled with a meat that seemed to be neither chicken nor tuna fish yet was reminiscent of both. To queries she gave no reply until each had eaten his fill. She then explained that what they had eaten was not chicken, not tuna fish, but the rich, white flesh of freshly killed rattlesnakes. The response was instantaneous—vomiting, often violent vomiting. A biological process is caught in a cultural web.

A highly intelligent teacher with long and successful experience in the public schools of Chicago was finishing her first year in an Indian school. When asked how her Navaho pupils compared in intelligence with Chicago youngsters, she replied, "Well, I just don't know. Sometimes the Indians seem just as bright. At other times they just act like dumb animals. The other night we had a dance in the high school. I saw a boy who is one of the best students in my English class standing off by himself. So I took him over to a pretty girl and told them to dance. But they just stood there with their heads down. They wouldn't even say anything." I inquired if she knew whether or not they were members of the same clan. "What difference would that make?"

"How would you feel about getting into bed with your brother?" The teacher walked off in a huff, but, actually, the two cases were quite comparable in principle. To the Indian the type of bodily contact involved in our social dancing has a directly sexual connotation. The incest taboos between members of the same clan are as severe as between true brothers and sisters. The shame of the Indians at the suggestion that a clan brother and sister should dance and the indignation of the white teacher at the idea that she should share a bed with an adult brother represent equally nonrational responses, culturally standardized unreason.

All this does not mean that there is no such thing as raw human nature. The very fact that certain of the same institutions are found in all known societies indicates that at bottom all human beings are very much alike. The files of the Cross-Cultural Survey at Yale University are organized according to categories such as "marriage ceremonies," "life crisis rites," "incest taboos." At least seventy-five of these categories are represented in every single one of the hundreds of cultures analyzed. This is hardly surprising. The members of all human groups have about the same biological equipment. All men undergo the same poignant life experiences such as birth, helplessness, illness, old age, and death. The biological potentialities of the species are the blocks with which cultures are built. Some patterns of every culture crystallize around focuses provided by the inevitables of biology: the difference between the sexes, the presence of persons of different ages, the varying physical strength and skill of individuals. The facts of nature also limit culture forms. No culture provides patterns for jumping over trees or for eating iron ore.

There is thus no "either-or" between nature and that special form of nurture called culture. Culture determinism is as one-sided as biological determinism. The two factors are interdependent. Culture arises out of human nature, and its forms are restricted both by man's biology and by natural laws. It is equally true that culture channels biological processes— vomiting, weeping, fainting, sneezing, the daily habits of food intake and waste elimination. When a man eats, he is reacting to an internal "drive," namely, hunger contractions consequent upon the lowering of blood sugar, but his precise reaction to these internal stimuli cannot be predicted by physiological knowledge alone. Whether a healthy adult feels hungry twice, three times, or four times a day and the hours at which this feeling recurs is a question of culture. *What* he eats is of course limited by availability, but is also partly regulated by culture. It is a biological fact that some types of berries are poisonous; it is a cultural fact that, a few generations ago, most Americans considered tomatoes to be poisonous and refused to eat them. Such selective, discriminative use of the environment is characteristically cultural. In a still more general sense, too, the process of eating is channeled by culture. Whether a man eats to live, lives to eat, or merely eats and lives is only in part an individual matter, for there are also cultural trends. Emotions are physiological events. Certain situations will evoke fear in people from any culture. But sensations of pleasure, anger, and lust may be stimulated by cultural cues that would leave unmoved someone who has been reared in a different social tradition.

Except in the case of newborn babies and of individuals born with clear-cut structural or functional abnormalities we can observe innate endowments only as modified by cultural training. In a hospital in New Mexico where Zuñi Indian, Navaho Indian, and white American babies are born, it is possible to classify the newly arrived infants as unusually active, average, and quiet. Some babies from each "racial" group will fall into each category, though a higher proportion of the white babies will fall into the unusually active class. But if a Navaho baby, a Zuñi baby, and a white baby —all classified as unusually active at birth—are again observed at the age of two years, the Zuñi baby will no longer seem given to quick and restless activity—*as compared with the white child*—though he may seem so as compared with the other Zuñis of the same age. The Navaho child is likely to fall in between as contrasted with the Zuñi and the white, though he will probably still seem more active than the average Navaho youngster.

It was remarked by many observers in the Japanese relocation centers that Japanese who were born and brought up in this country, especially those who were reared apart from any large colony of Japanese, resemble in behavior their white neighbors much more closely than they do their own parents who were educated in Japan.

I have said "culture channels biological processes." It is more accurate to say "the biological functioning of individuals is modified if they have been trained in certain ways and not in others." Culture is not a disembodied force. It is created and transmitted by people. However, culture, like well-known concepts of the physical sciences, is a convenient abstraction. One never sees gravity. One sees bodies falling in regular ways. One never sees an electromagnetic field. Yet certain happenings that can be seen may be given a neat abstract formulation by assuming that the electromagnetic field exists. Similarly, one never sees culture as such. What is seen are regularities in the behavior or artifacts of a group that has adhered to a common tradition. The regularities in style and technique of ancient Inca tapestries or stone axes from Melanesian islands are due to the existence of mental blueprints for the group.

Culture is a *way* of thinking, feeling, believing. It is the group's knowledge stored up (in memories of men; in books and objects) for future use. We study the products of this "mental" activity: the overt behavior, the speech and gestures and activities of people, and the tangible results of these things such as tools, houses, cornfields, and what not. It has been customary in lists of "culture traits" to include such things as watches or lawbooks. This is a convenient way of thinking about them, but in the solution of any important problem we must remember that they, in themselves, are nothing but metals, paper, and ink. What is important is that some men know how to make them, others set a value on them, are unhappy without them, direct their activities in relation to them, or disregard them.

It is only a helpful shorthand when we say "The cultural patterns of the Zulu were resistant to Christianization." In the directly observable world of course, it was individual Zulus who resisted. Nevertheless, if we do not forget that we are speaking at a high level of abstraction, it is justifiable to speak of culture as a cause. One may compare the practice of saying "syphilis caused the extinction of the native population of the island." Was it "syphilis" or "syphilis germs" or "human beings who were carriers of syphilis"?

"Culture," then, is "a theory." But if a theory is not contradicted by any relevant fact and if it helps us to understand a mass of otherwise chaotic facts, it is useful. Darwin's contribution was much less the accumulation of new knowledge than the creation of a theory which put in order data already known. An accumulation of facts, however large, is no more a science than a pile of bricks is a house. Anthropology's demonstration that the most weird set of customs has a consistency and an order is comparable to modern psychiatry's showing that there is meaning and purpose in the apparently incoherent talk of the insane. In fact, the inability of the older psychologies and philosophies to account for the strange behavior of madmen and heathens was the principal factor that forced psychiatry and anthropology to develop theories of the unconscious and of culture.

Since culture is an abstraction, it is important not to confuse culture with society. A "society" refers to a group of people who interact more with each other than they do with other individuals—who cooperate with each other for the attainment of certain ends. You can see and indeed count the individuals who make up a society. A "culture" refers to the distinctive ways of life of such a group of people. Not all social events are culturally patterned. New types of circumstances arise frequently.

A culture constitutes a storehouse of the pooled learning of the group. A rabbit starts life with some innate responses. He can learn from his own experience and perhaps from observing other rabbits. A human infant is born with fewer instincts and greater plasticity. His main task is to learn the answers that persons he will never see, persons long dead, have worked out. Once he has learned the formulas supplied by the culture of his group, most of his behavior becomes almost as automatic and unthinking as if it were instinctive. There is a tremendous amount of intelligence behind the making of a radio, but not much is required to learn to turn it on.

The members of all human societies face some of the same unavoidable dilemmas, posed by biology and other facts of the human situation. This is why the basic categories of all cultures are so similar. Human culture without language is unthinkable. No culture fails to provide for aesthetic expression and aesthetic delight. Every culture supplies standardized orientations toward the deeper problems, such as death. Every culture is designed to perpetuate the group and its solidarity, to meet the demands of individuals for an orderly way of life and for satisfaction of biological needs.

However, the variations on these basic themes are numberless. Some languages are built up out of twenty basic sounds, others out of forty. Nose plugs were considered beautiful by the predynastic Egyptians but are not by the modern French. Puberty is a biological fact. But one culture ignores it, another prescribes informal instructions about sex but no ceremony, a third has impressive rites for girls only, a fourth for boys and girls. In this culture, the first menstruation is welcomed as a happy, natural event; in that culture the atmosphere is full of dread and supernatural threat. Each culture dissects nature according to its own system of categories. The Navaho Indians apply the same word to the color of a robin's egg and to that of grass. A psychologist once assumed that this meant a difference in the sense organs, that Navahos didn't have the physiological equipment to distinguish "green" from "blue." However, when he showed them objects of the two colors and asked them if they were exactly the same colors, they looked at him with astonishment. His dream of discovering a new type of color blindness was shattered.

Every culture must deal with the sexual instinct. Some, however, seek to deny all sexual expression before marriage, whereas a Polynesian adolescent who was not promiscuous would be distinctly abnormal. Some cultures enforce lifelong monogamy, others, like our own, tolerate serial monogamy; in still other cultures, two or more women may be joined to one man or several men to a single woman. Homosexuality has been a permitted pattern in the Greco-Roman world, in parts of Islam, and in various primitive tribes. Large portions of the population of Tibet, and of Christendom at some places and periods, have practiced complete celibacy. To us marriage is first and foremost an arrangement between two individuals. In many more societies marriage is merely one facet of a complicated set of reciprocities, economic and otherwise, between two families or two clans.

The essence of the cultural process is selectivity. The selection is only exceptionally conscious and rational. Cultures are like Topsy. They just grew. Once, however, a way of handling a situation becomes institutionalized, there is ordinarily great resistance to chance or deviation. When we speak of "our sacred beliefs," we mean of course that they are beyond criticism and that the person who suggests modification or abandonment must be punished. No person is emotionally indifferent to his culture. Certain cultural premises may become totally out of accord with a new factual situation. Leaders may recognize this and reject the old ways in theory. Yet their emotional loyalty continues in the face of reason because of the intimate conditionings of early childhood.

A culture is learned by individuals as the result of belonging to some particular group, and it constitutes that part of learned behavior which is shared with others. It is our social legacy, as contrasted with our organic heredity. It is one of the important factors which permits us to live together in an organized society, giving us ready-made solutions to our problems, helping us to predict the behavior of others, and permitting others to know what to expect of us.

Culture regulates our lives at every turn. From the moment we are born until we die there is, whether we are conscious of it or not, constant pressure upon us to follow certain types of behavior that other men have created for us. Some paths we follow willingly, others we follow because we know no other way, still others we deviate from or go back to most unwillingly. Mothers of small children know how unnaturally most of this comes to us—how little regard we have, until we are "culturalized," for the "proper" place, time, and manner for certain acts such as eating, excreting, sleeping, getting dirty, and making loud noises. But by more or less adhering to a system of related designs for carrying out all the acts of living, a group of men and women feel themselves linked together by a powerful chain of sentiments. Ruth Benedict gave an almost complete definition of the concept when she said, "Culture is that which binds men together."

It is true any culture is a set of techniques for adjusting both to the external environment and to other men. However, cultures create problems as well as solve them. If the lore of a people states that frogs are dangerous creatures, or that it is not safe to go about at night because of witches or ghosts, threats are posed which do not arise out of the inexorable facts of the external world. Cultures produce needs as well as provide a means of fulfilling them. There exists for every group culturally defined, acquired drives that may be more powerful in ordinary daily life than the biologically inborn drives. Many Americans, for example, will work harder for "success" than they will for sexual satisfaction.

Most groups elaborate certain aspects of their culture far beyond maximum utility or survival value. In other words, not all culture promotes physical survival. At times, indeed, it does exactly the opposite. Aspects of culture which once were adaptive may persist long after they have ceased to be useful. An analysis of any culture will disclose many features which cannot possibly be construed as adaptations to the total environment in which the group now finds itself. However, it is altogether likely that these apparently useless features represent survivals, with modifications through time, of cultural forms once useful.

Any cultural practice must be functional or it will disappear before long. That is, it must somehow contribute to the survival of the society or to the adjustment of the individual. However, many cultural functions are not manifest but latent.* A cowboy will walk three

miles to catch a horse which he then rides one mile to the store. From the point of view of manifest function this is positively irrational. But the act has the latent function of maintaining the cowboy's prestige in the terms of his own subculture. One can instance the buttons on the sleeve of a man's coat, our absurd English spelling, the use of capital letters, and a host of other apparently nonfunctional customs. They serve mainly the latent function of assisting individuals to maintain their security by preserving continuity with the past and by making certain sectors of life familiar and predictable.

Every culture is a precipitate of history. In more than one sense history is a sieve. Each culture embraces those aspects of the past which, usually in altered form and with altered meanings, live on in the present. Discoveries and inventions, both material and ideological, are constantly being made available to a group through its historical contacts with other peoples or being created by its own members. However, only those that fit the total immediate situation in meeting the group's needs for survival or in promoting the psychological adjustment of individuals will become part of the culture. The process of culture building may be regarded as an addition to man's innate biological capacities, an addition providing instruments which enlarge, or may even substitute for, biological functions, and to a degree compensating for biological limitations—as in ensuring that death does not always result in the loss to humanity of what the deceased has learned.

Culture is like a map. Just as a map isn't the territory but an abstract representation of a particular area, so also a culture is an abstract description of trends toward uniformity in the words, deeds, and artifacts of a human group. If a map is accurate and you can read it, you won't get lost; if you know a culture you will know your way around in the life of a society.

Many educated people have the notion that culture applies only to exotic ways of life or to societies where relative simplicity and relative homogeneity prevail. Some sophisticated missionaries, for example, will use the anthropological conception in discussing the special modes of living of South Sea Islanders, but seem amazed at the idea that it could be applied equally to inhabitants of New York City. And social workers in Boston will talk about the culture of a colorful and well-knit immi-

---

* Roughly, recognized and unrecognized by participants in the culture.—Ed.

grant group but boggle at applying it to the behavior of staff members in the social-service agency itself.

In the primitive society the correspondence between the habits of individuals and the customs of the community is ordinarily greater. There is probably some truth in what an old Indian once said, "In the old days there was no law; everybody did what was right." The primitive tends to find happiness in the fulfillment of intricately involuted cultural patterns; the modern more often tends to feel the pattern as repressive to his individuality. It is also true that in a complex stratified society there are numerous exceptions to generalizations made about the culture as a whole. It is necessary to study regional, class, and occupational subcultures. Primitive cultures have greater stability than modern cultures; they change—but less rapidly.

However, modern men also are creators and carriers of culture. Only in some respects are they influenced differently from primitives by culture. Moreover, there are such wide variations in primitive cultures that any black-and-white contrast between the primitive and the civilized is altogether fictitious. The distinction which is most generally true lies in the field of conscious philosophy.

The publication of Paul Radin's *Primitive Man as a Philosopher* did much toward destroying the myth that an abstract analysis of experience was a peculiarity of literate societies. Speculation and reflection upon the nature of the universe and of man's place in the total scheme of things have been carried out in every known culture. Every people has its characteristic set of "primitive postulates." It remains true that critical examination of basic premises and fully explicit systematization of philosophical concepts are seldom found at the nonliterate level. The written word is an almost essential condition for free and extended discussion of fundamental philosophic issues. Where dependence on memory exists, there seems to be an inevitable tendency to emphasize the correct perpetuation of the precious oral tradition. Similarly, while it is all too easy to underestimate the extent to which ideas spread without books, it is in general true that tribal or folk societies do not possess competing philosophical systems. The major exception to this statement is, of course, the case where part of the tribe becomes converted to one of the great proselytizing religions such as Chris-

tianity or Mohammedanism. Before contact with rich and powerful civilizations, primitive peoples seem to have absorbed new ideas piecemeal, slowly integrating them with the previously existing ideology. The abstract thought of nonliterate societies is ordinarily less self-critical, less systematic, nor so intricately elaborated in purely logical dimensions. Primitive thinking is more concrete, more implicit—perhaps more completely coherent than the philosophy of most individuals in larger societies which have been influenced over long periods by disparate intellectual currents.

No participant in any culture knows all the details of the cultural map. The statement frequently heard that St. Thomas Aquinas was the last man to master all the knowledge of his society is intrinsically absurd. St. Thomas would have been hard put to make a pane of cathedral glass or to act as a midwife. In every culture there are what Ralph Linton has called "universals, alternatives, and specialties." Every Christian in the thirteenth century knew that it was necessary to attend mass, to go to confession, to ask the Mother of God to intercede with her Son. There were many other universals in the Christian culture of Western Europe. However, there were also alternative cultural patterns even in the realm of religion. Each individual had his own patron saint, and different towns developed the cults of different saints. The thirteenth-century anthropologist could have discovered the rudiments of Christian practice by questioning and observing whomever he happened to meet in Germany, France, Italy, or England. But to find out the details of the ceremonials honoring St. Hubert or St. Bridget he would have had to seek out certain individuals or special localities where these alternative patterns were practiced. Similarly, he could not learn about weaving from a professional soldier or about canon law from a farmer. Such cultural knowledge belongs in the realm of the specialities, voluntarily chosen by the individual or ascribed to him by birth. Thus, part of a culture must be learned by everyone, part may be selected from alternative patterns, part applies only to those who perform the roles in the society for which these patterns are designed.

Many aspects of a culture are explicit. The explicit culture consists in those regularities in word and deed that may be generalized straight from the evidence of the ear and the eye. The recognition of these is like the recognition of style in the art of a particular place and epoch. If we have examined twenty specimens of the wooden saints' images made in the Taos valley of New Mexico in the late eighteenth century, we can predict that any new images from the same locality and period will in most respects exhibit the same techniques of carving, about the same use of colors and choice of woods, a similar quality of artistic conception. Similarly, if, in a society of 2,000 members, we record 100 marriages at random and find that in 30 cases a man has married the sister of his brother's wife, we can anticipate that an additional sample of 100 marriages will show roughly the same number of cases of this pattern.

The above is an instance of what anthropologists call a behavioral pattern, the practices as opposed to the rules of the culture. There are also, however, regularities in what people say they do or should do. They do tend in fact to prefer to marry into a family already connected with their own by marriage, but this is not necessarily part of the official code of conduct. No disapproval whatsoever is attached to those who make another sort of marriage. On the other hand, it is explicitly forbidden to marry a member of one's own clan even though no biological relationship is traceable. This is a regulatory pattern—a Thou Shalt or a Thou Shalt Not. Such patterns may be violated often, but their existence is nevertheless important. A people's standards for conduct and belief define the socially approved aims and the acceptable means of attaining them. When the discrepancy between the theory and the practice of a culture is exceptionally great, this indicates that the culture is undergoing rapid change. It does not prove that ideals are unimportant, for ideals are but one of a number of factors determining action.

Cultures do not manifest themselves solely in observable customs and artifacts. No amount of questioning of any save the most articulate in the most self-conscious cultures will bring out some of the basic attitudes common to the members of the group. This is because these basic assumptions are taken so for granted that they normally do not enter into consciousness. This part of the cultural map must be inferred by the observer on the basis of consistencies in thought and action. Missionaries in various societies are often disturbed or puzzled because the natives do not regard "morals" and "sex code" as almost syn-

onymous. The natives seem to feel that morals are concerned with sex just about as much as with eating—no less and no more. No society fails to have some restrictions on sexual behavior, but sex activity outside of marriage need not necessarily be furtive or attended with guilt. The Christian tradition has tended to assume that sex is inherently nasty as well as dangerous. Other cultures assume that sex in itself is not only natural but one of the good things of life, even though sex acts with certain persons under certain circumstances are forbidden. This is implicit culture, for the natives do not announce their premises. The missionaries would get further if they said, in effect, "Look, our morality starts from different assumptions. Let's talk about those assumptions," rather than ranting about "immorality."

A factor implicit in a variety of diverse phenomena may be generalized as an underlying cultural principle. For example, the Navaho Indians always leave part of the design in a pot, a basket, or a blanket unfinished. When a medicine man instructs an apprentice he always leaves a little bit of the story untold. This "fear of closure" is a recurrent theme in Navaho culture. Its influence may be detected in many contexts that have no explicit connection.

If the observed cultural behavior is to be correctly understood, the categories and presuppositions constituting the implicit culture must be worked out. The "strain toward consistency" which Sumner noted in the folkways and mores[*] of all groups cannot be accounted for unless one grants a set of systematically interrelated implicit themes. For example, in American culture the themes of "effort and optimism," "the common man," "technology," and "virtuous materialism" have a functional interdependence, the origin of which is historically known. The relationship between themes may be that of conflict. One may instance the competition between Jefferson's theory of democracy and Hamilton's "government by the rich, the wellborn, and the able." In other cases most themes may be integrated under a single dominant theme. In Negro cultures of West Africa the mainspring of social life is religion; in East Africa almost all cultural behavior seems to be oriented toward certain premises and categories centered on

[*] Cultural rules. (See selection 21.)—Ed.

the cattle economy. If there be one master principle in the implicit culture, this is often called the "ethos" or *Zeitgeist*.

Every culture has organization as well as content. There is nothing mystical about this statement. One may compare ordinary experience. If I know that Smith, working alone, can shovel 10 cubic yards of dirt a day, Jones 12, and Brown 14, I would be foolish to predict that the three working together would move 36. The total might well be considerably more; it might be less. A whole is different from the sum of its parts. The same principle is familiar in athletic teams. A brilliant pitcher added to a nine may mean a pennant or may mean the cellar; it depends on how he fits in.

And so it is with cultures. A mere list of the behavioral and regulatory patterns and of the implicit themes and categories would be like a map on which all mountains, lakes, and rivers were included—but not in their actual relationship to one another. Two cultures could have almost identical inventories and still be extremely different. The full significance of any single element in a culture design will be seen only when that element is viewed in the total matrix of its relationship to other elements. Naturally, this includes accent or emphasis, as well as position. Accent is manifested sometimes through frequency, sometimes through intensity. The indispensable importance of these questions of arrangement and emphasis may be driven home by an analogy. Consider a musical sequence made up of three notes. If we are told that the three notes in question are *A*, *B*, and *G*, we receive information which is fundamental. But it will not enable us to predict the type of sensation which the playing of this sequence is likely to evoke. We need many different sorts of relationship data. Are the notes to be played in that or some other order? What duration will each receive? How will the emphasis, if any, be distributed? We also need, of course, to know whether the instrument used is to be a piano or an accordion.

Cultures vary greatly in their degree of integration. Synthesis is achieved partly through the overt statement of the dominant conceptions, assumptions, and aspirations of the group in its religious lore, secular thought, and ethical code; partly through habitual but unconscious ways of looking at the stream of events, ways of begging certain questions. To the naïve participant in the culture these modes of categorizing, of dissecting experience along these planes and not others, are as much "given" as the regular sequence of daylight and darkness or the necessity of air, water, and food for life. Had Americans not thought in terms of money and the market system during the depression they would have distributed unsalable goods rather than destroyed them.

Every group's way of life, then, is a structure—not a haphazard collection of all the different physically possible and functionally effective patterns of belief and action. A culture is an interdependent system based upon linked premises and categories whose influence is greater, rather than less, because they are seldom put in words. Some degree of internal coherence which is felt rather than rationally constructed seems to be demanded by most of the participants in any culture. As Whitehead has remarked, "Human life is driven forward by its dim apprehension of notions too general for its existing language."

In sum, the distinctive way of life that is handed down as the social heritage of a people does more than supply a set of skills for making a living and a set of blueprints for human relations. Each different way of life makes its own assumptions about the ends and purposes of human existence, about what human beings have a right to expect from each other and the gods, about what constitutes fulfillment or frustration. Some of these assumptions are made explicit in the lore of the folk; others are tacit premises which the observer must infer by finding consistent trends in word and deed.

In our highly self-conscious Western civilization that has recently made a business of studying itself, the number of assumptions that are literally implicit, in the sense of never having been stated or discussed by anyone, may be negligible. Yet only a trifling number of Americans could state even those implicit premises of our culture that have been brought to light by anthropologists. If one could bring to the American scene a Bushman who had been socialized in his own culture and then trained in anthropology, he would perceive all sorts of patterned regularities of which our anthropologists are completely unaware. In the case of the less sophisticated and less self-conscious societies, the unconscious assumptions characteristically made by individuals brought up under approximately the same social controls bulk even larger. But in any society, as Edward Sapir said, "Forms and significances which seem obvious to an outsider will be denied outright by those who carry out the patterns; outlines and implications that are perfectly clear to these may be absent to the eye of the onlooker."

All individuals in a culture tend to share common interpretations of the external world and man's place in it. To some degree every individual is affected by this conventional view of life. One group unconsciously assumes that every chain of actions has a goal and that when this goal is reached tension will be reduced or will disappear. To another group, thinking based upon this assumption is meaningless—they see life not as a series of purposive sequences, but as a complex of experiences which are satisfying in themselves, rather than as means to ends.

The concept of implicit culture is made necessary by certain eminently practical considerations. Programs of the British Colonial services or of our own Indian service, which have been carefully thought through for their continuity with the overt cultural patterns, nevertheless fail to work out. Nor does intensive investigation reveal any flaws in the setup at the technological level. The program is sabotaged by resistance which must be imputed to the manner in which the members of the group have been conditioned by their implicit designs for living to think and feel in ways which were unexpected to the administrator.

What good is the concept of culture so far as the contemporary world is concerned? What can you do with it? Much of the rest of this book will answer these questions, but some preliminary indications are in order.

Its use lies first in the aid the concept gives to man's endless quest to understand himself and his own behavior. For example, this new idea turns into pseudo problems some of the questions asked by one of the most learned and acute thinkers of our age, Reinhold Niebuhr. In his recent book *The Nature and Destiny of Man* Niebuhr argues that the universally human sense of guilt or shame and man's capacity for self-judgment necessitate the assumption of supernatural forces. These facts are susceptible of self-consistent and relatively simple explanation in purely naturalistic terms through the concept of culture. Social life among human beings never occurs without a system of conventional understandings which are transmitted more or less intact from generation to generation. Every individual is familiar with some of these and they constitute a set of standards against which he judges himself. To the extent that he fails to conform he experiences discomfort because his childhood training put great pressure on him to follow the accepted pattern, and his now unconscious tendency is to associate deviation with punishment or withdrawal of love and protection. This and other issues which have puzzled philosophers and scientists for so long become understandable through this fresh concept.

The principal claim which can be made for the culture concept as an aid to useful action is that it helps us enormously toward predicting human behavior. One of the factors limiting the success of such prediction thus far has been the naïve assumption of a minutely homogeneous "human nature." In the framework of this assumption all human thinking proceeds from the same premises; all human beings are motivated by the same needs and goals. In the cultural framework we see that, while the ultimate logic of all peoples may be the same (and thus communication and understanding are possible), the thought processes depart from radically different premises—especially unconscious or unstated premises. Those who have the cultural outlook are more likely to look beneath the surface and bring the culturally determined premises to the light of day. This may not bring about immediate agreement and harmony, but it will at least facilitate a *more* rational approach to the problem of international understanding and to diminishing friction between groups within a nation.

Knowledge of a culture makes it possible to predict a good many of the actions of any person who shares that culture. If the American Army was dropping paratroopers in Thailand in 1944, under what circumstances would they be knifed, under what circumstances would they be aided? If one knows how a given culture defines a certain situation, one can say that the betting odds are excellent that in a future comparable situation people will behave along certain lines and not along others. If we know a culture, we know what various classes of individuals within it expect from each other —and from outsiders of various categories. We know what types of activity are held to be inherently gratifying.

Many people in our society feel that the best way to get people to work harder is to increase their profits or their wages. They feel that it is just "human nature" to want to increase one's material possessions. This sort of dogma might well go unchallenged if we had no knowledge of other cultures. In certain societies, however, it has been found that the profit motive is not an effective incentive. After contact with whites the Trobriand Islanders in Melanesia could have become fabulously rich from pearl diving. They would, however, work only long enough to satisfy their immediate wants.

Administrators need to become conscious of the symbolic nature of many activities. American women will choose a job as hostess in a restaurant rather than one as waitress at a higher salary. In some societies the blacksmith is the most honored of individuals while in others only the lowest class of people are blacksmiths. White children in schools are motivated by grades; but children from some Indian tribe will work less hard under a system that singles the individual out from among his fellows.

Understanding of culture provides some detachment from the conscious and unconscious emotional values of one's own culture. The phrase, "some detachment," must be emphasized, however. An individual who viewed the designs for living of his group with complete detachment would be disoriented and unhappy. But I can prefer (i.e., feel affectively attached to) American manners while at the same time perceiving certain graces in English manners which are lacking or more grossly expressed in ours. Thus, while unwilling to forget that I am an American with no desire to ape English drawing-room behavior, I can still derive a lively pleasure from association with English people on social occasions. Whereas if I have no detachment, if I am utterly provincial, I am likely to regard English manners as utterly ridiculous, uncouth, perhaps even immoral. With that attitude I shall certainly not get on well with the English, and I am likely to resent bitterly any modification of our manners in the English or any other direction. Such attitudes clearly do not make for international understanding, friendship, and co-operation. They do, to the same extent, make for a too rigid social structure. Anthropological documents and anthropological teachings are valuable, therefore, in

that they tend to emancipate individuals from a too strong allegiance to every item in the cultural inventory. The person who has been exposed to the anthropological perspective is more likely to live and let live both within his own society and in his dealings with members of other societies; and he will probably be more flexible in regard to needful changes in social organization to meet changed technology and changed economy.

Perhaps the most important implication of culture for action is the profound truth that you can never start with a clean slate so far as human beings are concerned. Every person is born into a world defined by already existing culture patterns. Just as an individual who has lost his memory is no longer normal so the idea of a society's becoming completely emancipated from its past culture is inconceivable. This is one source of the tragic failure of the Weimar constitution in Germany. In the abstract it was an admirable document. But it failed miserably in actual life partly because it provided for no continuity with existent designs for acting, feeling, and thinking.

Since every culture has organization as well as content, administrators and lawmakers should know that one cannot isolate a custom to abolish or modify it. The most obvious example of failure caused by neglect of this principle was the Eighteenth Amendment. The legal sale of liquor was forbidden, but the repercussions in law enforcement, in family life, in politics, in the economy were staggering.

The concept of culture, like any other piece of knowledge, can be abused and misinterpreted. Some fear that the principle of cultural relativity will weaken morality. "If the Bugabuga do it why can't we? It's all relative anyway." But this is exactly what cultural relativity does *not* mean.

The principle of cultural relativity does not mean that because the members of some savage tribe are allowed to behave in a certain way that this fact gives intellectual warrant for such behavior in all groups. Cultural relativity means, on the contrary, that the appropriateness of any positive or negative custom must be evaluated with regard to how this habit fits with other group habits. Having several wives makes economic sense among herders, not among hunters. While breeding a healthy skepticism as to the eternity of any value prized by a particular people, anthropology does not as a matter of theory deny the existence of moral absolutes. Rather, the use of the comparative method provides a scientific means of discovering such absolutes. If all surviving societies have found it necessary to impose some of the same restrictions upon the behavior of their members, this makes a strong argument that these aspects of the moral code are indispensable.

Similarly, the fact that a Kwakiutl chief talks as if he had delusions of grandeur and of persecution does not mean that paranoia is not a real ailment in our cultural context. Anthropology has given a new perspective to the relativity of the normal that should bring greater tolerance and understanding of socially harmless deviations. But it has by no means destroyed standards or the useful tyranny of the normal. All cultures recognize some of the same forms of behavior as pathological. Where they differ in their distinctions, there is a relationship to the total framework of cultural life.

There is a legitimate objection to making culture explain too much. Lurking, however, in such criticism of the cultural point of view is often the ridiculous assumption that one must be loyal to a single master explanatory principle. On the contrary, there is no incompatibility between biological, environmental, cultural, historical, and economical approaches. All are necessary. The anthropologist feels that so much of history as is still a living force is embodied in the culture. He regards the economy as a specialized part of the culture. But he sees the value in having economists and historians, as specialists, abstract out their special aspects—so long as the complete context is not entirely lost to view. Take the problems of the American South, for example. The anthropologist would entirely agree that biological (social visibility of black skin, etc.), environmental (water power and other natural resources), historical (South settled by certain types of people, somewhat different governmental practices from the start, etc.), and narrowly cultural (original discrimination against Negroes as "heathen savages," etc.) issues are all inextricably involved. However, the cultural factor is involved in the actual working out of each influence—though culture is definitely not the whole of it. And to say that certain acts are culturally defined does not always and necessarily mean that they could be eliminated by changing the culture.

The needs and drives of biological man, and the physical environment to which he must adjust, provide the stuff of human life, but given culture determines the way this stuff is handled—the tailoring. In the eighteenth century a Neapolitan philosopher, Vico, uttered a profundity which was new, violent—and unnoticed. This was simply the discovery that "the social world is surely the work of man." Two generations of anthropologists have compelled thinkers to face this fact. Nor are anthropologists willing to allow the Marxists or other cultural determinists to make of culture another absolute as autocratic as the God or Fate portrayed by some philosophies. Anthropological knowledge does not permit so easy an evasion of man's responsibility for his own destiny. To be sure, culture is a compulsive force to most of us most of the time. To some extent, as Leslie White says, "Culture has a life and laws of its own." Some cultural changes are also compelled by economic or physical circumstances. But most of an economy is itself a cultural artifact. And it is men who change their cultures, even if—during most of past history—they have been acting as instruments of cultural processes of which they were largely unaware. The record shows that, while situation limits the range of possibility, there is always more than one workable alternative. The essence of the cultural process is selectivity; men may often make a choice. Lawrence Frank probably overstates the case:

> In the years to come it is possible that this discovery of the human origin and development of culture will be recognized as the greatest of all discoveries, since heretofore man has been helpless before these cultural and social formulations which generation after generation have perpetuated the same frustration and defeat of human values and aspirations. So long as he believed this was necessary and inevitable, he could not but accept this lot with resignation. Now man is beginning to realize that his culture and social organization are not unchanged cosmic processes, but are human creations which may be altered. For those who cherish the democratic faith this discovery means that they can, and must, undertake a continuing assay of our culture and our society in terms of its consequences for human life and human values. This is the historic origin and purpose of human culture, to create a human way of life. To our age falls the responsibility of utilizing the amazing new resources of science to meet these cultural tasks, to continue the great human tradition of man taking charge of his own destiny.

Nevertheless, to the extent that human beings discover the nature of the cultural process, they can anticipate, prepare, and—to at least a limited degree—control.

Americans are now at a period in history when they are faced with the facts of cultural differences more clearly than they can take with comfort. Recognition and tolerance of the deeper cultural assumptions of China, Russia, and Britain will require a difficult type of education. But the great lesson of culture is that the goals toward which men strive and fight and grope are not "given" in final form by biology nor yet entirely by the situation. If we understand our own culture and that of others, the political climate can be changed in a sur-

prisingly short time in this narrow contemporary world providing men are wise enough and articulate enough and energetic enough. The concept of culture carries a legitimate note of hope to troubled men. If the German and Japanese peoples behaved as they did because of their biological heredity, the outlook for restoring them as peaceful and cooperative nations would be hopeless. But if their propensities for cruelty and aggrandizement were primarily the result of situational factors and their cultures, then something can be done about it, though false hopes must not be encouraged as to the speed with which a culture can be planfully changed.

CULTURE AND EXPERIENCE

Prominent among the figures of speech used to describe culture is the analogy of a filter, which organizes and transforms perception. The filter's properties are seldom apparent to us in everyday life, but the profound effect of cultural assumptions on our experience and understanding of the world around us can be seen in situations like the one dealt with in this selection. The story of Hamlet is often thought to have universal appeal, as it deals with matters like love, hate, vengeance, and other passions which we consider to be primordial. Laura Bohannan's experience in recounting this famous Western myth to an audience with a very different cultural background illustrates the degree to which we depend on the assumptions and understandings given by culture to obtain meaning from the world of events.

> An African audience fails to grasp the intended meaning of the story of Hamlet because their understandings concerning human nature differ from those of the storyteller and, presumably, the author of the tale. Ophelia's death by drowning is understood in the context of the beliefs that drowning is caused only by witchcraft, and that witchcraft can be practiced upon one only by relatives in the male line. Thus, Laertes must be responsible for his sister's death. The audience speculates that the killing must have been caused by financial exigencies: being unable to sell Ophelia at a good bride price, because she is desired by a prince who apparently cannot marry her, Laertes sells her, dead, to the witches. Hamlet is killed when he tries to interfere with this plot.

Perhaps high school English teachers would evince less surprise than Bohannan at the Africans' inability to comprehend Hamlet as intended. In the classroom, as in the bush, it is not necessarily a lack of intelligence that impedes understanding. At least in part, in both instances, the problem is a divergence of shared cultural assumptions between the storyteller and the audience. On a more significant and more general level, these cultural gaps are responsible for many of the common misunderstandings between individuals, groups, and nations.

Selection 14
SHAKESPEARE IN THE BUSH
Laura Bohannan

Just before I left Oxford for the Tiv in West Africa, conversation turned to the season at Stratford. "You Americans," said a friend, "often have difficulty with Shakespeare. He was, after all, a very English poet, and one can easily misinterpret the universal by mis-understanding the particular."

I protested that human nature is pretty much the same the whole world over; at least the general plot and motivation of the greater tragedies would always be clear—everywhere—although some details of custom might have to be explained and difficulties of translation might produce other slight changes. To end an argument we could not conclude, my friend gave me a copy of *Hamlet* to study in the African bush: it would, he hoped, lift my mind above its primitive surroundings, and possibly I might, by prolonged meditation, achieve the grace of correct interpretation.

It was my second field trip to that African tribe and I thought myself ready to live in one of its remote sections—an area difficult to cross even on foot. I eventually settled on the hillock of a very knowledgeable old man, the head of a homestead of some hundred and forty people, all of whom were either his close relatives or their wives and children. Like the other elders of the vicinity, the old man spent most of his time performing ceremonies sel-dom seen these days in the more accessible parts of the tribe. I was delighted. Soon there would be three months of enforced isolation and leisure, between the harvest that takes place just before the rising of the swamps and the clearing of new farms when the water goes down. Then, I thought, they would have even more time to perform ceremonies and explain them to me.

I was quite mistaken. Most of the cere-monies demanded the presence of elders from several homesteads. As the swamps rose, the old men found it too difficult to walk from one homestead to the next, and the ceremonies gradually ceased. As the swamps rose even higher, all activities but one came to an end. The women brewed beer from maize and

Reprinted from *Natural History*, 75:7, 1966, pp. 28–33, with permission of the author.

millet. Men, women and children sat on their hillock and drank it.

People began to drink at dawn. By mid-morning the whole homestead was singing, dancing and drumming. When it rained, peo-ple had to sit inside their huts: there they drank and told stories. In any case, by noon, or before, I either had to join the party or retire to my own hut and my books. "One does not discuss serious matters when there is beer. Come, drink with us." Since I lacked their capacity for the thick native beer, I spent more and more time with *Hamlet*. Before the end of the second month, grace descended upon me. I was quite sure that *Hamlet* had only one possible interpretation, and that one univer-sally obvious.

Early every morning, in the hope of having some serious talk before the beer party, I used to call on the old man at his reception hut—a circle of posts supporting a thatched roof above a low mud wall to keep out the wind and rain. One day I crawled through the low doorway and found most of the men of the homestead sitting huddled in their ragged cloths on stools, low plank beds, and reclining chairs, warming themselves against the chill of the rain around a smoky fire. In the center were three pots of beer. The party had started.

The old man greeted me cordially. "Sit down and drink." I accepted a large calabash full of beer, poured some into a small drinking gourd, and tossed it down. Then I poured some more into the same gourd for the second man in seniority to my host before I handed my calabash over to a young man for further distribution. Important people shouldn't ladle beer themselves.

"It is better like this," the old man said, looking at me approvingly and plucking the thatch that had caught in my hair. "You should sit and drink with us more often. Your servants tell me that when you are not with us, you sit inside your hut looking at a paper."

The old man was acquainted with four kinds of "papers": tax receipts, bride price receipts, court fee receipts, and letters. The messenger who brought him letters from the chief used them mainly as a badge of office, for he always knew what was in them and told the old man. Personal letters for the few who had relatives in the government or mission stations were kept until someone went to a large market where there was a letter writer and reader. Since my arrival, letters were brought to me to be read. A few men also brought to me bride price receipts, privately, with requests to change the figures to a higher sum. I found moral arguments of no avail, since in-laws are fair game, and the technical hazards of forgery difficult to explain to an illiterate people. I did not wish them to think me silly enough to look at any such papers for days on end, and I hastily explained that my "paper" was one of the "things of long ago" of my country.

"Ah," said the old man. "Tell us."

I protested that I was not a storyteller. Storytelling is a skilled art among them; their standards are high, and the audiences critical —and vocal in their criticism. I protested in vain. This morning they wanted to hear a story while they drank. They threatened to tell me no more stories until I told them one of mine. Finally, the old man promised that no one would criticize my style "for we know you are struggling with our language." "But," put in one of the elders, "you must explain what we do not understand, as we do when we tell you our stories." Realizing that here was my chance to prove *Hamlet* universally intelligible, I agreed.

The old man handed me some more beer to help me on with my storytelling. Men filled their long wooden pipes and knocked coals from the fire to place in the pipe bowls; then, puffing contentedly, they sat back to listen. I began in the proper style, "Not yesterday, not yesterday, but long ago, a thing occurred. One night three men were keeping watch outside the homestead of the great chief, when suddenly they saw the former chief approach them."

"Why was he no longer chief?"

"He was dead," I explained. "That is why they were troubled and afraid when they saw him."

"Impossible," began one of the leaders, handing his pipe on to his neighbor, who interrupted, "Of course it wasn't the dead chief. It was an omen sent by a witch. Go on."

Slightly shaken, I continued. "One of these three was a man who knew things"—the closest translation for scholar, but unfortunately it also meant witch. The second elder looked

triumphantly at the first. "So he spoke to the dead chief saying 'Tell us what we must do so you may rest in your grave' but the dead chief did not answer. He vanished, and they could see him no more. Then the man who knew things—his name was Horatio—said this event was the affair of the dead chief's son, Hamlet."

There was a general shaking of heads round the circle. "Had the dead chief no living brothers? Or was this son the chief?"

"No," I replied. "That is, he had one living brother who became the chief when the elder brother died."

The old men muttered: such omens were matters for chiefs and elders, not for youngsters; no good could come of going behind a chief's back; clearly Horatio was not a man who knew things.

"Yes, he was," I insisted, shooing a chicken away from my beer. "In our country the son is next to the father. The dead chief's younger brother had become the great chief. He had also married his elder brother's widow only about a month after the funeral."

"He did well," the old man beamed and announced to the others, "I told you that if we knew more about Europeans we would find they really were very like us. In our country also," he added to me, "the younger brother marries the elder brother's widow and becomes the father of his children. Now, if your uncle, who is married to your widowed mother, is your father's full brother, then he will be real father to you. Did Hamlet's father and uncle have one mother?"

His question barely penetrated my mind; I was too upset and thrown too far off balance by having one of the most important elements of *Hamlet* knocked straight out of the picture. Rather uncertainly I said that I thought they had the same mother, but I wasn't sure—the story didn't say. The old man told me severely that these genealogical details made all the difference and that when I got home I must ask the elders about it. He shouted out the door to one of his younger wives to bring his goatskin bag.

Determined to save what I could of the mother motif, I took a deep breath and began again. "The son Hamlet was very sad because his mother married again so quickly. There was no need for her to do so, and it is our custom for a widow not to go to her next husband until she has mourned for two years."

"Two years is too long," objected the wife,

who had appeared with the old man's battered goatskin bag. "Who will hoe your farms for you while you have no husband?"

"Hamlet," I retorted without thinking, "was old enough to hoe his mother's farms himself. There was no need for her to remarry." No one looked convinced. I gave up. "His mother and the great chief told Hamlet not to be sad, for the great chief himself would be a father to Hamlet. Furthermore, Hamlet would be the next chief: therefore he must stay to learn the things of a chief. Hamlet agreed to remain, and all the rest went off to drink beer."

While I paused, perplexed at how to render Hamlet's disgusted soliloquy to an audience convinced that Claudius and Gertrude had behaved in the best possible manner, one of the younger men asked me who had married the other wives of the dead chief.

"He had no other wives," I told him.

"But a chief must have many wives. How else can he brew beer and prepare food for all his guests?"

I said firmly that in our country even chiefs had only one wife, that they had servants to do their work, and that they paid them from tax money.

It was better, they returned, for a chief to have many wives and sons who would help him hoe his farms and feed his people; then everyone loved the chief who gave much and took nothing—taxes were a bad thing.

I agreed with the last comment, but for the rest fell back on their favorite way of fobbing off my questions: "That is the way it is done, so that is how we do it." I decided to skip the soliloquy. Even if Claudius was here thought right to marry his brother's widow, there remained the poison motif, and I knew they would disapprove of fratricide. More hopefully I resumed, "That night Hamlet kept watch with the three who had seen his dead father. The dead chief appeared again, and although the others were afraid, Hamlet followed his dead father off to one side. When they were alone, Hamlet's dead father spoke."

"Omens can't talk!" The old man was emphatic.

"Hamlet's father wasn't an omen. Seeing him might have been an omen, but he was not." My audience looked as confused as I sounded. "It *was* Hamlet's dead father. It was a thing we call a 'ghost.'" I had to use the English word, for unlike many of the neighboring tribes, these people didn't believe in

the survival after death of any individuating part of the personality.

"What is a ghost? An omen?"

"No, a ghost is someone who is dead but who walks around and can talk, and people can hear him and see him but not touch him."

They objected. "One can touch zombis."

"No, no! It was not a dead body the witches had animated to sacrifice and eat. No one else made Hamlet's dead father walk. He did it himself."

"Dead men can't walk," protested my audience as one man.

I was quite willing to compromise. "A ghost is the dead man's shadow."

But again they objected. "Dead men cast no shadows."

"They do in my country," I snapped.

The old man quelled the babble of disbelief that arose immediately and told me with that insincere, but courteous, agreement one extends to the fancies of the young, ignorant and superstitious, "No doubt in your country the dead can also walk without being zombis." From the depths of his bag he produced a withered fragment of kola nut, bit off one end to show it wasn't poisoned, and handed me the rest as a peace offering.

"Anyhow," I resumed, "Hamlet's dead father said that his own brother, the one who became chief, had poisoned him. He wanted Hamlet to avenge him. Hamlet believed in his heart, for he did not like his father's brother." I took another swallow of beer. "In the country of the great chief, living in the same homestead, for it was a very large one, was an important elder who was often with the chief to advise and help him. His name was Polonius. Hamlet was courting his daughter, but her father and brother . . . (I cast hastily about for some tribal analogy) warned her not to let Hamlet visit her when she was alone on her farm, for he would be a great chief and so could not marry her."

"Why not?" asked the wife, who had settled down on the edge of the old man's chair. He frowned at her for asking stupid questions and growled, "They lived in the same homestead."

"That was not the reason," I informed them. "Polonius was a stranger who lived in the homestead because he helped the chief, not because he was a relative."

"Then why couldn't Hamlet marry her?"

"He could have," I explained, "but Polonius didn't think he would. After all, Hamlet was a man of great importance who ought to marry a chief's daughter, for in his country a man could have only one wife. Polonius was afraid that if Hamlet made love to his daughter, then no one else would give a high price for her."

"That might be true," remarked one of the shrewder elders, "but a chief's son would give his mistress' father enough presents and patronage to more than make up the difference. Polonius sounds like a fool to me."

"Many people think he was," I agreed. "Meanwhile, Polonius sent his son Laertes off to Paris to learn the things of that country, for it was the homestead of a very great chief indeed. Because he was afraid that Laertes might waste a lot of money on beer and women and gambling, or get into trouble by fighting, he sent one of his servants to Paris secretly, to spy out what Laertes was doing. One day Hamlet came upon Polonius' daughter Ophelia. He behaved so oddly he frightened her. Indeed,"—I was fumbling for words to express the dubious quality of Hamlet's madness—"the chief and many others had also noticed that when Hamlet talked one could understand the words, but not what they meant. Many people thought that he had become mad." My audience suddenly became much more attentive. "The great chief wanted to know what was wrong with Hamlet, so he sent for two of Hamlet's age mates (school friends would have taken long explanation) to talk to Hamlet and find out what troubled his heart. Hamlet, seeing that they had been bribed by the chief to betray him, told them nothing. Polonius, however, insisted that Hamlet was mad because he had been forbidden to see Ophelia, whom he loved."

"Why," inquired a bewildered voice, "should anyone bewitch Hamlet on that account?"

"Bewitch him?"

"Yes, only witchcraft can make anyone mad, unless of course, one sees the beings that lurk in the forest."

I stopped being a storyteller, took out my notebook and demanded to be told more about these two causes of madness. Even while they spoke, and I jotted notes, I tried to calculate the effect of this new factor on the plot. Hamlet had not been exposed to the beings that lurk in the forests. Only his relatives in the male line could bewitch him. Barring relatives not mentioned by Shakespeare, it had to be Claudius, who was attempting to harm him. And, of course, it was.

For the moment I staved off questions by saying that the great chief also refused to believe that Hamlet was mad for the love of Ophelia and nothing else. "He was sure that something much more important was troubling Hamlet's heart."

"Now Hamlet's age mates," I continued, "had brought with them a famous storyteller. Hamlet decided to have this man tell the chief and all his homestead a story about a man who had poisoned his brother because he desired his brother's wife and wished to be the chief himself. Hamlet was sure the great chief could not hear the story without making a sign if he was indeed guilty, and then he would discover whether his dead father had told the truth."

The old man interrupted, with deep cunning, "Why should a father lie to his son?" he asked.

I hedged: "Hamlet wasn't sure that it really was his dead father." It was impossible to say anything in that language, about devil-inspired visions.

"You mean," he said, "it actually was an omen, and he knew witches sometimes send false ones. Hamlet was a fool not to go to one skilled in reading omens and divining truth in the first place. A man-who-sees-truth could have told him how his father died, if he really had been poisoned, and if there was witchcraft in it; then Hamlet could have called the elders to settle the matter."

The shrewd elder ventured to disagree. "Because his father's brother was a great chief, one-who-sees-truth might therefore have been afraid to tell it. I think it was for reason that a friend of Hamlet's father—a witch and an elder—sent an omen so his friend's son would know. Was the omen true?"

"Yes," I said, abandoning ghosts and the devil; a witch-sent omen it would have to be.

"It was true, for when the storyteller was telling his tale before all the homestead, the great chief rose in fear. Afraid that Hamlet knew his secret he planned to have him killed."

The stage set of the next bit presented some difficulties of translation. I began cautiously. "The great chief told Hamlet's mother to find out from her son what he knew. But because a woman's children are always first in her heart, he had the important elder Polonius hide behind a cloth that hung against the wall of Hamlet's mother's sleeping hut. Hamlet started to scold his mother for what she had done."

There was a shocked murmur from everyone. A man should never scold his mother.

"She called out in fear, and Polonius moved behind the cloth. Shouting 'A rat' Hamlet took his machete and slashed through the cloth." I paused, for dramatic effect. "He had killed Polonius."

The old men looked at each other in supreme disgust. "That Polonius was truly a fool and a man who knew nothing! What child would not know enough to shout, 'It's me!'"

With a pang, I remembered that these people are ardent hunters, always armed with bow, arrow and machete; at the first rustle in the grass an arrow is aimed and ready, and the hunter shouts "Game!" If no human voice answers immediately, the arrow speeds on its way. Like a good hunter, Hamlet had shouted, "A rat!"

I rushed in to save Polonius' reputation. "Polonius did speak. Hamlet heard him. But he thought it was the chief and wished to kill him to avenge his father. He had meant to kill him earlier in the evening. . . ." I broke down, unable to describe to these pagans, who had no belief in individual afterlife, the difference between dying at one's prayers and dying "unhousell'd, disappointed, unaneled."

This time I had shocked my audience seriously. "For a man to raise his hand against his father's brother and the one who has become his father—that is a terrible thing. The elders ought to let such a man be bewitched."

I nibbled at my kola nut in some perplexity, then pointed out that after all the man had killed Hamlet's father.

"No," pronounced the old man, speaking less to me than to the young man sitting behind the elders. "If your father's brother has killed your father, you must appeal to your father's age mates; *they* must avenge him. No man may use violence against his senior relatives." Another thought struck him. "But if his father's brother had indeed been wicked enough to bewitch Hamlet and make him mad that would be a good story indeed, for it would be his fault, that Hamlet, being mad, no longer had any sense and thus was ready to kill his father's brother."

There was a murmur of applause. *Hamlet* was again a good story to them, but it no longer seemed quite the same story to me. As I thought over the coming complications of plot and motive, I lost courage and decided to skim over dangerous ground quickly. "The great chief," I went on, "was not sorry that Hamlet had killed Polonius. It gave him a reason to send Hamlet away, with his two treacherous age mates, with letters to a chief of a far country, saying that Hamlet should be killed. But Hamlet changed the writing on the papers, so that the chief killed his age mates instead."

I encountered a reproachful glare from one of the men whom I had told undetectable forgery was not merely immoral but beyond human skill. I looked the other way.

"Before Hamlet could return, Laertes came back for his father's funeral. The great chief told him Hamlet had killed Polonius. Laertes swore to kill Hamlet because of this, and because his sister Ophelia, hearing her father had been killed by the man she loved, went mad and drowned in the river."

"Have you already forgotten what we told you?" The old man was reproachful. "One cannot take vengeance on a madman! Hamlet killed Polonius in his madness. As for the girl, she not only went mad, she was drowned. Only witches can make people drown. Water itself can't hurt anything. It is merely something one drinks and bathes in."

I began to get cross. "If you don't like the story, I'll stop."

The old man made soothing noises and himself poured me some more beer. "You tell the story well, and we are listening. But it is clear that the elders of your country have never told you what the story really means. No, don't interrupt! We believe you when you say your marriage customs are different, or your clothes and weapons. But people are the same everywhere; therefore, there are always witches and it is we, the elders, who know how witches work. We told you it was the great chief who wished to kill Hamlet, and now your own words have proved us right. Who were Ophelia's male relatives?"

"There were only her father and her brother." Hamlet was clearly out of my hands.

"There must have been many more; this also you must ask of your elders when you get back to your country. From what you tell us, since Polonius was dead, it must have been Laertes who killed Ophelia, although I do not see the reason for it."

We had emptied one pot of beer, and the old men argued the point with slightly tipsy interest. Finally one of them demanded of me, "What did the servant of Polonius say on his return?"

With difficulty, I recollected Reynaldo and his mission. "I don't think he did return, before Polonius was killed."

"Listen," said the elder, "and I will tell you how it was and how your story will go, then you may tell me if I am right. Polonius knew his son would get into trouble, and so he did. He had many fines to pay for fighting, and debts from gambling. But he had only two ways of getting money quickly. One was to marry off his sister at once, but it is difficult to find a man who will marry a woman desired by the son of a chief. For if the chief's heir commits adultery with your wife, what can you do? Only a fool calls a case against a man who will someday be his judge. Therefore Laertes had to take the second way: he killed his sister by witchcraft, drowning her so he could secretly sell her body to the witches."

I raised an objection. "They found her body and buried it. Indeed Laertes jumped into the grave to see his sister once more—so, you see, the body was truly there. Hamlet, who had just come back, jumped in after him."

"What did I tell you?" The elder appealed to the others. "Laertes was up to no good with his sister's body. Hamlet prevented him, because the chief's heir, like a chief, does not wish any other man to grow rich and power-ful. Laertes would be angry, because he would have killed his sister with no benefit to himself. In our country he would try to kill Hamlet for that reason. Is this not what happened?"

"More or less," I admitted. "When the great chief found Hamlet was still alive, he encouraged Laertes to try to kill Hamlet and arranged a fight with machetes between them. In the fight both the young men were wounded to death. Hamlet's mother drank the poisoned beer that the chief meant for Hamlet in case he won the fight. When he saw his mother die of poison, Hamlet, dying, managed to kill his father's brother with his machete."

"You see, I was right!" exclaimed the elder.

"That was a very good story," added the old man, "and you told it with very few mistakes. There was just one more error, at the very end. The poison Hamlet's mother drank was obviously meant for the survivor of the fight, whichever it was. If Laertes had won, the great chief would have poisoned him, for no one would know that he had arranged Hamlet's death. Then too, he need not fear Laertes' witchcraft; it takes a strong heart to kill one's only sister by witchcraft.

"Sometime," concluded the old man, gathering his ragged toga about him, "you must tell us some more stories of your country. We, who are elders, will instruct you in their true meaning, so that when you return to your own land, your elders will see that you have not been sitting in the bush, but among those who know things and who have taught you wisdom."

Chapter 6

THE CONTENT OF CULTURE

THE CULTURE OF THE UNITED STATES
Selection 15

DEVIANCE AND SUBCULTURE
Selection 16

Culture can be regarded as consisting of three types of elements: values, beliefs, and norms. Values and beliefs are the "ideas" of a culture, and norms are the rules for behavior. It is also possible to consider material items—pots, baskets, tractors, and rockets—as a part of culture, but there is dispute regarding whether these items are not less confusingly considered as products of culture. The omission of material items simplifies the concept, because culture can then be defined as an abstraction from behavior rather than as an abstraction plus objects.

Values are ideas concerning the desirable, the beautiful, and the morally right. They define for the members of a culture what is worthwhile and what is not. As such, they can be said to be the very core of culture. Statements such as "Cleanliness is next to godliness" and "Abstract art is beautiful" are expressions of values.

Values are not provable by scientific means. A diamond can be shown to be hard, but it cannot be proved, in the same way, to be beautiful; for there is no test of beauty other than the agreement of people, either ordinary men or their "experts." For this reason, many sociologists have maintained that one cannot judge cultures. To say that culture A is good and is better than culture B requires definitions of "good" and "better" which can only come from the value system of some culture, presumably that of the judge. Since this value system cannot be proved to be true, there is no scientific way of supporting the statement. The conclusion that one should therefore refrain from attempting to judge cultures and, rather, assign equal worth to all cultures is called cultural relativism. Although a few people have taken serious objection to cultural relativism, it is generally accepted in sociology and anthropology.

Beliefs are ideas concerning facts and, as such, are distinguished from values by the possibility of testing them. This possibility may in some instances be quite hypothetical, as in the case of "Hell is a hot place," but at least hypothetically one could go to Hell with a thermometer and see. Beliefs can be either true or false, and a false belief, such as "Negroes are all lazy," is no less a part of culture than a true one, such as "American soldiers are brave men." Values, on the other hand, are neither true nor false, being untestable according to the rules of science.

146

Norms are cultural rules that guide behavior within the society, and as such they are the focus of the sociologist's concern with culture. Any statement that can be expressed as a commandment, either positive or negative, will exemplify a norm. "Thou shalt not smoke in class," "Thou shalt do thy homework diligently," statements about what is "done" and what is "not done," what is proper and what is not proper, all are normative statements.

Norms and beliefs, while not the same as values, are closely related to them. For instance, if a culture contains the value "Drinking is evil," it will probably contain norms like "One may not drink in public" and beliefs like "Drinking shortens life." (And it will not produce material items like wine cups.) A positive evaluation of wealth will tend to be accompanied by beliefs such as the idea that riches are the inevitable reward of talent, and by norms promoting work and saving.

One of the most important observations concerning culture is that it is patterned. The values, norms, and beliefs of a culture are arranged in a hierarchy, with some being considered more important than others. It is possible to learn about this hierarchy by finding out what people do in situations where they have a choice of actions, each of which is in accordance with a different norm. For instance, if men generally leave more money to their wives than to their universities, normative obligations to a wife are inferred to be more important than normative obligations to a university.

Patterning is also evident in the tendency of cultures to be self-consistent. In reality, cultures are not entirely consistent, but it is rare for a given culture to include a large number of contradictory elements, such as both the idea that man is inherently evil and the idea that man is inherently good. Consistency is also illustrated by the fact (referred to above) that a value is usually supported by several related beliefs and norms.

The content of a familiar culture, that of the United States, is described in an unusual way by Conrad M. Arensberg and Arthur H. Niehoff in Selection 15. Selection 16, by David Matza, suggests the complexity of actual cultures in the context of an essay concerning American youth.

THE CULTURE OF THE UNITED STATES

Perhaps the most difficult of cultures to comprehend is, paradoxically, one's own. From within a culture, it is difficult to distinguish the facts of culture from the facts of nature. Consequent confusions of the cultural and the biological are the source of many of the biologically based theories of social life that have been rejected by sociologists.

This problem is found not only in the context of sociology, but also in relations between members of groups with different cultures. A significant modern example occurs in the interaction between Western technical assistants who are trying to introduce modern technology and the populations of the developing countries where governments are seeking aid in industrializing and in improving the productivity of agriculture. This selection is taken from a handbook written to guide Americans engaged in this enterprise. The authors believe that by clearly specifying the values with which the workers as Americans are imbued, the workers will better be able to anticipate sources of misunderstanding that might otherwise frustrate their mission. This catalog of American values has been compiled by the anthropologist authors on the basis of their familiarity with non-Western cultures, providing a background against which the sometimes hidden and unrecognized values of their own society appear in contrast.

The culture of the United States is distinguished by the following characteristics: a tendency to dichotomous or twofold judgments; the division of life into distinct spheres of work and play; an extraordinary emphasis upon time; optimism concerning goals, the means being effort; the dominance of man over nature; materialism; moralism; equalitarianism; and humanitarianism. These characteristics are linked to the peculiar history and social structure of the West in general and America in particular. The non-Western people with whom Americans abroad come into contact are also possessed of values which may be hidden and unrecognized, and in the likely instance that the comparable values of the two cultures differ, the ground is laid for misunderstanding. Misunderstandings can be reduced when their source is shown to be unquestioned cultural assumptions, rather than ignorance, stupidity, or poor faith.

The picture drawn of American culture is specifically stated to be that of the middle classes, as it is people from this part of American society who are most likely to be recruited as technical assistants. Culture generally, and particularly that of a large, intricate, and varied society like the United States, is a complex matter which must of necessity be simplified in description. Especially in the lower classes, different patterns of culture prevail, and some of the misunderstandings referred to here in the context of cross-national contacts occur as well across class, ethnic, religious, regional and other boundaries within America.

Selection 15
FROM INTRODUCING SOCIAL CHANGE
Conrad M. Arensberg and Arthur H. Niehoff

Misinterpretation

In order to incorporate techniques from one culture into another one it is very important to understand the role and background of the innovator concerned. In this manual, several of the cases indicate that an innovator's failure was due to a misinterpretation of the motives and needs of the recipients. Such misinterpretations may rest on the innovator's failure to learn enough about the receiving culture; but they may also rest on false presuppositions, derived from assuming that conditions taken for granted at home also exist in the foreign situation.

It is true that men of all cultures, developed or underdeveloped, have much in common in the solution of their problems. A peasant farmer in India and a Texas corn farmer are both pragmatic and must be shown that an improvement is genuine before they will ac-

cept it; and a Laotian farmer tries to get help from the supernatural in producing unpredictable rain just as Americans turn to prayer in an unpredictable situation, such as the disappearance of an astronaut while re-entering the earth's atmosphere. Nevertheless, it still does not follow that all the basic assumptions of people with different cultures are the same. Although we may say that men everywhere are basically alike, the unlikenesses are still significant enough to block communication and thus impede change. If the innovator expects the people of the recipient culture to have precisely the same motivations as he or his countrymen, or to make the same distinctions of behavior, thought, and value, he is seriously risking failure of his plans.

The worst part of such a misapprehension of cultural realities is that it is unintentional. The individual does what is "natural" or what makes "common sense." He may not realize that his "natural" tendencies to action and decision are inevitably limited by his own cultural experience and by unconscious assumptions, based on the way of life of his own people. To examine the cultural premises of one's own actions and thought is a difficult

Reprinted from *Introducing Social Change: A Manual for Americans Overseas* by Conrad M. Arensberg and Arthur H. Niehoff (Chicago: Aldine Publishing Co., 1964), pp. 153–183, with permission. Copyright © 1964 by Conrad M. Arensberg and Arthur A. Niehoff.

process. In one's own culture it may never be necessary and most people probably think more freely and act better without ever doing it. However, in dealing with people of another culture, it is a necessity of the first importance.

In many of the cases in the previous chapters failures resulted from false presuppositions. Hybrid corn grown by Spanish-American farmers in Arizona was superior in terms of the Anglo-American economy. The innovator assumed that the value of corn was the same for Spanish-Americans as for Anglo-Americans, a false supposition. They valued it more in terms of taste and texture as human food rather than as animal feed. The United States administrators of the Pacific island of Palau assumed that if individuals participated in an American system of voting and electing public officials, democracy would thereby be absorbed into the culture. However, the Pacific islanders defined leadership quite differently than did Americans, and they had an imperfect understanding of the meaning of democratic elections.

In both of these cases the situation was not due to stupidity, but rather to the cultural blindness of the planners who were not aware that they needed information both about themselves and the people they wanted to help. Reliance was mistakenly placed upon "natural" and "common sense" assumptions relevant to the American scene, but inadequate in contacts with people of another culture.

Culture and professional specialization create unconscious blinders for all of mankind. Americans are prone to distortions arising from American attitudes; specialists are prone to be inattentive to whatever their expert training has led them to define as irrelevant. Experts are usually single-minded and specialized. When Americans deal with problems set against the known background of their own culture, specialization has resulted in great strength; but it has been gained only by training individuals to concentrate narrowly. However, in dealing with the problems of another culture, the conditions no longer arise from a familiar background and cannot be taken for granted. People no longer act "naturally."

The American specialist should be given some opportunity of knowing himself as a product of American and Western culture. He should be required to have some understanding not only of the behavior and values of the recipient peoples of foreign cultures, but also of his own assumptions and values. He needs to become aware of unconscious presuppositions from his own culture that tend to influence his decisions and actions in introducing new ideas. He should discover what his probable reactions will be to the difficulties he may encounter among the people with whom he will be working. In short, he needs to know how being an American may help or hinder him in his mission.

The social and psychological sciences, including cultural anthropology, can contribute to the knowledge required. They give a fairly adequate portrait of "the American character," as exemplified by most Americans.

The United States, like any other country, has a national culture. All people born and raised in this country have been strongly conditioned by it. This does not mean that they will all be alike, or that if some act differently from others they are more or less American than the others. It does mean, however, that among Americans of all regions, national origins, races, classes, and both sexes, there are some points of likeness in acting and thinking that turn up more frequently than among groups of people in other countries. The following characteristics will be drawn primarily from classes of the middle levels of income and status. It is from this sector of the population that most change agents are drawn.

The characteristics of American character have been traced to many sources. The values derived from life on the frontier, the great open spaces, the virgin wealth and the seemingly limitless resources of a new world appear to have affected our ideas of freedom. Individualism has been fostered by the inventive spirit and technical advances of the country, the successful expansion of capitalism, and as a result of the huge, free mass market. Much of our religious and ethical tradition seems to have been derived from Calvinist (Puritan) origin. We inherited Anglo-Saxon civil rights, rule of law, and representative institutions; the ideas of egalitarian democracy and a secular spirit sprang from the French and American Revolutions. The melting pot, the staggering trans-Atlantic migration of Europeans for over three centuries, has affected our national character. All these, and many other historical circumstances, have gone into the making of the modern American character.

It will be useful to describe some of the most important features of American culture, as one of the "developed" countries, in order to make clear the contrast with most of the "underdeveloped" countries which have been described previously. We make the contrast not to exalt our own conditions or belittle those that prevail elsewhere but to show why American assumptions differ from those of many other peoples. The contrast is based on facts. The conditions we picture hold good not only for the United States but also, to a large degree, for other developed countries—most of Western Europe, New Zealand, Canada, Australia, and some of the countries of South America. Many of these countries have had an historical or economic development similar to that of the United States; although none show the particularly American combination of cultural features.

American culture

The culture and people of the United States, then, have some special characteristics. Compared with other countries, the number of people is considerable, though they are spread rather thinly over a huge area of many diverse natural environments, most of which are rich, temperate, and still not intensively exploited. Americans command an exceedingly rich technology and a wealth in manufactured goods that is now the greatest in the world. The consumption rate of these goods is also high.

Although the country has a strong agrarian tradition in which farming was a family specialty, and though farming still produces an extraordinary yield of foodstuffs and fibers, the nation has become urbanized and dominated by its cities. The farming population consists of less than ten per cent of the total and agriculture has become so mechanized it can now be considered as merely another form of industry. Daily living for the majority is characteristically urban, regulated by the clock and the calendar, rather than by the seasons or an agricultural cycle. People live on money rather than on subsistence goods or property. They are mainly employees living on salaries paid by large and complex impersonal institutions. Money is the common denominator of exchange, even property usually having a value only in terms of its monetary worth.

Because of the high standard of living and the high level of technology in the country,

people have long lives. Their birth rate is also low, but their death rate is one of the lowest in the world; and this keeps the population from expanding as rapidly as in some of the underdeveloped countries.

Americans are a comparatively new group of people with a short history. Their origins are among the most diverse of the entire world, with a continuing variability of racial and ethnic stocks and a profusion of minority groups.

Americans exhibit wide ranges of wealth, property, education, manners, and tastes. Despite these diversities of origin, tradition, and economic level, there is a surprising conformity and almost continent-wide uniformity of language, diet, hygiene, dress, basic skills, land use, community settlement, recreational activities, use of mass communications, and innumerable other activities. The people share a rather small range of standard moral, political, economic, and social attitudes, being divided in opinion chiefly by their denominational, occupational and ethnic (race and national origin) interests. There are some regional variations, though these do not amount to a plurality of social views in the same sense as in some of the underdeveloped countries. There is a high degree of mobility, both geographically and occupationally.

There are status differences in America, based mainly on occupation, education and financial worth. Although in theory all persons have equal opportunities, there are certain limitations, particularly those based on racial or ethnic grounds, beyond which it is difficult for some individuals to go. Although a Negro may be appointed as a member of the Cabinet, it is improbable that one could become President and it is difficult for one to be elected to either house of Congress. Despite these limitations, most people change jobs, move from one city or region to another, or move up or down in status level with great frequency. They do not seem to mind being uprooted, a process so painful in other countries.

Husband, wife, and children constitute the basic American kinship unit, the nuclear family. There are high marriage rates, the couples setting up their own small households. Unlike many people in the underdeveloped areas, Americans have comparatively few children and rarely spend their lives as part of larger households. Family relationships are fluid and not particularly stable. Nowadays divorce is common and family custom usually requires old people and unmarried adults to live apart from their kin. In place of strong kinship ties, people tend to rely on an enormous number of voluntary associations of common interest, which they join—parent-teachers associations, women's clubs, social fraternities, church clubs, recreational teams, and many others.

The general level of education is high; literacy is high but by no means universal. From the age of six to sixteen the child is in an academic institution, learning the goals of good health, good character, and good citizenship. He is also taught to be competitive and adaptive to changing environments. He learns basic standard skills (driving cars, basic mechanics, reading, writing, arithmetic, typing, the liberal arts) rather than hereditary specializations. Specialization comes later in professional training.

The moral tone of the country is heavily Calvinist Protestant, but there are many other sects of Christianity. The religious beliefs are concerned almost as much with general morality as with man's search for the afterlife. Family relations, sexual customs, man's relationship to other men, and civic responsibility are all concerns of religion. A puritanic morality has become generalized and secular, part of the culture rather than the code of any single religious sect. No religious group is supported by the state. Formal religion is compartmentalized as are many other aspects of American life. A high percentage of the Protestants who form the bulk of America's population attend church sporadically and infrequently; and religious ideas seldom are mixed with secular ones. The church serves a strong social function, being the center of many clubs and groups. Religion is not a particularly unifying institution in American life. The spirit of the country is increasingly secular and rationalistic. It is not antireligious or even anticlerical, as is so often the case elsewhere; it is rather a spirit of religious indifference. The majority of individuals simply do not concern themselves with religion in the conduct of most matters.

The implication of this thumbnail sketch of American culture should now be clear. Neither the American complex of cultural conditions nor most of its important particulars can be relied upon to exist elsewhere, whether the other country is underdeveloped or developed.

To attribute the majority of our cultural characteristics to people of other cultures can only result in a chain of misunderstandings and mistakes.

Twofold judgments

The most hazardous tendency in the way of thinking that Americans take with them into other cultural situations is that of making twofold judgments based on principle. The structure of the Indo-European languages seems to foster this kind of categorization. Action in all situations is fostered by such judgments. An event or situation is assigned to a category believed high in value and thus a basis for positive action; or to one low in value and a basis for rejection, avoidance, or other negative action. Twofold judgments are the rule in American and Western life: moral-immoral, legal-illegal, right-wrong, success-failure, clean-dirty, modern-outmoded, civilized-primitive, developed-underdeveloped, practical-impractical, introvert-extrovert, secular-religious, Christian-pagan. The fact that such a method of dividing human activities into opposites is largely arbitrary is indicated by the necessity for Americans to compromise to solve problems. Compromising implies that neither side possesses "the truth" and that a just and proper solution can be achieved only by "splitting the difference."[1]

Judgment in terms of principle is very old and pervasive as a means of organizing thought in American and Western culture and is deeply rooted in the philosophy and religions of the West. It requires a very particular process and its special quality should be recognized. It is more than merely a habit of thinking in pairs. Other peoples have often invented dual ways of thinking: the Chinese Yin-and-Yang, the Zoroastrian dual (though equal) forces of good and evil, male and female principles, and forces of destruction and regeneration. However, other peoples do not usually rank one as superior and thus to be embraced on principle (the Christian God), while ranking the other as inferior and thus to be rejected on principle (the Christian Satan). Instead they will tend to rank the two categories as equal and say that each must have its due; or they may not connect them at all with principles guiding conduct.

In two of the world's largest religions, Buddhism and Hinduism, local beliefs which are quite distinct from those deriving from the theology of the dominant religion are permitted to live beside it. No one questions the fact that in Japan people may worship in a Buddhist temple and also in a Shinto shrine; or that they may observe the practices of Hinayana Buddhism in Laos and Thailand, while at the same time propitiating the "phi," the local non-Buddhist spirits. Actually, the normal religious practitioner in these countries has great difficulty in separating his Buddhist beliefs from his non-Buddhist ones. To him they all belong to the realm of the supernatural. This is quite different from the Christian attitude in which all that is supernatural, but not Christian, is superstition or paganism.

The average Western man, including the American, conducts his personal life and his maintenance of law and order in the community on principles of right and wrong, rather than on sanctions of shame, dishonor, ridicule, or horror of impropriety. He is forced to categorize his conduct in universal, impersonal terms. The "law is the law," and "right is right," regardless of other considerations.

Work and play

The habit of making twofold judgments based on principle is pervasive in American culture and is apt to distort interpretations of other ways of life. For instance, Americans maintain a twofold judgment of activity as either work or play. To most persons brought up in the present-day American environment of farming, business, or industry, work is what they do regularly, grimly, purposefully (for the money, or to do a good job, or to make a success) whether they enjoy it or not. It is a necessity, perhaps even more importantly, a duty, a "good thing in itself since one ought to keep occupied." A man is judged by his work. It is a serious adult business, for a man is supposed "to get ahead" or "make a contribution" to the community or mankind.

Play is different. It is fun, an outlet from work, without serious purpose except to make work more efficient. It is the lesser category and, though some of us may "enjoy our work," it is a matter of luck and by no means something that everyone can count on since all jobs contain some "dirty work," tedium, and tasks that one completes just by pushing on. Work and play are different worlds; there is a time and place for each; but, when it is time for work, then play and the lighter pursuits must be put aside.

The American habit of associating work with high purpose and grim effort, and play with frivolity and idleness (unless the play is considered as a therapeutic agent to do better work) is admirable at home, but it may be completely out of place in another culture. To insist on it, and to judge others negatively because they do not make the same distinction, can easily cause estrangement. In fact, for many peoples the times of most important work may also be the times of greatest festivity or highest ceremony. Work and play may be interwoven as thoroughly as two kinds of religious belief. A threshing floor may well be a dancing arena; building a new house or netting a school of fish may provide the occasion for a whole community to dance and sing together. Preparing the proper songs or dishes will be as "practical" an activity as the cutting of thatch or the care of the nets.

The combination of work and play is not a completely foreign idea to Americans, although urban, industrial society seems inimical to it. The American frontier, and even midwest farming communities until thirty and forty years ago, still combined the two in their husking bees, house-raising, and threshing parties. In the early part of this century, before wheat combines and farms of large acreage took over wheat threshing in midwestern states, farmers made the social and work rounds for several weeks in midsummer. Not only did they work together at these times; but they also feasted, socialized, and even managed a considerable amount of their courtships. It was a point of pride for each farmer's wife, with the help of the neighbor women, to have the largest and most elaborate quantities of food available for the men when they came in from the fields. The unmarried girls made a particular point of being there also, since most of the unmarried men were assembled. It was a gay time as well as a time of hard work.

Time is money

The way in which Americans distinguish between work and play can cause great difficulties in cultures. A good distinction of this sort is connected with American concepts of time. The more they are together, the sooner both foreigners and Americans become aware that their attitudes toward time vary. In many underdeveloped countries people speak of American time versus time of the country: *hora Americana–hora Mexicana,* or *mong Amelikan–mong Lao.* In general, American time is exact, people are punctual, activities are scheduled, and time is apportioned for separate activities.

Americans have frequent misunderstandings with the people of other nations because their attitude toward time is usually different, but nowhere is it more so than in relation to work. For Americans "time is money." Work is paid for in money and one balances his work against time or through regular periods for a set salary. Play or leisure time is before or after work time. An employer buys the time of his workers, schedules and assigns work as balanced against the time it will take, and budgets the wages against the time periods of his employees. Time can be turned into profit, for work turned out faster than planned can release extra time to do more work for extra gain.

The equating of work with time, using the least amount of time to produce the largest possible quantities, expecting that the time people are paid for be marked by sustained effort, and budgeting and planning man-hours in relation to cost of the end product are all central features of the American industrial economy and no small part of why it is so productive. Although they may complain about the necessity of routine and the tyranny of the clock in work, and even scheduled non-working hours, Americans are thoroughly used to such strictures. Eating, sleeping, playing, recreation, even courting must take place during "time off." No wonder time is scarce and worth saving.

Such a concept of time is usually quite foreign to peoples of non-Western or non-industrial cultures. In most agrarian, peasant societies, work is not equated with time and scheduled solely in terms of production, but instead is geared to seasonal emergencies, climatic threats, or sporadic exhaustion of supplies and resources. Many routines reflect, not hourly or daily repetitions based on wage labor, but the crises of individual and social life, the cycles of the crops, the fluctuations in daily temperature, and the round of ceremonial observances. Thus, difficulties seem to arise when Americans or other Westerners try to get non-Westerners to accept their kind of scheduling and routine. Often trouble may start if Americans expect exact, regular attendance or steady, unflagging effort through fixed periods of times.

In Bolivia, where some mines run by Americans require a full eight-hour day, and others run by the French offer no better working conditions, and equal or less pay, many Indian miners prefer to work for the latter. This is because the French managers pay only for work performed and let the Indians go home when they please.[2] In Islamic lands, Friday is the Sabbath, but it is not a day of rest. Western archaeologists, who hired local Muslims to dig on their sites, often gave their workers the day off (without pay). This only made the Muslims bewildered and indignant. They wanted the money and their religious beliefs did not prohibit them from working on their Sabbath.[3]

In Trinidad, no problem arose when East Indian workers had industrial jobs with a high incentive (and relatively good pay). In order to keep good jobs in the refineries and offices of oil companies they were willing to adjust to the British schedules. On impermanent jobs of low pay, however, they were highly unreliable. Some were hired as coolies, particularly to mow the lawn in the compounds. At first, this work was paid for by hourly wages, but the administrators soon realized that workers would stretch a day's work to last a week in order to get the maximum amount of pay. The problem was solved by hiring them on a piece work basis, and paying a set sum of money for cutting the grass in a given area. Then there was no dallying.

As industrialism increases in the non-Western countries, and relatively well-paying jobs become available to workers, Western time scheduling will necessarily become more widely and easily accepted. In Mexico, where industry is growing rapidly, American type time scheduling has already made considerable inroads. Increasing employment in factories and office buildings is causing the spread of the quick lunch, eliminating both the siesta and the midday meal at home.[4] However, until industry and urbanism become much more important in these countries, traditional attitudes of time will prevail.

Effort and optimism

Another aspect of work that influences Americans in their conduct and decisions is that tied up in the words, effort and optimism.

Effort is good in itself and with effort one can be optimistic about success. The high values connected with effort and activity pass quickly to the principle that, "It is better to do something than to sit back and do nothing." When there is an obstacle one should do something about it. Effort pays off with success. This thinking is based on the theory that the universe is mechanistic and man is its master and man is perfectible.[5] Thus, man can improve himself and control the part of the universe that is around him.

This national liking for effort and activity, and the optimism which holds that trying to do something about a condition or problem will almost invariably bring success in solving it, seems to be specifically American. Such attitudes are products of the continual expansion of culture during the past two hundred years, first along America's frontiers and later through its remarkable industrial growth. Obstacles exist to be overcome and bad conditions need only to be recognized in order to be rectified. Americans have confidence that, through effort, success will be achieved.

This traditional optimism of the American personality has been tempered to a certain extent in recent years because of international involvements, many of which present problems of a seriousness and complexity much greater than any faced previously. However, even if the optimism has been tempered (and perhaps realistically so), the method of overcoming obstacles has remained basically unchanged—put in a greater effort. If America has lagged in space achievements, or in the education of technical scientists, or in the development of successful international relations, the solution is to make a greater effort.

Effort and optimism also permeate the life of the individual American. Coming from an "open-class system" where status is usually achieved rather than inherited, both privilege and authority should be deserved and won. Effort, achievement, and success are woven throughout the fabric of American life and culture. Activist, pragmatist, and moralizing values rather than contemplative, theoretical, sensual, or mystical ones are integrated into the American character. Serious effort to achieve success is both a personal goal and an ethical imperative. The worthwhile man is the one who "gets results" and "gets ahead." A failure "gets nowhere," or "no results," for success is measured by results (though there

is some "credit for trying"). The successful man "tackles a problem," "does something about it," and in the process "gets ahead." His success is measured in terms of his positive solution of the problem. A failure is unsuccessful through his own fault. Even if he had "bad breaks," he should have "tried again." A failure in life "didn't have the guts" to "make a go of it" and "put himself ahead."

This is a very severe moral code. We do not know how widespread it is among Americans, but it is recognizable to all of us. It indicates a culture in which effort is rewarded, competition enforced, and merit and personal achievement recognized. Unfortunately, the code raises problems that occur even at home. For instance, it calls all those in high positions successes and all those in low ones failures, even though we know that there is "a need for Indians as well as chiefs."

We have rounded up these clichés, not only because they are so characteristic of Americans, but also because they illustrate the activist spirit that permeates our foreign work efforts. The drive to do something about bad conditions and to achieve success in overcoming them is particularly American. Like other traits of culture, we cannot expect to find an identical one among peoples elsewhere, particularly in non-industrial countries; and, like all virtues, this one has its pitfalls and can induce cultural blindness.

This American habit of evaluating effort, optimism, and practicality in terms of results and success means that merit is the main justification for authority or high position. When we observe that those in authority elsewhere have achieved their position through other values, we may react by bewilderment, anger, or cynicism. If we decide that they are wrong and that we should do something about it, we are surrendering to a typically American, activist judgment. We then not only risk alienating the only individuals who could work efficiently with us, but we also risk diluting and misdirecting our efforts. This is because the obstacles with which we must contend are not found in cultural differences but in specific technical and institutional problems.

Another pitfall caused by such judgments is the possibility of shifting (usually unconsciously) from a high evaluation of work, which many peoples may share in their own fashion, to a need for busywork, hurrying, and pressuring; in short, to encourage a love of activity for its own sake. This is easy to do. There is already a tendency among the civil servants in many of the underdeveloped countries to concentrate on paper work, a legacy of their colonial days; so a reinforcement of this attitude by a belief that work for its own sake is good will not help the situation.

To peoples in other parts of the world, a history of failure in recent decades and centuries is as commonplace as the successes of America. Their experiences may well have taught them to value not effort and optimism but endurance, passivity, pessimism, acceptance, pliancy, and evasion. It is not because they have no interest in getting things done, but because they had so many reversals during the period when America was achieving its greatness, that they lack the confidence of Americans.

Before undertaking a project, they may make many preparations which to Americans may seem extraneous; such as extensive consulting with others and the building up of a consensus; giving favors to win personal loyalties; trying to conciliate the proposed plans with religious and traditional beliefs; and considering minutely all alternatives, including the realistic alternative of not risking action at all. American demands for bustle and effort, for getting down to business, may not only be interpreted as nagging, pushing, and ill-mannered; but sometimes may also be downright frightening, especially when a wrong judgment could lead to disaster. After an initial failure the American determination to "try again" or to "try harder next time" may seem particularly foolhardy. Merely to intensify effort and try again on a bigger scale when resources are limited may appear to them as the most reckless compounding of original folly.

Misunderstandings have frequently occurred in international committee rooms between Americans or other Anglo-Saxons and Latin Americans because of the Latin use of rhetorical speech in discussions. Americans want to "get down to business," to confine themselves to the agenda at hand and to eliminate the flowery talk to which the Latins are accustomed. The Latins oppose such pressure. Such directness is not the way they settle problems.

American assumptions about effort and optimism include an active response to the challenge of obstacles and bad conditions and also a faith in progress and a constant view toward the future. American hopes for its families and communities are built around the children and the generation to follow. There is an accent on youthfulness. The ideals, as exemplified by commercial advertising and entertainment, almost always emphasize the young, and the old are not generally honored or sought out despite their experience. In general, elderly people are bypassed, either left in "old folks" homes or in retirement, and in either case, removed from the realm of practical life. This attitude differs greatly from that of non-Westerners, most of whom equate age with experience. The old are treated with deference and the oldest male is usually the arbiter of all family or community decisions.

American culture may be one of the few in which progress has long been a central value. This is because the American economy has progressed and expanded constantly ever since America emerged as an independent nation. In America, progress is equated with a better future, and with bigger and better successes; it also implies that the new and modern are explicitly better than the old and traditional. The experience of two world wars and the postwar international competition may have altered this view to a certain extent, but we still concentrate on the future and visualize it only as a better time than the present. Our technological and economic life must progress. No one expects it to be possible to keep America as it is today or as it was yesterday.

Americans should keep in mind that, for many peoples, their ages of glory were in the past, so the old ways are tried and true. Modernity and newness have no value in themselves for these peoples. Eventually they will change, because they know they must, but not because they feel life is constantly progressing.

Man and nature

The greater effort that marks the American response to obstacles may seem shallow, irreverent, or undignified to peoples of other cultures. Some obstacles do deserve respect and there are limitations to what man can do, even if he is the cleverest animal that has appeared so far. The American attitude toward nature is a case in point. For many Americans the natural environment is something to overcome, to improve, or to tear down and rebuild in a better way. American man attempts to conquer nature, so he breaks the soil, harnesses natural resources, and divides plants and animals into categories of useful and harmful. Harmful or undesirable plants are weeds and undesirable animals are vermin —the first to be uprooted or poisoned and the second to be trapped, shot, or poisoned. A botanical definition of a weed is "a plant growing out of place," from man's point of view, of course. The same yardstick could be applied to the definition of vermin.

Many of the American man's achievements are in a large measure due to his conquering attitude toward nature. The highest agricultural productivity in the world is only one of such achievements. This farming record, however, was also due to the very large expanses of land available in America. Even so, the American has paid, and is continuing to pay, certain prices for his agricultural success. Natural resources, particularly forests and waters, have been squandered and despoiled over large areas. Nature's balance has often been upset; and some conservationists now believe that the powerful insecticides being used to control such "pests" as the Japanese beetle and Dutch elm disease are destroying as many useful insects and birds as harmful ones.

This conquering attitude toward nature appears to rest on two assumptions: that the universe is mechanistic and man is its master; and that man is a categorically different form of ceature than all other forms of life. Specifically, they lack his unique attribute of a soul. In most of the non-Western world, nature is rarely conceived as being mechanistic and man is merely one form of life, different only in degree from the others. In most so-called animistic religions, all living creatures are believed to have something corresponding to a soul and there is no sharp dividing line between man, animals, and plants. Souls are even attributed to inanimate objects such as soil, rocks, mountains, and rivers. In the world of Hindus and Buddhists the belief in a cycle of rebirths strongly affirms man's kinship with nonhuman forms. In his endless cycle of life, a man can be an insect, an animal, another type of man, or a form of deity. Whether or not such beliefs are correct, many peoples' attitude toward nature is strongly influenced by them. Excluding Westerners, most people consider man and nature as one, and man works with nature rather than attempting to conquer it.

During long periods of trial and error, peoples of all cultures have worked out adaptations to their natural environment. Their adaptations may lack much by Western standards, but they do enable the inhabitants to get by, sometimes in quite difficult environments. Through experience, these peoples have evolved programs of conservation; methods of stretching and restoring their slim resources; and elaborate accommodations to climate, vegetation, and terrain. Some such adaptations, now embedded in tradition and religion, are: the Middle Eastern desert-derived patterns of Islamic ritual hygiene, austerity, and almsgiving; Japanese frugalities in house structure, farming, and woodworking technology; and Southeast Asian village economies in the measured use of rice, trees, and fish in the rainy lowlands. These and similar adaptations to natural environment are high developments in the balanced utilization of limited resources.

When, with a facile confidence that nature can be tamed by ever costlier, new mechanical devices, Americans or other Westerners attempt to brush aside the experience of centuries, it is perhaps exciting for the people being aided. However, they are not apt to be reassured if they have information concerning the realities of the environment that is ignored by the rushing, pushing, self-assured newcomers; particularly since the native solutions sometimes outlast the glamourous innovations. In environments that to us seem adverse, such as those of the rainy tropics, the arctics, or the desert, experience has shown that Western man's goods and machines do rot, rust, freeze, or grit up all too quickly, requiring huge and costly effort merely to keep them going. This is not surprising since our machinery has been developed primarily for use in a temperate zone where precipitation is spread more or less evenly throughout the year.

A graphic example of the lack of adaptability of Western machines occurred in recent years during the military struggles in Southeast Asia. Tanks and other mechanized land equipment were developed with the solid land of America and Europe in mind, but their use was drastically curtailed when the rice paddies of Vietnam and Laos became flooded. The mobile foot soldier, unencumbered with gear, could slip through the soggy fields and marshes and be constantly ready to fight, while the tank or halftrack was bogged down in mud. In 1960, a revolutionary faction in Laos merely waited until the rains had waterlogged the country to pull off a *coup d'état* in the capital.

They were well aware that the main army forces, equipped with tanks and other American machinery, could not reach the city until the land dried up six months later. Whether or not dog teams are preferable to snow tractors in the arctic, or black goatskin tents to expensively treated fabrics under the desert sun remain moot points.

Material well-being

The rich resources of America and the extraordinary growth of its industry and economy, have brought about a wide-spread wealth of material goods and possessions such as the world has never before seen. Among our people there has been a wholesale creation and diffusion of the marvels of modern comfort: swift, pleasant transportation, a great variety of foods, central heating, instantaneous hot water and electricity, labor-saving household devices, and comfortable homes. We like such comforts and continue to gear our industries to produce larger quantities and better versions of them. We have assigned a high value, almost a "right," to comfort.

Associated with this attitude toward comfort, and due to the state of our medical knowledge, we have also come to regard cleanliness as a virtue. "Cleanliness is next to Godliness," we say, and uncleanliness usually has undesirable.connotations or indicates low status. This does not mean that Americans have become "soft." In war and in overcoming obstacles or disaster we have proved our ability to face hardships. However, such times are only intermissions, endured in the belief that they will help us to re-establish the kind of life we value most, when our high standards of comfort and cleanliness will again prevail. In American civilization, such material well-being is both the criterion and the undeniable proof of success and progress.

Achievement and success are primarily measured in terms of material goods, both because they are abundant and because they are indicative of how much money an individual earns. Since there is little display value in the size of one's income or bank account, the average individual buys prestige articles that most people can readily observe: expensive clothing and furniture, fine cars, fancy houses and the endless variety of elaborate machinery with which they can be equipped—power mowers, barbecue paraphernalia, television and hi-fi sets, refrigerators, and dishwashing machines. A person's status is affected to a secondary extent by his level of education, type of occupation, and social behavior; but their value, too, is significant mainly in terms of how much income they help the individual obtain. For instance, a college professor who has earned his Ph.D. stands well below the status ranking of a business executive who may have no college education but who commands a much larger salary.

People other than Americans also value comfort and the saving of human labor but, not having been able to acquire as many labor-saving accessories as have Americans, they may have concentrated on the satisfactions of other needs. They may be more interested in achieving spiritual or esthetic goals than machines, which will shortly be outmoded anyway. Their choices are, of course, limited by their comparative poverty. Few other peoples have been able to have realistic hopes of obtaining all the varied devices that are available to the American. Therefore, comfort has not been so highly valued.

Given the opportunity, people of non-Western cultures may also turn to the satisfaction of their material wants. As they develop their productive capacity, this value will presumably grow with them. During the Mexican irrigation and road building program described previously, people tended to begin buying goods for their material well-being and comfort—better houses, new furniture, stoves, refrigerators, washing machines, air conditioners and motor vehicles. What they bought was dictated mainly by their financial position; that is, the wealthier people purchased more of the desired items; the poorer people less.[6] The demand for automobiles, better houses, and modern household devices is growing everywhere in the underdeveloped world. The emphasis on other values seems to outweigh those of material well-being and comfort only when the latter are unavailable, rather than being an indication of any basic preference for the less tangible values.

The world being as it is, divided roughly into have and have-not nations, there is one specific danger which the innovator may encounter. He will probably be quick to note the inferiority of comfort-producing mechanisms in the underdeveloped countries as compared to those to which he was accustomed at home. He may even tend to judge the host country by its possession or nonpossession of familiar conveniences, possibly punctuating his judgment by rude remarks about the state of the plumbing. He may have become so dependent on his native comforts as to spend a large share of his time and energy in achieving them or demanding them of his hosts.

There is no surer way to cut oneself off or gain the dislike of another people, particularly if they are poorer, than to insist ostentatiously and embarrassingly on the expensive luxuries of one's habitual way of life. Furthermore, to concentrate on creating an atmosphere of American comfort, a microcosm of American society and culture is thereby established, and it will tend to insulate itself from the local culture. It may be more convenient to buy all one's groceries in an American commissary. However, this means losing the opportunity to learn the buying patterns and dietary habits of the local people, a knowledge that could be partially learned by shopping at the local market. It may also be more convenient to travel in an American vehicle all the time; but this will eliminate the possibility of learning the bargaining procedures and transportation system of the local people.

In a study made in Trinidad, one of the authors usually travelled on the local jitneys along with a variety of Trinidadians. It turned out that the operation of such vehicles was quite a recent innovation, important economically as well as socially. A trip in one of these pirate taxis was a fine time and place to meet people and to gather information about the local culture. Total strangers, chatting with one another about local affairs, provided an excellent source of ethnographic information. There are many interesting and valuable experiences to be had in a non-Western culture, but material comfort is not apt to be one of them.

Moralizing

One of the most basic kinds of two-fold decisions Americans make is that of classifying actions and objects as good or bad. Whether discussing the conduct of foreign affairs or bringing up children, or any other action, it is generally agreed that Americans tend to moralize. While moralizing is one of the sources of America's great strength, it also creates pitfalls, particularly when it influences Americans in their relationships with other peoples.

Every people has its own code of morality as a part of its culture. A part of the inventory one must make to understand another people is the determination of the sort of judgments they habitually make about events, conduct and individuals. This can be difficult. We cannot assume that they will consider moral what we consider moral, or that their morals will be expressed as principles. Their moralities may rest on different bases from ours.

In many other cultures, rank or esteem, the dignity of a person, the honor of an individual, the compassion due an unfortunate, and the loyalty due a kinsman or co-religionist may all be important in moral judgments. Most forms of sexual behavior may not even be considered important in moral judgments; or where one sex (usually female) will be judged rigidly, the other will be judged very lightly. We are familiar with a morality based on the rule of law by a central government, and on a code of business and contract obligations of world commerce and industry. However, such concepts are new to most non-Western countries and often conflict with the old moralities.

The American habit of moralizing about behavior can lead to an even greater risk. It is more subtle and dangerous than mistaking a difference in moral standards as either amoral or "bad." It is the "cynicism" or "hard-boiled realism" acquired by Americans who over-react to the discovery that the model moral behavior they were taught to expect in parents, public servants, spouses, and other adults is not always present in real life. They react by becoming "tough," "cynical," and "wise" to the corruption of the world. Such reactions and recoil are dangerous because they encourage the cynic to believe that whatever varies from his version of the highest moral excellence is therefore of the lowest depravity. This view magnifies evil and turns what may merely be a difference in moral standards, or indifference to moralizing at all, into corruption. It leads an individual to seeing evil everywhere. The cynical moralizer who then goes on to action and decision may be pushing himself to wrong action that may be disastrous when working with another people.

An innovator should be particularly wary of one particular reaction that may develop from a cynical attitude. It is the anger that comes from the belief that many foreign countries, particularly the under-developed ones, are more graft-ridden, corrupt, dishonest, and unprincipled than our own. If one learns that educated officials divert a part of the American aid into their own pockets; that the policemen, clerks, and lesser functionaries make extra charges for processing forms through their offices; that businessmen connive at tax evasion or deal in black markets; or that landlords exact extortionary rents; it is all too easy to play the cynic. It is then easy to conclude that in these nations graft is universal, privilege unchecked, corruption general, and the situation hopeless. However, rather than making a moral judgment, it is much better to learn which customs, privileges, laws, obligations, immunities, and standards of value really prevail.

For example, the same merchant who connives at customs evasion may honor a debt within his guild for which no contract exists. Customs payments are a part of the Western system of collecting money, not comparable to guild responsibilities which involve traditional honor. A tribal chieftain in the Middle East may instigate a cattle raid (where he still can) yet tribal custom may oblige him to give his life to defend a guest's goods. On the other hand, the police law prohibiting cattle raiding is not a firm tradition, but a part of the new nationalism. In Muslim countries, a policeman may pocket a minor present. However, he may give his life trying to arrest a thief, because the religious laws of Islam prohibit stealing. All people have loyalties and a sense of responsibility, but in many countries these qualities are not yet tied in with their allegiance to the laws of the nation. In other words, nationhood has not yet been fully integrated into their lives.

When we make strong moral judgments about corrupt officials in other countries, we should keep in mind that in our own country such moral judgments are backed up by rigorous penalties. An official caught dealing in graft will have to face severe prosecution and an elaborate system of law designed to punish him. If this penalty system was not in force here, it is doubtful, despite all our moral indignation, that graft could be kept within reasonable bounds. Even with strong legal deterrents, there are still too many individuals willing to take bribes and risk detection. Our penalty system developed along with our culture during the period of America's expansion. Most of the underdeveloped countries, however, are too young as independent nations to

have yet elaborated similar systems. Where such systems do exist, they are still weak. Moreover, our codes of law and penalty, being largely based on European models, are for the most part foreign to their traditions. If the same weak penalties that prevail in the underdeveloped countries were the only legal deterrents in America, we might very well have even more graft and corruption than exists elsewhere.

Equality of men

The moralizing tendency is interrelated with another important trait of American culture—egalitarianism. Social equality is actually more of a moral idea than a fact of our lives. Great differences of wealth, education, influence, opportunity, and privilege exist in the United States. Nevertheless, the experiences that Americans underwent along the frontiers and through the process of immigration did represent a huge historical experiment in social leveling. Our legal and institutional heritage prescribes equal rights and condemns special privileges, and demands equal opportunity and representation for every citizen. Our national manners, with few exceptions (such as the old-fashioned racial etiquette of the once slave-holding South), are standardized for nearly all adult citizens. It is said that we make a cult of the Average Man. Inequality in achievement, merit, and worth is wrong, bad, or "unfair." When inequalities, based on hereditary status or special privilege, result in arrogant manners, or in an extravagant juxtaposition of wealth and misery or of pomp and abject humility, the average American is shocked and uncomfortable. He will often push to remedy such situations.

Egalitarian ideals are all to the good and they have certainly proven so on the American scene. However, people other than Americans have long since contributed to the common fund of such humanitarian concepts. The Muslims have always taught that all men are equal under Allah, and racial intolerance has been at a minimum among them. The Arabs have never refrained from marrying people of other racial groups. Most feelings of superiority found in Muslim countries are mainly a matter of supposed relationships with their prophet, Mohammed.

However, the majority of the world's societies are hierarchically organized, show marked class and caste differences, possess distinct aristocracies, elites, and other privileged groups, and most importantly, accept such inequalities as normal. In general, sociologists and anthropologists believe that the differences between whites and Negroes in the United States are of a caste-like nature. However, this has not changed the basic American value judgment of equality among men. Open patterns of subordination, deference, and acceptance of underprivilege call forth humanitarian sympathies (American style) for the "underdog," and American values call for efforts to do something about such matters. This impulse to act tempts us, on our own moral grounds, to interfere directly in the way of life and the systems of values of peoples. To the American's patience, it is trying to have to deal with persons whose authority seems neither justified nor deserved, or to wait for the ordinary man who will act only when he has received the go-ahead from his figures of prestige or respect. Yet, with hierarchically organized people, the traditional approvals must be obtained.

One of the more recent forms of egalitarianism on the American scene is that of the comparative equality of the sexes. In practice, women are barred from the highest positions in our nation and are discriminated against in certain professions. However, their treatment is more nearly equated with that of males than in practically all non-Western nations. Most Americans consider marriage a kind of partnership, an unusual kind of marriage among the cultures of the world. This is a product of our liberal history and, at least insofar as the economy is concerned, it has proved beneficial.

Some social commentators feel that, despite its economic advantages, this concept of marriage has brought about other sorts of disabilities. In any event, it has not yet been proven that equality of the sexes is best for all peoples in all cultures. Furthermore, this kind of equality may prove to be irrelevant in developing more efficient technologies and institutions in other lands. People in other societies may have strong feelings about the status of women. Therefore, unless inequalities between the sexes are definitely limiting development or change, it is usually best to work within the prevailing system of values. If change does come in this sphere, it will have to come from the local people themselves.

American ideals of equality tend to create

another difficulty. It is that of discerning local figures of aristocratic or prestige leadership when they do exist. If democratically-minded Americans find it hard to spot hierarchical patterns or organization, it is because too many of their own values and preconceptions stand in the way. For instance, that impoverished aristocrats or ascetic priests, beggarly in dress and looks, can still command respect and allegiance, despite their lack of outward signs of visible achievement and "success," is a difficult concept for Americans to grasp. Some people, like the Japanese, present another enigma; for they practice a kind of faceless leadership in which string-pullers exert their authority behind conspicuous but powerless puppet or ceremonial figures in public office.

A minor consequence of American egalitarianism is a preference for simple manners and for direct, informal, unpatronizing treatment of other persons. Americans are known for their informality and this can work to their genuine advantage if kept within limits. But, when abroad, a slavish adherence to simple, unaffected manners and forms of address can be disastrous. Especially in countries where people do differ in rank and prestige, Americans are likely to give offense if they are brusque, breezy and "kidding," treating all persons alike and impersonally. It is much better to try to acquire some of the local usages of long titles, flowery forms of address, language, and manners of courtesy and deference than to try to accustom foreigners to American ways. To neglect giving a man his due deference in countries where rank is important is to insult him. The American tendency of trying to make a foreigner into a regular or average guy by an informal, breezy, and "kidding" approach is dangerous. The informality of genuine kindness, courtesy, and unostentatious living is worth retaining. But when informality means belittling or disparaging a person whom his own society ranks high, then it is not advisable. American "kidding" and humor are very special products of an egalitarian culture. They are best kept at home.

In America, since all men are supposed to be potentially equal, and since success is an important individual goal, then a high value must be assigned to individuality. The characteristic is largely a heritage of our frontier days, when there was plenty of room and opportunity for the individual to achieve that of which he was capable. Due to the expansion of our industrial economy, and due to the increasing complexity and population of our society, individual action can no longer solve all problems. Cooperation is a necessity nowadays when large groups of people must work together. In the frontier days this was true to an extent, but the necessity became greater as the frontier became smaller and ultimately disappeared. Even then, because equality was a value, the manner of achieving individuality was not by accenting uniqueness but by stressing similarities. One might have more and better things than another, but they should be more or less the same kind of things. In this sense, even individuality evolved into a kind of conformity.

In America today, conformity has been emphasized even more by the necessity of living together in large groups, of accomplishing most of our aims through group effort (because it is more efficient). The organization man has superseded the rugged individualist. People are integrated into society through cooperation. Another indication of the weakening emphasis on individualistic action is the growing demand for security. There are only a few individuals who, through their own unaided efforts, are willing to risk an unknown future. Most Americans prefer to surround themselves with group insurances that cover all contingencies. In their efforts to attract new employees, employers advertise insurance benefits as much as the challenge of the work and the salary; and people buy insurance for the smallest items in their lives. Even household machines can be insured against breakdown. Government, too, becomes more and more involved in insuring the welfare of its citizens.

Humanitarianism

There is another value associated with egalitarianism that is also interrelated with our moralizing based on principles. It is the widespread and justly famous American trait of humanitarianism, which so often expresses itself as generosity. Americans respond liberally to calls for help and give all they can to others when disaster strikes. The amount of efficiency they can display at such times is amazing.

A dramatic illustration of American competence during a tragic aftermath of a battle occurred recently in Laos just after the capital city, Vientiane, had been heavily damaged by military action. The American technical aid efforts in the years preceding had not been particularly impressive. They had been bogged down to a considerable extent by cultural problems with the Lao, as well as by administrative problems in the American organization itself. But when the capital was attacked and heavily damaged, and the population was in difficult straits, the American aid organization (International Cooperation Administration), as well as other American groups in the city, went into action in a manner that was truly remarkable. After the attack, the city was badly damaged; but within two or three weeks it was on its feet again, primarily due to American planning and work. The Americans thought nothing of working day and night at this task and their organizational ability was clearly demonstrated. In three or four months the marks of the battle were almost obliterated, all primarily due to American action in emergency.

American humanitarianism is certainly one of the finest heritages from our pioneer ancestors. The only possible pitfall in our manner of expressing this quality is that it is usually highly organized, institutional, and impersonal. For many other peoples humanitarianism is highly personal and sometimes entails taking into one's house and social life the recipient of generosity. The people of poorer countries do not usually share with everyone; they cannot. However, they do have their own patterns of sharing: through personal and kinship obligations, by religious almsgiving, and in other ways. The American pattern of impersonal generosity need cause no difficulty if we do not let it blind us to the existence of other patterns; if we remember that other peoples are just not as rich as we are; and if we do not turn our method of giving into a harsh standard of judgment against the peoples who lack it.

Let us take an example from the traditional land of beggars, *baksheesh,* and the outstretched palm—the Middle East. Here the halt, lame, and blind line up at the mosque or church door. The naive American reaction is likely to be condemnatory. "All these poor people! This community must be very cruel or backward not to take care of these people!"

A deeper look into the realities of Middle Eastern social and cultural organization shows that these beggars are, in fact, being taken care of by the community. Every member of the faithful in Islam gives ten percent of his income (the *zaka*) in direct alms to the unfortunates who personally ask for it. "Give a little and get a blessing in return." This particular pattern of generosity is one that has been worked into the communal life of the society, in keeping with its meager resources. Do not conclude that the people who support such a system are heartless and ungenerous, or assume that the beggars are making a good thing of it. The difference between this kind of generosity and the Community Chest is mainly one of organization and personalization.

Notes

[1] Cora DuBois, "The Dominant Value Profile in American Culture," in *American Anthropologist*, Vol. 57, No. 6, Pt. 1: 1955, p. 1233.

[2] Richard N. Adams, "A Study of Labor Preferences in Peru," in *Human Organization*, Vol. 10, No. 3: 1951.

[3] Carleton Coon, *Caravan: The Story of the Middle East*, Henry Holt, New York 1951.

[4] Oscar Lewis, "Mexico since Cardenas," in *Social Change Today*, Harper and Bros., New York: 1960, p. 297.

[5] DuBois, *op. cit.*, pp. 1233–1234.

[6] Charles J. Erasmus, *Man Takes Control*, University of Minnesota Press, Minneapolis: 1961, pp. 240–242.

DEVIANCE AND SUBCULTURE

Just as large groups contain within them smaller subgroups, so do large-scale cultures contain subcultures. To each small group within the larger there pertains a subculture. Only in a general way can it be said that a complex society has a single culture.

The cultures of subgroups will depart to a greater or lesser extent from the general or dominant culture. Where the differences are relatively small, we speak of variant subcultures. For instance, Spanish-Americans place less stress on the value of time than the general American culture would lead one to expect.

Other groups within a society may possess subcultures that can be called deviant, insofar as they depart to a great extent from the dominant culture, and may even stress values that are in opposition to those of the dominant culture. "Professional" criminals, homosexuals, and narcotics addicts, for example, have well-developed subcultures containing values which are in contradiction to those of the dominant culture.

This selection concerns rebellious youth. Sociology and the related social sciences contain a great deal of discussion of the nature and causes of youthful rebellion. Matza here presents a very original analysis indicating that the deviant cultures of rebellious youth have close analogues in variant but respectable youth cultures, and that the deviant values of the rebels reflect subordinate or "subterranean" themes that exist even in the dominant culture.

> Most youth are not rebels, and the amount of rebelliousness in youth has not increased over the years in recent times. However, among all the age groups of society rebelliousness is greatest in young people, and the form of their rebellion requires explanation.
>
> Youthful rebellion takes place in three main forms: delinquency, radicalism, and Bohemianism. They are similar (and hence deviant) in their hostility to the "bourgeois" order of the dominant culture, but they differ in the matters of self-consciousness, social ambition, and rationale. Delinquency stresses the themes of excitement, material gain, and aggressive masculinity. Radicalism stresses idealism, populism, and evangelism. Bohe-

mianism stresses romanticism, expressionism, monasticism, and unconventionality. Variant versions of these deviant cultures, which are more acceptable in the dominant culture, are "teenage culture," doing good, and various forms of academic culture.

Unanswered questions in this essay concern why some youth are unable to weather the status crises associated with being young in our society by means of the variant subcultures, and what factors account for the choice among the deviant subcultures. The most current theories answer these questions not only in terms of the degrees of frustration that are experienced by youths of various backgrounds, but also in terms of the opportunities, whether deviant or variant, that are in fact open to them. Organized delinquency, for example, is not as easily available to alienated youth from middle-class neighborhoods as it is to those in the slums. At present the black nationalist movement is offering to the youth of the Negro ghetto an opportunity to engage in radicalism which was not available to the same extent in previous generations. The trends in youthful rebelliousness, then, may be expected to follow changes in the strainfulness of being young in various positions in the social structure, as well as changes in the relative opportunities for one form of rebellion as compared with others.

Selection 16
SUBTERRANEAN TRADITIONS OF YOUTH
David Matza

The rebellious character of youth has periodically troubled serious-minded adults since the appearance of modern civil life. While the major purpose of this paper is to describe some patterns of youthful rebelliousness, and not to inquire into their causes, it will be useful to begin with a brief discussion of some theories regarding youth's vulnerability to rebelliousness, and the evidence on which theories presumably rest.

The vulnerability of youth

The primary object of Kingsley Davis' two essays on youth written some twenty years ago was to explain the rebelliousness of youth in modern society as contrasted with the docility allegedly found in more primitive societies.[1] Among the reasons given was the fact that, although parents and youth remain together, the viewpoints of parents are primarily shaped during their own childhood; thus, friction is likely whenever the rate of change in customary attitudes is rapid. Furthermore, Davis suggested that the contemporary domination of the principle of merit results in tension and frustration by providing the basis for dispute regarding rightful incumbency in scarce positions and relative claims over scarce rights and perquisites. Moreover, he argued that adults tend to realism because of their greater stake in the system and because they are implicated in the compromises necessary in any ongoing social order. Youth, standing outside the establishment and not responsible for its defects, is likely to oscillate between what seems to adults an overdemanding idealism and a merciless cynicism.

Other writers have indicated additional sources of tension in the position of youth. Benedict, Erikson, Bloch and Niederhoffer, and many others, have stressed the crisis of identity inherent in a society which defines adolescence and youth ambiguously.[2] Parsons has emphasized the effects of an adult stress on performance.[3] Some have stressed the frustrating effects of a puritanical repression of sexuality, and others, of the post-Kinsey era, lament the effects of the stimulation provided by a sex-obsessed culture.[4] Whatever the dif-

Reprinted from the *Annals of the American Academy of Political and Social Science*, 338, 1961, pp. 102–118, with permission of the author and the publisher.

ference in opinion regarding the source, there seems to be a general consensus that something requires explaining, and this something usually turns out to be youthful rebelliousness.

Most empirical evidence seems to support this consensus, provided we limit our assertions in two ways. First, we may not contend that extremist versions of youthful rebelliousness characterize anything like a majority of the youthful population. Rather, it seems that the great majority of American youth behave either in a conventional manner[5] or participate in conventional versions[6] of deviant youth traditions; this, despite the fact that many youths are vulnerable to rebelliousness. Second, there seems no reason to believe that there have been any long-run increases or decreases in rates of youthful rebelliousness during the modern era. Rather, it seems likely that rates of some forms of youthful rebelliousness have increased somewhat over the last twenty-five years, whereas rates of other forms have declined. Even in those modes of rebelliousness like delinquency, where rates during the last twenty-five years have apparently increased, there is some evidence that rates fifty years ago were higher than those currently experienced.[7] During the decade of the fifties, a decline in youthful radicalism gave rise to the feeling that an age of conformity was upon us. There seems no firm ground for this suspicion. Periods of prosperity have often signaled a decline in radical activity.

What may we contend? First, within the life cycle, the apex of rebelliousness is reached during the period of youth, before and after which rates of rebelliousness seem considerably lower.[8] This holds, by hypothesis, for the three modes of youthful rebelliousness to be discussed in this paper: delinquency, radicalism, and Bohemianism. This means that the youthful spirit of rebelliousness coincides more or less with chronological youth.[9] Second, we contend that because of the persistent vulnerability of youth, traditions of each mode have emerged; distinctive viewpoints have remained relatively stable in content and location.[10] And, finally, that these traditions of youthful rebelliousness—delinquency, radicalism, and Bohemianism—are in the nature of subterranean traditions in American life.

The subterranean tradition

The major contribution of sociology to the understanding of deviance has consisted of two fundamental insights. First, persistent deviance is typically not a solitary enterprise; rather, it requires and most often receives group support. Second, deviance does not typically represent an historical innovation; rather, it has a history in particular neighborhoods and locales. Thus, the individual deviant is linked to the society in minimal fashion through companies of deviants and through localized traditions. To speak of subterranean traditions is to extend the notion of linking to the wider social system; it is to posit connections between localized deviant traditions and the broader traditions of conventional society. The notion of subterranean implies that there is an ongoing dialectic between conventional and deviant traditions and that, in the process of exchange, both are modified.[11]

Subterranean traditions of youth have a number of common aspects which suggest a definition of the concept. First, they are traditions which are publicly denounced. Second, the extreme versions of these traditions are adhered to by only a small proportion of the youthful population. Third, these traditions are familiar to and tolerated by broad segments of the adult population. Fourth, conventional versions of these traditions are experienced by broad segments of the youthful population. Fifth, these traditions are viewed with ambivalence in the privacy of contemplation by a majority of adults, and, thus, public reactions are subject to faddish oscillation ranging from sympathetic tolerance to outright suppression.[12] To point to the existence of subterranean traditions is to suggest that no one in any society is fully socialized or fully respondent to public expectations;[13] as a consequence, whenever there are available counterthemes there will be varying degrees of indulgence in these traditions ranging from relatively complete immersion to occasional vicarious appreciation.

Subterranean traditions of youth

Delinquency, radicalism, and Bohemianism are the extremist versions of subterranean youth traditions. They impart a spirit of rebelliousness and impetuosity that seems consistent with the sort of tensions ordinarily attributed to the position of youth. These kinds of behavior exhibit what is frequently termed immaturity or irresponsibility.[14] However, the lumping together of delinquency, radicalism, and Bohemianism requires more systematic justification. Thus, it will be useful to briefly discuss their similarities, over and above their apparent temperamental affinity, and to specify the differences between them.

Similarities. First, the traditions in question seem to have a greater appeal to youth than to the population at large. Second, all three have distinct anticivil implications, at least over the short run. All three are "threats" to the stability and order of an ongoing system. Third, all three are specifically antibourgeois, although in different ways. The delinquent, for instance, does not renounce bourgeois property arrangements, but he violates them. He does reject the bourgeois sentiments of methodism and routine, particularly as they are manifested within the school system. The Bohemian's attitude toward bourgeois property arrangements is typically one of indifference, although he is appalled by the commercialization ordinarily associated with these arrangements. His ire is especially reserved for the puritanical and methodical elements of the bourgeois ethos. Moreover, the Bohemian is typically antagonistic to recent trends in bourgeois society. He is opposed to the mechanized, organized, centralized, and increasingly collectivized nature of modern capitalism. The radical tradition envisages a less general denunciation. Particularly in the varieties of revolutionary Marxism, which represent the most important examples of modern radicalism, the primary focus of radical attack has been on the capitalist system of political and economic domination and on the imperialist role allegedly played by such systems in international affairs. The methodical, the puritanical, and, especially, the industrial aspects of the bourgeois order have been more or less embraced.

Thus, we see that each subterranean tradition has been hostile to the bourgeois order, but each has followed a somewhat different line of attack.

Differences. First, delinquency differs from both radicalism and Bohemianism with respect to the specific age of vulnerability. However, the stage of education seems a more decisive point of division than age per se. Delinquency is a high school phenomenon; it seems most pronounced among that section of youth which terminates its education during or at the end of high school. Radicalism and Bohemianism, particularly in the United States, are apparently enmeshed within the system of higher education. Its adherents are typically drawn from those whose education terminates during college, with the attainment of a bachelor's degree, or with some graduate work of indeterminable duration.

Second, they differ with respect to the degree of self-consciousness attained. Radicalism and Bohemianism are intellectually self-conscious and represent explicit and reasonably coherent critiques of modern society; the delinquent critique tends to be implicit. Furthermore, radicalism and Bohemianism possess a written literature; delinquency is almost by necessity an oral tradition.

Third, the modes of rebelliousness differ with respect to their ambitions. Delinquency has no designs on society; there is no desire on the part of delinquents to reconstruct it. Thus, in Merton's terms, they are aberrant.[15] Radicals, on the other hand, wish to reshape society in the form of their own ideological predilections. Thus, they are the archetype of Merton's nonconformist.[16] Bohemians fall somewhere between, typically wishing to develop a private and insulated way of life but rarely having any aspiration to convert the rest of society.

Fourth, the modes of rebelliousness differ with respect to assessments regarding their moral worth. In the case of delinquency, the judgments of its adherents seem to coincide with those belonging to conventional society.[17] There is no serious belief in either camp in the moral value of the delinquent enterprise. On the other hand, there has been considerable dispute regarding the moral value of radicalism and Bohemianism. Many intellectuals attribute varying degrees of moral value to them; those of lesser intellect have probably been less generous. Moreover, radicals and Bohemians, unlike delinquents, are convinced of the moral value of their enterprises.

Despite these differences, we have suggested that there is a spiritual affinity between delinquency, radicalism, and Bohemianism; all are modes of youthful rebelliousness. Each represents a subterranean tradition of American youth. Thus, an analysis of youthful deviance requires an examination of each tradition. It is to that task that we now turn.

Delinquency: spirit and substance[18]

There are many perceptive accounts describing the behavior of juvenile delinquents and their underlying values.[19] Although there have been important differences of opinion in the interpretation of this material and in the relative stress placed on various components, there exists a striking consensus on the content of delinquent values. Three themes describing the spirit of the delinquent enterprise and two defining its substance, or business, seem implicit in these accounts.

The distinctive feature of the spirit of delinquency is the celebration of prowess. Each of the themes in the delinquent tradition develops an aspect of the meaning of prowess. First, delinquents are deeply immersed in a restless search for excitement, "thrills" or "kicks." According to the delinquent code, the approved style of life is an adventurous one. Activities pervaded by displays of daring and charged with danger are highly valued in comparison with more mundane and routine patterns of behavior. Although delinquent acts do not exhaust the field of adventurous activities, they make up an important component of activities that may be feasibly viewed as adventurous. The fact that an activity involves breaking the law is often the fact that lends it its air of excitement. In fact, "kicks" or "action" may come to be defined with clear awareness as "any action tabooed by 'squares' that heightens and intensifies the present moment of experience and differentiates it as much as possible from the humdrum routines of daily life."[20] In courting physical danger, experimenting with the forbidden, and provoking the authorities, the delinquent is not simply enduring hazards; he is creating them in an attempt to manufacture excitement. For many delinquents, "the rhythm of life fluctuates between periods of relatively routine and repetitive activities and sought situations of greater emotional stimulation."[21]

Second, to attain prowess is to seek and receive the material rewards of society while avoiding, in the manner of a leisure class, the canons of school and work with their implicit commitments to methodism, security, and routine. Thus, delinquents commonly exhibit a disdain for "getting on" in the realms of school or work. In its place, there is a sort of aimless drifting or grandiose dreams of quick success.

However, the delinquent must be financed if he is to attain the luxury of the sporting life. Although some writers have coupled the delinquent's disdain of work with a disdain of money, it seems unlikely that money is renounced in the delinquent code; it would seem more accurate to say it is treated in a special way. Money is valued, but not for purposes of a careful series of expenditures or long-range objectives. Money, for the delinquent, is luxury and not regular income; and the modesty of the sums involved, for what are, after all, children, has obscured this fact. Money is viewed as something to be squandered in gestures of largesse, in patterns of conspicuous consumption. An age-old method of facilitating this is gambling among peers. A major function of this sort of gambling, whatever its motive, is to redistribute scarce finances so that, over the long run, each member of the group may play at luxury. This hardly exhausts the ways in which prowess may be used in the sudden acquisition of "large" sums of money. The other techniques involve incursions on the world of outsiders—the victims.

Simple expropriation—theft and its variants —must be included, of course; but it is only one of a variety of ways of "scoring" and does not always carry great prestige in the eyes of delinquents.[22] Other forms of prowess include chicanery or manipulation which may take the form of borrowing from social workers or more elaborate forms of "hustling"; an emphasis on "pull," frequently with reference to obtaining a "soft" job assumed to be available only to those with influential connections. Thus, there are a variety of means, ranging in legality from theft to the holding of a soft job, all of which are exhibitions of prowess, all of which may be applied in the pursuit of luxury.

A third theme running through the accounts of juvenile delinquency centers on aggression. This is the third component of prowess. The code of the warrior, which in many ways the delinquent code reflects, calls for an aggressive manliness, a reluctance to accept slights on one's honor.[23] The delinquent's readiness for aggression is particularly emphasized in the analysis of juvenile gangs in the slum areas of large cities. It is in such gangs that we find the struggles for "turf," and, thus, it is in these cases that the applicability of the warrior code is most apparent. Cloward and Ohlin have pointed out that we can be led into error by viewing these conflict-oriented delinquents as typical of all delinquents.[24] Yet, the gang delinquent's use of violence for the maintenance of honor, or "rep," and the proof of courage, or "heart," seems to express in extreme form the idea that aggression is a demonstration of toughness and, thus, of masculinity; and it is this idea which pervades delinquent thought. Whatever the degree of differentiation among delinquent subcultures, the concept of *machismo*,[25] of the path to manhood through the ability to take it and hand it out, is foreign to the average delinquent only in name.

Finally, let us turn to the substance of delinquency—the business of the delinquent enterprise. The substance of delinquency is defined by the legal code and contains two major elements. First, there is victimization. This includes larceny and all of its variants, assaults on persons or on property, that is, vandalism, and a host of less frequently committed offenses, all involving victims. Second, there are status offenses, activities which are expressly prohibited for juveniles but which may be performed by adults, within limits, with legal impunity. This includes truancy, drinking, gambling, driving cars, runaway, indulgence in sex, and, in some jurisdictions, smoking, swearing, staying out late, and a host of vaguely defined forms of misconduct. However, while these activities are officially delinquent, the law, particularly at the level of police enforcement, exhibits considerable discretionary tolerance with regard to youngsters exhibiting these forms of behavior, particularly if their dossiers are otherwise clean.[26]

Student radicalism: spirit and substance

Compared to the many accounts of delinquency, there are relatively few systematic descriptions of student radicalism in the United States.[27] Enough exists, however, to proceed with a tentative description of this tradition.[28]

Radicalism among students did not begin in the decade of the Thirties, although there is little question that it reached its height during that period. The Intercollegiate Socialist Society was organized in 1905, and by 1921 Calvin Coolidge decried student radicalism.[29] Despite the internecine struggles within the revolutionary socialist movement since 1905, some aspects of the radical tradition have remained relatively stable. What are the stable components of modern student radicalism?

First, there is the vision of apocalypse.[30] This refers to "the belief that the evil world as we know it, so full of temptation and corruption, will come to an end one day and will be replaced by a purer and better world."[31] This tradition has its origins in the apocalyptic outlook of the prophets of the Old Testament and has been passed down through the early Christians and adherents of heretical sects. Its modern recipients, suggests Shils, are "the modern revolutionary movements and above all the Marxian movements."[32] The tradition is best reflected in "doctrinaire politics, or the politics of the ideal."[33]

Whatever its general importance in revolutionary socialism, the politics of the ideal seems peculiarly well suited to the predispositions of youthful rebelliousness. This sort of politics seems perfectly consistent with Davis' description of youth's mixture of idealism and cynicism. In the politics of the ideal, perception and assessment become bifurcated with respect to idealism and cynicism. On this side of the apocalypse, one views and interprets events critically and cynically; on the other side, or in some contemporary foreshadowing of the future, one views and interprets events idealistically and generously.

The second component of the spirit of student radicalism is populism. "Populism is the belief in the creativity and in the superior worth of the ordinary people, of the uneducated and the unintellectual."[34] Because of the central role of populism in modern radicalism, revolutionary movements have tended to equate the apocalypse with the liberation of the folk. The particular folk celebrated has varied: in the Russian social revolutionary movement, it was the peasant; in traditional Marxism, it is the industrial proletariat; in the anarchism of Bakunin, it tended to be the *lumpenproletariat*. American student radicalism, largely unaware of these esoteric distinctions, has tended to lump these populist ideals together, arriving at a compote consisting of migrant farm workers, unskilled and semi-skilled industrial workers, and Negroes.

Among students, the appeal of populism is not simply an outgrowth of traditional radical propensities. Just as the apocalyptic mentality has a special appeal to youth, so, too, does populism. Students have a special affinity for populism because it serves an important function; populism, for students, is an effective attack on the presumption of professorial authority and a neat way of defending against unflattering assessment. For the radical, and for the Bohemian, too, a belief in populism allows students who perceive themselves as vanguard or avant garde to deflect the contrary judgments of their academic elders.

A third component of the student radical spirit is evangelism. Evangelism refers to excursions made by sectarians to the outside

world for the purpose of recruiting sympathizers, supporters, and members. It is an intensively active sort of belief. Thus, it is well
suited to the exuberance and impetuosity
characteristic of rebellious youth. Evangelism
plays an especially important role since, compared to Bohemianism, radicalism would
otherwise be too serious an enterprise to compete effectively for rebellious youth. Evangelism notwithstanding, student radicalism remains chronically vulnerable to Bohemianism
within its ranks.[35] Thus, evangelism seems as
important in the bolstering of internal enthusiasm as in its alleged purpose of gaining new
adherents. By encouraging excursion, it allows
student radicals to stray from the routine of
the radical enterprise,[36] and challenges his
capacities for argumentation, intimidation,
persuasion, and seduction.

The substance of student radicalism is unconventional political action. Its round-of-life
consists of taking stands on concrete issues,
circulation of petitions, distribution of leaflets,
sale of literature, raising funds, demonstrations and rallies, frequent meetings, discussions, debates, and the like. The mundane
character of most of these activities is more or
less obscured by the context within which they
are viewed. This context is provided by the
general characteristics of unconventional politics.

Radical politics is extremist rather than
moderate.[37] It is less attentive than conventional politics to the administrative bylaws
which govern collegiate activity. Thus, elements of excitement and risk are introduced.
Moreover, radical politics is revolutionary
rather than simply reformist. A revolutionary
orientation adds meaning and drama to concrete activities, and it provides a basis for
vicarious excitement by requiring identification with actual revolutions taking place elsewhere. Furthermore, radical politics is ideological rather than "market"[38] politics, and,
thus, a sense of moral superiority attaches to
the activities of the enterprise. Finally, radical
politics is year-round rather than seasonal,
and, thus, imparts a sense of urgency rarely
apparent in conventional politics. In summary,
each of the characteristics of unconventional
politics conspires to transform the mundane to
the extraordinary. Thus it is that what appears
to the uninitiated a serious and dull business is
converted to an enterprise with some appeal
for rebellious youth.

Bohemianism: spirit and substance

Bohemianism is a socioartistic enterprise
which appeared as a widespread phenomenon
in the first part of the nineteenth century in
France.[39] Since then, it has spread to many
parts of the world, particularly Europe and
the United States. Despite indigenous sources
in the United States and despite internal influences, the periods of rise and fall have coincided fairly well with its cycles in France.[40]
Beat, the most recent expression of American
Bohemianism, is best viewed as a response to
recurrent internal conditions which have typically favored its resurgence, most notably
prosperity of the postwar variety and as a reflection of developments on the French scene,
most notably the emergence of *café* existen-
tialism.

The failure to understand the traditional
character of Bohemianism in selected American locales and the failure to see its ebb and
flow as a reflection of recurrent social process,
internal and external, has been largely responsible for alarmist interpretations of beat. Beat
has been viewed, alternatively, as a sign of
incipient nihilist rebellion and a symbol of
hedonistic withdrawal from public life. It has
been interpreted as a symptom of some deeper
malady and a dark foreboding of what is to
come. Interpretations of this sort should be expected whenever deviant patterns are not
viewed in their historical context.[41] What are
the persistent components of the Bohemian
tradition, and why may beat be properly
viewed as its most recent American expression?

Romanticism. The first and major component of Bohemianism is romanticism. Romanticism, suggests Shils, "starts with the appreciation of the spontaneous manifestations of
the essence of concrete individuality. Hence it
values originality . . . that which is produced
from the 'genius' of the individual (or the
folk), in contrast with the stereotyped and
traditional actions of the philistine."[42] The
commitment to spontaneity and originality has
had many manifestations among traditional
Bohemians, particularly in the graphic arts.[43]
Among beats, however, greater stress has been
placed on development of originality and
spontaneity in other art forms. Most notable
among these have been the celebration of improvisation in modern jazz, poetry, and the

novel. For this reason, and for others, jazz and jazz musicians have occupied an exalted role in the beat point of view. Kerouac, the most notable literary exponent of improvisation, has occupied a similarly exalted position.[44]

The exaltation of spontaneity in artistic endeavor is reflected in the Bohemian view of the folk. Bohemianism, like radicalism, has a distinctive form of populism, which is best termed "primitivism." Its authentic folk hero is, of course, the gypsy. Due, perhaps, to the gypsy's chronic unavailability, it was not long before the notion of primitive folk was expanded to include more visible groupings. The closest approximation that could be found in urban society was the *lumpenproletariat*, and it is this group that has occupied a central place in the Bohemian's primitivist mystique.[45] In the modern rendition of Bohemianism, the mantle of idealized folk has largely fallen on the lower-class Negro.[46] However, the Negro is not the first American ethnic group to be granted this dubious honor. East European Jews, too, were perceived by previous Bohemians as the incarnation of primitive folk.[47]

Closely connected to the celebration of the primitive is the tradition of dedicated poverty. "A neighborhood where the poor live, the poor who are resigned to their poverty, is the best environment in which to live 'the life.' This is a cardinal principle which the beat share with the Bohemians of the past."[48] Although the dedication to poverty is, in part, a natural outgrowth of a commitment to primitivism, it is simultaneously a conscious way of avoiding the corrupting influence of the commercial world. Among beats, dedicated poverty is taken for granted. It is hardly a subject for debate. What is discussed are "ways of 'making it' . . . with as little commercial work as possible, or ideally, with no commercial work at all."[49]

A final aspect of romanticism seems wholly consistent with primitivism. It consists of a more or less complete rejection of bureaucratic-industrial society. This may be referred to as medievalism and is best described as an apocalyptic view without the apocalypse. Medievalism accepts the first part of the apocalyptic formula, man's fall from grace,[50] but makes no provision, as in radicalism, for man's redemption.[51]

In many respects, the beat's medievalism is similar to a more conventional intellectual view embodied in the theory of mass culture. Shils suggests:[52]

> The critical interpretation of mass culture rests on a distinct image of modern man, of modern society and of man in past ages. . . . According to this view, the ordinary consumer of popular culture is something new in the world. He is a "private atomic subject," utterly without religious beliefs, without any private life, without a family that means anything to him; he is standardized, ridden with anxiety, perpetually in a state of exacerbated unrest, his life emptied of meaning, trivialized, alienated from his past, his community, and possibly from himself, cretinized and brutalized.

Thus, the beat's rejection of modern life[53] is linked to the larger society through its affinity with the theory of mass culture, just as it is linked to the past through the tradition of what we shall call morose Bohemianism.

Expressive authenticity and the Bohemian moods. The second component of the Bohemian tradition is the insistence on the expression of authentic inner feelings. Thus, Bohemianism has been marked by an intense moodiness. Mood is not to be suppressed or obscured; rather, it is to be indulged, pursued, and exhibited. Mood is a crucial part of inner, or authentic, experience and, thus, deserves unhampered expression. Because of the dedication to the full expression of mood, Bohemianism has always been somewhat perplexing to the outsider who expects some consistency of temperament to accompany a reasonably coherent viewpoint.

Bohemianism has long had two faces which, although they are often combined in the career of the same person, have been manifested in two roughly differentiated streams. There is frivolous Bohemianism, reminiscent in many respects of aristocratic "dandyism"; and there is morose Bohemianism, initiated by Poe and popularized by Baudelaire.[54] After Baudelaire, the two moods persist and are reflected in beat in the modern distinction between "hot" and "cool."[55]

> By 1948 the hipsters, or beatsters, were divided into cool and hot. Much of the misunderstanding about . . . the Beat Generation . . . derives from the fact that there are two distinct styles of hipsterism; the cool today is your bearded laconic sage . . . before a hardly touched beer in

a beatnik dive, whose speech is low and unfriendly, whose girls say nothing and wear black: The "hot" today is the crazy talkative shining-eyed (often innocent and openhearted) nut who runs from bar to bar, pad to pad, looking for everybody, shouting, restless, lushy, trying to "make it" with subterranean beatniks who ignore him. Most beat generation artists belong to the hot school. . . . In many cases the mixture is 50–50. It was a hot hipster like myself who finally cooled it in Buddhist meditation, though when I go in a jazz joint I still feel like yelling "Blow, baby, Blow!"

Thus, in the insistence on the authentic display of mood, and in the development of frivolous and morose subtraditions, Bohemianism has pushed to the limits of human expression. It has had a manic and a depressive character.

Monasticism. Even for the morose, however, the solitary life receives little authorization in the Bohemian view. The unfriendly, laconic sage in Kerouac's description had, after all, "made the scene." Bohemias must have "scenes," since Bohemianism has always referred to a collecting of like-minded eccentrics.[56]

Monasticism, which refers to the formation of insulated communities of adherents, is an explicit attempt on the part of Bohemians to regain the sense of community which, according to their ideology, no longer exists in the broader society.[57] The clubs, *cafés*, dives, or pads, which are their monasteries, are places where the bonds of familiarity can be assumed and, except for the danger of the police interloper, one hardly need "check out" a scene before feeling secure in it. However, not all are welcome in the places of congregation. Monasticism refers to communities of authentic adherents. Thus, theirs is an exclusive community. Bohemians are not evangelists; on the contrary, the newcomer must prove in a variety of ways that he belongs.[58]

Bohemians have long realized that both the unauthentic (pretenders or "phonies") and the outright conventional (tourists or "squares") are greatly fascinated by the Bohemian life.[59] But because of their stress on authenticity, Bohemians have been guarded in their relations with phonies and squares. Moreover, they are guarded because they have been dimly aware of the fate that, sooner or later, befalls all Bohemias. The monasticism of Bo-

hemians, coupled with the persistence with which the squares and phonies discover their haunts, has meant that virtually no Bohemian "monastery" could long survive. Moreover, Bohemian neighborhoods, too, made up of garrets and *cafés*, in traditional Bohemian parlance, or pads and scenes, in modern Bohemian parlance, have been short-lived. When the phonies and squares arrive, some of the most zealous Bohemians leave. From that point on, the process seems irreversible; the phonies move in, the rents increase, many of the remaining Bohemians are forced to leave, and a new pseudo-Bohemia, in the manner of Greenwich Village, is created.[60]

Substance. The "business" of Bohemianism has two important and interrelated elements. First, there is the creation of unconventional art which may be distinguished from the conventional variety in three major ways. It is disaffiliated from the major institutions which provide the machinery for the production and distribution of art. Among these institutions are the modern university, with its direct and indirect subsidization of the arts, and the modern industries of mass communication which, alternatively, deal commercially in art (publishing firms) or deal in commercialized art (advertising). Second, stylistic innovation is characteristic of Bohemian art. In each of the arts, the Bohemian has been an experimenter in new styles of expression.

The third feature of unconventional art applies to its subject matter. Bohemian art has frequently dealt with the forbidden, the censorable. In his attempt to plumb the depths of human existence, the Bohemian has often been guilty of equivocation, of confusing or equating the two meanings of "depths." This equivocation was an outgrowth of the Bohemian's peculiar style of populism in which authentic life coincides with primitive life, with life as it is lived in the lowest orders of society and the underworld. His own descent into the lowest orders, resulting from his dedicated poverty, allowed him to extend the province of his subject matter in an important manner. If the Bohemian feared the *lumpenproletariat*, or if he discovered that their behavior was not always censorable, he could always turn to what is, after all, the most frequent subject matter of Bohemian art—Bohemians. This was fortunate, for if Bohemian life was not sufficiently censorable, there was always the possibility of making it so.

This brings us to the second and interrelated element of the Bohemian enterprise, the pursuit of unconventional personal experience It is interrelated, because, whatever its motive among Bohemians, it has persistently performed a crucial function for young, aspiring painters, poets, sculptors, and novelists. It has provided them with a subject matter to which to apply their variable talents.

In the pursuit of unconventional personal experience, there is no assurance of success. Some sorts of experience involve higher risks of failure than others—the pursuit of sexual conquest, for instance, is less likely to culminate successfully than the use of alcohol to lessen inhibitions. Thus, a cataloguing of the forms of experience traditionally pursued by Bohemians should not be mistaken for an accurate rendition of what Bohemians typically do. More time seems spent in pursuit than in actual experience.[61]

Two sorts of unconventional experience are pursued. First, there is the pursuit of hedonistic experiences which overlap considerably with activities that are currently deemed illegal in the United States. These are generally nonvictimizing offenses; included are such offenses as sexual excess, homosexuality, intemperate use of alcohol, disturbing the peace, use of narcotics, and speeding in automobiles. Many of these activities received celebration among Bohemians during the nineteenth century.[62] Thus, it should not be assumed that beats have attained a new threshold of hedonistic experience.

Second, there is a quest for transcendence. This is closely related to the problem of creativity and represents an experimenting with the limits to which human perception may be pushed. It is as an attempt to transcend the mundane limits on human perception that we can best understand three highly esoteric activities of beats: religious mysticism as manifested in Buddhist meditation, or the "Zen kick";[63] the flirtation with and acceptance of psychosis, or the "insanity bit";[64] and the hallucinogenic use of drugs.[65]

Rebellious youth: restoration and prevention

The integration of rebellious youth into conventional society hardly seems possible, particularly in view of the eccentricities inherent in each of the subterranean traditions. Yet, the great majority of vulnerable youth are barely touched by these traditions in their fullblown forms and, of those that are, the great majority seem able to re-enter conventional life with the attainment of social adulthood. Two questions must, therefore, be posed. Why, given the vulnerability of youth to modes of rebelliousness, do so few participate in full-blown deviant traditions? And by what process are those who do participate reintegrated into society? The first is the problem of prevention, the second of restoration.

Our concern, here, is not with programmatic solutions which, with respect to the problems of youthful rebelliousness, seem ineffective or nonexistent.[66] Instead, we are interested in a process on which the integration of youth seems far more dependent, and that is the crescive and unintended formation of arrangements which fortuitously expedite integration. One such arrangement may be found in the existence of conventional versions of subterranean traditions.[67]

Conventional versions are reasonable facsimiles of subterranean traditions in which their most offensive features are stripped away or tempered. As indicated above, this is not by design, but as a result of emergent syntheses of conventional and rebellious sentiments or as a consequence of the fortuitous existence of independent traditions.

A conventional version of the delinquent tradition is what has come to be called teenage culture. Here we find an emphasis on fun and adventure; a disdain for scholastic effort; the more or less persistent involvement in "tolerated" status offenses like drinking, gambling, occasional truancy, "making out" in the sense of sexual conquest, driving cars before the appropriate age, smoking, swearing, and staying out late. The elements of the delinquent tradition that are lacking or tempered are those that are least tolerated. Aggression is considerably tempered, but there is a persistent concern with the credentials on masculinity and femininity. Victimizing crimes are stripped away, and the forms of prowess used for getting money to play at luxury are usually limited to the "conning" of parents.

Many youngsters who would otherwise be vulnerable to the appeals of delinquency get caught up in the teen-age round-of-life. Because it has many inherent satisfactions, it tends to maintain the loyalty of its adherents. Furthermore, since it is allegedly capable of deflecting studious teenagers, it is probably at least as effective in deflecting youngsters who are prone to a tradition with which it has far greater affinity. Moreover, it is likely that the greatest proportion of exdelinquents do not fully reform and become "good boys" in the adult and scholastic sense of the term; more likely, they pass into the ranks of "corner boys" of the lower and middle classes. Thus, although teen-age culture may sometimes act as a preparation for the delinquent tradition, as its critics would have it, there seems little doubt that it often serves the functions of prevention and restoration.

A conventional version of the radical tradition may be found in the long-standing American posture of "doing good." This is a kind of inchoate and uninformed liberalism. It is vaguely radical in that it, too, laments the corruption of society and looks forward to improvement, but it does not envisage apocalypse. It, too, is populist, but only in the limited sense of being for the underdog. It, too, believes in evangelism, but the most frequent expression of its evangelism is guilty inaction. Though this group has long been recognized as a source of sympathizers for radical organizations, its functions in preventing radicalism by providing a tenable alternative, a facsimile, for rebelliously-inclined and idealistic youth has been frequently overlooked; so, too, has its function in the restoration of radical youth. It is not likely that the greatest number of ex-radicals become either McCarthyites or liberal anti-Communists; more likely, they slip into inactivity, pass into ranks of those committed to doing good, and neutralize the guilt of persistent political inactivity by pointing to the demands of scholarship.

In the Bohemian case, we must proceed cautiously. Because of the great emphasis placed on authenticity and, thus, the great sensitivity and hostility to phonies, the integrative effects of the conventional versions of Bohemianism may be partially neutralized. It is, perhaps, for this reason that Bohemians seem to linger further into the reaches of chronological adulthood than radicals or delinquents. A Bohemian, because of the stress on authenticity, is more likely than the radical or the delinquent to perceive the "duplicity of social systems" that lies behind each of the facsimiles. While this almost certainly holds with respect to the function of restoration, it is likely that conventional versions serve to deflect youth who are vulnerable to Bohemianism without yet being aware of its esoteric details. Nonetheless, we must leave open the

possibility that, because of the stress on authenticity, there can be no effective facsimile of Bohemianism.[68] Thus, it is with some hesitation that we suggest that fraternity life may be viewed as a conventional facsimile of frivolous Bohemianism and that student intellectuals stand in a similar relation to morose Bohemianism. Fraternity life frequently has a quality that is reminiscent of the most frivolous sorts of Bohemianism. There is the congregating and singing in student taverns, the round of larks and pranks, the aversion for cerebral activity, the exclusiveness and fraternalism of Bohemian monasticism, the pursuit of "weak" and typically inoffensive "kicks." The affinity between student intellectualism and morose Bohemianism may be found in the following: the student intellectual is concerned with creativity and free expression, which may be taken as a tempering of the Bohemian's commitment to unconventional art; he is concerned with integrity, which may be viewed as a routinized form of expressive authenticity; he is unwilling to join his conventional classmates in the celebration of material success, which is a tempered form of the Bohemian's dedication to poverty; he is prone to the medievalist view of Bohemians while rejecting primitivist populism; and, finally, he is temperamentally given to seriousness, which is a tempered version of the Bohemian's moroseness.

Our brief discussion of the integration of youth has focused on one set of mechanisms. These mechanisms, however, operate within a context of two other important features of modern society. First, there is the widespread sentiment of adult tolerance. Though the strength of this sentiment varies through time and by section of the population, there is a significant and influential portion of adult opinion that is ready to embrace prodigal youth if and when they return. Second, there is the waning of the tensions and frustrations making for youthful rebelliousness resulting from the onset of adulthood and the gaining of "first-class citizenship." As important as these are, they are not sufficient to provide a basis for the integration of youth. There is the further necessity for some systematic arrangement to exist through which the integrative potential of adult tolerance and social maturation of youth may be realized. One such arrangement may be found in the fortuitous existence of conventional versions of the subterranean traditions of youth.

Notes

1 Kingsley Davis, "Sociology of Parent-Youth Conflict," *American Sociological Review*, Vol. 5 (August 1940) and "Adolescence and the Social Structure," *The Annals of the American Academy of Political and Social Science*, Vol. 236 (November 1944).

2 Ruth Benedict, "Continuities and Discontinuities in Cultural Conditioning," *Psychiatry*, May 1933; Erik Erikson, in *New Perspectives for Research in Juvenile Delinquency*, eds. Helen Witmer and Ruth Kotinsky (Publication No. 356; Washington, D. C.: Children's Bureau, 1956); Herbert Bloch and Arthur Niederhoffer, *The Gang* (New York: Philosophical Library, 1958).

3 Talcott Parsons, "Age and Sex in the Social Structure of the United States," *American Sociological Review*, October, 1942.

4 Pitirim Sorokin, *The American Sex Revolution* (Boston: Sargent, 1956).

5 Frederick Elkin and William A. Westley, "The Myth of Adolescent Culture," *American Sociological Review*, December, 1955; also, Bennett M. Berger, "On the Youthfulness of Youth Cultures" (unpublished manuscript).

6 Conventional versions of deviant traditions are discussed in the final section of this paper.

7 Negley K. Teeters and David Matza, "The Extent of Delinquency in The United States," *The Journal of Negro Education* (Summer 1959), pp. 210–211; also Henry McKay's unpublished data on Chicago delinquency rates, cited in Albert K. Cohen and James F. Short, "Juvenile Delinquency," in *Contemporary Social Problems*, eds. Robert K. Merton and Robert A. Nisbet (New York: Harcourt, Brace and World, 1961), p. 84.

8 Evidence of this using national delinquency statistics may be found in most standard textbooks and the *Uniform Crime Reports* of any year. For instance, Cohen and Short, *op. cit.*, p. 85. More reliable evidence of "maturational reform," based on cohort analysis, appears in William McCord, Joan McCord, and Irving Zola, *Origins of Crime* (New York: Columbia University Press, 1959), p. 21; Jessie Bernard, *Social Problems at Mid-century* (New York: Dryden, 1957), pp. 421, 444; W. H. Dunham and M. E. Knauer, "The Juvenile Court and its Relationship to Adult Criminality," *Social Forces*, March 1954. The evidence for radicalism and Bohemianism are necessarily more impressionistic. For supportive but inconclusive evidence of "maturational defection" in radicalism, see Gabriel A. Almond, *The Appeals of Communism* (Princeton: Princeton University Press, 1954), pp. 218–220; James A. Wechsler, *The Age of Suspicion* (New York: Random House, 1953), p. 84; Robert E. Lane, *Political Life* (Glencoe: Free Press, 1959), pp. 216–217; Morris L. Ernst and David Loth, *Report on the American Communist* (New York: Holt, 1952). For impressionistic evidence on the drifting from Bohemianism with the gaining of adulthood, see Thomas Parkinson, "Phenomenon or Generation," in *A Casebook on the Beat*, ed. Thomas Parkinson (New York: Crowell, 1961), pp. 277–278; Albert Parry, *Garrets and Pretenders: A History of Bohemianism in America* (New York: Covici-Friede, 1933), p. 12.

9 Bennett Berger, *op. cit.*, rightly distinguishes between youthfulness in the spiritual sense and chronological youth. He suggests that there is no necessary correlation between the two. I agree but suggest that there is a rough empirical correlation.

10 The content of these viewpoints will be discussed below. With regard to stable ecological anchoring, the evidence varies in reliability. The ecological anchoring of the delinquent tradition has been documented in Clifford H. Shaw and Henry D. McKay, *Juvenile Delinquency and Urban Areas* (Chicago: University of Chicago Press, 1942); Albert K. Cohen, *Delinquent Boys* (Glencoe: Free Press, 1955). The widespread impression that youthful radicalism has been stably located on the campuses of a handful of typically large, prestigious, and cosmopolitan universities and colleges receives adequate documentary confirmation in Robert W. Iversen, *The Communists and the Schools* (New York: Harcourt, Brace, 1959), Chap. 6. The widespread impression that American Bohemianism has located in rundown sections of large cities or in areas adjacent to cosmopolitan campuses remains largely undocumented. However, there seems no urgent reason to question this impression.

11 Reinhard Bendix and Bennett Berger, "Images of Society and Problems of Concept Formation in Sociology," in *Symposium on Sociological Theory*, ed. Llewellyn Gross (Evanston: Row, Peterson, 1959).

12 Fads often involve the brief elevation of modified elements of subterranean traditions, most notably Bohemian traditions, to the status of eccentric but partially acceptable behavior. Perhaps the classic example of this in the United States was the "Trilby" fad in the 1890's when a modified form of fe-

male Bohemianism came in vogue. For a discussion of "Trilby," see Parry, *op. cit.*, Chap. 9.

[13] Dennis Wrong, "The Oversocialized Conception of Man in Modern Sociology," *American Sociological Review*, April 1961.

[14] Parsons, *op cit.*

[15] Robert K. Merton, "Social Problems and Sociological Theory," in *Contemporary Social Problems, op. cit.*, pp. 725–727.

[16] *Ibid.*

[17] Gresham M. Sykes and David Matza, "Techniques of Neutralization," *American Sociological Review*, December 1957.

[18] The following section is, with slight modification, based on David Matza and Gresham M. Sykes, "Juvenile Delinquency and Subterranean Values," *American Sociological Review*, forthcoming.

[19] Frederic M. Thrasher, *The Gang* (Chicago: University of Chicago Press, 1936); Clifford R. Shaw and M. E. Moore, *The Natural History of a Delinquent Career* (Chicago: University of Chicago Press, 1931); Albert K. Cohen, *Delinquent Boys, op. cit.*; Albert K. Cohen and James F. Short, "Research in Delinquent Subcultures," *The Journal of Social Issues*, Vol. 14 (1958), No. 3; Walter Miller, "Lower Class Culture as a Generating Milieu of Gang Delinquents," *The Journal of Social Issues*, Vol. 14 (1958), No. 3; Solomon Kobrin, "The Conflict of Values in Delinquent Areas," *American Sociological Review*, Vol. 16 (1951); Harold Finestone, "Cats, Kicks and Color," *Social Problems*, Vol. 5 (1957); Richard A. Cloward and Lloyd F. Ohlin, *Delinquency and Opportunity* (Glencoe: The Free Press, 1960); H. Bloch and Ar-

thur Niederhoffer, *The Gang, op. cit.;* Beatrice Griffith, *American Me* (Boston: Houghton Mifflin, 1948); Sheldon and Eleanor Glueck, *Unraveling Juvenile Delinquency* (New York: Commonwealth Fund, 1950).

[20] Finestone, *op. cit.*

[21] Miller, *op. cit.*

[22] Finestone, *op. cit.*

[23] Joseph Margolis, "Juvenile Delinquents: Latter-day Knights," *The American Scholar*, Spring 1960.

[24] Cloward and Ohlin, *op. cit.*

[25] Griffith, *op. cit.*

[26] Though it may appear obvious or unimportant, it is crucial to specify the substance of delinquency as well as its spirit. The basic process involved in the conventional versions of each tradition is the fortuitous stripping away of its most odious features. Thus, for instance, the conventional version of delinquency, teen-age culture, involves a continuing flirtation with its tolerable components; and among these tolerable components are the status offenses, to be discussed below.

[27] The most detailed and documented account is found in Iversen, *op. cit.;* for a good impressionistic account, see Wechsler, *op. cit.*

[28] While the Communists have never had a monopoly on student radicalism, their influence, particularly during the Thirties and early Forties, was considerable. Our discussion will focus primarily on Communists partially because of their prominence and partially because their activities have been best documented. See Iversen, *op. cit.*, Chap. 6.

[29] Iversen, *op. cit.*, p. 13.

[30] Edward A. Shils, "The Traditions of Intellectuals," in *The Intellectuals*, ed. George de Huszar (Glencoe: Free Press, 1960), pp. 55–61.

[31] *Ibid.*

[32] *Ibid.*

[33] *Ibid.*

[34] *Ibid.*

[35] The evidence for this is indirect but suggestive. The fear that Bohemianism is infecting the youth is a persistent fear among adult radicals. The classical radical case against Bohemian corruption was made by Lenin in his "sex is not a glass of water" dictum; the classical radical case for Bohemian joy was made by the anarchist Emma Goldman.

[36] For a discussion of the monotonous character of the round of student radical life, see Wechsler, *op. cit.*

[37] Seymour M. Lipset, *Political Man* (New York: Doubleday, 1960).

[38] Daniel Bell, *End of Ideology* (Glencoe: Free Press, 1960).

[39] Parry, *op. cit.*, ix.

[40] Parry, *ibid.*

[41] John P. Sisk, "Beatniks and Tradition," in Parkinson, *op. cit.*

[42] Shils, *op. cit.*, p. 57.

[43] Harold Rosenberg, *The Tradition of the New* (New York: Horizon, 1959); also, William Barrett, *Irrational Man* (New York: Doubleday, 1958), Chap. 3.

[44] Jack Kerouac's major publications include *On the Road* (New York: Viking, 1957); *Dharma Bums* (New York:

Viking, 1958); *The Subterraneans* (New York: Grove, 1958); *Excerpts from Visions of Cody*, 1958 (no further citation).

45 See the critique by Jean Malaquais of Norman Mailer's "The White Negro," in *Dissent*, Winter 1958.

46 The most explicit statement of this view is found in Norman Mailer, "The White Negro," *Dissent*, Summer 1957.

47 See Parry, *op. cit.*, p. 35, for a Bohemian's description of East European Jews on the Lower East Side in 1910 that is indistinguishable from the way in which lower-class Negro life is currently romanticized.

48 Laurence Lipton, *The Holy Barbarians* (New York: Messner, 1959), p. 59.

49 *Ibid.*, p. 54.

50 Typically dating from the Industrial Revolution.

51 Its only vision of apocalypse is the atomic holocaust, which, in a strict sense, is no apocalypse at all since there is little promise of redemption. See Gene Feldman and Max Gartenberg, *The Beat Generation and the Angry Young Men* (New York: Dell, 1958), p. 12.

52 Edward A. Shils, "Daydreams and Nightmares," *Sewanee Review*, Fall 1957, pp. 596–600.

53 For a somewhat obscene statement of the beat's rejection of modern progress, see Jack Kerouac, *Dharma Bums, op. cit.*, pp. 38–39; for a discussion of Poe and his rejection of society, see Parry, *op. cit.*, Chap. 1.

54 Parry, *op. cit.*, pp. 11–12.

55 Jack Kerouac, "The Origins of the Beat Generation," in Parkinson, *op. cit.*, p. 73.

56 For a discussion of the importance of "scenes," see Francis Rigney and L. Douglas Smith, *The Real Bohemia* (New York: Basic Books, 1961), Chap. 1; also Lipton, *op. cit.*, Chap. 1; and Parry, *op. cit.*

57 It is because of their peculiar commitment to community that beats often sound like "squares."

58 Rigney and Smith, *op. cit.*

59 Rigney and Smith, *op. cit.*, p. 181.

60 Parry, *op. cit.*, p. 58; Rigney and Smith, *op. cit.*, Chaps. 10–11.

61 Most novels of beat life written by beats, or those close to beats, confirm this point. Kerouac's novels particularly, may be taken as accurate replicas of beat life. Also, see Chandler Brossard, *Who Walk in Darkness* (New York: New Directions, 1952).

62 Parry, *op. cit.*, p. 11.

63 Kerouac, *Dharma Bums, op. cit.*

64 Seymour Krim, "The Insanity Bit," in *The Beats*, ed. Seymour Krim (Greenwich: Fawcett, 1960).

65 Lipton, *op. cit.*, p. 178.

66 The only subterranean tradition for which there is an ongoing correctional apparatus specializing in the restoration of youth is delinquency. Even in that case, however, there is considerable uncertainty as to whether the fact of official correction or the quality of that correction has any effect on the chances of reforming. See Edwin Powers and Helen Witmer, *An Experiment in the Prevention of Delinquency: The Cambridge-Somerville Youth Study* (New York: Columbia University Press, 1951).

67 Talcott Parsons, *The Social System* (Glencoe: The Free Press, 1951), pp. 305–306; also, Paul Goodman, *Growing Up Absurd* (New York: Random House, 1960); also, Bennett Berger, *op. cit.*

68 This does not mean that Bohemians cannot be restored to conventional society. There are other integrative processes. Bennett Berger points to the integrative effects of "youthful" roles within the adult system. See Berger, *op. cit.*

Chapter 7

THE ACQUISITION OF CULTURE

A THEORY OF PRIMARY SOCIALIZATION
Selection 17

UNSOCIALIZED MAN
Selection 18

SECONDARY SOCIALIZATION
Selection 19

Culture is carried and transmitted by individuals and is exhibited in their behavior. Its acquisition is the result of a process known as socialization, with
which this chapter is concerned. Socialization is the training process by which
an individual who is inexperienced in a given culture learns about and acquires
the culture as an aspect of his behavior. In using the term "socialization," we
usually, but not always, have in mind a child or a younger person who is taught
by his seniors.

Closely related to the concept of socialization are the concepts of assimilation
and acculturation. Assimilation generally refers to the learning of a culture on
the part of an individual already socialized into a culture different from the one
being learned. An example would be the experience of the immigrant. Assimilation may be thought of as "resocialization." Acculturation generally refers to a
similar process in which an entire group receives elements of another culture
and acquires a resemblance to the group from which the cultural elements are
received. An example would be an "underdeveloped" society that adopts
Western technology. One should be aware that although these distinctions can be
made among the concepts, the terms "socialization," "assimilation," and "acculturation" are at times used interchangeably.

The most important type of socialization is the initial or primary socialization
that children receive in all societies. Primary socialization receives its name
from the fact that it tends to take place in the context of a primary group—
parents, playmates, or neighbors (see Selection 27). The goals of primary socialization are the acquisition of language, the control of instinctual behavior
such as elimination and hunger, and the introduction of the child into the basic
ideas and norms of the socializing culture. It is through primary socialization
that the social forces of which Durkheim speaks are internalized, built into the
individual's personality so that he is unaware of their existence, yet subject
to their influence.

Most sociologists subscribe to the theory that attributes the origin of the conscious self to primary socialization. According to this theory, self-consciousness
(the act of regarding the self as an object) requires the possession of language,

as well as the ability to adopt the point of view of other people. Both of these are gained through the child's interaction with his parents and other socializing agents.

Primary socialization tends to be rather similar in all societies. This fact has been noted as an explanation for the existence of sympathetic understanding between human beings from radically different cultures. The Pilgrims and the Indians could understand each other in the absence of translators and bilingual dictionaries because members of both groups had undergone roughly similar experiences during primary socialization.

Socialization does not end with the primary stage, but continues throughout life. In complex societies, the socialization process beyond infancy is in part formalized and placed in the institutional context of education. Teachers are the socializing agents of this form of "secondary" socialization. Students are people who are acquiring cultural knowledge in the context of formal education. Your reading this book is a part of your socialization into the segment of American culture called sociology. Most secondary socialization, though, is not formalized, even in complex societies. It comes about informally and unconsciously in ordinary social interaction. When we are in new situations for which we have not learned the cultural expectations, as during a first visit to the opera, instructions are received by watching the behavior of others, and errors are corrected by the smiles and scowls of the others who are present.

In Selection 17, G. H. Mead states a theory of socialization that generally has been accorded acceptance in the field of sociology. Kingsley Davis, in Selection 18, describes a child who was grossly neglected while very young. This case exemplifies what the human animal may be like when it has not received primary socialization. In Selection 19, Howard S. Becker and Blanche Geer describe modifications in the idealism of medical students occurring in the course of and as an indirect result of socialization into the medical profession.

A THEORY OF PRIMARY SOCIALIZATION

The biological fact that human beings do not last forever establishes for societies the problem of replacing their members. The fact that children are born without culture establishes the additional problem of training these replacements. The training process which introduces children into the rudiments of their culture, imparting language, basic values and beliefs, and norms is called primary socialization.

Sociology's interest in primary socialization is shared with the discipline of psychology. Whereas psychology is concerned with this process as it results in the development of behavioral regularities characterizing individuals, the interest of sociology in this process is in the transmission of culture from one generation to the next. Since the process is one and the same, there has occurred in this area much cross-fertilization between the two disciplines; there has developed a set of theories called, from one viewpoint, theories of personality formation and, from the other viewpoint, theories of child socialization.

The reader will probably be familiar with some of the psychological theories in this area, most notably those of Freud and his followers. Traditionally, sociologists have preferred to think of socialization in the terms suggested by George Herbert Mead, which are presented in this selection. This preference is partly due to the fact that Mead taught at the University of Chicago during the early years of this century, and his influence was directly felt by the students in this first important department of sociology in America. Also, Mead's interests appeared to fit those of sociology more closely than did the interests of the Freudians, and it is still true that Mead is very compatible with a sociological outlook.

This selection is representative of Mead's thoughts on the development of children into social selves. It is a very difficult passage, partly because it is taken from a book that was put together by Mead's students from classroom notes, rather than being Mead's own manuscript. Close attention to the abstract may be helpful in locating the most important ideas in the selection.

The individual in large part is a product of society. The molding of this product takes place in childhood through two processes. The first of these is the acquisition of language which, in addition to serving as a medium of communication, imposes on the individual his culture's way of seeing things. For example, if a word like "sex" has nasty connotations in the language through its association with various cultural ideas, these nasty connotations are picked up by the child along with the word.

The other process molding the child is his acting, in play and games, like other people whom he sees and knows in the world around him. In so acting, the child adopts the point of view of the people whose behavior he is enacting. (A technique of psychological therapy, called psycho-drama, uses the same principle; "plays" are put on with the goal of understanding the characters whose roles are being played.)

There are thus two stages in the development of the child. The first stage is that of play, in which the child is able to take the role of one person at a time—his mother, his nurse, his brother, and similar "models" that he knows. In playing at being a particular person, the child is able to understand the attitudes of that person, and this understanding is incorporated into the child's self.

In the second stage, that of the game, the child must take the role not only of one person, but of many. Play, in the present sense, can take place when the child is alone. The game, on the other hand, is a social situation, requiring all the participants to know what the others expect of them. The child must see himself and other people not only from his own point of view or that of Mother or John or any single individual, but from the viewpoint of all the individuals involved in the game. This is a much more difficult task, called taking the role of the **generalized** other. When the child can take the role of the generalized other in a given group, he has completed his primary socialization and has begun to master the group's culture.

In sum, through play, the game, and the learning of language, the child acquires membership in a society and becomes in large part a product of that society and a bearer of its culture.

The considerations advanced in this selection are not incompatible with psychological approaches to the socialization process. In modern psychology, the extremely person-centered Freudian view has been modified to take greater account of the role of society in this process and of the consequently large social component in personality. Many recent sociologists have consciously adopted Freudian and neo-Freudian ideas in their studies of socialization.

It is unfortunate that Mead's theory, like Freud's, has proved to be somewhat difficult to test. Some empirical tests have been made, with results generally favorable to the theory. For instance, socialized individuals seem to be able to guess pretty well how others see them, a point implied in the discussion of role-taking. However, relatively few such tests have been performed, and it must be concluded that Mead's ideas are still largely in the realm of speculative theory.

Selection 17
FROM MIND, SELF AND SOCIETY
G. H. Mead

We were speaking of the social conditions under which the self arises as an object. In addition to language we found two illustrations, one in play and the other in the game, and I wish to summarize and expand my account on these points. I have spoken of these from the point of view of children. We can, of course, refer also to the attitudes of more primitive people out of which our civilization has arisen. A striking illustration of play as distinct from the game is found in the myths and various of the plays which primitive people carry out, especially in religious pageants. The pure play attitude which we find in the case of little children may not be found here, since the participants are adults, and undoubtedly the relationship of these play processes to that which they interpret is more or less in the minds of even the most primitive people. In the process of interpretation of such rituals, there is an organization of play which perhaps might be compared to that which is taking place in the kindergarten in dealing with the plays of little children, where these are made into a set that will have a definite structure or relationship. At least something of the same sort is found in the play of primitive people. This type of activity belongs, of course, not to the everyday life of the people in their dealing with the objects about them—there we have a more or less definitely developed self-consciousness— but in their attitudes toward the forces about them, the nature upon which they depend; in their attitude toward this nature which is vague and uncertain, there we have a much more primitive response; and that response finds its expression in taking the rôle of the other, playing at the expression of their gods and their heroes, going through certain rites which are the representation of what these individuals are supposed to be doing. The process is one which develops, to be sure, into a more or less definite technique and is controlled; and yet we can say that it has arisen out of situations similar to those in which little children play at being a parent, at being a

teacher—vague personalities that are about them and which affect them and on which they depend. These are personalities which they take, rôles they play, and in so far control the development of their own personality. This outcome is just what the kindergarten works toward. It takes the characters of these various vague beings and gets them into such an organized social relationship to each other that they build up the character of the little child.[1] The very introduction of organization from outside supposes a lack of organization at this period in the child's experience. Over against such a situation of the little child and primitive people, we have the game as such.

The fundamental difference between the game and play is that in the [former]* the child must have the attitude of all the others involved in that game. The attitudes of the other players which the participant assumes organize into a sort of unit, and it is that organization which controls the response of the individual. The illustration used was of a person playing baseball. Each one of his own acts is determined by his assumption of the action of the others who are playing the game. What he does is controlled by his being everyone else on that team, at least in so far as those attitudes affect his own particular response. We get then an "other" which is an organization of the attitudes of those involved in the same process.

The organized community or social group which gives to the individual his unity of self may be called "the generalized other." The attitude of the generalized other is the attitude of the whole community.[2] Thus, for example, in the case of such a social group as a ball team, the team is the generalized other insofar as it enters—as an organized process or social activity—into the experience of any one of the individual members of it.

If the given human individual is to develop a self in the fullest sense, it is not sufficient for him merely to take the attitudes of other human individuals toward himself and toward one another within the human social process,

Reprinted from *Mind, Self and Society* by G. H. Mead (Chicago: University of Chicago Press, 1934), with permission of the publisher.

* Editor's alteration of original text.

and to bring that social process as a whole into his individual experience merely in these terms: he must also, in the same way that he takes the attitudes of other individuals toward himself and toward one another, take their attitudes toward the various phases or aspects of the common social activity or set of social undertakings in which, as members of an organized society or social group, they are all engaged; and he must then, by generalizing these individual attitudes of that organized society or social group itself, as a whole, act toward different social projects which at any given time it is carrying out, or toward the various larger phases of the general social process which constitutes its life and of which these projects are specific manifestations. This getting of the broad activities of any given social whole or organized society as such within the experiential field of any one of the individuals involved or included in that whole is, in other words, the essential basis and prerequisite of the fullest development of that individual's self: only insofar as he takes the attitudes of the organized social group to which he belongs toward the organized, co-operative social activity or set of such activities in which that group as such is engaged, does he develop a complete self or possess the sort of complete self he has developed. And on the other hand, the complex co-operative processes and activities and institutional functionings of organized human society are also possible only insofar as every individual involved in them or belonging to that society can take the general attitudes of all other such individuals with reference to these processes and activities and institutional functionings, and to the organized social whole of experiential relations and interactions thereby constituted—and can direct his own behavior accordingly.

It is in the form of the generalized other that the social process influences the behavior of the individuals involved in it and carrying it on, i.e., that the community exercises control over the conduct of its individual members; for it is in this form that the social process of community enters as a determining factor into the individual's thinking. In abstract thought the individual takes the attitude of the generalized other[3] toward himself, without reference to its expression in any particular other individuals; and in concrete thought

he takes that attitude insofar as it is expressed in the attitudes toward his behavior of those other individuals with whom he is involved in the given social situation or act. But only by taking the attitude of the generalized other toward himself, in one or another of these ways, can he think at all; for only thus can thinking—or the internalized conversation of gestures which constitutes thinking—occur. And only through the taking by individuals of the attitude or attitudes of the generalized other toward themselves is the existence of a universe of discourse, as that system of common or social meanings which thinking presupposes at its context, rendered possible.

The self-conscious human individual, then, takes or assumes the organized social attitudes of the given social group or community (or of some one section thereof) to which he belongs, toward the social problems of various kinds which confront that group or community at any given time, and which arise in connection with the correspondingly different social projects or organized co-operative enterprises in which that group or community as such is engaged; and as an individual participant in these social projects or co-operative enterprises, he governs his own conduct accordingly. In politics, for example, the individual identifies himself with an entire political party and takes the organized attitudes of that entire party toward the rest of the given social community and toward the problems which confront the party within the given social situation; and he consequently reacts or responds in terms of the organized attitudes of the party as a whole. He thus enters into a special set of social relations with all the other individuals who belong to that political party; and in the same way he enters into various other special sets of social relations, with various other classes of individuals respectively, the individuals of each of these classes being the other members of some one of the particular organized subgroups (determined in socially functional terms) of which he himself is a member within the entire given society or social community. In the most highly developed, organized, and complicated human social communities—those evolved by civilized man—these various socially functional classes or subgroups of individuals to which any given individual belongs (and with the other individual members of which he thus enters into a special set of social relations) are of two kinds. Some of them are concrete social classes or subgroups, such as political parties, clubs, corporations, which are all actually functional social units, in terms of which their individual members are directly related to one another. The others are abstract social classes or subgroups, such as the class of debtors and the class of creditors, in terms of which their individual members are related to one another only more or less indirectly, and which only more or less indirectly function as social units, but which afford or represent unlimited possibilities for the widening and ramifying and enriching of the social relations among all the individual members of the given society as an organized and unified whole. The given individual's membership in several of these abstract social classes or subgroups makes possible his entrance into definite social relations (however indirect) with an almost infinite number of other individuals who also belong to or are included within one or another of these abstract social classes or subgroups cutting across functional lines of demarcation which divide different human social communities from one another, and including individual members from several (in some cases from all) such communities. Of these abstract social classes or subgroups of human individuals the one which is most inclusive and extensive is, of course, the one defined by the logical universe of discourse (or system of universally significant symbols)* determined by the participation and communicative interaction of individuals; for of all such classes or subgroups, it is the one which claims the largest number of individual members, and which enables the largest conceivable number of human individuals to enter into some sort of social relation, however indirect or abstract it may be, with one another—a relation arising from the universal functioning of gestures as significant symbols in the general human social process of communication.

I have pointed out, then, that there are two general stages in the full development of the self. At the first of these stages, the individual's self is constituted simply by an organization of the particular attitudes of other individuals toward himself and toward one another in the specific social acts in which he

* Roughly equivalent to "language."—Ed.

participates with them. But at the second stage in the full development of the individual's self that self is constituted not only by an organization of these particular individual attitudes, but also by an organization of the social attitudes of the generalized other or the social group as a whole to which he belongs. These social or group attitudes are brought within the individual's field of direct experience, and are included as elements in the structure or constitution of his self, in the same way that the attitudes of particular other individuals are; and the individual arrives at them, or succeeds in taking them, by means of further organizing, and then generalizing, the attitudes of particular other individuals in terms of their organized social bearings and implications. So the self reaches its full development by organizing these individual attitudes of others into the organized social or group attitudes, and by thus becoming an individual reflection of the general systematic pattern of social or group behavior in which it and the others are all involved—a pattern which enters as a whole into the individual's experience in terms of these organized group attitudes which, through the mechanism of his central nervous system, he takes toward himself, just as he takes the individual attitudes of others.

The game has a logic, so that such an organization of the self is rendered possible: there is a definite end to be obtained; the actions of the different individuals are all related to each other with reference to that end so that they do not conflict; one is not in conflict with himself in the attitude of another man on the team. If one has the attitude of the person throwing the ball he can also have the response of catching the ball. The two are related so that they further the purpose of the game itself. They are interrelated in a unitary, organic fashion. There is a definite unity, then, which is introduced into the organization of other selves when we reach such a stage as that of the game, as over against the situation of play where there is a simple succession of one rôle after another, a situation which is, of course, characteristic of the child's own personality. The child is one thing at one time and another at another, and what he is at one moment does not determine what he is at another. That is both the charm of childhood as well as its inadequacy. You cannot count on the child; you cannot assume that all the things he does are going to determine what he will do at any moment. He is not organized into a whole. The child has no definite character, no definite personality.

The game is then an illustration of the situation out of which an organized personality arises. Insofar as the child does take the attitude of the other and allows that attitude of the other to determine the thing he is going to do with reference to a common end, he is becoming an organic member of society. He is taking over the morale of that society and is becoming an essential member of it. He belongs to it insofar as he does allow the attitude of the other that he takes to control his own immediate expression. What is involved here is some sort of an organized process. That which is expressed in terms of the game is, of course, being continually expressed in the social life of the child, but this wider process goes beyond the immediate experience of the child himself. The importance of the game is that it lies entirely inside of the child's own experience, and the importance of our modern type of education is that it is brought as far as possible within this realm. The different attitudes that a child assumes are so organized that they exercise a definite control over his response, as the attitudes in a game control his own immediate response. In the game we get an organized other, a generalized other, which is found in the nature of the child itself, and finds its expression in the immediate experience of the child. And it is that organized activity in the child's own nature controlling the particular response which gives unity, and which builds up his own self.

What goes on in the game goes on in the life of the child all the time. He is continually taking the attitudes of those about him, especially the rôles of those who in some sense control him and on whom he depends. He gets the function of the process in an abstract sort of a way at first. It goes over from the play into the game in a real sense. He has to play the game. The morale of the game takes hold of the child more than the larger morale of the whole community. The child passes into the game and the game expresses a social situation in which he can completely enter; its morale may have a greater hold on him than that of the family to which he belongs or the community in which he lives. There are all sorts of social organizations, some of which are fairly lasting, some temporary, into which the child is entering, and he is playing a sort of social game in them. It is a period in which he likes "to belong," and he gets into organizations which come into existence and pass out of existence. He becomes a something which can function in the organized whole, and thus tends to determine himself in his relationship with the group to which he belongs. That process is one which is a striking stage in the development of the child's morale. It constitutes him a self-conscious member of the community to which he belongs.

Such is the process by which a personality arises. I have spoken of this as a process in which a child takes the rôle of the other, and said that it takes place essentially through the use of language. Language is predominantly based on the vocal gesture by means of which co-operative activities in a community are carried out. Language in its significant sense is that vocal gesture which tends to arouse in the individual the attitude which it arouses in others, and it is this perfecting of the self by the gesture which mediates the social activities that gives rise to the process of taking the rôle of the other. The latter phrase is a little unfortunate because it suggests an actor's attitude which is actually more sophisticated than that which is involved in our own experience. To this degree it does not correctly describe that which I have in mind. We see the process most definitely in a primitive form in those situations where the child's play takes different rôles. Here the very fact that he is ready to pay out money, for instance, arouses the attitude of the person who receives money; the very process is calling out in him the corresponding activities of the other person involved. The individual stimulates himself to the response which he is calling out in the other person, and then acts in some degree in response to that situation. In play the child does definitely act out the rôle which he himself has aroused in himself. It is that which gives, as I have said, a definite content in the individual which answers to the stimulus that affects him as it affects somebody else. The content of the other that enters into one personality is the response in the individual which his gesture calls out in the other.

We may illustrate our basic concept by a reference to the notion of property. If we say "This is my property, I shall control it," that affirmation calls out a certain set of responses which must be the same in any community in which property exists. It involves an organized attitude with reference to property which is common to all the members of the community. One must have a definite attitude of control of his own property and respect for the property of others. Those attitudes (as organized sets of responses) must be there on the part of all, so that when one says such a thing he calls out in himself the response of the others. He is calling out the response of what I have called a generalized other. That which makes society possible is such common responses, such organized attitudes, with reference to what we term property, the cults of religion, the process of education, and the relations of the family. Of course, the wider the society the more definitely universal these objects must be. In any case there must be a definite set of responses, which we may speak of as abstract, and which can belong to a very large group. Property is in itself a very abstract concept. It is that which the individual himself can control and nobody else can control. The attitude is different from that of a dog toward a bone. A dog will fight any other dog trying to take the bone. The dog is not taking the attitude of the other dog. A man who says "This is my property" is taking an attitude of the other person. The man is appealing to his rights because he is able to take the attitude which everybody else in the group has with reference to property, thus arousing in himself the attitude of others.

What goes to make up the organized self is the organization of the attitudes which are common to the group. A person is a personality because he belongs to a community, because he takes over the institutions of that community into his own conduct. He takes its language as a medium by which he gets his personality, and then through a process of taking the different rôles that all the others furnish he comes to get the attitude of the members of the community. Such, in a certain sense, is the structure of a man's personality. There are certain common responses which each individual has toward certain common things, and insofar as those common responses are awakened in the individual when he is affecting other persons he arouses his own self. The structure, then, on which the self is built is this response which is common to all, for one has to be a member of a community to be a self. Such responses are abstract atti-

tudes, but they constitute just what we term a man's character. They give him what we term his principles, the acknowledged attitudes of all members of the community toward what are the values of that community. He is putting himself in the place of the generalized other, which represents the organized responses of all the members of the group. It is that which guides conduct controlled by principles, and a person who has such an organized group of responses is a man whom we say has character, in the moral sense.

It is a structure of attitudes, then, which goes to make up a self, as distinct from a group of habits. We all of us have, for example, certain groups of habits, such as the particular intonations which a person uses in his speech. This is a set of habits of vocal expression which one has but which one does not know about. The sets of habits which we have of that sort mean nothing to us; we do not hear the intonations of our speech that others hear unless we are paying particular attention to them. The habits of emotional expression which belong to our speech are of the same sort. We may know that we have expressed ourselves in a joyous fashion but the detailed process is one which does not come back to our conscious selves. There are whole bundles of such habits which do not enter into a conscious self, but which help to make up what is termed the unconscious self.

After all, what we mean by self-consciousness is an awakening in ourselves of the group of attitudes which we are arousing in others, especially when it is an important set of responses which go to make up the members of the community. It is unfortunate to fuse or mix up consciousness, as we ordinarily use that term, and self-consciousness. Consciousness, as frequently used, simply has reference to the field of experience, but self-consciousness refers to the ability to call out in ourselves a set of definite responses which belong to the others of the group. Consciousness and self-consciousness are not on the same level. A man alone has, fortunately or unfortunately, access to his own toothache, but that is not what we mean by self-consciousness.

I have so far emphasized what I have called the structures upon which the self is constructed, the framework of the self, as it were. Of course we are not only what is common to all: each one of the selves is different from everyone else; but there has to be such a common structure as I have sketched in order that we may be members of a community at all. We cannot be ourselves unless we are also members in whom there is a community of attitudes which control the attitudes of all. We cannot have rights unless we have common attitudes. That which we have acquired as self-conscious persons makes us such members of society and gives us selves. Selves can only exist in definite relationships to other selves. No hard-and-fast line can be drawn between our own selves and the selves of others, since our own selves exist and enter as such into our experience only insofar as the selves of others exist and enter as such into our experience also. The individual possesses a self only in relation to the selves of the other members of his social group; and the structure of his self expresses or reflects the general behavior pattern of this social group to which he belongs, just as does the structure of the self of every other individual belonging to this social group.

Notes

[1] ["The Relation of Play to Education," *University of Chicago Record*, I (1886–97), 140 ff.]

[2] It is possible for inanimate objects, no less than for other human organisms, to form parts of the generalized and organized—the completely socialized—other for any given human individual, in so far as he responds to such objects socially or in a social fashion (by means of the mechanism of thought, the internalized conversation of gestures). Any thing—any object or set of objects, whether animate or inanimate, human or animal, or merely physical—toward which he acts, or to which he responds, socially, is an element in what for him is the generalized other; by taking the attitudes of which toward himself he becomes conscious of himself as an object or individual, and thus develops a self or personality. Thus, for example, the cult, in its primitive form, is merely the social embodiment of the relation between the given social group or community and its physical environment—an organized social means, adopted by the individual members of that group or community, of entering into social relations with that environment, or (in a sense) of carrying on conversations with it; and in this way that environment becomes part of the total generalized other for each of the individual members of the given social group or community.

[3] We have said that the internal conversation of the individual with himself in terms of words or significant gestures—the conversation which constitutes the process or activity of thinking—is carried on by the individual from the standpoint of the "generalized other." And the more abstract that conversation is, the more abstract thinking happens to be, the further removed is the generalized other from any connection with particular individuals. It is especially in abstract thinking, that is to say, that the conversation involved is carried on by the individual with the generalized other, rather than with any particular individuals. Thus it is, for example, that abstract concepts are concepts stated in terms of the attitudes of the entire social group or community; they are stated on the basis of the individual's consciousness of the attitudes of the generalized other toward them, as a result of his taking these attitudes of the generalized other and then responding to them. And thus it is also that abstract propositions are stated in a form which anyone—any other intelligent individual—will accept.

UNSOCIALIZED MAN

Biological and cultural development are so closely interwoven in men that it is difficult to be sure of their respective contributions to the adult human personality. Perhaps the ideal method of investigating this problem, if it were possible, would be to raise children in the absence of contact with culture. The resulting personalities would show the effects of biological development, along with non-cultural learning, while the differences between these individuals and people who have had an ordinary upbringing could be attributed to the cultural experiences of the latter. Such an experiment is impossible on the practical grounds that the infants would not be likely to survive the experience, as well as on ethical grounds. Lacking such an experiment, the next best thing is to study carefully those occasional creatures who are unfortunate enough to have been neglected in childhood, and fortunate enough to have survived this neglect.

Several cases that apparently illustrate this situation are known. Among them are the so-called "feral" children who, it is claimed, were brought up by wild animals when they were lost or abandoned in the woods. The claims of animal upbringing have been disputed, but it is clear that these children were not brought up in the normal family situations of their respective cultures. Similar-appearing individuals are known to have been raised by humans, yet to have been grossly neglected and supplied with little more than the food with which to remain alive. Although they had some exposure to a culture in their contact with food-givers, the contact was extremely limited, and these individuals are possibly not unlike the products of the hypothetical study described above.

The selection presents a description of the behavior of one such individual about whom a good deal is known. The child, Anna, was found in the United States and was studied by Kingsley Davis, who was teaching in the vicinity at the time of her discovery.

> Anna was rejected by her family because she was illegitimate and unwanted. She was not able to secure adoption and was returned to her mother, who maintained her physically over a period of years while neglecting her to an extreme degree. The description given of Anna at the time of her "discovery" may be taken as being close to what biology alone produced in the human being, lacking socialization. Although Anna's instinctual reflexes were in good order, she was in other respects an apathetic, vegetative creature.
>
> The introduction of cultural agents into Anna's life at the age of six produced some learning, which accelerated when the child was placed in a foster home with a parent substitute. Eventually, she acquired the rudiments of speech, and she was progressing slowly in the direction of normality for her culture at the time of her death.
>
> Cases such as this indicate the necessity of socialization, begun early enough in life, for the development of what we consider to be basic human nature. The similar case of Isabelle indicates that a capable child can overcome the effects of early social isolation if specialized care is given while the child is still young.

If Anna is accepted as an example of uncultured human nature, the conclusion follows that by far the largest part of what we usually accept as humanity is given by culture. This conclusion is in accord with Mead's theory, as well as with the ideas of the other theorists mentioned by Davis in the selection. It also lends plausibility to the assumption that man has had culture as long as he has existed on Earth.

Selection 18

FINAL NOTE ON A CASE OF EXTREME ISOLATION

Kingsley Davis

Early in 1940 there appeared [in the *American Journal of Sociology*] an account of a girl called Anna.[1] She had been deprived of normal contact and had received a minimum of human care for almost the whole of her first six years of life. At that time observations were not complete and the report had a tentative character. Now, however, the girl is dead, and, with more information available,[2] it is possible to give a fuller and more definitive description of the case from a sociological point of view.

Anna's death, caused by hemorrhagic jaundice, occurred on August 6, 1942. Having been born on March 1 or 6,[3] 1932, she was approximately ten and a half years of age when she died. The previous report covered her development up to the age of almost eight years; the present one recapitulates the earlier period on the basis of new evidence and then covers the last two and a half years of her life.

Early history

The first few days and weeks of Anna's life were complicated by frequent changes of domicile. It will be recalled that she was an illegitimate child, the second such child born to her mother, and that her grandfather, a widowed farmer in whose house her mother lived, strongly disapproved of this new evidence of the mother's indiscretion. This fact led to the baby's being shifted about.

Two weeks after being born in a nurse's private home, Anna was brought to the family farm, but the grandfather's antagonism was so great that she was shortly taken to the house of one of her mother's friends. At this time a local minister became interested in her and took her to his house with an idea of possible adoption. He decided against adoption, however, when he discovered that she had vaginitis. The infant was then taken to a children's home in the nearest large city. This agency found that at the age of only three weeks she was already in a miserable condition, being "terribly galled and otherwise in very bad shape." It did not regard her as a

Reprinted from the *American Journal of Sociology*, 52:5, 1947, pp. 432–437, with permission of the author and the publisher.

likely subject for adoption but took her in for a while anyway, hoping to benefit her. After Anna had spent nearly eight weeks in this place, the agency notified her mother to come to get her. The mother responded by sending a man and his wife to the children's home with a view to their adopting Anna, but they made such a poor impression on the agency that permission was refused. Later the mother came herself and took the child out of the home and then gave her to this couple. It was in the home of this pair that a social worker found the girl a short time thereafter. The social worker went to the mother's home and pleaded with Anna's grandfather to allow the mother to bring the child home. In spite of threats, he refused. The child, by then more than four months old, was next taken to another children's home in a near-by town. A medical examination at this time revealed that she had impetigo, vaginitis, umbilical hernia, and a skin rash.

Anna remained in this second children's home for nearly three weeks, at the end of which time she was transferred to a private foster-home. Since, however, the grandfather would not, and the mother could not, pay for the child's care, she was finally taken back as a last resort to the grandfather's house (at the age of five and a half months). There she remained, kept on the second floor in an attic-like room because her mother hesitated to incur the grandfather's wrath by bringing her downstairs.

The mother, a sturdy woman weighing about 180 pounds, did a man's work on the farm. She engaged in heavy work such as milking cows and tending hogs and had little time for her children. Sometimes she went out at night, in which case Anna was left entirely without attention. Ordinarily, it seems, Anna received only enough care to keep her barely alive. She appears to have been seldom moved from one position to another. Her clothing and bedding were filthy. She apparently had no instruction, no friendly attention.

It is little wonder that, when finally found and removed from the room in the grandfather's house at the age of nearly six years, the child could not talk, walk, or do anything that showed intelligence. She was in an extremely emaciated and undernourished condition, with skeleton-like legs and a bloated abdomen. She had been fed on virtually nothing except cow's milk during the years under her mother's care.

Anna's condition when found, and her subsequent improvement, have been described in the previous report. It now remains to say what happened to her after that.

Later history

In 1939, nearly two years after being discovered, Anna had progressed, as previously reported, to the point where she could walk, understand simple commands, feed herself, achieve some neatness, remember people, etc. But she still did not speak, and, though she was much more like a normal infant of something over one year of age in mentality, she was far from normal for her age.

On August 30, 1939, she was taken to a private home for retarded children, leaving the county home where she had been for more than a year and a half. In her new setting she made some further progress, but not a great deal. In a report of an examination made November 6 of the same year, the head of the institution pictured the child as follows:

> Anna walks about aimlessly, makes periodic rhythmic motions of her hands, and, at intervals, makes guttural and sucking noises. She regards her hands as if she had seen them for the first time. It was impossible to hold her attention for more than a few seconds at a time—not because of distraction due to external stimuli but because of her inability to concentrate. She ignored the task in hand to gaze vacantly about the room. Speech is entirely lacking. Numerous unsuccessful attempts have been made with her in the hope of developing initial sounds. I do not believe that this failure is due to negativism or deafness but that she is not sufficiently developed to accept speech at this time. . . . The prognosis is not favorable.

More than five months later, on April 25, 1940, a clinical psychologist, the late Professor Francis N. Maxfield, examined Anna and reported the following: large for her age; hearing "entirely normal"; vision apparently normal; able to climb stairs; speech in the "babbling stage" and "promise for developing intel-

ligible speech later seems to be good." He said further that "on the Merrill-Palmer scale she made a mental score of 19 months. On the Vineland social maturity scale she made a score of 23 months."[4]

Professor Maxfield very sensibly pointed out that prognosis is difficult in such cases of isolation. "It is very difficult to take scores on tests standardized under average conditions of environment and experience," he wrote, "and interpret them in a case where environment and experience have been so unusual." With this warning he gave it as his opinion at that time that Anna would eventually "attain an adult mental level of six or seven years."[5]

The school for retarded children, on July 1, 1941, reported that Anna had reached 46 inches in height and weighed 60 pounds. She could bounce and catch a ball and was said to conform to group socialization, though as a follower rather than a leader. Toilet habits were firmly established. Food habits were normal, except that she still used a spoon as her sole implement. She could dress herself except for fastening her clothes. Most remarkable of all, she had finally begun to develop speech. She was characterized as being at about the two-year level in this regard. She could call attendants by name and bring in one when she was asked to. She had a few complete sentences to express her wants. The report concluded that there was nothing peculiar about her, except that she was feeble-minded—"probably congenital in type."[6]

A final report from the school, made on June 22, 1942, and evidently the last report before the girl's death, pictured only a slight advance over that given above. It said that Anna could follow directions, string beads, identify a few colors, build with blocks, and differentiate between attractive and unattractive pictures. She had a good sense of rhythm and loved a doll. She talked mainly in phrases but would repeat words and try to carry on a conversation. She was clean about clothing. She habitually washed her hands and brushed her teeth. She would try to help other children. She walked well and could run fairly well, though clumsily. Although easily excited, she had a pleasant disposition.

Interpretation

Such was Anna's condition just before her death. It may seem as if she had not made much progress, but one must remember the condition in which she had been found. One must recall that she had no glimmering of speech, absolutely no ability to walk, no sense of gesture, not the least capacity to feed herself even when the food was put in front of her, and no comprehension of cleanliness. She was so apathetic that it was hard to tell whether or not she could hear. And all this at the age of nearly six years. Compared with this condition, her capacities at the time of her death seem striking indeed, though they do not amount to much more than a two-and-a-half-year mental level. One conclusion therefore seems safe, namely, that her isolation prevented a considerable amount of mental development that was undoubtedly part of her capacity. Just what her original capacity was, of course, is hard to say; but her development after her period of confinement (including the ability to walk and run, to play, dress, fit into a social situation, and, above all, to speak) shows that she had at least this much capacity —capacity that never could have been realized in her original condition of isolation.

A further question is this: What would she have been like if she had received a normal upbringing from the moment of birth? A definitive answer would have been impossible in any case, but even an approximate answer is made difficult by her early death. If one assumes, as was tentatively surmised in the previous report, that it is "almost impossible for any child to learn to speak, think, and act like a normal person after a long period of early isolation," it seems likely that Anna might have had a normal or near-normal capacity, genetically speaking. On the other hand, it was pointed out that Anna represented "a marginal case, [because] she was discovered before she had reached six years of age," an age "young enough to allow for some plasticity."[7] While admitting, then, that Anna's isolation *may* have been the major cause (and was certainly a minor cause) of her lack of rapid mental progress during the four and a half years following her rescue from neglect, it is necessary to entertain the hypothesis that she was congenitally deficient.

In connection with this hypothesis, one suggestive though by no means conclusive circumstance needs consideration, namely, the mentality of Anna's forebears. Information on this subject is easier to obtain, as one might guess, on the mother's than on the father's

side. Anna's maternal grandmother, for example, is said to have been college educated and wished to have her children receive a good education, but her husband, Anna's stern grandfather, apparently a shrewd, hard-driving, calculating farmowner, was so penurious that her ambitions in this direction were thwarted. Under the circumstances her daughter (Anna's mother) managed, despite having to do hard work on the farm, to complete the eighth grade in a country school. Even so, however, the daughter was evidently not very smart. "A schoolmate of [Anna's mother] stated that she was retarded in school work; was very gullible at this age; and that her morals even at this time were discussed by other students." Two tests administered to her on March 4, 1938, when she was thirty-two years of age, showed that she was mentally deficient. On the Stanford Revision of the Binet-Simon Scale her performance was equivalent to that of a child of eight years, giving her an I.Q. of 50 and indicating mental deficiency of "middle-grade moron type."[8]

As to the identity of Anna's father, the most persistent theory holds that he was an old man about seventy-four years of age at the time of the girl's birth. If he was the one, there is no indication of mental or other biological deficiency, whatever one may think of his morals. However, someone else may actually have been the father.

To sum up: Anna's heredity is the kind that *might* have given rise to innate mental deficiency, though not necessarily.

Comparison with another case

Perhaps more to the point than speculations about Anna's ancestry would be a case for comparison. If a child could be discovered who had been isolated about the same length of time as Anna but had achieved a much quicker recovery and a greater mental development, it would be a stronger indication that Anna was deficient to start with.

Such a case does exist. It is the case of a girl found at about the same time as Anna and under strikingly similar circumstances. A full description of the details of this case has not been published, but, in addition to newspaper reports, an excellent preliminary account by a speech specialist, Dr. Marie K. Mason, who played an important role in the handling of the child, has appeared.[9] Also the late Dr.

Francis N. Maxfield, clinical psychologist at Ohio State University, as was Dr. Mason, has written an as yet unpublished but penetrating analysis of the case.[10] Some of his observations have been included in Professor Zingg's book on feral man.[11] The following discussion is drawn mainly from these enlightening materials. The writer, through the kindness of Professors Mason and Maxfield, did have a chance to observe the girl in April, 1940, and to discuss the features of her case with them.

Born apparently one month later than Anna, the girl in question, who has been given the pseudonym Isabelle, was discovered in November, 1938, nine months after the discovery of Anna. At the time she was found she was approximately six and a half years of age. Like Anna, she was an illegitimate child and had been kept in seclusion for that reason. Her mother was a deaf-mute, having become so at the age of two, and it appears that she and Isabelle had spent most of their time together in a dark room shut off from the rest of the mother's family. As a result Isabelle had no chance to develop speech; when she communicated with her mother, it was by means of gestures. Lack of sunshine and inadequacy of diet had caused Isabelle to become rachitic. Her legs in particular were affected; they "were so bowed that as she stood erect the soles of her shoes came nearly flat together, and she got about with a skittering gait."[12] Her behavior toward strangers, especially men, was almost that of a wild animal, manifesting much fear and hostility. In lieu of speech she made only a strange croaking sound. In many ways she acted like an infant. "She was apparently utterly unaware of relationships of any kind. When presented with a ball for the first time, she held it in the palm of her hand, then reached out and stroked my face with it. Such behavior is comparable to that of a child of six months."[13] At first it was even hard to tell whether or not she could hear, so unused were her senses. Many of her actions resembled those of deaf children.

It is small wonder that, once it was established that she could hear, specialists working with her believed her to be feeble-minded. Even on nonverbal tests her performance was so low as to promise little for the future. Her first score on the Stanford-Binet was 19 months, practically at the zero point of the scale. On the Vineland social maturity scale her first score was 39, representing an age level of two and a half years.[14] "The general impression was that she was wholly uneducable and that any attempt to teach her to speak, after so long a period of silence, would meet with failure."[15]

In spite of this interpretation, the individuals in charge of Isabelle launched a systematic and skilful program of training. It seemed hopeless at first. The approach had to be through pantomime and dramatization, suitable to an infant. It required one week of intensive effort before she even made her first attempt at vocalization. Gradually she began to respond, however, and, after the first hurdles had at last been overcome, a curious thing happened. She went through the usual stages of learning characteristic of the years from one to six not only in proper succession but far more rapidly than normal. In a little over two months after her first vocalization she was putting sentences together. Nine months after that she could identify words and sentences on the printed page, could write well, could add to ten, and could retell a story after hearing it. Seven months beyond this point she had a vocabulary of 1,500–2,000 words and was asking complicated questions. Starting from an educational level of between one and three years (depending on what aspect one considers), she had reached a normal level by the time she was eight and a half years old. In short, she covered in two years the stages of learning that ordinarily require six.[16] Or, to put it another way, her I.Q. trebled in a year and a half.[17] The speed with which she reached the normal level of mental development seems analogous to the recovery of body weight in a growing child after an illness, the recovery being achieved by an extra fast rate of growth for a period after the illness until normal weight for the given age is again attained.

When the writer saw Isabelle a year and a half after her discovery, she gave him the impression of being a very bright, cheerful, energetic little girl. She spoke well, walked and ran without trouble, and sang with gusto and accuracy. Today she is over fourteen years old and has passed the sixth grade in a public school. Her teachers say that she participates in all school activities as normally as other children. Though older than her classmates, she has fortunately not physically matured too far beyond their level.[18]

Clearly the history of Isabelle's development

is different from that of Anna's. In both cases there was an exceedingly low, or rather blank, intellectual level to begin with. In both cases it seemed that the girl might be congenitally feeble minded. In both a considerably higher level was reached later on. But the Ohio girl achieved a normal mentality within two years, whereas Anna was still markedly inadequate at the end of four and a half years. This difference in achievement may suggest that Anna had less initial capacity. But an alternative hypothesis is possible.

One should remember that Anna never received the prolonged and expert attention that Isabelle received. The result of such attention, in the case of the Ohio girl, was to give her speech at an early stage, and her subsequent rapid development seems to have been a consequence of that. "Until Isabelle's speech and language development, she had all the characteristics of a feeble-minded child." Had Anna, who, from the standpoint of psychometric tests and early history, closely resembled this girl at the start, been given a mastery of speech at an earlier point by intensive training, her subsequent development might have been much more rapid.[19]

The hypothesis that Anna began with a sharply inferior mental capacity is therefore not established. Even if she were deficient to start with, we have no way of knowing how much so. Under ordinary conditions she might have been a dull normal or, like her mother, a moron. Even after the blight of her isolation, if she had lived to maturity, she might have finally reached virtually the full level of her capacity, whatever it may have been. That her isolation did have a profound effect upon her mentality, there can be no doubt. This is proved by the substantial degree of change during the four and a half years following her rescue.

Consideration of Isabelle's case serves to show, as Anna's case does not clearly show, that isolation up to the age of six, with failure to acquire any form of speech and hence failure to grasp nearly the whole world of cultural meaning, does not preclude the subsequent acquisition of these. Indeed, there seems to be a process of accelerated recovery in which the child goes through the mental stages at a more rapid rate than would be the case in normal development. Just what would be the maximum age at which a person could remain isolated and still retain the capacity for full cultural acquisition is hard to say. Almost certainly it would not be as high as age fifteen; it might possibly be as low as age ten. Undoubtedly various individuals would differ considerably as to the exact age.

Anna's is not an ideal case for showing the effects of extreme isolation, partly because she was possibly deficient to begin with, partly because she did not receive the best training available, and partly because she did not live long enough. Nevertheless, her case is instructive when placed in the record with numerous other cases of extreme isolation. This and the previous article about her are meant to place her in the record. It is to be hoped that other cases will be described in the scientific literature as they are discovered (as unfortunately they will be), for only in these rare cases of extreme isolation is it possible "to observe *concretely separated* two factors in the development of human personality which are always otherwise only analytically separated, the biogenic and the sociogenic factors."[20]

Notes

[1] Kingsley Davis, "Extreme Social Isolation of a Child," *American Journal of Sociology*, XLV (January, 1940), 554–65.

[2] Sincere appreciation is due to the officials in the Department of Welfare, Commonwealth of Pennsylvania, for their kind cooperation in making available the records concerning Anna and discussing the case frankly with the writer. Helen C. Hubbell, Florentine Hackbusch, and Eleanor Mecklenburg were particularly helpful, as was Fanny L. Matchette. Without their aid neither of the reports on Anna could have been written.

[3] The records are not clear as to which day.

[4] Letter to one of the state officials in charge of the case.

[5] *Ibid.*

[6] Progress report of the school.

[7] Davis, *op. cit.*, p. 564.

[8] The facts set forth here as to Anna's ancestry are taken chiefly

from a report of mental tests administered to Anna's mother by psychologists at a state hospital where she was taken for this purpose after the discovery of Anna's seclusion. This excellent report was not available to the writer when the previous paper on Anna was published.

[9] Marie K. Mason, "Learning to Speak after Six and One-half Years of Silence," *Journal of Speech Disorders*, VII (1942), 295–304.

[10] Frances N. Maxfield, "What Happens When the Social Environment of a Child Approaches Zero." The writer is greatly indebted to Mrs. Maxfield and to Professor Horace B. English, a colleague of Professor Maxfield, for the privilege of seeing this manuscript and other materials collected on isolated and feral individuals.

[11] J. A. L. Singh and Robert M. Zingg, *Wolf-children and Feral Man* (New York: Harper & Bros., 1941), pp. 248–251.

[12] Maxfield, unpublished manuscript cited above.

[13] Mason, *op. cit.*, p. 299.

[14] Maxfield, unpublished manuscript.

[15] Mason, *op. cit.*, p. 299.

[16] *Ibid.*, pp. 300–304.

[17] Maxfield, unpublished manuscript.

[18] Based on a personal letter from Dr. Mason to the writer, May 13, 1946.

[19] This point is suggested in a personal letter from Dr. Mason to the writer, October 22, 1946.

[20] Singh & Zingg, *op. cit.*, pp. xxi–xxii, in a foreword by the writer.

SECONDARY SOCIALIZATION

The acquisition of culture does not end with the completion of primary socialization. Particularly in a complex society, there is always more to culture than the individual already knows, and he is always learning and thus continuing his socialization. Moreover, culture is always changing, particularly quickly in complex societies, and it must be relearned. At the same time, the individual joins new groups with new subcultures and leaves old groups, abandoning former subcultures. Even late in life, socialization continues. The old person must learn the proper way to live in retirement and, at the end, the correct way in which to take his leave.

Secondary socialization is the focus of a whole institutional complex, formal education. A wide variety of culture is acquired in this way, and in contemporary society the scope of formal education is increasing. As the culture to be mastered becomes more complex, education becomes both more specialized and longer in duration, and the relative importance of education among social institutions increases.

The study of the socialization process and of educational institutions is one of the fastest growing sociological specialties. This selection concerns changes wrought in certain values of medical students by their experience in medical school. It should be noted that the fate of idealism is not formally among the considerations for which medical educators generally feel themselves responsible. The changes noted here are reflections of a curriculum which is planned without giving much thought to their possibility or importance.

> Medical students enter school as lay idealists: they believe that medicine is service to man, and that its study will give them the practical techniques to enter this service. During the two pre-clinical years, they find they have no opportunity to serve patients, and that knowledge they acquire is not only impractical, but comprises too large a body of facts to hope to master. The consequent reaction, strengthened by the formation of a student society and culture, is to select the facts to learn based on their usefulness in examinations, and to postpone idealism into the future.

> In the clinical years students find that they must work to understand medical problems, rather than help the bearers of these problems. Their

idealism becomes professionalized. The immediate concern of the young doctor is to gain technical competence, while the lay idealism recedes into the background but is not discarded.

The student culture of medical school, formed as a reaction to the demands of the educational situation, finds lay idealism irrelevant, but it builds a type of professional value. This is an unplanned but useful development that reconciles students to the realities of medicine and increases the motivation to technical competence. Sociologists have found that the student culture of the liberal arts college, rather than enhancing the goals of the college, defeats them by stressing intellectually irrelevant achievements in sports and dating, as well as substituting grades for learning as an academic goal. Positive or negative, student culture is a powerful influence on the motivation to learn and the manner of accomplishment in formal education.

Selection 19
THE FATE OF IDEALISM IN MEDICAL SCHOOL
Howard S. Becker and Blanche Geer

It makes some difference in a man's performance of his work whether he believes wholeheartedly in what he is doing or feels that in important respects it is a fraud, whether he feels convinced that it is a good thing or believes that it is not really of much use after all. The distinction we are making is the one people have in mind when they refer, for example, to their calling as a "noble profession" on the one hand or a "racket" on the other. In the one case they idealistically proclaim that their work is all that it claims on the surface to be; in the other they cynically concede that it is first and foremost a way of making a living and that its surface pretensions are just that and nothing more. Presumably, different modes of behavior are associated with these perspectives when wholeheartedly embraced. The cynic cuts corners with a feeling of inevitability while the idealist goes down fighting. *The Blackboard Jungle* and *Not as a Stranger* are only the most recent in a long tradition of fictional portrayals of the importance of this aspect of a man's adjustment to his work.

Professional schools often receive a major share of the blame for producing this kind of cynicism—and none more than the medical school. The idealistic young freshman changes

Reprinted from *American Sociological Review*, 23:1, 1958, pp. 50–56, with permission of the authors and the publisher.

into a tough, hardened, unfeeling doctor; or so the popular view has it. Teachers of medicine sometimes rephrase the distinction between the clinical and pre-clinical years into one between the "cynical" and "pre-cynical" years. Psychological research supports this view, presenting attitude surveys which show medical students year by year scoring lower on "idealism" and higher on "cynicism."[1] Typically, this cynicism is seen as developing in response to the shattering of ideals consequent on coming face-to-face with the realities of professional practice.

In this paper, we attempt to describe the kind of idealism that characterized the medical freshmen and to trace both the development of cynicism and the vicissitudes of that idealism in the course of the four years of medical training. Our main themes are that though they develop cynical feelings in specific situations directly associated with their medical school experience, the medical students never lose their original idealism about the practice of medicine; that the growth of both cynicism and idealism are not simple developments, but are instead complex transformations; and that the very notions "idealism" and "cynicism" need further analysis, and must be seen as situational in their expressions rather than as stable traits possessed by individuals in greater or lesser degree. Finally, we see the greater portion of these feelings as being collective rather than individual phenomena.

Our discussion is based on a study we are now conducting at a state medical school,[2] in which we have carried on participant observation with students of all four years in all of the courses and clinical work to which they are exposed. We joined the students in their activities in school and after school and watched them at work in labs, on the hospital wards, and in the clinic. Often spending as much as a month with a small group of from five to fifteen students assigned to a particular activity, we came to know them well and were able to gather information in informal interviews and by overhearing the ordinary daily conversation of the group.[3] In the course of our observation and interviewing we have gathered much information on the subject of idealism. Of necessity, we shall have to present the very briefest statement of our findings with little or no supporting evidence.[4] The problem of idealism is, of course, many-faceted and complex and we have dealt with it in a simplified way, describing only some of its grosser features.[5]

The freshmen

The medical students enter school with what we may think of as the idealistic notion, implicit in lay culture, that the practice of medicine is a wonderful thing and that they are going to devote their lives to service to mankind. They believe that medicine is made up of a great body of well-established facts that they will be taught from the first day on and that these facts will be of immediate practical use to them as physicians. They enter school expecting to work industriously and expecting that if they work hard enough they will be able to master this body of fact and thus become good doctors.

In several ways the first year of medical school does not live up to their expectations. They are disillusioned when they find they will not be near patients at all, that the first year will be just like another year of college. In fact, some feel that it is not even as good as college because their work in certain areas is not as thorough as courses in the same fields in undergraduate school. They come to think that their courses (with the exception of anatomy) are not worth much because, in the first place, the faculty (being Ph.D.'s) know noth-

ing about the practice of medicine, and, in the second place, the subject matter itself is irrelevant, or as the students say, "ancient history."

The freshmen are further disillusioned when the faculty tells them in a variety of ways that there is more to medicine than they can possibly learn. They realize it may be impossible for them to learn all they need to know in order to practice medicine properly. Their disillusionment becomes more profound when they discover that this statement of the faculty is literally true.[6] Experience in trying to master the details of the anatomy of the extremities convinces them that they cannot do so in the time they have. Their expectation of hard work is not disappointed; they put in an eight-hour day of classes and laboratories, and study four or five hours a night and most of the weekend as well.

Some of the students, the brightest, continue to attempt to learn it all, but succeed only in getting more and more worried about their work. The majority decide that, since they can't learn it all, they must select from among all the facts presented to them those they will attempt to learn. There are two ways of making this selection. On the one hand, the student may decide on the basis of his own uninformed notions about the nature of medical practice that many facts are not important, since they relate to things which seldom come up in the actual practice of medicine; therefore, he reasons, it is useless to learn them. On the other hand, the student can decide that the important facts are those which are likely to be asked on an examination; he uses this as a basis for selecting both facts to memorize and courses for intensive study. For example, the work in physiology is dismissed on both of these grounds, being considered neither relevant to the facts of medical life nor important in terms of the amount of time the faculty devotes to it and the number of examinations in the subject.

A student may use either or both of these bases of selection at the beginning of the year, before many tests have been given. But after a few tests have been taken, the student makes "what the faculty wants" the chief basis of his selection of what to learn, for he now has a better idea of what this is and also has become aware that it is possible to fail examinations and that he therefore must learn the expectations of the faculty if he wishes to stay in school. The fact that one group of students, that with the highest prestige in the class, took this view early and did well on examinations was decisive in swinging the whole class around to this position. The students were equally influenced to become "test-wise" by the fact that, although they had all been in the upper range in their colleges, the class average on the first examination was frighteningly low.

In becoming test-wise, the students begin to develop systems for discovering the faculty wishes and learning them. These systems are both methods for studying their texts and short-cuts that can be taken in laboratory work. For instance, they begin to select facts for memorization by looking over the files of old examinations maintained in each of the medical fraternity houses. They share tip-offs from the lectures and offhand remarks of the faculty as to what will be on the examinations. In anatomy, they agree not to bother to dissect out subcutaneous nerves, reasoning that it is both difficult and time-consuming and the information can be secured from books with less effort. The interaction involved in the development of such systems and short-cuts helps to create a social group of a class which had previously been only an aggregation of smaller and less organized groups.

In this medical school, the students learn in this way to distinguish between the activities of the first year and their original view that everything that happens to them in medical school will be important. Thus they become cynical about the value of their activities in the first year. They feel that the real thing—learning which will help them to help mankind—has been postponed, perhaps until the second year, or perhaps even farther, at which time they will be able again to act on idealistic premises. They believe that what they do in their later years in school under supervision will be about the same thing they will do, as physicians, on their own; the first year had disappointed this expectation.

There is one matter, however, about which the students are not disappointed during the first year: the so-called trauma of dealing with the cadaver. But this experience, rather than producing cynicism, reinforces the student's attachment to his idealistic view of medicine by making him feel that he is experiencing at least some of the necessary unpleasantness of the doctor's. Such difficulties, however, do not loom as large for the student as those of solving the problem of just what the faculty wants.

On this and other points, a working consensus develops in the new consolidated group about the interpretation of their experience in medical school and its norms of conduct. This consensus, which we call *student culture*,[7] focuses their attention almost completely on their day-to-day activities in school and obscures or sidetracks their earlier idealistic preoccupations. Cynicism, griping, and minor cheating become endemic, but the cynicism is specific to the educational situation, to the first year, and to only parts of it. Thus the students keep their cynicism separate from their idealistic feelings and by postponement protect their belief that medicine is a wonderful thing, that their school is a fine one, and that they will become good doctors.

Later years

The sophomore year does not differ greatly from the freshman year. Both the work load and anxiety over examinations probably increase. Though they begin some medical activities, as in their attendance at autopsies and particularly in their introductory course in physical diagnosis, most of what they do continues to repeat the pattern of the college science curriculum. Their attention still centers on the problem of getting through school by doing well in examinations.

During the third and fourth, or clinical years, teaching takes a new form. In place of lectures and laboratories, the students' work now consists of the study of actual patients admitted to the hospital or seen in the clinic. Each patient who enters the hospital is assigned to a student who interviews him about his illnesses, past and present, and performs a physical examination. He writes this up for the patient's chart, and appends the diagnosis and the treatment that he would use were he allowed actually to treat the patient. During conferences with faculty physicians, often held at the patient's bedside, the student is quizzed about items of his report and called upon to defend them or to explain their significance. Most of the teaching in the clinical years is of this order.

Contact with patients brings a new set of circumstances with which the student must deal. He no longer feels the great pressure created by tests, for he is told by the faculty, and this is confirmed by his daily experience, that examinations are now less important. His problems now become those of coping with a steady stream of patients in a way that will please the staff man under whom he is working, and of handling what is sometimes a tremendous load of clinical work so as to allow himself time for studying diseases and treatments that interest him and for play and family life.

The students earlier have expected that once they reach the clinical years they will be able to realize their idealistic ambitions to help people and to learn those things immediately useful in aiding people who are ill. But they find themselves working to understand cases as medical problems rather than working to help the sick and memorizing the relevant available facts so that these can be produced immediately for a questioning staff man. When they make ward rounds with a faculty member they are likely to be quizzed about any of the seemingly countless facts possibly related to the condition of the patient for whom they are "caring."

Observers speak of the cynicism that overtakes the student and the lack of concern for his patients as human beings. This change does take place, but it is not produced solely by "the anxiety brought about by the presence of death and suffering."[8] The student becomes preoccupied with the technical aspects of the cases with which he deals because the faculty requires him to do so. He is questioned about so many technical details that he must spend most of his time learning them.

The frustrations created by his position in the teaching hospital further divert the student from idealistic concerns. He finds himself low man in a hierarchy based on clinical experience, so that he is allowed very little of the medical responsibility he would like to assume. Because of his lack of experience, he cannot write orders, and he receives permission to perform medical and surgical procedures (if at all) at a rate he considers far too slow. He usually must content himself with "mere" vicarious participation in the drama of danger, life, and death that he sees as the core of medical practice. The student culture accents these difficulties so that events (and especially those involving patients) are interpreted and reacted to as they push him

toward or hold him back from further participation in this drama. He does not think in terms the layman might use.

As a result of the increasingly technical emphasis of his thinking the student appears cynical to the non-medical outsider, though from his own point of view he is simply seeing what is "really important." Instead of reacting with the layman's horror and sympathy for the patient to the sight of a cancerous organ that has been surgically removed, the student is more likely to regret that he was not allowed to close the incision at the completion of the operation, and to rue the hours that he must spend searching in the fatty flesh for the lymph nodes that will reveal how far the disease has spread. As in other lines of work, he drops lay attitudes for those more relevant to the way the event affects someone in his position.

This is not to say that the students lose their original idealism. When issues of idealism are openly raised in a situation they define as appropriate, they respond as they might have when they were freshmen. But the influence of the student culture is such that questions which might bring forth this idealism are not brought up. Students are often assigned patients for examination and follow-up whose conditions might be expected to provoke idealistic crises. Students discuss such patients, however, with reference to the problems they create for the student. Patients with terminal diseases who are a long time dying, and patients with chronic diseases who show little change from week to week, are more likely to be viewed as creating extra work without extra compensation in knowledge or the opportunity to practice new skills than as examples of illness which raise questions about euthanasia. Such cases require the student to spend time every day checking on progress which he feels will probably not take place and to write long "progress" notes in the patient's chart although little progress has occurred.

This apparent cynicism is a collective matter. Group activities are built around this kind of workaday perspective, constraining the students in two ways. First, they do not openly express the lay idealistic notions they may hold, for their culture does not sanction such expression; second, they are less likely to have thoughts of this deviant kind when they are engaged in group activity. The collective nature of this "cynicism" is indicated by the fact that students become more openly idealistic whenever they are removed from the influence of student culture—when they are alone with a sociologist as they near the finish of school and sense the approaching end of student life, for example, or when they are isolated from their classmates and therefore are less influenced by this culture.[9]

They still feel, as advanced students, though much less so than before, that school is irrelevant to actual medical practice. Many of their tasks, like running laboratory tests on patients newly admitted to the hospital or examining surgical specimens in the pathology laboratory, seem to them to have nothing to do with their visions of their future activity as doctors. As in their freshman year, they believe that perhaps they must obtain the knowledge they will need in spite of the school. They still conceive of medicine as a huge body of proven facts, but no longer believe that they will ever be able to master it all. They now say that they are going to try to apply the solution of the practicing M.D. to their own dilemma: learn a few things that they are interested in very well and know enough about other things to pass examinations while in school and, later on in practice, to know to which specialist to send difficult patients.

Their original medical idealism reasserts itself as the end of school approaches. Seniors show more interest than students in earlier years in serious ethical dilemmas of the kind they expect to face in practice. They have become aware of ethical problems laymen often see as crucial for the physician—whether it is right to keep patients with fatal diseases alive as long as possible, or what should be done if an influential patient demands an abortion—and worry about them. As they near graduation and student culture begins to break down as the soon-to-be doctors are about to go their separate ways, these questions are more and more openly discussed.

While in school, they have added to their earlier idealism a new and peculiarly professional idealism. Even though they know that few doctors live up to the standards they have been taught, they intend always to examine their patients thoroughly and to give treatment based on firm diagnosis rather than merely to relieve symptoms. This expansion and transformation of idealism appear most explicitly in their consideration of alternative careers, concerning both specialization and the kind of arrangements to be made for setting up practice. Many of their hypothetical choices aim at making it possible for them to be the kind of doctors their original idealism pictured. Many seniors consider specialty training so that they will be able to work in a limited field in which it will be more nearly possible to know all there is to know, thus avoiding the necessity of dealing in a more ignorant way with the wider range of problems general practice would present. In the same manner, they think of schemes to establish partnerships or other arrangements making it easier to avoid a work load which would prevent them from giving each patient the thorough examination and care they now see as ideal.

In other words, as school comes to an end, the cynicism specific to the school situation also comes to an end and their original and more general idealism about medicine comes to the fore again, though within a framework of more realistic alternatives. Their idealism is now more informed although no less selfless.

Discussion

We have used the words "idealism" and "cynicism" loosely in our description of the changeable state of mind of the medical student, playing on ambiguities we can now attempt to clear up. Retaining a core of common meaning, the dictionary definition, in our reference to the person's belief in the worth of his activity and the claims made for it, we have seen that this is not a generalized trait of the students we studied but rather an attitude which varies greatly, depending on the particular activity the worth of which is questioned and the situation in which the attitude is expressed.

This variability of the idealistic attitude suggests that in using such an element of personal perspective in sociological analysis one should not treat it as homogeneous but should make a determined search for subtypes which may arise under different conditions and have differing consequences. Such subtypes presumably can be constructed along many dimensions. There might, for instance, be consistent variations in the medical students' idealism through the four years of school that are related to their social class backgrounds. We have stressed in this report the subtypes that can be constructed according to variations in the object of the idealistic attitude and variations in the audience the person has in mind when he adopts the attitude. The medical students can be viewed as both idealistic and cynical, depending on whether one has in mind their view of their school activities or the future they envision for themselves as doctors. Further, they might take one or another of these positions depending on whether their implied audience is made up of other students, their instructors, or the lay public.

A final complication arises because cynicism and idealism are not merely attributes of the actor, but are as dependent on the person doing the attributing as they are on the qualities of the individual to whom they are attributed.[10] Though the student may see his own disregard of the unique personal troubles of a particular patient as proper scientific objectivity, the layman may view this objectivity as heartless cynicism.[11]

Having made these analytic distinctions, we can now summarize the transformations of these characteristics as we have seen them occurring among medical students. Some of the students' determined idealism at the outset is reaction against the lay notion, of which they are uncomfortably aware, that doctors are money-hungry cynics; they counter this with an idealism of similar lay origin stressing the doctor's devotion to service. But this idealism soon meets a setback, as students find that it will not be relevant for awhile, since medical school has, it seems, little relation to the practice of medicine, as they see it. As it has not been refuted, but only shown to be temporarily beside the point, the students "agree" to set this idealism aside in favor of a realistic approach to the problem of getting through school. This approach, which we have labeled as the cynicism specific to the school experience, serves as protection for the earlier grandiose feelings about medicine by postponing their exposure to reality to a distant future. As that future approaches near the end of the four years and its possible mistreatment of their ideals moves closer, the students again worry about maintaining their integrity, this time in actual medical practice. They use some of the knowledge they have gained to plan careers which, it is hoped, can best bring their ideals to realization.

We can put this in propositional form by saying that when a man's ideals are challenged by outsiders and then further strained by reality, he may salvage them by postponing their application to a future time when conditions are expected to be more propitious.

Notes

[1] Leonard D. Eron, "Effect of Medical Education on Medical Students," *Journal of Medical Education,* 10 (October, 1955), pp. 559–566.

[2] This study is sponsored by Community Studies, Inc., of Kansas City, Missouri, and is being carried on at the University of Kansas Medical School, to whose dean, staff, and students we are indebted for their wholehearted cooperation. Professor Everett C. Hughes of the University of Chicago is director of the project.

[3] The technique of participant observation has not been fully systematized, but some approaches to this have been made. See, for example, Florence R. Kluckhohn, "The Participant Observer Technique in Small Communities," *American Journal of Sociology,* 45 (November, 1940), pp. 331–343; Arthur Vidich, "Participant Observation and the Collection and Interpretation of Data," *ibid.,* 60 (January, 1955), pp. 354–360; William Foote Whyte, "Observational Fieldwork Methods," in Marie Jahoda, Morton Deutsch, and Stuart W. Cook (editors), *Research Methods in the Social Sciences,* New York: Dryden Press, 1951, II, pp. 393–514; and *Street Corner Society* (Enlarged Edition), Chicago: University of Chicago Press, 1955, pp. 279–358; Rosalie Hankey Wax, "Twelve Years Later: An Analysis of Field Experience," *American Journal of Sociology,* 63 (September, 1957), pp. 133–142; Morris S. Schwartz and Charlotte Green Schwartz, "Problems in Participant Observation," *ibid.,* 60 (January, 1955), pp. 343–353; and Howard S. Becker and Blanche Geer, "Participant Observation and Interviewing: A Comparison," *Human Organization.* The last item represents the first of a projected series of papers attempting to make explicit the operations involved in this method. For a short description of some techniques used in this

study, see Howard S. Becker, "Interviewing Medical Students," *American Journal of Sociology,* 62 (September, 1956), pp. 199–201.

[4] A fuller analysis and presentation of evidence will be contained in a volume on this study now being prepared by the authors in collaboration with Everett C. Hughes and Anselm L. Strauss.

[5] Renee Fox has shown how complex one aspect of this whole subject is in her analysis of the way medical students at Cornell become aware of and adjust to both their own failure to master all available knowledge and the gaps in current knowledge in many fields. See her "Training for Uncertainty," in Robert K. Merton, George C. Reader, and Patricia L. Kendall, *The Student Physician: Introductory Studies in the Sociology of Medical Education,* Cambridge: Harvard University Press, 1957, pp. 207–241.

[6] Compare Fox' description of student reaction to this problem at Cornell (*op. cit.,* pp. 209–221).

[7] The concept of student culture is analyzed in some detail in Howard S. Becker and Blanche Geer, "Student Culture in Medical School," *Harvard Educational Review.*

[8] Dana L. Farnsworth, "Some Observations on the Attitudes and Motivations of the Harvard Medical Student," *Harvard Medical Alumni Bulletin,* January, 1956, p. 34.

[9] See the discussion in Howard S. Becker, "Interviewing Medical Students," *op. cit.*

[10] See Philip Selznick's related discussion of fanaticism in *TVA and the Grass Roots,* Berkeley: University of California Press, 1953, pp. 205–213.

[11] George Orwell gives the layman's side in his essay, "How the Poor Die" in *Shooting an Elephant and Other Essays,* London: Secker and Warburg, 1950, pp. 18–32.

Part 4

SOCIAL ORGANIZATION

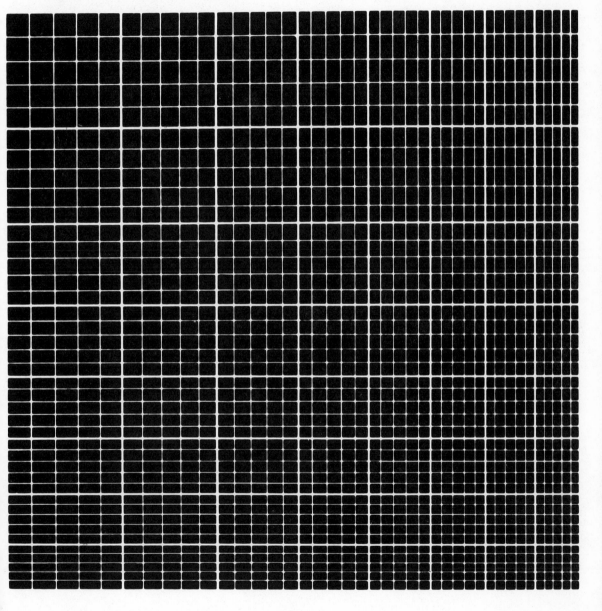

Chapter 8

NORMS

SOCIAL PRESSURE
Selection 20

FOLKWAYS AND MORES
Selection 21

BEHAVIOR SETTINGS
Selection 22

Norms are the focus of sociological interest in culture because they refer directly to behavior. Values are more central to culture than are norms, but they are farther removed from behavior and may be realized in different ways, whereas norms prescribe the specific ways in which values are to be realized in behavior.

Members of a group conform to its norms for two reasons. First, the norms of a group are internalized by its members in the socialization process (described in Chapter 7). People want to conform to norms that form a part of their social selves, and they feel uncomfortable, or guilty, when they violate these norms. Second, the members of a group form expectations of each other's behavior based on the norms. When these expectations are not fulfilled by one member, others in the group indicate their disapproval in various ways. Contrariwise, when one's behavior conforms closely to the norms, others indicate approval. These expressions of approval and disapproval of behavior, called sanctions, serve to direct behavior into normative channels.

The ultimate sanction available to any group is the expulsion of the norm-violator from the group. Therefore, a group's ability to force its members' behavior to correspond to the norms is related to the consequences of expulsion for the members. In the case of the total political society, this expulsion may take the form of imprisonment or exile (civil death) or capital punishment, and few people violate norms sanctioned in this fashion. Other groups are restricted to less extreme sanctions. If a group other than the total society ceases to be important to an individual, he is immune to the group's sanctions and can violate its norms with impunity.

Sociologists make several distinctions that are helpful in understanding the nature of norms. The distinction between prescriptive and proscriptive norms points to the fact that norms tell what is done and also what is not done in a society. The distinction between associational norms and communal norms points to the fact that some norms apply only to members of certain groups, while others are binding on all members of a society. The distinction between folkways and mores concerns the importance of norms as group members judge them. Mores are norms that the group defines as essential to social welfare and that are strongly sanctioned, whereas folkways are considered less important and are less strongly sanctioned. The distinction between ideal norms and real norms, the former not in fact considered binding on behavior, serves as a warning to the sociologist not to accept all verbalized culture at face value.

Although in general the behavior of members of a group follows the group norms, deviant behavior, violating the norms, is not uncommon. Few norms are followed by all group members at all times. Indeed, if this were so, it would be more difficult to identify norms, since one of the easiest and best ways of knowing a group's norms is to observe the instances in which sanctions are applied.

Sociology has a great interest in behavior that violates the norms, just as psychology is interested in disordered personalities. In both fields, the "abnormal" is interesting not only for itself, but for what it can tell about the "normal." Sociological theories of deviant behavior generally include the notion that what is deviant in one group is normal in another and that deviance in a complex society is a result of conforming to norms that are inappropriate in a particular context, rather than a result of lack of norms. The latter type of situation, called *anomie* by Durkheim, is assumed to be very rare, occurring for instance in periods of catastrophic social change, whereas deviance in general is very common. Thus, in most situations behavior is seen by sociologists to be conforming, and deviant behavior is explained as the result of conforming to deviant norms.

Selection 20, by Solomon E. Asch, suggests the role of group consensus in the origination and support of norms. Selection 21, by William Graham Sumner, presents a classic analysis of types of norms. Selection 22, by Sherri Cavan, introduces the concept of behavior settings and shows how it can add to the precision with which we are able to specify normative expectations.

SOCIAL PRESSURE

The socialized individual appears to want to conform. In such an individual, the internalized generalized other has become a part of the self. For instance, arriving at a restaurant where we find ourselves "underdressed," we feel uncomfortable. This discomfort springs from our perceptions of others' disapproval and also from within ourselves—from the disapproval of the internalized generalized other. The situation that brings about the discomfort is the contrast between our own behavior and the apparent consensus of others concerning the behavior that is appropriate in the situation. If the consensus of others is strong, if every man is wearing a suit and every woman is wearing a fashionable dress, our sport shirt or skirt and sweater will seem miserably conspicuous, and we will probably leave to seek a less pretentious establishment for dinner. However, if a few other diners appear in sport shirts and skirts and sweaters, the consensus of the majority is greatly weakened, and we dine on duck à *l'orange* tonight.

This selection investigates the power of group consensus to affect behavior in the context of a classical experiment. The size of the group and the strength of consensus are varied, with the different situations serving as control groups for each other.

The experiment concerned the very simple task of matching a "standard" line to one of three test lines, varying in length. There was always a correct answer, and the two wrong lines were considerably different from the standard line. The judgments took place in a group setting, where all members but one were previously instructed to give identical wrong answers. Among the subjects who did not know the "gimmick," approximately three-fourths agreed to the group's wrong answer at least once in a while, and many of them yielded consistently. Interviews of the subjects after the experiment indicated that some of the yielders reasoned that the others were wrong, but they felt that they should go along with the group; others of the yielders reasoned that the rest of the group was right, and that there must have been something wrong with themselves.

Variations on this basic experiment showed that the power of the unanimous majority was felt almost as strongly in groups of four as it was in much larger groups, and that the effect was greatly weakened by the presence of even one dissenter apart from the uninstructed subjects. The majority effect was weaker when the differences between the standard line and its alternatives were increased, but even when the error was glaring some subjects yielded to the majority.

The task in this experiment was simple and straightforward, and its performance was supported by cultural beliefs concerning the trustworthiness of sense data under ordinary circumstances and by normative obligations to tell the truth in scientific experiments. The subjects were college students, not simple, conformist oafs. The uneasiness with which we read this report stems from its demonstration of the weakness of personal standards and usual norms in the face of unanimous social opposition. The results of this study threaten our values concerning individualism and our beliefs concerning human rationality.

Perspective may be added to this experiment by comparing it to a similar one performed by Muzafer Sherif. Asch's experiment employed a simple perceptual task, to which there was an objective "right" answer. Sherif used an optical illusion for the experimental task. If a point of light is shown in a completely dark room, it appears to move, although it is in fact stationary. The impression as to how far the point "moves" varies from individual to individual. Sherif showed that when his subjects estimated the point's motion in the presence of others **all** of them shifted their estimates in the direction of the estimates given by the others. This occurred in spite of the fact that the subjects thought they were making judgments of an objective perceptual fact and did not realize that they were experiencing an optical illusion.

Most situations in life are neither so objective as those studied by Asch nor so illusory as those studied by Sherif, but fall somewhere between the two. The Asch experiment may be taken to represent the degree of conformity which can result when the situation is clear-cut and "factual," whereas the Sherif experiment may represent the extent of conformity under the conditions of illusion. These experiments help us understand why what is right, true, and proper in one culture is wrong, false, and improper in another. They remind us that norms, like the rest of culture, are the product of social definitions that are valid and remain so only in the presence of group consensus.

Selection 20
OPINIONS AND SOCIAL PRESSURE
Solomon E. Asch

That social influences shape every person's practices, judgments and beliefs is a truism to which anyone will readily assent. A child masters his "native" dialect down to the finest nuances; a member of a tribe of cannibals accepts cannibalism as altogether fitting and proper. All the social sciences take their departure from the observation of the profound effects that groups exert on their members. For psychologists, group pressure upon the minds of individuals raises a host of questions they would like to investigate in detail.

How, and to what extent, do social forces constrain people's opinions and attitudes? This question is especially pertinent in our day. The same epoch that has witnessed the unprecedented technical extension of communication has also brought into existence the deliberate manipulation of opinion and the "engineering of consent." There are many good reasons why, as citizens and as scientists, we should be concerned with studying the ways in which human beings form their opinions and the role that social conditions play.

Studies of these questions began with the interest in hypnosis aroused by the French physician Jean Martin Charcot (a teacher of Sigmund Freud) toward the end of the 19th century. Charcot believed that only hysterical patients could be fully hypnotized, but this view was soon challenged by two other physicians, Hyppolyte Bernheim and A. A. Liébault, who demonstrated that they could put most people under the hypnotic spell. Bernheim proposed that hypnosis was but an extreme form of a normal psychological process which became known as "suggestibility." It was shown that monotonous reiteration of instructions could induce in normal persons in the waking state involuntary bodily changes such as swaying or rigidity of the arms, and sensations such as warmth and odor.

It was not long before social thinkers seized

Reprinted from *Scientific American*, 193:5, 1955, pp. 31–35, with permission of the publisher. Copyright 1955 by Scientific American, Inc. All rights reserved.

upon these discoveries as a basis for explaining numerous social phenomena, from the spread of opinion to the formation of crowds and the following of leaders. The sociologist Gabriel Tarde summed it all up in the aphorism: "Social man is a somnambulist."

When the new discipline of social psychology was born at the beginning of this century, its first experiments were essentially adaptations of the suggestion demonstration. The technique generally followed a simple plan. The subjects, usually college students, were asked to give their opinions or preferences concerning various matters; some time later they were again asked to state their choices, but now they were also informed of the opinions held by authorities or large groups of their peers on the same matters. (Often the alleged consensus was fictitious.) Most of these studies had substantially the same result: confronted with opinions contrary to their own, many subjects apparently shifted their judgments in the direction of the views of the majorities or the experts. The late psychologist Edward L. Thorndike reported that he had succeeded in modifying the esthetic preferences of adults by this procedure. Other psychologists reported that people's evaluations of the merit of a literary passage could be raised or lowered by ascribing the passage to different authors. Apparently the sheer weight of numbers or authority sufficed to change opinions, even when no arguments for the opinions themselves were provided.

Now the very ease of success in these experiments arouses suspicion. Did the subjects actually change their opinions, or were the experimental victories scored only on paper? On grounds of common sense, one must question whether opinions are generally as watery as these studies indicate. There is some reason to wonder whether it was not the investigators who, in their enthusiasm for a theory, were suggestible, and whether the ostensibly gullible subjects were not providing answers which they thought good subjects were expected to give.

The investigations were guided by certain

underlying assumptions, which today are common currency and account for much that is thought and said about the operations of propaganda and public opinion. The assumptions are that people submit uncritically and painlessly to external manipulation by suggestion or prestige, and that any given idea or value can be "sold" or "unsold" without reference to its merits. We should be skeptical, however, of the supposition that the power of social pressure necessarily implies uncritical submission to it: independence and the capacity to rise above group passion are also open to human beings. Further, one may question on psychological grounds whether it is possible as a rule to change a person's judgment of a situation or an object without first changing his knowledge or assumptions about it.

In what follows I shall describe some experiments in an investigation of the effects of group pressure which was carried out recently with the help of a number of my associates. The tests not only demonstrate the operations of group pressure upon individuals but also illustrate a new kind of attack on the problem and some of the more subtle questions that it raises.

A group of seven to nine young men, all college students, are assembled in a classroom for a "psychological experiment" in visual judgment. The experimenter informs them that they will be comparing the lengths of lines. He shows two large white cards. On one is a single vertical black line—the standard whose length is to be matched. On the other card are three vertical lines of various lengths. The subjects are to choose the one that is of the same length as the line on the other card. One of the three actually is of the same length; the other two are substantially different, the difference ranging from three quarters of an inch to an inch and three quarters.

The experiment opens uneventfully. The subjects announce their answers in the order in which they have been seated in the room, and on the first round every person chooses the same matching line. Then a second set of cards is exposed; again the group is unanimous. The members appear ready to endure politely another boring experiment. On the third trial there is an unexpected disturbance. One person near the end of the group disagrees with all the others in his selection of the matching line. He looks surprised, indeed incredulous, about the disagreement. On the following trial he disagrees again, while the others remain unanimous in their choice. The dissenter becomes more and more worried and hesitant as the disagreement continues in succeeding trials; he may pause before announcing his answer and speak in a low voice, or he may smile in an embarrassed way.

What the dissenter does not know is that all the other members of the group were instructed by the experimenter beforehand to give incorrect answers in unanimity at certain points. The single individual who is not a party to this prearrangement is the focal subject of our experiment. He is placed in a position in which, while he is actually giving the correct answers, he finds himself unexpectedly in a minority of one, opposed by a unanimous and arbitrary majority with respect to a clear and simple fact. Upon him we have brought to bear two opposed forces: the evidence of his senses and the unanimous opinion of a group of his peers. Also, he must declare his judgments in public, before a majority which has also stated its position publicly.

The instructed majority occasionally reports correctly in order to reduce the possibility that the naïve subject will suspect collusion against him. (In only a few cases did the subject actually show suspicion; when this happened, the experiment was stopped and the results were not counted.) There are 18 trials in each series, and on 12 of these the majority responds erroneously.

How do people respond to group pressure in this situation? I shall report first the statistical results of a series in which a total of 123 subjects from three institutions of higher learning (not including my own, Swarthmore College) were placed in the minority situation described above.

Two alternatives were open to the subject: he could act independently, repudiating the majority, or he could go along with the majority, repudiating the evidence of his senses. Of the 123 put to the test, a considerable percentage yielded to the majority. Whereas in ordinary circumstances individuals matching the lines will make mistakes less than 1 per cent of the time, under group pressure the minority subjects swung to acceptance of the misleading majority's wrong judgments in 36.8 per cent of the selections.

Of course individuals differed in response.

At one extreme, about one quarter of the subjects were completely independent and never agreed with the erroneous judgments of the majority. At the other extreme, some individuals went with the majority nearly all the time. The performances of individuals in this experiment tend to be highly consistent. Those who strike out on the path of independence do not, as a rule, succumb to the majority even over an extended series of trials, while those who choose the path of compliance are unable to free themselves as the ordeal is prolonged.

The reasons for the startling individual differences have not yet been investigated in detail. At this point we can only report some tentative generalizations from talks with the subjects, each of whom was interviewed at the end of the experiment. Among the independent individuals were many who held fast because of staunch confidence in their own judgment. The most significant fact about them was not absence of responsiveness to the majority but a capacity to recover from doubt and to reestablish their equilibrium. Others who acted independently came to believe that the majority was correct in its answers, but they continued their dissent on the simple ground that it was their obligation to call the play as they saw it.

Among the extremely yielding persons we found a group who quickly reached the conclusion: "I am wrong, they are right." Others yielded in order "not to spoil your results." Many of the individuals who went along suspected that the majority were "sheep" following the first responder, or that the majority were victims of an optical illusion; nevertheless, these suspicions failed to free them at the moment of decision. More disquieting were the reactions of subjects who construed their difference from the majority as a sign of some general deficiency in themselves, which at all costs they must hide. On this basis they desperately tried to merge with the majority, not realizing the longer-range consequences to themselves. All the yielding subjects underestimated the frequency with which they conformed.

Which aspect of the influence of a majority is more important—the size of the majority or its unanimity? The experiment was modified to examine this question. In one series the size of the opposition was varied from one to 15 persons. The results showed a clear trend. When a subject was confronted with only a single individual who contradicted his answers, he was swayed little: he continued to answer independently and correctly in nearly all trials. When the opposition was increased to two the pressure became substantial: minority subjects now accepted the wrong answer 13.6 per cent of the time. Under the pressure of a majority of three, the subjects' errors jumped to 31.8 per cent. But further increases in the size of the majority apparently did not increase the weight of the pressure substantially. Clearly the size of the opposition is important only up to a point.

Disturbance of the majority's unanimity had a striking effect. In this experiment the subject was given the support of a truthful partner— either another individual who did not know of the pre-arranged agreement among the rest of the group, or a person who was instructed to give correct answers throughout.

The presence of a supporting partner depleted the majority of much of its power. Its pressure on the dissenting individual was reduced to one fourth: that is, subjects answered incorrectly only one fourth as often as under the pressure of a unanimous majority. The weakest persons did not yield as readily. Most interesting were the reactions to the partner. Generally the feeling toward him was one of warmth and closeness; he was credited with inspiring confidence. However, the subjects repudiated the suggestion that the partner decided them to be independent.

Was the partner's effect a consequence of his dissent, or was it related to his accuracy? We now introduced into the experimental group a person who was instructed to dissent from the majority but also to disagree with the subject. In some experiments the majority was always to choose the worst of the comparison lines and the instructed dissenter to pick the line that was closer to the length of the standard one; in others the majority was consistently intermediate and the dissenter most in error. In this manner we were able to study the relative influence of "compromising" and "extremist" dissenters.

Again the results are clear. When a moderate dissenter is present, the effect of the majority on the subject decreases by approximately one-third, and extremes of yielding disappear. Moreover, most of the errors the subjects do make are moderate, rather than flagrant. In short, the dissenter largely controls the choice of errors. To this extent the subjects broke away from the majority even while bending to it.

On the other hand, when the dissenter always chose the line that was more flagrantly different from the standard, the results were of quite a different kind. The extremist dissenter produced a remarkable freeing of the subjects; their errors dropped to only 9 per cent. Furthermore, all the errors were of the moderate variety. We were able to conclude that dissent *per se* increased independence and moderated the errors that occurred, and that the direction of dissent exerted consistent effects.

In all the foregoing experiments each subject was observed only in a single setting. We now turned to studying the effects upon a given individual of a change in the situation to which he was exposed. The first experiment examined the consequences of losing or gaining a partner. The instructed partner began by answering correctly on the first six trials. With his support the subject usually resisted pressure from the majority: 18 of 27 subjects were completely independent. But after six trials the partner joined the majority. As soon as he did so, there was an abrupt rise in the subjects' errors. Their submission to the majority was just about as frequent as when the minority subject was opposed by a unanimous majority throughout.

It was surprising to find that the experience of having had a partner and of having braved the majority opposition with him had failed to strengthen the individuals' independence. Questioning at the conclusion of the experiment suggested that we had overlooked an important circumstance; namely, the strong specific effect of "desertion" by the partner to the other side. We therefore changed the conditions so that the partner would simply leave the group at the proper point. (To allay suspicion it was announced in advance that he had an appointment with the dean.) In this form of the experiment, the partner's effect outlasted his presence. The errors increased after his departure, but less markedly than after a partner switched to the majority.

In a variant of this procedure the trials began with the majority unanimously giving correct answers. Then they gradually broke away until on the sixth trial the naive subject was alone and the group unanimously against him. As long as the subject had anyone on his side, he was almost invariably independent, but as soon as he found himself alone, the tendency to conform to the majority rose abruptly.

As might be expected, an individual's resistance to group pressure in these experiments depends to a considerable degree on how wrong the majority is. We varied the discrepancy between the standard line and the other lines systematically, with the hope of reaching a point where the error of the majority would be so glaring that every subject would repudiate it and choose independently. In this we regretfully did not succeed. Even when the difference between the lines was seven inches, there were still some who yielded to the error of the majority.

The study provides clear answers to a few relatively simple questions, and it raises many others that await investigation. We would like to know the degree of consistency of persons in situations which differ in content and structure. If consistency of independence or conformity in behavior is shown to be a fact, how is it functionally related to qualities of character and personality? In what ways is independence related to sociological or cultural conditions? Are leaders more independent than other people, or are they adept at following their followers? These and many other questions may perhaps be answerable by investigations of the type described here.

Life in society requires consensus as an indispensable condition. But consensus, to be productive, requires that each individual contribute independently out of his experience and insight. When consensus comes under the dominance of conformity, the social process is polluted and the individual at the same time surrenders the powers on which his functioning as a feeling and thinking being depends. That we have found the tendency to conformity in our society so strong that reasonably intelligent and well-meaning young people are willing to call white black is a matter of concern. It raises questions about our ways of education and about the values that guide our conduct.

Yet anyone inclined to draw too pessimistic conclusions from this report would do well to remind himself that the capacities for independence are not to be underestimated. He may also draw some consolation from a further observation: those who participated in this challenging experiment agreed nearly without exception that independence was preferable to conformity.

FOLKWAYS AND MORES

The norms that regulate behavior in a group are not all equally important. Rather, norms are evaluated according to the group's values, and some are considered more important than others. They range from the trivial, such as norms directing one to follow the fashion in dress, to those of great importance, such as the norms defining the conditions under which it is permissible to kill other people. Violations of trivial norms are punished by the application of mild sanctions, such as ridicule. The violation of norms that are considered vital to social welfare is punished with more extreme sanctions, including death. Correspondingly, conformity to the latter norms is more widespread than to the former.

This selection by the early American sociologist William Graham Sumner is the classic statement of the distinction among norms in terms of their importance to social welfare. In this famous work, Sumner introduced the terms "folkways" and "mores" into sociology and explained the relationship of norms to laws.

> Folkways originate in trial-and-error learning by group members, shared with the group as a whole. Folkways can be seen as individual habits or, on the group level, as customs. They are obeyed because they are traditional and have "always" existed. Sociological explanation ends when one has traced behavior to the folkways that demand it.
>
> Those folkways that are judged by the group to be important to social welfare are given the special name of "mores" (from the Latin; the singular is "mos"). The mores are concretized and rationalized in the laws, which, to retain their strength, must retain their harmony with the mores. A law that is not supported by the mores is not likely to be widely obeyed.
>
> Some mores are common to the whole society, but every subgroup has its own particular mores. On occasion, individuals will feel anxiety because they are members of groups with conflicting mores.

Modern sociology has found the distinctions made by Sumner to be very useful. However, there has been a slight change in the use of some of these terms. Sumner used the term "folkways" as the word "norms" is used today. A modern sociologist speaking of folkways refers to those norms that are not mores; that is, a folkway in the modern usage is a relatively minor norm, one which is not considered essential to social welfare. Mores are defined in modern sociology exactly as Sumner defined them. Sumner uses the term "institutions" in one of several acceptable contemporary meanings, but it is not the only established meaning of the term.

The fact that the distinction between folkways and mores is made as a dichotomy may be misleading. It is very hard to draw a line separating the two categories, since a norm can be considered to be more or less necessary to social welfare, rather than to be either necessary or dispensable. Likewise, sanctions cover a range of severity and are not limited to gentle reprisals on the one hand and death on the other. It is perhaps preferable to look at the terms "folkways" and "mores" as poles of a continuum along which norms can fall. The norms we call folkways lie closer to one end of the continuum, and the mores lie closer to the other end, with a great many norms in the middle. The same considerations apply to many other important dichotomous distinctions in sociology, such as those between "urban" and "rural" communities, "sacred" and "secular" cultures, and "primary" and "secondary" groups.

Selection 21
FROM FOLKWAYS
William Graham Sumner

Definition and mode of origin of the folkways. If we put together all that we have learned from anthropology and ethnography about primitive men and primitive society, we perceive that the first task of life is to live. Men begin with acts, not with thoughts. Every moment brings necessities which must be satisfied at once. Need was the first experience, and it was followed at once by a blundering effort to satisfy it. It is generally taken for granted that men inherited some guiding instincts from their beast ancestry, and it may be true, although it has never been proved. If there were such inheritances, they controlled and aided the first efforts to satisfy needs. Analogy makes it easy to assume that the ways of beasts had produced channels of habit and predisposition along which dexterities and other psychophysical activities would run easily. Experiments with newborn animals show that in the absence of any experience of the relation of means to ends, efforts to satisfy needs are clumsy and blundering. The method is that of trial and failure, which produces repeated pain, loss, and disappointments. Nevertheless, it is a method of rude experiment and selection. The earliest efforts of men were of this kind. Need was the impelling force. Pleasure and pain, on the one side and the other, were the rude constraints which defined the line on which efforts must proceed. The ability to distinguish between pleasure and pain is the only psychical power which is to be assumed. Thus ways of doing things were selected, which were expedient. They answered the purpose better than other ways, or with less toil and pain. Along the course on which efforts were compelled to go, habit, routine, and skill were developed. The struggle to maintain existence was carried on, not individually, but in groups. Each profited by the other's experience; hence there was concurrence towards that which proved to be most expedient. All at last adopted the same way for the same purpose; hence the ways turned into customs and be-

came mass phenomena. Instincts* were developed in connection with them. In this way folkways arise. The young learn them by tradition, imitation, and authority. The folkways, at a time, provide for all the needs of life then and there. They are uniform, universal in the group, imperative, and invariable. As time goes on, the folkways become more and more arbitrary, positive, and imperative. If asked why they act in a certain way in certain cases, primitive people always answer that it is because they and their ancestors always have done so. A sanction also arises from ghost fear. The ghosts of ancestors would be angry if the living should change the ancient folkways.

The folkways are a societal force. The operation by which folkways are produced consists in the frequent repetition of petty acts, often by great numbers acting in concert or, at least, acting in the same way when face to face with the same need. The immediate motive is interest. It produces habit in the individual and custom in the group. It is, therefore, in the highest degree original and primitive. By habit and custom it exerts a strain on every individual within its range; therefore it rises to a societal force to which great classes of societal phenomena are due. Its earliest stages, its course, and laws may be studied; also its influence on individuals and their reaction on it. It is our present purpose so to study it. We have to recognize it as one of the chief forces by which a society is made to be what it is. Out of the unconscious experiment which every repetition of the ways includes, there issues pleasure or pain, and then, so far as the men are capable of reflection, convictions that the ways are conducive to societal welfare. These two experiences are not the same. The most uncivilized men, both in the food quest and in war, do things which are painful, but which have been found to be expedient. Perhaps these cases teach the sense of social welfare better than those which are pleasurable

Reprinted from *Folkways* by William Graham Sumner (Boston: Ginn and Company, 1906), with permission of the publisher.

* Not used in the biological sense, but in the sense of behavior that takes place without conscious thought.—Ed.

and favorable to welfare. The former cases call for some intelligent reflection on experience. When this conviction as to the relation to welfare is added to the folkways they are converted into mores, and, by virtue of the philosophical and ethical element added to them, they win utility and importance and become the source of the science and the art of living.

Folkways are made unconsciously. It is of the first importance to notice that, from the first acts by which men try to satisfy needs, each act stands by itself, and looks no further than the immediate satisfaction. From recurrent needs arise habits for the individual and customs for the group, but these results are consequences which were never conscious, and never foreseen or intended. They are not noticed until they have long existed, and it is still longer before they are appreciated. Another long time must pass, and a higher stage of mental development must be reached, before they can be used as a basis from which to deduce rules for meeting, in the future, problems whose pressure can be foreseen. The folkways, therefore, are not creations of human purpose and wit. They are like products of natural forces which men unconsciously set in operation, or they are like the instinctive ways of animals, which are developed out of experience, which reach a final form of maximum adaptation to an interest, which are handed down by tradition and admit of no exception or variation, yet change to meet new conditions, still within the same limited methods, and without rational reflection or purpose. From this it results that all the life of human beings, in all ages and stages of culture, is primarily controlled by a vast mass of folkways handed down from the earliest existence of the race, having the nature of the ways of other animals, only the topmost layers of which are subject to change and control, and have been somewhat modified by human philosophy, ethics, and religion, or by other acts of intelligent reflection. We are told of savages that "It is difficult to exhaust the customs and small ceremonial usages of a savage people. Custom regulates the whole of a man's actions,—his bathing, washing, cutting his hair, eating, drinking, and fasting. From his cradle to his grave he is the slave of ancient usage. In his life there is nothing free, nothing original, nothing spontaneous, no progress towards

a higher and better life, and no attempt to improve his condition, mentally, morally, or spiritually."[1] All men act in this way with only a little wider margin of voluntary variation. . . .

The folkways are "right." Rights. Morals. The folkways are the "right" ways to satisfy all interests, because they are traditional, and exist in fact. They extend over the whole of life. There is a right way to catch game, to win a wife, to make one's self appear, to cure disease, to honor ghosts, to treat comrades or strangers, to behave when a child is born, on the warpath, in council, and so on in all cases which can arise. The ways are defined on the negative side, that is, by taboos. The "right" way is the way which the ancestors used and which has been handed down. The tradition is its own warrant. It is not held subject to verification by experience. The notion of right is in the folkways. It is not outside of them, of independent origin, and brought to them to test them. In the folkways, whatever is, is right. This is because they are traditional, and therefore contain in themselves the authority of the ancestral ghosts. When we come to the folkways we are at the end of our analysis. The notion of right and ought is the same in regard to all the folkways, but the degree of it varies with the importance of the interest at stake. The obligation of conformable and coöperative action is far greater under ghost fear and war than in other matters, and the social sanctions are severer, because group interests are supposed to be at stake. Some usages contain only a slight element of right and ought. It may well be believed that notions of right and duty, and of social welfare, were first developed in connection with ghost fear and otherworldliness, and therefore that, in that field also, folkways were first raised to mores. "Rights" are the rules of mutual give and take in the competition of life which are imposed on comrades in the in-group, in order that the peace may prevail there which is essential to the group strength. Therefore rights can never be "natural" or "God-given," or absolute in any sense. The morality of a group at a time is the sum of the taboos and prescriptions in the folkways by which right conduct is defined. Therefore morals can never be intuitive. They are historical, institutional, and empirical.

World philosophy, life policy, right, rights, and morality are all products of the folkways. They are reflections on, and generalizations from, the experience of pleasure and pain which is won in efforts to carry on the struggle for existence under actual life conditions. The generalizations are very crude and vague in their germinal forms. They are all embodied in folklore, and all our philosophy and science have been developed out of them. . . .

Definition of the mores. When the elements of truth and right are developed into doctrines of welfare, the folkways are raised to another plane. They then become capable of producing inferences, developing into new forms, and extending their constructive influence over men and society. Then we call them the mores. The mores are the folkways, including the philosophical and ethical generalizations as to societal welfare which are suggested by them, and inherent in them, as they grow. . . .

Why use the word mores. "Ethica," in the Greek sense, or "ethology," as above defined, would be good names for our present work. We aim to study the ethos of groups, in order to see how it arises, its power and influence, the modes of its operation on members of the group, and the various attributes of it (ethica). "Ethology" is a very unfamiliar word. It has been used for the mode of setting forth manners, customs, and mores in satirical comedy. The Latin word "mores" seems to be, on the whole, more practically convenient and available than any other for our purpose, as a name for the folkways with the connotations of right and truth in respect to welfare, embodied in them. The analysis and definition above given show that in the mores we must recognize a dominating force in history, constituting a condition as to what can be done, and as to the methods which can be employed.

Mores are a directive force. Of course the view which has been stated is antagonistic to the view that philosophy and ethics furnish creative and determining forces in society and history. That view comes down to us from the Greek philosophy and it has now prevailed so long that all current discussion conforms to it. Philosophy and ethics are pursued as independent disciplines, and the results are brought to the science of society and to statesmanship and legislation as authoritative dicta. We also have *Volkerpsychologie, Sozialpolitik,* and other intermediate forms which show the struggle of metaphysics to retain control of the science of society. The "historic sense," the *Zeitgeist,* and other terms of similar import are partial recognitions of the mores and their importance in the science of society. It can be seen also that philosophy and ethics are products of the folkways. They are taken out of the mores, but are never original and creative; they are secondary and derived. They often interfere in the second stage of the sequence, —act, thought, act. Then they produce harm, but some ground is furnished for the claim that they are creative or at least regulative. In fact, the real process in great bodies of men is not one of deduction from any great principle of philosophy or ethics. It is one of minute efforts to live well under existing conditions, which efforts are repeated indefinitely by great numbers, getting strength from habit and from the fellowship of united action. The resultant folkways become coercive. All are forced to conform, and the folkways dominate the societal life. Then they seem true and right, and arise into mores as the norm of welfare. Thence are produced faiths, ideas, doctrines, religions, and philosophies, according to the stage of civilization and the fashions of reflection and generalization.

The mores and institutions. Institutions and laws are produced out of mores. An institution consists of a concept (idea, notion, doctrine, interest) and a structure. The structure is a framework, or apparatus, or perhaps only a number of functionaries set to coöperate in prescribed ways at a certain conjuncture. The structure holds the concept and furnishes instrumentalities for bringing it into the world of facts and action in a way to serve the interests of men in society. Institutions are either crescive or enacted. They are crescive when they take shape in the mores, growing by the instinctive efforts by which the mores are produced. Then the efforts, through long use, become definite and specific. Property, marriage, and religion are the most primary institutions. They began in folkways. They became customs. They developed into mores by the addition of some philosophy of welfare, however crude. Then they were made more definite and specific as regards the rules, the prescribed acts, and the apparatus to be employed. This produced a structure and the institution was complete. Enacted institutions are products of rational invention and intention. They belong to high civilization. Banks are institutions of credit founded on usages which can be traced back to barbarism. There came a time when, guided by rational reflection on experience, men systematized and regulated the usages which had become current, and thus created positive institutions of credit, defined by law and sanctioned by the force of the state. Pure enacted institutions which are strong and prosperous are hard to find. It is too difficult to invent and create an institution, for a purpose, out of nothing. The electoral college in the constitution of the United States is an example. In that case the democratic mores of the people have seized upon the device and made of it something quite different from what the inventors planned. All institutions have come out of mores, although the rational element in them is sometimes so large that their origin in the mores is not to be ascertained except by an historical investigation (legislatures, courts, juries, joint stock companies, the stock exchange). Property, marriage, and religion are still almost entirely in the mores. Amongst nature men* any man might capture and hold a woman at any time, if he could. He did it by superior force which was its own supreme justification. But his act brought his group and her group into war, and produced harm to his comrades. They forbade capture, or set conditions for it. Beyond the limits, the individual might still use force, but his comrades were no longer responsible. The glory to him, if he succeeded, might be all the greater. His control over his captive was absolute. Within the prescribed conditions, "capture" became technical and institutional, and rights grew out of it. The woman had a status which was defined by custom, and was very different from the status of a real captive. Marriage was the institutional relation, in the society and under its sanction, of a woman to a man, where the woman had been obtained in the prescribed way. She was then a "wife." What her rights and duties were was defined by the mores, as they are to-day in all civilized society.

Laws. Acts of legislation come out of the mores. In low civilization all societal regulations are customs and taboos, the origin of which is unknown. Positive laws are impos-

---

* This concept is not accepted by modern sociologists.—Ed.

sible until the stage of verification, reflection, and criticism is reached. Until that point is reached there is only customary law, or common law. The customary law may be codified and systematized with respect to some philosophical principles, and yet remain customary. The codes of Manu and Justinian are examples. Enactment is not possible until reverence for ancestors has been so much weakened that it is no longer thought wrong to interfere with traditional customs by positive enactment. Even then there is reluctance to make enactments, and there is a stage of transition during which traditional customs are extended by interpretation to cover new cases and to prevent evils. Legislation, however, has to seek standing ground on the existing mores, and it soon becomes apparent that legislation, to be strong, must be consistent with the mores.[2] Things which have been in the mores are put under police regulation and later under positive law. It is sometimes said that "public opinion" must ratify and approve police regulations, but this statement rests on an imperfect analysis. The regulations must conform to the mores, so that the public will not think them too lax or too strict. The mores of our urban and rural populations are not the same; consequently legislation about intoxicants which is made by one of these sections of the population does not succeed when applied to the other. The regulation of drinking places, gambling places, and disorderly houses has passed through the above-mentioned stages. It is always a question of expediency whether to leave a subject under the mores, or to make a police regulation for it, or to put it into the criminal law. Betting, horse racing, dangerous sports, electric cars, and vehicles are cases now of things which seem to be passing under positive enactment and out of the unformulated control of the mores. When an enactment is made there is a sacrifice of the elasticity and automatic self-adaptation of custom, but an enactment is specific and is provided with sanctions. Enactments come into use when conscious purposes are formed, and it is believed that specific devices can be framed by which to realize such purposes in the society. Then also prohibitions take the place of taboos, and punishments are planned to be deterrent rather than revengeful. The mores of different societies, or of different ages, are characterized by greater or less readiness and confidence in regard to the use of positive enactments for the realization of societal purposes.

How laws and institutions differ from mores.
When folkways have become institutions or laws they have changed their character and are to be distinguished from the mores. The element of sentiment and faith inheres in the mores. Laws and institutions have a rational and practical character, and are more mechanical and utilitarian. The great difference is that institutions and laws have a positive character, while mores are unformulated and undefined. There is a philosophy implicit in the folkways; when it is made explicit it becomes technical philosophy. Objectively regarded, the mores are the customs which actually conduce to welfare under existing life conditions. Acts under the laws and institutions are conscious and voluntary; under the folkways they are always unconscious and involuntary, so that they have the character of natural necessity. Educated reflection and skepticism can disturb this spontaneous relation. The laws, being positive prescriptions, supersede the mores so far as they are adopted. It follows that the mores come into operation where laws and tribunals fail. The mores cover the great field of common life where there are no laws or police regulations. They cover an immense and undefined domain, and they break the way in new domains, not yet controlled at all. The mores, therefore, build up new laws and police regulations in time.

Notes

[1] JAI, XX, 140.

[2] "In the reigns of Theodosius and Honorius, imperial edicts and rescripts were paralyzed by the impalpable, quietly irresistible force of a universal social need or sentiment."—Dill, *Rome from Nero to M. Aurel.*, 255.

BEHAVIOR SETTINGS

It is evident that norms are properties of groups. What is right, proper, and correct depends on which group is being referred to. At times the group is the total society, in which case we speak of communal norms. At other times the group is more specific, and its norms, which we term "associational," are binding only on its members. All citizens must salute the flag; this is a communal norm. The requirement to kneel in church applies only to church members; this is an associational norm, and it is not applicable to all members of the society.

The point of the present selection is that just as norms are specific to groups, they are also specific to situations. Different times, different places, and different physical surroundings call for different types of behavior, even within the context of a single group. These various situations are known in sociology as behavior settings. They exercise an independent effect, separate from that of group membership, on the definition of appropriate and permissible activities, admissible personnel, the allocation of tasks, etc.

The public drinking place is a behavior setting in American society. This selection describes some of the norms specific to the behavior setting of the bar, based on the author's participant observation in a variety of drinking spots in a large metropolis.

The norms of bar behavior include freedom from deference and from good behavior. Behavior that could not ordinarily take place in public is permissible in the bar context. Examples are open quarrels, displays of

affection (except in homosexual bars), belching, falling asleep, and overindulgence in alcohol. Verbal and even bodily contact between strangers
is permissible.

This permissiveness is a result of the fact that the behavior setting is
localized in time and space, and possesses physical features that isolate
it from casual onlookers and offer the illusion of perpetual nighttime.

One's past history and the statuses that rest on past history are irrelevant in the bar. Names are not used, or are abbreviated to exclude
surnames. Exaggerated biographical claims are frequently made, without
efforts at refutation. Indeed, regular patrons attain reputations that are
limited to and valid within the context of the bar, and which may be
quite different from the reputations they hold in the outside world.

The selection presents a general characterization of bar behavior. However,
behavior settings can be quite specific. Behavior appropriate in one restaurant,
on one tennis court, or in one classroom can be quite different from that
appropriate in another example of the same category. Elsewhere, Cavan indicates that drinking places can be more finely categorized, and the appropriate
behavior more particularly specified, according to whether the main function
of the bar is merely to serve drinks (the convenience bar) or mainly to supply
entertainment (the nightspot), to offer an opportunity to meet strangers (the
marketplace bar) or to provide a "home" for a regular clientele (the home-
territory bar). Permissible behavior in each of these settings is somewhat different from the general pattern as defined in the selection.

In sum, information concerning behavior settings is valuable above and beyond information concerning group memberships in specifying the normative
expectations according to which social behavior can be understood.

Selection 22
FROM LIQUOR LICENSE
Sherri Cavan

If the openness of patrons and their encounters in the public drinking place and the cir-
cumscription of those encounters in time and
space give a tentative and superficial character to bar sociability, they also permit a latitude of behavior typically greater than that
permitted in many other public settings.[1] The
public drinking place is often treated as a setting where a variety of self-indulgent and
otherwise improper acts can be engaged in.
Insofar as one is freed from any expectations
of deference within the public drinking place,
one is freed of many of the converse expectations of demeanor as well.[2] What goes on in
the bar is localized in time and place, and one
need not anticipate being held accountable for

Reprinted from *Liquor License: An Ethnography
of Bar Behavior*, by Sherri Cavan (Chicago: Aldine
Publishing Co., 1966), by permission. Copyright
© 1966 by Sherri Cavan.

one's conduct at some later time or in some
other setting. As a result, behavior which is
either permissible or constitutes no more than
normal trouble in the bar encompasses a broad
range of activities that are often open to sanction in other, more serious public settings.

A variety of scenes and spectacles can ensue in public drinking places without penalty
for those involved. Short of physical violence,
little will provoke sanction from either management or other patrons, and even acts of
violence, if short and quickly over, may be
virtually ignored once they have happened.
The following incident, from a bar patronized
primarily by young middle-class people, provides an extreme example of the social *sang
froid* of the public drinking place.

A young man and a young woman had
been sitting together chatting and occasion-

ally dancing for about an hour and a half. Suddenly the man hit the girl in the face, knocking her from the bar stool onto the floor. The general hum of conversation that had been going on among the eight or ten people in the bar stopped for about thirty seconds, during which time the man walked out. No one made any attempt to stop him. One patron quite casually went over to the girl to help her up and the bartender held out a damp towel for her to put to her face. The rest of the patrons went back to their conversations as though nothing had happened. The girl got up, said something to the bartender, and then went to the bathroom. She came out, about ten minutes later, her face back in order, and sat down at the bar, where she remained for about fifteen minutes longer. No one made any further comment on the scene. After she had left, P. C. asked one of the patrons sitting next to him about it and was told, "They've been living together for months. That happens all the time."

Quarrels of varying intensity between patrons, which are sometimes almost routine events in public drinking places, may be casually attended to by other patrons or virtually ignored. But in either case there is typically little sense of impropriety accorded to the behavior of those involved.

A couple in their late forties who had been chatting with another couple at the far end of the bar suddenly burst into an argument that was audible throughout the bar. Neither of the bartenders nor any of the other patrons seated around the bar appeared bothered by their disturbance, and the six or seven patrons seated around the piano bar continued singing, without even glancing over at them.

Wives who enter in search of errant husbands may be accorded the tacit right to vent their anger there and then and treat the public drinking place as if it were no different from their own home.

Three men came in and had two rounds when the wife of one of them entered, visibly upset, and began yelling very loudly, "I don't care for all this and you know that. Drinking and running around." She continued haranguing him for five or ten minutes and then left. There were five other patrons in the bar at the time, but no one even glanced over at the disputants.

Sometimes an attempt is made to minimize the offense or embarrassment such scenes might provide for the patrons not involved. But typically this is done in a way that does not infringe on the right of those involved to carry on their altercation as they see fit. Thus activities handled in unequivocal terms in most settings may, in the public drinking place, be treated with a tact and finesse that seem unwarranted by their nature.

A man at the far end of the bar said something to the woman he was with and she began yelling, "You have no right to call me that I'll have your ass thrown out of here. I'll have you strung up." He responded in kind with the same volume, and the quarrel continued between them for about ten minutes. In the beginning none of the other patrons paid any attention to them and the bartender continued chatting with one of the other patrons. But after a while some of the patrons started glancing down at them and looking a bit uncomfortable. When this began to happen, the bartender went over and started the juke box, turning the volume up to mask their voices. When new patrons came in the bartender would indicate for them to sit away from the two, who sporadically continued their quarrel for over an hour.

There were thirteen people in the bar, a generally "refined" middle-class establishment. A woman in her forties, apparently very drunk, and her escort were arguing. Her voice began to get louder and louder, and then she demanded another beer. Ralph, the bartender, said to her, very quietly, that he wouldn't serve her. Then she became angry and yelled, "I've been his common law wife for two and a half years and he wants to go across the street for a piece of pussy."

Ralph tried to ignore them, but she kept shrieking angrily at her escort. Finally, the bartender went down to them and said to her escort, "Hank, take her out of here." The woman said that she would not go and screamed at Hank, "Why don't you fuck him (Ralph)." Ralph then went and turned the juke box volume up very loud, to cover their voices. He seemed very tense and one of the other women at the bar asked him if he wanted to play poker dice for the juke box with her. She won and he said, "Play anything, just as long as it's loud."

He went down to the woman again to talk

to her, but whatever he said was covered by music from the juke box. Soon thereafter her escort left, after first trying to pull her with him. Ralph then came down to where the majority of the other patrons were seated and tried to make a joke out of it, saying to one man, "Why don't you take old red-nose down there to some other bar for me. Do a bartender a favor." He repeated this two more times down the bar, changing the destination to a well-known, very elegant downtown bar.

When he went back to the woman she yelled at him, "If you want me to leave, call the police, call the police!" Ralph came back down the bar, shaking his head, and she finally left about ten minutes later.

The mutual involvement exhibited in displays of affection is equally permissible within the public drinking place. Although dark and secluded booths may provide areas where patrons can neck and pet unnoticed, such activity is not necessarily confined to unobservable regions but may be carried on in full view of all others present. It is not unusual to see couples dancing in close bodily contact or women sitting on the laps of their companions along the bar, nor is there a sense of impropriety associated with couples seated along the bar holding hands, resting their heads on one another's shoulders, hugging or kissing or occasionally fondling one another in even more intimate ways.

A couple in their mid-thirties were sitting along the bar, just to the right of me. They had been talking softly and holding hands when we got there, but soon he was fondling her breasts and kissing her —all quite openly.

An exception to the acceptability of displays of affection in public drinking places is found most notably in homosexual bars. This is apparently not because it is an affront to the others present but rather the sex of those involved provides legal grounds for the revocation of the establishment's license. Thus while the court may rule that regardless of whether they are heterosexual or homosexual in nature, "any public display which manifests sexual desires . . . may be and historically has been suppressed and regulated in a moral society,"[3] in actual practice the legal suppression and regulation of such activity in public drinking places is typically encountered only in homosexual bars. Quite obviously this does not

mean that there are no displays of affection in homosexual bars, but only that, in the interest of protecting the license of the establishment, management and patrons alike may actively attempt to control or conceal such activity if the likelihood of official discovery is great.

Like unmoderated mutual involvement, a variety of social faux pas may be committed with equanimity in the public drinking place. Patrons may belch, stumble, fall asleep, or fall off bar stools, and such activity is routinely accorded the same status as more socially acceptable activity. In one establishment, the bartender attempted to gently rouse a patron who had fallen asleep with his head and arms on the bar. When the bartender's efforts were unsuccessful, the patron was left to sleep quietly and without further comment on him or his activity. Finally, at closing time, he was aroused and accorded the same "Good night" as the other patrons who had been more actively attuned to the situation at hand. This is not to say that social mishaps may not serve as the basis for remarks. Almost any aspect of the passing scene may provide an item to be commented upon. But when remarks are made about such activities, they characteristically do not carry with them any negative evaluation of either the activity or the situational presence of the actor in question. In an elegant and well-known hotel bar one afternoon, a woman (seated at one of the tables with three companions) had been laughing for an extended period of time in a very shrill and audible manner. A man standing near me smiled and said rather pleasantly, "She sounds like she's having a good time."[4]

Overindulgence and a variety of activities typically characterized as effects of overindulgence, such as loss of motor control, excessive depression or elation, often carry little disapprobation in the public drinking place.[5]

A man in his late fifties, rather disheveled in appearance and quite apparently drunk, had been stumbling from one end of the bar to the other. Eventually he and another man who also appeared somewhat drunk began playing the bowling machine. Their game progressed in a slow and exaggerated manner, with a number of mishaps, such as dropping the ball and falling over the machine. There were others waiting to play, but no one interfered with their game. Finally the second man wandered off and the first man began asking some of the patrons standing around the machine to finish the game with him. When they declined he would offer to buy them a drink if they would play with him, and although no one complied, no one appeared offended by his actions or disturbed by his state.

Collin, one of the patrons seated at the bar, was visibly intoxicated, his body loose and somewhat out of control and his words loud and slurred. Whenever the bartender came down to where he was seated, Collin would engage in an elaborate pantomime of pouring a drink into his glass from a bottle which he had in the pocket of his jacket, and then demanded in a very loud voice that the bartender fill his glass for him. The bartender and the woman seated one stool away from him would play along with him. Occasionally, when he began to fall from his stool toward the woman, she would gently prop him up again. When she noticed me looking over at him she smiled and said, as though no further explanation for his behavior were necessary, "Collin's on vacation."

One of the men who could barely stand continued making the rounds of the women seated at the tables, asking them to dance. Some of the women would refuse him (as they would refuse some of the other men who evinced better motor control), but others would accept and go out on the dance floor with him.

Like overindulgence, other activities which in other settings might be considered demeaning may be treated in public drinking places as nothing more than "good, clean fun." In a crowded night spot, a portly gentleman got up on the stage one evening to dance with the young entertainers. Foregoing the customary movements of the dance, he simply strode around the entertainers on the stage and occasionally lifted his stomach with a heaving movement and smiled at the audience. At the end of his "number" he received a round of applause from the audience. In the same establishment on another occasion, the same indulgent treatment was accorded an attractive matron who got up on the stage and engaged in a mock strip tease before over two hundred patrons. In another bar, a patron who began to sing along with the guitar players in a rather thin and quavering voice received such a tremendous ovation from the other patrons that she went on with two encores, each of which was treated with the same apparent appreciation as her first attempt.

Not only may such role-releases be pleasurable to those who engage in them, but they may, in turn, be pleasurable for others to view. During the course of the study, one public drinking place which features a strip show instigated a policy by which one evening a week was to be "amateur night" when housewives, teachers, nurses, sales clerks and secretaries could be strippers for the evening at least. This amateur night became one of the most popular features of the establishment.

Indecorous conduct that might bring forth rather formidable sanctions outside the bar may pass without note inside the bar, as in the following example:

There were about nineteen people in the bar. A couple in their late thirties were dancing in the middle of the room. The woman began to posture in a mock-seductive way in front of the males along the bar, pulling her dress up above her stocking tops and the like, occasionally saying in an unserious tone of voice, "Oooo, aren't we awful!" But no one paid much attention to her.

In the same sense, not only is verbal contact between unacquainted males and females permissible in public drinking places but bodily contact is permissible as well. A woman in a public drinking place who finds a strange man's arm around her shoulder has little basis for expressing the kind of moral indignation she could express at the same conduct outside the bar; hence such behavior may be virtually ignored.

The limit on the range of behavior permissible in bars does, to a certain extent, vary from establishment to establishment, and this variation may constitute one dimension of the common-sense differentiation of types of public drinking places. There are some bars in which potential patrons may be refused admittance on the basis of improper dress, be ejected on the basis of using improper language, or, if need be, be turned over to the police if they act in an annoying manner. But there are other bars in which dress, language, or exacerbation may go virtually unnoticed. Knowledge of the actual range of permissible behavior in any given establishment provides the potential patron with information usable not only for determining the courses of action open to him within the establishment, but also as a guide to inform him of what he can expect on the part of others and how he is expected to respond to their course of activity.

Beyond the localization of encounters in time and space, additional support for the wide range of behavior permissible within the public drinking place is supplied by certain features of the physical milieu. With very few exceptions, the interior of the drinking place is at least obscured and is often completely shielded from the view of those outside the premises. The events within are thus exempted from any casual monitoring by nonparticipants. The street windows of bars are customarily painted, heavily curtained, or completely absent, and the door in most circumstances remains closed. For passers-by, casual observation of the happenings inside is virtually impossible. Anyone wishing to view the scene within must make his presence known to those who are there by at least partially, and often completely, entering the premises. Since the public drinking place is shielded from casual observation, there is little likelihood that those within or their activity will inadvertently become a matter of public knowledge. Hence, behavior need not be geared to the expectations governing the properties of public places that are more open to view.

Like the shielding of the interior from the street, the customary minimal illumination of the public drinking place also lends support to the range of behavior permissible within the setting by creating an atmosphere of perpetual nighttime within the bar and providing a protective covering of semidarkness for those who populate its interior. The differences in the proprieties governing daytime and nighttime behavior are effectively abridged and the visibility of one's activity is diminished. At the same time, part of the night atmosphere maintained in the public drinking place may be in deference to a more general expectation governing behavior—that drinking is more appropriate to the evening hours than to daylight and that evening behavior may be, if not more licentious, at least looser than daytime behavior.[6]

Where the public drinking place is contained as a subsetting within a larger setting, there may be variation in the extent to which its physical milieu supports a latitude of behavior greater than that permitted in the encompassing setting. When the bar is structurally separated by walls and doors from the setting within which it is contained—as is generally the case of bars located in transportation terminals and hotels and frequently the case of bars located in restaurants—the range of behavior permissible in the establishment may be identical with that in public drinking places that are structurally free-standing. However, even when the separation between the encompassing setting and the subsetting is almost complete, the larger setting may impart a special flavor to the public drinking places contained within it. Hotel bars, for example, are often characterized as "notorious pickup bars" (although in fact not all of them are used primarily in this way), presumably because of their location within the encompassing setting. The "moral holiday," as Hayner characterizes hotel behavior,[7] may be automatically applied to the subsetting as well.

In some public drinking places that are only partially or conventionally separated from the encompassing setting, the effective visibility of the behavior of the patrons of the subsetting may be reduced. Where full structural separation is absent, the maintenance of different degrees of illumination in the two settings is one of the prevalent means used to visually shield the bar from its surroundings. When the bar area is made substantially darker than the encompassing setting, not only is the night atmosphere of the public drinking place maintained, but the events that take place there are less visible to those present in the larger setting, although they may still be audible. Similarly, contained bars may be partially separated from a larger setting by partitions that expose no more than the legs and feet of those present.

When the structural separation between the two settings is not complete, the latitude of behavior is often less than in bars that are self-contained, particularly during the times when the encompassing setting is in use. In such situations, extensive mutual involvement of either an argumentative or an affectionate nature, as well as conduct which could be demeaning or indecorous in the encompassing setting, may be curtailed for a number of reasons.

In the first place, patrons may not care to

display the gamut of behavior fitting in the public drinking place before others not similarly engaged.

The definition of the subsetting as a public drinking place may of course imply that whatever is routinely expected within that setting is exempt from invidious comparison with what is fitting and proper in other settings. Even those who are not involved may be expected to treat events occurring in a bar as no less than the orderly and comprehensible behavior associated with such a setting. However, those outside but viewing the events within may not pay the respect to the setting that they should pay. Those who view the public drinking place as questionable, may, when they discover themselves sharing the encompassing premises, feel justified in displaying disdain for events in the subsetting and for the patrons in it. For these outsiders, the bar (as well as those who patronize it and their activities) may be beyond the boundaries of deference. For others whose opinion of the public drinking place as a conventional setting is less critical, their knowledge of the standing patterns of behavior associated with bars may be summary and incomplete. Hence in good faith they may take the behavior which they see as inappropriate to what they believe should take place within the setting. Thus the second curtailing factor affecting bar behavior is the possibility that those not involved may negatively evaluate the activity permissible to those who are involved, creating a source of possible embarrassment for the latter and restraining their activities accordingly.

Finally, setting deference and embarrassment may flow in the other direction as well. Those in a public drinking place may curtail the activities permissible to them because, although such activities may be appropriate within the subsetting, their nature may be such that they might disrupt the behavior patterns of the larger setting or embarrass those in the larger setting who are attuned to a different set of proprieties.

Biographies

In addition to the broader range of activities which can be treated as proper and fitting in the public drinking place, the localization of bar encounters in time and space may permit patrons to sever themselves from their biographies in a number of ways. This feature is general to public drinking places whether they are structurally self-contained or are a subsetting within some larger conventional setting.[8]

Since the operative rules merely restrict patronage to those who have reached legal drinking age, one need carry with him only those identity papers that establish his date of birth, and even these papers need not be shown unless his age is called into question by the management. Whatever the other characteristics of the patron's social identity, there is typically no call for them to be publicly proclaimed. If names are exchanged between interactants, they are typically given without benefit of surname. One's work rarely serves as a topic of conversation, and as a general rule, aspects of social position outside the bar carry little significance for those within the bar. Ideological commitment need not be declared, because issues of politics and religion generally are defined as outside the range of acceptable subject matter for bar discourse. Unless one imports his companions with him into the setting, to a great extent one can cut himself off within the bar from whatever rightful past, present, or future he has outside the bar.

At the same time, insofar as one's rightful biography need never be brought out in the bar, and insofar as one can expect that exchanges therein will rarely if ever subject one to encounters outside the bar, the patron is also at liberty to prefabricate an entire life for himself with little likelihood that it will later be exposed as a sham. Thus the patrons of the public drinking place can be people whose biographies are more socially satisfactory, more exciting, or more exotic than they could be in settings where more extensive and verifiable biographies are a requirement for entrance, or settings where encounters carry with them an obligation that present relationships be maintained or at least acknowledged at some future time or in some other place. This is not to say that within the bar no biographies with a factual referent ever exist, but only that within the bar biographies without a factual referent may very easily exist.

In part, the new biographies that can be spun for one's duration within the bar are typically limited only by the extent to which one can provide a coherent, internally consistent presentation of self. Thus the very homely woman may not be a high-priced model if her physical appearance would itself invalidate the claim, although the range of other biographical material—literary agent, vocalist, heiress—which she can put forth may be quite extensive. As one bar patron stated,

In a bar you can make all kinds of claims about yourself—just as long as you use enough sense not to say things that whoever you're talking to can see through immediately. I mean if I told you I was a writer you'd probably know right away that it was a lie because my English just isn't very good. But if I told you that I raced sports cars and then started telling you about cars and racing and the like I could probably snow you and you'd never know the difference.

But at the same time, there is a tacit agreement among bar patrons that a certain amount of contradictory biographical material will be ignored, so in fact bar patrons need not put too much effort into attempting to maintain a consistent line during the course of any encounter.

Seven of us (who were unacquainted outside the bar) were sitting around one of the tables for almost two-and-a-half hours. During this time Steve told us he was unemployed, that he was considering going to work for a stock brokerage firm, that he was working in some sort of management program, that he had never been abroad, and that he found you could make out better in Italy than in other European countries. The contradictions apparently bothered no one, and even though he was making himself somewhat objectionable on other grounds—specifically in his advances to one of the other men's female companion—no one called him down.

Thus while the number of former celebrities and people of note who may populate any given bar at any time may be far out of proportion to the number that actually exist outside the bar, little attention is paid to this discrepancy.

Since the creation of biographies in public drinking places is so inexpensive, as a general rule any biographical claims that are made are typically taken with a grain of salt by those to whom they are presented. When a patron is claiming a biography that is rightfully his, he may find that his statements are held in doubt and credit is not being given where it is due.

Henry said, "I used to be a logger. I don't care if you believe me or not, but it's true."

Every time Fred made a statement about himself either to me or to Gil, who had joined us somewhat later, he would pull out some kind of paper from his wallet in an attempt to document it. He pointed out very carefully that on his driver's license it was stated he was not married, showed a wage receipt as evidence that he did in fact work at a hospital, and he looked for almost five minutes for a seaman's passport. When he found it, he stated very pointedly, "You just can't buy these, you know!"[9]

While the patrons of public drinking places can exist without a valid biography (or without any biography at all) with respect to their lives in the outside world, some who patronize any given establishment regularly may create or have created for them a kind of biographical reputation within the bar. Regular patrons of a bar may find their presence and their activities within the bar being strung together in a kind of narrative, eventually to be read as a statement attesting to the kind of person they are. Sometimes this biography is localized only within the bar, but sometimes it contains imputations of more generalized attributes.

Those whose bar biography is localized to the bar itself form the general category of "bar characters" of which at least one instance may be found in almost every establishment. Their "character" status may be vested in them either by other patrons or by the employees of the establishment, or by both. They themselves may never be made aware of the fact that they have any special reputation within the bar.

The bartender and I had been talking for about half an hour when a couple came in. The woman sat down at the corner booth and the man ordered drinks for the two of them at the bar and carried them to the booth. The bartender nodded to them and said to me, "There's the lovers." When I asked him what he meant, he went on to say that they came in together every Friday after work, sat in the same booth, ordered the same drink, and always left by six o'clock. He went on to say that he and the waiter "kind of think they're carrying on an affair, but of course we've never said anything to them."

One of the patrons pointed an old man out

to me and said, "He's the character of this place. He comes in here every night, orders a pitcher of beer, takes it to the same place down there, and drinks the whole thing. . . . No, he never talks to anyone, just takes his pitcher of beer over there and drinks it down."

The apparent scheduled regularity of bar behavior is probably the most frequent basis for according bar character status to a patron. However, this regularity must include more than mere regularity of patronage; the patron's bar behavior must be in some way more broadly predictable. Merely to come in at the same time each day is not sufficient to maintain bar character status. Once inside, there must be no such variation in behavior as talking to the bartender one day and to another patron another day, or playing one song on the juke box one day and another the next time. Thus, while the bar character whose status is predicted on regularity may be indicated by the statement, "There he is, same time, same place, same drink," the statement carries the implication that everything else he will do in the bar will be similar to everything else he did last time and the time before, and that he can be counted on to enact the same repertoire of behavior in the future.

In establishments where such a bar character is among the clientele, recognized by bartender and patrons alike, he may form the basis of an ongoing joke between the bartender and the patrons. The time just before his arrival may be noted by the bartender or a patron, who may say something like, "Well, just about time for the mechanical man to arrive"; and the bartender may say to him as he leaves, with apparent sincerity, "See you again tomorrow," while he smiles at the patrons still seated at the bar and they grin at one another.[10]

The category of bar characters is not exhausted by the mechanical patron. It may also include those made notable by other types of activities, and sexuality, luck, generosity, pugnacity, wit and special knowledge may all be used as the basis for defining the bar character. Patrons may come to be labeled "the guy who always makes out with the chicks," "the big spender," "Arnie, who always has a bag of jokes," and the like. However, whether any particular bar character is to be treated as a hero, villain, or fool is to a great extent dependent upon the ethos of the particular es-

tablishment. The Don Juan who may be the hero of a pickup bar may be viewed as the fool, or more likely the villain, of the home-territory bar where sexual accessibility is held in abeyance.

In contradistinction to the bar character whose bar biography is localized to the establishment itself, patrons may also be invested with a biography that is based on their patronage but that carries with it implications of a character or way of life which exists outside the bar. Thus, for example, a woman who patronizes the same establishment regularly but arrives each time with a different male escort may eventually become known by others in the establishment as a "loose woman," even though her deportment within the bar is above question.[11]

Similarly, where there is a common set of biographical attributes shared by most of the patrons of an establishment, the same set of attributes may be attributed to others who patronize the bar and to those who work there as well. In one homosexual bar which I patronized on a regular basis during the course of study, I was introduced to the co-owner one night and informed that his wife was "a gay girl like you." In a skid-row bar where I worked for a while as a barmaid, customers would frequently ask me how long ago my husband ran off, apparently in an attempt to establish the nature of the crisis which could account for my present situation. In establishments where the clientele was generally "respectable," when I would arrive alone I would frequently be asked how long I had been in the city, the apparent implication of the question being that the only reason I was there alone was that I knew no one to accompany me.

In general, the rightful biographies of patrons in public drinking places can be held private, so that they are nobody else's business, or they can be created fictitiously on the spot out of almost nothing. In either case, one's existence outside the bar may be made discontinuous with his existence inside the bar, and whatever he could be held accountable for by virtue of a verifiable, rightful biography can be ignored in the public drinking place. And while within the bar one can be vested with a reputation of one sort or another, the characteristic feature of these bar-created reputations is that they have no consequences outside the public drinking place;

they are either irrelevant to one's life or discreetly treated as non-existent. Thus the events that take place within the public drinking place may become an item in the patron's diary, although not necessarily an item in his biography. The distinction between biography and diary here rests upon what is taken to constitute a "biographical fact." Goffman writes of biographies:

> Anything and everything an individual has done and can actually do is understood to be *containable* within his biography . . . even if we have to hire a biography specialist, a private detective, to fill in the missing facts and connect the discovered ones for us.[12]

However, although the totality of an individual's life may be containable within his biography, there is clearly a selective process which takes place, transforming some parts of his life into biographical facts and other parts into irrelevancies. The diary, unlike the biography, may contain the biographical facts and trivia as well. The retrospective construction of biographies may thus include a procedure of resorting, whereby information which was once contained only in the diary becomes information which is contained in both. But insofar as it can be assumed that what takes place within the bar is not to be treated in the same way as are events of serious life, it can also be assumed that behavior within the setting will be exempt from the resorting procedure. Hence the conduct of patrons within the bar need not be geared toward the anticipation of its possible biographical consequences.

Notes

[1] Woodard notes that dalliance and irresponsible enjoyment may well ensue in settings where the importance of continuing interaction is low and when conflicting interests are low. (James Woodard, "The Role of Fictions in Cultural Organizations," *Transactions of the New York Academy of Sciences*, Series II, 6 (June, 1944) pp. 311–344, p. 326. What takes place in the public drinking place, however, may be "allowable" only insofar as no one present feels he has the right or is willing to take the responsibility for sanctioning it. In this sense, what is treated here as latitude of behavior may in fact be normal trouble.

[2] Cf. Erving Goffman, "The Nature of Deference and Demeanor," *American Anthropologist*, 58 (1956), pp. 473–502.

[3] *San Francisco Chronicle*, January 21, 1960.

[4] The rule applicable in other public settings is found in Esquire Magazine, *The New Esquire Etiquette* (New York: J. B. Lippincott Co., 1959), p. 285: "In public the best manners are the quietest. Try not to attract attention to yourself or to your friends. You wouldn't commit the high school offense of loud talk and laughter in public."

[5] The question of poise is in this sense held in abeyance, and hence any embarrassment that might ensue from the loss of poise is out of the question. See Edward Gross and Gregory P. Stone, "Embarrassment and the Analysis of Role Requirements," *American Journal of Sociology*, 70 (1964), pp. 1–15; and Erving Goffman, "Embarrassment and Social Organization," *American Journal of Sociology*, 62 (1956), pp. 264–271.

[6] As de Grazia notes, "Evening has always been one of the most faithful friends of time. . . . Free-time activities may play on the edge of morality. Work has restraints that men react against; living in society involves restraints, too. Like petting, you might say, freetime activities have to fall on that narrow strip where fun exists and morality maintains a border in the law and the mores broadly conceived in their letter, spirit, application, history or anthropology." Sebastian de Grazia, *Of Time, Work and Leisure* (Garden City, N.Y.: Anchor Books, 1964), pp. 108, 404.

[7] Norman H. Hayner, *The Hotel* (Chapel Hill, N.C.: University of North Carolina Press, 1936), pp. 154–176.

[8] Like pleasure cruises and carnivals, vacation resorts also have a time-out aura about them like the public drinking place. Of such resorts in the Catskills, David Boroff writes, "For a minority of guests, the week at the resort is an exercise in role-playing. Released from the small Bronx apartment and engulfed in a more spacious life, the salesman sometimes becomes a sales manager, the small retailer a chainstore

magnate, and the stenographer an executive secretary." David Boroff, "The Catskills: Still Having a Wonderful Time," *Harper's Magazine* (July, 1958), p. 59.

[9] The provision of "concrete evidence," of course, need not be limited to the establishment of biographies with a factual referent. It may in fact be put out in an attempt to substantiate a "line." Cf. Margaret Chandler, *The Social Organization of Workers in a Rooming House Area* (unpublished Ph.D. dissertation, University of Chicago, 1948), p. 60.

[10] Cf. Erving Goffman, *The Presentation of Self in Everyday Life* (University of Edinburgh Social Sciences Research Centre Monograph No. 2, 1958), pp. 112–113, on team collusion.

[11] This possibility may account for the fact that single women, more than their married counterparts and more than males of either marital status, tend to be "bar-drifters," who frequent a variety of bars rather than one place in particular. In San Francisco, of those respondents who patronized public drinking places, 43 per cent of the unmarried men stated that they had a regular bar to which they went half the time or more, compared with 37 per cent of the married men, while only 26 per cent of the unmarried women had a regular bar, compared with 35 per cent of the married women. Alternatively, however, it may be that the single woman roams the terrain of public drinking places in the company of unmarried men, who are very likely to take her to their own regular bar, and hence she changes the locale in which she drinks as she changes her escort. (Details on the sample are found in Sherri Cavan, *Social Interaction in Public Drinking Places* [unpublished Ph.D. dissertation, University of California, Berkeley, 1965], footnote 68, Chapter 2.)

[12] Erving Goffman, *Stigma* (Englewood Cliffs, N.J.: Prentice Hall, Inc., 1963), pp. 62–63. Emphasis added.

Chapter 9

STATUSES

STATUS AND ROLE
Selection 23

SOCIAL TYPES
Selection 24

STATUS CONFLICT
Selection 25

Statuses, or social positions, are the units of social organization. It is they that "fasten down" norms by indicating which individuals are responsible for observing which norms. Statuses can be regarded as bundles of norms, and society can be seen as a bundle of statuses arranged in a particular manner.

Statuses must be distinguished from the individuals who fill them. A given status, such as male, may be filled by many individuals, and a given individual may fill several statuses, such as teacher, father, and citizen, simultaneously. A status may have no occupant at all, as when a chairman of the board retires and a new chairman has not yet been elected. However, these situations are generally very temporary, as is evidenced by the cry, "The King is dead! Long live the King!"

A status is meaningless without reference to other statuses. It makes no sense to talk of doctors without implying patients, of teachers without students, fathers without children, or governors without citizens. The norms that compose a status are the rights and duties of the occupants, and the behavior they prescribe is meaningful only if there are other people to grant these rights and receive these duties. For this reason, status is a completely sociological (relational) concept.

Statuses are ranked, some being considered higher than others. The rank of a status is variously expressed in prestige, power, or monetary reward. A group of statuses with the same rank is called a stratum. Classes and castes are familiar examples of strata.

The concept of role is invariably associated with that of status. Role has come to have many meanings in sociology, but in its classic and most common sense, it refers to the actual behavior performed in fulfillment of the norms of a status. Status is abstract, whereas role is concrete. Role is what we see in real behavior, and status is deduced from it.

Since role is the behavior of an individual, it is much less uniform than status. People occupying the same status and subject to the same norms will produce very different behavior. Lincoln, Grant, Coolidge, and Roosevelt were all Presidents of the United States, under a Constitution and set of laws that contained very similar status requirements, yet their behaviors, or roles, while occupying this status were quite different. Roles differ from each other in the degree of conformity to status norms, as well as in the manner or style of norm fulfillment.

Role behavior is evaluated as better or worse, just as status is evaluated as higher or lower, but these two evaluations must not be confused. Role behavior is considered good if the norms of the corresponding status are fulfilled. The reward for a well-done role performance is called esteem.

In contrast, status is evaluated regardless of whether or not its duties are well fulfilled. The typical reward for high status is called prestige. The office of Supreme Court justice merits prestige, even though a particular justice's behavior leads us to think that he is an ass. On the other hand, the reliable, efficient, and cheerful housemaid merits esteem on the basis of her good role performance; but she does not in our society gain prestige for her efforts, since she fills a low-status job.

Selection 23, by Ralph Linton, presents the classical definitions of status and role and makes the important distinction between achieved and ascribed statuses. Orrin Klapp, in Selection 24 on social types, suggests the ways in which statuses originate and develop. Selection 25, by William M. Evan and Ezra G. Levin, discusses the nature of status stresses and conflicts and suggests how the resultant problems are ameliorated.

STATUS AND ROLE

Perhaps the most important distinction made among statuses is that between ascribed statuses, which are independent of the individual's behavior, and achieved statuses, which are a consequence of prior acts. Both types of statuses are present in all societies, but their balance in number and importance varies considerably from society to society and has important consequences for the social order. Living in a society in which the number of ascribed statuses is minimal, we find it difficult to understand the functional benefits that accrue to societies depending heavily on such statuses; American values are opposed to favorable characterizations of such societies. This selection is important in pointing out the differences between these two types of societies and suggesting some consequences of these differences. The distinction between status and role, also contained in this selection, has likewise been found to be very useful in understanding social organization.

A status is a position in a pattern of social relations. It is a collection of rights and duties, or of norms. Role is the dynamic behavioral aspect of status, the acting out of the normatively prescribed behavior. A particular individual will occupy many statuses and play many roles. These terms are also used to indicate the sum of all statuses or all roles that an individual occupies or plays.

Ascribed statuses are those that depend on the accidents of birth, whereas achieved statuses are those that are open to competition. Age, sex, and biological relationships (kinship) serve as bases for the ascription of statuses in all societies. However, the norms constituting these statuses vary considerably from situation to situation. Although all societies recognize differences between men and women, old and young, and relatives and nonrelatives, the particular meaning of these terms and the behavior that is appropriate to the occupants of these ascribed statuses are quite different in different societies.

All social systems contain both ascribed and achieved statuses, and in all societies the bulk of statuses is ascribed. Moreover, competition for achieved statuses may be limited by ascription. Ascription of status may be more efficient than achievement in a relatively static society because it assures that necessary social positions will be filled and necessary roles undertaken, adequately if not always superbly. Training for an ascribed status can take the place of individual gifts in most instances. Ascription is not nearly so inefficient as Americans, with their individualistic values, might think.

This brilliant and fundamental statement contains some inadequacies that may prove confusing to the student. It is unfortunate that Linton uses the same term, "status," in both single and multiple senses. Status in the first sense, a position in a network of social relations, is a distinctly sociological concept, whereas in the multiple sense, as a combination of all single statuses of an individual, the term appears to be more psychological, and its proper use in sociology is not clear.

A further confusion is that the term "status" is used by other sociologists with yet a different meaning, that of prestige. All statuses, in Linton's sense, can be and generally are ranked relative to each other, some statuses being considered higher than others. The result of this evaluation in terms of prestige is often called by the same name—status. Thus the term "status" has become one of the most ambiguous of sociological terms, although it is in all senses a concept of great utility. The reader should be careful to distinguish the meaning of this term in the contexts in which he encounters it.

The distinction between ascription and achievement, although also of great utility, contains problems similar to those encountered in other sociological dichotomies, such as in the distinction between folkways and mores. Many statuses appear to be neither clearly achieved nor ascribed. For example, some statuses, such as religion in our society, are initially ascribed but are changeable, and therefore achieved, in adulthood. Some "achieved" statuses are the result of a competition so limited by ascription as to belie their label; an instance is the achievement of the presidency of a family-owned business. Furthermore, Linton's definition of achievement as related to competition appears inappropriate in the case of such evidently nonascribed statuses as prisoner and invalid. Linton intends these categories to be exhaustive of all statuses, but his use of the term "achievement" to describe the process of acquiring those statuses that are not ascribed represents an unfortunate choice.

Finally, one should note that not all writers maintain the distinction between status and role as presented here. These terms have frequently been used interchangeably and with various connotations not present in Linton's work.

Selection 23
FROM THE STUDY OF MAN
Ralph Linton

. . . we [have] discussed the nature of society and pointed out that the functioning of societies depends upon the presence of patterns for reciprocal behavior between individuals or

Reprinted from *The Study of Man* by Ralph Linton. Copyright, 1936, D. Appleton-Century Company, Inc. Reprinted by permission of Appleton-Century-Crofts, Inc.

groups of individuals. The polar positions in such patterns of reciprocal behavior are technically known as *statuses*. The term *status*, like the term *culture*, has come to be used with a double significance. A *status*, in the abstract, is a position in a particular pattern. It is thus quite correct to speak of each individual as having many statuses, since each individual participates in the expression of a number of patterns. However, unless the term is qualified in some way, *the status* of any individual means the sum total of all the statuses which he occupies. It represents his position with relation to the total society. Thus the status of Mr. Jones as a member of his community derives from a combination of all the statuses which he holds as a citizen, as an attorney, as a Mason, as a Methodist, as Mrs. Jones's husband, and so on.

A status, as distinct from the individual who may occupy it, is simply a collection of rights and duties. Since these rights and duties can find expression only through the medium of individuals, it is extremely hard for us to maintain a distinction in our thinking between statuses and the people who hold them and exercise the rights and duties which constitute them. The relation between any individual and any status he holds is somewhat like that between the driver of an automobile and the driver's place in the machine. The driver's seat with its steering wheel, accelerator, and other controls is a constant with ever-present potentialities for action and control, while the driver may be any member of the family and may exercise these potentialities very well or very badly.

A *rôle* represents the dynamic aspect of a status. The individual is socially assigned to a status and occupies it with relation to other statuses. When he puts the rights and duties which constitute the status into effect, he is performing a rôle. Rôle and status are quite inseparable, and the distinction between them is of only academic interest. There are no rôles without statuses or statuses without rôles. Just as in the case of *status,* the term *rôle* is used with a double significance. Every individual has a series of rôles deriving from the various patterns in which he participates and at the same time *a rôle,* general, which represents the sum total of these rôles and determines what he does for his society and what he can expect from it.

Although all statuses and rôles derive from social patterns and are integral parts of patterns, they have an independent function with relation to the individuals who occupy particular statuses and exercise their rôles. To such individuals the combined status and rôle represent the minimum of attitudes and behavior which he must assume if he is to participate in the overt expression of the pattern. Status

and rôle serve to reduce the ideal patterns for social life to individual terms. They become models for organizing the attitudes and behavior of the individual so that these will be congruous with those of the other individuals participating in the expression of the pattern. Thus if we are studying football teams in the abstract, the position of quarter-back is meaningless except in relation to the other positions. From the point of view of the quarter-back himself it is a distinct and important entity. It determines where he shall take his place in the line-up and what he shall do in various plays. His assignment to this position at once limits and defines his activities and establishes a minimum of things which he must learn. Similarly, in a social pattern such as that for the employer-employee relationship the statuses of employer and employee define what each has to know and do to put the pattern into operation. The employer does not need to know the techniques involved in the employee's labor, and the employee does not need to know the techniques for marketing or accounting.

It is obvious that, as long as there is no interference from external sources, the more perfectly the members of any society are adjusted to their statuses and rôles the more smoothly the society will function. In its attempts to bring about such adjustments every society finds itself caught on the horns of a dilemma. The individual's formation of habits and attitudes begins at birth, and, other things being equal, the earlier his training for a status can begin the more successful it is likely to be. At the same time, no two individuals are alike, and a status which will be congenial to one may be quite uncongenial to another. Also, there are in all social systems certain rôles which require more than training for their successful performance. Perfect technique does not make a great violinist, nor a thorough book knowledge of tactics an efficient general. The utilization of the special gifts of individuals may be highly important to society, as in the case of the general, yet these gifts usually show themselves rather late, and to wait upon their manifestation for the assignment of statuses would be to forfeit the advantages to be derived from commencing training early.

Fortunately, human beings are so mutable that almost any normal individual can be trained to the adequate performance of almost any rôle. Most of the business of living can be conducted on a basis of habit, with little need for intelligence and none for special gifts. Societies have met the dilemma by developing two types of statuses, the *ascribed* and the *achieved*. *Ascribed* statuses are those which are assigned to individuals without reference to their innate differences or abilities. They can be predicted and trained for from the moment of birth. The *achieved* statuses are, as a minimum, those requiring special qualities, although they are not necessarily limited to these. They are not assigned to individuals from birth but are left open to be filled through competition and individual effort. The majority of the statuses in all social systems are of the ascribed type and those which take care of the ordinary day-to-day business of living are practically always of this type.

In all societies certain things are selected as reference points for the ascription of status. The things chosen for this purpose are always of such a nature that they are ascertainable at birth, making it possible to begin the training of the individual for his potential statuses and rôles at once. The simplest and most universally used of these reference points is sex. Age is used with nearly equal frequency, since all individuals pass through the same cycle of growth, maturity, and decline, and the statuses whose occupation will be determined by age can be forecast and trained for with accuracy. Family relationships, the simplest and most obvious being that of the child to its mother, are also used in all societies as reference points for the establishment of a whole series of statuses. Lastly, there is the matter of birth into a particular socially established group, such as a class or caste. The use of this type of reference is common but not universal. In all societies the actual ascription of statuses to the individual is controlled by a series of these reference points which together serve to delimit the field of his future participation in the life of the group.

The division and ascription of statuses with relation to sex seems to be basic in all social systems. All societies prescribe different attitudes and activities to men and to women. Most of them try to rationalize these prescriptions in terms of the physiological differences between the sexes or their different rôles in reproduction. However, a comparative study of the statuses ascribed to women and men in different cultures seems to show that while such factors may have served as a starting point for the development of a division the actual ascriptions are almost entirely determined by culture. Even the psychological characteristics ascribed to men and women in different societies vary so much that they can have little physiological basis. Our own idea of women as ministering angels contrasts sharply with the ingenuity of women as torturers among the Iroquois and the sadistic delight they took in the process. Even the last two generations have seen a sharp change in the psychological patterns for women in our own society. The delicate, fainting lady of the middle eighteen-hundreds is as extinct as the dodo.

When it comes to the ascription of occupations, which is after all an integral part of status, we find the differences in various societies even more marked. Arapesh women regularly carry heavier loads than men "because their heads are so much harder and stronger." In some societies women do most of the manual labor; in others, as in the Marquesas, even cooking, housekeeping, and baby-tending are proper male occupations, and women spend most of their time primping. Even the general rule that women's handicap through pregnancy and nursing indicates the more active occupations as male and the less active ones as female has many exceptions. Thus among the Tasmanians seal-hunting was women's work. They swam out to the seal rocks, stalked the animals, and clubbed them. Tasmanian women also hunted opossums, which required the climbing of large trees.

Although the actual ascription of occupations along sex lines is highly variable, the pattern of sex division is constant. There are very few societies in which every important activity has not been definitely assigned to men or to women. Even when the two sexes cooperate in a particular occupation, the field of each is usually clearly delimited. Thus in Madagascar rice culture the men make the seed beds and terraces and prepare the fields for transplanting. The women do the work of transplanting, which is hard and back-breaking. The women weed the crop, but the men harvest it. The women then carry it to the threshing floors, where the men thresh it while the women winnow it. Lastly, the women pound the grain in mortars and cook it.

When a society takes over a new industry, there is often a period of uncertainty during which the work may be done by either sex, but it soon falls into the province of one or the other. In Madagascar, pottery is made by men in some tribes and by women in others. The only tribe in which it is made by both men and women is one into which the art has been introduced within the last sixty years. I was told that during the fifteen years preceding my visit there had been a marked decrease in the number of male potters, many men who had once practised the art having given it up. The factor of lowered wages, usually advanced as the reason for men leaving one of our own occupations when women enter it in force, certainly was not operative here. The field was not overcrowded, and the prices for men's and women's products were the same. Most of the men who had given up the trade were vague as to their reasons, but a few said frankly that they did not like to compete with women. Apparently the entry of women into the occupation had robbed it of a certain amount of prestige. It was no longer quite the thing for a man to be a potter, even though he was a very good one.

The use of age as a reference point for establishing status is as universal as the use of sex. All societies recognize three age groupings as a minimum: child, adult, and old. Certain societies have emphasized age as a basis for assigning status and have greatly amplified the divisions. Thus in certain African tribes the whole male population is divided into units composed of those born in the same years or within two- or three-year intervals. However, such extreme attention to age is unusual, and we need not discuss it here.

The physical differences between child and adult are easily recognizable, and the passage from childhood to maturity is marked by physiological events which make it possible to date it exactly for girls and within a few weeks or months for boys. However, the physical passage from childhood to maturity does not necessarily coincide with the social transfer of the individual from one category to the other. Thus in our own society both men and women remain legally children until long after they are physically adult. In most societies this difference between the physical and social transfer is more clearly marked than in our own. The child becomes a man not when he is physically mature but when he is formally recognized as a man by his society. This recognition is almost always given ceremonial expression in what are technically known as puberty rites. The most important element in these rites is not the determination of physical maturity but that of social maturity. Whether a boy is able to breed is less vital to his society than whether he is able to do a man's work and has a man's knowledge. Actually, most puberty ceremonies include tests of the boy's learning and fortitude, and if the aspirants are unable to pass these they are left in the child status until they can. For those who pass the tests, the ceremonies usually culminate in the transfer to them of certain secrets which the men guard from women and children.

The passage of individuals from adult to aged is harder to perceive. There is no clear physiological line for men, while even women may retain their full physical vigor and their ability to carry on all the activities of the adult status for several years after the menopause. The social transfer of men from the adult to the aged group is given ceremonial recognition in a few cultures, as when a father formally surrenders his official position and titles to his son, but such recognition is rare. As for women, there appears to be no society in which the menopause is given ceremonial recognition, although there are a few societies in which it does alter the individual's status. Thus Comanche women, after the menopause, were released from their disabilities with regard to the supernatural. They could handle sacred objects, obtain power through dreams and practise as shamans, all things forbidden to women of bearing age.

The general tendency for societies to emphasize the individual's first change in age status and largely ignore the second is no doubt due in part to the difficulty of determining the onset of old age. However, there are also psychological factors involved. The boy or girl is usually anxious to grow up, and this eagerness is heightened by the exclusion of children from certain activities and knowledge. Also, society welcomes new additions to the most active division of the group, that which contributes most to its perpetuation and well-being. Conversely, the individual who enjoys the thought of growing old is atypical in all societies. Even when age brings respect and a new measure of influence, it means the relinquishment of much that is pleasant. We can see among ourselves that the aging usually refuse to recognize the change until long after it has happened.

In the case of age, as in that of sex, the

biological factors involved appear to be secondary to the cultural ones in determining the content of status. There are certain activities which cannot be ascribed to children because children either lack the necessary strength or have not had time to acquire the necessary technical skills. However, the attitudes between parent and child and the importance given to the child in the family structure vary enormously from one culture to another. The status of the child among our Puritan ancestors, where he was seen and not heard and ate at the second table, represents one extreme. At the other might be placed the status of the eldest son of a Polynesian chief. All the *mana* (supernatural power) of the royal line converged upon such a child. He was socially superior to his own father and mother, and any attempt to discipline him would have been little short of sacrilege. I once visited the hereditary chief of a Marquesan tribe and found the whole family camping uncomfortably in their own front yard, although they had a good house built on European lines. Their eldest son, aged nine, had had a dispute with his father a few days before and had tabooed the house by naming it after his head. The family had thus been compelled to move out and could not use it again until he relented and lifted the taboo. As he could use the house himself and eat anywhere in the village, he was getting along quite well and seemed to enjoy the situation thoroughly.

The statuses ascribed to the old in various societies vary even more than those ascribed to children. In some cases they are relieved of all heavy labor and can settle back comfortably to live off their children. In others they perform most of the hard and monotonous tasks which do not require great physical strength, such as the gathering of firewood. In many societies the old women, in particular, take over most of the care of the younger children, leaving the younger women free to enjoy themselves. In some places the old are treated with consideration and respect; in others they are considered a useless incumbrance and removed as soon as they are incapable of heavy labor. In most societies their advice is sought even when little attention is paid to their wishes. This custom has a sound practical basis, for the individual who contrives to live to old age in an uncivilized group has usually been a person of ability and his memory constitutes a sort of reference library to which one

can turn for help under all sorts of circumstances.

In certain societies the change from the adult to the old status is made more difficult for the individual by the fact that the patterns for these statuses ascribe different types of personality to each. This was the case among the Comanche, as it seems to have been among most of the Plains tribes. The adult male was a warrior, vigorous, self-reliant, and pushing. Most of his social relationships were phrased in terms of competition. He took what he could get and held what he had without regard to any abstract rights of those weaker than himself. Any willingness to arbitrate differences or to ignore slights was a sign of weakness resulting in loss of prestige. The old man, on the other hand, was expected to be wise and gentle, willing to overlook slights and, if need be, to endure abuse. It was his task to work for the welfare of the tribe, giving sound advice, settling feuds between the warriors, and even preventing his tribe from making new enemies. Young men strove for war and honor, old men strove for peace and tranquillity. There is abundant evidence that among the Comanche the transition was often a difficult one for the individual. Warriors did not prepare for old age, thinking it a better fate to be killed in action. When waning physical powers forced them to assume the new rôle, many of them did so grudgingly, and those who had strong magic would go on trying to enforce the rights which belonged to the younger status. Such bad old men were a peril to young ones beginning their careers, for they were jealous of them simply because they were young and strong and admired by the women. The medicine power of these young men was still weak, and the old men could and did kill them by malevolent magic. It is significant that although benevolent medicine men might be of any age in Comanche folklore, malevolent ones were always old.

Before passing on, it might be well to mention still another social status which is closely related to the foregoing. This is the status of the dead. We do not think of the dead as still members of the community, and many societies follow us in this, but there are others in which death is simply another transfer, comparable to that from child to adult. When a man dies, he does not leave his society; he merely surrenders one set of rights and duties and assumes another. Thus a Tanala clan has two sections which are equally real to its members, the living and the dead. In spite of rather half-hearted attempts by the living to explain to the dead that they are dead and to discourage their return, they remain an integral part of the clan. They must be informed of all important events, invited to all clan ceremonies, and remembered at every meal. In return they allow themselves to be consulted, take an active and helpful interest in the affairs of the community, and act as highly efficient guardians of the group's mores. They carry over into their new status the conservatism characteristic of the aged, and their invisible presence and constant watchfulness does more than anything else to ensure the good behavior of the living and to discourage innovations. In a neighboring tribe there are even individual statuses among the dead which are open to achievement. Old Betsileo men and women will often promise that, after their deaths, they will give the living specific forms of help in return for specified offerings. After the death of one of these individuals, a monument will be erected and people will come to pray and make offerings there. If the new ghost performs his functions successfully, his worship may grow into a cult and may even have a priest. If he fails in their performance, he is soon forgotten.

Biological relationships are used to determine some statuses in all societies. The mere fact of birth immediately brings the individual within the scope of a whole series of social patterns which relate him to his parents, either real or ascribed, his brothers and sisters, and his parents' relatives. The biological basis for the ascription of these family statuses is likely to blind us to the fact that the physiological factors which may influence their content are almost exactly the same as those affecting the content of sex and age statuses. While there is a special relationship between the young child and its mother, based on the child's dependence on nursing, even this is soon broken off. After the second year any adult woman can do anything for the child that its mother can do, while any adult male can assume the complete rôle of the father at any time after the child is conceived. Similarly, the physiological factors which might affect the statuses of uncle and nephew, uncle and niece, or brother and sister are identical with those affecting the relations of persons in different age or sex groupings. This lack of physiological determinants may be responsible in part for the extraordinarily wide range of variation in the contents of the statuses ascribed on the basis of biological relationships in various societies.

Actually, the statuses associated with even such a close biological relationship as brother and sister are surprisingly varied. In some societies they avoid each other carefully and cannot even speak to each other except in the presence of a third party who relays the questions and answers. In some systems the eldest child ranks the others regardless of sex and must be respected and obeyed by them. In others the question of dominance is left to be settled by the children themselves, while in still others the youngest child ranks all those who preceded him. Practically every possible arrangement is represented in one society or another, suggesting that we have here a free field for variation, one in which one arrangement will work quite as well as another. The same sort of wide variation is found in the content of all the other statuses based on blood relationship with the exception of those relating to mother and child, and even here there is a fair degree of variation. There are a number of societies in which there is a more or less conscious attempt to break up the child's habits of dependence upon the mother and to alienate the child from her in order to bring it into closer association with its father's relatives. The child is taught that its mother really is not a member of the family, and hostility between mother and child is encouraged.

Not only do the statuses assigned by different societies to persons standing in the same blood relationships vary markedly, but there is also a high degree of variation in the sorts of blood relationship which are recognized and used as reference points for the assignment of status. Some societies, like our own, tend to recognize only close relatives and to be vague as to the reciprocal rights and duties of any relationship more remote than first cousin. Others select the line of the mother or the father and utilize relationships in this line to remote degrees while ignoring all but the closest relationships in the other line. In a very few cases, relationship in both lines is recognized to remote degrees, with a consequent assignment of status. Where this is the case the statuses based on relationship may actually include a whole tribe and determine the mutual rights and duties of all its members. Thus in certain Australian groups recognized blood relationships are extended to include not only the whole tribe but numerous individuals in other tribes as well. It is said that when a stranger visits such a tribe the old men investigate his genealogy until they find some point in common with one of the genealogies within their own group. When such a point of contact has been established, they can determine the relationship of the newcomer to all the various members of their own group and assign him a series of statuses which immediately fit him into the social body. If they are unable to find such a common point of relationship, they usually kill the stranger simply because they do not know what else to do with him. They have no reference points other than blood relationships by which statuses might be assigned to him.

There is another type of biologically conditioned relationship which is recognized in practically all societies. This is the relationship arising from the more or less continuous sexual association of individuals, i.e., marriage. The real importance of such associations lies in their continuity, in social recognition, and in the new series of blood relationships to which they give rise through the offspring which they produce. Casual or temporary sexual associations usually receive only a negative recognition from society, being ignored when not actually reprehended. Patterns may be developed to govern the behavior of individuals in such casual associations, but these patterns are usually extremely limited in their scope. They only affect the individuals who are directly involved and do not establish new statuses for the members of the families to which the contracting parties belong. Marriage, on the other hand, always establishes a series of such statuses. Thus the parents of a man and his mistress do not become parties to any reciprocal pattern of rights and duties, while the parents of a man and his wife always do become parties to such a pattern.

While relationships arising from sexual association are intrinsically different from those deriving from blood relationships, the two types have become interrelated in all societies. Blood relationships are everywhere used as reference points for delimiting the group of individuals within which marriage relationships may be contracted. This regulation is usually of a negative sort, certain blood relatives being prohibited from marrying but at the same time permitted freedom of choice among individuals not standing in these relationships. However, there are a fair number of societies in which such regulations assume a positive aspect. In such societies a man is not only forbidden to marry certain female relatives, such as his mother or sister, but is also enjoined to marry within a particular group of female relatives, as his mother's brother's or father's sister's daughters. In some cases these prescriptions are so strong that a man may have no alternatives except to marry a particular woman or remain a bachelor.

The causes which underlie such limitations on marriage, technically known as incest regulations, are very imperfectly understood. Since these regulations are of universal occurrence, it seems safe to assume that their causes are everywhere present, but biological factors can be ruled out at once. Close inbreeding is not necessarily injurious. Even when hereditary defects in the strain may make it so, its deleterious results require a long time to manifest themselves. Moreover, the average uncivilized group is small and rarely marries with outsiders. Within a few generations the heredity of its members becomes so uniform that there is little if any biological difference between marriage with a first cousin and marriage with a fourth cousin. Neither are purely social explanations of incest regulations altogether satisfactory, since the form which these regulations assume are extremely varied. The prohibition of marriage between mother and son is the only one universally present. Marriage between father and daughter is permitted in at least one society, the Azande, while several societies have recognized or even required marriage between brother and sister. This last seems to occur mainly in small ruling groups and seems to be designed to keep privilege and rank rigidly within the group. Thus in Hawaiian royal families brother and sister were required to marry and to cohabit until an heir had been born, although after this they might separate. It seems possible that there are certain psychological factors involved, but these can hardly be strong enough or constant enough to account for the institutionalization of incest regulations. This is proved by the fact that cases of incest between all the prohibited degrees do occur in all societies and that all societies have certain preventive regulations which would be unnecessary if the rules were self-enforcing. Incest regulations, once developed, are a valuable tool for preventing conflicts in the statuses held by individuals, but it is a little hard to imagine their invention for this purpose. They have probably originated from a combination of all these factors.

The bulk of the ascribed statuses in all social systems are parceled out to individuals on the basis of sex, age, and family relationships. However, there are many societies in which purely social factors are also used as a basis of ascription. There seems to be a general tendency for societies to divide their component individuals into a series of groups or categories and to ascribe to such categories differing degrees of social importance. Such divisions may originate in many different ways. They may grow out of individual differences in technical skill or other abilities, as in the case of craft groups or the aristocracies of certain Indian tribes, membership in which was determined by the individual's war record. They may also originate through the conscious formation of some social unit, such as the first college fraternity or the first business men's club, which is usually followed by the formation of a series of similar units organized upon nearly the same lines. Lastly, such divisions may originate through the subjugation of one society by another society, with the subsequent fusion of both into a single functional unit, as in the case of Old World aristocracies deriving from conquest. Even when the social divisions originate in individual differences of ability, there seems to be a strong tendency for such divisions to become hereditary. The members of a socially favored division try to transmit the advantages they have gained to their offspring and at the same time to prevent the entry into the division of individuals from lower divisions. In many cases these tendencies result in the organization of the society into a series of hereditary classes or castes. Such hereditary units are always used as reference points for the ascription of status.

The factor of social class or caste rarely if ever replaces the factors of sex, age, and biological relationship in the determination of status. Rather, it supplements these, defining the rôles of individuals still more clearly. Where the class system is strong, each class becomes almost a society in itself. It will have a series of sex, age, and relationship statuses which are peculiar to its members. These will differ from the statuses of other classes even when both are determined by the same bio-

logical factors. Not only is the commoner debarred from the occupation of aristocratic statuses, but the aristocrat is similarly debarred from the occupation of common statuses. It may be mentioned in passing that this arrangement is not always entirely to the advantage of the members of the upper class. During the nineteenth century the aristocratic prohibition against engaging in trade condemned many aristocrats to genteel poverty.

Feudal Europe offers an excellent example of the ascription of statuses on the basis of social class. A man born into the noble class could look forward to being a bachelor, in the technical sense of a boy beginning his training for knighthood, a squire, and lastly a knight and lord of a manor. The performance of the rôles connected with the final status required a long and arduous training both in the use of arms and in administration. The woman born into the same class could also look forward to being lady of a manor, a task which entailed special knowledge and administrative ability fully on a par with that of her husband. A man born into the peasant class could look forward only to becoming a tiller of the soil. He would pass through no statuses corresponding to those of bachelor or squire, and although he might be trained to the use of weapons, these would be different weapons from those used by the knight. The woman born in this class could only look forward to becoming a simple housewife, and her necessary training for this status was limited to a knowledge of housekeeping and baby-tending. The third class in medieval society, the burghers, also had its own series of statuses, the boy looking forward to becoming first an apprentice and then a master training apprentices in turn. All these divergent, class-determined statuses were mutually interdependent, and all contributed to the successful functioning of medieval society. The noble provided protection and direction, the peasant provided food, and the burgher took care of trade and manufactures.

Ascribed statuses, whether assigned according to biological or to social factors, compose the bulk of all social systems. However, all these systems also include a varying number of statuses which are open to individual achievement. It seems as though many statuses of this type were primarily designed to serve as baits for socially acceptable behavior or as escapes for the individual. All societies rely mainly on their ascribed statuses to take care of the ordinary business of living. Most of the statuses which are thrown open to achievement do not touch this business very deeply. The honored ones are extremely satisfying to the individuals who achieve them, but many of them are no more vital to the ordinary functioning of the society than are honorary degrees or inclusions in "Who's Who" among ourselves.

Most societies make only a grudging admission of the fact that a limited number of statuses do require special gifts for their successful performance. Since such gifts rarely manifest themselves in early childhood, these statuses are, of necessity, thrown open to competition. At the same time, the pattern of ascribing all vital statuses is so strong that all societies limit this competition with reference to sex, age, and social affiliations. Even in our own society, where the field open to individual achievement is theoretically unlimited, it is strictly limited in fact. No woman can become President of the United States. Neither could a Negro nor an Indian, although there is no formal rule on this point, while a Jew or even a Catholic entering the presidential race would be very seriously handicapped from the outset. Even with regard to achievable statuses which are of much less social importance and which, perhaps, require more specific gifts, the same sort of limited competition is evident. It would be nearly if not quite impossible for either a woman or a Negro to become conductor of our best symphony orchestra, even if better able to perform the duties involved than any one else in America. At the same time, no man could become president of the D. A. R., and it is doubtful whether any man, unless he adopted a feminine *nom de plume*, could even conduct a syndicated column on advice to the lovelorn, a field in which our society assumes, *a priori*, that women have greater skill.

These limitations upon the competition for achieved statuses no doubt entail a certain loss to society. Persons with special talents appear to be mutants and as such are likely to appear in either sex and in any social class. At the same time, the actual loss to societies through this failure to use their members' gifts to the full is probably a good deal less than persons reared in the American tradition would like to believe. Individual talent is too sporadic and too unpredictable to be allowed any important part in the organization of society. Social systems have to be built upon the potentialities

of the average individual, the person who has no special gifts or disabilities. Such individuals can be trained to occupy almost any status and to perform the associated rôle adequately if not brilliantly. The social ascription of a particular status, with the intensive training that such ascription makes possible, is a guarantee that the rôle will be performed even if the performance is mediocre. If a society waited to have its statuses filled by individuals with special gifts, certain statuses might not be filled at all. The ascription of status sacrifices the possibility of having certain rôles performed superlatively well to the certainty of having them performed passably well.

When a social system has achieved a good adjustment to the other sectors of the group's culture and, through these, to the group's environment, it can get along very well without utilizing special gifts. However, as soon as changes within the culture or in the external environment produce maladjustments, it has to recognize and utilize these gifts. The development of new social patterns calls for the individual qualities of thought and initiative, and the freer the rein given to these the more quickly new adjustments can be arrived at. For this reason, societies living under new or changing conditions are usually characterized by a wealth of achievable statuses and by very broad delimitations of the competition for them. Our own now extinct frontier offered an excellent example of this. Here the class lines of the European societies from which the frontier population had been drawn were completely discarded and individuals were given an unprecedented opportunity to find their place in the new society by their own abilities.

As social systems achieve adjustment to their settings, the social value of individual thought and initiative decreases. Thorough training of the component individuals becomes more necessary to the survival and successful functioning of society than the free expression of their individual abilities. Even leadership, which calls for marked ability under conditions of change, becomes largely a matter of routine activities. To ensure successful training, more and more statuses are transferred from the achieved to the ascribed group, and the competition for those which remain is more and more rigidly delimited. To put the same thing in different terms, individual opportunities decrease. There is not an absolute correlation between the degree of adjustment of a social system to its setting and the limitation of individual opportunity. Thus if the group attaches a high value to individual iniative and individual rights, certain statuses may be left open to competition when their ascription would result in greater social effiency. However, well-adjusted societies are, in general, characterized by a high preponderance of ascribed over achieved statuses, and increasing perfection of adjustment usually goes hand in hand with increasing rigidity of the social system.

Americans have been trained to attach such high values to individual initiative and achievement that they tend to look down upon societies which are rigidly organized and to pity the persons who live in them. However, the members of a society whose statuses are mainly prescribed are no less happy than ourselves and considerably more at peace. It would never occur to an orthodox Hindu that he was to be pitied because he could not change his caste. His whole life is arranged and oriented in terms of caste, and if he ever envies the members of other castes the emotion is on a par with our own envy of some animal's obvious comfort or satisfaction. His religion provides him with rationalizations of the whole system and with an explanation of his presence in the caste as a result of his soul's evolutionary status. It also holds out the hope of a better position in his next incarnation if his work in this is properly done. As a caste member his social and even emotional needs are amply provided for. There are even a small series of achievable statuses open to him if he is ambitious. He may become a member of the caste's governing body or the best goldsmith in a group of goldsmiths, admired by those whose admiration is based on a thorough knowledge of the work. In any struggle for advancement he knows exactly who his competitors are and what it is he wants to attain. He is much less likely to be disappointed than a man living under our own system, where every other man may be a rival and where the limits for ambition are not socially defined.

In India the idea of ceremonial pollution makes social intercourse between the castes difficult; but in societies which have strong class lines, without this idea, the presence of classes actually makes for ease of social intercourse. Here also, classes serve to delimit fields of competition. Where there can be no rivalry in vital matters and no social climbing, snubbing becomes unnecessary and indeed meaningless. Social status is something fixed and understood by both parties, so it can be ignored under circumstances where it has no direct bearing. Members of different classes can form friendships which are the stronger because their interests can never clash and they can evaluate each other as human beings with a clarity unclouded by fear of rivalry. Membership in a rigidly organized society may deprive the individual of opportunities to exercise his particular gifts, but it gives him an emotional security which is almost unknown among ourselves. Which of these is best or which makes for the greatest happiness to the greatest number the reader must decide for himself.

SOCIAL TYPES

A concept closely related to status is that of social type. Both statuses and types are positions in a social structure, but types are more informal, flexible, and changeable. Social types can be regarded as informal statuses or, since formal statuses often arise out of social types, as nascent statuses.

In this selection, Orrin Klapp discusses the relationship between statuses, types, and personalities. He regards social types as genetic links between the personality and the society. Social types derive from the idiosyncratic behavior of individual persons when this behavior is recognized as socially significant, as in the case of a Napoleon or a Florence Nightingale. Statuses in turn derive from social types through a process of formalizing, rationalizing, and institutionalizing the types.

Through social types, the society sets standards for a far wider variety of individual behaviors than could be recognized and controlled as formal statuses. Moreover, the diversity of individual behavior referred to here is a potential source of new culturally standardized behaviors when the need arises. In cases of rapid social change, a society can draw on its types as a source of new statuses.

> Social types are positions in the social structure that are not fully codified and rationalized. They are spontaneous, nondeliberate, and not fully spelled out. In contrast to statuses, social types are linked to personalities, and their requirements differ depending on who performs the behavior in question.
>
> Social types are useful or functional in several ways. First, in connection with statuses, they permit a more exact specification of the behavior to be expected from a person than the formal statuses alone generally provide. Second, they are a source of new formal statuses. Third, social types serve, as do statuses, to place individuals in society and to control their behavior when formal statuses are not available. Fourth, they aid in an individual's self-concept by pointing out those features of his behavior which the group finds significant.

With the exception of Klapp's second point, the functions of social types are duplicated in a more formalized manner by statuses. Thus, the essay adds to an appreciation of the functions of statuses as well as of social types. Statuses allocate particular rights and duties to various members of the society. They label individuals and control the behavior of those who occupy various positions in the society. Furthermore, statuses are internalized and become components of personality, in the manner suggested by Mead, Cooley, and others.

The reader should be aware that, in the course of this selection, Klapp is using the term "role" in much the same sense as the editor, following Linton, uses "status." Linton's "role" is Klapp's "role playing."

Selection 24
SOCIAL TYPES: PROCESS AND STRUCTURE
Orrin Klapp

Comparatively few of the hundreds of social types in American culture have received much attention and their general part in modern social systems has not been made clear. These collective concepts* have a function in role-definition and the organization of the self, for example, and hence are an important link between the person and the system. Their significance, if anything, is growing as our society becomes more mobile and anonymous, for it is more important to place people we do not know very well. The number of roles in modern systems is greater, and the individual has more choices and discriminations to make. Versatility in role playing is also probably greater, if we can judge by such things as the

Reprinted from *American Sociological Review*, 23:6, 1958, pp. 674–678, with permission of the author and the publisher.
* Roughly, "group ideas."—Ed.

development of human relations techniques and training. So we must know many roles in order to be "adjusted," and must be critics, if not connoisseurs, of social types in order to distinguish real from "phony" role-playing. Social types, as I shall try to suggest, are consensual concepts of roles that have not been fully codified and rationalized, which help us to find our way about in the social system. To put it another way, they are a chart to role-structures otherwise largely invisible and submerged.

The purpose of this paper is to try to show how the typing process serves the system and what aspects of structure are especially well reflected in social types. The following discussion considers four key structural-functional aspects of social types.

First, they make for finer discrimination of roles than the formal[1] structure recognizes. Between knowing a person's formal status only and knowing him intimately there is a kind of knowledge that "fills in." For example, bankers may be hard-headed but Mr. X is a "good Joe." This information can be quickly transmitted and serves to orient a person, say a loan-seeker, more effectively in the social structure. The social type[2] is his substitute for really knowing the person he deals with—and often not a poor substitute at that. Since any formal structure labels and recognizes only a limited number of roles, it is left to social typing to specify much of the informal structure and special situations that develop. One important function, then, is to label deviants within a status, for example, the character, the square, the troublemaker, the eager-beaver, the boon-doggler. *Sub rosa* and illicit organizations are also well indicated by social types, for example, the call-girl, pimp, pusher. Thus, unlike stereotypes, social types are cognitively valuable.* They aid perception and have "truth."

The social type, as here conceived, may be contrasted with the stereotype. A stereotype is often, if not generally, viewed as an inaccurate, rigid popular concept playing an important part in prejudice. It is not rational and interferes with insight.[3] The implicit aim of many of those who study stereotypes seems to be to analyze them so as to get rid of them. The conception of the social type presented here is in marked contrast with this view. Social types, according to the present argument, are as realistic as most concepts used in everyday life may be expected to be; they are needed for effective participation in modern secondary society, and are characteristically applied within the system to promote insightful relations rather than to hold people at a distance or portray outside groups in an inaccurate way. Take, for example, the way a bellhop, detective, or waiter uses social types to help him gauge the strangers with whom he deals; or the feeling we have of knowing people better when a social type "sums them up" or "hits the nail on the head." This is often a highly individual characterization rather than a "lumping" together. However valuable the concept of stereotype has been as a research tool,[4] it has served to obscure this functional side of the typing process by emphasizing its cognitive deficiencies.

To sum up the difference in emphasis of the two concepts: the stereotype is conceived as being in error whereas the social type is in a sense true (representative of real roles that are being played); one refers outside the group whereas the other refers inside the group to things with which people are familiar; one tends to be conceived as functionless or dysfunctional (or, if functional, serving prejudice and conflict mainly), whereas social types serve the structure of society at many points. People often speak as if they would like to be rid of stereotypes, but society as we know it would be inconceivable without social types. One goal of a functional study is to understand them so that we can live with and use them.

Since the concepts overlap, it is recommended as a step toward clarification, that the term stereotype be confined to the more rigid and inaccurate popular images and not be applied indiscriminately—probably not to the majority—of social types.

A second important function of social typing in a changing society is to define emergent roles and thus to play a role in the development of social structure. A changing social structure is marked by both emerging and disappearing types. Comparatively new American types, for example, are the egghead,[5] cat,[6] five-percenter, and hot-rodder. Obsolete types remain as linguistic fossils, such as Lord Fauntleroy, Lady Bountiful, vamp, and mugwump. For Negroes living in the northern United States, Uncle Tom is a fairly obsolescent type.

How does a role become defined and become merged with the social structure as a form of consensus? Suppose a person plays a new role that is important for a group. People may not be able to name the role at first, for they lack the vocabulary, remarking, for example, "He's an institution around here," or "You know Charlie." But in attempting to characterize the role, there is a kind of striving to hit the mark: some wit, perhaps, finds a name for it; or people may use the name of the person who first plays the role conspicuously (in life or fiction) and, in pointing out new players, say, "He's a Charlie." Many social type designations in our slang were originally proper names, for example, Babbitt, Uncle Bim, Judas, Fagin, Shylock, sloppy Jane. After a type becomes labeled, it can take on a formal status, even specify an office that may be occupied by others. A group may say, "We

* Add to knowledge.—Ed.

elect you Charlie." To use Weber's terminology, personal charisma becomes routinized by the typing process. So we can see a kind of continuum between a unique personal role and a formal organizational office, in which typing plays a part in the institutionalization of roles. But, let us repeat, the function of social types is not to supplant but to supplement formal social structure. While some types may become institutionalized as offices, their main ground is the informal area between the purely personal role and the rational social structure. They emerge as a kind of consensus on the level of "common sense" which, however, is not as rational as ideal bureaucratic structure.

A third important function of social typing is to help to place individuals within the social system. Typing a person gives him an informal status and brings him under controls otherwise absent. This occurs within the existent institutional framework; the new status is a modification of a formal status. For example, a boss may be discounted by employees as a fuddy-duddy, or a new employee as an eager-beaver. The controls brought into play by such typing are informal and supplement the formal sanctions. Here it should be noted that many social types have either a heroic, a villainous, or a foolish connotation and the person typed is treated accordingly.[7] In this way, to call a person a party-pooper, say, tells him, "Don't leave early," and subjects him to a certain amount of derision if he does so. People thus draw from the cultural repertoire of social types in order to control individuals and to modify their status. Every culture presumably includes such a repertoire; the American list is a long one.

A fourth function of social typing is personal orientation through self-typing and role-models. If the type becomes a major component of personality structure, it affects the individual's vulnerability to certain influences[8] and gives direction to his "gravitation"[9] from group to group. For example, a person may think of himself as a tough guy or a good Joe or a smart operator; seeing himself in such a role, he will reject suggestions and group-memberships inconsistent with his self-type and, conversely, he will seek those which build up his self-type.

An important ingredient of this orientation process is the institutionalization of certain types as role-models. The most significant social types for any institution or society may be expected to be found in its hero-cult.[10] Thus, in the United States, the cult of celebrities and the other dominating types presented by the mass communication media deserve careful sociological study.[11] Negative models are institutionalized in villain[12] and fool types.

Some aspects of social typing come out more clearly when a group or institution is formed of persons who belong to one predominant type, for example, a religious sect or brotherhood, or a clique of transvestites. The group exerts its own controls[13] in support of the type and it may become explicit, even formalized. (Indeed, the control of a cohesive group may be so strong that depersonalization occurs, that is, the uniqueness of personality disappears and only the type shows.) Associations with such names as The Optimists' Club and The Boosters' Club suggest that an effort has been made to formalize a type as an ideal status personality and that recruiting and socializing new members on the basis of this pattern has become institutionalized. As Whyte notes, good Joes are often selected by personality tests so as to meet the corporation's image.[14]

We have specified four key functions which social typing as a consensual process performs for a social system, especially in a society characterized by formality, anonymity, mobility, and change. These functions are: (1) role-discrimination; (2) definition and institutionalization of emergent roles; (3) modification of status and social control of incumbents through the influence of types as sanctions; and (4) personal orientation through self-typing and role-models provided by social types.

When such functions are needed, society may draw on people to fill appropriate types —it may cast them in the role or recruit them for the job. Where a need is recurrent or continuous, the type and recruitment procedures may become institutionalized, perhaps professionalized. Thus a city greeter's job probably calls for a glad-hander, a professional party-giver is likely to have been a "life of the party," a cafe-bouncer perhaps should be a tough guy, a confidence team needs a fast-talker, a conflict group often institutionalizes the type of the martyr.[15] The fool provides a clear example of a social type that has become an office and professionalized as the jester.[16] In mass entertainment, the standardized types of certain performers illustrate much the same thing, as in the cases of Jack Benny's "cheapskate" role, Humphrey Bogart's tough guy, and Mae West's sex queen. It may be said that the manifest function of such performers is entertainment, but a latent function is to supply social types. The selective influence of these types can be seen in such recruitment devices as beauty contests, amateur contests, movie-casting, studio build-ups of starlets, and popularity contests. Recruitment does not operate continuously in all cases, many types being seasonal or situational, for example, the agitator, the crusader, the man-on-a-white-horse, the authoritarian, the super-patriot, the scapegoat.[17] Heroes often serve to meet the emergency needs of society and at other times are "out of season."

This discussion merely shows some of the ways in which social types serve society. Viewed in their structural aspects, the ensemble of types constitutes a role-network undergirding, as it were, the formal structure. This role network is largely invisible and unspecified. Though not spelled out, it is based on consensus regarding roles: their nature, obligations and norms; what attitude to take toward them; and counter or reciprocal roles, including sanctions. Our slang registers this consensus. This "invisible" structure deserves study and inventory.[18]

Such an inventory would help to reveal submerged aspects of social structure and to diagnose important social phenomena. Examples of the latter include: mobility, as reflected in types like the climber, crasher, and joiner; stratification—top dog, big shot, low man, insider;[19] conformity—square, regular guy, egg-head, sissy, creep; group morale—boondoggler, eager beaver, goldbrick, fanatic; *anomie* and the exploitative ethics of *Gesellschaft**—chiseler,[20] smart operator, wolf, con man, pushover; and pseudo-*Gemeinschaft*†—glad hand, soft soaper.

Social types might also be used as an index of social change, registered by the number and kinds of emergent and obsolete types. For probably one mark of a modern dynamic culture is that it incorporates a large number of emergent types.

Moreover, societies can be compared in terms of social types. American types, for example, provide a distinctive *milieu*, which stands in contrast with those of Mexico, Canada, various European cultures, and so on. An inventory of each nation's (and ethnic group's) social types should help in the study of "national character."

Finally, the study of social types should be useful in the analysis of personality by indicating the types a person identifies with and by providing clues concerning his needs, reference groups, conflicts, and probable behavior. It may be the case that the ability of an individual to identify and discriminate social types is an index of his socialization, or, if an immigrant, of his degree of acculturation. In any event, this ability betokens in some measure the individual's capacity to find his way about in the informal social structure of his society.

* In this context, a group characterized by "impersonal" social relations.—Ed.
† Falsely intimate social relations, e.g., a book "club" in which the "members" are really customers.—Ed.

Notes

[1] By formal I mean role-behavior that is deliberate, prescribed, and subject to explicit rules and expectations, as contrasted with role-behavior that is spontaneous, non-deliberate, and not explicitly spelled out (though it may be normative). It is the distinction commonly made in sociology between formal and informal controls, and between certain aspects of primary and secondary group behavior. "Formality" in common speech also conveys the idea. It is not, however, the "empty" formalism defined by Cooley. Being explicitly prescribed, formal behavior necessarily has a rather high degree of rationality, whether traditional (e.g., etiquette, ritual, family organization), or legal or bureaucratic as Weber discusses these terms. In Parsons' terminology, formal behavior might be said to be universalistic and specific rather than particularistic and diffuse. Somewhat along the same line, E. T. Hiller writes, "Formality indicates a categorical rather than a unique personal footing," by which one conveys "a denial that affectional ideas are held" and a reminder that the other is to remain at a social distance "beyond the bounds of exclusive relations." (*Social Relations and Structures*, New York:

Harper and Brothers, 1947, pp. 105–106.) For these reasons, we may expect that formal structure will neglect many aspects of the persons with which social typing often deals more adequately, indeed, might be said to be especially concerned.

[2] A distinction between social type and social role is also in order. First, roles vary greatly in degree of consensus, ranging from those about which there is little consensus, perhaps because unique and personal, to those such as a doctor's obligation to administer emergency treatment—about which there is virtual unanimity throughout the society. Social types are roles which, though informal, have become rather well conceptualized and about which there is a comparatively high degree of consensus. Second, while many roles are widely allocated and do not "belong" to any particular kind of person who characteristically plays them, some get conceptually linked with a kind of person. At this point we may speak of the role-consensus as having developed into a social type. That is, a "tightwad" is not only a consensual concept of a stingy role but a kind of person who characteristically acts that way. This stress on the kind-of-person-who-acts-that-way helps also to clarify the distinction of social types from formal roles, which tend to be more abstract and impersonal.

[3] Walter Lippmann's remarks are typical: the "hallmark" of a stereotype is that it "precedes the use of reason; is a form of perception, imposes a certain character on the data of our senses before the data reach the intelligence." Where distance separates men who "are often in vital contact with each other . . . there is neither time nor opportunity for intimate acquaintance. Instead we notice a trait which marks a well known type, and fill in the rest of the picture by means of the stereotypes we carry about in our heads." *Public Opinion,* New York: Macmillan, 1922, pp. 67, 73.

[4] See, for example, the studies by Katz and Braly, Bettelheim and Janowitz, Campbell, Deutsch and Collins, Sargent, and Allport and Postman, collected in G. E. Swanson, T. M. Newcomb, and E. L. Hartley, editors, *Readings in Social Psychology,* New York: Henry Holt, 1952.

[5] The term egghead was apparently coined by John de Koven Alsop, to refer to supporters of Adlai Stevenson during the 1952 Presidential election. See Cleveland Amory, *Saturday Review,* Jan. 4, 1958, p. 5.

[6] See, e.g., Harold Finestone, "Cats, Kicks and Color," *Social Problems,* 5 (July, 1957), pp. 3–13.

[7] See O. E. Klapp, "Heroes, Villains and Fools as Agents of Social Control," *American Sociological Review,* 19 (February, 1954), pp. 56–62.

[8] See Walter C. Reckless, Simon Dinitz, and Barbara Kay, "The Self Component in Potential Delinquency and Potential Nondelinquency," *American Sociological Review,* 22 (October, 1957), pp. 566–570.

[9] The term is used by Albert K. Cohen to describe the movement of people with status-problems toward congenial groups in *Delinquent Boys,* Glencoe, Ill.: Free Press, 1955.

[10] See O. E. Klapp, "Hero Worship in America," *American Sociological Review,* 14 (February, 1949), pp. 53–62.

[11] Content-analysis of public images of celebrities should reveal their type. See, e.g., Thomas Harris, "The Building of Popular Images: Grace Kelly and Marilyn Monroe," *Studies in Public Communication,* University of Chicago, 1 (Summer, 1957), pp. 45–48.

[12] See O. E. Klapp, "American Villain-types," *American Sociological Review,* 21 (June, 1956), pp. 337–340.

[13] See, e.g., Edwin H. Sutherland, "The Professional Thief," *Readings in Social Psychology,* op. cit., pp. 271–279.

[14] William H. Whyte, Jr., *The Organization Man,* New York: Simon and Schuster, 1956. See especially Chapters 10 and 12.

[15] See Donald W. Riddle, *The Martyrs,* Chicago: University of Chicago Press, 1931.

[16] O. E. Klapp, "The Fool as a Social Type," *American Journal of Sociology,* 55 (September, 1949), pp. 157–162. Lucille Hoerr Charles finds clowning to be institutionalized in some cultures in all major areas of the world in "The Clown's Function," *Journal of American Folklore,* 58 (April–June, 1945), pp. 25–34.

[17] An unconventional way of looking at police and criminal court procedures is as a recruitment device for villains and scapegoats. See my "Vilification as a Social Process" (paper presented at the annual meeting of the American Sociological Society, Seattle, Wash., August, 1958).

[18] For one such inventory see Samuel M. Strong, "Social Types of the Negro Community of Chicago," unpublished Ph.D. thesis, The University of Chicago, 1940. I am at present making a survey of general social types in the United States.

[19] Floyd Hunter finds that social type labels help differentiate elite structure: upper leaders are referred to by names such as bigwig, big wheel, high

mogul, high boy, big operator, reactionary; those in the under-structure "trying to curry favor . . . by doing their bidding with too much alacrity" might include fire-ball, hot-shot, stoolie, punk, fall guy, hatchet man, See Hunter's *Community Power Structure*, Chapel Hill: Univer-

sity of North Carolina Press, 1953, p. 42.

[20] See Erwin O. Smigel, "Public Attitudes toward 'Chiseling' with Reference to Unemployment Compensation," *American Sociological Review*, 18 (February, 1953), pp. 59–67.

[Editor's Note: Professor Klapp suggests that students interested in social types refer to his book *Heroes, Villains and Fools: The Changing American Character*, Englewood Cliffs, N.J.: Prentice-Hall, Inc., 1962.]

STATUS CONFLICT

The social order by no means always functions smoothly. Conflict and stress are common and ordinary, and are so recognized in sociological theory. In this study of the stockbroker, Evan and Levin explain and comment upon the conflict that exists among different legitimate prescriptions for behavior that may apply to a single individual. Where behavior appropriate to one status violates the prescriptions applicable to another status that must also be fulfilled, the authors speak of "status conflict." Another type of conflict occurs when obligations in a given status with respect to one role partner conflict with comparable obligations in the same status to another role partner. This is termed "role conflict." Although the degree of status and role conflict appears particularly severe for the stockbroker, as described in this selection, the problems are in one degree or another present in a wide variety of social situations.

> The stockbroker in his most familiar aspect fills the status of commission merchant, who buys and sells as the agent of his client. Four other common statuses can be identified: the dealer, who buys and sells for his own account; the investment adviser; the underwriter, who helps a corporation sell its shares; and the director of corporations. These five statuses together constitute a status set. (In terms used in discussing Linton, this would be a status in the multiple sense.) Conflict can and does occur between the prescriptions of these statuses. For example, the broker as commission merchant must buy at the lowest possible price for his customers, whereas as dealer or underwriter he must sell his shares at the highest possible price. This represents status conflict.
>
> Another type of conflict occurs because in each status the broker must interact with many different role set members. This role conflict is exemplified by pressures to prefer large to small customers, for instance in allocating shares of a new stock issue which the broker is convinced will be profitable.
>
> Three mechanisms for coping with conflict are discussed. These are the segregation of statuses, the creation of regulatory and self-regulatory structures, and professionalization.

The means discussed here for the solution of status and role conflict are applicable in many other situations. The segregation of statuses allows a parent, friend, or neighbor to be an effective personnel director, tax auditor, or traffic court judge. Regulation, or formal control, provides outside support to strengthen one set of norms applicable in a particular situation against another. Professionalization as a form of conflict solution depends upon the creation of a particularly strong orientation to the norms of a special kind of colleague group. Efforts in this direction, modeled on the situation understood to prevail in medicine and law, have characterized increasing numbers of occupations in recent years. Real estate agents, life insurance salesmen, and librarians are examples of such occupations. Evan and Levin believe that various factors in the brokerage business, among them poor quality of personnel, lack of advanced training, and the commission method of payment, militate against the development of professionalization in this occupation. Similar factors in the other occupations mentioned have prevented the full development of professional controls. Professionalization as a means of solving status and role conflict has many advantages, but its development presumes a set of conditions that may take a long while to achieve.

Selection 25
STATUS-SET AND ROLE-SET CONFLICTS OF THE STOCKBROKER: A PROBLEM IN THE SOCIOLOGY OF LAW
William M. Evan and Ezra G. Levin

The securities industry may be viewed as a social system with a complex structure of interacting roles, a complex network of interacting organizations, and a complex system of legal norms derived from common law, statutory law, administrative regulations, and private legal systems.[1] It exemplifies what Riesman refers to as the "factual impenetrability of the law."[2] The complexity of this industry is documented in a recently-completed voluminous study entitled, *Report of Special Study of Securities Markets of the Securities and Exchange Commission*[3]—hereinafter referred to as the *Special Study*—which provides a wealth of data for sociological analysis.

The purpose of this paper is to (a) explore some of the structural sources of fiduciary and other role relationship problems of the stockbroker; (b) analyze alternative mechanisms for handling these problems; and (c) consider some implications of our analysis for role theory, for research on interorganizational relations, and for problems of social control.

The concept of the fiduciary relationship in law and sociology

The concept of a fiduciary relationship is common to both law and sociology and involves, basically, duties of loyalty and of trust. One who holds a position of trust, i.e., whose function it is to act for the benefit of another as to matters relevant to the relation between them, is deemed in law to be a fiduciary; as such, he is held to the highest standards of

Reprinted from *Social Forces*, 45:1, 1966, pp. 73–83, with permission of the publisher.

conduct—standards which are essentially different from the less demanding obligations imposed upon parties to a transaction which is negotiated at "arm's length," e.g., a buyer-seller relationship.[4] The transactions and statuses which give rise to the legal imposition of fiduciary standards are many and varied and may involve such diverse obligations as the employee who is prohibited from disclosing trade secrets, the guardian whose discretion must be exercised in the best interests of his ward, and the corporate director who may not divert corporate opportunities for himself.

Although fiduciary obligations have been legally imposed in a variety of *impersonal* situations, sociologists have tended to be concerned with the development of fiduciary standards primarily within the context of a *professional-client* relationship. Thus, Hughes, Goode, and others have pointed out in their studies of professions that there is a need to safeguard the client's interest by imposing certain restraints on the professional's conduct, inasmuch as the client does not have the requisite knowledge to determine whether the professional service is competent or sound.[5] Codes of ethics of the professions prescribe an ordinance of self-denial to insure that the professional does not exploit the client in the face of opportunities—and temptations—to do so.

A pervasive legal problem in the securities industry is whether and in what situations fiduciary responsibilities should be imposed and, if so, how they can be most effectively discharged.[6] Does the imposition of fiduciary responsibilities presuppose the professionalization of the stockbroker? The problems of endowing the buy-sell stockbroker-customer transaction with the characteristics of a fiduciary relationship are complicated by the various statuses which the stockbroker occupies, as will become apparent in examining his status-set and role-set.

The stockbroker's status-set and role-set

A stockbroker usually occupies various statuses at any point in his career or during the normal course of his occupational life. Preliminarily, it should be noted that each of the five principal statuses to be discussed may vary with the organizational context in which the stockbroker works. Thus, the stockbroker may be an employee in a large, medium, or small size firm; he may be a partner or stockholder of such a firm; or, he may be the sole proprietor of his own brokerage firm.

The investing public is most familiar with the *brokerage* function performed by the stockbroker as a commission merchant who executes securities transactions on behalf of his customers. As such, the broker is an agent vested with the fiduciary responsibility of acting for his principal, the customer.

The stockbroker may also function as a *dealer,* in which status he buys or sells for his own, rather than his customer's account. In this status as a principal, his compensation will result from the profit or "spread" which he is able to make on the various securities he sells.

The stockbroker may also render investment advice, either as an incidental service to his brokerage customers and without special compensation, or for a subscription or personal counseling fee, in which case he must separately register as an *investment adviser.*[7] Not infrequently, the investment adviser's fee for personal investment advice will be based on the size of the customer's account. Whether registered as an adviser or not, in some instances a broker may be given complete discretion to effect securities transactions.

From time to time, the stockbroker may act as an *underwriter,*[8] or wholesaler, in the offering to the public of the securities of a particular corporation.

As a representative of public shareholders to whom he may have sold such securities, the broker may be elected to the corporation's *board of directors.* Such election, of course, could take place on his own initiative or he could be asked to serve in this status because of the financial advisory services which he would be expected to render to the corporation.

These five major statuses which the stockbroker may occupy from time to time—broker, dealer, investment adviser, underwriter and director—comprise what might be referred to as his occupational "status-set."[9] In each of the statuses within the set, the stockbroker may interact with various persons in and out of the securities industry. The various persons with whom the stockbroker may come into contact in the course of performing his occupational functions, viz., his "role partners," collectively comprise what Merton has called his "role-set."[10] Thus, the role-set of the stockbroker qua broker would ordinarily include, among others, his employers (or employees), colleagues, customers, and other brokers, dealers, investment advisers, underwriters, and corporate directors.

The multiplicity of role partners with whom the stockbroker, as an occupant of one or another of his occupational statuses, interacts is a characteristic feature of the securities industry.[11] Figure 1 lists some elements in the status-set of the stockbroker and the corresponding role-set in each of his possible occupational statuses. The intricacies and complexities of the various role-sets to which the stockbroker is exposed because of his various statuses may give rise to two kinds of conflict —analytically distinguishable—which are designated as status-set conflict and role-set conflict. These conflicts, it should be noted, aggravate the more readily identifiable problems of maintaining high standards of trust imposed upon the stockbroker as a fiduciary—a problem that could arise for the stockbroker if he occupied but a single status and had but a single role partner.[12]

Status-set conflict, here used to mean the conflict to which the broker is exposed because of the multiple statuses he occupies in the securities industry, is exemplified by the fraud cases and proceedings brought in the courts and before the Securities and Exchange Commission (SEC). Most frequently, these involve conflicts deriving from the status of the broker as an undisclosed dealer, e.g., selling securities to a public brokerage customer without meeting the required disclosure of one's interest as a principal. Thus, the *Special Study* of the SEC learned that one brokerage firm which circulated a weekly market letter

STATUS–SET

ROLE–SET

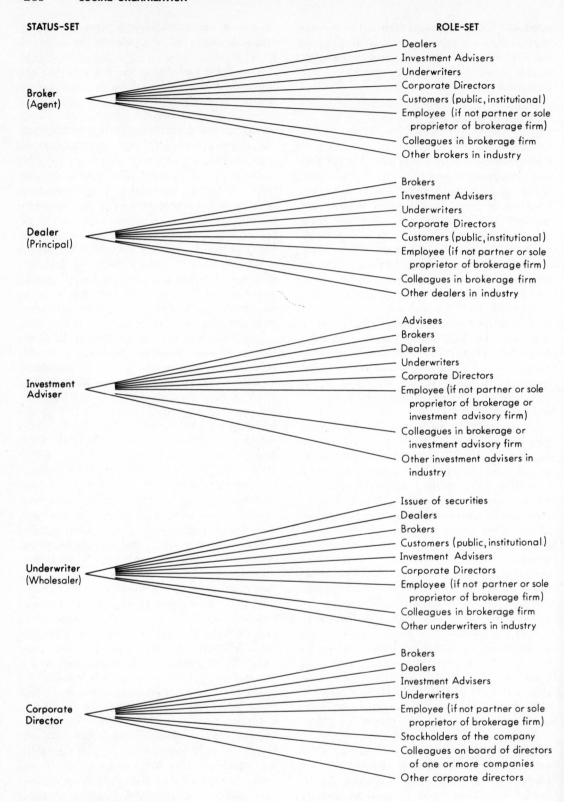

Figure 1.   Some Elements in the Status-set and Role-set of the Stockbroker.

to over 7,500 of its customers had made purchases of a security "on or immediately before the day on which it was recommended in the market letter, and sold it at a profit a day or so thereafter."[13]

Conflicts deriving from other status combinations are not uncommon, as the much discussed proceeding before the SEC, *In the Matter of Cady, Roberts & Co.*, indicates.[14] Here involved was the dual status of a broker and a corporate director. The partner of a brokerage firm had effected profitable transactions for certain of his customers' discretionary accounts on the basis of "inside information" of an impending dividend reduction of a company in which one of the broker's employees served as a director.[15] The partner, who acquired the information from his employee and acted on it prior to its public dissemination, sought to justify his action by claiming that he had a fiduciary obligation to those of his customers who had invested him with discretionary authority.[16] The SEC held that the broker, by virtue of his access to the inside information, had a higher obligation to the corporation itself and, in effect, to the investing public.

These status-set conflicts arise from the various statuses—e.g., broker, dealer, investment adviser, underwriter, and director—simultaneously occupied by a stockbroker. A second kind of conflict in the role-set involves conflicting obligations which the stockbroker may owe to his various role partners within a single status. Thus, in a recent proceeding before the SEC, a financial analyst, employed by a small brokerage concern, composed a fraudulent market letter about the merits of a stock offered by his broker-employer.[17] The financial analyst, who was then 24 years of age, protested not only that he was young and inexperienced but also that he had been ordered by his employer to prepare the letter and to include in it the false and misleading representations. The SEC rejected these contentions and held that he had, in effect, a higher obligation to the investing public than to his employer.

Role-set conflict for the stockbroker may also derive from differences in power of his various customers.[18] Power differentials may easily lead to preferential treatment by the broker of, for example, a large, institutional customer in such matters as the prior dissemination of investment advice rendered by the broker or in the allocation of new security issues to discretionary accounts.[19]

The factors promoting status-set and role-set conflicts derive from the extensive changes in the securities industry during the past 30 years, including the increase in number of stockholders to an estimated 17 million, many of whom are small investors with little knowledge of the intricacies of the stock market; the increase in the number of people employed in the securities industry (approximately 160,000 full-time employees in 1961); the increase in the number of corporations whose securities are publicly traded, an increase which has widened the investors' alternatives and thereby rendered his choice more difficult; and the large turnover of personnel in the securities industry.[20] In addition, status-set and role-set conflicts may be generated by the ease of entry of personnel into the industry, including the minimal educational and financial qualifications. As we shall see, these changes in the securities industry, together with the recruitment pattern and high turnover of personnel, pose many problems for the operation of the mechanisms which presently exist for resolving the status- and role-set conflicts of the stockbroker.

Mechanisms for resolving status-set and role-set conflicts

The potential status-set and role-set conflicts of the stockbroker pose social engineering questions of concern to legislators and administrators as well as theoretical questions concerning the conditions under which it is possible to implement the objectives of a legal system.

There are three alternative mechanisms, each differing in degree of effectiveness, which may help cope with fiduciary problems and status- and role-set conflicts of the stockbroker. These mechanisms are the segregation of statuses, the proliferation and functioning of regulatory and self-regulatory structures, and the professionalization of the stockholder.

Segregation of statuses. Segregation of statuses involves abridging the status-set of the stockbroker.[21] The London Exchange, as the *Special Study* notes,[22] has segregated broker and dealer statuses, and some form of status segregation also occurs in firms large enough to develop specialization of functions.[23] In addition, the SEC itself appears to believe that elimination of conflicting interests may reduce the likelihood of unlawful behavior, as is evidenced by its readmission to registration of former violators upon the condition that their activities be limited to a single status, e.g., by confirming transactions exclusively to acting as a dealer[24] or to the offering of advice on a fee basis.[25]

Indeed, the initial version of the Securities Exchange Act of 1934 provided for segregation of broker and dealer functions,[26] but this suggestion was omitted when the exchanges protested that the markets would be severely disrupted. As an alternative, Congress directed the SEC to "make a study of the feasibility and advisability of the complete segregation of the functions of dealer and broker."[27] Such a study was completed in 1936 by the SEC, which, although it did recommend certain limitations upon the broker functions rendered by specialists and floor traders, concluded that no legislative action with respect to the segregation of broker-dealer functions should be taken without further study. "To incorporate now into statutory law the requirement of complete segregation," the SEC noted, "would be to fail to utilize potentialities for flexible control and evolutionary development afforded by the administrative mechanism which the Congress has already created."[28]

The *Special Study* reaffirmed the earlier conclusion of the SEC, noting that complete segregation of functions . . . as a specific remedy for all the multifarious possibilities for conflicts in the complex securities business could not be a simple segregation in any traditional sense but would have to involve fragmentation of the business to a point where (as facetiously pointed out in a recent magazine article) each investor would have his own broker who would not be permitted to act for any other customer or for himself.[29]

In defense of status-duality, it is claimed, among other things, that trading by a broker as dealer (principal in the over-the-counter market is necessary to the maintenance of that market's liquidity, i.e., the ability of a willing buyer to find readily a willing seller, or vice versa, at a mutually agreeable price.[30] A reanalysis of the data in one of the tables in the *Special Study*, however, suggests that broker-dealer participation as a principal is concentrated in the more actively traded stocks, where liquidity is *least* needed; in-

deed, only 19 per cent of purchases over-the-counter effected by the public from or through broker-dealers as principals were made in the bottom 41 per cent of all stocks, as measured by share volume.[31] This finding suggests that the defense of status-duality in the over-the-counter markets—to the extent that it is based on a purported increase in liquidity by increasing the number of individuals engaged in trading[32]—may need to be re-examined. The data also suggest the appropriateness of asking the question raised by the *Special Study* in another context—in its section on floor traders —"Who is providing liquidity for whom?"[33]

In short, the potentialities of status segregation as a mechanism for resolving status- and role-set conflicts have not yet been fully exploited by the SEC. The argument against status segregation that it would have dysfunctional consequences for the securities industry has not been supported by empirical evidence. Systematic empirical study of status segregation would undoubtedly consider to whom and the circumstances under which its consequences would be functional or dysfunctional.

Regulatory and self-regulatory structures. A second mechanism for the resolution of status- and role-set conflicts consists of the functioning of regulatory and self-regulatory structures of the securities industry. These form an intricate polycentric system of controls which may be but briefly noted here.

The regulatory structure consists of federal statutes and various state laws. If a stockbroker violates any of these laws, he risks liability to a private investor and his conduct could come under the scrutiny of state regulatory bodies of the SEC,[34] which administers the federal laws as a quasi-judicial agency, promulgating rules and regulations as a direct regulatory body.

In addition to its direct regulatory activities, the SEC also functions as a supervisor of the self-regulatory bodies, which include the 14 exchanges registered with the SEC, and the National Association of Securities Dealers, Inc. (NASD)—the only association formed as a self-policing body pursuant to a 1938 amendment to the Securities Exchange Act of 1934.[35] The rules of these self-regulatory bodies are required by the Exchange Act to provide for the disciplining of members for conduct "consistent with just and equitable principles of trade."

The brokerage firms themselves may also serve as a self-regulatory mechanism for the resolution of status- and role-set conflicts of the stockbroker. Some firms prohibit the occupancy of dual statuses, such as broker and corporate director; some insist upon long training periods prior to permitting the assumption of full responsibilities as a broker; and some provide a substantial number of supervisory personnel to regulate the behavior of securities salesmen.[36]

The overall record of self-regulatory bodies in enforcing compliance by the securities industry with the applicable statutory provisions, as well as with ethical standards—and hence in resolving status- and role-set conflict—is an uneven one.[37] One conspicuous shortcoming to date has been in the failure of these bodies, particularly the NASD, to develop and extend adequately the philosophy of disclosure—on which the Securities Act of 1933, applicable to issuers of securities, is based—to the broker-dealer community, i.e., to communicate to investors in a meaningful way those facts which if known might affect their judgment with respect to a particular transaction. In part, the failure of these organizations to realize their regulatory potential may be due to the conflicting demands by which each is beset in confronting its dual tasks, i.e., as a self-regulatory agency charged with the protection of public investors from its members, and as an official representative of members dedicated to the advancement of their self-interests.[38] In addition, the self-regulatory agencies are faced with the danger that their actions may be excessive and exclusionary—and hence subject to the anti-trust laws.[39]

Thus, notwithstanding the assistance provided by self-regulatory and regulatory structures for the resolution of status- and role-set conflicts, the *Special Study* recognized that the fiduciary problems of the stockbroker would persist unless the members of the securities industry could achieve a level of conduct comparable to the ideal standards of the professions.

Professionalization of the stockbroker. In a professional-client relationship the burden of trustworthiness rests on the professional. To insure that the professional acts "ethically" toward the client, there is a system of colleague control and a code of ethics of the profession. The client, in turn, trusts the professional not for personal reasons but because he knows that the professional is *obligated* to be trustworthy. The client may manifest some elements of distrust in the professional if, for any reason, he has any questions about the professional's competence. The professional has to trust the client only to the extent of expecting the client to pay him his fee for services. Because of the functionally specific nature of the relationship and the preponderant dependence of the client on the professional, we may characterize the relationship as involving principally unilateral trust flowing from the client to the professional.

This relationship is in sharp contrast to the buyer-seller relationship. There is no burden of trustworthiness on the part of the seller, though if any transaction is to occur, the buyer must have a modicum of trust in the seller's representation of the commodity. If the stockbroker-customer relationship is to be transformed from a buyer-seller relationship into a professional-client relationship, the stockbroker would have to act in a manner which would convince the customer that he is trustworthy, that he is concerned with promoting the welfare of the customer—in short, that he would assume the status of, and accept the obligations imposed upon, a fiduciary.

The barriers to professionalization of the stockbroker occupation are formidable. In large measure, these barriers are inherent in the nature and structure of the securities industry itself; the commission and other profit opportunities of a brokerage firm and the method of compensation of its personnel.[40] The stockbroker is under great pressures to sell securities. Furthermore, his recommendation to customers of particular securities may be unduly influenced, among other things, by a higher rate of return to his brokerage firm (and, in turn, to its broker employees) on securities traded over-the-counter rather than on the exchange, on securities being distributed by his firm, and on lower rather than higher priced securities. Yet another source of pressure on the employee stockbroker is the policy of some brokerage firms to increase the employee's rate of compensation if he achieves a predetermined volume of transactions in a given period.[41]

Notwithstanding the economic pressures on the stockbroker, a New York Stock Exchange committee maintains that when a customer calls upon a stockbroker for investment information and advice, his obligations are analogous to those of a professional:

> Like a doctor or a lawyer, the representative should determine pertinent facts concerning his client's situation prior to giving advice. . . . (A) representative must never allow his personal investment actions to influence the advice he gives his clients, nor must he even permit his own order to buy or sell a security to affect his customers' order executions adversely.[42]

Unlike a doctor, who renders services to his patient and is ordinarily paid a fee irrespective of his diagnosis, the stockbroker's efforts are remunerated ordinarily only if his customer is moved to take market action and are therefore influenced by a motivation to sell securities. This merchandising orientation derives, in turn, from the dominance of a commission mode of compensation rather than a salary. In short, the stockbroker has a vested interest in consummating a sale, for otherwise his diagnosis, however brilliant, of the customer's financial condition, will not be immediately recompensed.

The stockbroker-doctor analogy drawn by the NYSE committee, although probably more in the spirit of a metaphor than a precise model for behavior, does raise the question of the prerequisites for transforming the stockbroker conduct vis-a-vis his customers from a buyer-seller into a professional-client relationship. There appear to be at least three prerequisites for effecting this transformation. The first is the need to change the recruitment process by raising the educational requirements for admission of personnel so as to reduce the high turnover—three out of every ten members of the NASD in 1961 were newcomers to the industry[43]—and to raise, thereby, the level of occupational commitment of the stockbroker. As the *Special Study* points out, the strictest enforcement of legal norms cannot significantly affect an individual whose educational and occupational background permits him to take on the job of selling securities as easily as that of selling used cars or vacuum cleaners. Furthermore, the statutory provisions prohibiting fraudulent selling activities may have little meaning to a high-pressure salesman or proprietor who is largely judgment-proof.[44]

A second prerequisite for the professionalization of the stockbroker is an increase of specialized training which could transmit not only knowledge and skills but also professional attitudes and values. As part of a deliberate socialization process, special courses of study of the securities industry would be intensified and extended to all would-be brokers. Moreover, some form of licensing would also probably increase the level of occupational commitment.[45]

A third prerequisite for the professionalization of the stockbroker might necessitate a fundamental revision of the present method of compensation by paying the stockbroker a salary rather than a percentage of earned commission fees. Such a revised compensation structure—the complexities entailed are not here minimized[46]—would probably reduce the temptations which presently beset the stockbroker qua broker.[47]

To the extent that some progress is achieved toward raising educational requirements for admission and providing specialized training that can also inculcate professional values, implementation of a new system of compensation would be facilitated. The potentially most significant manifestation of professionalism, however, is probably to be found in the rules promulgated by the NYSE and NASD with respect to the suitability of investment, made by customers. Thus, the NYSE has a "Know Your Customer" rule requiring partners or officers of its member organizations to "use due diligence to learn the essential facts relative to every customer."[48] Similarly, the NASD requires its members to have reasonable grounds to believe that any recommendation to a customer "is suitable upon the basis of the facts, if any, disclosed by such customer as to his other securities holdings and as to his financial situation and means."[49] Further development of these rules would be tantamount to achieving an early stage of professionalization, thus providing a mechanism for resolving status- and role-set conflicts of the stockbroker.

Conclusions and implications

The fiduciary problems of the stockbroker, the status-set and role-set conflicts to which he is exposed, and the organizational and legal structure of the securities industry raise several problems of interest to sociology in general and to the sociology of law in particular.

Our analysis suggests some implications for role theory, for the analysis of interorganizational relations, and for problems of social control.

Role theory. The stockbroker has been referred to as "a non-professional wearing many hats." Is this a unique feature of this occupation? Are the status-sets and role-sets of all professional and business occupations invariably more complex than those of nonprofessional or nonbusiness occupations? Neither the *Special Study* nor any social science investigation, with rare exceptions, has adequately mapped the role-sets and status-sets of an occupation.[50] Moreover, the concept of role-set would suggest that the members of an occupation have but one status. It is apparent from our analysis of the stockbroker functions that he may in fact simultaneously occupy several occupational statuses and that within each status he is involved in a somewhat different network of role-set relationships. In the absence of detailed, interactional data for an occupation, it may be impossible to ascertain the mechanisms that evolve or that can be devised to cope with role-set and status-set conflicts. In the case of the stockbroker, what combinations of status-sets and role-sets generate the highest number of strains? Although the broker *vs.* dealer statuses and the broker *vs.* director statuses have received most attention, it may turn out that other combinations of status-sets and role-sets are equally significant sources of fiduciary conflicts. Are role strains invariably more severe when fiduciary responsibilities are involved?[51]

Interorganizational relations. The securities industry exhibits what appears to be an immensely rich pattern of interactions of public and private organizations and their respective legal systems.[52] Until enactment of the Securities Acts Amendments of 1964, the unit of regulation by the SEC had not been the individual stockbroker but the brokerage firm; the unit of membership in the exchanges and NASD even now is principally a firm and not an individual. The SEC interacts with 14 exchanges which, in turn, interact with their member brokerage firms and the many thousands of corporations whose securities are traded on the exchanges. The NASD provides to the SEC an additional link with stockbrokers who are not associated with exchange member firms and who rely on trading in the over-the-counter market for their primary source of income.

These and other patterns of the interorganizational relations raise several significant questions.[53] First, what kinds of interorganizational relationships tend to generate new statuses or eliminate existing ones—whose function it is to interrelate organizations—and new legal norms, whether in the public or in the private legal sphere? The decision by the SEC in the *Cady, Roberts* proceeding cited earlier led some large brokerage firms to adopt a policy prohibiting service by their partners or employees as corporate directors so as to avoid the problem of conflicting fiduciary obligations.[54] It was because of a regulatory mechanism that made visible the disparity between the ideal (equal access to material investment facts) and the real (use of inside information) that the development and specification of a new rule of law—and its above noted resultant abridgment of statuses—was begun. To the extent that the regulatory mechanism succeeds in making such disparities observable, the process of development will be accelerated.

Second, what pattern of organizational interaction is functional or dysfunctional for the enforcement of legal norms? The SEC's efforts at regulating the exchanges apparently have been more effective than either the NASD's efforts in relation to its members or the efforts of the several exchanges in relation to their member brokerage firms. This difference in enforcement effectiveness of the law may be largely a function of the number of interacting organizational entities. The SEC's regulatory problems in relation to the 14 exchanges are considerably fewer than are those of the 14 exchanges vis-a-vis their thousands of brokerage firms, or of the NASD's problems in relation to its thousands of members.

One facet of the pattern of interorganizational relations that may significantly affect the enforcement efficiency of the SEC is the flow of personnel from the regulatory to the self-regulatory agencies and to the regulated organization. If the reference group of a substantial proportion of the personnel of the SEC is the brokerage community rather than the regulatory bodies, then the SEC's enforcement efficiency of legal norms is likely to be impaired. Moreover, the probability that SEC personnel will aspire to positions within the brokerage community will increase to the extent that opportunities for upward mobility in the regulatory structures are restricted.

Social control. From its inception, the policy of the SEC has been to foster self-regulation within the industry while performing its own regulatory functions. Given the large number of firms and the large number of individuals, and given the limited resources for enforcement at its disposal, a dilemma arises: how can powers be delegated to various subordinate organizations, regulatory and self-regula-

tory, each with limited resources, without running the risk of undermining the enforcement of the legal norms? This problem in the securities industry mirrors, in microcosm, the problem of maintaining social control via decentralization in a pluralistic democratic society.[55] If and to the extent that the professionalization of the stockbroker occupation increases, the decentralized system of control in the securities industry would probably increase in effectiveness. If these developments occur, the difficulties of implementing the various legal norms in the securities industry and of coping with the various status-set and role-set conflicts would be diminished.

Notes

[1] William M. Evan, "Public and Private Legal Systems," in William M. Evan (ed.), *Law and Sociology* (New York: The Free Press of Glencoe, 1962), pp. 165–184.

[2] David Riesman, "Law and Sociology: Recruitment, Training, and Colleagueship," in Evan, *op. cit.*, p. 14.

[3] *Report of Special Study of Securities Markets of the Securities and Exchange Commission,* H.R. Doc. No. 95, 88th Congress, 1st Session, Pts. 1–5 (Washington, D.C.: Government Printing Office, 1963). (In subsequent references to this study, we shall use the abbreviation *Special Study.*)

[4] The fiduciary responsibility ". . . is a legal concept containing the implicit principle that where power is exercised under the color of benefit to another, then the one who holds power must comport himself in ways consistent with the fiduciary basis of his authority. A fiduciary cannot treat his beneficiary as if he were merely his obligee in a contractual arrange-

ment. He owes duties of loyalty and good faith appropriate to the status assumed." Philip Selznick, "Sociology and Natural Law," *Natural Law Forum,* 6 (1961), p. 104.

[5] See, for example, Everett C. Hughes, *Men and Their Work* (Glencoe, Illinois: The Free Press, 1958), pp. 116–130, 139–144; Jerome E. Carlin, *Lawyers on Their Own* (New Brunswick, New Jersey: Rutgers University Press, 1962), pp. 161–164; William J. Goode, "Community within a Community: The Professions," *American Sociological Review,* 22 (April 1957), pp. 194–200.

[6] See, generally, Louis Loss, *Securities Regulation* (2d ed.: Boston: Little, Brown & Co.), Vol. 3, pp. 1500–1508, esp. p. 1505. This three-volume work constitutes the classic reference in the field.

[7] Investment Advisers Act of 1940, Section 202 (a) 11, 15 U.S.C. Section 80b–2(a)11; and see *Special Study,* Vol. 1, pp. 333–387; Loss, *op. cit.,* Vol. 2, pp. 1396, 1398–1402.

[8] See, *Special Study,* Vol. 1, pp. 481–595.

[9] Robert K. Merton, *Social Theory and Social Structure* (rev. ed.; Glencoe, Illinois: The Free Press, 1957), pp. 368–384.

[10] *Ibid.*

[11] "A striking phenomenon of the securities industry is the extent to which any one participant may engage in a variety of businesses or perform a variety of functions. A single firm with customers of many kinds and sizes, may, and often does, combine some or all of the functions of underwriter, commission house in listed securities, retailer of unlisted securities, custodian of funds and securities, investment adviser to discretionary accounts, to others on a fee basis, and to one or more investment companies, and financial adviser to one or more corporations. Its principals may invest or trade for their own accounts in securities also dealt in for others. In addition, as more particularly discussed above, principals and employees of the firm may serve on boards

of directors of issuers of securities, which the firm has underwritten, in which it makes a wholesale market, which it recommends to its retail customers, or all three." *Special Study*, Vol. 1, p. 439.

[12] *Special Study*, Vol. 1, p. 440.

[13] *Ibid.*, p. 372.

[14] Securities Exchange Act release No. 6668 (November 8, 1961). Many of the comments on this proceeding are collected in *University of Chicago Law Review*, 30:4 (1962), p. 122 at note 4.

[15] For purposes of our analysis we are imputing the employee's status as director to the brokerage partner.

[16] For another example of status-set conflict involving broker-directors, see *Blau v. Lehman*, 368 U.S. 403 (1962), discussed in *Special Study*, Vol. 3, p. 58.

[17] *In the Matter of Heft, Kahn & Infante, Inc.* Securities Exchange Act release no. 7020 (February 11, 1963), cited in *Special Study*, Vol. 1, p. 375.

[18] For a discussion of this attribute of the role-set, see Merton, *op. cit.*, pp. 372–374.

[19] *Special Study*, Vol. 1, p. 357.

[20] Cf. *Special Study*, Vol. 1, pp. 9–23.

[21] Merton, *op. cit.*, p. 379.

[22] *Special Study*, Vol. 2, p. 19.

[23] *Special Study*, Vol. 1, p. 434; Vol. 2, p. 615.

[24] Charles A. Massie, 18 SEC 32 (1945), cited in Loss, *op. cit.*, p. 1330.

[25] *In re Biesel*, Investment Advisors Act, release no. 145 (May 21, 1963).

[26] H.R. 7832, 78th Congressional Record 2378, Section 10 (1934), cited in *Special Study*, Vol. 2, p. 49.

[27] Section 11 (e), Securities Exchange Act of 1934.

[28] SEC *Report on the Feasibility and Advisability of the Complete Segregation of the Functions of Dealer and Broker* (Washington, D.C.: U.S. Government Printing Office, 1936), p. xiii.

[29] *Special Study*, Vol. 1, p. 440.

[30] *Special Study*, Vol. 2, p. 16.

[31] *Ibid.*, p. 706.

[32] A similar argument raised in defense of floor traders in the exchange markets is rejected in *Special Study*, Vol. 2, pp. 220–221.

[33] *Special Study*, Vol. 2, p. 221.

[34] For a review of what the Commission does, see the Commission's own pamphlet, SEC, *The Work of the Securities & Exchange Commission*, 1957; and see Loss, *op. cit.*, Vol. 1, pp. 129–131.

[35] See *Special Study*, Vol. 4, chap. 12, "The Regulatory Pattern," esp. pp. 501–504.

[36] *Special Study*, Vol. 1, pp. 290–302; and see New York Stock Exchange, "Supervision and Management of Registered Representatives and Customer Accounts" (1962).

[37] The New York Stock Exchange (NYSE), the *Special Study* noted, ". . . has fallen considerably short of its own best levels of achievement in many specific areas critically affecting the public, both in formulating rules and standards to meet changing needs and circumstances and also in providing effective enforcement of its

rules and standards." *Special Study, op. cit.*, Vol. 4, p. 576. Of the NASD's self-regulating performance, the *Special Study* said (Vol. 4, p. 679): "Despite many accomplishments in its relatively brief history, the NASD has fallen short of its potential as a self-regulatory agency—not only in sometimes failing to reach adequate results in areas that it has undertaken to deal with, but in failing to deal with some areas that well seemed to have called for self-regulatory attention." See also *Special Study*, Vol. 4, pp. 504–577 and 602–682.

[38] If the dual function of all of the self-regulatory institutions in the securities industry at least partially prevents them from full realization of their potential, there are nevertheless significant contrasts in the effectiveness of their attempts at self-regulation. The *Special Study* contrasted the organizational structure of the NASD—which relies primarily on member volunteers to review violations of the NASD Rules of Fair Practice—with the strong and well-paid administrative staff of the New York Stock Exchange which, the SEC found, is generally able to carry out its enforcement activities in an effective manner. The *Special Study* recommended an increase in size, stature and responsibility of the NASD paid staff as well as a diminished reliance on part-time volunteer committees whose members cannot be expected to discipline severely colleagues with whom they may have other and frequent contacts. See *Special Study*, Vol. 4, pp. 679–682.

[39] Cf. *Silver v. NYSE*, 373 U.S. 341 (1963).

[40] "An important and obvious feature of the securities industry which brings it closer to the world of business than of the profession is that most of its

members who deal with public customers normally and regularly engage in merchandising activities." *Special Study,* Vol. 1, p. 244. And cf. Bernard Barber, "Is American Business Becoming Professionalized? Analysis of a Social Ideology," in Edward A. Tiryakian (ed.), *Sociological Theory, Values, and Sociocultural Change* (New York: The Free Press of Glencoe, 1963).

[41] *Special Study,* Vol. 1, p. 261.

[42] NYSE Department of Member Firms, "Supervision and Management of Registered Representatives and Customer Accounts," p. 7 (1962), cited in *Special Study,* Vol. 1, p. 253.

[43] *Special Study,* Vol. 1, p. 96.

[44] *Ibid.,* p. 152.

[45] *Ibid.,* p. 160.

[46] Until 1949, members of the New York Stock Exchange were prohibited from paying other than a fixed salary to their employees; in practice, many firms circumvented this prohibition by varying the employee's salary each month on the basis of the brokerage transactions he effected. *Special Study,* Vol. 1, p. 225.

[47] The *Special Study* has suggested several measures pertain-ing to compensation designed to reduce the more extreme forms of pressure on the stockbroker. These measures would serve as additional protection to the public and remove some of the barriers to the professionalization of the stockbroker. The suggested measures include: ". . . making monthly compensation less specifically dependent on each month's production; eliminating a step-up of commission rates for transactions in a given month on reaching a stated volume for the month; discouraging undue compensation differentials for sales of different categories of securities where advisory bias may result from the compensation differential; and requiring disclosure of extra compensation in respect of particular types of transactions." *Special Study,* Vol. 1, p. 330.

[48] NYSE Constitution and Rules, Rule 405 (1), cited also in *Special Study,* Vol. 1, p. 316.

[49] NASD, *Manual,* Article 3, Section 2, NASD Rules of Fair Practice.

[50] See, for example, Robert K. Merton, George Reader, and Patricia Kendall (eds.), *Student Physician* (Cambridge: Harvard University Press, 1957).

[51] For a discussion of role strains in the professional-client relationship, see William M. Evan, "Role Strains and the Norm of Reciprocity in Research Organizations," *American Journal of Sociology,* 68 (November 1962), pp. 350–353.

[52] Evan, "Public and Private Legal Systems," in Evan (ed.), *Law and Sociology,* pp. 165–184.

[53] William M. Evan, "The Organization-set: Toward a Theory of Inter-organization Relations," in James D. Thompson (ed.), *Approaches to Organizational Design* (Pittsburgh: University of Pittsburgh Press, 1966), pp. 174–190.

[54] *Special Study,* Vol. 1, p. 437.

[55] Two other problems are also implicitly raised: the correlative problem of maintaining, under any self-regulatory scheme, the autonomy of the self-regulators and the regulated; and the more basic problem as to the conditions limiting self-regulation generally. For a discussion of data collected by the *Special Study* bearing on the latter problem, see Ezra G. Levin and William M. Evan, "Professionalism and the Stockbroker: Some Observations on the SEC Special Study," *The Business Lawyer,* 21 (January 1966), pp. 358–359.

Chapter 10

GROUPS

A group is a collection of people with certain common properties. Consideration of the nature of these common properties enables one to distinguish between statistical groups, societal groups, social groups, and associations. Each of these varieties of groups has different meanings for sociology.

A statistical group is a group only in the logical sense of the word and does not necessarily have a sociological meaning. The things that members of a statistical group have in common can be anything at all and may be completely subjective, meaningful only to the observer. For example, all girls whose faces I consider pretty form a statistical group, which is of interest probably only to myself. Their membership in this group alone has absolutely no effect on their behavior and is irrelevant to sociology. It is only in those cases where a statistical group is also a societal group, a social group, or an association that membership in it affects behavior and becomes of sociological interest. For this reason, some people prefer to speak of statistical aggregates or categories, rather than of statistical groups.

Members of societal groups recognize their memberships, and this recognition affects their behavior. Figuratively, they say "I belong; I am one of them," and they recognize certain rights and duties in consequence. Traditionally, sociologists have said that societal group members possess "consciousness of kind"; but such "consciousness" should not be interpreted as continual awareness, and in fact it may be quite unconscious in the Freudian sense.

Since societal group membership affects behavior, such membership is of great interest to sociology. For example, by knowing that some people are American Catholics it is possible to make fairly good guesses concerning their occupations, where they live, their educational attainments, how they vote, and many other facets of their social lives. However, membership in a societal group alone does not necessarily imply interaction with other members of the group, nor the demands for conformity and experiences of sanctions that go along with social interaction. Generalizations based on societal group membership are usually subject to large amounts of error in individual cases.

Members of a social group have in common social interaction, or behavior which is directed to one another. A social group consists of people playing interacting roles. It is the realization in concrete form of abstract status relations.

Social groups occur in almost infinite variety, as each one is in some respects unique. They can be classified according to content, or the purpose of the group, and according to form, or the structure of the group. Among the formal dimensions of social groups are: the nature of social relations within the group (primary groups distinguished from secondary groups), the size of the group (large or small), the achieved or ascribed basis of membership (voluntary groups distinguished from involuntary), characteristics of the group boundaries (open or closed), the scope of the group (unibonded or multibonded), and the type of organization (associations distinguished from informal groups). Sociology is generally more interested in these distinctions of form than in distinctions of content, but both can be important. For example, although a large university has many points of similarity to a large corporation, which it resembles in form, it also bears similarity to a small college, which it resembles in content.

Selections concerning statistical groups, which are not in themselves of interest to sociology, are not included in this chapter. Selection 26, by Bernard Berelson, Paul F. Lazarsfeld, and William N. McPhee, deals with classes and ethnic or minority groups and is presented as an example of the sociological treatment of societal groups. The theoretical statement by Charles Horton Cooley in Selection 27 and the descriptive research study by George C. Homans in Selection 28 illustrate sociological concern with informal social groups. The treatment of formally organized social groups, or associations, is reserved for the next chapter.

SOCIETAL GROUPS

A statistical group is a number of people who have something in common according to an outside observer, and it may be a useful concept for categorizing behavior. In contrast, members of a societal group have something in common that they themselves recognize, and this fact makes it a useful concept for explaining behavior. Sociology has a far greater interest in explanation than in mere categorization; therefore the present chapter begins with a consideration of societal groups.

The selection deals with two well-known examples of societal groups: social classes and ethnic ("minority") groups. Membership in a social class or an ethnic group does not require social interaction. A person can consider himself a Jew although he has never entered a synagogue, or consider himself a member of the middle class even though he lives on welfare and is shunned by people on the "right" side of the tracks. Berelson, Lazarsfeld, and McPhee here show that membership in a societal group affects the decision to vote for one party or the other in an American election. The selection is taken from their large-scale study of the 1948 election in Elmira, New York.

> The higher the social class, the more likely are people to vote Republican. The societal group basis of this generalization is both inferred from occupation and ascertained directly by asking people to which class they belong. Consciousness of kind with respect to class can be demonstrated by direct questions; however, it appears not to be very strong among the citizens of Elmira. (Chart 2 makes the interesting point that people who are statistically in the lower class but who are conscious of being in the middle class are more likely to vote Republican than people who are statistically in the middle class but who are conscious of being in the lower class.)

Catholics and other members of ethnic groups are relatively likely to vote Democratic. Greater consciousness of ethnic group membership increases the tendency of these individuals to vote Democratic.

Conclusions are that class and ethnic status (and location of residence) furnish a social basis for political interest; that party preferences are transmitted along with political opinions in the family; and that membership in these societal groups channels communication and insulates one from hearing contradictory points of view.

Implicit in this discussion is the idea that the effect of societal group membership on behavior, in this case voting, depends at least in part on interaction in the context of social groups. The authors note elsewhere that during the campaign people discuss their voting intentions with their family and friends and that voting intentions are directly influenced by this interaction. People do not generally sit in isolation and wonder to themselves which candidate is better for the working class. In other words, consciousness of kind and its effects are not magic, but are the psychological reflection of social group membership. Although, as noted above, a state of consciousness of kind can exist in the absence of social group membership, such a situation is rare and may be considered temporary in most cases. People generally give up their illusions of membership in a social elite if they are not invited to join the elite clubs or asked to the homes of the leading citizens.

An interesting question that may occur to the reader is what happens when an individual is conscious of membership in societal groups with different political predispositions. How, for instance, does a rich Catholic vote? Berelson, Lazarsfeld, and McPhee provide the answer in another chapter. People in a position of "cross-pressures" from membership in conflicting groups have difficulty in making up their minds. They tend to be disinterested in the campaign, to change their voting intentions very often, and to come to a final decision between candidates very late in the campaign. Other studies have indicated that people under cross-pressures bulk large among the citizens who avoid a decision by choosing not to vote.

Selection 26
FROM VOTING

Bernard Berelson, Paul F. Lazarsfeld, and William N. McPhee

. . . In contemporary America, political events and social differentiation have combined to produce three major types of political cleavage: (1) occupational, income, and status cleavages; (2) religious, racial, and ethnic cleavages; and (3) regional and urban-rural cleavages.[1] For the large majority of the population political experience is organized around major social identifications, associations, and memberships. One's own private political convictions are not so private or so much one's own as they may seem—or as one might wish them to be. In political affairs of the mid-twentieth century the kinds of social experience most persistently underlying political choices are those centering on class, ethnic, and ecological* differences. Such social bases of political traditions are the subject matter of the present chapter.

Socioeconomic status

In our discussion of social differentiation in politics, the place to start is the "obvious" place: the effect of differing socioeconomic

* In this usage, areal.—Ed.

status* upon political attitudes. If there is one social characteristic that is generally admitted to affect opinion on public affairs, at least since 1932, this is it. Although voting along socioeconomic lines is generally recognized as characteristic of this country since the depression of the 1930's, it is much older than that—as old, in fact, as the Republic itself.

Class affiliation. Socioeconomic status—as measured here by an index composed of the breadwinner's occupation, education, and interviewer's rating—is directly related to the final vote decision (Chart 1). The higher the socioeconomic status (SES), the more Republican the vote; put crudely, richer people vote Republican more than poorer people.

Class identification. Nor is this relationship by any means limited to the so-called objective measures of socioeconomic status. It also appears when socioeconomic status is measured in terms of the respondent's own class identification—his own feeling as to the class in which he belongs. With socioeconomic status controlled, class identification exerts an independent influence upon the vote, especially on the lower socioeconomic status level (Chart 2).

"Class-consciousness." Since the norms of the general community are more favorable to

*Class.—Ed.

middle-class and business groups, it is more likely that they will achieve political solidarity than the working class, especially in this small-town environment. Particularly in towns like Elmira, the development of a "class-conscious" vote is inhibited by the status of the dominant community ideology centered in the middle class and its rural forebears. As a result the workers show less political solidarity and more political ambivalence. In 1948 Elmira the business, professional, and white-collar groups supported the Republicans fully 75 per cent; the workers split their vote almost fifty-fifty. There is a more cohesive business vote than labor vote. Were this not the case generally, the closeness of the Republican-Democratic vote in this country would not exist because of the strong numerical majority held by wage workers over salaried employees and independent entrepreneurs and professionals. The working class splits its vote more than does the business class.[2]

This fact can be explained in at least two ways. On the one hand, the workers could have a class-conscious ideology but be split on which party expresses it better. On the other hand, the workers could be themselves split on the matter of ideology itself, especially in a middle-class community like Elmira. The latter seems to be the case. There is little class-consciousness among workers in Elmira and hence no great tendency toward uniform political action.

Now this matter of ideology is not easy to

Chart 1   Socioeconomic Status Index Differentiates Vote (Percentage Republican of two-party vote)

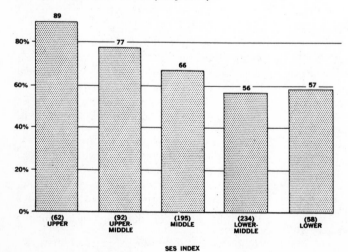

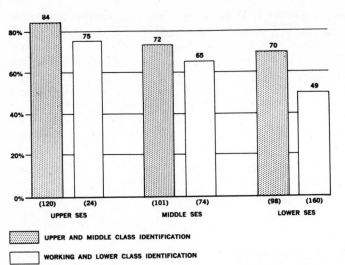

UPPER AND MIDDLE CLASS IDENTIFICATION

WORKING AND LOWER CLASS IDENTIFICATION

Chart 2   Subjective Class Identification Differentiates Vote in Addition to Objective Socioeconomic Status (Percentage Republican of two-party vote)

gauge in a few survey questions. What would class-consciousness mean in a town like Elmira? Presumably it would be manifested by such elements as these: response to verbal symbols like "big business" (negative) and "labor" (positive); a conviction that existing institutions are managed in disregard of the workers' rights and interests; a feeling of solidarity with other workers that would express itself in a desire to associate with them in leisure-time and other private activities; and, finally, the desire for a political movement specifically dedicated to the interest of the working class. Accordingly a number of questions were devised to see whether workers consider themselves a special group in the population by such criteria. At least by this test there is little class-consciousness in Elmira. While there are some differences between the workers and other occupations on these items, they are slight (except in the case of attitudes toward labor unions). Workers do not particularly distrust social institutions, or feel unduly handicapped by their social position, or show interest in their own rather than other groups, or have deviant ambitions for their children, or advocate a political party for labor. At bottom, the working class is loyal to the dominant middle-class ideology symbolized by the "American way of life" (Table 1).[3]

Yet the political history of the last twenty years in this country reveals a number of ac-

tual and potential clashes between economic interests of the different classes. What this seems to mean in Elmira is that the workers are in an ambivalent position in which their political values are derived from the dominant culture at the same time that their interest in social prestige and economic security is to some extent blocked by the interests of the dominant groups. American cultural values and actual life-experience are mutually reinforcing for upper and middle classes in the society, and accordingly they exhibit a high degree of political consensus. But cultural values and life-experience are often in contradiction for the workers, and accordingly they are more ambivalent and, as we shall see, more unstable in their political support. It takes a depression or a heated political campaign directly aimed at economic interest to bring out their "class vote" sharply against the norms of the "larger community."

Political generations. The relationship between socioeconomic status (SES) and vote is partly a function of the political conditions under which each generation comes of age. The younger generation raised in the New Deal era showed a high tendency to vote along the socioeconomic class lines associated with the Roosevelt elections (Chart 3).[4] Their elders, introduced to politics in the Republican 1920's, are not so far apart on class lines. Ac-

Table 1*   Elmira Workers Display Little Indication of Working-class-consciousness (Per Cent)

| Theoretical manifestations of working-class-consciousness | BREADWINNER'S OCCUPATION | | |
	Business, profession, self-employed	White collar	Labor
Reactions to symbols:			
Favorable to "billion-dollar corporations"	74	85	75
Favorable to "labor unions"	44	53	66
Images of social institutions:			
Believe "most city governments make the welfare of all citizens their main concern"	63	60	50
Believe most successful people have "gotten ahead" because of "ability"	86	88	74
Styles of life:			
Prefer clubs whose members are "all of my own class"	34	36	41
Like to read or hear stories about			
"working people"	79	86	80
"business people"	74	70	55
If son were a lawyer, would like him to work "for himself," "in private law firm," or "for business corporation" (instead of for "labor union" or "government")	95	90	82
If son were a doctor, would like him to be "specialist with private practice" or "head of private hospital" (instead of "head of government medical service")	96	96	92
Political militancy:			
Believe "it would be good for country if labor unions had a political party of their own"	8	7	13
Total no. of cases	171	106	340

*These data were obtained from a mail survey conducted after the election; about 75 per cent of our original sample responded. The questions appear in Appendix B [of *Voting*].

ceptance of the political norms current at the time of political initiation does not stop there; it tends to perpetuate itself through succeeding elections. Recognizing that young voters of the 1930's and later were more Democratic than their elders, many observers concluded that young "liberals" would grow up into old "conservatives." But a whole "political generation" may have been developing for whom the socioeconomic problems of their youth served as bases for permanent political norms—a semipermanent generation that would later bulge the ranks of the Democrats in certain age groups much as the crop of postwar babies is bulging different grades in school as they grow up. Presumably an age generation can be transformed by political events and social conditions into a political generation

based on class considerations—a generation that retains its allegiances and norms while succeeding generations are moving in another direction.[5] In addition, in a community like Elmira there is no difference by age at the higher socioeconomic status levels, but at the middle and lower levels there is a tendency for people to become more Republican as they grow older—as the political climate of the community "rubs off" on them.

Minority religious and ethnic status[6]

Now let us turn to another basic differentiation within the electorate. The United States has been characterized by many political observers as a nation composed of blocs of minority voters. While the history of American

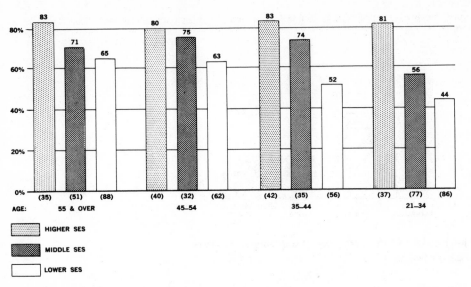

80% ── 83 ── 71 ── 65 ── ── 80 ── 75 ── 63 ── ── 83 ── 74 ── 52 ── ── 81 ── 56 ── 44

AGE: (35) (51) (88)   (40) (32) (62)   (42) (35) (56)   (37) (77) (86)
55 & OVER   45–54   35–44   21–34

HIGHER SES

MIDDLE SES

LOWER SES

Chart 3   Age Differences Indicate a Trend toward Greater Class Voting in the New Deal Generation (Percentage Republican of two-party vote)

politics attests to the general ineffectiveness of minority political parties, it also demonstrates the importance of the minority social vote—an electorate composed of so-called "hyphenated Americans." Racial, religious, and ethnic groups have demonstrated a unity in their voting allegiance that has led some observers to assign them a place of increasing importance in determining the outcome of elections. For example, Samuel Lubell, in *The Future of American Politics,* concludes that "for the immediate future the prospects point to an intensification of 'League of Nations' politics. . . . Virtually none of the underdog groups has obtained the full recognition of its numbers" (p. 79). Politicians have always been concerned with organizing the "Negro vote" or the "Jewish vote" or the "Italian vote." Such minority voters are quite numerous, especially in crucial metropolitan areas; they offer a common characteristic to which the politician can appeal; and they possess the internal cohesion, and often organization, essential for delivering a solid bloc vote.

A basic difference in political support within the electorate exists between the white native-born Protestant voters, representing the "majority" group in American society, on the one hand, and a number of racial, ethnic, and religious minority groups, on the other (Chart 4).

Now it is generally recognized that such minority groups are tied to the Democratic machine in the big cities, where they constitute a large segment of the party's support. But Elmira is a small upstate town with little machine politics and not a great deal of organized minority activity.[7] Even in this small, quiet community there is a sharp differential in vote between minority ethnic groups and "pure Americans." Even here the election can be clearly seen as a contest between the minority groups and the dominant majority—the former supporting the Democrats and the latter the Republicans. Let us analyze first the Catholic group and then review the situation for the other minority groups.

The Catholic vote.[8] The relation between votes and socioeconomic status is, after all, "reasonable" in view of the acknowledged relationship between politics and economic problems. In aiding or retarding unionism, in levying taxes upon incomes and profits, in distributing public aid, in financing social security—in these and countless other ways the government participates in what is called "class legislation." No wonder, then, that different classes vote differently.

But what of Catholicism? At first glance it seems to have no direct connection with American politics in 1948. The political issues indirectly involving Catholics were such matters as United States relations with Spain, the Vati-

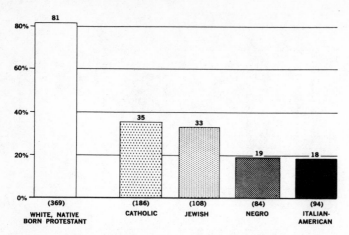

Chart 4   The Minorities and the "Majority" Vote Differently (Percentage Republican of two-party vote)

ican envoy, and the treatment of parochial schools under proposed federal aid to education. These were not salient in the 1948 campaign. Yet Catholics in the Republican community of Elmira voted Republican less than half as much as the Protestants.

To some extent, of course, this tendency reflects a historical identification. The Democratic party in New York State has been traditionally associated with the Catholics (Tammany Hall, Al Smith, Jim Farley, Ed Flynn, *et al.*), and national party leaders have been Catholics, particularly the chairmen of the Democratic National Committee over the last twenty-five years. In addition, there is a long-term connection between the party and the church stemming from the great immigration waves of the nineteenth century. But such considerations do not account for *contemporary* Catholic allegiance to the Democrats.

Independent of other factors. Now, in the first place, the Catholic vote is not simply a spurious reflection of other demographic factors. For example, Catholics are on a lower (average) income level than Protestants, and this condition is sometimes thought to be responsible for the apparent correlation between religion and political attitudes. However, the correlation in Elmira is genuine. No matter what demographic variable is controlled, the relationship between Catholic affiliation and party preference significantly remains (Chart 5). Not only that, but the religious affiliation (and the ethnic differences it represents) appears to be a stronger influence upon vote than any other single factor. For example, on each socioeconomic status level about half as many Catholics vote Republican as Protestants. Catholics of high status vote more Democratic than do Protestants of low status; thus Catholic affiliation is stronger than socioeconomic status in determining vote. In Elmira the Catholics have almost achieved the socioeconomic position of the Protestants, but this has not basically deflected their vote from the Democratic candidate.

Here, then, we find a condition not anticipated nor endorsed by classical political theorists: a nonpolitical, associative factor with strong influence upon the electoral decision. Regardless of other demographic characteristics—and despite democratic claims, protestations, or theories to the contrary—there is a strong "religious vote" in this country.

Independent of attitudes. And, still more, ideological or attitudinal position on the issues is no more powerful an influence than religion. An index of "liberalism," based on socioeconomic issues of the time, illustrates the matter. Conservative Catholics—that is, those who agree in substance with the Republican position on big business, unions, and price control—are no more Republican than liberal Protestants (Chart 6). At each step of this liberalism-conservatism score Catholics are much more Democratic than Protestants. In this respect vote is as much conditioned by who one is as by what one believes.

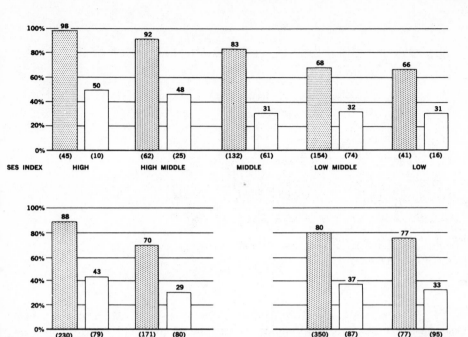

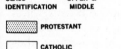

PROTESTANT

CATHOLIC

Chart 5 Regardless of What Other Demographic Factors Are Taken into Account, There Is a Basic Difference in Vote between Catholics and Protestants (Percentage Republican of two-party vote)

Catholics and "Catholics." The importance of religious affiliation in affecting political decision can be tested still further. To this point we have dealt simply with the report that one "belongs" to a religion; but there is belonging and belonging. If religious affiliation is operative, it should be even stronger among the more deeply religious or among those more intimately connected with the church. And that is so. The longer Catholics have lived in Elmira (i.e., the longer they have been associated with their co-religionists in this institution), the more Democratic do they vote (Chart 7). Similarly, the longer Protestants have lived in Elmira, the more Republican they become, probably in response to the predominantly Republican climate of opinion in the town. But Catholics become more Democratic despite the prevailing opinion climate, illustrating to some extent their group isolation, at least as far as politics is concerned. And the more intimately Catholic they feel, as indicated by their assertion that their religious group is among their "most important" identifications, the more Democratic they vote. (The fact that this is not so for the Protestants suggests the lack of a particular religious orientation to their vote.)[9]

Thus, the more intensely religious status is felt or the more pervasive its influence, the more powerful its effect upon vote. (This effect, incidentally, derives from in-group association and mutual reinforcement—in ways we shall analyze later—rather than from direct suggestion or pressure. Close observation of political activity among formal Catholic organizations, including the local church, failed to reveal any attempt to "deliver" the Catholic vote. The result derived from informal social relations, not formal institutional pressure.)

Religion and political involvement. Actually the effect of religious affiliation depends also upon the voter's involvement in politics. The more deeply Catholics are involved, the less effect religion as such has upon their vote. It

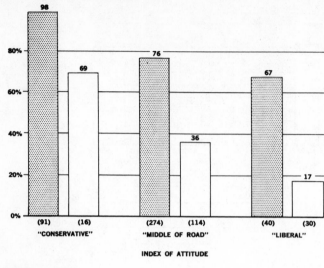

PROTESTANT

CATHOLIC

Chart 6   Religious Affiliation Is as Strong an Influence upon Vote as "Liberalism-Conservatism" (Percentage Republican of two-party vote)

was the politically *uninterested* Catholics who followed religious affiliation most frequently in determining their vote. The more involved Catholics had certain political considerations on which to base their decision as to how to vote; the less involved simply followed the lead of the religious group (see Chart 8).

Long-term age trend. With all this, 1948 marked a weakening of the Catholic vote in Elmira. In 1940 and again in 1944 about 85 per cent of Elmira Catholics claimed to have voted Democratic, and in 1948 this proportion had fallen to about 65 per cent. The likelihood of a trend away from the Democratic party on

Chart 7   The Closer the Religious Affiliation, the Stronger Its Effect upon Vote (Percentage Republican of two-party vote)

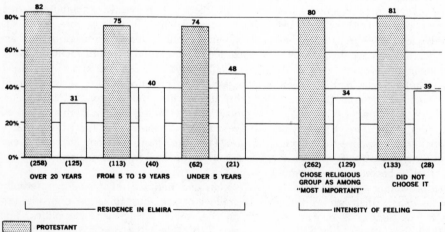

PROTESTANT

CATHOLIC

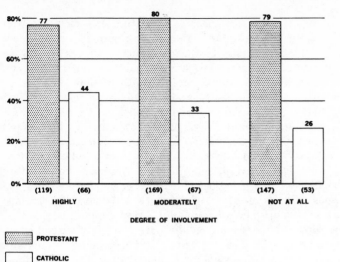

Chart 8   Percentage Republican of Two-party Vote

the part of Catholics is further suggested by the vote of different age groups. Political observers generally seem to believe that younger people—out of greater "liberalism"—have been more Democratic in recent years. But this is a complicated matter. The younger Protestants do vote more Democratic, but the younger Catholics vote more Republican (Chart 9). Thus the younger generation of Catholics voted less by religion than their elders, and in time this may diminish the difference between the two religious groups. The largest differ-

ence between Protestants and Catholics exists among the older people (70 percentage points); among the middle-aged this difference has fallen to about 40 percentage points and among the younger people to less than 30. The succession of generations seems to be softening the religious difference.

To recapitulate, here is a social characteristic that is not directly involved in political issues but nevertheless makes a big difference in vote. Catholics vote differently from Protestants, and this difference is not simply a func-

Chart 9   The Religious Difference Is Greatest among the Older People and Least among the Younger (Percentage Republican of two-party vote)

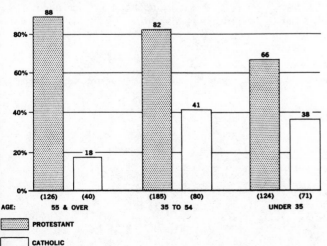

tion of differing demographic or ideological positions. Regardless of socioeconomic status level or age or even political attitude, Catholics vote more Democratic than do Protestants. And the more closely they are bound to their religion, the more Democratic they are.

Other minorities. What about the other minority groups in Elmira? In most respects the story is the same. As we have noted, Italians, Negroes, and Jews voted heavily Democratic in Elmira in 1948—82 per cent of the Italian-Americans, 81 per cent of the Negroes, and 67 of the Jews. And, as in the case of the Catholics, the vote for Truman is not particularly affected by differences in socioeconomic status. Even among the highest-income Jewish voters the ratio of Truman to Dewey voters is about three to one. There is little variance by socioeconomic status level within the Negro group, and on each socioeconomic status level the Italians are more Democratic than the non-ethnic native-born.

Contrary to the tendency among Catholics, however, the younger Negroes and Jews supported the Democrats even more strongly than their elders. Thus the educated youth may serve as the standard-bearers of these more newly active minorities, just as youth led the disintegration of older cleavages between Catholics and Protestants. In any case, the younger generation in these minority groups is more Democratic than the younger generation of Catholics (see Chart 10).

But in the case of psychological identification and social interaction with the group, these minorities are the same as the Catholics —the more closely the members identified with their minority group, the stronger their Democratic vote (Chart 11). Regardless of the particular measure, those minority members who feel close to their own group (or who feel hostile to the out-group) are more likely to express the group's political preference (i.e., vote Democratic) than their fellows.

Minority voting patterns are closely linked to the social and psychological forces that determine intergroup relations in the United States today. In the political arena, as in other spheres of community life, the intergroup tension present in most American communities results in a difference of opinion between the members of minority and "majority" groups. This division of political support is expected behavior on the part of both groups. During an election campaign it becomes an overtly expressed and openly recognized political alignment, reinforced by the stereotyped expectations of both sides. Different voting patterns become one of the prevailing practices of the community—"the way we do things around here."

The social transmission of political choices

In Elmira, then, it is the socioeconomic classes, on the one hand, and the religious and ethnic groups, on the other, that serve as the social carriers of political traditions. In the country at large, to these two kinds of differentiation in the population is added the ecological division of region or size of community (e.g., the metropolitan area as against the small town). In contrast, there are only minor differences in voting between men and women or between young and old or, indeed, on any other characteristic.

Why do certain characteristics make a difference and not others? Why is there not a

Chart 10   Percentage Republican of Two-party Vote

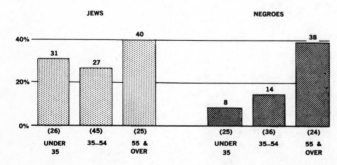

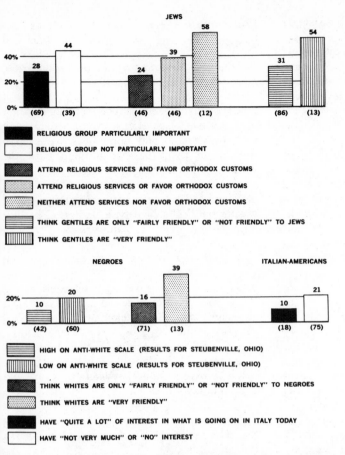

RELIGIOUS GROUP PARTICULARLY IMPORTANT

RELIGIOUS GROUP NOT PARTICULARLY IMPORTANT

ATTEND RELIGIOUS SERVICES AND FAVOR ORTHODOX CUSTOMS

ATTEND RELIGIOUS SERVICES OR FAVOR ORTHODOX CUSTOMS

NEITHER ATTEND SERVICES NOR FAVOR ORTHODOX CUSTOMS

THINK GENTILES ARE ONLY "FAIRLY FRIENDLY" OR "NOT FRIENDLY" TO JEWS

THINK GENTILES ARE "VERY FRIENDLY"

NEGROES   ITALIAN-AMERICANS

HIGH ON ANTI-WHITE SCALE (RESULTS FOR STEUBENVILLE, OHIO)

LOW ON ANTI-WHITE SCALE (RESULTS FOR STEUBENVILLE, OHIO)

THINK WHITES ARE ONLY "FAIRLY FRIENDLY" OR "NOT FRIENDLY" TO NEGROES

THINK WHITES ARE "VERY FRIENDLY"

HAVE "QUITE A LOT" OF INTEREST IN WHAT IS GOING ON IN ITALY TODAY

HAVE "NOT VERY MUCH" OR "NO" INTEREST

Chart 11 The Closer the Minority Group Affiliation, the Stronger the Democratic Vote (Percentage Republican of two-party vote)

distinctive women's vote or a sharp cleavage along age lines or, for that matter, a more or less random dispersal of the votes of individuals? In part this is a matter of timing, that is, of the historical period in which our study happens to be made. But, if a number of such studies had been made over the entire span of the two-party system, it is likely that most of them would have found similar differences in voting by class, ethnic, and ecological blocs of the American population. Why are such bases of political cleavage so persistent?

Explanations of a political character are prominent; for example, the explanation that such people have group interests in common and represent convenient blocs for political appeal and mobilization. Thus, in simplified terms, Jews vote Democratic "because" of Roosevelt's interventionist stand against Hitler; Negroes, "because" of the relief and wel-

fare program of the New Deal; and both "because" of civil rights legislation. Less understood, however, are the social conditions that contribute to the success of such political mobilization—and, more importantly, to its persistence. Voting blocs are often perpetuated so long after group needs and political alternatives have changed that it is unrealistic to speak of active, contemporary "interests" being involved in more than a few of the voting differences between groups that exist in the country at a given time. Why do the others persist with such force?

There appear to be three ways in which social relations contribute to the maintenance of political differences.

First, there is the necessary condition of an economic division of labor or a physical separation or a social differentiation in the population such that people of unlike characteristics are affected in different ways by a single political policy. In other words, it is necessary to have a social basis for a political interest. It would be difficult in contemporary America, for example, to maintain strong voting differences by sex, because there are few policy issues persisting over a period of time that affect men and women differently. *Differentiation* is a condition for disagreement.

Second, a necessary condition for the persistence of political differences is their *transmission* to succeeding generations. Parents and children sharing the same characteristics provide a condition of continuity in which political choices can be taught, however, subtly and unconsciously, by the one to the other. Some such transmission is necessary so that voting traditions do not die out. This presumably is a reason why youth movements in politics are often less stable or persistent than other bases of voting traditions that can more easily be transmitted from generation to generation.

Similarly, a political movement based on the special interests of old age (e.g., pensions) has difficulty in maintaining itself because of the necessary absence of a generational tie. *Transmission* is a condition for persistence.

Finally, given the origin of a voting difference in one generation and the transmittibility of it to the next, another condition is necessary for it to survive in the succeeding generation. Members of the social groups involved must be substantially more in contact with one another, socially and physically, than they are with opposing groups. This condition will be analyzed in some detail in Chapter 6 [of *Voting*] where we will try to show how political traditions are maintained through marriage and through living and working with socially alike, and hence politically like-minded, people. *Contact* is a condition for consensus.

In sum, the conditions underlying persistent voting cleavages seem to be (1) initial social differentiation such that the consequences of political policy are materially or symbolically different for different groups; (2) conditions of transmittability from generation to generation; and (3) conditions of physical and social proximity providing for continued in-group contact in succeeding generations. In contemporary America these conditions are best met in *class*, in *ethnic*, and in *ecological* divisions of the population. They continue to provide, then, the most durable social bases for political cleavage.

Summary

Socioeconomic status

1. Higher socioeconomic status groups vote more Republican than lower.

2. Class identification affects vote in addition to objective class status: voters identifying with the middle and upper class vote more Republican than those identifying with the working or lower class.

3. White-collar and business groups have greater political solidarity, as indicated by uniform party preference, than workers.

4. Workers are not particularly class-conscious.

5. Age differences reveal greater class voting in the younger groups raised in the New Deal era—suggesting the development of a "political generation."
   and (*a*) Young Catholics and Protestants are more likely than older voters to resolve the cross-pressure between religion and class in favor of class.

6. Women, less politicized than men, follow the class tendency in voting less than men in the current era.

Ethnic status

7. White native-born Protestants vote Republican more than minority ethnic groups—specifically, Catholics, Italian-Americans, Jews, and Negroes.

8. Catholics vote more Democratic than Protestants regardless of class status or class identification or national origin.

9. Catholics vote more Democratic than Protestants regardless of the "liberalism" or "conservatism" of their attitudes on political issues.

10. Catholics closely identified with their religion vote Democratic more than Catholics not so identified.

11. Catholics personally involved in political affairs follow the religious lead in voting less than Catholics not so involved.

12. The difference between Catholics and Protestants in voting is strongest among older people; young Catholics are more Republican than their elders, and young Protestants more Democratic.

13. The Democratic vote of Italian-Americans, Jews, and Negroes is not eliminated by class controls.

14. Contrary to the case with Catholics, younger members of the currently active minorities, Jews and Negroes, are more Democratic than their elders.

15. As in the case of Catholics, the more closely members of minorities identify with their ethnic group, the more Democratic their vote.

Notes

[1] By virtue of the design of this community study, this factor of place of residence was not included. However, occasional comparisons with other regions or the country as a whole are made, and the influence of the Republican predominance in Elmira is evident at many points.

[2] An important circumstance making for greater political harmony within the business group is simply their greater rate of political activity within the community. They belong to more organizations than the labor group, they talk politics more, and they are looked to more for political advice. They not only reassure themselves through such activities; they also set a political "tone" for the entire community. And they were in positions to do so: about 80 per cent of the occupational elite of the community were Republicans and about 75 per cent of the officers of clubs and organizations.

[3] What is more, the analysis of interrelations among these opinions reveals that the few signs of working-class alienation from middle-class norms do not tend to come from the same people. There are only a handful of "radical" workers in Elmira (and some of them seem to represent more of a personality deviation). Worker complaints against "the system" are isolated and individualized, not diffused within a core group of class-conscious workers.

[4] In addition, there is a suggestion in the Elmira data that younger people resolve the cross-pressure of religion and class status more in favor of the latter. Younger Catholics of the business and white-collar group are more Republican than older Catholics; and younger Protestants of the union labor group are more Democratic than older Protestants. The data [follow in Table 1].

[5] Just as age has a revealing relationship to vote when associated with SES, so does sex. As indicated by a measure like interest, women are less politicized than men—they follow the vote of their SES level less than men, on both extremes. High SES men are more Republican than high SES women; low SES men are more Democratic than low SES women. The data [follow in Table 2].

[6] Some material in this section was originally prepared by Edward Suchman and was edited for this volume by the authors.

[7] The minority groups under study here differ somewhat in the extent to which they constitute meaningful "community groups" in Elmira. Only the Negroes and the Jews have associational and organizational ties. The Catholics and the foreign-born do not form noticeably separate community groups within the town. The Negroes form the most distinctive separate community, with their own social and welfare organizations, an active NAACP chapter, a Negro church, Negro leadership, and a strong sense of being a group set apart from

TABLE 1

| Age | Percentage Republican of two-party vote | |
	Business and white-collar Catholics	Union labor Protestants
Up to 44	48 (48)	48 (65)
45 and over	32 (31)	70 (50)

TABLE 2

	Percentage Republican of two-party vote	
SES	Men	Women
High	88 (75)	76 (79)
Middle	64 (75)	67 (120)
Low	51 (145)	61 (147)

the majority community. The Jewish group was next clear cut in its own in-group organization, with its own Jewish center, recognized Jewish leaders, and a feeling of minority-group membership. Both the Italian-American group and the Catholic group were rather closely integrated into the main stream of community life and neither viewed itself, nor was either viewed by the majority group, as a separate community. For this reason, the Catholics and the ethnic groups serve as examples of demographic voting based upon membership in a common population class with strong *informal* relations, whereas the Negroes and the Jews are examples of more organized groups based upon membership in a physically separated as well as a psychological and social community.

The original sample of the Elmira community contained 297 Catholics, but only 48 foreign-born, 15 Jews, and 17 Negroes. There was an additional group of 224 second-generation Americans (at least one parent foreign-born). A postelection survey, conducted as part of a larger study of intergroup relations in Elmira by the Social Science Research Center of Cornell University, included cross-sectional samples of Jews, Negroes, and Italian-Americans—150 in each group —and this augmented sample permits a comparison of the final vote decision of these minority groups with the votes of the "majority group." (While the Italian-Americans are also Catholic, the Catholic group includes only a minority who are of Italian descent. The results presented are based upon two independent samples of Italian-Americans and Catholics.)

[8] For a fuller treatment of the Catholic vote in Elmira see David Gold, "The Influence of Religious Affiliation on Voting Behavior" (Ph.D. dissertation, Department of Sociology, University of Chicago, 1953).

[9] This is also reflected in the greater family solidarity of the lower-educated Catholic household, as expressed in intrafamily discussion of politics. The data [follow in Table 3].

TABLE 3

	Among those with some high school or less	
Percentage who	Catholic	Protestant
Last discussed politics with family member (June)	33 (32)	7 (72)
Last discussed politics with family member (October)	50 (94)	43 (221)

PRIMARY GROUPS

On some occasions, especially in complex societies, social interaction takes place among people who are strangers. In the sale of a pair of gloves in a department store, both customer and clerk are usually unaware of such elemental facts as each other's name. It suffices for this relationship that they know each other's statuses and act according to the norms. The professor lecturing to a class of three hundred students is in an essentially similar situation, although the interaction is not so fleeting and impermanent. In contrast to groups such as these, called secondary groups, are the primary groups that are the subject of this selection.

Always in simple societies, and very commonly even in highly complex civilizations, social interaction takes place among people who "know" each other. The corner gang, the office crowd, the "boys" at the barbershop, and the girls at the supermarket are examples of what sociologists mean by primary groups. Primary groups are characterized by intimate and cooperative social relations. They are of necessity small groups, but they exist within the confines of the most impersonal bureaucracies of complex societies, as well as in the circles of small and isolated tribes. In this selection Charles Horton Cooley, who coined the term, defines the primary group and indicates its importance for psychology as well as sociology.

> Primary groups are characterized by intimate face-to-face association and cooperation. These groups are primary in many senses, the most important of which is their formation of personality (primary socialization).
>
> In all societies, the child acquires his culture in the context of primary groups. Since these primary groups are similar the world over, socialized human beings display common elements of personality, including the capacity to feel sympathy, regardless of the society in which they were raised. This is what people mean when they speak of human nature.
>
> The most important primary groups are the family, the play group, and the neighborhood. They occur in nearly all societies, and their effects are seen in all socialized human beings.

Despite some anachronisms, such as the passage concerning race, this work has endured as the classic definition of primary groups. Some sociologists have taken exception to Cooley's requirement that primary groups be face-to-face, suggesting that very intimate social interaction can be carried on by mail or by telephone. Defenders of Cooley's definition point out that such groups tend to die out if it becomes obvious to the members that they will never see each other again.

It is also possible to question the sharp distinction between primary and secondary groups implied by the dichotomous terminology. (The term "secondary group" was not used by Cooley, but was introduced by later sociologists.) Since intimacy can be greater or less and the balance between cooperation and competition is not an all-or-none affair, it seems plausible to consider these terms as poles of a continuum, with groups being more or less primary and secondary, rather than either one or the other.

Cooley's discussion of the primary group fits well with, and in fact was implied in, Mead's theory of socialization, discussed in Selection 19. The universal presence of primary groups can explain uniformities among men which might otherwise, erroneously, be attributed to biology.

Selection 27
FROM SOCIAL ORGANIZATION
Charles Horton Cooley

By primary groups I mean those characterized by intimate face-to-face association and cooperation. They are primary in several senses, but chiefly in that they are fundamental in forming the social nature and ideals of the

individual. The result of intimate association, psychologically, is a certain fusion of individualities in a common whole, so that one's very self, for many purposes at least, is the common life and purpose of the group. Perhaps the simplest way of describing this wholeness is by saying that it is a "we"; it involves the sort of sympathy and mutual identification for which "we" is the natural expression. One lives in the feeling of the whole and finds the chief aims of his will in that feeling.

It is not to be supposed that the unity of the primary group is one of mere harmony and love. It is always a differentiated and usually a competitive unity, admitting of self-assertion and various appropriative passions; but these passions are socialized by sympathy, and come, or tend to come, under the discipline of a common spirit. The individual will be ambitious, but the chief object of his ambition will be some desired place in the thought of the others, and he will feel allegiance to common standards of service and fair play. So the boy will dispute with his fellows a place on the team, but above such disputes will place the common glory of his class and school.

The most important spheres of this intimate association and cooperation—though by no means the only ones—are the family, the play-group of children, and the neighborhood or community group of elders. These are practically universal, belonging to all times and all stages of development; and are accordingly a chief basis of what is universal in human nature and human ideals. The best comparative studies of the family, such as those of Westermarck[1] or Howard,[2] show it to us as not only a universal institution, but as more alike the world over than the exaggeration of exceptional customs by an earlier school had led us to suppose. Nor can any one doubt the general prevalence of play-groups among children or of informal assemblies of various kinds among their elders. Such association is clearly the nursery of human nature in the world about us, and there is no apparent reason to suppose that the case has anywhere or at any time been essentially different.

As regards play, I might, were it not a matter of common observation, multiply illustrations of the universality and spontaneity of the group discussion and cooperation to which it gives rise. The general fact is that children, especially boys after about their twelfth year, live in fellowships in which their sympathy, ambition and honor are engaged even more, often, than they are in the family. Most of us can recall examples of the endurance by boys of injustice and even cruelty, rather than appeal from their fellows to parents or teachers—as, for instance, in the hazing so prevalent at schools, and so difficult, for this very reason, to repress. And how elaborate the discussion,

how cogent the public opinion, how hot the ambitions in these fellowships.

Nor is this facility of juvenile association, as is sometimes supposed, a trait peculiar to English and American boys; since experience among our immigrant population seems to show that the offspring of the more restrictive civilizations of the continent of Europe form self-governing play-groups with almost equal readiness. Thus Miss Jane Addams, after pointing out that the "gang" is almost universal, speaks of the interminable discussion which every detail of the gang's activity receives, remarking that "in these social folk-motes, so to speak, the young citizen learns to act upon his own determination."[3]

Of the neighborhood group it may be said, in general, that from the time men formed permanent settlements upon the land, down, at least, to the rise of modern industrial cities, it has played a main part in the primary, heart-to-heart life of the people. Among our Teutonic forefathers the village community was apparently the chief sphere of sympathy and mutual aid for the commons all through the "dark" and middle ages, and for many purposes it remains so in rural districts at the present day. In some countries we still find it with all its ancient vitality, notably in Russia, where the mir, or self-governing village group, is the main theatre of life, along with the family, for perhaps fifty millions of peasants.

In our own life the intimacy of the neighborhood has been broken up by the growth of an intricate mesh of wider contacts which leaves us strangers to people who live in the same house. And even in the country the same principle is at work, though less obviously, diminishing our economic and spiritual community with our neighbors. How far this change is a healthy development, and how far a disease, is perhaps still uncertain.

Besides these almost universal kinds of primary association, there are many others whose form depends upon the particular state of civilization; the only essential thing, as I have said, being a certain intimacy and fusion of personalities. In our own society, being little bound by place, people easily form clubs, fraternal societies and the like, based on congeniality, which may give rise to real intimacy. Many such relations are formed at school and college, and among men and women brought together in the first instance by their occupations—as workmen in the same trade, or the like. Where there is a little common interest and activity, kindness grows like weeds by the roadside.

But the fact that the family and neighborhood groups are ascendant in the open and plastic time of childhood makes them even now incomparably more influential than all the rest.

Primary groups are primary in the sense that they give the individual his earliest and completest experience of social unity, and also in the sense that they do not change in the same degree as more elaborate relations, but form a comparatively permanent source out of which the latter are ever springing. Of course they are not independent of the larger society, but to some extent reflect its spirit; as the German family and the German school bear somewhat distinctly the print of German militarism. But this, after all, is like the tide setting back into creeks, and does not commonly go very far. Among the German, and still more among the Russian, peasantry are found habits of free cooperation and discussion almost uninfluenced by the character of the state; and it is a familiar and well-supported view that the village commune, self-governing as regards local affairs and habituated to discussion, is a very widespread institution in settled communities, and the continuator of a similar autonomy previously existing in the clan. "It is man who makes monarchies and establishes republics, but the commune seems to come directly from the hand of God."[4]

In our own cities the crowded tenements and the general economic and social confusion have sorely wounded the family and the neighborhood, but it is remarkable, in view of these conditions, what vitality they show; and there is nothing upon which the conscience of the time is more determined than upon restoring them to health.

These groups, then, are springs of life, not only for the individual but for social institutions. They are only in part moulded by special traditions, and, in larger degree, express a universal nature. The religion or government of other civilizations may seem alien to us, but the children or the family group wear the common life, and with them we can always make ourselves at home.

By human nature, I suppose, we may understand those sentiments and impulses that are human in being superior to those of lower animals, and also in the sense that they belong to mankind at large, and not to any particular race or time. It means, particularly, sympathy and the innumerable sentiments into which sympathy enters, such as love, resentment, ambition, vanity, hero-worship, and the feeling of social right and wrong.[5]

Human nature in this sense is justly regarded as a comparatively permanent element in society. Always and everywhere men seek honor and dread ridicule, defer to public opinion, cherish their goods and their children, and admire courage, generosity, and success. It is always safe to assume that people are and have been human.

It is true, no doubt, that there are differences of race capacity, so great that a large part of mankind are possibly incapable of any high kind of social organization. But those differences, like those among individuals of the same race, are subtle, depending upon some obscure intellectual deficiency, some want of vigor, or slackness of moral fibre, and do not involve unlikeness in the generic impulses of human nature. In these all races are very much alike. The more insight one gets into the life of savages, even those that are reckoned the lowest, the more human, the more like ourselves, they appear. Take for instance the natives of Central Australia, as described by Spencer and Gillen,[6] tribes having no definite government or worship and scarcely able to count to five. They are generous to one another, emulous of virtue as they understand it, kind to their children and to the aged, and by no means harsh to women. Their faces as shown in the photographs are wholly human and many of them attractive.

And when we come to a comparison between different stages in the development of the same race, between ourselves, for instance, and the Teutonic tribes of the time of Caesar, the difference is neither in human nature nor in capacity, but in organization, in the range and complexity of relations, in the diverse expression of powers and passions essentially much the same.

There is no better proof of this generic likeness of human nature than in the ease and joy with which the modern man makes himself at home in literature depicting the most remote and varied phases of life—in Homer, in the Nibelung tales, in the Hebrew Scriptures, in the legends of the American Indians, in the stories of frontier life, of soldiers and sailors, of criminals and tramps, and so on. The more penetratingly any phase of human life is studied the more an essential likeness to ourselves is revealed.

To return to primary groups: the view here maintained is that human nature is not something existing separately in the individual, but *a group-nature or primary phase of society,* a relatively simple and general condition of the social mind. It is something more, on the one hand, than the mere instinct that is born in us —though that enters into it—and something less, on the other, than the more elaborate development of ideas and sentiments that makes up institutions. It is the nature which is developed and expressed in those simple, face-to-face groups that are somewhat alike in all societies; groups of the family, the playground, and the neighborhood. In the essential similarity of these is to be found the basis, in experience, for similar ideas and sentiments in the human mind. In these, everywhere, human nature comes into existence. Man does not have it at birth; he cannot acquire it except through fellowship, and it decays in isolation.

If this view does not recommend itself to common sense I do not know that elaboration will be of much avail. It simply means the application at this point of the idea that society and individuals are inseparable phases of a common whole, so that wherever we find an individual fact we may look for a social fact to go with it. If there is a universal nature in persons there must be something universal in association to correspond to it.

What else can human nature be than a trait of primary groups? Surely not an attribute of the separate individual—supposing there were any such thing—since its typical characteristics, such as affection, ambition, vanity, and resentment, are inconceivable apart from society. If it belongs, then, to man in association what kind or degree of association is required to develop it? Evidently nothing elaborate, because elaborate phases of society are transient and diverse, while human nature is comparatively stable and universal. In short the family and neighborhood life is essential to its genesis and nothing more is.

Here as everywhere in the study of society we must learn to see mankind in psychical wholes, rather than in artificial separation. We must see and feel the communal life of family and local groups as immediate facts, not as combinations of something else. And perhaps we shall do this best by recalling our own experience and extending it through sympathetic observation. What, in our life, is the family and the fellowship; what do we know of the we-feeling? Thought of this kind may help us to get a concrete perception of that primary group-nature of which everything social is the outgrowth.

Notes

[1] The History of Human Marriage.

[2] A History of Matrimonial Institutions.

[3] Newer Ideals of Peace, 177.

[4] De Tocqueville, Democracy in America, vol. i, chap. 5.

[5] These matters are expounded at some length in the writer's Human Nature and the Social Order.

[6] The Native Tribes of Central Australia. Compare also Darwin's views and examples given in chap. 7 of his Descent of Man.

A SOCIAL GROUP

Primary groups are basic components of all larger groups. Even such giant and "impersonal" groups as armies, corporations, and states contain myriads of primary groups in the form of office and shop cliques. This fact is generally unrecognized on a formal or official level. It nonetheless has important consequences most easily recognized when they are felt to be undesirable.

A well-known example of the consequences of primary groups for large associations is the almost universal presence of restriction of output in industry. Restriction of output refers to pressures exerted on members by primary groups to keep their production within certain limits. For instance, although workers at the American Widget-Welding Works may be paid for each piece they produce, primary-group pressures may prevent any worker from producing more than fifty widgets per day, even if some workers must therefore spend half the day idle at their benches. A worker who consistently produces more than fifty pieces will be labeled a "rate buster"; as a sanction, the satisfactions of primary group relations with other workers will be denied to him. Under these circumstances, management may find it difficult to increase production by such techniques as raising the piece rate, since the source of the limited production is in the primary-group norms and not in the economic motivation of the workers.

Primary groups can also be of great utility to larger groups. They provide an important source of motivation to work; in some cases adherence to primary-group norms far surpasses the more commonly understood sources of motivation. During World War II, Army officials were surprised to learn of the importance of loyalty to one's "buddies" as a motivation to fight, in contrast to such factors as hatred of the enemy or devotion to one's country. The other side of the coin concerning restriction of output is that a minimum, as well as a maximum, is applied to each worker's production, thus assuring a constant output. We can go so far as to say that primary groups are necessary to larger groups, and that, in general, large formal associations require corresponding informal organizations of primary groups.

This selection is a study of one small work group. The group is unusual in its apparent lack of restriction of output, but the typical satisfactions of primary-group life in an otherwise uninteresting job are highlighted in this study.

> The job of the cash posters is a dull, routine clerical task shared by ten girls. The cash posters form a social group, which is delineated in terms of greater interaction among these girls than with girls who are not cash posters. The social satisfactions of the job are considerable for most of the girls, compensating in part for the dullness of the work.
>
> The group is divided into two cliques, along with a few isolates who belong to neither clique. This division appears in reported behavior, both on and off the job, and in observed behavior on the job.
>
> Among the findings reported concerning this group are that popularity varies along with social interaction, but that production bears no relationship to either popularity or interaction. The isolate, the low producer, the accurate worker, the high producer, and the popular girl are discussed as social types, relating work effectiveness to social position in the group and in the wider society, as well as to the individual's past work history.

The study uses three different research methods—objective indices of production, systematic observation of behavior, and interviewing—in a very intensive study of one small group. Caution in interpretation is indicated because this is a study of a single case which may not be typical of other work groups. For instance, the finding that popularity and interaction are unrelated to productivity might not apply in a group where there was restriction of output.

Particular attention might be paid to the sociogram, reproduced on page 278, which illustrates a very useful technique for learning about group structure. The girls were asked to name their friends, and their choices were plotted in this figure. The cliques appear very clearly, as do the isolates, who were not named by anybody. People who receive many sociometric choices, like Burke in this example, may be expected to possess influence in the group and to exercise a kind of leadership. Homans tested the validity of this sociogram by comparing it with another one based on observed social interaction. The two sociograms indicated the same group structure.

Homans's conclusions concerning the processes at work in this group are unpretentious, down-to-earth explanations, which are appealing in a discipline that sometimes goes to excesses of florid terminology. However, it is important to observe his warning that the scope of this study is too narrow to establish the observed relationships as general hypotheses.

Selection 28
THE CASH POSTERS: A STUDY OF A GROUP OF WORKING GIRLS
George C. Homans

Since the Western Electric researches, few studies of single groups of workers have been reported, and even fewer that combined the measurement of individual effectiveness with the systematic observation of social behavior and the interviewing of all the group members. I shall describe briefly here a study that did combine these features.[1] It is a study of the ten girl "cash posters" in an accounting division of a certain company, and it formed part of a study of the division as a whole, which I carried on from December 1949 through April 1950. Since it deals with only one group and that group had only ten members, it can hardly hope to establish general hypotheses about small group behavior. Several such studies, made with comparable methods, might hope to do so, and they would provide the indispensable background to more macroscopic studies of worker behavior, made by questionnaires. But by itself the present one can only be called a case study of the relations between repetitive work, individual behavior, and social organization in a clerical group.

Method of study

I have described elsewhere my procedure in introducing myself into the company and the division.[2] I chose to study this particular division largely because the nature of some of the jobs allowed the keeping of reliable output records, and because the layout of the "floor" allowed an unobstructed view of what went on. My first step was to occupy a small table

Reprinted from *American Sociological Review*, 19:6, 1954, pp. 724–733, with permission of the author and the publisher. This article is also reprinted in George C. Homans, *Sentiments and Activities* (New York: The Free Press of Glencoe, 1962), pp. 75–90.

at the back of the room. With this as a base of operations, I spent about a month introducing myself to each of the workers, learning the various clerical procedures, and getting a general impression of behavior in the division. Any constraint due to the presence of a stranger seemed to end after I attended the Christmas office party, and from then on I could get no evidence that the workers' behavior was different from what it had been before I came in.

The second stage of the study, which took 14 working days, was systematic observation of interaction in the room, specifically of who talked to whom, and how often. With 60 persons in the room, I soon found I could not keep a continuous interaction record, and so I adopted a sampling procedure. Every 15 minutes I scanned the room like a radar beam and made a note of which persons were talking together at that time. This method, plus the distances at which most of the observations were made, precluded systematic recording of originations, receipts, and durations of interaction. I could only see *which persons* were interacting. It also precluded recording the content of interaction, except when it took place, as it often did, right in front of me. In this case I did not record content systematically, but only if it seemed to throw light on social relations.

The third and longest phase of the study consisted of individual interviews with the supervisors and workers, conducted on company time in a private room away from the office floor. Before the interview, I asked each worker if she was willing to talk to me; they all agreed except one, whom I did not press further, and who was not one of the cash posters. The interviews, which lasted from one to two hours, were non-directive except in two respects. After explaining again the purpose of the study, I always began the main body of the interview with the question: "How do you like your job?" That is, the initial focus of the interview was on attitudes toward the job. I did not press for information on "personal problems," which rarely came up, or on life outside the job, which often did, but I did not discourage talking about these matters if they arose. Then at some point in the course of the interview, as the question came up naturally, I asked, "Who are your close friends in here?" I wanted to get further systematic information on social organization. I recorded each interview, as I remembered it, as soon as possible after it ended.

During the interviewing period, I kept in touch with the division every day, to make arrangements for the next interviews and to hear the latest gossip. When the interviews were over, I returned for two weeks to my table on the floor, to check my first impressions and to make further brief interaction records to determine whether my original results were badly out of line. They were not.

The management also gave me the basic personnel data on the workers and, if they were kept, their output and accuracy records. The whole study took four months and a half. Let me say here, as I have said before, that I enjoyed my association with a fine body of American men and women. In fact I had a wonderful time.

The cash posting job

The division contained sixty persons, doing several different clerical jobs. I am concerned here with only ten of the workers and only one of the jobs—the ten girls that did the "cash posting."

The cash posting job was next to the bottom of the grades that made up the usual channel of advancement in the division. At the time of the study, a poster made 42.23 dollars for a 40-hour, 5-day week. The posters were all high-school graduates, young in age, and relatively new to the company, as promotion to cash poster from lower grades came fairly rapidly. The reason for this was that the company required girls to leave the company when they married, and most marrying takes place at the ages represented by the cash posters. So vacancies on the job were frequent, but promotion to higher grades took place much more

slowly. None of the girls looked forward to cash posting or to work in the company as a permanent job.

The day before a girl left the company to get married, the others, in the afternoon "relief" period, decorated her desk and covered it with candy and presents. Since none of the supervisors felt he should take it on, the girls assigned me the job of handing out the presents and, far more unnerving, of pinning a corsage on the girl who was leaving. In this way I came to be of some use in division society.

One supervisor, who also had special clerical work to do, was in charge of cash posters, and he reported to the division head.

All the reader needs to know about the company is that it had a large number of customers to whom it sent out monthly bills. It was the business of the division to account for the payment of these bills. Because there were so many of them, they were not all sent out on the first of the month but some on every working day. The bills were printed by machine from punchcards, whereupon the cards were brought to the division and placed in files, ten in number, which ran in four rows up and down the floor. Although old-fashioned bookkeeping had long disappeared from the company, its language was still preserved, and so the files were called "ledgers," and the cards, since they represented unpaid bills, were called the "arrears."

As customers paid their bills, their cash and checks, together with the bill stubs, went to the cashier's office, not on the floor. There the receipts were added, and from there bundles of stubs, each wrapped in an adding-machine tape showing the total of each bundle, came to the desk occupied by the posters' supervisor, which was close in front of my own. He arranged them on the desk in order of size. A cash poster took the first bundle in order, went to the appropriate ledger and, flipping through the arrears cards, pulled out the cards whose printed numbers corresponded to those on the stubs in her "tape." This was called "pulling cash" or more formally "cash posting"—another survival of the language of ledgerbooks. The removal of a card from the arrears meant that a customer would not be billed again for that amount next month.

When she had pulled all the cards corresponding to stubs in her bundle ("tape"), the cash poster brought cards, stubs, and tape back to the supervisor's desk, took the first new tape, and repeated the process. The pulled cards and tape were sent down to the machine room, where the cards were mechanically counted and added. This addition revealed any failure of cards and tape to balance and thus any mistakes—wrong cards pulled—that the poster had made. Since each poster kept a record of which tapes she had worked on, it was easy to calculate how many cards she pulled and how many errors she made per hour of work. These output and accuracy records were written up daily and placed in a drawer of the supervisor's desk for the posters to see. The cash posters did look at them, and in summary form they were made available to me.

Ninety per cent of all bills were paid in the exact amount shown on the stub. In the case of over- or under-payments, the posters had to perform certain operations on the cards besides simply pulling them, but for the sake of brevity these will not be described. The number of such payments in a tape, the number of stubs in a tape, and the degree to which the cards corresponding to the stubs were concentrated in a single ledger affected the speed at which the tape could be completed. But the order in which the tapes were picked up equalized these variations, in the long run, among the cash posters.

Besides cash posting, the girls spent some time every afternoon working on "collection stubs." This was a job of determining, before the company put pressure on delinquent customers, whether long-overdue bills had been recently paid. No output records could be kept of this work. When they finished it, the girls returned to pulling what they illogically called "next day's cash."

Cash posting was the only "production" job in the division—the only one it had to stay caught up with every day. And no girl was accepted as a cash poster unless, by the end of her training period, she could pull, on the average, 300 cards an hour. This was called the "quota," and it served as a standard of minimum output. The records show that all the girls did, on the average, make the quota; most of them did not find this hard to do, and some of them made a great deal more. In theory, the supervisor "bawled out" a girl if she failed for two days in a row to make the quota. In fact, he rarely had to, and when he did the bawling out was gentle. But neither

did he praise a girl when she made a high record, and there was no incentive payment. The public output records themselves seemed to suffice to keep output up. One of my field notes reads as follows: "Murphy, LoPresti,[3] and others gathered around their boss's desk looking at the output records with cries of 'I made it!' " The fact is that cash posting looked to an outsider like a hard and dull job. A number of girls who were offered it had turned it down. The supervisors wisely felt that they would have a still harder time getting recruits and getting out production if they tried to bear down on a group of young girls like this one.

The girls liked their immediate boss. He never tried to use "human relations skills." He was frank and outspoken when they broke the rules, but they felt they knew where they stood with him and said—which is the highest of all praise from workers—"He's fair." Or even, "He's a *man!*" For his part he said, "I have a good bunch of girls working for me. I really don't think you could get a better one anywhere. Of course, some of them carry the others. They're not all equally fast. But they do a good job, even the slowest of them. Some of them are so good they really ought to have something better than they have now."

The cash posters were on their feet most of the day, moving, "tapes" in hand, from ledger to ledger. This gave them many chances for social contact, both with members of their own job group and with other workers, many of whom also worked at the ledgers. They made the most of their opportunities, especially as they were convinced they could do their work without concentrating on it—they could work and talk at the same time. In theory, talking was discouraged. In practice, the supervisors made little effort to stop it, except when it got so loud they thought it disturbed some of the older workers. In part, they felt that they could not stop it; in part, that talking did not always get in the way of work. As one of them said, "If you get them on the carpet for talking or making mistakes, you usually find that the girl who talks most or has made the mistake is one of your best girls."

The cash posters spent most of their time on their feet, but they were also assigned small tables, four in one place and six in another, where they could work on collection stubs or where, if they had to pull many cards in a single ledger, they could bring the card tray to work on it seated. Assignment to neighboring tables was an important factor in the formation of friendships. In the last half-hour of the last working day of the year, all tables were reassigned in accordance with the supervisor's plan, secret until then. The girls took their new seats to the accompaniment of squealing and giggling. This move was supposed, among other things, to break up cliques that might get in the way of work.

The characteristics of the cash posting job should by now be clear. It was an exceedingly routine and repetitive clerical job, which could be done with little concentration by girls whose main interests were not in the job itself and who were not deeply concerned with promotion in the company. In view of the fact that it required no previous outside training, such as stenography, it paid well. It required no cooperation among the girls but allowed much social interaction. Little pressure was put on the girls to work fast, and morale was generally good.

Attitudes toward the job

I opened the interviews with the question, "How do you like your job?" And nine out of the ten cash posters said they liked it, the next comment usually being, "It's a job," *i.e.* better than no job at all. Since the interviews were non-directive, I got no further systematic information on the reasons why they liked the job, but I suspect that the frequency with which they spontaneously mentioned some of its features is a pretty good index of their importance to the posters. Only one feature of the job was mentioned favorably by more than half (6) of the girls, and that was the general friendliness of the group and the "niceness" of the people in the division. The only other attitude expressed by more than half (6) may be summed up as: "I do my work and get my quota and that's all."

A characteristic comment was Elizabeth Rourke's: "Then there was an opening on cash posting. I learned the job in three weeks. Most of them take four. I got so I could do 297, so they qualified me and forgot about the last three. After all, a job's a job. It really isn't hard to get the quota. Of course, you have to keep working, but if you do, you don't have any trouble getting over 300. That's all I worry about. As long as I get over 300 I don't care. Sometimes they bawl you out, if you

don't make 300 two days in a row. But half the time I think Al Johnson (former boss of the cash posters) is kidding. He says, 'Aren't you ever going to stop talking?' I have to talk, and I think that a lot of the time it helps you to talk. You speed up a little afterwards so's to be sure to make your quota. It makes you feel better. Half the time you can do your work with your eyes and talk at the same time. The other day I wasn't thinking of what I was doing—I guess I was thinking of something else—and I made 400. I don't usually do that, but Dotty Murphy does it all the time. It's just as easy for her to get 400 as it is for me to get 300. But if you do make 400 no one says anything. You don't get anything for it. You don't get any more pay, so what good does it do you to get 400? Then they might expect you to get 400 all the time."

This last remark is characteristic of situations where restriction of output exists. And other remarks of the same kind were made, for instance: "If you pull a lot of cards, you spoil the job for the other girls. They're expected to pull that many too." In point of fact no one in the room remembered a time when the quota had been anything but 300: it had never been raised. It served as a floor under output, but a glance at the output records later in this paper will show that output varied greatly above the quota. No group norm put a ceiling on output. A couple of years before, when relations between the posters and a former division head were strained, there may have been some restriction. And when Lillian Granara became the first cash poster in recent history to pull over 400 cards an hour, she said she was criticised for doing so. But such behavior seems to have disappeared at the time of my study. When Murphy began to match Granara's performance, she escaped attack. Only the two posters, Asnault and Burke, who had been on the job in the old days expressed, in interviews, disapproval of the speed at which others were working; and on the floor no girl brought effective pressure on any other to keep her output down.

The attitudes characteristic of restriction of output were present in the group; the thing itself was not, certainly not as an organized group practice. But neither did the girls feel under any pressure to work particularly fast. Indeed the lack of pressure may have been the very thing that helped some of them to work, in fact, very fast indeed.

Social organization

Besides forming a job-group, the cash posters formed a distinct social group, in the following sense. The interaction count showed that only one cash poster (Burke) interacted more often with members of other job groups than with her own. The so-called ledger clerks formed the largest job-group in the division and the one next above the posters in the ladder of promotion, though their pay was the same. Only one of the ledger clerks interacted more often with the cash posters than with members of her own group. This was O'Brien, the youngest of the ledger clerks and the one who had been most recently a cash poster. This tendency of the cash posters to interact with one another took place in spite of the fact that nothing in the work itself or in the layout of the room prevented their interacting more often with members of other job-groups.

Within this over-all unity of the posters, sub-groups could be mapped out both by sociometric choice and by interaction. The sociogram resulting from answers to the interview question: "Who are your close friends in here?" is shown in Figure 1. It reveals two main trios: Donovan, LoPresti, and Murphy on one side and Asnault, Coughlin, and Granara on the other, with Rourke a link between the two. The first trio was linked by Coughlin to O'Brien, the newest of the ledger clerks. Burke, though generally popular and friendly, did not express close friendship with any cash poster but was attached to a ledger clerk clique centering around Brooks. Urquhart, the newest cash poster, chose three of this clique

but was chosen by none. And Shaugnessy, a true isolate, neither chose nor was chosen.

That these choices represented real social groupings is best shown by data of another sort. Once in the morning and once in the afternoon, the girls left the floor for ten minutes to take their "relief" periods. At these times the same girls regularly gathered at the same places. O'Brien, Coughlin, Asnault, Granara, and Rourke regularly went "downstairs," and Shaugnessy attached herself to them. Murphy, LoPresti, and Donovan went to the "wash room." Burke went to the "vault" with the group that included Allen and Brooks, and more and more often, as time went on, Urquhart attached herself to this group. Not surprisingly, friendship choice and interaction off the floor were closely related.

The most important determinant of clique formation was the position of a poster's table during her first year on the job. Girls who sat near one another then had many chances to interact and tended to become friends, and the friendships once made were apt to persist even after seating arrangements were changed, as they were every New Year's Eve. This was true of both the main trios of the sociogram. As Granara said, "The girls I go around with in here are Ann (Coughlin) and Marie (Asnault). We sat together last year and we used to talk. We'd pass by and call each other 'stupid' and things like that. Other people would think it was an insult, but it's just a joke with us. Ann used to go and have lunch with Shirley (Allen) and Kay (Burke) and Susan (Brooks) and people like that, but now she goes around with us."

Figure 1   Sociogram of the Cash Posters

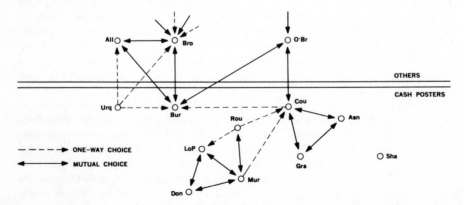

Although the girls were observably and by their own recognition divided into cliques, I could observe no hostility between them, and most of the posters spoke favorably of the general friendliness in the division. Murphy said there had been some hostility in the past: "In those days there was a lot of jealousy in here. We were divided into two sides—the girls with their chairs over by the window and the girls inside. You know the way we were set up last year. We would speak to each other, but one group would think the others were trying to get ahead of them." She mentioned the matter of overtime. In that year, Murphy, Donovan, LoPresti, and Urquhart sat together "inside," the others "by the window." While I was in the room, the posters got no overtime work.

Just as I could observe no hostility between the posters' cliques, so I could observe no systematic differences between them in off-the-job activities. But there were some differences between the two groups—they might almost be called moieties*—that provided the larger social structure of the division. The older women were not much interested in organized social activities, and leadership in them fell to the younger ledger clerks, notably Brooks and O'Brien. When the office gave a party, these two were elected co-chairmen. Two bowling teams from the office occasionally played against one another, and Brooks and O'Brien were captains of the teams. A tall and beautiful girl and a good bowler, Brooks received more friendship choices than any other person in the division, and was fourth in total interactions. O'Brien interacted more than anyone save Murphy, whom I shall speak of later. The sociogram shows that each headed a different circle of friends, though there were important links of friendship, notably that of Burke with O'Brien, between the two groups.

Compared to the O'Brien group, the Brooks group contained a higher proportion of girls that lived in the suburbs of the city—particularly the "better" suburbs—and they engaged in what were, in their view, somewhat more sophisticated activities, for instance, a skiing week-end. O'Brien, Coughlin, Asnault, and Granara were asked on this party but did not go. As one of the Brooks group (Allen) said: "I used to think that city girls were sophisticated, but when I came in here I found that

the country girls knew twice as much as the city girls. By country girls I mean people like Susan Brooks, Kay Burke and myself. Kay likes classical music. The city girls haven't been anywhere, and all they are interested in is getting married when they are 18, sitting at home, and going out to the movies once a week. When I talk about music, they just say, 'Don't say those names to me.' " It is easy to exaggerate these differences and in any event they were not very important to the cash posters, as only two of their number were members of the Brooks group: Burke centrally and Urquhart peripherally.

All I need say in summary of this brief section on social organization is that certain familiar relationships between the distributions of interaction, interpersonal sentiment,† and differences in off-the-job activity have turned up here as they turn up in many observational studies of working groups.[4] Friendship choice was associated with interaction off the job. Cliques, defined by frequent interaction and friendship choice between members, tended to display mutual hostility and different styles of off-the-job activity, though the tendencies were slight. Note also the influence of "external" factors, such as differences in social background and assignments to seats and job, in setting initial values of interaction and activity variables.

Individual effectiveness

I turn now to the behavior of individual cash posters, especially in relation to effectiveness on the job. Table 1 summarizes the quantitative data I obtained in the study. The "time on job" column gives in years and months the length of time each girl had been cash posting at the time I began the study. The "lateness" column gives the total number of times each girl was late in the five months of the study. Absences are not included, because they seemed, far more than latenesses, to be determined by forces beyond the girls' control. The "cards per hour" column gives the five-months' average of output. The output of only one of the girls, Urquhart, showed the characteristics of a learning curve by being higher every successive month. "Errors per hour" is the same kind of figure as "cards per hour." The "interaction" columns show the

---

* Denotes the division of a tribe into two equal parts, as in many "primitive" societies.—Ed.

† Liking and disliking.—Ed.

Table 1   Cash Posters

	Age	Time on job	Late-ness	Cards per hour	Errors per hour	INTERACTION JAN. 9–26				SOC. CHOICES		
						In	Out	Total	Range	In	Out	Total
Asnault	22	3–5	6	363	.57	38	8	46	13	2	0	2
Burke	26	2–5	3	306	.66	11	53	64	24	2	3	5
Coughlin	20	2–0	4	342	.40	38	20	58	17	4	1	5
Donovan	20	1–9	7	308	.79	20	10	32	14	2	0	2
Granara	21	1–3	6	438	.65	27	10	40	16	2	0	2
LoPresti	25	−11	8	317	.03	40	8	56	14	3	0	3
Murphy	19	−7	0	439	.62	52	34	92	22	3	0	3
Rourke	17	−4	3	323	.82	33	27	60	16	1	0	1
Shaugnessy	23	−2	16	333	.44	13	2	16	9	0	0	0
Urquhart	18	−2	11	361	.49	21	9	32	13	0	0	0

number of times a girl was seen talking to another girl during the period in which I counted interactions by the method described above. The figures show the times she talked to another cash poster (in) and the times she talked to some other worker (out). These are raw scores. The "total" figures are corrected to make up for the absences of certain of the girls. "Range" is the number of *different* persons a girl talked to. "Sociometric choices" are those *received* by a girl, either from other cash posters (in) or from other workers in the division (out). The way choices were *given* is shown in the sociogram (Figure 1).

Ten cases is a small number on which to base statistical relationships. Yet there is at least one significant correlation among these figures: frequency of interaction is significantly related to sociometric choices received.[5] Popular girls talked, and were talked to, a great deal. This finding may seem to run counter to one of Bales and his associates. Tabulating the data from twelve meetings of five-man discussion groups, these investigators appear to have found an over-all relationship between interactions *initiated* and "liking" choices received. But the *top* men in interaction initiated were not highly chosen on a "liking" question. Indeed they were only third, on the average, in likes, and received *most* dislikes. Unlike my finding, high interactors were not popular. What can account for the difference in the findings?

The members of the Bales groups were working on problems, common to all the members, which they were to solve by discussion. In moving towards a solution, the most fre-

quent interactors seem to have taken control of their groups. At least they were the most highly chosen on the question, "Who gave the most guidance?" And as Bales writes, "The more 'directive' and 'constricting' the quality of activity, the more likely it is to arouse negative reactions."[6] Or as I should put it, the authority, recognized or unrecognized, of one person over another will tend to cut down the other's liking for the person in authority.[7]

Unlike the Bales groups, the cash posters were working on individual jobs. Their interactions were largely "social": not directed to common tasks. The person in authority over them was their boss; no one of them had much occasion to exercise control over the others. These differences in the conditions (external system) under which the groups were brought together go far to account for differences in the findings. Let us remember Claude Bernard's *dictum:* "The experimenter will be convinced that phenomena can never be contradictory if they are observed under the same conditions, and he will know that, if they show variations, this necessarily results from the intervention or interference of other conditions, which mask or modify these phenomena."[8]

To return to the data on the cash posters, one relationship that would be important if it did exist is in fact absent. Contrary to the theory that talking interfered with work, the figures show no correlation—for this kind of work and this kind of workers—between output and frequency of interaction. Indeed the lowest producer and the highest were the two most frequent talkers.

Inspection of the table shows that a girl whose score was extreme on one of the measures was also extreme on the others. The number of individuals is too small to establish as general hypotheses the relationships thus suggested. Instead I shall briefly describe a few of the posters as each exhibiting a distinct constellation of traits, in the hope that other researchers will discover similar constellations.

The isolate

Mildred Shaugnessy was more often late than the others. She interacted far less than they. She named no one, and was named by no one, as a close friend. Her low interaction was not just the result of her having been in the division a short time. Urquhart had been a cash poster just as briefly, interacted quite a lot, named three girls as friends, and was gaining acceptance. Shaugnessy was the only girl the others expressed any hostility toward, usually giving the reason that she made personal remarks she thought were funny but they did not. She came from a "poor" section of the city, and appeared to this observer less well-dressed than the others. She was not married, but it was believed in the division that she was not living at home, that she had had some kind of quarrel with her family. In her interview, she expressed more attitudes that differed from the modal ones in her group than did any of the others. In particular, she expressed general approval of all the bosses, in spite of the fact that they often "called" her for being late—the other girls were much more selective in their approval—and she said that talking got in the way of posting. She had to concentrate; the other girls were more apt to feel that talking helped work. How far this was a rationalization of the circumstance that people did not in fact talk to her I cannot tell. As a job she would like to have, she mentioned a telephone switchboard of her own in a small hotel, that is, an isolated job. Other studies have found a relationship between absenteeism and failure to be accepted as a member of an organized group at work.[9] In this case I believe lateness to be more closely linked to acceptance. If one is not liked at work, one will be that much less eager to go to work—though Shaugnessy did not make this connection. She has since left the employ of the company to get another job.

The low producer

Catherine Burke was a tall, heavy girl, but I doubt that her physical slowness had much to do with the fact that her output was lower than that of any other cash poster. She had been a cash poster longer than any other girl but one; she expressed no liking for the job, but she had several times refused "promotion" to ledger clerk, saying "It's too much trouble." (The job did not carry any more pay.) Her choice and interaction pattern reflected the facts that she was popular and that many of her friendships were with girls who had moved out of cash posting. Only one poster talked more than she did, but unlike all the others, Burke talked far more with other members of the division than with posters. She tied with Coughlin on sociometric choices, but again, and unlike Coughlin, her choices came more from the others than from the posters. She talked to more *different* people not only than any other poster but than any other person in the whole division. She was also the only cash poster who had any higher education—two years at a Catholic junior college. She got a job in the company because her father had worked in it for many years. The family had done well, lived in a "good" suburb, and her brother had an excellent job in public relations. By reputation she had the most active social life outside the office; she belonged to more outside organizations and spoke of herself as "the traveller of the division": "In the summer I'm always coming in on Friday with a bag and coming in with it again on Monday morning." Popular though she was, she believed in keeping her social life at the office and her social life outside separate. "I don't believe in having your friends come from the office. Most of my close friends are not in here. They are the girls I went to college with. When I talk to them I find out that I am getting a lot more pay than they are. I tell them that cash posting is something pretty wonderful. I don't let them in on the truth." Perhaps the best way to sum up this fine and able girl is to say that she was bored with the work of the division and wasted on it. Even more than the others, her deepest interests were outside cash posting and indeed the company—just as her interactions were.

She was also a survivor of days when relations with the bosses were much less good than they were in my time. As she said, "Some of the girls that have come in recently think that we (Asnault and herself) are silly. They try to get four or five hundred and walk their legs off. I tell them they don't know how we had to fight to get things the way they are now." She has since left the company to enter a Catholic religious order.

The accurate worker

Helen LoPresti's record was remarkable for her extraordinarily small number of mistakes. This cannot be related to her social position; her interaction and sociometric scores were in no way extreme. She herself explained her accuracy by an experience in her past. During the war she had worked for a firm, famous for its efficiency and high-pressure methods, that runs a chain of department stores. As she said, "I worked for a man who was a buyer in jewelry, and kept his figures for him. If I didn't have them right, he would be out hundreds of dollars. He couldn't do the work himself. He had to trust me. So when I work here, I try to be accurate . . . and of course that slows me down on production." Intelligent and conscientious, she won rapid promotion in the firm and became supervisor of a small number of other girls. She went on to say: "The girls were inexperienced, and it got so that I was doing all the work. I tried to do it all myself. I was too efficient for my own good. I would do the work after hours and take it home with me. Finally it got to be too much for me. I'm sensitive. I was worrying about everything and I couldn't stand it, so I quit." A girl who wants everything done just right may have trouble delegating work to others. Certainly she is under specially heavy strain in a firm like the one LoPresti worked for. Not only does the firm put her under pressure, but she puts it on herself. Cash posting allowed LoPresti to do everything right without being under pressure, and she liked it: "You have nothing to worry about. You do your work and that's that. I worry about a lot of things. Am I normal, you must be asking yourself? Well, *am* I normal?"—Interviewer: "Don't be silly." (Giggle from both.)—LoPresti: "I don't want to get into a spot like I was in at ———." (Note the interviewer's non-directive technique.) LoPresti has since been promoted in the company.

The high producer

I could never develop any subtle social or psychological theory to account for the behavior of Dorothy Murphy. For me, she simply had a high activity rate: she had the highest output among the posters, and she also talked more than anyone else in the room. Her interview was the longest: I had to stop it so that she could take her "relief" period. She was never late. A stocky girl, she never, unlike her nearest rival, gave the slightest appearance of making an effort to work fast, and she herself felt that if she concentrated she did not do so well. It may be significant that she reported a very energetic mother, active in association work, and a father who probably, as production manager of a factory, had a better job than the fathers of the other cash posters. She was easily intelligent enough to go to college. Both her brothers had gone, and her family could have afforded it, but she did not want to. And yet she cannot have been without ambition. Although she liked her present job, she was the only poster who had formally applied for transfer to some other division. She has since transferred to a division where the chances for advancement were greater than they were in ours, and as a result this very effective girl has moved higher in the company than any of the former cash posters.

The popular girl

Ann Coughlin received most sociometric choices from other cash posters and tied with Burke in total choices received. In other respects her record was not remarkable. She talked often but not very often; her output was neither low nor high—and this fact itself may be significant. Unlike Murphy, she had wanted to go to college, but her family could not afford it. She can best be described as a sweetheart—strong in all the less sophisticated and more familial virtues. She stands in sharp contrast to the social isolate, and she was the only girl who said, "I *love* my job." She has since left the company to get married.

I have tried to describe a small group of working girls—a study clinical in intent but employing some systematic observations of work effectiveness and social organization. I have described the attitudes of the girls toward a job that was highly repetitive, done without restriction of output or pressure for production from supervision. The analysis of social organization brought out again some familiar generalizations. Finally, I have tried to describe certain constellations of traits in individual behavior, related to work effectiveness, to social position in the group and outside, and to the worker's past history, that may prove suggestive to other researchers. In conclusion, let me express the hope that the kind of research described here will not be wholly abandoned in favor of more macroscopic investigations.

Notes

[1] The research reported here was made possible financially by the Laboratory of Social Relations, Harvard University.

[2] G. C. Homans, "Status among Clerical Workers," *Human Organization*, 12 (Spring, 1953), pp. 5–10.

[3] All names are fictitious but faithful to ethnic background.

[4] See G. C. Homans, *The Human Group*, New York: Harcourt, Brace, and Co., 1950, especially Chs. 4 and 5.

[5] $P = .024$ by Fisher's Exact Test; population divided into those above the median and those below on each variable.

[6] R. F. Bales, "The Equilibrium Problem in Small Groups," in T. Parsons, R. F. Bales, and E. A. Shils, *Working Papers in the Theory of Action*, Glencoe, Ill.: The Free Press, 1953, pp. 146–147.

[7] G. C. Homans, *The Human Group*, pp. 244–248.

[8] C. Bernard, *Introduction à l'Étude de la Médecine Expérimentale*, Paris: Flammarion, 1952, p. 113.

[9] See especially E. Mayo, *The Social Problems of an Industrial Civilization*, Boston: Harvard Graduate School of Business Administration, 1945, Ch. V.

Chapter 11

ASSOCIATIONS

Associations are social groups that may be said to have constitutions. A constitution is a set of principles defining the norms and statuses of a particular group. It may be unwritten, as exemplified by the famous Constitution of the British state, but sometimes it takes the form of a document, such as the American Constitution or the articles of incorporation and table of organization of a manufacturing company. The constitution of an association, even when not written, defines the fundamental associational norms which group members are expected to follow and indicates the associational statuses they are expected to fill.

Associations as they exist in the real world have been found by sociologists to contain two levels of organization, the formal and the informal. Whereas the formal organization reflects the letter of the constitution, the informal organization is generally not provided for in the constitution, but it develops as the members play their roles. This duality of organization has been said to give associations a two-faced character; the formal organization is relatively rigid, inflexible, and impersonal, whereas the informal organization is flexible and provides for personal needs. The constitution, through the formal organization, provides the main outlines of associational structure, and the informal organization, developing through time, fills in the details. Both are always present in associations, and it appears that both are needed for an association to function.

The distinction between formal and informal organization should be evident to the student in his experiences with a college or university, which is an associational group. The formal status of a department secretary, for instance, requires her to answer correspondence and type manuscripts for the professors in her department. Her informal status, on the other hand, often allows her to advise students on all varieties of matters, from the academic to the personal. Similarly, anyone experienced in applying for jobs can testify to the importance of impressing the lowly receptionist, who often occupies an important place in the informal structure of an office.

There are many varieties of associations—small and large, voluntary and involuntary—with a range of goals that covers the universe of human interests. Sociology has traditionally been most deeply concerned with the form of association known as bureaucracy. Regardless of its goals, a group is a bureaucracy if it is organized to apply general rules to individual cases in a rational manner. Since the time of Max Weber, sociologists have regarded bureaucracy as the increasingly "typical" form of association in modern industrial societies. In countries like the United States, bureaucracy extends from government down through the production of food for our tables to house-cleaning, medical care, and baby-sitting in many instances. Traditional social groups, such as families and friendship groups, have lost many of their former functions to bureaucratic associations, and institutions like the church and school have become increasingly bureaucratized.

Selection 29, by Joseph R. Gusfield, discusses a voluntary association in the situation of change. It points to the interdependence of associations (and other groups) and the larger society. Selections 30, 31, and 32, by Max Weber, Ralph H. Turner, and Erwin O. Smigel, illustrate sociology's interest in the bureaucratic form of organization that characterizes many modern associations.

VOLUNTARY ASSOCIATIONS

Associations vary in the degree to which they fill their members' lives. At one extreme are the "total institutions," exemplified by armies and prisons, which are actually both associations and communities because they encompass all aspects of the members' lives including physical needs. Less extreme are associations like corporate firms, which demand the commitment of a very substantial portion of the employees' lives, but which, at least in their contemporary bureaucratic form, allow room for a considerable sphere of private behavior in which the association has, in theory, no interest. In contrast are the numerous associations that demand only a small porportion of the typical member's total activities, but which may in the aggregate have important social consequences. In this category are the ordinary voluntary associations with which everyone is familiar—Boy Scouts, PTA, Lions, Rotary, etc. Not all voluntary associations demand a minor commitment—some religious sects furnish glaring examples—and not all part-time activities are strictly voluntary, as illustrated by the Army Reserve, but the correlation is typical.

The term "voluntary" stresses the fact that commitment to these associations is conditional on member satisfaction. If a voluntary association fails to meet the needs of its membership it will go out of existence. Gusfield discusses here a situation in which, because of broad social changes, the program of a voluntary association was thrown out of line with the interests of its membership. In this situation, two basic alternatives were open to the association: to change its goals to accord with the needs of its existing membership or to maintain its goals and search for a new source of members. The latter course was taken, and the association is now in the position of attacking the very people who formerly constituted the core of its membership.

Prior to the Prohibitionist era, the Woman's Christian Temperance Union was a middle-class association engaged in a broad program of reformist action in which abstinence from alcohol was but one goal among several which were conceived as alleviating a condition of misery prevalent among the lower classes. With the early twentieth-century decline in "rural culture," middle-class people found themselves divided on the issue of abstinence, and the WCTU began to lose its prestige and power. Instead of modifying the association's goals by stressing moderation rather than abstinence, or by emphasizing some other reform goal, the leaders maintained and increased the Union's emphasis upon abstinence, losing some members and attracting new ones from among lower middle and working-class abstainers. The association has shifted its attack from the working class to the church-going but indulging upper middle class, who are viewed as traitors to the values of the "rural culture."

The research hypothesis of this study, that the WCTU has changed its organizational character, is very nicely supported because it is demonstrated in three independent ways. Gusfield analyzes the literature of the association for the period under discussion, presents interviews with current members, and examines statistics concerning the occupational level of the leaders (or their husbands). One point, perhaps, may stand greater emphasis than Gusfield gives it. Many voluntary associations have no goals other than mere sociability, or "socializing." A college fraternity is an example; the members remain satisfied as long as people continue to come to meetings, regardless of whether anything is accomplished. In contrast, instrumental associations, attracting members on other bases than sociability alone, face additional problems both in failure and in success with respect to their goals. Perhaps the best illustrations of associations that fail to achieve their goals are the religious sects whose prophecies fail. The most famous burlesque show in Boston for many years occupied an edifice that had been built by the Millerite church, which declined when the world failed to end on several successive occasions. On the other hand, officials of the National Foundation for Infantile Paralysis, which had found a rich source of funds in the annual March of Dimes, were in a way almost embarrassed as delighted by the discoveries of Jonas Salk. The price of either success or failure in achieving goals by an instrumental association is the requirement to change them or cease to exist. The transformation of the WCTU into what is for practical purposes a new association may be laid at the door of the success and simultaneous failure of Prohibition, to which the WCTU was firmly committed.

Selection 29
SOCIAL STRUCTURE AND MORAL REFORM: A STUDY OF THE WOMAN'S CHRISTIAN TEMPERANCE UNION
Joseph R. Gusfield

Social changes affect the fortunes of organizations and movements no less than they do the fate of individuals. Movements which try to alter the manners, tastes, and daily habits of large numbers of people are peculiarly vulnerable to shifts in the culture of the population. Few social movements in American history have achieved as many successes and witnessed as many disappointments as the temperance movement. In the one hundred and fifty years during which the organized move-

Reprinted from *American Journal of Sociology*, 61:3, 1955, pp. 221–232, with permission of the author and the publisher.

ment has been a significant part of American life, it has gone through a process of "boom and bust," from activity and success to quiescence and failure. The last seventy-five years have been particularly beset with steep rise and equally steep fall. The high point of the movement was reached in the passage of the Eighteenth Amendment and the nadir in Repeal and the period following.

This paper examines the Woman's Christian Temperance Union, one important segment of the temperance movement, during the last eighty years. We have tried to discover the way in which the movement has changed and some of the reasons which help explain that change.

The problem

Previous studies of social movements have dealt largely with organizations that have decreased in numbers and influence. Such studies have indicated a gradual modification in the structure and ideology of the movement. As the movement grows, it tends to adapt itself to its society and to substitute the values of organizational power and prestige for its original goals. This process has been described in the now familiar theory of the "institutionalization of social movements."[1]

Recently, Messinger has shown how the adaptive process has affected a declining social movement, the Townsend Movement.[2] Here the adaptation to loss of influence and adherents was in terms of the loss of the movement's actual mission and the emphasis on the preservation of the organization as such. New activities of the Townsend clubs are understandable only as devices to perpetuate the organization's membership, income, and power.

The WCTU cannot be called a "successful" movement. Its fundamental goal, the changing of American drinking habits, is less realizable today than in earlier periods. Neither is it analogous to the movement in decline. Membership figures indicate that the size of the organization, while less than before Repeal, is still above two hundred thousand and actually growing now in membership (Table 1).

While the WCTU is far from decline or death, temperance norms have lost a great deal of their power in American culture. Their political power, as pressure groups, is far less

Table 1 WCTU Membership by Decades

Year	Membership
1881	22,800
1891	138,377
1901	158,477
1911	245,299
1921	344,892
1931	372,355
1941	216,843
1951	257,548

Source: Treasurer's reports in Annual Report of the National Woman's Christian Temperance Union, 1881–1951.

than before and during Prohibition.[3] The percentage of "dry" communities in the United States is far less than in the period before the passage of Prohibition, and fewer Americans are abstainers today.[4]

The change in American drinking habits and the increased permissiveness of drinking norms have presented the WCTU with an environment more hostile to the doctrine of total abstinence than was true in the years of the organization's formation and development. The reaction of the WCTU to this changed situation forms the subject of this paper. We want to know whether the change in environment has led to changes in the goals and doctrine of the movement. We further seek to explain changes, or lack of change, in the organization.

Several possible modes of reaction suggest themselves to us. Faced with a now more hostile environment, the WCTU might change to achieve greater acceptance within the new norms. This would entail giving up much of the earlier mission for the sake of organizational values, which is the adaptation suggested by the Townsend Movement cited above. Second, it is conceivable that we may find little change in the face of changed conditions. Third, it is also conceivable that we may find changes which increase the gap between the public and the organization.

The pre-Prohibition period: temperance as social welfare

Moral reform and social welfare. The American temperance movement during the nineteenth century was a part of a general effort toward the improvement of the worth of the human being through improved morality as well as economic conditions. The mixture of the religious, the equalitarian, and the humanitarian was an outstanding facet of the moral reformism of many movements.[5] Temperance supporters formed a large segment of movements such as sabbatarianism, abolition, woman's rights, agrarianism, and humanitarian attempts to improve the lot of the poor.

In these efforts there is evident a satisfaction with the basic outlines of the economic and social system. What is attempted is the extension of the system to include the underprivileged. The reforms proposed attempt to alleviate suffering through humanitarian actions by those in advantageous positions or to reform the habits of the suffering as a way to the improvement of both their character *and* their material situation. There was clearly a relationship between the two.[6] Moral reformism of this type suggests the approach of a dominant class toward those less favorably situated in the economic and social structure. Barnes has pointed out that many of the social movements of the nineteenth century were composed of people bent on reforming others rather than themselves.[7] Abolitionists were rarely former slaveowners. Except for one short episode in the 1840's,[8] the temperance movement has drawn to it people of little or no experience with drinking.

The goals and doctrine of the WCTU were part of this humanitarian moral reform movement in the period before Prohibition. This is most evident in the late nineteenth century but remained a strong aspect of WCTU activities well into the Prohibition period.

In its auxiliary interests the WCTU revealed a great concern for the improvement of the welfare of the lower classes. It was active in campaigns to secure penal reform, to shorten working hours and raise wages for workers, and to abolish child labor and in a number of other humanitarian and equalitarian activities. In the 1880's the WCTU worked to bring about legislation for the protection of working girls against the exploitation by men. During the late nineteenth century several committees were active among lower-class groups, among them the Department of Work with Miners, the Department of Work with Lumberers, and the Department of Work among Railroadmen,[9] which directed their efforts toward converting the worker to Christianity, bringing him material comforts, and spreading the gospel of temperance.

The activities of the WCTU in the pre-Prohibition era appear to be the actions of a socially dominant group, essentially satisfied with the major outlines of the social structure. The social welfare efforts can be viewed as attempts to raise the lower classes to a level of behavior held out to them by the dominant middle-class citizen. This view is supported by the paternalistic character of much of WCTU social welfare activity during this period. For example, in 1882 the WCTU established a Kitchen Gardens Department to train "uneducated and untrained girls" in the arts of cooking and household management. The aim of this activity was explicitly stated as the prep-

aration of housemaids, and it was hoped that occupational training would protect the girl from the temptations of city life.[10] The same training and the same rationale are found in the WCTU industrial schools established to aid "fallen women."[11]

The WCTU played an important role in the leadership of the woman's movement in the late nineteenth century, but this was not the only concern of the organization with questions of social justice. The labor movement had strong support from the WCTU. The Knights of Labor aided the temperance activities of the WCTU. The WCTU supported the struggle for the eight-hour day and the six-day week[12] and many of the strikes of the 1890's, though it balked at the use of violence. Its support of the labor cause is illustrated in the report of the Committee on the Relations between Temperance and Labor for 1894. Employers were urged to refrain from "kindling the spirit of animosity among those already struggling under the iron heel of oppression" and thus provoking violence.[13]

These are illustrations of the interest of the WCTU during the nineteenth century in economic and social reform. It is difficult to find activities in which moral reform is clearly distinct from economic or social reform. Prison reform, for example, was stressed as a way to rehabilitate character, to convert men to Christianity, and to prevent the suffering of prisoners.

After 1900 this humanitarian interest appears less frequently, although it is still an important aspect of WCTU activities. Two things become evident. First, the humanitarianism and the equalitarian concern for the poor have greatly decreased. The Committee on the Relation of Temperance and Labor, for example, has shifted its major concern from labor issues to the propagation of the temperance cause among workers. The reports of this committee after 1900 show an interest in the morals and character of the worker. Thus in 1909 the report of this committee stated: "Urge working men and women who work for wages to cultivate a sense of responsibility in the thoroughness of their work and to consider their employer's welfare as well as their own."

The second point is that humanitarian concerns are not ignored, although decreased in emphasis, prison reform and child welfare receiving considerable attention. Between 1900 and 1920 the WCTU allotted one of the largest segments of its budget for its center at Ellis Island devoted to aiding incoming immigrants. In 1919 a huge Americanization project was begun, reminiscent of the paternalistic pattern described above. It set aside $40,000 for the purpose, the second largest single appropriation in its history.

After 1900, however, the moral reformism of the WCTU is more frequently separated from a concern with the underprivileged. With the development of the Anti-Saloon League after 1900, temperance aims become important in the campaign for legal sanctions against the sale of alcoholic beverages. Yet the emphasis on the lower classes as the object of WCTU reform is still present.

Temperance as reform of the underprivileged. An effort to improve the lot of the poor and the underprivileged was not only displayed in the WCTU's auxiliary concerns. The very doctrine of temperance can be seen as directed toward changing the habits of the lower classes. The materials usually depict the drunkard as a worker. Temperance is frequently presented as the solution to economic problems, the route to success, whereas drinking is seen as the path to economic and social ruin. The WCTU did make some efforts to promote temperance sentiment among socially elite groups through a Department of Drawing Room Conversion. These proved unsuccessful and were abandoned.

A popular slogan of the temperance movement, in the nineteenth century, was that "drink is the curse of the working classes." Total abstinence was viewed as the solution to the problem of poverty. A story entitled "The Strike at Dennis Moriarity's" illustrates how the WCTU saw temperance as the answer to the worker's problems.[14] Dennis, son of a workman on strike, refuses to fetch beer for the strikers, insisting that they could pay their bills, even while on strike, if they didn't drink. The strikers are impressed by his reasoning. One says, "It's the saloon that hurts and keeps us poor. I've been wondering all this while why Debs and the rest of the leaders didn't see it."

In the above story the immigrant as well as the laborer is the central character. Irish and German immigrants were often depicted in the fiction of the WCTU as drunkards or shown in the process of reformation. Often it was the son or daughter of the immigrant who

effected the reformation through his or her experiences with the WCTU.[15] This type of story again presents the idea that acceptance of temperance is a mode of assimilation into middle-class life.

That temperance is a key to class position is seen in the fates of the middle-class man who violates the temperance norms and the lower-class immigrant who accepts such norms. Lapses are punished by the loss of economic and social position. The WCTU was active, both before and after the turn of the century, in spreading the idea that "lips that have touched liquor shall never touch mine." Through its young girls' groups it tried to make sobriety in the male a prerequisite for marriage. The following story from a WCTU journal illustrates the awful consequences of drink for the middle-class male:

Ned has applied for a job, but he is not chosen. He finds that the potential employer has judged him to be like his Uncle Jack. Jack is a kindly man but he spends his money on drink and cigarettes. Ned has also been seen drinking and smoking. The employer thinks that Ned lacks the necessary traits of industriousness which he associates with abstinence and self-control.[16]

The implications of the above story seem clear. The man who wants to succeed must have the requisite character. He must appear to possess the characteristics of sobriety which indicate the other virtues of thrift, industry, and self-control. Temperance is thus a way not only to conform to morality but to achieve social and economic welfare. The WCTU was acting as a vehicle of progress and improvement of the poor and underprivileged.

Analysis of committee reports. We have classified the various committee reports found in the *Annual Reports* of the WCTU. The treatment of issues in these reports demonstrates the existence of the humanitarian reformist orientation in earlier periods. As Prohibition struggles became fiercer, the WCTU decreased its humanitarian interest. Moral conformity appeared apart from a concern with the welfare of the downtrodden. For example, the Department of Rescue Work had been interested in the improvement of the working girls' morality, wages, and living conditions as one consistent goal. By 1916 this department was chiefly concerned with efforts to limit fashion changes in the name of morality. The social welfare interest had disappeared. The interest in temperance more frequently appears unrelated to other welfare considerations. It is not until after Repeal, however, that the reports indicate unalloyed moral reform and temperance interests more frequently than humanitarian reform unalloyed or mixed with other interests (Table 2).

Humanitarian reform and social dominance. The great concern of the WCTU with the lower classes was a dominant feature of its aims during the period from its formation in 1874 to the passage of Prohibition. It is not drinking per se that is emphasized but the drinking problems of the poor and the working classes. Even where drinking in upper classes is berated, a prime concern is the impact of upper-class drinking patterns on the lower classes.

In its temperance doctrine as well as in its alliances with social movements of a reformist nature, the WCTU attempted to cope with the problems posed for urban America by the advent of urbanism, immigration, and industry in the late nineteenth century. The large industrial working class with its alien culture clashed with the rural image of virtue. A social group whose own position was relatively secure could best react to this threat by ameliorative reforms.

The doctrine of temperance appears to function in this fashion in the pre-Prohibition period. Implicit in the logic of the activities and the doctrine of the WCTU was a basic satisfaction with the social order.[17] The problems of the underprivileged can be solved in two ways. In one, greater kindness and humanitarianism can be extended to those who have not been fortunate. This is the motif in activities such as prison reform, work with "fallen women," better labor conditions, and other reform measures described. The demand for greater equality for women is an attack on the system of male superiority, but this is not generalized into an attack on other parts of the social and economic system.

Second, the doctrine of temperance itself suggests a solution consonant with the dominance of the group and the concern with injustice and suffering. If the lower classes and the immigrants will acquire the habits and social codes of the native middle classes, their problems will be solved. In short, assimilation into middle-class, Protestant culture is the reformist solution the WCTU offered in the pre-Prohibitionist period.

It is noteworthy that, prior to the 1920's, we find no condemnation of the American middle classes in WCTU literature. The good, churchgoing people of American Protestantism are seldom depicted as drinking. It is to this class that the WCTU looks for support of its aims. In defending the canons of sobriety, the WCTU could act as a representative of this class. An article in the *Union Signal* in 1889 put this as follows: "The class least touched by the evil thus far is that which here, as elsewhere in the land, forms its bone and sinew—the self-respecting and self-supporting class whose chief pleasures in life center in and about the home."[18]

The "moralizer-in-retreat"

The political strength of the temperance movement in America has been greatest in those states with large proportions of Protestant and rural populations.[19] With the decline in supremacy of the rural culture, both in city and in country, the norms of temperance have become less respectable. The advocates of temperance now face a more hostile environment in which they cannot enunciate a moral code and assume large segments of population in agreement with them. In the phrase of David Riesman, they are "moralizers-in-retreat."[20]

Table 2*   **Classification of WCTU Committee Reports by Period and by Interests**

	INTERESTS (PER CENT OF TOTAL REPORTS)				
Period	Humanitarian reform (%)	Moral reform (unalloyed) (%)	Temperance (unalloyed) (%)	Other (%)	N†
1879– 1903	78.6	23.5	26.5	15.3	98
1904–28	45.7	30.7	33.1	18.0	127
1929–49	25.8	37.0	48.2	1.2	81

* Source: Sample of every fifth *Annual Report* of the WCTU.
† Percentages total more than 100 per cent due to several interests in some committee reports.

With the repeal of the Eighteenth Amendment, the WCTU found itself in a radically new situation. It could no longer assume that the norms of abstinence were really supported by the dominant middle-class elements in American life. The total abstainer became a figure of disapproval and ridicule rather than a figure of power and respect.

WCTU leaders interviewed generally felt that the total abstainer no longer had a position of respect in the community.[21] They saw this as a change which has affected the churchgoing middle classes as well as the secularized groups. The same theme is evident in the journals and in the speeches and reports from convention proceedings. The following interview excerpts are fairly typical:

There has been a breakdown in the middle classes. The upper classes have always used liquor. The lower classes have always used liquor. Now the middle class has taken it over. The thing is slopping over from both sides.

You know that today church people drink. That's the reason for the poor showing of the WCTU. It's been that way since Prohibition. There are many that believe but won't sign the pledge. They are afraid that they might want to take a drink.

The WCTU was seen, by the leaders interviewed, as lower in prestige today than in an earlier period when temperance norms held a stronger position in the American society. Leaders contrasted the prestigeful social composition of earlier periods with the present composition. Examples such as the following appear frequently in the interviews:

When this union was first organized, we had many of the most influential ladies of the city. But now they have got the idea that we ladies who are against taking a cocktail are a little queer. We have an undertaker's wife and a minister's wife, but the lawyer's and the doctor's wives shun us. They don't want to be thought queer.

I remember when the X's lived in the house that is now the Hotel W. They were the finest people in the town, and they were temperance people.

When I joined, women of prominence and social prestige were in it. They were the backbone of the churches and the schools.

The WCTU is recognized by its membership as having retreated from a past position of greater influence, power, and prestige. To be a member of the WCTU is therefore harmful to social acceptability in many groups. It opens her to ridicule from people whose opinion is important to her.

This is frankly realized by the WCTU. The literature of the organization does not hide the fact. For example, a membership drive pamphlet contained the following description of one type of WCTU member, Mrs. I-Would-if-I-Could: "She wouldn't think of asking for money or inviting anyone to join. She knows the organization is not especially popular in some groups. . . . There are times when she prefers not to mention her membership."

Local leaders also described the low esteem of the WCTU in their communities:

People don't like us. Some of the churches don't respect us.

Well, as you have probably learned, this isn't the organization it used to be. It isn't popular, you know. The public thinks of us —let's face it—as a bunch of old women, as frowzy fanatics. I've been viewed as queer, as an old fogy, for belonging to the WCTU. . . . This attitude was not true thirty years ago.

The WCTU is acutely aware of what it has been and of what it has become. The present position of unpopularity might lead to several different types of reaction. One possible position would be a reversal of past doctrine and the embracing of a doctrine of moderate drinking. This would be the acceptance of the new standard of the middle classes. Another possibility might be a de-emphasis of temperance aims and a substitution of other aims, such as those of a social welfare nature or an attack on "popular" enemies, such as drug addiction or juvenile delinquency.

The alternatives considered above all imply the importance of maintaining the popularity and acceptance of the organization in middle-class circles. If the organization should attempt to maintain its old doctrines, it could no longer be representative of prestigeful segments of American life. With the social base of dominance undetermined, can the WCTU continue a reformist attitude toward lower classes, or must it become a sectarian critic of the class it once represented?

Moral indignation: censure of the new middle class

The characteristic doctrine of the WCTU is no longer humanitarian reform of the under-privileged. Instead it is an indignation directed against the middle-class moderate drinker. Total abstinence is presented as behavior morally demanded, apart from social welfare considerations. The new standards of the middle class are seen as defections from the traditional morality of abstinence.

"Moral indignation" as used here is not equivalent to the use of the term by Ranulf.[22] We are not concerned with the "disinterested tendency to inflict punishment" but rather with the quality of anger generated by the failure of others to recognize standards of morality which the actor recognizes. The definition of "indignation" given by *Webster's New Collegiate Dictionary* accurately conveys our meaning. It is "righteous wrath" and "anger excited by that which is unworthy, base, or disgraceful." In understanding this emotion in the WCTU, we must keep in mind the fact that abstinence was once a respectable middle-class doctrine. The middle-class drinking habits are not only in conflict with WCTU norms; they are defections from past standards.

A fiction story in the *Union Signal* illustrates this sense of moral indignation toward the new doctrine of temperance.[23] The story is entitled "Today's Daughter." Ruth, sixteen, is taken to a party at the home of a new boy who has just moved into the neighborhood. The boy has told Ruth's family that he is glad the new house has a game room in the basement. Aunt Liz is suspicious. She knows that many of the houses in the neighborhood now have bars in the basement game rooms. Ruth's mother tries to still these suspicions: "We're not living in the Victorian period. . . . I'm sure the Barrets are alright [sic]. They joined the church last Sunday." Aunt Liz's reply greatly unnerves Ruth's mother: "As if that meant respectability *these days!* Many's the church member who drinks and smokes and thinks nothing of it."

This episode contains the significant parts of the current position of the WCTU. Here are people of moderate incomes, in the same neighborhood and members of the same church as the WCTU adherent, yet the indexes of social class, religion, and ethnicity are no longer good assurances of abstinence.

Conflict between the doctrine of the total abstainer and a new "middle-class psychology" is evident. The following story is an apt illustration in which the new middle class is criticized for defection from the Protestant norms which supported and sustained the temperance doctrine. The story is entitled "When Yesterday Returned."[24] Jane, the heroine, reveres her "old-fashioned, Christian grandmother" who taught her the temperance pledge. Jane's mother ridicules temperance as prudishness and says that it hinders her social position. The struggle between the two groups, the newer and more prestigeful moderate drinkers and the old-fashioned abstainers, is epitomized after Jane scolds a visitor who asked for whiskey before dinner.

> When the guest had gone her mother informed her in no uncertain tones that "such plebeian mannerisms" were rude. And furthermore if there were to be any more such old-fashioned, prudish notions exploited before such persons as Mr. Forsythe, the family's opportunities for social prestige would be lost forever and Jane's visits to her grandmother curtailed.

The figures of the underprivileged poor and the laborer no longer appear as the center of WCTU interest. In their place is the middle-class, churchgoing moderate drinker. Toward him the WCTU displays resentment rather than reformist concern. Typical remarks of interviewees stress the moderate drinker:

> We fear moderation more than anything. Drinking has become so much a part of everything—even in our church life and our colleges.

> Since Repeal, people are drinking who wouldn't have before. They are held in great regard. The social drinker has a greater effect on children than the drunkards.

In past decades moderate drinking might have subjected the drinker to fear of loss of reputation or damaged career.[25] Some writers have lately maintained that career routes more and more demand the skills of fellowship, personal attachments, and the ability to be the "good fellow."[26] This means that the culture may place great value on tolerance of others, in drinking as well as in other behavior. This makes the moral reformer even more reprehensible in the life of the new middle-class culture.

In reaction to this, the WCTU has poured out wrath against the defector from standards of abstinence who talks of taking an "objective" stand toward the problem. One interviewee complained of the Yale School of Alcohol Studies:

You as a teacher must take a stand against smoking and drinking. Do you know of the Yale center? Well, I went down there one night. When they were through, you didn't know whether they were for it or against it. They didn't want to commit themselves. What can they expect students to do?

This attitude has made it difficult for the WCTU to co-operate with organizations which viewed drinking from a social welfare interest in curing or preventing alcoholism. Insistence on the vital importance of legal restriction of the sale of drink has continued. The president of the WCTU took an "unbending" position when she said: "Between right and wrong only one ground is possible and that is a battle ground."[27]

The fact that "good people" are drinking is a chronic complaint among interviewees and in the pages of WCTU literature. One membership pamphlet voices this lament as follows:

The greatest difficulty to be found today among youth, in anti-alcohol education, is the fact that "good people" are using liquor. Beautifully gowned women sipping their cocktails in lavish cocktail lounges give the impression that it is an extremely cultured thing to do. . . . Even within some of the best homes, the bar is set up.[28]

The social position of the moderate drinker in the concern of the WCTU is not that of the poverty-stricken, the socially elite, or the non-churchgoer. It is rather the class from which the WCTU formerly drew its power and which formed the base for a doctrine of social reformism. Interviewees stressed the change in the churchgoer as the cause for the new respectability of drinking:

The churches aren't helping, some of them. We went to the home of a professor for a church meeting, and she [his wife] served sherry. The football coach's wife makes no bones about it. She serves liquor.

It creeps into the official church boards. They keep it in their iceboxes. . . . The minister here thinks that the church has gone too far, that they are doing too much to help the temperance cause. He's afraid that he'll stub some influential toes.

The churches aren't doing enough. . . . Many nominally take a stand, but many don't follow it locally. There was one churchman in L. who had beer at his daughter's wedding. Another churchman in H. had wine at a wedding that really flowed. And this was the Church of the Brethren!

The WCTU has not attempted to reformulate its previous temperance doctrine in the direction of popular acceptance, despite the changed milieu in which it must operate. Rather it has swung in the direction of a greater sectarianism which carries it strongly into conflict with previous sources of adherence. How can we explain this? Why has it not accommodated to the new situation? Some light may be shed on this question by the analysis of the social composition of the movement between the years 1885 and 1949.

Increasing class distance. We have studied the social composition of local leaders in the WCTU through the use of directories of officers published in annual state WCTU reports. These list the local officers and their addresses for each city, town, and village in which there is a unit. With these lists, we then utilized city business directories, which gave us the occupation of the husband of the officer.[29] We were limited in choice of cities by availability of state reports for each of the four years chosen—1885, 1910, 1925, 1950—and by the availability of city directories for each of the cities and years. However, we were able to compile comparative data for thirty-eight cities in five states (Table 3).

The results of this study indicate that the socioeconomic status of the local leadership has diminished during the period 1885–1950. There has been a relatively steady decrease in the percentage of professional people, proprietors, managers, and officials and a relatively steady increase in the skilled and unskilled groups. More and more, the social base of the WCTU appears to be lower middle class and lower class rather than the earlier picture of upper middle and lower middle classes.

This suggests an answer to the question posed above. The present social composition of the movement cannot duplicate the pre-

Table 3   WCTU Local Leaders Classified by Husband's Occupation for State and Year

| | HUSBAND'S OCCUPATION | | | | | | | |
State and year	Professional and semi-professional	Proprietors, managers, and officials	Clerical and sales	Skilled labor	Unskilled and semi-skilled	Farm	Total (%)	N
Connecticut:								
1885	25.7	20.0	22.9	22.9	5.8	2.9	100	68
1910	21.0	31.6	13.2	21.0	10.6	2.6	100	34
1925	3.8	15.4	21.2	36.6	21.1	1.9	100	51
1950	12.4	18.6	25.0	29.2	14.8	0.0	100	52
Michigan:								
1885	17.8	33.3	6.7	28.9	8.9	4.4	100	42
1910	15.3	19.4	19.4	26.4	15.3	4.1	100	72
1925	13.0	14.6	18.8	24.6	27.6	1.4	100	66
1950	13.2	7.1	16.6	26.2	36.9	0.0	100	77
Illinois:								
1885	20.0	35.6	11.2	24.4	8.8	0.0	100	50
1910	14.5	22.0	20.4	25.4	15.2	2.5	100	136
1925	11.8	19.3	23.5	19.3	24.4	1.7	100	124
1950	12.4	14.2	16.8	25.6	31.0	0.0	100	127
Minnesota:								
1885	25.6	33.3	15.4	17.9	5.2	2.6	100	38
1910	14.0	19.3	27.3	28.9	9.6	0.9	100	116
1925	12.7	22.8	20.1	28.9	15.5	0.0	100	151
1950	10.3	17.6	23.6	31.5	17.0	0.0	100	164
Maryland:								
1885	22.2	44.4	27.8	5.6	0.0	0.0	100	15
1910	13.6	36.4	40.9	9.1	0.0	0.0	100	22
1925	16.7	35.2	20.4	18.4	9.3	0.0	100	57
1950	21.4	33.3	21.4	16.8	7.1	0.0	100	41
Total:								
1885	22.6	30.4	26.1	22.1	6.5	2.3	100	193
1910	15.1	22.0	21.8	26.6	12.3	2.2	100	348
1925	12.0	21.2	21.0	25.3	19.6	0.9	100	392
1950	12.4	16.3	20.3	28.2	22.8	0.9	100	408

tense to social dominance from which a reformist position is possible. Further, the very class structure of the movement accentuates the split between the upper and the lower middle classes which appears in the interviews and documentary materials. A uniform middle-class culture is less of a reality than it was in earlier periods.

One would anticipate that the groups most susceptible to norms encouraging drinking are precisely those upper-middle-class groups making up the world of the professional, business executive, and salesman—the new middle classes whose religion is less evangelical and whose norms emphasize fellowship, toleration,

and leisure. These seem to be the groups who have left the WCTU. Their higher socioeconomic status would have afforded them leadership had they remained.

The data suggest that temperance norms have filtered down to lower socioeconomic groups. The moral indignation of the movement is explainable by the resentment engendered by the defection of the upper middle class. These are no longer available as models with which the religiously oriented in America can identify. The quality of "moralizing" has ceased to be respectable. The adherents of rural nineteenth-century values epitomized in the doctrine of total abstinence do not have available tangible models of success and prestige in social levels above them. Nevertheless, they nourish expectation that the values on which they have been raised will be the values of groups above them in status. Their resentment is understandable as a response to the realization that their expectations are no longer true.

Conclusion

This study has demonstrated a shift in the doctrine and social composition of a moral reform movement. The earlier stages of the WCTU were shown to have been characterized by an attitude of moral reform directed toward the lower classes. In this stage, social composition data indicate that the WCTU represented a socially dominant class.

Today the WCTU is an organization in retreat. Contrary to the expectations of theories of institutionalization, the movement has not acted to preserve organizational values at the expense of past doctrine. In adhering to less popular positions, it has played the role of the sect and widened the gap between WCTU membership and middle-class respectability. Analysis of social composition in this stage indicates that the movement is today less upper middle class in composition than in earlier periods and more lower middle and lower class in composition. In this respect, as well as in the changed drinking norms of the upper middle classes, the split within American Protestant middle classes has been widened.

The moral indignation of the WCTU today is a very different approach to temperance and to the American scene from the reformism and progressivism of the late nineteenth and early twentieth centuries. The plight of the "moralizer-in-retreat" is the plight of the once powerful but now rejected suitor. The symbols at his command no longer ring true in the halls where once they were heard with great respect. He cannot identify easily with those above him in status, because they now repudiate his morality. It is the sense of the historical shift, fully as much as the absolute clash in values, that has soured his reformism and generated his resentment.

Notes

[1] The basic statements of this approach can be found in Ernst Troeltsch, *The Social Teachings of the Christian Churches*, trans. Olive Wyon (London: George Allen & Unwin, Ltd., 1911), I, 331–43; Max Weber, *The Theory of Social and Economic Organization*, trans. A. M. Henderson and Talcott Parsons (New York: Oxford University Press, 1947), pp. 363–86; Robert Park and Ernest W. Burgess, *Introduction to the Science of Sociology* (Chicago: University of Chicago Press, 1921), pp. 865–74; Herbert Blumer, "Collective Behavior," in *Principles of Sociology*, ed. Robert Park (New York: Barnes & Noble, 1939), pp. 167–222. The general approach has been utilized in many studies. Examples of these are H. Richard Niebuhr, *Social Sources of Denominationalism* (New York: Henry Holt & Co., 1929); Liston Pope, *Millhands and Preachers* (New Haven: Yale University Press, 1943); S. D. Clark, *Church and Sect in Canada* (Toronto: University of Toronto Press, 1949); Roberto Michels, *Political Parties*, trans. Eden and Cedar Pal (new ed.; Glencoe, Ill.: Free Press, 1949); Seymour Lipset, *Agrarian Socialism* (Berkeley and Los Angeles: University of California Press, 1950); A. J. Muste, "Factional Fights in Trade Unions," in *American Labor Dynamics*, ed. J. B. S. Hardman (New York: Harcourt, Brace & Co., 1929).

[2] Sheldon Messinger, "Organizational Transformation: A Case Study of a Declining Social Movement," *American Sociological Review*, XX (February, 1955), 3–10.

[3] Odegard has analyzed the extensive power of the Anti-Saloon League during the Prohibition and pre-prohibition periods (Peter Odegard, *Pressure Politics* [New York: Columbia University Press, 1928]).

[4] E. M. Jellinek, "Recent Trends in Alcoholism and in Alcohol Consumption," *Quarterly Journal of Studies on Alcohol*, VIII (1947), 1–43; "How Hard Do Americans Drink?" *Fortune*, XLVII (1953), 121–25, 146–48, 153–54. The trend toward greater permissiveness in American drinking norms is, as we shall show, clearly recognized by the WCTU as well as by other temperance leaders. In this regard see Harry S. Warner, *The Liquor Cult and Its Culture* (Columbus, Ohio: Intercollegiate Association, 1946), and Albion Roy King, "Drinking in Colleges," *Christian Century*, July 18, 1951, pp. 842–43, and July 25, 1951, pp. 864–68.

[5] Cf. Arthur Schlesinger, *The American as Reformer* (Cambridge: Harvard University Press, 1950), pp. 3–15; Gilbert Hobbs Barnes, *The Anti-Slavery Impulse* (New York: D. Appleton-Century Co., 1933); Arthur Bestor, Jr., "The Ferment of Reform," in *Problems in American History,* ed. Richard Leopold and Arthur Link (New York: Prentice-Hall, Inc., 1952).

[6] Everett C. Hughes has pointed out the moralistic elements in the attitude of George Pullman in the construction of Pullman, Illinois, in the late nineteenth century. The material conditions of the town would, Pullman felt, develop the moral qualities which made better human beings as well as better workers. Such workers would have the traits of sobriety, industry, thrift, and loyalty (cf. Everett C. Hughes, "A Calvinistic Utopia" [unpublished manuscript]).

[7] *Op. cit.*

[8] The Washingtonian movement was the response of former drunkards, who made an organized attempt to reform drunkards. The rest of the temperance movement would not unite with them (cf. John Krout, *The Origins of Prohibition* [New York: Columbia University Press, 1928], pp. 182–222).

[9] Historical material of the paper is largely based on reading of the annual reports of the National Woman's Christian Temperance Union and samples of the WCTU journal, the *Union Signal.* The data cover the years 1874–1953. For a complete statement of the material presented here cf. Joseph Gusfield, "Organizational Change: A Study of the Woman's Christian Temperance Union" (unpublished Ph.D. dissertation, University of Chicago).

[10] *Annual Report of the WCTU* (1884), pp. 47–51.

[11] *Annual Report of the WCTU* (1889), p. 62.

[12] Not only were the speeches of Frances Willard, President of the WCTU from 1879 to 1898, very favorable to labor but the committee reports reveal similar prolabor sentiments (cf. *Annual Report of the WCTU* [1889], p. 144; *Annual Report of the WCTU* [1894], p. 147). The general attitude of the WCTU toward the six-day week was a mixture of religious sabbatarianism and social justice (cf. *Union Signal,* January 1, 1885). For a fuller treatment of the relations between the WCTU and the labor movement see Mary Earhart, *Frances Willard: From Prayers to Politics* (Chicago: University of Chicago Press, 1944), pp. 245–59.

[13] *Annual Report of the WCTU* (1894), p. 447.

[14] *Union Signal,* October 11, 1894, pp. 2–3.

[15] During the agitation of the Woman's Crusades of 1873, out of which the WCTU emerged, the struggle against "demon rum" was often carried out as one between the churchwomen and German and Irish saloon-keepers. The accounts of the crusades contain many examples of the immigrant as the opponent of sobriety (cf. Annie Wittenmyer, *History of the Woman's Temperance Crusade* [Philadelphia: Mrs. Annie Wittenmyer, 1878]; Eliza Stewart, *Members of the Crusade* [Columbus, Ohio: William G. Hubbard Co., 1888]).

[16] *Union Signal,* January 1, 1883, p. 6.

[17] There were some efforts toward a more revolutionary position in the late nineteenth century. Frances Willard, the leader of the WCTU from 1879 to 1898, was an outspoken Socialist and tried to make the WCTU follow her position. Despite her great power and influence in the movement, she did not succeed.

[18] May 16, 1889, p. 3.

[19] Odegard, *op. cit.,* pp. 24–35; cf. Harold Gosnell, *Grass Roots Politics* (Washington, D. C.: American Council on Public Affairs, 1942), pp. 101–2; André Siegfried, *America Comes of Age* (New York: Harcourt, Brace & Co., 1927), pp. 70–90.

[20] David Riesman, *The Lonely Crowd* (New Haven: Yale University Press, 1950), p. 195; cf. Alfred M. Lee, "Techniques of Social Reform: An Analysis of the New Prohibition Drive," *American Sociological Review,* IX (1944), 65–77.

[21] Interviews were conducted with forty-six local and national WCTU leaders. The local leaders were active in upstate New York and in Chicago; the national leaders, members of the staff of the WCTU National Headquarters in Evanston, Illinois.

[22] Svend Ranulf, *Moral Indignation and Middle Class Psychology* (Copenhagen: Levin & Munksgaard, 1938), p. 13.

[23] *Union Signal,* December 25, 1937, pp. 5–6.

[24] *Ibid.,* June 3, 1939–July 29, 1939.

[25] In some American industries this still remains true, as in the International Business Machines Corporation, under the leadership of Thomas Watson (cf. *Time,* March 28, 1955, p. 83). Watson may be taken as one of the last of the temperance reformers in positions of dominance. His attitude of strong

disapproval toward employee drinking on or off the job is viewed as unusual enough to warrant comment both in *Time* and in the IBM communities.

26 Cf. Riesman, *op. cit.*, pp. 130–44; C. Wright Mills, *White Collar* (New York: Oxford University Press, 1951), pp. 91–100, 182–88.

27 *Annual Report of the WCTU*

(1952), p. 87. Recently, with the retirement of the past president, there has been a "softer" attitude toward the Prohibition question and toward co-operation with non-Prohibitionist antialcohol groups. The general condemnation of the middle-class drinker still remains the focus of WCTU doctrine, however.

28 Roy L. Smith, *Young Mothers*

Must Enlist (Evanston, Ill.: National WCTU Publishing House, 1953).

29 In the case of widows we used the last occupation of the husband. In classifying occupations, we utilized United States Employment Service, *Dictionary of Occupational Titles* (Washington, D. C.: Government Printing Office, 1944).

BUREAUCRACY IN THEORY

Max Weber was one of the most influential sociologists of all times. His many interests centered about the question of how and why men voluntarily obey authority, which is one of the most profound and basic of sociological questions. The answer he suggested had three components, related to three types of authority. Men obey "traditional" authority "because it has always been," that is, because they have been socialized to accept it. They obey "charismatic" authority because its source is felt to be above men, supernatural, awesome, or fearful. They obey "rational-legal" authority because it achieves valued goals in a rational or, roughly, an efficient manner. The latter type of authority Weber believed to be most clearly expressed in the form of association he termed bureaucracy.

The model or picture that Weber draws of bureaucracy, which is presented in this selection, is not a description of any real existing association. It is rather a theoretical device known as an ideal type. An ideal type is created by the sociologist to embody the unique characteristics that are present in a number of real groups, which are assumed to contain the principles of the ideal type in a form somewhat adulterated by particular circumstances. The ideal type is what the sociologist believes these associations would be like if the adulterations had not occurred. In the present instance, Weber surveyed a number of efficient associations throughout history, paying special attention to the Prussian bureaucracy of his own time, which he felt came especially close to the ideal type of a most efficient association. However, all of them contained elements of inefficiency, and Weber constructed the ideal type of bureaucracy by imagining these groups without the elements of inefficiency that he actually found. Having constructed the ideal type, Weber was able to judge existing associations as more or less bureaucratic, depending on how closely they fitted his model.

An ideal bureaucracy is organized according to the following principles: each official is responsible for a particular task; there is a hierarchy of supervision; work proceeds with the use of records or files; officials receive training in their jobs; the job constitutes the full-time duty of every official; and all officials know and follow general rules.

An organization run in this fashion reaps the advantage of technical superiority, of efficiency in attaining whatever goal is sought. This advantage can be thought of in terms of speed, precision, and continuity, among other things.

Bureaucracies can prosper only under certain social conditions. Among these are the development of a money economy and a quantitative and qualitative profusion of tasks to be performed. These conditions are historically rare, being characteristic principally of modern Western states and business firms. Where these conditions are not fully present, the associations that are found are less bureaucratic, and are therefore less efficient or rational.

Weber supports his hypotheses concerning the efficiency of bureaucracy with a wide variety of observations taken from various periods of history and from diverse cultures. However, modern sociologists, while generally admiring Weber's thesis, have subjected it to much criticism. Most notably it has been observed that since the ideal type does not really exist, Weber's propositions concerning bureaucracy are not really testable. If it is shown that a given association does not yield the efficiency that Weber says a bureaucracy yields, the test can be discarded by claiming that the association isn't bureaucratic enough.

Additional criticisms of Weber's formulation occur in the selection that follows. Granted the plausibility and usefulness of the criticisms, Weber's thesis still remains an impressive one, which has perhaps stimulated more research than any other sociological work ever written.

Selection 30
BUREAUCRACY
Max Weber

Modern officialdom functions in the following specific manner:

I. There is the principle of fixed and official jurisdictional areas, which are generally ordered by rules, that is, by laws or administrative regulations.

1. The regular activities required for the purposes of the bureaucratically governed structure are distributed in a fixed way as official duties.

2. The authority to give the commands required for the discharge of these duties is distributed in a stable way and is strictly delimited by rules concerning the coercive means, physical, sacerdotal,* or otherwise, which may be placed at the disposal of officials.

3. Methodical provision is made for the regular and continuous fulfilment of these duties and for the execution of the corresponding rights; only persons who have the generally regulated qualifications to serve are employed.

In public and lawful government these three

Reprinted from *From Max Weber: Essays in Sociology,* edited and translated by H. H. Gerth and C. Wright Mills. Copyright 1946 by Oxford University Press. Reprinted by permission. This chapter has been abridged as noted.
* Priestly, i.e., religious.—Ed.

elements constitute "bureaucratic authority." In private economic domination, they constitute bureaucratic "management." Bureaucracy, thus understood, is fully developed in political and ecclesiastical communities only in the modern state, and, in the private economy, only in the most advanced institutions of capitalism. Permanent and public office authority, with fixed jurisdiction, is not the historical rule but rather the exception. This is so even in large political structures such as those of the ancient Orient, the Germanic and Mongolian empires of conquest, or of many feudal structures of state. In all these cases, the ruler executes the most important measures through personal trustees, table-companions, or court-servants. Their commissions and authority are not precisely delimited and are temporarily called into being for each case.

II. The principles of office hierarchy and of levels of graded authority mean a firmly ordered system of super- and subordination in which there is a supervision of the lower offices by the higher ones. Such a system offers the governed the possibility of appealing the decision of a lower office to its higher authority, in a definitely regulated manner. With the full development of the bureaucratic type, the office hierarachy is monocratically organized.† The principle of hierarchical office authority is found in all bureaucratic structures: in state and ecclesiastical structures as well as in large party organizations and private enterprises. It does not matter for the character of bureaucracy whether its authority is called "private" or "public."

When the principle of jurisdictional "competency" is fully carried through, hierarchical subordination—at least in public office—does not mean that the "higher" authority is simply authorized to take over the business of the "lower." Indeed, the opposite is the rule. Once established and having fulfilled its task, an office tends to continue in existence and be held by another incumbent.

III. The management of the modern office is based upon written documents ("the files"), which are preserved in their original or draught form. There is, therefore, a staff of subaltern officials and scribes of all sorts. The body of officials actively engaged in a "public" office, along with the respective apparatus of material implements and the files, make up a "bureau." In private enterprise, "the bureau" is often called "the office."

In principle, the modern organization of the civil service separates the bureau from the private domicile of the official, and, in general, bureaucracy segregates official activity as something distinct from the sphere of private life. Public monies and equipment are divorced from the private property of the official. This condition is everywhere the product of a long development. Nowadays, it is found in public as well as in private enterprises; in the latter, the principle extends even to the leading entrepreneur. In principle, the executive office is separated from the household, business from private correspondence, and business assets from private fortunes. The more consistently the modern type of business management has been carried through the more are these separations the case. The beginnings of this process are to be found as early as the Middle Ages.

It is the peculiarity of the modern entrepreneur that he conducts himself as the "first official" of his enterprise, in the very same way in which the ruler of a specifically modern bureaucratic state spoke of himself as "the first servant" of the state.[1] The idea that the bureau

activities of the state are intrinsically different in character from the management of private economic offices is a continental European notion and, by way of contrast, is totally foreign to the American way.

IV. Office management, at least all specialized office management—and such management is distinctly modern—usually presupposes thorough and expert training. This increasingly holds for the modern executive and employee of private enterprises, in the same manner as it holds for the state official.

V. When the office is fully developed, official activity demands the full working capacity of the official, irrespective of the fact that his obligatory time in the bureau may be firmly delimited. In the normal case, this is only the product of a long development, in the public as well as in the private office. Formerly, in all cases, the normal state of affairs was reversed: official business was discharged as a secondary activity.

VI. The management of the office follows general rules, which are more or less stable, more or less exhaustive, and which can be learned. Knowledge of these rules represents a special technical learning which the officials possess. It involves jurisprudence, or administrative or business management.

The reduction of modern office management to rules is deeply embedded in its very nature. The theory of modern public administration, for instance, assumes that the authority to order certain matters by decree—which has been legally granted to public authorities—does not entitle the bureau to regulate the matter by commands given for each case, but only to regulate the matter abstractly. This stands in extreme contrast to the regulation of all relationships through individual privileges and bestowals of favor, which is absolutely dominant in patrimonialism,* at least insofar as such relationships are not fixed by sacred tradition.

All this results in the following for the internal and external position of the official:

I. Office holding is a "vocation." This is shown, first, in the requirement of a firmly prescribed course of training, which demands the entire capacity for work for a long period of time, and in the generally prescribed and

† Governed by a single political authority.—Ed.

* A contrasting type of social organization emphasizing the will of the ruler instead of impersonal rules.—Ed.

special examinations which are prerequisites of employment. Furthermore, the position of the official is in the nature of a duty. This determines the internal structure of his relations, in the following manner: Legally and actually, office holding is not considered a source to be exploited for rents or emoluments, as was normally the case during the Middle Ages and frequently up to the threshold of recent times. Nor is office holding considered a usual exchange of services for equivalents, as is the case with free labor contracts. Entrance into an office, including one in the private economy, is considered an acceptance of a specific obligation of faithful management in return for a secure existence. It is decisive for the specific nature of modern loyalty to an office that, in the pure type, it does not establish a relationship to a *person*, like the vassal's or disciple's faith in feudal or in patrimonial relations of authority. Modern loyalty is devoted to impersonal and functional purposes. Behind the functional purposes, of course, "ideas of culture-values" usually stand. These are *ersatz** for the earthly or supra-mundane personal master: ideas such as "state," "church," "community," "party," or "enterprise" are thought of as being realized in a community; they provide an ideological halo for the master.

The political official—at least in the fully developed modern state—is not considered the personal servant of a ruler. Today, the bishop, the priest, and the preacher are in fact no longer, as in early Christian times, holders of purely personal charisma. The supra-mundane and sacred values which they offer are given to everybody who seems to be worthy of them and who asks for them. In former times, such leaders acted upon the personal command of their master; in principle, they were responsible only to him. Nowadays, in spite of the partial survival of the old theory, such religious leaders are officials in the service of a functional purpose, which in the present-day "church" has become routinized and, in turn, ideologically hallowed.

II. The personal position of the official is patterned in the following way:

1. Whether he is in a private office or a public bureau, the modern official always strives and usually enjoys a distinct *social esteem* as compared with the governed. His social position is guaranteed by the prescrip-

tive rules of rank order and, for the political official, by special definitions of the criminal code against "insults of officials" and "contempt" of state and church authorities.

The actual social position of the official is normally highest where, as in old civilized countries, the following conditions prevail: a strong demand for administration by trained experts; a strong and stable social differentiation, where the official predominantly derives from socially and economically privileged strata because of the social distribution of power; or where the costliness of the required training and status conventions are binding upon him. The possession of educational certificates—to be discussed elsewhere[2]—is usually linked with qualification for office. Naturally, such certificates or patents enhance the "status element" in the social position of the official. For the rest this status factor in individual cases is explicitly and impassively acknowledged; for example, in the prescription that the acceptance or rejection of an aspirant to an official career depends upon the consent ("election") of the members of the official body. This is the case in the German army with the officer corps. Similar phenomena, which promote this guild-like closure of officialdom, are typically found in patrimonial and, particularly, in prebendal† officialdoms of the past. The desire to resurrect such phenomena in changed forms is by no means infrequent among modern bureaucrats. For instance, they have played a role among the demands of the quite proletarian and expert officials (the *tretyj* element) during the Russian revolution.

Usually the social esteem of the officials as such is especially low where the demand for expert administration and the dominance of status conventions are weak. This is especially the case in the United States; it is often the case in new settlements by virtue of their wide fields for profit-making and the great instability of their social stratification.

2. The pure type of bureaucratic official is *appointed* by a superior authority. An official elected by the governed is not a purely bureaucratic figure. Of course, the formal existence of an election does not by itself mean that no appointment hides behind the election —in the state, especially, appointment by party

---

* Roughly, artificial substitutes.—Ed.

† Collegiate, in the sense of an academic faculty which chooses its own members.—Ed.

chiefs. Whether or not this is the case does not depend upon legal statutes but upon the way in which the party mechanism functions. Once firmly organized, the parties can turn a formally free election into the mere acclamation of a candidate designated by the party chief. As a rule, however, a formally free election is turned into a fight, conducted according to definite rules, for votes in favor of one of two designated candidates.

In all circumstances, the designation of officials by means of an election among the governed modifies the strictness of hierarchical subordination. In principle, an official who is so elected has an autonomous position opposite the superordinate official. The elected official does not derive his position "from above" but "from below," or at least not from a superior authority of the official hierarchy but from powerful party men ("bosses"), who also determine his further career. The career of the elected official is not, or at least not primarily, dependent upon his chief in the administration. The official who is not elected but appointed by a chief normally functions more exactly, from a technical point of view, because, all other circumstances being equal, it is more likely that purely functional points of consideration and qualities will determine his selection and career. As laymen, the governed can become acquainted with the extent to which a candidate is expertly qualified for office only in terms of experience, and hence only after his service. Moreover, in every sort of selection of officials by election, parties quite naturally give decisive weight not to expert considerations but to the services a follower renders to the party boss. This holds for all kinds of procurement of officials by elections, for the designation of formally free, elected officials by party bosses when they determine the slate of candidates, or the free appointment by a chief who has himself been elected. The contrast, however, is relative: substantially similar conditions hold where legitimate monarchs and their subordinates appoint officials, except that the influence of the followings are then less controllable.

Where the demand for administration by trained experts is considerable, and the party followings have to recognize an intellectually developed, educated, and freely moving "public opinion," the use of unqualified officials falls back upon the party in power at the next election. Naturally, this is more likely to happen when the officials are appointed by the chief. The demand for a trained administration now exists in the United States, but in the large cities, where immigrant votes are "corralled," there is, of course, no educated public opinion. Therefore, popular elections of the administrative chief and also of his subordinate officials usually endanger the expert qualification of the official as well as the precise functioning of the bureaucratic mechanism. It also weakens the dependence of the officials upon the hierarchy. This holds at least for the large administrative bodies that are difficult to supervise. The superior qualification and integrity of federal judges, appointed by the President, as over against elected judges in the United States is well known, although both types of officials have been selected primarily in terms of party considerations. The great changes in American metropolitan administrations demanded by reformers have proceeded essentially from elected mayors working with an apparatus of officials who were appointed by them. These reforms have thus come about in a "Caesarist" fashion. Viewed technically, as an organized form of authority, the efficiency of "Caesarism," which often grows out of democracy, rests in general upon the position of the "Caesar" as a free trustee of the masses (of the army or of the citizenry), who is unfettered by tradition. The "Caesar" is thus the unrestrained master of a body of highly qualified military officers and officials whom he selects freely and personally without regard to tradition or to any other considerations. This "rule of the personal genius," however, stands in contradiction to the formally "democratic" principle of a universally elected officialdom.

3. Normally, the position of the official is held for life, at least in public bureaucracies; and this is increasingly the case for all similar structures. As a factual rule, *tenure for life* is presupposed, even where the giving of notice or periodic reappointment occurs. In contrast to the worker in a private enterprise, the official normally holds tenure. Legal or actual life-tenure, however, is not recognized as the official's right to the possession of office, as was the case with many structures of authority in the past. Where legal guarantees against arbitrary dismissal or transfer are developed, they merely serve to guarantee a strictly objective discharge of specific office duties free from all personal considerations. In Germany, this is

the case for all juridical and, increasingly, for all administrative officials.

Within the bureaucracy, therefore, the measure of "independence," legally guaranteed by tenure, is not always a source of increased status for the official whose position is thus secured. Indeed, often the reverse holds, especially in old cultures and communities that are highly differentiated. In such communities, the stricter the subordination under the arbitrary rule of the master, the more it guarantees the maintenance of the conventional seigneurial style of living for the official. Because of the very absence of these legal guarantees of tenure, the conventional esteem for the official may rise in the same way as, during the Middle Ages, the esteem of the nobility of office[3] rose at the expense of esteem for the freemen, and as the king's judge surpassed that of the people's judge. In Germany, the military officer or the administrative official can be removed from office at any time, or at least far more readily than the "independent judge," who never pays with loss of his office for even the grossest offense against the "code of honor" or against social conventions of the salon. For this very reason, if other things are equal, in the eyes of the master stratum the judge is considered less qualified for social intercourse than are officers and administrative officials, whose greater dependence on the master is a greater guarantee of their conformity with status conventions. Of course, the average official strives for a civil-service law, which would materially secure his old age and provide increased guarantees against his arbitrary removal from office. This striving, however, has its limits. A very strong development of the "right to the office" naturally makes it more difficult to staff them with regard to technical efficiency, for such a development decreases the career-opportunities of ambitious candidates for office. This makes for the fact that officials, on the whole, do not feel their dependency upon those at the top. This lack of a feeling of dependency, however, rests primarily upon the inclination to depend upon one's equals rather than upon the socially inferior and governed strata. The present conservative movement among the Badenia clergy, occasioned by the anxiety of a presumably threatening separation of church and state, has been expressly determined by the desire not to be turned "from a master into a servant of the parish."[4]

4. The official receives the regular *pecuniary* compensation of a normally fixed *salary* and the old age security provided by a pension. The salary is not measured like a wage in terms of work done, but according to "status," that is, according to the kind of function (the "rank") and, in addition, possibly, according to the length of service. The relatively great security of the official's income, as well as the rewards of social esteem, make the office a sought-after position, especially in countries which no longer provide opportunities for colonial profits. In such countries, this situation permits relatively low salaries for officials.

5. The official is set for a *"career"* within the hierarchical order of the public service. He moves from the lower, less important, and lower paid to the higher positions. The average official naturally desires a mechanical fixing of the conditions of promotion: if not of the offices, at least of the salary levels. He wants these conditions fixed in terms of "seniority," or possibly according to grades achieved in a developed system of expert examinations. Here and there, such examinations actually form a character *indelebilis** of the official and have lifelong effects on his career. To this is joined the desire to qualify the right to office and the increasing tendency toward status group closure and economic security. All of this makes for a tendency to consider the offices as "prebends"† of those who are qualified by educational certificates. The necessity of taking general personal and intellectual qualifications into consideration, irrespective of the often subaltern character of the educational certificate, has led to a condition in which the highest political offices, especially the positions of "ministers," are principally filled without reference to such certificates.

The social and economic presuppositions of the modern structure of the office are as follows:

The development of the *money economy*, insofar as a pecuniary compensation of the officials is concerned, is a presupposition of bureaucracy. Today it not only prevails but is predominant. This fact is of very great importance for the whole bearing of bureaucracy,

* What is indelible, that is, on the permanent record.—Ed.
† Stipends to members of the "college."—Ed.

yet by itself it is by no means decisive for the existence of bureaucracy. . . .

The proper soil for the bureaucratization of an administration has always been the specific developments of administrative tasks. We shall first discuss the quantitative extension of such tasks. In the field of politics, the great state and the mass party are the classic soil for bureaucratization. . . .

Bureaucratization is occasioned by intensive and qualitative enlargement and internal deployment of the scope of administrative tasks more than by their extensive and quantitative increase. But the direction that bureaucratization takes and the reasons that occasion it vary widely. . . .

The decisive reason for the advance of bureaucratic organization has always been its purely technical superiority over any other form of organization. The fully developed bureaucratic mechanism compares with other organizations exactly as does the machine with the non-mechanical modes of production.

Precision, speed, unambiguity, knowledge of the files, continuity, discretion, unity, strict subordination, reduction of friction and of material and personal costs—these are raised to the optimum point in the strictly bureaucratic administration, and especially in its monocratic form. As compared with all collegiate, honorific, and avocational forms of administration, trained bureaucracy is superior on all these points. And as far as complicated tasks are concerned, paid bureaucratic work is not only more precise but, in the last analysis, it is often cheaper than even formally unremunerated honorific service.

Honorific arrangements make administrative work an avocation and, for this reason alone, honorific service normally functions more slowly; being less bound to schemata and being more formless. Hence it is less precise and less unified than bureaucratic work because it is less dependent upon superiors and because the establishment and exploitation of the apparatus of subordinate officials and filing services are almost unavoidably less economical. Honorific service is less continuous than bureaucratic and frequently quite expensive. This is especially the case if one thinks not only of the money costs to the public treasury —costs which bureaucratic administration, in comparison with administration by notables, usually substantially increases—but also of the frequent economic losses of the governed

caused by delays and lack of precision. The possibility of administration by notables normally and permanently exists only where official management can be satisfactorily discharged as an avocation. With the qualitative increase of tasks the administration has to face, administration by notables reaches its limits— today, even in England. Work organized by collegiate bodies causes friction and delay and requires compromises between colliding interests and views. The administration, therefore, runs less precisely and is more independent of superiors; hence, it is less unified and slower. All advances of the Prussian administrative organization have been and will in the future be advances of the bureaucratic, and especially of the monocratic, principle.

Today, it is primarily the capitalist market economy which demands that the official business of the administration be discharged precisely, unambiguously, continuously, and with as much speed as possible. Normally, the very large, modern capitalist enterprises are themselves unequalled models of strict bureaucratic organization. Business management throughout rests on increasing precision, steadiness, and, above all, the speed of operations. This, in turn, is determined by the peculiar nature of the modern means of communication, including, among other things, the news service of the press. The extraordinary increase in the speed by which public announcements, as well as economic and political facts, are transmitted exerts a steady and sharp pressure in the direction of speeding up the tempo of administrative reaction towards various situations. The optimum of such reaction time is normally attained only by a strictly bureaucratic organization.

Bureaucratization offers above all the optimum possibility for carrying through the principle of specializing administrative functions according to purely objective considerations. Individual performances are allocated to functionaries who have specialized training and who by constant practice learn more and more. The "objective" discharge of business primarily means a discharge of business according to *calculable rules* and "without regard for persons."

"Without regard for persons" is also the watchword of the "market" and, in general, of all pursuits of naked economic interests. A consistent execution of bureaucratic domination means the leveling of status "honor."

Hence, if the principle of the free-market is not at the same time restricted, it means the universal domination of the "class situation." That this consequence of bureaucratic domination has not set in everywhere, parallel to the extent of bureaucratization, is due to the differences among possible principles by which polities may meet their demands.

The second element mentioned, "calculable rules," also is of paramount importance for modern bureaucracy. The peculiarity of modern culture, and specifically of its technical and economic basis, demands this very "calculability" of results. When fully developed, bureaucracy also stands, in a specific sense, under the principle of *sine ira ac studio*.* Its specific nature, which is welcomed by capitalism, develops the more perfectly the more the bureaucracy is "dehumanized," the more completely it succeeds in eliminating from official business love, hatred, and all purely personal, irrational, and emotional elements which es-

* Calm and rational action.—Ed.

cape calculation. This is the specific nature of bureaucracy and it is appraised as its special virtue.

The more complicated and specialized modern culture becomes, the more its external supporting apparatus demands the personally detached and strictly "objective" *expert*, in lieu of the master of older social structures, who was moved by personal sympathy and favor, by grace and gratitude. Bureaucracy offers the attitudes demanded by the external apparatus of modern culture in the most favorable combination. As a rule, only bureaucracy has established the foundation for the administration of a rational law conceptually systematized on the basis of such enactments as the latter Roman imperial period first created with a high degree of technical perfection. During the Middle Ages, this law was received along with the bureaucratization of legal administration, that is to say, with the displacement of the old trial procedure which was bound to tradition or to irrational presuppositions, by the rationally trained and specialized expert.

Notes

¹ Frederick II of Prussia.

² Cf. Wirtschaft und Gesellschaft, pp. 73 ff. and part II. (German Editor.)

³ 'Ministerialen.'

⁴ Written before 1914. (German editor's note.)

BUREAUCRACY IN PRACTICE

In response to Weber's suggestion that bureaucracy represents the most efficient form of social organization, his critics have noted some sources of inefficiency that appear to be built into the model presented in the last selection. Perhaps the best known criticism appears in Robert Merton's essay, "Bureaucratic Structure and Personality" (1940). Merton stresses the inefficiency that can result when officials pay too much attention to the rules, which are only supposed to be means but which tend to become ends in themselves because of the way in which bureaucrats are supervised. The resulting inflexibility can interfere with the achievement of the very ends the bureaucracy is set up to achieve. His argument is well documented with examples of apparent inefficiency in bureaucracies, most memorably that of a Navy pilot whose application for American citizenship was denied because he had left the limits of the United States while piloting a plane for the Antarctic expedition of Admiral Byrd.

A second type of problem in the achieving of efficiency by bureaucracies is found in the informal organization, which under certain conditions tends to subvert the formal, rule-oriented organization. The informal aspect of bureaucracy is by no means always obstructionist, but it introduces goals into the organization that may be independent of or even in conflict with the formal goals. This selection, based on the author's personal experiences during World War II, illustrates the problems that may occur, and the resolutions that are effected in one typical bureaucracy.

> The Navy disbursing officer occupies a middle-level position in a highly bureaucratic structure. He is subject to two types of bureaucratic rules— the written procedures of his manual, and the commands of his superiors. In addition, he is subject to especially strong informal pressures because of the centrality of his function as paymaster to the "clients" that he serves. Conflicts occur between the written and oral rules, and although formal procedures exist to resolve these conflicts, the informal organization precludes their use in most situations. In addition, conflicts occur between rules of both types and demands generated by friendships and obligations incurred informally but imperatively.
>
> Four types of responses to this conflict are noted. The "regulation type" of disbursing officer follows the written rules narrowly. An "obliging type" in contrast leans with the informal pressures. A "sincere type" overlooks the conflict and manages successfully to pretend that it does not exist. Most common is the "realist," who solves the conflict by giving in to informal pressures where he judges the results to be in the spirit of the regulations, and by concealing the resultant technical breaches of the formal rules.

Turner does not completely explain the reasons for the predominance of the realist solution to the status conflict illustrated here. Reading between the lines, it would seem that the realist solution is the most successful in terms of minimizing refusals and hence further demands upon the bureaucrat. The solutions reached by the disbursing officer in this case, and by bureaucrats more generally, would seem to fit the model of the "lazy man," who will solve conflict in the manner that minimizes the disruptions to his routine. If the Navy were to change its auditing system in the direction of closer supervision of disbursing officers, the realists would come more to resemble the "regulation types." If, on the other hand, more discretion were given to the disbursing officer, the "obliging type" would doubtless be more prominent. The balance between types could also be shifted by such changes as more (or less) clearly separating the chain of command in the disbursing officer's department from that of the rest of the ship; raising (or lowering) the rank of the disbursing officer in the Navy; or introducing changes in the formal rules regularizing (or specifically punishing) some of the exceptions now made informally.

Selection 31
THE NAVY DISBURSING OFFICER AS A BUREAUCRAT
Ralph H. Turner

Every administrative structure exists in order to achieve certain goals, which goals normally originate outside the structure and are imposed on it from the top. A bureaucratic administrative system is supposed to function as

Reprinted from *American Sociological Review,* 12:3, 1947, pp. 342–348, with permission of the author and the publisher.

a nearly impersonal machine, individual discretion entering only when alternate procedures are compatible with the system. The ordinary official is expected to apply procedures with blind precision, irrespective of the degree to which they achieve or subvert the general goals.

Needless to say, actual administration often

fails to adhere closely to the goals of the organization. Reasons for the divergence may be inadequacies of the procedural pattern and conflicting procedures, conflicting goals within the organization, inadequacies of the bureaucrats themselves, and, most important, the position of each functionary as not only a square on the organization chart but also as a focus of pressures applied by a number of informal structures not envisaged in the formal pattern.

The purpose of this paper is to describe a few of the sociologically relevant influences which bear on a certain type of bureaucratic official, namely, the Navy disbursing officer. Bureaucracy is conceived as defined by Max Weber.[1] Though certain types of influence are more clearly displayed in the position of the disbursing officer, most of what is said will also apply to any Supply Corps officer and, to a lesser degree, to all naval officers. The findings are the result of participant observation by the writer, both as a disbursing officer during the war and as an observer of other officers in a similar position.

From the standpoint of the present analysis there are three characteristics which distinguish the disbursing officer in degree from the remainder of the naval organization. First, disbursing officers handle matters of immediate personal importance to their clients. Navigation, gunnery, etc., may be more vital to the lives of the men, but their problems are vague to those not directly concerned. An error in a pay account or a delay in pay day is more quickly recognized and more loudly protested by the rank and file than deficiencies in most other departments aboard ship. Consequently the disbursing officer and his staff are under constant bombardment for favors and incessant criticism for their mistakes—real or imagined—or failures to grant favors.

Second, the disbursing officer is a bureaucrat serving a larger bureaucracy of which he is an integral part. Robert Merton has noted the important fact that a government servant is usually superordinate to his clients,[2] not in any formal sense, but because the client has no direct authority over him and no effective access to anyone of superior authority. Superordination and subordination are clearly defined in the Navy by the label which each man carries on his uniform. Though most of the disbursing officer's clients are enlisted men and hence subordinate, a good many will be officers of senior rank who are thereby empow-

ered to reward or punish him in various ways. Thus in adhering to the formal patterns relating to disbursing the officer must often act counter to the larger formal pattern by defying a senior officer.

Finally, the disbursing officer, unlike most other bureaucrats, is personally accountable and financially liable for any deviation from regulations in the expenditure of government funds in spite of any contrary order from a superior officer.

Three characteristics of the social structure in which the disbursing officer finds himself which make it difficult for him to behave as the ideal bureaucrat will be discussed. First is the frequent conflict between regulations (as interpreted by the disbursing officer) and orders from superiors, both of which are supposed to be obeyed. Second is the subordination of the disbursing officer through rank to many of his clients. Third is the network of informal structures, which exert particular pressure on the disbursing officer because of the crucial services which he dispenses. The facilitating conditions for the operation of these influences include the following: The disbursing officer's incomplete command of voluminous and rapidly changing regulations; the ambiguousness or incompleteness of regulations with respect to many situations; acceptance of properly signed vouchers as proof of fact by the General Accounting Office in auditing disbursing accounts, so that certain documents can be falsified with impunity; those personality traits of the officer which resist strictly impersonal behavior.

Within the formal structure the distinctive problem of the disbursing officer is that of reconciling orders from superiors with regulations when they seem to conflict. Orders may be issued by senior officers in the supply department (of which disbursing is a part) or by the commanding and executive officers of the activity. Conflicts with superior officers in the supply department are usually reconciled fairly smoothly because the supply officer understands the problem of disbursing accountability, often from earlier experience as a disbursing officer, and because of fairly close relationships between them. Conflicts stemming from orders by the commanding and executive officers, who have little knowledge of and little patience with disbursing regulations, and who are generally not accustomed to being asked by a subordinate to discuss the advisability of an order they have issued, present a ticklish problem. If the order seems to be at all important to the officer in question, the senior supply officer can usually be expected to add his pressure, through threats and suggested devices for "getting around" the law. The subsequent careers of disbursing and supply officers can be materially affected by notations which the commanding officer may enter in "fitness reports" submitted periodically to the Bureau of Naval Personnel.

The conflict between regulations (as interpreted) and orders from superiors is not limited to the disbursing function or even to military organizations. The conflict is incipient in every bureaucratic structure because the rational type of authority, as Weber has indicated, involves recognition both of rules and the right of officials to issue orders.[3] Though the hierarchy of officials exists only to administer the rules, which in turn express the purposes of the organization, it is patent that official behavior and commands may often counter the rules. In the small informal organization of a business hiring only a handful of employees, rules may be largely unformulated and procedures passed verbally down the hierarchy as required, thereby eliminating the conflict by making orders supreme. Or the opposite extreme in which authority is expressed solely through a code of rules, each functionary being left to apply the rules without supervision, might be imagined but hardly realized in an actual situation. Because of the inadequacy of either rules or hierarchical authority alone to serve the purposes of bureaucratic administration, both must be present. Thus the ideal type, bureaucracy, is itself a compromise between two ideal extremes, utilizing and compromising two channels of authority, which may be in conflict.

Bureaucracies differ, however, in the degree to which they emphasize chain of command or rules. Business organizations tend to vest greater authority in the chain of command, minimizing numbers of rules and winking at violations if the official achieves results. "Cutting through red tape" is the popular phrase for the emphasizing rules. Government bureaucracies stress rules more strongly because of their different aims and because of fear of abuse of authority by officials, and through civil service regulations functionaries are given more authority to defy superiors in the application and interpretation of rules.

Many a former business executive serving as a naval officer in charge of civilian employees in navy yards has been startled to find his orders called into question by subordinates, and to find himself powerless to enforce his orders. As businesses get larger the emphasis on rules to insure uniform practice reduces the contrast with government bureaucracy. Custodians of funds in business or government are more tightly bound by rules and less subject to arbitrary orders from superiors.

In the Navy, and probably in other bureaucratic structures, the intensity of the conflict varies with different levels in the hierarchy. For the lower ranks of enlisted men the conflict hardly exists because they are explicitly denied the right to make decisions on their own.[4] At the higher levels the official is confronted with fewer and broader orders so that in the top ranks the conflict arises less frequently. Thus the conflict between orders and regulations is most acute at the intermediate levels, from ensign to lieutenant in particular.

In business and in most naval positions, this conflict is resolved in favor of the order, the functionary not being held responsible for violating a rule in compliance with an order from a superior official. As indicated previously, the personal accountability of the disbursing officer denies this way out. Consequently, the Navy, recognizing the possibility of conflict, has provided two procedures for its resolution. The disbursing officer is to point out the apparent discrepancy to the superior and, if no understanding is reached, an inquiry may be sent to the Bureau of Supplies and Accounts. Or, the matter may be referred to the commanding officer who may order the disbursing officer to make the expenditure "under protest," the commanding officer thereby assuming full financial liability. The former procedure was used often during the war for minor issues, but senior officers are often unwilling to wait several months for answers and a disbursing officer who frequently resorts to this tactic is soon in poor standing. A disbursing officer considering the second method invariably pictures himself being transferred to "amphibs" and suffering various awful fates at the hands of a wrathful commanding officer, so the method is seldom employed. However, the occasional disbursing officer who has courage enough to threaten its use usually finds the commanding officer unwilling to assume the personal risk involved in defying him.

The very training given the disbursing officer in the supply corps school teaches him that the above methods are not approved ways of handling such difficulties. The young officer is taught that he must be a "Can do paymaster," in contradistinction to the type of officer who is always ready to cite the paragraph in the Manual which prevents any par-officer can almost always find a way to do any-ticular action being taken. The "Can do" thing he is ordered to do. This emphasis, of course, partly reflects a general de-emphasis of rules fostered by the war. But it further reinforces the tendency for the disbursing officer to find "informal" ways of dealing with matters and to deviate from the ideal pattern of a bureaucrat.

The second obstacle to impersonal functioning by the disbursing officer is the system of rank. As indicated by Weber, military officers are marked off by class distinction.[5] And Talcott Parson has observed that, "there is no legitimate order without a charismatic element."[6] It is the union of class distinctions with a strong element of "charisma of office" which gives the rank structure its peculiar and powerful nature. Senior officers are expected to be treated with deference irrespective of their actions. Because of "class" levels, senior officers are usually able to punish or reward a lesser officer indirectly. However, through their charisma officers are generally held in far greater awe than their actual powers or inclinations warrant, and a lesser officer is often afraid even to suggest to a superior that his request is not in keeping with regulations. One of the problems of military organization lies in the rather widespread fear of superiors which creates extra labor and ill-feeling on the part of men who feel that they must find some way to conform to an erroneous or careless order. Rank has been too widely discussed to need further elaboration here except to note that the disbursing officer, who is at once both a functionary with specified duties and a position in a system of levels, sometimes finds that he cannot act without violating one of these rules.

A third obstacle to bureaucratic impartiality is the system of informal social groupings. Philip Selznick's three characteristics of the informal structure as found in business and labor union bureaucracies, namely, spontaneity, network of personal relations, and orientation toward control,[7] apply equally to naval situations.

These informal structures are of three sorts. Relatively enduring friendship patterns weigh heavily where the disbursing officer belongs to the same primary associations as do many of his clients. Particularly aboard ship where a relatively small number of officers live, eat and play poker together in a small space is this true. "Say, 'Pay,' I sure could use about twenty dollars before payday," or, "Isn't there some way I can get flight pay this month?" is the sort of appeal which comes constantly from friends. As a human being, the disbursing officer wants to help his friends, and the penalty for brusque disposal of such requests is social ostracism.

A second type of simulated friendship or, in Navy jargon, "carbanging," relationships includes less enduring and more uncertain influences. Nevertheless, these are in many cases sufficiently persistent and organized relations among persons to justify the term "structure." They take a multitude of well-known forms: an officer treats one of lesser rank as an equal, he compliments the disbursing officer on the good reputation of his office, he jokes and attempts to appear as an old friend. The aim is always, first, to be defined as a person rather than an applicant in the disbursing officer's eyes, and second, to be defined favorably.

The third and most extensive sort of informal structure is that which may be called an exchange system. The officer who assigns staterooms aboard ship finds it easy to get extra food from the galley. The ship's photographer who makes some personal pictures of the supply officer gets first choice when the next shipment of fountain pens reaches "ship's store." Such exchanges are not usually verbalized as such among officers, but the officer who does another a favor has no doubt that there will be a return. However, there also exist extensive and well-verbalized systems for distribution of favors and certain types of supplies, especially at shore stations. The exchange structures extend so far that it is often difficult for a man to secure those services and equipment which are essential to his job unless he can promise some return. Aboard a large ship one attempt was made in the ship's store to sell the limited stock of watches and cigarette lighters on the basis of impartial drawings. Complaints were so many and vigorous from persons who claimed they had been promised a watch or were owed one that thereafter the "spoils" system was used, with much less complaint. Even some enlisted men in key positions, such as the mail clerk and carpenter's mates, are able to exercise influence over officers because of the services at their disposal. Needless to remark, any resort to strictly formal procedure impairs the disbursing officer's potentially exceptionally good position in the system of mutual benefits. Denunciations of these exchange structures are periodically issued by some commands, but such pronouncements are read by only a few and are seldom implemented by more than one or two courts-martial for petty thievery. Furthermore, commanding officers are frequently among the beneficiaries of such systems.

To the participants these exchange systems are widely different from bribery. Bribery is impersonal and is recognized as contrary to law and morals. Favor exchange systems are eminently personal. As long as the system functions smoothly it is just one man doing a favor for a "buddy," and only when a return favor is not forthcoming will the idea of exchange be stressed. And secondly, the exchange system incorporates its own code of behavior. The individual who puts legal technicality ahead of reciprocity is reprehensible, is spoken of with almost moral indignation. The system is not "wrong" or "crooked"; it is a moral system of its own and anyone who puts legality first is a hypocrite. However, there is an ambivalence of attitude toward the system. The official who follows it deliberately and impersonally in order to acquire too great a quantity of goods is disliked, though with a mixture of envy. The system is supposed to operate in leisurely fashion, maintaining the appearance that the goods acquired are secondary to the friendships involved.

The three sorts of systems described operate not only to grant favors to some but to withhold fair consideration from others. Since disbursing officers generally are stereotyped as acting slowly, being tied up in red tape and giving unsatisfactory assistance, prompt careful attention to the business of a client is often defined as a favor. Persons not favorably placed in the informal structures may be deprived of pay because of inadequate attention to their accounts or may suffer undue delay in the handling of their business.

The influence of these systems is felt not only directly by the disbursing officer but also through the enlisted men in his office. Because of their lack of official status, enlisted men develop especially elaborate and powerful in-

formal structures. A new disbursing officer, in the interest of fairness, stopped the dispensing of favors by his enlisted men. A serious morale problem ensued because the disbursing office personnel, no longer able to contribute services, were simply dropped from the status producing structures, or, as they complained, they had lost their "drag."

Under the combined impact of the informal structures and his formal office, what solutions does the disbursing officer reach? Four types of disbursing officer will be suggested on the basis of their divergent resolutions of the conflicting forces at work. These will be ideal constructs, but have sufficient empirical validity that any disbursing officer should be able to recognize them as applying to other officers he has known and also to tendencies within himself.

The Regulation type approximates the true bureaucrat in that he remains impervious to rank, informal structures, and orders of his superiors, but goes further in employing the narrowest possible interpretation of every regulation. For fear of the General Accounting Office his rule is, "When in doubt, don't." He is the stereotyped disbursing officer and the stereotyped bureaucrat.[8] This type is not in a majority during wartime, and consists chiefly of "green" officers who have not yet felt the full pressure of the contrary influences or have not yet learned how easily regulations may be manipulated, and of "mustangs," former enlisted men who have secured commissions.

Opposite is the type who doubts the potency of the General Accounting Office and feels that, "They can't hold me," if money is expended loosely. He will do anything for a friend or superior without debate. This type is limited to a very few reserve officers who seldom last very long, though many officers have sought escape from the anxieties of their position in the assurance that after the war Congress will pass a "relieving act."

On a different axis, and also fairly infrequent, is the Sincere type. He fails to recognize conflicts between regulations and orders from superiors and is unaware of the importance of the informal systems. Apparent conflicts he attributes to his own incomplete understanding of regulations, and rules are seen less as controls than as tools for the execution of orders. He is 100 per cent "sold" on the Navy, is well liked by his superiors and will be assigned positions of favor and responsibility so long as he is a junior officer. His naivete places him in less favor when he reaches higher levels.

The commonest type is the Realist. Regulations are seen as illogical concatenations of procedures, restrictions and interpretations, frequently ambiguous, sometimes contradictory, and often, when strictly applied, defeating the purpose for which they were constructed. Rules specify chiefly the papers which must be filed in support of expenditures, and these may be correct without the payment being correct. The most successful career men of the supply corps include many of this type. They assume the regulation facade when the client is not fortunately placed in the informal or rank structure, but know how any payment may be made "legally" if the request comes from an important enough source.

Many conscientious officials join this type when they come to recognize that strict interpretation of rules often works injustice in terms of the rules' obvious intent and that efforts at strict enforcement are frequently nullified because other people know how to prepare papers "in correct form." Such an official begins by helping a client whose claim is payable within the intent of the law but is invalidated by a technicality to give the "right" information to insure payment. Differential

treatment of clients on this basis is hard to maintain, so the officer soon finds himself giving such aid without reference to justification, or more frequently, under varying pressures and moods, wavering between a regulation attitude and an opportunistic attitude.

Two general tendencies emerge among disbursing officers as the consequences of orders conflicting with regulations and the pressures of rank and informal structure.

One is differential treatment of clientele. Because of the time consumed in extra-routine treatment of persons on the "in," others get summary treatment. The second tendency is for loopholes in regulations to become tools in the hand of the disbursing officer to elevate his own status. Thus he may become more concerned with his own bargaining power than with correct application of rules.

In sum, what has been shown is that during this last war powerful influences were at work on the navy disbursing officer, diverting him from functioning as an ideal-typical bureaucrat. These influences move him, not in the direction of ultra-formalism so frequently observed for bureaucrats in other contexts,[9] but toward personal functioning within systems of power and status in which rules become of secondary importance.

Notes

[1] Cf. H. H. Gerth and C. Wright Mills, translators and editors. *From Max Weber: Essays in Sociology* (New York: Oxford University Press, 1946), pp. 196–244.

[2] "Bureaucratic Structure and Personality," *Social Forces*, 18: 567, May 1940.

[3] Max Weber, *Wirtschaft und Gesellschaft* (Tubingen: J. C. B. Mohr, 1925), p. 124.

[4] Cf. United States Navy, *The Bluejackets' Manual* (Annapolis: U.S. Naval Institute, 1940), p. 32.

[5] Max Weber, *op. cit.*, p. 128.

[6] *The Structure of Social Action* (New York: McGraw-Hill, 1937), p. 665.

[7] "An Approach to a Theory of Bureaucracy," *American Sociological Review*, 8: 47–54, 1943. Selznick uses a different definition of bureaucracy, referring to deviations from the Weber construct which become informally organized and routinized.

[8] Cf. Ludwig Von Mises, *Bureaucracy* (New Haven: Yale University Press, 1944), p. 41.

[9] Cf. Robert Merton, *op. cit.*, pp. 560–568.

BUREAUCRATIC PATTERNS

Much work in sociology since Weber's time has been devoted to producing a deeper understanding and a more complex theory of bureaucracy. A major advance in this line was a study of a gypsum plant by Alvin Gouldner (1954), in which Weber's ideal type was refined and a classification developed according to the nature of the regulations applied. In mock bureaucracy, Weber's rules and hierarchy are found, but the rules are not evident in behavior, because they are totally external and no members of the hierarchy assume responsibility for their application. An academic illustration might be a classroom where a "No Smoking" sign is prominently displayed, yet in which professor and students smoke freely. In punishment-centered bureaucracy, the rules are accepted by part of the hierarchy and resisted by the remainder. The assignment of outside reading sometimes constitutes an area in which a college bureaucracy appears punishment centered. In representative bureaucracy, the rules are endorsed throughout the hierarchy because they accord with the values of all levels. Rules concerning conscientious and fair grading constitute an academic example. In this classification, Weber is being not disavowed, but developed.

This selection continues Gouldner's approach to Weber. Smigel believes that the bureaucratic Wall Street law firms he studied exemplify a fourth "pattern," which he terms "professional bureaucracy." Although it closely resembles representative bureaucracy, the origin of the accepted rules is not within the organization, but rather in the extensive socialization undergone by members of a profession.

> The formal structure of the large Wall Street law firm, which is described, is minimal. Compared with a typical corporation or Government bureau, the rules are sparse and sketchy, and the hierarchy is vaguely defined. Moreover, the members of the firms, when questioned, perceive their organizations to be loosely structured, and they like what they feel to be an unbureaucratic organization. It would seem that this is a very imperfect and hence inefficient bureaucracy, yet the Wall Street law firm, which guides the most important businesses in the country, functions efficiently.

> The paradox is explained by the fact that in these law firms, rules of the profession fill in for rules of the organization and render the latter unnecessary. Since the Bar Association canons of ethics prohibit a lawyer's knowingly entering a conflict-of-interest situation, the law firm does not need a rule to this effect. Since the rules of the courts tell how pleas are to be filed, rules of the firm in this matter are unnecessary. These formal external rules are buttressed by an informal professional milieu, which makes it unnecessary to use formal enforcement proceedings when the rules are violated.

> Professional rules originate in the socialization of lawyers, and are legitimated in the informal milieu of fellow-professionals with whom lawyers practice. Violations of the rules are interpreted as inadvertent, although they diminish the status of the violator, since the rules are endorsed at all levels of the hierarchy.

Smigel suggests as a possible generalization from this instance that the existence of external rules sufficiently powerful to substitute for organizational rules is one of the differences between a profession and other occupations. The comparison with the stockbroker, described in Selection 25, supports Smigel's position. The higher intellectual caliber of the legal bureaucrats, their longer and common period of training, and compensation on a less market-oriented basis distinguish the professionals, and provide the basis for both formal and informal normative codes.

Selection 32

PROFESSIONAL BUREAUCRACY AND THE LARGE WALL STREET LAW FIRMS

Erwin O. Smigel

Much has been written about the importance of formal rules for the smooth functioning of large-scale organizations. Max Weber,[1] for example, thought bureaucracy—which is founded on formal rules—to be the most rational and effective way to run large organizations. Examination of the social structure of large law firms presents an opportunity to see how an organization can function smoothly with far fewer rules than would normally be expected.

This report is based on an extensive study of the Wall Street lawyer and his firm. To investigate this subject, an analysis was made of law firms composed of fifty or more lawyers. The main sample consisted of 18 of the 20 largest New York firms. In addition, four similar firms outside New York were studied. From the New York firms 188 attorneys were interviewed, as were 44 from the other offices.

Large law firms are not without formal structure. To begin with, they are departmentalized. Generally they are divided into five sections: business law, litigation, estates and trusts, real estate and tax law. Each of these departments has a head lawyer, though neither he nor the department are usually given formal titles. In fact it was more customary for respondents to deny departmentalization. Complicating matters somewhat for some firms is the existence of permanent and temporary teams of lawyers for special clients, which overlap the main organizational structure. Lawyers in this system are members of both departments and teams.

The firms are also stratified. At the top are the senior partners or executive partners. Under them are the general partners and in some firms at the very bottom of this category are limited partners, who are junior or retiring members of the firm. The next stratum is made up of associate lawyers. These men are employees, and they informally divide, mainly on the basis of age, into permanent associates, senior associates and junior associates. Except

Reprinted by permission of the author and the publisher. A revision of an article which appeared in *Estudios de Sociologia*, Vol. 2, published by Bibliografica Omeba in Buenos Aires, Argentina, n.d., pp. 155–163.

for the beginning associates, who may be placed in a pool of lawyers, the associates are to be found in the various departments. The last major stratum is composed of non-professional employees, such as secretaries and clerks. We are not concerned with the non-professional worker here.

There are some managerial positions in the Wall Street firm. First, an executive committee or a senior partner usually has control of salaries and the sharing of profits, as well as having the final word on the management of the firm. Second, a managing partner takes care of work assignments and other everyday tasks. Third, in some organizations there is also a hiring partner who does a great deal of the initial recruitment, although this position is sometimes filled by a committee. Finally, there is an office manager, not usually a lawyer, who supervises the non-professional staff. He reports either to the managing partner or to a committee charged with looking after and setting policy concerning this group.

The firms have some formal, written rules, but they are very few. The main ones are found in the partnership agreements. These agreements generally concern who can make decisions, who gets what proportion of the profits, and what happens in the event of the death or retirement of a partner or in case there is a split in the firm (who keeps the firm's name, what happens to the assets, etc.). There are other formal precepts, mainly concerning procedures for billing and filing, keeping diaries, withdrawing for expenses, signing opinion letters and taking outside legal work.

That the organization of their firms was loose was spontaneously mentioned by 27 per cent of the sample. Only a very few thought this unfortunate. Most felt there was some advantage in having a loosely organized office. It was more professional, they said, and allowed for greater independence. It also promoted creativity and provided organizational flexibility. Most lawyers were pleased that their offices were loosely organized, and they did what they could to perpetuate the image of a small, informal firm. As the statement of one very busy and famous senior partner illustrates in the extreme: "Come in anytime! My door is always open. We are like a country law firm here."

Although the large law firms are not quite so loosely structured as the lawyers in them would like to believe, they are quite loosely structured as compared, for instance, with most corporations. Yet despite this looseness, the firms are effective. They serve the client well and keep him contented. In addition, and perhaps as a prerequisite for effectiveness, they also keep their own lawyers happy.

Among the lawyers interviewed, 101 were asked to explain why their organizations worked, even though loosely structured. The following factors, based upon their answers, seem to be adequate explanations in combination: homogeneity of the personnel; special (i.e., law review) training of many attorneys; development of esprit de corps; control of competition; stability and easy recognition of some informal rules; the use of judgment (which in some instances involves a knowledge of regulations not considered to be such); the special role of the client; informal external professional rules, including responsibility; and formal external professional controls. Among these items, external professional controls, both formal and informal, seem to be the most important. It is to these factors that the rest of this paper is devoted. They are especially salient for the discussion, for they point to one major weapon in the arsenal of control techniques available to professional large-scale organizations which is not available, or certainly not to the same degree, to non-professional institutions.

The impact of the formal rules of the profession on the organization of the large firms is demonstrable. These formal rules, however, would probably be less successful if professional people did not also have informal codes and a professional milieu. The acceptance of professional norms for the lawyer probably starts with the decision to enter the law, is speeded by entrance into law school and, depending on the type of practice, receives a further boost when he starts to work. During the course of this investigation numerous examples of informal professional rules were observed. They ranged from attorneys helping other attorneys, even though they were in competition, to a reluctance to talk about other lawyers (especially in derogatory

terms), to the encouragement of disputatious behavior.

The informal professional rules cited here serve the function of rendering formal organizational rules less crucial. They furthermore buttress the formal rules of the profession, thus vitiating the need for rules internal to the organization. That this connection is recognized is seen in the statements of those respondents who said that professional responsibility was what made the loosely organized law firms work.

Formal professional rules are numerous. A primary source is the canons of ethics. Lawyers did not always have written prescriptions. George Sharwood, in his 1854 essay, *Professional Ethics,* is considered responsible for formalizing these ideals. Sharwood felt the function of the canons was to define high moral principles which every lawyer needs:

> There is certainly, without any exception, no profession in which so many temptations beset the path to swerve from the line of strict integrity, in which so many delicate and difficult questions of duty are continually arising. There are pitfalls and mantraps at every step, and the mere youth, at the very outset of his career, needs often the prudence and self-denial as well as the moral courage, which belongs commonly to riper years. High moral principle is the only safe guide, the only torch to light his way amidst darkness and obstruction.

It was not until 1908, however, that the canons of professional ethics were adopted by the American Bar Association. The principal additions were passed in 1928. Essentially the 47 canons furnished, as do most professional codes, the clues to proper behavior in three main areas of social relationship: between the professional and the client, the professional and the fellow professional, and between the professional and society at large. Trumbull, in his book, *Materials on the Lawyer's Professional Responsibility,* places the canons into categories which provide an opportunity to see quickly what they generally cover: responsibility, the right to practice law, fiduciary relationship to the client, limitations on duty to clients, freedom to serve or not to serve, professional fees, solicitation and advertising, and relations with lawyers, clients and the public.[2] What the canons say has been added to by what the courts and bar associations have said when trying to enforce them. Drinker[3] lists some of the cases and decisions, thereby furnishing the bar with a type of professional common law.

It is true, as MacKinnon says,[4] that the canons are behind the times, and this is especially the case for the work of large law firms. None the less, they do have an effect on the Wall Street firms. Part of the canons are reflected in the firms' formal rules, but this is true only for the most important mandates. All firms, for example, are careful to avoid conflict-of-interest situations. Most law offices send a list of all new clients to all partners, and if a partner feels that a conflict of interest will arise, the problem is discussed at the firm meeting where the decision may be made to take or refuse the client's case.

The law firms also take a hand in seeing that the canons of ethics are enforced. This is not too difficult a task. The caliber of men hired by these firms makes it unlikely that many would be willing to risk their reputation by being unethical. In addition, these firms can afford to be ethical, and they avoid legal matters where the temptation to violate is probably greatest: divorce, criminal and negligence work.

Of equal importance in enforcing the canons are the bar associations. Whereas it is the state's highest court that actually disciplines a lawyer for a breach of the canons, it is the bar association that formally initiates the complaint. The Committee on Grievances of the state Bar Association checks into the merits of complaints and then determines whether to refer them to the court. In most cases, complaints terminate with these committees. In Chicago, Trumbull found that of 56 complaints filed with the Committee on Grievances, 42 were disposed of as follows: ten respondents were disbarred, one was suspended, five had their names stricken from the roll of attorneys, and the rest received lesser sentences or had their cases dismissed.[5] While not many lawyers were punished, and only 192 complaints were filed with the Committee in the eleven months studied, the threat of disbarment did exist, and the stigma for a lawyer of even having his name listed was great. Thus, the task of the law firm in policing its own members is made much less difficult.

The courts play a direct role in the organization of law firms by prescribing acceptable modes of behaving in court and setting schedules that determine a firm's working calendar, and they can and do discipline lawyers who do not obey their dictates. For example, the Supreme Court of the United States lists 36 rules which affect the lawyer. Rule 10, for instance, states in detail just how an attorney must proceed to file a notice of appeal. Rule 33 offers a number of options regarding how a pleading, motion, notice or other document must be served. Part 4 of this rule reads:

> Whenever proof of service is required by these rules, it must accompany or be endorsed upon the document in question at the time such document is presented to the clerk for filing. Any document filed with the clerk by or on behalf of counsel of record whose appearance has not previously been entered must be accompanied by an entry of appearance.

To the extent that large law firms are still involved in litigation these rules make it unnecessary for the firms to create their own regulations to cover the required behavior. It is furthermore unnecessary for the law office to do any extensive policing, for the courts have the power to enforce their own standards. This statement can be generalized to other external rules for what all of them do is to provide guides for behavior and thus make it unnecessary for the law firm to formulate regulations. The minimization of internal rules and the fact that external prescriptions do not usually have to be monitored by the firm gives the associate the desired feeling of independence and responsibility (a necessary part of the informal professional milieu) and makes the task of managing easier and more pleasant. So that though the large law firm has few formal rules, its organization is effective, in part, because it has accepted, and its lawyers have internalized, the rules, both formal and informal, of the legal profession.

These observations bring to the sociologist's attention a new, previously unrecognized dimension of bureaucracy. Following Alvin Gouldner's study of bureaucracy in the context of a gypsum plant,[6] we currently recognize three "patterns" of bureaucracy—Mock, Punishment-Centered, and Representative. Insofar as a bureaucracy is Mock, there is little obedience to the rules because the rules are imposed from outside and, in the gypsum plant case, neither management nor labor agrees with the regulations. The Punishment-Centered dimension involves rules formulated by either labor or management and enforced by one side upon the other. Insofar as a bureaucracy is Representative, all groups involved endorse and follow the formal rules.

The present study finds a fourth "pattern," Professional bureaucracy. Insofar as a bureaucracy is Professional, it relies on external formal rules formulated, in this case, by professional associations and government, and in contrast to Mock bureaucracy these rules are supported by a professional milieu which is favorable to their enforcement. The professional regulations are external to the organization but internal to the personnel. Further, while the rules are representative, they are not Representative in the way described by Gouldner, i.e., in terms of some common agreement between workers and management. Most of the canons are accepted because lawyers have been trained to accept them. This is especially true today because present-day lawyers have had little to do with deciding the rules and have learned them in almost a subliminal fashion. Only to the extent that external formal rules are currently being fashioned and represent the present sentiment of lawyers can these professional standards be considered similar to Gouldner's Representative rules. For some attorneys, of course, some rules are Punishment-Centered, in that the law firm, the courts, or the elites see to it that others follow them.

Let us compare systematically this fourth dimension of bureaucracy with the three previously isolated by Gouldner in the gypsum plant study:

1. Where Mock rules are imposed from the outside (and ignored), Representative are initiated from both top and bottom, and Punishment-Centered arise from one side only. Professional rules are adopted from the outside through socialization.

2. In the case of Mock rules, there is no legitimation; the rules called Representative are legitimized throughout the hierarchy; Punishment-Centered rules are legitimized at one level only; and the formal Professional rules are legitimized in the informal professional milieu.

3. Enforcement of Mock rules violates values of all participants. In the case of Representative rules, enforcement is supported by all. One level of the hierarchy supports, and another opposes, the enforcement of Punishment-Centered rules. Enforcement of Professional rules is endorsed by all levels of the hierarchy.

4. Where Mock rules are broken, this is explained as a result of human nature. Violation of Representative rules is explained as ignorance or well-intentioned error. Violation of Punishment-Centered rules is understood to be willful. Reactions to violating Professional rules resemble those to violating Representative rules—the deviance is believed to be innocent error.

5. Deviation from Mock rules is status-enhancing, and from Representative rules is status-impairing. The effects of deviance in Punishment-Centered cases varies with the position of the party and the reasons for the deviance. Deviance from Professional rules is status-impairing.

6. In sum, Mock rules are not enforced. Representative rules are enforced throughout the hierarchy. Punishment-Centered rules are enforced by only a part of the hierarchy. Professional rules are occasionally directly enforced from outside, but the enforcement is informal more often than it is formal.

The identification of a Professional dimension of bureaucracy has a number of other implications. For example, it leads to the hypothesis that the greater the external control, the less the need for internal control. Is there then an inverse relationship between the extent to which a given occupation, such as a profession, establishes a set of rules and the necessity for an organization to create its own formal internal rules? We may eventually find that external occupational rules exist for all occupations but that they do not exist in the same quantities, and this is probably one of the factors that differentiate an occupation from a profession. In this study it was found that whereas the law firms were relatively free of internal formal rules, the legal profession itself is highly codified and these external rules take the place of the internal. This is probably true for all professions and of some other occupations. It is possibly true in descending degree from the highest prestige occupations to the lowest. This type of examination places a given institution within a larger societal context, instead of trying to understand it in isolation.

The large Wall Street law firms function effectively though they are loosely organized, in large part, because they are controlled by formal and informal professional rules, external to the organization. This fact, in turn, strengthens the impression that the firms are loosely organized, since the lawyers do not consider the outside rules as rules of this firm.

The result of this complex is that management does not have to enforce many rules, and lawyers working in what they consider a relatively rule-free environment feel that initiative and independence and professional responsibility are being sponsored.

Notes

[1] Hans H. Gerth and C. Wright Mills (trs. and eds.), *From Max Weber: Essays in Sociology*, New York: Oxford University Press, 1958, Chap. 8.

[2] William M. Trumbull, *Materials on the Lawyer's Professional Responsibility*, Englewood Cliffs, N.J.: Prentice Hall, 1957, p. 348.

[3] Henry Drinker, *Legal Ethics*, New York: Columbia University Press, 1953.

[4] F. B. MacKinnon, "Ethical Problems of Lawyers in Large Law Firms and House Counsel" (Mimeographed), April 19, 1956.

[5] Trumbull, *op. cit.*, p. 77.

[6] Alvin W. Gouldner, *Patterns of Industrial Bureaucracy*, Glencoe, Illinois: The Free Press, 1954.

Part 5

SOCIAL DIFFERENTIATION

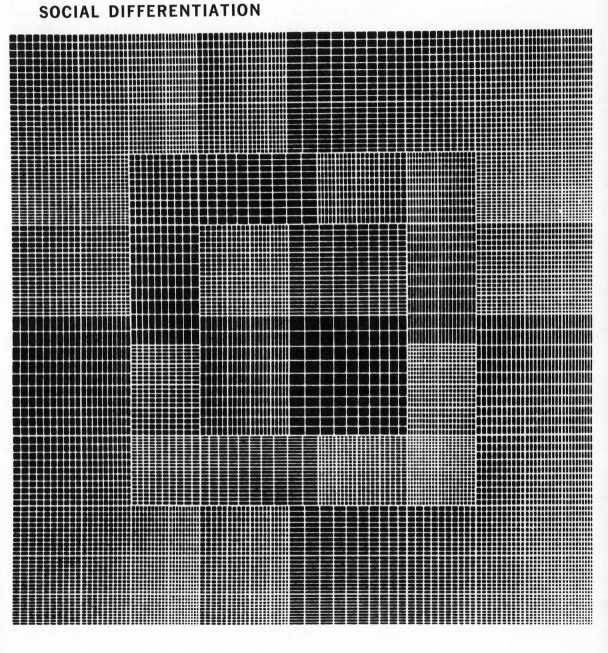

Chapter 12

WOMEN AND MEN

SEX AS A SOCIAL STATUS
Selection 33

THE WOMAN IN AMERICA
Selection 34

Some societies do not distinguish social classes, and many do not recognize what we call races, but all societies distinguish between men and women. Sex is a biological fact, and it is among the most obvious of physical distinctions that occur among members of any society. It is, moreover, a true dichotomy; a person is physically either male or female and not, except in rare pathological cases, at some point on a scale between these two poles.

This physical distinction is seized on by all societies as a basis for assigning ascribed statuses. In all societies, the norms for the behavior of men differ at least to some extent from those applicable to women. Moreover, the physical basis of the sex distinction has led to a general belief, even in very sophisticated societies, that the behavior prescribed for the two sexes is "natural" and entirely based on biology. The norms for behavior of the two sexes are generally very strongly binding, and deviation in sex roles is usually severely censured.

While acknowledging the biological basis of the distinction between the sexes, sociologists and anthropologists are generally skeptical concerning claims that biological differences between the sexes cause significant behavioral differences. Although in a single society the differences between masculinity and femininity are usually very great, what is considered appropriate behavior for a man or woman in one society may bear little relationship to behavior appropriate for the same sex in a different society. These differences from society to society in behavior appropriate to either sex must be largely cultural in origin. Whatever the biological differences are between men and women, it is obvious that culture distorts and magnifies them many times.

American society, no less than many others, makes important distinctions between the sexes. Men are expected to be strong, competitive, aggressive, and rugged, whereas women are expected to be tender, sympathetic, and sensitive. These are norms of ascribed sex statuses. An important feature of these statuses in America is a large amount of conflict among the norms pertaining to each sex. This is particularly true for the middle-class woman. The same person who dusts, scrubs, cooks, and cleans up after the children is expected to appear fresh and alluring at six o'clock when her husband brings the boss home for dinner. She may then be expected to discuss the latest books or the political situation in an informed way. Moreover, if she is also employed, as are an increasing number of married women in our society, additional demands, such as aggressive salesmanship, may be added to this conflict of norms.

Regardless of the supreme effort needed to keep up with its demands, the female status is less highly valued in America than is that of the male. Statistics show that women occupy the low-prestige jobs far more than do men, and that in jobs of equal prestige women are paid less. Many unpleasant stereotypes are applied to women. Women are fickle, weak, and impractical in a society that values the strong, steadfast, and practical properties of the stereotyped male. Women are segregated from the "superior" sex in commuter suburbs during the day and in groups abandoned to "woman talk" at evening social gatherings. Based on this kind of data, a parallel has been suggested between the status of women and the similarly ascribed status of the Negro in America.

Selection 33, by Margaret Mead, sheds light on the cultural nature of the difference between masculinity and femininity through the study of sex statuses in three societies widely different from our own. In Selection 34, Fred Davis and Virginia L. Olesen discuss the status of women in America, in the context of a study of career orientations of young nurses.

SEX AS A SOCIAL STATUS

In Western society, masculinity and femininity are strongly distinguished, and the norms prescribing appropriate behavior for the members of each sex are very different. Moreover, these norms are quite pervasive. In few situations is one's sex completely irrelevant. Men dress, drink, greet, sit, walk, and even talk in a manner considerably different from that of women in our society.

These pervasive differences (of impressive magnitude) in behavior between the sexes are commonly ascribed to differences in biological constitutions. It is argued, for instance, that because women must bear children they are naturally fit to be passive and to engage in sedentary activities. Men, being free of this physiological burden, are therefore naturally active and aggressive. The premises of such arguments cannot be questioned, but the conclusions do not necessarily follow. Men and women do differ, physically and physiologically, and there is a strong correlation between biological sex and the behavior observed in our society; but one must not, here as elsewhere, accept correlation as proof of causation.

One of the greatest challenges to the belief that sex differences in behavior are a simple function of biology is Margaret Mead's book, *Sex and Temperament in Three Primitive Societies*, from which this selection is drawn. It is a study of three societies that are very unlike our own. In two of the societies, the Arapesh and Mundugumor, the sexes are only to a slight extent differentiated in their behavior. Both men and women among the Arapesh tend to be cooperative and sympathetic. Among the Mundugumor both sexes are aggressive and ruthless. In the third society, Tchambuli, the behavior of men and women is different, with the men being weak and dependent and the women being independent and impersonal. These societies present, in different ways, three ideas other than our own concerning the expected behavior of the sexes and three refutations of the bio-social theories mentioned above.

The contrasts between the Arapesh, Mundugumor, Tchambuli, and Americans in the behavior of the two sexes mean that differential behavior of men and women is the result of differential socialization. Where behavior prescribed for the sexes refers to variables of personality or character, not all individuals of a given sex will possess hereditary inclinations to fill their statuses; yet all will be under pressure to conform. Conformity to sex-linked norms is in this case achieved in socialization by encouraging some hereditary traits and suppressing others, presumably with the use of sanc-tions by the socializing agents.

Yet some individuals will adjust to their sex statuses with difficulty, if at all. Innate dispositions, accidents of primary socialization, or socializa-tion in a deviant subculture can be factors in this situation. The resulting problems will be more serious if the sex statuses are sharply differentiated, as among the Tchambuli or the Americans. In these cases, the deviant individual runs the risk of being considered unnatural. The consequences are most unpleasant when the deviant is a member of the sex with the greater prestige, such as a male in our society. By failing to conform to and adopt his sex status this deviant is analogous to a prince who rejects his crown—his action casts doubt on fundamental social values.

Mead's argument may be somewhat overstated. Assuming the validity of her descriptions of the three New Guinea societies (concerning which there is some doubt), the patterning of sex roles in these instances is rather exceptional. The rule is closer to the American pattern than to any of the others. The predomi-nant understanding today is that there exists a common association of sex differences with personality traits, reflecting not a genetic association between sex and temperament, but a relative good fit and lack of strain between inherited sex-linked physical traits and certain socially given temperamental traits. This view does accord with Mead's thesis to the extent of recognizing that sex is a social status as well as a fact of biology, and that differences in behavior ac-cording to sex appear in most instances to be the result of conformity to cul-tural norms, rather than of direct biological determination. It differs in that it leads to the expectation that cultures generally will tend to select similar traits as components of the two sex statuses. Male aggressiveness and female tender-ness, for example, are predicted to be the norm in most societies.

Selection 33
FROM SEX AND TEMPERAMENT IN THREE PRIMITIVE SOCIETIES
Margaret Mead

We have now considered in detail the ap-proved personalities of each sex among three primitive peoples. We found the Arapesh—both men and women—displaying a personal-ity that, out of our historically limited preoc-cupations, we would call maternal in its paren-tal aspects, and feminine in its sexual aspects. We found men, as well as women, trained to be cooperative, unaggressive, responsive to the needs and demands of others. We found no idea that sex was a powerful driving force either for men or for women. In marked con-

trast to these attitudes, we found among the Mundugumor that both men and women de-veloped as ruthless, aggressive, positively sexed individuals, with the maternal cherish-ing aspects of personality at a minimum. Both men and women approximated to a personal-ity type that we in our culture would find only in an undisciplined and very violent male. Neither the Arapesh nor the Mundugumor profit by a contrast between the sexes; the Arapesh ideal is the mild, responsive man married to the mild, responsive woman; the Mundugumor ideal is the violent aggressive man married to the violent aggressive woman. In the third tribe, the Tchambuli, we found a genuine reversal of the sex-attitudes of our own culture, with the woman the dominant, impersonal, managing partner, the man the less responsible and the emotionally dependent person. These three situations suggest, then, a very definite conclusion. If those temperamental attitudes which we have traditionally regarded as feminine—such as passivity, responsiveness, and a willingness to cherish children—can so easily be set up as the masculine pattern in one tribe, and in another be outlawed for the majority of women as well as for the majority of men, we no longer have any basis for regarding such aspects of behaviour as sex-linked. And this conclusion becomes even stronger when we consider the actual reversal in Tchambuli of the position of dominance of the two sexes, in spite of the existence of formal patrilineal institutions.*

The material suggests that we may say that many, if not all, of the personality traits which we have called masculine or feminine are as lightly linked to sex as are the clothing, the manners, and the form of head-dress that a society at a given period assigns to either sex. When we consider the behaviour of the typical Arapesh man or woman as contrasted with the behaviour of the typical Mundugumor man or woman, the evidence is overwhelmingly in favour of the strength of social conditioning. In no other way can we account for the almost complete uniformity with which Arapesh children develop into contented, passive, secure persons, while Mundugumor children develop as characteristically into violent, aggressive, insecure persons. Only to the impact of the whole of the integrated culture upon the growing child can we lay the formation of the contrasting types. There is no other explanation of race, or diet, or selection that can be adduced to explain them. We are forced to conclude that human nature is almost unbelievably malleable, responding accurately and contrastingly to contrasting cultural conditions. The differences between individuals who are members of different cultures, like the differences between individuals within a culture, are almost entirely to be laid to differences in conditioning, especially during early childhood, and the form of this conditioning is culturally determined. Standardized personality differences between the sexes are of this order, cultural creations to which each generation, male and female, is trained to

* Descent, succession, and inheritance in the male line.—Ed.

conform. There remains, however, the problem of the origin of these socially standardized differences.

While the basic importance of social conditioning is still imperfectly recognized—not only in lay thought, but even by the scientist specifically concerned with such matters—to go beyond it and consider the possible influence of variations in hereditary equipment is a hazardous matter. The following pages will read very differently to one who has made a part of his thinking a recognition of the whole amazing mechanism of cultural conditioning—who has really accepted the fact that the same infant could be developed into a full participant in any one of these three cultures—than they will read to one who still believes that the minutiae of cultural behaviour are carried in the individual germ-plasm. If it is said, therefore, that when we have grasped the full significance of the malleability of the human organism and the preponderant importance of cultural conditioning, there are still further problems to solve, it must be remembered that these problems come *after* such a comprehension of the force of conditioning; they cannot precede it. The forces that make children born among the Arapesh grow into typical Arapesh personalities are entirely social, and any discussion of the variations which do occur must be looked at against this social background.

With this warning firmly in mind, we can ask a further question. Granting the malleability of human nature, whence arise the differences between the standardized personalities that different cultures decree for all of their members, or which one culture decrees for the members of one sex as contrasted with the members of the opposite sex? If such differences are culturally created, as this material would most strongly suggest that they are, if the new-born child can be shaped with equal ease into an unaggressive Arapesh or an aggressive Mundugumor, why do these striking contrasts occur at all? If the clues to the different personalities decreed for men and women in Tchambuli do not lie in the physical constitution of the two sexes—an assumption that we must reject both for the Tchambuli and for our own society—where can we find the clues upon which the Tchambuli, the Arapesh, the Mundugumer, have built? Cultures are man-made, they are built of human materials; they are diverse but comparable structures within which human beings can attain full human stature. Upon what have they built their diversities?

We recognize that a homogeneous culture committed in all of its gravest institutions and slight usages to a co-operative unaggressive course can bend every child to that emphasis, some to a perfect accord with it, the majority to an easy acceptance, while only a few deviants fail to receive the cultural imprint. To consider such traits as aggressiveness or passivity to be sex-linked is not possible in the light of the facts. Have such traits, then, as aggressiveness or passivity, pride or humility, objectivity or a preoccupation with personal relationships, an easy response to the needs of the young and the weak or a hostility to the young and the weak, a tendency to initiate sex-relations or merely to respond to the dictates of a situation or another person's advances—have these traits any basis in temperament at all? Are they potentialities of all human temperaments that can be developed by different kinds of social conditioning and which will not appear if the necessary conditioning is absent?

When we ask this question we shift our emphasis. If we ask why an Arapesh man or an Arapesh woman shows the kind of personality that we have considered in the first section of this book, the answer is: Because of the Arapesh culture, because of the intricate, elaborate, and unfailing fashion in which a culture is able to shape each new-born child to the cultural image. And if we ask the same question about a Mundugumor man or woman, or about a Tchambuli man as compared with a Tchambuli woman, the answer is of the same kind. They display the personalities that are peculiar to the cultures in which they were born and educated. Our attention has been on the differences between Arapesh men and women as a group and Mundugumor men and women as a group. It is as if we had represented the Arapesh personality by a soft yellow, the Mundugumor by a deep red, while the Tchambuli female personality was deep orange, and that of the Tchambuli male, pale green. But if we now ask whence came the original direction in each culture, so that one now shows yellow, another red, the third orange and green by sex, then we must peer more closely. And leaning closer to the picture, it is as if behind the bright consistent yellow of the Arapesh, and the deep equally consistent red of the Mundugumor, behind the orange and green that are Tchambuli, we found in each case the delicate, just discernible outlines of the whole spectrum, differently overlaid in each case by the monotone which covers it. This spectrum is the range of individual differences which lie back of the so much more conspicuous cultural emphases, and it is to this that we must turn to find the explanation of cultural inspiration, of the source from which each culture has drawn.

There appears to be about the same range of basic temperamental variation among the Arapesh and among the Mundugumor, although the violent man is a misfit in the first society and a leader in the second. If human nature were completely homogeneous raw material, lacking specific drives and characterized by no important constitutional differences between individuals, then individuals who display personality traits so antithetical to the social pressure should not reappear in societies of such differing emphases. If the variations between individuals were to be set down to accidents in the genetic process, the same accidents should not be repeated with similar frequency in strikingly different cultures, with strongly contrasting methods of education.

But because this same relative distribution of individual differences does appear in culture after culture, in spite of the divergence between the cultures, it seems pertinent to offer a hypothesis to explain upon what basis the personalities of men and women have been differently standardized so often in the history of the human race. This hypothesis is an extension of that advanced by Ruth Benedict in her *Patterns of Culture*. Let us assume that there are definite temperamental differences between human beings which if not entirely hereditary at least are established on a hereditary base very soon after birth. (Further than this we cannot at present narrow the matter.) These differences finally embodied in the character structure of adults, then, are the clues from which culture works, selecting one temperament, or a combination of related and congruent types, as desirable, and embodying this choice in every thread of the social fabric —in the care of the young child, the games the children play, the songs the people sing, the structure of political organization, the religious observance, the art and the philosophy.

Some primitive societies have had the time and the robustness to revamp all of their institutions to fit one extreme type, and to develop educational techniques which will ensure that the majority of each generation will show a personality congruent with this extreme emphasis. Other societies have pursued a less definitive course, selecting their models not from the most extreme, most highly differentiated individuals, but from the less marked types. In such societies the approved personality is less pronounced, and the culture often contains the types of inconsistencies that many human beings display also; one institution may be adjusted to the uses of pride, another to a casual humility that is congruent neither with pride nor with inverted pride. Such societies, which have taken the more usual and less sharply defined types as models, often show also a less definitely patterned social structure. The culture of such societies may be likened to a house the decoration of which has been formed by no definite and precise taste, no exclusive emphasis upon dignity or comfort or pretentiousness or beauty, but in which a little of each effect has been included.

Alternatively, a culture may take its clues not from one temperament, but from several temperaments. But instead of mixing together into an inconsistent hotchpotch the choices and emphases of different temperaments, or blending them together into a smooth but not particularly distinguished whole, it may isolate each type by making it the basis for the approved social personality for an age-group, a sex-group, a caste-group, or an occupational group. In this way society becomes not a monotone with a few discrepant patches of an intrusive colour, but a mosaic, with different groups displaying different personality traits. Such specializations as these may be based upon any facet of human endowment—different intellectual abilities, different artistic abilities, different emotional traits. So the Samoans decree that all young people must show the personality traits of unaggressiveness and punish with opprobrium the aggressive child who displays traits regarded as appropriate only in titled middle-aged men. In societies based upon elaborate ideas of rank, members of the aristocracy will be permitted, even compelled, to display a pride, a sensitivity to insult, that would be deprecated as inappropriate in members of the plebeian class. So also in professional groups or in religious sects some temperamental traits are selected and institutionalized, and taught to each new member who enters the profession or sect. Thus the physi-

cian learns the bed-side manner, which is the natural behaviour of some temperaments and the standard behaviour of the general practitioner in the medical profession; the Quaker learns at least the outward behaviour and the rudiments of meditation, the capacity for which is not necessarily an innate characteristic of many of the members of the Society of Friends.

So it is with the social personalities of the two sexes. The traits that occur in some members of each sex are specially assigned to one sex, and disallowed in the other. The history of the social definition of sex-differences is filled with such arbitrary arrangements in the intellectual and artistic field, but because of the assumed congruence between physiological sex and emotional endowment we have been less able to recognize that a similar arbitrary selection is being made among emotional traits also. We have assumed that because it is convenient for a mother to wish to care for her child, this is a trait with which women have been more generously endowed by a carefully teleological process of evolution. We have assumed that because men have hunted, an activity requiring enterprise, bravery and initiative, they have been endowed with these useful attitudes as part of their sex-temperament.

Societies have made these assumptions both overtly and implicitly. If a society insists that warfare is the major occupation for the male sex, it is therefore insisting that all male children display bravery and pugnacity. Even if the insistence upon the differential bravery of men and women is not made articulate, the difference in occupation makes this point implicitly. When, however, a society goes further and defines men as brave and women as timorous, when men are forbidden to show fear and women are indulged in the most flagrant display of fear, a more explicit element enters in. Bravery, hatred of any weakness, of flinching before pain or danger—this attitude which is so strong a component of *some human* temperaments has been selected as the key to masculine behaviour. The easy unashamed display of fear or suffering that is congenial to a different temperament has been made the key to feminine behaviour.

Originally two variations of human temperament, a hatred of fear or willingness to display fear, they have been socially translated into inalienable aspects of the personalities of the two sexes. And to that defined sex-personality every child will be educated, if a boy, to suppress fear, if a girl, to show it. If there has been no social selection in regard to this trait, the proud temperament that is repelled by any betrayal of feeling will display itself, regardless of sex, by keeping a stiff upper lip. Without an express prohibition of such behaviour the expressive unashamed man or woman will weep, or comment upon fear or suffering. Such attitudes, strongly marked in certain temperaments, may by social selection be standardized for everyone, or outlawed for everyone, or ignored by society, or made the exclusive and approved behaviour of one sex only.

Neither the Arapesh nor the Mundugumor have made any attitude specific for one sex. All of the energies of the culture have gone towards the creation of a single human type, regardless of class, age, or sex. There is no division into age-classes for which different motives or different moral attitudes are regarded as suitable. There is no class of seers or mediums who stand apart drawing inspiration from psychological sources not available to the majority of the people. The Mundugumor have, it is true, made one arbitrary selection, in that they recognize artistic ability only among individuals born with the cord about their necks, and firmly deny the happy exercise of artistic ability to those less unusually born. The Arapesh boy with a tinea infection has been socially selected to be a disgruntled, antisocial individual, and the society forces upon sunny co-operative children cursed with this affliction a final approximation to the behaviour appropriate to a pariah. With these two exceptions no emotional rôle is forced upon an individual because of birth or accident. As there is no idea of rank which declares that some are of high estate and some of low, so there is no idea of sex-difference which declares that one sex must feel differently from the other. One possible imaginative social construct, the attribution of different personalities to different members of the community classified into sex-, age-, or caste-groups, is lacking.

When we turn however to the Tchambuli, we find a situation that while bizarre in one respect, seems nevertheless more intelligible in another. The Tchambuli have at least made the point of sex-difference; they have used the obvious fact of sex as an organizing point for the information of social personality, even though they seem to us to have reversed the normal picture. While there is reason to believe that not every Tchambuli woman is born with a dominating, organizing, administrative temperament, actively sexed and willing to initiate sex-relations, possessive, definite, robust, practical and impersonal in outlook, still most Tchambuli girls grow up to display these traits. And while there is definite evidence to show that all Tchambuli men are not, by native endowment, the delicate responsive actors of a play staged for the women's benefit, still most Tchambuli boys manifest this coquettish play-acting personality most of the time. Because the Tchambuli formulation of sex-attitudes contradicts our usual premises, we can see clearly that Tchambuli culture has arbitrarily permitted certain human traits to women, and allotted others, equally arbitrarily, to men.

If we then accept this evidence drawn from these simple societies which through centuries of isolation from the main stream of human history have been able to develop more extreme, more striking cultures than is possible under historical conditions of great intercommunication between peoples and the resulting heterogeneity, what are the implications of these results? What conclusions can we draw from a study of the way in which a culture can select a few traits from the wide gamut of human endowment and specialize these traits, either for one sex or for the entire community? What relevance have these results to social thinking? Before we consider this question it will be necessary to discuss in more detail the position of the deviant, the individual whose innate disposition is too alien to the social personality required by his culture for his age, or sex, or caste ever to wear perfectly the garment of personality that his society has fashioned for him.

What are the implications for an understanding of the social deviant of the point of view outlined in the last chapter? Under the term "deviant" I include any individual who because of innate disposition or accident of early training, or through the contradictory influences of a heterogeneous cultural situation, has been culturally disenfranchised, the individual to whom the major emphases of his society seem nonsensical, unreal, untenable, or downright wrong. The average man in any society looks into his heart and finds there a reflection of the world about him. The delicate educational process that has made him into an adult has assured him this spiritual membership in his own society. But this is not true of the individual for whose temperamental gifts his society has no use, nor even tolerance. The most cursory survey of our history is enough to demonstrate that gifts honoured in one century are disallowed in the next. Men who would have been saints in the Middle Ages are without vocation in modern England and America. When we take into account primitive societies that have selected far more extreme and contrasting attitudes than did our own ancestral cultures, the matter becomes even clearer. To the extent that a culture is integrated and definite in its goals, uncompromising in its moral and spiritual preferences, to that very extent it condemns some of its members—members by birth only—to live alien to it, in perplexity at the best, at the worst in a rebellion that may turn to madness.

It has become the fashion to group together all of those by whom the cultural norm is not accepted as neurotics, individuals who have turned from "reality" (that is, the present-day solutions of their own society) to the comfort or inspiration of fantasy situations, taking refuge in some transcendental philosophy, in art, in political radicalism, or merely in sexual inversion or some other elaborated idiosyncrasy of behaviour—vegetarianism or the wearing of a hair shirt. The neurotic is furthermore regarded as immature; he has not grown up sufficiently to understand the obviously realistic and commendable motivations of his own society.

In this blanket definition two quite different concepts have become blurred and confused, each one rendering the other nugatory. Among the deviants in any society, it is possible to distinguish those who are physiologically inadequate. They may have weak intellects or defective glands; any one of a number of possible organic weaknesses may predetermine them to failure in any but the simplest tasks. They may—very, very rarely such an individual is found—have practically all of the physiological equipment of the opposite sex. None of these individuals are suffering from any discrepancy between a purely temperamental bent and social emphasis; they are merely the weak and the defective, or they are abnormal in the sense that they are in a group which deviates too far from human cultural standards—not particular cultural standards—for effective functioning. For such individuals any society must provide a softer, more limited, or a more special environment than that which it provides for the majority of its members.

But there is another type of neurotic that is continually being confused with these physiologically handicapped individuals, and this is the cultural deviant, the individual who is at variance with the values of his society. Modern psychiatric thought tends to attribute all of his maladjustment to early conditioning and so places him in the invidious category of the psychically maimed. A study of primitive conditions does not bear out such a simple explanation. It does not account for the fact that it is always those individuals who show marked temperamental proclivities in opposition to the cultural emphases who are in each society the maladjusted persons; or for the fact that it is a different type of individual which is maladjusted among the Mundugumor from the type which is maladjusted among the Arapesh. It does not explain why materialistic, bustling America and a materialistic, bustling tribe in the Admiralty Islands both produce hoboes, or why it is the individual endowed with a capacity to feel strongly who is maladjusted in Zuñi and Samoa. Such material suggests that there is another type of unadjusted person, whose failure to adjust should be referred not to his own weakness and defect, not to accident or to disease, but to a fundamental discrepancy between his innate disposition and his society's standards.

When society is unstratified and the social personalities of both sexes are fundamentally alike, these deviants are drawn indiscriminately from both sexes. Among the Arapesh the violent man and the violent woman, among the Mundugumor the trustful, co-operative man and the trustful, co-operative woman, are the deviants. Too much positive self-feeling predetermines one to maladjustment among the Arapesh, too much negative self-feeling is an equal liability among the Mundugumor. In earlier chapters we have discussed the personalities of some of these deviating individuals, and shown how the very gifts that Mundugumor society would have honoured were disallowed among the Arapesh, how Wabe and Temos and Amitoa would have found Mundugumor life intelligible, and Ombléan and Kwenda would have been well placed among the Arapesh. But the alienness of both these groups in their own cultures, although it impaired their social functioning, reducing the ises to which their gifts might have been put, nevertheless left their psycho-sexual functioning unimpaired. Amitoa's positive drive made her behave not like a man, but like a woman of the Plains. Ombléan's love for children and willingness to work strenuously in order to care for a number of dependents did not make him suspect that he was like a woman, nor did it provoke in his associates an accusation of effeminacy. In loving children and peace and order, he might be behaving like some white men or some tribe they had never seen, but certainly no more like a Mundugumor woman than like a Mundugumor man. There was no homosexuality among either the Arapesh or the Mundugumor.

But any society that specializes its personality types by sex, which insists that any trait—love for children, interest in art, bravery in the face of danger, garrulity, lack of interest in personal relations, passiveness in sex-relations; there are hundreds of traits of very different kinds that have been so specialized—is inalienably bound up with sex, paves the way for a kind of maladjustment of a worse order. Where there is no such dichotomy, a man may stare sadly at his world and find it essentially meaningless but still marry and rear children, finding perhaps a definite mitigation of his misery in this one whole-hearted participation in a recognized social form. A woman may daydream all her life of a world where there is dignity and pride instead of the mean shopkeeping morality that she finds all about her, and yet greet her husband with an easy smile and nurse her children through the croup. The deviant may translate his sense of remoteness into painting or music or revolutionary activity and yet remain in his personal life, in his relations to members of his own and the opposite sex, essentially unconfused. Not so, however, in a society which, like that of the Tchambuli or that of historical Europe and America, defines some temperamental traits as masculine, some as feminine. In addition to, or aside from, the pain of being born into a culture whose acknowledged ends he can never make his own, many a man has now the added misery of being disturbed in his psycho-sexual life. He not only has the wrong feelings but, far worse and more confusing, he has the feelings of a woman. The significant point is not whether this malorientation, which makes the defined goals of women in his society intelligible to him and the goals of the man alien and

distasteful, results in inversion or not. In extreme cases in which a man's temperament conforms very closely to the approved feminine personality, and if there is in existence a social form behind which he can shelter himself, a man may turn to avowed inversion and transvesticism. Among the Plains Indians, the individual who preferred the placid activities of the women to the dangerous, nerve-racking activities of the men could phrase his preference in sex terms; he could assume women's dress and occupations, and proclaim that he really was more a woman than a man. In Mundugumor, where there is no such pattern, a man may engage in feminine activities, such as fishing, without its occurring to him to symbolize his behaviour in female attire. Without any contrast between the sexes and without any tradition of transvesticism, a variation in temperamental preference does not result in either homosexuality or transvesticism. As it is unevenly distributed over the world, it seems clear that transvesticism is not only a variation that occurs when there are different personalities decreed for men and women, but that it need not occur even there. It is in fact a social invention that has become stabilized among the American Indians and in Siberia, but not in Oceania.

I observed in some detail the behaviour of an American Indian youth who was in all probability a congenital invert, during the period when he was just making his transvesticism explicit. This man had, as a small boy, showed such marked feminine physical traits that a group of women had once captured him and undressed him to discover whether he was really a boy at all. As he grew older he began to specialize in women's occupations and to wear female underclothing, although he still affected the outer costume of a male. He carried in his pockets, however, a variety of rings and bangles such as were worn only by women. At dances in which the sexes danced separately, he would begin the evening dressed as a man and dancing with the men, and then, as if acting under some irresistible compulsion, he would begin to move closer and closer to the women, as he did so putting on one piece of jewelry after another. Finally a shawl would appear, and at the end of the evening he would be dressed as a *berdache*, a transvestite. The people were just beginning to speak of him as "she." I have cited his case in this connexion to make clear that this is the type of maladjusted individual with which this discussion is not concerned. His aberrancy appeared to have a specific physiologic origin; it was not a mere temperamental variation that his society had decided to define as feminine.

This discussion is concerned neither with the congenital invert nor with overt behaviour of the practising homosexual. There are, it is true, ways in which the different types of maladjustment intersect and reinforce each other, and the congenital invert may be found among those who have found shelter in transvesticism. But the deviants with whom we are concerned here are those individuals whose adjustment to life is conditioned by their temperamental affinity for a type of behaviour that is regarded as unnatural for their own sex and natural for the opposite sex. To produce this type of maladjustment, not only is it necessary to have a definite approved social personality, but also this personality must be rigidly limited to one of the two sexes. The coercion to behave like a member of one's own sex becomes one of the strongest implements with which the society attempts to mould the growing child into accepted forms. A society without a rigid sex-dichotomy merely says to the child who shows aberrant behaviour traits: "Don't behave like that." "People don't do that." "If you behave like that, people won't like you." "If you behave like that you will never get married." "If you behave like that, people will sorcerize you"—and so on. It invokes—as against the child's natural inclination to laugh or cry or sulk in the wrong places, to see insult where there is none, or fail to see insult that is intended—considerations of human conduct as socially defined, not of sex-determined conduct. The burden of the disciplinary song is: "You will not be a real human being unless you suppress these tendencies which are incompatible with our definition of humanity." But it does not occur to either the Arapesh or the Mundugumor to add: "You aren't behaving like a boy at all. You are behaving like a girl"—even when actually this may be the case. It will be remembered that among the Arapesh, boys, owing to their slightly different parental care, do cry more than girls and have temper tantrums until a later age. Yet because the idea of sex-difference in emotional behaviour is lacking, this real difference was never invoked. In societies without a sex-dichotomy of temperament, one aspect, one very basic aspect, of the child's sense of its position in

the universe is left unchallenged—the genuineness of its membership in its own sex. It can continue to watch the mating behaviour of its elders and pattern its hopes and expectations upon it. It is not forced to identify with a parent of opposite sex by being told that its own sex is very much in question. Some slight imitation of a father by a daughter, or of a mother by a son, is not seized upon and converted into a reproach, or a prophecy that the girl will grow up to be a tomboy or the boy a sissy. The Arapesh and Mundugumor children are spared this form of confusion.

Consider in contrast the way in which children in our culture are pressed into conformity: "Don't act like a girl." "Little girls don't do that." The threat of failing to behave like a member of one's own sex is used to enforce a thousand details of nursery routine and cleanliness, ways of sitting or relaxing, ideas of sportsmanship and fair play, patterns of expressing emotions, and a multitude of other points in which we recognize socially defined sex-differences, such as limits of personal vanity, interest in clothes, or interest in current events. Back and forth weaves the shuttle of comment: "Girls don't do that." "Don't you want to grow up to be a real man like Daddy?" —tangling the child's emotions in a confusion that, if the child is unfortunate enough to possess even in some slight degree the temperament approved for the opposite sex, may well prevent the establishment of any adequate adjustment to its world. Every time the point of sex-conformity is made, every time the child's sex is invoked as the reason why it should prefer trousers to petticoats, baseball-bats to dolls, fisticuffs to tears, there is planted in the child's mind a fear that indeed, in spite of anatomical evidence to the contrary, it may not really belong to its own sex at all.

How little weight the anatomical evidence of own sex has, as over against the social conditioning, was vividly dramatized recently in a case in a Middle Western city, where a boy was found who had lived twelve years as a girl, under the name of Maggie, doing a girl's tasks and wearing a girl's clothes. He had discovered several years before that his anatomy was that of a boy, but that did not suggest to him the possibility of being classified as a boy socially: Yet when social workers discovered the case and effected the change of his classification, he did not show any traits of inversion; he was merely a boy who had been mistakenly classified as a girl, and whose parents, for some reasons that were not discovered, refused to recognize and rectify their error. This bizarre case reveals the strength of social classification as over against merely anatomical membership in a sex, and it is this social classification which makes it possible for society to plant in children's minds doubts and confusions about their sex-position.

Such social pressure exerts itself in a number of ways. There is first the threat of sex-disenfranchisement against the child who shows aberrant tendencies, the boy who dislikes rough-and-tumble play or weeps when he is rebuked, the girl who is only interested in adventures, or prefers battering her playmates to dissolving in tears. Second, there is the attribution of the emotions defined as feminine to the boy who shows the mildest preference for one of the superficial sex-limited occupations or avocations. A small boy's interest in knitting may arise from a delight in his own ability to manipulate a needle; his interest in cooking may derive from a type of interest that might later make him a first-class chemist; his interest in dolls may spring from no tender cherishing feelings but from a desire to dramatize some incident. Similarly, a girl's overwhelming interest in horseback-riding may come from a delight in her own physical coordination on horseback, her interest in her brother's wireless set may come from pride in her proficiency in handling the Morse code. Some physical or intellectual or artistic potentiality may accidentally express itself in an activity deemed appropriate to the opposite sex. This has two results: The child is reproached for his choice and accused of having the emotions of the opposite sex, and also, because the occupational choice or hobby throws him more with the opposite sex, he may come in time to take on much of the socially sex-limited behaviour of that opposite sex.

A third way in which our dichotomy of social personality by sex affects the growing child is the basis it provides for a cross-sex identification with the parents. The invocation of a boy's identification with his mother to explain his subsequent assumption of a passive rôle towards members of his own sex is familiar enough in modern psychiatric theory. It is assumed that through a distortion of the normal course of personality development the boy fails to identify with his father and so loses the clue to normal "masculine" behaviour. Now there is no doubt that the developing child searching for clues to his social rôle in life usually finds his most important models in those who stand in a parental relationship to him during his early years. But I would suggest that we have still to explain why these identifications occur, and that the cause lies not in any basic femininity in the small boy's temperament, but in the existence of a dichotomy between the standardized behaviour of the sexes. We have to discover why a given child identifies with a parent of opposite sex rather than with the parent of its own sex. The most conspicuous social categories in our society—in most societies—are the two sexes. Clothes, occupation, vocabulary, all serve to concentrate the child's attention upon its similarity with the parent of the same sex. Nevertheless some children, in defiance of all this pressure, choose the parents of opposite sex, not to love best, but as the persons with whose motives and purposes they feel most at one, whose choices they feel they can make their own when they are grown.

Before considering this question further, let me restate my hypothesis. I have suggested that certain human traits have been socially specialized as the appropriate attitudes and behaviour of only one sex, while other human traits have been specialized for the opposite sex. This social specialization is then rationalized into a theory that the socially decreed behaviour is natural for one sex and unnatural for the other, and that the deviant is a deviant because of glandular defect, or development accident. Let us take a hypothetical case. Attitudes towards physical intimacy vary enormously among individuals and have been very differently standardized in different societies. We find primitive societies, such as those of the Dobu and the Manus, where casual physical contact is so interdicted for both sexes, so hedged about with rules and categories, that only the insane will touch another person lightly and casually. Other societies, such as that of the Arapesh, permit a great deal of easy physical intimacy between individuals of different ages and both sexes. Now let us consider a society that has specialized to one sex this particular temperamental trait. To men has been assigned the behaviour characteristic of the individual who finds casual physical contact intolerable, to women, as their "natural" behaviour, that of individuals who accept it easily. To men, the hand on the arm or across the shoulder, sleeping in the same room with another man, having to hold another man on the lap in a crowded automobile—every contact of this kind would be, by definition, repellent, possibly even, if the social conditioning were strong enough, disgusting or frightening. To women in this given society, however, physical contact that was easy and unstylized would be, by definition, welcome. They would embrace each other, caress each other's hair, arrange each other's clothes, sleep in the same bed, comfortably and without embarrassment. Now let us take a marriage between a well-brought-up man in this society, who would be intolerant of any physical casualness, and a well-brought-up woman, who would consider it as natural when displayed by women and never expect it among boys or men. To this couple is born a girl who displays from birth a *noli me tangere* attitude that nothing her mother can do will dispel. The little girl slips off her mother's lap, wriggles away when her mother tries to kiss her. She turns with relief to her father, who will not embarrass her with demonstrations of affection, who does not even insist upon holding her hand when he takes her for a walk. From such a simple clue as this, a preference that in the child is temperamental, in the father is socially stabilized male behaviour, the little girl may build up an identification with her father, and a theory that she is more like a boy than like a girl. She may come in time to be actually better adjusted in many other ways to the behaviour of the opposite sex. The psychiatrist who finds her later in life wearing mannish attire, following a male occupation, and unable to find happiness in marriage may say that identification with the opposite sex was the cause of her failure to adjust as a woman. But this explanation does not reveal the fact that the identification would not have occurred in these terms if there had been no dichotomy of sex-attitudes in the society. The Arapesh child who is more like a reserved father than like a demonstrative mother may feel that it resembles its father more than its mother, but this has no further effects on its personality in a society in which it is not possible to "feel like a man" or "feel like a woman." The accident of a differentiation of sex-attitudes makes these chance identifications dynamic in the adjustment of the child.

This example is admittedly hypothetical and simple. The actual conditions in a modern society are infinitely more complicated. To list merely some of the kinds of confusions that occur should be sufficient to focus attention upon the problem. One of the child's parents may be aberrant, and therefore be a false guide to the child in its attempt to find its rôle. Both the children's parents may deviate from the norm in opposite ways, the mother showing more pronounced temperamental traits usually specialized as male, the father showing the opposite traits. This condition is very likely to occur in modern society, in which, because it is believed marriage must be based upon contrasting personalities, deviant men often choose deviant women. So the child, groping for clues, may make a false identification because its own temperament is like that decreed for the opposite sex, or a false identification because, while it is itself fitted for easy adjustment, the parent of its own sex is maladjusted.

I have discussed first identification along temperamental lines, but the identification may also be made in other terms. The original identification may be through intelligence or specific artistic gifts, the gifted child identifying with the more gifted parent, regardless of sex. Then, if the double standard of personality exists, this simple identification on the basis of ability or interest will be translated into sex terms, and the mother will lament: "Mary is always working with Will's drafting instruments. She hasn't any more normal girl's interests at all. Will says it's a pity she wasn't born a boy." From this comment, it is very easy for Mary to come to the same conclusion.

Worth mentioning here is the way in which the boy's plight differs from the girl's in almost every known society. Whatever the arrangements in regard to descent or ownership of property, and even if these formal outward arrangements are reflected in the temperamental relationships between the two sexes, the prestige values always attach to the occupations of men, if not entirely at the expense of the women's occupations, at least to a great extent. It almost always follows, therefore, that the girl "who should have been a boy" has at least the possibility of a partial participation in activities that are surrounded by the aura of masculine prestige. For the boy "who should have been a girl" there is no such possibility open. His participation in women's activities is almost always a matter for double reproach: he has shown himself unworthy to be categorized as a man, and has thereby condemned himself to activities with a low prestige value.

Furthermore, it is seldom that the particular attitudes and interests which have been classified as feminine in any society have been given any very rich expression in art or in literature. The girl who finds the defined masculine interests closer to her own can find for herself forms of vicarious expression; the boy who might have found similar outlets if there were a comparable feminine art and literature is denied such satisfactory escape. Kenneth Grahame has immortalized the perplexity of all small boys before the special and limited interests of girls in his famous chapter, "What They Talked About":

"She's off with those Vicarage girls again," said Edward, regarding Selina's long black legs twinkling down the path. "She goes out with them every day now; and as soon as ever they start, all their heads go together and they chatter, chatter, chatter, the whole blessed time! I can't make out what they find to talk about. . . ."

"P'raps they talk about birds'-eggs," I suggested sleepily . . . "and about ships, and buffaloes, and desert islands; and why rabbits have white tails; and whether they'd sooner have a schooner or a cutter; and what they'll be when they're men—at least, I mean there's a lot of things to talk about, if you *want* to talk."

"Yes; but they don't talk about those sort of things at all," Edward persisted. "How *can* they? They don't *know* anything; they can't do anything—except play the piano, and nobody would want to talk about *that;* and they don't care about anything—anything sensible, I mean. So what *do* they talk about? . . . But it's these girls I can't make out. If they've anything really sensible to talk about, how is it nobody knows what it is? And if they haven't—and we know they *can't* have, naturally—why don't they shut up their jaw? This old rabbit here—*he* doesn't want to talk. . . ."

"O but rabbits *do* talk!" interposed Harold. "I've watched them often in their hutch. They put their heads together and their noses go up and down, just like Selina's and the Vicarage girls'!" . . .

"Well, if they do," said Edward unwillingly, "I'll bet they don't talk such rot as those girls do!" Which was ungenerous, as well as unfair; for it has not yet transpired —nor has it to this day—*what* Selina and her friends talked about.[1]

This perplexity is likely to remain throughout life. The woman who either by temperament or accident of training has become more identified with the interests of men, if she cannot adjust to the current sex-standards, loses out in her essentially feminine rôle of childbearing. The man who has been disenfranchised from his own sex's interests suffers a subtler disenfranchisement, since a great part of the artistic symbolism of his society is rendered unavailable and there is no substitute to which he can turn. He remains a confused and bewildered person, unable to feel as men "naturally" feel in his society, and equally unable to find any satisfaction in rôles that have been defined by women, although their social personality is more akin to his temperament.

And so, in a thousand ways, the fact that it is necessary to feel not only like a member of a given society in a given period, but like a member of one sex and not like a member of the other, conditions the development of the child, and produces individuals who are unplaced in their society. Many students of personality lay these multiple, imponderable maladjustments to "latent homosexuality." But such a judgment is fathered by our two-sex standard; it is *post hoc* diagnosis of a result, not diagnosis of a cause. It is a judgment that is applied not only to the invert but to the infinitely more numerous individuals who deviate from the social definition of ~ppropriate behaviour for their sex.

If these contradictory traits of temperament which different societies have regarded as sex-linked are not sex-linked, but are merely human potentialities specialized as the behaviour of one sex, the presence of the deviant, who need no longer be branded as a latent homosexual, is inevitable in every society that insists upon artificial connexions between sex and bravery, or between sex and positive self-feeling, or between sex and a preference for personal relations. Furthermore, the lack of correspondence between the actual temperamental constitution of members of each sex and the rôle that a culture has assigned to them has its reverberations in the lives of those individuals who were born with the expected and correct temperament. It is often assumed that in a society which designates men as aggressive and dominating, women as responsive and submissive, the maladjusted individuals will be the dominant, aggressive woman and the responsive, submissive man. Theirs is, indubitably, the most difficult position. Human contacts of all sorts, and especially courtship and marriage, may present insoluble problems to them. But consider also the position of the boy naturally endowed with an aggressive, dominating temperament and reared to believe that it is his masculine rôle to dominate submissive females. He is trained to respond to responsive and submissive behaviour in others by a display of his self-conscious aggressiveness. And then he encounters not only submissive females, but also submissive males. The stimulus to dominating behaviour, to an insistence upon unquestioning loyalty and reiterated statements of his importance, is presented to him in one-sex groups, and a "latent homosexual" situation is created. Similarly, such a man has been taught that his ability to dominate is the measure of his manhood, so that submissiveness in his associates continually reassures him. When he encounters a woman who is as naturally dominating as he is himself, or even a woman who, although not dominating temperamentally, is able to outdistance him in some special skill or type of work, a doubt of his own manhood is set up in his mind. This is one of the reasons why men who conform most closely to the accepted temperament for males in their society are most suspicious and hostile towards deviating women who, in spite of a contrary training, show the same temperamental traits. Their hold upon their conviction of their own sex-membership rests upon the non-occurrence of similar personalities in the opposite sex.

And the submissive, responsive woman may find herself in an equally anomalous position, even though her culture has defined her temperament as the proper one for women. Trained from childhood to yield to the authority of a dominant voice, to bend all of her energies to please the more vulnerable egotism of dominant persons, she may often encounter the same authoritative note in a feminine voice and thus she, who is by temperament the ideal woman in her society, may find women so engrossing that marriage adjustments never enter the picture. Her involvement in devotion to members of her own sex may in turn set up in her doubts and questions as to her essential femininity.

Thus the existence in a given society of a dichotomy of social personality, of a sex-determined, sex-limited personality, penalizes in greater or less degree every individual born within it. Those whose temperaments are indubitably aberrant fail to adjust to the accepted standards, and by their very presence, by the anomalousness of their responses, confuse those whose temperaments are the expected ones for their sex. So in practically every mind a seed of doubt, of anxiety, is planted, which interferes with the normal course of life.

But the tale of confusions is not ended here. The Tchambuli, and in a milder degree parts of modern America, represent a further difficulty that a culture which defines personality in terms of sex can invent for its members. It will be remembered that while Tchambuli theory is patrilineal, Tchambuli practice gives the dominant position to women, so that the position of the man with aberrant—that is, dominating—temperament is rendered doubly difficult by the cultural forms. The cultural formulation that a man has paid for his wife and can therefore control her continually misleads these aberrant individuals into fresh attempts to such control, and brings them into conflict with all their childhood training to obey and respect women, and their wives' training to expect such respect. Tchambuli institutions and the emphases of their society are, to a certain extent, at odds with one another. Native history attributes a high development of dominating temperaments to various neighbouring tribes, whose women have for many generations run away and married the Tchambuli. In explanation of its own inconsistencies, it invokes the situation that was just frequent enough among the Arapesh to confuse the adjustments of men and women there. These inconsistencies in Tchambuli culture were probably increased by a diminished interest in war and head-hunting and a greater interest in the delicate arts of peace. The importance of the women's economic activities may also have increased without any corresponding enhancement of the men's economic rôle. Whatever the historical causes, and they are undoubtedly multiple and complex, Tchambuli today presents a striking confusion between institutions and cultural emphasis. And it also contains a larger number of neurotic males than I have seen in any other primitive culture. To have one's aberrancy, one's temperamental inability to conform to the prescribed rôle of responsive dancing attendance upon women, apparently confirmed by institutions—this is too much, even for members of a primitive society living under conditions far simpler than our own.

Modern cultures that are in the throes of adjusting to women's changing economic position present comparable difficulties. Men find that one of the props of their dominance, a prop which they have often come to think of as synonymous with that dominance itself—the ability to be the sole support of their families—has been pulled from beneath them. Women trained to believe that the possession of earned income gave the right to dictate, a doctrine which worked well enough as long as women had no incomes, find themselves more and more often in a confused state between their real position in the household and the one to which they have been trained. Men who have been trained to believe that their sex is always a little in question and who believe that their earning power is a proof of their manhood are plunged into a double uncertainty by unemployment; and this is further complicated by the fact that their wives have been able to secure employment.

All such conditions are aggravated in America also by the large number of different patterns of decreed behaviour for each sex that obtain in different national and regional groups, and by the supreme importance of the pattern of intersex behaviour that children en-counter within the closed four walls of their homes. Each small part of our complex and stratified culture has its own set of rules by which the power and complementary balance between the sexes is maintained. But these rules differ, and are sometimes even contradictory, as between different national groups or economic classes. So, because there is no tradition which insists that individuals should marry in the group within which they were reared, men and women are continually marrying whose pictures of the interrelationships between the sexes are entirely different. Their confusions are in turn transmitted to their children. The result is a society in which hardly anyone doubts the existence of a different "natural" behaviour for the sexes, but no one is very sure what that "natural" behaviour is. Within the conflicting definitions of appropriate behaviour for each sex, almost every type of individual is left room to doubt the completeness of his or her possession of a really masculine or a really feminine nature. We have kept the emphasis, the sense of the importance of the adjustment, and at the same time we have lost the ability to enforce the adjustment.

Note

[1] From *The Golden Age,* by Kenneth Grahame. Copyright 1895, 1922, by Dodd, Mead and Company, Inc.

THE WOMAN IN AMERICA

In the United States today it is clear that part of the traditional status of women is breaking down. Traditionally, women were expected to devote their lives to the care of the family, and to enter only indirectly into economic institutions. An exception was made for certain occupations such as teaching, nursing, and social work, but by and large it was unmarried women who were free to enter these fields as a kind of "second-best" alternative to marriage. At present, sizable and growing numbers of women are in the labor force, and many of these women workers are married. The change observed in this aspect of the female status raises the question of whether other changes may not also be occurring in the direction of lessening the distinction between appropriate behavior for women and men. Many social reformers feel that such changes would be desirable, and they place faith in the increasing entry of women into the economy as a means of achieving these changes. This selection examines the issue in the context of a professionally oriented school of nursing.

> The reformers' faith is groundless. The student nurses possess a very traditional view of the female role. The percentage ranking work and career as an important goal for women, far from increasing, declines during nursing school from entry to graduation, despite the students' exposure to contrary values on the part of the teachers. Furthermore, the young nurses' attitude towards their work is narrowly vocational, rather than professional, and professionalism declines over time, again despite the efforts of the teaching staff. That there is no increase in the percentage planning graduate work supports the validity of the other findings.

This pessimistic news for the reformers is subject to various qualifications, as the authors note. Perhaps experience beyond nursing school may have a different effect, or perhaps the fact that nursing is after all a traditionally female profession exercises adverse selection in terms of a lack of predisposition to "emancipation." In the absence of data in support of these explanations, it seems best to speculate that the aspects of the traditional female status concerning commitment to family and related values are still firmly engrained in middle-class American girls, despite their entering the labor force at a professional level.

Selection 34
THE CAREER OUTLOOK OF PROFESSIONALLY EDUCATED WOMEN
Fred Davis and Virginia L. Olesen

Despite the pronounced trend since World War II for more American women to secure employment outside the home, social critics continue to express misgivings over the range and distribution of their participation in the labor force, the quality of their commitment to vocations, and the manner in which they are attempting to integrate modern work roles with more traditional feminine roles.[1] Proponents of a new emancipation for women focus such concern mainly on college women, seeing them as most able to help meet the skill requirements of an advanced industrial society and to innovate versions of the female role which better synthesize vocational commitments with marriage, child-rearing, and home-making. A widely held view of such reformers is that greatly expanded recruitment of college women into the professions would act as a social stimulus toward effecting a more emancipated reconstitution of women's status in

Reprinted from *Psychiatry*, 28:4, 1965, pp. 334–345, by permission of the authors and by special permission of The William Alanson White Psychiatric Foundation, Inc., which holds the copyright.

American society. It is this thesis which we attempt to assay here by an analysis of longitudinal questionnaire data from five classes of collegiate student nurses, evaluating our findings in the light of possibly qualifying influences such as the students' membership in a female profession, their predominantly middle- and upper-middle-class backgrounds, and the trustworthiness of present career orientations for predicting future work behavior.

Those who urge college women to prepare themselves for careers in the professions and higher technical occupations recognize—and, indeed, approve of—the fact that most of them will marry and have children, activities which in the orthodox view are sufficient unto themselves and preclude any serious commitment to vocation.[2] But, of course, it is exactly the orthodox view that reformers seek to amend, regarding it as inherently fallacious and seeing it as perhaps the chief barrier to a needed redefinition of woman's status in society.

We shall not here do justice to the whole breadth and tenor of the critique directed by reformers against the conventional ideology of the woman's role, nor set forth in detail the many interrelated values that are seen as accruing to women, the family, and society through their assuming a more vital commitment to professional work. The following, however, are some of the values usually cited.

First, many professions—medicine, nursing, teaching, engineering, to mention a few—are already, or shortly will be, facing critical shortages of personnel which could in large part be relieved by the recruitment of women to these fields. Second, unlike clerical or unskilled service work into which many capable women now drift for want of preparation in intellectually more exacting pursuits, the professions represent a meaningful extension of the liberal education that most college women receive. Moreover, some observers speculate that with the increase of automation in the clerical, service, and manufacturing sectors of the economy, the day may not be far off when the woman college graduate without professional skills will be virtually unemployable, except possibly at tasks so mindless as to make a mockery of her higher education. Third, save for the unusually talented few who can achieve a career in the creative or performing arts, the professions, broadly speaking, are the only fields that can motivate, engage, and adequately reward women who might want to combine a career with family life. Indeed, it is the reformer's vision that were some such development to transpire on a large enough scale, women might gradually alter their self-concept as the "weaker" or "second" sex and sufficiently recast the cultural definition of their role to facilitate a freer and less guilt-ridden commitment to vocation. Since this kind of redefinition of the adult female role would entail an adaptive redefinition in the adult male role as well, new norms and understandings of a more flexible and equalitarian cast would in time come to govern the relations of the sexes, not only in marriage but, derivatively, in courtship and child-rearing.[3] Needless to say, many adjustments other than these ideational ones would also have to come to pass in order for the family and occupational system to assimilate cultural change of this magnitude.[4] But these as a rule are regarded as less of an obstacle by reformers than is the overhauling of those rentier-based Victorian attitudes which still exert so pronounced an influence on the ethos of family life and on the articulation of feminine roles therein.[5]

Like most broadly conceived programs of social action, the one we have described above defies any concrete empirical assessment of its implicit validity, for its attainment is in large measure contingent on major changes in cultural values. Whether values will change in the desired direction and will bring with them corresponding modifications in the institutional forms that now structure women's roles can be argued, speculated upon, or, at best, inferred; they cannot be scientifically predicted with any certainty, much less proved or disproved. A mode of inquiry which can, however, throw light on the issue is that of isolating institutional segments of the contemporaneous society wherein certain, if not all, of the requisites posited by the reformer's program can be located, and then assessing the extent to which predicated alterations in role conceptions and value perspectives are being realized. This procedure, which is the one we have followed, approximates a small-scale "natural experiment" which, despite its numerous methodological shortcomings for the larger problem at hand, offers some empirical basis for weighing the assumptions, assertions, and prognostications contained in the reformer's critique. Certainly our method will afford no secure basis for generalizing on the situation and prospects of women in American society. But, if one bears in mind the circumstances wherein our natural experiment meets and falls short of the programmatic prescriptions of reformers, some insight may be gained into the current validity of certain of their assumptions. Our procedure may also uncover as yet unanticipated opportunities and obstacles in the realization of their prospectus.

The study

Our data are drawn from a three-year study of the development of professional identities among student nurses attending a university school of nursing in a large metropolitan area.[6] Although several kinds of data were gathered (namely, fieldwork observations, longitudinal panel interviews, questionnaires, and personality inventories), those we shall report on here derive mainly from questionnaires administered to five classes of students who were in residence at the school for varying periods during the time span of the study.

As indicated above, a prime focus of the study has been to determine whether, and in what ways, professional education in nursing influences the student's basic attitudes toward and imagery of work in relation to women's roles—that is, the relative value accorded work in her projected life scheme, the meanings she attaches to work generally and to work in nursing in particular, the quality of her commitment to nursing, and her general views on the situation of American women. Our interest in these topics was spurred not only by the broad social issues alluded to above, but by certain local, indigenous matters as well.

As our fieldwork with students and faculty early revealed, the school in which this study was made is one which, because of the high standing it enjoys among collegiate schools of nursing, places strong emphasis on the development of career and leadership orientations in its students. From the outset, they are urged to consider graduate work in nursing. Much stress is given to career planning in general and to the role that graduates of the school are expected to play as innovators of nursing practice, as bearers of advanced doctrine and techniques, and as potential contributors to knowledge in the field.[7] While an old-fashioned feminist position is carefully eschewed, repeated reference is made to the possibility and social desirability of combining a *career* (not simply work) in nursing with marriage and children, if not during the preschool child phase of the family life cycle, then soon thereafter. In a course given in the senior year these themes are amplified in the context of a broad survey of the sociohistorical development of the profession, its problems, and prospects.

Clearly, something other than an orthodox definition of the adult female role is implied by these institutional emphases.[8] The obvious question, though, is what impact, if any, do they make on the students. These are by and large girls of middle-class and upper-middle-class background, reared in large and medium-sized cities and affiliated predominantly with the more socially prestigeful Protestant denominations, such as Episcopal, Congregational, or Unitarian. Less than fifteen per cent classify as working-class according to Hollingshead's Index of Social Position,[9] and an equally small proportion is Catholic. Except for a handful of Orientals and even fewer Negroes, all are white. Prior to enrollment in the school all had attended college for at least two years, the majority of them at a campus noted for its high academic standards. Their grade point averages at entry place them as fully on a scholastic par with students completing the normal four-year undergraduate college curriculum.

Findings

In this section we shall deal with various facets of what, for want of a better term, we designate as the *career outlook* of the students —that is, an attitudinal complex of opinions, aspirations, and plans concerning the place they are prepared to accord to work in their adult lives. In particular, we will be concerned with the direction and magnitude of change in career outlook from time of entry into the school to graduation.

The relevant data derive from responses to identical questionnaire items administered to four (and, in the case of one item, to five) classes of students at entry and/or graduation. With one class, that of 1963, it was possible to secure both entry and graduation data. With the other four classes, it was possible, given the time span of the study, to secure only entry data (classes of 1964 and 1965) or graduation data (classes of 1961 and 1962). In the tables that follow, therefore, two kinds of statistical comparisons will be made: Those between the entry and graduation responses of the thirty-eight students who comprise the class of 1963,[10] and those between the *entry* responses of two post-1963 classes (1964 and 1965) and the *graduation* responses of one or both pre-1963 classes (1961 and 1962). Despite the larger number in the latter comparison, we view the findings resulting from it as primarily corroborative or qualifying of those registered by the class of 1963 wherein the responses of *the same people* are compared at two points in time.[11]

In presenting our findings on students' career outlooks we shall proceed from the general to the specific, beginning with those which, at one extreme, reflect a rather broad ideological orientation to issues concerning the proper role of adult women in American society, and ending with those which, at the other extreme, bear on so concrete a matter as plans to seek graduate education in nursing. In between we shall consider such intermediate attitudinal dimensions as the balance among possible womanly roles which students hope to achieve in their adult lives and the values (professional or vocational) that they seek to realize from work in nursing. This "several-layered" analysis of career outlook affords, in our estimate, a well-rounded picture of the place of a professional career in the projected life schemes of the students, and also uncovers points of consistency or strain among the component attitudes that make up career outlook. And, since changes in conceptions of the self and in role definition are often preceded by sensed strain among aspirations and expectations, we would regard such a finding as potentially supportive of the claim that professional education can lead women to important reformulations of their adult life role.

Table 1 summarizes in score form students' responses (*agree in the main, have mixed feelings, disagree in the main, no opinion*) to a series of ten value-laden allegations on the life situation of the contemporary American woman. Five of these were phrased so that they would accord with "reform" sentiments on the matter, while the other five gave voice to sentiments of a decidedly orthodox tendency.[12] A score was derived for each student by weighting (from zero to two) each of her ten responses according to how nearly it corresponded with a "reform" opinion toward the item in question. Means were then calculated for each class.

As may be inferred from Table 1, both at entry and at or near graduation students for the most part assume an orthodox stance on issues pertaining to the situation of American women. Had they on the average conceded so little as harboring "mixed feelings" toward most of the allegations, the mean reform scores registered by the several classes would have fallen in the vicinity of ten. As it is, none of the class means approaches this figure. What is even more significant, though, is the absence of change from entry to graduation despite the intervening three years of professional education. The class of 1963 registers much the same "low" score at both time points, and there is no significant difference between the mean scores of the combined classes of 1964 and 1965 at entry and of the class of 1962 a year prior to graduation. Thus it would seem fair to conclude that a professional education in nursing in no way alters the fundamentally conventional orientation to the adult female role that these students bring with them initially.

But it may be argued that items of so strident an ideological tendency as those included in the question hold little meaning for young women and that the responses elicited in no way reflect their tangible preoccupations with future life roles. Table 2 bears on this possible criticism, since it considers still another facet of the students' career outlook—namely, the relative value they attach to different thematic components in the adult female role.

Here, students were asked to rank, from one to four, four different attributes commonly associated with the adult female role. The question read: "Here are four kinds of womanly qualities admired in America today. Ideally, if you could arrange your life, which quality would you choose to emphasize *most*, which second most, which third, and which last: (1)

Table 1 Reform versus Orthodoxy in Students' Views of the Situation of American Women, at Entry and at Graduation

		At Entry				At Graduation			
Class	N	Mean Score*	S.D.		Class	N	Mean Score*	S.D.	P
1963	38	6.76	3.17		1963	38	7.79	3.56	NS‡
1964	28	6.86	3.16						
1965	49	6.24	3.21						
1964 and 1965	77	6.47	3.20		1962†	31	6.39	2.74	NS§

* The score range is 0 to 20, 20 signifying the maximum attainable "reform" score.
† Measured a year prior to actual graduation.
‡ Two-tailed *t* test for correlated samples. See Quinn McNemar, *Psychological Statistics* (second edition); New York, 1955; pp. 108–109.
§ Two-tailed *t* test for independent samples. (See McNemar, in ‡ footnote.)

Table 2   Percentages of Students, at Entry and Graduation, Assigning "Work and Career" to at Least Second Rank* in Their Projected Life Scheme

At Entry			At Graduation			
Class	N	Percent	Class	N	Percent	P
1963	38	82	1963	38	61	.10>p>.05†
1964	28	61				
1965	49	79				
1964 and 1965	77	73	1962	31	54	NS‡

* The one or two students in each class who rank "work and career" in first place are included in these proportions.

† Two-tailed McNemar test for change in related samples. See Sidney Siegel, *Non-parametric Statistics;* New York, McGraw-Hill, 1956; pp. 63–67.

‡ Two-tailed chi-square test for independent samples.

Great attractiveness to men, dresses stunningly, has charm and sophistication; (2) Devoted to her family, manages her home with great interest, cares well for her husband and children, enriches their lives; (3) Active in community affairs and performs good works which give her a position of leadership in the community; (4) Dedicated to work and career, believes that her work is significant in its own right, and is respected in her field." Since, as might be expected, overwhelming majorities at both time points—in every instance over 87 per cent—rank "home and family" in first place, Table 2 examines the more modest question of how many students assigned "work and career" to at least second place in their projected life scheme. In other words, granted that a professional nursing education as such stands little chance of displacing "home and family" from its ideational hegemony, does it at least enhance the *relative* value accorded "work and career"?

Again, the results are, at best, inconclusive for those who would maintain that professional education as such induces women to realign values attaching to the adult female role. Whereas majorities of students at both time points do in fact rank "work and career" second, after first selecting "home and family," there is no increase in the proportion doing so from time of entry to graduation. On the contrary, Table 2 reveals a distinct trend in the opposite direction, and for the class of 1963 the percentage drop in those prepared to accord "work and career" as much as second place is large enough to approach statistical significance.

Still it may be claimed that, while "work and career" do not come to occupy a more prominent place in the projected life scheme of these students, to the extent that they attach any importance to them at all, the quality of their commitment is strengthened by virtue of having received a *professional* education. To test this assumption, entering and graduating students were asked how important (*highly, fairly, slightly, not at all*) they would regard each of nine items when contemplating "work in nursing following graduation." Five of the items were of a distinctly vocational bent (for example, good pay, regular hours, built-in promotion) while the other four reflected work goals which are regarded customarily as professional (for example, to be a spokesman and representative of the field, to follow through on that which interests and excites one in the field). On the basis of her responses a professional values score was calculated for each entering and graduating student.

These data are summarized in Table 3, which shows a close parallel between this facet of the students' career outlook and those already presented in Tables 1 and 2. None of the class means approaches what could be thought of as a high professional values score. Moreover, there is strong evidence that the rather middling scores registered at entry "deteriorate" toward vocationalism by the time of graduation; both time point comparisons, that involving the class of 1963 alone and that between two later entering classes (1964 and 1965) and one prior graduating class (1962), show significant declines in professional values scores. The attenuation of professional perspec-

Table 3   Professional Values Scores of Students, at Entry and Graduation

		At Entry				At Graduation			
Class	N	Mean Score*	S.D.	Class	N	Mean Score*	S.D.	P
1963	38	14.76	2.88	1963	38	12.18	2.88	.001 †
1964	28	13.50	2.58					
1965	49	13.65	2.53					
1964 and 1965	77	13.60	2.53	1962	31	12.39	3.46	.05 ‡

* Two score range is 0 to 27, 27 signifying the maximum attainable "professional" score.
† Two-tailed t test for correlated samples. See Quinn McNemar, *Psychological Statistics* (second edition); New York, Wiley, 1955; pp. 108–109.
‡ Two-tailed t test for independent samples. (See McNemar, in † footnote.)

tives, and the corresponding encroachment of vocational attitudes, occur despite the strenuous attempts which we have observed on the part of the school to instill strong professional commitments in its students.

Finally, to round out the inquiry into developmental trends in the students' career outlook, we thought it worthwhile to examine some very tangible facet of the issue to see whether at this level of specificity a contrary or qualifying tendency (as is often the case with complex attitudinal sets) would reveal itself. The question selected dealt with the student's estimate of the likelihood that she would seek graduate education in nursing "at some time in the foreseeable future" following graduation. A five-point scale was used ranging from "highly probable" to "highly improbable," with a sixth residual category for students who "have not given any thought to it." Our working hypothesis was that if larger proportions of students at graduation than at entry declared it highly or fairly probable that they would go on to graduate school, then it could be assumed that in certain respects at least the curriculum does engender more positive career commitments. But, as Table 4 shows, there is no warrant for this assumption. The proportions so declaring remain about the same at both time points, roughly between a quarter and a third; no significant increase or decrease is recorded in either of the time point comparisons. At this level too, then, we are unable to qualify our general finding that professional education in nursing in no way inclines these young college women to reformulate their essentially orthodox perspectives on the adult female role.

Table 4   Percentages of Students, at Entry and Graduation, Declaring That It Is "Highly" or "Fairly" Probable That They Will Seek Graduate Education in Nursing

	At Entry				At Graduation			
Class	N	Percent Highly or Fairly		Class	N	Percent Highly or Fairly	P
1963	38	21		1963	38	26	NS*
1964	28	29		1961	41	32	
1965	49	39		1962	31	23	
1964 and 1965	77	35		1961 and 1962	72	28	NS†

* Two-tailed McNemar test for change in related samples. See Sidney Siegel, *Non-Parametric Statistics*; New York, McGraw-Hill, 1956; pp. 63–67.
† Two-tailed chi-square test for independent samples.

Discussion

What implications do these apparently negative findings hold for those who look to the education of college women in the professions as a primary means for eventually altering the status of women in American society? At least three issues implicit in our study merit discussion before even the most tentative of conclusions can be drawn. These are: (1) The significance to be attributed to the fact that the young women in our study have entered a predominantly female rather than a male profession or one more nearly balanced as to sex; (2) The relationship, if any, of their preponderantly middle-class social origins to the orthodoxy of their sex-role orientation; and (3) the predictive value of current attitudes toward work and career for estimating actual behavior in these spheres at some later phase in the students' life cycle.

The female professions. A number of recent studies of women electing, studying, or working in such predominantly female professions as teaching, nursing, social work, and librarianship have been fairly consistent in noting that whatever else motivates and sustains women in these pursuits, it is rarely the aim of furthering a career. Or, to put the matter somewhat more circumspectly, it has in general been noted that whereas large majorities of women in these fields are genuinely attached to (that is, neither alienated nor disaffected from) the day-by-day work of their field, such attachment only rarely embraces a deep career commitment to the profession per se.[13] Thus, on the basis of findings wholly consistent with our own, Mason, Dressel, and Bain conclude that, compared to beginning men teachers, beginning women teachers are considerably less intent on a continuing career of professional advancement in the field of education.[14] Katz and Martin in a study of student nurses observe that there is little about their recruitment to nursing which testifies to an unfolding process of commitment to the field.[15] Rather, they point to the important influence of apparently extraneous situational factors in the decision to study nursing. Still other studies of nurses, both student and graduate, concur in the finding that relatively small numbers contract long-range career commitments or regard their profession as a major organizing focus of their lives.[16]

It would seem reasonable to suggest, therefore, that at present membership in a female profession as such in no way entails a primary life commitment to career or any substantial modification in the traditional conception of the adult female role. Despite the sometimes considerable demands in time, training, and effort which these professions exact, women in them continue to gear their major life decisions to the rewards and exigencies emanating from such extraoccupational roles as wife, mother, and homemaker. Only a small minority—typically the older, unmarried, and childless—evidences serious career commitments, a circumstance which, incidentally, helps account for the fact that it is they who are most commonly found in leadership positions in the women's professions.[17] This has led to the speculation that, unlike the more homogeneous marital and familial status configurations obtaining in the male professions, the discrepancy in life-situation between leaders and rank and file in the female professions has acted in circuitous ways to further attenuate the fostering of strong career commitments. Because so many young women in the female professions are married or can still entertain a reasonable hope of marrying and raising a family, they are prone, despite modest career achievements, to view their own situation as peculiarly advantaged in comparison with that of leaders in their field. Hence, the "costs" of career success are often seen as incommensurate with the gains. Needless to say, this hardly encourages the kind of career modeling necessary for advancement in a profession. Second, the absence of this type of career stimulus further spares the rank and file from any necessity to radically refurbish their concept of their social role as women.

Some evidence has begun to accumulate which suggests that girls who choose the female professions are perhaps even more feminine (in the conventional sense), even more committed to traditional values, than are their vocationally more indifferent peers—not to mention the scant few who aspire to a predominantly male field of work. On the basis of a series of studies on adolescent and college girls inaugurated in the mid-fifties, Douvan holds that, by and large, girls who enter a field such as nursing or teaching are further along than those who have not decided on any occupation in resolving the issue of feminine identity in terms consonant with the *traditional* cultural definition of the adult female role.[18] Having worked through this troublesome aspect of growing up, such girls are psychologically freer to pursue secondary goals of an occupational sort which can complement, and perhaps even facilitate, the realization of their feminine ego ideal. (The qualities of nurturance, succorance, and expressiveness so widely attributed to such fields as nursing and grade-school teaching comprise but one facet of this assumed complementarity in sexual and occupational roles.) Patently sensible though such a stance may be for a young woman entering a female profession, it is hardly the mettle from which innovation, much less revolution, in sexual roles is fashioned.

While the as yet incomplete data of Douvan warrant caution concerning full acceptance of her thesis, the absence of any strongly contradictory findings lends it more than a purely hypothetical status. Until disproven, it can only augment the mass of existing evidence that casts doubt on the ability of the female professions to serve as wellsprings, as it were, for altering presently prescribed cultural definitions of the adult female role. At minimum, this recognition should qualify somewhat the urgings of reformers for greater participation by college women in the professions. Instead, greater attention might be paid to the varieties of professional milieus and their differing potentials for reconstituting the social-psychological forces that shape the role of women in American society.

Does this imply, then, that the reformer's goal would stand a better chance of attainment if more college women were to enter the professions now dominated by men? Plausible though the suggestion sounds, the data that might illuminate it are extremely sparse, if only because so few American women undertake professional studies in these fields and even fewer have careers in them. It is known, for instance, that since the nineteen-thirties the proportion of women graduates from schools of medicine, law, engineering, and architecture, as well as the proportion receiving Ph.D.'s in academic disciplines, has either declined or, at best, remained stable. In absolute numbers, too, what few increases have been recorded have been far from substantial.[19] Clearly, the postwar trends toward earlier marriage, particularly among college youth, and toward an increase in middle-class family size have much to do with the loss of women recruits to male fields. As for the small number of women who are actually studying or working in them, very little is known. Judging from some scattered, small-scale studies, it appears that a comparatively large proportion are unmarried. But whether they are unmarried or married, the admittedly scant evidence suggests that even these highly trained professional women are constrained, both by circumstance and inner conviction, to forego many of the career opportunities open to their male counterparts.[20]

Be that as it may, there has not as yet accumulated in America a sufficient fund of historical experience by which to judge the consequences for family and economic life that might result from greatly broadened participation by women in the male professions, the sciences, and other spheres of advanced intellectual endeavor. The prospect remains an open and promising one which merits the careful consideration and planning of those who seek a new status for women in society.

Class recruitment sources and career outlook. Early in this paper we noted that the social background of the collegiate nursing students were largely urban, Protestant, and middle-class or upper-middle-class. Since it is likely that for some time to come the large majority of college women entering professional schools of *either* the male or female stripe will possess essentially this kind of background, it is worth speculating on the relationship of middle-class social origins to the maintenance of orthodox sex-role orientations among professionally educated women. Since there is usually a broad correspondence between a dominant cultural group in a society and the prevailing morality of that society, it might be argued that the experiential base for restructuring a core social role like that of woman lies not with the ideologically dominant middle classes, but elsewhere in the social structure, perhaps among upwardly mobile working-class or marginally ethnic girls who may not have fully assimilated the prevailing morality. Accordingly, it could be argued that middle-class girls, like those so heavily represented in our study, are *least* likely to renounce the traditional imagery of the adult female role. Such may well be the case; at the same time, however, what evidence is there that upwardly mobile working-class girls, for example, develop a different outlook on their future adult roles than do middle-class girls?

Our own study thus far includes so few girls of working-class and ethnically marginal origins that we are unable to shed any light on the question. Nevertheless, the surprisingly few studies that treat this issue even tangentially indicate that socioeconomic origins make little if any difference in the career orientations or sex-role definitions of college girls. Thus, Goldsen in her study of Cornell women concludes, "no definite set of social characteristics appears to predispose a girl toward a career."[21] Similarly, the Simpsons find that among girls attending two Southern universities "career orientation is not affected by socioeconomic background *per se*."[22] In apparent contradiction is a 1951 study by Rose of women undergraduates at Minnesota in which he reports that economically "better off" students are less likely than "poorer" students to be preparing for a specific vocation in the professions and semi-professions.[23] Rose's classification of "poorer" students, however, is highly relative and includes, the reader gathers, few of working-class background.

It would seem, then, that the intriguing notion that upwardly mobile girls constitute a promising source for effecting change in adult women's roles through recruitment to the professions is at this juncture unsupported, at best. This can probably be accounted for by the dynamics of upward mobility in our society, in particular as experienced by females. It may be true that during adolescence the upwardly mobile girl reacts negatively to the low occupational status of her parents and begins to imagine attaining a more prestigeful place for herself through education and a career; yet in the course of achieving mobility, and through coming into close contact with middle-class youngsters, she doubtless also assimilates other values and perspectives associated with middle-class life styles. Chief among these, perhaps, is the belief that a too strong commitment to career is, inter alia, inimical to a happy marriage and feminine self-fulfillment. Hence, whatever career aspirations she may have entertained earlier are by late adolescence or early adulthood muted, and come increasingly to be displaced onto a prospective mate.

Present career outlook and future behavior.
Last we must consider whether presently perceived career orientation is a trustworthy index of future work behavior. Will, for example, the young student nurses in our study—who now seem so fixated on the traditional image of adult womanhood, who eschew any serious commitment to career, who contemplate future work mainly in terms of short-run situational benefits—be as attached to these views ten to fifteen years hence as they are today? Naturally, no certain answers can at this time be furnished to these questions. To accept, though, the students' present statements on work, career, and life-goals as determining their future behavior jars not only our commonsense understanding of an everyday world in which projects unfold, are abandoned, and again pursued, but denies as well any significant possibilities for change, for a reevaluation of life goals and a reemergence of arrested facets of the self at later stages in the life passage. On these grounds alone, the predictive value of our data must be treated with caution. Compounding the hazards of prediction in this area further, however, is much that is beginning to be learned about the general life situation of the married educated woman.

Especially relevant in this connection is the recurrent theme found in much recent sociological and psychological writing on American women concerning the reappraisal of life goals and self-concepts which occurs following the last child's entrance into grade school, typically when the mother is in her mid-thirties or early forties. Apparently, it is then that many educated women find themselves in the predicament of rediscovering aspirations for careers for which they have had little preparation. Indeed, so widespread is this phenomenon alleged to be that it has already earned the by now fashionably awesome and overworked appellation of "an identity crisis." Whether it is an identity crisis or, more simply, a sudden coping with problematic life alternatives, the phenomenon does testify to an important and, until recently, little appreciated psychocultural discontinuity in the adult woman's life cycle— a discontinuity which for educated women in particular engenders perhaps as much psychic turmoil as is attributed to the well-chronicled transition from adolescence to adulthood.

A remarkable aspect of this discontinuity— which, incidentally, has considerable bearing on the predictive value of our data—is the seeming incapacity of nubile Americans, be they college girls or not, to emphatically envision and plan for life contingencies as little removed in time as ten to fifteen years hence, when for all but a few the romantic aura of the connubial state and the domestic confinements of child-rearing will have passed.[24] In short, what is so deftly evaded at fair twenty returns to haunt at dispirited thirty-five.

How can we account for this anomaly in adult female socialization, especially in view of the widespread attention that the "discontented educated housewife" has received in recent years and the growing public awareness of the propensity of married women in their thirties and forties to return to the labor force? (And, while college girls can hardly be expected to show an interest in demographic phenomena, the fact is that the more education a married woman has, the more likely she is to be in the labor force in her middle to late adult years.)[25] Obviously, some of the problem must be attributed to a failure in transmission of values and life-style imagery between successive female generations. But whether this failure is due to a dearth or distortion of information given young women concerning contingencies they are likely to confront later in life, or to a kind of systemically induced selective inattention which is somehow functional for the transitional status of mate-seeker and prospective mother, is difficult to determine in the absence of any sustained research on the question.[26] On the one hand, it seems apparent, for example, that the working mother is neither a prominent nor a heroic figure in contemporary popular literature.[27] Also testifying in some part to an information gap is the evidence that college daughters of working and work-oriented mothers take a more positive view toward future employment, if not necessarily toward a career, than do those whose mothers have not worked or, if they have, view work by married women dimly.[28] On the other hand, arguing against an overly rationalistic "information-gap" explanation is the abundant testimony of educators and researchers on how peculiarly resistant young college women are, including the most intellectually gifted among them, to urgings that they prepare themselves for higher academic or professional pursuits, and how imperturbable they remain in the face of awesome warnings of the "reality shock" that awaits them should they fail to do so.[29]

In any case, these considerations constrain us not to take at face value what the collegiate nursing students now say about the place and meaning work will have for them later in life. As with countless women before them, and doubtlessly many more to follow, the gradual recognition with age that home and family, central though they be for woman, as for man, are neither all-consuming nor all-fulfilling will cause many to reformulate in action those orthodox life perspectives which now arrest them.[30] And, in the course of this reformulation, as new possibilities emerge and old expectancies fade, it is possible that a deeper engagement with career and profession might ensue. Granting even the attenuated career commitments that at present seem to be associated with the female professions, little in this realm of possibility can as yet be ruled out, so embryonic is the American experience of women's full participation in society.

Notes

[1] Alva Myrdal and Viola Klein, *Women's Two Roles;* London, Routledge and Kegan Paul, 1956; Betty Friedan, *The Feminine Mystique;* New York, Norton, 1963; Simone de Beauvoir, *The Second Sex;* London, Jonathan Cape, 1953; Issue on "The Woman in America," *Daedalus* (1964) 93.

[2] Mirra Komarovsky, "Cultural Contradictions and Sex Roles," *Amer. J. Sociology* (1946) 52: 184–189.

[3] See Alice S. Rossi, "Equality between the Sexes," in *Daedalus* (see footnote 1); pp. 607–652.

[4] For example: Extensive and low-cost nursery facilities in the community and at places of employment; greater ease of transport between home and job; more flexible work schedules for mothers of small children; liberally subsidized schemes of adult professional education for married women preparing to launch or return to careers.

[5] See Myrdal and Klein, in footnote 1.

[6] Admission into the school is preceded by two years of college liberal arts studies. Com-

pletion of the nursing curriculum entails another three years, at the end of which the student receives a B.S. degree and is eligible for an R.N. certificate.

[7] Fred Davis and Virginia L. Olesen, "Baccalaureate Students' Images of Nursing," *Nursing Research* (1964) 13: 8–15.

[8] Elvi Whittaker and Virginia L. Olesen, "The Faces of Florence Nightingale: Functions of the Heroine Legend in an Occupational Sub-culture," *Human Organization* (1964) 23: 123–130.

[9] August B. Hollingshead and Fredrick C. Redlich, *Social Class and Mental Illness: A Community Study;* New York, Wiley, 1958; pp. 387–397.

[10] Because we are here interested mainly in the effects of a *completed* professional education on the career outlooks of young women, we have eliminated from consideration all entering students in the classes of 1963, 1964, and 1965 who subsequently dropped out of school, a combined total of 28 out of 143. However, in a preliminary comparison of the entry questionnaire responses of dropouts and continuing students no important differences could be detected in their responses on a variety of items.

[11] Nonetheless, on the basis of their background characteristics and their responses, the five classes are strikingly similar.

[12] Examples of "reform" statements included in the question were: "Some radical alterations in the division of labor in the family ought to be made so that women can make their full contribution to social progress." "If society did not make women feel so guilty about outside agencies helping them in the care and upbringing of their children, more women would

want to work and neither they nor their children would suffer for it." Examples of "orthodox" statements were: "Regardless of her worldly accomplishments, a woman who never marries is more to be pitied than emulated." "There is something unnatural and unattractive about women who seem to be more preoccupied with their work and careers than they are with their homes."

[13] By career commitment we mean a relatively high propensity to sacrifice other life values in behalf of those represented by vocation. See Howard S. Becker, "Notes on the Concept of Commitment," *Amer. J. Sociology* (1960) 66: 32–40.

[14] Ward S. Mason, Robert J. Dressel, and Robert K. Bain, "Sex Role and the Career Orientation of Beginning Teachers," *Harvard Educ. Review* (1959) 29: 370–383.

[15] Fred E. Katz and Harry W. Martin, "Career Choice Processes," *Social Forces* (1962) 41: 149–154.

[16] See Everett C. Hughes, Helen M. Hughes, and Irwin Deutscher, *Twenty Thousand Nurses Tell Their Story;* Philadelphia, Lippincott, 1958; pp. 232–267; Ronald G. Corwin and Marvin J. Taves, "Nursing and Other Health Professions," in *Handbook of Medical Sociology,* edited by Howard E. Freeman, Sol Levine, and Leo G. Reeder; Englewood Cliffs, N.J., Prentice-Hall, 1963, pp. 204–206; Fred Davis and Virginia L. Olesen, "Initiation into a Women's Profession," *Sociometry* (1963) 26: 89–101.

[17] William A. Glaser, "Nursing Policy: Some Cross-National Comparisons," in *The Nursing Profession,* edited by Fred Davis; New York, Wiley (in press).

[18] Personal communication. See

also Elizabeth Douvan and Carol Kay, *Adolescent Girls;* Ann Arbor, Mich., Survey Research Center, Univ. of Mich. (undated); pp. 20–57.

[19] John B. Parrish, "Professional Womanpower as a National Resource," *Quart. Review Economics and Business* (1961) 1: 54–63.

[20] See Alberta E. Siegel and Miriam B. Haas, "The Working Mother: A Review of Research," *Child Development* (1963) 34: 513–542; p. 526; John Kosa and Robert E. Coker, Jr., "The Female Physician in Public Health," paper presented at the Annual Meeting of the American Sociological Association, Los Angeles, California, August, 1963; Jewell C. Field, "Factors Associated with Graduate School Attendance and Role Definitions of the Women Doctoral Candidates at the Pennsylvania State University," unpublished Master's Thesis, Pennsylvania State University, 1961.

[21] Rose K. Goldsen, Morris Rosenberg, Robin M. Williams, Jr., and Edward A. Suchman, *What College Students Think;* New York, Van Nostrand, 1960; p. 51.

[22] Richard L. Simpson and Ida H. Simpson, "Occupational Choice Among Career-Oriented College Women," *Marriage and Family Living* (1961) 23: 377–383; p. 379. See also Alberta E. Siegel and Elizabeth A. Curtis, "Familial Correlates of Orientation Toward Future Employment Among College Women," *J. Educ. Psychology* (1963) 54: 33–37; p. 36.

[23] Arnold M. Rose, "The Adequacy of Women's Expectations for Adult Roles," *Social Forces* (1951) 30: 73.

[24] See Paul Heist, "A Commentary on the Motivation and Education of College Women,"

J. Natl. Assn. Women Deans and Counselors (1962) 25: 59; and Mabel Newcomer, "Women's Education," *J. Natl. Assn. Women Deans and Counselors* (1960) 23: 38.

25 In a 1957 survey the highest rate of labor force participation among all groups of married women was the 44 percent recorded by college graduates aged 35 to 64. U.S. Department of Commerce, Bureau of the Census, *Educational Attainment of Workers, March 1957* (Current Population Reports, Labor Force, Series P–50), 1957. See also Mildred W. Weil, "An Analysis of the Factors Influencing Married Women's Actual or Planned Work Participation," *Amer. Sociol. Review* (1961) 26: 91–96.

26 For a discussion of categories of ignorance relevant in sociological analysis, see Louis Schneider, "The Role of the Category of Ignorance in Sociological Theory: An Explanatory Statement," *Amer. Sociol. Review* (1962) 27: 492–508.

27 Mary Hatch and David L. Hatch, "Problems of Married Working Women as Presented by Three Popular Working Women's Magazines," *Social Forces* (1958) 37: 148–153.

28 See Siegel and Curtis, in footnote 22.

29 See Heist, in footnote 24; John H. Bushnell, "Student Culture at Vassar," in *The American College*, edited by R. Nevitt Sanford; New York, Wiley, 1962; pp. 512–513.

From a programmatic standpoint, a crucial problem in engendering more positive career orientations among college women is that of deflating the "mystique" (see Friedan, in footnote 1) that now envelops the traditional version of the married middle-class woman's role, while simultaneously fostering in fact and in imagination emotionally viable representations of "the new woman" with whom young girls can identify. These are far from easy projects, and once undertaken are likely to produce effects in such spheres as childhood socialization, sex mores, and the division of labor in the family. How this would happen and with what emergent consequences for social life in general constitute, however, a vast terra incognita for the sociologist. This perhaps also suggests that the whole problem of discontinuity in adult female socialization holds much theoretical relevance for such central sociological issues as the dynamics of social change, the mechanisms of value transmission, and the ontological bonds between successive generations.

30 Some slight indication that the psychological expectancy of combining work—not necessarily a career—with marriage is being fostered among the student nurses is found in their responses to another of our questionnaire items. Asked how long they would choose to remain away from work in the event of having children, only 30 percent of 115 entering students said they would return as soon as their children entered grade school or sooner. Among 69 graduating students, however, 44 percent so indicated.

Chapter 13

THE FAMILY

FUNCTIONS OF THE FAMILY
Selection 35

CHANGING FUNCTIONS
Selection 36

A DYING INSTITUTION?
Selection 37

The family is an institution, by which is meant a recognized and accepted way of doing things. It is to be distinguished from a family, which is a group. The family is the set of norms pertaining to such groups.

The family takes many forms in different societies, although it is always focused about conjugal (man-and-wife) and parental relationships. It can be based upon one marriage or upon many. It can emphasize paternal, maternal, or both lines of descent. It can be highly extended, including people we might not think of as relatives, or, as in our own society, extend no farther than the isolated nuclear family of husband, wife, and children. The variation in family form among societies indicates that kinship is not only biological but is a social status, which, as in adoption, "blood brotherhood," and even marriage, can be entirely independent of biological relatedness.

The American family is very small and simple in comparison with family institutions in many other societies. Some of the most "primitive" societies have kinship systems so intricate and elaborate that ours looks quite "under-developed" in comparison. The isolated nuclear family which is the American ideal consists of parents and their children living independent from in-laws, grandparents, uncles, cousins, and other extended kin.

A consequence of the restriction in size and the independence of the American family is its relative instability. In many societies, the nuclear family is held together by a plethora of kin with an interest in its maintenance. These relatives exert pressure on the parents to stay together, and provide moral support in times of stress. The relatively high divorce rate in American society is related to the lack of these supports and pressures. A corresponding advantage of the isolated nuclear family is its great potential mobility, since it can relocate where there is an economic demand without having to move scores of additional relatives. Thus, the instability of the American family can be seen as a price paid for a free labor market.

An additional source of instability in the American family is its loss of functions to other institutions. The rural farm family of earlier Western societies was largely self-sufficient. It produced its own food, clothing, and shelter and educated its children in both secular and religious culture. The modern urban family has lost most of these functions. Even that phase of economic production known as housework—sewing, cooking, washing, and cleaning—is gradually. being taken over by other institutions, such as frozen food corporations and dry cleaners. It is easier today than ever before for an individual to live alone and dispense entirely with the family—for example, "Sara Lee" cooks much better and is far cheaper to support than the majority of American women. The only family functions that have thus far gone unchallenged by other institutions are the provision of affection and the primary socialization of children. Thus, the instability of the family can be seen as a price paid for a high standard of living.

The selections in this chapter concern the causes of the changing functions and growing instability of the family in America. All three authors direct their attention to the possibility of the disappearance of the family. In his study of the kibbutz, Selection 35, Melford Spiro lists the functions performed by the traditional family, and suggests that these functions have been totally taken over by other institutions in the kibbutz; however, in a later work he modifies his conclusion, holding that the institution of the couple in the kibbutz is equivalent to the family. W. F. Ogburn in Selection 36 indicates some reasons for changes experienced by the contemporary American family, but he is convinced that the family, though changing, is a vital and permanent institution in society. Barrington Moore thinks otherwise. In Selection 37 he predicts the ultimate demise of the family and its replacement by other, more efficient institutions.

FUNCTIONS OF THE FAMILY

Sociologists traditionally have considered the family to be a universal institution. Although there are significant variations in family structure from society to society, the nuclear family—husband, wife, and children—is said to exist everywhere. The reason usually given for the universality of the family is its suitability for the fulfillment of four basic needs of any society: regulation of sex, creation of children, their socialization, and their support.

In this selection, Melford Spiro suggests that although these four needs must be fulfilled everywhere, there is no logical reason why they have to be fulfilled by the family. Conceivably, a society may be found that utilizes other institutions for these purposes and dispenses with the family. No unambiguous example of such a society has been found so far, but Spiro thinks that the Israeli kibbutz may be interpreted as an exception to the universality of the family.

> Marriage and the family as usually understood in the social sciences are absent in the kibbutz (but not in Israeli society as a whole). The institution of the "couple" fulfills some of the needs filled by the family in other societies, but the "couple" is not an economic unit and plays a very small role in socializing the children. Economic activities involve the entire kibbutz, and socialization of the children is delegated to professional nurses and teachers.
>
> The family is not needed because the entire community is a very strong primary group. Kibbutz members feel obligations similar to those of kinship towards all the other members. The communist principles of mutual welfare that appear so unworkable in the large-scale European societies from which these people originally came are workable in the intense primary-group atmosphere of the kibbutz. This familylike social atmosphere allows the community to take over some of the duties of the family, which then vanishes, leaving the "couple" as a residue to fill sexual and affectional needs.

Spiro is a conscientiously self-critical scientist. In a later work (1958) he finds that his conclusion in this selection "does not leave me entirely satisfied." Concerning the "couple" and its children he notes that they constitute a unique group in the kibbutz: Children are both desired and planned; the kinship terms "father," "son," "mother," and "daughter" are used exclusively by this group; parents and children comprise a social group; the nature of interaction within this group is unique; the rate of interaction is especially high; and psychological ties are more intense than in any similar situation within the kibbutz. Spiro concludes, "We can either perceive [the couple] in cross-cultural perspective, as a unique group and invent a new term to refer to it, or we can revise Murdock's definition of family in order to accommodate it." Whichever of these alternatives the reader may prefer, both lend support to the hypothesis that the nuclear family, or something very closely resembling it, is necessary to any society because it is apparently uniquely qualified to handle the universal demand of human beings for affection and intimacy.

Selection 35
IS THE FAMILY UNIVERSAL?
Melford Spiro

Introduction

The universality of the family has always been accepted as a sound hypothesis in anthropology; recently, Murdock has been able to confirm this hypothesis on the basis of his important cross-cultural study of kinship. Moreover, Murdock reports that the "nuclear" family is also universal, and that typically it has four functions: sexual, economic, reproductive, and educational. What is more important is his finding that no society "has succeeded in finding an adequate substitute for the nuclear family, to which it might transfer these functions."[1] In the light of this evidence there would be little reason to question his prediction that "it is highly doubtful whether any society ever will succeed in such an attempt, utopian proposals for the abolition of the family to the contrary notwithstanding."[2]

The functions served by the nuclear family are, of course, universal prerequisites for the survival of any society; and it is on this basis that Murdock accounts for its universality.

Without provision for the first and third [sexual and reproductive], society would become extinct; for the second [economic], life itself would cease; for the fourth [edu-

Reprinted from *American Anthropologist*, 56:5, 1954, pp. 839–846, with permission of the author and the publisher.

cational], culture would come to an end. The immense social utility of the nuclear family and the basic reason for its universality thus begins to emerge in strong relief.[3]

Although sexual, economic, reproductive, and educational activities are the functional prerequisites of any society, it comes as somewhat of a surprise, nevertheless, that all four functions are served by the same social group. One would normally assume, on purely a priori grounds, that within the tremendous variability to be found among human cultures, there would be some cultures in which these four functions were distributed among more than one group. Logically, at least, it is entirely possible for these functions to be divided among various social groups within a society; and it is, indeed, difficult to believe that somewhere man's inventive ingenuity should not have actualized this logical possibility. As a matter of fact this possibility has been actualized in certain utopian communities—and it has succeeded within the narrow confines of these communities. The latter, however, have always constituted subgroups within a larger society, and the basic question remains as to whether such attempts could succeed when applied to the larger society.

Rather than speculate about the answer to this question, however, this paper presents a case study of a community which, like the utopian communities, constitutes a subgroup within a larger society and which, like some utopian communities, has also evolved a social structure which does not include the family. It is hoped that an examination of this community—the Israeli *kibbutz*—can shed some light on this question.

Marriage and the family in the kibbutz

A *kibbutz* (plural, *kibbutzim*) is an agricultural collective in Israel, whose main features include communal living, collective ownership of all property (and, hence, the absence of "free enterprise" and the "profit motive"), and the communal rearing of children. *Kibbutz* culture is informed by its explicit, guiding principle of: "from each according to his ability, to each according to his needs." The "family," as that term is defined in *Social Structure*, does not exist in the *kibbutz,* in either its nuclear, polygamous, or extended forms. It should be emphasized, however, that the *kibbutzim* are organized into three separate national federations, and though the basic structure of *kibbutz* society is similar in all three, there are important differences among them. Hence, the term *kibbutz,* as used in this paper, refers exclusively to those *kibbutzim* that are members of the federation studied by the author.[4]

As Murdock defines it,[5] the "family":

is a social group characterized by common residence, economic cooperation, and reproduction. It includes adults of both sexes, at least two of whom maintain a socially approved sexual relationship, and one or more children, own or adopted, of the sexually cohabiting adults.

The social group in the *kibbutz* that includes adults of both sexes and their children, although characterized by reproduction, is not characterized by common residence or by economic co-operation. Before examining this entire social group, however, we shall first analyze the relationship between the two adults in the group who maintain a "socially approved sexual relationship," in order to determine whether their relationship constitutes a "marriage."

Murdock's findings reveal that marriage entails an interaction of persons of opposite sex such that a relatively permanent sexual relationship is maintained and an economic division of labor is practised. Where either of these behavior patterns is absent, there is no marriage. As Murdock puts it:[6]

Sexual unions without economic cooperation are common, and there are relationships between men and women involving a division of labor without sexual gratification . . . but marriage exists only when the economic and the sexual are united in one relationship, and this combination occurs only in marriage.

In examining the relationship of the couple in the *kibbutz* who share a common marriage, and whose sexual union is socially sanctioned, it is discovered that only one of these two criteria—the sexual—applies. Their relationship does not entail economic co-operation. If this be so—and the facts will be examined in a moment—there is no marriage in the *kibbutz,* if by "marriage" is meant a relationship between adults of opposite sex, characterized by sexual and economic activities. Hence, the generalization that "marriage, thus defined, exists in every known society,"[7] has found an exception.

A *kibbutz* couple lives in a single room, which serves as a combined bedroom-living room. Their meals are eaten in a communal dining room, and their children are reared in a communal children's dormitory. Both the man and the woman work in the *kibbutz,* and either one may work in one of its agricultural branches or in one of the "service" branches. The latter include clerical work, education, work in the kitchen, laundry, etc. In actual fact, however, men preponderate in the agricultural branches, and women, in the service branches of the economy. There are no men, for example, in that part of the educational system which extends from infancy to the junior-high level. Nor do women work in those agricultural branches that require the use of heavy machinery, such as trucks, tractors, or combines. It should be noted, however, that some women play major roles in agricultural branches, such as the vegetable garden and the fruit orchards; and some men are indispensable in service branches such as the high school. Nevertheless, it is accurate to state that a division of labor based on sex is characteristic of the *kibbutz* society as a whole. This division of labor, however, does not characterize the relationship that exists between couples. Each mate works in some branch of the *kibbutz* economy and each, as a member (*chaver*) of the *kibbutz* receives his equal share of the goods and services that the *kibbutz* distributes. Neither, however, engages in economic activities that are exclusively directed to the satisfaction of the needs of his mate. Women cook, sew, launder, etc., for the entire *kibbutz*, and not for their mates exclusively. Men produce goods, but the economic returns from their labor go to the *kibbutz*, not to their mates and themselves, although they, like all members of the *kibbutz*, share in these economic returns. Hence though there is economic co-operation between the sexes within the community as a whole, this co-operation does not take place between mates because the social structure of this society precludes the necessity for such co-operation.

What then is the nature of the relationship of the *kibbutz* couple? What are the motives for their union? What functions, other than sex, does it serve? What distinguishes such a union from an ordinary love affair?

In attempting to answer these questions it should first be noted that pre-marital sexual relations are not taboo. It is expected, however, that youth of high-school age refrain from sexual activity; sexual intercourse between high-school students is strongly discouraged. After graduation from high school, however, and their election to membership in the *kibbutz*, there are no sanctions against sexual relations among these young people. While still single, *kibbutz* members live in small private rooms, and their sexual activities may take place in the room of either the male or the female, or in any other convenient location. Lovers do not ask the *kibbutz* for permission to move into a (larger) common room, nor, if they did, would this permission be granted if it were assumed that their relationship was merely that of lovers. When a couple asks for permission to share a room, they do so—and the *kibbutz* assumes that they do so—not because they are lovers, but because they are in love. The request for a room, then, is the sign that they wish to become a "couple" (*zug*), the term the *kibbutz* has substituted for the traditional "marriage." This union does not require the sanction of a marriage ceremony, or of any other event. When a couple requests a room, and the *kibbutz* grants the request, their union is *ipso facto* sanctioned by society. It should be noted, however, that all *kibbutz* "couples" eventually "get married" in accordance with the marriage laws of the state—usually just before, or soon after, their first child is born—

because children born out of wedlock have no legal rights, according to state law.

But becoming a "couple" affects neither the status nor the responsibilities of either the male or the female in the *kibbutz*. Both continue to work in whichever branch of the economy they had worked in before their union. The legal and social status of both the male and the female remain the same. The female retains her maiden name. She not only is viewed as a member of the *kibbutz* in her own right, but her official registration card in the *kibbutz* files remains separate from that of her "friend" (*chaver*)—the term used to designate spouses.[8]

But if sexual satisfaction may be obtained outside of this union, and if the union does not entail economic co-operation, what motivates people to become "couples"? It seems that the motivation is the desire to satisfy certain needs for intimacy, using that term in both its physical and psychological meanings. In the first place, from the sexual point of view, the average *chaver* is not content to engage in a constant series of casual affairs. After a certain period of sexual experimentation, he desires to establish a relatively permanent relationship with one person. But in addition to the physical intimacy of sex, the union also provides a psychological intimacy that may be expressed by notions such as "comradeship," "security," "dependency," "succorance," etc. And it is this psychological intimacy, primarily, that distinguishes "couples" from lovers. The criterion of the "couple" relationship, then, that which distinguishes it from a relationship between adults of the same sex who enjoy psychological intimacy, or from that of adults of opposite sex who enjoy physical intimacy, is love. A "couple" comes into being when these two kinds of intimacy are united in one relationship.

Since the *kibbutz* "couple" does not constitute a marriage because it does not satisfy the economic criterion of "marriage," it follows that the "couple" and their children do not constitute a family, economic co-operation being part of the definition of the "family." Furthermore, as has already been indicated, this group of adults and children does not satisfy the criterion of "common residence." For though the children visit their parents in the latter's room every day, their residence is in one of the "children's houses" (*bet yeladim*), where they sleep, eat, and spend most of their time.

More important, however, in determining whether or not the family exists in the *kibbutz* is the fact that the "physical care" and the "social rearing" of the children are not the responsibilities of their own parents. But these responsibilities, according to Murdock's findings, are the most important functions that the adults in the "family" have with respect to the children.

Before entering into a discussion of the *kibbutz* system of "collective education" (*chinuch meshutaf*), it should be emphasized that the *kibbutz* is a child-centered society, *par excellence*. The importance of children, characteristic of traditional Jewish culture, has been retained as one of the primary values in this avowedly antitraditional society. "The Parents' Crown" is the title given to the chapter on children in an ethnography of the Eastern European Jewish village. The authors of this ethnography write:[9]

> Aside from the scriptural and social reasons, children are welcomed for the joy they bring beyond the gratification due to the parents—the pleasure of having a child in the house. A baby is a toy, the treasure, and the pride of the house.

This description, except for the scriptural reference, applies without qualification to the *kibbutz*.

But the *kibbutz* has still another reason for cherishing its children. The *kibbutz* views itself as an attempt to revolutionize the structure of human society and its basic social relations. Its faith in its ability to achieve this end can be vindicated only if it can raise a generation that will choose to live in this communal society, and will, thus, carry on the work that was initiated by the founders of this society—their parents.

For both these reasons the child is king. Children are lavished with attention and with care to the point where many adults admit that the children are "spoiled." Adult housing may be poor, but the children live in good houses; adult food may be meager and monotonous, but the children enjoy a variety of excellent food; there may be a shortage of clothes for adults, but the children's clothing is both good and plentiful.

Despite this emphasis on children, however, it is not their own parents who provide directly for their physical care. Indeed, the latter have no responsibility in this regard. The *kibbutz* as a whole assumes this responsibility for all its children. The latter sleep and eat in special "children's houses"; they obtain their clothes from a communal store; when ill, they are taken care of by their "nurses." This does not mean that parents are not concerned about the physical welfare of their own children. On the contrary, this is one of their primary concerns. But it does mean that the active responsibility for their care has been delegated to a community institution. Nor does it mean that parents do not work for the physical care of their children, for this is one of their strongest drives. But the fruits of their labor are not given directly to their children; they are given instead to the community which, in turn, provides for all the children. A bachelor or a "couple" without children contribute as much to the children's physical care as a "couple" with children of their own.

The family's responsibility for the socialization of children, Murdock reports, is "no less important than the physical care of the children."

> The burden of education and socialization everywhere falls primarily upon the nuclear family. . . . Perhaps more than any other single factor collective responsibility for education and socialization welds the various relationships of the family firmly together [p. 10].

But the education and socialization of *kibbutz* children are the function of their "nurses" and teachers, and not of their parents. The infant is placed in the "infants' house" upon the mother's return from the hospital, where it remains in the care of nurses. Both parents see the infant there; the mother when she feeds it, the father upon return from work. The infant is not taken to its parents' room until its sixth month, after which it stays with them for an hour. As the child grows older, the amount of time he spends with his parents increases, and he may go to their room whenever he chooses during the day, though he must return to his "children's house" before lights-out. Since the children are in school most of the day, however, and since both parents work during the day, the children—even during their school vacations—are with their parents for a (approximately) two-hour period in the evening—from the time that the parents return from work until they go to eat their evening meal. The children may also be with their parents all day Saturday—the day of rest—if they desire.

As the child grows older he advances through a succession of "children's houses" with children of his own age, where he is supervised by a "nurse." The "nurse" institutes most of the disciplines, teaches the child his basic social skills, and is responsible for the "socialization of the instincts." The child also learns from his parents, to be sure, and they too are agents in the socialization process. But the bulk of his socialization is both entrusted, and deliberately delegated, to the "nurses" and teachers. There is little doubt but that a *kibbutz* child, bereft of the contributions of his parents to his socialization, would know his culture; deprived of the contributions of his "nurses" and teachers, however, he would remain an unsocialized individual.

As they enter the juvenile period, preadolescence, and adolescence, the children are gradually inducted into the economic life of the *kibbutz*. They work from an hour (gradeschool students) to three hours (high school seniors) a day in one of the economic branches under the supervision of adults. Thus, their economic skills, like most of their early social skills, are taught them by adults other than their parents. This generalization applies to the learning of values, as well. In the early ages, the *kibbutz* values are inculcated by "nurses," and later by teachers. When the children enter junior high, this function, which the *kibbutz* views as paramount in importance, is delegated to the "homeroom teacher," known as the "educator" (*mechanech*), and to a "leader" (*madrich*) of the inter-*kibbutz* youth movement. The parents, of course, are also influential in the teaching of values, but the formal division of labor in the *kibbutz* has delegated this responsibility to other authorities.

Although the parents do not play an outstanding role in the socialization of their children, or in providing for their physical needs, it would be erroneous to conclude that they are unimportant figures in their children's lives. Parents are of crucial importance in the *psychological* development of the child. They serve as the objects of his most important identifications, and they provide him with a certain security and love that he obtains from no one else. If anything, the attachment of the young children to their parents is greater than it is in our own society. But this is irrelevant to the main consideration of this paper. Its purpose is to call attention to the fact that those functions of parents that constitute the *conditio sine qua non* for the existence of the "family"—the physical care and socialization of children—are not the functions of the *kibbutz* parents. It can only be concluded that in the absence of the economic and educational functions of the typical family, as well as of its characteristic of common residence, that the family does not exist in the *kibbutz*.

Interpretation

It is apparent from this brief description of the *kibbutz* that most of the functions characteristic of the typical nuclear family have become the functions of the entire *kibbutz* society. This is so much the case that the *kibbutz* as a whole can almost satisfy the criteria by which Murdock defines the "family." This observation is not meant to imply that the *kibbutz* is a nuclear family. Its structure and that of the nuclear family are dissimilar. This observation does suggest, however, that the *kibbutz* can function without the family because it functions as if it, itself, were a family; and it can so function because its members perceive each other as kin, in the psychological implications of that term. The latter statement requires some explanation.

The members of the *kibbutz* do not view each other merely as fellow citizens, or as coresidents in a village, or as co-operators of an agricultural economy. Rather do they view each other as *chaverim*, or comrades, who comprise a group in which each is intimately related to the other, and in which the welfare of the one is bound up with the welfare of the other. This is a society in which the principle, "from each according to his ability, to each according to his needs," can be practised not because its members are more altruistic than the members of other societies, but because each member views his fellow as a kinsman, psychologically speaking. And just as a father in the family does not complain because he works much harder than his children, and yet he may receive no more, or even less, of the family income than they, so the *kibbutz* member whose economic productivity is high does not complain because he receives no more, and sometimes less, than a member whose productivity is low. This "principle" is taken for granted as the normal way of doing things. Since they are all *chaverim*, "it's all in the family," psychologically speaking.

In short, the *kibbutz* constitutes a *gemeinschaft*.* Its patterns of interaction are interpersonal patterns; its ties are kin ties, without the biological tie of kinship. In this one respect it is the "folk society," in almost its pure form. The following quotation from Redfield[10] could have been written with the *kibbutz* in mind, so accurately does it describe the social-psychological basis of *kibbutz* culture.

> The members of the folk society have a strong sense of belonging together. The group . . . see their own resemblances and feel correspondingly united. Communicating intimately with each other, each has a strong claim on the sympathies of the others.[11] . . . the personal and intimate life of the child in the family is extended, in the folk society, into the social world of the adults. . . . It is not merely that relations in such a society are personal; it is also that they are familial. . . . the result is a group of people among whom prevail the personal and categorized relationships that characterize families as we know them, and in which the patterns of kinship tend to be extended outward from the group of genealogically connected individuals into the whole society. The kin are the type persons for all experience.[12]

Hence it is that the bachelor and the childless "couple" do not feel that an injustice is being done them when they contribute to the support of the children of others. The children *in* the *kibbutz* are viewed as the children *of* the *kibbutz*. Parents (who are much more attached to their own children than they are to the children of others) and bachelors, alike, refer to all the *kibbutz* children as "our children."

* Primary-group community.—Ed.

The social perception of one's fellows as kin, psychologically speaking, is reflected in another important aspect of *kibbutz* behavior. It is a striking and significant fact that those individuals who were born and raised in the *kibbutz* tend to practise group exogamy, although there are no rules that either compel or encourage them to do so. Indeed, in the *kibbutz* in which our field work was carried out, all such individuals married outside their own *kibbutz*. When they are asked for an explanation of this behavior, these individuals reply that they cannot marry those persons with whom they have been raised and whom they, consequently, view as siblings. This suggests, as Murdock has pointed out, that "the *kibbutz* to its members *is* viewed psychologically as a family to the extent that it generates the same sort of unconscious incest-avoidance tendencies" (private communication).

What is suggested by this discussion is the following proposition: although the *kibbutz* constitutes an exception to the generalization concerning the universality of the family, structurally viewed, it serves to confirm this generalization, functionally and psychologically viewed. In the absence of a specific social group—the family—to whom society delegates the functions of socialization, reproduction, etc., it has become necessary for the entire society to become a large extended family. But only in a society whose members perceive each other psychologically as kin can it function as a family. And there would seem to be a population limit beyond which point individuals are no longer perceived as kin. That point is probably reached when the interaction of its members is no longer face-to-face; in short, when it ceases to be a primary group. It would seem probable, therefore, that only in a "familial" society, such as the *kibbutz*, is it possible to dispense with the family.

Notes

1 G. P. Murdock, *Social Structure* (New York: Macmillan, 1949).

2 *Ibid.*, p .11.

3 *Ibid.*, p. 10.

4 The field work, on which statements concerning the *kibbutz* are based, was conducted in the year 1951–1952, and was made possible by a postdoctoral fellowship awarded by the Social Science Research Council.

5 Murdock, *op. cit.*, p. 1.

6 *Ibid.*, p. 8.

7 *Ibid.*, p. 8.

8 Other terms, "young man"

(*bachur*) and "young woman" (*bachura*), are also used in place of "husband" and "wife." If more than one person in the *kibbutz* has the same proper name, and there is some question as to who is being referred to when the name is mentioned in conversation, the person is

identified by adding, "the *bachur* of so-and-so," or "the *bachura* of so-and-so."

[9] M. Zborowski and E. Herzog, *Life Is with People* (New York: International Universities Press, 1952), p. 308.

[10] R. Redfield, "The Folk Society," *American Journal of Sociology* 52, pp. 293–308.

[11] *Ibid.*, p. 297.

[12] *Ibid.*, p. 101.

CHANGING FUNCTIONS

The family is a highly valued institution, in most societies, including our own. However, evidence from the past fifty years indicates that the American family has become much less stable than it used to be. Increasing divorce rates, along with more permissive attitudes toward divorce, are among the data that point to this conclusion. W. F. Ogburn is among those observers who believe that this instability is not in the long run threatening to the family. This selection presents his diagnosis of the causes of family instability. His thesis implies that the concern people feel for the future of the family, although unwarranted, is understandable because ideals concerning the family have not changed to the same extent as its functions.

   The structure of the family is changing because of changes in economics and technology. Technological innovations, applied by economic institutions, have given the manufacturing firm a competitive advantage over the family in the field of production. In a similar fashion, the family is losing its protective functions to government, recreational to the commercial entertainment industry, educational to the school, and religious to the church.

   However, no other institutions pose serious competition to the family in the realm of affection, including sexual experience, and in the primary-socialization aspect of education. It is in these activities that the family is becoming specialized.

   Because there are fewer activities within the family, it is less stable than formerly, but this instability is less socially disruptive for the same reason. Since ideals, social controls, and valuations concerning the family are changing less rapidly than functions, this instability is often seen as a social problem; but it is much less problematic than many people believe.

Social institutions have been known to vanish. Witchcraft and slavery are American examples of this fact. Institutions have also been known to change to the point that they are unrecognizable, which is the situation that Spiro believed he had found with regard to the family on the Israeli kibbutz. Ogburn denies that either of these fates awaits the family. In accord with the opinion of most sociologists, he believes that the family is uniquely qualified to provide affection to its members, thus explaining the universality of the family and providing a basis for optimism concerning its future.

Selection 36
WHY THE FAMILY IS CHANGING
W. F. Ogburn

The family as a social institution is changing, as are other institutions. These changes differ somewhat in countries according to the degree of their industrialization, of their urbanization and of their isolation. But whatever these changes may be, they can be better seen after an analysis of the factors that affect the form and functions of the family. Five such factors are selected as of especial importance.

Community size

The first factor is the numbers of people living within the area of the community in which the family exists. Among many peoples who hunt and gather food without cultivation of plants and domestication of animals the community is small, sometimes consisting of very few families, say, five or six. The community is a band that often occupies an area for only a short time. In other cases the number of families may be 25 to 50, and the occupation of a site, as for instance near the sea coast or a water fall, may be larger.

In any case, the population is not large enough to support many social organizations. A band of 25 persons with six or seven men and eight or nine women living in relative isolation could not support a baseball team, a debating society or a luncheon club. Since, say, ten such single purpose organizations must necessarily have the same personnel in membership, it is more probable that there will be one organization with ten functions.

Among such primitive hunters there are always two social organizations, the family and the community. The functions that people have are then divided between these two organizations. These functions are such as eating, working, loving, procreating, fighting, playing, educating, safeguarding and worshipping. Theoretically, the family could have had only one of these functions, procreation, and the community all the remainder. Actually the family in such small communities is an organization that procreates, educates, prepares food, eats together, with members working for it, and

Reprinted from *Sociologus*, 4:2 (New Series), 1954, pp. 160–170, with permission of the publisher.

thus has multiple functions. So does the community which may organize hunting parties; make provision for worship, provide recreation, aid in informal education and furnish the parties to feuds or factional disputes. There may be other organizations such as men's clubs or age societies. But in general most of the activities of life are divided between the family and the community, the proportionate distribution varying among different peoples according to situations and circumstances. The emphasis to be noted is that in such small communities the family is a multi-purpose organization with many functions and not one for procreation and child rearing only.

In a large community such as a modern city, these various human activities may become functions of specialized institutions. Thus, factories produce cloth and clothing, restaurants serve food, churches are places of worship, and schools educate. Hence many family functions either leave the family for such specialized institutions as when spinning and weaving left the family for the factory or the family function may be surpassed by those single purpose organizations, as when recreation in the family is relatively less than in places of commercial recreation such as motion picture theatres, at athletic events, at school playgrounds, or in parks. Large communities therefore make it possible for various other organizations to take over and develop functions exercised by the family in very small communities. Hence, relatively, it is possible for the family to lose functions to outside organizations.

The economic factor

There is one activity in society that has proved to be of exceptional importance in affecting other activities. This is the production of food, and other goods and services, which we call the economic function. For instance, it may determine the location of a community, as for instance in a fertile valley, or near to the fish beds of the ocean, or where a person lives as in a city or the open country, or in a mining community in the hills. The economic factor provides the standard of living of a family either of wealth or poverty. It is a source of power socially, politically and militarily. It is a factor in the choice of a mate, in the rearing of children, in the provision of recreation, in safeguarding against life's adversities, and affects status in a society.

The extent that the family as a social institution has an economic function, then, is of great importance. The family has an economic function in all societies and in all sizes of communities in that members of the family work and provide for what the family consumes, and some are better providers than others. The variation that is important is in the relative extent that other organizations than the family exercise the function of production of goods and services. Thus in cities today the great centers of production—and trade is a production of place utilities*—are factories, stores, offices, banks, railways and highways, while in farms that are isolated the family is a center of production, which in commercial farming is yielding to other economic institutions.

By contrast, self-sufficient family farms of the open country are the main economic centers. The household is the forerunner of the factory. Where farming families live in villages, as is the case in most of the agricultural nations, some economic functions are shared more readily with other non-farming families of handicraftsmen who make wheels, model iron, tan hides of animals etc. Before trade was very much developed and technology had not advanced very far, and where the agricultural family possessed the plough and had domesticated animals, with some knowledge of fertilizers, the family was the outstanding economic organization. That is to say, in the household economy, few other economic institutions could compare with the family as a producing organization. Some families took on a military function and with private armies were able to levy upon other families for their produce and labor. In such cases these military farmers, the lords and dukes, became the centers of very powerful family organizations. Out of such families grew kinship, which was modelled after the authoritarian head of a family. The status of families was at its zenith.

There were at this time some families that existed without farming, by trade, by handi-

craft production, and by transporting goods especially in boats and sometimes in caravans. There were at those times towns and an occasional city on a waterway, which developed specialized organizations such as guilds. Traders used market places and peddlers carried goods from place to place but manufacturing was much in cottages, and hence manufacturing tended to remain in the family even in urban communities. Since the handicraftsmen worked in their homes, the economic function of the family was still an important one as compared with the economic function of other institutions, as, for instance, those of religious organizations such as monasteries.

Not a great deal is known about family life in towns and cities in the era of the household economy. We may infer, however, that there was more division of labor between families there than on farms in the open country or perhaps in hamlets and small villages and hence more purchase or exchange. Yet, if the population of towns and cities was drawn from village and rural areas, and if much handicraft was a family function, then very likely the customs of marriage and the family in towns and cities were not greatly different from that of the general culture area which was predominantly rural. The type tended still to be set by the conditions of the predominant occupation which was farming with a moderately high grade of equipment and knowledge and with a variety of domestic animals, some of which may have been fairly numerous.

We assume that the high development of the economic function of the family of the farming population and very probably of the towns too, had its influence on other activities such as protection, recreation, status creation, education, religion and the other great classes of human activity.

It is possible that the economic functions in the time of the household economy based on the use of the plough and domesticated animals made the family the greatest social institution in power and influence that it has ever been, greater than in earlier hunting and hoe cultures and greater than in later cities of the age of mechanical power.

With the coming of factories and transport run by mechanical power and the great multiplication of communities of very large size, relative diminution of the economic function of the family and of other correlated functions is an often told story.

* Roughly, putting things where they are needed. —Ed.

The role of technology

Two great influences shaping the structure of the family have been signalized, these are the size of the community and the performance of economic functions. While economic production and community size are causes, they are also results of preceding causes. We think that an important cause of changes in community size and of economic production is technology, which is used here as a general term to include the knowledge and use of inventions and of material culture, as well as the application of science.

For instance, it was the discovery that seeds could be planted and cultivated by human beings and the invention of the digging stick or hoe that changed the hunting cultures with their wandering bands into larger settled agricultural communities. It was the plough and the domestication of animals that led to still larger communities, which became still more large if they were on water where boats could be used. Finally, the many big cities of today are the result of factories and railroads which expand into large metropolitan areas with the invention of automotive transportation.

Similarly it may be argued that the economic organization is changed from time to time by invention and discovery. We think the large household which sometimes included kin, both vertical and lateral, as well as parents and children was more prevalent in the plough culture than in the hoe culture or the hunting culture. The skills of the handicraftsmen in making stone tools, boats, working with metals, in household construction, in preparing skins for use, in making wheels, in furniture making, in creating fine fabrics expanded with technological development leading to division of labor, exchange, trade and transportation, even when production remained in the household. With mechanical power applied to moving metals there came mass production and many cities with a galaxy of institutions.

Technology then by affecting community size and by developing and transferring the economic functions of the family, is an indirect once removed factor of great importance affecting the family.

Social control

A useful institution becomes socially valued. Such is the case with the family. If there be disruption or disorganizing tendencies connected with such an institution there will be agencies of regulation and control. One of the disruptive forces in the family is the sex appeal to one or both of the mates by individuals outside the family. There is thus a tendency for society to channelize sex activity particularly for mates in families. Without such controls not all mates would confine their sexual relations to each other, which might result in an unstable family organization. Family stability is considered to be especially important where there are young children to rear. Otherwise they might not be reared so well. Hence there are laws regarding divorce, and against adultery, and codes approving chastity and moral disapproval of deviant sex practices. To the support of these controls there are marshalled the forces of religious sanction. So powerful an urge as sex is difficult to keep in the authorized and ideal bounds, so various societies have provided for various outlets or escapes from the approved regimen, where they do not prove too disruptive.

Controls are also needed for the family not only as a procreative institution, but also as an institution of economic production. The members of the family must be held to their various duties which should be performed regularly and frequently even though arduous, monotonous and fatiguing. Goods must be produced on schedule. Hence an economic institution needs a head, a boss, with the authority to compel obedience on the part of the labor.

Then, too, families have property that must be guarded, divided, transmitted or otherwise disposed of. So there are laws regarding property which were often a family as well as an individual matter. Property, especially landed property, has had a good deal to do with the continuity of families over generations and with the residence of brides and grooms.

Property, production and sex are important to society, and hence are subject to controls taking the form of laws, morals, religious sanctions, and informal customs, the infraction of which is accompanied by some form of punishment.

Cultural lags

When a complex institution of inter-related parts is changing, not all parts change at the same time or at the same rate. Thus the family in one locality may lose many of its economic functions, but legal controls of production and property may remain unchanged or change more slowly. Similarly, if cities cover the land rapidly, say within a century, families therein have a different daily life from what they had in rural areas from which the urban families came. This daily life may differ as to where the members of the family work, or spend their time, or as to the times of going to work, or their methods of recreation. Yet the social codes suited to rural life may persist with little change into the new urban setting. Thus it may be considered that "woman's place is in the home." Or still valued may be the old adage "early to bed and early to rise makes a man healthy, wealthy and wise," which was very well suited to a rural family life that dealt with domesticated animals. Or, again, man is still considered the head, the boss, as he was in reality when production was in the home.

In cities the family bonds weaken and the members of the families emerge as individuals with rights as independent persons. Yet the laws regarding property rights for women are changed very slowly.

In general the social valuations that take the form of laws, sanctions, moral codes and ideologies are singularly resistant to change. The economic or technological aspects of families often change first and the ideational aspects change later, thus remaining for a time out of harmony. This fact that the structural parts of a family do not fit well during a period of rapid change makes an understanding difficult unless this phenomenon of cultural lag is recognised and worked into the analysis.

Five factors

We have reviewed five factors that influence the structure and functions of the family. The size of a community and the location of economic functions are seen to influence the family greatly. Where the size of the community increases much, the family is expected to change particularly in its functions. The change, however, is not immediate. For the family is likely to try to maintain for a time its old ways. So too when the family loses or gains a large proportion of the economic functions in a society or community, its structure changes as do also various other functions correlated with economic functions. Particularly are its power and prestige affected. The prime mover of these changes is frequently techno-

logical development operating on community size and economic activity.

This process is complicated by the sanctions and controls which society places on a family and which have so much to do with conduct, since they affect ideas of right and wrong and evaluations based upon emotions and sentiments. And back of these are often law and punishment.

These sanctions and controls change often more slowly than the other factors affecting the family as an institution, such as material culture, population density, and economic production.

The foregoing represents an attempt to generalize over a very large and complex field. As generalizations for which little evidence has been given and for which satisfactory evidence does not exist especially of families in the prehistorical eras and areas they should be taken as theory, family theory.

Looking at this theory critically, it could be true only in general. In the first place there are more than five factors affecting the family. For instance the sex ratio of adults has an influence, and the widely spread polygamy* among preliterate people is probably related to the hazards of life to the men who follow the more dangerous activities, which thus lead to an excess of women. But here again polygamy and monogamy change slowly and would not quickly be adapted to a fluctuating sex ratio. The existence of polygamy is also the result of other factors than the sex ratio.

Then again the sequence may not always be as set forth in the preceding paragraphs, that is from technology, to economics, to the structure of the family with ideational lags. It may be that ideas, as for instance in the western urban world on the position of women, their freedom and rights, may be imported and adopted into rural areas of the Orient by the carriers of some ideology of a semi-religious nature or otherwise, and adopted first before the economic structure is harmoniously suited to the change. Such may be the case for instance of the revision of the Hindu code proposed by Ambedkar in the Indian parliament, but not as yet adopted.

There are types of minds that dislike averages and even refuse to use them. They insist on the presentation of the whole frequency dis-

---

* In this case specifically, polygyny, or the marriage of one man to several wives.–Ed.

tribution, of which the average is a most inadequate condensation. Such types of mind will renounce the foregoing generalizations.

But where theory has not been proven it still serves the useful purpose of being a tool of analysis and a source of hypothesis. We shall apply, then, some of these generalizations to the changing family of the modern Western World.

The modern family of the West

The urban families of the nations of Western Europe and the United States have common features as well as differences.

Most important is the loss of functions to other social institutions which have developed these functions much further than the family has. Thus production has been transferred to the factory, though consumption remains as an important family function, with men, women and children spending much of their time away from home. With the shift of economic functions there have been transferred other functions. Protection has increasingly become less a family function in cities and more a function of police, courts, governmental insurance, private pension plans, old age bureaus, and health regulations. Recreation has become commercial and hence outside the home. Religious worship is rare in homes, though religion is something of a barrier in formation of families for persons of different faiths. Marriage ceremonies are increasingly civil ones. Particularly in cities have the power and prestige of families as such declined. Power is in government and industry rather than in the family as it was in feudal times. Women and children are less under family discipline.

The most vigorous functions remaining to the family are affectional and educational. The affectional function here includes procreation, as well as affection between parents and children. Educational functions in the family here are those that shape the personality of children before they are of school age. Affection may exist between members of different families and schools share part of the educational function.

The family and household are becoming smaller[1] in size partly because of the diminution of economic production in the household and partly because of the costs of rearing children which must be paid to agencies outside the family. This reduction in size is made possible by discoveries in methods of avoiding conception other than abstinence. The invention of contraceptives is the particular technological development that is largely responsible for the reduction in size of the family.

In many countries there is a tendency to form families at earlier ages, which seems to be due in part to the possibility of marriage without necessarily having children to support and also possibly to the employment of young wives, without children, who add to the family income. Early marriage is also favoured by prosperous phases of the business cycle. Thus earlier marriage is influenced by the invention of contraceptives and the technological and economic developments which furnished remunerative employment to wives outside the home.

In the formation of families the choice of mates is based less and less on economic qualifications such as good housekeeping skills and on business capacities and more and more on personality considerations characterized by romance and companionship. These trends are obviously due to the decrease of the economic functions of families.

The authoritarian family with powers of discipline and punishment centered primarily in the male head is declining with consequent freedom to wives and children and the granting of more legal rights and economic and social opportunities to women. This change is due to the inventions that moved production from the household to the factory and that built cities which furnished economic opportunities outside the home.

The restriction of sex activity to the family on the part of women, and possibly of men is becoming less. This increased sexual freedom seems to be due to the technological and scientific developments that led to the use of contraceptives, to the conquest of venereal diseases, to opportunities of privacy and anonymity in cities, to the decrease of religious authority over sex control, and to the naturalistic conceptions of biological functions.

The instability of families is increasing in that there is more permanent separation of mates and more marriages among those who have been previously married. This increased separation, divorce, and annulment occurs because there are fewer bonds that hold two persons together through life. If formerly there were seven ties, i.e. functions, that held the family together and now there are only one and a half, more disruption is to be expected. Permanent separation of mates is more common in cities where there are fewer family functions than in rural areas, more common among childless couples where contraceptives have been effectively used, more common among the young with more imperative demands of sex compatibility and affection, and less common among religious groups whose codes are less affected by modern science.

Family social status and family pride are decreasing, as would be expected where wealth is concentrated in industry and power in government, and where families are becoming less stable with emphasis upon romance rather than upon social virtues and achievements.

The ideals, social controls and valuations of the family are changing, too, but much less rapidly; and newer ideals are slow to arise. Thus the professed attitude towards divorce seems to be to make a husband and wife live together whether they want to or not. Compulsory habitation of husband and wife together seems to be a goal, though in practice the courts do not always act accordingly, even though the legal statutes remain unchanged. Compulsory habitation together in pre-industrial revolution days was not a goal but a means to a goal which was to keep the production of the household going without too much labor turnover and to rear successfully a large family. But where there is no family production and many childless couples or families with few children living at home, the dangers and hazards of disruption, though existing, are much less. The social valuations of the family as found in laws, moral codes and religious rules, do not make distinctions between families without children and families with children. Under the new urban conditions there are many wives who have never had a child and many whose few children have been reared and left the nest. If the remaining functions of the family are those largely producing happiness and companionship for mates and rearing children, then obviously these functions are quite different for families without children and families with them. But such differences are not yet formulated into social codes and widely recognised social valuations. The precedents of court action seem to be moving in the direction less slowly than legislative action.

The sloughing off of various functions of the family except the personality functions has meant a focussing of attention upon the happiness and companionship of mates and on the rearing of little children. An inventory of the researches of sociologists shows that their investigations are increasingly concerned with such topics as mate selection, courting procedures, sex aspects of marriage and family, sex education, education for marriage and family, happiness in marriage, personalities of children where there are only one or two in the family, factors affecting compatibility, the resolution of marital conflicts, and the success or failure of remarriage. These interests are quite in harmony with the analyses of the factors affecting the family as set forth in this paper and with the trends herein described. The welfare of the future families depends much upon the successes of the researches and wide diffusion of the knowledge derived therefrom.

Note

[1] The evidence for this statement and others which follow are found in a forthcoming book "Technology and the Changing Family" by W. F. Ogburn and M. F. Nimkoff, published by Houghton Mifflin and Co., Boston.

A DYING INSTITUTION?

This selection demonstrates how the same data can be quite differently interpreted and lead to very different theoretical and policy-oriented conclusions. Barrington Moore believes that predictions of continued importance for the family as an institution specializing in affection and socialization represent ideals and hopes of sociologists as middle-class Americans, rather than the most straightforward interpretation of the masses of data now available. The plausibility of this criticism is related to the fact that sociologists, like all observers, are social beings imbued with culture, and complete detachment from this culture is impossible. Bearing this fact in mind, let the reader evaluate the merits of this argument as compared with Ogburn's, and decide for himself which is more faithful to the data.

> The specialization of the family in affection would be an illogical and unnecessary development, for affection develops best among people who choose each other, rather than among people related by the circumstances of ascribed kinship statuses. The intimate confessions of friends and of great writers provide data suggesting that the family is perhaps more of a painful burden than a source of affection, and if this is general the family is certain to fail as specialized in affection. Likewise, the functions of the family in primary socialization are being rendered superfluous, and whatever socializing influences remain seem more to run from children to parents than vice versa.

> These facts suggest trends, if not current realities, but statistics on marriage and divorce show that the latter is increasing more rapidly than the former, and if this continues the family will eventually die out. Its functions in handling affection would be taken over by friendship and similar institutions, and it could be replaced for socialization by properly constituted bureaucratic organizations that might function very well if given generous resources.

The intimate data on which Moore rests his argument are certainly genuine. Apparently some families are quite unsuccessful. To broaden the criticism of these families to the family as an institution, it is necessary to assume that the reported conditions are general. Available information does not support this assumption, but Moore replies that these are conditions which most people are unwilling to admit and discuss. His argument is plausible but unproved.

On the other hand, Moore's interpretation of marriage and divorce statistics seems less defensible. Part of the rising divorce rate must be laid to an increased ability and willingness of the poor to undertake legal divorce, where in previous times legalized or informal separation, unrecorded in the divorce statistics, had the same effect. Moreover, the divorce rate, though high, has fallen from its historic peak in the late 1940s; and most divorced people remarry, indicating that although they may consider a particular marriage to have been a failure, they do not therefore reject the family as an institution.

Selection 37
THOUGHTS ON THE FUTURE OF THE FAMILY
Barrington Moore, Jr.

Among social scientists today it is almost axiomatic that the family is a universally necessary social institution and will remain such through any foreseeable future. Changes in its struc-

Reprinted by permission of the publishers from Barrington Moore, Jr., *Political Power and Social Theory*, Cambridge, Mass.: Harvard University Press. Copyright, 1958, by the President and Fellows of Harvard College.

ture to be sure, receive wide recognition. The major theme, however, in the appraisal American sociologists present is that the family is making up for lost economic functions by providing better emotional service. One work announces as its central thesis that "the family in historical times has been, and at present is, in transition from an institution to a companionship." In the past, the authors explain, the forces holding the family together were external, formal, and authoritarian, such as law, public opinion, and the authority of the father. Now, it is claimed, unity inheres in the mutual affection and comradeship of its members.[1] Another recent work by a leading American sociologist makes a similar point. The trend under industrialism, we are told, does not constitute a decline of the family as such, but mainly a decline of its importance in the performance of economic functions. Meanwhile, the author tells us, the family has become a more specialized agency for the performance of other functions, namely, the socialization of children and the stabilization of adult personalities. For this reason, the author continues, social arrangements corresponding rather closely to the modern family may be expected to remain with us indefinitely.[2]

In reading these and similar statements by American sociologists about other aspects of American society, I have the uncomfortable feeling that the authors, despite all their elaborate theories and technical research devices, are doing little more than projecting certain middle-class hopes and ideals onto a refractory reality. If they just looked a little more carefully at what was going on around them, I think they might come to different conclusions. This is, of course, a very difficult point to prove, though C. Wright Mills, in a brilliant essay, has shown how one area of American sociology, the study of crime, is suffused with such preconceptions.[3] While personal observations have some value, one can always argue that a single observer is biased. Here all I propose to do, therefore, is to raise certain questions about the current sociological assessment of the family on the basis of such evidence as has come my way rather casually. In addition, I should like to set this evidence in the framework of an intellectual tradition, represented, so far as the family is concerned, by Bertrand Russell's *Marriage and Morals*, that sees the family in an evolutionary perspective,[4] and raises the possibility that it may be an obsolete institution or become one before long. I would suggest then that conditions have arisen which, in many cases, prevent the family from performing the social and psychological functions ascribed to it by modern sociologists. The same conditions may also make it possible for the advanced industrial societies of the world to do away with the family and substitute other social arrangements that impose fewer unnecessary and painful restrictions on humanity. Whether or not society actually would take advantage of such an opportunity is, of course, another question.

It may be best to begin with one observation that is not in itself conclusive but at least opens the door to considering these possibilities. In discussions of the family, one frequently encounters the argument that Soviet experience demonstrates the necessity of this institution in modern society. The Soviets, so the argument runs, were compelled to adopt the family as a device to carry part of the burden of making Soviet citizens, especially after they perceived the undesirable consequences of savage homeless children, largely the outcome of the Civil War. This explanation is probably an accurate one as far as it goes. But it needs to be filled out by at least two further considerations that greatly reduce its force as a general argument. In the first place, the Soviets, I think, adopted their conservative policy toward the family *faute de mieux*. That is to say, with their very limited resources, and with other more pressing objectives, they had no genuine alternatives. Steel mills had to be built before creches, or at least before creches on a large enough scale to make any real difference in regard to child care. In the meantime the services of the family, and especially of grandma (*babushka*), had to be called upon. In the second place, with the consolidation of the regime in the middle thirties, Soviet totalitarianism may have succeeded in capturing the family and subverting this institution to its own uses. At any rate the confidence and vigor with which the regime supported this institution from the early thirties onward suggests such an explanation. Thus the Soviet experience does not constitute by itself very strong evidence in favor of the "functional necessity" of the family.

If the Soviet case does not dispose of the possibility that the family may be obsolete, we may examine other considerations with greater confidence, and begin by widening our historical perspective. By now it is a familiar observation that the stricter Puritan ethics of productive work and productive sex have accomplished their historical purposes in the more advanced sections of the Western world. These developments have rendered other earlier elements of Western culture and society, such as slavery, quite obsolete, and constitute at least prima facie evidence for a similar argument concerning the family. Let us ask then to what extent may we regard the family as a repressive survival under the conditions of an advanced technology? And to what extent does the modern family perform the function of making human beings out of babies and small children either badly or not at all?

One of the most obviously obsolete features of the family is the obligation to give affection as a duty to a particular set of persons on account of the accident of birth. This is a true relic of barbarism. It is a survival from human prehistory, when kinship was the basic form of social organization. In early times it was expedient to organize the division of labor and affection in human society through real or imagined kinship bonds. As civilization became technically more advanced, there has been less and less of a tendency to allocate both labor and affection according to slots in a kinship system, and an increasing tendency to award them on the basis of the actual qualities and capacities that the individual possesses.

Popular consciousness is at least dimly aware of the barbaric nature of the duty of family affection and the pain it produces, as shown by the familiar remark, "You can choose your friends, but you can't choose your relatives." Even if partly concealed by ethical imperatives with the weight of age-old traditions, the strain is nevertheless real and visible. Children are often a burden to their parents. One absolutely un-Bohemian couple I know agreed in the privacy of their own home that if people ever talked to each other openly about the sufferings brought on by raising a family today, the birth rate would drop to zero. It is, of course, legitimate to wonder how widespread such sentiments are. But this couple is in no sense "abnormal." Furthermore, a revealing remark like this made to a friend is worth more as evidence than reams of scientific questionnaires subjected to elaborate statistical analyses. Again, how many young couples, harassed by the problems of getting started in life, have not wished that their parents could be quietly and cheaply taken care of in some institution for the aged? Such facts are readily accessible to anyone who listens to the conversations in his own home or among the neighbors.

The exploitation of socially sanctioned demands for gratitude, when the existing social situation no longer generates any genuine feeling of warmth, is a subtle and heavily tabooed result of this barbaric heritage. It is also one of the most painful. Perhaps no feeling is more excruciating than the feeling that we ought to love a person whom we actually detest. The Greek tragedians knew about the problem, but veiled it under religion and mythology, perhaps because the men and women of that time felt there was no escape. In the nineteenth century the theme again became a dominant one in European literature, but with the clear implication that the situation was unnecessary. Even these authors, Tolstoi, Samuel Butler, Strindberg, and Ibsen, in exposing the horrors and hypocrisies of family life, wove most of their stories around the marital relationship, where there is an element of free choice in the partner selected. Kafka's little gem, *Das Urteil,* is a significant exception. With magnificent insight into the tragedy on both sides, it treats the frustrations of a grown-up son forced to cherish a helpless but domineering father. Henry James' short story, *Europe,* is an effective treatment of the same relationship between a mother and her daughters. Despite some blind spots and limitations, the artists, it appears, have seen vital aspects of the family that have largely escaped the sociologists.

In addition to these obsolete and barbaric features one can point to certain trends in modern society that have sharply reduced rather than increased the effectiveness of the home as an agency for bringing up children. In former times the family was a visibly coherent economic unit, as well as the group that served to produce and raise legitimate children. The father had definite and visible economic tasks, before the household became separated from the place of work. When the children could see what he did, the father had a role to be copied and envied. The source and justification of his authority was clear. Internal conflicts had to be resolved. This is much less the case now.

It is reasonably plain that today's children are much less willing than those of pre-industrial society to take their parents as models for conduct. Today they take them from the mass media and from gangs. Radio and television heroes, with their copies among neighborhood gangs, now play a vital part in the socialization process. Parents have an uphill and none too successful struggle against these sources. Like adult mobs, children's groups readily adopt the sensational, the cruel, and the most easily understood for their models and standards. These influences then corrupt and lower adult standards, as parents become increasingly afraid to assert their own authority for fear of turning out "maladjusted" children.[*]

The mass media have largely succeeded in battering down the walls of the social cell the family once constituted in the larger structure of society. Privacy has greatly diminished. Newspapers, radios, and television have very largely destroyed the flow of private communications within the family that were once the basis of socialization. Even meals are now much less of a family affair. Small children are frequently plumped in front of the television set with their supper on a tray before them to keep them quiet. Since the family does less as a unit genuine emotional ties among its members do not spring up so readily.[5] The advertising campaign for "togetherness" provides rather concrete evidence that family members would rather not be together.

The mother, at least in American society, is generally supposed to be the homemaker and the center of the family. Has she been able to take up the slack produced by the change in the father's role? Is she, perhaps, the happy person whose face smiles at us from every advertisement and whose arts justify the sociologists' case? A more accurate assessment may be that the wife suffers most in the modern middle-class family, because the demands our culture puts upon her are impossible to meet. As indicated by advertisements, fiction, and even the theories of sociologists, the wife is expected to be companion, confidante, and ever youthful mistress of her husband.

If the demands could be met, many wives might feel very happy in this fulfillment of their personality. The actual situation is very different. The father is out of the house all day and therefore can be neither overlord nor companion. With the father absent, radio and television provide the mother with a watery substitute for adult companionship. A young colleague told me recently that his wife leaves

the radio on all day merely to hear the sound of a grown-up voice. The continual chatter of little children can be profoundly irritating, even to a naturally affectionate person. The absence of servants from nearly all American middle-class households brings the wife face to face with the brutalizing features of motherhood and housework. If she had the mentality of a peasant, she might be able to cope with them more easily. Then, however, she could not fulfill the decorative functions her husband expects. As it is now, diapers, dishes, and the state of the baby's bowels absorb the day's quota of energy. There is scarcely any strength left for sharing emotions and experiences with the husband, for which there is often no opportunity until the late hours of the evening. It is hardly a wonder that the psychiatrists' anterooms are crowded, or that both husband and wife seek escapes from psychological and sexual boredom, the cabin fever of the modern family. For the wife, either a job or an affair may serve equally well as a release from domesticity.

A further sign of the modern family's inadequacy in stabilizing the human personality may be seen in the troubled times of adolescence. This stage of growing up has been interpreted as a rejection of adult standards of responsibility and work by youngsters who are about to enter adult life. It seems to me that this period is more significantly one of pseudo-rebellion, when the youngsters copy what they see to be the real values of adult life instead of the professed ones. Even in the more extreme forms of youthful rebellion, relatively rare among respectable middle-class children, such as roaring around in noisy cars to drinking and seduction parties, the adolescents are aping actual adult behavior. Adolescents then do things they know many grown-ups do when the latter think they are escaping the observant eyes of the young. A "hot-rod" is, after all, nothing but an immature Cadillac. Where the Cadillac is the symbol of success, what else could be expected? Adult standards too are made tolerable through commercialized eroticism that lures us on to greater consumption from every billboard and magazine cover. Thus the whole miasma of sexual and psychological boredom in the older generation, pseudo-rebellion and brutality in the younger one, is covered over by a sentimental and suggestive genre art based on commercial sentiment.

[*] It is sometimes claimed that the modern family still represents a bulwark against mass and totalitarian pressures. No doubt this is true in the best cases, those few where parents are still able to combine authority and affection. These are, however, mainly a relic of Victorian times. By and large it seems more likely that the family constitutes the "transmission belt" through which totalitarian pressures toward conformity are transmitted to the parents through the influence of the children.

No doubt many will think that these lines paint too black a picture. Statistics could perhaps be accumulated to show that families such as the type sketched here are far from a representative cross-section of American middle-class life. Such facts, however, would not be relevant to the argument. As pointed out elsewhere in these essays, the representative character of certain types of social behavior is not necessarily relevant to estimates of current and future trends. This kind of statistical defense of the status quo represents that of a certain maiden's virtue by the claim, "After all, she is only a little bit pregnant."

To refute the appraisal offered in these pages it would be necessary to demonstrate that they misrepresent basic structural trends in the family in advanced industrial countries. The most important argument of this type that I have encountered asserts that the proportion of married people in the population has steadily risen while the proportion of single individuals has steadily dropped. Therefore, people obviously prefer family life to bachelorhood, and the gloomy picture sketched above must be nothing more than vaporings of sour-bellied intellectuals thrown on the dumpheap by the advance of American society.

Before discussing the question further, let us look at some of the relevant facts. The table below shows changes in the proportions of single, married, and divorced persons in the United States from the age of fourteen onward. The source, an authoritative and very recent statistical survey of the American family, has standardized the proportions for age, using the 1940 age distribution as a standard, in order to eliminate changes due merely to shifts in the age composition of our population, which would merely confuse the issue.[6] The figures do show a rise in the proportion of married persons and a decline in the proportion of single ones. They also show that the proportion of married persons is overwhelmingly larger than the number of divorced ones. But the biggest change has been in the proportion of divorced people. For men it has risen ninefold since 1890 and for women more than fivefold. A bigger proportion of people are married now than in 1890, but a *much* bigger proportion have abandoned the marital state. In the long run, the latter change might turn out to be the more important one.

Even the statistical evidence, in other words, does not uphold in a completely unambiguous manner the sociologists' argument for the family. Sometimes an attempt to save the case is made by interpreting the rise in divorce as something that allows greater freedom for the individual to choose marital partners on the basis of congeniality. Thereby divorce allegedly strengthens the family's function as a source of emotional support.[7] By talking about greater freedom for the individual in this fashion one has already taken a long step toward the opponents' view that marriage as such may be superfluous.

The point cannot be considered merely in the light of the facts as they exist now or have existed in the past. To do this in social questions is basically unscientific. Those who dismiss negative appraisals of the family with the crude observation that they reflect personal bias or mere "European decadence" deserve an equally crude reply: "So what if Americans prefer to get married! That simply shows how stupid they are."

Acrimony here unfortunately conceals a genuine issue. It is perfectly possible that conditions exist, perhaps even now, that permit better institutional arrangements than most people would be willing to accept. The word better, of course, implies a definite standard of judgment. One can debate such standards

Percentage Distribution of Persons 14 Years and Over by Marital Status and Sex in the Civilian Population

1890–1954

Year	Single	Male Married	Divorced	Single	Female Married	Divorced
1954	28.4	66.7	1.8	22	65.8	2.2
1950	29.4	65.5	1.5	22.5	64.8	2.1
1940	34.8	59.7	1.2	27.6	59.5	1.6
1930	34.7	59.1	1.1	26.9	59.7	1.3
1890	36.7	57.9	0.2	27.8	57.7	0.4

endlessly, and perhaps cannot reach agreement without at some point making arbitrary assumptions. I shall not enter this debate here except to say that any social institution is a bad one that imposes more suffering on people than is necessary when they have sufficient material resources and scientific knowledge to do away with this suffering. This standard, anthropologists tell us, is that not only of Western culture, but of all culture.[8]

What then, are the prospects for the future? We need not take a completely determinist view. Indeed, the perceptions that both plain people and opinion makers have about the present enter in as a significant component among the forces shaping the future and thereby provide an entering wedge for rational adaptation.

Among those who accept a substantial part of the preceding image of the family as basically correct, one frequently hears the prescription that what American culture really needs is a higher evaluation of the social role of the housewife and of motherhood. The trouble with this prescription, I would suggest, is that it merely increases the element of self-deception already so prevalent in our culture. Under present conditions motherhood *is* frequently a degrading experience. There is nothing to be gained by concealing facts in the manner of an advertising campaign designed to raise the prestige of a particular occupation. We would not think of trying to eliminate the hazards of coal mining in this way. Why should we try to do it with motherhood? If it is true that under present circumstances the experience of motherhood narrows and cramps the personality rather than promotes the development of its capacities, some other way will have to be found if it is to be a real solution.

The trend towards a continually more efficient technology and greater specialization, which dominates the rest of our culture, may conceivably provide an answer. In regard to the division of labor it is important to recall one widely known but neglected fact. In the past, whenever human beings have acquired sufficient resources and power, as among aristocracies, they have put the burden of child-rearing on other shoulders. Twenty years ago Ralph Linton pointed out that "aristocrats the world over . . . are reluctant to take care of their own children. Anyone who has had to take care of two or three infants simultaneously

will understand why. This arduous business is turned over to slaves or servants. . . ."[9]

Since the decline of slavery, a basic trend in European society has been to transfer to machines more and more tasks formerly carried out by slaves. By and large, this change has been accompanied by the growth of large organizations to perform tasks formerly scattered among many small groups. This trend may well affect the family. Specialized human agencies, developing from such contemporary forms as the creche, play school, and boarding school, might assume a much larger share of the burden of child rearing, a task that could in any case be greatly lightened by machinery for feeding and the removal of waste products. Can one sensibly argue that the technical ingenuity and resources required to solve this problem are greater than those necessary for nuclear warfare? Are we to regard as permanent and "natural" a civilization that develops its most advanced technology for killing people and leaves their replacement to the methods of the Stone Age?

Against this viewpoint it is usually argued that human infants require some minimum of human affection, even fondling, if they are to survive, and that therefore some form of the family is bound to remain. The premises may be correct, but the conclusion does not follow. A nurse can perform these tasks of giving affection and early socialization just as well as the parents, often better. The argument does not prove anything therefore about the inevitable necessity of the family.

At the same time this point of view does call attention to certain important problems. Industrial society is not likely to produce household nurses, or any form of "servant class" in abundance. On the other hand, as everyone knows who has been in a hospital, nurses in a bureaucratic setting have a strong tendency to treat persons under their care "by the book," without much regard for their individual tasks and requirements. This is a well-known trait of bureaucracy, which tends to treat people and situations alike in order to achieve precision and efficiency. Infants and small children on the contrary require individual attention. For some years they may need to feel that they are the center of the universe. How then can the characteristics of bureaucracy be brought in line with those of maternal affection?

Though this may be the most difficult problem facing any qualitative transformation of the family, it is not necessarily insoluble. In the first place, as Bertrand Russell points out, a good institutional environment may be better for the development of the human personality than a bad family one.[10] In the second place, an increase in the resources allocated to a bureaucratic organization can greatly increase its flexibility and capacity to satisfy variations in individual temperament. Any first-class hotel knows how to cope with this problem. In a few of the best ones in Europe the guest can have privacy and the illusion of being the center of the universe. Finally, one might legitimately expect that the persons who are drawn to serve in any such child-rearing institutions of the future would have more than the average amount of fondness for children, as well as general human warmth and kindliness. Under proper circumstances and management such institutions could give full scope to these benevolent sentiments.

Certain other considerations suggest an alternative that has at least the merit of being much more palatable to the vast majority of people today, since it is more in line with our deep-rooted cultural traditions. These considerations are essentially two. One is the possibility of some innate biological trait roughly resembling the "maternal instinct." The other lies in technological developments that might allow for wider dissemination of machinery to lighten household tasks and to take over the more routine aspects of child rearing. The dish-washing machine, laundromat, and as a much more extreme device, the "Skinner box" represent prototypes of this technological development that could strengthen decentralized arrangements for rearing children.

I do not know what students of human physiology now believe about the maternal instinct. Common observation is enough to show that it cannot be an instinct like sex or hunger. There are many women who never become fond of children, or who soon cease to be fond of them. For them the institutional outlet just sketched would be the most satisfactory way of providing for their offspring. But for others, possibly the majority, the gestation period with its trials and burdens may be enough to create in the mother a desire to retain the infant under her care, after which she could become reluctant to give it up. If machinery were available to lighten child-rearing and household tasks on a far wider scale than is now the case, mothers might be able to satisfy the more positive desires of motherhood. One that seems to be quite important in the middle-class is the desire to mold the child according to some ideal image, though it is now contradicted by fears of damaging the child that derive from superficial popularizations of Freud.

For the home to become again the place where human beings take the first important steps toward realizing their creative potentialities, parents would have to become willing once more to assert their authority. In turn this authority would have to acquire a rational and objective basis, freed of current attempts to revive religious taboos. Thus there would have to be a philosophical as well as a social revolution whose implications we cannot here pursue. One aspect, nevertheless, deserves to be stressed. Rational arguments can be given only to persons competent to understand them. For obvious reasons children are not able to absorb all rational arguments at once, though the present system of education undoubtedly postpones the development of this faculty where it does not destroy it altogether. Therefore parents will have to learn not to be afraid of saying to a child, "You are not old enough yet to understand why you have to do this. But you must do it anyway." The "progressive" family, where every decision turns into an incoherent and rancorous debate, actually contributes to reactionary tendencies in society by failing to equip the next generation with adequate standards of judgment.

There are, however, some grounds for doubting that this conservative solution will eventually prevail as the dominant one. The disappearance of the wider economic functions of the family would make it very difficult, and probably impossible to restore the emotional atmosphere of a cooperative group in which the father has a respected authority. Furthermore, the bureaucratic division of labor has proved the most effective way of solving recurring and routine problems in other areas of life. Though a considerable part of the task of raising children is not routine, a very great portion is repetitive. For these reasons one may expect that semi-bureaucratic arrangements will continue to encroach on the traditional structure of the family. No doubt many individual variations, combinations, and compromises will remain for some time to come. Yet one fine day human society may realize that the part-time family, already a prominent part of our social landscape, has undergone a qualitative transformation into a system of mechanized and bureaucratized child rearing, cleansed of the standardized overtones these words now imply. As already pointed out, an institutional environment can be warm and supporting, often warmer than a family torn by obligations its members resent.

Such a state of affairs, if it comes at all, is well over the visible horizon now. Quite possibly it may never come at all. If it does come, there is not the slightest guarantee that it will solve all personal problems and land us in a state of air-conditioned euphoria. Values that many people hold high today may go by the board, such as the affection older couples show for one another who have shared the same pains in life until they have grown but a single scar. It is also possible that a world of reduced family burdens might be one of shallow and fleeting erotic intrigues, based really on commercial interests.[11] Hollywood could conceivably be the ugly prototype of such a future world, especially in its earlier transitional phases. The most that might be claimed by any future apologist for such institutions, if they ever come to pass, is that they gave greater scope to the development of the creative aspects of the human personality than did the family, which had begun to damage rather than develop this personality under advancing industrialism. And the most that can be claimed for the arguments supporting this possibility is that they correspond to some important trends visible in the family itself as well as in the rest of society. Nevertheless, it would appear that the burden of proof falls on those who maintain that the family is a social institution whose fate will differ in its essentials from that which has befallen all the others.

Notes

[1] Ernest W. Burgess and Harvey J. Locke, *The Family* (2nd ed.; New York, 1953), p. vii. Though this work bears the earmarks of a college text, it is nevertheless authoritative. Burgess is one of the best known American students of the family.

[2] Talcott Parsons, Robert F. Bales, et al., *The Family: Socialization and Interaction Process* (Glencoe, 1955), pp. 9–10, 16–19. In an earlier work, *The Social System* (Glencoe, 1951), p. 156, Parsons raises the possibility of the breakup of the family, mainly to. indicate how improbable such an eventuality seems.

[3] "Professional Ideology of Social Pathologists," *American Journal of Sociology*, vol. XLIX,

No. 2 (September 1943), 165–180.

[4] New York, 1929.

[5] Compare George C. Homans, *The Human Group* (New York, 1950), pp. 444, 450.

[6] The figures used in the accompanying table were adapted from the table in Paul C. Glick, *American Families* (New York, 1957), p. 104.

[7] Compare Parsons, *The Family*, pp. 24–25.

[8] "No culture places a value upon suffering as an end in itself; as a means to the ends of the society (punishment, discipline, etc.), yes; as a means to the ends of the individual (purification, mystical exaltation, etc.), yes; but of and for itself, never." A. L. Kroeber and Clyde Kluckhohn, "Culture: A Critical Review of Concepts and Definitions," *Papers of the Peabody Museum of American Archaeology and Ethnology*, vol. XLVII, No. 1 (1952), 177.

[9] Ralph Linton, *The Study of Man* (New York, 1936), p. 246.

[10] *Marriage and Morals*, p. 169. For Russell's qualifications see pp. 219–220.

[11] For some suggestive counter arguments to this view, see Herbert Marcuse, *Eros and Civilization* (Boston, 1955), pp. 201–202.

Chapter 14

CITY, COUNTRY, AND SUBURB

AN URBAN AREA
Selection 38

A SMALL TOWN
Selection 39

THE SUBURBS
Selection 40

Unlike sex statuses or the institution of the family, cities are not found in all societies. Cities require for their existence the presence of an agricultural surplus, so that people who devote themselves to nonagricultural pursuits can be fed in exchange for political, economic, or other services. This surplus appeared in Neolithic times in connection with several improvements in agriculture. There were no cities in previous societies, and none exist among contemporary "primitives." However, cities are universal in industrial societies and are also found in many preindustrial societies such as medieval Europe, ancient China, pre-Columbian Central America, and present-day "underdeveloped" countries.

Cities are of interest to sociology for two reasons. First, cities possess a distinctive social order. From this point of view much research has been performed investigating the origin, growth, and structure of urban communities. Second, cities are specialized social environments, and the fact that social relations take place in an urban context has an effect upon behavior that must be taken into account by social science. This interest is illustrated by the many studies of differences between the urban and rural family, church, school, and other institutions.

Urban society can be differentiated from rural society by its relatively great specialization and complexity. The city is the site of the greatest division of labor in any society. It is here that the specialists live, are trained, and perform their jobs. A glance at a metropolitan classified telephone directory suggests impressively the extent to which the division of labor has proceeded in the city, and this specialization applies not only to occupations, but to all statuses within the society. This extreme specialization poses great problems of coordination and is the subject of a very complex social order, relying heavily on formal organization.

Among the consequences of specialization and complexity in the city are contrast, segregation, and formal control. The heterogeneous performers of highly specialized roles mingle together in the densely populated city, leading to the impression of contrast. Segregated residential and occupational subcommunities bring together those who occupy interrelated statuses and keep them

369

apart from others. The diversity of norms, values, and beliefs among urban populations requires the institution of formal law, administered by bureaucracies composed of police, lawyers, judges, and legislators. Even psychological processes take a different form under urban conditions. A large number of social relations in the city are by necessity secondary relations. One consequence is the possibility of loneliness, in the midst of the crowd, far greater than that which could be felt on an isolated farm.

The city is a permanent and growing part of the American and indeed the world scene. Throughout the world, cities are growing in number and size. More than 1 out of 8 people now live in cities of 100,000 or more, compared with less than 2 per cent in 1800. The United States, 5 per cent urban in 1790, is now more than two-thirds urban and may shortly equal the four-fifths that the urban population comprises in England and Wales. Moreover, throughout the world, urban culture is being diffused to rural places. Television, the mail-order catalog, and higher education for children are familiar symbols of this process in our own country. The rural culture and social relations of our grandfathers yesterday and the "primitive" tribes of New Guinea today are both in a sense distinctly of the past.

A facet of urban development that has caught the attention of many Americans is the growth of suburbs. Originally conceived as a phenomenon in some sense midway between city and country, suburbs are today being considered as a distinctly urban phenomenon, bearing little resemblance to the rural models they claim as inspiration. However, it is true that the nineteenth-century stereotype of the city is becoming increasingly outdated as suburbs form a larger proportion of the total urban settlement in America. Suburbanization in other societies has not proceeded to nearly the same extent, and it remains to be seen whether the suburban form is destined to be an American, and secondarily British, peculiarity or whether world urbanization will take the same course.

Selection 38, by Harvey Warren Zorbaugh, describes a part of the metropolis that displays the marked characteristics of variety and contrast that have traditionally been associated with urbanism. Arthur Vidich and Joseph Bensman, in Selection 39, describe a small American town from the viewpoint of its residents. Dennis Wrong, in Selection 40, discusses and evaluates the image of the suburbs prevalent among intellectuals.

AN URBAN AREA

The social order of the city has been characterized as "a mosaic of social worlds." This is indeed the picture presented in this selection by Harvey Zorbaugh. It is from a study of a central area of Chicago, which is in turn part of a series of urban studies done at the University of Chicago in the 1920s and 1930s under the direction of Robert Park. Park loved this growing, lusty metropolis and stimulated his students to produce a set of research monographs that remains unsurpassed for insight into the meaning of urbanism.

> The Near North Side of Chicago is immediately adjacent to the Loop, or the commercial core. It is a changing area, with commerce displacing residence at one end and working-class residence disintegrating into slums at the other. Perhaps because of this transition, the area is one of contrasts and extremes. Within a very few blocks can be found the Gold Coast, which is the most exclusive residential area of Chicago; Little Italy, one of the worst slums; Towertown, the habitat of the artist; the "world of furnished rooms"; and the "hobohemia" of Clark Street.
>
> Paradoxically, in view of the geographical mixture of these various groups, they are extremely isolated from each other and fail to understand

each other. The riddle of the city is how these contrasting and mutually ignorant groups can exist without conflict in the absence of community organization.

The riddle would be a much greater one if the community Zorbaugh studied were not so unusual. Even for a large metropolis, this is not a typical area. It is representative at most of what is usually called "the zone of transition," the ring of residential areas mixed with commerce that tends to surround the central business districts of large industrial cities. This is an exciting and fascinating area which can exist only in a great metropolis, and it deserves the kind of attention that Zorbaugh brings to it. It is, however, a small segment of the city, and the extremes of glitter and depression found here are not, for better or worse, the lot of the average city dweller.

As a postscript, it may be noted that Zorbaugh overestimated the amount of change occurring in this area and may have exaggerated the role of transition in producing the conditions of which he writes. It is many years since this research was performed and the city has continued its rapid growth; yet the visitor to Chicago will still find the gleaming facades on the Lake, the slum by the River, and the hoboes on Clark Street. Towertown has abandoned its symbolic water tower to the commercial development of Michigan Avenue, but its former inhabitants cling to the fringes of the district. The slum is now Negro instead of Italian, and the Persians and Greeks are no more; but the most impressive changes are the result of a force nowhere mentioned by Zorbaugh— the bulldozers of urban redevelopment.

Selection 38
FROM THE GOLD COAST AND THE SLUM
Harvey Warren Zorbaugh

The Chicago River, its waters stained by industry, flows back upon itself, branching to divide the city into the South Side, the North Side, and "the great West Side." In the river's southward bend lies the Loop, its skyline looming toward Lake Michigan. The Loop is the heart of Chicago, the knot in the steel arteries of elevated structure which pump in a ceaseless stream the three millions of population of the city into and out of its central business district. The canyon-like streets of the Loop rumble with the traffic of commerce. On its sidewalks throng people of every nation, pushing unseeingly past one another, into and out of office buildings, shops, theaters, hotels, and ultimately back to the north, south, and west "sides" from which they came. For miles over what once was prairie now sprawls in endless blocks the city.

Reprinted from *The Gold Coast and the Slum* by Harvey Warren Zorbaugh (Chicago: University of Chicago Press, 1929), with permission of the publisher.

The city's conquest of the prairie has proceeded stride for stride with the development of transportation. The outskirts of the city have always been about forty-five minutes from the heart of the Loop. In the days of the horse-drawn car they were not beyond Twenty-second Street on the South Side. With the coming of the cable car they were extended to the vicinity of Thirty-sixth Street. The electric car—surface and elevated—again extended the city's outskirts, this time well past Seventieth Street. How far "rapid transit" will take them, no one can predict.

Apace with the expansion of the city has gone the ascendancy of the Loop. Every development in transportation, drawing increasing throngs of people into the central business district, has tended to centralize there not only commerce and finance, but all the vital activities of the city's life. The development of communication has further tightened the Loop's grip on the life of the city. The telephone has at once enormously increased the area over which the central business district can exert control and centralized that control. The newspaper, through the medium of advertising, has firmly established the supremacy of the Loop and, through the news, focused the attention of the city upon the Loop. The skyscraper is the visible symbol of the Loop's domination of the city's life. The central business district of the old city—like that of modern London—with its six- and eight-story buildings, sprawled over an unwieldy area. But the skyscraper, thrusting the Loop skyward thirty, forty, fifty stories, has made possible an extraordinary centralization and articulation of the central business district of the modern city. Drawing thousands daily into the heart of the city, where the old type of building drew hundreds, the cluster of skyscrapers within the Loop has become the city's vortex.

As the Loop expands it literally submerges the areas about it with the traffic of its commerce. Business and industry encroach upon residential neighborhoods. As the roar of traffic swells, and the smoke of industry begrimes buildings, land values rise. The old population moves slowly out, to be replaced by a mobile, shifting, anonymous population bringing with it transitional forms of social life. Within the looming shadow of the skyscraper, in Chicago as in every great city, is found a zone of instability and change—the tidelands of city life.

In a part of these tidelands, within ten minutes' walk of the Loop and the central business district, within five minutes by street car or bus, just across the Chicago River, lies the Near North Side, sometimes called "North Town." Within this area, a mile and a half long and scarcely a mile wide, bounded by Lake Michigan on the east and by the Chicago River on the south and west, under the shadow of the Tribune Tower, a part of the inner city, live ninety thousand people, a population representing all the types and contrasts that lend to the great city its glamor and romance.

The first settlers of Chicago built upon the north bank of the Chicago River, and Chicago's first business house and first railroad were on Kinzie street. But early in Chicago's history destiny took its great commercial and industrial development southward, and for several decades the North Side was a residential district, well-to-do and fashionable. The story of early Chicago society centers about homes on

Ohio, Erie, Cass, and Rush streets; and street after street of old stone fronts, curious streets some of them, still breathe an air of respectability reminiscent of earlier and better days and belying the slow conquest of the slum.

Here change has followed fast upon change. With the growth of the city commerce has encroached upon residential property, relentlessly pushing it northward or crowding it along the lake shore, until now the Near North Side is chequered with business streets. Into this area, where commerce is completing the conquest of the community, has crept the slum. Meantime great industries have sprung up along the river, and peoples speaking foreign tongues have come to labor in them. The slum has offered these alien peoples a place to live cheaply and to themselves; and wave upon wave of immigrants has swept over the area—Irish, Swedish, German, Italian, Persian, Greek, and Negro—forming colonies, staying for a while, then giving way to others. But each has left its impress and its stragglers, and today there live on the Near North Side twenty-nine or more nationalities, many of them with their Old World tongues and customs.

The city's streets can be read as can the geological record in the rock. The old stone fronts of the houses on the side streets; old residences along lower Rush and State, crowded between new business blocks, or with shops built along the street in front of them; a garage with "Riding Academy" in faded letters above its doors; the many old churches along La Salle and Dearborn streets; an office building growing out of a block of rooming-houses; "Deutsche Apotheke" on the window of a store in a neighborhood long since Italian— these are signs that record the changes brought about by the passing decades, changes still taking place today.

The Near North Side is an area of high light and shadow, of vivid contrasts—contrasts not only between the old and the new, between the native and the foreign, but between wealth and poverty, vice and respectability, the conventional and the bohemian, luxury and toil.

Variety is the spice of life, as depicted in the books of the Board of Assessors; autocracy and democracy mingle on the same pages; aphorisms are borne out; and "art for art's sake" remains the slogan of the twentieth century.

On one page of North District Book 18,

the record of the worldly holdings of James C. Ewell, artist, 4 Ohio Street, is set down as "Total personal property, $19." So-and-so, artists, are reported thruout the district with this notation. "Attic room, ill-furnished, many paintings: unable to estimate."

The art colony is located in this section, as is the colony of the rich and the nearly rich. And on the same page are the following three entries which span the stream of life:

Cyrus H. McCormick, 50 E. Huron St., $895,000; taxable assessment, $447,500.
Mary V. McCormick, 678 Rush St., $480,000; taxable assessment, $240,000.

And then—as another contrast—the following entry appears on record:

United States Senator Medill McCormick, guest at the Drake Hotel, $——,000,000,-000.[1]

At the corner of Division Street and the Lake Shore Drive stands a tall apartment building in which seventeen-room apartments rent at one thousand dollars a month. One mile west, near Division Street and the river, Italian families are living in squalid basement rooms for which they pay six dollars a month. The greatest wealth in Chicago is concentrated along the Lake Shore Drive, in what is called the "Gold Coast." Almost at its back door, in "Little Hell," is the greatest concentration of poverty in Chicago. Respectability, it would seem, is measured by rentals and land values.[2]

The Near North Side is not merely an area of contrasts; it is an area of extremes. All the phenomena characteristic of the city are clearly segregated and appear in exaggerated form. Not only are there extremes of wealth and poverty. The Near North Side has the highest residential land values in the city, and among the lowest; it has more professional men, more politicians, more suicides, more persons in *Who's Who*, than any other "community" in Chicago.[3]

The turgid stream of the Chicago River, which bounds the Near North Side on the south and the west, has played a prominent part in its history. A great deal of shipping once went up the river, and tugs, coal barges, tramp freighters, and occasional ore boats still whistle at its bridges and steam slowly around its bends. This shipping caused commerce and industry to locate along the river, and today wharves, lumber and coal yards, iron works,

gas works, sheet metal works, light manufacturing plants and storage plants, wholesale houses for spices, furs, groceries, butter, and imported oils line both sides of the river for miles, and with the noise and smoke of the railroads make a great barrier that half encircles the Near North Side, renders the part of it along the river undesirable to live in, and slowly encroaches northward and eastward.

"North Town" is divided into east and west by State Street. East of State Street lies the Gold Coast, Chicago's most exclusive residential district, turning its face to the lake and its back upon what may lie west toward the river. West of State Street lies a nondescript area of furnished rooms: Clark Street, the Rialto of the half-world; "Little Sicily," the slum.

The Lake Shore Drive is the Mayfair of the Gold Coast. It runs north and south along Lake Michigan, with a wide parkway, bridle path, and promenade. On its western side rise the imposing stone mansions, with their green lawns and wrought-iron-grilled doorways, of Chicago's wealthy aristocracy and her industrial and financial kings. South of these is Streeterville, a "restricted" district of tall apartments and hotels. Here are the Drake Hotel and the Lake Shore Drive Hotel, Chicago's most exclusive. And here apartments rent for from three hundred fifty to a thousand dollars a month. Indeed, the Lake Shore Drive is a street more of wealth than of aristocracy; for in this midwest metropolis money counts for more than does family, and the aristocracy is largely that of the financially successful.

South of Oak Street the Lake Shore Drive, as it turns, becomes North Michigan Avenue, an avenue of fashionable hotels and restaurants, of smart clubs and shops. North Michigan Avenue is the Fifth Avenue of the Middle West; and already it looks forward to the day when Fifth Avenue will be the North Michigan Avenue of the East.

On a warm spring Sunday "Vanity Fair" glides along "the Drive" in motor cars of expensive mark, makes colorful the bridlepaths, or saunters up the promenade between "the Drake" and Lincoln Park. The tops of the tan motor busses are crowded with those who live farther out, going home from church—those of a different world who look at "Vanity Fair" with curious or envious eyes. Even here the element of contrast is not lacking, for a mother from back west, with a shawl over her head, waits for a pause in the stream of motors to lead her eager child across to the beach, while beside her stand a collarless man in a brown derby and his girl in Sunday gingham, from some roominghouse back on La Salle Street.

For a few blocks back of the "the Drive"—on Belleview Place, East Division Street, Stone, Astor, Banks, and North State Parkway, streets less pretentious but equally aristocratic—live more than a third of the people in Chicago's social register, "of good family and not employed." Here are the families that lived on the once fashionable Prairie Avenue, and later Ashland Boulevard, on the South and West sides. These streets, with the Lake Shore Drive, constitute Chicago's much vaunted Gold Coast, a little world to itself, which the city, failing to dislodge, has grown around and passed by.

At the back door of the Gold Coast, on Dearborn, Clark, and La Salle streets, and on the side streets extending south to the business and industrial area, is a strange world, painfully plain by contrast, a world that lives in houses with neatly lettered cards in the window: "Furnished Rooms." In these houses, from midnight to dawn, sleep some twenty-five thousand people. But by day houses and streets are practically deserted. For early in the morning this population hurries from its houses and down its streets, boarding cars and busses, to work in the Loop. It is a childless area, an area of young men and young women, most of whom are single, though some are married, and others are living together unmarried. It is a world of constant comings and goings, of dull routine and little romance, a world of unsatisfied longings.

The Near North Side shades from light to shadow, and from shadow to dark. The Gold Coast gives way to the world of furnished rooms; and the rooming-house area, to the west again, imperceptibly becomes the slum. The common denominator of the slum is its submerged aspect and its detachment from the city as a whole. The slum is a bleak area of segregation of the sediment of society; an area of extreme poverty, tenements, ramshackle buildings, of evictions and evaded rents; an area of working mothers and children, of high rates of birth, infant mortality, illegitimacy, and death; an area of pawnshops and second-hand stores, of gangs, of "flops" where every bed is a vote. As distinguished from the vice area, the disintegrating neighborhood, the slum is an area which has reached the limit of decay and is on the verge of reorganization as missions, settlements, playparks, and business come in.

The Near North Side, west of Clark Street from North Avenue to the river, and east of Clark Street from Chicago Avenue to the river, we may describe as a slum, without fear of contradiction. For this area, cut off by the barrier of river and industry, and for years without adequate transportation, has long been a backwater in the life of the city. This slum district is drab and mean. In ten months the United Charities here had 460 relief cases. Poverty is extreme. Many families are living in one or two basement rooms for which they pay less than ten dollars a month. These rooms are stove heated, and wood is sold on the streets in bundles, and coal in small sacks. The majority of houses, back toward the river, are of wood, and not a few have windows broken out. Smoke, the odor from the gas works, and the smell of dirty alleys is in the air. Both rooms and lots are overcrowded. Back tenements, especially north of Division Street, are common.[4]

Life in the slum is strenuous and precarious. One reads in the paper of a mother on North Avenue giving away her baby that the rest of her children may live. Frequently babies are found in alleyways. A nurse at the Passavant Hospital on North La Salle tells of a dirty little gamin, brought in from Wells Street, whose toe had been bitten off by a rat while he slept. Many women from this neighborhood are in the maternity ward four times in three years. A girl, a waitress, living at the Albany Hotel on lower Rush Street, recently committed suicide leaving the brief note, "I am tired of everything. I have seen too much. That is all."[5]

Clark Street is the Rialto of the slum. Deteriorated store buildings, cheap dance halls and movies, cabarets and doubtful hotels, missions, "flops," pawnshops and second-hand stores, innumerable restaurants, soft-drink parlors and "fellowship" saloons, where men sit about and talk, and which are hangouts for criminal gangs that live back in the slum, fence at the pawnshops, and consort with the transient prostitutes so characteristic of the North Side—such is "the Street." It is an all-night street, a street upon which one meets all the varied types that go to make up the slum.

The slum harbors many sorts of people: the criminal, the radical, the bohemian, the migratory worker, the immigrant, the unsuccessful, the queer and unadjusted. The migratory worker is attracted by the cheap hotels on State, Clark, Wells, and the streets along the river. The criminal and underworld find anonymity in the transient life of the cheaper rooming-houses such as exist on North La Salle Street. The bohemian and the unsuccessful are attracted by cheap attic or basement rooms. The radical is sure of a sympathetic audience in Washington Square. The foreign colony, on the other hand, is found in the slum, not because the immigrant seeks the slum, nor because he makes a slum of the area in which he settles, but merely because he finds there cheap quarters in which to live, and relatively little opposition to his coming. From Sedgwick Street west to the river is a colony of some fifteen thousand Italians, familiarly known as "Little Hell." Here the immigrant has settled blocks by villages, bringing with him his language, his customs, and his traditions, many of which persist.

Other foreign groups have come into this area. North of "Little Sicily," between Wells and Milton streets, there is a large admixture of Poles with Americans, Irish, and Slavs. The Negro, too, is moving into this area and pushing on into "Little Hell." There is a small colony of Greeks grouped about West Chicago Avenue, with its picturesque coffee houses on Clark Street. Finally, there has come in within the past few years a considerable colony of Persians, which has also settled in the vicinity of Chicago Avenue. The slum on the Near North Side is truly cosmopolitan.

In the slum, but not of it, is "Towertown," or "the village." South of Chicago Avenue, along east Erie, Ohio, Huron, and Superior streets, is a considerable colony of artists and of would-be artists. The artists have located here because old buildings can be cheaply converted into studios. The would-be artists have followed the artists. And the hangers-on of bohemia have come for atmosphere, and because the old residences in the district have stables. "The village" is full of picturesque people and resorts—tearooms with such names as the Wind Blew Inn, the Blue Mouse, and the Green Mask. And many interesting art stores, antique shops, and stalls with rare books are tucked away among the old buildings. All in all, the picturesque and unconventional life of "the village" is again in striking contrast to the formal and conventional life of the Gold Coast, a few short blocks to the north.

One has but to walk the streets of the Near North Side to sense the cultural isolation beneath these contrasts. Indeed, the color and picturesqueness of the city exists in the intimations of what lies behind the superficial contrasts of its life. How various are the thoughts of the individuals who throng up Michigan Avenue from the Loop at the close of the day—artists, shop girls, immigrants, inventors, men of affairs, women of fashion, waitresses, clerks, entertainers. How many are their vocational interests; how different are their ambitions. How vastly multiplied are the chances of life in a great city, as compared with those of the American towns and European peasant villages from which most of these individuals have come. What plans, plots, conspiracies, and dreams for taking advantage of these chances different individuals must harbor under their hats. Yet they have little in common beyond the fact that they jostle one another on the same street. Experience has taught them different languages. How far they are from understanding one another, or from being able to communicate save upon the most obvious material matters!

As one walks from the Drake Hotel and the Lake Shore Drive west along Oak street, through the world of rooming-houses, into the slum and the streets of the Italian Colony one has a sense of distance as between the Gold Coast and Little Hell—distance that is not geographical but social. There are distances of language and custom. There are distances represented by wealth and the luster it adds to human existence. There are distances of horizon—the Gold Coast living throughout the world while Little Hell is still only slowly emerging out of its old Sicilian villages. There are distances represented by the Gold Coast's absorbing professional interests. It is one world that revolves about the Lake Shore Drive, with its mansions, clubs, and motors, its benefits and assemblies. It is another world that revolves about the Dill Pickle Club, the soap boxes of Washington Square, or the shop of Romano the Barber. And each little world is absorbed in its own affairs.

For the great majority of the people on the Gold Coast—excepting those few individuals who remember, or whose parents remember, the immigrant communities out of which they have succeeded in climbing—the district west of State Street exists only in the newspapers. And from the newspapers they learn nothing reassuring. The metropolitan press pictures this district as a bizarre world of gang wars, of exploding stills, of radical plots, of "lost" girls, of suicides, of bombings, of murder.

The resident of the Lake Shore Drive forms his conceptions of Little Sicily from such items as these:

"LITTLE ITALY" STORE WRECKED BY BOMB

For the eighth consecutive Sunday the North Side "Little Italy" was awakened by its usual "alarm clock." The "alarm clock" was a large black powder bomb. The detonation was heard throughout the colony. A part of the grocery store of Mrs. Beatrice Diengello was wrecked, and the eight families living in the adjoining tenement were rudely awakened.

TWO SHOT TO DEATH IN WHISKEY FEUD

Two bullet-ridden bodies were found yesterday near "Death Corner," Cambridge and Oak streets. Police investigation developed the theory that a feud among whiskey runners was responsible for the murders.

KIN'S SILENCE AGAIN HIDES ITALIAN SLAYER

The usual shrugging of shoulders answered detectives who are trying to clear up Chicago's latest Italian murder—that of Frank Mariata, a laborer, who was shot to death as he was leaving his flat, 462 Division Street, yesterday morning. Three men were seen rushing from the building after the shooting, but relatives of the dead man claim they have no idea who the slayers are. Although three guns were found under Mariata's pillow, his wife insists he had no enemies.

FIFTY-THREE PER CENT OF CHICAGO'S KILLING OCCURRED IN LITTLE ITALY AND BLACK BELT

More than half of the violent deaths in Chicago in the first ninety days of this year occurred among Negroes or Italians, two groups constituting about 7 per cent of the population. The Italian blackhand zone is on the Near North Side, bounded by Erie, Dearborn, Division, and the river.

Similarly, the "Gold Coaster" concludes from his morning paper that the Persian col-ony is a place of feuds, flashing knives, flying chairs, and shattering glass:

TWO COPS END WAR OF 200 PERSIANS: THREE MEN STABBED

Three men were stabbed, several badly beaten, and ten arrested during a pitched battle between rival factions of Persians in a coffee shop at 706 North Clark Street early yesterday evening. Police in answering a riot call had to fight their way through more than two hundred fighting men.

For several years there has been an unwritten law that no Syrian Persian was allowed north of Huron Street on Clark Street. Five members of the race wandered into the coffee shop of Titian and Sayad and sat down at a table to play cards. In a short time six Assyrian Persians entered the place and saw them. They walked to the table, it is said, and remarked that the Syrians had better get off the street. At that the five Syrians started to fight.

In a moment other men in the place drew knives and advanced on the battlers. Chairs were overturned and windows broken. The fight led out to the street. Finally more than two hundred had taken up the fight. Then someone sent in a riot call.

Beyond these newspaper reports, little is known of the world west of State Street by the people of the Gold Coast. Their affairs rarely take them into the river district. The reports of social agencies are little read. It is a region remote.

But to the people who live west of State Street the Gold Coast is immediate and real. It is one of the sights of the town. They throng its streets in going down to the lake on hot summer days. From the beach they gaze up at the magnificent hotels and apartments of Streeterville, and at the luxurious and forbidding mansions of the Lake Shore Drive. They watch the streams of costly automobiles and fashionably dressed men and women. The front pages of the newspapers they read as they hang to straps on the street cars in the evening are filled with pictures of the inhabitants of the Gold Coast, and with accounts of their comings and goings. It all enlists the imagination. Consequently the people from "back west" enormously idealize the Gold Coast's life. They imitate its styles and manners. The imagination of the shop girl, of the immigrant, of the hobo plays with these externals of its life. In the movie they see realistic pictures of "high society." These they take to be the inner, intimate life of which they see the externals along the Lake Shore Drive. As a result the social distance from Death Corner to the Drake Hotel is no less than the distance from Casino Club to Bughouse Square.

The isolation of the populations crowded together within these few hundred blocks, the superficiality and externality of their contacts, the social distances that separate them, their absorption in the affairs of their own little worlds—these, and not mere size and numbers, constitute the social problem of the inner city. The community, represented by the town or peasant village where everyone knows everyone else clear down to the ground, is gone. Over large areas of the city "community" is little more than a geographical expression. Yet the old tradition of control persists despite changed conditions of life. The inevitable result is cultural disorganization.

Notes

[1] *Chicago Herald and Examiner,* July, 1923.

[2] United Charities of Chicago: *Sixty Years of Service.* In 1920–21 there were 90 contributions to the United Charities in less than a square mile on the Gold Coast, and 460 poverty cases in the square mile behind it.

[3] Taking figures for five widely differing "communities" in Chicago, this fact is clearly brought out [in the table below]:

[4] A five-room house on Hill Street, the rooms in which are $9 \times 12 \times 10$ feet high, has thirty occupants. Another nurse told the writer of being called on a case on Sedgwick Street and finding two couples living in one room. One couple worked days, the other nights; one couple went to bed when the other couple got up. Mrs. Louise De Koven Bowen (*Growing Up with a City*), reminiscing of her United Charities experiences, tells of a woman who for three years existed on the food she procured from garbage cans and from the samples of department store demonstration counters. She adds:

"Sometimes fate seems to be relentless to the point of absurdity, as in one case I remember of an Italian family. . . . The man was riding on a street car and was suddenly assaulted by an irate passenger. . . . His nose was broken and he was badly disfigured. . . . A few days later, on his way home from a dispensary where he had gone to have his wound dressed, he fell off a sidewalk and broke his leg. The mother gave birth to a child the same day. Another child died the following day, and the eldest girl, only fourteen years old, who had been sent out to look for work, was foully assaulted on the street."

Such is the life of the slum!

[5] *Chicago Evening American,* December 21, 1923.

Community	Population	Who's Who	Physicians	Politicians	Poverty cases	Suicides
Back of the Yards *	39,908	1	28	4	185	8
Bridgeport †	64,875	0	44	12	180	3
Lawndale ‡	105,819	1	212	14	251	6
Woodlawn ¶	69,504	31	185	14	48	8
Near North	83,819	151	212	30	555	28

* Immigrant community back of the Stockyards.
† Polish "area of first settlement" on the Southwest Side.
‡ Jewish "area of second settlement" on the West Side.
¶ South Side residential community, surrounding the University of Chicago, containing many professional men and women.

A SMALL TOWN

Discussion of country and city in America involves one in an ideological debate that has continued since our nation's founding. Basic economic and political differences between these two segments of society have led to a battle of imagery in which the urban virtues of cosmopolitanism and opportunity are contrasted with vices like snobbery and unwholesomeness, and the peace and friendliness asserted for the country have their foils in provinciality and dullness. Although

sociologists claim to be interested in facts and not virtues, in this area of discussion, as in many others, the facts have value consequences that are impossible
to avoid.

This selection is from a sociological study of a small town in rural New York
State. This particular chapter presents the image that residents of Springdale
have of their community. As is the case with many sets of beliefs, the facts as
the social scientist finds them are not always in accordance with the imagined
state of affairs, but the latter is highly valued, and its realization is the function of many community norms. In other words, Springdale's image of itself is
in many ways a fiction, but this fiction exercises an influence on the behavior of
its residents.

> Springdale people think of themselves as "just plain folks." This term has
> many connotations, including morality and democratic equalitarianism.
> "Folks" are contrasted with "city people," who are stereotyped in an un-
> favorable fashion. Springdale's image of itself is supported by norms pre-
> scribing friendship with neighbors, and the resulting behavior has the ef-
> fect of reinforcing the friendly image of the town. The image is somewhat
> compromised by gossip, but the gossip takes place on a private level and is
> not publicly acknowledged.
>
> The repertory of statuses in this small town is very limited. There is
> no provision, either positive or negative, for the integration of intel-
> lectuals or introverts into the social organization of the community.
> Springdale is tolerant of deviants, typing them as characters, but it makes
> no social use of them.

This passage is a superb illustration of the themes that rural America has used
in its ideological battle with the city. However, Vidich and Bensman in the
body of their book suggest that all is not as Springdalers imagine, despite the
normative structure supporting this image. They note that the claimed social
homogeneity of the community hides five distinct social classes with grossly different interests. Local government is largely a matter of machine politics, rather
than the idealized democracy that is asserted. Most significantly, they find
Springdale to be in a position of economic and social dependence upon the encompassing city-dominated society. Through the mass media (radio, television,
magazines, movies, etc.), through immigrants from the cities, and especially
through the integration of local economic activities into a national economy,
Springdale has become an extension of Albany, New York City, and Washington. This dependence, so much in contrast with the proclaimed image of Springdale, has been increased by the abdication of local government to larger units
because of the prevailing commitment to low local taxes. Springdale has sold
its autonomy and can claim independence only because its residents are able to
deceive themselves.

This is, of course, a case study. Springdale cannot necessarily be assumed to
be typical of rural communities in general. The truly isolated, self-supporting
rural community, hidden away in an Appalachian valley, might bear a much
closer likeness in reality to Springdale's self-image whereas the degree of dependence actually noted in Springdale might be considerably greater in a town of
central Illinois that is tied more closely to national commodities markets. For
the most part, however, rural America has increasingly lost its isolation, becoming integrated with the total, urban-dominated society, and adopting urban
culture. Differences that used to mark the distinction between city and country
have been disappearing, and the folk society that small towns still proclaim exists
no more.

Selection 39

FROM SMALL TOWN IN MASS SOCIETY

Arthur J. Vidich and Joseph Bensman

When one becomes more intimately acquainted with the people of Springdale, and especially with the more verbal and more prominent inhabitants, one finds that they like to think of themselves as "just plain folks." The editor of the paper, in urging people to attend public meetings or in reporting a social event, says, "all folks with an interest" should attend or "the folks who came certainly had a good time." Almost any chairman of a public gathering addresses his audience as folks—"all right folks, the meeting will get underway"— and the interviewer in his work frequently encounters the same expression—"the folks in this community," "the townfolk," "the country folk," "good folks," and "bad folks." Depending on context, the term carries with it a number of quite different connotations.

First and foremost, the term serves to distinguish Springdalers from urban dwellers, who are called "city people," an expression which by the tone in which it is used implies the less fortunate, those who are denied the wholesome virtues of rural life. City people are separated from nature and soil, from field and stream, and are caught up in the inexorable web of impersonality and loneliness, of which the public statement in Springdale is: "How can people stand to live in cities?" In an understandable and ultimate extension of this valuation one may occasionally hear references to the rural or country folk, in contrast to the villagers, the former being regarded by Springdalers as the "true folk."

The self-designation as "folk" includes everyone in the community; by its generality of reference it excludes neither the rich nor the poor, for everyone can share equally in the genuine qualities ascribed by the term. This is not to say that the community does not recognize scoundrels and wastrels in its own environment; quite the contrary, the scoundrel and allied types become all the more noticeable in the light of the dominant genuineness of rural life. It is rather to say that the standard of judgment by which character is assessed in Springdale includes no false or artificial values. To be one of the folks requires neither money, status, family background, learning, nor refined manners. It is, in short, a way of referring to the equalitarianism of rural life.

The term also includes a whole set of moral values; honesty, fair play, trustworthiness, good-neighborliness, helpfulness, sobriety, and clean-living. To the Springdaler it suggests a wholesome family life, a man whose spoken word is as good as a written contract, a community of religious-minded people, and a place where "everybody knows everybody" and "where you can say hello to anybody." The background image of urban society and city people gives force and meaning to the preferred rural way of life.

Rural virtues and city life

The sense of community-mindedness and identification has its roots in a belief in the inherent difference between Springdale and all other places, particularly the nearby towns and big cities. For the Springdaler surrounding towns all carry stigmata which are not found in Springdale: the county seat is the locus of vice and corruption, the Finnish settlement is "red," University Town is snobbish and aloof, and Industrial Town is inhuman, slummy and foreign. In the big city the individual is anonymously lost in a hostile and dog-eat-dog environment. Being in the community gives one a distinct feeling of living in a protected and better place, so that in spite of occasional internal quarrels and the presence of some unwholesome characters, one frequently hears it said that "there's no place I'd rather live . . . there isn't a better place to raise a family . . . this is the best little town in the whole country." In the face of the outer world, Springdalers "stick up for their town."

The best example of community identification occurs when newspapers of neighboring towns choose to publicize negative aspects of Springdale life: making banner headlines over the dismissal of a school principal, publishing the names of youthful criminal offenders who come from good families. In such instances, irrespective of issue or factional position, any-one with an interest in the community comes to its defense: "We may have our troubles, but it's nothing we can't handle by ourselves—and quicker and better if they'd leave us alone." A challenge to the image of Springdale as a preferred place cuts deep and helps to re-create the sense of community when it is tem-porarily lost.

It is interesting that the belief in the su-periority of local ways of living actually condi-tions the way of life. Springdalers *"make an effort* to be friendly" and *"go out of their way* to help newcomers." The newspaper always emphasizes the positive side of life; it never reports local arrests, shotgun weddings, mort-gage foreclosures, lawsuits, bitter exchanges in public meetings, suicides or any other unpleas-ant happening. By this constant focus on warm and human qualities in all public situations, the public character of the community takes on those qualities and, hence, it has a tone which is distinctly different from city life.

Relationships with nearby towns, in spite of the occasional voicing of hostility, also have a sympathetic and friendly competitive aspect. No one in Springdale would gloat over another town's misfortunes, such as a serious fire or the loss of an industry. Athletic rivalries have long histories and although there is a vocabu-lary of names and yells for "enemies," these simply stimulate competitiveness and arouse emotions for the night of the contest. No one takes victory or defeat seriously for more than a day or two and only in a very rare instance is there a public incident when outsiders visit the town. "Nobody really wants trouble with other towns."

When one goes beyond neighboring com-munities, the Springdaler leaps from concrete images of people and places to a more general-ized image of metropolitan life. His everyday experiences give him a feeling of remoteness from the major centers of industry, commerce and politics. His images are apt to be as ste-reotyped as those that city people hold con-cerning the country. Any composite of these images would certainly include the following:

1. Cities breed corruption and have grown so big and impersonal that they are not able to solve the problems they create.

2. Cities are an unwholesome environment for children and families, and have had an unhealthy effect on family morals.

3. Urban politicians and labor leaders are corrupt and represent anti-democratic forces in American life.

4. Washington is a place overridden with bureaucrats and the sharp deal, fast-buck op-erator, both of whom live like parasites off hard-working country folk.

5. Industrial workers are highly paid for doing little work. Their leaders foment trou-ble and work against the good of the country.

6. Cities are hotbeds of un-American senti-ment, harbor the reds and are incapable of educating their youth to Christian values.

7. Big universities and city churches are centers of atheism and secularism and in spite of occasional exceptions have lost touch with the spiritual lesson taught by rural life.

8. Most of the problems of country life have their origin in the effects which urban life has on rural ways.

What is central, however, is the feeling of the Springdaler that these things do not basi-cally affect him. While he realizes that machin-ery and factory products are essential to his standard of life and that taxation and agricul-tural policy are important, he feels that he is independent of other features of industrial and urban life, or, better, that he can choose and select only the best parts. The simple physical separation from the city and the open rural atmosphere make it possible to avoid the prob-lems inherent in city life. Personal relations are face-to-face and social gatherings are intimate, churchgoing retains the quality of a family af-fair, the merchant is known as a person, and you can experience the "thrill of watching na-ture and the growth of your garden." Spring-dalers firmly believe in the virtues of rural living, strive to maintain them and defend them against anyone who would criticize them.

"Neighbors are friends"

Almost all of rural life receives its justifica-tion on the basis of the direct and personal and human feelings that guide people's rela-tions with each other. No one, not even a stranger, is a stranger to the circumambience of the community. It is as if the people in a deeply felt communion bring themselves to-gether for the purposes of mutual self-help and protection. To this end the community is organized for friendliness and neighborliness, so much so that the terms "friends" and "neighbors" almost stand as synonyms for "folk."

In its most typical form neighborliness occurs in time of personal and family crisis—birth, death, illness, fire, catastrophe. On such occasions friends and neighbors mobilize to support those in distress: collections of money are taken, meals are prepared by others, cards of condolence are sent. A man whose house or barn has burned may unexpectedly find an organized "bee" aiding in reconstruction. Practically all organizations have "sunshine" committees whose sole purpose is to send greeting cards. These practices are so widespread and ultimately may include so many people that an individual, unable to acknowledge all this friendliness personally, will utilize the newspaper's "card of thanks" column to express his public appreciation.

Borrowing and "lending back and forth" is perhaps the most widespread act of neighborliness. Farmers say they like to feel that "in a pinch" there is always someone whom they can count upon for help—to borrow tools, get advice, ask for labor. In spite of the advent of mechanized and self-sufficient farming and consequently the reduction of the need for mutual aid, the high public value placed on mutual help is not diminished. Though a farmer may want to be independent and wish to avoid getting involved in other people's problems and, in fact, may privately resent lending his machinery, it is quite difficult for him to refuse to assist his neighbor if asked. Even where technological advance has made inroads on the need for the practice, to support the public creed remains a necessity.

For housewives in a community where "stores don't carry everything" domestic trading and borrowing is still a reality; they exchange children's clothing and *do* borrow salt and sugar. In Springdale they say "you never have to be without . . . if you need something bad enough you can always get it: of course, sometimes people overdo it and that makes it bad for everybody, but after a while you find out who they are." The process of selectively eliminating the bad practitioners makes it possible to keep the operation of the practice on a high plane.

Neighborliness has its institutional supports and so is given a firm foundation. Ministers and church groups make it a practice to visit the sick in hospitals and homes and to remember them with cards and letters, and all other organizations—the Legion, Masons, Community Club, book clubs—designate special committees to insure that remembrance is extended to the bereaved and ill. The Legion and Community Club "help our own" with baskets of food and clothing at Christmas time and organize fund drives to assist those who are "burned out." The ideology of neighborliness is reflected in and reinforced by the organized life of the community.

To a great extent these arrangements between friends and neighbors have a reciprocal character: a man who helps others may himself expect to be helped later on. In a way the whole system takes on the character of insurance. Of course some people are more conscious of their premium payments than others and keep a kind of mental bookkeeping on "what they owe and who owes them what," which is a perfectly permissible practice so long as one does not openly confront others with unbalanced accounts. In fact, the man who knows "exactly where he stands" with his friends and neighbors is better advised than the one who "forgets and can't keep track." The person who is unconsciously oblivious of what others do for him and distributes his own kindness and favor without thinking is apt to alienate both those whom he owes and doesn't owe. The etiquette for getting and giving in Springdale is an art that requires sensitive adjustments to the moods, needs and expectations of others. This ability to respond appropriately in given situations is the sign of the good neighbor. That this sensitivity is possessed by large numbers of people is attested to by the fact that friendliness and neighborliness contribute substantially to the community's dominant tone of personalness and warmth.

Of course, everyone does not participate equally or at the same level in being a good friend and neighbor. Deviations and exceptions are numerous. Neighborliness is often confined to geographical areas and to socially compatible groups. The wife of the lawyer is on neighborly terms with others like herself rather than with the wife of a carpenter. Farmers necessarily have less to do with people in the village and teachers are more apt to carry on friendly relations with each other. Those who are not willing to both give and take find themselves courteously eliminated from this aspect of local life. "People who are better off" simply by possessing sufficient resources do not find it necessary to call on friends and neighbors for help, though "everyone knows that if you went and asked them for something, they'd give it to you right away." Others have a more "independent turn of mind" and "will get by with what they have, no matter what, just to be free of mind"; the ideology of neighborliness is broad enough to include them "so long as they don't do anyone harm." The foreign elements, particularly the Poles, limit their everyday neighboring to their own group, but still by community definitions they are good neighbors because "you can always trust a Pole to deal square . . . if they owe you anything, they will always pay you back on time." Some folks are known as "just good people" who by choice "keep to themselves." By isolating themselves within the community they neither add to nor detract from the neighborly quality of community life and so do not have an effect on the public character of the town.

The only group which does not fall within the purview of the conception of friend and neighbor is the 10 per cent of the population that live "in shacks in the hills." The people who live in shacks "can't be trusted"; "they steal you blind"; "if you're friendly to them, they'll take advantage of you"; "if you lend them something you'll never see it again"; "they're bad . . . no good people . . . live like animals." Hence by appropriately extending the social definition to give it a broader base than mutual aid, all groups in the community, except the shack people, fulfill the image of good friend and neighbor. The self-conception then reinforces itself, serves as a model for achievement and adds to the essential appearance of community warmth.

Good folks and bad folks

"Of course, there are some people who just naturally have a dirty mouth. You'll find them anywhere you go and I'd be lying if I said we didn't have a few here." The "dirty mouth" is a person who not only fabricates malicious gossip about his enemies but also wantonly and carelessly spreads his fabrications. He commits the double *faux pas* of being deliberately malicious and of not observing the etiquette of interpersonal relations, and he is

perhaps the most despised person in the community.

There are a whole range of personal qualities which are almost unanimously disapproved in Springdale. These are identified in the person

"who holds a grudge . . . who won't ever forget a wrong done to him."

"who can't get along with other people . . . who won't ever try to be friendly and sociable."

"who gives the town a bad name . . . always raising up a ruckus . . . always trying to stir up trouble."

"who tries to be something he isn't . . . the show-off . . . the braggart."

"who thinks he's better than everybody else . . . who thinks he's too good for the town . . . who thinks he's a cut above ordinary folks."

"who is bossy . . . thinks his ideas are always the best . . . tries to run everything . . . wants to be the center of attention all the time without working for it."

"who makes money by cheating people . . . who hasn't made his money honestly . . . you can't figure out where he got all that money."

"whom you can't trust . . . whose word is no good . . . who doesn't do what he says he was going to do . . . who doesn't carry through on anything."

In almost the exact reverse, the qualities of a good member of the community are found in the person who

"forgives and forgets . . . lets bygones be bygones . . . never dredges up the past . . . lets you know that he isn't going to hold it against you."

"is always doing something for the good of the town . . . gives willingly of his time and money . . . supports community projects . . . never shirks when there's work to be done."

"gets along with everybody . . . always has a good word . . . goes out of his way to do a good turn . . . never tries to hurt anybody . . . always has a smile for everybody."

"is just a natural person . . . even if you know he's better than you, he never lets you know it . . . never tries to impress anybody just because he has a little more money . . . acts like an ordinary person."

"always waits his turn . . . is modest . . . will work along with everybody else . . . isn't out for his own glory . . . takes a job and does it well without making a lot of noise."

"worked hard for what he's got . . . deserves every penny he has . . . doesn't come around to collect the first day of the month . . . you know he could be a lot richer."

"stands on his word . . . never has to have it in writing . . . does what he says . . . if he can't do it he says so and if he can he does it . . . always does it on time."

Springdalers affirm that on the whole most people in the community have these qualities. They are the qualities of "average folk" and "we like to think of ourselves as just a little above the average." "Average people can get things done because nobody has any high-blown ideas and they can all work together to make the community a better place to live."

What is interesting about the usual definitions of good and bad people are the types that are excluded entirely. At this level those who go unrecognized, even in the negative statements, are the intellectuals, the bookish and the introverts. In a community that places a high premium on being demonstrably average, friendly and open, the person who appears in public and "doesn't say much" is a difficult character to understand: "he's a good fellow, but you never know what he's thinking." "Book reading and studying all the time," while they have a place, "shouldn't be carried too far . . . you have to keep your feet on the ground, be practical." The intellectual is respected for his education, is admired for his verbal facility and sometimes can provide the right idea, but nevertheless he is suspect and "shouldn't be allowed to get into positions of responsibility." It is apparent that where stereotyped public definitions do not easily fit, non-conformity is still tolerated so long as it does not seriously interfere with the workings of the town.

In the community setting the test case of the toleration and sympathy for non-conformity lies in attitudes toward cranks, psychotics and "odd" personalities: the ex-minister who writes poetry, the hermit who lives in the woods, the woman obsessed with the legal correctness of her husband's will, the spinster who screams at callers, the town moron and the clinical catatonic. Needless to say these represent only a small percentage of the population. The point is that Springdale is able to absorb, protect and care for them; when in the infrequent instance they intrude on the public scene, they are treated with the same sympathy and kindness accorded a child. So long as non-conformity does not interfere with the normal functioning of the town, no price is exacted from the non-conformist. At the worst, the non-conforming types are surrounded by humor. They become local "characters" who add color and interest to the everyday life of the community; because they are odd and different, they are always available as a standard conversational piece. In this way the community demonstrates its kindness and "lives and lets live."

"We're all equal"

With the exception of a few "old cranks" and "no goods," it is unthinkable for anyone to pass a person on the street without exchanging greetings. Customarily one stops for a moment of conversation to discuss the weather and make inquiries about health; even the newcomer finds others stopping to greet him. The pattern of everyone talking to everyone is especially characteristic when people congregate in groups. Meetings and social gatherings do not begin until greetings have been exchanged all around. The person who feels he is above associating with everyone, as is the case with some newcomers from the city, runs the risk of being regarded a snob, for the taint of snobbishness is most easily acquired by failing to be friendly to everyone.

It is the policy of the Community Club to be open to "everyone, whether dues are paid or not" and hardly a meeting passes without a repetition of this statement. Those who are the leaders of the community take pride in this organization specifically because it excludes no one, and this fact is emphasized time and again in public situations. Wherever they can, community leaders encourage broad participation in all spheres of public life: everyone is urged and invited to attend public meetings and everyone is urged to "vote not as a duty, but as a privilege." The equality at the ballot box of all men, each according to his own conscience, in a community where you know all the candidates personally, where votes can't be bought and where you know the poll-keepers, is the hallmark of equality that underpins all other equality. "Here no man counts more than any other"; this is stated in every affirmation of rural political equality—"if you don't like the rascals, use your vote to kick them out."

The social force of the idea finds its most positive expression in a negative way. The ladies of the book clubs, the most exclusive and limited membership groups in Springdale, find themselves in the ambiguous position of having to be apologetic for their exclusiveness. Because they are select in a community which devalues standoffishness, they are the only groups that are defensive in meeting the rest of the public. To the observer, they explain, "It's not that we want to be exclusive. It's just that sixteen is all you can manage in a book club. If anybody wants to be in a book club, she can start her own, like the Wednesday Group." By the same token they receive a large share of resentment; any number of vulgar expressions refer to this feminine section of the community.

The public ideology of equality has its economic correlates. One must not suppose that inequalities in income and wealth go unnoticed; rather, they are quite closely watched and known in Springdale. However, such differences, as in the image of the frontier community, are not publicly weighed and evaluated as the measure of the man.

In everyday social intercourse it is a social *faux pas* to act as if economic inequalities make a difference. The wealthiest people in town, though they have big homes, live quite simply without servants. The serviceman, the delivery boy and the door-to-door canvasser knock at the front door and, though they may feel somewhat awkward on carpeted floors, are asked to enter even before stating their business. A man who flaunts his wealth, or demands deference because of it, is out of tune with a community whose "upper class" devalues conspicuous consumption and works at honest pursuits. "What makes the difference is not the wealth but the character behind it."

It is not a distortion to say that the good man is the working man and in the public estimation the fact of working transcends, indeed explains, economic differentials; work has its own social day of judgment and the judgment conferred is self-respect and respectability. Work, in the first instance, is the great social equalizer, and the purest form of work which serves as a yardstick for all other work is farm work. By this mechanism the "hard-working poor man" is superior to the "lazy rich man." The quotation marks are advised and indicate the hypotheticalness of the case because in common usage the two, work and wealth, go together. Where they don't it is because of misfortune, catastrophe, bad luck or simply because the man is young and work has not yet had a chance to pay its dividends. But even wealth is the wrong word. Work is rather juxtaposed beside such terms as rich, solvent, well-off; wealth implies more economic differentiation than Springdalers like to think exists in their community. Thus, the measure of a man, for all public social purposes, is the diligence and perseverance with which he pursues his economic ends; the "steady worker," the "good worker," the "hard worker" in contrast to the "fly-by-night schemer," the "band-wagon jumper," and the "johnny-come-lately." For the Springdaler the test case is the vulgar social climber, the person who tries to "get in with the better people" by aping them in dress and possessions which only money can buy. In spite of the social and economic differences visible to the outside observer, the pervading appearance of the community is that of a social equality based on the humanness of rural life.

Like other small rural communities Springdale must face the classic problem of preserving individual privacy in the face of a public ideology which places a high valuation on positive expressions of equalitarianism and neighborliness. The impression of community warmheartedness which is given by the free exchange of public greetings and the easy way "everybody gets along with everybody else" has its counterpart in the absence of privacy implied by the factor of gossip. The observer who has been in the community for a length of time realizes that "everybody isn't really neighborly . . . that some people haven't talked to each other for years . . . that people whom you might think are friends hate each other . . . that there are some people who are just naturally troublemakers . . . that he'd skin his own grandmother for a buck." However, such statements are never made in public situations. The intimate, the negative and the private are spoken in interpersonal situations involving only two or three people. Gossip exists as a separate and hidden layer of community life.

That is why it is at first difficult for the observer to believe the often-repeated statement that "everybody knows everything about everybody else in Springdale," or, as stated otherwise, "in a small town you live in a glass house." It develops that the statements are true only to a degree: while one learns intimate and verifiable details of people's private lives, these never become the subject of open, public discussion.

In the private sphere—at what is commonly regarded as the level of gossip, either malicious or harmless—Springdalers tend to emphasize the negative and competitive qualities of life. One learns about domestic discords, sexual aberrations, family skeletons, ill-gained wealth, feuds, spite fences, black sheep, criminal records and alcoholism. The major preoccupation, however, is reserved for "what he's worth" in the strictly monetary and material meaning of the expression. The image of the sharp trading farmer, the penny-wise homemaker and the thrifty country folk is reflected in reverse in this concern with the state of other people's finances and possessions. All men, from the bartender to the clergyman, are capable of such concern typically expressed as follows:

"I'd say he's worth at least $30,000. Why the cows and buildings are worth that alone."

"You'd think a man with his money would give more than $50 to the church."

"The reason he's got so much is because he never spends any, hasn't taken a vacation for thirty years, never contributes a cent to anything."

"There's a man who's got a fortune and you'd never guess it."

"What I couldn't do with his dough."

"The way they spend money, you'd think it was like picking leaves off a tree."

"There's a guy making $2,800 and he's got a new Pontiac."

"Up to his neck in debt and he walks around like he had a million."

"Lend him a cent and you'll never see it again."

"He cleaned up during the war."

"There isn't anything he can't turn into a dollar."

"Figure it out. He's working, his wife's working, they haven't got any kids and they're collecting rent on two houses besides."

"He could be doing well if he stopped drinking."

"He may be taking in more than me, but then he's killing himself doing it."

"If he'd loosen up and be human, this town would be a better place for everybody."

"But, then, I haven't done so bad myself. There's the car, only four years left on the house and two kids through school."

These and similar statements, however, serve the function of enabling a person to calculate his relative financial standing. They are encountered almost everywhere in private gossip, but remain unspoken and hidden in ordinary public situations.

What is interesting about gossip is that in Springdale it seldom hurts anyone. Because it occurs in small temporarily closed circles and concerns those who are not present, the subject of the gossip need never be aware of it. Moreover, the *mores* demand, or better still one should say that it is an iron law of community life, that one not confront the subject of gossip with what is said about him. For this reason, though everyone engages in the practice, no one *has* to learn what things are being said about him. In the rare instance where one hears about gossip about oneself, it comes as a distinct shock "to think that so-and-so could have said that about me."

In a way, then, it is true that everyone knows everything about everyone else but, because of the way the information is learned, it does not ordinarily affect the everyday inter-personal relations of people; in public view even enemies speak to each other. When the victim meets the gossiper, he does not see him as a gossip and the gossiper does not let the privately gained information affect his public gestures; both greet each other in a friendly and neighborly manner and, perhaps, talk about someone else. Because the people of the community have this consideration for other people's feelings ("we like to think of our-selves as considerate and kind, not out to hurt anybody . . . that's one of the main reasons you live in a small town") relationships be-tween people always give the impression of personalness and warmth.

The etiquette of gossip which makes pos-sible the public suppression of the negative and competitive aspects of life has its counter-part in the etiquette of public conversation which always emphasizes the positive. There are thus two channels of communication that serve quite different purposes. In public con-versation one hears comments only on the good things about people—"a man who has always done good things for the town"; "a swell guy"; "she's always doing good things for people"; "a person who never asks any-thing in return." More than this, the level of public conversation always focuses on the col-lective success of the community and the indi-vidual successes of its members. People com-ment on the success of a charitable drive, on the way a money-raising project "went over the top," on "what a good program it was," on the excellence of the actors' performance. These same themes become the subject of self-congratulatory newspaper articles. When fail-ures occur, when the play "was a flop," as of course must happen from time to time, one senses what is almost a communal conspiracy against any further public mention of it. So too with the successes of individuals—the man who after many years of diligence finally gets a good job, the person who completes a corre-spondence course, the local girl who gets a college degree, the local boy who makes good in the city, the man who finally succeeds in establishing himself in business, the winner of a contest, the high scorer, the person who has his name in a city newspaper—all such suc-cesses are given recognition in conventional conversation and in the press. At the public level all types of success are given public recognition while failure is treated with si-lence. It is because of the double and separate set of communication channels that negative gossip seldom colors the friendly ethos and the successful mood of the public life of the com-munity.

IMAGES OF THE SUBURBS

There has always been an edge to the city, where it borders rural land; but in for-mer times the city outskirts were often built up to full urban density. Medieval cities frequently were surrounded by walls, within which the landscape was unmistakably urban, while sheep grazed on the opposite side. Even today, the outskirts of many European cities contain blocks of apartments that look out over tilled fields. Thus, it is not only the peripheral location but also the physical and social structure of an area that qualifies it as suburban. In speak-ing of a suburb in this country we usually have in mind a residential area which is peripheral to and socially dependent upon a city and which is characterized by single-family houses surrounded by lawns or yards.

Although suburban development is generally pictured as a very new phenomenon, it has existed in the United States since the opening of the first railroads in the early nineteenth century made commutation a practical pos-sibility. The first suburbs were located along railroad lines and clustered near the stations, and open country was seldom far away. The development and diffusion of the automobile in the twentieth century changed this pattern of settlement and was a factor in the enormous growth of suburbia in this cen-tury; but in many ways the new communities are not greatly different from what preceded them more than a hundred years ago. However, in recent decades the suburbs have become the focus of a barrage of social criticism. In this selection, Dennis Wrong examines the disparaging image held by the critics, and finds it inaccurate.

The critical image holds that suburbanites have fled the cities to escape their urban origins, and have settled down to the pursuit of material status symbols in the context of a standardized, yet transient, environment. Social science data suggest that suburbanizing migrants brought with them such cultural phenomena as Republican voting, a high birth rate, church-going and other traits associated with the suburbs. The suburbs did not cause these traits, which developed independently of the move. Moreover, many of these traits now seem to have been temporary, and they no longer characterize the suburbs.

The reason for the acceptance of the myth of suburbia would seem to have been an extraordinary visibility of behavior which in a central city context was hidden from sight. The criticism of suburbia is more properly criticism of middle-class America, and not necessarily of a peculiar life-style generated by suburban residence.

The idea of a distinctive suburban life style has been tested and found wanting in many studies. Suburbanites live very much as people of comparable social class and ethnic status live in the central city. Likewise, suburban problems differ little from those of the central city, though they may be slower to be recognized and are complicated by the fact that political solutions are more difficult because of a lack of central government. Suburbs can be dingy, grimy places on occasion, and the best of them are often poorly planned and inadequately serviced. Traffic problems, machine politics, and high taxes are not monopolies of central cities. What suburbs do seem to offer to Americans, which some central cities cannot offer, is the highly valued opportunity to own a single-family home.

Selection 40
SUBURBS AND MYTHS OF SUBURBIA
Dennis H. Wrong

Suburbia is no longer a very fashionable topic. In the 1950's, social critics and sociologists subjected the growing numbers of suburban dwellers to endless scrutiny, seeing them as especially representative of an affluent postwar America whose complacency and flaccidity were mirrored in Eisenhower's Presidency. The suburb was the new habitat of the American middle class, whose taste, intellect, spiritual vigor and mental health were savagely attacked in best-selling assaults, both journalistic and fictional, on "split-level traps," "cracks in the picture window," and "gray flannel-suited" commuters. Social scientists, meanwhile, dis-

Reprinted from *Readings in Introductory Sociology*, edited by Dennis H. Wrong and Harry L. Gracey, New York: The Macmillan Company, 1967, by permission of the author and the publisher.

covered new "styles of life" developing in the suburbs and linked suburban expansion to the revival of the Republican party, higher birth rates and the upward mobility of the erstwhile urban masses.

An image of the suburbanite as a new kind of American possessing a distinctive outlook shaped by his residential environment emerged from these accounts. He was pictured as a former plebeian city-dweller who, benefiting from postwar prosperity, fled to the suburbs to escape his origins. He changed his political affiliation from Democratic to Republican to express his sense of social elevation and refurbished his religious and ethnic loyalties by rejoining the church and choosing to live among those of like background, seeking in particular communities that excluded Negroes and other minorities. His insecurity about his newly won higher status revealed itself, however, in the frantic pursuit of material status symbols purchased to impress his neighbors, who were similarly striving to impress him. The inevitable result was a pervasive standardization of life externally manifested in the monotonous similarity of houses, furnishings, clothing, gardens, and cars. The cultural and leisure pursuits of suburbanites were also uniform: watching TV, reading mass magazines and the latest bestsellers, gardening, and outdoor barbecuing.

But common interests and possessions failed to create true "togetherness" in suburbia, for they existed in the context of the wary status-seeking that had motivated the move to the suburbs in the first place. And in spite of the proclaimed virtues of roots and local community spirit, each suburb remained a temporary resting place for many of its residents, who on climbing still higher up the social ladder were apt to move to a more prestigious, higher-income suburb and start the whole process all over again. This transience gave the busy suburban social life, both informal and in such organized groups as the church, the PTA, the women's clubs, a synthetic and compulsive quality, belying the vaunted neighborliness so often extolled in contrast to the cold impersonality of city life.

This portrait of the suburban lifestyle possessed an initial plausibility, because it managed to link all the new developments in American life during the late 1940's and the 1950's to suburbanization. The postwar economic boom was bringing relative affluence to many who had not previously known it, the moderation of class conflicts in our politics enabled the Republicans to win office under Eisenhower, obsession with the Cold War created a spirit of political timidity, marriage rates and birth rates were soaring to the highest levels in two generations, there was evidence of a religious revival in the land, and the mass media, particularly the new medium of television, were reaching more and more Americans. All of these trends seemed to attain their maximum intensity in suburbia and the mass migration to the suburbs after 1945 represented one of the largest and most visible population movements in American history. Whether described in the neutral language of the sociologists or in the satirical and rejecting epithets of social critics deprived temporarily of their usual targets of political attack, the suburbs seemed to exhibit all that was most contemporary and most typical in American life. Thus was born a composite portrait of suburbanism as a way of life that has been dubbed by those who have recently challenged its accuracy the "myth of suburbia."

All this seems very passé nowadays. With the return to power of the Democratic party in 1960, the growth of the civil rights movement, and the rediscovery of poverty, our attention today is directed to social problems arising out of inequality and economic deprivation rather than to the psychological burdens of newly won affluence. The Negroes and the poor are overwhelmingly concentrated in the center of the city or in such rural slums as those in Appalachia rather than in the outlying metropolitan districts. Moreover, the cities, responding to the flight of so many of their former inhabitants to the suburbs, have launched programs of urban renewal that have created a host of new and hotly debated political issues. Sociologists have turned to the investigation of blue-collar rather than white-collar ways of life. And social critics now assail middle-class America less for its allegedly trivial leisure pursuits and compulsive conformism than on moral grounds, charging it with racial bigotry and insensitivity to the sufferings of the urban poor and the Negroes trapped in black ghettoes.

Yet a social reality does not simply disappear when the spotlight of publicity is no longer focused upon it. The suburbs are still very much with us. Nor has the process of suburbanization slowed up: there is every indication that the movement of population to the suburbs has continued and will continue during the sixties at a rate equal to or surpassing that of the forties and fifties. By 1960, just over one fifth of the American people (roughly forty million of them) lived in the suburbs; by 1970 the proportion is likely to be closer to one third. Politically, the suburbs stand to gain the most from the reapportionment of congressional and state legislative districts required by recent Supreme Court and lower court decisions, even though few of the cases heard by the courts were suits brought by suburban voters. It is therefore worth taking another look at received views of the suburban way of life, examining not only their validity when first put forward but also how continuing suburban growth and change affects their accuracy as descriptions of social reality.

A suburb is an area adjacent to the political boundaries of a city that is more densely settled than the open countryside, but less so than the central city. It depends on the city economically and culturally; politically, however, it is a self-governing municipality. A suburb, then, is a *place* defined by its location in relation to a city, both geographically and along transportation lines. This elementary fact needs to be stressed in view of the prevalent tendency to treat suburbia as if it were a state of mind or a moral and spiritual condition. Thus defined, virtually all cities and towns in the United States—large, middle-sized, and small—have in the present century produced suburbs forming a population belt encircling their original political boundaries. But the distinctive social and political outlook that commentators have attributed to suburbia is clearly intended to characterize chiefly the suburban populations surrounding the metropolitan giants among American cities. At the 1960 census, twenty-one million people (about 12 per cent of the total American population) lived in the suburban belt surrounding the central cities of our ten largest metropolitan areas. This figure, however, includes residents of industrial suburbs with working-class populations engaged in varied economic activities, whereas the popular generalizations about suburbia apply only to middle-class residential or "dormitory" suburbs whose inhabitants commute some distance to work, usually to the central city.

Most of the earlier accounts of the suburbs failed to distinguish between the traits of the residents that were acquired as a result of living in suburban communities with their special relation to cities, and traits that suburban migrants possessed before moving to the suburbs and continued to share after moving with fellow-citizens who remained in the city. Just as "urban" attitudes may exist in rural areas—say, among Great Plains farmers, a fair number of whom are today sufficiently prosperous and literate to own private planes, vacation in Hawaii, and subscribe to the Book-of-the-Month Club—so may the so-called suburban way of life flourish outside of the suburbs. Urban tastes and attitudes, nevertheless, could scarcely have *originated* outside of those dense concentrations of people of different occupations that we call cities. It is far less certain, on the other hand, that the outlook imputed to suburbia could have developed only in the special physical and demographic setting of the suburbs.

Sociologists who have continued to study the suburbs have recently concentrated their efforts on debunking the so-called "myth of suburbia" created by the popular writers of the 1950's and earlier sociological studies. Bennett Berger, for example, investigated a new working-class "mass-produced" suburb in California and found little evidence among its residents of the changes in attitudes and behavior alleged to result from the move to the suburbs. Their class identification remained working-class, their occupational and income aspirations were no higher than formerly, they did not participate more actively in the church or in other local community affairs, they regarded the suburb as their permanent home, and they continued to vote regularly for the Democratic party. William Dobriner, studying Levittown, Long Island, found that since 1950 Levittown has been "steadily drifting from monolithic homogeneity into heterogeneity" as far as the income, occupational, and even ethnic and religious composition of its population is concerned. S. D. Clark, a Canadian sociologist, has, in effect, insisted that the move to the suburbs is largely a search for cheap family housing and that status-seeking and mobility striving do not have to be invoked to account for it. Finally, Herbert Gans has criticized the general proposition that location, population density, and housing have the influence on attitudes and ways of life assumed by many writers on urban communities, whether slums, residential neighborhoods in the city or suburbs. Gans argues that the styles of life associated with the upper-middle, lower-middle, and working classes are determined by social and economic conditions having little to do with place of residence within the metropolitan community.

The enormous pluralities won by Eisenhower in the two Presidential elections of the 1950's gave rise to the claim that migrants to the suburbs were prone to change their party preferences from Democratic to Republican. But detailed analyses of the vote in 1952 and 1956 suggest that most of the suburban Republicans would have voted for Eisenhower even if they had remained in the city. Indeed, voters resembling the migrants in their social and economic characteristics who did remain voted just as overwhelmingly for Eisenhower, cutting deeply into the "normal" Democratic big-city majorities. Moreover, it is now plain that 1952 and 1956 were what Angus Campbell and his associates at the University of Michigan Survey Research Center call "deviating elections," elections in which the result was determined largely by the personal popularity of one candidate rather than by regular party preferences. In the more normal 1960 Presidential election, Nixon was unable to hold the huge suburban margins run up by Eisenhower, and in 1964, central cities and suburbs alike, outside of the South, were carried by the Democrats in the Johnson landslide.

Both Angus Campbell and political scientist Robert C. Wood have shown that migrants to the suburbs in the 1950's were indeed more likely to vote Republican, but not because of the impact of suburbia on their political preferences. Rather, Republicans were more likely to move to the suburbs than Democrats with the same social and economic characteristics, perhaps because big-city Republicans more often came from families who had grown up in traditionally Republican small towns and rural areas a generation or more ago. Such family histories would explain both their Republicanism and their greater disposition to move to the suburbs in an attempt to recapture something of the uncongested, small-town atmosphere of their forebears. Angus Campbell has also shown that movers to the suburbs, though preponderantly Republican, had not achieved greater upward social mobility than those they left behind them in the city. So much for the view that suburban Republicanism is the result of party-switching reflecting the new conservatism of the upward mobile.

The high birth rates of the 1950's, linked by many commentators to the family and child-centered way of life of suburbanites, have declined in the 1960's and many demographers expect them to decline still further. TV sets are now as ubiquitous in city neighborhoods and even in the slums as in the suburbs. Studies of local government have shown suburbanites to be just as apathetic as residents of city wards and small towns when it comes to voting in local elections and participating in civic affairs. The trend toward increased church attendance by Americans has leveled off in recent years. Sociological studies have shown that *all* Americans, whether they live in the suburbs, the city, or the country, attach greater significance to their religious affiliations than was the case before World War II. More new churches and synagogues have certainly been built in the suburbs, but this is to be expected, because the suburbs have been growing more rapidly than other areas and does not result from any stimulus to greater religious activity peculiar to the suburban environment.

Social scientists, of course, greatly enjoy debunking popular myths. Some of them, indeed, appear to believe that the refutation of common beliefs about contemporary society provides the main justification for the existence of social science. (Sometimes it almost seems as if social scientists initially help create new stereotypes in order to make work for other social scientists in testing and correcting them.) Debunking is clearly not enough, for one also wants to know why a particular myth won such wide currency. The myth of suburbia may be no more than a mid-twentieth-century version of the old intellectual's game of deriding the middle class (*épater le bourgeois*), but even so it possessed and still possesses in many circles a surface plausibility that needs to be accounted for.

The myth partly owes its origin to emphasis on extreme and vivid cases in the earlier accounts of the suburbs. The various Levittowns, Park Forest, Illinois, as described by William H. Whyte in *The Organization Man*, the mass-produced housing developments quickly thrown up by private realtors described by John Keats in *The Crack in the Picture Window*—these are the initial sources of the myth. It is relatively easy to show that mass-produced or "packaged" suburbs, springing up overnight like earlier boomtowns, are not the only, or even the most typical, kind of suburb. Their standardized house-types all similarly priced and the absence of the contrasts between old and new residents found in most communities obviously promote the social homogeneity and the busy creation of new formal and informal groups that have been seen as characteristic of suburbia in general. Yet there are many other kinds of suburbs: traditional, upper-class suburbs, often dating back to the turn of the century; old rural towns that have gradually been engulfed by migrants from the city; stable, middle-income residential suburbs with individually styled houses, in addition to industrial satellites with noncommuting working-class populations. All have been increasing in population in the past two decades, though not necessarily at the same rate.

If the suburbs have long been more heterogeneous than the myths of suburbia suggest, it is also the case that they have been becoming even more heterogeneous. Suburbanization is, after all, a *process*, and one that is by no means completed. William Dobriner's study of Levittown, Long Island, built in the late 1940's, finds that commuting to the central city—that presumably universal characteristic of suburbanites—is less common than formerly as a growing number of Levittown residents take shorter journeys to work, often to new industrial cities within the suburban ring. Dobriner concludes that the suburbs are losing their sociological distinctiveness and becoming merely the most recent extensions of the city. "In our efforts to capture the sociological soul of the suburbs," he writes, "perhaps we turned away from the basic and most fascinating question . . . the way in which cities create suburbs only to turn them into cities in their own image."

Yet suburban life possesses one unique feature that helps explain the resonance of the myth: what Dobriner calls the "visibility principle." Middle-class ways of life that are concealed from public view in city apartments or residential backstreets become highly visible in the suburbs, with their open lawns and gardens, on-the-street parking, backyard barbecue pits and swimming pools and more important, the more informal visiting and friendship patterns that are possible in a smaller, less-densely settled and more like-minded community than a city neighborhood. The suburb is middle-class America fully exposed to public observation. Take the status-seeking, for example, that is alleged to be a peculiar trait of the suburban style of life. In the city there is not only less opportunity publicly to display one's possessions as "status symbols," but there is far less incentive to do so when they will be observed by the vulgar throng in all its variety, as well as by one's own circle of class and ethnic equals, one's own "reference group," to use the sociological term. In the suburb, sur-

rounded by neighbors of similar class and ethnic background, this inhibition disappears. It is not that suburban life breeds a frenetic concern with status lacking in city-dwellers; it is merely that the status-seeking propensities of the latter must necessarily be expressed in more limited, less public ways.

Although there is little difference between suburban communities and many home-owning middle-class residential neighborhoods inside the city line (except for the local government independence of the former), the suburbs are more visible to strangers. They are located in proximity to major highways and transportation lines into the city and, in the case of new subdivisions, have been suddenly and dramatically created by bulldozing out of exisence areas of the nearby countryside long visited by city-dwellers for picnics and walks through the woods on Sunday outings. On the other hand, middle-class residential neighborhoods in the city are often isolated from the rest of the city and protected from close contact with it by ecological barriers: hills in San Francisco or Montreal, ravines in Washington or Toronto, lake-shore enclaves in Chicago or Detroit.

From a broader perspective, it is clear that the myth of suburbia very well suited the prevailing style of cultural criticism during the politically quiescent 1950's. In the 1920's, also a decade of political complacency, intellectuals assailed the philistinism, sexual puritanism, and moral hypocrisy of the American middle class, seeing the small town or city as the place of residence of most Americans and the breeding ground of these attitudes. Suburbia played a similar role in the 1950's with Whyte's organization man replacing Sinclair Lewis' Babbitt, and the oppressive togetherness of the suburb supplanting the xenophobic provinciality of Main Street, as targets of satire. Conversely, celebrators of the American way of life saw the small town in the 1920's and the suburb in the 1950's as the locus of its virtues: in the earlier period *Saturday Evening Post* covers of frame houses and tree-lined streets played the same symbolic role as glossy advertising lay-outs depicting ranchhouse living thirty years later. With civil rights, poverty, and international peace becoming major political issues in the 1960's, delineations of the suburban life-cycle have lost the immediacy and sense of relevance they possessed a decade ago, just as the Depression and the New Deal ended the *Zeitgeist* of the 1920's and the cultural revolt against the small town that played so large a part in it.

Yet the small town was indeed becoming a backwater of American life by the 1930's as more and more Americans moved to metropolitan areas, whereas the suburbs are still expanding and even now contain more Americans than central cities, small urban communities, or rural areas. We cannot therefore dismiss them as objects of interest, regarding the obsession with them in the 1950's as no more than a fad of yesterday. The image of a homogenized suburban sameness was always a caricature and is becoming an even more distorted one with the passage of time. The increasing heterogeneity of suburbia, however, means merely that the distinction between *suburbanization* and *urbanization* as social processes is becoming a less meaningful one. The continuing growth and differentiation of cities remains one of the most significant social trends of our time.

Chapter 15

CLASS AND CASTE

A THEORY OF STRATIFICATION
Selection 41

THE CASTE SYSTEM
Selection 42

THE CLASS SYSTEM
Selection 43

CLASS AND CULTURE
Selection 44

Stratification refers to the differential ranking of statuses whereby some are considered higher and others lower. It is an aspect of all social differentiation, existing everywhere. A class structure, however, is more than this. Class is a status in its own right, and classes or strata are, at a minimum, societal groups. A class structure is not universal; but it appears in all societies of any complexity.

Class is one of the most important social statuses partly because it nearly always exercises a strong influence on behavior. Different classes possess different cultures, with sets of values, beliefs, and norms that are often quite different and sometimes opposed. Juvenile delinquency, for instance, is regarded by some sociologists as normal and conforming behavior for members of the urban lower classes, behavior which is problematic only because middle-class culture defines it so. The pervasiveness of class influences on behavior is suggested by the fact that among the first questions we ask of an acquaintance is "What do you do?" The answer to this question indicates our new friend's social class and suggests the kind of manners, topics of conversation, and language that we should expect from him and that he may be expecting of us.

Despite its importance in sociology, class is an ambiguous concept. One approach to determining the several meanings of class is through examination of the methods that are used to ascertain the class status of individuals. Each of three different methods implies a corresponding concept of class.

A common method, called "reputational," assigns class status through a knowledge of reputed social interaction. The reputational method determines who associates with whom and relates this information to a model of class structure that is recognized by members of the society. If residents of a community agree, for instance, that there are six social classes, in each of which certain "specimen" families belong, the class status of other families can be known by determining with which of the specimen families they associate. This procedure is similar to determining from a sociogram the cliques into which various individuals fall.

The model of class underlying this method is a social group. Classes in this sense consist of people who share social interaction; they maintain separate cultures by restricting interaction with members of other classes. The major problem with this conception is the difficulty of applying it to large-scale and complex societies in which people do not interact with (or may not even know) a large proportion of the population.

A second method, called "subjective," merely asks people the class to which they belong. The subjective method implies that classes are societal groups and that their members have consciousness of kind. This conception meets with difficulty because people's answers differ considerably depending on how the question is asked. When asked if they are in the upper, middle, or lower class, most Americans say they are in the middle class; but when given a choice between that term and "working class" about half will choose the latter. This may indicate a vagueness of class lines or an indisposition to talk in class terms or simply a lack of the class consciousness that subjective methods assume to be present.

The most frequently used method for assigning class status is called "objective," but this complimentary label should not obscure its difficulties. The objective method assigns class status as a function of some other more easily measured statuses, the most common being occupation, education, and income. Class is assumed to be a simple reflection of whatever variable, such as occupation, is used to assign it. Among the problems of this method are the differences that appear between the "objective" variables in particular cases. For example, the rich butcher and the underpaid professor will be placed in different classes depending on whether they are rated by occupation or by income. Some sociologists have sought to meet this problem by combining several variables in an objective class "index."

Real differences exist between these concepts, and none seems to be completely satisfactory. If the state of knowledge in this area is not hopelessly muddied by different meanings and different measures for ostensibly the same phenomena, it is because there are strong empirical relationships between these various meanings and measures. People who occupy positions of prestige or who earn large sums of money tend to think of themselves as upper class or middle class and to associate with others like themselves. Possible conclusions are either that the reputational, subjective, and objective concepts of class are strongly related to some fundamental concept which has proved to be elusive in definition, or else that class has not one, but three or more related yet distinct meanings.

Systems of stratification are generally considered to fall on a continuum between two ideal types called caste and open class. The principal differences between these types are the degree of social distance between adjacent groups and the degree of social mobility (achievement of class status). In the ideal caste system, social distance is extreme. No social intercourse of an intimate or primary type can cross the lines dividing castes. Caste status is totally ascribed and cannot be changed, so mobility is nonexistent. No real society possesses an ideal type caste structure, but India has been taken as a fair approximation.

The American system is considered to be relatively close to the open-class ideal type. Social distance in the ideal type is minimal, so that classes merge with those above and below them, and mobility occurs frequently. Class is ascribed only in the first few years of life, after which it is entirely achieved. Although other differences have been posited between caste and open class, these seem to be the most important.

Selection 41, by Kingsley Davis and Wilbert E. Moore, suggests an explanation for the universality of stratification, as well as for other facts concerning class systems. Mason Olcott's article, Selection 42, discusses the caste system. In Selection 43, W. Lloyd Warner, Marchia Meecker, and Kenneth Eells illustrate the open-class system, emphasizing the differences between the ideal type and American reality. Richard Hoggart describes the world view of the British working classes in Selection 44, thus illustrating the cultural differences that exist among social classes.

A THEORY OF STRATIFICATION

This selection is addressed to three important facts concerning stratification. First, the ranking of statuses exists in all known societies. Scholars have claimed that social classes are absent in some very small "primitive" groups, but even in these cases there appear to be individual statuses that are considered better than others. Second, certain statuses tend to be highly rated in all societies. These are statuses associated with religious, political, and economic leadership and with technical skill. Third, beyond the uniformities just mentioned, stratification systems differ greatly in the extent and nature of inequality they contain.

Davis and Moore propose a theory of stratification based on the assumption that all societies face the twin problems of placement—getting people to fill statuses—and performance—getting them to act out the associated roles. They suggest that inequality is universally used as a motivational incentive in meeting these problems. The particular statuses that are generally favored in stratification systems are so privileged because they are vital to the social order and because they require exceptional skill. Differences among stratification systems are explained with reference to particular problems faced by different societies, as well as to related features of a society's organization.

> Social statuses differ in their importance to society and in the skill necessary to the performance of the associated roles. To induce talented individuals to fill important skilled statuses which must not go unfilled and which may require long and arduous training, these statuses must contain a motivational inducement in the form of rights and indirectly associated perquisites. The differential treatment of statuses introduces stratification into all societies.

> Religious, political, and economic leadership statuses tend to be highly evaluated or prestigious in all societies because they are generally of great social import. Statuses demanding technical competence and rare skills likewise tend to be highly evaluated. However, differences in the sizes of societies, the stage of cultural development, and the presence or absence of other societies in the environment produce different needs that lead to corresponding variations in stratification systems. These differences lead to the suggestion that the common typology of caste, estate, and class may be too simple a model for the many distinctions that need to be made among systems of stratification.

Davis and Moore have presented an important and seminal contribution to sociological theory in this work. As might be expected in the case of a short statement with broad implications, it has been strongly criticized, and with considerable reason. Among the most cogent criticisms are these:

1. The definition of importance, contained in footnote 3, is not altogether satisfactory. Many menial jobs appear to fill the requirements given by Davis and Moore, whereas the contrary is true for many high-status positions (like that of a film star in our society). The designation of a status as important may simply be a way of sayng that it has prestige, in which case the Davis and Moore theory would be an example of circular reasoning.

2. Many critics have noted that scarcity of talent is itself a result of a system of stratification, instead of or in addition to being a cause as these authors sug-

gest. For example, lower-class people lack the talent to be corporation presidents, partly because the neighborhood schools they attend are inferior to those in middle-class suburbs.

3. The same rewards supposedly used to motivate skilled people to fill important statuses are in fact often granted for pure ownership. The rich playboy's wealth has no motivational power. This fact is not given sufficient emphasis by Davis and Moore.

4. The magnitude of differences in income, prestige, and power between the statuses of existing societies seems extreme if motivational purposes are the only ones served by stratification. Is it really necessary to pay a corporation executive fifty times as much as a common laborer in order for anyone to be motivated to fill the former status? The theory obviously needs supplementation to account for this fact.

In sum, the selection presents a lucid and reasonable theory, but some important questions remain to be answered before it can be considered a fully satisfactory explanation of the facts with which it deals.

Selection 41
SOME PRINCIPLES OF STRATIFICATION
Kingsley Davis and Wilbert E. Moore

In a previous paper some concepts for handling the phenomena of social inequality were presented.[1] In the present paper a further step in stratification theory is undertaken—an attempt to show the relationship between stratification and the rest of the social order.[2] Starting from the proposition that no society is "classless," or unstratified, an effort is made to explain, in functional terms, the universal necessity which calls forth stratification in any social system. Next, an attempt is made to explain the roughly uniform distribution of prestige as between the major types of positions in every society. Since, however, there occur between one society and another great differences in the degree and kind of stratification, some attention is also given to the varieties of social inequality and the variable factors that give rise to them.

Clearly, the present task requires two different lines of analysis—one to understand the universal, the other to understand the variable features of stratification. Naturally each line of inquiry aids the other and is indispensable, and in the treatment that follows the two will be interwoven, although, because of space limitations, the emphasis will be on the universals.

Reprinted from *American Sociological Review*, 10:2, 1945, pp. 242–249, with permission of the authors and the publisher.

Throughout, it will be necessary to keep in mind one thing—namely, that the discussion relates to the system of positions, not to the individuals occupying those positions. It is one thing to ask why different positions carry different degrees of prestige, and quite another to ask how certain individuals get into those positions. Although, as the argument will try to show, both questions are related, it is essential to keep them separate in our thinking. Most of the literature on stratification has tried to answer the second question (particularly with regard to the ease or difficulty of mobility between strata) without tackling the first. The first question, however, is logically prior and, in the case of any particular individual or group, factually prior.

The functional necessity of stratification

Curiously, however, the main functional necessity explaining the universal presence of stratification is precisely the requirement faced by any society of placing and motivating individuals in the social structure. As a functioning mechanism a society must somehow distribute its members in social positions and induce them to perform the duties of these positions. It must thus concern itself with motivation at two different levels: to instill in the proper individuals the desire to fill certain positions, and, once in these positions, the desire to perform the duties attached to them. Even though the social order may be relatively static in form, there is a continuous process of metabolism as new individuals are born into it, shift with age, and die off. Their absorption into the positional system must somehow be arranged and motivated. This is true whether the system is competitive or non-competitive. A competitive system gives greater importance to the motivation to achieve positions, whereas a non-competitive system gives perhaps greater importance to the motivation to perform the duties of the positions; but in any system both types of motivation are required.

If the duties associated with the various positions were all equally pleasant to the human organism, all equally important to societal survival, and all equally in need of the same ability or talent, it would make no difference who got into which positions, and the problem of social placement would be greatly reduced. But actually it does make a great deal of difference who gets into which positions, not only because some positions are inherently more agreeable than others, but also because some require special talents or training and some are functionally more important than others. Also, it is essential that the duties of the positions be performed with the diligence that their importance requires. Inevitably, then, a society must have, first, some kind of rewards that it can use as inducements, and, second, some way of distributing these rewards differentially according to positions. The rewards and their distribution become a part of the social order, and thus give rise to stratification.

One may ask what kind of rewards a society has at its disposal in distributing its personnel and securing essential services. It has, first of all, the things that contribute to sustenance and comfort. It has, second, the things that contribute to humor and diversion. And it has, finally, the things that contribute to self respect and ego expansion. The last, because of the peculiarly social character of the self, is largely a function of the opinion of others, but it nonetheless ranks in importance with the first two. In any social system all three kinds of rewards must be dispensed differentially according to positions.

In a sense the rewards are "built into" the position. They consist in the "rights" associated with the position, plus what may be called its accompaniments or perquisites. Often the rights, and sometimes the accompaniments, are functionally related to the duties of the position. (Rights as viewed by the incumbent are usually duties as viewed by other members of the community.) However, there may be a host of subsidiary rights and perquisites that are not essential to the function of the position and have only an indirect and symbolic connection with its duties, but which still may be of considerable importance in inducing people to seek the positions and fulfil the essential duties.

If the rights and perquisites of different positions in a society must be unequal, then the society must be stratified, because that is precisely what stratification means. Social inequality is thus an unconsciously evolved device by which societies insure that the most important positions are conscientiously filled by the most qualified persons. Hence every society, no matter how simple or complex, must differentiate persons in terms of both prestige and esteem, and must therefore possess a certain amount of institutionalized inequality.

It does not follow that the amount or type of inequality need be the same in all societies. This is largely a function of factors that will be discussed presently.

The two determinants of positional rank

Granting the general function that inequality subserves, one can specify the two factors that determine the relative rank of different positions. In general those positions convey the best reward, and hence have the highest rank, which (a) have the greatest importance for the society and (b) require the greatest training or talent. The first factor concerns function and is a matter of relative significance; the second concerns means and is a matter of scarcity.

Differential functional importance. Actually a society does not need to reward positions in proportion to their functional importance. It merely needs to give sufficient reward to them to insure that they will be filled competently. In other words, it must see that less essential positions do not compete successfully with more essential ones. If a position is easily filled, it need not be heavily rewarded, even though important. On the other hand, if it is important but hard to fill, the reward must be high enough to get it filled anyway. Functional importance is therefore a necessary but not a sufficient cause of high rank being assigned to a position.[3]

Differential scarcity of personnel. Practically all positions, no matter how acquired, require some form of skill or capacity for performance. This is implicit in the very notion of position, which implies that the incumbent must, by virtue of his incumbency, accomplish certain things.

There are, ultimately, only two ways in which a person's qualifications come about: through inherent capacity or through training. Obviously, in concrete activities both are always necessary, but from a practical standpoint the scarcity may lie primarily in one or the other, as well as in both. Some positions require innate talents of such high degree that the persons who fill them are bound to be rare. In many cases, however, talent is fairly abundant in the population but the training process is so long, costly, and elaborate that relatively few can qualify. Modern medicine, for example, is within the mental capacity of most individuals, but a medical education is so burdensome and expensive that virtually none would undertake it if the position of the M.D. did not carry a reward commensurate with the sacrifice.

If the talents required for a position are abundant and the training easy, the method of acquiring the position may have little to do with its duties. There may be, in fact, a virtually accidental relationship. But if the skills required are scarce by reason of the rarity of talent or the costliness of training, the position, if functionally important, must have an attractive power that will draw the necessary skills in competition with other positions. This means, in effect, that the position must be high in the social scale—must command great prestige, high salary, ample leisure, and the like.

How variations are to be understood. In so far as there is a difference between one system of stratification and another, it is attributable to whatever factors affect the two determinants of differential reward—namely, functional importance and scarcity of personnel. Positions important in one society may not be important in another, because the conditions faced by the societies, or their degree of internal development, may be different. The same conditions, in turn, may affect the question of scarcity; for in some societies the stage of development, or the external situation, may wholly obviate the necessity of certain kinds of skill or talent. Any particular system of stratification, then, can be understood as a product of the special conditions affecting the two aforementioned grounds of differential reward.

Major societal functions and stratification

Religion. The reason why religion is necessary is apparently to be found in the fact that human society achieves its unity primarily through the possession by its members of certain ultimate values and ends in common. Although these values and ends are subjective, they influence behavior, and their integration enables the society to operate as a system. Derived neither from inherited nor from external nature, they have evolved as a part of culture by communication and moral pressure. They must, however, appear to the members of the society to have some reality, and it is the role of religious belief and ritual to supply and reinforce this appearance of reality. Through belief and ritual the common ends and values are connected with an imaginary world symbolized by concrete sacred objects, which world in turn is related in a meaningful way to the facts and trials of the individual's life. Through the worship of the sacred objects and the beings they symbolize, and the acceptance of supernatural prescriptions that are at the same time codes of behavior, a powerful control over human conduct is exercised, guiding it along lines sustaining the institutional structure and conforming to the ultimate ends and values.

If this conception of the role of religion is true, one can understand why in every known society the religious activities tend to be under the charge of particular persons, who tend thereby to enjoy greater rewards than the ordinary societal member. Certain of the rewards and special privileges may attach to only the highest religious functionaries, but others usually apply, if such exists, to the entire sacerdotal class.

Moreover, there is a peculiar relation between the duties of the religious official and the special privileges he enjoys. If the supernatural world governs the destinies of men more ultimately than does the real world, its earthly representative, the person through whom one may communicate with the supernatural, must be a powerful individual. He is a keeper of sacred tradition, a skilled performer of the ritual, and an interpreter of lore and myth. He is in such close contact with the gods that he is viewed as possessing some of their characteristics. He is, in short, a bit sacred, and hence free from some of the more vulgar necessities and controls.

It is no accident, therefore, that religious functionaries have been associated with the very highest positions of power, as in theocratic regimes. Indeed, looking at it from this point of view, one may wonder why it is that they do not get *entire* control over their societies. The factors that prevent this are worthy of note.

In the first place, the amount of technical competence necessary for the performance of religious duties is small. Scientific or artistic capacity is not required. Anyone can set himself up as enjoying an intimate relation with deities, and nobody can successfully dispute him. Therefore, the factor of scarcity of personnel does not operate in the technical sense.

One may assert, on the other hand, that religious ritual is often elaborate and religious lore abstruse, and that priestly ministrations require tact, if not intelligence. This is true, but the technical requirements of the profession are for the most part adventitious, not related to the end in the same way that science is related to air travel. The priest can never be free from competition, since the criteria of whether or not one has genuine contact with the supernatural are never strictly clear. It is this competition that debases the priestly position below what might be expected at first glance. That is why priestly prestige is highest in those societies where membership in the profession is rigidly controlled by the priestly guild itself. That is why, in part at least, elaborate devices are utilized to stress the identification of the person with his office—spectacular costume, abnormal conduct, special diet, segregated residence, celibacy, conspicuous leisure, and the like. In fact, the priest is always in danger of becoming somewhat discredited —as happens in a secularized society—because in a world of stubborn fact, ritual and sacred knowledge alone will not grow crops or build houses. Furthermore, unless he is protected by a professional guild, the priest's identification with the supernatural tends to preclude his acquisition of abundant worldly goods.

As between one society and another it seems that the highest general position awarded the priest occurs in the medieval type of social order. Here there is enough economic production to afford a surplus, which can be used to support a numerous and highly organized priesthood; and yet the populace is unlettered and therefore credulous to a high degree. Perhaps the most extreme example is to be found in the Buddhism of Tibet, but others are encountered in the Catholicism of feudal Europe, the Inca regime of Peru, the Brahminism of India, and the Mayan priesthood of Yucatan. On the other hand, if the society is so crude as to have no surplus and little differentiation, so that every priest must be also a cultivator or hunter, the separation of the priestly status from the others has hardly gone far enough for priestly prestige to mean much. When the priest actually has high prestige under these circumstances, it is because he also performs other important functions (usually political and medical).

In an extremely advanced society built on scientific technology, the priesthood tends to lose status, because sacred tradition and supernaturalism drop into the background. The ultimate values and common ends of the society tend to be expressed in less anthropomorphic ways, by officials who occupy fundamentally political, economic, or educational rather than religious positions. Nevertheless, it is easily possible for intellectuals to exaggerate the degree to which the priesthood in a presumably secular milieu has lost prestige. When the matter is closely examined the urban proletariat, as well as the rural citizenry, proves to be surprisingly god-fearing and priest-ridden. No society has become so completely secularized as to liquidate entirely the belief in transcendental ends and supernatural entities. Even in a secularized society some system must exist for the integration of ultimate values, for their ritualistic expression, and for the emotional adjustments required by disappointment, death, and disaster.

Government. Like religion, government plays a unique and indispensable part in society. But in contrast to religion, which provides integration in terms of sentiments, beliefs, and rituals, it organizes the society in terms of law and authority. Furthermore, it orients the society to the actual rather than the unseen world.

The main functions of government are, internally, the ultimate enforcement of norms, the final arbitration of conflicting interests, and the overall planning and direction of society; and externally, the handling of war and diplomacy. To carry out these functions it acts as the agent of the entire people, enjoys a monopoly of force, and controls all individuals within its territory.

Political action, by definition, implies authority. An official can command because he has authority, and the citizen must obey because he is subject to that authority. For this reason stratification is inherent in the nature of political relationships.

So clear is the power embodied in political position that political inequality is sometimes thought to comprise all inequality. But it can be shown that there are other bases of stratification, that the following controls operate in practice to keep political power from becoming complete: (a) The fact that the actual holders of political office, and especially those determining top policy must necessarily be few in number compared to the total population. (b) The fact that the rulers represent the interest of the group rather than of themselves, and are therefore restricted in their behavior by rules and mores designed to enforce this limitation of interest. (c) The fact that the holder of political office has his authority by virtue of his office and nothing else, and therefore any special knowledge, talent, or capacity he may claim is purely incidental, so that he often has to depend upon others for technical assistance.

In view of these limiting factors, it is not strange that the rulers often have less power and prestige than a literal enumeration of their formal rights would lead one to expect.

Wealth, property, and labor. Every position that secures for its incumbent a livelihood is, by definition, economically rewarded. For this reason there is an economic aspect to those positions (e.g. political and religious) the main function of which is not economic. It therefore becomes convenient for the society to use unequal economic returns as a principal means of controlling the entrance of persons into positions and stimulating the performance of their duties. The amount of the economic return therefore becomes one of the main indices of social status.

It should be stressed, however, that a position does not bring power and prestige *because* it draws a high income. Rather, it draws a high income because it is functionally important and the available personnel is for one reason or another scarce. It is therefore superficial and erroneous to regard high income as the cause of a man's power and prestige, just as it is erroneous to think that a man's fever is the cause of his disease.[4]

The economic source of power and prestige is not income primarily, but the ownership of capital goods (including patents, good will, and professional reputation). Such ownership should be distinguished from the possession of consumers' goods, which is an index rather than a cause of social standing. In other words, the ownership of producers' goods is properly speaking, a source of income like other positions, the income itself remaining an index. Even in situations where social values are widely commercialized and earnings are the readiest method of judging social position, income does not confer prestige on a position so much as it induces people to compete for the position. It is true that a man who has a high income as a result of one position may find this money helpful in climbing into another position as well, but this again reflects the effect of his initial, economically advantageous status, which exercises its influence through the medium of money.

In a system of private property in productive enterprise, an income above what an individual spends can give rise to possession of capital wealth. Presumably such possession is a reward for the proper management of one's finances originally and of the productive enterprise later. But as social differentiation becomes highly advanced and yet the institution of inheritance persists, the phenomenon of pure ownership, and reward for pure ownership, emerges. In such a case it is difficult to prove that the position is functionally important or that the scarcity involved is anything other than extrinsic and accidental. It is for this reason, doubtless, that the institution of private property in productive goods becomes more subject to criticism as social development proceeds toward industrialization. It is only this pure, that is, strictly legal and functionless ownership, however, that is open to attack; for some form of active ownership, whether private or public, is indispensable.

One kind of ownership of production goods consists in rights over the labor of others. The most extremely concentrated and exclusive of such rights are found in slavery, but the essential principle remains in serfdom, peonage, encomienda,* and indenture. Naturally this kind of ownership has the greatest significance for stratification, because it necessarily entails an unequal relationship.

But property in capital goods inevitably introduces a compulsive element even into the nominally free contractual relationship. Indeed, in some respects the authority of the contractual employer is greater than that of the feudal landlord, inasmuch as the latter is more limited by traditional reciprocities. Even the classical economics recognized that competitors would fare unequally, but it did not pursue this fact to its necessary conclusion that, however it might be acquired, unequal control of goods and services must give unequal advantage to the parties to a contract.

Technical knowledge. The function of finding means to single goals, without any concern with the choice between goals, is the exclusively technical sphere. The explanation of why positions requiring great technical skill receive fairly high rewards is easy to see, for it is the simplest case of the rewards being so distributed as to draw talent and motivate training. Why they seldom if ever receive the highest rewards is also clear: the importance of technical knowledge from a societal point of view is never so great as the integration of goals, which takes place on the religious, political, and economic levels. Since the technological level is concerned solely with means, a purely technical position must ultimately be subordinate to other positions that are religious, political, or economic in character.

Nevertheless, the distinction between expert and layman in any social order is fundamental, and cannot be entirely reduced to other terms. Methods of recruitment, as well as of reward, sometimes lead to the erroneous interpretation that technical positions are economically determined. Actually, however, the acquisition of knowledge and skill cannot be accomplished by purchase, although the opportunity to learn may be. The control of the avenues of training may inhere as a sort of property right in certain families or classes, giving them power and prestige in consequence. Such a situation adds an artificial scarcity to the natural scarcity of skills and talents. On the other hand, it is possible for an opposite situation to arise. The rewards of technical position may be so great that a condition of excess supply is created, leading to at least temporary devaluation of the rewards. Thus "unemployment in the learned professions" may result in a debasement of the prestige of those positions. Such adjustments and readjustments are constantly occurring in changing societies; and it is always well to bear in mind that the efficiency of a stratified structure may be affected by the modes of recruitment for positions. The social order itself, however, sets limits to the inflation or deflation of the prestige of experts: an oversupply tends to debase the rewards and discourage recruitment or produce revolution, whereas an under-supply tends to increase the rewards or weaken the society in competition with other societies.

Particular systems of stratification show a wide range with respect to the exact position of technically competent persons. This range is perhaps more evident in the degree of specialization. Extreme division of labor tends to create many specialists without high prestige since the training is short and the required native capacity relatively small. On the other hand it also tends to accentuate the high position of the true experts—scientists, engineers, and administrators—by increasing their authority relative to other functionally important positions. But the idea of a technocratic social order or a government or priesthood of engineers or social scientists neglects the limitations of knowledge and skills as a basic for performing social functions. To the extent that the social structure is truly specialized the prestige of the technical person must also be circumscribed.

Variation in stratified systems

The generalized principles of stratification here suggested form a necessary preliminary to a consideration of types of stratified sys-

---

* An estate granted by the Spanish crown, including rights to the labor of the Indians living on the territory.—Ed.

tems, because it is in terms of these principles that the types must be described. This can be seen by trying to delineate types according to certain modes of variation. For instance, some of the most important modes (together with the polar types in terms of them) seem to be as follows:

(a) The degree of specialization. The degree of specialization affects the fineness and multiplicity of the gradations in power and prestige. It also influences the extent to which particular functions may be emphasized in the invidious system, since a given function cannot receive much emphasis in the hierarchy until it has achieved structural separation from the other functions. Finally, the amount of specialization influences the bases of selection. Polar types: *Specialized, Unspecialized.*

(b) The nature of the functional emphasis. In general when emphasis is put on sacred matters, a rigidity is introduced that tends to limit specialization and hence the development of technology. In addition, a brake is placed on social mobility, and on the development of bureaucracy. When the preoccupation with the sacred is withdrawn, leaving greater scope for purely secular preoccupations, a great development, and rise in status, of economic and technological positions seemingly takes place. Curiously, a concomitant rise in political position is not likely, because it has usually been allied with the religious and stands to gain little by the decline of the latter. It is also possible for a society to emphasize family functions—as in relatively undifferentiated societies where high mortality requires high fertility and kinship forms the main basis of social organization. Main types: *Familistic, Authoritarian* (*Theocratic* or sacred, and *Totalitarian* or secular), *Capitalistic.*

(c) The magnitude of invidious differences. What may be called the amount of social distance between positions, taking into account the entire scale, is something that should lend itself to quantitative measurement. Considerable differences apparently exist between different societies in this regard, and also between parts of the same society. Polar types: *Equalitarian, Inequalitarian.*

(d) The degree of opportunity. The familiar question of the amount of mobility is different

from the question of the comparative equality or inequality of rewards posed above, because the two criteria may vary independently up to a point. For instance, the tremendous divergences in monetary income in the United States are far greater than those found in primitive societies, yet the equality of opportunity to move from one rung to the other in the social scale may also be greater in the United States than in a hereditary tribal kingdom. Polar types: *Mobile* (open), *Immobile* (closed).

(e) The degree of stratum solidarity. Again the degree of "class solidarity" (or the presence of specific organizations to promote class interests) may vary to some extent independently of the other criteria, and hence is an important principle in classifying systems of stratification. Polar types: *Class organized, Class unorganized.*

External conditions

What state any particular system of stratification is in with reference to each of these modes of variation depends on two things: (1) its state with reference to the other ranges of variation, and (2) the conditions outside the system of stratification which nevertheless influence that system. Among the latter are the following:

(a) The stage of cultural development. As the cultural heritage grows, increased specialization becomes necessary, which in turn contributes to the enhancement of mobility, a decline of stratum solidarity, and a change of functional emphasis.

(b) Situation with respect to other societies. The presence or absence of open conflict with other societies, of free trade relations or cultural diffusion, all influence the class structure to some extent. A chronic state of warfare tends to place emphasis upon the military functions, especially when the opponents are more or less equal. Free trade, on the other hand, strengthens the hand of the trader at the expense of the warrior and priest. Free movement of ideas generally has an equalitarian effect. Migration and conquest create special circumstances.

(c) Size of the society. A small society limits the degree to which functional specialization can go, the degree of segregation of different strata, and the magnitude of inequality.

Composite types

Much of the literature on stratification has attempted to classify concrete systems into a certain number of types. This task is deceptively simple, however, and should come at the end of an analysis of elements and principles, rather than at the beginning. If the preceding discussion has any validity, it indicates that there are a number of modes of variation between different systems, and that any one system is a composite of the society's status with reference to all these modes of variation. The danger of trying to classify whole societies under such rubrics as *caste, feudal,* or *open class* is that one or two criteria are selected and others ignored, the result being an unsatisfactory solution to the problem posed. The present discussion has been offered as a possible approach to the more systematic classification of composite types.

Notes

[1] Kingsley Davis, "A Conceptual Analysis of Stratification," *American Sociological Review.* 7: 309–321, June, 1942.

[2] The writers regret (and beg indulgence) that the present essay, a condensation of a longer study, covers so much in such short space that adequate evidence and qualification cannot be given and that as a result what is actually very tentative is presented in an unfortunately dogmatic manner.

[3] Unfortunately, functional importance is difficult to establish. To use the position's prestige to establish it, as is often unconsciously done, constitutes circular reasoning from our point of view. There are, however, two independent clues: (a) the degree to which a position is functionally unique, there being no other positions that can perform the same function satisfactorily; (b) the degree to which other positions are dependent on the one in question. Both clues are best exemplified in organized systems of positions built around one major function. Thus, in most complex societies the religious, political, economic, and educational functions are handled by distinct structures not easily interchangeable. In addition, each structure possesses many different positions, some clearly dependent on, if not subordinate to, others. In sum, when an institutional nucleus becomes differentiated around one main function, and at the same time organizes a large portion of the population into its relationships, the *key* positions in it are of the highest functional importance. The absence of such specialization does not prove functional unimportance, for the whole society may be relatively unspecialized; but it is safe to assume that the more important functions receive the first and clearest structural differentiation.

[4] The symbolic rather than intrinsic role of income in social stratification has been succinctly summarized by Talcott Parsons, "An Analytical Approach to the Theory of Social Stratification," *American Journal of Sociology,* 45:841–862, May, 1940.

THE CASTE SYSTEM

The concept of caste usually appears in sociology as an ideal type, to which no real society is expected to conform completely. However, the term brings to mind the society of India, especially during the period of British colonialism, when the ideal type was approached more closely than in any other known society. Indeed, the formulation of the ideal type has depended heavily on the study of the Indian system of stratification in much the same way as Weber's description of bureaucracy derived largely from his familiarity with the contemporary Prussian administration.

This selection presents a summary view of the Indian system of stratification as it existed before Independence. Olcott offers a description of the system, suggests its functions, and notes the effects of changes taking place toward the end of the Colonial period.

The Indian system of stratification is described by Olcott as permitting marriage only within a stratum (endogamy), as possessing a religious basis, rigorously ascribing statuses, assigning many fixed rights and duties to each status, and excluding a certain proportion of the population from social participation at any level. Among the functions of the system are the modification of conflict between strata; the support of Hindu culture, including the arts and crafts; social integration on an intraclass basis; and the facilitation of personal adjustment. Implicit is the idea that some of the problems the caste system helps to solve are themselves products of the system; for instance, personal maladjustment can arise where the rules of caste prevent a person from using his native talents. Moreover the deprivations that the system imposes on the outcastes can be seen as dysfunctional for the total society.

Gradual modernization and industrialization of India under the late Colonial regime have led to a rise in the position of the outcastes, but these forces have not weakened the caste system in all aspects. In fact, modern communications techniques add to the effectiveness of intracaste social organization.

Some recent research suggests that the picture of the Indian system of stratification presented here is somewhat overstated in the direction of the ideal type. That is, the earlier studies of India by Western observers, on which this article is partly based, tended to neglect the differences between ideal and real norms, between what is said and what is in fact done. We now believe that even in its most rigid state the caste system permitted more variance than this description implies.

The caste system has also changed considerably over time. A rigid system approximating the ideal type was associated with the period of British colonialism, for the British successfully followed a policy of maintaining control by winning over and strengthening the traditional centers of power. The association of the caste system with colonialism resulted in a considerable weakening of caste when India achieved her independence. The constitution of the Republic of India eliminated the discrimination in rights and duties that had existed previously under Hindu civil law, and brought universal suffrage. An increased tempo of social change, including the effort to industrialize, has made the dysfunctions of the system more evident and has further weakened its place in Hindu culture. The caste system has not yet disappeared, nor must it necessarily vanish in a modern industrial Indian society. It must, however, adapt and change.

A comparison of stratification in the Indian system with that in the American South is of considerable interest, since some observers have claimed that the latter can also be described as a caste system. The systems are similar in the high degree of ascription they both involve. An American of known Negro ancestry is automatically considered to be Negro, and although "passing" for white occasionally takes place in urban centers, very few Negroes are able to do this because of their color. Endogamy is also part of the mores in both societies. Although these similarities may justify applying the caste label to the American case, there are remarkable differences to consider. In America there are far fewer rights and duties linked to "caste." Negroes occupy a wide range of low-prestige statuses, and individual choice within this range is far greater than that available to a member of an Indian caste. Moreover, there are no outcastes in the American situation. A person is either white or Negro, and a product of stratum intermarriage is assigned to the lower stratum, rather than being made an outcaste. Most important, the stratification system of the American South lacks religious sanctions. The religious structure has accommodated to the biracial society, and segregated churches are the rule, but there are few accepted religious principles supporting the system. In point of fact, much of the leadership for changing the stratification system has come from religion, which is the very institution that most notably frustrates change in the Indian case.

Selection 42
THE CASTE SYSTEM OF INDIA
Mason Olcott

I. *What are the essentials of the system?*

1. Endogamy.* The Caste system is a hierarchy of endogamous groups that individuals enter only by birth. A caste differs from a clan or sib† in being endogamous and recognizing various ranks. It differs from a class in its strict enforcement of permanent endogamy within caste groups.

The largest enumeration of castes was in the 1901 *Census* which listed "2,378 main castes and tribes" (No. 1, 537, 557) some of which in turn are divided into endogamous subcastes of which the Brahmans are said to have 800. All ancient occupations used to be organized on a caste basis, even those now considered anti-social. The *Census* speaks of 4,500,000 persons belonging to castes and tribes "whose hereditary occupation is crime of one kind or another—theft, burglary, highway robbery, or even assassination, combined in many instances with prostitution."

2. Compelling religious sanctions. The caste system of India differs from the class systems of other countries mainly in being invested with the mighty sanctions of the ancient Hindu religion, as is evidenced by the very name given to the system, *varna ashrama dharma.* *Varna* means color, *ashrama* may be translated religious discipline, while *dharma* covers religio-social righteousness, obligations and mores. The families of a caste often have a common name and occupation. To be a good Hindu a man may believe anything or nothing but he

must fulfill his caste obligations. Orthodox Hinduism prohibits him from marrying his child to a person of another caste, from eating and drinking with an outsider, from eating unfit or unclean food, from touching an Outcaste or letting his shadow fall upon him, and from following an unsuitable occupation. A villager's failure to observe minutely all the taboos and elaborate ceremonial rules usually leads to his being boycotted by his fellow caste-men as to marriage and food, and sometimes as to companionship, drink and tobacco. Even the village artisans will not deign to serve him. Until a few decades ago no strict Hindu might cross the "black waters" of the ocean with impunity. To be received back into caste he had to make atonement by swallowing a pellet of the five products of the sacred cow, including the dung and urine.

In the authoritative Bhagavadgita, when Arjuna hesitates to slay his distant relatives, his divine charioteer Lord Krishna reminds him that he is a Kshatriya (warrior) and that he must never swerve from his caste *dharma:*

> Better to do the duty of one's caste,
> Though bad and ill-performed and fraught
>   with evil,
> Than undertake the business of another,
> However good it be. For better far
> Abandon life at once than not fulfill
> One's own appointed work.[1]

3. Hierarchy based on birth and reincarnation. The caste system recognizes an indefinite number of groups of different ranks, each one standing on the shoulders of the castes below it. Every aspect of the life of an orthodox Hindu hinges on what the Westerner calls the accident of birth. His domestic ceremonies and customs, his home and temple worship, his circle of friends and relatives, his occupa-

---

* Marriage within a group.—Ed.
† Kinship groups that are exogamous; members marry nonmembers.—Ed.

Reprinted from *American Sociological Review*, 9:6, 1944, pp. 648–657, with permission of the author and the publisher.

tion and trade union, all depend upon the level of the group into which he was born. His pay, his perquisites, and benefits to be received in times of distress are also largely determined by birth.

Hinduism lends weighty support to the hierarchy of caste by declaring that a man's caste is the exact index of his soul's behavior and piety in previous births. If born a Brahman, the so-called "pinnacle of perfection," "lord of creation," his soul has been scrupulous in its observances and ceremonials during countless earlier lives. But if he is born a lowly Sudra, he has not fulfilled his caste *dharma,* while if he is born a despised Outcaste, that is convincing proof of the foulness of his deeds in previous incarnations.

4. *Social-economic interdependence.* The far reaching mutual relationships at the heart of the caste system are well brought out by Dr. W. H. Wiser whose minute daily observations during his several months of residence during each of five years in Karimpur in the United Provinces are summed up in his excellent study from which I quote:

> In a Hindu village in North India, each individual has a fixed economic and social status established by his birth in a given caste. If he is born into a carpenter family, he finds himself related by blood to carpenters exclusively. . . . The men in all these families earn their livelihood through the carpentry trade, sometimes supplemented by agriculture. Each carpenter has his own clientele (or jajman), which has become established through custom and which continues from generation to generation. . . . This relationship once established cannot be broken except by the carpenter himself who may choose to sell his rights to another carpenter. . . . The relationship fixes responsibilities both on the carpenter and on the one whom he serves. The carpenter during the sowing season must remove and sharpen the plow point once or twice a week. During the harvest he must keep sickles sharp and renew handles as often as demanded. He must be ready to repair a cart whenever called upon by a customer, or to make minor repairs on a customer's house. In exchange he receives at each harvest 28 pounds of grain for every plow owned by his client. Similar relationships of mutual service exist between practically all the 24 castes of the village of Karimpur. In return for services rendered, payments in cash or kind are made daily, monthly, semi-annually, or on special occasions. Even more important are the various concessions granted, usually without payment: residence site, rent-free land, funeral-pyre plot, food for family and fodder for animals, clothing, timber, cattle dung fuel, credit facilities, supplementary employment, use of raw materials, tools, implements or draft animals, hides, casual leave and aid in litigation. These rights are valued so highly that many a villager prefers them to a steady cash income from a neighboring mill.[2]

In large cities such custom-fixed interdependence has been breaking down.

5. *The Outcaste substratum.* The cultured Hindu has his menial and defiling drudgery performed for him by forty to seventy millions called Outcastes, Depressed Classes, or Untouchables. Divided into 280 sections often struggling one against the other, they are mostly descended from the ancient races who inhabited India before the invasion of the Dravidian-speaking Mediterraneans and the Aryan peoples. Later they accepted servitude on the lowest fringes of Hindu society. They commonly live outside the village in unspeakable filth, eking out their existence by menial and polluting labor. Carrion is the only meat that millions of them can obtain. In dry areas they find it difficult to find water for bathing, and even for drinking. They sacrifice animals to appease the dreaded demons and demonesses that dominate their dreary lives. Their touch, their very presence is thought to contaminate others. Caste mores have held them down in abysmal ignorance and degradation on the assumption that they suffer justly for their vicious deeds in previous lives. The 1931 *Census* spoke of their being debarred from the use of tax-supported roads, reservoirs, wells and schools, from temples, burning grounds and other religious institutions, and from private tea shops, hotels and theatres. In some places such prohibitions are now being relaxed.

II. *What factors molded the caste system?*

Many studies of caste have suffered from the single-cause fallacy. Ibbetson proposed his theory of the tribal origin of caste. Risley thought that caste was caused by race and hypergamy (marrying women into higher groups), while Nesfield and Dahlmann propounded occupation as the chief reason for its origin, and Senart said that the family worship of the gens* was the cause of caste. There is an element of truth in each of these theories but none is complete in itself. We cannot make the generalization that there is any single cause for caste. Nor can we assume that the entire caste system took definite shape at one particular time and was not later modified. Rather we can trace many diverse factors working together with various potency at different times and places.

1. *Food and occupational taboos.* The 1931 *Census* argues that "the essential ingredients which made the growth of caste possible were of pre-Aryan origin, without them the development of caste would not and could not have taken place."[3] Caste is weakest in North India and especially in the Panjab where the Aryan racial element is strongest. The animistic† Nagas of Assam are modern representatives of very ancient aboriginal tribes. These people taboo alien food on the ground that it is connected with the strangers' soul matter and thus has a dangerous magical effect on the Nagas who eat it. Other unassimilated tribes in inaccessible parts of Assam have taboos against visitors following their former handicrafts since they would offset the logical mana or magic. "The sentiments and beliefs on which caste is based presumably go back to the totemistic‡ Proto-Australoid and Austro-Asiatic inhabitants of pre-Dravidian India, and we may conceive of their becoming effective in contact with Dravidian-speaking strangers bringing new crafts from the West. Hence would arise local taboos against certain crafts and persons, taboos which tended to become tribal and to erect rigid divisions between communities."[4] The same authority regards these taboos as the main source for the untouchability of the Outcastes.

2. *Tribal cohesion.* The aboriginal tribes, as they become accessible, gradually entered the religious and social systems of the more civ-

ilized peoples with whom they came in contact. In doing so they retained their original unity based on socio-religious mores and folkways. The tribe thus became an endogamous caste. This slow process of assimilation may be seen in various stages of development in different parts of India. The fact that so many of the old customs have been retained is due to the Hindu's spirit of compromise and tolerance of strange ideas and practices. These two factors may easily have been at work for centuries before the advent of the Aryan. They have certainly been effective ever since.

3. *The Aryan desire for racial purity.* When the Aryans entered India from the northwest during the second millennium before Christ, they were divided into three social classes similar to those of their Iranian kinsmen: the ruling or military, the priestly, and the Aryan commonality, but it was possible for a person to pass from one class to another. The Aryans, wishing to preserve their fair color, seem to have prohibited intermarriage with the aborigines not long after their invasion. To this day the higher castes generally have lighter skins and narrower noses than the castes lower on the scale, though many North Indian Outcastes are fair.

4. *Guild perpetuation.* The existence of different cultures side by side and the gradual development of industry brought division of labor. The Aryans with better paying occupations protected the interests of their children by apprenticeship combined with guild endogamy, and forced on some of India's previous inhabitants heavy manual labor, scavenging and working with the hides and carcasses of dead cattle. Those who were compelled to carry on such demeaning occupations were prohibited from marrying those whose work was honored. The desire to perpetuate the guild and its rights is still a factor that strengthens caste in those places that have been little touched by the forces of modern life.

5. *Priestly supremacy and religious dogmas.* As the Aryans came into India the priesthood was admitting recruits from other classes, and was subordinate to the military class. Before very long the Brahmans, by gaining a monopoly of magic, learning, professional work and statecraft, gained the supremacy. But about

---

* Clan.—Ed.
†Refers to religious belief that objects have souls. —Ed.
‡ Religion linking animal and other symbols to kinship groups.—Ed.

550 B.C. a Kshatriya prince, Gautama, founded Buddhism, which was accepted by other warrior nobles and many commoners and became the state religion. It opposed the caste system by emphasizing virtue rather than birth as the means of salvation. The Buddhists struggled for twelve centuries with the Brahmans, who regained the ascendancy only after the Kshatriyas had been bled white by continual warfare and after the Brahmans had accepted elements of Buddhist philosophy. The Brahmans imposed their control over state and religion, and promulgated dogmas to perpetuate their supremacy. For example, the great Hindu lawgiver Manu, following earlier writers, proclaimed as one of his basic doctrines that the resplendent One had assigned distinctive occupations and duties to each of four great orders: to the Brahmans who issued from his mouth, teaching, receiving alms and sacrificing for others; to the Kshatriyas who sprang from his arms, protection of the people; to the Vaisyas who came from his thighs, trading, money lending and land cultivation; and to the Sudras who were made of his feet, service of the other three orders.[5] This clever scheme outlined what the Brahmans wanted every one to accept, but it probably never accurately corresponded to actual conditions, even when it was elaborated by theories about hundreds of other castes springing from unlawful marriages between the four great orders. Below these a fifth order of Outcastes was later added to do the menial and scavenging work of the Sudras and the others. Fiction though these teachings were, they were piously believed and gave strong religious backing to the maintenance of caste barriers throughout the ages. The imitation of religious ideas has been infectious. On account of their stabilizing effect on a heterogeneous people, the vested interests of the priests have for centuries been supported by the civil powers.

Holding an established monopoly of teaching and priestcraft, the Brahmans kept enlarging upon the necessity of elaborate rituals to be performed by themselves. New genealogies and fables of the origin of new castes were ingeniously fabricated and quickly accepted. Armed with one of these and some new rituals, many a subcaste has ventured forth to claim full status as an endogamous caste, with stereotyped ideas of its own superiority. In no land did group snobbery become such a basic and permanent principle of life as in India.

The lower caste groups, being ill treated by the higher castes, wanted some one on whom they could project their spite and contempt and thus raise their own social prestige. This made them join in walling off the Outcastes as despicable and untouchable.

6. *Migration.* As groups moved to new places, they were soon isolated from their relatives, since travel by foot or oxcart was the only means of keeping in touch. Their food, work, customs and rituals gradually changed through the years. These variations gave rise to new caste groups.

III.   To what extent is caste being modified in modern times?

1. *The British hands off policy tends to produce gradual change.* After defeating the French, the East India Company took over the remnants of the Mogul Empire at bargain prices. The Company exercised the political power needed to maintain law and order, its trade with India, and its exploitation of the country's fabulous wealth. Except for abolishing the Thugs (clever gangsters inflamed by religion) and the practice of Suttee (the immolation of widows on their husbands' funeral pyres), the British did little to modify India's religious and social customs. Queen Victoria in 1857 promised her new subjects complete religious neutrality and freedom of worship. Like their predecessors the Great Moguls, the British have sought out and strengthened the existing vested interests as the best means of preserving law and order. The collectors of land taxes whom they found have been elevated into Zamindars and Maharajahs. Men at the top of the caste hierarchy have been confirmed in their prerogatives and powers over the destinies of their fellows. The sacred laws and customs of the Hindus are largely recognized in civil law. Under such conditions many of the customs connected with caste continue to flourish. Some exceptions are that the civil statutes (for example, Removal of Caste Disabilities Act) and courts sometimes regulate marriage, and that the criminal courts, instead of the caste councils, decide cases of assault, adultery and rape. In spite of the legalization of intercaste marriages by the Special Marriage Act of 1872, these have never become numerically important.

2. *Many minor rules are losing hold under the harsh impact of modern industrial civilization.* For strategic and commercial purposes the British early established a good system of highways and railroads. The new transportation facilities, especially crowded busses and third-class train compartments jammed to the doors and ceilings, throw together millions of people of all castes and of no caste, and leave little room for the niceties of ceremonial purity.

City factories and slums also force people of various castes close together. Modern machinery is destroying the old crafts and providing unheard of ways to earn a livelihood. Occupational mobility and movement from the compact ancestral village are breaking down those caste rules which do not concern marriage. A new money economy is destroying age-old customs and offering novel changes to win social recognition.

About a century ago the British started schools with English as the medium of instruction to train clerks and subordinate officials. Secularist teachings, scientific questionings and ideals of individual freedom soon took root and brought forth the fruit of criticism of the ancient mores. The telegraph, the newspaper, and the radio have also rapidly spread fresh concepts and standards throughout India. Professional men have come to disobey dietary and commensal restrictions on activities outside their homes, while their illiterate wives and mothers at home have scrupulously observed the sacred traditions. The sweeping advance of women's education in recent years is now accelerating the tempo of change.

The notion that a person is defiled by a lower caste man coming in contact with him is no longer universally held by Hindus. Some castes that were formerly split in two by migration are now tending to amalgamate.

People who have crossed the deep ocean are almost never required to make atonement by swallowing the five products of the cow. Taboos against some foods and against accepting food and water from persons of other castes are also gradually being weakened under the weight of modern conditions. Such changes are taking place most rapidly in city-dominated areas among English-educated and business people.

3. *Caste organizations are being definitely strengthened.* At the same time that modern transportation, communication and education are weakening the prohibitions regarding food and drink, they are also tending to strengthen other features of caste. Millions of devotees jam the buses and trains every year to visit distant sacred places they once could not reach. These expanded mass pilgrimages, the printed page, the radio, popular education and keen competition for jobs have worked to strengthen caste solidarity and the influence of caste customs regarding marriage.

Ghurye claims that the studies of caste in the *Indian Census* have strengthened the caste system. The author of the 1931 *Census* argues against this view, but admits that every census "gives rise to a pestiferous deluge of representations, accompanied by highly problematical histories, asking for recognition of some alleged fact or hypothesis. . . . As often as not, deterrent action is requested against the corresponding hypothesis of other castes. . . . Its standing is to be obtained by standing upon others rather than with them."[6]

The first caste conference was that of the Kayasths or accountants in 1887. Since then hundreds of castes have met and organized themselves to perpetuate and extend their special privileges, to raise their social status by reforms, to provide for the education of their needy and deserving children, to help their poor, and to petition for larger employment in government service. Most provinces have been forced by such pressures to pass rules that a definite proportion of the posts in the various services shall be filled from members of different castes, provided that they have the minimum qualifications. Sometimes even those who have failed in the examinations are admitted to office.

Castes having similar occupations and those residing in different parts of a language area are consolidating to secure greater social and political power. Together with this broader basis of caste life and endogamy goes the claim to higher rank in the caste hierarchy. For example, the Kamars called themselves Kshatriyas in 1921 and Brahmans in 1931. Some outcaste leather workers of the United Provinces have returned themselves as Rajputs (princely warriors). Such social ambitions have given rise to new forms of inter-caste competition. Each caste, fearing that some other caste will gain an advantage over it, seeks to build up its educational, economic and religious position and to tear down its hated rivals.

4. *The Outcastes' lot is being slowly improved.* Ever since the beginning of the modern missionary movement, most Christians have treated these people as human beings and children of the Heavenly Father. They have offered them medical, educational and economic service on the same basis as anyone else. Outcastes joining Protestant Churches have lost the stigma with which they had formerly been stamped, even in the eyes of most Hindus. Since 1906 liberal Hindus have had their own missions to provide these exploited people with education and work, to remedy their social disabilities and to preach to them. In recent years the Government has issued rules that all public wells, roads, railways, schools, post offices and other public buildings be opened to the Depressed Classes on equal terms with other people, but the enforcement of these rules rests upon local public opinion, which is often hostile. Not many years ago the only schooling allowed to Outcaste children was what they could get as they stood outside the school door. If they were admitted inside, the caste parents would withdraw their children. But between 1917 and 1926 the number of India's Outcaste pupils rose from 195,000 to 667,000, the latter figure being barely over one per cent of the Outcaste population. With thousands of the Depressed Classes being admitted to the franchise on property or literacy qualifications, and with their special representation in the legislatures, their votes are becoming an important political prize. This fact tends to improve their treatment by caste-men.

The lasting solution of the problem rests, not with missions or with Government, but rather with the Depressed Classes themselves and with the Hindu majority. Many Outcaste groups have organized themselves for their educational, social and political advancement. One of the best developed of these movements has been that started during the last century among three related groups of outcaste origin in Travancore, Malabar and South Kanara by the great religious leader, Sri Narayana Guruswami. He united them into a single Union for the Protection of the Sri Narayana religion, which has its own temples and priests but worships in the orthodox Hindu fashion. A few years ago these same Izhuvars not only were deprived of temple entry but had to stay 325 feet from the Hindu temple at Guruvayur, though they were well to do and well edu-

cated. However, as a result of the passive resistance and suffering of nationalist Hindus, the state temples of Travancore were opened to all cleanly dressed Hindus. Temples in the Madras Presidency have also been thrown open. Under Gandhi's inspiring leadership the National Congress has struggled hard and long to have the Untouchables admitted to the Hindu temples, on the ground that if this were conceded all other disabilities would in time disappear.

A number of years ago the national leader, Lajpat Rai, wrote, "National decline has its origin in the oppression of others. If we Indians desire to achieve national self-respect and dignity, we should open our arms to our unfortunate brothers and sisters of the Depressed Classes."[7] More recently Gandhi writes, "This untouchability will soon be a thing of the past. Hindu society has become conscious of the hideous wrong done to man by this sinful doctrine. Hundreds of Hindu workers are devoting themselves to the uplift of these suppressed classes. . . . The masses give intellectual assent to the reformer's plea; but are slow to grant equality in practice to their Outcaste brethren."[8]

IV. What were the outcomes when India was relatively static?

An evaluation of India's caste system depends entirely on whether we look at it from the standards of a static or of a dynamic society. Until about a century ago, India's life was largely static, though not so stagnant as the self-satisfied West has contemptuously assumed.

1. *Caste furnished a recognized pattern for numberless competing groups to dwell side by side with little or no strife.* For at least 5000 years India was the meeting point for the most diverse racial strains, we know from the recent Indus Valley discoveries. Geographical, linguistic and cultural factors made for the widest variety. This long period saw many wars between local kings, but few acute conflicts between different social groups, on account of the restraining hand of caste. It often served as a *Pax Indica* enabling the most heterogeneous peoples to live contentedly side by side in recognized, stable relationships. Not war but clever compromise was the desire of the Brahman priests who dominated the Hindu caste system after their overthrow of Buddhism about 650 A.D.

2. Caste and its religious basis gave strong continuity to Hindu life and learning. Sir Valentine Chirol speaks of "the Hindu's fine conception of the continuity of the family as one unbroken chain, sanctified by common worship, which stretches back to remote ancestors and forward to all the future generations."[9] This was one of the factors making it possible to preserve the high contributions of Indian culture in spite of Moslem incursions, repeated wars, famines and catastrophes. Most of these traditions were linked with religion and maintained by the Brahmans. On this point, R. P. Masani says, "The mystic and miraculous hymns and liturgies had to be preserved and handed down from father to son by word of mouth. Their sanctity depended not merely on their words or general sense, but on every accent rightly placed. There was need for men who could specialize in the study of the texts, comprehend the symbolic meaning of the ritual, and assist in the perpetuation of this textual tradition."[10] A whole literature of this philosophic insight and great beauty was thus memorized and transmitted orally from father to son for many centuries. This would have been impossible without specialization and very difficult unless that specialization had been hereditary.

3. A wide range of beautiful arts and crafts were preserved through father-son apprenticeship. In the Indus Valley sites inhabited fifty centuries ago, almost every household had its hand spindles. Archeologists have ascertained that these people were the first to spin and weave fiber from the real cotton plant. *Sindon*, the Greek word for cotton, is named after the Sind or Indus Valley. They and the Romans admiringly imported the fabrics made by the weaving castes of India. India's arts and crafts survived until they were destroyed by the competition of Western machine goods during the past 150 years. With little population growth and almost stationary demand for the products of each craft the system of occupational endogamy supplied the number of workers needed in every craft. If there came to be excess of families in one village, they could move to a neighboring place.

4. Within each caste grew up a firm group solidarity and sense of responsibility, which lasted throughout the centuries, in spite of war and confusion. This close bond of kinship brought together socially the rich and poor members of a caste in the prolonged marriage and funeral rites and all other festivals and solemnities. In addition the wealthier members of a caste saw that the poorer did not starve, thus taking care of dependents and defectives and largely obviating the need of public charity. This system of relief worked fairly well except when the whole country-side was suffering from famine or epidemic, or in the case of the Outcastes and lower castes where all the members were poor and downtrodden. Class lines were never sharply drawn until modern times. As opposed to Western individualism and its frequently excessive mobility, Hinduism always exalted the static caste and the welfare of all its conformist members. Gandhi feels very keenly about this: "Free competition is excessive individualism, enabling the strong to exploit the weak, whether this is done within the same race, between capitalists and laborers, or among the colored races by the white man. This free competition is threatening India. Therefore I want to protect my country through a reformed caste system, removing untouchability and retaining the group loyalty and the hereditary craftsmanship of the castes."[11]

5. Caste status prevented personal choice and lessened maladjustment. No problems arose of choosing occupation or career. Every man inherited his work from his father and continued it using the traditional methods and serving the ancestral patrons. Almost all women followed in their mothers' footsteps of ministering to husband and children. Friends and companions did not have to be carefully selected by the individual, but were decided for him by birth. A person did not have to struggle to make a niche for himself; his place was already made for him when he was born. In all these ways a person had none of the troubled effort of striking out and choosing for himself. His path was already determined for him. His status was clearly defined by birth and ancient custom. This hampered broad personality development, but at the same time obviated many conflicts and frustrations.

6. The caste system involved unjust treatment of the Outcastes and some low-caste people.

The men at the top could command servile obedience from the lowest castes, while all the groups at the bottom were deprived of human rights and made subordinate to higher groups. Men and women may have resented their misfortunes and hated their oppressors, but in a stable society ruled by the aged with their age-old ideas, injustice seemed part of a divinely established order. What could they do about their lot? They meekly resigned themselves to the fate written on their foreheads. Orthodox Hinduism, with its promises of rewards in future births for caste conformity in this birth, was truly "the opiate of the people," dulling the senses of the oppressed to their terrible degradation and lulling them into silent acquiescence. For centuries it produced the slave mentality, which Gandhi has blamed on the British.

V. What are the present outcomes in a dynamic society?

The intellectual, religious, political, and industrial revolutions, each of which in turn shook Europe to its foundations between the Renaissance and the present day, have all been telescoped together in India during scarcely more than a century. Save for inaccessible mountains and jungles, "the unchanging East," no longer exists. India is on the move. The leaven of Western ideas, discoveries and inventions is so powerfully at work in the lump of India's four hundred millions that no one can fully control the outcome. World War II is greatly expanding India's industries. The first major famine in thirty years is shaking India to its foundations. For these reasons the only accurate standard by which to measure the caste system at present is based on its outcomes in a society that is becoming more dynamic with every passing year.

1. Recent changes are giving rise to extremely bitter inter-caste strife. The old taboos that kept every one in the position where he was born are noticeably weakening, and no fresh controls are taking their place. Members of castes are branching out into occupations infringing on the prerogatives of other castes. Each caste seeks by all possible means to gain the ascendancy over the castes that used to be of equal or slightly superior rank. Some caste councils obtain higher educational degrees and better paying jobs for their young men, while others increase their prestige by new prohibitions on diet. According to the former Maharajah Gaekwar of Baroda, a progressive Hindu, "the eternal struggle between caste and caste for social superiority has become a source of constant ill-feeling in these days. The human desire to help the members of one's caste leads to nepotism, heart-burning and consequent mutual distrust."

2. Latent injustices are rendered patent by new social ideals and the acids of modernity. The theory that everyone in the village would be served by every one else, and in turn would equally serve him through his special occupation, does not correspond to the facts. The interrelationships are extremely asymmetrical, the Brahmans, the big landlords, the grain dealers, and the money lenders (sometimes the same people) being scrupulously served but not giving commensurate service. At least they do little or nothing that costs them exertion or loss of prestige. At the other end of the scale the lowest castes and the Outcastes are badly maltreated and forced into most degrading servitude.

3. The Outcastes are feeling most bitterly the inhumanities heaped upon them. For centuries they have been constantly subject to the mental and moral degradation of serfdom. Direct overt reaction would be least harmful to their mental health, but this course is usually blocked by disadvantages real or imagined. The direct covert reaction of resentment is extremely common, but may be completely concealed from the members of the oppressing castes. At other times the impulse to strike back is forced into some indirect channel. This whole matter has been ably treated by Dr. J. C. Heinrich in his *Psychology of a Suppressed People*.

In recent years the Kallars of South India, whose caste occupation was robbery, attempted to enforce the following among other rules upon the Outcastes: "No males shall be allowed to wear clothes below the knees or above the hips. The men shall not use umbrellas and should not wear sandals. Their children should not get themselves educated. The children should be asked only to tend the cattle of the Mirasidars (a class of landlords). Their men and women should work as slaves of the Mirasidars. They must sell away their own lands to Mirasidars at very cheap rates, and if they won't do so, no water will be allowed to them to irrigate their lands. Even if something is grown by the help of rain water, the crops should be robbed away when they are ripe for harvest." When the Outcastes disregarded these regulations, the caste men burned their huts, destroyed their property and looted their livestock.[12]

Restrictions of this kind used to be enforced as part of the unwritten mores, but now in many cases they are no longer carried into effect. But serfdom for debt continues, the debt being passed on from father to son. In Travancore several branches of the Depressed Classes must never approach nearer than forty or eighty feet of a caste person, and must always call out before they enter a main road. The Mahars of Western India wrote to the British Secretary of State, "We are sick of the bondage which the barbarism of Hindu customs imposes upon us. . . . We have long submitted to the Jaganaut of caste; we have for ages been crushed under its wheels. But we can no longer submit to the tyranny." Gandhi has said, "I consider untouchability to be a heinous crime against humanity. It is . . . an arrogant assumption of superiority. . . . It has suppressed vast numbers of the human race. . . . I know of no argument in favor of its retention."[13] M. D. Altekar writes of the effects of injustice, "At present a sudden and terrific explosion of resentment is being witnessed all over the country. The outburst is so great that the political unity, laboriously built up for half a century by patriotic men, has been consumed in the twinkling of an eye."[14]

4. Sacred traditions are stifling needed social progress.   At a time when social customs must change rapidly to keep pace with modern business and technology, the caste system with its cramping restrictions prevents men from making adequate adjustment. The system is one of the means by which the gerontocracy* maintains its power. Everyone is required to remain within the caste status in which he was born. No matter how little he has to occupy him, a man may not engage in the occupation of another caste. If a caste man has insufficient land, he cannot weave or work for hire out of fear that he will lower his status. Constructive social experimentation has been seriously hampered by the divisive tendencies of caste exclusiveness and by the fatalism and the absorption in petty trifles brought about by caste. Mahatma Gandhi has this to say, "India is a country of nonsense. It is nonsensical to parch one's throat with thirst when a kindly Mohammedan is ready to offer pure water to drink, and yet thousands of Hindus would sooner die of thirst than drink water from a Mohammedan household."

5. Caste seriously restricts newly valued individual freedom.   For a man to take his place in modern society, a certain amount of liberty of action is necessary. But caste, with its multitudinous, burdensome regulations based on the accident of birth, hampers a person's freedom to experiment and even to lead his own life according to his better judgment. Rabindranath Tagore, world-famous poet, has said, "The regeneration of the Indian people, to my mind, directly and perhaps solely depends upon the removal of this condition of caste."

* Government by elders.—Ed.

Notes

[1] *Gita*, 3, 35.

[2] *The Hindu Jajmani System*, Lucknow, Lucknow Publishing House, 1936, pp. 5–6.

[3] Vol. I, Part I, pp. 436–438.

[4] *Ibid.*

[5] Book I, lines 87–89.

[6] Vol. I, Part I, p. 433.

[7] *The Arya Samaj*, p. 232.

[8] *Annals of the American Academy of Political and Social Science*, Vol. 145, No. 2, p. 181.

[9] *India*, p. 25.

[10] R. P. Masani, *The Legacy of India*, Oxford: Clarendon Press, 1937, p. 128.

[11] Quoted in *National Christian Council Review*, December, 1937.

[12] *Census*, 1931, Vol. I, Part I, p. 485.

[13] *Young India, 1919–22*, New York, Huebsch, 1924, p. 482.

[14] *Annals of the American Academy of Political and Social Sciences*, Vol. 145, No. 2, p. 186.

THE CLASS SYSTEM

The United States stands in the same relation to the ideal type of an open-class society as India does to the ideal type of a caste society. As in India, there is a tendency on the part of observers of America to confuse the real and the ideal, and to distort the picture of American stratification in the direction of the ideal type, depicting less inequality and more social mobility than in fact exists. This distortion is fostered by the ideological pressures of the American Dream, which both denies the existence of social classes in any form and implicitly recognizes them by maintaining that anyone can rise to the top.

Sociologists, because of their training, have been less affected by these pressures to distortion in describing the American class system. Sociological theory posits the existence of classes in all complex societies, including our own. The goal of sociological research in this area has not been to determine whether stratification exists in America but rather to determine the form that it takes. A very large number of studies have been directed to this question, and a great deal is known, although many disagreements remain to be resolved.

The senior author of this selection was one of the first social scientists to attempt a systematic study of American stratification, and much of what is known about this subject today derives from work of W. Lloyd Warner and his students. Among their most notable accomplishments are the "Yankee City Series," a detailed study of class in a New England town, and *Democracy in Jonesville* and *Deep South,* which deal with communities in the Middle West and in Mississippi. The present selection gives a brief overview of these major studies and summarizes Warner's ideas concerning class in America.

> At the top of Yankee City's class structure are a group of old families (the upper-upper class) whose status is based on inherited wealth. Directly beneath these are families who are equally wealthy, but whose wealth has more recent origins (the lower-upper class). The third group in the hierarchy is the solid, respectable group of business proprietors and professional men (the upper-middle class). These groups are relatively small and represent the cream of society, above the level of the common man.
>
> The level of the common man is divided into two classes (lower-middle and upper-lower), the one consisting largely of clerks and white-collar workers and the other of semiskilled "poor but honest" workmen. A final class (lower-lower) lies below the common man in a position analogous to that of Indian outcastes. The epithets directed at these people suggest that they lack the elements of decency, and to a large degree they are isolated from the rest of the community.
>
> The findings from Jonesville and Old City (*Deep South*) are cited to indicate both general similarities and regional differences. Jonesville lacks the old families of Yankee City, and Warner suggests that this situation may prevail throughout the later-settled parts of the country. Stratification in the South is complicated by the presence of Negroes, who form a separate caste. Although class varies from community to community, a general pattern can be discerned that fits the country as a whole.

Warner's work on American stratification can justifiably be called pioneering. It has been extensively criticized, partly because many people are ideologically opposed to Warner's findings. The following two criticisms are recurrent, and their validity is a subject of debate among sociologists.

First, the picture of class in America presented in this selection rests on the study of three communities. All three are small cities. The critics assert that these communities cannot be assumed to be representative of the great metropolitan centers in which an increasing proportion of Americans reside and that

Warner's concept of class may be valid only in small cities. Warner replies to this criticism by noting that several recent works by his students indicate that the validity of his conception of class is even more apparent in large than in small cities.

Second, the reputational method of measurement used in the early Warner studies cannot easily be applied in a society of millions, and many critics intimate that the model of class underlying this method is therefore rendered invalid. They believe that Warner's idea of class oversimplifies a much more complex class structure. On the other hand, Warner has devised a method that combines measures of occupation, source of income, type of dwelling, and area of residence into an objective index that is easily applicable to very large populations. He has shown that this Index of Status Characteristics correlates well with the reputational method of measurement, and he believes that the same model of class underlies both. On this basis he asserts that the six-fold class structure described in the selection is valid for the total society.

In sum, both supporters and critics of Warner's approach to social class in America are in general agreement on the validity of his description of the class structure in the communities he studies. The degree to which these results can be generalized remains a matter of disagreement among sociologists. However, even Warner's most severe critics recognize the value of the Yankee City, Old City, and Jonesville studies in posing the problem of class to sociology and in stimulating one of the most fruitful traditions of research in American sociology.

Selection 43
FROM SOCIAL CLASS IN AMERICA
W. Lloyd Warner, Marchia Meecker, and Kenneth Eells

Class among the New England Yankees

Studies of communities in New England clearly demonstrate the presence of a well-defined social-class system.[1] At the top is an aristocracy of birth and wealth. This is the so-called "old family" class. The people of Yankee City say the families who belong to it have been in the community for a long time—for at least three generations and preferably many generations more than three. "Old family" means not only old to the community but old to the class. Present members of the class were born into it; the families into which they were born can trace their lineage through many generations participating in a way of life characteristic of the upper class back to a generation marking the lowly beginnings out of

Reprinted from *Social Class in America* by W. Lloyd Warner, Marchia Meecker, and Kenneth Eells (Chicago: Science Research Associates, 1949), with permission of W. Lloyd Warner.

which their family came. Although the men of this level are occupied gainfully, usually as large merchants, financiers, or in the higher professions, the wealth of the family, inherited from the husband's or the wife's side, and often from both, has been in the family for a long time. Ideally, it should stem from the sea trade when Yankee City's merchants and sea captains made large fortunes, built great Georgian houses on elm-lined Hill Street, and filled their houses and gardens with the proper symbols of their high position. They became the 400, the Brahmins, the Hill Streeters to whom others looked up; and they, well-mannered or not, looked down on the rest. They counted themselves, and were so counted, equals of similar levels in Salem, Boston, Providence, and other New England cities. Their sons and daughters married into the old families from these towns and at times, when family fortune was low or love was great, they married wealthy sons and daughters from the newly rich who occupied the class level below them.

This was a happy event for the fathers and mothers of such fortunate young people in the lower half of the upper class, an event well publicized and sometimes not too discreetly bragged about by the parents of the lower-upper-class children, an occasion to be explained by the mothers from the old families in terms of the spiritual demands of romantic love and by their friends as "a good deal and a fair exchange all the way around for everyone concerned."

The new families, the lower level of the upper class, came up through the new industries—shoes, textiles, silverware—and finance. Their fathers were some of the men who established New England's trading and financial dominance throughout America. When New York's Wall Street rose to power, many of them transferred their activities to this new center of dominance. Except that they aspire to old-family status, if not for themselves then for their children, these men and their families have a design for living similar to the old-family group. But they are consciously aware that their money is too new and too recently earned to have the sacrosanct quality of wealth inherited from a long line of ancestors. They know, as do those about them, that, while a certain amount of wealth is necessary, birth and old family are what really matter. Each of them can cite critical cases to prove that particular individuals have no money at all, yet belong to the top class because they have the right lineage and right name. While they recognize the worth and importance of birth, they feel that somehow their family's achievements should be better rewarded than by a mere second place in relation to those who need do little more than be born and stay alive.

The presence of an old-family class in a community forces the newly rich to wait their turn if they aspire to "higher things." Meanwhile, they must learn how to act, fill their lives with good deeds, spend their money on approved philanthropy, and reduce their arrogance to manageable proportions.

The families of the upper and lower strata of the upper classes are organized into social cliques and exclusive clubs. The men gather fortnightly in dining clubs where they discuss matters that concern them. The women belong to small clubs or to the Garden Club and give their interest to subjects which symbolize their high status and evoke those sentiments necessary in each individual if the class is to maintain itself. Both sexes join philanthropic organizations whose good deeds are an asset to the community and an expression of the dominance and importance of the top class to those socially beneath them. They are the members of the Episcopalian and Unitarian and, occasionally, the Congregational and Presbyterian churches.

Below them are the members of the solid, highly respectable upper-middle class, the people who get things done and provide the active front in civic affairs for the classes above them. They aspire to the classes above and hope their good deeds, civic activities, and high moral principles will somehow be recognized far beyond the usual pat on the back and that they will be invited by those above them into the intimacies of upper-class cliques and exclusive clubs. Such recognition might increase their status and would be likely to make them members of the lower-upper group. The fact that this rarely happens seldom stops members of this level, once activated, from continuing to try. The men tend to be owners of stores and belong to the large proprietor and professional levels. Their incomes average less than those of the lower-upper class, this latter group having a larger income than any other group, including the old-family level.

These three strata, the two upper classes and the upper-middle, constitute the levels above the Common Man. There is a considerable distance socially between them and the mass of the people immediately below them. They comprise three of the six classes present in the community. Although in number of levels they constitute half the community, in population they have no more than a sixth, and sometimes less, of the Common Man's population. The three levels combined include approximately 13 per cent of the total population.

The lower-middle class, the top of the Common Man level, is composed of clerks and other white-collar workers, small tradesmen, and a fraction of skilled workers. Their small houses fill "the side streets" down from Hill Street, where the upper classes and some of the upper-middle live, and are noticeably absent from the better suburbs where the upper-middle concentrate. "Side Streeter" is a term often used by those above them to imply an inferior way of life and an inconsequential status. They have accumulated little property but are frequently home owners. Some of the more successful members of ethnic groups, such as the Italians, Irish, French-Canadians, have reached this level. Only a few members of these cultural minorities have gone beyond it; none of them has reached the old-family level.

The old-family class (upper-upper) is smaller in size than the new-family class (lower-upper) below them. It has 1.4 per cent, while the lower-upper class has 1.6 per cent, of the total population. Ten per cent of the population belongs to the upper-middle class, and 28 per cent to the lower-middle level. The upper-lower is the most populous class, with 34 per cent, and the lower-lower has 25 per cent of all the people in the town.

The prospects of the upper-middle-class children for higher education are not as good as those of the classes above. One hundred per cent of the children of the two upper classes take courses in the local high school that prepare them for college, and 88 per cent of the upper-middle do; but only 44 per cent of the lower-middle take these courses, 28 per cent of the upper-lower, and 26 per cent of the lower-lower. These percentages provide a good index of the position of the lower-middle class, ranking it well below the three upper classes, but placing it well above the upper-lower and the lower-lower.[2]

The upper-lower class, least differentiated from the adjacent levels and hardest to distinguish in the hierarchy, but clearly present, is composed of the "poor but honest workers" who more often than not are only semi-skilled or unskilled. Their relative place in the hierarchy of class is well portrayed by comparing them with the classes superior to them and with the lower-lower class beneath them in the category of how they spend their money.

A glance at the ranking of the proportion of the incomes of each class spent on ten items (including such things as rent and shelter, food, clothing, and education, among others) shows, for example, that this class ranks second for the percentage of the money spent on food, the lower-lower class being first and the rank order of the other classes following lower-middle according to their place in the social hierarchy. The money spent on rent and shelter by upper-lower class is also second to the lower-lower's first, the other classes' rank order and position in the hierarchy being in exact correspondence. To give a bird's-eye view of the way this class spends its money, the rank of the upper-lower, for the percentage of its

budget spent on a number of common and important items, has been placed in parentheses after every item in the list which follows: food (2), rent (2), clothing (4), automobiles (5), education (4), and amusements (4-5). For the major items of expenditure the amount of money spent by this class out of its budget corresponds fairly closely with its place in the class hierarchy, second to the first of the lower-lower class for the major necessities of food and shelter, and ordinarily, but not always, fourth or fifth to the classes above for the items that give an opportunity for cutting down the amounts spent on them. Their feelings about doing the right thing, of being respectable and rearing their children to do better than they have, coupled with the limitations of their income, are well reflected in how they select and reject what can be purchased on the American market.[3]

The lower-lower class, referred to as "Riverbrookers" or the "low-down Yankees who live in the clam flats," have a "bad reputation" among those who are socially above them. This evaluation includes beliefs that they are lazy, shiftless, and won't work, all opposites of the good middle-class virtues belonging to the essence of the Protestant ethic. They are thought to be improvident and unwilling or unable to save their money for a rainy day and, therefore, often dependent on the philanthropy of the private or public agency and on poor relief. They are sometimes said to "live like animals" because it is believed that their sexual mores are not too exacting and that pre-marital intercourse, post-marital infidelity, and high rates of illegitimacy, sometimes too publicly mixed with incest, characterize their personal and family lives. It is certain that they deserve only part of this reputation. Research shows many of them guilty of no more than being poor and lacking in the desire to get ahead, this latter trait being common among those above them. For these reasons and others, this class is ranked in Yankee City below the level of the Common Man (lower-middle and upper-lower). For most of the indexes of status it ranks sixth and last.

Class in the democratic Middle West and Far West

Cities large and small in the states west of the Alleghenies sometimes have class systems which do not possess an old-family (upper-upper) class. The period of settlement has not always been sufficient for an old-family level, based on the security of birth and inherited wealth, to entrench itself. Ordinarily, it takes several generations for an old-family class to gain and hold the prestige and power necessary to impress the rest of the community sufficiently with the marks of its "breeding" to be able to confer top status on those born into it. The family, its name, and its lineage must have had time to become identified in the public mind as being above ordinary mortals.

While such identification is necessary for the emergence of an old-family (upper-upper) class and for its establishment, it is also necessary for the community to be large enough for the principles of exclusion to operate. For example, those in the old-family group must be sufficiently numerous for all the varieties of social participation to be possible without the use of new-family members; the family names must be old enough to be easily identified; and above all there should always be present young people of marriageable age to become mates of others of their own class and a sufficient number of children to allow mothers to select playmates and companions of their own class for their children.

When a community in the more recently settled regions of the United States is sufficiently large, when it has grown slowly and at an average rate, the chances are higher that it has an old-family class. If it lacks any one of these factors, including size, social and economic complexity, and steady and normal growth, the old-family class is not likely to develop.

One of the best tests of the presence of an old-family level is to determine whether members of the new-family category admit, perhaps grudgingly and enviously and with hostile derogatory remarks, that the old-family level looks down on them and that it is considered a mark of advancement and prestige by those in the new-family group to move into it and be invited to the homes and social affairs of the old families. When a member of the new-family class says, "We've only been here two generations, but we still aren't old-family," and when he or she goes on to say that "they (old family) consider themselves better than people like us and the poor dopes around here let them get away with it," such evidence indicates that an old-family group is present and able to enforce recognition of its superior position upon its most aggressive and

hostile competitors, the members of the lower-upper, or new-family, class.

When the old-family group is present and its position is not recognized as superordinate to the new families, the two tend to be co-ordinate and view each other as equals. The old-family people adroitly let it be known that their riches are not material possessions alone but are old-family lineage; the new families display their wealth, accent their power, and prepare their children for the development of a future lineage by giving them the proper training at home and later sending them to the "right" schools and marrying them into the "right" families.

Such communities usually have a five-class pyramid, including an upper class, two middle, and two lower classes.[4]

Jonesville, located in the Middle West, approximately a hundred years old, is an example of a typical five-class community. The farmers around Jonesville use it as their market, and it is the seat of government for Abraham County. Its population of over 6,000 people is supported by servicing the needs of the farmers and by one large and a few small factories.

At the top of the status structure is an upper class commonly referred to as "the 400." It is composed of old-family and new-family segments. Neither can successfully claim superiority to the other. Below this level is an upper-middle class which functions like the same level in Yankee City and is composed of the same kind of people, the only difference being the recognition that the distance to the top is shorter for them and the time necessary to get there much less. The Common Man level, composed of lower-middle- and upper-lower-class people, and the lower-lower level are replicas of the same classes in Yankee City. The only difference is that the Jonesville ethnics in these classes are Norwegian Lutherans and Catholic Poles, the Catholic Irish and Germans having been absorbed for the most part in the larger population; whereas in Yankee City the ethnic population is far more heterogeneous, and the Catholic Irish are less assimilated largely because of more opposition to them, and because the church has more control over their private lives.

The present description of Jonesville's class order can be brief and no more than introductory because all the materials used to demonstrate how to measure social class are taken from Jonesville. The interested reader will obtain a clear picture in the chapters which follow [in *Social Class in America*] of what the classes are, who is in them, the social and economic characteristics of each class, and how the people of the town think about their status order.

The communities of the mountain states and Pacific Coast are new, and many of them have changed their economic form from mining to other enterprises; consequently, their class orders are similar to those found in the Middle West. The older and larger far western communities which have had a continuing, solid growth of population which has not destroyed the original group are likely to have the old-family level at the top with the other classes present; the newer and smaller communities and those disturbed by the destruction of their original status structure by large population gains are less likely to have an old-family class reigning above all others. San Francisco is a clear example of the old-family type; Los Angeles, of the more amorphous, less well-organized class structure.

Class in the Deep South

Studies in the Deep South demonstrate that, in the older regions where social changes until recently have been less rapid and less disturbing to the status order, most of the towns above a few thousand population have a six-class system in which an old-family elite is socially dominant.

For example, in a study of a Mississippi community, a market town for a cotton-growing region around it, Davis and the Gardners found a six-class system. . . .[5]

The people of the two upper classes make a clear distinction between an old aristocracy and an aristocracy which is not old. There is no doubt that the first is above the other; the upper-middle class views the two upper ones much as the upper classes do themselves but groups them in one level with two divisions, the older level above the other; the lower-middle class separates them but considers them co-ordinate; the bottom two classes, at a greater social distance than the others, group all the levels above the Common Man as "society" and one class. An examination of the terms used by the several classes for the other classes shows that similar principles are operating.

The status system of most communities in the South is further complicated by a color-caste system which orders and systematically controls the relations of those categorized as Negroes and whites.

Although color-caste in America is a separate problem and the present volume does not deal with this American status system, it is necessary that we describe it briefly to be sure a clear distinction is made between it and social class. Color-caste is a system of values and behavior which places all people who are thought to be white in a superior position and those who are thought of as black in an inferior status.

Characteristics of American Negroes vary from very dark hair and skin and Negroid features to blond hair, fair skin, and Caucasian features, yet all of them are placed in the "racial" category of Negro. The skin and physical features of American Caucasians vary from Nordic blond types to the dark, swarthy skin and Negroid features of some eastern Mediterranean stocks, yet all are classed as socially white, despite the fact that a sizable proportion of Negroes are "whiter" in appearance than a goodly proportion of whites. The members of the two groups are severely punished by the formal and informal rules of our society if they intermarry, and when they break this rule of "caste endogamy," their children suffer the penalties of our caste-like system by being placed in the lower color caste. Furthermore, unlike class, the rules of this system forbid the members of the lower caste from climbing out of it. Their status and that of their children are fixed forever. This is true no matter how much money they have, how great the prestige and power they may accumulate, or how well they have acquired correct manners and proper behavior. There can be no social mobility out of the lower caste into the higher one. (There may, of course, be class mobility within the Negro or white caste.) The rigor of caste rules varies from region to region in the United States.[6]

The Mexicans, Spanish Americans, and Orientals occupy a somewhat different status from that of the Negro, but many of the characteristics of their social place in America are similar.[7]

The social-class and color-caste hypotheses, inductively established as working principles for understanding American society, were developed in the researches which were reported in the "Yankee City" volumes, *Deep South*, and *Caste and Class in a Southern Town.* Gunnar Myrdal borrowed them, particularly color-caste, and made them known to a large, non-professional American audience.[8]

The generalities of American class

It is now time to ask what are the basic characteristics of social status common to the communities of all regions in the United States and, once we have answered this question, to inquire what the variations are among the several systems. Economic factors are significant and important in determining the class position of any family or person, influencing the kind of behavior we find in any class, and contributing their share to the present form of our status system. But, while significant and necessary, the economic factors are not sufficient to predict where a particular family or individual will be or to explain completely the phenomena of social class. Something more than a large income is necessary for high social position. Money must be translated into socially approved behavior and possessions, and they in turn must be translated into intimate participation with, and acceptance by, members of a superior class.

This is well illustrated by what is supposed to be a true story of what happened to a Mr. John Smith, a newly rich man in a far western community. He wanted to get into a particular social club of some distinction and significance in the city. By indirection he let it be known, and was told by his friends in the club they had submitted his name to the membership committee.

Mr. Abner Grey, one of the leading members of the club and active on its membership committee, was a warm supporter of an important philanthropy in this city. It was brought to his attention that Mr. Smith, rather than contributing the large donation that had been expected of him, had given only a nominal sum to the charity.

When Mr. Smith heard nothing more about his application, he again approached one of the board members. After much evasion, he was told that Mr. Grey was the most influential man on the board and he would be wise to see that gentleman. After trying several times to make an appointment with Mr. Grey, he finally burst into Grey's offices unannounced.

"Why the hell, Abner, am I being kept out of the X club?"

Mr. Grey politely evaded the question. He asked Mr. Smith to be seated. He inquired after Mr. Smith's health, about the health of his wife, and inquired about other matters of simple convention.

Finally, Mr. Smith said, "Ab, why the hell am I being kept out of your club?"

"But, John, you're not. Everyone in the X club thinks you're a fine fellow."

"Well, what's wrong?"

"Well, John, we don't think you've got the *kind* of money necessary for being a good member of the X club. We don't think you'd be happy in the X club."

"Like hell I haven't. I could buy and sell a half dozen of some of your board members."

"I know that, John, but that isn't what I said. I did not say the amount of money. I said the kind of money."

"What do you mean?"

"Well, John, my co-workers on the charity drive tell me you only gave a few dollars to our campaign, and we had you down for a few thousand."

For a moment Mr. Smith was silent. Then he grinned. So did Mr. Grey. Smith took out his fountain pen and checkbook. "How much?"

At the next meeting of the X club Mr. Smith was unanimously elected to its membership.

Mr. Smith translated his money into philanthropy acceptable to the dominant group, he received their sponsorship, and finally became a participant in the club. The "right" kind of house, the "right" neighborhood, the "right" furniture, the proper behavior—all are symbols that can ultimately be translated into social acceptance by those who have sufficient money to aspire to higher levels than they presently enjoy.

To belong to a particular level in the social-class system of America means that a family or individual has gained acceptance as an equal by those who belong in the class. The behavior in this class and the participation of those in it must be rated by the rest of the community as being at a particular place in the social scale.

Although our democratic heritage makes us disapprove, our class order helps control a number of important functions. It unequally divides the highly and lowly valued things of our society among the several classes according to their rank. Our marriage rules conform to the rules of class, for the majority of marriages are between people of the same class. No class system, however, is so rigid that it completely prohibits marriages above and below one's own class. Furthermore, an open class system such as ours permits a person during his lifetime to move up or down from the level into which he was born. Vertical social mobility for individuals or families is characteristic of all class systems. The principal forms of mobility in this country are through the use of money, education, occupation, talent, skill, philanthropy, sex, and marriage. Although economic mobility is still important, it seems likely now that more people move to higher positions by education than by any other route. We have indicated before this that the mere possession of money is insufficient for gaining and keeping a higher social position. This is equally true of all other forms of mobility. In every case there must be social acceptance.

Class varies from community to community.

The new city is less likely than an old one to have a well-organized class order; this is also true for cities whose growth has been rapid as compared with those which have not been disturbed by huge increases in population from other regions or countries or by the rapid displacement of old industries by new ones. The mill town's status hierarchy is more likely to follow the occupational hierarchy of the mill than the levels of valuated participation found in market towns or those with diversified industries. Suburbs of large metropolises tend to respond to selective factors which reduce the number of classes to one or a very few. They do not represent or express all the cultural factors which make up the social pattern of an ordinary city.

Yet systematic studies from coast to coast, in cities large and small and of many economic types, indicate that, despite the variations and diversity, class levels do exist and that they conform to a particular pattern of organization.

Notes

[1] See Chapter 15 [of *Social Class in America*] for a description of the several volumes of "Yankee City Series." New and poorly organized towns sometimes have class systems which have no old-family (upper-upper) class.

[2] See W. Lloyd Warner and Paul S. Lunt, *The Social Life of a Modern Community*, Vol. I, "Yankee City Series" (New Haven: Yale University Press, 1941), pp. 58–72.

[3] The evidence for the statements in the paragraph can be found in *The Social Life of a Modern Community*, pp. 287–300.

[4] It is conceivable that in smaller communities there may be only three, or even two, classes present.

[5] Allison Davis, Burleigh B. Gardner, and Mary R. Gardner, *Deep South* (Chicago: University of Chicago Press, 1941). Also read: John Dollard, *Caste and Class in a Southern Town* (New Haven: Yale University Press, 1937); Mozell Hill, "The All-Negro Society in Oklahoma" (Unpublished Ph.D. dissertation, University of Chicago, 1936); Harry J. Walker, "Changes in Race Accommodation in a Southern Community" (Unpublished Ph.D. dissertation, University of Chicago, 1945).

[6] See St. Clair Drake and Horace R. Cayton, *Black Metropolis* (New York: Harcourt, Brace & Co., 1945), for studies of two contrasting caste orders; read the "Methodological Note" by Warner in *Black Metropolis* for an analysis of the difference between the two systems.

[7] See W. Lloyd Warner and Leo Srole, *The Social Systems of American Ethnic Groups*, Vol. III, "Yankee City Series" (New Haven: Yale University Press, 1945). Chapter X discusses the similarities and differences and presents a table of predictability on their probable assimilation and gives the principles governing these phenomena.

[8] Gunnar Myrdal, *An American Dilemma* (New York: Harper & Bros., 1944). For an early publication on color-caste, see W. Lloyd Warner, "American Caste and Class," *American Journal of Sociology*, XLII, No. 2 (September, 1936), 234–37, and "Formal Education and the Social Structure," *Journal of Educational Sociology*, IX (May, 1936), 524–531.

CLASS AND CULTURE

Among the most notable effects of stratification is that through the differential distribution of wealth, prestige, and power it produces a variety of subcultures. Whether the system be castelike or open class, the social categories produced by stratification differ in some degree in a very large number of significant ways. For example, research on classes in the United States reveals differences between them in the matters of physical and mental health, educational and occupational goals and aspirations, sex behavior, family structure, child-raising patterns, voting habits, buying preferences, aesthetic taste, associational patterns and neighboring, and literally dozens of other forms of social behavior. Social classes can almost be said to inhabit different worlds. If the interaction between them is not usually as adverse as Marx suggested, misunderstandings and hostilities are fairly common occurrences in situations in which members of different classes interact, because of strong cross-cultural differences. That these differences are often ignored and, in equalitarian societies like the United States, disavowed can exacerbate the problems of interclass communication.

This selection, by a British scholar with working-class origins, attempts to present a picture of the world as working-class people view it. The selection is from a larger work which inquires into the effect of mass literacy and mass communications upon the culture of the British working classes.

> British workers see the world as divided into "them" and "us." Utterly different attitudes relate to each category. Towards "them," the outsiders, the attitude is one of wary distrust, of deference combined with dislike. "Them" are resisted in petty ways, but are blamed for all social inadequacies.
>
> "Us" brings forth a feeling of in-group solidarity, engendered by the close and intimate conditions of working-class life. Within the group there is harsh pressure to conform to a stable, unchanging, and therefore secure if also coarse and elemental pattern for behavior.
>
> The life situation of "us" leads to patterns of acceptance, toleration, and fatalism in the face of difficulties.

This description of the British working classes corresponds well with what is known about the working classes in the United States and other industrial countries. This is understandable in that the origins of these attitudes and beliefs are in the provincial and personal nature of the life experiences of such people. Hoggart's larger work makes the point that in Britain as well as elsewhere, some changes in this pattern are occurring as a result of the near-universal exposure to mass media, but the changes are generally modifications of this basic pattern, rather than revolutionary innovations.

The general world view described in the selection helps explain many of the particular findings of sociologists concerning class-related differences in behavior. If the poor pay more because they insist on buying higher-priced nationally advertised brands, if they lose their homes because they are unable to resist the forces of middle-class urban redevelopment, if they are the last to receive the benefits of newly discovered medical technology, these facts are the predictable consequences of the parochial and limited life experiences that their class position provides.

Selection 44
FROM THE USES OF LITERACY
Richard Hoggart

A. *"Them": "self-respect"*

Presumably most groups gain some of their strength from their exclusiveness, from a sense of people outside who are not "Us." How does this express itself in working-class people? I have emphasised the strength of home and neighbourhood, and have suggested that this strength arises partly from a feeling that the world outside is strange and often unhelpful, that it has most of the counters stacked on its side, that to meet it on its own terms is difficult. One may call this, making use of a word commonly used by the working-classes, the world of "Them." "Them" is a composite dramatic figure, the chief character in modern urban forms of the rural peasant–big-house relationships. The world of "Them" is the world of the bosses, whether those bosses are private individuals or, as is increasingly the case today, public officials. "Them" may be, as occasion requires, anyone from the classes outside other than the few individuals from those classes whom working-people know as individuals. A general practitioner, if he wins his way by his devotion to his patients, is not, as a general practitioner, one of "Them"; he and his wife, as social beings, are. A parson may or may not be regarded as one of "Them," according to his behaviour. "Them" includes the policemen and those civil servants or local-authority employees whom the working-classes meet—teachers, the school attendance man, "the Corporation," the local bench. Once the Means Test Official, the man from "the Guardians" and the Employment Exchange officer were notable figures here. To the very poor, especially, they compose a shadowy but numerous and powerful group affecting their lives at almost every point: the world is divided into "Them" and "Us."

"They" are "the people at the top," "the higher-ups," the people who give you your dole, call you up, tell you to go to war, fine

Reprinted from *The Uses of Literacy* by Richard Hoggart. New York: Oxford University Press, Inc., 1957, by permission of the publisher. Canadian permission by Chatto & Windus Ltd., publishers.

you, made you split the family in the 'thirties to avoid a reduction in the Means Test allowance, "get yer in the end," "aren't really to be trusted," "talk posh," "are all twisters really," "never tell yer owt" (e.g., about a relative in hospital), "clap yer in clink," "will do y' down if they can," "summons yer," "are all in a click (clique) together," "treat y' like muck."

There has been plenty of violent action by the authorities in England, especially during the first half of the nineteenth century. But on the whole, and particularly in this century, the sense of "Them" among working-class people is not of a violent or harsh thing. This is not the "Them" of some European proletariats, of secret police, open brutality and sudden disappearances. Yet there exists, with some reason, a feeling among working-class people that they are often at a disadvantage, that the law is in some things readier against them than against others, and that petty laws weigh more heavily against them than against some other groups. Their street-corner betting, it is often remarked, is a risky business; if they ran an account with a "Commission Agent" it would not be. If they celebrate and get drunk they are likely to do so in a public bar, and run more risk of being picked up than the man who keeps his drinks at home. Their relations with the police tend to be rather different from those of the middle-classes. Often they are good, but good or bad, they tend to regard the policeman primarily as someone who is watching them, who represents the authority which has its eye on them, rather than as a member of the public services whose job it is to help and protect them. They are close to the police and know something of the bullying and petty corruption that can sometimes exist. "Oh, the police always look after themselves. They'll stick by one another till they're blue in the face, and the magistrates always believe them," they have said for years, and go on saying.

Towards "Them" generally, as towards the police, the primary attitude is not so much fear as mistrust; mistrust accompanied by a lack of illusions about what "They" will do for one, and for the complicated way—the apparently unnecessarily complicated way—in which "They" order one's life when it touches them. Working-class people have had years of experience of waiting at labour-exchanges, at the panel doctor's and at hospitals. They get something of their own back by always blaming the experts, with or without justification, if something goes wrong—"Ah never ought to 'ave lost that child if that doctor 'ad known what 'e was doing." They suspect that public services are not so readily and effectively given to them as to the people who can telephone or send a stiff letter.

So often their contacts are with the minor officials, with those in the lower grades of uniformed and pensioned jobs. Again, as with the police, these may be to other classes servants, but to the working-classes they seem the agents of "Them" and are mistrusted, even though they may be kindly and well disposed. If they are ill disposed, they can display to working-class people all the insolence of minor office, the brusqueness of the pettily uniformed; they can be "bosses' men." So, when working-class people are asked to become foremen or N.C.O.s they often hesitate. Whatever their motives, they will be regarded now as on the side of "Them." Some minor officials have a doubleness in their attitudes. They tend to be sharp towards the working-classes because they would like to feel more securely separate from them; they know in their hearts by just how little they are separated and do not like to think of dropping back. Their deference towards the middle-classes can conceal an animosity; they would like to be one of them but realise they are not.

By all this working-class women are easily made unhappy, and so are usually more deferential than their menfolk towards small officials. A man is more likely to kick against it, and his kicking often takes the form of becoming really "vulgar." He is liable, if driven, to offer to "knock 'is bloody block off if 'e doesn't cut out 'is bloody chelp."

Perhaps no place so well illustrates the division into "Them" and "Us" as a typical North Country Magistrates' Court. It so often has an air of sour, scrubbed, provincial puritanism and mortification, from the stench of carbolic which meets you at the door, past the lavatories still marked MALES and FEMALES, to the huge pitch-pine bench lighted by high and narrow windows. The policemen may themselves feel nervous under the eye of superior officials, but to the working-class people in the well of the court they look like the hired and menacing—the more menacing because now on their own ground, with their helmets off—assistants of that anonymous authority which the bench symbolises. The magistrates' clerk may be one who likes to "run people around a bit"; the figures on the bench seem to peer down from a distant world of middle-class security and local importance. Listening to a series of cases I usually find myself admiring the success of the bench in seeing through the incapacity and often evasiveness of working-class witnesses to a genuinely human view of the cases. They have to make most of the allowances, since the working-class people involved are aware of almost nothing but the vast apparatus of authority which has somehow got hold of them, and which they cannot understand.

To these major attitudes towards "Them" may be added one or two minor but recurrent ones. The "Orlick" spirit first, the "I ain't a gentleman, you see" attitude; a dull dog-in-the-manger refusal to accept anything higher that one's own level of response, which throws out decent attempts at using authority and debases them with the rest. Or the peculiarly mean form of trickery which goes with some forms of working-class deference, the kind of obvious "fiddling" of someone from another class which accompanies an over-readiness to say "sir," but assumes—in the very obviousness with which it is practised—that it is all a contemptuous game, that one can rely on the middle-class distaste for a scene to allow one to cheat easily. Or the attitude which grows when self-respect is low, and results in a series of "They oughts." Like primitive kings, "They ought" to bring rain when it is needed, and are to be blamed if rain comes inopportunely; after all, "that's what They're there for." "They" ought to look after you when you are in trouble, to "do something about it," to "take care that sort of thing doesn't happen," to "lock 'em up." The contrast is sharp with that much more common attitude which causes working-class people only to make use of "Them" when absolutely forced: don't get into the hands of authority, and, if you must have help, only "trust yer own sort."

The "Them/Us" attitudes seem to me strongest in those over thirty-five, those with memories of unemployment in the 'thirties and of all the "Thems" of those days. Younger people, even if they are not active in the unions, here inhabit a different atmosphere from that their fathers grew up in: at least, the atmosphere has a different emotional temperature. At bottom the division is still there, and little changed in its sharpness. Young people are likely to be less actively hostile, or contemptuous or fearful towards the bosses' world; nor are they likely to be deferential. But this is not always because they are better able than their parents to cope with that world, that they have come to terms with the great outside in a way their parents have not; they often seem to be simply ignoring it, to have "contracted out" of any belief in its importance; they have gone into their own worlds, supported now by a greater body of entertaining and flattering provision than their parents knew. When they have to meet the other world sharply, as on many occasions after marriage, they often do their best to go on ignoring it, or draw upon attitudes similar to those of their parents. Ask at a baby clinic what proportion of working-class mothers can even now be persuaded to take full advantage of the services. I know some who will not "go near" the clinic, not even for their orange juice; they mistrust anything authority provides and prefer to go to the chemists', even though this is more expensive.

Behind all this is a problem of which we are acutely conscious today—that everyone is expected to have a double eye, one for his duties as an individual person, and another for those as a citizen in a democracy. Most of us, even the more-or-less intellectual, find it difficult to relate these worlds to each other. Working-class people, with their roots so strongly in the homely and personal and local, and with little training in more general thinking, are even less likely to be able to bring the two worlds into focus. They are, if they think of it, ill at ease; this second and complex world cannot easily be dramatised, is too vast, too much "beyond" them. They do much to bring it within their own scope, usually by simplification: for the rest they continue to say, as their grandparents said, "I don't know what the world's coming to."

One traditional release of working-class people in their dealings with authority is more positive than this. I mean their debunking-art, their putting-a-finger-to-the-nose at authority by deflating it, by guying it. The policeman may sometimes be a trouble; he can also have

songs written about his feet. My impression is that this reaction is less strong than it used to be. No doubt the change is due in part to the greatly improved position of working-class people in society. It can also be an expression of the "contracting-out" mentioned earlier, of a feeling that "we get on alright as we are"; we ask "Them" for nothing and feel no particular resentment towards them. Such an attitude may be encouraged by the great quantity of entertainment offered today. These entertainments are of such a kind that they render their consumers less likely to make the ironically vigourous protest contained in debunking-art.

The old manner survives to some degree in the Services, where the division between "Them" and "Us" is still clear and formal. Most of the debunking songs heard there are at least forty years old. I have in mind songs such as, "Left, left. I had a good job when I left," "When this bloody war is over," and "I don't want to be a soldier."

More than a vigour, there is a clear dignity in that reaction to the pressures of the outside world which takes the form of insisting on "keeping y' self-respect." And the moment this idea of "self-respect" and "self-reliance" comes to mind, it begins to flower into related ideas: into that of "respectability" first, which itself spreads outwards and upwards from some thin-lipped forms, through the pride of a skilled workman, to the integrity of those who have practically nothing except a determination not to allow themselves to be dragged down by circumstances. At the centre is a resolution to hold on to that of which one can be rightly proud; in a world which puts so many stumbling-blocks in the way, to hold on at least to "self-respect." "At least, ah've got me self-respect"; the right to be able to say that, though it can be said meanly, makes up for a lot. It is at work constantly in the hatred of "going on the parish," in the worry to keep up sick payments, in the big insurances to avoid a parish burial, in thrift and the cult of cleanliness. There is, I think, a tendency among some writers on the working-classes to think of all those who aim at thrift and cleanliness as imitators of the lower middle-classes, as in some way traitors to their own class, anxious to get out of it. Conversely, those who do not make this effort tend to be regarded as more honest and less servile than those who do. But cleanliness, thrift and self-respect arise more from a concern not to drop down, not to succumb to the environment, than from an anxiety to go up; and among those who altogether ignore these criteria, the uninhibited, generous and carefree spirits are outnumbered by the slovenly and shiftless whose homes and habits reflect their inner lack of grip. Even the urge for children to "get on" and the respect for the value of "book-learning" is not most importantly produced by the wish to reach another class out of snobbery. It is associated much more with the thought of a reduction in the numerous troubles which the poor have to meet, simply because they are poor:

> I have seen him that is beaten, him that is beaten: thou art to set thine heart on books. I have beheld him that is set free from forced labour: behold, nothing surpasseth books.

"How narrow the gap, how slight the chance," for keeping the raft afloat and being able to "look people in the face." It is therefore important to have that sense of independence which arises from a respect for oneself, because that is what no one can physically take away. "Ah've worked 'ard all me life," people will· say, "and ah owe no man anything." They own nothing either, except a few sticks of furniture, but they never expected to own more. Hence the survival of all kinds of apparent oddities, especially among those now over fifty. I know several families which have elected to keep their electricity supply on the shilling-in-the-slot system. They pay more that way and frequently find themselves in the dark because no one has a shilling; they have enough money coming in now to pay quarterly bills easily. But they cannot bear the thought of having a debt outstanding longer than a week. (Clothing club "draws" and the grocery bill often come in another category—they do not seem like debts owed to "Them.")

Here, too, lies the origin of the clinging, whatever straits people have reached, to the "little bit of something" which speaks of a time when they had tastes of their own and the freedom to make gestures. No doubt these things are better arranged now, but when I was a boy our area was shocked by the clumsiness of a Board of Guardians visitor who suggested to an old woman that, since she was living on charity, she ought to sell a fine teapot she never used but always had on show. "Just fancy," people went around say-

ing, and no further analysis was needed. Everyone knew that the man had been guilty of an insensitive affront to human dignity. . . . "Oh, reason not the need; . . ./ . . . Allow not nature more than nature needs,/Man's life is cheap as beast's."

We may understand why working-class people often seem not "oncoming" to social workers, seem evasive and prepared to give answers designed to put off rather than to clarify. At the back of the announcement that "Ah keep meself to meself" there can be a hurt pride. It is difficult to believe that a visitor from another class could ever realise imaginatively all the ins-and-outs of one's difficulties—there is an anxiety not to "show y'self up," to defend one-self against patronage.

It is still important to "have a trade in your hands," and this not merely because a skilled tradesman has, until recently, almost always earned more. The skilled workman can say more firmly than the unskilled labourer that he is "as good as the next chap." He is out of the ruck of those who receive the first shock of large labour cuts; he has remnants of a journeyman's pride. He may never seriously think of moving, but at the back of his mind is the idea that he is at liberty to pack his tools and go. Fathers who are anxious to "do right" by the boys still try to have them apprenticed.

B. "Us"—the best and the worst of it

In any discussion of working-class attitudes much is said about the group-sense, that feeling of being not so much an individual with "a way to make" as one of a group whose members are all roughly level and likely to remain so. I avoid the word "community" at this stage because its overtones seem too simply favourable; they may lead to an under-estimation of the harsher tensions and sanctions of working-class groups.

Certainly working-class people have a strong sense of being members of a group, and just as certainly that sense involves the assumption that it is important to be friendly, cooperative, neighbourly. "We are all in the same boat"; "it is no use fighting one another"; but "in unity is strength." One's mind goes back to the movements of the last century, to the hundreds of "Friendly" societies, to the mottoes of the unions: the Amalgamated Society of Engineers, with "Be United and Industrious"; the Provisional Committee of the National Union of Gas Workers and General Labourers choosing, in the late 'nineties, "Love, Unity and Fidelity." And the "Love" in the last recalls the strength which this sense of unity acquired from a Christian background.

The friendly group tradition seems to me to have its strength initially from the ever-present evidence, in the close, huddled, intimate conditions of life, that we are, in fact, all in the same position. You are bound to be close to people with whom, for example, you share a lavatory in a common yard. That "luv" which is still the most common form of address, and not only to people in their own class, by tram and bus conductors and by shop-keepers, is used automatically, but still indicates something. To call anyone "neighbourly" or "right sociable" is to offer a high compliment; a club may be praised because it is a "real sociable place"; the most important recommendation for lodgings or seaside "digs" is that they are "sociable," and this outweights over-crowding; and a church is just as likely to be weighed in the same scales. "Ar' Elsie got married at All Saints'," they will say, of the church they chose from several nearby, not one of which can claim them as parishioners—"it's a nice friendly church." The story of a Christmas party at the local will end, "It was a luvly night. Everybody got real friendly." Good neighbourliness consists not just in "doing fair by each other," but in being "obliging" or "always ready to oblige." If the neighbours in a new area seem to lack the right kind of neighbourliness, the newcomer will insist that she "just can't settle."

The sense of a group warmth exercises a powerful hold, and continues to be missed when individuals have moved, financially and probably geographically, out of the working-classes. I have noticed that self-made men now living in villas—grocers who have done well and own a small chain of local shops; jobbing builders who have advanced so far as to be putting up fields of private "semis"—like to join the crowd at football matches. They drive up in a car now and wear shaggily prosperous Harris tweed, but many of them still go on the terraces rather than in the stands. I imagine they enjoy recapturing something of the mateyness of the ranks, much as a commissioned Q.M. will usually be found in the non-commissioned bar at a unit dance.

This is not a very self-conscious sense of community; it is worlds away from the "fellowship in service" of some of the socially purposive movements. It does not draw its main strength from—indeed, it precedes, and is more elementary than—the belief in the need to improve each other's lot jointly which gave rise to such organisations as the Co-operative movement. It arises chiefly from a knowledge, born of living close together, that one is inescapably part of a group, from the warmth and security that knowledge can give, from the lack of change in the group and from the frequent need to "turn to a neighbour" since services cannot often be bought. It starts from the feeling that life is hard, and that "our sort" will usually get "the dirty end of the stick." In most people it does not develop into a conscious sense of being part of "the working-class movement": the "co-ops" are today less typical of the outlook of the majority in the working-classes than the small privately-owned cornershops serving a couple of streets. The attitude finds expression in a great number of formal phrases—"Y've got to share and share alike"; "y've got to 'elp one another out"; "y've got to 'elp lame dogs"; "we must all pull together"; "it's sink or swim together." But for the most part these are actually spoken only on special occasions, at singsongs and festivals.

The solidarity is helped by the lack of scope for the growth of ambition. After the age of eleven, when the scholarship boys and girls go off to the grammar-school, the rest look increasingly outward to the real life which will begin at fifteen, to the life with the group of older men and women which, for the first few years after school, forms the most powerfully educative force they know. Once at work there is for most no sense of a career, of the possibilities of promotion. Jobs are spread around horizontally, not vertically; life is not seen as a climb, nor work as the main interest in it. There is still a respect for the good craftsman. But the man on the next bench is not regarded as an actual or potential competitor. It is not difficult to understand, therefore, the strong emotional hold of the "go slow —don't put the other man out of a job" attitude. Working-class people number several vices among their occupational attitudes, but not those of the "go-getter" or the "livewire," nor those of "the successful smilers the city can use"; "keen types" are mistrusted.

Whatever one does, horizons are likely to be limited; in any case, working-class people add quickly, money doesn't seem to make people happier, nor does power. The "real" things are the human and companionable things— home and family affection, friendship and being able to "enjoy y'self"; "money's not the real thing," they say, and "Life isn't worth living if y'sweating for extra money all t' time." Working-class songs often ask for love, friends, a good home; they always insist that money does not matter.

There are exceptions: those who still hold to the line Matthew Arnold satirised—"Ever remember, my dear Dan, that you should look forward to being one day manager of that concern." Among some of the more avidly respectable this shows in the way boys are urged to "get on," to pass that scholarship, to be careful of their "penmanship" since gentlemen in offices like "a neat hand." And there are sharp-eyed little men whom the rest regard with charity as wrong-headed, who "never let a penny go." They take on extra work at nights and weekends and are always anxious to make an extra bob-or-two at the hour when others are having a good time. These people are not usually moving upward or out of their class; they are running agitatedly round inside it, amassing the unconsidered trifles which are always about.

The attitude to bachelors probably shows as well as anything the tolerance which is extended to established exceptions within the group. The occasional bachelor in any neighbourhood is likely to be living at home with a widowed mother or in the family of a married sister. Such a bachelor can usually be found on most nights in a fixed corner of the local pub or club, since he is likely to be quiet and regular in his habits. Perhaps a certain kind of shyness has helped to make him a bachelor; he is in some ways a lone bird, but he cannot be called lonely. He is respected in the neighbourhood. He is not thought of as a man-on-the-loose and therefore as a potential Don Juan. He probably figures, rather, as a harmless uncle of indeterminate age, one who is "always very polite" and "quiet-spoken" and is said to be good to his mother or sister. There is sometimes a touch of amusement in this attitude, as though behind it is a feeling that old So-and-so has been a little scared of the physical relations with a woman which marriage entails. But this is not normally an expression of scorn; nor is such a bachelor likely to be regarded as selfish or queer or antisocial. Some men, it is felt, are born bachelors; they are therefore a real part of the neighbourhood.

That minority who become conscious of their class-limitations and take up some educational activity—so as to "work for their class" or "improve themselves"—tend to be ambiguously regarded. The respect for the "scholar" (like the doctor and the parson) to some extent remains. I remember sitting, not long after I had won a scholarship, next to a middle-aged bachelor miner in a workingmen's club. Whenever he paid for his rum-and-hot-milk he passed me a half-crown from the change. I tried to refuse: "Tek it, lad, and use it for thee education," he said. "Ah'm like all miners. Ah only waste t'bluddy stuff." On the other hand, there is often a mistrust of "book-learning." What good does it do you? Are you any better off (i.e., happier) as a clerk? or as a teacher? Parents who refuse, as a few still do, to allow their children to take up scholarships are not always thinking of the fact that they would have to be fed and clothed for much longer; at the back is this vaguely formulated but strong doubt of the value of education. That doubt acquires some of its force from the group-sense itself; for the group seeks to conserve, and may impede an inclination in any of its members to make a change, to leave the group, to be different.

The group, I suggested, works against the idea of change. It does more than this: it imposes on its members an extensive and sometimes harsh pressure to conform. Those who become different, through education and in one or two other ways, may often be allowed for, and I do not want to suggest a strong automatic hostility to any departure at all from the group or its attitudes. Indeed, one of the marked qualities of working-class groups is a wide tolerance in some things; but it is a tolerance which works freely only if the chief class assumptions are shared.

The group is close: it is likely to regard someone originally from a town forty miles away as "not one of us" for years; and I have seen it unconsciously and insensitively cruel for a long time—and kind, too, in many things —towards a foreign wife. The group watches, often with a low unallowingness, an unimaginative cruelty which can make for much unhappiness. "Ah wunder what she meant by that?"; "Ooh, don't things get about!"; "It doesn't do to let others know too much" are common phrases. Wondering what the neighbours will say is as common here as elsewhere; perhaps more common, in its own way. Working-class people watch and are watched in a manner which, because horizons are limited, will often result in a mistaken, and lowering, interpretation of what the neighbours do. A working-class woman may be known to act as a "sitter-in" at the place where she cleans all day; but if she is brought home at the end of the evening she is likely to ask to be left a couple of streets away. What would the neighbours say if they saw her coming home with a man?

The group does not like to be shocked or attacked from within. There may be little of the competitive urge to keep up with the Joneses, but just as powerful can be the pressure to keep down with the Atkinses. Hence the frequent use, long before advertisers made so much of its value, of the appeal to the ordinary and the unextreme, "any decent man would . . .," "it's not natural," "I like 'im; 'e's always the same." If you want to be one of the group you must not try to "alter people's ways," and you will be disliked if you imply a criticism of their ways by acting differently yourself; if you infringe the taboos you will run into disfavour:

> There's such a thing as mass thought, you know. If you think the same as the man next to you, you're all right. But if you don't, if you're seen bringing in a book (i.e., into work) or anything like that, you're not. It's very difficult to stand up to ridicule.

All classes require conformity to some degree; it needs to be stressed here because there is a tendency to stress upper- and middle-class conformity and to regard the working-classes as more free from it.

Acting beyond the ideas of the group, "acting posh," "giving y'self airs," "getting above y'self," "being lah-de-dah," "thinking y'self too good for other people," "being stuck-up," "turning y'nose up at other people," "acting like Lady Muck"—all these are much disliked and not very sensitively discriminated. The genuine "toff" might be found amusing, as he was fifty years ago, and the "real gentleman" (who will talk to you "just like I'm talking to you now") is still likely to be admired, even though he is obviously one of "Them." Neither inspires a feeling as strong as that aroused by the person who is putting on "posh" airs be-

cause he thinks they are better than working-class airs. "Ay, and what do you dislike most, then?" asks Wilfred Pickles. "Stuck-up fowk." Roars of applause. "Jolly good! and will you just tell me what you like most?" "Good neighbourly fowk." Increased applause. ". . . and very right too. Give her the money."

Whatever their origins, Gracie Fields and Wilfred Pickles hardly qualify as members of the working-classes now. But both are still warmly "alright" because they remain of them in spirit and have conquered the "moneyed classes" with their working-class wit and attitudes. "They love Wilfred Pickles down South," working-class people will say, meaning that people not of their class love him: there is some pride that their values, those of the unpolished and "straight," are appreciated by other classes. Their "comics" have stormed the posh citadels; "good luck to 'em!"

We frequently hear that the English working-classes are gentle, gentler than those of almost any other country, gentler today than their own parents and grandparents. Undoubtedly there has been a decrease in the amount of sheer brutality in the towns during the last fifty years, a decline in the rough and savage stuff which sometimes made the streets at night and particularly at weekends places to avoid. The hooliganism and rowdyism which caused the police to work in pairs in several areas of many towns have almost gone. We no longer hear, except very occasionally, of bare-fist fights on bits of waste-ground, of broken bottle fights inside bars, of regular assaults by gangs on girls at fairgrounds, of so much animal drunkenness.

It would be a deluding and foolish archaism which regretted the loss of all this, which assumed that its decline meant the loss of some gusto among the working-classes, that the gentleness is merely a passivity. But that same generation which was often coarse and savage could also be gentle: I think again of my grandmother, who saw brutalities which would shock a woman of almost any class today and was herself often harshly crude. But she, in common with many of her generation, had in some things an admirable gentleness and fineness of discrimination. Perhaps the gentleness we notice is not so much a new feature as an old strain which is more evident, has been allowed more room to operate today. It must have taken generations to develop, is the product of centuries in which people got along pretty well together, were not persistently harassed by the more violent evidences of the powers above them, and felt—however severe their troubles—that law was fairly generally applicable and authority not hopelessly corrupt. I have not forgotten the experiences of the "Hungry Forties" of the last century; but I think also of the Russian serfs and of the Italian attitude towards civil servants even to-day. All this has no doubt bred a reasonableness, a remarkably quiet assumption that violence is the last ditch.

If I draw further attention, then, to the strain of coarseness and insensitivity running through working-class life, I do so not to infer that other classes have not their own forms, nor to deny all that is usually said about gentleness, but to restore a balance which we have been inclined to lose during the last twenty years. The evidence must be chosen with unusual care, must not include habits which simply seem coarse by the usage of other classes. Thus, working-class speech and manners in conversation are more abrupt, less provided with emollient phrases than those of other groups: their arguments are often conducted in so rude a way that a stranger might well think that after this, at the worst, fighting would follow, and at the best a permanent ending of relations. I find that even now, if I am not to be misunderstood, I have to modify a habit of carrying on discussion in an "unlubricated" way, in short sharp jabs that are meant to go home—and yet not meant really to hurt. Neither the phrasing nor the rhythms of working-class speech have the easing and modified quality which, in varying degrees, is characteristic of other classes. The pattern of their speech follows more closely the pattern of emotions they are feeling at the time, whether it be exasperation, as in the rows, or gaiety, as in that occasional shrieking of working-class housewives out for a day at the sea which dismays some who sit in the front gardens of private hotels. There is, of course, a "calling a spade a spade" arrogance which makes a few working-class people overdo the rougher elements in their speech when with others from a different class.

But working-class life, whatever changes there may have been, is still closer to the ground than that of most other people. The prevalent grime, the closeness and the difficulties of home life, I have sufficiently described; we have to remember as well that the physical conditions of the working-lives of men, and of some women, are often noisy, dirty and smelly. We all know this in our heads, but realise it freshly only if we have to pass through some of those deep caverns in Leeds where the engines clang and hammer ceaselessly and the sparks fly out of huge doorways and men can be seen, black to the shoulders, heaving and straining at hot pieces of metal: or through the huge area in Hull which has a permanent pall of cooking fish-meal over it, seeping through the packed houses. The heavy, rough and beast-of-burden work is still there to be done and working-class people do it. These are not conditions which produce measured tones or the more padded conversational allowances.

Thus the rows which are so much a part of the life of any working-class neighbourhood, and of many working-class families, can be easily misinterpreted. They are understandably a part of the neighbourhood's life: in narrow, terraced streets, with thin party-walls, they could hardly be kept private anyhow, unless they were conducted in very subdued voices. They certainly are not quietly conducted, and so they become one of the interests of the neighbourhood. Children, hearing that "Old So-and-so's up t' street are 'aving a right row," will gather in a group as near as they can. And if a row goes on too long or too noisily for the patience of a neighbour, he can always hammer on the party-wall or rattle a poker on the fire-back.

It could be wrong to assume from this that working-class people are congenitally quarrelsome and continually rowing. Some rows are nasty and distressing, and some families are known to be "always 'aving rows," and these will probably not be regarded as the most respectable. Many families—perhaps most—will have an occasional row. All this will not be automatically regarded as bringing disrepute to the neighbourhood. It is accepted that disputes—perhaps about the amount of money spent on drinking, perhaps among womenfolk about the sharing of household duties, perhaps about "another woman"—will arise from time to time, and that they will erupt into vivid, quick, noisy war. In my experience, rows about drinking are the most common, and those about the "other woman" (or man) the least common.

If I may digress for a moment on this latter aspect: these affairs, as I knew them, seemed generally to concern a man in his late thirties or early forties, a man who was slightly more dapper than his acquaintances, though in the same sort of work. His wife would have lost her physical appeal, so he sought interest elsewhere. Yet the woman he "took up with" was likely enough to be married herself and of roughly the same age as his own wife—and to a stranger no more attractive physically. The two would probably become drinking companions in a known place. The wife would soon learn what was going on and fierce rows would blow up (on more than one occasion I remember a much more serious development— an early-morning "bashing" of the man by the injured husband on a piece of waste-ground). The oddest feature of all was that sometimes the two women became friendly, and settled into a relationship which the connections of the husband with each of the women not only did not preclude but seemed to nourish.

Most of the rows I experienced were not thought of as shocking occurrences. Rows of that kind took place in the truly slummy areas, with drunken fights between the menfolk or, worse, between men and women or, worst of all, between women alone. Such events would really shock an ordinary working-class neighbourhood.

I remember too that in our neighbourhood we accepted suicides as a moderately common occurrence. Every so often one heard that So-and-so had "done 'erself in," or "done away with 'imself," or "put 'er 'ead in the gas-oven," since the gas-oven was the most convenient means of self-destruction. I do not know whether suicide took place more often in the sort of groups I am speaking of than in middle-class groups. It did not happen monthly or even every season, and not all attempts succeeded; but it happened sufficiently often to be part of the pattern of life. Among the working-classes it could not be concealed, of course, any more than a row could; everyone quickly knew about it. The fact I want to stress is that suicide was not felt to be simply a personal matter or one confined to the family concerned, but that it was felt to be bound up with the conditions of the common life. Sometimes the cause was that a girl had "got 'erself into trouble" and for one reason or another could not go through with it; just as often it was that, for those who put their heads on a pillow inside the oven-door, life had become unendurable; they were ill and treatment seemed to be doing no good; they were out of work; or, whatever they did, the debts piled up. This was not long ago. The fact that suicide could be accepted—pitifully but with little suggestion of blame—as a part of the order of existence shows how hard and elemental that life could be.

Does this altogether explain, for example, the way many working-class men speak when no women are present? In part, perhaps; but one has to be careful of special pleading here. George Orwell, noting that working-class men use four-letter words for natural functions freely, says they are obscene but not immoral. But there are degrees and kinds of obscenity, and this sort of conversation is often obscene and nothing else, obscene for the sake of obscenity in a dull, repetitive and brute way. And there are kinds of immorality; such men may use short and direct words about sex which at first are a relief after the allusion of cabaret shows and the literature of sexual sophistication. But they use those words so indiscriminately and talk so preponderantly about sex as often to reveal a calloused sensibility. Listen to them speaking of their sexual adventures and plans; you are likely to feel smothered by the boring animality, the mongrel-dogs-rutting-in-alleyways quality. It is a quality which owes as much to an insensitivity in relations as to a freedom from hypocrisy. To each class its own forms of cruelty and dirt; that of working-class people is sometimes of a gratuitously debasing coarseness.

C. "Putting up with things": "living and letting live"

I have spoken of a world and a life whose main lines are almost predictable, of work for a man which is probably not interesting, of years of "making-do" for a woman, of the lack in most people of any feeling that some change can, or indeed ought to, be made in the general pattern of life.

By and large, seems to be the note that is struck, we are not asked to be the great doers in this world; our kind of life offers little of splendour or of calls for the more striking heroisms, and its tragedies are not of the dramatic or rhetorical kind. At least, that is the sort of view this world seems to invite us to take: to do its heavier work, with sights fixed at short distance.

When people feel that they cannot do much

about the main elements in their situation, feel it not necessarily with despair or disappointment or resentment but simply as a fact of life, they adopt attitudes towards that situation which allow them to have a liveable life under its shadow, a life without a constant and pressing sense of the larger situation. The attitudes remove the main elements in the situation to the realm of natural laws, the given and raw, the almost implacable, material from which a living has to be carved. Such attitudes, at their least-adorned a fatalism or plain accepting, are generally below the tragic level; they have too much of the conscript's lack of choice about them. But in some of their forms they have dignity.

At the lowest is the acceptance of life as hard, with nothing to be done about it: put up with it and don't aggravate the situation: "what is to be, will be"; "if y' don't like it, y' mun lump it"; "that's just the way things are"; "it's no good kicking against the pricks"; "what can't be mended must be made do with"; "y've got to tek life as it cums—day in, day out." In many of these is a note of dull fatalism; life is always like that for people like us. But the really flat ones are a minority among the phrases of roughly cognate type; in most the note is of a cheerful patience: "y've got to get on wi' it best way y' can"; "grin and bear it"; "ah well, least said, soonest mended"; "oh, it'll all be the same in a hundred years' time"; "all such things are sent to try us" (here, as in some others, the connection with religion is evident); "it isn't always dark at six"; "we're short o' nowt we've got"; "worse things 'appen at sea"; "ah well, we live in 'opes." It's all bound to be ups-and-downs, the rough with the smooth, roundabouts and swings: "it's no good moaning"; "mek the best of it—stick—soldier on—"; "don't meet trouble 'alf-way." You may sort-of-hope for a windfall or a sudden, wonderful surprise, but not really; you've got to go on and "mek yer own life"; "keep yer end up"; "life is what y' mek it"; "Mek shift and fadge" and you'll be "alright"—as private soldiers were when they knocked up something like a living-space out of the most unpromising conditions.

This is not so much the cheerfulness of the stiff upper lip as of the unexpecting, partly stoic, partly take-life-as-it-comes "lower orders." T. S. Eliot says somewhere that stoicism can be a kind of arrogance, a refusal to be humble before God: working-class stoicism is rather a self-defence, against being altogether humbled before men. There may be little you can do about life; there is at any rate something you can be. A working-class housewife, if she finds over a period that she has a shilling a week spare from house-keeping for emergencies, can say that she is "quite happy"; and the adverb does not modify the adjective, but makes it absolute.

So to tolerance, to "living and letting live"; a tolerance bred both from a charity, in that all are in the same lower situation together, and from the larger unidealism which that situation creates. The larger unexpectancy encourages a slowness to moral indignation: after all, it's no good creating problems; there are plenty as it is: "anything for a quiet life." The tolerance exists along with the conservatism and conformity already described; they clash only rarely. They co-exist, are drawn upon at different times and for different purposes, and people know instinctively which is relevant at any time. Far from contradicting, they thus mutually reinforce each other.

The stress on tolerance arises, then, chiefly from the unexpectant, unfanatic, unidealistic group sense, from the basic acceptance by most people of the larger terms of their life. Working-class people are generally suspicious of principles before practice (in the more articulate this occasionally becomes a thrusting brass-tacks "realism" which is in fact a self-glorification, masking a disinclination to probe uncomfortably—"let's get on with the job. All this theory gets you nowhere"). Most are likely to assume that you will lie rather than disappoint or hurt; you may thereby be going against a principle, but that is something outside, and people are here and now. You have to get along with them, to "rub along" and "mind yer own business" as you expect other people to mind theirs. Life is never perfect: avoid extremes; most things are "alright up to a point," or "alright if y'don't go too far"; and, after all, "it all depends." You may have views, but should never "push them down people's throats." Views never matter enough, but people do: you should not judge by rules but by facts, not by creed but by character. "Y' can't change 'uman nature"; "it teks all sorts to mek a world"; you should "tek people as y' find 'em"; "there's good and bad wherever y' go"; "'uman nature's the same wherever y' go," and "a man's a man wherever y' go"; "everyone's got a right to live."

All this supports the general lack of patriotism, the mistrust of the public or official things. The "fear of freedom" may have tempted the middle-classes towards authoritarianism; it affects the working-classes differently. They still feel in their bones that the public and the generalised life is wrong. This rudimentary internationalism can co-exist with anti-Semitism or with strong feeling against Roman Catholicism (as representing Authoritarianism in its "worst" form); but such intolerance comes out only occasionally, and the two worlds do not often meet.

We know that the pressure to conform expresses itself in an intricate network not of ideas but of prejudices which seek to impose a rigid propriety. They gain strength from the remains of the puritanism which once so strongly affected the working-classes, and which still rules fairly strictly a number of working-class lives. On most the puritanism, buttressing itself against the hard facts of working-class conditions, even now has some effect, lives to some degree among those in whom can be found the wider forms of tolerance. We may see this better by looking at attitudes towards drink and, more fully, sex.

On the one hand, drinking is accepted as part of the normal life, or at least of the normal man's life, like smoking. "A man needs 'is pint"; it helps to make life worth while; if one can't have a bit of pleasure like that, then what is there to live for? It is "natural" for a man to like his beer. Women seem to be drinking more easily now than they did a generation ago; even as late as my adolescence the "gin-and-It" woman was regarded as a near-tart. But still, after the children have arrived, women's drinking is not usually considerable; the weekends are their big "let-out." Just how much beer-drinking a man may be allowed without incurring disapproval depends on his circumstances; there is a finely-graded scale of allowances. A widower might be expected to drink more than most, since he has not got a wife and comfortable home to go back to. A man and wife with no children can be allowed regular drinking, since they are not taking the bread from their children's mouths, and home without kids is not very inviting. A husband with a family should drink "within reason,"

that is, should know when he has had enough, and should always "provide." There are occasions—festivals, celebrations, cup-ties, trips—when anyone might be expected to drink quite a lot. It is understandable that certain situations might "drive anyone to drink." On the whole, the emphasis is a double one: on the rightness of drinking in itself, and on the realisation that, if it once "gets hold," complete collapse—a near-literal home-breaking as the furniture is sold—may well follow.

It was clearly this latter side which gave such force to the anti-drink movement during the last century and in the first decade or so of this. It was easy to see how even a family which had had as good food as it wished and a few extras could be down to bread-and-scrape off an orange-box inside a month if the "demon drink" took hold. Economically a working-class home has always been, and to a large extent remains, a raft on the sea of society. So the Temperance Movement was still going strong as late, at least, as the early 'thirties, when I signed the pledge twice at intervals of a year or so. I was between ten and twelve at the time, and signed with the rest of my Sunday school acquaintances; we felt in an obscure way that it affected our eligibility for places on the Whitsuntide "treat." I had a drunken uncle, the last of a line which stretched well back to the 'seventies, and had its counterpart in many of the families around us. We did not by then sing songs like, "Please sell no more drink to my Father," or, "Don't go out tonight, dear Father," or, "Father, dear Father, come home with me now," or—my own favourite—"My drink is water bright" (which went something like this: "Merry Dick, you soon would know,/If you lived in Jackson's Row/My drink is water bright,/My drink is water bright,/From the crystal spring"). We heard those only as amusement from our elders, who had been taught them as children: but we saw their point. We knew that too much drinking, even as little as three shillings a week more than a family could afford, meant quick poverty, "tick" mounting until the final bust-up, clothing rapidly and obviously deteriorating, desperately worried mothers, lost jobs, rows of increasing force and frequency. "Thank goodness, 'e's never been a drinker," housewives will still say regularly. There is little violent drunkenness nowadays, and much less drinking of all kinds, but drink is still regarded as the main pitfall for a working-class husband. Drink, then, is "alright," is "natural," in moderation. Once the boundary, which varies with different kinds of family, is crossed, disaster may follow. On the other hand, the man who does not drink at all is a bit unusual—most working-class people would not ask for a majority of men like that, whatever the perils of drink.

A friend of mine from a nearby street was an only child and seemed to have no father; his mother was a tailoress, but always able to dress him well, and he had more pocket-money than the rest of us. He went to the pictures a couple of times a week, and could usually produce a penny for some chips. It was only in my teens that I discovered that his mother was a prostitute, operating in the city centre. She needed more money to bring up the boy than tailoring offered. (I think her husband had simply disappeared.) More, she was anxious that he should not "suffer" because he had "no father behind him," and the way of ensuring this which presented itself to her imagination was to provide him with the financial superiority which counts so much among boys. Much of what has been said already may go some way towards explaining why she thought so little of the sale of her body; my particular concern here is to point out that she was not ostracised, except by a few who talked of "giving the street a bad name." Most nodded at or talked to her as to anyone else, even though they would never have had recourse to prostitution, would indeed have been horrified at the thought for themselves. "After all, she's got to live," they used to say; they understood the pressure of the situation, and could see how some people were led to this solution. They did not "turn against them" because of it: and although I heard from such people many a judgment on what they regarded in others as wanton and dirty behaviour, I do not remember hearing a moral judgment on this woman.

A few years later she was joined, on another "beat" in the same area, by the younger daughter in a family of six children whose father had brought them up after his wife's death. They lived not far from the first woman, and often came in for adverse comment. But it was inspired more by the fact that the father did not clothe or feed them as

well as the neighbours thought possible, even in his difficult circumstances, than because one of the girls went out to prostitution.

Later, I served a spell as overnight dispatch-clerk to a long-distance transport firm, taking over from a youth who lived a couple of streets away from us. About four times a night the big lorries and their trailers pulled in from Newcastle, dropped some goods, and perhaps a road "floozie," re-loaded, and headed for London. For the rest of the night-shift I was alone in the back streets of the city centre, except for the policemen, the night watchman and an occasional late prostitute. As I took over, my predecessor told me that he was sometimes visited, about half-past eleven, by a prostitute called Irene, who liked to have a cup of tea. She was a good sort and would occasionally "give you a blow-through" in the furniture-van at the back, if she were not too tired. I met her only once, and she talked most of the time about the pain in her feet. She was almost completely unselfconscious about her occupation and might have been selling papers, so matter-of-fact and dull did she find it. I suppose my rock-climbing-under-graduate look put her off, for she made no offers and came back no more whilst I was there. Later, I used to see her looking into the windows of the posh corner-shops, when I passed through town occasionally at night. The poor girl must have had customers—young bloods from the better districts, visiting commercial travellers, students proving their manhood, broken-down salesmen, young labourers with money and ale inside them, or those homeless labourers who move from town to town following the big jobs—but I never saw her with one. I remember she told me of a sister on the stage—"she's luvly to look at." There seemed to be a steady trickle of good-looking working-class girls into the choruses of the traveling revues.

I do not mean to suggest, in relating these incidents, that working-class people are sexually more licentious than others: I think it doubtful whether they are. But sexual matters do seem nearer the surface, and sexual experience in the working-classes is probably more easily and earlier acquired than in other social groups. The nearness to the surface accompanies, as social workers sometimes point out, a great shyness about some aspects of sex— about discussing it "sensibly," about being seen naked, or even about undressing for the act of sex, or about sophistications in sexual behaviour. Even today few working-class parents seem to tell their children anything about sex. They know they will quickly pick it all up from the street-corner. But they are not deliberately leaving it aside because they know the street-gang will do the work for them; indeed, they are likely to be greatly upset if they find their children talking or acting "dirty." They leave it, I think, partly because they are not good teachers, are neither competent in nor fond of exposition, prefer knowledge to come incidentally, by means of apothegm and proverb; and partly because of this shyness about bringing sex to the conscious and "sensible" level. And this will apply as much to the man who, in a suitable context, will talk sex as freely as his mates, as to his perfectly "clean-mouthed" wife.

But children after the age of ten, and especially boys, learn from the older ones in their groups and later at work. With boys the emphasis is, inevitably, on both the enjoyment of sexual experience and on its dreadful and exciting dangers; and particularly in the early stages, on the pleasures and dangers of masturbation. For many, masturbation soon gives place to some actual hetero-sexual experience. Obviously this is where a working-class boy's pattern in sexual life is likely to differ from that of, say, a public-schoolboy, living until he is eighteen largely in an all-boy community. From thirteen onwards working-class boys' talk, then, is very often of sex adventures, of how easy such and such a girl is to "feel" or to "get down" and so on. By eighteen those who wish it can have had a great deal of sexual experience. A group of bricklayers for whom I acted as labourer during a University vacation quickly elicited the information that I was virgin and thereafter regarded me, in a friendly way, as less than a man, as another kind of monk, dedicated to books rather than to religion. They all claimed to be "getting it regular," though I am sure there was much exaggeration. The married men joined in the frequent sex talk as readily as the rest and regularly lamented their lost freedom, but in an expected kind of way.

How would one sum up the attitude of such men, in general, to their irregular sexual experiences? I should perhaps add that there are, of course, many men to whom the foregoing does not apply. They have little sense of guilt or sin in connection with their sex-life; they make much of sex, but not because underneath they feel lost and anonymous in the great urban mass. That would be to attribute the attitudes of other kinds of people to them. They are not indulging in the bravado of immorality about which much was heard in the behaviour of some groups during the 'twenties. Yet they do feel vaguely that "scientific discovery" has made it all more legitimate as well as, with cheap contraceptives, easier. They are not happily amoral savages disporting in some slumland Marquesas Melville never knew. They take their sex-life easily, but do not rollick through it like citified versions of the "apples be ripe" bucolics of T. F. Powys, or like contemporary versions of the great tuppers of the past. In some respects their attitude towards promiscuous sex activity does come from a long way back. But for them it is all rather scrabbily hole-and-corner. In most cases such activity does not seem to be continued after marriage, or to affect strongly the likelihood of a good marriage relationship.

My impression, though here I may be falling into a romantic error myself, is that more girls than boys escape altogether this bitty, promiscuous sexual experience. The names of the same girls who are willing crop up again and again; the easy ones are soon well known. Of course, the girls have much more to lose at the game; they are liable to "get caught."

To me the surprising thing is that so many girls are able to remain unaffected, to retain both an ignorance about the facts of sex and an air of inviolability towards its whole atmosphere that would not have been unbecoming in a mid-nineteenth-century young lady of the middle-classes. It is wonderful how, without evident prudishness or apparent struggle, many of them can walk through the howling valley of sex-approaches from the local lads and probably of sex-talk at work, and come through to the boy they are going to marry quite untouched mentally and physically. Their best light has been the implicit assurance that they would marry, that they were "keeping themselves for one man," and this not in a merely calculating sense.

My experience suggests, then, that most girls do not move from man to man, picking up fragmentary experience on the way, but that they begin courting early and go on steadily until an early marriage. Some still "get into trouble" from fifteen onwards, but they are the exceptions. Many have had some sexual experience before marriage, but usually with the boy they eventually marry; they have not been promiscuous. Nor are they sheltered: from sixteen they are regarded as in most respects adult; they meet the boy they "fall for" and start courting. They are probably almost completely ignorant of the practice of sex. They feel romantically towards the boy; he presses; it does not seem all that important to wait until marriage, and they yield. He will perhaps take precautions, but a proportion of the men will not, being unprepared or inexpert. If a baby is conceived, the marriage takes place sooner than was expected, but the girl is unlikely to feel that she has been caught. My impression is that most of the girls who lose their virginity before marriage lose it in this way—with boys they are genuinely fond of, when circumstances conspire—rather than from any deliberate passing from boy to boy "for the fun of it."

On the whole, once they are "going steady," loyalty is assumed on each side, and there is little infidelity. The girls are not likely to regard themselves as wicked in anticipating the marriage. They are following a line which will quite soon land them with the attitudes and habits of their mothers, as "decent" working-class housewives. Meanwhile, one may as well allow it: "it 'urts nobody. It's only natural, 'i'nt it?"

Chapter 16

COLOR AND CREED

THE JEWISH EXPERIENCE
Selection 45

THE NEGRO EXPERIENCE
Selection 46

COLOR AND CLASS
Selection 47

Race, religion, and nationality are frequent bases of social differentiation in human societies. Although there exist societies without these distinctions, they tend to be small isolated societies where only one religion is known and where the members have all descended from a common biological stock.

Some nineteenth-century writers fixed their attention on presumed biological differences to account for behavioral differences among these groups, but contemporary sociology discounts this emphasis and focuses on cultural explanations. Indeed, the thing that races, religious groups, and nationalities have in common from a sociological point of view is a culture significantly different from that of their neighbors. The term "ethnic group" is used to designate groups such as these, that are differentiated from a "dominant" group in the same society primarily on cultural grounds, whether or not other bases of differentiation, such as skin color, are also present. (At one time sociologists talked of "minorities," instead of ethnic groups, but the term is now seldom used because of instances, like that in South Africa, in which the "minority" forms a numerical majority of the population.)

Ethnic groups tend to be subordinated to dominant groups. This subordination takes the form of prejudice and discrimination, which are related but distinct concepts. Prejudice refers to beliefs and evaluations concerning ethnic groups and their members. Discrimination refers to overt behavior and the real norms governing this behavior. Although these concepts are generally closely linked, Robert Merton has pointed to some significant instances in which they are not, in which the social (normative) context inhibits the behavioral expression of prejudice in discrimination. For example, observers have noted that some Southerners in the North, while maintaining their beliefs concerning the inferiority of the Negro, act in a less discriminatory fashion toward Negroes than do most Northerners. Merton calls these people fair-weather illiberals, meaning that although they are prejudiced they refrain from discrimination because of their (exaggerated) perception of the disapproval that discrimination would bring out in a Northern context. A Southerner who continues to discriminate in the North would be an all-weather illiberal. Likewise, someone who discriminates under no circumstances is an all-weather liberal, and a Northerner who discriminates while he is in the South is a fair-weather liberal.

The study of ethnic groups in the United States has focused on Negroes, who form the largest and probably the least privileged group in our society. Another object of intensive study has been the Jews, who in this country present a paradoxical reversal of class and ethnic statuses. (Jews earn more and have higher-type occupations than Americans of Old Yankee origins.) Because prejudice and discrimination are in conflict with some fundamental American values (designated by Gunnar Myrdal as the American Creed), much of this research has been "applied" research, performed with the goal of possible use to diminish discrimination. Recently, much has been made of the applicability of generalizations concerning Negroes and Jews to groups in general, including women, the lower classes, adolescents, and even foreign states considered as members of an international society. The basis for this extension in theory of ethnic-group research is the fact that all groups are culturally differentiated. Moreover, there is the realization that some degree of hostility toward members of out-groups is an inevitable accompaniment of in-group self-consciousness, whether these feelings are expressed as race pride or nationalism, etc. The broad implications of research on ethnic groups make it one of the most significant fields of sociological inquiry.

Selection 45, by Louis Wirth, describes the history of the Jewish ghetto, and presents a model that sociologists have traditionally used in viewing the history of ethnic groups in the United States. Selection 46, by Karl E. and Alma F. Taeuber, describes the segregation of Negroes in Chicago, and indicates some limitations of Wirth's model. In Selection 47, E. Franklin Frazier traces the history of the class structure in the American Negro group.

THE JEWISH EXPERIENCE

When ethnic groups live in the same community as the dominant group, there is a general tendency for residential segregation to develop. The residentially segregated area is often referred to as the ghetto, which is the name that was applied to the Jewish quarter in the towns and villages of medieval Europe.

This selection deals with the Jews in Europe and in the cities of the United States. Wirth shows how the residential segregation of Jews in the ghetto bolstered segregation in other spheres, and how the ghetto benefited as well as restricted the group it contained. He reminds us that the medieval ghetto was voluntary in its origins, that modern ghettos are in large part voluntary and unplanned, and that ghettos are as much a product of in-group attraction as of out-group exclusion.

Wirth believes that twentieth-century developments have lessened the functional value of the Jewish ghetto in the West and that the ghetto is in the process of disintegration. He predicts the end of the Jewish ghetto in Chicago (and other American cities) and implies the ultimate assimilation and amalgamation of Western Jewry.

> The Jewish ghetto originated in voluntary residential segregation in medieval Europe. It became enacted into law long after its establishment and persists as a local community in American cities without being legally required. It permits accommodation between dissenting groups by maintaining social isolation through spatial isolation, and its complex of specialized institutions reinforces the culture of the ethnic group. Strong parallels in these regards exist between the Jewish ghetto and other ethnic communities in the American city.
>
> As ethnic groups assimilate, their ghettos begin to disintegrate. The Jewish ghetto in the American city would not have survived into the twen-

tieth century except for its being renewed by immigration from the unenlightened countries of eastern Europe. The more assimilated Jews flee the ghetto, but their escape is retarded because they find a new, second-generation ghetto or "Deutschland" in the areas to which they move. In time, new flights occur to still more assimilated areas, where the ethnic culture is increasingly diluted and the ethnic group begins to merge with the dominant group.

Wirth's argument is interesting both in its specific reference to Jews and in its general reference to ethnic groups in American cities. Particularly noteworthy is his model of assimilation in which the descendants of immigrants proceed from ghetto to ghetto, each move leading to somewhat greater assimilation until total assimilation is achieved.

Wirth's specific predictions concerning the assimilation of the Jews can be strongly criticized. He implies in this 1927 article that the Jews will be amalgamated with the dominant group and lose their Jewish identity. This event is still far from taking place. That Wirth's model can be applied unselectively on a more general level is even more doubtful, as the next selection will indicate.

Selection 45
THE GHETTO
Louis Wirth

I

For the past five hundred years the Jewish settlements in the Western world have been known as ghettos. The modern ghetto, some evidence of which is found in every city of even moderate size, traces its ancestry back to the medieval European urban institution by means of which the Jews were segregated from the rest of the population. In the East, until recently, the ghetto took the form of the "pale" of settlement, which represents a ghetto within a ghetto. The ghetto is no longer the place of officially regulated settlement of the Jews, but rather a local cultural area which has arisen quite informally. In the American cities the name "ghetto" applies particularly to those areas where the poorest and most backward groups of the Jewish population, usually the recently arrived immigrants, find their home.

From the standpoint of the sociologist the ghetto as an institution is of interest first of all because it represents a prolonged case study in isolation. It may be regarded as a form of accommodation through which a minority has effectually been subordinated to a

Reprinted from American Journal of Sociology, 33:1, 1927, pp. 57–71, with permission of the publisher.

dominant group. The ghetto exhibits at least one historical form of dealing with a dissenting minority within a larger population, and as such has served as an instrument of control. At the same time the ghetto represents a form of toleration through which a modus vivendi is established between groups that are in conflict with each other on fundamental issues. Some of these functions are still served by the modern ghetto, which, in other respects, has a character quite distinct from that of the medieval institution. In Western Europe and America, however, it is of primary interest because it shows the actual processes of distribution and grouping of the population in urban communities. It indicates the ways in which cultural groups give expression to their heritages when transplanted to a strange habitat; it evidences the constant sifting and resifting that goes on in a population, the factors that are operative in assigning locations to each section, and the forces through which the community maintains its integrity and continuity. Finally, it demonstrates the subtle ways in which this cultural community is transformed by degrees until it blends with the larger community about it, meanwhile reappearing in various altered guises of its old and unmistakable atmosphere.

This paper concerns itself, not with the history of the ghetto, but with its natural history. Viewed from this angle the study of the ghetto is likely to throw light on a number of related phenomena, such as the origin of segregated areas and the development of local communities in general; for, while the ghetto is, strictly speaking, a Jewish institution, there are forms of ghettos that concern not merely Jews. Our cities contain Little Sicilies, Little Polands, Chinatowns, and Black Belts. There are Bohemias and Hobohemias, slums and Gold Coasts, vice areas and Rialtos in every metropolitan community. The forces that underlie the formation and development of these areas bear a close resemblance to those at work in the ghetto. These forms of community life are likely to become more intelligible if we know something of the Jewish ghetto.

II

The concentration of the Jews into segregated local areas in the medieval cities did not originate with any formal edict of church or state. The ghetto was not, as is sometimes mistakenly believed, the arbitrary creation of the authorities, designed to deal with an alien people. The ghetto was not the product of design on the part of anyone, but rather the unwitting crystallization of needs and practices rooted in the customs and heritages, religious and secular, of the Jews themselves. Long before it was made compulsory the Jews lived in separate parts of the cities in the Western lands of their own accord. The Jews drifted into separate cultural areas, not by external pressure or by deliberate design. The factors that operated toward the founding of locally separated communities by the Jews are to be sought in the character of Jewish traditions, in the habits and customs, not only of the Jews themselves, but of the medieval town-dweller in general. To the Jews the spatially separated and socially isolated community seemed to offer the best opportunity for following their religious precepts, their established ritual and diet, and the numerous functions which tied the individual to familial and communal institutions. In some instances it was the fear of the remainder of the population, no doubt, which induced them to seek each other's company, or the ruler under whose protection they stood found it desirable, for purposes of revenue and control, to grant them a separate

quarter. The general tenor of medieval life no doubt played an important rôle, for it was customary for members of the same occupational group to live in the same locality, and the Jews, forming, as a whole, a separate vocational class and having a distinct economic status, were merely falling in line, therefore, with the framework of medieval society, in which everyone was tied to some locality. In addition, there were the numerous ties of kinship and acquaintanceship which developed an *esprit de corps* as a significant factor in community life. There was the item of a common language, of community of ideas and interests, and the mere congeniality that arises even between strangers who, coming from the same locality, meet in a strange place. Finally, the segregation of the Jews in ghettos is identical in many respects with the development of segregated areas in general. The tolerance that strange modes of life need and find in immigrant settlements, in Latin quarters, in vice districts, and in racial colonies is a powerful factor in the sifting of the urban population and its allocation in separate local areas where one obtains freedom from hostile criticism and the backing of a group of kindred spirits.

Corresponding to the local separateness of the Jew from his Christian neighbors there is to be noted the functional separation of the two groups. Just as the world beyond the ghetto wall was external to the life within the ghetto, so the personal relationships between Jews and non-Jews were those of externality and utility. The Jews supplemented the economic complex of medieval European life. They served a number of functions which the inhabitants of the town were incapable of exercising. The Jews were allowed to trade and engage in exchange, occupations which the church did not permit Christians to engage in. Besides, the Jews were valuable taxable property and could be relied on to furnish much-needed revenue. On the other hand, the Jews, too, regarded the Christian population as a means to an end, as a utility. The Christians could perform functions such as eating the hind quarter of beef, and could purchase the commodities that the Jews had for sale; they could borrow money from the Jew, and pay interest; they could perform innumerable services for him which he could not perform himself. In the rigid structure of medieval life the Jews found a strategic place. The attitude of the medieval church had coupled trade and finance with sin. The Jews were free from this taboo, which made the occupation of merchant and banker seem undesirable to the Christian population. The Christian churchmen were not troubled about the "perils of the Jewish soul," for, so far as they knew, he had no soul to be saved. What made the trade relation possible, however, was not merely the fact that it was mutually advantageous, but the fact that trade relationships are possible when no other form of contact between two peoples can take place. The Jew, being a stranger,* and belonging, as he did, to a separate and distinct class, was admirably fitted to become the merchant and banker. He drifted to the towns and cities where trade was possible and profitable. Here he could utilize all the distant contacts that he had developed in the course of his wandering. His attachment to the community at large was slight, and when necessity demanded it he could migrate to a locality where opportunities were greater. He owned no real property to which he was tied, nor was he the serf of a feudal lord. His mobility in turn developed versatility. He saw opportunities in places where no native could see them. While the ghetto was never more than a temporary stopping-place, the Jew was never a hobo, for he had an aim, a destination, and his community went with him in his migrations.

While the Jew's contacts with the outside world were categorical and abstract, within his own community he was at home. Here he could relax from etiquette and formalism. His contacts with his fellow-Jews were warm, intimate, and free. Especially was this true of his family life, within the inner circle of which he received that appreciation and sympathetic understanding which the larger world could not offer. In his own community, which was based upon the solidarity of the families that composed it, he was a person with status. Whenever he returned from a journey to a distant market, or from his daily work, he came back to the family fold, there to be recreated and reaffirmed as a man and as a Jew. Even when he was far removed from his kin, he lived his real inner life in his dreams and hopes with them. He could converse with his own kind in that familiar tongue which the rest of the world could not understand. He was

bound by common troubles, by numerous ceremonies and sentiments to his small group that lived its own life oblivious of the world beyond the confines of the ghetto. Without the backing of his group, without the security that he enjoyed in his inner circle of friends and countrymen, life would have been intolerable.

Through the instrumentality of the ghetto there gradually developed that social distance which effectually isolated the Jew from the remainder of the population. These barriers did not completely inhibit contact, but they reduced it to the type of relationships which were of a secondary and formal nature. As these barriers crystallized and his life was lived more and more removed from the rest of the world, the solidarity of his own little community was enhanced until it became strictly divorced from the larger world without.

III

The forms of community life that had arisen naturally and spontaneously in the course of the attempt of the Jews to adapt themselves to their surroundings gradually became formalized in custom and precedent, and finally crystallized into legal enactment. What the Jews had sought as a privilege was soon to be imposed upon them by law. As the Jews had come to occupy a more important position in medieval economy, and as the church at about the time of the Crusades became more militant, there set in a period of active regulation. The ghetto became compulsory. But the institution of the ghetto had by this time become firmly rooted in the habits and attitudes of the Jews. The historians of the ghetto are usually inclined to overemphasize the confining effect of the barriers that were set up around the Jew, and the provincial and stagnant character of ghetto existence. They forget that there was nevertheless a teeming life within the ghetto which was probably more active than life outside.

The laws that came to regulate the conduct of the Jews and Christians were merely the formal expressions of social distances that had already been ingrained in the people. While on the one hand the Jew was coming to be more and more a member of a class—an abstraction—on the other hand there persisted the tendency to react to him as a human being. The ghetto made the Jew self-conscious.

* "In, but not of, the society."—Ed.

Life in the ghetto was bearable only because there was a larger world outside, of which many Jews often got more than a passing glimpse. As a result they often lived on the fringe of two worlds. There was always some movement to get out of the ghetto on the part of those who were attracted by the wide world that lay beyond the horizon of the ghetto walls and who were cramped by the seemingly narrow life within. Sometimes a Jew would leave the ghetto and become converted; and sometimes these converts, broken and humiliated, would return to the ghetto to taste again of the warm, intimate, tribal life that was to be found nowhere but among their people. On such occasions the romance of the renegade would be told in the ghetto streets, and the whole community would thereby be welded into a solid mass amid the solemn ceremonies by which the stray member was reincorporated into the community.

The inner solidarity of the ghetto community always lay in the ties of family life, and through the organization in the synagogue these families gained status within a community. Confined as the province of the ghetto was, there was ample opportunity for the display of capacity for leadership. The ghetto community was minutely specialized and highly integrated. There were probably more distinct types of personality and institutions within the narrow ghetto streets than in the larger world outside.

The typical ghetto is a densely populated, walled-in area usually found near the arteries of commerce or in the vicinity of a market. The Jewish quarter, even before the days of the compulsory ghetto, seems to have grown up round the synagogue, which was the center of Jewish life, locally as well as religiously. A common feature of all ghettos was also the cemetery, which was a communal responsibility and to which unusual sentimental interest was attached. There were a number of educational, recreational, and hygienic institutions, such as a school for the young, a bath, a slaughter house, a bakehouse, and a dance hall. In the close life within the ghetto walls almost nothing was left to the devices of the individual. Life was well organized, and custom and ritual played an institutionalizing rôle which still accounts for the high degree of organization of Jewish communities, often verging on overorganization. These institutions did not arise ready made. They represent what

life always is, an adaptation to the physical and social needs of a people. In this case particularly, those institutions that had to deal with the conflict and disorder within the group and the pressure from without were the characteristic form of accommodation to the isolation which the ghetto symbolized and enforced. This holds good not merely for the institutions of the ghetto, but for the functionaries and personalities that center around them. The Jews as a race as we know them today are themselves a product of the ghetto.

The ghetto, from the standpoint of biology, was a closely inbreeding, self-perpetuating group to such an extent that it may properly be called a closed community. Not that there was no intermarriage, but these mixed marriages as a rule were lost to the ghetto. The Jews have frequently and rightly been pointed out as the classic example of the great force of religious and racial prejudices, of segregation and isolation, in giving rise to distinct physical and social types. These types persist roughly to the extent that ghetto life and its effects have continued relatively unchanged, which is most true of Eastern Europe and the Orient. The difference in community life accounts in large part for the differences between various local groupings within the Jewish population.

The Russian, Polish, and in part the Roumanian, Jews differ from those of Western Europe—the German, French, Dutch, and English Jews—in several fundamental respects. For a long period the Jews of the East were merely a cultural dependency—an outpost—of Western Jewry. When an independent cultural life did develop in Russia, Poland, and Lithuania, it was self-sufficient and self-contained, set apart from the larger world. Not so with the Jews of Western Europe. They were never quite impervious to the currents of thought and the social changes that characterized the life of Europe since the Renaissance. While the Jews of the East lived in large part in rural communities, in a village world, those of the West were predominantly a city people, in touch with the centers of trade and finance near and far, and in touch at least for some time with the pulsating intellectual life of the world. While the Jews of the Rhine cities were associating with men of thought and of affairs, their brethren in Russia were dealing with peasants and an uncultured, decadent, feudal nobility. When the Jewries of the West were already seething with modernist religious, political, and social movements, those of the East were still steeped in mysticism and medieval ritual. While the Western Jews were moving along with the tide of progress, those of the East were still sharing the backwardness and isolation of the gentile world of villagers and peasants. Although until the middle of the last century the Jews of the East were never quite so confined in their physical movements as were the ghetto Jews of the West, the former lived in a smaller world, a world characterized by rigidity and stability; and when they were herded into cities, in which they constituted the preponderant bulk of the total population, they merely turned these cities into large villages that had little in common with the urban centers of the West. Many features of local life in the modern Jewish community bear the imprint of the successive waves of immigrants first from the West and then from the East.

The formal enactments that made the ghetto the legal dwelling-place of the Jews were abolished toward the middle of the last century in most of the countries of the world. Strangely enough, the abolition of the legal ghetto was opposed by a great portion of Jews as late as a hundred years ago, for they had a premonition that the leveling of the ghetto walls would mean the wiping out of separate community life, which the formal ghetto rules merely symbolized. Those who saw in the new freedom the waning influence of the Jewish religion and the ultimate dissolution of Jewish life in separate communities had two things left to console them: (1) the formal equality decreed by law did not at once gain for the Jew ready acceptance and a parallel social status among his fellow-citizens; and (2) although Western Jewry seemed to be crumbling, there were approximately six millions of Jews left on the other side of the Vistula who were still clinging to the old bonds that exclusion and oppression had fashioned. But since that time even Russia has been revolutionized, and the so-called "last bulwark" of Judaism threatens to disappear.

IV

Just as the ghetto arose before formal decrees forced the Jews into segregated areas, so the ghetto persists after these decrees have been annulled. Mr. Zangwill has said: "People who have been living in a ghetto for a couple of centuries are not able to step outside merely because the gates are thrown down, nor to efface the brands on their souls by putting off their yellow badges. The isolation from without will have come to seem the law of their being."[1] The formal abolition of the ghetto and the granting of citizenship did for the Jews about what the emancipation proclamation did for the Negro. Slavery was more than a mere legal relationship, and the ghetto was more than a statute. It had become an institution. Though the physical walls of the ghetto have been torn down, an invisible wall of isolation still maintains the distance between the Jew and his neighbors.

Even in towns containing only a handful of Jews, there will be found in all parts of the world some more or less definitely organized community. The ecological factors that enter into its development are essentially those of the medieval ghetto. There are several items besides the continuity of traditions from within and prejudice from without that account for the persistence of the modern ghetto, particularly in American cities. One of these is the colonization movement among the Jews, by which Old World communities are sometimes kept intact in the New World. But even where no such organized effort exists, it is remarkable to what extent the Jewish community tends to perpetuate its old surroundings.

To a large extent the modern ghetto is necessitated by the precepts and practices of orthodox Judaism, by the need of dwelling within easy reach of the synagogue, the schoolroom, and the ritual bath, the kosher butcher shop and the kosher dairy. But even for those who are indifferent to religious observances and ritual practices, residence in the ghetto is necessitated by social and economic circumstances. Ignorance of the language of the new country, of its labour conditions, and of its general habits and ways of thought, as well as the natural timidity of a fugitive from a land of persecution, compels the immigrant Jew to settle in the colony of his co-religionists. Among them he is perfectly at home; he finds the path of employment comparatively smooth, and if his efforts to attain it be delayed, he is helped in the interval by charity from a dozen hands.[2]

In countries where the contact between Jew and non-Jew has been continued for a few generations, and where no new immigration

from other countries in which the Jews retained their old status has taken place, the
ghetto has to a large extent disintegrated.
Under these circumstances, not only does the
ghetto tend to disappear, but the race tends
to disappear with it. Contact with the world
through education, commerce, and the arts
tends to bring about a substitution of the cultural values of the world at large for those of
the ghetto. This contact, moreover, frequently
brings about intermarriage, which is most frequent in those localities where intercourse between Jew and Gentile is least restricted. It is
safe to say that the present fifteen and a half
million Jews in the world constitute only a
small proportion of the living descendants of
the original Jewish settlers in the Western
world at the beginning of the Christian era.
They are merely the residue of a much larger
group whose Jewish identity has been lost in
the general stream of population. What has
happened in the case of the Jews is essentially
what has happened in all minority groups in
recent times. As the barriers of isolation have
receded, social intercourse and interbreeding
have decimated the size of the group and leveled its distinguishing characteristics to those
of the milieu.

A Jewish community may in some respects
be said to exist after the obstacles to ready
intercourse with the world outside have been
removed, but it tends to become a nondescript
community. Where, however, as is the case in
most large cities of Western Europe and especially the United States, a steady influx of
new immigrants has replenished the disintegrating community, there a ghetto, with all the
characteristic local color, has grown up and
maintains itself. It is with such a community,
as found in the Chicago ghetto, that this study
has dealt.

V

Western ghettos differ from those of the
East in that the former comprise at least two
sections, the native and the foreign. The native
section lives in some sort of concentration
within convenient distance from the communal
institutions. A rise in material prosperity is
generally followed by a removal to a better
district, where a new Jewish area is created,
but one less distinguished from its environment by external tokens. The foreign section,
however, lives in a state of dense concentra-

tion. Their poverty makes them settle in the
poor quarter of the town, where they reproduce the social conditions in which they have
been born and bred, so far as the new environment will allow. The ghetto in the East may
be a symbol of political bondage; but in the
West the only bondage that it typifies is that
exercised by economic status, by sentiment and
tradition.[3]

If you would know what kind of Jew a man
is, ask him where he lives; for no single factor
indicates as much about the character of the
Jew as the area in which he lives. It is an index
not only to his economic status, his occupation, his religion, but to his politics and his
outlook on life, and the stage in the assimila-
tive process that he has reached.

West of the Chicago River, in the shadow
of the central business district, lies a densely
populated rectangle of crowded tenements
representing the greater part of Chicago's immigrant colonies, among them the ghetto. It
contains the most varied assortment of people
to be found in any similar area of the world.
This area has been the stamping-ground of virtually every immigrant group that has come
to Chicago. The occupation of this area by
the Jews is, it seems, merely a passing phase
of a long process of succession in which one
population group has been crowded out by
another. There is, however, an unmistakable
regularity in this process. In the course of the
growth of the city and the invasion of the
slums by new groups of immigrants there has
resulted a constancy of association between
Jews and other ethnic groups. Each racial and
cultural group tends to settle in that part of
the city which, from the point of view of
rents, standards of living, accessibility, and tolerance, makes the reproduction of the Old
World life easiest. In the course of the invasion of these tides of immigrants the ghetto has
become converted from the outskirts of an
overgrown village to the slum of a great city
in little more than one generation. The Jews
have successively displaced the Germans, the
Irish, and the Bohemians, and have themselves
been displaced by the Poles and Lithuanians,
the Italians, the Greeks and Turks, and finally
the Negro. The Poles and Jews detest each
other thoroughly, but they can trade with
each other very successfully. They have transferred the accommodation to each other from
the Old World to the New. The latest invasion of the ghetto by the Negro is of more

than passing interest. The Negro, like the immigrant, is segregated in the city into a racial colony; economic factors, race prejudice, and cultural differences combine to set him apart. The Negro has drifted to the abandoned sections of the ghetto for precisely the same reasons that the Jews and the Italians came there. Unlike the white landlords and residents of former days and in other parts of the city, the Jews have offered no appreciable resistance to the invasion of the Negroes. The Negroes pay good rent and spend their money readily. Many of the immigrants of the ghetto have not as yet discovered the color line.

The transition and deterioration of the ghetto has been proceeding at such speed that the complexion of the area changes from day to day. Dilapidated structures that a decade ago were Lutheran and Catholic churches have since become synagogues, and have now been turned into African M. E. churches. Under the latest coat of paint of a store-front colored mission there are vestiges of signs reading "Kosher Butchershop" and "Deutsche Apotheke."

True to the ancient pattern, the most colorful and active section of the ghetto is the street market, which resembles a medieval fair more than the shopping district of a modern city. But this institution, together with the rest of ghetto culture, is fast declining. The life of the immigrants in the ghetto is so circumscribed and they are so integrally a part of it that they are unaware of its existence. It is the children of the immigrant who discover the ghetto and then . . . flee. What a few years ago was a steady but slow outward movement has now developed into a veritable stampede to get out of the ghetto; for, with all its varied activities and its colorful atmosphere, the ghetto nevertheless is a small world. It throbs with a life which is provincial and sectarian. Its successes are measured on a small scale, and its range of expression is limited.

Not until the immigrant leaves the ghetto does he become fully conscious of himself and his status. He feels a sense of personal freedom and expansion as he takes up his residence in the more modern and less Jewish area of second settlement. As late as twenty years ago, when the first Jewish fugitives from the ghetto invaded Lawndale, an area about two miles west, which in Chicago represents the area of second settlement, they came into collision with the Irish and the Germans, who

had turned what was recently a prairie into something like a park. It took the Jews about ten years to convert it into a densely settled apartment-house area. At first they could not rent. Experience in the ghetto from which the Irish and Germans had been displaced had given these residents a vision of what was in store for their homes. But this time the Jews could afford to buy, and they bought in blocks. By 1910 Lawndale had become a second ghetto. Its synagogues were a little more modern than those of Maxwell street; the beards of the Lawndale Jews were a little trimmer, and their coats a little shorter, than in the original ghetto; but Lawndale had become Jewish. Those residents of the ghetto who stayed behind derisively called Lawndale "Deutschland," and its inhabitants "Deutschuks," because they were affecting German ways.

But the Lawndale Jews found little rest and satisfaction. Their erstwhile neighbors, impelled by identical motives—to flee from their fellow-Jews, and be less Jewish—had given Lawndale a new complexion, unmistakably Jewish, though not quite as genuine as that of the ghetto itself.

In their attempt to flee from the ghetto, the partially assimilated Jews have found that the ghetto has followed them, and a new exodus sets in. The plans of those who fled from the ghetto in order to obtain status as human beings—as successful business or professional men, rather than as Jews—have been frustrated by the similar plans of others. So it is with the third settlement in the fashionable apartment hotels and the suburbs. As the area becomes predominantly Jewish, the non-Jewish settlers move, and the Jews begin the pursuit anew. Scarcely does the Jew get a glimpse of the freer world that looms beyond the ghetto when he becomes irritated by the presence of his fellow-Jews, more Jewish than himself; he is bored, disgusted, and resumes his flight.

In the process he changes his character and his institutions. But what has held the community together in spite of all disintegrating forces from within and without is not only the replenishment of the ghetto by new immigrants—for this is a waning factor—but rather the return to the ghetto of those who have fled but have been disappointed and disillusioned about the results of their flight. They have found the outside world cold and unresponsive to their claims, and return to the warmth and the intimacy of the ghetto. Finally, the Jewish community has been kept intact by the fact that the outside world has treated it as an entity. The Jewish problem, if there be one, consists in the fact that the ghetto persists in spite of the attempt of so many to flee. As long as the nucleus remains, it will serve as a symbol of community life to which even those who are far removed in space and in sympathies belong and by which they are identified.

The Jews as individuals do not always find the way to assimilation blocked. They make friends as well as enemies. The contacts between cultural and racial groups inevitably produce harmony as well as friction; and the one cannot be promoted nor the other prevented by nostrums and ready-made programs and administrative devices. Interaction is life, and life is a growth which defies attempts at control and direction, however rational they may be, that do not take account of this dynamic process. In the struggle for status, personality arises. The Jew, like every other human being, owes his unique character to this struggle, and that character will change and perhaps disappear as the struggle changes or subsides.

What makes the Jewish community—composed as it is of heterogeneous cultural elements and distributed in separate areas of our cities—a community is its capacity to act corporately. It is a cultural community and constitutes as near an approach to communal life as the modern city has to offer. The ghetto, be it Chinese, Negro, Sicilian, or Jewish, can be completely understood only if it is viewed as a socio-psychological, as well as an ecological, phenomenon; for it is not merely a physical fact, but also a state of mind.

Notes

[1] Israel Zangwill, *Children of the Ghetto*, p. 6.

[2] Israel Cohen, *Jewish Life in Modern Times*, pp. 27–38.

[3] See Cohen, *op. cit.*, p. 37.

THE NEGRO EXPERIENCE

Ethnic groups generally originate at a given time, through such developments as conquest, as in the case of South Africa; internal differentiation, as in the case of American Mormons; or migration, as in the case of most American groups. Sociologists have noted that the longer an ethnic group is in existence, the more it tends to become assimilated, socially and culturally, into the dominant society. Often, members of an ethnic group marry into the dominant group, a phenomenon which in the aggregate is called amalgamation. If these processes of assimilation and amalgamation continue unchecked, and no new ethnic group members are introduced into the society, the group will disappear by merging into the dominant group. This seems to be occurring in the United States in the case of nationalities originating in northwest Europe, such as the Scandinavians and Irish, who immigrated in large numbers during the 1840s. In a slower fashion, many European groups that immigrated in the period 1890–1910 show signs of assimilation and amalgamation. The process of immigration and assimilation has been thought to describe the history of ethnic groups generally.

One striking exception to this pattern has been the American Negroes, who represent our oldest immigrant group (although in the context of Northern cities they are a rather new group). The facts of their low social status and continued segregation are generally known, but it is not clear whether Negroes are following the pattern of European immigrant groups, albeit at a much, much slower pace, or whether they are traveling a different road which will not lead to assimilation and amalgamation.

In this selection the Taeubers inquire into the problem using data from recent decades. They use a methodological tool called the Index of Residential Segregation. This tells roughly the percentage of the population in one group that would have to move if the group's residential distribution were to be made similar to that of another group. To illustrate, in Chicago this index for Negroes and all whites in 1960 was 83. This means that 83 per cent of the Negroes in Chicago would have had to change residences in order for the pattern of Negro settlement to be the same as that of whites. This is obviously a very high figure, indicating extreme segregation.

> The Index of Residential Segregation between Negroes and whites in Chicago was 85 in 1930 and 83 in 1960. The Negro is the most segregated of ethnic groups, and there has been little change in this segregation over the past 30 years (although segregation was less in decades before 1930). Moreover, segregation has continued even though the Negro has progressed considerably in some other ways, and this is an unprecedented occurrence in the history of American ethnic groups.
>
> Earlier Negro migrants are no less segregated from whites than are newer migrants, thus ruling out one possible explanation of this fact. Nor are explanations in terms of the size of the migration or rural origins convincing. The visibility of the Negro due to his skin color is paralleled among the Japanese, and since the Japanese are less segregated from whites and are further desegregating, visibility does not seem an adequate explanation. The poverty of the Negro can account for only a small proportion of the segregation.
>
> Even the newest immigrant group, the Puerto Ricans, who are lower than Negroes in wealth, education, and all other indexes of prosperity, are less segregated. A reasonable conclusion is that because of factors still not well understood, the Negro is not following the general model of immigrant groups, and predictions of gradual integration based on this model are invalid.

The model of "automatic" assimilation and amalgamation over time is too simple to account for the experience of the Negro. It is also less than adequate in several other situations. As we saw in the last selection, Wirth in 1927 predicted the disappearance of the Jews, an event that now seems distant if even likely. Whereas the Japanese in America seem to be following the model, the Chinese, who migrated to the United States at about the same time, are not. It would seem that pluralistic accommodation, a stable relationship between groups in which each retains its separate identity and distinct culture, is an alternative to assimilation and amalgamation. This situation has been observed over time in places as different as Switzerland and the Ituri Forest of Africa. It need not imply subordination of one or more groups, although such subordination on a permanent basis is not ruled out either. One of the major questions in sociology concerns what conditions in the ethnic group, the dominant group, and their interrelations lead to these alternatives.

The Taeubers note that residential segregation has a fundamental impact upon segregation in many other institutions: religion, education, political power, and economic benefits are also likely to be segregated when residences are segregated. Many social critics share this concern. The data of this article suggest that integration of Negroes in the United States will not be achieved by reliance on the unaided social forces that have helped other groups.

Selection 46

THE NEGRO AS AN IMMIGRANT GROUP: RECENT TRENDS IN RACIAL AND
ETHNIC SEGREGATION IN CHICAGO

Karl E. Taeuber and Alma F. Taeuber

During the last half of the nineteenth century and the early decades of the twentieth, millions of immigrants from Europe entered the United States. Many of these immigrants settled initially in ethnic colonies in large northern cities and found jobs as unskilled laborers in burgeoning mass-production industries. With the onset of World War I in Europe, and with the passage of restrictive legislation in the United States in the early 1920's, the period of massive overseas migration came to an end. At the same time, however, there developed a large-scale migration of Negroes from the South to the same large northern industrial cities. Like the immigrants from abroad, the Negro migrants to northern cities filled the lowest occupational niches and rapidly developed highly segregated patterns of residence within the central cities.

In view of many obvious similarities between the Negro migrants and the various immigrant groups preceding them, it has been suggested that northern urban Negroes are but the latest of the immigrant groups, undergoing much the same processes of adaptation to city life and of assimilation into the general social structure as the European groups preceding them.[1] The persistence of Negroes as a residentially segregated and underprivileged group at the lowest levels of socioeconomic status, however, is frequently interpreted in terms of distinctive aspects of the Negro experience, particularly their historical position in American society.[2]

The question of whether or not a northern urban Negro population can fruitfully be viewed as an immigrant population, comparable to European immigrant populations of earlier decades with respect to the nature and speed of assimilation, will be explored on the basis of data permitting analysis of recent trends in racial and ethnic segregation in Chicago.

The processes by which various immigrant groups have been absorbed into American so-

Reprinted from *American Journal of Sociology*, 69:4, 1964, pp. 374–382, by permission of The University of Chicago Press. Copyright 1964 by the University of Chicago.

ciety are complex and have been studied from a variety of viewpoints. Unfortunately there is no sociological consensus on a definition of assimilation and there is nothing approaching a definitive study of the processes of assimilation for any one immigrant group. It is beyond the scope of our task here to attempt to provide such a definition. We feel that a distinctively sociological approach to the topic must view assimilation as a process of dispersion of members of the group throughout the social structure. Cultural and psychological processes, we feel, should not be incorporated into a sociological definition, although their relationship to institutional dispersion should, of course, be retained as one focus of research on assimilation.

For our purposes, it will suffice to have a working definition of the process of assimilation considerably less sophisticated than that required for a general sociological theory. Accepting the view that both immigrant groups and Negro migrants originally settled in segregated patterns in central areas of cities and ranked very low in terms of socioeconomic measures, assimilation then consisted in large part of a process of social and economic advancement on the part of the original members of the group and their descendants, along with a decreasing residential concentration in ethnic colonies. Our concern with diminishing residential segregation as a necessary concomitant of the assimilation process derives from Myrdal's discussion of the "mechanical" importance of residential segregation in facilitating other forms of segregation and discrimination, and Hawley's discussion of the impact of spatial patterns on race relations.[3] Our concern with socioeconomic advance reflects the initially low status of the groups with which we are concerned, whereas a more general treatment would need to reckon with the unusually high status of some immigrant stocks, as well as with other aspects of social status and institutional dispersion than those for which we have data.

The data in Table 1 illustrate for selected immigrant groups the patterns of socioeconomic advance and residential dispersion from highly segregated ethnic colonies. For each of the larger ethnic groups, data for 1950 show the average standing on three measures of socioeconomic status, standardized for age,[*] of the first generation (the foreign-born white, FBW) and the second generation (native white of foreign or mixed parentage, NWFMP). The nationality groups are split into "old," "new," and "newer" groups in an extension of the traditional system. On the average, comparing within the first or within the second generation, the "old" immigrant groups are the best off on these measures, the "new" groups are intermediate, and the "newer" groups are the worst off. It cannot be determined from these data to what extent the old immigrants are better off by virtue of their longer average length of residence in the United States, or to what extent they may have been better off at their time of immigration than the newer immigrants were at the time of their move.

Comparisons between the first and second generations might appear to be a more direct means for assessing the extent of socioeconomic advance, particularly since the emphasis in the literature on assimilation is on inter-generational processes rather than simply on processes of upward mobility through time in the status of the original immigrants. Comparisons of corresponding status measures for the first and second generations in Table 1 reveal, in general, the expected pattern of intergenerational advance. Data such as these, however, do not refer directly to a specific set of immigrant parents and their native-born children and must be interpreted with great caution.[4] For instance, it would be unwarranted on the basis of these data to assume that descendants of German immigrants are not as well off as their parents in terms of education. It is more credible that recent immigrants from Germany, under our immigration laws, include a large proportion of persons of high socioeconomic status.

Measures of the changing residential patterns of the immigrant groups are given in columns 7–9 of Table 1. The measure, an index of residential segregation between the total foreign stock (FBW + NWFMP) of each

nationality and the total native whites of native parentage (NWNP), assumes a value of 100 for maximum residential segregation and a value of 0 if the residential distributions are identical.[5] The indexes were computed from the distribution of each group among the seventy-five community areas of the city of Chicago for 1930 (the last previous census year that included information on the total foreign stock) and 1960. The degree of residential segregation from the native population is highest for the "newer" immigrants and lowest for the "old" immigrants. Between 1930 and 1960, most of the ethnic groups became less segregated from the native population. Only for England, Ireland and Sweden did the indexes fail to decline, and these were already at relatively low levels.[6]

This general approach to the measurement or assimilation of immigrant groups has been pursued for a number of cities and longer time periods by Lieberson. He found a remarkably persistent and consistent association through time between residential desegregation of an ethnic group and increasing socioeconomic similarity to native whites, and cross-sectionally between the position of each group as compared to others on measures of residential segregation and its relative levels on status measures.[7]

The index of residential segregation between Negroes and NWNP for 1930 was 84, and for 1960, 82. These values are higher than any of those for specific immigrant stocks. Furthermore, each of the immigrant stocks was highly segregated from Negroes in 1930 and 1960. There is relatively little intermixture of Negro residences with those of any group of whites. Even the "newer" immigrant groups, the Puerto Ricans and Mexicans, are not joining or replacing Negroes in established Negro areas but are moving into separate ethnic colonies of their own at the periphery of Negro areas. Negroes clearly occupy a distinctive position as the most residentially segregated of the principal migrant groups. The separation of Negroes from all groups of whites is sharper than any of the patterns of residential segregation between ethnic groups or between socioeconomic groups within the white population.[8] Apparently this pattern has developed during the last few decades. Lieberson has demonstrated that, although prior to the great Negro migrations of World War I there were instances of immigrant stocks being more seg-

[*] Since age affects such matters as education (e.g., older people are less well educated than young people), and immigrant groups differ in the age of members (e.g., newer groups tend to be younger), it is necessary to make a statistical correction of the data to eliminate the effects of age. This is called standardization.—Ed.

Table 1   Selected Characteristics (Age-standardized) of Foreign-born and Native Ethnic Populations in 1950, and Indexes of Residential Segregation of Selected Groups of Foreign Stock from
Native Whites of Native Parentage, 1930 and 1960, Chicago*

Country of origin	Per cent high school graduates (males age 25 and over)		Per cent with income above $3,000 (persons with income)		Per cent with white-collar jobs (employed males)		Index of residential segregation (compared with NWNP)		
	FBW	NWFMP	FBW	NWFMP	FBW	NWFMP	1930	1960	Change
"Old" immigrant groups:									
England and Wales	45	50	53	58	49	51	11	18	+7
Ireland	27	47	47	56	22	47	23	31	+8
Norway	31	47	54	57	24	51	44	37	−7
Sweden	25	48	59	60	23	51	26	30	+4
Germany	37	34	53	55	34	42	22	19	−3
"New" immigrant groups:									
Austria	29	40	54	57	33	44	30	16	−14
Czechoslovakia	25	33	44	54	22	36	59	37	−22
Italy	15	27	47	53	24	37	52	32	−20
Poland	18	25	42	49	25	30	63	38	−25
U.S.S.R.	35	60	60	69	59	74	51	44	−7
"Newer" immigrant groups:									
Mexico	14	16	38	29	8	13	71	54	−17
Puerto Rico†	13	29	16	37	22	36	†	67	†

* Data for 1930 and 1950 refer to foreign white stock (foreign-born plus native of foreign or mixed parentage);
data for 1960 refer to total foreign stock. Abbreviations used are FBW for foreign-born white, NWFMP for native
white of foreign or mixed parentage, and NWNP for native white of native parentage. The three socioeconomic
characteristics refer to the Standard Metropolitan Area population, while the segregation indexes are based on
community areas within the city. Age-standardization was by the direct method, using age groups 25–44 and 45
and over, with the Standard Metropolitan Area age composition as a standard.
† Socioeconomic characteristics for Puerto Rican population refer to total United States; Puerto Rican population
by community areas for Chicago available for 1960 only.
Source: Characteristics from U.S. Bureau of the Census, U.S. Census of Population: Vol. IV, Special Reports, Pt. 3.
chap. A, "Nativity and Parentage," and chap. D, "Puerto Ricans in Continental United States." Distributions of
population by community areas for 1930 and 1960 from data on file at Chicago Community Inventory, University
of Chicago.

regated from native whites than were Negroes,
since 1920 there has been a general tendency
for Negro residential segregation to be highest.[9]

Data pertaining specifically to the comparison between whites and non-whites (97 per
cent of Chicago's non-whites are Negroes)
on measures of socioeconomic status and of
residential segregation are presented in Table
2. For each of four measures reflecting socioeconomic status, there was improvement in the
status of the non-white population between
1940 and 1960. (For whites, improving status
would be more clearly evident if the data
referred to the entire metropolitan area rather

than just the city of Chicago.) The indexes of
residential segregation between whites and
Negroes, in the top panel of the table show
minor fluctuations around an extremely high
level and give no indication of the declines
anticipated on the basis of the socioeconomic
advancement of the Negro population. That
this is not an atypical finding is indicated by
reference to other data showing a long term
historical trend toward increasing residential
segregation between whites and non-whites.
Increasing racial residential segregation was
evident in most large cities of the United
States between 1940 and 1950, while during
the 1950's, southern cities continued to in-

Table 2 Selected Socioeconomic Characteristics (Unstandardized) of Whites and Non-whites, Chicago, 1940, 1950, and 1960

Characteristic	Non-white	White
Residential segregation index whites vs. Negroes: *		
1930	85	
1940	85	
1950	79	
1960	83	
Per cent high school graduates, ages 25+:		
1940	16	25
1950	25	37
1960	29	37
Per cent white collar, male:		
1940	17	40
1950	17	41
1960	21	40
Per cent home-owners:		
1940	7	26
1950	12	33
1960	16	39
Per cent multiple-person households with 1.01 or more persons per room:		
1940	41	17
1950	46	14
1960	34	10

* These values differ slightly from those cited in the text for Negroes as compared to native whites of native parentage.
Source: Data for 1940 from the 1940 Census Tract Bulletin for Chicago; for 1950 from Philip M. Hauser and Evelyn M. Kitagawa (eds.), *Local Community Fact Book for Chicago, 1950* (Chicago: Chicago Community Inventory, 1953); and for 1960 from the 1960 Census Tract Bulletin for Chicago.

crease in segregation and northern cities generally registered modest declines.[10]

In broad perspective, the historical trend toward improving socioeconomic status of immigrant groups has gone hand in hand with decreasing residential segregation. In contrast, Negro residential segregation from whites has increased steadily over past decades until it has reached universally high levels in cities throughout the United States, despite advances in the socioeconomic status of Negroes.

We have been unable to locate any data permitting a comparison between Negroes long resident in Chicago, or born and raised in the North, and Negroes with lesser periods of residence in the city. Thus we are not able to make even the crude intergenerational comparisons for Negroes that are possible for the immigrant groups. The only analysis of this type possible with census data is a comparison between recent migrants and the rest of the population, and the only published data are residential distributions, with no socioeconomic characteristics. For 1960, with the seventy-five community areas of Chicago as units, the index of residential segregation between non-whites resident in the metropolitan area for five years or more and native whites of native parents is 80.5. Comparing non-whites with less than five years' residence in the metropolitan area and NWNP, the index was 81.0. Comparing the recent in-migrants with the non-whites who were resident in the metropolitan area five years or more, the index was 13. Thus the recent non-white in-migrants are distributed differently from the rest of the non-white population, but each group is highly segregated from the native whites. Unfortunately, these results cannot be readily interpreted in terms of the general assimilation and dispersion processes under consideration. Possibly there are trends toward socioeconomic advancement and residential dispersion on the part of "second generation" Negroes in Chicago that are confounded in the data for the total Negro population.

Decreasing residential concentration of immigrant groups occurred despite the efforts of many nationality organizations to maintain the ethnic colonies.[11] Few Negro organizations have been as explicitly segregationist. In some immigrant groups, many members were dispersing from the ethnic colonies even while large-scale immigration of that group was still under way. For every immigrant group, diminishing residential segregation has been evident since the cessation of large-scale immigration. For Negroes, however, residential segregation has increased since the first period of large-scale immigration to northern cities, and this increase in residential segregation continued during the late 1920's and 1930's when the volume of migration was at a low level. These observations tend to discredit the argument that a major barrier to residential dispersion of the Negro population of Chicago is its continuing rapid increase. However, the size of the Negro population and the magnitude of its annual increase are larger than for any single ethnic group in the past, and comparisons with smaller groups are not completely convincing. That rapid increase leads to increasing residential segregation was demonstrated directly in the intercity comparative study previously cited. There was no definite relationship between increase in Negro population and increase in the value of the segregation index. Indeed, during the 1950–60 decade, there appeared to be a slight relationship in the opposite direction.[12]

More significant in accounting for the divergent trends in residential segregation may be the different urban contexts in which the immigrant and Negro populations found themselves. Comparing the residential locations of Italian-born and Polish-born in Chicago in 1899 and in 1920, Wallace observed:

> . . . it can be seen that the areas of greatest dispersion, low proportion, and presumably of "second" settlement for many immigrants were those which were not settled at all in 1899.
>
> The implication of this fact is that the so-called "assimilation" process was not reflected by the geographic dispersion of the immigrant populations into "cosmopolitan American areas." The dispersal was more directly related to an increase in housing alternatives as the city grew at the periphery.[13]

By the time the Negro concentrations were forming near the central areas of Chicago, the city was built up and the urbanized area extended well beyond the present boundaries. Residential alternatives at a price Negroes could afford and located sufficiently close in to permit inexpensive commuting were no longer available.

It has been suggested that considerable time is required for Negroes to make the transition from a "primitive folk culture" to "urbanism as a way of life."[14] Several types of data indicate that large and increasing proportions of the Negro urban population are city-born and raised. For instance, there is a rapidly decreasing color differential in the percentage of the Chicago population born in the state of Illinois. In 1960, 44 per cent of the native-born, non-white residents of Chicago were born in Illinois, as contrasted to 66 per cent of the

white population.[15] National estimates for 1958 showed that of all males aged 45–64 living in metropolitan places of 500,000 or more population, 65 per cent of the non-whites, as compared to 77 per cent of the whites, had lived in this size city for twenty years or longer.[16] Estimates of the components of growth of the non-white population of Chicago indicate that between 1950 and 1960 natural increase was as important as net immigration, and that natural increase will in the future account for rapidly increasing proportions of the growth of the non-white population.[17]

Unfortunately there is inadequate knowledge of the specific length of time under specified conditions for the required cultural transformation to occur. Wallace's observations indicate a significant degree of dispersal over time among first-generation immigrants. Such processes are more often conceived as primarily intergenerational. That many of the "first generation" Negro migrants to northern cities have lived there for twenty years or more and that in the younger adult ages there are sizable numbers of "second generation" urban Negroes suggested that there has been ample time for any necessary adjustment to urban living, at least for large proportions of the Negro population. It is also clear that if northern Negroes remain inadequately educated for urban living and fail to participate fully in the urban economy, the "primitive folk culture" of the South can less and less and less be assigned responsibility, and northern cities will be suffering from the neglect of their own human resources.

The "visibility" of Negroes due to skin color and other features which make the large majority of second-, third-, and later-generation descendants readily identifiable as Negroes is often cited as a basic factor in accounting for the distinctive position of Negroes in our society. It is exceedingly difficult to assess the significance of visibility. There is no other group that is strictly comparable to Negroes regarding every factor except visibility. It is not completely irrelevant, however, to note that non-white skin color, by itself, is not an insurmountable handicap in our society. The socioeconomic status of the Japanese population of Chicago in 1950 substantially exceeded that of the Negro population; and their residential segregation from whites, although high, was considerably lower than that between Negroes and whites.[18] Unfortunately there are no trend data available on the characteristics of the Japanese in Chicago. A more appropriate Japanese population for comparison, however, is the much larger one in the San Francisco area. A recent study there affirmed that "ethnic colonies of Japanese are gone or rapidly going" and documented their rapid socioeconomic advance.[19]

In the traditional immigrant pattern, the more recent immigrants displaced the older groups at the bottom socioeconomic levels. How do the Negroes compare with the other "newer" immigrant groups, the Mexicans and the Puerto Ricans? The limited data now available suggest that the Negroes will soon be left alone at the bottom of the social and economic scale. We have already noted (from data in Table 1) that the "newer" groups were, in 1950, of very low status compared to the other immigrant groups, and that their residential segregation from the native whites of native parentage was the highest of all the immigrant groups. For 1960, data on distribution within Chicago of persons born in Puerto Rico are available separately from data on those persons born in the United States of Puerto Rican parentage. Thus it is possible to compute indexes of residential segregation for first- and second-generation Puerto Ricans. For Chicago in 1960, these index values were 68.4 for the first generation and 64.9 for the second generation, indicating that residential dispersion has already begun for the Puerto Ricans. This difference actually understates the amount of dispersion, since the second generation consists in large proportion of children still living with their first-generation parents.

Selected socioeconomic measures for the Puerto Rican and the non-white populations of Chicago in 1960 are shown in Table 3. On every measure, the Puerto Rican population is less well off—it is less educated, has lower income, is more crowded, is less likely to own homes, is less well housed, and lives in older buildings. Yet the index of residential segregation (computed with respect to NWNP) for Puerto Ricans is 67 as compared with 82 for Negroes.

Up to now we have been making comparisons between Negroes and immigrant groups, demonstrating that residential dispersion has not accompanied socioeconomic advance by Negroes in the way that it did for immigrant groups. Economic status and expenditure for housing, however, are clearly

Table 3 Selected Socioeconomic Characteristics (Unstandardized) of Puerto Ricans and Nonwhites, Chicago, 1960

Characteristic	Non-white	Puerto-Rican
Residential segregation vs. whites	83	67
Per cent high school graduates total	29	11
Median family income	$4,742	$4,161
Per cent families earning less than $3,000	28	27
Per cent families earning more than $10,000	9	4
Per cent home-owners	16	6
Per cent substandard dwellings	26	33
Per cent 1.01 or more persons per room	34	52
Per cent housing units built since 1940	12	6
Median gross rent	$88	$79
Median number of rooms	3.9	3.7
Median number of persons	3.0	4.0

Source: Data are from the 1960 Census Tract Bulletin for Chicago.

correlated between economic status and residential segregation. By virtue of variations in the type, age, and quality of housing, and in the patterns of residential choice by persons of varying socioeconomic status, the subareas of a city are differentiated in terms of the average status of their residents. Since Negroes are of much lower average status than whites, they would be expected to be disproportionately represented in low-status residential areas. In fact, an extreme position regarding the relationships between patterns of socioeconomic residential segregation and racial residential segregation would attribute all of the latter to the former. Such a position is sometimes offered as a counterargument to charges of racial discrimination against the real estate business. To the extent that this position is correct, it might be expected that future economic advances on the part of the Negro population should be translated into decreased residential segregation.

The task of partialing out a component of racial segregation due to economic factors involves some difficult methodological problems, and no method is entirely satisfactory.[20] Our approach utilizes indirect standardization of available census data. Let us delineate the status of a residential area in terms of, say, the income distribution of its residents. Specifically, consider for each community area of Chicago the number of families with incomes below $1,000, from $1,000–1,999, from $2,000–2,999, and so forth. For the city as a whole in 1960, 44 per cent of all families with an income below $1,000 were non-white, as were 44 per cent of families with incomes from $1,000–1,999, and 40 per cent of families with incomes from $2,000–2,999. For each community area, we can apply these city-wide percentages to the observed income distribution to obtain the number of non-white families expected if income alone determined the residential locations of whites and non-whites.

By the method of indirect standardization just outlined, we obtain an expected number of non-white and white families for each of the seventy-five community areas. We can then compute an index of residential segregation between expected numbers of non-white and white families. This index can be regarded as the amount of racial residential segregation attributable to patterns of residential differentiation of income groups. For 1950, the index of residential segregation between the numbers of whites and non-whites expected on the basis of income was 11, as compared with the actual segregation index of 79. As a rough measure, then, we can attribute 11/79, or 14 per cent, of the observed racial residential segregation in Chicago in 1950 to income differentials between whites and non-whites. For 1960, the corresponding values are 10 for the expected index, 83 for the observed index, and 12 per cent for the racial segregation attributable to income differentials.

In a recent study of the relationships between housing consumption and income, Reid has demonstrated many pitfalls in the uncritical use of income distributions in the analysis of housing patterns.[21] We have therefore repeated the above analyses, using distributions by major occupational groups and distributions by educational attainment. For 1960, the index of residential segregation computed from the numbers of whites and non-whites expected on the basis of patterns of occupational differentiation is 9, and that expected on that basis of patterns of educational differentiation is 3. The results using income distribu-

tions are thus supported by the results from other measures of socioeconomic status, and the conclusion seems clear that patterns of socioeconomic differentiation of residential areas can account for only a small proportion of observed racial residential segregation.

Reid demonstrated that differences between whites and non-whites in observed patterns of housing consumption are largely attributable to income differentials between whites and non-whites. Our analysis suggests that residential segregation cannot be attributed to these differentials. Apparently the economic structure of the housing market for whites is similar to that for non-whites, even though non-whites are excluded from a large share of the housing supply for which their economic circumstances would allow them to compete.

The judicious conclusion from our review of a variety of pieces of data is that we simply do not yet know enough about immigrant assimilation processes and any corresponding processes among Negro migrants to northern cities to be able to compare the two. We believe that this very lack of knowledge makes questionable any attempt to reason from presumed patterns of assimilation among immigrants in the past to current racial problems in northern cities. Furthermore, such evidence as we could compile indicates that it is more likely to be misleading than instructive to make such comparisons.

Our definition of assimilation as involving socioeconomic advancement and residential dispersion is simple, and greater differences between groups would appear were a more complex definition adopted. Restriction of portions of the analysis to the city of Chicago had little effect on the measures for non-whites, but probably led to an understatement of the degree of assimilation of the immigrant stocks insofar as higher-status members of these groups have moved to the suburbs. The segregation indexes probably overstate somewhat the residential isolation of small groups, such as particular immigrant stocks, as compared with large groups such as total native whites of native parents. Taking account of any of these limitations in our data would tend to increase the differences between Negroes and immigrant groups. Even so, our data showed that second-generation persons from several countries are of higher socioeconomic status than the total native whites of native parentage. Relatively few Negroes in Chicago have white-collar jobs or incomes above the median level for whites, and yet there are large numbers of adult Negroes who were born in the city. Basic differences between the Negroes and the immigrant groups seems to us implicit in the failure of residential desegregation to occur for Negroes while it has continued for the immigrant groups.

In view of the fundamental impact of residential segregation on extralegal segregation of schools, hospitals, parks, stores, and numerous other facilities, the failure of residential dispersion to occur strikes us as an especially serious social problem. Socioeconomic advance and residential dispersion occurred simultaneously for the various immigrant groups. It is apparent that the continued residential segregation of the Negro population is an impediment to the continued "assimilation" of Negroes into full and equal participation in the economy and the society at large.

Notes

[1] Philip M. Hauser, "On the Impact of Urbanism on Social Organization, Human Nature and the Political Order," *Confluence*, VII (Spring, 1958), 65. Elsewhere Hauser has expressed a more cautious view, emphasizing the lack of definitive knowledge; see his *Population Perspectives* (New Brunswick, New Jersey: Rutgers University Press, 1960), p. 129.

[2] D. J. Bogue, "Chicago's Growing Population Problem," *Commerce*, LIX (July, 1962), 31.

[3] Gunnar Myrdal, *An American Dilemma* (New York: Harper & Bros., 1944), I, 618; Amos H. Hawley, "Dispersion versus Segregation: Apropos of a Solution of Race Problems," *Papers of the Michigan Academy of Science, Arts, and Letters*, XXX (1944), 667–674.

[4] For an enumeration of some of the difficulties see C. A. Price and J. Zubrzycki, "The Use of Inter-marriage Statistics as an Index of Assimilation," *Population Studies*, XVI (July, 1962), 58–69.

[5] The index of residential segregation is an index of dissimilarity between the residential distributions of each group. For further discussion, see Otis Dudley Duncan and Beverly Duncan, "A Methodological Analysis of Segregation Indexes," *American Sociological Review*, XX (April, 1955), 210–217.

[6] For a more detailed discussion of these patterns, using data for 1930 and 1950, see Otis Dudley Duncan and Stanley Lieberson, "Ethnic Segregation and Assimilation," *American Journal of Sociology*, LXIV (January, 1959), 364–374.

[7] Stanley Lieberson, *Ethnic Patterns in American Cities* (New York: Free Press of Glencoe, 1963).

[8] For a discussion of class residential segregation in Chicago see Otis Dudley Duncan and Beverly Duncan, "Residential Distribution and Occupational Stratification," *American Journal of Sociology*, LX (March, 1955), 493–503.

[9] Lieberson, *op. cit.*, pp. 120–132.

[10] Karl E. Taeuber, "Negro Residential Segregation, 1940–1960: Changing Trends in the Large Cities of the United States" (paper read at the Annual Meetings of the American Sociological Association, 1962).

[11] David A. Wallace "Residential Concentration of Negroes in Chicago" (unpublished Ph.D. dissertation, Harvard University, 1953).

[12] Taeuber, *op. cit.*

[13] Wallace, *op. cit.*, p. 205.

[14] Philip M. Hauser, "The Challenge of Metropolitan Growth," *Urban Land*, XVII (December, 1958), 5.

[15] Data from U.S. Bureau of the Census, *U.S. Census of Population, 1960: General Social and Economic Characteristics, Illinois.* Final Report PC (1)–15C, Tables 72 and 77.

[16] Karl E. Taeuber, "Duration-of-residence Analysis of Internal Migration in the United States," *Milbank Memorial Fund Quarterly*, XXXIX (January, 1961), Table 3.

[17] D. J. Bogue and D. P. Dandekar, *Population Trends and Prospects for the Chicago-Northwestern Indiana Consolidated Metropolitan Area: 1960 to 1990* (Chicago: Population Research and Training Center, University of Chicago, 1962).

[18] Although the maximum value of the residential segregation index is less than 100 for ethnic groups of small size, this is not sufficient to vitiate the Negro-Japanese comparison.

[19] Harry H. L. Kitano, "Housing Japanese-Americans in the San Francisco Bay Area," in Nathan Glazer and Davis McEntire (eds.), *Studies in Housing and Minority Groups* (Berkeley: University of California Press, 1960), p. 184.

[20] A general discussion of this problem can be found in the section on explanation of a real variation in Otis Dudley Duncan, Ray P. Cuzzort, and Beverly Duncan, *Statistical Geography* (Glencoe, Ill.; Free Press, 1961).

[21] Margaret G. Reid, *Housing and Income* (Chicago: University of Chicago Press, 1962).

COLOR AND CLASS

The present racial situation in the United States is the product of a historical process. The gulf between whites and Negroes has been both greater and less in past periods than now. Likewise, there has been considerable change in the internal structure of the Negro group. These processes were studied in detail by the author of this selection and are described in his book *The Negro in the United States* (1949). This selection briefly summarizes the main points of that book and introduces the argument of Frazier's second major work, *Black Bourgeoisie*. Here he shows how the class structure of the Negro group reinforces the segregation and, indirectly, the discrimination which Negroes as a whole experience.

The institution of slavery in the United States was a response to an economic need, and its characteristics differed with changes in the economic uses to which slaves were put. At the height of the cotton-plantation system in the South, the whites dominated a three-tiered Negro society consisting of field slaves, house slaves, and free Negroes, in ascending order. This system was disrupted by the Civil War and Reconstruction, during which there was a tendency for lower-class whites and Negroes to merge politically because of common economic interests. Reestablishment of the formerly dominant white middle classes was made possible by allocating privileges to the lower-class whites at the expense of the Negroes, the whole system being supported by a racist ideology. The liberated Negroes of the postbellum South retained their antebellum class system in slightly modified form; the Negro upper classes were those who had descended from the free Negroes and house slaves; and education and conventional behavior, rather than occupation and income, were the accepted symbols of this status.

The "Great Migration" of Negroes from Southern farms to Northern cities following 1915 created a new Negro class, based on occupation and income, that Frazier calls the black bourgeoisie. This new Negro middle class lacks roots in Negro culture, which it rejects, and is denied participation in the white middle-class culture. Members therefore live in a "world of make-believe" based on an unrealistic faith in Negro business and supported by the Negro press.

It is not difficult to see that Frazier's interpretation of Negro history and his critique of the black bourgeoisie are essentially Marxist. He sees the relations of dominant and ethnic groups and the internal structure of Negro society as determined by economic factors, and his critique of the black bourgeoisie is reminiscent of Marx's criticism of the European laboring classes. Marx believed that the potential leaders of labor had unknowingly "sold out" to the capitalists for a very small handful of silver. They had acquired a "false consciousness" that opposed their own true interests as well as those of their fellows, since they had not been adequately rewarded for their loyalty to the status quo and had not been admitted to the capitalist class. Frazier in very similar language points to the fact that the privileges of the black bourgeoisie are petty, in comparison to the privileges of the white middle classes, and that the world of make-believe is ultimately disadvantageous for the black bourgeoisie themselves as well as for lower-class Negroes.

Although Marx proved to be a rather poor prophet, he was in many ways an excellent sociologist, and his insight rings true in this work. Frazier may have been a better prophet than Marx, for as he would have predicted the leadership of the current Negro movement has been less evidently recruited from the middle classes than from the vast lower ranks of this subordinate people.

Selection 47
FROM BLACK BOURGEOISIE
E. Franklin Frazier

The presence of at least 15,000,000 persons of Negro ancestry[1] among the people of the United States is the outcome of the expansion of Europe which began in the fifteenth century and became firmly established during the succeeding two centuries.[2] As the result of this expansion Europeans met and conquered many primitive peoples, laid the basis for European settlements, and established commercial relations with the old civilizations of Asia and Africa. European expansion in the Americas became especially important for the economic development of Europe, since the production of tobacco, sugar, and cotton, which were exchanged for European manufactures, increased world trade and brought untold wealth to Europe. For the production of these raw materials and articles of commerce Negro slaves were transported to the New World and became the main support of the "triangular trade" involving the metropolis, Africa, and the colonies. Negro slaves thus became the creators of the wealth that made the flowering of capitalism possible in the nineteenth century.[3]

1. Negro slavery and the plantation

In the southern sections of what became the United States, the plantation system of agriculture developed on the basis of enslaved

Negro labor. After the failure of the attempt to utilize the native Indian as a source of forced labor, white indentured servants were introduced into the colonies.[4] But they were soon supplanted by Negro slaves, who proved a more efficient and a more economical source of labor. During the seventeenth and eighteenth centuries the importation of Negroes gradually increased to meet the growing need for laborers in the production of tobacco, rice, and indigo. But with the invention of the cotton gin, which enabled American producers to supply the increased demands of English manufacturers, the importation of Negro slaves was accelerated. As a result, the agitation against slavery, which had found expression along with the idealism respecting liberty during the American Revolution, died down when the declining productivity of slave labor on tobacco plantations was followed by a period of unprecedented profits in cotton production.

The condition of the Negro slaves on the southern plantations varied considerably. In the lower South, where the large cotton plantation tended to take on the character of a purely industrial organization, the treatment of the slaves was extremely brutal since they were regarded as mere work animals. They were treated even more inhumanly by the slave traders who supplied the needs of a commercial system of agriculture. As articles of commerce, the Negro slaves were treated in the same manner as the mules which were advertised for sale along with them. On the other hand, where the plantation became a social as well as an economic organization, under a semi-patriarchal regime, more consideration was shown for the personalities of the slaves. The lives of the masters and slaves became intertwined in a system of social relationships. The relations between whites and blacks thus came to be regulated by a complex system of social rituals and etiquette permitting a maximum degree of intimacy while maintaining the complete subordination of the blacks. The traditions governing race relations on the plantation became so firmly rooted in the South that they have persisted until the present day.[5]

2. The impact of Western civilization

Where the plantation acquired the character of a social institution, it provided the means by which the Negro slaves could rapidly take over European culture. The basis for the rapid acculturation of the Negro slaves was created by the manner in which the slaves had been captured in Africa, sold on the slave markets, and integrated into the plantation system. The Negro slaves, who represented many different tribal backgrounds, had been captured in Africa during tribal wars and slave-hunting expeditions. They had been herded into the *baracoons* on the coast to await the arrival of slave ships. Then, during the Middle Passage they were transported in ships, in which they were packed spoon-fashion, to the West Indies where they were sold on the slave markets. In the West Indies they underwent a period of being "broken into" slavery before they were shipped to local plantations or to the plantations on the mainland. In the English colonies on the mainland, and later in the United States, they were widely scattered on plantations which had fewer slaves on the whole than did the plantations in the West Indies.

On the plantations in the southern states the Negro slave sloughed off almost completely his African cultural heritage.[6] The African family system was destroyed and the slave was separated from his kinsmen and friends. Moreover, in the United States there was little chance that he could reknit the ties of kinship and old associations. If by chance he encountered fellow slaves with whom he could communicate in his native tongue, he was separated from them. From the very beginning he was forced to learn English in order to obey the commands of his white mas-

ters. Whatever memories he might have retained of his native land and native customs became meaningless in the New World. The very fact that the majority of the slaves were young males practically eliminated the possibility of recreating a social organization that could perpetuate and transmit the African cultural heritage.

While all of the slaves were always under the surveillance of the whites, the house servants lived constantly in close association with their masters. Very often these house servants had associated from childhood with their masters. Consequently, they early acquired the speech of their masters, a fact which set them off from the more isolated field hands, who spoke a dialect. Living in close association with whites, the house servants were subject to a type of discipline which caused them to identify themselves with their masters. This discipline included both moral and religious instruction. The slaves participated in the religious life of their white masters—including family prayers and attendance at the white churches, where a section was reserved for them.

Some recognition had to be given the individual qualities of the slaves, and it was most often among the house servants that these differences were recognized. For example, there was a division of labor on the plantation in which the intelligence and talents of the slaves found expression. Generally, the son of a house servant was apprenticed to some artisan to learn a skilled trade. These skilled mechanics, who constituted a large section of the artisans in the South, formed with the house servants a sort of privileged class in the slave community. The greater the integration of the slaves into the activities and family life of their white masters, the more nearly their behavior and ideals approximated those of the whites. On the other hand, the field hands, who had few intimate contacts with the whites and were subject to a more formal type of social control, could give expression to a more spontaneous type of behavior—especially in their religious life and in their musical creations. The field hands were especially attracted by the Methodist and Baptist missionaries who, in their revival meetings, preached a simple doctrine of salvation through conversion in which a highly emotional experience was of primary importance. Although the slaves were under the surveillance of the whites in order to prevent conspiracies and revolts, they were able to engage in a form of worship different from that of the whites and the more disciplined house servants. The Spirituals, or religious folksongs, grew out of these relatively independent religious meetings. The new slaves who were brought to the plantations from Africa had to adjust to a social world quite different from that from which they had come.

The close association of the races on the plantation, especially in the same household, resulted in considerable race mixture. The interbreeding of the races had begun in the seventeenth century soon after the introduction of Negroes into Virginia, and continued on a large scale as long as slavery existed. Many of the mulattoes were emancipated by their white fathers and formed the basis of the free Negro population that grew up in the South before the Civil War.[7] In 1850, mulattoes or mixed-bloods constituted 37 per cent of the free Negro population but only 8 per cent of the slave population.

The free Negroes were not evenly distributed over the South, but were concentrated principally in cities and in those states where the plantation system of agriculture did not flourish. In Maryland and Virginia, where there were 83,942 and 58,042 free Negroes, respectively, in 1860,[8] many of these free Negroes owed their freedom to the fact that they had been permitted to "hire their time" and work as semi-free laborers. With the money which they were able to accumulate after paying their masters for their "time" they bought their freedom. Although the majority of the free Negroes in the South did not live much above a subsistence level, many of them bought land and became independent farmers, or became successful mechanics and skilled artisans. In Charleston, South Carolina, and in New Orleans, the free Negroes or "free people of color" accumulated considerable wealth as skilled artisans, and as owners of plantations included slaves among their possessions.[9]

The free Negroes constituted, in fact, the element in the Negro population that had made the greatest progress in acquiring European culture. The pattern of family life of the well-to-do free Negroes in the plantation South was the same as the patriarchal family pattern of the slave-holding whites. Moreover, their outlook on life and their values were the same as the white models. They occupied the position of an intermediate caste in some parts of the South, especially in New Orleans. As a group the free Negroes of the South were much better off economically than the free Negroes of the North, who had not been able to compete with the European immigrants. At one time the free Negroes in the South outnumbered the free Negroes in the North, but as the result of persecutions following the anti-slavery agitation in the North many of them migrated to the North. Nevertheless, half of the nearly 500,000 free Negroes in the United States at the outbreak of the Civil War were in the South.

3. A nation within a nation?

As the result of the Civil War and Emancipation, the future status of the Negro in American society became one of the most pressing problems facing the American government. This problem was tied up with the problem of re-integrating the southern states into the federal Union. Lincoln, although opposed to slavery, had never believed that Negroes and whites could be citizens of the same community. He had cautiously suggested that the educated free mulattoes in Louisiana who had fought on the Union side should be permitted to qualify as citizens in the reconstructed government of Louisiana. The assassination of Lincoln followed too soon for him to make known his general program for the future of the Negro. The successor of Lincoln, Andrew Johnson, who as a representative of the non-slaveholding "poor whites" had remained loyal to the Union, soon made it clear that he wanted to build a "democracy" in the South consisting only of white citizens, or white men of property. As the result of this policy, he was opposed by two factions of the Republican Party—the abolitionists among the Old Radicals, who were genuinely interested in creating a democracy in the South based upon the political participation of whites and Negroes; and the Republicans who, fearing that a white farming class would nullify the victory of the North, wanted to use Negro voters to support legislation that would give a legal basis to triumphant industrial capitalism.[10]

The program of the Republican Congress for the reconstruction of the southern states gave promise of a democratic revolution in an area that had been ruled by a slaveholding oligarchy. Under the protection of the Union Army, the black freedmen along with the non-slaveholding whites were given the right to vote and hold office. Three amendments to the federal Constitution were necessary, however, to provide a legal basis for the citizenship of the Negro: the Thirteenth, abolishing slavery; the Fourteenth, making him a citizen, and the Fifteenth, forbidding restrictions upon his rights as a citizen on account of race or his previous status as a slave. Some of the more radical Republicans proposed that the plantations be divided in order to create a class of black and white small landowners. In fact, the black freedmen had been promised land by the federal government as a guarantee of their freedom. But since this program appeared too revolutionary for the majority of the Republican leaders, the vast majority of ex-slaves remained landless, except for a relatively small number of Negroes who had secured land during the Civil War.

The Negro has been blamed for the disorders and the graft on the part of politicians and speculators during the Reconstruction Period. But unprejudiced historians, who place the behavior of the Negro during this period in its proper perspective, agree that the Negro was the victim of the conflict of economic interests over which he had no control and that he exhibited considerable wisdom in attempting to help formulate social policies.[11] The Negro gave his support to the establishment of a system of public education and sought to make land available to the great masses of black and white farmers. But the question of race was utilized to divide the whites and the Negroes. The "redemption" of the South in 1876, which was hailed as the restoration of "white supremacy," really resulted in the political ascendancy of the "Bourbons," or the new middle classes and the planters. The state constitutions, which were supposed to be the legal instruments by which the "barbarous blacks" maintained their power but were, in fact, nothing more than the expression of middle-class interests, were retained for decades after the restoration of "white supremacy."

The restoration of "white supremacy" did not resolve the class conflict among whites in the South. In fact, the white planters sometimes used Negro voters to defeat the aspirations of the disinherited whites. When agrarian unrest among the "poor whites" of the South joined forces with the Populist movement, which represented the general unrest among American farmers, the question of race was used to defeat the co-operation of "poor whites" and Negroes. It was then that the demagogues assumed leadership of the "poor

whites" and provided a solution of the class conflict among whites that offered no challenge to the political power and economic privileges of the industrialists and the planter class. The program, which made the Negro the scapegoat, contained the following provisions: (1) the Negro was completely disfranchised by all sorts of legal subterfuges, with the threat of force in the background; (2) the funds which were appropriated on a per capita basis for Negro school children were diverted to white schools; and (3) a legal system of segregation in all phases of public life was instituted. In order to justify this program, the demagogues, who were supported by the white propertied classes, engaged for twenty-five years in a campaign to prove that the Negro was subhuman, morally degenerate, and intellectually incapable of being educated.[12]

The North acquiesced in this program as a solution of the race problem. The rise to prominence of Booker T. Washington as the leader of the Negroes from 1895 onward was due to his apparent acceptance of racial segregation as a solution of the "Negro problem." Under his leadership, support of so-called "industrial education" for the Negro was provided by northern capitalists. During the quarter of a century from 1890 to 1915, when lynchings and mob violence were used to put the Negro "in his place" in the South, Negroes gave up their hope for freedom and equality in American life. Only a small group of northern Negro intellectuals, led by W. E. Burghardt Dubois and a few northern white "radicals" (on racial issues), attacked the so-called "solution" of the race problem. But more important than the attack of the radicals were changes in race relations which were set in motion by the northward migration of the Negro masses that began in 1915 as a result of the first World War.

But before analyzing the changes which occurred in race relations as the result of the northern migrations, let us consider the nature of the social world of the Negro which emerged as the result of the system of racial segregation.[13] Until the first World War only about a tenth of the Negroes in the United States were in the North, and seven-eighths of those in the North lived in cities. The residents of the relatively small Negro communities in the northern cities gained their livelihood in domestic and personal service. Although they were restricted in their opportunities for employment in industry and white-collar occupations, they did not suffer much discrimination in utilizing public institutions. However, they had their own churches and their social life revolved chiefly about their own clubs and other organizations. In the South, on the other hand, the entire life of the Negro—except for his contacts with whites as a domestic or personal servant, or as a laborer —was restricted to the Negro community. Although this rigid system of racial segregation grew up in a region where, until 1920, more than three-fourths of the Negroes lived on farms and plantations, the "color line" in southern cities was as rigid as in rural areas. In the rural areas the majority of the Negroes worked as sharecroppers under a system closely resembling serfdom, while the majority of those in the cities gained a livelihood as domestic servants and as unskilled laborers. The church was the chief center of the Negro's social life in both the cities and in the rural areas. It provided the chief means for self-expression and leadership and erected a shelter against a hostile white world. In conjunction with the church there were the numerous mutual aid societies and fraternal organizations that offered not only an opportunity for social life, but provided aid in the time of sickness and death.

In this segregated world, especially in cities, a class structure slowly emerged which was based upon social distinctions such as education and conventional behavior, rather than upon occupation and income. At the top of the social pyramid there was a small upper class. The superior status of this class was due chiefly to its differentiation from the great mass of the Negro population because of a family heritage which resulted partly from its mixed ancestry. The family heritage consisted of traditions of civilized behavior and economic efficiency. The members' light skin-color was indicative not only of their white ancestry, but of their descent from the Negroes who were free before the Civil War, or those who had enjoyed the advantages of having served in the houses of their masters. This upper class constantly incorporated those Negroes who were able to acquire an education in the schools supported by northern philanthropy. The members of the upper class depended on a number of skilled occupations for a living, though there was a sprinkling of teachers, doctors, educated ministers, and small businessmen among them.

It was from this isolated social world that thousands of Negroes began migrating to northern industrial centers during the first World War.[14] Although the migrants were attracted to northern cities because of opportunities for employment, the migrations were, in part, a flight from oppression to a Promised Land of freedom and equality. But many of the Negro migrants became disillusioned about the North when, without neighbors and friends, they faced the keen competition and racial discrimination of the cold, impersonal environment of northern cities. In their disillusionment many of them joined the Garvey Movement, the only serious Negro nationalist movement to arise in the United States. According to the leader of this movement, Marcus Garvey, who was a Negro of West Indian origin, the Negro would never achieve equality in America, a white man's country, and therefore the only salvation for the Negro was to return to Africa. Negro intellectuals and the middle-class Negroes generally were hostile to this movement, which gradually dissolved when the leader was sent to the federal penitentiary in Atlanta.[15]

Despite the failure of the Negro to find a Promised Land in the North, the Negro enjoyed certain advantages in the North that changed his outlook on the world as well as his status in American society. In the North the Negro worker gained a foothold for the first time in American industry. Negro children had access for the first time on a large scale to a standard American education, generally in nonsegregated schools. Negroes enjoyed the right to vote and hold office, and as the result of their political power could resist racial discrimination. Through their experience with city life, Negroes acquired a certain sophistication towards the world and tended to redefine their problems in America. They did not seek a solution in a narrow program of racial exclusiveness such as the Garvey Movement. Especially during the Depression years some of them joined the Communist Party, which defined the Negro problem as a problem of "national liberation" from capitalist oppression.[16] The vast majority of Negroes, however, gave up their sentimental allegiance to the Republican Party and supported the Democratic Party and the New Deal Program, which offered concrete economic advantages and a promise of satisfying their aspirations as citizens.

The greater economic and social freedom of the North accelerated the slow occupational differentiation of the Negro population. The rise of the industrial unions (C.I.O.) with their more liberal racial policy helped the integration of Negro workers into industry.[17] But Negroes did not share immediately in the benefits of the economic revival that followed the decision of the United States to become the "arsenal of democracy." It was the result of agitation and the demand for manpower in a war against Nazism with its racial policy, that the Negro began to enjoy some of the fruits of an expanding American economy. Since the second World War, Negroes have continued to receive a larger share of the national income than they did before the War. Moreover, the racial barriers in the North, where nearly a third of the Negroes now live, have tended to be lowered in all phases of public life. Even in the South, the segregation of the Negro has been less rigid in public transportation, and Negro students have been admitted to some of the public universities. As the result of the changes in the economic status of the Negro, the Negro middle class, or the "black bourgeoisie" has grown in size and acquired a dominant position among Negroes. . . .

[The black bourgeoisie]

As the result of the break with its cultural past, the black bourgeoisie is without cultural roots in either the Negro world with which it refuses to identify, or the white world which refuses to permit the black bourgeoisie to share its life. . . . Lacking a cultural tradition and rejecting identification with the Negro masses on the one hand, and suffering from the contempt of the white world on the other, the black bourgeoisie has developed a deepseated inferiority complex. In order to compensate for this feeling of inferiority, the black bourgeoisie has created in its isolation what might be described as a world of make-believe in which it attempts to escape the disdain of whites and fulfill its wish for status in American life. One of the most striking indications of the unreality of the social world which the black bourgeoisie created is its faith in the importance of "Negro business," i.e., the business enterprises owned by Negroes and catering to Negro customers. Although these enterprises have little significance either from the standpoint of the American economy or the economic life of the Negro, a social myth has

been created that they provide a solution to the Negro's economic problems. Faith in this social myth and others is perpetuated by the Negro newspapers, which represent the largest and most successful business enterprises established by Negroes. Moreover, the Negro newspapers help to create and maintain the world of make-believe in which Negroes can realize their desires for recognition and status in a white world that regards them with contempt and amusement. Much of the news featured in the Negro newspapers is concerned with the activities of the members of Negro "society," or it tends to make "socialites" out of most Negroes whose activities are considered newsworthy. "Society" is a phase of the world of make-believe which represents in an acute form the Negro's long preoccupation with "social life" as an escape from his subordinate status in America.

Since the world of make-believe can not insulate the black bourgeoisie completely from the world of reality, the members of this class exhibit considerable confusion and conflict in their personalities. Their emotional and mental conflicts arise partly from their constant striving for status within the Negro world, as well as in the estimation of whites. Moreover, they have accepted unconditionally the values of the white bourgeois world: its morals and its canons of respectability, its standards of beauty and consumption. In fact, they have tended to overemphasize their conformity to white ideals. Nevertheless, they are rejected by the white world, and this rejection has created considerable self-hatred, since it is attributed to their Negro characteristics. At the same time, because of their ambivalence towards Negroes, they are extremely sensitive to slights and discriminations which Negroes suffer. Since they do not truly identify themselves with Negroes, the hollowness of the black bourgeoisie's pretended "racial pride" is revealed in the value which it places upon a white or light complexion. Because of their social isolation and lack of a cultural tradition, the members of the black bourgeoisie in the United States seem to be in the process of becoming NOBODY. What significance, then, does the fate of the black bourgeoisie in the United States have for the bourgeoisie of other racial or cultural minorities that have come into existence as the result of the expansion of western civilization and European capitalism?

Notes

[1] According to the United States Census for 1950, the Negro population numbered 15,026,-675. This figure does not include, of course, an unknown number of Negroes who have "passed" into the white race, or their offspring and descendants who have no knowledge of their Negro ancestry.

[2] J. H. Parry, *Europe and a Wider World, 1415–1745* (London: Hutchinson, 1949).

[3] Eric Williams, *Capitalism and Slavery* (Chapel Hill: University of North Carolina Press, 1944), *passim*.

[4] E. Franklin Frazier, *The Negro in the United States* (New York: Macmillan, 1949), Chapter II, "Evolution of the Slave System."

[5] Frazier, *op. cit.*, Chapter III, "The Plantation as a Social Institution."

[6] See Frazier, *op. cit.*, Chapter I. The position stated here has been challenged by Melville J. Herskovits, *The Myth of the Negro's Past* (New York: Harper, 1942). According to Herskovits, who has made a systematic and comprehensive study of African cultural survivals in the New World, many of the social characteristics of Negroes in the United States are attributable to African survivals. Nevertheless, Herskovits admits that there are fewer of these survivals, that they have become more attenuated, and that they are less easily recognized in the United States than in Brazil and the West Indies.

[7] John H. Russell, *The Free Negro in Virginia: 1619–1865* (Baltimore: Johns Hopkins University Press, 1913), *passim*. On the free Negroes in the South before the Civil War, the following works may be consulted: Carter G. Woodson, *Free Negro Heads of Families in the United States in 1830* (Washington, D.C.: The Association for the Study of Negro Life and History, 1925); John Hope Franklin, *The Free Negro in North Carolina* (Chapel Hill: University of North Carolina Press, 1943); Luther P. Jackson, *Free Negro Labor and Property Holding in Virginia, 1830–1860* (New York: Appleton-Century-Crofts, 1942); Edward R. Turner, *The Negro in Pennsylvania* (Washington, D.C.: American Historical Association, 1911); James M. Wright, *The Free Negro in Maryland, 1634–1860* (New York: Columbia University Press, 1921); Frazier, *op. cit.*, Chapter IV, "The Free Negro."

[8] See Russell, *op. cit.*, and Wright, *op. cit.*

[9] E. Horace Fitchett, "The Traditions of the Free Negroes in Charleston, South Carolina," *Journal of Negro History*, XXV, pp. 139–152.

[10] Louis M. Hacker, *The Triumph of American Capitalism* (New York: Simon and Schuster, 1940).

[11] John Hope Franklin, "Reconstruction," in Richard Leopold and Arthur Link (eds.), *Problems in American History* (New York: Prentice-Hall, 1952). See also W. E. Burghardt DuBois, *Black Reconstruction* (New York: Harcourt, Brace, 1935), and Paul Lewison, *Race, Class and Party* (New York: Oxford University Press, 1932).

[12] Frazier, *op. cit.*, pp. 155–164.

[13] W. E. Burghardt DuBois, "The Negro in the Black Belt: Some Social Sketches," *Bulletin of the [U.S.] Department of Labor*, No. 22, May, 1899. See also the sixteen monographs in the *Atlanta University Studies*, edited by W. E. B. DuBois, on the various aspects of Negro life.

[14] The Chicago Commission on Race Relations, *The Negro in Chicago* (Chicago: University of Chicago Press, 1922). See also, for later developments, St. Clair Drake and Horace R. Cayton, *Black Metropolis* (New York: Harcourt, Brace, 1945).

[15] T. G. Standing, "Nationalism in Negro Leadership," *American Journal of Sociology*, XI, pp. 180–192. See also W. E. B. DuBois, "Marcus Garvey," *The Crisis*, December 1920 and January 1921, and E. Franklin Frazier, "Garvey: A Mass Leader," *The Nation*, August 18, 1926.

[16] See Wilson Record, *The Negro and the Communist Party* (Chapel Hill: University of North Carolina Press, 1951), Chapter III.

[17] See Herbert R. Northrop, *Organized Labor and the Negro* (New York: Harper, 1949); Horace R. Cayton and George R. Mitchell, *Black Workers and the New Unions* (Chapel Hill: University of North Carolina Press, 1939).

Chapter 17

SOCIETY AND ITS INSTITUTIONS

Institutions are the major large-scale components of the social order. In sociology the word refers not to prisons and mental hospitals, which are associations, but to organized ways of filling the needs and accomplishing the goals of individuals and societies. One way of looking at institutions is as organized sets of statuses, just as statuses can be regarded as complexes of norms. In turn, society can be seen as an organization of institutions. Among the most important are the family, the economy, the political system, education, and religion. Materials on the family were presented in Chapter 13 and on education in Selection 19. The selections in this chapter deal with the political, economic, and religious institutions of contemporary society.

The norms and statuses that enter into institutions are said to be "institutionalized." Such norms and statuses are established, or subject to a great amount of agreement on the part of the members of the society. They become a part of tradition, and are thus authoritative. One does not question an institutionalized norm, and sanctions are swift and sure if it is violated. Institutions, similarly, are established. They tend to be more stable than the specific norms and statuses that comprise them. To illustrate, consider that changes in laws are a daily occurrence, at least while legislatures are in session, but changes in forms of government are generally rare and catastrophic events. However, institutions are not completely static; like all social phenomena, they are subject to change. Moreover, although institutional change is generally slow, on occasion it is extremely rapid, in which case we speak of revolution. The term is usually associated with rapid change in the political system, but it is also applied to other fields. For instance, we speak of agricultural, commercial, and industrial revolutions in the economy, as well as of revolutions in education, religion, etc.

In the study of institutions, sociology shares an interest with economics and political science, which are specialized social sciences devoted to the intensive study of particular institutions. If the interest of sociology in institutions can

be differentiated from that of economics and political science, it is in sociology's emphasis on comparative studies. Contemporary economics, for instance,
proceeds from several assumptions concerning the nature of the market, the
goals of buyer and seller, the medium of exchange, etc. Sociologists are often
more concerned with variations in these given conditions—for instance, where
barter rather than money is the basis of exchange or where exchange is between
kinship groups instead of between individuals—and with conditions in other
institutions that are responsible for these variations.

Sociological perspectives on institutions are very hard to formulate, because
the scope of the concept exceeds that of the more precise research tools that
are presently available for the study of society. Thus, the study of institutions
is one of the more speculative areas of sociology, as can be seen in the following selections. Selection 48, John Kenneth Galbraith on the economic system,
Selection 49, C. Wright Mills on the political system, and Selection 50, Will
Herberg on the religious system of the contemporary United States, present
points of view that are controversial because none are supported by a detailed
and unambiguous body of data, and all have important ideological implications. Selection 51, by W. Phillips Davison, is an attempt to deal with one of
the most vexing problems in this field, the relationship between social institutions and the individual members of the society.

THE AMERICAN ECONOMIC SYSTEM

The classical economist's description of the market contained buyers and sellers so numerous that any single individual was powerless to affect the market
price of a commodity by adding or withdrawing his contribution to supply and
demand. This situation of "free competition" once accurately described the
vast bulk of the economic system of the United States, and it has been retained
as a part of American ideology.

However, by requiring large numbers of producers and consumers, the model
of free competition assumes very small units of production and consumption.
In most sectors of American industry this is no longer the case. In 1962, the
500 largest industrial corporations possessed over two-thirds of all the manufacturing assets in the country. In many industries the entire output was a
product of but a few large corporations. The scale of the enterprises and their
entrenched power made it nearly impossible for new corporations to enter the
field, and the model of free competition, according to which the actions of a
single producer or consumer could not affect the market, was rendered invalid.

A long-recognized exception to the model of free competition is monopoly,
in which a single corporation dominates an industry. The monopolist's power
over price is limited only by the relative need of the buyers. The monopolist
uses his "market power" to maximize his profit by keeping the supply of the
commodity small enough that a high price can be obtained, but not allowing
the price to go so high that only a few units are sold.

The general situation in the American economy is not that of monopoly,
but neither is it that of free competition. Rather, the number of buyers and
sellers of most commodities is small enough that each can influence the market
price, but none has complete control. This situation is termed "oligopoly" by
economists. Oligopoly as thus conceived also presents market power, and
many concerned people have suggested that government should try to restore
free competition in industries that have developed oligopoly. In *American Capitalism*, from which this selection is taken, John Kenneth Galbraith holds that
such concern is often unnecessary because market power tends to exist on
both sides of an oligopolistic market, with oligopolistic sellers selling to "oli-
gopsonistic" buyers. In this state, which Galbraith calls countervailing power,

the market advantages of buyer and seller cancel each other out, reducing the negative effects of concentration of power in the economy.

> Market power is curtailed by countervailing power through much of the American economy. Where a market advantage is being gained by a monopoly or oligopoly there is an opportunity for the other side of the economic transaction to exercise countervailing power, and this opportunity is often seized. Labor and retailing are presented as examples of the operation of this principle, whereas the building industry is presented as a negative case.

> Countervailing power on the part of buyers can best occur where demand is not too strong, and it fails to form in inflationary periods. The proper role of government is to aid in the development of countervailing power, in part through the pursuit of anti-inflationary policies.

Galbraith implies that government policy aimed at the creation or restoration of free competition is based on a faulty understanding of markets. Free competition in industries that need enormous assets may be wasteful, whereas countervailing power allows the economies of scale while preventing the exploitation of the consumer.

A major problem in this formulation is the meager specification of conditions under which countervailing power occurs. Galbraith says that inflation must be avoided in general, but he is very sketchy in explaining why some industries lacking strong demand have been unable to develop countervailing power. His example of the building industry, for instance, raises unanswered questions.

Moreover, the conditions under which countervailing power is maintained are not fully specified. Surely, pressure may appear for merger or collusion between the opposing buyers and sellers. May not countervailing power be a stage in the development of large firms that produce, distribute, and sell commodities in an oligopolistic fashion?

Selection 48
FROM AMERICAN CAPITALISM
John Kenneth Galbraith

I

On the night of November 2, 1907, the elder Morgan played solitaire in his library while the panic gripped Wall Street. When the other bankers had divided up the cost of saving the tottering Trust Company of America, he presided at the signing of the agreement, authorized the purchase of the Tennessee Coal & Iron Company by the Steel Corporation to encourage the market, cleared the transaction with President Roosevelt and the panic was over. There, as legend has preserved and

Reprinted from *American Capitalism* by John Kenneth Galbraith (Boston: Houghton Mifflin Company, 1952), with permission of the publisher.

doubtless improved the story, was a man with power a self-respecting man could fear.

A mere two decades later, in the crash of 1929, it was evident that the Wall Street bankers were as helpless as everyone else. Their effort in the autumn of that year to check the collapse in the market is now recalled as an amusing anecdote; the heads of the New York Stock Exchange and the National City Bank fell into the toils of the law and the first went to prison; the son of the Great Morgan went to a Congressional hearing in Washington and acquired fame, not for his authority, but for his embarrassment when a circus midget was placed on his knee.

As the banker, as a symbol of economic

power, passed into the shadows his place was taken by the giant industrial corporation. The substitute was much more plausible. The association of power with the banker had always depended on the somewhat tenuous belief in a "money trust"—on the notion that the means for financing the initiation and expansion of business enterprises was concentrated in the hands of a few men. The ancestry of this idea was in Marx's doctrine of finance capital; it was not susceptible to statistical or other empirical verification at least in the United States.

By contrast, the fact that a substantial proportion of all production was concentrated in the hands of a relatively small number of huge firms was readily verified. That three or four giant firms in an industry might exercise power analogous to that of a monopoly, and not different in consequences, was an idea that had the most respectable of ancestry in classical economics. So as the J. P. Morgan Company left the stage, it was replaced by the two hundred largest corporations—giant devils in company strength. Here was economic power identified by the greatest and most conservative tradition in economic theory. Here was power to control the prices the citizen paid, the wages he received, and which interposed the most formidable of obstacles of size and experience to the aspiring new firm. What more might it accomplish were it to turn its vast resources to corrupting politics and controlling access to public opinion?

Yet, as was so dramatically revealed to be the case with the omnipotence of the banker in 1929, there are considerable gaps between the myth and the fact. The comparative importance of a small number of great corporations in the American economy cannot be denied except by those who have a singular immunity to statistical evidence or striking capacity to manipulate it. In principle the American is controlled, livelihood and soul, by the large corporation; in practice he seems not to be completely enslaved. Once again the danger is in the future; the present is still tolerable. Once again there may be lessons from the present which, if learned, will save us in the future.

II

As with social efficiency, and its neglect of technical dynamics, the paradox of the unexercised power of the large corporation begins with an important oversight in the underlying economic theory. In the competitive model— the economy of many sellers each with a small share of the total market—the restraint on the private exercise of economic power was provided by other firms on the same side of the market. It was the eagerness of competitors to sell, not the complaints of buyers, that saved the latter from spoliation. It was assumed, no doubt accurately, that the nineteenth-century textile manufacturer who overcharged for his product would promptly lose his market to another manufacturer who did not. If all manufacturers found themselves in a position where they could exploit a strong demand, and mark up their prices accordingly, there would soon be an inflow of new competitors. The resulting increase in supply would bring prices and profits back to normal.

As with the seller who was tempted to use his economic power against the customer, so with the buyer who was tempted to use it against his labor or suppliers. The man who paid less than the prevailing wage would lose his labor force to those who paid the worker his full (marginal) contribution to earnings. In all cases the incentive to socially desirable behavior was provided by the competitor. It was to the same side of the market and thus to competition that economists came to look for the self-regulatory mechanism of the economy.

They also came to look to competition exclusively and in formal theory still do. The notion that there might be another regulatory mechanism in the economy has been almost completely excluded from economic thought. Thus, with the widespread disappearance of competition in its classical form and its replacement by the small group of firms if not in overt, at least in conventional or tacit collusion, it was easy to suppose that since competition had disappeared, all effective restraint on private power had disappeared. Indeed this conclusion was all but inevitable if no search was made for other restraints and so complete was the preoccupation with competition that none was made.

In fact, new restraints on private power did appear to replace competition. They were nurtured by the same process of concentration which impaired or destroyed competition. But they appeared not on the same side of the market but on the opposite side, not with competitors but with customers or suppliers. It will be convenient to have a name for this counterpart of competition and I shall call it *countervailing power*.[1]

To begin with a broad and somewhat too dogmatically stated proposition, private economic power is held in check by the countervailing power of those who are subject to it. The first begets the second. The long trend toward concentration of industrial enterprise in the hands of a relatively few firms has brought into existence not only strong sellers, as economists have supposed, but also strong buyers as they have failed to see. The two develop together, not in precise step but in such manner that there can be no doubt that the one is in response to the other.

The fact that a seller enjoys a measure of monopoly power, and is reaping a measure of monopoly return as a result, means that there is an inducement to those firms from whom he buys or those to whom he sells to develop the power with which they can defend themselves against exploitation. It means also that there is a reward to them, in the form of a share of the gains of their opponents' market power, if they are able to do so. In this way the existence of market power creates an incentive to the organization of another position of power that neutralizes it.

The contention I am here making is a formidable one. It comes to this: Competition which, at least since the time of Adam Smith, has been viewed as the autonomous regulator of economic activity and as the only available regulatory mechanism apart from the state, has, in fact, been superseded. Not entirely, to be sure. There are still important markets where the power of the firm as (say) a seller is checked or circumscribed by those who provide a similar or a substitute product or service. This, in the broadest sense that can be meaningful, is the meaning of competition. The role of the buyer on the other side of such markets is essentially a passive one. It consists in looking for, perhaps asking for, and responding to the best bargain. The active restraint is provided by the competitor who offers, or threatens to offer, a better bargain. By contrast, in the typical modern market of few sellers, the active restraint is provided not by competitors but from the other side of the market by strong buyers. Given the convention against price competition, it is the role of the competitor that becomes passive.

It was always one of the basic presupposi-

tions of competition that market power exercised in its absence would invite the competitors who would eliminate such exercise of power. In other words competition was regarded as a *self-generating* regulatory force. The doubt whether this was in fact so after a market had been pre-empted by a few large sellers, after entry of new firms had become difficult and after existing firms had accepted a convention against price competition, was what destroyed the faith in competition as a regulatory mechanism. Countervailing power is also a self-generating force and this is a matter of great importance. Something, although not very much, could be claimed for the regulatory role of the strong buyer in relation to the market power of sellers, did it happen that, as an accident of economic development, such strong buyers were frequently juxtaposed to strong sellers. However it is far more important that, as with the ancient presupposition concerning competition, the regulatory role of the strong buyer, in relation to the market power of the strong seller, is also self-generating. As noted, power on one side of a market creates both the need for, and the prospect of reward to, the exercise of countervailing power from the other side.[2] In the market of small numbers, the self-generating power, by contrast, is readily assimilated to the common sense of the situation and its existence, once we have learned to look for it, is readily subject to empirical verification.

Market power can be exercised by strong buyers against weak sellers as well as by strong sellers against weak buyers. In the competitive model, competition acted as a restraint on both kinds of exercise of power. This is also the case with countervailing power. In turning to its practical manifestations, it will be convenient, in fact, to begin with a case where it is exercised by weak sellers against strong buyers.

III

The operation of countervailing power is to be seen with the greatest clarity in the labor market where it is also most fully developed. Because of his comparative immobility, the worker has long been highly vulnerable to private economic power. The customer of any particular steel mill, at the turn of the century, could always take himself elsewhere if he felt he was being overcharged. Or he could exercise his sovereign privilege of not buying steel at all. The worker had no comparable freedom if he felt he was being underpaid. Normally he could not move and he had to have work. Not often has the power of one man over another been used more callously than in the American labor market after the rise of the large corporation. As late as the early twenties, the steel industry worked a twelve-hour day and seventy-two-hour week with an incredible twenty-four-hour stint every fortnight when the shift was changed.

No such power is exercised today and for the reason that its earlier exercise stimulated the counteraction that brought it to an end. In the ultimate sense it was the power of the steel industry, not the organizing abilities of John L. Lewis and Philip Murray, that brought the United Steel Workers into being. The economic power that the worker faced in the sale of his labor—the competition of many sellers dealing with few buyers—made it necessary that he organize for his own protection. There were rewards to the power of the steel companies in which, when he had successfully developed countervailing power, he could share.

As a general though not invariable rule there are strong unions in the United States only where markets are served by strong corporations. And it is not an accident that the large automobile, steel, electrical, rubber, farm-machinery and non-ferrous metal-mining and smelting companies all bargain with powerful CIO unions. Not only has the strength of the corporations in these industries made it necessary for workers to develop the protection of countervailing power, it has provided unions with the opportunity for getting something more as well. If successful they could share in the fruits of the corporation's market power. By contrast there is not a single union of any consequence in American agriculture, the country's closest approach to the competitive model. The reason lies not in the difficulties in organization; these are considerable, but greater difficulties in organization have been overcome. The reason is that the farmer has not possessed any power over his labor force, and at least until recent times has not had any rewards from market power, which it was worth the while of a union to seek. As an interesting verification of the point, in the Great Valley of California, the large farmers of that area have had considerable power vis-à-vis their labor force. Almost uniquely in the United States, that region has been marked by persistent attempts at organization by farm workers.

The other industries which are not marked by any high degree of concentration, and accordingly are not especially powerful in their labor market, do not normally have strong unions. The textile industry, boot and shoe manufacture, lumbering and other forest industries in most parts of the country, and smaller wholesale and retail enterprises, are all cases in point. I do not advance the theory of countervailing power as a monolithic explanation of trade-union organization; in the case of bituminous-coal mining and the clothing industry, for example, the unions have emerged as a supplement to the weak market position of the operators and manufacturers. They have assumed price- and market-regulating functions that are the normal functions of management. Nevertheless, as an explanation of the incidence of trade-union strength in the American economy, the theory of countervailing power clearly fits the broad contours of experience.

IV

The labor market serves admirably to illustrate the incentives to the development of countervailing power and it is of great importance in this market. However, its development, in response to positions of market power, is pervasive in the economy. As a regulatory device one of its most important manifestations is in the relation of the large retailer to the firms from which it buys. The way in which countervailing power operates in these markets is worth examining in some detail.

One of the seemingly harmless simplifications of formal economic theory has been the assumption that producers of consumers' goods sell their products directly to consumers. All business units are held, for this reason, to have broadly parallel interests. Each buys labor and materials, combines them and passes them along to the public at prices that, in some sense, maximize returns. Were this in fact the case, the lot of the consumer would be an unhappy one.

In practice, goods pass to retailers whose interests, normally,[3] are at sharp variance with those of their suppliers. The typical retailer is deeply concerned with his volume of sales. This is uniquely important for minimizing inventory risk, it is a prime factor in the prestige of the concern, and, of course, it is one of the dimensions of profit. The convention that excludes cutthroat price competition—in the case of retailers the cutting of gross margins—is observed by retailers as by other firms. Nonetheless, lower prices—a low level in general as well as low prices in relation to those of other firms—are regarded by one whole class of retailers as the major device for obtaining and maintaining volume. It is in their interest accordingly to resist any exercise of market power by their suppliers that results in higher prices. More important, any power retailers can exercise to reduce their supplier's prices will redound to their benefit. It will enable them to use price as an inducement without breaking the convention against destructive cutting of their own margins.

Such an opportunity exists only when their suppliers are enjoying the fruits of market power from which they can be separated. Thus, in precise parallel with the labor market, we find the retailer with both a protective and profit incentive to develop countervailing power whenever his supplier is in possession of market power. The practical manifestation of this, over the last half-century, has been the spectacular rise of the food chains, the variety chains, the mail-order houses (now graduated into chain stores), the department-store chains, and the co-operative buying organizations of the surviving independent department and food stores.

This development has been the countervailing response to previously established positions of power. The gains from invading these positions have been considerable. The rubber tire industry is a fairly commonplace example of oligopoly. Four large firms are dominant in the market. In the thirties, Sears, Roebuck & Co. was able, by exploiting its role as a large and indispensable customer, to procure tires from Goodyear Tire & Rubber company at a price from twenty-nine to forty per cent lower than the going market. These it resold to thrifty motorists for from a fifth to a quarter less than the same tires carrying the regular Goodyear brand.

One consequence of the failure of the government to recognize the role of countervailing power is that many hundreds of pages of court records have detailed the exercise of this power by the Great Atlantic & Pacific Tea Company. There is little doubt that this firm has used the countervailing power it has developed with considerable artistry. In 1937, a survey by the company indicated that, for an investment of $175,000, it could supply itself with corn flakes. Assuming that it charged itself the price it then was paying to one of the three companies manufacturing this delicacy, it could earn a modest sixty-eight per cent on the outlay. Armed with this information, and the threat to go into the business which its power could readily make effective, it had no difficulty in bringing down the price by approximately ten per cent.[4] Such gains from the exercise of countervailing power, it will be clear, could only occur where there is an exercise of original market power with which to contend. The A & P could have reaped no comparable gains in buying staple products from the farmer. Committed as he is to the competition of the competitive model, the farmer has no gains to surrender. Provided, as he is, with the opportunity of selling all he produces at the impersonally determined market price, he has not the slightest incentive to make a special price to A & P beyond that which might be associated with the simple economies of bulk sale.

The examples of the exercise of countervailing power by Sears, Roebuck and A & P just cited show how this power is deployed in its most dramatic form. The day-to-day exercise of the buyer's power is a good deal less spectacular but also a good deal more significant. At the end of virtually every channel by which consumers' goods reach the public there is, in practice, a layer of powerful buyers. In the food market there are the great food chains, in clothing there are the department stores, the chain department stores and the department store buying organizations; in appliances there are Sears, Roebuck, and Montgomery Ward and the department stores; these latter firms are also important outlets for furniture and other house furnishings; the drug and cosmetic manufacturer has to seek part of his market through the large drug chains and the department stores; a vast miscellany of consumers' goods pass to the public through Woolworth's, Kresge's and the other variety chains.

In all of these cases buyers deal directly with the manufacturer and there are few of the latter who, in setting prices, do not have to reckon with the attitude and reaction of their powerful customers. The retail buyers have a variety of weapons at their disposal to use against the market power of their suppliers. Their ultimate sanction is to develop their own source of supply as the food chains, Sears, Roebuck, and Montgomery Ward have extensively done. They can also concentrate their entire patronage on a single supplier and, in return for a lower price, give him security in his volume and relieve him of selling and advertising costs.

The more commonplace but more important exercise of countervailing power consists, merely, in keeping the seller in a state of uncertainty as to the intentions of a buyer who is indispensable to him. The larger of the retail buying organizations place orders around which the production schedules and occasionally the investment of even the largest manufacturers become organized. A shift in this custom imposes prompt and heavy loss. The threat or even the fear of this sanction is enough to cause the supplier to surrender some or all of the rewards of his market power. He must, frequently, make a more conditional surrender to less potent buyers if he is not to be more than ever in the power of his large customers. It will be clear that in this operation there are rare opportunities for playing one supplier off against another.

A measure of the importance which large retailing organizations attach to the deployment of their countervailing power is the prestige they accord to their buyers. These men (and women) are the key employees of the modern large retail organization; they are highly paid and they are among the most intelligent and resourceful people to be found anywhere in business. In the everyday course of business, they are considerably better known, both for their capacities and their power, than the salesmen from whom they buy.

There are producers of consumers' goods who have secured themselves from exercise of countervailing power. Some, like the automobile and the oil industry, have done so either by integrating their distribution through to the consumer or because they have an organization of small and dependent and therefore fairly powerless dealers. It seems probable that in a few industries, tobacco manufacture for example, the members are strong enough and have sufficient solidarity to withstand any pressure applied to them even by the most powerful buyer. However, even the tobacco manufacturers, under conditions that were especially favorable to the exercise of countervailing power in the thirties, were forced to make liberal price concessions, in the form of advertising allowances, to the A & P[5] and possibly also to other large customers. When the comprehensive representation of large retailers in the various fields of consumers' goods distribution is considered, it is reasonable to conclude —the reader is warned that this is an important generalization—that most positions of market power in the production of consumers' goods are covered by positions of countervailing power.

Countervailing power also manifests itself, although less visibly, in producers' goods markets. For many years the power of the automobile companies, as purchasers of steel, has sharply curbed the power of the steel mills as sellers. Detroit is the only city where the recently outlawed basing-point system was not used to price steel. Under the basing-point system, all producers regardless of location quoted the same price at any particular point of delivery. This minimized the opportunity of a strong buyer to play one seller off against the other. The large firms in the automobile industry had developed the countervailing power which enabled them to do precisely this. They were not disposed to tolerate any limitations on their exercise of such power. In explaining the quotation of "arbitrary prices" on Detroit steel, a leading student of the basing-point system has recently recognized, implicitly, the role of countervailing power by observing that "it is difficult to apply high cartel prices to particularly large and strong customers such as the automobile manufacturers in Detroit."[6]

The more normal operation of countervailing power in producers' goods markets turns on the relatively small number of customers which firms in these industries typically have. Where the cigarette or soap manufacturer numbers his retail outlets by the hundreds of thousands and his final consumers by the millions, the machinery or equipment manufacturer counts his customers by the hundreds or thousands and, very often, his important ones by the dozen. The latter are important to the seller as individuals and are able to collect the rewards of that importance. As elsewhere, the market pays a premium to those who develop power as buyers that is equivalent to the market power of those from whom they buy. The reverse is true where weak sellers do business with strong buyers.

V

There is an old saying, or should be, that it is a wise economist who recognizes the scope of his own generalizations. While countervailing power is of decisive importance in regulating the exercise of private economic power, it is not universally effective. Some industries, because they are integrated through to the consumer or because their product passes through a dependent dealer organization, have not been faced with countervailing power. As noted, there are a few cases where a very strong market position has proven impregnable even against the attacks of strong buyers. And there are cases where the dangers from countervailing power have, apparently, been recognized and where it has been successfully resisted.

An example of successful resistance to countervailing power is the residential-building industry. No segment of American capitalism evokes less pride. Yet anyone approaching the industry with the preconceptions of competition in mind is unlikely to see, very accurately, the reasons for its shortcomings. There are many thousands of individual firms in the business of building houses. Nearly all are small—the capital of the typical housebuilder runs from a few hundred to a few thousand dollars. The members of the industry oppose little market power to the would-be house owner. Except in times of extremely high building activity there is aggressive competition for business.

The industry does show many detailed manifestations of guild restraint. Builders are frequently in alliance with each other, the unions, and local politicians to protect prices, wages and to maintain established building techniques. These derelictions have been seized upon avidly by the critics of the industry. Since they represent its major departure from the competitive model, they have been assumed to be the cause of the poor performance of the housing industry.

Unhappily, were the restraints on contract prices, materials and techniques in the industry swept away, it seems improbable that the prices of new houses would be much changed and the satisfaction of customers with what they get for what they pay much enhanced. The reason is that the typical builder would still be a small and powerless figure contending with unions that are far stronger than he and buying his building materials in small quantities at high cost from suppliers with effective market power. It is these factors which, very largely, determine the cost of the house.

The builder is kept without power. With few exceptions, the manufacturers of building supplies decline to sell direct to the builder. This prevents any one of the latter from bringing pressure to bear on his source of supply; at the same time it helps keep all builders relatively small and powerless by uniformly denying them the economies of direct purchase. All must pay jobbers' and retailers' margins. A few builders—a spectacular case is Levitt & Sons of Long Island—have managed to circumvent this ban.[7] As the result of more effective buying, a much stronger position in dealing with labor, and the savings from large-scale production of houses, they have notably increased the satisfaction of customers with what they receive for their money. Few can doubt that the future of the industry, if its future is to improve on its past, lies with such firms.

Thus it is the notion of countervailing power, not of competition, which points the way to progress in the housing industry. What is needed is fewer firms of far greater scale with resulting capacity to bring power to bear upon unions and suppliers. It is the absence of such firms, and of the resulting economies, which helps explain why one sector of this industry—low-cost housing where cost is especially important in relation to ability-to-pay—has passed under government management. In the absence of an effective regulating mechanism within the industry in the form of countervailing power, private entrepreneurship has been superseded.

VI

The development of countervailing power requires a certain minimum opportunity and capacity for organization, corporate or otherwise. If the large retail buying organizations had not developed the countervailing power which they have used, by proxy, on behalf of the individual consumer, consumers would have been faced with the need to organize the equivalent of the retailer's power. This would be a formidable task but it has been accomplished in Scandinavia and, in lesser measure, in England where the consumer's co-operative, instead of the chain store, is the dominant instrument of countervailing power in consumers' goods markets.[8] Quite probably there would have been similar organization in the United States. The fact that there are no consumer co-operatives of any importance in the United States is to be explained, not by any inherent incapacity of the American for such organization, but because the chain stores preempted the gains of countervailing power first. The counterpart of the Swedish Kooperativa Forbundet or the British Cooperative Wholesale Societies has not appeared in the United States simply because it could not compete with the A & P and the other large food chains. The meaning of this, which incidentally has been lost on devotees of the theology of cooperation, is that the chain stores are approximately as efficient in the exercise of countervailing power as a co-operative would be. In parts of the American economy where proprietary mass buyers have not made their appearance, notably in the purchase of farm supplies, individuals (who are also individualists) have shown as much capacity to organize as the Scandinavians and the British and have similarly obtained the protection and rewards of countervailing power. The Grange League Federation, the Eastern States Farmers' Exchange and the Illinois Farm Supply Company, co-operatives with annual sales running to multi-million-dollar figures, are among the illustrations of the point.

However, it must not be assumed that it is easy for great numbers of individuals to coalesce and organize countervailing power. In less developed communities, Puerto Rico for example, one finds people fully exposed to the exactions of strategically situated importers, merchants and wholesalers and without the apparent capacity to develop countervailing power in their own behalf. (Anyone, incidentally, who doubts the force of the countervailing power exercised by large retailer-buying organizations would do well to consider the revolution which the entry of the large chain stores would work in an economy like that of Puerto Rico and also how such an intrusion would be resented and perhaps resisted by importers and merchants now able to exercise

their market power with impunity against the thousands of small, independent and inefficient retailers who are their present outlets.)

In light of the difficulty in organizing countervailing power, it is not surprising that the assistance of government has repeatedly been sought in this task. Without the phenomenon itself being fully recognized, the provision of state assistance to the development of countervailing power has been a major function of government—perhaps *the* major domestic function of government. Much of the domestic legislation of the last twenty years, that of the New Deal episode in particular, only becomes fully comprehensible when it is viewed in this light. . . .

VII

I come now to the major limitation on the operation of countervailing power—a matter of much importance in our time. Countervailing power is not exercised uniformly under all conditions of demand. It does not function at all as a restraint on market power when there is inflation or inflationary pressure on markets.

Because the competitive model, in association with Say's Law, was assumed to find its equilibrium at or near full employment levels, economists for a long time were little inclined to inquire whether markets in general, or competition in particular, might behave differently at different levels of economic activity, i.e., whether they might behave differently in prosperity and depression. In any case the conventional division of labor in economics has assigned to one group of scholars the task of examining markets and competitive behavior, to another a consideration of the causes of fluctuations in the economy. The two fields of exploration are even today separated by watertight bulkheads, or, more accurately, by professorial division of labor and course requirements. Those who have taught and written on market behavior have assumed a condition of general stability in the economy in which sellers were eager for buyers. To the extent, as in recent years, that they have had to do their teaching or thinking in a time of inflation—in a time when, as the result of strong demand, eager buyers were besieging reluctant sellers —they have dismissed the circumstance as abnormal. They have drawn their classroom and textbook illustrations from the last period of deflation, severe or mild.

So long as competition was assumed to be the basic regulatory force in the economy these simplifications, although they led to some error, were not too serious. There is a broad continuity in competitive behavior from conditions of weak to conditions of strong demand. At any given moment there is a going price in competitive markets that reflects the current equilibrium of supply-and-demand relationships. Even though demand is strong and prices are high and rising, the seller who prices above the going or equilibrium level is punished by the loss of his customers. The buyer still has an incentive to look for the lowest price he can find. Thus market behavior is not fundamentally different from what it is when demand is low and prices are falling.

There are, by contrast, differences of considerable importance in market behavior between conditions of insufficient and excessive demand when there is oligopoly, i.e., when the market has only a small number of sellers. The convention against price competition, when small numbers of sellers share a market, is obviously not very difficult to maintain if all can sell all they produce and none is subject to the temptation to cut prices. Such a device for maintaining the convention against price competition as the basing-point system only has significance when demand is insufficient in relation to capacity. The basing-point system by making known, or easily calculable, the approved prices at every possible point of delivery in the country provided protection against accidental or surreptitious price-cutting. Such protection is not necessary when there is no temptation to cut prices. By an interesting paradox when the basing-point system was attacked by the government in the late depression years it was of great consequence to the steel, cement and other industries that employed it. When, after the deliberate processes of the law, the system was finally abolished by the courts in April 1948, the consequences for the industries in question were rather slight. The steel and cement companies were then straining to meet demand that was in excess of their capacity. They were under no temptation to cut prices and thus had no *current* reason to regret the passing of the basing-point system.

These differences in market behavior under conditions of strong and of weak demand are important and there are grounds for criticizing their neglect—or rather the assumption that there is normally a shortage of buyers—in the conventional market analysis. However, the effect of changes in demand on market behavior becomes of really profound importance only when the role of countervailing power is recognized. Countervailing power, as a restraint on market power, *only* operates when there is a relative scarcity of demand. Only then is the buyer important to the seller and this is an obvious prerequisite for his bringing his power to bear on the market power of the seller. If buyers are plentiful, that is, if supply is small in relation to current demand, the seller is under no compulsion to surrender to the bargaining power of any customer. The countervailing power of the buyer, however great, disappears with an excess of demand. With it goes the regulatory or restraining role of countervailing power in general. Indeed, the best hope of the buyer, under conditions of excess demand, may be to form a coalition with a seller to bring about an agreed division of returns.[9]

Following the useful practice of testing theory against experience, it is worth noting that it was the twenties and the thirties which were the periods of great growth of chain and group buying enterprises.[10] In sharp contrast with most other types of business, the early depression years especially were favorable to the great chain stores. These were years when demand, generally, fell short of the capacity of suppliers to meet it. Thus they were favorable to the exercise of countervailing power. The intensity of the trade agitation against the mass retailers, culminating in 1936 in the passage of the Robinson-Patman Act (designed as we shall see presently to limit their exercise of this power), was itself a measure of the chain's advantage in this period. By contrast, during the years of strong demand and short supply during World War II, the chain stores lost ground, relatively, to independents. As this strong demand in relation to supply destroyed their capacity to exercise countervailing power, their advantage disappeared. It is interesting to note that the trade agitation and resentment against the chains almost completely disappeared during the war and postwar years.

However, it is again in the labor market where the change in the pattern of exercise of countervailing power that accompanies changes in demand can be seen with greatest clarity. Here also it has the most portentous consequences. In industries where strong firms bargain with strong unions, the management of the former has what has come to be considered a normal resistance to wage increases when demand is not pressing upon capacity. To yield is to increase unit costs. The firm cannot with impunity pass along these higher costs to its customers. There may be a question as to whether other firms in the industry will follow suit; there will always be a question of the effect of the higher prices on sales. If the demand for the products is in any measure elastic the consequence of the higher prices will be a loss of volume. This, with its effect on employment in the industry, is something of which modern union leadership, as well as management, is usually conscious. Thus the trial of strength between union and management associated with collective bargaining is, essentially, over the division of profits. When demand is limited, we have, in other words, an essentially healthy manifestation of countervailing power. The union opposes its power as a seller of labor to that of management as a buyer: At stake is the division of the returns. An occasional strike is an indication that countervailing power is being employed in a sound context where the costs of any wage increase cannot readily be passed along to someone else. It should be an occasion for mild rejoicing in the conservative press. The *Daily Worker*, eagerly contemplating the downfall of capitalism, should regret this manifestation of the system.

Under conditions of strong demand, however, collective bargaining takes on a radically different form. The management is no longer constrained to resist union demands on the grounds that higher prices will be reflected in shrinking volume. There is now an adequate supply of eager buyers. The firm that first surrenders to the union need not worry lest it be either the first or the only one to increase prices. There are buyers for all. No one has

occasion, as the result of price increases, to worry about a general shrinkage in volume. A strong demand means an inelastic demand. On the other hand, there are grave disadvantages for management in resisting the union. Since profits are not at stake, any time lost as the result of a strike is a dead loss. Worker morale and the actual loss of part of the working force to employers who offer better wages must be reckoned with. Thus when demand is sufficiently strong to press upon the capacity of industry generally to supply it, there is no real conflict of interest between union and employer. It is to their mutual advantage to effect a coalition and to pass the costs of their agreement along in higher prices. Other buyers along the line, who under other circumstances might have exercised their countervailing power against the price increases, are similarly inhibited. Thus under inflationary pressure of demand, the whole structure of countervailing power in the economy dissolves.

We have already seen an example of this dissolution of countervailing power in the continuing rounds of wage and price increases following World War II. The full coalition between management and labor, under the conditions of inflationary demand of these years, was partly disguised by the conventional expressions of animosity and by the uncertainty of management as to how long the inflation would last. However, the "Fifth Round" in 1950–51 was negotiated with scarcely an important strike. The President of the United States Steel Corporation, in yielding to the union in November 1950, indicated a *de facto* coalition when he pointed out that the "half-cent" inflation in steel prices, which would be passed along to customers, was a small price to pay for "uninterrupted and expanded" production. The consequences of this failure of countervailing power in times of inflation are considerable. . . .

Notes

[1] I have been tempted to coin a new word for this which would have the same convenience as the term competition and had I done so my choice would have been "countervailance." However, the phrase "countervailing

power" is more descriptive and does not have the raw sound of any newly fabricated word.

[2] This has been one of the reasons I have rejected the terminology of bilateral monopoly in characterizing this phenomenon. As bilateral monopoly is treated in economic literature, it is an adventitious occurrence. This, obviously, missed the point and it is one of the reasons that the

investigations of bilateral monopoly, which one would have thought might have been an avenue to the regulatory mechanisms here isolated, have in fact been a blind alley. However, this line of investigation has also been sterilized by the confining formality of the assumptions of monopolistic and (more rarely) oligopolistic motivation and behavior with which it has been approached. (Cf. for example, William H. Nicholls, *Imperfect Competition within Agricultural Industries,* Ames, Iowa: 1941, pp. 58 ff.) As noted later, oligopoly facilitates the exercise of countervailing market power by enabling the strong buyer to play one seller off against another.

[3] An exception of great importance will be stressed presently.

[4] I am indebted to my friend Professor M. A. Adelman for these details which are from his forthcoming book, on the A & P Case, to be published by the Harvard University Press.

[5] Richard B. Tennant, *The American Cigarette Industry* (New Haven: Yale University Press, 1950), p. 312.

[6] Fritz Machlup, *The Basing Point System* (Philadelphia: Blakiston Co., 1949), p. 115.

[7] Levitt has established a wholly-owned building-supply company to buy materials for its projects. *Fortune,* August 1947, p. 168.

[8] Especially in Scandinavia the co-operative has been explicitly viewed as a device for countering the power of the cartels— i.e., as an instrument for the exercise of countervailing power.

[9] The everyday distinction between a "buyers" and a "sellers" market and the frequency of its use reflect the importance which participants in actual markets attach to the ebb and flow of countervailing power. That this distinction has no standing in formal economics follows from the fact that countervailing power has not been recognized by economists. As frequently happens, practical men have devised a terminology to denote a phenomenon of great significance to themselves but which, since it has not been assimilated to economic theory, has never appeared in the textbooks. The concept of the "break-even point," generally employed by businessmen but largely ignored in economic theory, is another case in point.

[10] See Temporary National Economic Committee, *Large Scale Organization in the Food Industries,* Monograph No. 35 by A. C. Hoffman (Washington: U.S. Government Printing Office), pp. 5 ff.

THE AMERICAN POLITICAL SYSTEM

A number of students of modern industrial societies are worried and pessimistic concerning the possibility of progress toward democratic ideals in these societies. They note that democratic ideology originated in preindustrial societies, including the England of the Puritans and the France of Rousseau, in which the organizational distance between the primary group and the state was very small, and the structure of government was relatively simple. The democratic states of the eighteenth century, most notably the French Republic, were founded on a faith in the intelligence and worth of the common man and on a belief in the possibility of an institutional structure that would allow the common man to apply his common sense to political affairs.

Succeeding events, particularly the demonstrated instability of many democratically instituted states such as the Weimar Republic of Germany, and the involvement of popular governments in two world wars and the current cold war, have strained belief in these eighteenth century principles. The more pessimistic of modern observers point to the difficulty of maintaining popular control in rapidly growing societies with even more rapidly growing governments. They believe furthermore that complex technology may be making common sense obsolete. Some, including C. Wright Mills, posit that a power vacuum has correspondingly opened and that democracy has been bypassed by the entry into this vacuum of a power elite composed of the heads of political, military, and industrial bureaucracies. The view presented in this selection is more fully spelled out in Mills's book *The Power Elite* (1956).

In certain societies, notably the United States and the Soviet Union, the average citizen is politically unconcerned, and power is highly concentrated. Recent history in the United States indicates an increasing centralization of power in economic, political, and military institutions, along with an unprecedented increase in the means of violence available to the holders of power.

Three levels of power are distinguished in American society. At the top is a power elite fusing economic, political, and military institutions and excluding other institutions such as education and religion. This elite is based on psychological and sociological similarity of personnel, interrelations of the institutional hierarchies which they head, and deliberate coordination of activities.

The middle level of power, represented in "politics" and focused in the Congress, is increasingly parochial and stalemated, yielding up important decisions to the power elite. The lower level, the public, no longer influences, but is guided along by the mass media. In sum, the United States now lacks the prerequisites for the democratic state that is envisaged in its ideology.

The implications of Mills's description are ominous, but its validity has been challenged. The chief reply to Mills is that in a society that is admittedly so complex, things can hardly be as simple as he describes them at the top or at any level. However, the evidence on both sides of the question is of necessity sketchy since information concerning levels of power is always difficult to obtain and the secrecy necessitated by the cold war further obscures the facts, although Mills takes this secrecy itself to be evidence for his thesis.

The manifest truth in Mills's thesis, amply supported by empirical research, is that the average American citizen is politically uninterested and is shortsighted concerning events outside his immediate experience. That this situation may lead to a power vacuum appears to be a reasonable assumption, but that the vacuum will be filled by a power elite does not necessarily follow. Moreover, the question of whether a more enlightened government would result from a greater participation of the common man, although answered affirmatively by American ideology, is still empirically an open one.

Selection 49
THE STRUCTURE OF POWER IN AMERICAN SOCIETY
C. Wright Mills

I

Power has to do with whatever decisions men make about the arrangements under which they live, and about the events which make up the history of their times. Events that are beyond human decision do happen; social arrangements do change without benefit of explicit decision. But insofar as such decisions

Reprinted from "The Structure of Power in American Society," by C. Wright Mills, in *The British Journal of Sociology*, Vol. XI, No. 1, March 1958, copyright by Routledge and Kegan Paul Ltd., 1958. Reprinted by permission of Brandt & Brandt.

are made, the problem of who is involved in making them is the basic problem of power. Insofar as they could be made but are not, the problem becomes who fails to make them?

We cannot today merely assume that in the last resort men must always be governed by their own consent. For among the means of power which now prevail is the power to manage and to manipulate the consent of men. That we do not know the limits of such power, and that we hope it does have limits, does not remove the fact that much power today is successfully employed without the sanction of the reason or the conscience of the obedient.

Surely nowadays we need not argue that, in

the last resort, coercion is the "final" form of power. But then, we are by no means constantly at the last resort. Authority (power that is justified by the beliefs of the voluntarily obedient) and manipulation (power that is wielded unbeknown to the powerless)—must also be considered, along with coercion. In fact, the three types must be sorted out whenever we think about power.

In the modern world, we must bear in mind, power is often not so authoritative as it seemed to be in the medieval epoch: ideas which justify rulers no longer seem so necessary to their exercise of power. At least for many of the great decisions of our time—especially those of an international sort—mass "persuasion" has not been "necessary"; the fact is simply accomplished. Furthermore, such ideas as are available to the powerful are often neither taken up nor used by them. Such ideologies usually arise as a response to an effective debunking of power; in the United States such opposition has not been effective enough recently to create the felt need for new ideologies of rule.

There has, in fact, come about a situation in which many who have lost faith in prevailing loyalties have not acquired new ones, and so pay no attention to politics of any kind. They are not radical, not liberal, not conservative, not reactionary. They are inactionary. They are out of it. If we accept the Greek's definition of the idiot as an altogether private man, then we must conclude that many American citizens are now idiots. And I should not be surprised, although I do not know, if there were not some such idiots even in Germany. This—and I use the word with care—this spiritual condition seems to me the key to many modern troubles of political intellectuals, as well as the key to much political bewilderment in modern society. Intellectual "conviction" and moral "belief" are not necessary, in either the rulers or the ruled, for a ruling power to persist and even to flourish. So far as the role of ideologies is concerned, their frequent absences and the prevalence of mass indifference are surely two of the major political facts about the western societies today.

How large a role any explicit decisions do play in the making of history is itself an historical problem. For how large that role may be depends very much upon the means of power that are available at any given time in any given society. In some societies, the innumerable actions of innumerable men modify their milieux, and so gradually modify the structure itself. These modifications—the course of history—go on behind the backs of men. History is drift, although in total "men make it." Thus, innumerable entrepreneurs and innumerable consumers by ten-thousand decisions per minute may shape and re-shape the free-market economy. Perhaps this was the chief kind of limitation Marx had in mind when he wrote, in *The 18th Brumaire*: that "Men make their own history, but they do not make it just as they please; they do not make it under circumstances chosen by themselves. . . ."

But in other societies—certainly in the United States and in the Soviet Union today—a few men may be so placed within the structure that by their decisions they modify the milieux of many other men, and in fact nowadays the structural conditions under which most men live. Such elites of power also make history under circumstances not chosen altogether by themselves, yet compared with other men, and compared with other periods of world history, these circumstances do indeed seem less limiting.

I should contend that "men are free to make history," but that some men are indeed much freer than others. For such freedom requires access to the means of decision and of power by which history can now be made. It has not always been so made; but in the later phases of the modern epoch it is. It is with reference to this epoch that I am contending that if men do not make history, they tend increasingly to become the utensils of history-makers.

The history of modern society may readily be understood as the story of the enlargement and the centralization of the means of power—in economic, in political, and in military institutions. The rise of industrial society has involved these developments in the means of economic production. The rise of the nation-state has involved similar developments in the means of violence and in those of political administration.

In the western societies, such transformations have generally occurred gradually, and many cultural traditions have restrained and shaped them. In most of the Soviet societies, they are happening very rapidly indeed and without the great discourse of western civilization, without the Renaissance and without the Reformation, which so greatly strengthened and gave political focus to the idea of freedom. In those societies, the enlargement and the co-ordination of all the means of power has occurred more brutally, and from the beginning under tightly centralized authority. But in both types, the means of power have now become international in scope and similar in form. To be sure, each of them has its own ups and downs; neither is as yet absolute; how they are run differs quite sharply.

Yet so great is the reach of the means of violence, and so great the economy required to produce and support them, that we have in the immediate past witnessed the consolidation of these two world centres, either of which dwarfs the power of Ancient Rome. As we pay attention to the awesome means of power now available to quite small groups of men we come to realize that Caesar could do less with Rome than Napoleon with France; Napoleon less with France than Lenin with Russia. But what was Caesar's power at its height compared with the power of the changing inner circles of Soviet Russia and the temporary administrations of the United States? We come to realize—indeed they continually remind us—how a few men have access to the means by which in a few days continents can be turned into thermonuclear wastelands. That the facilities of power are so enormously enlarged and so decisively centralized surely means that the powers of quite small groups of men, which we may call elites, are now of literally inhuman consequence.

My concern here is not with the international scene but with the United States in the middle of the twentieth century. I must emphasize "in the middle of the twentieth century" because in our attempt to understand any society we come upon images which have been drawn from its past and which often confuse our attempt to confront its present reality. That is one minor reason why history is the shank of any social science: we must study it if only to rid ourselves of it. In the United States, there are indeed many such images and usually they have to do with the first half of the nineteenth century. At that time the economic facilities of the United States were very widely dispersed and subject to little or to no central authority.

The state watched in the night but was without decisive voice in the day.

One man meant one rifle and the militia were without centralized orders.

Any American as old-fashioned as I can only agree with R. H. Tawney that "Whatever the future may contain, the past has shown no more excellent social order than that in which the mass of the people were the masters of the holdings which they ploughed and the tools with which they worked, and could boast . . . 'It is a quietness to a man's mind to live upon his own and to know his heir certain.'"

But then we must immediately add: all that is of the past and of little relevance to our understanding of the United States today. Within this society three broad levels of power may now be distinguished. I shall begin at the top and move downward.

II

The power to make decisions of national and international consequence is now so clearly seated in political, military, and economic institutions that other areas of society seem off to the side and, on occasion, readily subordinated to these. The scattered institutions of religion, education and family are increasingly shaped by the big three, in which history-making decisions now regularly occur. Behind this fact there is all the push and drive of a fabulous technology; for these three institutional orders have incorporated this technology and now guide it, even as it shapes and paces their development.

As each has assumed its modern shape, its effects upon the other two have become greater, and the traffic between the three has increased. There is no longer, on the one hand, an economy, and, on the other, a political order, containing a military establishment unimportant to politics and to money-making. There is a political economy numerously linked with military order and decision. This triangle of power is now a structural fact, and it is the key to any understanding of the higher circles in America today. For as each of these domains has coincided with the others, as decisions in each have become broader, the leading men of each—the high military, the corporation executives, the political directorate—have tended to come together to form the power elite of America.

The political order, once composed of several dozen states with a weak federal-centre, has become an executive apparatus which has taken up into itself many powers previously scattered, legislative as well as administrative, and which now reaches into all parts of the social structure. The long-time tendency of business and government to become more closely connected has since World War II reached a new point of explicitness. Neither can now be seen clearly as a distinct world. The growth of executive government does not mean merely the "enlargement of government" as some kind of autonomous bureaucracy: under American conditions, it has meant the ascendency of the corporation man into political eminence. Already during the New Deal, such men had joined the political directorate; as of World War II they came to dominate it. Long involved with government, now they have moved into quite full direction of the economy of the war effort and of the post-war era.

The economy, once a great scatter of small productive units in somewhat automatic balance, has become internally dominated by a few hundred corporations, administratively and politically interrelated, which together hold the keys to economic decision. This economy is at once a permanent-war economy and a private-corporation economy. The most important relations of the corporation to the state now rest on the coincidence between military and corporate interests, as defined by the military and the corporate rich, and accepted by politicians and public. Within the elite as a whole, this coincidence of military domain and corporate realm strengthens both of them and further subordinates the merely political man. Not the party politician, but the corporation executive, is now more likely to sit with the military to answer the question: what is to be done?

The military order, once a slim establishment in a context of civilian distrust, has become the largest and most expensive feature of government; behind smiling public relations, it has all the grim and clumsy efficiency of a great and sprawling bureaucracy. The high military have gained decisive political and economic relevance. The seemingly permanent military threat places a premium upon them and virtually all political and economic actions are now judged in terms of military definitions of reality: the higher military have ascended to a firm position within the power elite of our time.

In part at least this is a result of an historical fact, pivotal for the years since 1939: the attention of the elite has shifted from domestic problems—centered in the 'thirties around slump—to international problems—centered in the 'forties and 'fifties around war. By long historical usage, the government of the United States has been shaped by domestic clash and balance; it does not have suitable agencies and traditions for the democratic handling of international affairs. In considerable part, it is in this vacuum that the power elite has grown.

(i) To understand the unity of this power elite, we must pay attention to the psychology of its several members in their respective milieux. Insofar as the power elite is composed of men of similar origin and education, of similar career and style of life, their unity may be said to rest upon the fact that they are of similar social type, and to lead to the fact of their easy intermingling. This kind of unity reaches its frothier apex in the sharing of that prestige which is to be had in the world of the celebrity. It achieves a more solid culmination in the fact of the interchangeability of positions between the three dominant institutional orders. It is revealed by considerable traffic of personnel within and between these three, as well as by the rise of specialized go-betweens as in the new style high-level lobbying.

(ii) Behind such psychological and social unity are the structure and the mechanics of those institutional hierarchies over which the political directorate, the corporate rich, and the high military now preside. How each of these hierarchies is shaped and what relations it has with the others determine in large part the relations of their rulers. Were these hierarchies scattered and disjointed, then their respective elites might tend to be scattered and disjointed; but if they have many interconnections and points of coinciding interest, then their elites tend to form a coherent kind of grouping. The unity of the elite is not a simple reflection of the unity of institutions, but men and institutions are always related; that is why we must understand the elite today in connection with such institutional trends as the development of a permanent-war establishment, alongside a privately incorporated economy, inside a virtual political vacuum. For the men at the top have been selected and formed by such institutional trends.

(iii) Their unity, however, does not rest solely upon psychological similarity and social intermingling, nor entirely upon the structural blending of commanding positions and common interests. At times it is the unity of a more explicit co-ordination.

To say that these higher circles are increasingly co-ordinated, that this is *one* basis of their unity, and that at times—as during open war—such co-ordination is quite wilful, is not to say that the co-ordination is total or continuous, or even that it is very surefooted. Much less is it to say that the power elite has emerged as the realization of a plot. Its rise cannot be adequately explained in any psychological terms.

Yet we must remember that institutional trends may be defined as opportunities by those who occupy the command posts. Once such opportunities are recognized, men may avail themselves of them. Certain types of men from each of these three areas, more farsighted than others, have actively promoted the liaison even before it took its truly modern shape. Now more have come to see that their several interests can more easily be realized if they work together, in informal as well as in formal ways, and accordingly they have done so.

The idea of the power elite is of course an interpretation. It rests upon and it enables us to make sense of major institutional trends, the social similarities and psychological affinities of the men at the top. But the idea is also based upon what has been happening on the middle and lower levels of power, to which I now turn.

III

There are of course other interpretations of the American system of power. The most usual is that it is a moving balance of many competing interests. The image of balance, at least in America, is derived from the idea of the economic market: in the nineteenth century, the balance was thought to occur between a great scatter of individuals and enterprises; in the twentieth century, it is thought to occur between great interest blocs. In both views, the politician is the key man of power because he is the broker of many conflicting powers.

I believe that the balance and the compromise in American society—the "countervailing powers" and the "veto groups," of parties and associations, of strata and unions—must now be seen as having mainly to do with the middle levels of power. It is these middle levels

that the political journalist and the scholar of politics are most likely to understand and to write about—if only because, being mainly middle class themselves, they are closer to them. Moreover these levels provide the noisy content of most "political" news and gossip; the images of these levels are more or less in accord with the folklore of how democracy works; and, if the master-image of balance is accepted, many intellectuals, especially in their current patrioteering, are readily able to satisfy such political optimism as they wish to feel. Accordingly, liberal interpretations of what is happening in the United States are now virtually the only interpretations that are widely distributed.

But to believe that the power system reflects a balancing society is, I think, to confuse the present era with earlier times, and to confuse its top and bottom with its middle levels.

By the top levels, as distinguished from the middle, I intend to refer, first of all, to the scope of the decisions that are made. At the top today, these decisions have to do with all the issues of war and peace. They have also to do with slump and poverty which are now so very much problems of international scope. I intend also to refer to whether or not the groups that struggle politically have a chance to gain the positions from which such top decisions are made, and indeed whether their members do usually hope for such top national command. Most of the competing interests which make up the clang and clash of American politics are strictly concerned with their slice of the existing pie. Labour unions, for example, certainly have no policies of an international sort other than those which given unions adopt for the strict economic protection of their members. Neither do farm organizations. The actions of such middle-level powers may indeed have consequence for top-level policy; certainly at times they hamper these policies. But they are not truly concerned with them, which means of course that their influence tends to be quite irresponsible.

The facts of the middle levels may in part be understood in terms of the rise of the power elite. The expanded and centralized and interlocked hierarchies over which the power elite preside have encroached upon the old balance and relegated it to the middle level. But there are also independent developments of the middle levels. These, it seems to me, are better understood as an affair of intrenched and provincial demands than as a centre of national decision. As such, the middle level often seems much more of a stalemate than a moving balance.

(i) The middle level of politics is not a forum in which there are debated the big decisions of national and international life. Such debate is not carried on by nationally responsible parties representing and clarifying alternative policies. There are no such parties in the United States. More and more, fundamental issues never come to any point or decision before the Congress, much less before the electorate in party campaigns. In the case of Formosa, in the spring of 1955, the Congress abdicated all debate concerning events and decisions which surely bordered on war. The same is largely true of the 1957 crisis in the Middle East. Such decisions now regularly by-pass the Congress, and are never clearly focused issues for public decision.

The American political campaign distracts attention from national and international issues, but that is not to say that there are no issues in these campaigns. In each district and state, issues are set up and watched by organized interests of sovereign local importance. The professional politician is of course a party politician, and the two parties are semi-feudal organizations: they trade patronage and other favours for votes and for protection. The differences between them, so far as national issues are concerned, are very narrow and very mixed up. Often each seems to be forty-eight parties, one to each state; and accordingly, the politician as campaigner and as Congressman is not concerned with national party lines, if any are discernible. Often he is not subject to any effective national party discipline. He speaks for the interests of his own constituency, and he is concerned with national issues only insofar as they affect the interests effectively organized there, and hence his chances of re-election. That is why, when he does speak of national matters, the result is so often such an empty rhetoric. Seated in his sovereign locality, the politician is not at the national summit. He is on and of the middle levels of power.

(ii) Politics is not an arena in which free and independent organizations truly connect the lower and middle levels of society with the top levels of decision. Such organizations are not an effective and major part of American life today. As more people are drawn into the political arena, their associations become mass in scale, and the power of the individual becomes dependent upon them; to the extent that they are effective, they have become larger, and to that extent they have become less accessible to the influence of the individual. This is a central fact about associations in any mass society: it is of most consequence for political parties and for trade unions.

In the 'thirties, it often seemed that labour would become an insurgent power independent of corporation and state. Organized labour was then emerging for the first time on an American scale, and the only political sense of direction it needed was the slogan, "organize the unorganized." Now without the mandate of the slump, labour remains without political direction. Instead of economic and political struggles it has become deeply entangled in administrative routines with both corporation and state. One of its major functions, as a vested interest of the new society, is the regulation of such irregular tendencies as may occur among the rank and file.

There is nothing, it seems to me, in the make-up of the current labour leadership to allow us to expect that it can or that it will lead, rather than merely react. Insofar as it fights at all it fights over a share of the goods of a single way of life and not over that way of life itself. The typical labour leader in the U.S.A. today is better understood as an adaptive creature of the main business drift than as an independent actor in a truly national context.

(iii) The idea that this society is a balance of powers requires us to assume that the units in balance are of more or less equal power and that they are truly independent of one another. These assumptions have rested, it seems clear, upon the historical importance of a large and independent middle class. In the later nineteenth century and during the Progressive Era, such a class of farmers and small businessmen fought politically—and lost—their last struggle for a paramount role in national decision. Even then, their aspirations seemed bound to their own imagined past.

This old, independent middle class has of course declined. On the most generous count, it is now 40 per cent of the total middle class (at most 20 per cent of the total labour force).

Moreover, it has become politically as well as economically dependent upon the state, most notably in the case of the subsidized farmer.

The *new* middle class of white-collar employees is certainly not the political pivot of any balancing society. It is in no way politically unified. Its unions, such as they are, often serve merely to incorporate it as hanger-on of the labour interest. For a considerable period, the old middle class *was* an independent base of power; the new middle class cannot be. Political freedom and economic security *were* anchored in small and independent properties; they are not anchored in the worlds of the white-collar job. Scattered property holders were economically united by more or less free markets; the jobs of the new middle class are integrated by corporate authority. Economically, the white-collar classes are in the same condition as wage workers; politically, they are in a worse condition, for they are not organized. They are no vanguard of historic change; they are at best a rearguard of the welfare state.

The agrarian revolt of the 'nineties, the small-business revolt that has been more or less continuous since the 'eighties, the labour revolt of the 'thirties—each of these has failed as an independent movement which could countervail against the powers that be; they have failed as politically autonomous third parties. But they have succeeded, in varying degree, as interests vested in the expanded corporation and state; they have succeeded as parochial interests seated in particular districts, in local divisions of the two parties, and in the Congress. What they would become, in short, are well-established features of the *middle* levels of balancing power, on which we may now observe all those strata and interests which in the course of American history have been defeated in their bids for top power or which have never made such bids.

Fifty years ago many observers thought of the American state as a mask behind which an invisible government operated. But nowadays, much of what was called the old lobby, visible or invisible, is part of the quite visible government. The "governmentalization of the lobby" has proceeded in both the legislative and the executive domain, as well as between them. The executive bureaucracy becomes not only the centre of decision but also the arena within which major conflicts of power are resolved or denied resolution. "Administration" replaces electoral politics; the manœuvring of cliques (which include leading Senators as well as civil servants) replaces the open clash of parties.

The shift of corporation men into the political directorate has accelerated the decline of the politicians in the Congress to the middle levels of power; the formation of the power elite rests in part upon this relegation. It rests also upon the semi-organized stalemate of the interests of sovereign localities, into which the legislative function has so largely fallen; upon the virtually complete absence of a civil service that is a politically neutral but politically relevant depository of brain-power and executive skill; and it rests upon the increased official secrecy behind which great decisions are made without benefit of public or even of Congressional debate.

IV

There is one last belief upon which liberal observers everywhere base their interpretations and rest their hopes. That is the idea of the public and the associated idea of public opinion. Conservative thinkers, since the French Revolution, have of course Viewed With Alarm the rise of the public, which they have usually called the masses, or something to that effect. "The populace is sovereign," wrote Gustave Le Bon, "and the tide of barbarism mounts." But surely those who have supposed the masses to be well on their way to triumph are mistaken. In our time, the influence of publics or of masses within political life is in fact decreasing, and such influence as on occasion they do have tends, to an unknown but increasing degree, to be guided by the means of mass communication.

In a society of publics, discussion is the ascendant means of communication, and the mass media, if they exist, simply enlarge and animate this discussion, linking one face-to-face public with the discussions of another. In a mass society, the dominant type of communication is the formal media, and publics become mere markets for these media: the "public" of a radio programme consists of all those exposed to it. When we try to look upon the United States today as a society of publics, we realize that it has moved a considerable distance along the road to the mass society.

In official circles, the very term, "the public," has come to have a phantom meaning, which dramatically reveals its eclipse. The deciding elite can identify some of those who clamour publicly as "Labour," others as "Business," still others as "Farmer." But these are not the public. "The public" consists of the unidentified and the non-partisan in a world of defined and partisan interests. In this faint echo of the classic notion, the public is composed of these remnants of the old and new middle classes whose interests are not explicitly defined, organized, or clamorous. In a curious adaptation, "The public" often becomes, in administrative fact, "the disengaged expert," who, although ever so well informed, has never taken a clear-cut and public stand on controversial issues. He is the "public" member of the board, the commission, the committee. What "the public" stands for, accordingly, is often a vagueness of policy (called "openmindedness"), a lack of involvement in public affairs (known as "reasonableness"), and a professional disinterest (known as "tolerance").

All this is indeed far removed from the eighteenth-century idea of the public of public opinion. That idea parallels the economic idea of the magical market. Here is the market composed of freely competing entrepreneurs; there is the public composed of circles of people in discussion. As price is the result of anonymous, equally weighted, bargaining individuals, so public opinion is the result of each man's having thought things out for himself and then contributing his voice to the great chorus. To be sure, some may have more influence on the state of opinion than others, but no one group monopolizes the discussion, or by itself determines the opinions that prevail.

In this classic image, the people are presented with problems. They discuss them. They formulate viewpoints. These viewpoints are organized, and they compete. One viewpoint "wins out." Then the people act on this view, or their representatives are instructed to act it out, and this they promptly do.

Such are the images of democracy which are still used as working justifications of power in America. We must now recognize this description as more a fairy tale than a useful approximation. The issues that now shape man's fate are neither raised nor decided by any public at large. The idea of a society that is at bottom composed of publics is not a matter of fact; it is the proclamation of an ideal, and as well the assertion of a legitimation masquerading as fact.

I cannot here describe the several great forces within American society as well as elsewhere which have been at work in the debilitation of the public. I want only to remind you that publics, like free associations, can be deliberately and suddenly smashed, or they can more slowly wither away. But whether smashed in a week or withered in a generation, the demise of the public must be seen in connection with the rise of centralized organizations, with all their new means of power, including those of the mass media of distraction. These, we now know, often seem to expropriate the rationality and the will of the terrorized or—as the case may be—the voluntarily indifferent society of masses. In the more democratic process of indifference the remnants of such publics as remain may only occasionally be intimidated by fanatics in search of "disloyalty." But regardless of that, they lose their will for decision because they do not possess the instruments for decision; they lose their sense of political belonging because they do not belong; they lose their political will because they see no way to realize it.

The political structure of a modern democratic state requires that such a public as is projected by democratic theorists not only exist but that it be the very forum within which a politics of real issues is enacted.

It requires a civil service that is firmly linked with the world of knowledge and sensibility, and which is composed of skilled men who, in their careers and in their aspirations, are truly independent of any private, which is to say, corporation, interests.

It requires nationally responsible parties which debate openly and clearly the issues which the nation, and indeed the world, now so rigidly confronts.

It requires an intelligentsia, inside as well as outside the universities, who carry on the big discourse of the western world, and whose work is relevant to and influential among parties and movements and publics.

And it certainly requires, as a fact of power, that there be free associations standing between families and smaller communities and publics, on the one hand, and the state, the military, the corporation, on the other. For unless these do exist, there are no vehicles for reasoned opinion, no instruments for the rational exertion of public will.

Such democratic formations are not now ascendant in the power structure of the United States, and accordingly the men of decision are not men selected and formed by careers within such associations and by their performance before such publics. The top of modern American society is increasingly unified, and often seems wilfully co-ordinated: at the top there has emerged an elite whose power probably exceeds that of any small group of men in world history. The middle levels are often a drifting set of stalemated forces: the middle does not link the bottom with the top. The bottom of this society is politically fragmented, and even as a passive fact, increasingly powerless; at the bottom there is emerging a mass society.

These developments, I believe, can be correctly understood neither in terms of the lib-eral nor the marxian interpretation of politics and history. Both of these ways of thought arose as guidelines to reflection about a type of society which does not now exist in the United States. We confront there a new kind of social structure, which embodies elements and tendencies of all modern society, but in which they have assumed a more naked and flamboyant prominence.

That does not mean that we must give up the ideals of these classic political expectations. I believe that both have been concerned with the problem of rationality and of freedom: liberalism, with freedom and rationality as supreme facts about the individual; marxism, as supreme facts about man's role in the political making of history. What I have said here, I suppose, may be taken as an attempt to make evident why the ideas of freedom and of rationality now so often seem so ambiguous in the new society of the United States of America.

AMERICAN RELIGION

The paradox to which this selection is addressed is that in symbols Americans are a highly religious people, but in attitudes they are not. Ours is a secular society, yet one in which religious participation as measured by church affiliation, attendance, contributions, and buildings is remarkably high and is growing. At the beginning of the nineteenth century, no more than a fifth of Americans were church members. By 1958, 63 per cent were listed on church rolls, and even more thought of themselves as church members although their names were not inscribed in the membership lists. In striking contrast is the fact that business and politics remain the central concern of Americans, and people do not see that religious principles are relevant to these aspects of their lives. This selection presents one attempt to come to terms with these disparate facts.

Americans believe in God, regard themselves as church members, adhere to orthodox beliefs and perform orthodox duties. They have a high respect for religion and for ministers. Nonetheless, religion remains peripheral to the main concerns of modern society, business and politics.

More relevant to the central concerns of Americans is a body of beliefs that can be labeled the American Way of Life, a kind of all-embracing faith that spans the three religious communities of Catholicism, Protestantism, and Judaism. Important themes in this body of beliefs are the Constitution, free enterprise, equalitarianism, and idealism. (Note the parallel with the principal themes in American culture described in Selection 15.)

The American Way of Life is intertwined with formal religion. It reflects the beliefs of dissenting Protestantism with which many of the early settlers were imbued, and in turn it has secularized and Americanized the traditional religions as they have developed on these shores. For example, American counterparts of European religion are likely to disparage theology and ritual and to stress social activism to a greater degree than these same religions in their original settings.

The sociology of religion has traditionally thought in terms of either established and institutionalized churches or dissident, charismatic sects. The American experience fits neither of these models. American religions, whether they originate in churches or sects, tend to a different model, that of the denomination, which is stable, settled, recognized, but tolerant and pluralist.

If the American Way of Life is a type of superfaith embracing all Americans, why is it not adequate in itself? Why do Americans persist in adhering to denominations that are less relevant to their main concerns? Herberg's answer to this question is that religious faith in the form of participation in a denomination of some kind is one of the duties prescribed by the superfaith. To lack religion, at least in the form of identifying with one of the three great religious communities, is felt to be un-American. A distinctive and peculiar characteristic of American society is the moral obligation in the larger sense to have faith in the narrower sense of a minimal participation in orthodox religion.

Other explanations can and have been offered of the tendency of Americans to identify with and to join religious denominations. Perhaps the most important recognizes that the American church is multifunctional. In a society where geographical mobility is common (a fifth of all families move during any given year), the role of religious organizations in matters like education, welfare, and sociability ought not to be ignored.

Selection 50
FROM PROTESTANT, CATHOLIC, JEW
Will Herberg

I

What do Americans believe? Most emphatically, they "believe in God": 97 per cent according to one survey, 96 per cent according to another, 95 per cent according to a third.[1] About 75 per cent of them, as we have seen, regard themselves as members of churches, and a sizable proportion attend divine services with some frequency and regularity.[2] They believe in prayer: about 90 per cent say they pray on various occasions.[3] They believe in life after death, even in heaven and hell.[4] They think well of the church and of ministers.[5] They hold the Bible to be an inspired book, the "word of God."[6] By a large majority, they think children should be given religious instruction and raised as church members.[7] By a large majority, too, they hold religion to be of very great importance.[8] In all of these respects their attitudes are as religious

as those of any people today, or, for that matter, as those of any Western people in recent history.

Yet these indications are after all relatively superficial; they tell us what Americans say (and no doubt believe) about themselves and their religious views; they do not tell us what in actuality these religious views are. Nowhere are surface appearances more deceptive, nowhere is it more necessary to try to penetrate beyond mere assertions of belief than in such ultimate matters as religion.

We do penetrate a little deeper, it would seem, when we take note of certain curious discrepancies the surveys reveal in the responses people make to questions about their religion. Thus, according to one trustworthy source, 73 per cent said they believed in an afterlife, with God as judge, but "only 5 per cent [had] any fear, not to say expectation, of going [to hell]."[9] Indeed, about 80 per cent, according to another source, admitted that what they were "most serious about" was not the life after death in which they said they believed, but in trying to live as comfortably in this life as possible.[10] And in their opinion they were not doing so badly even from the point of view of the divine judgment: 91 per cent felt that they could honestly say that they were trying to lead a good life, and 78 per cent felt no hesitation in saying that they more than half measured up to their own standards of goodness, over 50 per cent asserting that they were in fact following the rule of loving one's neighbor as oneself "all the way"![11] This amazingly high valuation that most Americans appear to place on their own virtue would seem to offer a better insight into the basic religion of the American people than any figures as to their formal beliefs can provide, however important in themselves these figures may be.

But perhaps the most significant discrepancy in the assertions Americans make about their religious views is to be found in another area. When asked, "Would you say your religious beliefs have any effect on your ideas of politics and business?", a majority of the same Americans who had testified that they regarded religion as something "very important" answered that their religious beliefs had no real effect on their ideas or conduct in these decisive areas of everyday life; specifically, 54 per cent said no, 39 per cent said yes, and 7 per cent refused to reply or didn't know.[12] This disconcerting confession of the irrelevance of religion to business and politics was attributed by those who appraised the results of the survey as pointing to a calamitous divorce between the "private" and the "public" realms in the religious thinking of Americans.[13] There is certainly a great deal of truth in this opinion, and we shall have occasion to explore it in a different context, but in the present connection it would seem that another aspect of the matter is more immediately pertinent. *Some* ideas and standards undeniably govern the conduct of Americans in their affairs of business and politics; if they are not ideas and standards associated with the teachings of religion, what are they? It will not do to say that people just act "selfishly" without reference to moral standards of any kind. All people act "selfishly," of course; but it is no less true of all people, Americans included, that their "selfishness" is controlled, mitigated, or, at worst, justified by some sort of moral commitment, by some sort of belief in a system of values beyond immediate self-interest. The fact that more than half the people openly admit that their religious

beliefs have no effect on their ideas of politics and business would seem to indicate very strongly that, over and above conventional religion, there is to be found among Americans some sort of faith or belief or set of convictions, not generally designated as religion but definitely operative as such in their lives in the sense of providing them with some fundamental context of normativity and meaning. What this unacknowledged "religion" of the American people is, and how it manages to coexist with their formal religious affirmations and affiliations, it is now our task to investigate.

II

"Every functioning society," Robin M. Williams, Jr. points out, "has to an important degree a *common* religion. The possession of a common set of ideas, rituals, and symbols can supply an overarching sense of unity even in a society riddled with conflicts."[14] What is this "common religion" of American society, the "common set of ideas, rituals, and symbols" that give it its "overarching sense of unity"? Williams provides us with a further clue when he suggests that "men are always likely to be intolerant of opposition to their central ultimate values."[15] What are these "central ultimate values" about which Americans are "intolerant"? No one who knows anything about the religious situation in this country would be likely to suggest that the things Americans are "intolerant" about are the beliefs, standards, or teachings of the religions they "officially" acknowledge as theirs. Americans are proud of their tolerance in matters of religion: one is expected to "believe in God," but otherwise religion is not supposed to be a ground of "discrimination." This is, no doubt, admirable, but is it not "at least in part, a sign that the crucial values of the system are no longer couched in a religious framework"?[16]

What, then, is the "framework" in which they *are* couched? What, to return to our original question, is the "common religion" of the American people, as it may be inferred not only from their words but also from their behavior?

It seems to me that a realistic appraisal of the values, ideas, and behavior of the American people leads to the conclusion that Americans, by and large, do have their "common religion" and that that "religion" is the system familiarly known as the American Way of Life. It is the American Way of Life that supplies American society with an "overarching sense of unity" amid conflict. It is the American Way of Life about which Americans are admittedly and unashamedly "intolerant." It is the American Way of Life that provides the framework in terms of which the crucial values of American existence are couched. By every realistic criterion the American Way of Life is the operative faith of the American people.

It would be the crudest kind of misunderstanding to dismiss the American Way of Life as no more than a political formula or propagandist slogan, or to regard it as simply an expression of the "materialistic" impulses of the American people. Americans are "materialistic," no doubt, but surely not more so than other people, than the French peasant or petty bourgeois, for example. All such labels are irrelevant, if not meaningless. The American Way of Life is, at bottom, a spiritual structure, a structure of ideas and ideals, of aspirations and values, of beliefs and standards; it synthesizes all that commends itself to the American as the right, the good, and the true in actual life. It embraces such seemingly incongruous elements as sanitary plumbing and freedom of opportunity, Coca-Cola and an intense faith in education—all felt as moral questions relating to the proper way of life.[17] The very expression "way of life" points to its religious essence, for one's ultimate, over-all way of life is one's religion.

The American Way of Life is, of course, conceived as the corporate "way" of the American people, but it has its implications for the American as an individual as well. It is something really operative in his actual life. When in the *Ladies' Home Journal* poll, Americans were asked "to look within [themselves] and state honestly whether [they] thought [they] really obeyed the law of love under certain special conditions," 90 per cent said yes and 5 per cent no when the one to be "loved" was a person belonging to a different religion; 80 per cent said yes and 12 per cent no when it was the case of a member of a different race; 78 per cent said yes and 10 per cent no when it concerned a business competitor—but only 27 per cent said yes and 57 per cent no in the case of "a member of a political party that you think is dangerous," while 25 per cent said yes and 63 per cent said no when it concerned an enemy of the nation.[18] These figures

are most illuminating, first because of the incredible self-assurance they reveal with which the average American believes he fulfills the "impossible" law of love, but also because of the light they cast on the differential impact of the violation of this law on the American conscience. For it is obvious that the figures reflect not so much the actual behavior of the American people—no people on earth ever loved their neighbors as themselves as much as the American people say they do—as how seriously Americans take transgressions against the law of love in various cases. Americans feel they *ought* to love their fellow men despite differences of race or creed or business interest; that is what the American Way of Life emphatically prescribes.[19] But the American Way of Life almost explicitly sanctions hating a member of a "dangerous" political party (Communists and fascists are obviously meant here) or an enemy of one's country, and therefore an overwhelming majority avow their hate. In both situations, while the Jewish-Christian law of love is formally acknowledged, the truly operative factor is the value system embodied in the American Way of Life. Where the American Way of Life approves of love of one's fellow man, most Americans confidently assert that they practice such love; where the American Way of Life disapproves, the great mass of Americans do not hesitate to confess that they do not practice it, and apparently feel very little guilt for their failure. No better pragmatic test as to what the operative religion of the American people actually is could be desired.[20]

It is not suggested here that the ideals Americans feel to be indicated in the American Way of Life are scrupulously observed in the practice of Americans; they are in fact constantly violated, often grossly. But violated or not, they are felt to be normative and relevant to "business and politics" in a way that the formal tenets of "official" religion are not. That is what makes the American Way of Life the "common religion" of American society in the sense here intended.

It should be clear that what is being designated under the American Way of Life is not the so-called "common denominator" religion; it is not a synthetic system composed of beliefs to be found in all or in a group of religions. It is an organic structure of ideas, values, and beliefs that constitutes a faith common to Americans and genuinely operative in their lives, a faith that markedly influences, and is influenced by, the "official" religions of American society. Sociologically, anthropologically, if one pleases, it is the characteristic American religion, undergirding American life and overarching American society despite all indubitable differences of region, section, culture, and class.

Yet qualifications are immediately in order. Not for all Americans is this American religion, this "common religion" of American society, equally operative; some indeed explicitly repudiate it as religion. By and large, it would seem that what is resistive in contemporary American society to the American Way of Life as religion may be understood under three heads. First, there are the churches of immigrant-ethnic background that still cherish their traditional creeds and confessions as a sign of their distinctive origin and are unwilling to let these be dissolved into an over-all "American religion"; certain Lutheran and Reformed churches in this country[21] as well as sections of the Catholic Church would fall into this classification. Then there are groups, not large but increasing, that have an explicit and conscious theological concern, whether it be "orthodox," "neo-orthodox," or "liberal"; in varying degrees, they find their theologies at odds with the implied "theology" of the American Way of Life. Finally, there are the ill-defined, though by all accounts numerous and influential, "religions of the disinherited," the many "holiness," pentecostal, and millenarian sects of the socially and culturally submerged segments of our society;[22] for them, their "peculiar" religion is frequently still too vital and all-absorbing to be easily subordinated to some "common faith." All of these cases, it will be noted, constitute "hold outs" against the sweep of religious Americanism; in each case there is an element of alienation which generates a certain amount of tension in social life.

What is this American Way of Life that we have said constitutes the "common religion" of American society? An adequate description and analysis of what is implied in this phrase still remains to be attempted, and certainly it will not be ventured here; but some indications may not be out of place.

The American Way of Life is the symbol by which Americans define themselves and establish their unity. German unity, it would seem, is felt to be largely racial-folkish, French unity largely cultural; but neither of these ways is open to the American people, the most diverse in racial and cultural origins of any in the world. As American unity has emerged, it has emerged more and more clearly as a unity embodied in, and symbolized by, the complex structure known as the American Way of Life.

If the American Way of Life had to be defined in one word, "democracy" would undoubtedly be the word, but democracy in a peculiarly American sense. On its political side it means the Constitution; on its economic side, "free enterprise"; on its social side, an equalitarianism which is not only compatible with but indeed actually implies vigorous economic competition and high mobility. Spiritually, the American Way of Life is best expressed in a certain kind of "idealism" which has come to be recognized as characteristically American. It is a faith that has its symbols and its rituals, its holidays and its liturgy, its saints and its sancta;[23] and it is a faith that every American, to the degree that he is an American, knows and understands.

The American Way of Life is individualistic, dynamic, pragmatic. It affirms the supreme value and dignity of the individual; it stresses incessant activity on his part, for he is never to rest but is always to be striving to "get ahead"; it defines an ethic of self-reliance, merit, and character, and judges by achievement: "deeds, not creeds" are what count. The American Way of Life is humanitarian, "forward looking," optimistic. Americans are easily the most generous and philanthropic people in the world, in terms of their ready and unstinting response to suffering anywhere on the globe. The American believes in progress, in self-improvement, and quite fanatically in education. But above all, the American is idealistic. Americans cannot go on making money or achieving worldly success simply on its own merits; such "materialistic" things must, in the American mind, be justified in "higher" terms, in terms of "service" or "stewardship" or "general welfare." Because Americans are so idealistic, they tend to confuse espousing an ideal with fulfilling it and are always tempted to regard themselves as good as the ideals they entertain: hence the amazingly high valuation most Americans quite sincerely place on their own virtue. And because they are so idealistic, Americans tend to be moralistic: they are inclined to see all issues as plain and simple, black and white, issues of morality. Every struggle in which they are seriously engaged becomes a "crusade." To Mr. Eisenhower, who in many ways exemplifies American religion in a particularly representative way, the second world war was a "crusade" (as was the first to Woodrow Wilson); so was his campaign for the presidency ("I am engaged in a crusade . . . to substitute good government for what we most earnestly believe has been bad government"); and so is his administration —a "battle for the republic" against "godless Communism" abroad and against "corruption and materialism" at home. It was Woodrow Wilson who once said, "Sometimes people call me an idealist. Well, that is the way I know I'm an American: America is the most idealistic nation in the world"; Eisenhower was but saying the same thing when he solemnly affirmed: "The things that make us proud to be Americans are of the soul and of the spirit."[24]

The American Way of Life is, of course, anchored in the American's vision of America. The Puritan's dream of a new "Israel" and a new "Promised Land" in the New World, the "novus ordo seclorum" on the Great Seal of the United States reflect the perennial American conviction that in the New World a new beginning has been made, a new order of things established, vastly different from and superior to the decadent institutions of the Old World. This conviction, emerging out of the earliest reality of American history, was continuously nourished through the many decades of immigration into the present century by the residual hopes and expectations of the immigrants, for whom the New World had to be really something new if it was to be anything at all. And this conviction still remains pervasive in American life, hardly shaken by the new shape of the world and the challenge of the "new orders" of the twentieth century, Nazism and Communism. It is the secret of what outsiders must take to be the incredible self-righteousness of the American people, who tend to see the world divided into an innocent, virtuous America confronted with a corrupt, devious, and guileful Europe and Asia. The self-righteousness, however, if self-righteousness it be, is by no means simple, if only because virtually all Americans are themselves derived from the foreign parts they so distrust. In any case, this feeling about America as really and truly the "new order" of things at last established is the heart of the outlook defined by the American Way of Life.[25]

In her *Vermont Tradition*, Dorothy Canfield

Fisher lists as that tradition's principal ingredients: individual freedom, personal independence, human dignity, community responsibility, social and political democracy, sincerity, restraint in outward conduct, and thrift.[26] With some amplification—particularly emphasis on the uniqueness of the American "order" and the great importance assigned to religion—this may be taken as a pretty fair summary of some of the "values" embodied in the American Way of Life. It will not escape the reader that this account is essentially an idealized description of the middle-class ethos. And, indeed, that is just what it is. The American Way of Life is a middle-class way, just as the American people in their entire outlook and feeling are a middle-class people.[27] But the American Way of Life as it has come down to us is not merely middle-class; it is emphatically inner-directed. Indeed, it is probably one of the best expressions of inner-direction in history. As such, it now seems to be undergoing some degree of modification—perhaps at certain points disintegration—under the impact of the spread of other direction in our society. For the foreseeable future, however, we may with some confidence expect the continuance in strength of the American Way of Life as both the tradition and the "common faith" of the American people.[28]

III

The American Way of Life as the "common faith" of American society has coexisted for some centuries with the historic faiths of the American people, and the two have influenced each other in many profound and subtle ways. The influence has been complex and reciprocal, to the point where causal priority becomes impossible to assign if indeed it does not become altogether meaningless. From the very beginning the American Way of Life was shaped by the contours of American Protestantism; it may, indeed, best be understood as a kind of secularized Puritanism, a Puritanism without transcendence, without sense of sin or judgment. The Puritan's vision of a new "Promised Land" in the wilderness of the New World has become, as we have suggested, the American's deep sense of the newness and uniqueness of things in the Western Hemisphere. The Puritan's sense of vocation and "inner-worldly asceticism" can still be detected in the American's gospel of action and service, and his consciousness of high responsibility before God in the American's "idealism." The Puritan's abiding awareness of the ambiguity of all human motivations and his insight into the corruptions of inordinate power have left their mark not only on the basic structure of our constitutional system but also on the entire social philosophy of the American people.[29] Nor have other strands of early American Protestantism been without their effect. There can be little doubt that Pietism co-operated with frontier revivalism in breaking down the earlier concern with dogma and doctrine, so that the slogan, "deeds, not creeds," soon became the hallmark both of American religion and of the American Way of Life.[30] These are but aspects of an influence that is often easier to see than to define.

The reciprocal action of the American Way of Life in shaping and reshaping the historic faiths of Christianity and Judaism on American soil is perhaps more readily discerned. By and large, we may say that these historic religions have all tended to become "Americanized" under the pervasive influence of the American environment. This "Americanization" has been the product not so much of conscious direction as of a "diffuse convergence" operating spontaneously in the context of the totality of American life. What it has brought, however, is none the less clear: "religious groupings throughout [American] society [have been] stamped with recognizably 'American' qualities,"[31] to an extent indeed where foreign observers sometimes find the various American religions more like each other than they are like their European counterparts.[32]

Under the influence of the American environment the historic Jewish and Christian faiths have tended to become secularized in the sense of becoming integrated as parts within a larger whole defined by the American Way of Life. "There is a marked tendency," Williams writes in his discussion of the relations of religion to other institutions in the United States, "to regard religion as a good because it is useful in furthering other major values—in other words, to reverse the ends-means relation implied in the conception of religion as an ultimate value."[33] In this reversal the Christian and Jewish faiths tend to be prized because they help promote ideals and standards that all Americans are expected to share on a deeper level than merely "official" religion. Insofar as any reference is made to

the God in whom all Americans "believe" and of whom the "official" religions speak, it is primarily as sanction and underpinning for the supreme values of the faith embodied in the American Way of Life. Secularization of religion could hardly go further.

As a consequence, in some cases of its own origins, but primarily of the widespread influence of the American environment, religion in America has tended toward a marked disparagement of "forms," whether theological or liturgical. Even the highly liturgical and theological churches have felt the effects of this spirit to the degree that they have become thoroughly acculturated. Indeed, the anti-theological, anti-liturgical bias is still pervasive despite the recent upsurge of theological concern and despite the greater interest being shown in liturgy because of its psychological power and "emotional richness."

American religion is (within the limits set by the particular traditions of the churches) non-theological and non-liturgical; it is activistic and occupied with the things of the world to a degree that has become a byword among European churchmen. With this activism has gone a certain "latitudinarianism," associated with the de-emphasis of theology and doctrine: Americans tend to believe that "ethical behavior and a good life, rather than adherence to a specific creed, [will] earn a share in the heavenly kingdom."[34] The activism of American religion has manifested itself in many forms throughout our history: in the Puritan concern for the total life of the community; in the passionate championing of all sorts of reform causes by the evangelical movements of the first half of the nineteenth century; in the "social gospel" of more recent times; in the ill-starred Prohibition "crusade"; in the advanced "progressive" attitudes on social questions taken by the National Council of Churches, the National Catholic Welfare Conference, and the various rabbinical associations; in the strong social emphasis of American Protestant "neo-orthodoxy." This activism, which many Europeans seem to regard as the distinguishing feature of American religion, both reflects the dynamic temper of the American Way of Life and has been a principal factor in its development.

It is hardly necessary to continue this analysis much farther along these general lines. The optimism, moralism, and idealism of Jewish and Christian faith in America are plain evidence of the profound effect of the American outlook on American religion. Indeed, such evidence is amply provided by any tabulation of the distinctive features of religion in America,[35] and needs no special emphasis at this point.

What is perhaps of crucial importance, and requires a more detailed examination, is the new attitude toward religion and the new conception of the church that have emerged in America.[36]

Americans believe in religion in a way that perhaps no other people do. It may indeed be said that the primary religious affirmation of the American people, in harmony with the American Way of Life, is that religion is a "good thing," a supremely "good thing," for the individual and the community. And "religion" here means not so much any particular religion, but religion as such, religion-in-general. "Our government makes no sense," President Eisenhower recently declared, "unless it is founded in a deeply felt religious faith—*and I don't care what it is*" (emphasis added).[37] In saying this, the President was saying something that almost any American could understand and approve, but which must seem like a deplorable heresy to the European churchman. Every American could understand, first, that Mr Eisenhower's apparent indifferentism ("and I don't care what it is") was not indifferentism at all, but the expression of the conviction that at bottom the "three great faiths" were really "saying the same thing" in affirming the "spiritual ideals" and "moral values" of the American Way of Life. Every American, moreover, could understand that what Mr. Eisenhower was emphasizing so vehemently was the indispensability of religion as the foundation of society. This is one aspect of what Americans mean when they say that they "believe in religion." The object of devotion of this kind of religion, however, is "not God but 'religion.' . . . The faith is not in God but in faith; we worship not God but our own worshiping."[38] When Americans think of themselves as profoundly religious people, whose "first allegiance" is "reserved . . . to the kingdom of the spirit,"[39] this is, by and large, what they mean, and not any commitment to the doctrines or traditions of the historic faiths.

With this view of religion is associated a closely analogous view of the church. For America, the celebrated dichotomy of "church" and "sect,"[40] however pertinent it may be to

European conditions, has only a secondary significance. The concept of the church as the nation religiously organized, established socially, if not always legally, has only an oblique relevance to American reality; and though America does know sects in the sense of "fringe" groups of the "disinherited," it does not understand these groups and their relation to the more conventional churches the way Europe does. An entirely new conception of church and church institutions has emerged in America.

It must be remembered that in America the variety and multiplicity of churches did not, as in Europe, come with the breakdown of a single established national church; in America, taking the nation as a whole, the variety and multiplicity of churches was almost the original condition and coeval with the emergence of the new society. In America religious pluralism is thus not merely a historical and political fact; it is, in the mind of the American, the primordial condition of things, an essential aspect of the American Way of Life, and therefore in itself an aspect of religious belief.[41] Americans, in other words, believe that the plurality of religious groups is a proper and legitimate condition. However much he may be attached to his own church, however dimly he may regard the beliefs and practices of other churches, the American tends to feel rather strongly that total religious uniformity, even with his own church benefiting thereby, would be something undesirable and wrong, indeed scarcely conceivable. Pluralism of religions and churches is something quite axiomatic to the American. This feeling, more than anything else, is the foundation of the American doctrine of the "separation of church and state," for it is the heart of this doctrine that the government may not do anything that implies the pre-eminence or superior legitimacy of one church over another.

This means that outside the Old World distinction of church and sect America has given birth to a new type of religious structure—the denomination.[42] The denomination as we know it is a stable, settled church, enjoying a legitimate and recognized place in a larger aggregate of churches, each recognizing the proper status of the others.[43] The denomination is the "non-conformist sect" become central and normative. It differs from the church in the European understanding of the term in that it would never dream of claiming to be *the* national ecclesiastical institution; it differs from the sect in that it is socially established, thoroughly institutionalized, and nuclear to the society in which it is found. The European dichotomy becomes meaningless, and instead we have the nuclear denomination on the one side, and the peripheral sect on the way to becoming a denomination on the other. So firmly entrenched is this denominational idea in the mind of the American that even American Catholics have come to think in such terms; theologically the Catholic Church of course continues to regard itself as the one true church, but in their actual social attitudes American Catholics, hardly less than American Protestants or Jews, tend to think of their church as a denomination existing side by side with other denominations in a pluralistic harmony that is felt to be somehow of the texture of American life.[44]

Denominational pluralism, as the American idea of the church may be called, obviously implies that no church can look to the state for its members or support. Voluntarism and evangelism are thus the immediate consequences of the American idea: for their maintenance, for their very existence, churches must depend on the voluntary adherence of their members, and they are therefore moved to pursue a vigorous evangelistic work to win people to their ranks. The accommodation of the church to American reality extends even to its inner polity. "As the polity of the Roman church followed the pattern of the Roman empire," H. Richard Niebuhr points out, "so the American churches incline to organize themselves [along representative lines] in conformity with the system of state and national legislatures and executives."[45] Even the Roman Catholic Church, with its fixed hierarchical structure, has not been totally immune to American influence of this kind.[46]

The denominational idea is fundamental to American thinking about religion, but it is not the last word. Americans think of their various churches as denominations, but they also feel that somehow the denominations fall into larger wholes which we have called religious communities. This kind of denominational aggregation is, of course, something that pertains primarily to Protestantism and to a lesser degree to Judaism; both have more or less organized denominations which, taken together, form the religious communities. Catholicism, on the other hand, has no such overt inner divisions, but American Catholics readily understand the phenomenon when they see it among Protestants and Jews. Denominations are felt to be somehow a matter of individual preference, and movement between denominations is not uncommon; the religious community, on the other hand, is taken as something more objective and given, something in which, by and large, one is born, lives, and dies, something that (to recall our earlier analysis) identifies and defines one's position in American society.[47] Since the religious community in its present form is a recent social emergent, its relations to the denominations properly so-called are still relatively fluid and undefined but the main lines of development would seem to be fairly clear.

When the plurality of denominations comprehended in religious communities is seen from the standpoint of the "common faith" of American society, what emerges is the conception of the three "communions"—Protestantism, Catholicism, Judaism—as three diverse, but equally legitimate, equally American, expressions of an over-all American religion, standing for essentially the same "moral ideals" and "spiritual values." This conception, whatever may be thought of it theologically, is in fact held, though hardly in explicit form, by many devout and religiously sophisticated Americans. It would seem to be the obvious meaning of the title, *The Religions of Democracy*, given to a recent authoritative statement of the Protestant, Catholic, and Jewish positions.[48] "Democracy" apparently has its religions which fall under it as species fall under the genus of which they are part. And in this usage "democracy" is obviously a synonym for the American Way of Life.

It is but one more step, though a most fateful one, to proceed from "the religions of democracy" to "democracy as religion" and consciously to erect "democracy" into a superfaith above and embracing the three recognized religions. This step has been taken by a number of thinkers in recent years. Thus, Professor J. Paul Williams has been urging a program of religious reconstruction in which he insists that: "Americans must come to look on the democratic ideal (not necessarily the American practice of it) as the Will of God, or if they please, of Nature. . . . Americans must be brought to the conviction that democracy is the very Law of Life. . . . The state must be brought into the picture; governmental agencies must teach the democratic ideal *as religion* . . . primary responsibility for teaching democracy as religion must be given to the public school, for instance. . . ."[49]

Professor Horace M. Kallen reaches very much the same conclusion from another direction. "For the communicants of the democratic faith," he writes, "it is the religion *of* and *for* religions. . . . [It is] the religion of religions, all may freely come together in it."[50]

It is not our purpose, at this point, to draw the theological implications of this super-religion of "democracy" as the "religion of religions"; it is only necessary to point out that it marks a radical break with the fundamental presuppositions of both Judaism and Christianity, to which it must appear as a particularly insidious kind of idolatry. What is merely implicit and perhaps never intended in the acceptance of the American Way of Life as the "common religion" of American society is here brought to its logical conclusion and made to reveal its true inner meaning.

By and large, the "common faith" of American society remains implicit and is never carried to the logical conclusion to which a few ideologists have pushed it. By the great mass of the American people the American Way of Life is not avowed as a super-faith above and embracing the historic religions. It operates as a "common faith" at deeper levels, through its pervasive influence on the patterns of American thought and feeling. It makes no pretensions to override or supplant the recognized religions, to which it assigns a place of great eminence and honor in the American scheme of things. But all the implications are there. . . .

IV

The "common faith" of American society is not merely a civic religion to celebrate the values and convictions of the American people as a corporate entity. It has its inner, personal aspects as well; or rather, side by side and in intimate relation with the civic religion of the American Way of Life, there has developed, primarily through a devitalization of the historic faiths, an inner, personal religion that promises salvation to the disoriented, tormented souls of a society in crisis.

This inner, personal religion is based on the American's *faith in faith*. We have seen that a primary religious affirmation of the American is his belief in religion. The American believes that religion is something very important for the community; he also believes that "faith," or what we may call religiosity, is a kind of "miracle drug" that can cure all the ailments of the spirit. It is not faith in *anything* that is so powerful, just faith, the "magic of believing." "It was back in those days," a prominent American churchman writes, recalling his early years, "that I formed a habit that I have never broken. I began saying in the morning two words, 'I believe.' Those two words *with nothing added* . . . give me a running start for my day, and for every day" (emphasis not in original).[51]

The cult of faith takes two forms, which we might designate as introvert and extrovert. In its introvert form faith is trusted to bring mental health and "peace of mind," to dissipate anxiety and guilt, and to translate the soul to the blessed land of "normality" and "self-acceptance." In earlier times this cult of faith was quite literally a cult of "faith healing," best expressed in what H. Richard Niebuhr has described as the "man-centered, this-worldly, lift-yourselves-by-your-own-bootstraps doctrine of New Thought and Christian Science."[52] Latterly it has come to vest itself in the fashionable vocabulary of psychoanalysis and is offering a synthesis of religion and psychiatry.[53] But at bottom it is the same cult of faith in faith, the same promise that through "those two words, 'I believe,' with nothing added," all our troubles will be dissipated and inner peace and harmony restored.

The cult of faith has also its extrovert form, and that is known as "positive thinking." "Positive thinking," thinking that is "affirmative" and avoids the corrosions of "negativity" and "skepticism," thinking that "has faith," is recommended as a powerful force in the world of struggle and achievement.[54] Here again it is not so much faith in anything, certainly not the theocentric faith of the historic religions, that is supposed to confer this power—but just faith, the psychological attitude of having faith, so to speak. And here too the cult is largely the product of the inner disintegration and enfeeblement of the historic religions; the familiar words are retained, but the old meaning is voided. "Have faith," "don't lose faith," and the like, were once injunctions to preserve one's unwavering trust in the God from Whom comes both the power to live and the "peace that passeth understanding." Gradually these phrases have come to be an appeal to maintain a "positive" attitude to life and not to lose confidence in oneself and one's activities. "To believe in yourself and in everything you do": such, at bottom, is the meaning of the contemporary cult of faith, whether it is proclaimed by devout men from distinguished pulpits or offered as the "secret of success" by self-styled psychologists who claim to have discovered the "hidden powers" of man.[55] What is important is faith, faith in faith. Even where the classical symbols and

formulas are still retained, that is very often what is meant and what is understood.

Such are some major aspects of the social, cultural, and spiritual environment in which religion in America moves and has its being. And religion in America means the three great religious communities, the Protestant, the Catholic, and the Jewish. These three religious communities must now be examined and the main features characterizing each of them in turn described.

Notes

[1] *Belief in God:* 97 per cent— "Do Americans Believe in God?" *The Catholic Digest,* November 1952; 96 per cent— Gallup poll, *Public Opinion News Service,* December 18, 1954; 95 per cent—Lincoln Barnett, "God and the American People," *Ladies' Home Journal,* November 1948, p. 37. According to the *Catholic Digest* poll 89 per cent of Americans believe in the Trinity ("How Many in the U.S. Believe in the Trinity?" *The Catholic Digest,* July 1953) and 80 per cent think of Christ as divine ("What We Americans Think of Our Lord," *The Catholic Digest,* August 1953).

[2] *Church membership and attendance:* see above, chap. iv, pp. 47–50.

[3] *Prayer:* 92 per cent answer yes to the question, "Do you ever pray to God?" ("Americans and Prayer," *The Catholic Digest,* November 1953); 90 per cent say they pray, 56 per cent "frequently"—Barnett, "God and the American People," *Ladies' Home Journal,* November 1948, p. 37.

[4] *Life after death:* 77 per cent believe in afterlife, 7 per cent don't, 16 per cent don't know— "What Do Americans Think of Heaven and Hell?" *The Cath-*

olic Digest, March 1953; 76 per cent say yes, 13 per cent no, 11 per cent don't know—Gallup poll, *Public Opinion News Service,* December 11, 1944; 73 per cent say yes, 15 per cent no, 12 per cent no opinion— Barnett, "God and the American People," *Ladies' Home Journal,* November 1948, pp. 230–231; 74 per cent believe in life after death—Gallup poll, *Public Opinion News Service,* April 19, 1957.

Heaven and Hell: 72 per cent believe in heaven, 58 per cent in hell—*The Catholic Digest,* as above; 52 per cent think that "life after death is divided into heaven and hell," though heaven looms larger in their minds than hell—Barnett, "God and the American People," *Ladies' Home Journal,* November 1948, p. 231; 61 per cent believe there is a devil—Gallup poll, *Public Opinion News Service,* April 19, 1957.

[5] *Opinion about church and clergymen:* 75 per cent deny the allegation that the church is too much concerned about money—"Is the Church Too Much Concerned about Money?" *The Catholic Digest,* March 1954; 68 per cent regard clergymen as "very understanding," 21 per cent as "fairly understanding"—"How Understanding Are Clergymen?" *The*

Catholic Digest, December 1953; clergymen rank at the top in the scale of those who "do most good"—see above, chap. iv, p. 51.

[6] *Bible:* 86 per cent regard it as divinely inspired, the "word of God"—"What Do Americans Think of the Bible?" *The Catholic Digest,* May 1954; a survey conducted by the *British Weekly* gives the figure for Americans who regard the Bible as divinely inspired as 86.5 per cent (see *Information Service* [National Council of Churches of Christ], December 27, 1952).

[7] *Religious instruction:* 98 per cent say yes—"Do Americans Want Their Children to Receive Religious Instruction?" *The Catholic Digest,* September 1953. *Children raised as church members:* 72 per cent say yes— "How Important Is Religion to Americans?" *The Catholic Digest,* February 1953.

[8] *Importance of religion:* 75 per cent regard it as "very important," 20 per cent as "fairly important"—"How Important Is Religion to Americans?" *The Catholic Digest,* February 1953; 69 per cent think that the influence of religion is increasing and 81 per cent believe that religion can answer "most of today's problems"—Gallup poll,

Public Opinion News Service, April 21, 1957. The religiosity of the American people appears even more striking when it is contrasted with the much more "skeptical" views held by the British; see the series of comparative surveys conducted by the Gallup organization, *Public Opinion News Service,* April 16, 17, 18, 19, 21, 1957.

⁹ Barnett, "God and the American People," *Ladies' Home Journal,* November 1948, p. 234.

¹⁰ "What the U.S. Thinks of Life Here and Hereafter," *The Catholic Digest,* May 1953.

¹¹ Barnett, "God and the American People," *Ladies' Home Journal,* November 1948, pp. 233, 234, 235.

¹² Barnett, "God and the American People," *Ladies' Home Journal,* November 1948, p. 234.

¹³ See particularly the statement of Father George B. Ford, in Barnett, "God and the American People," *Ladies' Home Journal,* November 1948, p. 237.

¹⁴ Robin M. Williams, Jr., *American Society: A Sociological Interpretation* (Knopf, 1951), p. 312.

¹⁵ Williams, *American Society,* p. 320 n.

¹⁶ Williams, *American Society,* p. 344.

¹⁷ When an American tourist comes upon the inadequate sanitary arrangements in certain parts of Europe and discovers what seems to him the careless attitude of the inhabitants in matters of personal hygiene, he is inclined to feel what he experiences not simply as a shortcoming in modern living conveniences but as a *moral defect,* on a par with irreligion, caste rigidity, and the absence of

American representative democracy. Cp. the following placard displayed by many restaurants in the midwest: "Sanitation is a way of life. As a way of life, it must be nourished from within and grow as an ideal in human relations."

¹⁸ Barnett, "God and the American People," *Ladies' Home Journal,* November 1948, pp. 235–236.

¹⁹ Where this "principle" of the American Way of Life is flagrantly violated by local prescription, as in the case of racial attitudes in the south and elsewhere, festering "bad conscience" and a destructive defensive aggressiveness are the result.

²⁰ "Differences in religion make a difference in social conduct" (Williams, *American Society,* p. 311). Investigating belief-systems from this angle would seem to be a good way of discovering what the "religion" of an individual or a group really is.

²¹ Discussing the European background of such churches, H. Richard Niebuhr writes: "These churches are doctrinal and liturgical in character, regarding conformity to creed and ritual as the essential requirements of Christianity" (*The Social Sources of Denominationalism* [Holt, 1929], p. 126).

²² For a discussion of the "religions of the disinherited," see below, chap. vi, pp. 122–123, chap. ix, pp. 216–219.

²³ See the illuminating account of Memorial Day as an "American sacred ceremony" in W. Lloyd Warner, *Structure of American Life* (Edinburgh, 1952), chap. x. Warner writes: "The Memorial Day ceremonies and subsidiary rites, such as those of Armistice Day, of today, yesterday, and tomorrow,

are rituals which are a sacred symbol system which functions periodically to integrate the whole community, with its conflicting symbols and its opposing autonomous churches and associations. . . . Memorial Day is a cult of the dead which organizes and integrates the various faiths, ethnic and class groups, into a sacred unity" (p. 214). As to the "saints" of the American Way of Life, Warner quotes a Memorial Day orator: "No character except the Carpenter of Nazareth has ever been honored the way Washington and Lincoln have been in New England. Virtue, freedom from sin, and righteousness were qualities possessed by Washington and Lincoln, and in possessing these qualities both were true Americans" (p. 220). The theological implications of this statement are sensational: Washington and Lincoln, as "true Americans," are credited with the moral and spiritual qualities ("virtue, freedom from sin, and righteousness") traditionally associated with Christ, and we are all urged to "emulate" them!

²⁴ For the quotations, as well as a general account of Mr. Eisenhower's religion, see Paul Hutchinson, "The President's Religious Faith," *The Christian Century,* March 24, 1954. For a sharp critique, see William Lee Miller, "Piety along the Potomac," *The Reporter,* August 17, 1954.

²⁵ For a penetrating examination of the sources and expressions of the American conviction of a "new order of things" in the New World, see Reinhold Niebuhr, *The Irony of American History* (Scribner's, 1952).

²⁶ Dorothy Canfield Fisher, *Vermont Tradition* (Little, Brown, 1953). For a comprehensive

survey of American life, see Max Lerner, *America as a Civilization: Life and Thought in the United States Today* (Simon and Schuster, 1957); see also Elting E. Morison, ed., *The American Style: Essays in Value and Performance* (Harper, 1958).

27 "America is a middle-class country, and the middle-class values and styles of perception reach into all levels except perhaps the fringes at the very top and the very bottom" (David Riesman, *Individualism Reconsidered* [Free Press, 1954], p. 499).

28 Riesman sees the immigrant generations as an important source of replenishment of old-line middle-class inner-directedness in American society (*Individualism Reconsidered*, pp. 289, 290).

29 See H. Richard Niebuhr, *The Kingdom of God in America* (Willett, Clark, 1937), pp. 76–83.

30 See F. E. Mayer, *The Religious Bodies of America* (Concordia, 1954), pp. 352–353, 354, 378 n.

31 Williams, *American Society*, p. 319. See also Roy F. Nichols, *Religion and American Democracy* (Louisiana State University Press, 1959) and William Lee Miller, "Religion and the American Way of Life," in *Religion and the Free Society* (Fund for the Republic, 1958).

32 "European visitors are able to detect better than we ourselves the emergence of a 'typically American' form of Christian worship" (Herbert Wallace Schneider, *Religion in 20th Century America* [Harvard, 1952], p. 170). "As many have noticed, the Protestant churches in America, even though brought from Europe, show more qualities in common than any one

retains with its European stem. And they feel that in America, the synagogue is no longer an alien. Even the Catholic Church in America acquires a tone unlike Catholicism in Europe" (Perry Miller, "The Location of American Religious Freedom," in *Religion and Freedom of Thought* [Doubleday, 1954], p. 21).

33 Williams, *American Society*, p. 337. Something of the shift involved in this secularization of Jewish-Christian faith is suggested by Ralph Barton Perry in his apologia for Protestant "liberalism": "If it does not stress the love of God, it does at least embrace the love of neighbor. If it neglects the fatherhood of God, it at any rate proclaims the fraternity of men. If it disparages the church along with other corporate entities, it is because it is so insistent on the finality of the human person. The independence of this moral ideal in no way argues *against* theism. . . ." (Ralph Barton Perry, *Characteristically American* [Knopf, 1949], p. 117).

34 Oscar Handlin, *The Uprooted* (Little, Brown, 1951), p. 128.

35 See, e.g., the section, "Relatively Distinctive Features of American Religious Institutions," in Williams, *American Society*, pp. 315–351.

36 Two recent studies of contemporary American religion are of major importance: A. Roy Eckardt, *The Surge of American Piety* (Association Press, 1958) and Martin E. Marty, *The New Shape of American Religion* (Harper, 1959). See also Lerner, *America as a Civilization*, chap. x, sec. 1, "God and the Churches" (pp. 703–717), and William H. Whyte, Jr., *The Organization Man* (Simon and Schuster, 1956), Part VII, chap. 26, "The Church of Suburbia" (pp. 365–381).

37 *The New York Times*, December 23, 1952; see also G. Elson Ruff, *The Dilemma of Church and State* (Muhlenberg, 1954), p. 85. Cp. the very similar sentiment expressed by Robert C. Ruark: "Although I am not a practicing religionist, I have a great respect for organized religion, no matter what shape it takes" ("Scoff-religious," *New York World Telegram*, October 10, 1955).

38 Miller, "Piety along the Potomac," *The Reporter*, August 17, 1954. Mr. Miller continues: "If the object of devotion is not God but 'religion' . . . then the resulting religiosity may become simply the instrument of more substantial commitments." The most "substantial" commitment of the American people, to which their "religiosity" is instrumental, is the American Way of Life. Once more to quote Mr. Eisenhower: "I am the most intensely religious man I know. Nobody goes through six years of war without faith. A democracy cannot exist without a religious base. I believe in democracy" (*New York Times*, May 4, 1948).

39 Dwight D. Eisenhower, quoted in Paul Hutchinson, "The President's Religious Faith," *The Christian Century*, March 24, 1954.

40 See Ernst Troeltsch, *The Social Teaching of the Christian Churches* (1911; tr. by Olive Wyon, Macmillan, 1931), Vol. I, pp. 331–349, Vol. II, pp. 691–728; also J. Milton Yinger, *Religion in the Struggle for Power* (Duke, 1946), pp. 16–50.

41 Williams speaks of a "value-consensus in which religious differences are subsidiary to the values of religious liberty" (*American Society*, p. 345).

42 "The Mormons, the Orthodox Jews, and a few small religious

communities are religiously organized peoples, but almost all other religious bodies in the United States, including the Roman Catholic Church, are neither national churches nor sects; they are commonly known as denominations or 'communions'" (Schneider, *Religion in 20th Century America*, p. 22). Even the groups Schneider mentions as exceptions, insofar as they have become acculturated to American life, would seem to fall into the same pattern.

[43] Since most American denominations emerged from earlier sects, denominations have sometimes been defined as "simply sects in an advanced stage of development and adjustment to each other and the secular world" (Leopold von Wiese, *Systematic Sociology*, adapted and amplified by Howard Becker [Wiley, 1932], p. 626). There is, of course, a good deal of truth in this definition; its defect, however, is that it regards the denomination as essentially transitional between sect and church, which is emphatically not the case with denominations in the American sense. American denominations have indeed, by and large, developed out of sects, but they represent the final stage of development, rather than a transitional stage to something else ("church" in the European sense). For a more general discussion, see Joachim Wach, *Types of Religious Experience* (Routledge and Kegan Paul, 1951), chap. ix, "Church, Denomination, and Sect."

[44] In a number of European countries (Germany, Holland, Switzerland), Protestant and Catholic churches have reached a kind of balance in which neither can pretend to be "the" national church. But where this is the case, it is simply a social and historical fact, not the proper and normative condition.

In America, on the other hand, the plurality of churches is held to be proper and normative; in this the American situation differs fundamentally from the European, even where the latter seems to resemble it most.

[45] H. Richard Niebuhr, *The Social Sources of Denominationalism*, p. 207. "The Church in our time, like the Church in any place at any time, is deeply influenced in its institutional forms by the political and economic society with which it lives in conjunction. As the polity of all the churches, whether they are episcopal, presbyterian, or congregational by tradition, has been modified in the direction of the political structure of Canada and the United States, so the institutional status and authority of the ministry are being modified in the direction of the democratic type of political, educational, and economic executive or managerial authority" (H. Richard Niebuhr, *The Purpose of the Church and Its Ministry* [Harper, 1956], p. 90). Cf. the statement of Franklin Clark Fry, president of the United Lutheran Church of America: "The polity of our church as a whole is frankly constructed on a secular model. Its prototype is the government of the United States" (quoted in H.E.F., "Lutherans Centralize," *The Christian Century*, October 27, 1954).

[46] Thus McAvoy speaks of the "practical and parochial character of American Catholicism"; the "parochial" character he relates to the "American tradition of disestablishment," while for the "practical" aspect of American Catholicism, he notes that "some observers have claimed that [it] is the product of the puritanism dominant in American Protestantism" (Thomas T. McAvoy, "The Catholic Church in the United States," in Waldemar Gurian and M. A. Fitz-

simons, *The Catholic Church in World Affairs* [Notre Dame, 1954], pp. 361, 364).

[47] Despite all the instability of American life, fully 96 per cent of Americans were found in 1955 still belonging to the religious community of their birth (see *Public Opinion News Service*, March 20, 1955).

[48] Louis Finkelstein, J. Elliot Ross, and William Adams Brown, *The Religions of Democracy: Judaism, Catholicism, and Protestantism in Creed and Life* (Devin-Adair, 1946). One of the clearest expressions of this conception by a layman was voiced by Admiral William F. Halsey, principal speaker at the fifth annual "four chaplains award dinner." "This picture," Admiral Halsey declared, "is symbolic of our national life. Protestant, Catholic, and Jew, each group has given, when called upon, the full measure of devotion in defense of our [American democratic] way of life" (*The New York Times*, February 6, 1955).

[49] J. Paul Williams, *What Americans Believe and How They Worship* (Harper, 1952), pp. 71, 78, 368, 374; see the critical review of this book by J. H. Nichols, *The Christian Century*, September 3, 1952. (A strong tendency toward this kind of "religion of democracy" is to be found in Jewish Reconstructionism; see Ira Eisenstein and Eugene Kohn, *Mordecai M. Kaplan: An Evaluation* [Jewish Reconstructionist Foundation, 1952], p. 259). "The religion of the American majority is democracy. . . . In fact, the religion of public education is a more powerful factor in American life today than that of the churches. The only religion with which the great majority of American youth have ever come in contact is the religion of public education" (Conrad Moehlman, *School and*

Church: The American Way [Harper, 1944], pp. ix, x). David Riesman speaks of "new ways of using the school as a kind of community center, as the chapel of a secular religion perhaps" (*Individualism Reconsidered*, p. 211).

50 H. M. Kallen, "Democracy's True Religion," *Saturday Review of Literature*, July 28, 1951.

51 Daniel A. Poling, "A Running Start for Every Day," *Parade: The Sunday Picture Magazine*, September 19, 1954.

52 H. Richard Niebuhr, *The Social Sources of Denominationalism*, p. 104. Niebuhr thus describes this type of religiosity in which the old Puritan spirituality has terminated: "In its final phase, the development of this religious movement exhibits the complete enervation of the once virile force . . . the problem of evil [has been] simplified out of existence, and for the mysterious will of the Sov-

ereign of life and death and sin and salvation [has been substituted] the sweet benevolence of a Father-Mother God or the vague goodness of the All. Here the concern for self has been secularized to its last degree; the conflicts of sick souls have been replaced by the struggles of sick minds and bodies; the Puritan passion for perfection has become a seeking after the kingdom of health and mental peace and its comforts" (p. 105).

53 The most celebrated effort along these lines is undoubtedly Joshua Loth Liebman, *Peace of Mind* (Simon and Schuster, 1946).

54 Norman Vincent Peale, *The Power of Positive Thinking* (Prentice-Hall, 1952). For a careful study of American religious literature reflecting both the "peace of mind" and the "positive thinking" gospels, see Louis Schneider and Sanford M. Dornbusch, *Popular Reli-*

gion: Inspirational Books in America (University of Chicago Press, 1958).

55 A salesman writes to Norman Vincent Peale in the latter's regular question page in *Look:* "I have lost my faith and enthusiasm. How can I get them back?" To which Dr. Peale replies: "Every morning, give thanks for the new day and its opportunities. Think outgoingly of every prospect you will call on. . . . Affirm aloud that you are going to have a great day. Flush out all depressing, negative, and tired thoughts. Start thinking faith, enthusiasm and joy. . . ." ("Norman Vincent Peale Answers Your Questions," *Look*, August 10, 1954). This may be compared with an advertisement for a quite "secular" self-help book in *The New York Times Magazine* for May 8, 1949:

DON'T WORRY
If you don't acknowledge it, it isn't so!
Develop the Art of Adaptability

THE INDIVIDUAL AND THE SOCIETY

One of the oldest problems in social science is to understand the nature of the relationship between the abstract institutions and the concrete groups and individuals that make up a society. One approach to this problem is through the related concepts of "the public" and "public opinion." Public opinion is seen as organizing individuals and groups to influence and change the institutions of society.

A major barrier to the use of these concepts is their extreme vagueness. Although statements concerning the public and public opinion are common in sociology, there is no standard definition of either of these concepts, and only a few attempts have thus far been made to state how opinion develops within a public. This selection is a welcome exception to the neglect of the subject.

Davison conceives of publics as based on primary groups and as organized by community leadership. Although publics may be very large, they can still be regarded as social groups. Members of publics engage in social interaction, creating the impression of unanimity of attitude on which public opinion depends.

A public is a group of individuals who do not know each other but who have formed beliefs concerning each other's attitudes on a particular subject and modify their behavior in accordance with these beliefs. Public opinion refers to the attitudes that are held in consequence of these beliefs. Not all opinions on public issues are a part of public opinion; only those opinions that are maintained in the light of the perceived opinions of others qualify for this designation.

Public opinion originates as personal opinions. These develop into public opinion through circulation in primary groups and transmission, with the help of community leaders, to other primary groups. Their acceptance is conditioned by their harmony with previously established opinions and, through "personal sampling," by their relationship to people's estimates of what members of other groups think. An opinion becomes public opinion when it becomes so widespread that people shape their behavior in accordance with it.

Public opinion is a temporary phenomenon related to the issue at hand. If the point is won or if the issue disappears because it is displaced by a new one or because it becomes hopelessly lost, public opinion disappears. Prior to its disintegration, it may leave a residue in the form of changed institutions or novel norms.

The selection offers both definitions and a set of integrated hypotheses, or theory, concerning public opinion. As there are no standard definitions in this area, acceptance of those suggested by Davison may be considered a matter of taste. The hypotheses are based on a large number of studies of behavior in small groups and in crowds, and they are applied by analogy to the case of publics. The similarities between publics and crowds, and even small groups, are strong enough to make this theory a reasonable one, but it needs direct testing on publics.

A remaining question is why public opinion varies in its effectiveness in influencing institutions. On some occasions, even in a liberal democracy, strong public opinion meets implacable resistance from the occupants of powerful statuses, and the issue is lost. In contrast, even autocratic tyranny must apparently yield at times to strong public opinion. There is a discrepancy between the implications of Mills (Selection 49) and those of Davison that suggests an important opportunity for research.

Selection 51
THE PUBLIC OPINION PROCESS
W. Phillips Davison

Although the term "public opinion" was not used until the eighteenth century, the phenomenon itself has been noted and described by writers in ancient, medieval, and early modern times. Public opinion appears most often in urban societies and in those with relatively well-developed communication facilities, as for instance in the Greek city states, but it can also be observed, even if more rarely, in pre-

Reprinted from *Public Opinion Quarterly*, 22:2, 1958, pp. 91–106, with permission of the author and the publisher.

dominantly rural societies with rudimentary communications.[1] The existence of phenomena bearing strong resemblances to public opinion has been noted by anthropologists in primitive societies of widely varying characteristics.[2]

In ancient and medieval times writers who mention public opinion often refer to it as having mystical or divine properties. Early modern writers regard it as perceptible but indefinable. They usually agree on two of its aspects: that it is a consensus among a large number of people, and that this consensus somehow exercises force. The German poet

Wieland has given us one of the first formal discussions of public opinion in his *Gespräch unter vier Augen* (1798):

I, for my part, understand by it an opinion that gradually takes root among a whole people; especially among those who have the most influence when they work together as a group. In this way it wins the upper hand to such an extent that one meets it everywhere. It is an opinion that without being noticed takes possession of most heads, and even in situations where it does not dare to express itself out loud it can be recognized by a louder and louder muffled murmur. It then only requires some small opening that will allow it air, and it will break out with force. Then it can change whole nations in a brief time and give whole parts of the world a new configuration.

Wieland's description is similar to many others given in writings of approximately the same period.[3]

More recently, students have been able to agree substantially on a number of distinguishing marks of public opinion. A list of characteristics, which is still one of the best, was given by Floyd Allport more than twenty years ago.[4] He noted that public opinion involved verbalization and communication among many individuals, that some widely known issue was always involved, that public opinion represented action or a readiness for action by individuals who were aware that others were reacting to the same situation, and that it was ordinarily a transitory phenomenon. Other writers have pointed out that a majority is not necessarily involved, that public opinion must be distinguished from norms and customs, and that the effectiveness of public opinion in bringing about change depends on the political and societal context in which it operates.

In spite of a considerable measure of agreement on these and other characteristics of public opinion, social scientists have been unable either to link these characteristics together into a theoretical framework or to offer a satisfactory definition of the phenomenon they are attempting to describe. Having rejected the "collective mind" explanation, which provided a theoretical basis for public opinion study even if one that was manifestly incorrect, students have been left without any concept that

adequately serves to interrelate the various observed aspects of the phenomenon.

This gap has been pointed out with increasing frequency. In the twentieth anniversary issue of this journal a number of authorities noted that especially during the past two decades progress in measuring and describing various aspects of public opinion has greatly outstripped conceptualization.[5] Our ability to measure the distribution of individual opinions in a population or the thematic content of communications is now far greater than our capacity to explain how the phenomenon that we call public opinion arises in the first place or why sustained propaganda will have very little effect in one situation while in another a series of whispers will produce a riot.

While lamentable, the primitive state of public opinion theory is not surprising. The extent to which a satisfactory explanation of the phenomenon as a whole has eluded serious thinkers indicates that factors of considerable complexity are involved. And since this problem has been attacked repeatedly by psychologists, sociologists, political scientists, and representatives of other disciplines, we may suspect that insight from all these fields will be required if a solution is to be found.

Nevertheless, although the hazards are sufficiently apparent to discourage speculation in the realm of public opinion theory, and obviously have done so, the importance of the phenomenon suggested by its close relationship to major problems of political, social, and economic behavior is ample justification for renewed attempts. This article represents such an attempt.

A definition of public opinion

The term "public opinion" will be used here in a sense suggested by Allport and will refer to action or readiness for action with regard to a given issue on the part of members of a public who are reacting in the expectation that others in the public are similarly oriented toward the same issue.

If we accept this definition as a tool for use in further inquiry, it raises a number of questions for investigation. How is the central issue in the public opinion process defined? What is a public? How are expectations as to the behavior of others formed? What effect do these expectations have on the attitudes and behavior of individual members of the public? What is the usual sequence of steps in the process by which public opinion is formed?

That the suggested definition is not completely adequate is indicated by the fact that a number of other questions are not immediately raised. The definition says nothing about communication, about opinion leadership, or about the role of primary groups. Yet we strongly suspect that these are somehow involved in the phenomenon under study. The part they play may be illuminated, however, if we examine the process by which public opinion is formed.

Genesis of an issue in the primary group

A familiar allegory uses the analogy of seeds to illustrate the growth of ideas. The seeds are numbered in thousands, and are scattered over the landscape. Some fall on the rocks and fail to germinate. Others start to take root but some die because they lack soil in sufficient depth or because they are smothered by faster-growing weeds. Only a few fall on earth where the conditions are right for continued growth and multiplication.

Similarly, there are many more issues that might provide the basis for mass movements than ever see the light of day. All men have grievances, inspirations, and ideas for improving society, but most of these die away in mutterings or casual conversations. An issue begins to take root only when it is communicated from one person to a second, who then carries it further in his own conversation. Most potential issues disappear from attention before this human chain grows to an appreciable length, but the few that survive form the basis for public opinions.

Let us take the hypothetical case of Center City. This is a town of some 30,000 persons, situated in a predominantly agricultural region. It serves as the market place for a wide area and has a relatively large population of small business men and white collar workers. It also has a few small factories and a junior college. Center City is governed by a mayor who was returned at the last election, in which the principal issue was a proposed sales tax. The mayor successfully opposed this tax, and the issue is now less controversial.

But one day a new factor is injected into the political life of the town. Mr. Jones, who runs a dry goods store on Main Street, re-

ceives a notice that the value of his residence has been reassessed. From now on he will have to pay almost half as much again in real estate tax as he has paid in previous years. He hurries down to the assessor's office to protest, but receives no satisfaction. He complains loud and long to his wife, his brother-in-law, his neighbors, and his friends on Main Street. The valuation of his property, he says, is way out of line with that placed on similar properties in the neighborhood.

As it happens, Mr. Jones is a popular man. He has many friends and is not known as one who constantly complains or makes hasty judgments. When he discusses his grievance against the city government with others, some of them remember grievances of their own: one has been treated inconsiderately by municipal employees, another has had difficulties with trash collection, a third dislikes the mayor personally because of a family squabble several years ago. In the minds of all those who interact in these discussions a generalized picture of maladministration is built up. Soon one cannot mention the city government in the circle frequented by Mr. Jones without eliciting the opinion that it is time for a change in city hall. A political issue has arisen.

Actually, we know very little about the formative stage of issues. This part of the public opinion process is usually buried in obscurity because it is unlikely to attract the attention of historians or journalists. Students of public opinion have ordinarily given attention to issues only after they have exploded into public view. Observation of small group behavior does, however, suggest the kind of process that is at work.[6]

The history of issues is complicated further by the fact that important ideas often appear independently at various times and places.[7] To which one of these points of origin should the idea that eventually emerges into public discussion be traced? Or is it the very fact that an idea has a number of apparently independent points of origin that is in part responsible for its subsequent growth?

But, however an issue germinates, we know that in order to survive and spread it must find one or more human groupings that are hospitable to it.[8] Otherwise, the originator will usually discard it or keep it to himself, since it interferes with the harmony of his social relationships. Those few who persist in expressing ideas that find no resonance among their daily associates are usually the lonely and embittered members of society.

Emergence of leadership

Let us return to Mr. Jones and his friends in Center City. Their dissatisfaction with the local government soon comes to the attention of the Opposition Party. This party knows that several similarly disaffected groups exist in the city and, since an election is scheduled for the following year, decides it is time to fan the flames of dissatisfaction. Leaders of the Opposition Party are on good terms with the publisher of the *Center City Bugle* and arrange with him for a series of articles, based largely on leads supplied by the party, on inefficiency in the local government. These deal not only with tax valuations and trash collection, but also with police protection, street lighting, and other subjects about which there have been complaints. One result of these articles is that the mayor and city councilmen prepare to defend themselves. Another is that additional complaints and more information about alleged shortcomings of the city administration flow into the offices of the *Bugle* and the Opposition Party.

While the series of articles on local mismanagement is appearing, and as indignant responses can be heard from the mayor and his friends, the leader of the Opposition Party makes a series of speeches before trade and fraternal groups. His problem is that dissatisfaction with the government comes both from those who think tax valuations are too high and from those who favor extended city services, and who therefore are inferentially in favor of added taxes. To solve this problem, the opposition leader avoids mentioning the tax problem at all and concentrates on two slogans:

PUT CENTER CITY ON A BUSINESS BASIS

and

GIVE THE CITIZEN HIS MONEY'S WORTH

He states that the aims of both these slogans can be accomplished by returning the Opposition Party to office at the next election.

Thus, at this stage of the public opinion process, leadership transcending the original primary group or groups can be distinguished. Sometimes this leadership is provided by the original exponent of the issue in question, whose influence then begins to extend beyond the circle of those he knows personally. An example of such a situation is given in a recent study of a fluoridation controversy in Northampton, Massachusetts, where one of the original opponents of fluoridation succeeded in winning election as mayor and then continued his campaign from the mayor's office.[9] A similar situation is noted in an older study of a controversy over the location of a new school in a rural community. Here the men who had personal interests in the location of the new school, and who first expressed opinions about it, became community leaders as far as this issue was concerned.[10]

More often, however, ideas that are agitating small, face-to-face groups are taken up by men who are already concerned with mass manipulation and who have at their disposal the means of organization and publicity. Such ideas may be collected and exploited by leaders in one field or another with considerable self-consciousness. Before the last presidential election a speech writer for a prominent politician asked the author whether he could suggest any lively foreign policy issue that had not recently been dealt with by some national figure. Political parties are increasingly ascertaining by public opinion polls what issues are most talked about throughout the population and then are tailoring their campaigns to fit these issues.

When leadership takes over, simplification and generalization of the original ideas can usually be observed. The leader attempts to formulate the issues in such a manner that they will be understood by and be of interest to the largest possible number of people. A classic example of this adaptation process has been provided by Walter Lippmann in his analysis of a speech made by Charles Evans Hughes following his acceptance of the Republican presidential nomination in 1916.[11]

At this point it is possible to suggest a definition of leadership that may be useful in this discussion. A leader is one who, in the course of interacting with others, influences their attitudes and behavior more than they influence his. He can be distinguished from a spokesman, who merely registers the opinions of a group, and from a prestigeful follower, who lends authority to an existing pattern of attitudes and behavior. In practice, a leader often serves as spokesman and may seek to appear as a prestigeful follower, but if he actually is limited to one or the other of these roles he cannot be regarded as a leader. This definition is illustrated by the rapidly shifting patterns of leadership that can be observed in mob action. A mob leader falls from power and a new leader emerges when the behavior of the latter exerts more influence on the actions of the mob members than does the behavior of the former, who may then become a follower.[12]

Inter-group communications

The most important characteristic of communications at this stage of the public opinion process is their ability to transmit facts and opinions about the issue concerned to members of many primary groups. Mass communications have the advantage of being able to reach large numbers of people simultaneously, but even when they are not available the same effect may be achieved, although more slowly and with infinitely more difficulty, through person-to-person communication systems. It is probably because of this fact that we are able to discern public opinion phenomena in societies where mass communications are poorly developed, or are under the rigid control of the state, even though we see these phenomena more rarely than in societies where mass communication systems are easily available to all currents of opinion.

Through inter-group communications the ideas that were originally developed as a result of interaction within face-to-face groups, and were then rationalized by opinion leaders, become available to large numbers of people who are not personally acquainted with each other. Some of those exposed pay no attention. Others find the new ideas incompatible with existing ideas on which they already base their behavior or with the norms of the groups to which they belong, and either consciously or unconsciously reject the new notions. If all, or nearly all, of the audience falls into one of these two categories, then the phenomenon we call public opinion never appears. If, on the other hand, a substantial number of individuals accept the new ideas there is a chance that public opinion may develop.

Those who agree or disagree with an issue propounded in inter-group communications are not scattered at random throughout the audience but are clustered in certain population categories. Those who agree may, for example, be concentrated in the ranks of low income groups, younger people, Baptists, and Midwesterners; while those who disagree may be found more frequently among higher income groups, Episcopalians, and Easterners. Studies of public opinion have repeatedly found that the distribution of individual opinions on any given issue is correlated with the group composition of the audience in question.[13]

Personal opinions on public issues

When a controversial idea is received by a significant number of persons in any segment of an audience, face-to-face discussions are likely to start again.[14] This process resembles the one that takes place in the original primary group where the issue is generated, except that this time group discussion proceeds in the awareness that many other people are thinking and talking about the same thing. Out of these discussions new formulations and leaders may emerge and these may modify the formulation presented in the first wave of inter-group communication or may merely reinforce it. A circular process is thus set up: an increasing volume of public communications stimulates more and more discussions, and the involvement of new groups and individuals leads to more public communication.

It is at this point that most of us enter the public opinion process. We rarely take part in the discussions that lead to the initial emergence of an issue, nor do we attempt to formulate or manipulate it. But we are constantly bombarded with ideas originating outside the realm of our personal acquaintanceship (although these may be relayed to us by relatives or friends) and we must disregard, reject, or consider each of these ideas. If we think about the issues involved and form attitudes about them, these attitudes are likely to be shaped not only by our existing attitudes but also by the attitudes prevalent among those with whom we have day to day relationships.[15]

Our attitudes and opinions about issues under public discussion are, however, also conditioned by our knowledge of the opinions and behavior of other groups. The statement attributed to Winston Churchill to the effect that if Hitler invaded Hell, he (Churchill) would say a favourable word for the Devil in the House of Commons is an extreme example of the way in which the actions or opinions of those outside our immediate group help to shape our attitudes on broader issues. "If they are fur it, then I'm agin' it." Studies of prestige suggestion have shown that our attitudes may be shaped by the views of those with whom we have few personal contacts as well as by the attitudes of those with whom we live our daily lives. This is particularly true of people who would like to raise their social status and who therefore model their behavior on that of others with whom they may be acquainted only through press, radio, or television.

The process just described occurred in Center City. As a result of the agitation of the Opposition Party, informal discussions took place along Main Street, especially at lunch time, and in service clubs and fraternal organizations. Small businessmen tended to subscribe to the Opposition Party's slogans. Many white collar workers, who hoped some day to become store owners or managers, adjusted their opinions to those of the boss. In numerous cases their relatives and friends followed suit. Only among the mayor's immediate political following and in the ranks of labor was there strong sentiment in favor of the incumbent administration. A local union leader wrote the *Bugle* in support of the mayor, pointing out that the city government had successfully avoided a sales tax. But since the Opposition Party had said nothing about imposing such a tax most skilled and unskilled workers did not feel themselves threatened. As a matter of fact, only a minority joined in the lively discussions; most citizens were not greatly concerned with local politics. They remained silent during the discussions at which they were present, and at this point did not form any personal opinions at all.

Expectations as to the behavior of others

In the process of forming their own attitudes on public issues, people usually learn about the opinions of others beyond their own immediate circle of acquaintances. Indeed, they often attempt self-consciously to ascertain what these opinions are. They note views reported in the mass media and may even question taxi drivers or casual acquaintances they meet on the train as to the prevailing opinion on a given issue in one part of the country or another. More often, however, people learn about the opinion of others without realizing that they are seeking them.

This process might be called "personal sampling." It leads to a picture of the way members of other groups may be expected to react. From the few opinions that are accessible to us we generalize as to the opinions of large groups or whole populations. We decide, after three or four conversations, that "all the better people in town" feel in such and such a way about a given issue; or we may read a few Paris newspapers and conclude that Frenchmen are overwhelmingly in favor of halting atom bomb tests.

A study of reactions to a radio dramatization of H. G. Wells' *War of the Worlds* provides some excellent examples of the way the personal sampling process may be carried out, although in this case the sampling was in reference to a question of fact (whether or not there had really been an invasion from Mars) rather than to a question of opinion.[16] Walter Lippmann also notes this personal sampling process.[17]

The way in which expectations are formed, and the resulting nature of these expectations, varies greatly from individual to individual and from case to case. Some people feel that they know how a given group will react even without sampling the opinions of any members of this group. ("Labor will never stand for that.") The less educated are likely to sample poorly or to project their own opinions onto the whole human race. ("Everybody knows that the earth is flat.") Or a very simple differentiation may be made between the probable difference in the views of good and bad people, or rich and poor. Those with more education are likely to make finer differentiations. But, however accurate or inaccurate these expectations are, they serve to provide an individual with a picture of the way people beyond the reach of his personal observation are likely to behave on any issue in which he is interested.

Practical propagandists are aware of the importance of the picture people form of the attitudes of others and seek to influence this, often by "rigging" the sample. During the Berlin blockade, for instance, East German communists sought to convince West Berliners that pro-communist opinion was strong in the city. They therefore started sending groups of three or four agitators, dressed in work clothes, into West Berlin. One of these would engage a passer-by in conversation on political questions and then, if another West Berliner joined in, the second communist would come up as if by chance, and so on.[18] Similarly, during the South Sea Bubble in 18th century London, the directors of the South Sea Company sent agents into Exchange Alley, where they attempted to create the impression that the stock of the company was in great demand.[19] It has been alleged that advertising agencies have resorted to analogous tactics by stationing operatives in rush-hour subways, with instructions to make loud-voiced comments to each other about the virtues of a given product or service. Such efforts to influence an individual's picture of public attitudes are more often unsuccessful than successful, since they usually are outweighed by other observations a person can easily make in the course of his everyday life.

As a result of prior information, observation, and personal sampling, people are able to locate their own position and the position of the groups to which they belong with regard to an issue. "We" are for it, "they" are against it, and the rest don't care.

The formation of expectations about the opinions and probable behavior of others could be seen in our hypothetical case of Center City. As a result of conversations, discussions, and reading of the *Bugle,* people who were interested in local politics decided that nearly all the business and professional men, and most of the better-paid white collar employees would vote for the Opposition Party at the next election. The politically-conscious segment of labor clearly supported the mayor, but most factory workers showed little interest. White collar girls and housewives were also seen as indifferent. There were in fact very appreciable deviations from these patterns, but those who discussed politics in Center City ordinarily spoke as if the various population groups would vote as a unit.

Adjustment of opinions and behavior

Once expectations about the attitudes and behavior of others on a given issue have been formed, these expectations tend to influence the opinions and behavior, and even the attitudes, of the people who entertain them. They know that expressions in favor of an issue are likely to win respect or affection for them in one group and may provoke hostile reactions or indifference in other groups. Therefore, they are likely to speak or act in one way if they anticipate approbation and to remain silent or act in another way if they anticipate hostility or indifference. When emotions run high, people may even express support for a position they privately oppose.

This process can be observed most clearly in a crowd that is organized around a given issue. People who do not share the opinions as expressed by the crowd's leaders are likely to remain silent, fearing the disapproval of those around them. This very silence isolates others who may be opposed, since they conclude that, with the exception of themselves, all those present share the same attitudes. Even some who oppose the dominant opinion, or who do not care about it, may express approval by applauding, and thus adjust their behavior to the expected reactions of others present. Crowd members who gain cheers by riotous behavior will be encouraged to even greater excesses. A process is set up in which expectations produce behavioral adjustments, and these in turn reinforce expectations. When this has happened, public opinion has been formed.

It is at this last stage of the public opinion process that individuals who may be unconcerned with the issue at hand are drawn in. Although they may not have formed a personal attitude about the issue, and indeed may not be aware of its nature, they still cannot ignore the behavior of those about them who *do* feel strongly about it. They therefore adopt the opinions of these others. Most often they are involved through some primary group to which they belong, as when one politically-concerned member of a family insists that the others vote, but they may also feel the impact of the opinions of those with whom they are not acquainted.[20] Jules Verne's imperturbable hero, Phineas Fogg, who arrived in San Francisco during an election rally in the course of girdling the world in eighty days, found that having no opinion about the local election left him in a highly exposed position. Women who have little interest in the latest trends of fashion still find themselves influenced by the dominant opinion among other women as to what is suitable attire for a given occasion. The fairy tale of the emperor's new clothes is also a case in point, in that all who were sensitive to the opinions of others maintained that they saw the clothes, while only the child, belonging to a population category that is often insensitive to grown-up opinions, announced that the emperor was naked.

In Center City, the process of behavioral adjustment on the basis of expectations was clearly observable. Speakers at business men's luncheons learned that jokes at the expense of the mayor were likely to provoke laughter. Even those who did not share the views of the Opposition Party usually joined politely in the merriment, although somewhat less heartily. Office seekers whose observations convinced them that the mayor would be defeated made small contributions to the Opposition Party, or offered their services as party workers. The minority along Main Street who favored the mayor kept discreetly silent on the subject of local politics, except when talking to personal friends.

When election day came, most of those who supported the Opposition Party marched to the polls, taking with them their relatives of voting age and their friends. A good turn-out was assured by the fact that these people felt the eyes of their neighbors and associates upon them. The supporters of the mayor, who did not feel an equal degree of pressure from the less-interested members of their own group, showed a much lower incidence of voting. The headline in the *Center City Bugle* on the following morning ran:

PUBLIC OPINION SWEEPS MAYOR FROM OFFICE

Before leaving this final stage of the public opinion process, it may be useful to attempt a definition of a public in the sense that it has been referred to here. A public is a large collection of individuals (either assembled at one point or scattered throughout a wide area) who do not know each other personally but who react to an issue with the expectation that certain categories of others will display similar attitudes on the same issue. It thus includes those whose behavior is influenced by the expected approval or expected similar actions of others, even if they themselves have no strongly-held attitude about the issue in question. This definition does not, however, include those who, even if they take the ex-

pected behavior of the public into account in shaping their overt actions, feel no community of interest with it. For example, social scientists studying a riot or a political rally are not members of the rioting or rallying public when the term is used in this sense.

As this last reservation suggests, the behavior of those who are not members of a given public may still be influenced by the public opinion that has taken root there. Thus, the social scientists in question may be especially discreet in their note-taking because they do not wish to arouse hostility or suspicion on the part of the members of the public they are studying. Similarly, military or political planners often take public opinion into account as one datum, along with many others of both a social and a non-social nature. They may be concerned with public opinions in a given area along with the geographic location, raw materials, industrial plant, and political leadership of this area.

It is clear, of course, that the expression "public" is also used frequently in other ways: to refer to a population, to an audience, or to any collection of persons distinguished by a single characteristic (e.g., the stockholders of a company). In connection with discussions of public opinion, however, we believe that a definition along the lines of the one we have offered is the most useful. To use one of the other possible definitions leads to the anomaly that one can distinguish several public opinions among members of a single public.

The dissolution of public opinion

One of the characteristics of public opinion that has been noted since early times is that it is a transitory phenomenon. It seems to arise spontaneously and to disappear imperceptibly. With the benefit of the scheme outlined above, we can offer some suggestions as to the various ways it disappears.

Since public opinion refers to attitudes and behavior polarized around an issue, it is clear that if the issue disappears the behavioral adjustment that characterizes public opinion will cease to have any purpose. A mob, for instance, will break up if the occasion for its gathering ceases to exist. Sometimes new goals are found as, for instance, when the mob turns its attention to destruction of property if the victim escapes, but this can be only a temporary stay. The mob members soon resume their normal patterns of life. A similar pattern of developments can be observed in the case of a political public after an election is over.

In other instances, public opinion on one issue is displaced by public opinion on another. At the same time that behavioral adjustment with regard to the first issue is at its height, a new wave of public opinion based on a different issue may be starting to form. This new issue attracts the attention of many members of the first public and a new public, possibly more powerful, is formed. Democratic statesmen who take actions that they know will be opposed by public opinion at the time often do so with the expectation that they will subsequently receive popular support when all the facts are known, or when the situation has been changed by new developments.

Public opinion may sometimes be broken up by superior physical force. The ringleaders may be arrested, all known adherents of a given viewpoint may be subjected to harsh penalties, or all communication among members of a public may be halted. If this repression is carried through relentlessly, individuals who initially composed the public may find their former behavioral adjustment incompatible with their personal safety or with the attainment of other values and adjust their behavior and even their attitudes to the new situation.

Public opinion may lead to the formation of customs or social norms before it is dissipated. The feminist movement managed to organize public opinion in such a manner that many of those who privately disagreed or who didn't care were led to adjust their behavior to conform to the pattern demanded by the militant minority. This pattern, subsequently buttressed by political and economic changes in many areas, then became established as a custom or norm. Feminism was no longer an issue, but people behaved in the manner demanded by the feminists because this was the way they had learned to behave. Their actions were no longer taken with reference to expected approval or hostility from others but either with no thought at all or else with reference to custom or social norms.

Finally, public opinion may also cease to exist when it has succeeded in having the issue around which it was organized embedded in formal laws or constitutions. The writers of *The Federalist* struggled hard to organize public opinion in favor of the constitution of the United States. After the constitution had been ratified, political behavior on many questions then became governed by reference to this formal instrument rather than by public opinion. It is only when a custom or law is seriously threatened that individual behavior may once again become polarized by reference to expectation of mass reactions.

A postscript on terminology

Partially because of its long history and undefined character the term "public opinion" has been used to refer to a great many phenomena, in addition to phenomena of the type that have been described above. It may serve to clarify our discussion if we mention some of these usages and explain why they cannot be applied to the phenomenon we have attempted to describe.

A common usage is to refer to the findings of opinion polls as public opinion. If, for example, it is found that 80 per cent of eligible voters are in favor of increased federal grants for certain public works, it is sometimes said that public opinion supports legislation to this effect. But it may be that the issue has not been generally discussed. A majority of individual citizens may favor increased federal aid for highways, but their position is taken without reference to the expected behavior of others, because they have not been able to form an expectation about this behavior. They may not know that others share their opinions. In this case, the poll gives us the sum of individual opinions, but the process described in this article has not taken place, or has taken place among the members of only a relatively small public.

This, of course, is not to say that such survey findings are inaccurate or of no value. In some cases they enable us to predict (although not with very great accuracy) what majority and minority public opinion on an issue would be if it were to be formed. Furthermore, they may provide a useful guide for legislators, since in a democracy individual opinions may be as suitable a basis for legislative action as public opinion. The political leader who takes the sum of individual opinions as a guide, however, runs the risk that public opinion when formed later may be of a substantially different character.

An older usage treats public opinion as if

it were represented by the dominant ideas expressed in public communications. This approach has been shaken by the observation that successful political candidates in hotly contested elections are often opposed by a heavy proportion of the mass media. It was dealt an even heavier blow when in 1956 the Hungarians rebelled against those who had enjoyed a near monopoly of the communication media for ten years. We are fairly certain that public communications do not necessarily reflect what people talk about in small groups, and even if the issues mentioned in headlines are discussed either approvingly or disapprovingly they may not serve as issues around which a public opinion process is centered.

A third usage refers to public opinion as an agent that enforces social norms, taboos, and so on. In a few cases this may be true, but ordinarily the process we have described does not appear to take place in such situations. A person who breaks a norm or violates a taboo is usually punished without reference to the expected attitudes or behavior of others in the group, and very little communication may take place. Those who administer the punishment play a role more like that of the traffic policeman who gives a ticket when he sees a law violated, while most group members who adhere to established norms or taboos do so not because of the expected behavior of those around them but because they feel that it is the right thing to do. That is, they will behave in the same manner even in private.

The most difficult distinction to maintain is the one between the public opinion process as we have described it here and the process that takes place in relatively small groups. In both cases we can see that similar individual predispositions and environmental influences may be involved, that communication and interaction take place, that expectations as to the attitudes and behavior of others are formed, and that the overt behavior of the self is adjusted to the expected behavior of others with respect to a given issue. At first sight it would appear that a distinction between the public opinion process and what we might call the group opinion process would be difficult to make.

Nevertheless, we believe that there are very important differences. Perhaps most important is the fact that a public is formed around a single issue, or a number of closely related issues, while the range of issues on which a small group may demand conformity from its members can be very great indeed.

A second difference is that the interaction process leading to the formation of group opinions takes place among people who are in frequent association, while the public opinion process involves people who may be united in a particular interaction process only once. Consequently, behavioral adjustment with regard to an issue on which there is consensus in a small group may actually be brought about more because of the past relations and expected future relations among members of the group than because of the dominant stand of the group members on this particular issue. Thus a faculty member may express agreement with a course of action suggested by his colleagues not because of the immediate appreciation he anticipates but because he feels he owes this support to his colleagues in view of their past indulgence to him, or perhaps because he is planning on submitting a proposal himself at a later meeting and does not want to prejudice its chances. Log-rolling in Congress is a similar case in point. A transitory public has no comparable past and future, but only a present.

A related distinction is that group members usually know each other, while members of a public may be total strangers. Adjustment in the group may therefore take place with reference to specific people ("these are my friends and I don't want to hurt their feelings"), while such a process is unlikely in a faceless public.

Indeed, the importance of the public in social processes seems to be related to the fact that, as distinct from the small group, it is a transitory, impersonal aggregate that is organized around a particular issue. These characteristics give it a great suppleness and versatility. The group opinion process is an extremely important component of the public opinion process, but the distinction between the two must be maintained if public opinion phenomena are to be explained adequately.

Notes

[1] Wilhelm Bauer, *Die Öffenliche Meinung in der Weltgeschichte,* Potsdam, 1930.

[2] Felix M. and Marie Keesing, *Elite Communication in Samoa: A Study of Leadership,* Stanford University Press, 1956; Margaret Mead, "Public Opinion Mechanisms among Primitive Peoples," *Public Opinion Quarterly,* July 1937.

[3] Cf. Hans Speier, "Historical Development of Public Opinion," *Social Order and the Risks of War,* New York, Stewart, 1952.

[4] "Toward a Science of Public Opinion," *Public Opinion Quarterly,* January 1937.

[5] See especially William Albig, "Two Decades of Opinion Study: 1936–1956," *Public Opinion Quarterly,* Spring 1957.

[6] See especially the excellent summary of small group research in Elihu Katz and Paul F. Lazarsfeld, *Personal Influence,* The Free Press, 1955, pp. 31–116.

[7] The frequency of independent, but almost simultaneous, discoveries has been noted by historians of science. Cf. Robert K. Merton, "Priorities in Scientific Discovery," *American Sociological Review,* December 1957.

[8] Harold D. Lasswell has pointed to the significance of the small group as "a radiating nucleus for an idea." Cf. *Psychopathology and Politics,* University of Chicago Press, 1930, p. 187.

[9] Bernard and Judith Mausner, "A Study of the Anti-scientific Attitude," *Scientific American,* February 1955.

[10] Richard L. Schank, "Testtube for Public Opinion: A Rural Community," *Public Opinion Quarterly,* January 1938.

[11] *Public Opinion,* Penguin Books, 1946, pp. 150–154; also p. 156.

[12] Robert C. Myers, "Anti-Communist Mob Action: A Case Study," *Public Opinion Quarterly,* Spring 1948.

[13] A familiar example is provided by Paul F. Lazarsfeld, Bernard Berelson, and Hazel Gaudet, in *The People's Choice,* Columbia University Press, 1948, pp. 25–27.

[14] Cf. Elihu Katz, "The Two-step Process of Communication: An Up-to-date Report on an Hypothesis," *Public Opinion Quarterly,* Spring 1957.

[15] This process is illustrated by a great many studies. See especially the remarks on voting changes by social units in Bernard R. Berelson, Paul F. Lazarsfeld and William N. McPhee, *Voting,* University of Chicago Press, 1954, pp. 118–132.

[16] Hadley Cantril, *The Invasion from Mars,* Princeton University Press, 1947.

[17] *Op. cit.,* pp. 112–13.

[18] Berlin *Tagesspiegel,* July 1, 1948.

[19] Charles Mackay, *Extraordinary Popular Delusions and the Madness of Crowds,* L. C. Page and Company, 1932, p. 53.

[20] Cf. Lazarsfeld, Berelson and Gaudet, *op. cit.,* p. 149.

Chapter 18

THE PROBLEM OF SOCIAL CHANGE

AN ECONOMIC THEORY OF REVOLUTION
Selection 52

A CRITIQUE OF THE ECONOMIC THEORY OF REVOLUTION
Selection 53

REVOLUTION AND NEED SATISFACTION
Selection 54

Although sociological research studies generally investigate conditions in a single society at a single time, sociologists recognize that the static pictures thus obtained are but a part of a constantly changing configuration. The search for general principles of behavior does not deny social change, but seeks to incorporate understanding of this change.

Admittedly, most sociological knowledge concerns contemporary Western societies. Among the reasons for this fact is the inapplicability of very recently developed research techniques to the data available from previous times and other societies. Consciousness of the problems of validity and reliability in social observation was not highly developed until the appearance of modern social science in nineteenth-century Europe. The survey method, which, with its promise of representativeness, is the most important tool of contemporary sociology, was poorly developed until World War II. Large-scale statistical information is even today available in trustworthy form only in the most bureaucratized states; even the United States Census contains inaccuracies that militate against its use for many research purposes. Furthermore, sociologists investigating the past must rely on the interests of people no longer living to provide the data. The topic of interest to the sociologists may never have occurred to past observers, or the records of whatever knowledge on the topic existed may be lost.

Despite the problems involved, studies of social change are common in sociology, and there would seem to be no basis in fact for the criticism sometimes made that sociologists are ahistorical or neglectful of change. Perhaps the most common type of sociological research embodying attention to change is the study of present or recent social trends. This interest is apparent in many of the selections contained in Part V of this book: for example, the writings of Ogburn on changes in the family (Selection 36), Olcott on changes in the caste system (Selection 42), and Frazier on changes in the Negro class system (Selection 47). The other common concern with change is historical sociology, the sociological study of history. It is from this tradition that the selections in this chapter are drawn.

Because, as mentioned above, historical data are difficult materials for modern research methods and because the scope of the subject is so large, historical sociology remains, among the branches of sociology, perhaps the closest to traditional social philosophy. It is in general an interpretative, speculative field of thought. However, historical sociology has been marked recently by several attempts to clarify concepts, to render data more precise, to formulate more general theories, and to test them in a manner analogous to that used for contemporary data. This trend is exemplified in this chapter.

The selections have been chosen to illustrate the treatment of one of the most perplexing problems in the field of historical sociology: the causes of revolution. General sociological theory relatively easily encompasses such changes as the vacillations of fad and fashion, as well as the slow, progressive trends that are usually found in the norms, statuses and institutions of a society. However, the rare but not unique occasions in history when traditional institutions are at least temporarily upset "overnight" do not accord with our usual understanding of the social order, nor can they readily be explained, as in the case of war, in terms of outside forces impinging on a society. The classic theory in this field is that of Karl Marx, sketched in Selection 52. Selection 53, by Crane Brinton, and Selection 54, by James C. Davies, may be regarded as commentaries on Marx, testing and revising his theory as it applies to revolutions in general.

AN ECONOMIC THEORY OF REVOLUTION

Perhaps the most famous theory of revolution is that of Karl Marx. Although Marx is usually considered an economist, this label is too narrow for a man who made inestimable contributions to political theory, social philosophy, and sociology, in addition to economics. The economic order is stressed in his theory not only as a phenomenon to be explained, but as an explanation in turn for all other social phenomena. Work of this scope cannot be called economic theory.

The crux of Marx's general theory is that certain economic factors, the "instruments of production," greatly influence the rest of society and that inevitable changes in the economy are reflected in all other parts of the social order. Although there are many places in which Marx intimates that noneconomic factors may in turn influence the economy, his stress is certainly on economic causation.

Marx believed that he saw reflected in the proletariat the particular source of social change in a capitalist society. He predicted that capitalism would be succeeded by a new and terminal stage of social development, called communism, through a proletarian revolution. The immediate cause of the proletarian revolution was stated to be an inevitable and increasing economic deprivation of the working classes under capitalism. The success of the revolution was expected to depend on the education of the proletariat by the bourgeoisie, so that the bourgeoisie could be said to be preparing its own overthrow.

The Communist Manifesto, from which this selection is drawn, is a political tract as well as a sociological essay. It is a clear and concise statement of most of Marx's insights, but it lacks the detailed supporting facts that appear in his major work, *Capital* (1867).

> History is class struggle, in which there is always an oppressed social class in conflict with an oppressing class. The history of the bourgeoisie is traced first in terms of economic factors alone——manufacturing, new sources of power, and extension of commerce——and then in terms of "consequent" social factors——the growth of cities, civilization of remote societies, political centralization, etc. As the instruments of production change, so do economic relations and so do all social relations and institutions.

The facts of commercial crises and overproduction indicate that now, in the nineteenth century, the bourgeois class has lost control over the processes that brought it into power. The proletariat, which is a creation of the bourgeoisie, is becoming more oppressed, not through malice on the part of the bourgeoisie, but because of economic necessity under the capitalist system. Moreover, the proletariat is being educated and is obtaining the means with which to effect the inevitable overthrow of the bourgeoisie. It is simply a matter of time until conditions for the proletariat under capitalism will be unbearable. The revolution that will then occur will lead to a new form of social existence, communism.

The history of "Communist" revolutions does not seem to support Marx's theory. The first of these occurred in Russia, where Marx would least have expected a proletarian revolution because of the poorly developed state of capitalism at the time. Not only were Poland, Hungary, China, and even Czechoslovakia hardly good examples of overripe capitalism, but the resultant societies bear little resemblance to Marx's utopia.

An equally impressive refutation of Marx's theory of revolution is its own success. Ironically, it is this theory, in its ideological aspects, that has been one of the greatest sources of social change the world has ever known. The man who minimized the role of ideas in changing the social order would have had great difficulty in explaining this fact.

However, these events have not denied Marx's theory an academic legitimacy. It seems reasonable to assume that economic deprivation will be reflected in social unrest, and it is true that revolutions are unlikely to occur in surplus-ridden societies. From the time Marx propounded his theory, various thinkers have tried not only to refute it, but to separate the truth from the falsehood within it. The remaining selections in this chapter are strongly indebted to Marx's original insights.

Selection 52
FROM THE COMMUNIST MANIFESTO
Karl Marx and Friedrich Engels

Bourgeois and proletarians[1]

The history of all hitherto existing society[2] is the history of class struggles.

Freeman and slave, patrician and plebeian, lord and serf, guildmaster[3] and journeyman, in a word, oppressor and oppressed, stood in constant opposition to one another, carried on an uninterrupted, now hidden, now open fight, that each time ended, either in the revolutionary reconstitution of society at large, or in the common ruin of the contending classes.

In the earlier epochs of history we find almost everywhere a complicated arrangement of society into various orders, a manifold gradation of social rank. In ancient Rome we have patricians, knights, plebeians, slaves; in the middle ages, feudal lords, vassals, guildmasters, journeymen, apprentices, serfs; in almost all of these classes, again, subordinate gradations.

The modern bourgeois society that has sprouted from the ruins of feudal society, has not done away with class antagonisms. It has but established new classes, new conditions of oppression, new forms of struggle in place of the old ones.

Our epoch, the epoch of the bourgeois, possesses, however, this distinctive feature: it has

Reprinted from *The Communist Manifesto* by Karl Marx and Friedrich Engels (1848).

simplified the class antagonisms. Society as a whole is more and more splitting up into two great hostile camps, into two great classes directly facing each other: Bourgeoisie and Proletariat.

From the serfs of the middle ages sprang the chartered burghers of the earliest towns. From these burgesses the first elements of the bourgeoisie were developed.

The discovery of America, the rounding of the Cape, opened up fresh ground for the rising bourgeoisie. The East Indian and Chinese markets, the colonization of America, trade with the colonies, the increase in the means of exchange and in commodities generally, gave to commerce, to navigation, to industry, an impulse never before known, and thereby, to the revolutionary element in the tottering feudal society, a rapid development.

The feudal system of industry, under which industrial production was monopolized by closed guilds, now no longer sufficed for the growing wants of the new markets. The manufacturing system took its place. The guild masters were pushed on one side by the manufacturing middle class; division of labor between the different corporate guilds vanished in the face of division of labor in each single workshop.

Meantime the markets kept ever growing, the demand ever rising. Even manufacture no longer sufficed. Thereupon steam and machinery revolutionized industrial production. The place of manufacture was taken by the giant, Modern Industry, the place of the industrial middle class, by industrial millionaires, the leaders of whole industrial armies, the modern bourgeois.

Modern industry has established the world's market, for which the discovery of America paved the way. The market has given an immense development to commerce, to navigation, to communication by land. This development has, in its turn, reacted on the extension of industry; and in proportion as industry, commerce, navigation and railways extended, in the same proportion the bourgeoisie developed, increased its capital, and pushed into the background every class handed down from the middle ages.

We see, therefore, how the modern bourgeoisie is itself the product of a long course of development, of a series of revolutions in the modes of production and of exchange.

Each step in the development of the bourgeoisie was accompanied by a corresponding political advance of that class. An oppressed class under the sway of the feudal nobility, an armed and self-governing association in the mediæval commune,[4] here independent urban republic (as in Italy and Germany), there taxable "third estate" of the monarchy (as in France), afterwards, in the period of manufacture proper, serving either the semi-feudal or the absolute monarchy as a counterpoise against the nobility, and, in fact, corner-stone of the great monarchies in general, the bourgeoisie has at last, since the establishment of Modern Industry and of the world's market, conquered for itself, in the modern representative State, exclusive political sway. The executive of the modern State is but a committee for managing the common affairs of the whole bourgeoisie.

The bourgeoisie, historically, has played a most revolutionary part.

The bourgeoisie, wherever it has got the upper hand, has put an end to all feudal, patriarchal, idyllic relations. It has pitilessly torn asunder the motley feudal ties that bound man to his "natural superiors," and has left remaining no other nexus between man and man than naked self-interest, callous "cash payment." It has drowned the most heavenly ecstacies of religious fervor, of chivalrous enthusiasm, of philistine sentimentalism, in the icy water of egotistical calculation. It has resolved personal worth into exchange value, and in place of the numberless indefeasible chartered freedoms, has set up that single, unconscionable freedom—Free Trade. In one word, for exploitation, veiled by religious and political illusions, it has substituted naked, shameless, direct, brutal exploitation.

The bourgeoisie has stripped of its halo every occupation hitherto honored and looked up to with reverent awe. It has converted the physician, the lawyer, the priest, the poet, the man of science, into its paid wage laborers.

The bourgeoisie has torn away from the family its sentimental veil, and has reduced the family relation to a mere money relation.

The bourgeoisie has disclosed how it came to pass that the brutal display of vigor in the middle ages, which Reactionists so much admire, found its fitting complement in the most slothful indolence. It has been the first to show what man's activity can bring about. It has accomplished wonders far surpassing Egyptian pyramids, Roman aqueducts, and Gothic cathedrals; it has conducted expeditions that put in the shade all former Exoduses of nations and crusades.

The bourgeoisie cannot exist without constantly revolutionizing the instruments of production, and thereby the relations of production, and with them the whole relations of society. Conservation of the old modes of production in unaltered forms, was, on the contrary, the first condition of existence for all earlier industrial classes. Constant revolutionizing of production, uninterrupted disturbance of all social conditions, everlasting uncertainty and agitation, distinguish the bourgeois epoch from all earlier ones. All fixed, fast-frozen relations, with their train of ancient and venerable prejudices and opinions, are swept away; all new-formed ones become antiquated before they can ossify. All that is solid melts into air, all that is holy is profaned, and man is at last compelled to face with sober senses his real conditions of life and his relations with his kind.

The need of a constantly expanding market for its products chases the bourgeoisie over the whole surface of the globe. It must nestle everywhere, settle everywhere, establish connections everywhere.

The bourgeoisie has through its exploitation of the world's market given a cosmopolitan character to production and consumption in every country. To the great chagrin of Reactionists, it has drawn from under the feet of industry the national ground on which it stood. All old-established national industries have been destroyed or are daily being destroyed. They are dislodged by new industries, whose introduction becomes a life and death question for all civilized nations, by industries that no longer work up indigenous raw material, but raw material drawn from the remotest zones, industries whose products are consumed, not only at home, but in every quarter of the globe. In place of the old wants, satisfied by the productions of the country, we find new wants, requiring for their satisfaction the products of distant lands and climes. In place of the old local and national seclusion and self-sufficiency, we have intercourse in every direction, universal inter-dependence of nations. And as in material, so also in intellectual production. The intellectual creations of individual nations become common property. National one-sidedness and narrow-mindedness become more and more impossible, and from the numerous national and local literatures, there arises a world literature.

The bourgeoisie, by the rapid improvement of all instruments of production, by the immensely facilitated means of communication, draws all, even the most barbarian, nations into civilization. The cheap prices of its commodities are the heavy artillery with which it batters down all Chinese walls, with which it forces the barbarians' intensely obstinate hatred of foreigners to capitulate. It compels all nations, on pain of extinction, to adopt the bourgeois mode of production; it compels them to introduce what it calls civilization into their midst, i.e., to become bourgeois themselves. In one word, it creates a world after its own image.

The bourgeoisie has subjected the country to the rule of the towns. It has created enormous cities, has greatly increased the urban population as compared with the rural, and has thus rescued a considerable part of the population from the idiocy of rural life. Just as it has made the country dependent on the towns, so it has made barbarian and semi-barbarian countries dependent on the civilized ones, nations of peasants on nations of bourgeois, the East on the West.

The bourgeoisie keeps more and more doing away with the scattered state of the population, of the means of production, and of property. It has agglomerated population, centralized means of production, and has concentrated property in a few hands. The necessary consequence of this was political centralization. Independent, or but loosely connected provinces, with separate interests, laws, governments and systems of taxation, became lumped together into one nation, with one government, one code of laws, one national class interest, one frontier, and one customs tariff.

The bourgeoisie, during its rule of scarce one hundred years, has created more massive and more colossal productive forces than have all preceding generations together. Subjection of Nature's forces to man, machinery, application of chemistry to industry and agriculture, steam navigation, railways, electric telegraphs, clearing of whole continents for cultivation, canalization of rivers, whole populations conjured out of the ground—what earlier century had even a presentiment that such productive forces slumbered in the lap of social labor?

We see then: the means of production and

of exchange on whose foundation the bourgeoisie built itself up, were generated in feudal society. At a certain stage in the development of these means of production and of exchange, the conditions under which feudal society produced and exchanged, the feudal organization of agriculture and manufacturing industry, in one word, the feudal relations of property, became no longer compatible with the already developed productive forces; they became so many fetters. They had to be burst asunder.

Into their place stepped free competition, accompanied by a social and political constitution adapted to it, and by the economical and political sway of the bourgeois class.

A similar movement is going on before our own eyes. Modern bourgeois society with its relations of production, of exchange, and of property, a society that has conjured up such gigantic means of production and of exchange, is like the sorcerer, who is no longer able to control the powers of the nether world whom he has called up by his spells. For many a decade past the history of industry and commerce is but the history of the revolt of modern productive forces against modern conditions of production, against the property relations that are the conditions for the existence of the bourgeoisie and of its rule. It is enough to mention the commercial crises that by their periodical return put on its trial, each time more threateningly, the existence of the bourgeois society. In these crises a great part not only of the existing products, but also of the previously created productive forces, is periodically destroyed. In these crises there breaks out an epidemic that, in all earlier epochs, would have seemed an absurdity—the epidemic of overproduction. Society suddenly finds itself put back into a state of momentary barbarism; it appears as if a famine, a universal war of devastation had cut off the supply of every means of subsistence; industry and commerce seem to be destroyed; and why? because there is too much civilization, too much means of subsistence, too much industry, too much commerce. The productive forces at the disposal of society no longer tend to further the development of the conditions of bourgeois property; on the contrary, they have become too powerful for these conditions, by which they are fettered, and so soon as they overcome these fetters, they bring disorder into the whole of bourgeois society, endanger the existence of bourgeois property. The conditions of bourgeois society are too narrow to comprise the wealth created by them. And how does the bourgeoisie get over these crises? On the one hand by enforced destruction of a mass of productive forces; on the other, by the conquest of new markets, and by the more thorough exploitation of the old ones. That is to say, by paving the way for more extensive and more destructive crises, and by diminishing the means whereby crises are prevented.

The weapons with which the bourgeoisie felled feudalism to the ground are now turned against the bourgeoisie itself.

But not only has the bourgeoisie forged the weapons that bring death to itself; it has also called into existence the men who are to wield those weapons—the modern working class—the proletarians.

In proportion as the bourgeoisie, *i.e.*, capital, is developed, in the same proportion is the proletariat, the modern working class, developed; a class of laborers, who live only so long as they find work, and who find work only so long as their labor increases capital. These laborers, who must sell themselves piecemeal, are a commodity, like every other article of commerce, and are consequently exposed to all the vicissitudes of competition, to all the fluctuations of the market.

Owing to the extensive use of machinery and to division of labor, the work of the proletarians has lost all individual character, and, consequently, all charm for the workman. He becomes an appendage of the machine, and it is only the most simple, most monotonous, and most easily acquired knack, that is required of him. Hence, the cost of production of a workman is restricted almost entirely to the means of subsistence that he requires for his maintenance, and for the propagation of his race. But the price of a commodity, and therefore also of labor, is equal, in the long run, to its cost of production. In proportion, therefore, as the repulsiveness of the work increases, the wage decreases. Nay, more, in proportion as the use of machinery and division of labor increase, in the same proportion the burden of toil also increases, whether by prolongation of the working hours, by increase of the work exacted in a given time, or by increased speed of the machinery, etc.

Modern industry has converted the little workshop of the patriarchal master into the great factory of the industrial capitalist. Masses of laborers, crowded into the factory, are organized like soldiers. As privates of the industrial army they are placed under the command of a perfect hierarchy of officers and sergeants. Not only are they slaves of the bourgeois class, and of the bourgeois State, they are daily and hourly enslaved by the machine, by the over-seer, and, above all, by the individual bourgeois manufacturer himself. The more openly this despotism proclaims gain to be its end and aim, the more petty, the more hateful and the more embittering it is.

The less skill and exertion of strength is implied in manual labor, in other words, the more modern industry becomes developed, the more is the labor of men superseded by that of women. Differences of age and sex have no longer any distinctive social validity for the working class. All are instruments of labor, more or less expensive to use, according to age and sex.

No sooner is the exploitation of the laborer by the manufacturer so far at an end that he receives his wages in cash, than he is set upon by the other portions of the bourgeoisie, the landlord, the shopkeeper, the pawnbroker, etc.

The lower strata of the middle class—the small tradespeople, shopkeepers, and retired tradesmen generally, the handicraftsmen and peasants—all these sink gradually into the proletariat, partly because their diminutive capital does not suffice for the scale on which modern industry is carried on, and is swamped in the competition with the large capitalists, partly because their specialized skill is rendered worthless by new methods of production. Thus the proletariat is recruited from all classes of the population.

The proletariat goes through various stages of development. With its birth begins its struggle with the bourgeoisie. At first the contest is carried on by individual laborers, then by the workpeople of a factory, then by the operatives of one trade, in one locality, against the individual bourgeois who directly exploits them. They direct their attacks not against the bourgeois conditions of production, but against the instruments of production themselves; they destroy imported wares that compete with their labor, they smash to pieces machinery, they set factories ablaze, they seek to restore by force the vanished status of the workman of the middle ages.

At this stage the laborers still form an inco-herent mass scattered over the whole country, and broken up by their mutual competition. If anywhere they unite to form more compact bodies, this is not yet the consequence of their own active union, but of the union of the bourgeoisie, which class, in order to attain its own political ends, is compelled to set the whole proletariat in motion, and is moreover yet, for a time, able to do so. At this stage, therefore, the proletarians do not fight their enemies, but the enemies of their enemies, the remnants of absolute monarchy, and land owners, the nonindustrial bourgeois, the petty bourgeoisie. Thus the whole historical movement is concentrated in the hands of the bourgeoisie; every victory so obtained is a victory for the bourgeoisie.

But with the development of industry the proletariat not only increases in number; it becomes concentrated in greater masses, its strength grows and it feels that strength more. The various interests and conditions of life within the ranks of the proletariat are more and more equalized, in proportion as machinery obliterates all distinctions of labor, and nearly everywhere reduces wages to the same low level. The growing competition among the bourgeois, and the resulting commercial crises, make the wages of the workers ever more fluctuating. The unceasing improvement of machinery, ever more rapidly developing, makes their livelihood more and more precarious; the collisions between individual workman and individual bourgeois take more and more the character of collisions between two classes. Thereupon the workers begin to form combinations (Trades' Unions) against the bourgeois; they club together in order to keep up the rate of wages; they found permanent associations in order to make provision beforehand for these occasional revolts. Here and there the contest breaks out into riots.

Now and then the workers are victorious, but only for a time. The real fruit of their battles lies not in the immediate result but in the ever improved means of communication that are created in modern industry and that place the workers of different localities in contact with one another. It was just this contact that was needed to centralize the numerous local struggles, all of the same character, into one national struggle between classes. But every class struggle is a political struggle. And that union, to attain which the burghers of the middle ages, with their miserable highways, required centuries, the modern proletarians, thanks to railways, achieve in a few years.

This organization of the proletarians into a class and consequently into a political party, is continually being upset again by the competition between the workers themselves. But it ever rises up again; stronger, firmer, mightier. It compels legislative recognition of particular interests of the workers, by taking advantage of the divisions among the bourgeoisie itself. Thus the ten-hours' bill in England was carried.

Altogether collisions between the classes of the old society further, in many ways, the course of the development of the proletariat. The bourgeoisie finds itself involved in a constant battle. At first with the aristocracy; later on, with those portions of the bourgeoisie itself whose interests have become antagonistic to the progress of industry; at all times with the bourgeoisie of foreign countries. In all these countries it sees itself compelled to appeal to the proletariat, to ask for its help, and thus to drag it into the political arena. The bourgeoisie itself, therefore, supplies the proletariat with weapons for fighting the bourgeoisie.

Further, as we have already seen, entire sections of the ruling classes are, by the advance of industry, precipitated into the proletariat, or are at least threatened in their conditions of existence. These also supply the proletariat with fresh elements of enlightenment and progress.

Finally, in times when the class struggle nears the decisive hour, the process of dissolution going on within the ruling class, in fact within the whole range of old society, assumes such a violent, glaring character, that a small section of the ruling class cuts itself adrift, and joins the revolutionary class, the class that holds the future in its hands. Just as, therefore, at an earlier period, a section of the nobility went over to the bourgeoisie, so now a portion of the bourgeoisie goes over to the proletariat, and in particular, a portion of the bourgeois ideologists, who have raised themselves to the level of comprehending theoretically the historical movement as a whole.

Of all the classes that stand face to face with the bourgeoisie to-day, the proletariat alone is a really revolutionary class. The other classes decay and finally disappear in the face of modern industry; the proletariat is its special and essential product.

The lower middle class, the small manufacturer, the shopkeeper, the artisan, the peasant, all these fight against the bourgeoisie to save from extinction their existence as fractions of the middle class. They are therefore not revolutionary, but conservative. Nay, more, they are reactionary, for they try to roll back the wheel of history. If by chance they are revolutionary, they are so only in view of their impending transfer into the proletariat; they thus defend not their present, but their future interests, they desert their own standpoint to place themselves at that of the proletariat.

The "dangerous class," the social scum, that passively rotting class thrown off by the lowest layers of old society, may, here and there, be swept into the movement by a proletarian revolution; its conditions of life, however, prepare it far more for the part of a bribed tool of reactionary intrigue.

In the conditions of the proletariat, those of old society at large are already virtually swamped. The proletarian is without property; his relation to his wife and children has no longer anything in common with the bourgeois family relations; modern industrial labor, modern subjection to capital, the same in England as in France, in America as in Germany, has stripped him of every trace of national character. Law, morality, religion, are to him so many bourgeois prejudices, behind which lurk in ambush just as many bourgeois interests.

All the preceding classes that got the upper hand sought to fortify their already acquired status by subjecting society at large to their conditions of appropriation. The proletarians cannot become masters of the productive forces of society, except by abolishing their own previous mode of appropriation, and thereby also every other previous mode of appropriation. They have nothing of their own to secure and to fortify; their mission is to destroy all previous securities for, and insurances of, individual property.

All previous historical movements were movements of minorities, or in the interest of minorities. The proletarian movement is the self-conscious, independent movement of the immense majority, in the interest of the immense majority. The proletariat, the lowest stratum of our present society, cannot stir, cannot raise itself up, without the whole superincumbent strata of official society being sprung into the air.

Though not in substance, yet in form, the

struggle of the proletariat with the bourgeoisie is at first a national struggle. The proletariat of each country must, of course, first of all settle matters with its own bourgeoisie.

In depicting the most general phases of the development of the proletariat, we traced the more or less veiled civil war, raging within existing society, up to the point where that war breaks out into open revolution, and where the violent overthrow of the bourgeoisie lays the foundation for the sway of the proletariat.

Hitherto every form of society has been based, as we have already seen, on the antagonism of oppressing and oppressed classes. But in order to oppress a class certain conditions must be assured to it under which it can, at least, continue its slavish existence. The serf, in the period of serfdom, raised himself to membership in the commune, just as the petty bourgeois, under the yoke of feudal absolutism, managed to develop into a bourgeois. The modern laborer, on the contrary, instead of rising with the progress of industry, sinks deeper and deeper below the conditions of existence of his own class. He becomes a pauper, and pauperism develops more rapidly than population and wealth. And here it be-comes evident that the bourgeoisie is unfit any longer to be the ruling class in society and to impose its conditions of existence upon society as an over-riding law. It is unfit to rule because it is incompetent to assure an existence to its slave within his slavery, because it cannot help letting him sink into such a state that it has to feed him instead of being fed by him. Society can no longer live under this bourgeoisie; in other words, its existence is no longer compatible with society.

The essential condition for the existence, and for the sway of the bourgeois class, is the formation and augmentation of capital; the condition for capital is wage-labor. Wage-labor rests exclusively on competition between the laborers. The advance of industry, whose involuntary promoter is the bourgeoisie, replaces the isolation of the laborers, due to competition, by their revolutionary combination, due to association. The development of modern industry, therefore, cuts from under its feet the very foundation on which the bourgeoisie produces and appropriates products. What the bourgeoisie therefore produces, above all, are its own grave diggers. Its fall and the victory of the proletariat are equally inevitable.

Notes

[1] By bourgeoisie is meant the class of modern Capitalists, owners of the means of social production and employers of wage-labor. By proletariat, the class of modern wage-laborers who, having no means of production of their own, are reduced to selling their labor-power in order to live.

[2] That is, all written history. In 1847, the pre-history of society, the social organization existing previous to recorded history, was all but unknown. Since then, Haxthausen discovered common ownership of land in Russia, Maurer proved it to be the social foundation from which all Teutonic races started in history, and by and by village communities were found to be, or to have been the primitive form of society everywhere from India to Ireland. The inner organization of this primitive Communistic society was laid bare, in its typical form, by Morgan's crowning discovery of the true nature of the Gens and its relation to the Tribe. With the dissolution of these primaeval communities society begins to be differentiated into separate and finally antagonistic classes. I have attempted to retrace this process of dissolution in: "Der Ursprung der Familie, des Privateigenthums und des Staats," 2nd edit., Stuttgart, 1886.

[3] Guildmaster, that is a full member of a guild, a master within, not a head of a guild.

[4] "Commune" was the name taken, in France, by the nascent towns even before they had conquered from their feudal lords and masters, local self-government and political rights as the "Third Estate." Generally speaking, for the economical development of the bourgeoisie, England is here taken as the typical country; for its political development, France.

A CRITIQUE OF THE ECONOMIC THEORY OF REVOLUTION

Among the best-known works to take issue with Marx's interpretation of the origins of revolution is Crane Brinton's *Anatomy of Revolution,* from which this selection is taken. Brinton studied four revolutions—the English of the seventeenth century, the American and French of the eighteenth, and the Russian of the twentieth century—in a search for common traits which may be characteristic of revolution as a social phenomenon.

In carefully guarded language, Brinton claims to observe similarities in the courses of these revolutions, which he presents as a hypothetical model for other revolutions. He notes that the instances he has studied may not be representative of all revolutions but perhaps of those revolutions that share the following characteristics with his four: taking place in the post-medieval West; being of a "popular" nature and undertaken in the name of freedom for a repressed minority; and ending ultimately in the successful transfer of power.

This selection presents Brinton's findings concerning economic conditions during the last years of the old regimes, prior to the outbreak of the revolutions. It is of particular interest in its bearing on Marx's theory.

> The societies of England, America, France, and Russia prior to their respective revolutions do not show evidence of economic decline. Not even on the local level of particular provinces or social classes can exceptional poverty be found. Rather, these societies seem to have in common a condition of disaffection on the part of some relatively prosperous groups who want more than they are getting. Class antagonism does exist, but it does not appear to have a clear economic basis. The only poverty apparent in these societies seems to be in their governments, which experience severe financial difficulties that resist efforts to reform.

Brinton also finds a "desertion of the intellectuals" from the old regime, inefficient and lagging machinery of government, and demoralization of the old ruling class in each of these prerevolutionary societies. In three of the four revolutions, the initiating events are connected with financial collapse; but in Russia governmental collapse is total and not just financial. The revolution is inaugurated when the dissatisfied groups seize on the government's difficulties to make demands for power and are opposed by means of force, but ineffectively so.

Brinton's admirable caution in interpreting his data makes it difficult to say precisely what he considers to be the cause or causes of revolution. He simply indicates what conditions were present when the revolutions he studied broke out. It is clear, however, that he rejects Marx's suggestion that increasing economic poverty characterizes the onset of revolution. In these societies, prior to revolution, progress rather than poverty is general; the revolutionary party appears to emerge, not from the downtrodden masses, but from near the top of the social structure.

Brinton makes his point very well, but perhaps the juxtaposition of his careful research with the glittering generalities of *The Communist Manifesto* is unfair to Marx, whose knowledge of historical fact was considerable. Moreover, it is perhaps unfair to require Marx's theory to fit the data of these revolutions, which are, with the possible exception of the Russian, patently nonproletarian in origin, and even the latter might be disavowed by Marx. Brinton has not included the abortive Revolutions of 1848 and 1870, which so thoroughly convinced Marx that he was right. One may reasonably conclude, however, that Brinton has shifted the "burden of proof" of their theory onto the Marxists.

Selection 53
FROM ANATOMY OF REVOLUTION
Crane Brinton

As good children of our age, we are bound to start any such study as this with the economic situation. All of us, no matter how little sympathy we may have with organized communism, betray the extent of Marx's influence in the social studies—and of the influences that influenced Marx—by the naturalness with which we ask the question: "What had economic interests to do with it all?" Now it is incontestable that in all four of the societies we are studying the years preceding the outbreak of revolution witnessed unusually serious economic, or at least financial, difficulties of a special kind. The first two Stuarts were in perpetual conflict with their parliaments over taxes, and the years just before 1640 resounded with complaints about Ship Money, benevolences, tonnage and poundage and other terms now strange to us, but once capable of making a hero of a very rich Buckinghamshire gentleman named John Hampden, who was financially quite able to pay much larger taxes than he did. Americans need not be reminded of the part trouble over taxation played in the years just before the shot fired at Concord defied all the laws of acoustics. "No taxation without representation" may be rejected by all up-to-date historians as in itself an adequate explanation of the beginnings of the American revolution, but the fact remains that it was in the 1770's a slogan capable of exciting our fathers to action. In 1789 the French Estates-General, the calling of which precipitated the revolution, was made unavoidable by the bad financial state of the government. Official France in 1789 was financially in as unhappy a way as, until our own times, one would have believed it possible for a government to be. In Russia in 1917 financial collapse did not perhaps stand out so prominently because the Czarist regime had achieved an all-round collapse in all fields of governmental activity, from war to village administration. But three years of war had put such a strain on Russian finances that, even with the support of the Allies, high prices and

scarcity were by 1917 most obvious factors in the general tension.

Yet in all of these societies, it is the *government* that is in financial difficulties, not the societies themselves. To put the matter negatively, our revolutions did not occur in societies economically backward, nor in societies undergoing widespread economic misery or depression. You will not find in these societies of the old regime anything like unusually widespread economic want. In a specific instance, of course, the standard against which want or depression is measured must be the standard of living more or less acceptable to a given group at a given time. What satisfied an English peasant in 1640 would be misery and want for an Iowa farmer of 1938. It is possible that certain groups in a society may be in unusual want even though statistically that abstraction "society as a whole" is enjoying an increasing—and almost equally abstract—"national income." Nevertheless, when national income is rapidly increasing, someone does get the benefit. We must look more carefully at our four societies in this respect.

France in 1789 was a very striking example of a rich society with an impoverished government. The eighteenth century had begun to collect statistics about itself, and though these would not satisfy a modern economist they enable us to be very certain about the increasing prosperity of eighteenth-century France. Any series of indices—foreign trade, population growth, building, manufactures, agricultural production—will show a general upward trend all through the eighteenth century. Here are a few examples: wastelands all over France were being brought under the plow and in the *élection* of Melun alone in two years from 1783 to 1785 uncultivated land was reduced from 14,500 to 10,000 *arpents;* Rouen in 1787 produced annually cotton cloth worth fifty millions of *livres,* having at least doubled its production in a generation; French trade with North Africa (the Barbary Coast) increased from about 1,000,000 *livres* in 1740 to 6,216,-000 *livres* in 1788; the total French foreign trade had in 1787 increased nearly 100,000,-000 *livres* in the dozen years since the death of Louis XV in 1774.

Reprinted from *Anatomy of Revolution* by Crane Brinton (New York: W. W. Norton, 1938) with permission of the author and Prentice-Hall, Inc.

Even in our imperfect statistics we can distinguish short-term cyclical variations, and it seems clear that in some respects, notably in the wheat harvest, 1788–89 was a bad year. It was, however, by no means a deep trough year like 1932 for this country. If business men in eighteenth-century France had kept charts and made graphs, the lines would have mounted with gratifying consistency through most of the period preceding the French revolution. Now this prosperity was certainly most unevenly shared. The people who got the lion's share of it seem to have been the merchants, bankers, business men, lawyers, peasants who ran their own farms as businesses; the middle class, as we have come to call it. It was precisely these prosperous people who in the 1780's were loudest against the government, most reluctant to save it by paying taxes.

In America, of course, with an empty continent available for the distressed, general economic conditions in the eighteenth century show increasing wealth and population, with economic distress a purely relative matter. There can be no talk of starvation, of grinding poverty in the New England of the Stamp Act. Even the minor fluctuations of the business cycle fail to coincide with the revolution, and the early years of the 1770's were distinctly years of prosperity. There were economic stresses and strains in colonial America, as we shall soon see, but no class ground down with poverty.

Nor is it easy to argue that early Stuart England was less prosperous than late Tudor England had been. There is rather evidence that, especially in the years of personal government which preceded the Long Parliament, England was notably prosperous. Ramsay Muir writes that "England had never known a more steady or more widely diffused prosperity and the burden of taxation was less than in any other country. The coming revolution was certainly not due to economic distress." Even in the Russia of 1917, apart from the shocking breakdown of the machinery of government under war-strain, the productive capacity of society as a whole was certainly greater than at any other time in Russian history; and to take again the long view, the economic graphs had all been mounting for Russia as a whole in the late nineteenth and early twentieth centuries, and the progress in trade and production since the abortive revolution of 1905 had been notable.

Our revolutions, then, clearly were not born in societies economically retrograde; on the contrary, they took place in societies economically progressive. This does not, of course, mean that no groups within these societies cherished grievances mainly economic in character. Two main foci for economic motives of discontent seem to stand out. First, and much the less important, is the actual misery of certain groups in a given society. No doubt in all our societies, even in America, there was a sort of submarginal group of poor people whose release from certain forms of restraint is a very important feature of revolution itself. But in studying the preliminary signs of revolution, these people are not very important. French republican historians have long insisted on the importance of the bad harvest of 1788, the cold winter of 1788–89, and the consequent sufferings of the poor. Bread was relatively dear in that spring when the Estates-General first assembled. There was apparently a tightening up of business conditions in America in 1774–75, but certainly nothing like widespread distress or unemployment. The local sufferings of Boston, considerable under the Port Bill, were really a part of the revolution itself, and not a sign. The winter of 1916–17 was certainly a bad one in Russia, with food rationing in all the cities.

The important thing to note, however, is that French and Russian history are filled with famines, plagues, bad harvests, sometimes local, sometimes national in sweep, many of which were accompanied by sporadic rioting, but in each case only one by revolution. In neither the English nor the American revolution do we find even this degree of localized want or famine. Clearly, then, the economic distress of the underprivileged, though it may well accompany a revolutionary situation, is not one of the symptoms we need dwell upon. This the subtler Marxists themselves recognize, and Trotsky has written: "In reality the mere existence of privations is not enough to cause an insurrection; if it were, the masses would always be in revolt."

Of much greater importance is the existence among a group, or groups, of a feeling that prevailing conditions limit or hinder their economic activity. We are especially aware of this element in our American revolution, and Professor A. M. Schlesinger has shown how the prosperous merchants, their immediate interests damaged by the new imperial policy of the British government, led an agitation against the legislation of 1764 and 1765 and helped stir up a discontent among the less well-to-do which these merchants later found a bit embarrassing. No doubt, too, that many of the firm spots in the very uneven and wavering policy of the British government—the Stamp Act and subsequent disorders, the announced intention of enforcing the Navigation Act, and so on—did have momentary ill effects on business, did throw men out of work. The currency question was of course mismanaged in a day when common sense did not very effectively supplement ignorance of economic processes. The colonies were always lacking in specie, and business enterprise suffered from this lack. Paper money, to which recourse was inevitable, was also an inevitable source of further quarrels between governors and governed.

The working of economic motives to revolt among possessing classes normally inclined to support existing institutions is especially clear among the aristocrats of tidewater Virginia. Largely dependent on a single crop, tobacco, used to a high standard of living, increasingly indebted to London bankers, many of the planters hoped to recoup their fortunes in the western lands they regarded as clearly belonging to Virginia. George Washington's own involvements in western land speculations make one of the favorite topics of the debunkers. By the Quebec Act of 1774, however, the British government took the trans-Allegheny lands north of the Ohio from Virginia and other claimant colonies, and incorporated them with Canada. This act gave a grievance to others besides the planter-speculator. The closing of this frontier was also an offense to a class perhaps normally more inclined to revolt—the restless woodsmen and fur traders, and the only slightly less restless small pioneer farmers who had already occupied the Appalachian valleys, and were ready to pour over into the Kentucky and Ohio country. The Quebec Act in itself does not, of course, explain the American revolution; but taken with a long series of other acts, the Stamp Act, the Navigation Act, the Molasses Act, it accounts for the feeling so evident among active and ambitious groups in America that British rule was an unnecessary and incalculable restraint, an obstacle to their full success in life.

In France the years preceding 1789 are marked by a series of measures which antag-onized different groups. With striking awkwardness, the government offered with one hand what it withdrew with the other. Tax-reform efforts, never carried through, offended privileged groups, without pleasing the unprivileged. Turgot's attempted introduction of laissez-faire into labor relations offended all the vested interests of the old guilds. The famous tariff reduction treaty with England in 1786 directly affected French textiles for the worse, increased unemployment in Normandy and other regions, and gave the employer class a grievance against the government. So, too, in seventeenth-century England, there is no doubt that the attempt to revive obsolete forms of taxation seemed to London or Bristol merchants a threat to their rising prosperity and importance.

Thus we see that certain economic grievances—usually not in the form of economic distress, but rather a feeling on the part of some of the chief enterprising groups that their opportunities for getting on in this world are unduly limited by political arrangements—would seem to be one of the symptoms of revolution. These feelings must, of course, be raised to an effective social pitch by propaganda, pressure-group action, public meetings, and preferably a few good dramatic riots, like the Boston Tea Party. As we shall see, these grievances, however close they are to the pocketbook, must be made respectable, must touch the soul. What is really but a restraint on a rising and already successful group, or on several such groups, must appear as rank injustice towards everyone in the society. Men may revolt partly or even mainly because they are hindered, or, to use Dr. George Pettee's expressive word, cramped; but to the world—and, save for a very few hypocrites, also to themselves—they must appear wronged. Revolutions cannot do without the word "justice."

All this, however, is rather less than what the Marxists seem to mean when they talk about the revolutions of the seventeenth, eighteenth, and nineteenth centuries as deliberately the work of a class-conscious bourgeoisie. Not having the benefit of the writings of Marx to go by, nor indeed those of the still little known Adam Smith, even eighteenth-century revolutionists and discontented spirits used a very non-economic vocabulary. Of course the Marxist, aided by Freud, can reply neatly that economic motivation drove these bourgeois at an un- or sub-conscious level. The trouble with this, from the point of view of the person brought up in the conventions of professional historical research, is that the subconscious never, or rarely, writes documents or makes speeches. If we confine ourselves to what these bourgeois said and did, we find plenty of evidence that separate groups—the American merchants, for instance—felt specific economic grievances, but no signs that bourgeois, entrepreneurs, business men, were aware that as a class their interests in free economic expansion were blocked by existing "feudal" arrangements. Indeed in France a great many business men were more annoyed by the semi-free trade treaty of 1786 with England than by any other governmental step. Certainly one finds no trace of men in England or America or France saying: "Organized feudalism is preventing the triumph of middle-class capitalism. Let us rise against it." Nor, as a matter of fact, were there in these countries just before the revolutions any serious *economic* barriers to prevent the clever lad, even in the lower classes, from making money if he possessed the money-making gifts. Dozens of careers—a Pâris-Duverney, an Edmund Burke, a John Law, a John Hancock—show this. Certainly one cannot deny that class antagonisms existed in these countries; but so far as we can judge, these class antagonisms do not seem to have a clear and simple economic basis. In twentieth-century Russia, of course, these antagonisms were expressed in the language of economics, even though here we shall probably also find that human sentiments as well as human interests are involved.

To sum up so far, if we look at economic life in these societies in the years preceding revolution, we note first, that they have been on the whole prosperous; second, that their governments are chronically short of money—shorter, that is, than most governments usually are; third, that certain groups feel that governmental policies are against their particular economic interests; fourth, that, except in Russia, class economic interests are not openly advanced in propaganda as a motive for attempting to overturn existing political and social arrangements. It is interesting to note here that Professor R. B. Merriman, in a study of six seventeenth-century revolutions in England, France, the Netherlands, Spain, Portugal, and Naples, finds that they all had in common a financial origin, all began as protests against taxation.

If now we turn from the stresses and strains of economic life to the actual workings of the machinery of government, we find a much clearer situation. Here again, we must not posit a normal condition in which this machinery works perfectly. Government here on earth is at best a rough and ready thing, and the governed will always find something to grumble about, from favoritism in distributing low-number automobile license plates to post-office pen points. But there are obviously degrees of governmental inefficiency, and degrees of patience on the part of the governed. In our four societies the governments seem to have been relatively inefficient, and the governed relatively impatient.

Indeed, the near-bankruptcy of a government in a prosperous society might be regarded as good *a priori* evidence of its inefficiency, at least in the old days when government undertook few social or "socialized" services. France in 1789 is a striking example of a society the government of which simply no longer works well. For generations French kings and their ministers had fought the particularistic tendencies of the provinces to get out of the control of Paris by devising a whole series of agencies of centralization, which may be said in a sense to run from the *missi dominici* of Charlemagne to the *intendants* of Richelieu and Louis XIV. Almost as if they had been Anglo-Saxons, however, they destroyed very little of the old in the process, so that France in 1789 was like an attic stuffed full of all kinds of old furniture—including some fine new chairs that just wouldn't fit in the living room. We need not go too deeply into the details of the situation, which can perhaps be summed up graphically by saying that in the sense in which you could make a map of the United States showing all our administrative areas—townships, counties, states—you could not possibly make *one* map of the administrative areas of old France. Even the confusion added to an administrative map of the United States by the various, and relatively new, federal commissions, bureaus, agencies, administrations, does not begin to equal that of France in 1789. You would need at least half a dozen maps to show the crisscross units of *paroisse, seigneurie, baillage, sénéchaussée, généralité, gouvernement, pays d'état et d'élection, les cinq grosses fermes, pays de grande et de petite gabelle*—and this is but a beginning.

There is told about Louis XV one of those

revealing anecdotes, the actual historical truth of which is unimportant, since they reflect contemporary opinion of a concrete condition. Traveling in the provinces, his majesty saw that a town hall or some such building in which he was to be received had a leaky roof. "Ah, if I were only a minister, I'd have that fixed," he remarked. A government of which such a tale could be told was perhaps despotic, but most certainly inefficient. In general, it would seem the inefficiency is more readily recognized by those who suffer from it than is the despotism.

The incompetence of the English government under the first two Stuarts is much less clear, but one can safely say that the central government was not as well run, especially under James I, as it had been under Elizabeth. What is most striking in the English situation is the total inadequacy to modern government of a tax system based on the modest needs of a feudal central government. For the government of James I was beginning to be a modern government, to undertake certain elementary social services, and to rest on a bureaucracy and an army that had to be paid in cash. The chronic need for money which confronted James I and Charles I was by no means a result of riotous living and courtly extravagance, but was for the most part brought on by expenses no modern government could have avoided. And yet their income was on the whole determined and collected by old-fashioned medieval methods. At any rate it is clear that the Stuarts needed money; but their attempts to fill their coffers were awkward, hand-to-mouth expedients that brought them into sharp quarrels with the only people from whom they could collect money—the gentry and the middle class. Their struggles with Parliament threw the whole machinery of English government out of gear.

In America the failure of the machinery was a double one. First, the central colonial administration in Westminster had been allowed to grow in the hit-or-miss fashion Anglophiles have long regarded as the height of political wisdom. In this crisis, however, muddling through clearly was not enough. The attempted reform in colonial administration after the Seven Years' War only made matters worse, as did Turgot's attempted reforms in France, since it was carried out in a series of advances and retreats, cajolings and menaces, blowings-hot and blowings-cold. Second, within most of the colonies the machinery of gov-

ernment had never been properly adjusted to the frontier. The newer western regions of many colonies complained that representation, courts, administrative areas, were rigged in favor of the older seaboard settlements.

The breakdown of Czarist administration is now so much a commonplace that one is tempted to suspect that it has been a bit exaggerated. Looking at the decades preceding 1917—for in all these countries we have been considering the background of the revolutions and not their actual outbreaks—it seems possible to maintain that the government of Russia in peacetime, at least, was perhaps a bit more of a going concern than the other governments we have been studying. From Catherine the Great to Stolypin a great deal of actual improvement can be seen in Russian government. But one thing is clear from the hundred years preceding 1914. Russia could not organize herself for war, and failure in war had, especially in 1905, brought with it a partial collapse of the machinery of internal administration. We must be very careful here to stick to facts and to avoid judgments which have so insinuated themselves into our awareness of Russia that we regard them as facts. It may be that there is some wild oriental element in the Russian soul that makes Russians both incompetent and submissive politically, subject, however, to fits of alcoholic rebellion. This soul is certainly very hard to observe scientifically; and even in literature one may hesitate to label Dostoevski more Russian than Turgenev, who seems far from wild, oriental, drunken or mystic. For our purposes, it is sufficient to note that the Russian *governmental* breakdown, clear in 1917 or even 1916, was by no means clear, say, in 1912.

Finally, one of the most evident uniformities we can record is the effort made in each of our societies to reform the machinery of government. Nothing can be more erroneous than the picture of the old regime as an unregenerate tyranny, sweeping to its end in a climax of despotic indifference to the clamor of its abused subjects. Charles I was working to "modernize" his government, to introduce into England some of the efficient methods of the French. Strafford is in some ways but an unlucky Richelieu. George III and his ministers were trying very hard to pull together the scattered organs of British colonial government. Indeed, it was this attempt at reform, this desire to work out a new colonial "system," that gave the revolutionary movement in America a start. In both France and Russia, there is a series of attempted reforms, associated with names like Turgot, Malesherbes, Necker, and Stolypin. It is true that these reforms were incomplete, that they were repealed or nullified by sabotage on the part of the privileged. But they are on the record, an essential part of the process that issued in revolution in these countries.

REVOLUTION AND NEED SATISFACTION

This selection illustrates a more recent attempt to separate the truth from the falsehood of Marx and to utilize the former. Two major qualifications are placed upon the Marxist theory. First, Davies replaces Marx's economic determinism with a multifactor cause. The state of dissatisfaction that results in revolution may have economic bases, but it may also have noneconomic bases. (In a private communication to the Editor he cites the American Revolution, the Civil War, and the Congo violence in the 1960s as examples of revolutions with significant noneconomic causes.)

Second, Davies believes that for a revolution to occur, dissatisfaction must appear on a background of progressive social improvement. A long decline in welfare, stressed by Marx, will not produce a revolution. On the other hand, a relatively brief setback in the context of steadily increasing welfare may very well bring about a revolution.

> Marx believed that revolutions result from increasing impoverishment. An opposing idea, espoused by De Tocqueville, is that revolutions occur in periods of economic progress. These two ideas are linked by positing that the crucial condition for the occurrence of a revolution is a sharp decline following a long period of economic and social improvement. These conditions lead to a revolution by creating a state of psychological dissatisfaction, an intolerable gap between what people want and what they actually get, for which the government is blamed. Three revolutions are discussed in detail and several others are briefly mentioned in support of this theory.

Davies' theory is supported by some impressive data. However, the paper is a preliminary statement and contains some ambiguities that must be clarified before the theory can be evaluated reasonably. An important problem is in the relationship between the psychological factor of need satisfaction, which is Davies' immediate, or proximal, causal variable, and the "economic and social" (sociological) factors in terms of which he attempts to validate the theory. Exactly what needs are involved and how they are satisfied or frustrated is not clear, nor are the respective contributions of economic and other factors adequately specified.

Davies admits that he does not know the limits of his theory. He is not sure whether it applies to all revolutions or only to some of them, presumably the "progressive" ones. In this respect the statement is similar to that of Brinton (Selection 53). Moreover, it is not clear whether the posited causes of revolution are necessary (a revolution requires their presence) or sufficient (their presence requires a revolution) or both.

In sum, Davies' theory of revolution as stated here in preliminary form perhaps raises more questions than it answers. However, this is a common situation among theories at an early stage in their formulation, and the apparent support that this formulation receives from historical data suggests that it may eventually prove to be very fruitful.

Selection 54
TOWARDS A THEORY OF REVOLUTION
James C. Davies

In exhorting proletarians of all nations to unite in revolution, because they had nothing to lose but their chains, Marx and Engels most succinctly presented that theory of revolution which is recognized as their brain child. But this most famed thesis, that progressive degradation of the industrial working class would finally reach the point of despair and inevitable revolt, is not the only one that Marx fathered. In at least one essay he gave life to a quite antithetical idea. He described, as a precondition of widespread unrest, not progressive degradation of the proletariat but rather an improvement in workers' economic condition which did not keep pace with the growing welfare of capitalists and therefore produced social tension.

A noticeable increase in wages presupposes a rapid growth of productive capital. The rapid growth of productive capital brings about an equally rapid growth of wealth, luxury, social wants, social enjoyments. Thus, although the enjoyments of the workers have risen, the social satisfaction that they give has fallen in comparison with the increased enjoyments of the capitalist, which are inaccessible to the worker, in comparison with the state of development of society in general. Our desires and pleasures spring from society; we measure them, therefore, by society and not by the objects which serve for their satisfaction. Because they are of a social nature, they are of a relative nature.[1]

Marx's qualification here of his more frequent belief that degradation produces revolution is expressed as the main thesis by de Tocqueville in his study of the French Revolution. After a long review of economic and social decline in the seventeenth century and dynamic growth in the eighteenth, de Tocqueville concludes:

So it would appear that the French found their condition the more unsupportable in proportion to its improvement. . . . Revolutions are not always brought about by a gradual decline from bad to worse. Na-

Reprinted from *American Sociological Review*, 27:1, 1962, pp. 5–19, with permission of the author and publisher.

tions that have endured patiently and almost unconsciously the most overwhelming oppression often burst into rebellion against the yoke the moment it begins to grow lighter. The regime which is destroyed by a revolution is almost always an improvement on its immediate predecessor. . . . Evils which are patiently endured when they seem inevitable become intolerable when once the idea of escape from them is suggested.[2]

On the basis of de Tocqueville and Marx, we can choose one of these ideas or the other, which makes it hard to decide just when revolutions are more likely to occur—when there has been social and economic progress or when there has been regress. It appears that both ideas have explanatory and possibly predictive value, if they are juxtaposed and put in the proper time sequence.

Revolutions are most likely to occur when a prolonged period of objective economic and social development is followed by a short period of sharp reversal.[3] The all-important effect on the minds of people in a particular society is to produce, during the former period, an expectation of continued ability to satisfy needs—which continue to rise—and, during the latter, a mental state of anxiety and frustration when manifest reality breaks away from anticipated reality. The actual state of socio-economic development is less significant than the expectation that past progress, now blocked, can and must continue in the future.

Political stability and instability are ultimately dependent on a state of mind, a mood, in a society. Satisfied or apathetic people who are poor in goods, status, and power can remain politically quiet and their opposites can revolt, just as, correlatively and more probably, dissatisfied poor can revolt and satisfied rich oppose revolution. It is the dissatisfied state of mind rather than the tangible provision of "adequate" or "inadequate" supplies of food, equality, or liberty which produces the revolution. In actuality, there must be a joining of forces between dissatisfied, frustrated people who differ in their degree of objective, tangible welfare and status. Well-fed, well-educated, high-status individuals who rebel in the face of apathy among the objectively deprived can accomplish at most a coup d'état. The objectively deprived, when faced with solid opposition of people of wealth, status, and power, will be smashed in their rebellion as were peasants and Anabaptists by German noblemen in 1525 and East Germans by the Communist élite in 1953.

Before appraising this general notion in light of a series of revolutions, a word is in order as to why revolutions ordinarily do not occur when a society is generally impoverished —when, as de Tocqueville put it, evils that seem inevitable are patiently endured. They are endured in the extreme case because the physical and mental energies of people are totally employed in the process of merely staying alive. The Minnesota starvation studies conducted during World War II[4] indicate clearly the constant pre-occupation of very hungry individuals with fantasies and thoughts of food. In extremis, as the Minnesota research poignantly demonstrates, the individual withdraws into a life of his own, withdraws from society, withdraws from any significant kind of activity unrelated to staying alive. Reports of behavior in Nazi concentration camps indicate the same preoccupation.[5] In less extreme and barbarous circumstances, where minimal survival is possible but little more, the preoccupation of individuals with staying alive is only mitigated. Social action takes place for the most part on a local, face-to-face basis. In such circumstances the family is a— perhaps the major—solidary unit[6] and even the local community exists primarily to the extent families need to act together to secure their separate survival. Such was life on the American frontier in the sixteenth through nineteenth centuries. In very much attenuated form, but with a substantial degree of social isolation persisting, such evidently is rural life even today. This is clearly related to a relatively low level of political participation in elections.[7] As Zawadzki and Lazarsfeld have indicated,[8] preoccupation with physical survival, even in industrial areas, is a force strongly militating against the establishment of the community-sense and consensus on joint political action which are necessary to induce a revolutionary state of mind. Far from making people into revolutionaries, enduring poverty makes for concern with one's solitary self or solitary family at best and resignation or mute despair at worst. When it is a choice between losing their chains or their lives, people will mostly choose to keep their chains, a fact which Marx seems to have overlooked.[9]

It is when the chains have been loosened somewhat, so that they can be cast off without a high probability of losing life, that people are put in a condition of proto-rebelliousness. I use the term proto-rebelliousness because the mood of discontent may be dissipated before a violent outbreak occurs. The causes for such dissipation may be natural or social (including economic and political). A bad crop year that

Figure 1   Need Satisfaction and Revolution

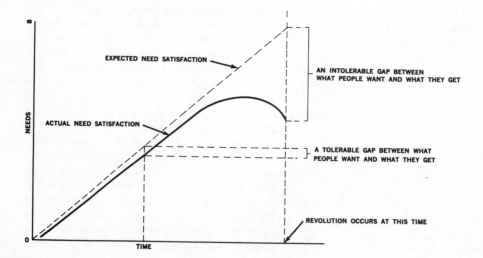

threatens a return to chronic hunger may be succeeded by a year of natural abundance. Recovery from sharp economic dislocation may take the steam from the boiler of rebellion.[10] The slow, grudging grant of reforms, which has been the political history of England since at least the Industrial Revolution, may effectively and continuously prevent the degree of frustration that produces revolt.

A revolutionary state of mind requires the continued, even habitual but dynamic expectation of greater opportunity to satisfy basic needs, which may range from merely physical (food, clothing, shelter, health, and safety from bodily harm) to social (the affectional ties of family and friends) to the need for equal dignity and justice. But the necessary additional ingredient is a persistent, unrelenting threat to the satisfaction of these needs: not a threat which actually returns people to a state of sheer survival but which puts them in the mental state where they believe they will not be able to satisfy one or more basic needs. Although physical deprivation in some degree may be threatened on the eve of all revolutions, it need not be the prime factor, as it surely was not in the American Revolution of 1775. The crucial factor is the vague or specific fear that ground gained over a long period of time will be quickly lost. This fear does not generate if there is continued opportunity to satisfy continually emerging needs; it generates when the existing government suppresses or is blamed for suppressing such opportunity.

Three rebellions or revolutions are given considerable attention in the sections that follow: Dorr's Rebellion of 1842, the Russian Revolution of 1917, and the Egyptian Revolution of 1952. Brief mention is then made of several other major civil disturbances, all of which appear to fit the J-curve pattern.[11]* After considering these specific disturbances, some general theoretical and research problems are discussed.

No claim is made that all rebellions follow the pattern, but just that the ones here presented do. All of these are "progressive" revolutions in behalf of greater equality and liberty. The question is open whether the pattern occurs in such markedly retrogressive revolutions as Nazism in Germany or the 1861 Southern rebellion in the United States. It will

surely be necessary to examine other progressive revolutions before one can judge how universal the J-curve is. And it will be necessary, in the interests of scientific validation, to examine cases of serious civil disturbance that fell short of producing profound revolution—such as the Sepoy Rebellion of 1857 in India, the Pullman Strike of 1894 in America, the Boxer Rebellion of 1900 in China, and the Great Depression of the 1920s and 1930s as it was experienced in Austria, France, Great Britain, and the United States. The explanation for such still-born rebellions—for revolutions that might have occurred—is inevitably more complicated than for those that come to term in the "normal" course of political gestation.

Dorr's Rebellion of 1842

Dorr's Rebellion[12] in nineteenth-century America was perhaps the first of many civil disturbances to occur in America as a consequence, in part, of the Industrial Revolution. It followed by three years an outbreak in England that had similar roots and a similar program—the Chartist agitation. A machine-operated textile industry was first established in Rhode Island in 1790 and grew rapidly as a consequence of domestic and international demand, notably during the Napoleonic Wars. Jefferson's Embargo Act of 1807, the War of 1812, and a high tariff in 1816 further stimulated American industry.

Rapid industrial growth meant the movement of people from farms to cities. In Massachusetts the practice developed of hiring mainly the wives and daughters of farmers, whose income was thereby supplemented but not displaced by wages. In Rhode Island whole families moved to the cities and became committed to the factory system. When times were good, industrialized families earned two or three times what they got from the soil; when the mills were idle, there was not enough money for bread.[13] From 1807 to 1815 textiles enjoyed great prosperity; from 1834 to 1842 they suffered depression, most severely from 1835 to 1840. Prosperity raised expectations and depression frustrated them, particularly when accompanied by stubborn resistance to suffrage demands that first stirred in 1790 and recurred in a wave-like pattern in 1811 and then in 1818 and 1820 following suffrage extension in Connecticut and Massa-

---

* Actually an inverted "J," as in Figure 1.—Ed.

chusetts. The final crest was reached in 1841, when suffrage associations met and called for a constitutional convention.[14]

Against the will of the government, the suffragists held an election in which all adult males were eligible to vote, held a constitutional convention composed of delegates so elected and in December 1841 submitted the People's Constitution to the same electorate, which approved it and the call for an election of state officers the following April, to form a new government under this unconstitutional constitution.[15]

These actions joined the conflict with the established government. When asked—by the dissidents—the state supreme court rendered its private judgment in March 1842 that the new constitution was "of no binding force whatever" and any act "to carry it into effect by force will be treason against the state." The legislature passed what became known as the Algerian law, making it an offense punishable by a year in jail to vote in the April election, and by life imprisonment to hold office under the People's Constitution.

The rebels went stoutly ahead with the election, and on May 3, 1842 inaugurated the new government. The next day the People's legislature met and respectfully requested the sheriff to take possession of state buildings, which he failed to do. Violence broke out on the 17th of May in an attempt to take over a state arsenal with two British cannon left over from the Revolutionary War. When the cannon misfired, the People's government resigned. Sporadic violence continued for another month, resulting in the arrest of over 500 men, mostly textile workers, mechanics, and laborers. The official legislature called for a

new constitutional convention, chosen by universal manhood suffrage, and a new constitution went into effect in January, 1843. Altogether only one person was killed in this little revolution, which experienced violence, failure, and then success within the space of nine months.

It is impossible altogether to separate the experience of rising expectations among people in Rhode Island from that among Americans generally. They all shared historically the struggle against a stubborn but ultimately rewarding frontier where their self-confidence gained strength not only in the daily process of tilling the soil and harvesting the crops but also by improving their skill at self-government. Winning their war of independence, Americans continued to press for more goods and more democracy. The pursuit of economic expectations was greatly facilitated by the growth of domestic and foreign trade and the gradual establishment of industry. Equalitarian expectations in politics were satisfied and without severe struggle—in most Northern states—by suffrage reforms.

In Rhode Island, these rising expectations—more goods, more equality, more self-rule—were countered by a series of containing forces which built up such a head of steam that the boiler cracked a little in 1842. The textile depression hit hard in 1835 and its consequences were aggravated by the Panic of 1837. In addition to the frustration of seeing their peers get the right to vote in other states, poor people in Rhode Island were now beset by industrial dislocation in which the machines that brought them prosperity they had never before enjoyed now were bringing economic disaster. The machines could not be converted

Figure 2

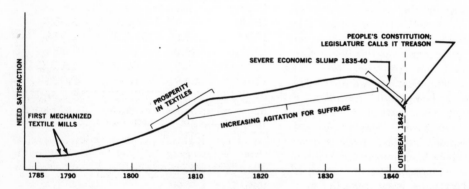

to produce food and in Rhode Island the machine tenders could not go back to the farm.

When they had recovered from the preoccupation with staying alive, they turned in earnest to their demands for constitutional reform. But these were met first with indifference and then by a growing intransigence on the part of the government representing the propertied class. Hostile action by the state supreme court and then the legislature with its Algerian law proved just enough to break briefly the constitutional structure which in stable societies has the measure of power and resilience necessary to absorb social tension.

The Russian Revolution of 1917

In Russia's tangled history it is hard to decide when began the final upsurge of expectations that, when frustrated, produced the cataclysmic events of 1917. One can truly say that the real beginning was the slow modernization process begun by Peter the Great over two hundred years before the revolution. And surely the rationalist currents from France that slowly penetrated Russian intellectual life during the reign of Catherine the Great a hundred years before the revolution were necessary, lineal antecedents of the 1917 revolution.

Without denying that there was an accumulation of forces over at least a 200-year period,[16] we may nonetheless date the final upsurge as beginning with the 1861 emancipation of serfs and reaching a crest in the 1905 revolution.

The chronic and growing unrest of serfs before their emancipation in 1861 is an ironic commentary on the Marxian notion that human beings are what social institutions make them. Although serfdom had been shaping their personality since 1647, peasants became increasingly restive in the second quarter of the nineteenth century.[17] The continued discontent of peasants after emancipation is an equally ironic commentary on the belief that relieving one profound frustration produces enduring contentment. Peasants rather quickly got over their joy at being untied from the soil after two hundred years. Instead of declining, rural violence increased.[18] Having gained freedom but not much free land, peasants now had to rent or buy land to survive: virtual personal slavery was exchanged for financial servitude. Land pressure grew, reflected in a doubling of land prices between 1868 and 1897.

It is hard thus to tell whether the economic plight of peasants was much lessened after emancipation. A 1903 government study indicated that even with a normal harvest, average food intake per peasant was 30 per cent below the minimum for health. The only sure contrary item of evidence is that the peasant population grew, indicating at least increased ability of the land to support life, as the following table shows.

The land-population pressure pushed people into towns and cities, where the rapid growth of industry truly afforded the chance for economic betterment. One estimate of net annual income for a peasant family of five in the rich blackearth area in the late nineteenth century was 82 rubles. In contrast, a "good" wage for a male factory worker was about 168 rubles per year. It was this difference in the degree of poverty that produced almost a doubling of the urban population between 1878 and 1897. The number of industrial workers increased almost as rapidly. The city and the factory gave new hope. Strikes in the 1880s were met with brutal suppression but also with the beginning of factory legislation, including the requirement that wages be paid regularly and the abolition of child labor. The burgeoning proletariat remained comparatively contented until the eve of the 1905 revolution.[19]

Table 1   Population of European Russia (1480–1895)

	Population in millions	Increase in millions	Average annual rate of increase*
1480	2.1		
1580	4.3	2.2	1.05%
1680	12.6	8.3	1.93%
1780	26.8	14.2	1.13%
1880	84.5	57.7	2.15%
1895	110.0	25.5	2.02%

* Computed as follows: dividing the increase by the number of years and then dividing this hypothetical annual increase by the population at the end of the preceding 100-year period.
Source for gross population data: *Entsiklopedicheskii Slovar*, St. Petersburg, 1897, vol. 40, p. 631. Russia's population was about 97% rural in 1784, 91% in 1878, and 87% in 1897. See Masaryk, *op. cit.*, p. 162n.

There is additional, non-economic evidence to support the view that 1861 to 1905 was the period of rising expectations that preceded the 1917 revolution. The administration of justice before the emancipation had largely been carried out by noblemen and landowners who embodied the law for their peasants. In 1864 justice was in principle no longer delegated to such private individuals. Trials became public, the jury system was introduced, and judges got tenure. Corporal punishment was alleviated by the elimination of running the gauntlet, lashing, and branding; caning persisted until 1904. Public joy at these reforms was widespread. For the intelligentsia, there was increased opportunity to think and write and to criticize established institutions, even sacrosanct absolutism itself.

But Tsarist autocracy had not quite abandoned the scene. Having inclined but not bowed, in granting the inevitable emancipation as an act not of justice but grace, it sought to maintain its absolutist principle by conceding reform without accepting anything like democratic authority. Radical political and economic criticism surged higher. Some strong efforts to raise the somewhat lowered floodgates began as early as 1866, after an unsuccessful attempt was made on the life of Alexander II, in whose name serfs had just gained emancipation. When the attempt succeeded fifteen years later, there was increasing state action under Alexander III to limit constantly rising expectations. By suppression and concession, the last Alexander succeeded in dying naturally in 1894.

When it became apparent that Nicholas II shared his father's ideas but not his forcefulness, opposition of the intelligentsia to absolutism joined with the demands of peasants and workers, who remained loyal to the Tsar but demanded economic reforms. Starting in 1904, there developed a "League of Deliverance" that coordinated efforts of at least seventeen other revolutionary, proletarian, or nationalist groups within the empire. Consensus on the need for drastic reform, both political and economic, established a many-ringed circus of groups sharing the same tent. These groups were geographically distributed from Finland to Armenia and ideologically from liberal constitutionalists to revolutionaries made prudent by the contrast between their own small forces and the power of Tsardom.

Events of 1904–5 mark the general downward turning point of expectations, which people increasingly saw as frustrated by the continuation of Tsardom. Two major and related occurrences made 1905 the point of no return. The first took place on the Bloody Sunday of January 22, 1905, when peaceful proletarian petitioners marched on the St. Petersburg palace and were killed by the hundreds. The myth that the Tsar was the gracious protector of his subjects, however surrounded he might be by malicious advisers, was quite shattered. The reaction was immediate, bitter, and prolonged and was not at all confined to the working class. Employers, merchants, and white-collar officials joined in the burgeoning of strikes which brought the economy to a virtual standstill in October. Some employers even continued to pay wages to strikers. University students and faculties joined the revolution. After the great October strike, the peasants ominously sided with the workers and engaged in riots and assaults on landowners. Until peasants became involved, even some landowners had sided with the revolution.

The other major occurrence was the disastrous defeat of the Russian army and navy in the 1904–5 war with Japan. Fundamentally an imperialist venture aspiring to hegemony over the people of Asia, the war was not regarded as a people's but as a Tsar's war, to save and spread absolutism. The military defeat itself probably had less portent than the return of shattered soldiers from a fight that was not for them. Hundreds of thousands, wounded or not, returned from the war as a visible, vocal, and ugly reminder to the entire populace of the weakness and selfishness of Tsarist absolutism.

The years from 1905 to 1917 formed an almost relentless procession of increasing misery and despair. Promising at last a constitutional government, the Tsar, in October, 1905, issued from on high a proclamation renouncing absolutism, granting law-making power to a duma, and guaranteeing freedom of speech, assembly, and association. The first two dumas, of 1906 and 1907, were dissolved for recalcitrance. The third was made pliant by reduced representation of workers and peasants and by the prosecution and conviction of protestants in the first two. The brief period of a free press was succeeded in 1907 by a reinstatement of censorship and confiscation of prohibited publications. Trial of offenders against the Tsar was now conducted by courts martial. Whereas there had been only 26 executions of the death sentence, in the 13 years of Alexander II's firm rule (1881–94), there were 4,449 in the years 1905–10, in six years of Nicholas II's soft regimen.[20]

But this "white terror," which caused despair among the workers and intelligentsia in the cities, was not the only face of misery. For the peasants, there was a bad harvest in 1906 followed by continued crop failures in several areas in 1907. To forestall action by the dumas, Stolypin decreed a series of agrarian reforms designed to break up the power of the rural communes by individualizing land ownership. Between these acts of God and government, peasants were so preoccupied with hunger or self-aggrandizement as to be dulled in their sensitivity to the revolutionary appeals of radical organizers.

After more than five years of degrading terror and misery, in 1910 the country appeared to have reached a condition of exhaustion. Political strikes had fallen off to a new low. As the economy recovered, the insouciance of hopelessness set in. Amongst the intelligentsia the mood was hedonism, or despair that often ended in suicide. Industrialists aligned themselves with the government. Workers worked. But an upturn of expectations, inadequately quashed by the police, was evidenced by a recrudescence of political strikes which, in the first half of 1914—on the eve of war—approached the peak of 1905. They sharply diminished during 1915 but grew again in 1916 and became a general strike in February 1917.[21]

Figure 3 indicates the lesser waves in the tidal wave whose first trough is at the end of serfdom in 1861 and whose second is at the end of Tsardom in 1917. This fifty-six year period appears to constitute a single long phase in which popular gratification at the termination of one institution (serfdom) rather quickly was replaced with rising expectations which resulted from intensified industrialization and which were incompatible with the continuation of the inequitable and capricious power structure of Tsarist society. The small trough of frustration during the repression that followed the assassination of Alexander II seems to have only briefly interrupted the rise in popular demand for more goods and more power. The trough in 1904 indicates the consequences of war with Japan. The 1905–6 trough reflects the repression of January 22, and after, and is followed by economic recovery. The final downturn, after the first year of war, was a consequence of the dislocations of the German attack on all kinds of concerted activities other than production for the prosecution of the war. Patriotism and governmental repression for a time smothered discontent. The inflation that developed in 1916 when goods, including food, became severely scarce began to make workers self-consciously discontented. The conduct of the war, including the growing brutality against reluctant, ill-provisioned troops, and the enormous loss of life, produced the same bitter frustration in the army.[22] When civilian discontent reached the breaking point in February, 1917, it did not take long for it to spread rapidly into the armed forces. Thus began the second phase of

Figure 3

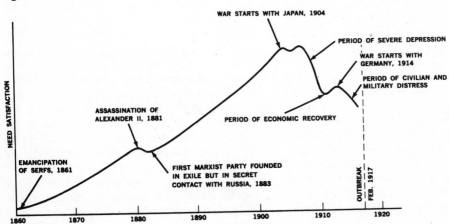

the revolution that really started in 1905 and ended in death to the Tsar and Tsardom—but not to absolutism—when the Bolsheviks gained ascendancy over the moderates in October. A centuries-long history of absolutism appears to have made this post-Tsarist phase of it tragically inevitable.

The Egyptian Revolution of 1952

The final slow upsurge of expectations in Egypt that culminated in the revolution began when that society became a nation in 1922, with the British grant of limited independence. British troops remained in Egypt to protect not only the Suez Canal but also, ostensibly, to prevent foreign aggression. The presence of foreign troops served only to heighten nationalist expectations, which were excited by the Wafd, the political organization that formed public opinion on national rather than religious grounds and helped establish a fairly unified community—in striking contrast to late-nineteenth century Russia.

But nationalist aspirations were not the only rising expectations in Egypt of the 1920s and 1930s. World War I had spurred industrialization, which opened opportunities for peasants to improve, somewhat, their way of life by working for wages in the cities and also opened great opportunities for entrepreneurs to get rich. The moderately wealthy got immoderately so in commodity market speculation, finance, and manufacture, and the uprooted peasants who were now employed, or at any rate living, in cities were relieved of at least the notion that poverty and boredom must be the will of Allah. But the incongruity

of a money-based modern semi-feudality that was like a chariot with a gasoline engine evidently escaped the attention of ordinary people. The generation of the 1930s could see more rapid progress, even for themselves, than their parents had even envisioned. If conditions remained poor, they could always be blamed on the British, whose economic and military power remained visible and strong.

Economic progress continued, though unevenly, during World War II. Conventional exports, mostly cotton, actually declined, not even reaching depression levels until 1945, but direct employment by Allied military forces reached a peak of over 200,000 during the most intense part of the African war. Exports after the war rose steadily until 1948, dipped, and then rose sharply to a peak in 1951 as a consequence of the Korean war. But in 1945 over 250,000 wage earners[23]—probably over a third of the working force—became jobless. The cost of living by 1945 had risen to three times the index of 1937.[24] Manual laborers were hit by unemployment; white collar workers and professionals probably more by inflation than unemployment. Meanwhile the number of millionaires in pounds sterling had increased eight times during the war.[25]

Frustrations, exacerbated during the war by German and thereafter by Soviet propaganda, were at first deflected against the Birtish[26] but gradually shifted closer to home. Egyptian agitators began quoting the Koran in favor of a just, equalitarian society and against great differences in individual wealth. There was an ominous series of strikes, mostly in the textile mills, from 1946–8.

At least two factors stand out in the post-

Figure 4

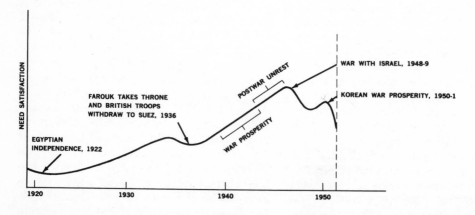

ponement of revolution. The first was the insatiable postwar world demand for cotton and textiles and the second was the surge of solidarity with king and country that followed the 1948 invasion of the new state of Israel. Israel now supplemented England as an object of deflected frustration. The disastrous defeat a year later, by a new nation with but a fifteenth of Egypt's population, was the beginning of the end. This little war had struck the peasant at his hearth, when a shortage of wheat and of oil for stoves provided a daily reminder of a weak and corrupt government. The defeat frustrated popular hopes for national glory and—with even more portent— humiliated the army and solidified it against the bureaucracy and the palace which had profiteered at the expense of national honor. In 1950 began for the first time a direct and open propaganda attack against the king himself. A series of peasant uprisings, even on the lands of the king, took place in 1951 along with some 49 strikes in the cities. The skyrocketing demand for cotton after the start of the Korean War in June, 1950 was followed by a collapse in March, 1952. The uncontrollable or uncontrolled riots in Cairo, on January 26, 1952, marked the fiery start of the revolution. The officers' coup in the early morning of July 23 only made it official.

Other civil disturbances

The J-curve of rising expectations followed by their effective frustration is applicable to other revolutions and rebellions than just the three already considered. Leisler's Rebellion in the royal colony of New York in 1689 was a brief dress-rehearsal for the American Revolution eighty-six years later. In an effort to make the colony serve the crown better, duties had been raised and were being vigorously collected. The tanning of hides in the colony was forbidden, as was the distillation of liquor. An embargo was placed on unmilled grain, which hurt the farmers. After a long period of economic growth and substantial political autonomy, these new and burdensome regulations produced a popular rebellion that for a year displaced British sovereignty.[27]

The American Revolution itself fits the J-curve and deserves more than the brief mention here given. Again prolonged economic growth and political autonomy produced continually rising expectations. They became acutely frustrated when, following the French and Indian War (which had cost England so much and the colonies so little), England began a series of largely economic regulations having the same purpose as those directed against New York in the preceding century. From the 1763 Proclamation (closing to settlement land west of the Appalachians) to the Coercive Acts of April, 1774 (which among other things, in response to the December, 1773 Boston Tea Party, closed tight the port of Boston), Americans were beset with unaccustomed manifestations of British power and began to resist forcibly in 1775, on the Lexington-Concord road. A significant decline in trade with England in 1772[28] may have hastened the maturation of colonial rebelliousness.

The curve also fits the French Revolution, which again merits more mention than space here permits. Growing rural prosperity, marked by steadily rising land values in the eighteenth century, had progressed to the point where a third of French land was owned by peasant-proprietors. There were the beginnings of large-scale manufacture in the factory system. Constant pressure by the bourgeoisie against the state for reforms was met with considerable hospitality by a government already shifting from its old landed-aristocratic and clerical base to the growing middle class. Counter to these trends, which would *per se* avoid revolution, was the feudal reaction of the mid-eighteenth century, in which the dying nobility sought in numerous nagging ways to retain and reactivate its perquisites against a resentful peasantry and importunate bourgeoisie.

But expectations apparently continued rising until the growing opportunities and prosperity rather abruptly halted, about 1787. The fiscal crisis of the government is well known, much of it a consequence of a 1.5 billion livre deficit following intervention against Britain in the American war of independence. The threat to tax the nobility severely—after its virtual tax immunity—and the bourgeoisie more severely may indeed be said to have precipitated the revolution. But less well-known is the fact that 1787 was a bad harvest year and 1788 even worse; that by July, 1789 bread prices were higher than they had been in over 70 years; that an ill-timed trade treaty with England depressed the prices of French textiles; that a concurrent bumper grape crop depressed wine prices—all with the result of making desperate the plight of the large segment of the population now dependent on other producers for food. They had little money to buy even less bread. Nobles and bourgoisie were alienated from the government by the threat of taxation; workers and some peasants by the threat of starvation. A long period of halting but real progress for virtually all segments of the population was now abruptly ended in consequence of the government's efforts to meet its deficit and of economic crisis resulting from poor crops and poor tariff policy.[29]

The draft riots that turned the city of New York upside down for five days in July, 1863 also follow the J-curve. This severe local disturbance began when conscription threatened the lives and fortunes of workingmen whose enjoyment of wartime prosperity was now frustrated not only by military service (which could be avoided by paying $300 or furnishing a substitute—neither means being available to poor people) but also by inflation.[30]

Even the riots in Nyasaland, in February and March, 1959, appear to follow the pattern of a period of frustration after expectations and satisfactions have risen. Nyasaland workers who had enjoyed the high wages they were paid during the construction of the Kariba dam in Rhodesia returned to their homes and to unemployment, or to jobs paying $5 per month at a time when $15 was considered a bare minimum wage.[31]

One negative case—of a revolution that did not occur—is the depression of the 1930s in the United States. It was severe enough, at least on economic grounds, to have produced a revolution. Total national private production income in 1932 reverted to what it had been in 1916. Farm income in the same year was as low as in 1900; manufacturing as low as in 1913. Construction had not been as low since 1908. Mining and quarrying was back at the 1909 level.[32] For much of the population, two decades of economic progress had been wiped out. There were more than sporadic demonstrations of unemployed, hunger marchers, and veterans. In New York City, at least 29 people died of starvation. Poor people could vividly contrast their own past condition with the present—and their own present condition with that of those who were not seriously suffering. There were clearly audible rumbles of revolt. Why, then, no revolution?

Several forces worked strongly against it. Among the most depressed, the mood was one of apathy and despair, like that observed in Austria by Zawadzki and Lazarsfeld. It was not until the 1936 election that there was an increased turnout in the national election. The great majority of the public shared a set of values which since 1776 had been official dogma—not the dissident program of an alienated intelligentsia. People by and large were in agreement, whether or not they had succeeded economically, in a belief in individual hard work, self-reliance, and the promise of success. (Among workers, this non-class orientation had greatly impeded the establishment of trade unions, for example.) Those least hit by the depression—the upper-middle-class businessmen, clergymen, lawyer, and intellectuals—remained rather solidly committed not only to equalitarian values and to the established economic system but also to constitutional processes. There was no such widespread or profound alienation as that which had cracked the loyalty of the nobility, clergy, bourgeoisie, armed forces, and intelligentsia in Russia. And the national political leadership that emerged had constitutionalism almost bred in its bones. The major threat to constitutionalism came in Louisiana; this leadership was unable to capture a national party organization, in part because Huey Long's arbitrariness and demagogy were mistrusted.

The major reason that revolution did not nonetheless develop probably remains the vigor with which the national government attacked the depression in 1933, when it became no longer possible to blame the government. The ambivalent popular hostility to the business community was contained by both the action of government against the depression and the government's practice of publicly and successfully eliciting the cooperation of businessmen during the crucial months of 1933. A failure then of cooperation could have intensified rather than lessened popular hostility to business. There was no longer an economic or a political class that could be the object of widespread intense hatred because of its indifference or hostility to the downtrodden. Had Roosevelt adopted a demagogic stance in the 1932 campaign and gained the loyalty to himself personally of the Army and the F.B.I., there might have been a Nazi-type "revolution," with a potpourri of equalitarian reform, nationalism, imperialism, and domestic scapegoats. Because of a conservatism in America stemming from strong and long attachment to a value system shared by all classes, an anti-capitalist, leftist revolution in the 1930s is very difficult to imagine.

Some conclusions

The notion that revolutions need both a period of rising expectations and a succeeding period in which they are frustrated qualifies substantially the main Marxian notion that revolutions occur after progressive degradation and the de Tocqueville notion that they occur when conditions are improving. By putting de Tocqueville before Marx but without abandoning either theory, we are better able to plot the antecedents of at least the disturbances here described.

Half of the general, if not common, sense of this revised notion lies in the utter improbability of a revolution occurring in a society where there is the continued, unimpeded opportunity to satisfy new needs, new hopes, new expectations. Would Dorr's rebellion have become such if the established electorate and government had readily acceded to the suffrage demands of the unpropertied? Would the Russian Revolution have taken place if the Tsarist autocracy had, quite out of character, truly granted the popular demands for constitutional democracy in 1905? Would the Cairo riots of January, 1952 and the subsequent coup actually have occurred if Britain had departed from Egypt and if the Egyptian monarchy had established an equitable tax system and in other ways alleviated the poverty of urban masses and the shame of the military?

The other half of the sense of the notion has to do with the improbability of revolution taking place where there has been no hope, no period in which expectations have risen. Such a stability of expectations presupposes a static state of human aspirations that sometimes exists but is rare. Stability of expectations is not a stable social condition. Such was the case of American Indians (at least from our perspective) and perhaps Africans before white men with Bibles, guns, and other goods interrupted the stability of African society. Egypt was in such a condition, vis-à-vis modern aspirations, before Europe became interested in building a canal. Such stasis was the case in Nazi concentration camps, where conformism reached the point of inmates cooperating with guards even when the inmates were told to lie down so that they could be shot.[33]

But in the latter case there was a society with externally induced complete despair, and even in these camps there were occasional rebellions of sheer desperation. It is of course true that in a society less regimented than concentration camps, the rise of expectations can be frustrated successfully, thereby defeating rebellion just as the satisfaction of expectations does. This, however, requires the uninhibited exercise of brute force as it was used in suppressing the Hungarian rebellion of 1956. Failing the continued ability and persistent will of a ruling power to use such force, there appears to be no sure way to avoid revolution short of an effective, affirmative, and continuous response on the part of established governments to the almost continuously emerging needs of the governed.

To be predictive, my notion requires the assessment of the state of mind—or more precisely, the mood—of a people. This is always difficult, even by techniques of systematic public opinion analysis. Respondents interviewed in a country with a repressive government are not likely to be responsive. But there has been considerable progress in gathering first-hand data about the state of mind of peoples in politically unstable circumstances. One instance of this involved interviewing in West Berlin, during and after the 1948 blockade, as reported by Buchanan and Cantril. They were able to ascertain, however crudely, the sense of security that people in Berlin felt. There was a significant increase in security after the blockade. [34]

Another instance comes out of the Middle Eastern study conducted by the Columbia University Bureau of Applied Social Research and reported by Lerner.[35] By directly asking respondents whether they were happy or unhappy with the way things had turned out in their life, the interviewers turned up data indicating marked differences in the frequency of a sense of unhappiness between countries and between "traditional," "transitional," and "modern" individuals in these countries.[36] There is no technical reason why such comparisons could not be made chronologically as well as they have been geographically.

Other than interview data are available with which we can, from past experience, make reasonable inferences about the mood of a people. It was surely the sense for the relevance of such data that led Thomas Masaryk before the first World War to gather facts about peasant uprisings and industrial strikes and about the writings and actions of the intelligentsia in nineteenth-century Russia. In the present report, I have used not only such data —in the collection of which other social scientists have been less assiduous than Masaryk— but also such indexes as comparative size of vote as between Rhode Island and the United States, employment, exports, and cost of living. Some such indexes, like strikes and cost of living, may be rather closely related to the mood of a people; others, like value of exports, are much cruder indications. Lest we shy away from the gathering of crude data, we should bear in mind that Durkheim developed his remarkable insights into modern society in large part by his analysis of suicide rates. He was unable to rely on the interviewing technique. We need not always ask people whether they are grievously frustrated by their government; their actions can tell us as well and sometimes better.

In his *Anatomy of Revolution*, Crane Brinton describes "some tentative uniformities" that he discovered in the Puritan, American, French, and Russian revolutions.[37] The uniformities were: an economically advancing society, class antagonism, desertion of intellectuals, inefficient government, a ruling class that has lost self-confidence, financial failure of government, and the inept use of force against rebels. All but the last two of these are long-range phenomena that lend themselves to studies over extended time periods. The first two lend themselves to statistical analysis. If they serve the purpose, techniques of content analysis could be used to ascertain trends in alienation of intellectuals. Less rigorous methods would perhaps serve better to ascertain the effectiveness of government and the self-confidence of rulers. Because tensions and frustrations are present at all times in every society, what is most seriously needed are data that cover an extended time period in a particular society, so that one can say there is evidence that tension is greater or less than it was N years or months previously.

We need also to know how long is a long cycle of rising expectations and how long is a brief cycle of frustration. We noted a brief period of frustration in Russia after the 1881 assassination of Alexander II and a longer period after the 1904 beginning of the Russo-Japanese War. Why did not the revolution occur at either of these times rather than in 1917? Had expectations before these two times not risen high enough? Had the subsequent decline not been sufficiently sharp and deep? Measuring techniques have not yet been devised to answer these questions. But their unavailability now does not forecast their eternal inaccessibility. Physicists devised useful temperature scales long before they came as close to absolute zero as they have recently in laboratory conditions. The far more complex problems of scaling in social science inescapably are harder to solve..

We therefore are still not at the point of being able to predict revolution, but the closer we can get to data indicating by inference the prevailing mood in a society, the closer we will be to understanding the change from gratification to frustration in people's minds. That is the part of the anatomy, we are forever being told with truth and futility, in which wars and revolutions always start. We should eventually be able to escape the embarrassment that may have come to Lenin six weeks after he made the statement in Switzerland, in January, 1917, that he doubted whether "we, the old [will] live to see the decisive battles of the coming revolution."[38]

Notes

[1] The Communist Manifesto of 1848 evidently antedates the opposing idea by about a year. See Edmund Wilson, *To The Finland Station* (Anchor Books edition), New York: Doubleday & Co. (n.d.), p. 157; Lewis S. Feuer, Karl Marx and Friedrich Engels: *Basic Writings on Politics and Philosophy*, N. Y.: Doubleday & Co., Inc., 1959, p. 1. The above quotation is from Karl Marx and Frederick Engels, "Wage Labour and Capital," *Selected Works in Two Volumes*, Moscow: Foreign Languages Publishing House, 1955, vol. 1, p. 94.

[2] A. de Tocqueville, *The Old Regime and the French Revolution* (trans. by John Bonner), N. Y.: Harper & Bros., 1856, p. 214. The Stuart Gilbert translation, Garden City: Doubleday & Co., Inc., 1955, pp. 176–177, gives a somewhat less pungent version of the same comment.

L'Ancien Régime was first published in 1856.

[3] Revolutions are here defined as violent civil disturbances that cause the displacement of one ruling group by another that has a broader popular basis for support.

[4] The full report is Ancel Keys *et al.*, *The Biology of Human Starvation*, Minneapolis: University of Minnesota Press, 1950. See J. Brozek, "Semi-starvation and Nutritional Rehabilitation," *Journal of Clinical Nutrition*, 1 (January, 1953), pp. 107–118 for a brief analysis.

[5] E. A. Cohen, *Human Behavior in the Concentration Camp*, New York: W. W. Norton & Co., 1953, pp. 123–125, 131–140.

[6] For community life in such poverty, in Mezzogiorno Italy, see E. C. Banfield, *The Moral Basis of a Backward Society*, Glencoe, Ill.: The Free Press, 1958. The author emphasizes that the nuclear family is a solidary, consensual, moral unit (see p. 85) but even within it, consensus appears to break down, in outbreaks of pure, individual amorality—notably between parents and children (see p. 117).

[7] See Angus Campbell *et al.*, *The American Voter*, New York: John Wiley & Sons, 1960, Chap. 15, "Agrarian Political Behavior."

[8] B. Zawadzki and P. F. Lazarsfeld, "The Psychological Consequences of Unemployment," *Journal of Social Psychology*, 6 (May, 1935), pp. 224–251.

[9] A remarkable and awesome exception to this phenomenon occurred occasionally in some Nazi concentration camps, e.g., in a Buchenwald revolt against capricious rule by criminal prisoners. During this revolt, one hundred criminal prisoners were killed by political prisoners. See Cohen, *op. cit.*, p. 200.

[10] See W. W. Rostow, "Business Cycles, Harvests, and Politics: 1790–1850," *Journal of Economic History*, 1 (November, 1941), pp. 206–221 for the relation between economic fluctuation and the activities of the Chartists in the 1830s and 1840s.

[11] This curve is of course not to be confused with its prior and altogether different use of Floyd Allport in his study of social conformity. See F. H. Allport, "The J-curve Hypothesis of Conforming Behavior," *Journal of Social Psychology*, 5 (May, 1934), pp. 141–183, reprinted in T. H. Newcomb & E. L. Hartley, *Readings in Social Psychology*, N. Y.: Henry Holt & Co., 1947, pp. 55–67.

[12] I am indebted to Beryl L. Crowe for his extensive research on Dorr's Rebellion while he was a participant in my political behavior seminar at the University of California, Berkeley, Spring 1960.

[13] Joseph Brennan, *Social Conditions in Industrial Rhode Island: 1820–1860*, Washington, D. C.: Catholic University of America, 1940, p. 33.

[14] The persistent demand for suffrage may be understood in light of election data for 1828 and 1840. In the former year, only 3600 votes were cast in Rhode Island, whose total population was about 94,000. (Of these votes, 23 per cent were cast for Jackson and 77 per cent for Adams, in contrast to a total national division of 56 per cent for Jackson and 44 per cent for Adams). All votes cast in the 1828 election amount to 4 per cent of the total Rhode Island population and 11 per cent of the total U.S. population excluding slaves. In 1840, with a total population of 109,000 only 8300 votes—8 per cent—were cast in Rhode Island, in contrast to 17 per cent of the national population excluding slaves.

[15] A. M. Mowry, *The Dorr War*, Providence, R. I.: Preston & Rounds Co., 1901, p. 114.

[16] There is an excellent summary in B. Brutzkus, "The Historical Peculiarities of the Social and Economic Development of Russia," in R. Bendix and S. M. Lipset, *Class, Status, and Power*, Glencoe, Ill.: The Free Press, 1953, pp. 517–540.

[17] Jacqueries rose from an average of 8 per year in 1826–30 to 34 per year in 1845–49. T. G. Masaryk, *The Spirit of Russia*, London: Allen and Unwin, Ltd., 1919, Vol. 1, p. 130. This long, careful, and rather neglected analysis was first published in German in 1913 under the title *Zur Russischen Geschichts- und Religionsphilosophie*.

[18] Jacqueries averaged 350 per year for the first three years after emancipation. *Ibid.*, pp. 140–141.

[19] The proportion of workers who struck from 1895 through 1902 varied between 1.7 per cent and 4.0 per cent per year. In 1903 the proportion rose to 5.1 per cent but dropped a year later to 1.5 per cent. In 1905 the proportion rose to 163.8 per cent, indicating that the total working force struck, on the average, closer to twice than to once during that portentous year. In 1960 the proportion dropped to 65.8 per cent; in 1907 to 41.9 per cent; and by 1909 was down to a "normal" 3.5 per cent. *Ibid.*, p. 175n.

[20] *Ibid.*, p. 189n.

[21] In his *History of the Russian Revolution*, Leon Trotsky presents data on political strikes from 1903 to 1917. In his *Spirit of Russia*, Masaryk presents comparable data from 1905 through 1912. The figures are not identical but the reported yearly trends are consistent. Masaryk's figures are somewhat lower, except for 1912. Cf. Trot-

sky, *op. cit.*, Doubleday Anchor Books ed., 1959, p. 32 and Masaryk, *op. cit. supra*, p. 197n.

[22] See Trotsky, *op. cit.*, pp. 18–21 for a vivid picture of rising discontent in the army.

[23] C. Issawi, *Egypt at Mid-century: An Economic Survey*, London: Oxford University Press, 1954, p. 262. J. & S. Lacouture in their *Egypt in Transition*, New York: Criterion Books, 1958, p. 100, give a figure of over 300,000. Sir R. Bullard, editor, *The Middle East: A Political and Economic Survey*, London: Oxford University Press, 1958, p. 221 estimates total employment in industry, transport and commerce in 1957 to have been 750,000.

[24] International Monetary Fund, *International Financial Statistics*, Washington, D. C. See monthly issues of this report 1950–53.

[25] J. and S. Lacouture, *op. cit.*, p. 99.

[26] England threatened to depose Farouk in February 1942, by force if necessary, if Egypt did not support the Allies. Capitulation by the government and the Wafd caused widespread popular disaffection. When Egypt finally declared war on the Axis in 1945, the prime minister was assassinated. See J. & S. Lacouture, *op. cit.*, pp. 97–98 and Issawi, *op. cit.*, p. 268.

[27] See J. R. Reich, *Leisler's Rebellion*, Chicago: University of Chicago Press, 1953.

[28] See U. S. Bureau of the Census, *Historical Statistics of the United States, Colonial Times to 1957*, Washington, D. C., 1960, p. 757.

[29] See G. Lefebvre, *The Coming of the French Revolution*, Princeton: Princeton University Press, 1947, pp. 101–109, 145–148, 196. G. Le Bon, *The Psychology of Revolution*, New York: G. Putnam's Sons, 1913, p. 143.

[30] The account by Irving Werstein, *July 1863*, New York: Julian Messner, Inc., 1957, is journalistic but to my knowledge the fullest yet available.

[31] E. S. Munger, "The Tragedy of Nyasaland," American Universities Field Staff Reports Service, vol. 7, no. 4 (August 1, 1959), p. 9.

[32] See U. S. Bureau of the Census, *Historical Statistics of the United States: 1789–1945*, Washington, D. C.: 1949, p. 14.

[33] Eugen Kogon, *The Theory and Practice of Hell*, New York: Farrar, Straus & Co., 1950, pp. 284–286.

[34] W. Buchanan, "Mass Communication in Reverse," *International Social Science Bulletin*, 5 (1953), pp. 577–583, at p. 578. The full study is W. Buchanan and H. Cantril, *How Nations See Each Other*, Urbana: University of Illinois Press, 1953, esp. pp. 85–90.

[35] Daniel Lerner, *The Passing of Traditional Society*, Glencoe, Ill.: Free Press, 1958.

[36] *Ibid.*, pp. 101–103. See also F. P. Kilpatrick & H. Cantril, "Self-anchoring Scaling, A Measure of Individuals' Unique Reality Words," *Journal of Individual Psychology*, 16 (November, 1960), pp. 158–173.

[37] See the revised edition of 1952 as reprinted by Vintage Books, Inc., 1957, pp. 264–275.

[38] Quoted in E. H. Carr, *A History of Soviet Russia*, vol. 1, *The Bolshevik Revolution: 1917–23*, London: Macmillan, 1950, p. 69.

INVENTORY OF CONCEPTS